ISBN 978-0-365-21416-8
PIBN 10836304

The
Smith Alumnae
Quarterly

INDEX

TO

VOLUMES XVI TO XX

NOVEMBER, 1924—JULY, 1929

Published by the
Alumnae Association of Smith College
• • •
November, 1929

INDEX TO VOLUMES XVI–XX OF THE
SMITH ALUMNAE QUARTERLY

EXPLANATORY

In addition to the usual abbreviations, the following are used:

A. A. C., American Alumni Council

S. C., Smith College.

S . C. A. C. W., Smith College Association for Christian Work.

S. C. R. U., Smith College Relief Unit.

Names of alumnae, when occurring as main entries, have class designations appended.

In the case of married alumnae, all entries are put under the married name, but reference is made from the maiden name and the class designation is given under both headings.

Names of active members of the faculty (except the President) have (f) appended, and if alumnae, have also class designation.

Names of the departments at the back of the magazine are not indexed, nor is much of the constantly recurring news which appears in them. The Bulletin Board contains regularly notes of vespers, concerts, lectures; Art Museum and Library exhibitions and gifts; departmental and faculty news; also undergraduate news, of athletics, Outing Club activities, dramatics, elections, prizes and honors. The Note Room is a running commentary on college happenings. Current Alumnae Publications and Alumnae Notes need no explanation. Most of the communications in Let Us Talk of Many Things are indexed under author and subject.

Under the heading Obituary (with the proper subdivisions) are listed the names of alumnae, non-graduates, undergraduates, faculty, officers, and notable friends of the college, whose deaths are recorded in the volumes indexed. These items are not repeated in the main alphabet.

Under the general heading Smith College (and not elsewhere) may be found all entries relating directly to the college: as, Faculty, Trustees, Dormitories, etc.

References are to volume and page, but that possessors of unbound volumes may use the index conveniently, a table is appended showing what pages are in each number:

Vol. XVI.	Nov. 1924	pp.	1–132	May 1927	pp.	257–400
	Feb. 1925		133–264	July 1927		401–552
	May 1925		265–400			
	July 1925		401–568	Vol. XIX.	Nov. 1927	pp.	1–132
				Feb. 1928		133–260
Vol. XVII.	Nov. 1925	pp.	1–140	May 1928		261–412
	Feb. 1926		141–268	July 1928		413–576
	May 1926		269–404			
	July 1926		405–548	Vol. XX.	Nov. 1928	pp.	1–132
				Feb. 1929		133–260
Vol. XVIII.	Nov. 1926	pp.	1–132	May 1929		261–408
	Feb. 1927		133–256	July 1929		409–560

INDEX

.PAGE

— "Laurenus Clark Seelye" [a note on
  Mrs. Rhees's biography].............   20: 262
— In Memoriam: Herbert Vaughan Ab-
  bott; Inez Whipple Wilder...........   20: 266
— The Retirement of Professor Wood ...   20: 412
— Commencement and the A. A. C......   20: 493
— and Condit, Marion (Carr) 07, The
  Cleveland Party....................   20: 304
Hill, Richard S., assists K. Koffka 19: 190
Hill, Susan L. 03, article on her work in
  handmade jewelry, by M. M. Howey..   20: 160
Hills, James M., The Exhibit of 1904 .... 20: 495
Hills, Therese C., note of appreciation for
  public use of S. C. swimming pool..... 17: 22
Hillyer family, and S. C. Art Department
                              16: 462; 17: 448
Hincks, Sarah, dean of S. C. class of 1928 16: 57
Hoblit, Louise (Barber) 99, an interview
  with, as President of the Pasadena
  Board of Education.................   20: 168
Hodge, Lucy M. 23, Junior Colleges to the
  Rescue?..........................   19: 181
Holden, Alice M. 05 (f), report on Alum-
  nae Directed Reading..............   17: 73
Holland, Dr. and Mrs. J. G...........   16: 270
Holt, Ellen 90, sketch of, as candidate for
  Alumnae Trustee...................   19: 349
Homans, S. M. 90, see Woodruff, Susan
  (Homans)
Hombleux, France, Smith contribution to
  communal buildings of.............   20: 349
—mayor of, cablegram from, at dedication
  of Grécourt gates..................   16: 10
—sends good wishes for 1925 to "dames du
  Smith Collège"....................   16: 209
Homemaking........................   17: 146
Homestead Orchards, A. M. Comstock ..   18: 295
Hopkins, Mrs. Elizabeth J., head of
  Dewey House, 1875–90.............   18: 258
Hotaling, Amita (Fairgrieve) 12, The
  "Ten-Cent Magazine"...............   17: 44
Houck, Bertha A., The Lady Who Built
  the Architects' Building............   20: 39
Houghton, Ruth 29, elected Chairman of
  Judicial Board....................   19: 342
How I Coördinate all my Interests, D.
  (A.) Oates........................   19: 184
How I Do It, G. (B.) Stearns..........   18: 163
How one Husband Does It [Anon.].......   18: 484
How Well Are the Seniors? A. M. Rich-
  ardson, M.D......................   19: 425
Howes, Ethel (Puffer) 91, The Handi-
  capped Candidate.................   16: 149
— Freshman Curriculum Discussion.....   16: 187
— The Institute for the Coördination of
  Women's Interests.............17: 1; 19: 308
— The First Institute Conference......   17: 434
— note on the Nursery School.........   18: 155
Howey, Martha M. 01, Susan Leland Hill,
  Master Craftsman.................   20: 160
Hubbell, Henry S., second portrait of
  Pres. Seelye by, presented to S. C...... 20: 474
Huberth, Helen 28, and others, Smith Col-
  lege Goes out to Meet the World......   19: 12
Humanizing the Registrar's Office, J. C.
  Cahoon..........................   17: 277
Humphrey, Sarah W. (f)..............   18: 257
Hyde, George P., appointed Treasurer of
  S. C.............................   16: 518
— Financial Supervision of Student Or-
  ganizations......................   17: 151
— Is Smith College Playing Poor? 20: 8

I

Illustrations:
— Academic procession, 50th anniversary
                              16: 402, 488
— All-Smith hockey team.............   20: 197
— All-Smith swimming team..........   19: 340
— Alumnae Frolic tableaux, 1929......   20: 471
— Alumnae parade, 1925.........16: 473, 474
                  1926.............   17: 456
                  1927.........18: 443, 445
                  1928.............   19: 462
                  1929.........20: 409, 452
— Alumnae's reception, The, in North-
  ampton, 1925....................   16: 336
— Androcles and the Lion............   19: 448
— Antique gymnastics...............   17: 180

PAGE

— Arcturus, The, off Cocos Island.....   17: 42
— Armchairs and nice books...........   20: 431
— As the press sees us...............   18: 189
— At Mürren with the camera 17: 323
— Audience in John M. Greene Hall, 1925 16: 475
— Autumn..........................   17: 1
— Baggage.........................   18: 71
— Beaux' Stratagem, The...........18: 324, 427
— Beggar's Opera, The..............   19: 340
— Birch tree, The..................   19: 438
— "Birthday party" (three pictures) ....
                              16: 493, 494
— Blazed Trail (Outing Club's raft).....   16: 524
— Bookplates in S. C. Library........   17: 323
— Burton Hall.....................   16: 293
— Campus scenes......16: 200, 266, 482, 483, 485
                  487; 17: 340, 465, 467, 475; 18: 193, 195, 332
                  433, 453, 456; 19: 195, 343, 475, 478; 20: 337
                              449, 465, 493, 504, 506
— "Cathedral-like forests"...........   19: 167
— Chicago College Club.............   16: 184
— Christmas miracle play............   20: 197
— Chrysanthemum exhibitions ...17: 205; 20: 197
— Circling Years, The (many small pic-
  tures and portraits)............16: 430 *et seq*
  See also Sophia and the Circling Years
— Class in calisthenics (reproduction of
  the 80s).........................   16: 480
— Class of 83......................   19: 485
— Class of 85, forty years after........   16: 471
— Class of 1927, officers of 18: 421
— Class of 1929....................   20: 467
— "Class of 76"....................   18: 439
— Class on roof of swimming pool.......   16: 335
— Clay models of prehistoric monsters ..   20: 197
— Coffee 10c.......................   19: 198
— College Hall tower................   18: 424
— College theatre, plans for.......18: 27, 29, 31
— Commencement scenes 17: 405, 452, 455
                              456, 457, 459, 466, 469
— Commencement weather..........18: 454, 455
— Competitive cups.................   18: 333
— Costumes.................16: 136, 440, 447
                  19: 413, 444, 485; 20: 148
— Costumes, class.................17: 455; 18: 441
                              19: 460; 20: 451
  See also, above, Alumnae parade
— Cots in Gymnasium, 50th anniversary   16: 507
— Crews in form of letter S 16: 525
— Cross word puzzle................   16: 197
— Cups, competitive, awarded for com-
  mencement attendance, costume, etc. .. 18: 333
  The same picture may be found at
  19: 345 and 20: 346
— Czar, the, holds court at Carnival 20: 197
— Dewey House.................16: 265, 431
— Dewey House and some of its occupants
  (several views)................18: 257, 258
— Doorway of Burton Hall...........   19: 278
— Dormitories, two new [as planned]....   20: 265
  See also, below, Quadrangle
— Eclipse, as seen by Smith College at
  Windsor, Conn...................   16: 133
— Elephant hunting, Belgian Congo 17: 302
— Elm tree on campus..............   19: 455
— Ethel de Long Zande's home 19: 433
— Faculty soccer team..............   17: 208
— Fiftieth Anniversary gift of alumnae ..   18: 1
— Fiftieth Anniversary scenes ...16: 465, 469, 493
— Fifty-two superwomen with Mrs. Ford
  and Mrs. Teagle..................   18: 463
— "Fill every glass"................   19: 337
— Foreign students, 1924............   16: 60
                  1925.............   17: 66
                  1926.............   18: 15
                  1927.............   19: 33
                  1928.............   20: 64
— Freshman Entrance Prize Winners,
  1927............................   19: 1
— Freshman granddaughters, 1924......   17: 64
                  1926......   18: 62
                  1927......   19: 60
                  1928......   20: 68
— From the Hadley bridge............   19: 489
— Front row in chapel, with the President
  in France.......................   19: 71
— with the President home.........   19: 197
— Furniture Exchange pleasantries 17: 67
— Furniture renovation..............   19: 68

The Smith Alumnae Quarterly

Published by the
Alumnae Association of Smith College
• • •
November, 1926

THE SMITH ALUMNAE QUARTERLY

November, 1926

TABLE OF CONTENTS

Published by the Alumnae Association of Smith College
at Rumford Building, 10 Ferry St., Concord, N. H.

Member of Alumni Magazines Associated

Florence Homer Snow 1904, Business Manager ...... { Rumford Building, 10 Ferry St., Concord, N. H., or
Marion E. Graves 1915, Advertising Manager .... { College Hall, Northampton, Mass.

BOARD OF EDITORS

Edith Naomi Hill 1903 .... College Hall, Northampton .... Editor-in-Chief
Elizabeth H. Kingsley 1919 .... Assistant to the Editor

Ethel Puffer Howes 1891	Anna T. Kitchel 1903
Jean Fine Spahr 1883	Marie E. Gilchrist 1916
Elizabeth Lewis Day 1895	Clara Savage Littledale 1913

Bernice Sanborn 1918

Price $1.50 per year (four numbers) in advance

Volume XVIII .... No. 1

*Entered as second-class matter at the post office at Concord, N. H., under the act of March 3, 1879:
Copyright, 1926, by the Alumnae Association of Smith College.*

Smith College Fiftieth Anniversary Publications

The following volumes are being issued under the auspices of the College as part of the Anniversary celebration

THE STUDY OF MUSIC IN THE AMERICAN COLLEGE
By Roy Dickinson Welch, A.B.   *Price* $2.00 · *Postage* 15c

BEN JONSON'S ART: ELIZABETHAN LIFE AND LITERATURE AS REFLECTED THEREIN
By Esther Cloudman Dunn, Ph.D.   *Price* $3.00 · *Postage* 15c

SOPHIA SMITH, AND THE BEGINNINGS OF SMITH COLLEGE
By Elizabeth Deering Hanscom, Ph.D. *and*
Helen French Greene, M.A.   *Price* $2.00 · *Postage* 15c

A BIBLIOGRAPHY OF THE NORTH AMERICAN HEMIPTERA-HETEROPTERA
By Howard Madison Parshley, Sc.D.   *Price* $3.50 · *Postage* 15c

THE PLANTATION OVERSEER AS REVEALED IN HIS LETTERS
By John Spencer Bassett, Ph.D., LL.D.   *Price* $3.50 · *Postage* 15c

THE MORPHOLOGY OF AMPHIBIAN METAMORPHOSIS
By Inez Whipple Wilder, A.M.   *Price* $3.00 · *Postage* 15c

THE SALAMANDERS OF THE FAMILY PLETHODONTIDAE
By Emmett Reid Dunn, Ph.D.   *Price* $6.00 · *Postage* 15c

THE SHORT STORY IN SPAIN IN THE XVII CENTURY
By Caroline Brown Bourland, Ph.D.   *In Press*

JEAN-JACQUES ROUSSEAU, ESSAI D'INTERPRETATION NOUVELLE
By Albert Schinz, Ph.D., O.A.   *In Preparation*

On Sale at the President's Office, *College Hall, Northampton, Mass.*

Morrow   Martha Wilson   Gardiner

THE FIFTIETH ANNIVERSARY GIFT OF THE ALUMNAE

The Smith Alumnae Quarterly

Vol. XVIII   NOVEMBER, 1926   No. 1

Entered as second class matter at the Post Office at Concord, New Hampshire, under the Act of March 3, 1879.

The Quadrangle

Laura W. L. Scales and Elizabeth Cutter Morrow

Mrs. Scales, Warden of the College, writes what she has called a "general article' about the dormitories, giving certain data which she knows better than anyone else; and Mrs. Morrow tells the story of the furnishings of the living- and dining-rooms. The Trustees delegated the task of furnishing to a Committee of which Mrs. Morrow was the chairman and trustee member, and Katherine Garrison Norton 1895 and Amey Aldrich 1895 the alumnae members.

"YOU have labored and others have entered into your labors." In 1921 the alumnae and friends of the College raised $4,000,000 and as one result Cushing, Ellen Emerson, and Jordan were built; in 1925 at the Fiftieth Birthday celebration the alumnae made their birthday gift of $600,000. Now Morrow, Martha Wilson, and Gardiner face the earlier group across the court of the quadrangle.*

The architects, Messrs. Ames and Dodge, have described their plans for these buildings in the QUARTERLY for May 1925. The completed buildings carry out our hopes. The tower, the terrace, the connecting stairway (may there soon be another), the vaulted dining-rooms, the segregated service quarters, all contribute their share of dignity and beauty and service. The "monotonous bedrooms" are there, 190 for undergraduates, but so satisfactory are they in their opportunities for space, light, closet room, and privacy, that they are the coveted lodgings of a large part of the College. The furnishing of these rooms, done by Miss Leonard, seems to be surprisingly acceptable even to the varied tastes of their occupants—and indeed one would be hard to please who did not enjoy their comfort and harmony of color. A chest of drawers, mirror, desk and desk chair in walnut finish, the usual couch, brown wicker chair with gay chintz, and a harmonizing rug make up the equipment of each room. Downstairs has been put to uses familiar and otherwise: besides the large living-rooms and dining-rooms there are the two "lounges," each with a little stage, there are two small libraries, four rooms for graduate students, and four guest rooms. These guest rooms may be rented by anyone connected with the college community and perhaps are a slight compensation to the students for the strict ruling against overnight guests in their own rooms, though in times of stress these guest rooms will be reserved for the use of the College and the

* The dimensions of the inclosed quadrangle are 269' x 370'.

Alumnae Office.   The description of this floor will be given elsewhere by Mrs. Morrow, who, as one of the committee of alumnae, has undertaken the arduous task of furnishing this large territory.

Martha Wilson and Morrow, like Cushing and Ellen Emerson, form one housekeeping unit, with one kitchen serving two dining-rooms.   Miss Kathleen M. Robertson, who came to us from Girton College, England, is Head of Martha Wilson and also housekeeping head of Morrow.   Miss Vera Brown, Assistant Professor of History, is the social head of Morrow.   Miss Brown was last year social head of Hatfield House, which was then managed in conjunction with Wallace House.   She and all the students of Hatfield moved together to Morrow House.   Miss Myra Sampson, Associate Professor of Zoölogy, and Miss Inez Scott of the Latin Department are the two resident members of the faculty in Martha Wilson and Morrow.   In Gardiner House Mrs. Marie Dugan of New York is the Head, feeling herself already more a part of the College because she was the "nominee" of one of our alumnae; Miss Mabelle Blake, Personnel Director, is the resident faculty member.   These and a staff of some 27 maids, the graduate students—two American, one French, and one Japanese girl—and undergraduates of the four classes well distributed make up the human content of this portion of the quadrangle.   They have the happy lot of being the pioneers in these new habitations of Smith.

The architects tell us that an inclosed quadrangle is rare in this country, and an inclosed quadrangle of colonial design all but unique.   We are already proud of ours.   In the life of Smith we have a new pleasure to the eye, a new

The Memorial Steps

These steps are between Cushing and Morrow Houses and were erected by the Class of 1905 in
memory of its alumnae president, Marian Rumsey Ewing.

stimulus to the imagination, a new center of interest, and a new field for effort. Three hundred and seventy undergraduates live here in the six houses, a unit almost the size of the undergraduate body at Bryn Mawr. In the tower which dominates the scene is a clock, the quadrangle's own time, and a bell, the old College Hall bell, the quadrangle's own voice of summons and warning. The terrace may be the stage for outdoor pageant or play, the corners and stairways and porticoes meeting places for large receptions of the President and Faculty, the lawns (one need scarcely use the phrase "to be," so forehanded is the work of Mr. King) the scene of Junior Promenade garden parties. At least here is ready a setting of dignity and beauty. Even memory and tradition are not lacking. The names of the houses and of the memorial steps given by the Class of 1905 for one of its members provide them—Gardiner, Martha Wilson, Morrow, and Marian Rumsey Ewing. Scholarly tastes, wide service, home building, public-mindedness, and devotion to the purpose of the College, these the names suggest to us.

Yet these names never can belong to the quadrangle alone. The quadrangle is after all only a part of the whole. Observe the bicycle as symbol! In the basement of Gardiner House is a storeroom for all the bicycles of the quadrangle, that large flotilla which, starting out in the morning, brings this farthest outpost of the campus within quick reach of all the varied centers of college activity. The quadrangle is the expansion of our college life, an added space for growing gentlewomen.

LAURA W. L. SCALES 1901, *Warden*

Mrs. Morrow, our new permanent trustee and the chairman of the Furnishing Committee, uses as the text of her article her report submitted last June as senior alumnae trustee:

"IN the last report of the senior alumnae trustee she asked a rhetorical question,—'Can dignity, good taste, and economy meet in all our college interiors?' and the Board of Trustees a few months later requested her to find the answer herself by becoming chairman of the Furnishing Committee for the three new dormitories. If this report deals only with this special piece of work it is because the chairman has been so absorbed by it.

"The committee carries great responsibility because the money it is spending represents the loyalty and sacrifice of the alumnae poured out so generously last year in the Fiftieth Anniversary Gift. We are conscious of the trust reposed in us and we are trying to use the money wisely.

"In the attempt to find out what is most needed in the living-rooms of the dormitories, we have had many conferences with Mrs. Scales and Miss Leonard, and we have talked with Heads of Houses, Resident Faculty, the girls themselves, and anxious mothers. The work of furnishing is exceedingly interesting and somewhat complicated. The question of upkeep in the dormitories is a serious one, for the College operates on a close budget and cannot spend much for repairs or cleaning. This means that delicate colors cannot be used in upholstery or hangings and that furniture must be strong and serviceable. Yet we do not want drab, iron-clad rooms but cheerful, homelike interiors. It

would be wonderful if every single alumna who gave to the Birthday Gift could
be satisfied with the finished product, the furnished dormitories, but as furnishing is so largely a matter of personal taste the committee does not look for that
miracle.   We only bespeak your sympathetic consideration of our problem.
So far as we have worked out the answer to the rhetorical question we find
that 'dignity, good taste, and economy' do not naturally walk hand in hand.
They have to be forced a little into one another's company.

"ELIZABETH (CUTTER) MORROW 1896, *Senior Alumnae Trustee*"

When Miss Hill asked me to write something for the QUARTERLY about the
furnishing of the three new dormitories I told her that I had expressed my
feelings in the alumnae trustee report in June.   She was not satisfied with this
bare outline, however, and has persuaded me that the text of my report needs
a little amplification.

Mrs. Norton, Miss Aldrich, and I agreed at the outset that we wanted the
furnished dormitories to be cheerful, bright, and homelike in appearance, that
we would buy only really good furniture for them, and that we would not
exceed our budget.   (The influence of a Scotch president is far reaching.)
This statement will not seem a platitude to anyone who knows the cost of good
furnishing and also the sum put at our disposal for filling the spacious rooms
on the first floor of the new buildings.   We realized that living up to our
principles might result in a little dignified bareness, but that we felt was not
out of keeping with New England ideals.   For color and cheerfulness we resolved to depend upon light paint on the walls and woodwork and the gayest
chintz we dared buy for the curtains.   Tables, chairs, and sofas must be strong
and serviceable and upholstered for the most part in dark shades, but their
shapeliness would show well against a warm background.

After consultation with Mrs. Scales and Miss Leonard the refectory style
of table was chosen for all three dining-rooms as an agreeable change and in
the hope that conversation across a narrow table might be easier than over a
round one and reduce the inevitable noise at mealtime.   The chairs are Windsor.   All the furniture is of butternut color which contrasts pleasantly with the
dark green linoleum on the floor.   In the flanking dormitories archways divide
the dining-room into two parts, and the grouping of benches and chairs by the
fireplace in the front room give a homelike look to the entrance.   The high
ceiling, eleven feet to peak, has been filled with a handsome chandelier of black
and gold crystal drops.   It is an interesting example of direct and indirect
lighting for the circle of colonial lamps gives one light and the large bowl beneath
the other.   The chintz in the Gardiner dining-room is blue in tone; in Morrow
and Martha Wilson heavy English linen is used, the former a mandarin red, the
latter a medley of red and green.

Living-rooms are of three sorts in the flanking dormitories: a main living-
room almost square with a big fireplace and many windows, a long narrow room

EDITOR'S NOTE.—It was very difficult to choose from the many attractive pictures which Mr. Stahlberg took of
the new dormitories.   At some future time we hope to publish more: for instance, there is a delightful view of the
little Morrow library and we have in mind also a double panel of the beautiful grandfather clocks in Gardiner and
Morrow, and the dining-room in Martha Wilson which is quite different from the rooms in the flanking dormitories.

Above: Kitchen serving Morrow and Martha Wilson

Below: Gardiner Dining-Room

Martha Wilson and Gardiner showing Gardiner Dining-Room

The Living-Room in Gardiner

The Lounge in Morrow

The Tower Bedroom in Martha Wilson

A Typical Bedroom

The Living-Room in Martha Wilson
Inset: Entering the Gardiner Living-Room

The Living-Room in Morrow

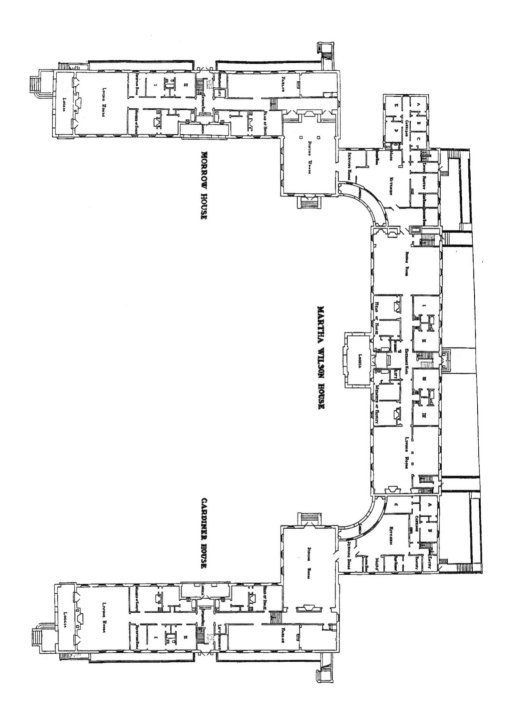

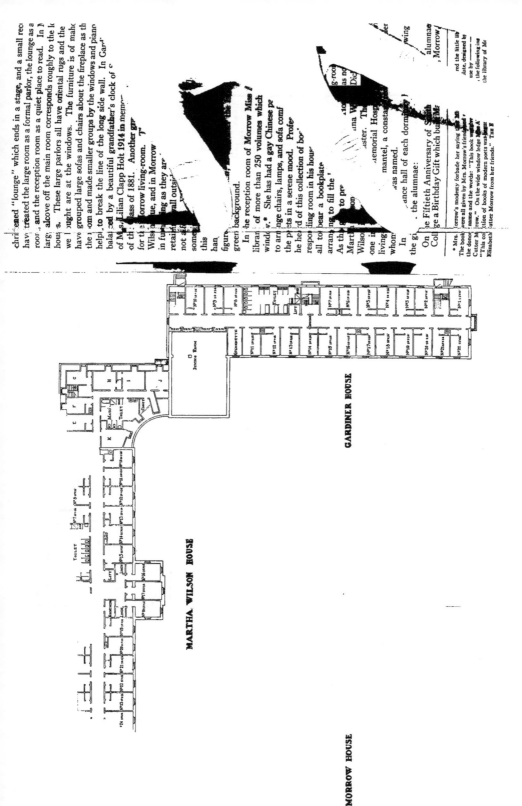

chri...ned "lounge" which ends in a stage, and a small rec
hav...treated the large room as a formal parlor, the lounge as a
roo...and the reception room as a quiet place to read. In M
larg; above off the main room corresponds roughly to the k
hous's. These large parlors all have oriental rugs and the
we l ught are at the windows. The furniture is of mahc
have grouped large sofas and chairs about the fireplace as th
the ...om and made smaller groups by the windows and piano
helpl...to break the line of the long side wall. In Gar
bala...ced by a beautiful grandfather's clock of c
of M...Lilian Clapp Holt 1914 in memo—
of th...ass of 1881. Another gr
for th...orrow living-room. T
Wils...ue, and in Morrow
in fu...ing as they are
retai...all outsi
not a
some
this
han
figur
green background.

In the reception room of Morrow Miss !
librar...of more than 250 volumes which
wind...w.* She has had a gay Chinese pe
to arr...nge chairs, lamps, and sofa comf
the p...ets in a serene mood. Profe
he he...d of this collection of bo
respo...ding room in his hous
all to...bear a bookplate
arran...ng to fill the
As th...to pre
Mart...son
Wilso
one i
living
whom
In
...ance hall of each dormi
...the alumnae:
On...e Fiftieth Anniversary of S...th
Col...ge a Birthday Gift which bu...M

g-roo...
as no
Dic
una W
...aster. The
...emorial Hosp
mantel, a consta
...was named.
In

...er
...wing
alumnae
, Morrow
...red the little lil
...late, designed by
...use by
, the following in
the library of M

* Mrs...orrow's modesty forbade her saying th... M
The book...were all given by Mrs. Morrow's frien...r
the dono...ame and the words: "This book w...he
Cutter M...ow." On the wide window ledge M...A
"This col...ction of books of modern poets wa...nt
Elizabeth...tter Morrow from her friends." Th...F

MARTHA WILSON HOUSE

GARDINER HOUSE

MORROW HOUSE

christened "lounge" which ends in a stage, and a small reception room. We have treated the large room as a formal parlor, the lounge as an informal sitting-room, and the reception room as a quiet place to read. In Martha Wilson the large alcove off the main room corresponds roughly to the lounge in the other houses. These large parlors all have oriental rugs and the proudest chintzes we bought are at the windows. The furniture is of mahogany finish. We have grouped large sofas and chairs about the fireplace as the natural heart of the room and made smaller groups by the windows and piano. A tall secretary helps to break the line of the long side wall. In Gardiner this high piece is balanced by a beautiful grandfather's clock of Scotch workmanship, the gift of Mrs. Lilian Clapp Holt 1914 in memory of her aunt, Mrs. Lucia Clapp Noyes of the Class of 1881. Another grandfather's clock is on its way from England for the Morrow living-room. The prevailing color in Gardiner is red, in Martha Wilson blue, and in Morrow yellow. The lounges presented a difficult problem in furnishing as they are long and narrow in shape, somewhat darkened by the retaining wall outside, and end in a stage which cried out for properties we could not afford. We have provided stage curtains that pull smoothly and we hope sometime to see them part for a performance. Normandy chairs are used in this room which could be easily moved up to the footlights. In Morrow the hangings are of raspberry red with some of the chairs and sofa pillows done in figured English linen; in Gardiner the hangings are of flowered chintz with a green background.

In the reception room of Morrow Miss Aldrich has gathered a little poetry library of more than 250 volumes which fills the space on either side of the window.* She has had a gay Chinese paper put on the walls and we have tried to arrange chairs, lamps, and sofa comfortably so that the girls may sit down to the poets in a serene mood. Professor Gardiner was so much interested when he heard of this collection of books that he decided to give a library to the corresponding room in his house. He plans to present us with about 500 volumes, all to bear a bookplate saying: *Hortum animi colendo*. The Class of '95 is arranging to fill the bookshelves in the living-room of Martha Wilson House. As this goes to press Martha Wilson House has not yet received the portrait of Martha Wilson given by Mrs. Anna Wilson Dickinson 1906 and Mr. John P. Wilson in memory of their sister. The portrait is by Seifert, a replica of the one in the Children's Memorial Hospital in Chicago. It will hang in the living-room over the mantel, a constant reminder of the splendid woman for whom the house was named.

In the entrance hall of each dormitory hangs the following appreciation of the gift of the alumnae:

On the Fiftieth Anniversary of Smith College the alumnae made to the College a Birthday Gift which built Martha Wilson, Morrow, and Gardiner

---

* Mrs. Morrow's modesty forbade her saying that Miss Aldrich gathered the little library as a tribute to her. The books were all given by Mrs. Morrow's friends and each has a bookplate, designed by Chester Aldrich, bearing the donor's name and the words: "This book was given to Morrow House by ——— ———, a friend of Elizabeth Cutter Morrow." On the wide window ledge Miss Aldrich has placed the following inscription in a narrow frame: "This collection of books of modern poets was begun and placed in the library of Morrow House as a tribute to Elizabeth Cutter Morrow from her friends." THE EDITOR.

houses. Alumnae from all classes from 1879 to 1925 inclusive and the under graduates of the College gave to this Fund, and of the following classes every member made a contribution to the Gift.

1880	1884	1893
1881	1886	1895
1882	1888	1897
1883.	1889	1905
	1890	

"And are the dormitories finished?" several visitors have asked as they made the grand tour of the three new buildings.   The furnishing is done in the sense that this appropriation for buying furniture is spent, but so far as the new college unit is a living thing it is decidedly unfinished—it is only beginning to be.   The Committee feels that the essentials are all there for comfort and pleasant living.   There is beauty too in the rooms though none is completely filled.   Good things beget good things and we are sure that Gardiner, Martha Wilson, and Morrow dormitories will gradually acquire more if these already provided are appreciated and cared for.   It takes time and loyalty to make a real home, on a college campus or anywhere else, for houses like people *grow* in grace.

ELIZABETH (CUTTER) MORROW 1896

*Looking towards Martha Wilson through the
Ellen Emerson Arch*

The Curriculum—Why Bother?

WILLIAM ORTON

Mr. Orton, Professor of Economics and Sociology, is too well known to Smith alumnae to need introduction here. He is much sought after by alumnae clubs and other organizations as a lecturer on current economic, social, and education problems; he has conducted courses on International Relations in Springfield, and is a frequent contributor to the *New Age*, *New Republic*, *American Economical Review*, and other periodicals. It is in his capacity as member of the Committee on the Course of Study that he writes this article. This Committee has been given a commission by the Faculty to make a study of our curriculum and to report in time for the course of study work for next year. The Committee is taking great pains to get ideas and suggestions from academic departments and has received a number of helpful contributions from the Faculty as well as from two alumnae classes circularized and from the student questionnaire. Professor Orton does not discuss the Smith curriculum in this paper, but, in view of the fact that the question of curricula is confronting educators everywhere, his summary of this contemporary problem as it faces our own and similar colleges should be interesting and profitable.

A RECENT article by Mr. H. G. Wells, inspired by an intellectual irascibility characteristic of the half-educated, bears the startling title: "The four years at college are wasted." Anyone who has watched the course of education during the past ten years might be tempted to exclaim, "I was waiting for somebody to say just that!" for the period has been one of cumulative criticism and experiment touching every phase of educational activity. Fundamental principles and traditions have everywhere been attacked, and from the kindergarten to the great universities change seems to be the order of the day. The school, the trade union, the library, the community center, the extension agencies, even public education authorities, have all felt the influence of new theory and the passion for experiment. The general field of adult education has been elaborately surveyed and made the object of a special campaign by one of the great semi-public foundations of America. Popular as well as technical discussions of education constitute an unusually large proportion of the publishers' announcements; and the college and the university, as the natural foci of so much educational effort, have a prominent position in the general movement. Both Oxford and Cambridge—apart from the report of the Royal Commission—have recently made fundamental alterations in their curricula, modifying the scope of the classical basis, introducing important new schools outside it, and recasting the disciplines required of that perennial problem, the "pass man." London is so altered by the introduction of new degrees and new schools that large sections of it are unrecognizable to an older generation; while American higher education has become involved in what is really nothing less than an attempt to reshape not merely its processes but its ends—an attempt of which innumerable experiments mark little more than the beginning.

In a short view all this seems very unusual and perhaps somewhat disconcerting. But—aside from the fact that a longer perspective shows educational practice coming up for some such general overhaul about once in every generation—there are decisive reasons for the prevalent post-war "unrest."

Not merely education, but every field of social organization—economics, government, philosophy, ethics, art, science, religion—is being submitted to a process of stocktaking incidental to the recovery from the war; and while on the one hand education is eagerly following the advance in scientific understanding of the mind and its processes, on the other it is endeavoring to find an answer to the demands of a society that dare not, even if it would, accept unchallenged the assumptions that prevailed before that great disaster. Accordingly, it is not merely the speculations of professional pedagogues or the bleating of innumerable hungry sheep that "look up and are not fed," that move the teaching world. It is essays like those of Russell, Inge, Lippman, Wallas, Martin: the novels of Anderson, Lewis, Galsworthy, Barbusse, Rolland, and many another; for in these lies a body of social criticism to which, almost in despair of other reply, more and more thinking people are turning to education for an answer.

This criticism is reinforced from within the college. What the Yale Committee (1919) described as "the new spirit in the nation and in the university which requires of every institution and agency that it take account of stock, consider the lessons taught by the war, and seek to improve its methods to meet the new conditions" has found expression among teachers and students from every quarter. Even to summarize that criticism would require more space than is here available; but some of its salient aspects may be noted in so far as they relate to our immediate problem.

First, from every side comes a reëmphasis upon what was perhaps President Eliot's basic idea, namely, "spontaneous personal interest and enthusiasm, rather than compulsion, as the driving force in education." As the Dartmouth seniors put it in their almost famous report of 1924, "Possibly the heart of the educational problem lies in this question of how to awaken the initiative of the student—to get him going, as it were, under his own steam. . . . We discard as the greatest demerit of our present educational system the theory and practice of professorial activity to compensate for and care for student apathy." Naturally, as President Eliot realized long ago, this implies guidance rather than compulsion as the principle obligation of the college to the student; and it imposes upon the student an intellectual responsibility and a necessity for self-knowledge more akin to what is demanded by Oxford and Cambridge, and perhaps more fitted to the needs of useful citizenship in a modern democracy. A signal merit claimed by the Dartmouth students for their revision is "that the student is being—to a greater extent than at present—turned loose in the world of books and ideas, facing more nearly the same conditions that will confront him after graduation, feeling more keenly the need for those qualities of initiative and resourcefulness which he will later need so intensely." A recent ballot of Rhodes scholars as to the qualifications of the finest teacher they had known gave first place to the statement: "He expected more initiative and allowed more independence to students." "Our liberal curricula are still governed far too much by the theory of discipline," says a recent vice-president of the Association of University Professors.

Discipline, we may add, in both senses of the word; for the need of revising and supplementing the older academic "disciplines" in the light of our modern situation is felt by many who profess those disciplines themselves—as, for example, by the classical "dons" at Cambridge who supported the proposal to abolish the Greek requirement for matriculation. It is possible too that new disciplines, new sequences and syntheses of study, may be required by a society so shaken and changing as is ours: of which need the recent emphasis upon the social sciences is symptomatic. College faculties have no such assurance of the inspired and final character of the traditions delivered unto them that they can safely disregard the appeals of the ever-increasing mass of students who come from, and must speedily return to, a world more recent than their own. Nor is there, after all, any ground for undue distrust of these appeals. One and all evince a willingness, nay, an eagerness, to study, provided interest is aroused and some reference to life made evident. Is it an unreasonable demand? "Teachers who have a vision of what education may do for society," says Dr. H. W. Holmes, "will wish to organize their teaching material in such a way as to make the values of their subjects clear, and achievement in them a fascination and delight." In the medieval universities student patronage was a much more powerful determinant than it has since become; and our honored traditions are based upon the results of it. Mr. Gavit, in his extensive study of the modern college, formed the conclusion that student judgment as to the value of courses and instructors is "unerring and searching to the marrow of the bones, *especially when it was done by the girls.*" In which connection, the questionnaire recently submitted to Smith students asking, *inter alia*, what courses they would have chosen in place of certain present requirements, showed the following results (in order):—English, Art, Sociology, Music, History, Modern Languages, Economics—a selection which seems reasonable and significant enough, all things considered, to merit some consideration!

To discuss the attempts to deal with some of the foregoing considerations now in progress or contemplation at Barnard, Bennington, Pomona, Dartmouth, Smith, and elsewhere is beyond the province of this article. It may be said with confidence that the final task of combining the adaptations necessary to the present social order with what is finest and of most enduring value in our academic tradition, is one which cannot be done for, but must be done by, the college faculties themselves. It calls for an idealism and an open-mindedness high enough to transcend vested departmental interests and beloved traditions in the service of life itself; and it demands an intuitive appreciation of those qualities of mind and character which are equally necessary to fine achievement in both life and scholarship.

Exchange of Students with Foreign Countries

Margaret B. Crook

The QUARTERLY is very glad to publish the picture of the students who have come from foreign countries and to print information about them and a brief résumé of those who have been with us in the past five or six years. Miss Crook, Associate Professor of Biblical Literature, is from England. She has her B.A. hons., London, the diploma in anthropology with distinction from Oxford, and the three-year certificate from Manchester College, Oxford. In a later QUARTERLY she will give us some material on the work of her committee with Smith students who seek entrance to foreign universities.

ELEVEN foreign students now at Smith College, representing nine countries, make 1926–27 the banner year in the history of the Committee on Exchange of Students with Foreign Countries. From 1921 to the summer of 1925 the average number was eight and the countries represented numbered five each year and once six. In 1925–26 there were ten foreign students representing seven countries. Hence our pride as we survey the home field at the beginning of the academic year. The number is not large when all is said, but it is sufficient unto the day; for with these students coming from settings so widely various and from universities with methods so different from each other as well as from our own, we must not accept more than we can assimilate.

Since 1921, seemingly the age of our files for dealing with incoming students, at least seventeen nations have been represented at Smith College. China, prominent until this year, has sent us students holding the Boxer Indemnity Scholarships. The Armenians are with us all the time. A succession of Spanish students vanishes after 1922 and the name of Italy is no more heard in the land. French students, holding French-American Scholarships, instituted during the war, are present in twos and threes at first, for two years there are none, and in the present year France figures again on the list with one student. Czecho-Slovakia, Finland, Latvia, Sweden, and the Philippines furnish one student each since 1921. The first English woman appears in 1924 and there are two for 1925, a quota that is maintained for the present year. The fact that the Trustee Fellowships, and more recently the Fellowships in Education, are open to applicants from Great Britain accounts for their presence. Oxford has sent us one graduate, London two, Manchester University one, and Cambridge one. Germany, absent at first from the list, has three representatives for 1925–26, and two (one a returning undergraduate) for the present year. Our first Hungarian appears in 1925–26 and one is here this year. The French, German, and Hungarian students now come to us through the Exchange Bureau of the Institute of International Education as guests of the College. Students coming upon these terms have numbered not more than one a year from each nation. For the first time in our stated period we have a Japanese student sent over by the American Friends Service Committee. Also for the first time Soviet Russia figures upon our lists associated with the name of a vigorous young freshman.

Among the eleven foreign students of this year three are returning to continue work taken up last year and eight are entering for the first time. Countries represented are Armenia, Brazil, England, France, Germany, Hungary, Japan, Russia, and Porto Rico. Students who have been at Smith before are Margarete Klumpp, now a senior, who expects to return to Germany at the end of next summer and to take up graduate work at one or more European universities for the following winter. Kate Pinsdorf '28, of Brazil, educated at Buenos Aires, Argentine, is a Special Honors student in History. Miss Pinsdorf is president of the foreign students' association, known as the Cosmopolitan

Stella Eskin, Clara Fetter, Paulette Mayot, Kiyo Harano, Louise Goepfert, Margarete Klumpp, Beatrix Tudor-Hart, Nora Edmed, Tsoghik Zarifian, María Pintado, Ingeborg Jonsson (N.C.), Kate Pinsdorf

Club. María Pintado '29, of Porto Rico, is the holder of the Latin American Scholarship. Of the eight entering students five are graduates from Great Britain and Europe. Two British students are fellows in Education. Gwendoline Nora Edmed is a graduate of King's College, London, Assistant Head of Rotherham High School (a school of 500 girls), an officer of the Women's Royal Naval Service, and is interested in the British Girl Guide movement. Helena Beatrix Tudor-Hart, the daughter of an English artist, was born in Paris, educated there and in London, graduated with honors from Newnham College, Cambridge, and has done graduate work at Vienna and at Giessen. Paulette Mayot of France was educated at the University of Neuilly-Coll. Ste. Marie, taking her Bacc. latin-langues, 1921, Bacc. philo. 1922. She studied at the Sorbonne 1924–26, securing certificates for advanced work in English and in Sociology. She has written articles for French journals. At Smith she is working for her A.M. in Sociology. Louise Goepfert, from Germany, was born in Switzerland and educated at the universities of Frankfort-on-Main and of Berlin. She is a journalist and art critic who writes for many important German papers. She is studying Art and English at Smith College and is a zealous student of many sides of American life, showing especial interest in American Art Galleries, in the activities of the Smith Press Board, and in the Workshop productions. Clara Yolan Fetter, of Hungary, holds her doctorate of Philosophy from the University of Budapest; she is a brilliant student of

Hungarian history, concentrating here upon studies that are new to her in Government and for the improvement of her English.   Kiyo Harano, of Japan, has taken the Special English Course of four years' duration at the Women's Christian College of Tokio.   She is also studying English at Smith.   Stella Eskin, after a year at the University of Boston, is entering as a member of the freshman class; she is a Russian, born near Moscow, whose home is in Northern China at Harbin, a Russian city, where she received her school education.   She selected Smith College for herself when her brother, a graduate of M. I. T., decided to return to China during the past summer.   Tsoghik Zarifian completes the list.   She is an Armenian, born at Alexandropol, who has had a high school education in the United States.   There are Canadian students in College who have technically the right to swell the numbers of the "foreign" students, but they present no problems to the Committee.

The Committee on Exchange of Students is greatly interested in making the stay in this country of overseas students as beneficial as possible.   It seems most desirable that each girl see a few of the chief cities of the Eastern States, visiting those centers whose interests bear most directly upon her academic career.   Foreign students invariably find that money does not go so far here as they expected it to go; they find it out of the question to meet hotel expenses in the big cities during vacations, and as a result they have frequently to forego visits to libraries, museums, and art galleries that would be of great value to them.   It occurs to the Committee that Smith alumnae might be interested in inviting the foreign students to visit them for a few days at a time during vacations.   Students would provide their own traveling expenses to cities not too far from Northampton and thus could spend their vacations in centers offering some special academic attraction.

At Christmas, invitations to Boston would be most welcome for one student who wishes to study educational institutions there, and for another who is eager to study the Boston and Cambridge art galleries.   A third would like to be near New York for Christmas week.   During Easter vacation, several students would be very glad to visit Philadelphia and Washington to work in the art galleries and the Library of Congress, while another would welcome the opportunity to spend a few days studying an educational institution in Baltimore.   Alumnae interested, by courtesy of the QUARTERLY, are invited to write for further information to the Chairman of the Committee on Exchange of Students.

Another side to the work of the Committee is the task of serving as a bureau of information for Smith students who, as they leave Smith, wish to continue their studies abroad.   The Committee helps these graduates to gain admission to foreign universities, especially in cases where the openings are limited.

And so we begin a new year with eleven foreign students living in our dormitories, teaching the Americans much and learning much in exchange.   That the Americans, at least, value every opportunity for foreign contact is proved by the great numbers who strive to enter the Cosmopolitan Club, many more than can possibly be admitted.   The educational value of the exchange is unlimited, and we hope the numbers of our foreign students will increase as the Committee, with added experience, is able to expand its machinery.

How Did the New Admission Rules Work?

ERNST H. MENSEL

Chairman of the Board of Admission

The editors have learned that an article on the latest developments in the problem of admission to college is indispensable for the fall issue and present the third paper by Professor Mensel on that subject.

THIS article is not a discussion of principles underlying admission to college or of new regulations devised by the Faculty; it is merely a report on the workings of the machinery set up, with special reference to the new features introduced last year, and a brief survey of some phases of the situation as revealed by the make-up of the freshman class.

The new rules that went into effect for the first time this year cover the elimination of all other examining agencies except the College Entrance Examination Board, the abolition of the September examinations for admission, and the introduction of the "scholastic aptitude test." The expectations based on these innovations have been amply fulfilled, more particularly with reference to the first two. The operation of the first new rule has helped to reduce the number of examination periods of which a candidate for admission might avail herself. Regents' grades were accepted through January, but there was no opportunity for anyone to take the May examinations given by another institution and, in case of failure to pass them, make another attempt after a little cramming to show adequacy of preparation in the June examinations of the College Entrance Board. This rule and the second one that does away with the September examinations for admission made it possible for our Board at the July meeting to proceed immediately with the selection of the entire freshman class. The information required was at hand for all candidates and all available places could be filled at once without the necessity of providing for a certain fairly large, but indeterminate number of persons who, not having entered the June examinations or not having completed the requirements at that time, might successfully pass the September tests. This uncertainty regarding the results of the later examinations has always been a source of trouble and has made it difficult to give equitable treatment to all concerned. Not only did these new regulations prove of decided advantage to the various administrative offices, our own, that of the Warden, and that of the Registrar, they were also of benefit to the students whom the College could not admit in acquainting them with this fact in the early part of the summer and in thus affording them the opportunity of seeking admission elsewhere.

Two items of uncertainty, however, could not be eliminated: that of a possible last minute change on the part of students just admitted, and that caused by the withdrawal, during the summer months, of members of the three upper classes —both items of considerable importance inasmuch as the second helps to determine the size of the freshman class, and both affect the exclusion or admission of a number of properly qualified students. In order to take care of these numerical fluctuations, which were to be expected although not in so large a measure as they did occur this summer, the Board of Admission established a waiting list of students who, although not having attained so high a rank as those definitely admitted, had given evidence of ability to do college work in a creditable manner.   This list was carefully compiled on the basis of relative merit, so far as it was humanly possible, and from this list the vacancies that occurred were immediately filled.

The ever increasing number of aspirants for a college education, the limited facilities of the higher institutions and their physical inability to take care of all who wish to come and may seem to be able to profit from what the colleges have to offer, have directed increased attention to the problems of admission and are calling for the best educational guidance and the best available machinery for use in the process of selection.   Whatever means can be found to establish the potential success or failure of an applicant for admission has a claim to careful consideration and possible utilization if it promises to be of actual help in predicting the future worth of a student.   To the category of such means of measurement belongs the "scholastic aptitude test," a test of the type already in use in a large number of institutions and applied to students after entrance to college, called by various names such as "psychological examination," "intelligence test," "mental alertness test."   An examination of this kind has been given for some years past at Smith College; it was this year for the first time administered to those still outside its gates.   It does not suit the purpose of this paper to go into the details of this test; I may say, however, that its adoption by the College is quite in line with the personnel work carried on among our students, the reason for which is to be found in a genuine interest in rendering greater service to the individual student.   The new test was made available through the instrumentality of the College Entrance Examination Board; it was formulated by a committee appointed by the Board and conducted by it in June along with the other examinations in the usual academic subjects.   Mount Holyoke, Vassar, Wellesley, Smith were among the institutions requiring that this test be taken by all their candidates for admission.   It is too early to express a definite opinion on the success of this new venture; its usability, however, has been demonstrated, not as a substitute for other examinations that measure "the adequacy of preparation on a standard scale," nor as a means of exclusion from college—for a low test score does not always mean inability to do college work—but as a supplement to all other information concerning a given candidate.*   In this way the Board of Admission has utilized the data furnished through this test and has found this information particularly helpful in borderline cases and when it was a question of gauging the relative merits of students placed on the waiting list.   Its value will also be apparent for post-entrance personnel work when those with relatively low scores may have to be watched and helped in order to avert possible academic disaster or may have to be weeded out, in good season, as academic misfits, and when the more brilliant student may show signs of falling from her high estate and should be urged to better performance.

"Once upon a time" more than 2000 names had accumulated on our books as those of persons who, in the course of years, had declared their intention, or

---

* The QUARTERLY is promised more data in a later issue. Cf. "The Scholastic Aptitude Test," in *The Work of the College Entrance Examination Board*, 1901–1925. Ginn and Co., 1926.

their parents had done so for them, of entering College this fall. Of a good many little more has been heard. Their number gradually decreased when, in consequence of repeated communications received from the office of the Board of Admission, they were confronted with the necessity of making a decision. For various reasons, often not communicated to us, nearly one-half of them were found to have changed their plans or to be behind in their preparation and desirous of having their names transferred to another year. About 1200 decided to take the final plunge and go in for the examinations, and not quite all of these sent in their records after taking the examinations. The Class of 1930 numbers 630 members; since the examination requirement for admission went into effect, only two freshman classes have been larger, that of 1922 with 638 and that of 1923 with 632. Of this year's class 331 entered by the New Plan, 298 by the Old, one was the special case of a foreign student. It is of interest to notice that the New Plan has gained ground; last year 100 more students entered by the Old Plan than by the New. This preference for the latter method of entrance has always been strong among students coming from the public high schools, while those from the private schools very largely chose the Old Plan which allowed them gradually to accumulate the necessary number of credits; last year private school candidates did so in the ratio of nearly three to one, 66 to 179; this year 118 entered by the New Plan from private schools, 180 by the Old. It is difficult to assign a definite reason for this striking change; it may be connected with the elimination of the Barnard and Bryn Mawr examinations for our candidates and with the discontinuance of the September examinations for admission. If this drift continues in the same direction we may gradually and naturally come to the one method of entrance, that of the New Plan. Of the 630 members of the entering class, 164 had all their preparation in the public schools, 298 were prepared entirely in private schools, and 167 in both public and private schools, and of this latter class by far the greater number had had at least three years in the public high schools so that still at least one-half our incoming students had the larger part of their pre-college training in the public schools.

Two more classes of students should be mentioned, those admitted under the Old Plan with a condition and those coming from other institutions with advanced standing. The Board of Admission has not yet come to the point where it would say that a student is not college material if she has not passed in all subjects in which she was examined, and that the doors of the College should be shut to her. Among such students may be those who have attained excellent grades in some subjects while not reaching a passing grade in a one-unit, rarely a two-unit, subject, or those in whose cases, for good reasons, allowance could be made. A number of such candidates were admitted in July, with the expectation that the deficit should and would be made up before college opened. September examinations were conducted for the removal of these conditions, and 90% of those entering them passed the tests creditably and thereby vindicated the Board's judgment of their ability.

Students wishing to transfer from other institutions have always been a problem both because they had perhaps entered the other institutions on certificate and also because, repeatedly, our experience with such students had not been very satisfactory.   The Board last year adopted rather stringent rules for the admission of students with advanced standing and likewise limited their number. In consequence, we have this year only 32 students of this type entering college, either on examination by the Old or the New Plan, or admitted without examination (16) because they had done their work with distinction at the institutions from which they come.   These advanced standing students represent 26 colleges and universities.

It remains only to give the names of the students who won the two entrance prizes of two hundred dollars each.   The prize for the best record under the Old Plan was awarded to Susan Albright of Buffalo, N. Y., prepared at Miss Hall's School in Pittsfield, Mass., and the Franklin School; the prize for the best record under the New Plan went to Marjorie Lawson of East Orange, N. J., prepared at the East Orange High School, with honorable mention given to Alleen Kelly of Cleveland Heights, Ohio, prepared at the Laurel School, Cleveland.

The Smith College Experimental Schools

Seth Wakeman
Chairman of the Department of Education

SMITH COLLEGE inaugurated a program of experimental education several years ago with the Smith College School for Exceptional Children. This school is intended for public school children with special educational disabilities and children of retarded mental development.   It is conducted by the Department of Education in coöperation with the Board of Education of the city of Northampton under a plan which is somewhat unique.   Each fall the Superintendent of Schools of Northampton makes a report to the Department of Education of all children in the elementary schools of the city who are several years retarded in their school progress.   Members of the staff and graduate students in the Department go into the public schools, examine and study each child that has been reported.   A selection is then made of those children who can most profitably be taught in the School for Exceptional Children.   The present policy is to select from among the children of the first three grades so that the group in the school will be as homogeneous as possible.   For the past three years the work of the school has been most successful under the direction of Miss Frances E. Cheney, the principal.   In the past there has usually been difficulty in persuading parents that a child is in need of specialized educational treatment.   We encountered the feeling that it marked and designated a child in sending it to a special school.   This fall, however, the school has its full number and there have been several unsolicited applications for admission. This, surely, is an excellent criterion of the success of the school for it means that the work of the school in the past few years has been justified by the benefits it has brought to individual children.

In connection with this school, two fellowships of five hundred dollars each are offered to graduate students each year.   The graduate students have, along with the theoretical courses, practical, supervised teaching of a specialized type. The course offered by Miss Cheney is conducted with special reference to the problems of the school, the use of experimental methods in teaching, and the absolute necessity for the study of the individual child. A second course is offered in the Classification of School Children. Here again there is the practical problem with a whole school system as a laboratory.

This fall a second experimental school has been opened—the Smith College Day School. A group of parents had conducted the Northampton Day School in the parish house of St. John's Church. In the spring this school was taken over by the Department of Education. Some necessary changes have been made in Gill Hall and the Day School is now most comfortably and adequately at home there. Instruction is offered to children from five years of age through the work of the Junior High School. Twenty-seven children entered the school when it opened this fall—a most satisfactory number for the first year.

The Smith College Day School is an experimental school of the progressive type. The charge that is often brought against progressive and experimental schools is that the work of such schools is often hazy and vague—at least to the child, if not to the administrator. Parents, we know, sometimes feel that educational experiments are being made at the cost of the proper educational progress of the child. There is no need for this and we hope to demonstrate that the elementary education which is truly progressive, liberal, and experimental is really education of the soundest and most worthwhile type. After all a school is a place for learning! The school cannot now be described in detail: we are working out a course of study and making other definite plans.

The Day School is under the direction of Miss Elizabeth M. Collins, the principal. Miss Collins is offering a course, primarily for graduate students, upon the progressive theory of elementary education. In this school, there are also offered two graduate fellowships of five hundred dollars each for graduate students who carry on their observation and practice teaching under Miss Collins's direction. The teachers in the school are, in each case, thoroughly experienced and trained women who understand the experimental type of education and the problems and responsibilities which progressive experimental education presents to the teacher.

The third venture in experimental education is the project and plan of the Institute for the Coördination of Women's Interests—the Smith College Nursery School. The Department of Education is interested in the educational side of this school and in the experimental and research work. Through a most generous gift to the Institute, two fellowships are offered for study in the Nursery School by the Department of Education and the fellows carry on their graduate work under the direction of the Department. The school, I believe, has already been described by the Institute.* Nursery schools in this country are decidedly experimental in nature and no one, I am sure, would be inclined to make dogmatic assertions about them. There is no doubt of the fact, however, that the nursery school movement is the most important educational development in years. A course is offered by the Department on the Pre-School

---

* The Institute promises an article after the school has been in operation for a few months. It reports an enrollment of 27 and a waiting list.—THE EDITORS.

Child, which includes a study of the physical and mental development of the pre-school child and the theory and educational value of play. The course is conducted with observation and study in the Nursery School.

Smith College is now prepared to offer instruction in education of a type that is rarely found—instruction of a college grade in elementary and pre-school education which is actually based upon the practical work of the school. Educational theory based upon practice is something quite different from the educational theory of the lecture room. Each advanced student is actually observing and teaching and putting the theory and method to the test. In the three schools there is a great range and variability of children and the graduate students concentrating their work in one school will be given opportunity to observe and work in each of the other schools. A graduate student undertakes a problem for investigation which serves as the thesis for the Master's degree.

This year the work is largely with graduate students—an excellent group, two of whom have come from England. We hope, however, as our schools progress, that this will not continue for we are extremely concerned with the problem of interesting college undergraduates in elementary school work. At the present time, women college graduates who wish to teach usually enter secondary school work. The salary offered the college graduate in the secondary school is greater than in the elementary school. This condition is changing and there are signs that in the next few years it will change much more rapidly. A few cities now offer the same salary to the college graduate for teaching in the elementary school as in the secondary school. The newer progressive schools and nursery schools, needing the most capable type of teacher, are now looking for college graduates.

The college graduate feels it to be much less difficult to step into the secondary school and teach the subjects in which she majored in college even though she may be better adapted to and really more interested in younger children. Considering only the fact that the average woman college graduate entering teaching has a rather brief career, it would often be much more valuable and beneficial for her to understand elementary education and to have experience with younger children. Necessary reforms and changes in elementary education need the most intelligent and the most able teachers. It is a real challenge to the women's colleges at the present time. The Smith College Experimental Schools can justify their existence in Smith College if they succeed in interesting undergraduates in elementary and pre-school education.

. . . . .

In this brief article, I am, at the present time, necessarily limited to a mere description of the Experimental Schools. I have left unanswered several questions—Why experimental? Why progressive? These, with Miss Hill's permission, I should like to answer at a later time.

As soon as the schools are organized and the children have become accustomed to visitors, we shall be glad to welcome alumnae as visitors. We would ask, however, that when possible, arrangements for visiting be made with the principals or with me in advance. S. W.

The College in Residence

IN President Seelye's "Early History of Smith College" we read in the chapter in which he outlines the building plans for the College:

Instead of a mammoth structure, large enough to meet both academic and domestic necessities, it was determined to erect one central building exclusively for academic instruction and to group around it, as might be needed, comparatively small dwelling-houses which should be conducted as far as possible like well-ordered private homes.

In other words, from the very outset it was planned to have Smith College a resident college. For a time that hope was realized, but students thronged in larger and larger numbers and before we quite realized it that little phrase, "as might be needed," was entirely snowed under and we found ourselves a college in which from one-third to one-half of our students were living in houses neither owned nor operated by the College—"off-campus houses" as they have been called these many years. We still called ourselves a resident college but deep in our hearts we hoped that no one would contradict us, and not only did we long for the day in which we could hold up our heads and proclaim that in truth as well as in spirit were we a college in residence, but we resolved to do something about it! The answer, as all the world of Smiths knows, was the $4,000,000 campaign and then the Birthday Gift; and now as the College opens for its fifty-second year the words "off-campus houses" are stricken from the *Catalog* and we announce with pride and unspeakable relief that the College can house "on campus"—which means in its own houses and three houses rented and operated by it—1725 students. This is rather more than twice as many as could be housed when President Neilson came in 1917. There are besides, in houses closely affiliated with the College, places for 293 students, and about 35 live at home.

So great is our satisfaction in this condition (although, as the President says, we haven't finished yet, of course) that we have thought it would be interesting to publish a campus map and give sundry details concerning our houses of residence and our methods of administering them. For instance: Where did they get their names? What does it mean when we say Morrow House, and Baldwin, and Ellen Emerson? It is time we knew more definitely the men and women who have been and are such close friends of the College that we have identified their names with our daily living. It is our policy to have fairly equal representation of the four classes in the houses owned by the College, and even in the "approved" houses a great effort is being made to have four-class representation. There are eleven of these approved houses, two of which are houses for self-help students, and two are senior houses. This year will be the last year of their continuance as invitation houses. Although most emphatically favoring four-class houses the Administration recognizes the desire of friends to live together, and for several years past groups of four girls have been allowed to draw for places and "go in," as college vernacular has it, as a group on the lowest number. It is also possible for a girl to change her campus house once during her course. This year, of the

630 freshmen, 545 are on campus—a proportion which a few years ago would have seemed possible only upon the arrival of the millennium.

The material which follows these introductory paragraphs has been prepared with meticulous care. We have searched through *Presidents' Reports* for years back, we have used much data gathered by President Seelye for the QUARTERLY a dozen years ago, and we have severely taxed the patience of the Warden's office with our importunate demand for figures. The "dem'd total" we here submit, sure that when next you return you will find your way about the campus and its environs with a new sense of ownership if you have a little more intimate knowledge of our "comparatively small dwelling-houses" which we are conducting as far as possible "like well-ordered homes."

DEWEY HOUSE (Miss Harriette Kingsley, head) houses 48 students. It was bought by the College in 1871 and named after its former owner, Judge Charles A. Dewey.

WASHBURN HOUSE (Mrs. Mary K. Howes, head) houses 40 students. It was built in 1878 and named for William B. Washburn, LL.D., one of the original trustees appointed by Sophia Smith in her will. Mr. Washburn served the State as Governor and as Senator in Congress and was a liberal supporter of the College.

HUBBARD HOUSE (Mrs. Phebe Mulford, head) houses 48 students. It was built in 1879 and named for George W. Hubbard of Hatfield, also one of the original trustees and the first treasurer of Smith College. It was Mr. Hubbard who induced Miss Smith to change the location of the College from Hatfield to Northampton. At his death he bequeathed the bulk of his property to the College.

WALLACE HOUSE (Mrs. Elizabeth C. Bliss, head) houses 52 students. It was built in 1889 and was named after Rodney Wallace of Fitchburg, for nearly twenty-five years a trustee and generous benefactor. He served the State in the General Court, in the Governor's Council, and in Congress.

LAWRENCE HOUSE (Mrs. Carol N. Cisler, head) houses 62 students. It was built in 1893 and named for Elizabeth (Lawrence) Clarke 1883, an alumnae trustee.

MORRIS HOUSE (Mrs. Helen Pratt, head) houses 50 students. This also was built in 1893 and named for an alumnae trustee, Kate (Morris) Cone 1879.

DICKINSON HOUSE (Miss Alice Eames, head) houses 59 students. It was built in 1894 and named in consequence of a gift of $10,000 from Mr. Samuel Dickinson of Hatfield, as a memorial to his sister, the widow of George W. Hubbard. That the memorials might not be separated, it was placed by the side of the Hubbard House.

TENNEY HOUSE (Dr. Florence Gilman, head) houses 14 students. It was bequeathed to the College by Mrs. Mary Smith Tenney at her death in 1895. Her brother, Justin Smith, had previously bequeathed his share in the undivided half of their estate to the College, on condition that his sister should have the use of it during her life. The house was built in 1710 by Isaac Clark, Mrs. Tenney's great grandfather, and was occupied by four generations of the same family for nearly two hundred years.

TYLER HOUSE (Miss Edith Parmelee, head) houses 61 students. It was built in 1898 and named for Professor William S. Tyler, D.D., LL.D., of Amherst College and father of Dean Henry M. Tyler of Smith. Professor Tyler was the first president of the Board of Trustees. The small house which already stood on the land was retained and called Tyler Annex.

HAVEN HOUSE (Mrs. Louise S. Dake, head) houses 61 students. It was bought in 1898, enlarged, and named for Miss Elizabeth Appleton Haven,

searched through *President's* ...
gathered by President Seelye for the
e have severely taxed the patience of
site demand for figures. The "dem'd
ext you return you will find your way
new sense of ownership if you have
comparatively small dwelling-houses"
"like well-ordered homes."

y, head) houses 48 students. It was
after its former owner, Judge Charles

owes, head) houses 40 students. It
m B. Washburn, LL.D., one of the
Smith in her will. Mr. Washburn
enator in Congress and was a liberal

ord, head) houses 48 students. It
e W. Hubbard of Hatfield, also one of
urer of Smith College. It was Mr.
ange the location of the College from
he bequeathed the bulk of his prop-

Bliss, head) houses 52 students. It
Rodney Wallace of Fitchburg, for
enerous benefactor. He served the
nor's Council, and in Congress.
, head) houses 62 students. It was
wrence) Clarke 1883, an alumnae

) houses 50 students. This also
ee trustee, Kate (Morris) Cone 1879.
...nths, head) houses 59 students. It was
ience of a gift of $10,000 from Mr. Samuel
rial to his sister, the widow of George W.
ght not be separated, it was placed by the

iman, head) houses 14 students. It was
previously bequeathed his share in the undi-
Mary Smith Tenney at her death in 1895.
the College, on condition that his sister should have
e. The house was built in 1710 by Isaac Clark,
two hundred years.
ilth Parmelee, head) houses 61 students. It was
for Professor William S. Tyler, D.D., LL.D., of
of Dean Henry M. Tyler of Smith. Professor Tyler
he Board of Trustees. The small house which al-
s retained and called Tyler Annex.
nuse S. Dake, head) houses 61 students. It was
and named for Miss Elizabeth Appleton Haven,

SMITH COLLEGE
NORTHAMPTON, MASS.
PLAN OF THE GROUNDS
MAY, 1923
THE PROPERTY TO THE COLLEGE
IS SHADED
SCALE OF FEET
TOTAL ACREAGE 87.25

who bequeathed to the College about $50,000 for the benefit of the Astronomy Department. Wesley House, its annex, was acquired on the same property and so named because it had previously been the Methodist parsonage.

ALBRIGHT HOUSE (Miss Alice E. Putnam, head) houses 59 students. It was built in 1900 and named for Mr. J. J. Albright of Buffalo, founder of the Albright Art Gallery there and a generous contributor to the funds of the College.

CHAPIN HOUSE (Miss Lucy Fitch, head) houses 58 students. It was built in 1903 and was named after President Seelye's wife, Henrietta Sheldon Chapin.

SUNNYSIDE (Miss Catharine Koch, head) houses 12 students. It was given to the College in 1906 by its owner, Mrs. John Storrer Cobb, as a place where students and teachers might secure rest and medical care by paying the cost of its maintenance. Since 1921 it has been used as a coöperative house.

BALDWIN HOUSE (Mrs. Margaret Duffield, head) houses 57 students. It was built in 1908 and named after William H. Baldwin Jr., a civic reformer of national reputation and for seven years a valued trustee of the College.

GILLETT HOUSE (Mrs. Ruth Field, head) houses 64 students. It was built in 1910 and named for Edward B. Gillett, LL.D., one of the most talented lawyers of the State and one of the original trustees appointed by Sophia Smith.

NORTHROP HOUSE (Miss Wilhelmina Phelps, head) houses 64 students. This also was built in 1910 and named after an original trustee, Birdseye G. Northrop, LL.D. Mr. Northrop acquired so high a reputation as a member of the Boards of Education of Massachusetts and Connecticut that Japan entrusted to him the education of the first Japanese youths who were sent to this country.

156 ELM ST. GROUP (Mrs. Esther Carman, head) houses 52 students. It consists of four houses: 150 Elm, bought in 1915, 156 and 164 Elm, bought in 1916, and 168 Elm, bought in 1922.

HOPKINS GROUP (Miss Mary T. Bergen, head) houses 53 students. It consists of the three Maltby houses and was bought in 1919–20 and named in honor of Mrs. Elizabeth J. Hopkins, the first lady in charge at the opening of the College in 1875.

SESSIONS HOUSE (Miss Anna E. Preston, head) houses 36 students. It was bought in 1920 and retains the name of its former owner, Mrs. Ruth Sessions.

CAPEN HOUSE (Mrs. Martha B. Parker, head) houses 50 students. The College came into possession of the Capen School property in June 1921, being the residuary legatee of Miss Bessie T. Capen through the terms of her will. There is a small annex to both Capen and Faunce.

FAUNCE HOUSE (Miss Edith Forrest, head) houses 54 students. This also was part of the Capen School, acquired in 1921, and it has retained its former name.

TALBOT HOUSE (Mrs. Alice Palmer, head) houses 67 students. This is the third dormitory acquired in 1921 in the property of the Capen School, and this too retains its old name.

JORDAN HOUSE (Mrs. Margaret McV. Smith, head) houses 71 students. It was built in 1922 and named after Mary Augusta Jordan, Professor Emeritus of English, head of the English Department from 1884 to her retirement in 1921. It includes a small annex, the former Edwards Church parsonage.

ELLEN EMERSON HOUSE (Miss Ellen M. Cook, head) houses 62 students. It was built in 1922 and named for Ellen (Emerson) Davenport 1901, who died in 1921. Mrs. Davenport, among other activities, served as president of the Alumnae Association, member of the Board of Trustees, chairman of the War Service Board, and associate director of the S. C. R. U.

CUSHING HOUSE (Mrs. Marie A. Battis, head) houses 59 students. This is the third of the quadrangle dormitories built in 1922. It was named in honor of Eleanor Philbrook Cushing 1879, Professor Emeritus of Mathematics, who was the first Smith alumna to have a place on the faculty, where she taught from 1881–1922. No one was so long actively connected with Smith College in the whole course of its history as was Miss Cushing. She was also a former president of the Alumnae Association. She died in 1925.

HENSHAW GROUP (Miss Grace Kierstede, head) houses 57 students. It was bought in 1923 from Mrs. Mary V. Burgess, and consists of four houses, two on Elm St. and two on Henshaw Av.

PARK HOUSE (Miss Jean Wylie, head) houses 58 students. It was bought from Mrs. Mabon in 1923–24 and named in memory of the Reverend Edwards A. Park of Andover, a member of the original Board of Trustees. Its annex is the Look house, bought with the Maltby property in 1919–20.

GARDINER HOUSE (Mrs. Marie R. Dugan, head) houses 63 students. It was built in 1926 and named for Harry Norman Gardiner, Professor Emeritus, who retired in 1924 after forty years of service as professor of Philosophy and Psychology.

MARTHA WILSON HOUSE (Miss Kathleen Robertson, head) houses 64 students. This also was built in 1926 and was named in memory of Martha Wilson 1895, who, as president of the Alumnae Association, was instrumental in establishing the Alumnae Council, opening the Alumnae Office, and starting the SMITH ALUMNAE QUARTERLY. She died in 1923.

MORROW HOUSE (Miss Vera Brown, head) houses 63 students. This also was built in 1926, completing the quadrangle, and is named for Elizabeth (Cutter) Morrow 1896, a former president of the Alumnae Association, an alumnae trustee from 1920–26, and now a permanent trustee. Gardiner, Martha Wilson, and Morrow houses are the Fiftieth Anniversary Gift from the alumnae.

DAWES HOUSE (Mrs. Ida Walker, head) houses 31 students. It was bought in 1926 from Mrs. Gertrude Clapp and named in honor of Miss Anna Dawes of Pittsfield, the first woman to serve on the Board of Trustees.

Three houses are rented and operated by the College but privately owned:

22 BELMONT AV. (Mrs. Mary Williamson, head) houses 28 students.
13 BELMONT AV. (Miss Ruth Young, head) houses 30 students.
36 GREEN ST. (Miss Leta Kirk, head) houses 18 students.

There are 293 girls in houses approved by the College but privately owned, as follows:

9 BELMONT AV. (Miss Julia Sherman, head) houses 31 students.
12 BELMONT AV. (Mrs. Mary M. Parker, head) houses 42 students.
84 ELM ST. (Miss Abby Tucker, head) houses 19 students.
26 GREEN ST. (Mrs. Ellen Houghton, head) houses 30 students.
10 HENSHAW AV. (Mrs. Dana Pearson, head) houses 39 students.
75 WEST ST. (Mrs. John Dickerman, head) houses 36 students.
16 BELMONT AV. (Mrs. J. G. Sherburne, head) houses 16 students.
30 BELMONT AV. (Miss Bertha Medlicott, head) houses 18 students.
30 GREEN ST. (Miss Josephine Sellars, head) houses 30 students.
54 BELMONT AV. (Miss Mary A. Peffers, head) houses 16 students.
6 BELMONT PL. (Mrs. John Selden, head) houses 16 students.

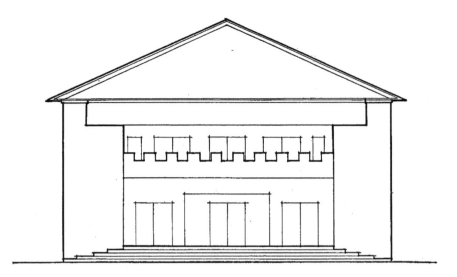

A College Theatre*

SAMUEL A. ELIOT JR.

THERE are two different principles underlying the architecture of theatres devised for educational (rather than commercial or primarily artistic) purposes: one, that of conformity to the best practice in the conventional theatre, so that workers can pass readily from educational to professional dramatics, and playwrights learn to suit their plays to the usual theatre of their time; the other, that of research both into the past and into the future of theatric art, converting the theatre-building into a laboratory for the investigation of and experimentation with all conceivable varieties of drama and theatric expression.

Archeologically, a college theatre should be able to present, without violent distortion, the masterpieces of Greek and Shakespearean drama in something like their original setting, and to approximate the manner of staging of medieval plays, No plays and other Asiatic types.   If it is sufficiently flexible for this, it will need but little more to be flexible enough for futuristic forms and experiments.   The student, whether of playwriting or of production, will have an instrument he can adapt to his fresh vision, not merely one to which he must adapt himself.

Specifically there should be provision for spacious outdoor performances, for behind-curtain productions of the utmost realism, and for before-curtain presentations upon a permanent (but changeable) arrangement of steps and levels, suggestive of the Shakespearean fore-stage but useful for many other sorts of

*ₜThrough the courtesy of *Theatre Arts Monthly* we are reprinting this article from its August issue.   Professor Eliot has revised the article a trifle and appends a paragraph which is addressed particularly to Smith readers. —THE EDITOR.

drama. And these three requirements must be met by a comparatively small building, not only to save expense but because student-performers are disadvantaged when straining for broad technique or "big" effects.

The ideal building I have been thinking out, ever since I began to teach, accordingly has at its rear a sky dome, indispensable for perfectly realistic exterior settings, and at its front a porch and balcony adapted for open-air productions, Greek or modern. Its interior is based on the unique "stage" I was privileged to experiment with as the first director of the Little Theatre at Indianapolis. Let me describe the façade first.

The theatre faces west, or perhaps southwest, to catch the radiance, and the lengthening shadows, of a declining sun. It faces a gradually steepening slope of ground, at the top of which, about 100 feet away, is a building whence searchlights can play upon its front during evening performances. Upon this slope seats would be erected for special occasions, not permanently constructed,— rows of seats terminating in front in a semicircle or an obtuse angle, to leave a level area before the theatre's steps for choric evolutions in Greek plays. For the façade proper is a replica (though far narrower and higher) of the *skênê* built at Athens in 427 B.C. Its front porch, approached by six or seven easy steps, is a "stage" 36 feet long by 10 feet deep. The steps curve forward and at either side bend back against the blank faces of towers (*paraskênia*) that flank the porch. These towers contain the stairs by which are reached not only the balcony of the indoor auditorium but also the two levels on the façade required by such plays as Euripides' "Orestes," and they are pierced, on the side toward the porch, both with a door and with a window useful for lighting and (in comedy) for acting. Twelve feet above the porch is a battlemented upper-stage some six or seven feet deep. (There are panels to fit in the battlements when a straight parapet is more appropriate.) At its rear is a slightly convex wall with five or six French windows—the back wall of the indoor auditorium's balcony. Above this juts out the pediment, from the base of which may hang painted cloths to mask the French windows. The side-towers slant back against the corners of this pediment like giant buttresses, hiding steep stairs by which the floor of the deep pediment may be reached.

This pediment is a modern substitute for the Greek *mêchanê*, by which divinities were revealed in mid-air. Against its concave, sky-blue background may be set life-sized images of the gods who appear in extant Greek plays: patron Dionysus in the middle, for honor's sake, Athena and Apollo on either hand, and so forth, and before the performance begins a living actor may take the statue's place and at his cue advance, gesture, and speak; or otherwise the front of the pediment will be covered with a skyey curtain continuing upward the painted prospect below, which at a word will part or drop to discover a deity standing as upon clouds in a blue void. Perhaps a steam-pipe along the pediment's edge may add an illusive mist—whereon by night beautiful lights may play. On these four levels: before the steps (*orchêstra*), on the main porch, on the walled roof (*episkênion*), and in the lofty pediment (*theologeion*), all the plays of Aristophanes and nearly all of Euripides and Sophocles will find themselves at home, and we know that the earlier plays were revived (sometimes adapted) in this same environment after 427.

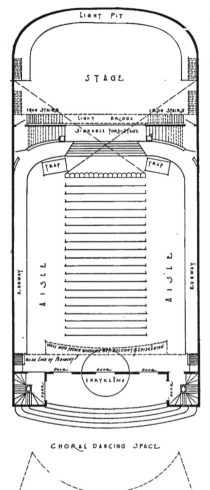

One Greek device, the *ekkyklêma*, remains to be described. It is exceedingly important in Aeschylus, and frequent in Aristophanes. It is set in the middle of the theatre's front wall (the rear wall of the porch or Greek "stage"), and consists of a turntable, 14 feet in diameter, flush with the floor, and half within, half without, the wall. A section of the wall, that is, 14 feet wide by perhaps 9 feet high, is pivoted and revolves *with* the turntable. On the inner half-circle little scenes and tableaux are prepared, or the whole chorus grouped (Aeschylus' "Furies," or Aristophanes' "Thesmophoriazusai" and at cue are electrically swung around onto the outdoor platform, by means of a cable about the disk's circumference, controlled from within. The section of front wall that revolves thus may perfectly well contain a door, and there will be doors on either side of the separate segment.

Passing through these doors into the auditorium, we find a lobby eight or nine feet wide, and then an unbroken mass of seats, with spacious aisles to either side. Instead of the wide auditoriums of most commercial theatres, or the tunnel-like narrowness of many artistic theatres, these seats scarcely extend beyond the sides of the proscenium arch, so that each spectator may see every part of a rectangular stage-set, and yet the room is wide and easeful, with walls that curve toward the proscenium. Between the side-aisles and these walls are the runways—adapted from the "Flowery paths" of the Japanese theatre but here without seats on both sides—four feet wide, and the same height as the stage above the slanting floor between them. They are reached by stairs from below, at the rear corners of the auditorium, and lighted by lamps in the ceiling entirely masked from the central area of seats. Actors passing to and fro on these runways may be seen either against the gray-felted wall or against black or gayer hangings special to the particular play in hand. Whereas in former ages intimacy between performer and spectator was attained by more or less surrounding the former with onlookers, here the compact mass of spectators may have performers on three sides at once.

The front row of seats is a considerable distance away from the curtain.   This not only permits room for elaborate fore-stage arrangements, but simplifies sight-line problems back of the curtain. · Actors within the proscenium-frame, consequently, have less intimate contact with their audience than is usual in our apronless modern theatres, but pictorial illusion and representational objectivity gain.   In the case of realistic plays depending on close contact between actor and spectator—such plays perhaps as Schnitzler's or Pirandello's—ways can be found of bringing both setting and action out onto the fore-stage.

This fore-stage consists of a platform, 25'x5', directly in front of the proscenium.   It is on hydraulic plungers and can be level with the stage proper, or one step lower; or it can sink into the basement and rise again with plastic settings, or properties; or it can stay below, and an orchestra assemble in the resulting pit, concealed from the audience by the permanent steps that link the fore-stage platform and the auditorium floor.   If fore-stage and orchestra are needed simultaneously, the musicians can still assemble underneath, and be heard, albeit muffledly, through openings in the risers of these steps.   To the ends of the steps, at each side, come the runways, affording horizontal access to the fore-stage.   Below and before the ends of the runways, at the foot of the side-aisles, are trapdoors, giving actors an approach to the fore-stage from below (cf. the devil in Hofmannsthal's "Everyman," or the evil angel in Marlowe's "Faustus"); the present stage at Smith College provides such approaches, which have proved often of great effect.   And from the ends of the fore-stage stairways ascend to corner-balconies, accessible from within the proscenium-wall, thus giving a downward approach as well.   Under the balconies, opening upon the runways at the point where they bend sharply toward the fore-stage steps, are doors also connecting with the backstage area.   The parapets of the balconies, some nine inches wide, continue down the stair-sides, with fewer and huger steps, and terminate in solid square posts, five feet high and two feet wide, which are open on their upstage side and provide convenient nooks and outlooks for prompter and electrician.   Leaping down this parapet, to the post-top, and thence to the fore-stage, instead of descending soberly by the stair, may come many a Mercury, Harlequin, or sudden fugitive.   Finally, above the proscenium arch, there is a wide, low aperture, usually closed tight, but openable when actors standing on the light-bridge within wish to look or speak down to the fore-stage eighteen or twenty feet below.   To permit this, the stage-house must of course be high enough to let the asbestos curtain ascend six feet above the light-bridge.   The act-drop, which is pierced at the center and at each side to allow free passage through it between stage and fore-stage, must likewise, hanging as it does between asbestos curtain and light-bridge, descend below the latter and not intervene between it and this window.

Behind these two front curtains, there are structures or drapes at either side, deepening the proscenium as the light-bridge itself does across the top of the arch, or swinging forward to narrow the proscenium frame a trifle, and in either case masking the proscenium spotlights that cluster thickly, one above another, at each side.   From the ends of the light-bridge, narrow iron stairs descend to little iron landings in the downstage corners of the stage-house, where are the doors to the fore-stage balconies, and continue thence, rearward, to the stage

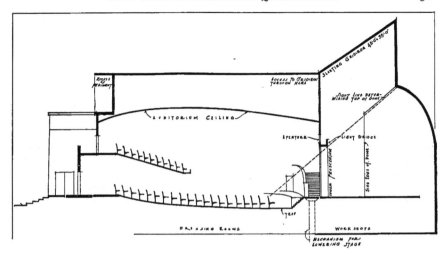

floor and on down into the light-pit that encircles its rear two-thirds. Down-stage of these stairways, under the fore-stage balconies and stairs, are on one side the electrician's storeroom and on the other the room for small properties and tools.. There are no fly-galleries: as in the Guild theatre, the fly-lines de-scend to the stage floor and are worked by counterweights more than by muscular effort. The lines from the rear part of the gridiron, which if they were vertical would be visible against the sky dome, are slanted forward to pulleys downstage of the dome's side, and worked from the side of the stage opposite to the lines from the front half of the grid.

The sky dome is the principal "sight," back-stage. More than 50 feet wide, 30 feet deep, and correspondingly high, it is larger than any dome yet seen in this country. In Germany, before the war, I was made to realize unforgetably the incomparable illusion-value of a solid, domed, plaster "sky"; and in "Cali-ban" at Boston in 1917 I was taught the tremendous expressive value of un-realistic lighting in a dome. Hence, this is the feature in my ideal theatre that I value beyond all others. It is lit partly by lights suspended above, where its top is cut back, but mostly from the five-foot-wide light-pit that separates its bottom from the stage floor. This opening will be useful for much besides: bringing characters, or armies, up over the horizon-line, against the sky; passing up plastic scenery and heavy properties from their storage place under the stage; and in general affording instant access from the stage to the regions below, where are located the workshops and (further forward, under the auditorium) the dressing-rooms and greenroom.

On this stage, equipped both with a dome and with a gridiron as deep as most stages possess, more realism, more subtle lighting effects, more atmosphere, will be possible than on any other stage in America that I have seen. Before this stage, on the diverse levels and various approaches, unrealistic drama of every type can be flexibly and intimately presented, and, by a temporary arrangement of poles and hangings, realistic plays also brought forward into closer relationship with the audience.   And against the classic façade, in the long evenings, Greek plays can be reproduced occasionally with extraordinary truth to the scenic intentions of their authors.   The theatre is an educational instrument of unmatched value, and also a laboratory where new effects can be tried out and a new drama and theatric art brought into existence.

Author's Note.—This article has been revised a trifle, since it appeared in *Theatre Arts.*   I wish that its illustrative drawings could have been revised, too. The façade should have a lower, wider aspect: its pediment less steep, and its sides flanked by low chorus-rooms with *parodos* entrances, level with the lawn. The seating-plan should be more fan-shaped and provide a greater number of orchestra chairs and a wider balcony.   The egg-shaped groundplan thus suggested, rather than this one with parallel side-walls, would also allow more roomy corner-balconies for the actors and more easy stairs to them, besides doubtless a more interesting exterior elevation.   The site at Smith on which I should best like to see this theatre built, is that confronting the Students' Building:—the choral dancing-space at the foot of that gentle hollow, the sky dome backed up into the angle at its eastern end between the main campus thoroughfare and the road that skirts the Alumnae Gymnasium.   The egg-shaped plan fits this plot admirably, and the length of the building, 125 feet, is not such as to intrude upon the great sweep of open ground between the '83 Seat and the Fountain— upon which, indeed, the outdoor audience would be seated just as it is nowadays on Illumination Nights, only facing downhill and eastward, instead of uphill and westward as now.

The Government Under Which We Live

KATHARINE STETSON BINGHAM

President of the Student Government Association

The November QUARTERLY goes with our compliments to the parents of all freshmen, and it is chiefly for them that Katharine Bingham 1927 has explained the ideals, principles, and latest developments of our Student Government.   She is the daughter of Ethel (Stetson) Bingham 1901, and we suspect that her audience will include many hundreds of alumnae who, although not the mothers of Smith daughters, are, nevertheless, keen to keep informed on any "latest developments" of student life.

STUDENT government is no longer an experiment in our schools and colleges, and probably the majority of parents and alumnae have come in contact with this movement.   Some form of student government has existed at Smith for a long time, but we have been organized under our present constitution only since 1919.   This movement is by no means confined to the colleges and most girls have lived under its regulations in school.   Its ideals are similar wherever such an organization is found.   Each group, however, has its own problems, limitations, and immediate goals.   Last year Smith was asked to fill out a questionnaire which included the query, "At what stage of development is Student Government at Smith?"   It proved a particularly hard question to answer, but it also seemed to be one which demanded an answer if we ourselves were to understand the Student Government Association of Smith College.

If we attempt to define the purpose of Student Government at Smith it seems inevitable to quote from our constitution:

The purpose of this Association shall be to encourage active coöperation in the work of self-government; to uphold the highest standards of honor and integrity in matters of personal conduct; to strengthen cordial relations between faculty and students; to make and enforce laws according to the Grant of Powers; to provide for the formation of an official body to give adequate and effective expression to the opinion of the student body in matters of general college interest.

The Grant of Powers referred to was given by the President and Faculty and they "reserve the right to revoke all or any part of these authorizations at any time, if the exercise of them by the Student Government Association shall prove to be unsatisfactory or impracticable."

Furthermore, to understand our problems it is necessary to know a little of the organization and machinery of our government. The legislative power is exercised jointly by the Student Council and House of Representatives. The executive power is vested in the Council and the judicial power in the Judicial Board. The Student Council is composed of 11 members (also the chairman of Judicial Board and the president of the House of Representatives who sit with the Council as non-voting members); the Judicial Board of 8 members; and the House of Representatives of all the house presidents, and in addition one extra representative from each house having thirty students or over, and two extra representatives from each house having sixty students or over. The House elects two of its number to be members of Judicial Board. The other members of Judicial Board and the Council members are elected by the classes, with the exception of the president of Council and the chairman of Judicial Board, who are elected by the Council from nominees presented by the entire undergraduate body.

Representative government is always difficult—it never portrays accurately all opinions, and yet this is not the most trying thing we have to face. Although every student upon entering Smith automatically becomes a member of the Student Government Association, the responsibility is not universally accepted.

When our Grant of Powers was given, the legislative powers assumed a very prominent place. The Student Government Association has power to legislate in practically "all matters not affecting the academic work of the college, its health regulations, its financial affairs, or its relation with the world outside the college." This lawmaking power and the responsibility of law enforcement is the most difficult problem we have to meet.

A community of two thousand necessitates the making and keeping of many rules that would be superfluous in a smaller group. It is the weakest member of the group that we have to consider, and the stronger members, who would be able to take care of themselves without these restrictions, cannot help feeling that certain rules are unjust and unnecessary.

Last spring, Council, with the approval of the House of Representatives, changed the method of law enforcement. Before this the laws were enforced by a very definite Honor System which made every student

(a) On her honor to report herself if she had broken a rule.
(b) On her honor to remind another who failed to report herself for the violation of the rules, of her obligation to do so.

For several years people had felt that this plan was not working as it should, that its implications escaped a great many people, and that in such a very large group as that at Smith, it was not feasible. The Judicial Board was such a very small group that its members seemed to be out of touch with the situation in college, and most of the infractions of rules which were brought to their attention did not come through the working of this Honor System. It did not seem to fulfill the purpose of the organization "to encourage active coöperation in the work of self-government; to uphold the highest standards of honor and integrity in all matters of personal conduct." If, as sometimes happened, the Honor System was flagrantly violated, the power of the Association seemed thereby to be weakened and the morale of the college lowered in other matters. We felt the need of more people who would take a definite responsibility in the operation of the affairs of the Association.

It seems to us that the general statement of the responsibility of Student Government given in the foreword to the Rules and Regulations this year is all that is necessary for any intelligent citizen:

Every student entering Smith College automatically becomes a member of the Student Government Association and as such is required to conform to its rules and regulations. These rules are based on the general principle that every student shall conduct herself at all times in such a way as to uphold her own good name and that of the College. They are framed to insure the safety and general welfare of the student body. These regulations cannot, in the nature of things, be equally acceptable to every student, for they have been drawn up with a view to the interests of the individual as a member of a community, and therefore recognize certain rights of the community over the individual. The obligation of the student to conform to these regulations is not lessened by this consideration. Because the Student Government Association believes that a willing and intelligent support of a few fundamental and comprehensive rules can be given by everyone, it has not attempted to lay down specific rules of conduct. In situations not explicitly provided for the student should be guided by the principles upon which the rules are based.

It is obvious from this statement that any change in the machinery of our government in no way relieves the individual of personal responsibility in regard to the support of the rules of the Association.

We have, however, made plans for a more important house government. There are to be House Councils which are to deal with certain disciplinary matters in their own houses and to be responsible for the general attitude of the house toward Student Government. The House Council of any house is composed of approximately 10% of its members headed by the house president. The other members are elected by the Student Council from nominations made by the house. It is hoped that these House Councils will not only act as judicial bodies, but will be the group to which suggestions may be brought, and the center of many new house interests and enterprises. They will work and coöperate with Council. It is believed that they will foster a more general interest in the affairs of the Association. It is extremely necessary to have a centralized government, but without frequent reports from many interested subordinate groups, a Student Council of thirteen cannot adequately judge of the opinion of the whole, nor can it have an intelligent idea to what extent the Association is supported. We are constantly seeking new methods for binding the students more closely to the Association, and these House Councils are thus being inaugurated to strengthen the organization and put it on a firmer footing.

This is a definite delegation of judicial authority, and for that reason not capable of being handled by the House of Representatives. President Neilson, at first chapel, made it clear that very often it was difficult for the Administration to stand behind the policies of the Student Government Association. The Administration bears the brunt of the criticism which our mistakes or apparent mistakes bring forth, and he showed quite clearly the obligation which lies with each student to uphold the highest standards of student government in order that the total result may be of the highest order.

The Student Government Association has a very different side from that of a purely judiciary and lawmaking body. It does "strengthen the cordial relations between faculty and students" and it hopes more and more to act as an official body "to give adequate and effective expression to the opinion of the student body in matters of general college interest."

This is the second year that we have made a special effort to reach the freshmen. A great many of the infractions of rules came through absolute ignorance of the rules and general lack of interest in them. A commission of thirty seniors, chosen by Council, is intrusted with the responsibility of teaching the rules to the freshmen. The freshman class is divided among this group and they meet several times for reading and discussion of the regulations. At the end of a certain period the freshmen are given an examination. The questions are all of the problem type—given a situation, they are expected to indicate the proper course of action. Every girl is required to pass this examination, for it is the only way we have of assuring ourselves that the freshmen know the rules which they are $e_xpe_cte_d$ to keep.

We wonder at what stage of development Student Government is at Smith, and the question with which we started seems very pertinent. It is without doubt in a transitional state. Before the ideal for which Student Government is working may be attained, it is inevitable that we pass through many experiments. We hope that our latest step will make it easier for us to reach this goal, by making Student Government a more vital issue to the student body.

Epitaph for a Perfect Lady

She was majestic and tall,
She always kept an appointment,
She considered the feelings of all,
Even the fly in the ointment.

ELEANOR GOLDEN 1926, *from the 1926 Class Book*

"O 1930, to You We Sing"

MARY L. CLARK

President of the S. C. A. C. W.

IT was with qualms, as well as with great hopes, that the S. C. A. Welcoming Committee awaited the arrival of the twenty-five freshmen coming early for the Christian Association Conference. The few freshmen who had already come to Hamp for examinations seemed to have passed beyond the range of mere "welcoming," and were ready, rather, to learn the next lesson about Smith and Smithites. So we played games and danced, and discovered, by the way, a great deal of talent in these sub-freshmen. But Friday morning the Committee, arrayed in white and badges, were more than eager to begin the real work of meeting trains. The Class of 1930 still seemed so nebulous a quantity that it was not until we had actually met and registered most of the Conference freshmen that we breathed a sigh of belief.

The Conference for Incoming Freshmen had been planned by the S. C. A. C. W. Cabinet late in the spring last year. It grew out of our conviction that there was a need of spiritual awakening on the college campus. We hoped that by really coming to know twenty-five out of the six hundred newcomers, and by acquainting them with the many branches of the Christian Association work in the college, we might have a responsible and responsive unit to work with through the year, and might gain a new vision with them of how this freshman class might help to "deepen the Christ-life in the college." The problem of membership in the Conference was a large one. We wrote to the heads of the schools sending the greatest number of girls to Smith this year, asking them to recommend girls who would be interested and able to attend the Conference. So much for the preliminaries.

On Friday, September 24, they came. And we were sure, once for all, that there was most certainly going to be a Class of 1930 with strength and personality all its own. The Welcoming Committee and the Conference members were entertained together at Wallace House. Our real début was the welcoming tea Friday afternoon, open to all freshmen then in Northampton and to their parents and friends. Friday evening came the first Conference meeting, at which Mrs. Scales gave the group a welcoming word, and the President of Student Council, the head of Welcoming Committee, and the President of S. C. A. C. W. spoke. Mr. Darr, minister of the First Congregational Church, led us in a splendid devotional talk. The meeting over, we danced and sang and laughed, and finally went home after singing together "Alma Mater." Saturday morning Mr. Welles, minister of Edwards Church, spoke to the group

EDITOR'S NOTE.—There were no fall "exams" as in other years to harrow the souls of would-be freshmen and their sympathetic older sisters, who welcomed them with one hand while preparing to pack their trunks with the other should the Board of Admission be adamant, and so the task of the Welcoming Committee this year was one of pure joy. There are few alumnae who are not familiar with the usual work of this committee, but the creation of the Freshman Conference is entirely new. The drawing is by Saraellen Richardson '27, a member of the Committee.

about the need of a renewed God-consciousness on the campus, and of the opportunity open to these freshmen to accomplish all things. Then the President of S. C. A. told of the different departments in the Association. Through the kindness of friends the group was then able to divide up and actually to see the Children's Home, Alms House, and Old Ladies' Home where the Social Work is carried on. We learned a great deal in those two short hours.

Saturday afternoon we discussed, formally and informally. We also took a tour of the campus, teaching names and places to the freshmen who were to act as an extension of the Welcoming Committee on Monday. And such a revelation of our upper class ignorance as it was! The Sorbonnites, especially, felt like freshmen raised to the nth degree. But we all felt superbly proud of our lovely campus. After supper, in the cool of the evening, we walked up to the home of one of the professors for an evening of stunts and games, closing with a simple candle-light service.

The Weatherman got out of the wintry side of bed Sunday morning. Nevertheless, we bundled up and went in groups to the different town churches. It afforded an opportunity for the freshmen to meet the ministers and to begin to feel at home in coöperating with the churches. Sunday dinner was an impressive occasion, in true collegiate style. Sunday afternoon the group that had become so well acquainted in this very short time spread to the four ends of the campus to settle in their permanent college homes. We came together again for an afternoon service addressed by Mr. Harlow, and a Sunday night sing at the home of Mr. and Mrs. Welles.

The rest of the 630 came on Monday; but no sudden influx of college girls could affect the thermometer's December aspect. Trains were met, and the white badges saved us from congealing completely when we happened to offer our services to a sophomore—or a senior! A few freshmen "had learned almost everything in prep school, and expected to make up for any lack now by experience." Others were "more than ready to call on Mrs. Scales," and take the President out to tea. There was the pressing question of whether they must suppress school sweaters, pins, and badges. But all these lesser matters faded into insignificance when they accepted the challenge to heroism, and, despite the cold, were willing to consume ice cream on the steps of Studes. The icy atmosphere around and within only made a more striking contrast to the warm welcome afforded them by the Committee and the Conference.

It is in the coming college generation that the value of this Freshman Conference will be tested. Will 1930 have a head start on true evaluations, leadership, peace, and power? We believe it will, and we will vision a like opportunity for 1931.

Cologne Cathedral

Here the faint pealing of a distant bell
Speaks the performance of a miracle.
Here, by a crucifix and flickering lights
He stands, bewildered by the solemn rites.
He hears, through aisles of stone, as in a dream
Winds of New England and a tumbling stream.

BETH MacDUFFIE 1920

Juniper Lodge—a Question and an Answer

IT was with some trepidation that the new Faculty Committee took up the management of Juniper Lodge for the season of 1926. Each member had served as Faculty Resident under Miss Cutler and knew that she had been the heart and soul of the enterprise. She was to be abroad and not available even for consultation in an emergency. But the history of the season bears out, as applied to Miss Cutler, the saying that the test of a really great organizer is that his work can go on without him.

Each season two or three members of the household seem to have justified the whole enterprise—the exhausted student with no home to turn to, whom a whole summer of rest and milk and eggs finally put on her feet, or the young faculty members who, after doing graduate study and teaching simultaneously, caught their breath there for fresh summer work. Of no less import was the testimony of a student who came half worn out with a piece of unfinished work and who said she had never found a place where she could turn off work so easily.

But when the managing committee is asked not only for rosy stories but for an answer to a reasonable question, it welcomes the opportunity.

One of those reasonable questions is, "Are we being asked to raise money to board at less than cost certain people who might pay the full cost?"

Our answer begins with an explanation of the eligibility list. In carrying out Mr. Reynolds's wish, the committee may fill the house from
1. Graduate students at Smith College.
2. Smith women doing graduate work at Smith or at other colleges.
3. Women graduate students at Yale. (This last class does not enter into our financial problem as the cost of their maintenance is fully covered by the Reynolds fund at Yale.)

How recent in the past or how immediate in the future the graduate work must be, is determined by the committee, which is also allowed to fill unexpected vacancies from outside the panel.

The residents drawn from classes 1 and 2 will then be either
a. Smith Fellows whose board is paid by the chairman out of the fund, or
b. Residents who pay their own board—at the present rate, $10 per week.

It is evident that $10 covers only table board and a minor share of operating expenses. The "overhead"—taxes, insurance, major repairs—for groups a and b alike, must be met out of the fund.

Probably no one objects to meeting this deficit for students who can really pay no more. But where shall this line be drawn? What of the student who can indeed lay up fifty dollars for a two weeks' vacation, but who really needs five weeks at ten dollars? What of those who need our type of leisure and quiet and cannot buy it elsewhere for any money? Other things being equal, financial need has the right of way. But we share the difficulty of our own and other colleges in assessing costs on a sliding scale of financial ability. Even on a correct theory we shall make mistakes in practice. But so far the generosity of individuals who thought they were getting too much for their money has generally outrun any reasonable expectations—though in telling this we are violating their confidence.   JULIA HARWOOD CAVERNO

WHAT ALUMNAE ARE DOING

A Part-time Psychologist with a Family

JOSEPHINE DORMITZER ABBOTT

Mrs. Abbott graduated in 1911; she has five children of her own besides a stepson, and will receive her M.A. in psychology from Radcliffe in February. This statement surely justifies us in saying that she is "coördinating women's interests." She has been working for her degree as a part-time psychologist (twenty hours a week) at the Judge Baker Foundation in Boston since February under the Department of Social Ethics at Harvard; Dr. Richard Cabot directing from Harvard and Dr. Healy supervising at the Foundation. From September to February she will work at the Foundation under the direction of the Department of Psychology at Harvard.

WHAT I have to say on this subject might well be rewritten from an entirely different point of view, namely, from the angle of the Coördination of Women's Interests as demonstrating the type of part-time work which may be undertaken by a woman running a home and family. In fact, the more married one is, and the more children one has, helps decidedly in this particular field, for here is the opportunity to amalgamate all one's knowledge and experience, practical and theoretical. The greater one's understanding of normal children, the more readily can one enter into the behavior problems of delinquent and adolescent youth.

The essential requirements for such a part-time position—the minimum time being twenty hours a week—are first of all a smoothly running household and healthy, well supervised children, plus an understanding and coöperative husband. Then, in addition, a course in Mental Measurements and practical work in Clinical Psychometrics and, as added valuable background, a course in Abnormal Psychology. Having once acquired the technical training necessary, one is sufficiently equipped to start in on this field.

Perhaps just a word about the Judge Baker Foundation may not be out of place at this point. This Foundation was established about ten years ago as a memorial by his friends to Judge Baker—the first Judge of the Juvenile Court in Boston. Here are studied "educational, vocational, and conduct problems of young people who are brought for study by parents or who come through the Juvenile Court, school, and all types of agencies which deal with the young. Aiming to make extensive and all round studies, its staff comprises those working from the standpoint of psychological, medical, and social sciences."

In detail there are employed three full-time and two part-time psychologists (to which latter group the writer belongs), three social service workers, two to three doctors, usually from the Rockefeller Foundation, a psychoanalyst, and two psychiatrists. The actual time I have spent per week at the Foundation has been one whole day, from nine to five, and three half days from either nine to one or one to five, a minimum of twenty hours per week. This is a more easily adapted program for a housekeeper than might at first appear, for it allows plenty of time at home in which to catch up with domestic duties.

It would be sufficient inspiration alone to work under the supervision of such master minds as those of Dr. Healy and Dr. Bronner but, in addition, one acquires an infinite variety of experience and an insight and knowledge of human life that is in itself a never to be forgotten acquisition. All the previous experiences in social case work or other varieties of social service, and all the accumulated knowledge one can store up from any source whatsoever, stand here in good stead as background upon which one may draw for possible solutions of the perplexing problems which are constantly presenting themselves for solution, for direction, prognosis, and counsel.

To the psychologist at the Foundation is given a very definite and important piece of work. Hers is the duty of administering to each child the various tests comprising what is called there the Minimum Schedule. These consist of tests for learning ability (of auditory and visual rote), of tests for motor coördination, for manual dexterity, for social and moral apperceptions, for school work, for speed and accuracy, for common sense information, and of course include as well the Stanford Binet Test for mental levels and intelligence quotients. The tests generally take about two and a half hours to administer. If special abilities or disabilities are noted, further testing is given in order to find out in which capacities the child excels. The contrast between the psychological point of view at the Judge Baker Foundation and that of a Psychopathic Hospital is most interesting. Having been working in both places this winter at the same time, the different angles were most apparent. At the latter place, mental retardation and psychotic symptoms were of paramount importance for the mental diagnosis. At the Judge Baker Foundation, on the other hand, the best mental abilities and qualities were those of most interest; and all this evidence was formulated with a view to preventing delinquencies and explaining behavior problems and anti-social attitudes; the mental make-up being just one of the aspects relating to the whole problem of adjustment. Social, hereditary, and physical causes are of equal value, and all these together lead to the summary by Dr. Healy of each case on its own merits, as to direct causation, progress, and ameliatory measures.

This field offers a distinct challenge to any one interested in the personal equation and in studying the problems which beset youth—youth in conflict with tradition, with social customs, and with restrictions superimposed by family attitudes and moral conventions. The more one has to bring to it, the more one can abstract from it, which of course is a truism applicable to any sphere of social, case, or philanthropic work.

After the tests have been administered, the psychologist is responsible for obtaining from the child his own story; that is to say, his own account of the particular situation in which he finds himself the subject for study. We try by sympathetic understanding, by tactful questioning, and by a friendly, coöperative, unjudicial attitude to see the situation as through the eyes of the child, to sympathize with him in his lack of being understood, to see the lure of bad companions as they appeal to him, to realize how slightly ambushed are the pitfalls which surround us all—all of us who, except by the Grace of God, might be in his shoes—a terrified, misunderstood little child who has in some unaccountable way offended against the social or moral laws of society. To be really efficient in this field one must have a real love for children, a sympathetic understanding of childhood and the problems of adolescence, the ability to recognize traits not normal which might possibly later develop into a psychosis, to become again a child but with an adult point of view. The point of view must be a scientific one, however, not swayed by maudlin sentiment and warped by foolish, unwise sympathy; but one looking for points to strengthen in the child's character, obstacles to avoid, and a synthesis of abilities which will make reconstruction possible.

If the child is inhibited, these inhibitions must be overcome in order that his overburdened heart may find release and that he may pour out into sympathetic ears all the troubles that beset him. Rarely do we meet a child who will not become friendly and, after realizing that we are there to advise, counsel, and direct, not to censure and condemn, talk about his problem with ease.

The psychologist also assists in recording for the Doctor the child's physical condition. At the staff conferences which are held three times a week, the cases are presented and summarized according to the evidence as presented by the psychologist, doctors, and social workers. The Juvenile Court cases are always given precedence as the sentence is suspended by the judge pending the findings and recommendations of the Foundation. Cases vary in age and variety from six to seventeen years and from petty larceny to serious moral and anti-social offenses. There are four distinct headings under which the cases may be classified: (1) Court Cases, (2) Educational, (3) Vocational, (4) Behavior Problems. We have special tests for these of differing types of vocational ability, clerical, mechanical, and so forth, tests for non-readers, for defective hearers, too numerous to mention here.

There is much opportunity at the Foundation for original research, especially in the field of behavior problems of school children, which is the writer's special objective and very naturally works in well with a home laboratory of five active children. To illustrate what I mean by individual research, I might cite the following cases: a boy was sent to us by a teacher in one of the ungraded classes to see if we could tell her how best to handle him. In her opinion he was not only deficient mentally, but a very trying behavior problem as well. He had lately made two vicious attacks upon children, one with a knitting needle and the other with a knife. She felt at her wits' end. Upon careful study, we discovered that he presented a very definite picture of schizophrenia —a positive psychosis—which warranted hospital commitment. His stereotyped responses, his mental blocking on visual designs and imagery, his phantasy formation, his hallucinations, both auditory and visual, and his withdrawal from reality, all were conclusive evidences of his mental unbalance.

Another time a girl came in to us for vocational advice as she was unable to keep a position more than a few weeks at a time. What really was the basis of this instability was a very definite inferiority complex of which she was entirely unaware. By careful analysis we were able to trace its psycho-genetic origin and definitely to help her to overcome it. There are too many varieties of cases to begin to enumerate them but they are all interesting and most of them afford definite chances for help.

For a concrete example of the practical value of such an experience, one has only to see with what ease one can abstract herself from her immediate relationship as a mother, and view her children with a critical, impartial eye; thus seeing things in their true relationships in spite of the "close up" which four home walls tend to create. The ability to recognize symptoms of adolescent rebellion when they appear and not to misconstrue tendencies which have no deep import, is a great help to any mother. I recommend most heartily this field—the psychological and psychometric one—for anyone interested in the guidance of young people. There is never any monotony, but an ever changing procession of life's cross sections all equally fascinating and worthy of intense and constructive study.

To have been allowed this opportunity—the first time it has been done for credit from Radcliffe toward a Master's degree in Psychology—is a most inspiring experience and I am deeply grateful both to the Departments of Psychology and Social Ethics which have allowed me credit for this work, and to Dr. William Healy and Dr. Augusta Bronner, the heads of the Foundation, for their interest and coöperation in making this venture possible.

Smith Women on School Boards

Data compiled by Eleanor L. Lord 1887

ALTHOUGH the alumnae biographical blanks did not call for information on the point, further search in the QUARTERLY class news items discovered at least seventeen alumnae who are now members of school boards or have recently served in that capacity. A brief questionnaire drew forth some very interesting comments upon their experiences.

Geographically, three alumnae have served in New England, five in New York or New Jersey, two in the south, five in Ohio and Illinois, and one on the Pacific Coast. Three report from rural villages, six from large cities, eight from suburban or residential communities. Seven have served more than one term, three have been chairman of the board, one having been president since 1922, and this in a city and university center of 190,000 inhabitants with a school population of 28,000; while another in a smaller community has had full responsibility for months at a time when the other two members were away.

All have served as members, in several cases chairmen, of committees in charge of such matters as the engaging of teachers, salaries, buildings, curriculum, housing of teachers, lunch room, textbooks, and provision for meeting college entrance requirements. The question, "Have you been able to push any measures that the men members would perhaps not have been interested to put through?" elicited some interesting replies too detailed for quotation here. Among the measures mentioned were: medical inspection, provision for physical education and athletic equipment for girls as well as boys, contacts with museums of art and natural history, cheap tickets for orchestral concerts, improvement in sanitation and up-keep of buildings, safety of children on the streets and in the school yard, improvement in the caliber of teachers (in one case through the requirement of physical examinations), better accommodations for teachers, "equal pay," and in one town the appointment of a much needed supervisor of home economics. Apart from committee work, several alumnae report that through interest and activity in Parent-Teacher Associations and Mothers' Clubs they have been able to bring teachers, school board, parents, and pupils into closer and more sympathetic relations—no small contribution to educational progress.

All but two of the Smith women were elected by popular vote in town meeting or on regular party tickets in municipal elections. In one city the board is appointed by the mayor and in another by commissioners. In one wealthy and progressive New York suburban village candidates are nominated by a committee composed of representatives of the town group, the Woman's Club, and the Parent-Teacher Association. In spite of this plan, however, the present Smith member does not consider the status of women members especially favorable, since "the essential plans are pretty well worked up by the business members and the business manager previous to the meetings, the trend being for women to be of a Victorian meekness," although there is free discussion and women are listened to, especially in matters of health or ethics. As to the status of women on school boards, opinions and experiences differ somewhat. Most of the writers appear to believe that matters of a strictly business nature such as those concerned with building contracts and the like should fall to the men, but that the women are at least as much concerned as the men with the appointment of teachers, the curriculum, sanitation, health, safety, lunches, planning of buildings, and in most cases better fitted to pass upon these matters since they have more time to visit schools, investigate conditions, study educational trends, and deal with parents who need soothing. As one alumna points out, changes in instruction or course of study, problems of overcrowded buildings or classes make far less impression upon a business man's board than the addition of a few cents to the school tax. The traditional attitude appears in one report which says: "We have no woman member on our board at present, owing chiefly to the fact that an extensive building program promised so much responsibility that no woman who would be sufficiently competent could be induced to accept the office." To balance this an alumna from a much smaller town writes: "I went on to the board in order to build a new school house. With the hearty support of my fellow members we got through a bond issue of $10,000—the first which had ever been passed in the community for any purpose—and built an up-to-date four-room school, and a two-room school for the colored children."

Not all women members are college graduates, of course, but all the Smith members agree that there is great need of women in this field of public service and that it is especially important for college women, who of all others should be best qualified by training and experience, to take advantage of every opportunity to serve on the school board of their community. Six of the Smith alumnae reporting were graduated in the nineties and the others between 1905 and 1914 and all but one are married women. This seems to show that for those who once taught or whose children have ceased to be in constant need of parental oversight, service on a school board offers an unusually congenial and valuable activity for the continuance or revival of educational interests. Prejudices and customs of an almost medieval darkness survive in some quarters and there is need of courage and tact. One Smith woman dealing with an inconceivably ignorant and prejudiced rural board was unable to secure vaccination or to abolish corporal punishment by means of *an end of rubber hose kept in the desk of every principal and teacher.*

The testimony even of this random group would seem to substantiate the claim of one alumna that in many communities "college women constitute the progressive local element and from them must come new ideas." The following excerpts will indicate the importance of this form of civic service for college women and the changing attitude with respect to their appointment.

"Some non-college graduates could probably have done as well as I have, but college women seem to be more willing to undertake responsibilities. Last June the Smith commandment, 'Thou shalt not shirk,' was emphasized. It is a good commandment for every member of a community."

"I believe the greatest improvement in school boards that could now be made would be to have at least half of them women. . . . In our village it is the women who are interested in educational activities."

"During my eight years of service I was a member of many sub-committees— in fact, the tendency was to give me too much to do, first, because I had leisure (being only a housewife and the mother of four children!) and, secondly, because the men had confidence in me. I really feel that I made a contribution to a growing school. In addition, my four children were in the school and my ambition that they should have the same if not better opportunities than a private school could give in courses of study, citizenship, and democracy made me eager to investigate at every opportunity."

"In this town it is almost a liability to admit a college education. I ran as an independent candidate without pledge or commitment, was backed by the best people (educated) of town, and by a narrow margin led the field. It makes an interesting situation."

"We give permanent tenure to a teacher after three years' service and I feel it is a very necessary step to know the teacher and her (or his) qualifications before giving her to the town for life. I feel that work on the teachers committee is valuable because I can spare the time to visit the classes. The men with whom I am associated could not be nicer. They are interested in my point of view and there has never been a disagreeable moment in our relations."

"I retired with many regrets as the work was the most interesting I have been engaged in since leaving college, but it is too big a job to be half done."

"As chairman of the Vocational Training and Trade School I am making an intensive study of trade training for the sub-normal. The girls would surely suffer if there was no woman interested, as the men think only in terms of boys or that dressmaking is the only trade a girl is interested in."

Leisure Made Profitable

MARY GREENE PATCH

Mrs. Patch, Smith 1893, has found an occupation for her leisure hours which, once understood, should make a strong appeal to many home-keeping alumnae. She tells us that although
still a novice at Braille transcribing she is convinced that it offers an opportunity for real social
service and is at the same time an engrossing way of occupying leisure moments.

"Won't you help the blind?"

THIS question was asked me by a friend several years ago. I replied that
I'd be glad to do so but that I could not, being unable to give instruction
in any handicraft or money to support the work. When informed that the
request meant only using part of my leisure to transcribe into Braille reading
matter for the blind, I consented at once, and was soon launched in what has
proved so fascinating an occupation that it is often difficult to keep it from
interfering with other duties.

Very little preparation is required for the work. A few lessons to master
the Braille group or cell are given free of charge by the Red Cross, through
correspondence or, where possible, a local teacher, their Braille manual being
used as a textbook. This cell consists of six raised dots arranged in parallel
rows three high and two wide. Each Braille character is formed by one or more
of these dots and occupies a full cell space. They represent single letters,
groups of letters, numerals, and punctuation marks. On completing the course
of lessons a test article is written and sent to the headquarters in Washington.
In a short time a certificate arrives and, as an accredited transcriber, the pupil
begins her work—short stories or magazine articles at first, books, when more
experienced.

Although the necessary equipment cannot be carried in a pocket, like the
ubiquitous war-time sock, many odd moments at home can have a few lines
of Braille to show for themselves if the work table is always ready. Mine
stands by a window from which I can see anyone approaching the house, and
during frequent waits for a friend who has no sense of time, I find Braille a
satisfactory outlet for my feelings.

Braille is done by hand either with a writer or with a stylus and a small metal
slate, the sheet of heavy paper being clamped to a backboard on which the
slate is adjusted. It is well to decide between them at the outset, as it is confusing to change later, because with the slate the reverse side of the paper is
toward one and the characters are punched from right to left, the arrangement
of the dots being reversed. The Braille writer is used like an ordinary typewriter. It has six keys, one for each dot, and all the dots of a character are
made simultaneously, so that it has the advantage of speed, and is also less
trying to the eyes. On it an expert can do from ten to twelve pages in an hour;
but it is expensive, the cheapest type being $35.00 as compared to $1.90 for a
slate on which from four to six pages can be done in the same length of time.

Personally, I find it more satisfactory to write only two pages on my slate and to reread each carefully before starting the next. Accuracy is the first requirement in transcribing. There is no way of inserting an omitted letter or punctuation mark. With an eraser—a blunt piece of metal shaped like a short pencil—dots can be flattened and small mistakes corrected, but one must always bear in mind that the future reader is to *feel* the page, not *see* it.

My constant companion while working is Funk and Wagnall's "Standard Dictionary." One might well wonder why a dictionary is necessary when merely copying from a printed page. The reason is this: a contraction can be used only when all the letters which it represents are in the same syllable. Early in my work, I wrote "even-ing" as Webster, my former guide, gives it, but the "Standard Dictionary" has "eve-ning," so the use of the "en" sign was incorrect. Since that experience, I look up every doubtful word. One mistake may necessitate rewriting the entire page.

While volunteers do all the transcribing, the proof reading is usually done by the sightless, to many of whom the small sum thus earned is a great help—yet not so much, perhaps, as the pleasure of taking an active part in the work. After the proof reading, each page is shellacked on the reverse side to strengthen it. The pages are then bound eighty to one hundred in a volume. An average novel makes from seven to nine volumes, while Thomas Hardy's "A Pair of Blue Eyes" is in twelve.

Braille takes its name from a Frenchman, Louis Braille, who, with his system of dots in relief, gave books to the blind nearly a century ago. After much changing and adapting, the form now used in this country, known as Grade One and a Half, was adopted in 1917. The first volunteer Braillists in America were enlisted to increase the number of books available for the soldiers at Evergreen Hospital near Baltimore, who were blinded in the World War. The Red Cross was interested and several chapters began transcribing. Then in 1921 the National organization assumed responsibility for the rapidly growing work, and Headquarters, with a Director of Braille, were established in the Library of Congress. Braille volumes ready to bind are sent from all over the country to this Room for the Blind, and they are mailed by the Government to ex-service men anywhere in the United States. In some large cities the public library contains a collection of over a thousand such books for their local needs. There are states also, like California, where transcribers can send their work to the capitol, there to be bound and circulated through the state library.

There is a so-called press Braille, embossed with a stereotyper on metal sheets from which not to exceed forty impressions can be taken, but the cost of such work is so great that very few books could be supplied if no hand copying were done by volunteers.

Much time and effort have been spent in trying to find some method of transcribing two or more pages of this hand copied Braille at a time, but thus far no device has been wholly successful. Even if one should be found, I am sure the call for more workers would be as insistent as it is now, and I am equally sure that anyone who will devote even a little time each day to Braille will find it splendid drill in concentration and patience, as well as a real pleasure. So I repeat the question that was put to me, "Won't you help the blind?"

Making Jam for the Railroads

Janet Mary Burns

Since 1915 Janet Burns, Smith 1896, has been engaged in the fascinating business of making jams and jellies, and now she is supplying the dining-cars of six railroads with jam and marmalade. Look for her label, ye peripatetic alumnae! She tells us that last year she had about 1496 pounds of oranges and grapefruit and about 2486 pounds of marmalade. She works in her own home in St. Paul and only in rush times does she employ more than one assistant.

ONCE upon a time, after living for many years in an apartment, we moved into a house—a house with grounds for a garden. What is more attractive than a house and garden enclosed by a hedge? That had long been one of my dreams and, wishing to pay for the garden and hedge myself, I decided to take orders for orange marmalade, the kind my mother and my grandmother had made for many years. Mother had made it not only for her family, but often filled orders at Easter time that her Easter offering might be more generous. Both garden and hedge were planted and they and the business, which financed them, have had a more or less checkered career during the last twelve years.

I little realized, at the time, that I was starting out on a vocation as professional cook, but the people who bought the marmalade began to ask for currant jelly, raspberry jam, pickled and brandy peaches, and so forth, and soon I had to have a separate kitchen and storeroom, so as not to monopolize the family stove and preserve closet. Gradually the number of fruits grew until, one year, I discovered on my little printed folder that there were 37 varieties, not far short of Heinz's famous 57.

One July I received an order from one of the clubs for fifty 5-lb. crocks of currant jelly. Currants had already been in the market for some time; I did not feel sure that I could get enough to complete the order, but I succeeded in doing so. Never had I seen anything "jell" in such large containers and I used to wake up in the night in agony for fear it had not stiffened, and early in the morning I would go down to test my sample glasses. Evidently the jelly was sufficiently firm, for the large jars still go every year to the club, though not so many as before prohibition became the law.

During the summers of 1917 and '18, when housewives could not get the necessary amount of sugar and many did not have maids to help with their preserving, my kitchen was busy from ten to fifteen hours a day, usually six days a week, and many of those days the thermometer outside was over 95 degrees. I never tested it within.

Those summers were quite thrilling. The fruits seemed to vie with each other to see which one could be done first and which could cost the most. There was much red tape necessary in order to get the required amount of sugar and heartbreaking prices to pay for it.

Quite early in the work, I began to fill individual jars and one of my cousins, appreciating the advantage of making the package as attractive as possible, had some charming labels designed for me, for both large and small jars. For many years I filled gift boxes and baskets for the Christmas trade, shipping many to the soldiers in France. That was before the days of the "Shop Early" slogan, and many a time have I worked till two or three o'clock in the morning filling hurry calls the last few days before Christmas.

In the fall of 1916 I received my first order for marmalade for the dining-cars of the Great Northern Railroad, and in all these ten years but one month has passed without my receiving at least one order from them. The Northern Pacific, the Soo Line, the Duluth, South Shore and Atlantic, the Omaha, and the Northwestern Railways are also supplied with my little jars of orange and of grapefruit marmalade. You cannot fail to recognize them, as the maker's name is plain to see with her monogram with the tiny thistle for her Scotch ancestry and the wee moccasin flower for Minnesota.

The oranges and the grapefruit can be put up all through the year, so, gradually, I have given up many of the other fruits and made marmalades my specialty, catering particularly to the dining-car trade, handling hundreds of little jars each month. Incidentally, as a warning to any one who thinks this an easy job, each jar is handled eleven times before being shipped. Often I receive letters from people who have had my marmalade on the trains, asking where they can buy more of it, or, if they are also in the business, where they can purchase the same kind of jars. I must confess the latter requests are the more frequent of the two.

Financially, I have not made a startling success, possibly because my products are made too much by hand. There have been many worries, frequent failures, many discouragements, much hard work, but in spite of all these the business has been full of interest and has given me the kind of occupation I wanted, one I could carry on in my own home, so as to be near my mother as long as she needed me.

Current Alumnae Publications

Compiled by Nina E. Browne

ANGELL, FLORENCE A. 1911. The International Federation Meets at Amsterdam, in A. A. U. W. Jour., Oct.

BARRETT, LILLIAN F. 1906. The Crowd Out Front, in Theatre Mag., June. Adventures of a Woman Playwright, in T. M. Aug.—More Chills and Thrills of a Playwright, in T. M. Sept.

†BATCHELDER, ALICE L. 1901. "People by the World Forgot," in The Four Cs, July.

BATCHELDER, ANNIE, 1913. A Cross-section of a Busy Life, in Chicago Public Library Staff News, June.

BOYD, MARION M. 1916. There is an Island, in Bookman, June.

BRADFORD, ANNA H. 1986-97, 98-00 (Mrs. Hubbard). Personality, in Congregationalist, Aug. 26.

†CARPENTER, FRANCES A. 1912 (Mrs. Huntington). The Clothes We Wear.—The Foods We Eat.—The Houses We Live In. N. Y. Amer. Book Co.

† Already in collection.

CHALMERS, MARJORIE, 1917 (Mrs. Carleton). Swinging Goddess. Boston. Small, Maynard.

CUTTER, ELIZABETH R. 1896 (Mrs. Morrow). Kings' Color, in Scribner's, Aug.

DASKAM, JOSEPHINE D. 1898 (Mrs. Bacon). Medusa's Head. N. Y. Appleton.

DREW, EMILY F. 1903. A History of the Industries of Kingston. Two Hundredth Anniv. Com.

EGBERT, CAROLYN L. 1915 (Mrs. Sailer). Yenching's Recent Sorrow, in Missionary Herald, July.

FERGUS, PHYLLIS, 1913 (Mrs. Hoyt). "Intreat Me Not to Leave Thee." Phila. T. Presser.—23d Psalm; Ruth; 121st Psalm. N. Y. Aeolian Co.—Spring's a Coming. Chic. C. F. Summy.

†FRAME, VIRGINIA W. 1899 (Mrs. Church). Teaching Young People to Love Books, in International Book Review, July.

FULLER, EUNICE, 1908 (Mrs. Barnard). G. B. S.: The Father of the Flapper, in New

Republic, July 28.—Does the American Baby Need a School? in N. R. Aug. 11.

GILCHRIST, MARIE E. 1916. Au Revoir, in Forum, Aug.

HALL, CLARISSA M. 1910–Dec. 12 (Mrs. Hammond). At Chion-In, in Amer. Poetry Assoc. Yearbook of Poems for 1926.

HAWKINS, ETHEL W. 1901. The Stream of Consciousness Novel, in Atlantic, Sept.

HAZARD, GRACE W. 1899 (Mrs. Conkling). Flying Fish. N. Y. Knopf.—Steamer Letter, in New Republic, July 21.

JUDSON, ALICE C. 1925. C. L. Sewing Circle, in Child Life, Aug. 1925–Sept. 1926.

LEONARD, FLORENCE, 1888. How Can I Raise the Standard of my Playing, in Étude, Sept.

LEWIS, MARY S. 1893–Apr. 1895 (Mrs. Leitch). The Unrisen Morrow. Phila., Dorrance.—The Gods are Dead, in Lyric, July.—He Who Has Known a River; The Scoffer, in Independent Anthology, Aug.— Pity the Great, in North Amer. Review, Sept.–Nov.—The Sea Invades the Hills, in Lyric West, May–June.

MCAFEE, HELEN, 1903. On a Turkish Screen, in Saturday Rev. of Lit., June 26.

MAXSON, RUTH P. 1905 (Mrs. Aughiltree). City Slave, in Country Bard, Summer.

NICHOLL, LOUISE T. 1913. Identity, in N. Y. Herald Tribune.—"Renaissance" (After Pater), in Amer. Parade, July.

SCUDDER, VIDA D. 1884. Review of Education and the Good Life, in Atlantic Bookshelf, July.

SHERMAN, ELLEN B. 1891. The Cry of the Children, in Springfield Republican, May 27. —The Dice of the Gods, in Gammadion, June.—In the Twilight of Faith; The Seven Devils of Militarism, in Gammadion, Fall. —The Empty Room, Misnomer, Winged Prophets, Wornout Words, Upstairs to Bed, in Boston Herald, Sept. 16, 17, 20, 22, 24.—Letting One's Self Go, in Saturday Rev. of Lit., July 31.

STAPLES, MARY A. 1910 (Mrs. Kirkpatrick). Income and Outgo. N. Y. Crowell Pub. Co.—"Balance on Hand," in Woman's Home Comp., Oct.

STOREY, VIOLET A. 1920. To an Older Woman, in Harper's, Sept.

STORM, MARIAN, 1913. A Woman Champion of Cortes and Drake, in Our World, Sept.—

The Fixed Light, in Country Gentleman, Mar.

†STREETER, HILDA E. 1917. Historic Cherry Valley.

SWETT, MARGERY, 1917. A Cabinet System, in Writer's Monthly, July.—†The Elusive Lyric, in W. M. Aug.—A Dancing Tragedian; Fable of a Little Sister, in Poetry, Sept.—A Memorial Poem from India, in P. Oct.—The Girl in the Gallery, in Southwest Rev., Oct.—The Mountain Dwellers, in New Leader, June 12.—The Question of New York, in Author and Journalist, Feb.— Review of the Dancing of Anna Duncan, in Dance, July.—Intelligence, Girls, not Beauty, in Dance, Aug.—Innocents on Tour, in Dance, Oct. [A story of Portia Mansfield's Company of Dancers]—The Truth about Canned Foods, in Progress, Apr.—Loss of Nutrition in Cooking, in P. July–Aug.— What is a Poet Anyhow? Atlantic Contributors' Club, Mar.

TINKER, GRACE E. 1894–96 (Mrs. Davis). Neighbors in Christ Around the World. Chic. Women's Board of Missions.

TRENT, LUCIA, 1919. One Lonely Dreamer, in The Crisis, July.—Only One Lover Shall be True, in Greenwich Village Quill, July.

VALLENTINE, JESSIE, 1906 (Mrs. Thayer). The Farmer's Wife [class supper speech], in Forum, July.

†VAN DEMAN, RUTH, 1911. A Guide to Good Meals for the Junior Homemaker. U. S. Dept. of Agriculture. Misc. Circular, no. 49.—Uncle Sam Undertakes Calorie Counting, in Western Dietitian, July.

†VAN KLEECK, MARY, 1904. Modern Industry and Society, in Amer. Federationist, June.—What Industry Can Do to Raise Standards of Work for Women, in Penn. Dept. of Labor and Industry. Conference on Women in Industry, 1925.—The Women's Industrial Conference, in Bulletin of the Taylor Society, Feb.

WATTS, MARTHA, 1912–14 (Mrs. Frey). To Albert Spaulding from the Ladies, in Club Fellow and Washington Mirror, Apr. 21.

WILD, LAURA H. 1892. The Church, the Book and the Youth Movement, in Congregationalist, July 1.

†WILLIAMS, CORA M. 1883. Lines and Lyrics. Los Angeles, Times-Mirror Press.

Notes on Publications

With the first chapters of "Medusa's Head," by Josephine Daskam Bacon, the author tells the occasion for her writing of this story. "The real true reason why I joined up with the sleuths," she says, "is not literary. It is entirely a matter of family pride. One of my children who was passing a pleasant evening at home reading my books looked up at me and said thoughtfully, 'You've written about every kind of story there is, haven't you, mother?' 'Quite so,' said I with simple modesty. 'Only I never read a mystery story of yours,' said the child. 'You don't seem able to do that kind, do you, mother?' 'I don't see where you get that idea,' said I coldly. 'But could you think of a mystery to write about?' persisted the cynical infant. 'Could I?' said I. 'Could I? Watch me!'"

Hide and Seek

THE "hiders" are becoming fewer and fewer as the "seekers" wax enthusiastic, and we look forward to the day when the alumnae hymn book will have no use at all for that good old song, "Where is my wandering boy [girl] tonight?"

Name	*Mail returned from*
Alice A. Allen 91	313 Champion St., Battle Creek, Mich.
Katharine Brewster 85	Box 418, Derby, Conn.
Mrs. Alexander Cameron 17 (Edna Stickel)	139 Hugo Av., San Francisco, Calif.
Mrs. Frank M. Clark 08 (Mary Keenan)	Box 46, Andes, N. Y.
Adelaide Cozzens 22	310 W. 86 St., N. Y. C.
Mrs. B. V. Davies 91 (Mary Aikens)	Bryngolan, Claremont, Cape Colony, South Africa
Mrs. Courtney Davis 21 (Mary Kelly)	Box 73, Houston, Tex.
Mrs. W. C. Dexter 06 (Helen Fillebrown)	Woodstock, N. Y.
Elizabeth Donnell 22	24 Flushing Pl., Flushing, N. Y.
Mrs. Henry F. Eddy 07 (Ethel Willard)	14 Bither Av., Springfield, Mass.
Mrs. Alfred H. Ehrenclou 17 (Olive Nisley)	Boston Psychopathic Hospital, Boston, Mass.
Esther Eisler M.A. 23	Illinois Woman's College, Jacksonville, Ill.
Annah Haake 88	Indianapolis, Ind.
Eileen Hafey 10	West Haven, Conn.
Gladys Hall 14	241 Maple St., Holyoke, Mass.
Clara Hallock 06	259 S. Cherry St., Galesburg, Ill.
Mrs. Harry K. Hamilton 06 (Esther Searle)	R. F. D. 6, Greensboro, N. C.
Clara Hart 18	128 W. 13 St., N. Y. C.
Mrs. Paul Hart 13 (Mary Walker)	1018 Burton Av., Cincinnati, O.
Dora Hastings 91	Southwick, Mass.
Edith Holman 08	1114 Park Pl., Brooklyn, N. Y.
Margaret Ickes 12	12582 Clifton Blvd., Cleveland, O.
Mrs. William B. Imlach 12 (Genevieve Wilson)	228 W. 71 St., N. Y. C.
Harriet Jacobs 92	Stephens College, Columbia, Mo.
Mrs. Fernando Lavenas 11 (Margaret Sullivan)	14 Westland Av., Boston, Mass.
Louise Leland 23	Virginia Hotel, Chicago, Ill.
Rosamond Lent 01	159 W. 103 St., N. Y. C.
Mary Long 22	11 Gorham Av., Brookline, Mass.
Christine McCarthy 17	145 Park Av., West Springfield, Mass.
Mrs. George L. Neuhoff Jr. 11 (Myrtle Alderman)	925 Beach Av., St. Louis, Mo.
Edith Nicholls 19	19 Haine St., New Haven, Conn.
Dorothy Prescott 22	Northboro, Mass.
Mabel Schnurr 09	123 Waverly Pl., N. Y. C.
Marjorie Smith 24	Washington Seminary, Washington, Pa.
Persis Weaver 24	5433 Greenwood Av., Chicago, Ill.
Mrs. Paul D. White 23 (Ina Reid)	110 Charles St., Boston, Mass.
Jessie C. Williams 18	130 E. 57 St., N. Y. C.

LET US TALK OF MANY THINGS

THE FRESHMEN— GOD BLESS 'EM!

WE have just been up to the new dormitories— the newest new dormitories, that is—and we are so excited about them that it doesn't seem as though we could bear it because we were born too soon! We want to start all over again (barring the Entrance Examinations, *if* you please) and buy a bicycle and come whizzing out of the Quadrangle archway, past the President's House, and down the sweet elmarched walk that skirts Paradise, and so to chapel and the gym and, yes, even to Seelye and the Libe. Alas and alack, it is not so to be, for there have been other birthdays besides the College's Fiftieth since the days when we were freshmen, and now the best we can do is to settle ourselves down in our corner of College Hall and watch the pageant of the campus from out our ivy-framed window and through the sun-flecked yellow leaves of our own particular New England Elm. And no one need be too sorry for our middle-aged fate at that, for we have been to Freshman Frolic and freshman song trials, and we have seen the sun on the river and on Mt. Tom on Mountain Day and, moreover, we have scanned the gallery at chapel time and counted 630 freshmen who are challenging us older members of the Smith family to walk with them in our old familiar ways. In fact, as far as we can see, this, the fifty-second of our circling years, has started out as busily and as joyously as all the fifty-one that have gone before.

And as for the QUARTERLY—well, it like the majority of the freshmen is eighteen years old, and, in so far forth, begs to share in the blessing we invoke in our title, because each year when we think of the task it is called upon to perform with just a few pictures and the printed word we get a kind of freshman panic and wonder whether we ought not to turn the job over to younger hands or older hands, but, in any case, different hands. And then

we get so enthusiastic about student activities, or college policies, or tales of the alumnae, that, presto, the panic goes, and the typewriter and blue pencil begin to work overtime; and somehow or other we manage to distribute some 7500—or maybe by reason of the freshman parents to whom with deep salaams we send this complimentary issue, it is 8000—modest brown magazines throughout the length and breadth of this and other lands to people who really care about Smith College and its past and its present and, most important of all, its future.

Its future! That's the reason we dedicate this November editorial to the freshmen, because as long as there are Smith College freshmen there is bound to be a Smith College future. We say this with our hands on our hearts to the three upper classes because of course we know as well as they do that they are every bit as essential to the college as the freshmen (for the matter of that, whatever would become of the freshmen if they didn't have older sisters to bring them up in the way they should go?). But, after all, why bother to build new dormitories if the circling years should bring no freshmen to their doors? Why bother about the curriculum (and of course, O alumnae, you will read Mr. Orton's paper) if freshmen came no longer to be taught? Why—well, anyway, by the time you have read this QUARTERLY through (and we are not going to dangle any alluring bait before any of the articles because you can't really get up to date on Smith College without reading them all, especially that Parent Letter on page 57) and have seen the freshman dean and the granddaughters, and heard all about the registration data, you won't have any doubt that the Class of 1930 (it *is* a bit paralyzing that!) is just as important to Smith College as was each of the one-time freshman classes you see tabulated over in the Alumnae Notes section where the circling years and the continents go round and round and the alumnae stars flit perpetually between. And even here the freshman daughters and sisters and cousins and nieces shine forth in item after item with a promise all their own.

And so, here's to the freshmen, God bless 'em—the freshmen of 1930, and those erstwhile freshmen of 1929 and '28 and back and back and back to those pioneer freshmen of '79; and as for the QUARTERLY—may it take up the tale of the strivings and achievements of them all, and with Smith College as a text and certain goal make the record of this fifty-second year of freshman classes the proudest of them all.

E. N. H. 1903

RENDER UNTO CAESAR

"IT pays to advertise" is no doubt the producer's chief commandment. The consumer has come to believe that it pays to read advertisements. Certainly to read (and heed) the advertisements in one's favorite magazine is profitable. Taking it for granted that the QUARTERLY is the favorite magazine of all who read this page, noting and acting upon the advertisements appearing regularly therein must prove advantageous. Q. E. D. Concerning one such advertisement at any rate, I can personally testify that the "demonstration" just given proved cogent.

During the summer of 1925 I was somewhat vaguely planning a trip abroad for this year of 1926. I had noticed in several issues of the QUARTERLY the dignified and carefully worded advertisement of Mr. Charles Ashmun, with the alluring finale, "No charge for our service." So I wrote to his office requesting information. I have not yet ceased to marvel at the response. At my age, I had to make a number of rather fussy requirements —and I'd none too much money to spend. Nevertheless from the time of first writing until my return after a five months' tour, we (my niece, Smith '95, and I) felt guarded and guided everywhere we went. For instance, on arriving in New York, two days before sailing, a note from Mr. Ashmun's office awaited us at our hotel proffering personal attention in any way we might need during our stay in the city. On visiting the office, where, in the absence of Mr. Ashmun, we were most courteously received by his assistant, Mr. John Squibb, we were given notes of introduction to their representatives in Paris and in London. Arriving in Naples, we were met by their representative there, who took us

through the customs office without delay and had a cab in waiting to take us to the hotel where rooms had been already engaged for us. Through the two offices to which we were sent in Paris and in London were planned many details of our weeks in France and in England, relieving us of much irksome correspondence. And still we were met with the same assurance, "No charge for the service." Our return passage was engaged through Mr. Ashmun's office by letter from France just as soon as we could fix on a date. In each case, going and returning, every detail received attention and on request we even were informed of the customary amount to be given in "tips" on leaving the ship. With all this we were not dependent upon any "coupons," but were quite free to alter plans from day to day as suited our momentary fancy. Whenever we were sure as to any procedure, we went ahead, but whenever there was any doubt in our minds, we at once consulted the Paris or the London firm to which we had introductions. The uniform patience, courtesy, and helpfulness which we met in both instances will always be remembered with gratitude.

ANNIE B. JACKSON 1882

HOW ABOUT ALUMNAE ASSEMBLY?

E. N. H. asks: "What are your ideas about the Alumnae Assembly? Of course we can't always have 50th Birthday Parties and cakes and things, but can't we be joyful nevertheless?"

"That's just what I say," I reply in all haste. 'What's an Alumnae Assembly for, if not to make you everlastingly glad you're an alumna, and since it's the Smith way to be gay rather than sentimental about it, and do it with a dash of paprika and not with little drops of salt water, there's no earthly reason why we shouldn't have a giddy time every time."

I continue brightly, just to keep E. Hill's spirits up, "Let's see, what are the things most likely to make the oldest at the Assembly feel young and the youngest not too sad at being among the old? First of all of course there's President Neilson and then the cups for the best costumes and best attendance—that's always exciting. Then do you remember how thrilling it was last year to see a representative from every single class march up to the platform in giddy array? Let's have that. There'd be sure to be almost a complete set at every Commencement.

"Then let's have something more than the usual words of kindly greeting, some kind of special ceremony of welcome to the newest alumnae, nothing stiff or solemn of course, and they would probably want to retort in kind.

"For a stunt—a satire on current college events—why not transfer the stunt usually given by the ten-year-out class at the alumnae business meeting to the Alumnae Assembly?

"It would be nice," I suggest diplomatically, "to invite, as we did this year, the new honorary degrees, whether or no we invite them to speak. And don't let us forget to gay up the President himself by having on hand some encouraging results from our Alumnae Fund.

"And finally do not let us plunge the meeting in gloom in spite of our best efforts! Let there be no singing, unless we can have a brass band to drown the usual pathetic alumnae quaver. No, on second thoughts, why not render one or two of our official songs, with the magnificent encouragement of the organ at full blast?

"One thing more, Edith, although you didn't ask me to cover all the Commencement functions. If we subtract the stunt from the Saturday business meeting, why not fill up the gap with some real give-and-take between us and our Alumnae Trustees? We don't know them half well enough—what they do, in general, what special responsibility each one has, what they see the college becoming, how they're representing us, 'n'everything. It would surely be the appropriate time and place and the loved one all together. And they might even enjoy it! And no one would really miss the stunts and costumes. Most of us are quite funny, just as we are!"

H. C. B. F.

2 To those of us who were at the Fiftieth Birthday Party the Alumnae Assembly in 1926 seemed too much of a let down. We went in hoping for another short and snappy meeting like the Birthday Party. What we got was short, but it wasn't snappy. Of course we want President Neilson's speech, and the awarding of the cups, and the welcome to the senior class, and perhaps a few good songs. But after that we want a STUNT: something peppy and funny to bring Commencement to a real climax. And, incidentally, how about holding the meeting in Sage Hall where the audience wouldn't be scattered and where everyone could hear? 1919

THE QUESTION OF "IN MEMORIAMS" *Dear Editor:* Would you consider omitting "In Memoriams" of deceased graduates and give only the death notice in Alumnae Notes?

All eulogies sound alike to readers who did not know the departed and I am fed up on "radiant personality" and "irreparable loss." The custom of using the QUARTERLY for broadcasting testimonials no doubt started with a sincere desire to pay a fitting tribute, but has it not become a burdensome and meaningless convention? Class letters provide the suitable channel for intimate and personal remarks and I should like to see QUARTERLY space saved for news of the living.

Respectfully yours,
ANTI-OBITUARY

THIS letter came to the editor after she had attended a convention at Ohio State University and heard a paper entitled, "The Problem of the Obituary Notice." It was a psychological moment, for the editor of the QUARTERLY in common with editors of all alumni-ae publications is becoming very much concerned over that very problem. Smith College is not an old college as colleges go, nevertheless, in the four issues of the QUARTERLY for last year the death of 52 alumnae and non-graduates was announced, and if we continue to be as generous of space as heretofore in the matter of In Memoriams it is easy to see that the older we grow the more gloomy the columns of the Alumnae Notes will become. It is in the hope that you will consider the problem in all seriousness and offer suggestions that we print the foregoing letter and reprint portions of the Convention paper. It's depressing business but inevitable.

The author is the editor of the *Cornell Alumni News* and bases his awful prognostications on Cornell but he claims that the ratio will hold good for any college. We print only the portions which seem particularly relevant to our problem although the entire paper is extremely interesting:

The alumni publication is faced with the prospect of a problem of vast magnitude in its obituaries and may well begin early to consider it with open eyes. Whether the full force of the problem is felt in ten years or in forty is unimportant. The editor who continues to view obituary notices simply as the last compliment that he can pay to his departed subscriber is going to be overwhelmed with a mass of material in the future that will tax his ingenuity to the utmost. For the individual magazine the date of this flood is not a movable feast. It can be determined by inflexible mathematics, but a review of the history of the material is necessary before we can construct the mathematical formula for the forecast.

. . . . .

After a class has been out of college between forty-five and fifty years, deaths in its ranks are quite to be expected. Consequently when the dying classes, if I may so designate them, become enough larger relatively so that their original membership equals the matriculation of the then entering classes, it is easily seen that at that time the number of obituaries in all classes in a given year should about equal the matriculation of the incoming freshman class. That this has not been obvious before is because none of the larger colleges of to-day were more than a small fraction of their present size fifty years ago.

The author then proceeds to demonstrate by means of a chart and tables that when the classes which were in Cornell in 1913–14 attain the average age of 65 years, or about 1958, Cornell may expect an obituary list of about 2400 names a year. Figures are based on an annual enrollment of 5000. At the present time the *Cornell Alumni News* runs about 200 obituary notices a year. The extent of the problem is apparent without further comment. The Smith situation is not going to become so acute as this for many years and yet, as the editor of the *Cornell Alumni News* says, "Unless we begin to cut down now before the dike begins to leak we shall have a deluge on our hands that will soon have many times the volume that it would have if we began at once to cut down our long obituary notices."

We invite your consideration of the probblem. Do you agree with Anti-Obituary or can you suggest a compromise?

THE EDITOR

A YEAR IN FRANCE WITH YOUR FAMILY

IN the article "Our Juniors in France,"* Miss Breck reveals how valuable the year in France is proving to her and we owe much to the wise direction of President Neilson that our juniors can have this broadening experience. I have just returned from a year in France spent with the entire family and so I wish to bring to you the good news that those of you who cannot again be juniors can nevertheless have a year in France and an even finer year, for it can be with your husband and children.

Perhaps the first objection that comes to your mind is the one of expense, and to this let me answer that if you take $4000 as an average cost of living for a family of six, the

* SMITH QUARTERLY, Feb. 1926.

same sum, apart from the ocean voyage, will enable this same family to have a year of *la civilisation française*. This sum will as completely cover your expenses for a year as it does in this country. It means careful planning and will not permit you to patronize those enticing patisserie shops as freely as I should judge our juniors did, but it does not mean denying yourself all pleasures. We lived in pensions averaging $1.25 a day; followed courses in the University; attended the theater; had trips by the day and a few longer ones; and in addition to our French books brought home a few treasures.

The French respect those who must economize and so there is absolutely nothing unpleasant from that point of view in traveling on limited funds. The wealthy American tends to raise a barrier between himself and the French. The French are very quick to feel the slightest lack of delicacy or attempt to push forward, but if you have a sincere desire to find what France has to offer you and do not wish to criticize what she lacks you will find the French people kind and helpful to a degree that touches your heart.

Your next remark will be, "But what about the children?" Our four were a girl 14 years and boys 12, 10, and 4 years old. If your idea of learning *la civilisation française* is to rush from one place to another I frankly admit children are a hindrance, but if it is of the French people, their mode of life, of study, their rich culture you wish to learn, your children will aid you. Traveling with your family is traveling in earnest and the French are quick to see it and to respond to it. When a French person would not have spoken to us he would speak to the children and some of our pleasantest friendships we owe to them.

On account of the children we only stayed five weeks in Paris and chose Grenoble for the remainder of the time. Of this city, the interesting trips in its vicinity and of what the university offers Miss Breck has given you a by no means exaggerated account. But to this must be added the excellent schools for children. The Lycée de Garçons is one of the best in France and the Lycée de Filles is also good. The lycée is a government school preparing directly for the university and in some instances having common professors. To one from the United States the tuition seems nominal, about $3.00 a quarter, and textbooks are correspondingly reasonable. To the lycée are sent primarily the children of the educated classes and the instruction is on a plane hardly conceivable to one not conversant with English and Continental methods. The method of teaching is perhaps over impersonal but the challenge to one's intellect is a stimulus no ambitious child will ever cease to feel.

With no previous knowledge of French the children commenced regular school work after six weeks of private instruction and on leaving France could understand French as easily as English, could read and talk fluently. It is a fine thing for a child to acquire French while he is young and before his reasoning faculties beset him each time he tries to form a sentence. But of even greater value than this facility of speech is the intimacy with the French life which the children got unconsciously through their play with the French children, as they went back and forth to school with them, as they joined in their pranks and in their study, and as they took part in their all day tramps.

Though my husband was with me I am convinced that a mother alone could make a similar trip with her children. While we were in Grenoble there was an American woman with four children doing that very thing.

What the year meant to me and my husband need not be dwelt upon. It enables us to form correct impressions gathered from the newspapers and throws a flood of light on the background of all literature. The French have learned the fine art of living on its intellectual side at a very moderate expense and I wish that more of my fellow alumnae might see this civilization at first hand.

ELISABETH (SOUTHWORTH) HARRISON 1904

WE TRAVEL IN KOREA Once again we stay-at-home alumnae travel vicariously in foreign parts; this time under the tutelage of Jeanne Sloan 1906, who is teaching in Pyengyang, Korea.

AS one leaves China for Mukden, the home of the dynasty which captured China in 1618, the change is very gradual. One realizes that we are going north by the much better built houses, all having chimneys.

Korea is a country with many titles. It has often been called the "Hermit Nation"; the "Land of the Morning Calm," because there is no wind early in the day; "The Land of the Topknots," because formerly all married men twisted their long hair in a knot on top of the head, which was easily seen through the queer little black hats perched like cans on the tops of their heads and held there by strings tied

under their chins. That the climate is better than either China or Japan, is acknowledged generally, I believe. The country is beautiful but so mountainous that only 18% can be cultivated.

The Japanese are now ruling this country, as everyone knows. Their mistakes at first were numerous but I understand that they are sincerely trying to avoid making more, and much can be said to their credit. In a very short time Korea has changed from a primitive country, with no roads or bridges worthy of the name, with no sanitation, nor with any apparent organization, into a surprisingly modern country. The energy of the Japanese is amazing. The railroads are fine. There is a splendid system of auto roads. The streets have been straightened, electric cars and electric lights installed, and modern buildings are springing up in every direction. The best plots of land are saved for the most important buildings, and the tops of hills or other suitable places are made into parks, for the Japanese are very artistic. The Koreans are very likable but as a race they are shiftless. They seem glad to follow a good example but lack the initiative to better their own conditions. The unfortunate thing is that the Japanese are gradually getting control of the land, and driving the Koreans out of business. They are here by the thousands and intend to stay. The Koreans dislike the Japanese intensely because Japan in the early ages came in contact with civilization via Korea so the Koreans consider them upstarts. On the other hand the Koreans look toward China with the greatest affection.

A recent cause for irritation between the races is that Shinto Shrines are being built throughout the country. At the one recently dedicated at Seoul all were expected to officiate. Since this is strictly Japanese—the worship of their imperial ancestors—the Koreans rebel at the idea. During the five weeks that we were in Japan this year we were very fortunate to be at Nara, one of the most important of Shinto Shrines, when the name of the new Imperial Baby was announced to her ancestors' spirits. At the close of the ceremony much food was offered to the spirits and left on the shrine for them. A Japanese who had studied abroad was once asked if he thought the spirits ate the food. "Yes," he replied, "to the same extent that the spirits of your ancestors smell the flowers you leave on their graves."

Although both Japan and Korea are noted silk producers, we can only buy it in quantities of twelve yards, fifteen inches wide, for that is the amount needed for a kimona or Korean coat. They always use that amount whether small or large, and the extra is turned up to be used when made over for another.

Silk is often brought to the door by women who have raised the silk worms and have done all the preparation and weaving themselves, but scarcely two yards look alike. Pongee is not manufactured. The worms feed on oak leaves to produce that color.

JEANNE SLOAN 1906

INTERCOLLEGIATE ALUMNI HOTELS

IN the alumni publications of some eighty-five colleges and universities is appearing this fall four pages of advertising that mark a new era not only for the publications themselves as a medium for national advertising but in the coöperation between the colleges for men and women. The pages have to do with the intercollegiate alumni hotels and will be found beginning on page 129 of this issue. We believe that Smith alumnae will be well repaid for giving them a careful reading. The colleges and universities coöperating in this movement have already named certain hotels in some thirty-five cities that shall be known as Intercollegiate Alumni Hotels, equipped with everything tending to make it easy for the college man or woman to connect with college mates living in that city. A careful list of names and addresses of graduates of all participating colleges will be at the desk so that even if time is short and one's *Alumnae Register* left at home it will take no time at all to locate the classmate whose married name has slipped your mind (thereby making a city directory hopeless). Alumni and alumnae will be found there and the management will make every effort to give college men and women special service and courtesy. These intercollegiate alumni hotels, in short, will serve as college clubs for the traveler and if one stays in any city will prove helpful in making connections with one's local college club.

It was in California about three years ago that the intercollegiate idea originated. It grew out of a very definite need. The growth of travel by automobile combined with the gigantic growth in numbers of university and college men has brought to light the necessity for some place to which the visiting alumnus may go when in a strange city to find the names and addresses of his fellow alumni living in the community. It was formerly the policy of the University of California Alumni Association, for instance, to have the president or secretary of the local alumni club keep on file these names and addresses. Often, however, when the list was most desired the local president or secretary could not be found, so by keeping an accurate list on file at a prominent hotel this list became available at all hours of the day and night, and consequently it has resulted that a new means has been found whereby alumni spirit can be engendered in centers distant from the immediate influence of the University.

Many eminent university leaders have followed the growth of the hotel headquarters movement in the Far West. President Ray Lyman Wilbur of Stanford University says: "We have found by experience that by having an outstanding hotel in a local community act as a depository for names and addresses of local alumni and as general headquarters for our association activities, the morale of our alumni association has been greatly strengthened. And as for the hotels, Halsey E. Manwaring, manager of the famous Palace Hotel of San Francisco, says: "For three years we have acted as official headquarters for University of California and Stanford University Alumni Associations. From our experience we believe that a nation-wide establishment of Intercollegiate Alumni Hotels will prove an excellent move and one in which the hotel industry may well be proud of playing a part."

For over a year a large committee representing eighty college and university alumni associations has been working to make this national movement possible. The committee is named on the fourth page of the advertisement and we note here only the fact that Marion Graves, advertising manager of the SMITH QUARTERLY, is one of its members. The American continent has been traveled back and forth by its representatives many times in order to have coördinated action in the establishment of intercollegiate alumni headquarters.

And the moral of this tale comes at the end, like all morals. The success of the project lies in the coöperation between the hotels and the college graduates. We commend our Smith share in the undertaking to Smith alumnae and urge them as individuals and as local club units to make as many contacts with the hotels designated in their localities as possible.

TO THE PARENTS OF SMITH COLLEGE STUDENTS

This letter was mailed in August to all parents of Smith students.

"IT has been our custom these last few years to send to the parents of our students towards the end of the summer a short communication dealing with some of the problems in the solution of which we desired their understanding and help. This year we wish to discuss a matter of policy in which we may have seemed to them inconsistent.

"It is a fundamental principle at Smith College that we seek to develop in the students the power of self-direction. The freedom necessary for such a development inevitably involves the possibility of mistakes and a certain amount of waste, but without such risk character cannot grow. In accordance with this principle, the faculty last year returned to an early practice of the college, and voted to make attendance at the regular class exercises voluntary. The assumption underlying this decision was that the students should be treated as adults who came to college for intellectual gain, and that a better attitude towards classroom instruction would be induced if we abandoned compulsory attendance and placed on the student's shoulders the responsibility for using her opportunities to the greatest advantage. It was hoped also that there would result an additional stimulus to the teachers to make their lectures interesting and essential.

"In returning to this earlier policy we apparently underestimated the changes in social customs which have taken place in recent years. The American people travel a great deal more than formerly, and afford their children much more opportunity for travel. The freedom from compulsory attendance resulted in a disconcerting increase in the practice of spending week-ends away from college, and in the duration of these week-ends. The attraction of the social excitements of the cities proved to a considerable number of girls an ever increasing rival of the soberer intellectual interests provided by the college, and it became clear that unless these girls lived more continuously in Northampton the college had not a fair chance to create round them the appropriate atmosphere for its purposes.

"We have therefore decided that we must make it clear that this is a resident college, and that while an occasional absence may be permissible, a student in coming here must make up her mind that apart from vacations the center of her interest during her four years must lie in the campus. To make this effective it has been voted that residence in college for eight semesters is a requirement for the degree, and that this requirement will not ordinarily be regarded as fulfilled if the student is absent more than seven nights in the semester. Cases of protracted illness and the like will, of course, be dealt with on their merits.

"Saturday afternoon and Sunday, though free from class appointments, are none the less valuable and important in college life. They afford time for country walks, quiet reading and friendly intercourse, religious exercises, and that solitary contemplation the lack of which more and more tends to impoverish our lives. After such a pause, work is resumed with relish on Monday. But if this interval is spent in a whirl of excitement in New York, and still more if the week-end begins on Friday and lasts till Monday afternoon, the student returns exhausted to a feverish attempt to cram a week's academic activities into four days. Even the girls who do not indulge in such dissipation of time and energy are disturbed by the atmosphere brought back by the others from these too frequent excursions.

"Already we are receiving protests from parents against the proposed restrictions, with allusions to 'dreary week-ends in Northampton' and requests for permission for additional leaves of absence as a reward for scholarship or good conduct. Let it be clearly understood that we regard it as a privilege to live in this community, not to be away from it as much as possible. The pur-

pose of this letter is to ask parents to have this point of view firmly in their minds in their dealings with their daughters in matters of allowances and permission to pay visits in term time, and to urge upon them the importance of acting on the principle that the opportunities afforded by the college are privileges to be seized, not tasks to be evaded. The students who refuse to accept this view are wasting their time and ours, and usurping places eagerly coveted by many who cannot be admitted on account of the necessary limitations of our numbers.

"LAURA W. L. SCALES, *Warden*
W. A. NEILSON, *President*"

THE FALL REGISTRATION

THIS year there are 2033 undergraduates at Smith and 34 juniors in France. There are also 64 Graduate Students (plus one in France) and 4 non-collegiate students. The distribution is: Seniors, 478; Juniors, 409 (and 34 in France); Sophomores, 516; Freshmen, 630. Total, 2033 and 34 in France. (Total for last year, 2061 and 32 in France.) This includes the students who have entered on advanced standing. There are 1725 students living in campus houses.

Advanced Standing.—There are 32 advanced standing students representing 26 different institutions. The 8 universities represented are: Colorado, Manitoba, Michigan, Minnesota, Ohio State, Pittsburgh, Southern Methodist, Wyoming; and the 18 colleges: Adelphi, Allegheny, Beloit, Carleton, Connecticut, Elmira, Jackson (Tufts), Lake Erie, Mills, Milwaukee-Downer, Pennsylvania State, Radcliffe, Rice Institute, St. Mary's Junior, Springfield Junior, Superior Normal, Virginia, Wilson.

Thirty-three former students have been readmitted to Smith this fall, 9 of them as freshmen and 24 as upperclassmen. Of these 24 upperclassmen 2 are offering credit for a year's work at the University of Chicago, 1 at Pittsburgh, 1 at the University of Minnesota, 1 at Skidmore, and 1 for more than a year's work at the University of California.

Graduate Students.—There are 65 graduate students, one of whom is studying under the supervision of Mlle. Delpit, Director of the Junior Group in France. Twenty-three are full time graduate students; the rest, including 28 members of the faculty, as well as local public and private school teachers, are taking

one or more graduate courses. Of the total number 25 are candidates for the M.A. degree in June 1927; of the remaining 40 ten already possess advanced degrees and one of these is a candidate for the degree of Ph.D. in French here. Of the remaining number 22 are also registered for the M.A. degree. These students come from the following institutions in this country and abroad: Allegheny College, Barnard, Bridgewater Normal School, Brown, Budapest (Hungary), Butler, Carleton, Colby, College of St. Catherine, Colorado College, Columbia, Connecticut, Earlham (Canada), Berlin and Frankfurt (Germany), George Washington University, Guilford, Kings College (University of London, England), Middlebury, Mount Holyoke, Ohio Wesleyan, Pennsylvania State College, Smith (20), Sorbonne (France), Southern Methodist College, Springfield (Mo.) Normal School, State University of Iowa, Teachers College of Boston, Tokyo Woman's Christian College (Japan), the universities of Indiana, Illinois, Minnesota, South Dakota, Southern California, and Vermont, Wellesley, Western College (Ohio), Western Ontario.

Registration by States and Countries.—In the entire college 45 of the 48 states are represented, and also the District of Columbia. There are no students from Nevada, South Carolina, or Utah. Foreign countries represented are: Brazil, Russia, Cuba, England, France, Germany, Hungary, Japan, Porto Rico, Sweden, Syria. Canada is also represented in the enrollment.

Foreign Students.—There are 11 foreign students at Smith this year, representing 9 countries. See article in front of magazine.

FRESHMAN STATISTICS

FIRST of all we introduce Miss Mary McElwain, the Dean of the Class of 1930. We wax ecclesiastical when we think of what a dean means to a class. She is theirs "to have and to hold, for richer for poorer, in sickness and in health," and not even the diploma at the end of their four years together breaks the relationship, for returning alumnae find their way very quickly to the homes of their class deans — providing they are young enough to have graduated in the halcyon days since class deans were created in our Smith scheme of things. That, to be strictly accurate, was in 1918, and Miss McElwain ushered the Class of 1920 through its junior and senior years; she then took 1924 under her wing, and since seeing them out into the wide, wide world has spent one year with a full teaching schedule in her own field (Latin) and another on sabbatical leave in Europe. She returned this fall to shepherd young 1930, and she is busier than the proverbial old woman who lived in a shoe.

MISS MARY McELWAIN

Figures compiled from the Freshman Class show distribution as follows: from New York come 144; Massachusetts 112; New Jersey 55; Ohio 53; Connecticut 51; Pennsylvania 45; Illinois 33; Michigan and New Hampshire 10; Minnesota 9; California 8; Texas 7; Colorado, Indiana, Maryland, Missouri, Rhode Island, Vermont, and Washington 6 each; Florida and Maine 5; Iowa, Virginia, and Wisconsin 4; Alabama, District of Columbia, Georgia, and Tennessee 3; Arkansas, Delaware, and West Virginia 2; Arizona, Idaho, Kansas, Kentucky, Mississippi, Montana, New Mexico, North Dakota, Oklahoma, Oregon 1. The class also includes one student from Russia. See the article on page 16.

Of these 331 entered by the New Plan and 298 by the Old Plan, not counting the 1 foreign (special) student. See article on page 17.

From public schools come 164; from private schools 298; from both public and private schools, 167; special student, 1. Total, 630.

Questionnaires as usual were circulated among the freshmen this fall. The returns were not complete but the cards that came in show various interesting statistics as follows: Denominational preferences show that 198 are Episcopalians, 103 Congregationalists, and 99 Presbyterians. There are 38 Unitarians, 51 Jews, 30 Catholics, the remainder being scattered among many other denominations.

The answers show that artists, authors, carpenters, judges, manufacturers, barbers, and merchants have sent their daughters to Smith. One hundred thirty-six are professional men, including lawyers, doctors, teachers, and ministers. The merchants, of whom there are 92, come next in number; and the manufacturers are third, with 59. There are 32 bankers, 22 brokers, 37 managers, and 21 insurance agents. One freshman is the daughter of a retired whaling captain, and another is the daughter of a rancher in California.

There are 292 college graduates among the fathers and 115 among the mothers. The freshman class last year recorded 270 fathers and 111 mothers who were college graduates. Forty-six are Smith granddaughters.

SMITH GRANDDAUGHTERS

"THE coming generations are following swift and sure," writes Miss Woodward in The Circling Years, and so they are for we record 177 names in our Smith granddaughters' list with mothers ranging all down the line from '87 to '08· There are only 46 freshmen as against the 58 of last year (we expect the rest of the eighteen-year-old alumnae children have gone to Harvard or Yale!) but these, 46 are most amazingly accommodating, for most of them turned up smiling for their pictures, and we are sure the others were unavoidably detained. The picture is on page 62 and the afternoon of the very day on which we write these words the originals are coming to our granddaughters' party.

SENIORS (1927)

Virginia Silsbee Allen............................Margaret (Lusch) Allen 02
Rebekah Purves Armstrong.......................Rebekah (Purves) Armstrong ex-05
Katharine Bannon................................Edith (Leeds) Bannon 96

Elizabeth Tew Becker............................Elizabeth (Coakley) Becker ex-01
Katharine Stetson Bingham.......................Ethel (Stetson) Bingham 01
Charlotte Rogers Brown..........................Margaret (Tucker) Brown ex-01
Kathleen Sanford Brown..........................Stella (Sanford) Brown 94
Elizabeth Waity Chase...........................Lena (Tyler) Chase 92
Mary Lawrence Clark.............................Mary (Whitcomb) Clark 00
Catherine Cole..................................Christine (Mansfield) Cole 92
Marian Axtell Cowperthwait......................Emma (Byles) Cowperthwait 98
Rita Creighton Curran...........................Mae (Fuller) Curran 97
Louise Parsons Dakin............................Bertha (Kirkland) Dakin 97
Margaret Day....................................Elizabeth (Lewis) Day 95
Mary Adelaide De Groat..........................Helen (Goodrich) De Groat 95
Eleanor Cochran Deland..........................Isabel (Adams) Deland 96
Caroline Doane..................................Lucy (Daniels) Doane 96
Antoinette Dodge................................Isabel (Adams) Dodge ex-01
Jessie Downing..................................Jessica (Burnham) Downing 90
Selma Erving....................................Emma (Lootz) Erving 97
Janet Fowler Geer...............................Jeanette (Fowler) Geer 96
Rachel Hall.....................................Gertrude (Porter) Hall ex-96
Myra Louise Halligan............................Mary (Ballard) Halligan ex-98
Elizabeth Hamburger.............................Amy (Stein) Hamburger 04
Pauline Hitchcock...............................Charlotte (Emerson) Hitchcock 95
Margaret Atherton Jacobus.......................Marion (Chapman) Jacobus 98
Lucia Elizabeth Jordan..........................Elsie (Pratt) Jordan 92
Katharine Condé Knowlton........................Kathrina (Condé) Knowlton ex-02
Margaret Larkin.................................Caroline (Gleason) Larkin 02
Frances Shackelford McConnell...................Genevieve (Knapp) McConnell 97
Anna Bell Marble................................Annie (Russell) Marble 86
Janet Olmsted...................................Marguerite (Prescott) Olmsted 03
Mary Candace Pangborn...........................Georgia (Wood) Pangborn ex-96
Alice Louise Phelps.............................Ella (Shaver) Phelps 95
Doris Pinkham...................................Isabella (Foote) Pinkham 96
Catherine Welles Steane.........................Alice (Curtis) Steane 02
Martha Sullivan.................................Amelia (Owen) Sullivan 81
Dorothy Tebbetts................................Frances (Ayer) Tebbetts 93
Ruth Lockwood Thompson..........................Jeanne (Lockwood) Thompson 94

JUNIORS (1928)

Dorothy Wright Adams............................Mary (Humphrey) Adams 94
Mary Anne Adams.................................Leona (Haywood) Adams ex-04
Lucy Emma Allen.................................Mabel (Calef) Allen 96
Elizabeth Mitchell Bacon........................Caroline (Mitchell) Bacon 97
Nancy Catherine Barnett.........................Lucy (Kurtz) Barnett 05
Eloise Barrangon................................Lucy (Lord) Barrangon 00
Elizabeth Kingsley Blake *......................Helen (Putnam) Blake 93
Alice Blodgett..................................Alice (Foster) Blodgett ex-99
Eleanor Brown...................................Margaret (Tucker) Brown ex-01
Mary Came.......................................Florence (Barker) Came 92
Harriet Westbrook Dunning.......................Mary (Ward) Dunning 97
Beatrice Clyde Edwards..........................Frances (McCarroll) Edwards 03
Lucia Mary Elmer................................Helen (Shoemaker) Elmer 01
Elizabeth Cole Fleming..........................Elizabeth (Cole) Fleming 97
Frances Franklin Galt...........................Clarace (Eaton) Galt 99
Helen Geromanos.................................Alice (Bradley) Geromanos 03
Frances Gilbert.................................Florence (Cook) Gilbert ex-04
Mary Elizabeth Godfrey..........................Emma (Eastman) Godfrey 99
Sally Peabody Goodell *.........................Helen (Peabody) Downing 04
Elizabeth Graham................................Alice (McClintock) Graham 99
Virginia Coyle Hall.............................Georgianna (Coyle) Hall 98
Katharine Ide Haskell *.........................Bertha (Groesbeck) Haskell 00
Imogene Hyde†...................................Florence (Keith) Hyde 97
Martha Kellogg..................................Cyrena (Case) Kellogg ex-07
Elizabeth Lewis.................................Elizabeth (Bradley) Lewis ex-00
Jane McEldowney.................................Anne (McConway) McEldowney 93
Anne Spencer Morrow.............................Elizabeth (Cutter) Morrow 96
Mary Cassandra Munroe...........................Rebecca (Kinsman) Munroe 95
Margaret Lucia Olney............................Bertha (Holden) Olney 02
Katherine Owsley *..............................Katherine (McKelvey) Owsley 04
Priscilla Paine.................................Mary (Tillinghast) Paine B.M. 99

* In France for the year.   † Stepchild.

Alice Edgerton Parsons...........................Alice (Lord) Parsons 97
Katherine Phelps................................Clara (Chapin) Phelps 98
Katharine Bush Salmon...........................Myra (Smith) Salmon B.M. 00
Barbara Helen Sherman...........................Helen (Harsha) Sherman 01
Emma Sutton Stewart †...........................Caroline (Daugherty) Stewart 13
Margaret Anna Stone.............................Harriet (Westinghouse) Stone 99
Margaret Morse Tarbox...........................Louise (Higgins) Tarbox 98
Ellenor Thorndike Trull.........................Ellen (Duckworth) Trull 96
Anne Sedgwick Wade..............................Margaret (Silsbee) Wade 99
Helen Ardell Wickwire...........................Mabel (Fitzgerald) Wickwire ex-01
Agnes Patton Woodhull...........................Agnes (Patton) Woodhull 01

SOPHOMORES (1929)

Frances Potter Adams............................Margaret (Potter) Adams ex-04
Clara Allen.....................................Frances (Young) Allen ex-96
Louise Bennett..................................Ethelwyn (Foote) Bennett 97
Barbara Blackmore Birge.........................Edna (Riddle) Birge ex-02
Eleanor Withington Boardman.....................Dorcas (Leese) Boardman 01 (00)
Katherine Southwick Bolman......................Florence (Tullock) Bolman 03
Caroline Buck...................................Annie (Allen) Buck 95
Mary-Frances Butler.............................Cora (Waldo) Butler 98
Helen Cheney....................................Ethel (Brooks) Cheney 05
Dorothy Preston Clark...........................Julia (Bourland) Clark 05
Elizabeth Louise Clough.........................Sara (Hunt) Clough 95
Sophie Connett..................................Carol (Morrow) Connett 98
Ruth Leicester Connolly.........................Nellie (Cuseck) Connolly 04
Carolyn Cummings................................Helen (Boss) Cummings 97
Alice Allen Eaton...............................Abby (Allen) Eaton 99
Marian Burton Giles.............................Mary (Vanderbeek) Giles 93
Lucie Culver Gould..............................Anna (Smith) Gould 00
Elizabeth Graham................................Alice (McClintock) Graham 99
Evelyn Hatch....................................Elisabeth (Smith) Hatch ex-93
Mary Hollister..................................Ruth (Albright) Hollister 00
Ida Elizabeth Holt †............................Dorothea (Wells) Holt 04
Cornelia Jenney.................................Caroline (King) Jenney 00
Ruth Rodney King................................Florence (Lord) King 95
Teresa Lawlor Kirby.............................Alice (Lawlor) Kirby 05
Mary Lane.......................................Mary (Comer) Lane 04
Elizabeth Wheeler Lumbard.......................Elizabeth (Tarbox) Lumbard 98
Effie Comey Manson..............................Effie (Comey) Manson 98
Kathryn Elizabeth Olp...........................Florence (Dowling) Olp 02
Frances Louise Page.............................Mathilde (Heidrich) Page 01
Margaret Germaine Palfrey.......................Methyl (Oakes) Palfrey 01
Eleanor Adelaide Pier...........................Pearl (Wilson) Pier 97
Marjorie Wentworth Pitts........................Edith (Suffren) Pitts 03
Mary Frances Potter.............................Eleanor (Hotchkiss) Potter 01
Ellen Emmeline Robinson.........................Mary (Wallace) Robinson 02
Phyllis Rust....................................Litz (Dustin) Rust 96
Frances Louise Seaman...........................Grace (Whiting) Seaman ex-90
Harriet Armington Seelye........................Anne (Barrows) Seelye 97
Barbara Damon Simison...........................Josephine (Damon) Simison ex-03
Lalia Barnes Simison............................Josephine (Damon) Simison ex-03
Eleanor Elizabeth Spottiswoode..................Grace (Field) Spottiswoode 93
Margaret Linton Streit..........................Margaret (Hotchkiss) Streit 04
Lucelia Wakefield Taussig.......................Harriet (Learned) Taussig 96
Eleanor Wiley Thayer............................Mary (Wiley) Thayer 00
Susan Tully.....................................Susan (Kennedy) Tully 03
Eunice Winchester Warnock.......................Una (Winchester) Warnock 04
Polla Rawson Watkins............................Nellie (Lunt) Watkins ex-01
Shirley Prence White............................Mabel (Moore) White 94
Alice Winchester................................Pearl (Gunn) Winchester 95
Mary Louise Young...............................Grace (Wiard) Young 97

FRESHMEN (1930)   The Freshman picture is over the page.

37 Susan Albright...............................Susan (Fuller) Albright 91
 6 Mary Alexander...............................Katherine (Harter) Alexander 02
31 Mary Thornton Barker.........................Mariana (Higbie) Barker 01
15 Frances Bascom...............................Lucy (Tufts) Bascom 99
25 Martha Buckham Benedict......................Ada (Platt) Benedict 94
16 Marjorie Starr Best..........................Marjorie (Ayres) Best 95
35 Mary Ten Eyck Bradley........................Corinne (Davis) Bradley 04

```
 8 Dorothy Brooks..............................Mary (Read) Brooks 00
   Elizabeth Covington Campbell..................Elizabeth (Fish) Campbell ex-02
 7 Christine Chace.............................Christine (MacLeod) Chace 01
 1 Grace Cheney...............................Helen (Hatch) Cheney ex-05
19 Mary Hunt Clough...........................Sara (Hunt) Clough 95
34 Elizabeth Abbot Copeland....................Annie (Young) Copeland 96
39 Eleanor Dodge..............................Florence (Grey) Dodge 08
28 Alma Louise Dunning.........................Eunice (Klock) Dunning 99
 5 Mary Erety Elmer............................Helen (Shoemaker) Elmer 01
40 Ruth Emeline Farrington......................Blanche (Clough) Farrington 01
41 Clarissa Breckenridge Fisk...................Grace (Breckenridge) Fisk 97
44 Janet Gordon...............................Janet (Sheldon) Gordon 01
33 Ruth Christine Griffenhagen..................Christine (Gloeckler) Griffenhagen 08
13 Adelaide Smith Hall.........................Georgianna (Coyle) Hall 98
22 Ruth Albro Hill.............................Annie (Cranska) Hill 02
14 Susan Garvin Hopkins........................Marie (Cunningham) Hopkins ex-05
20 Beatrice Howell.............................Alice (Egbert) Howell 02
24 Elizabeth May Howland.......................Elizabeth (Mason) Howland 04
42 Helen Zerbe Hunt............................Anna (Day) Hunt 96
27 Jane Bruce Loomis...........................Helen (Bruce) Loomis 05
26 Helen Mary MacKenzie........................Helen (Kennard) MacKenzie ex-97
17 Eugenia Mewborn............................Gertrude (Fiedler) Mewborn ex-06
 4 Alida Donnell Milliken.......................Alida (Leese) Milliken 00
23 Elinor Reed Morris..........................Gertrude (Powell) Morris ex-06
43 Rachel Eve Neely...........................Rachel (Schlesinger) Neely ex-07
45 Katharine Lincoln Newell....................Helen (Lincoln) Newell ex-04
36 Nancy Wynne Parker.........................Beulah (Johnson) Parker 03
29 Paula Lyle Patch............................Helen (Andrew) Patch 99
 2 Nathalie Worthington Penrose.................Mazy (Worthington) Penrose ex-00
21 Frances Perry..............................Margaret (Watson) Perry 04
   Eleanor Adelaide Pier.......................Pearl (Wilson) Pier 97
32 Carol Riegelman............................Lillian (Ehrich) Riegelman 04
11 Lydia Goodwin Ross.........................Mabel (Landers) Ross 96
 9 Teresina Rowell (1929)......................Teresina (Peck) Rowell 94
12 Elizabeth Harriet Sherman...................Helen (Harsha) Sherman 01
10 Jane Semple Stewart.........................Elizabeth (Barnard) Stewart 04
 3 Helen Wright Teagle.........................Alice (Wright) Teagle 04
38 Dorothy Page Walker.........................Lucinda (Holt) Walker 00
18 Emily Alden White...........................Jessie (Carter) White 87
   Charlotte Rouse Wickwire....................Mabel (Fitzgerald) Wickwire ex-01
```

THE FRESHMAN GRANDDAUGHTERS

BULLETIN BOARD

VESPERS.—The vesper speakers this year have been President Neilson, R. Bruce Taylor, D.D., LL.D., of Queen's University, Kingston, Ont., Rev. John Haynes Holmes of New York, Rev. George A. Gordon of Old South Church, Boston, and Rev. Sidney A. Lovett of Boston.

CONCERTS.—A concert was given by Mary Lewis, lyric soprano, in John M. Greene Hall on Oct. 15 under the auspices of the Veterans of Foreign Wars.

The Smith College Concert Course was opened Oct. 19 by the New York Philharmonic Orchestra, conducted by Willem Mengelberg. The following artists will appear later in the season: Richard Crooks, tenor, Nov. 24; The English Singers, Dec. 15; Walter Gieseking, pianist, Jan. 25; Pablo Casals, cellist, Feb. 21; the Boston Symphony Orchestra, Mar. 8; Fritz Kreisler, violinist, Mar. 21; Cleveland Symphony Orchestra, Apr. 29; Harvard and Smith Glee Clubs, May 7.

The Hampton Institute Quartet gave a concert on Oct. 22.

The Chamber Music Series this year includes a recital by the Flonzaley Quartet on Nov. 3; the Paul Shirley Ensemble, Feb. 9; and the London String Quartet on Mar. 16; also two concerts by the Elshuco Trio on Nov. 17 and Jan. 19, as the gift to the College of Mrs. E. S. Coolidge.

Mr. Moog gave his first organ recital of the year on Oct. 17.

LECTURES.—The following lectures have been given: "Philosophy and Civilization" by Professor S. Radnakrishman of the University of Calcutta; "Russia, a Warning and a Challenge" by Sherwood Eddy, LL.D.; "Matter and Spirit" by John Alexander Smith, Waynflete Professor of Philosophy at Oxford.

Lectures by Hugh Walpole were given Oct. 27 and 28 under the auspices of the Hampshire Bookshop.

See another column for the program of the School of Politics held Oct. 29 and 30.

THE SMITH COLLEGE MUSEUM OF ART.—The Tryon Gallery was formally opened on Oct. 8 by a reception for members of the faculty and staff and their wives. The February QUARTERLY will publish an extensive article on this building and the Department of Art.

The First Special Exhibition on display in the Special Exhibition room in the Tryon Gallery consisted of a group of small sculptures mostly by American artists, loaned through the courtesy of Mr. Frank Purdy of the Ferargil Galleries, New York.

THE LIBRARY.—Miss Dunham has been spending part of her year's leave of absence doing research work in Cambridge, England. She will probably go to Italy for the winter.

THE GYMNASIUM.—This summer for the second time the College coöperated with the Red Cross in conducting classes in swimming in the Scott Gymnasium. Professor McArdle with the assistance of Miss Trow, executive secretary of the Hampshire County Branch of the Red Cross, planned all the schedules, Miss McInnes of the faculty was in charge in July, and Miss Bruce, her first assistant, through August. Suits and all bath linen were furnished by the College and were taken care of by the college laundry. Miss Trow has expressed the great appreciation of the people of Northampton for the generosity of the College. There were 606 people enrolled in the classes, divided as follows: girl scouts 59, children 71, adults 476. There were 14 candidates for the Red Cross Life Saving Corps of whom eight successfully passed the tests. It is interesting to note that nearly all of these eight learned to swim in the Red Cross classes in the Smith swimming pool only the summer before.

Departmental Notes

Dean Bernard was secretary of the Conference of the Five Colleges held at Bryn Mawr, Oct. 22 and 23. The five colleges are Bryn Mawr, Mount Holyoke, Vassar, Wellesley, and Smith. Conferences are held twice yearly. Their purpose is to provide opportunity for the discussion of matters both educational and social which affect all five of the institutions and to form a common ground on which to meet and discuss difficulties. Professor Mensel, as chairman of the Board of Admission, also attended.

ENGLISH.—During the latter part of the summer, Professor Eliot conducted six Smith students on a six weeks' tour through Germany, Austria, and Czecho-Slovakia to study theater conditions there. The party became the guests of the German Government and had a Prussian attaché at their service. The six girls were: Margaret Wall, Irma Burkhardt, Beatrice Plumer, Aletta Freile, Elsie Anderson '27, and Miss Pickard (Spoken English).

Miss Hughes taught during the summer at the Bryn Mawr Summer School for industrial girls.

GOVERNMENT.—Professor Kimball delivered the first of a series of lectures on current events before the Rhode Island Women's Republican Club of Providence, Oct. 8. He will deliver the second one on Nov. 12. Mr. Kimball will also lecture before the Boston Smith Club on Nov. 5.

SOCIOLOGY.—Professor Barnes spent the summer abroad where he interviewed various officials and ex-officials, including the former Kaiser, on the subject of the blame for the World War. He also lectured in Germany. He plans to speak for the first time in this country since his return before the Hampshire County Progressive Club on Sunday evening, Oct. 31.

ZOÖLOGY.—Professor Dunn returned early in September from "one of the most remarkable scientific expeditions of modern times," with two giant lizards from the Dutch East Indies. The specimens are reputed to be the only living ones in captivity. They have been placed in the New York Zoölogical Gardens.

DIED.—Elizabeth Shand Allison, Oct. 19, after a short illness. Miss Allison graduated from Smith in 1909, was assistant registrar here from 1913–22, secretary to the warden 1922–23, and curator in the Art Department 1923–26.

APPOINTMENTS.—There are 48 new members of the faculty and staff this year. Below is a list of those of professorial rank.

Art: Peter Teigen, assistant professor. Mr. Teigen has an A.B. 1917 from the University of Minnesota and M.Arch. 1919 Harvard. He held the Robert Bacon Fine Arts Fellowship from 1922–24 and was assistant in Fine Arts at Harvard 1921–22.

Education: Elizabeth M. Collins, assistant professor. Miss Collins has studied at the Gorham Normal School and done College Extension work with the University of Maine, Bates, Simmons, and Sargent School. She was a public school teacher 1895–1917, principal of the Somerset Private Day School 1917–21, primary supervisor Augusta Public Schools 1921–23, primary and elementary supervisor Melrose Public Schools 1923–26.

Olive B. Gilchrist, assistant professor. Miss Gilchrist has her A.B. 1898, A.M. 1900, and Ph.D. 1916 from Boston University, as well as an Ed.M. 1926 from the Harvard Graduate School of Education. She has taught German, French, History, and English in France and in various high schools in this country.

Elene M. Michell, assistant professor. Miss Michell has a B.S. 1907 from Teachers College, Ed.M. 1925 and Ed.D. 1926 from Harvard. She held the Austen Scholarship from the Graduate School of Education at Harvard, 1925–26, and has had wide experience in social welfare and high school work.

English: Mary Ellen Chase, associate professor. Miss Chase has the degrees of A.B. 1909 University of Maine, A.M. 1918 and Ph.D. 1922 University of Minnesota. She taught History and English in various schools from 1909–17, and from 1917–25 was assistant professor of English at the University of Minnesota.

Marjorie Nicolson, associate professor (absent for the year). Miss Nicolson graduated from the University of Michigan in 1914 and took her A.M. there in 1918 and her Ph.D. in 1920 at Yale. She was a fellow at Yale from 1918–20 and at Johns Hopkins 1923–26. She took graduate courses in English at the University of Minnesota 1920–23. She was a librarian in the Detroit Public Library 1911–14, taught in high and normal schools 1914–18, was assistant professor of English at the University of Minnesota 1920–23 and at Goucher 1923–26.

Margaret Macgregor, assistant professor. Miss Macgregor graduated from Goucher in 1917 and took her A.M. at the University of Pennsylvania in 1921. She has held scholarships at Johns Hopkins and the University of Pennsylvania, has done work in high schools and in the English department at the University of Minnesota 1921–26.

French: René Guiet, associate professor. M. Guiet took his A.M. at the University of Illinois in 1921, and Licence-ès-Lettres at the Sorbonne in 1924. He was an instructor at the University of Illinois 1920–24, at Hunter College 1925–26, and was professor of French at the summer school of Middlebury College in 1925.

Hygiene and Physical Education: Dorothy Ainsworth, assistant professor. Announced in the July QUARTERLY. Miss Ainsworth is Head of the Gymnasium.

Philosophy: Alexander J. D. Porteous, professor. See comment in another column.

Psychology: William Sentman Taylor,

professor. See comment in another column.

Spanish: Miguel Zapata y Torres, assistant professor. Mr. Torres graduated from Cornell in 1922, took his A.M. there in 1924 and his Ph.D. in 1926. He held the University Fellowship in Romance Languages for travel and study abroad in 1924–25. He has been foreign correspondent for several New York firms and was a student and instructor at Cornell from 1919–26.

Spoken English: Frederick W. Brown, assistant professor. Mr. Brown holds a Ph.D. 1914 from Heidelberg University (Tiffin, O.) and A.M. 1917 Princeton. He has taught history and politics in high school and colleges, was instructor in speech at the State University of Iowa 1920–21 and research assistant in psychology 1921–22. From 1922–25 he was professor of English speech at Hokkaido Imperial University, Sapporo, Japan.

Personnel Office: Frances Knapp, Placement Secretary. Miss Knapp was Smith 1918 and took her Ed.M. at Harvard in 1924. She taught in 1918–19, 20–23, and 25–26, was assistant psychologist, Boston Psychopathic Hospital 1924–25, and psychologist, Division of Mental Hygiene, Boston, 1924–25.

Ruby B. Litchfield, Associate Director. Miss Litchfield graduated from Smith in 1910 and took a B.S. from Simmons in 1916. She was supervisor of deportment, Boston Society for the Care of Girls, 1915–23, did research work for the Children's Aid Association of Boston in 1923, and was General Secretary for the Brookline Friendly Society, 1923–26.

SABBATICAL ABSENCES have been granted as follows: for the year, Professors John Spencer Bassett, Howard R. Patch, Harris H. Wilder, Inez W. Wilder, Associate Professor Eleanor S. Duckett, Mary A. Dunham, Librarian. For the first semester, Associate Professor Arthur T. Jones.

PUBLICATIONS.—Chenot, Anna, and Bourgoin, Louise. Editors "Pierre," the autobiography of the early life of Anatole France. Allan and Bacon.

Conkling, Grace H. "Flying Fish." A. A. Knopf.

Dunn, Emmett Reid. "The Salamanders of the Family Plethodontidae." Smith College, Fiftieth Anniversary Series. (To be reviewed in a later issue.)

Grant, Elliott M. "French Poetry and Modern Industry." Harvard University Press.

Hankins, F. H. "An Introduction to the Study of Society." To appear soon.

Schinz, Albert. Editor "Nêne" by Ernest Pérchon. Ginn and Co.

Titchener, Frances. "L'Ecole Auvergnate." Champion, in Paris.

HEADS OF HOUSES.—There are six new appointments, as follows: Mrs. Marie A. Battis, Cushing; Miss Mary T. Bergen, Hopkins B; Mrs. Marie R. Dugan, Gardiner; Mrs. Alice Palmer, Talbot; Mrs. Ida Walker, Dawes; Mrs. Mary B. Williamson, 22 Belmont.

Undergraduate News

The annual entrance examination prizes were awarded as follows: Under the Old Plan to Susan Albright of Buffalo (N. Y.) who prepared at the Franklin School, Buffalo, and Miss Hall's School, Pittsfield. She is a Smith granddaughter, the daughter of Susan (Fuller) Albright '91, and a member of the family for which the Albright House was named. Under the New Plan the prize was awarded to Marjorie Lawson of East Orange (N. J.) who prepared for college at the East Orange High School. Honorable mention under the New Plan was accorded Alleen Kelly of Cleveland Heights (O.) who prepared at the Laurel School in Cleveland.

Eighteen members of the junior class have been admitted to candidacy for Special Honors. They are: in Classics, Elizabeth McCard; in English, Nancy Barnett, Florence Bill, Helen Huberth, Martha Kellogg, Florence Lyon, Frances Reed, Roberta Seaver, Sarah Taylor; in History, Ruth De Young, Louise Mayer, Kate Pinsdorf; in History, Government, and Economics, Frances Galt, Elizabeth Rosenberg, Elizabeth Stoffregen; in Mathematics, Rachel Howe; in Music, Gertrude P. Smith; in Spanish, Marion Kuhn. Twelve members of the senior class are continuing their work for Special Honors.

The Honor Roll from the class of 1929, consisting of students with an average of B or higher for the academic year 1925–26, is as follows: Mary Arnott, Mary Elizabeth Belcher, Carolyn Bixler, *Katherine Bolman*, Nancy Brenner, Elizabeth Carroll, Ruth Cook, Ruth Culp, Margaret Dunne, Marjorie Fales, Elizabeth French, *Marian Giles*, Jane Grinnan, Adele Hamerschlag, Dorothy Harger, Inez Hill, Marian Holden, Ruth Houghton, Elizabeth Howard, *Cornelia Jenney*, Cordelia Job, Barbara Johnston, Miriam Lee, Claire Levin, Christina Lochman, Mary McClintock, Janet MacInnes, Elizabeth Mack, Rosa

Mitchell, Mary Osborn, *Margaret Palfrey*, Althea Payson, Mary Petermann, Ida Raisbeck, Margaret Rheinberger, Mary Roblin, Wilhelmina Schoellkopf, *Barbara Simison*, *Lalia Simison*, Marjorie Stern, Frances Strakosch, Ruth Sumner, Elin Teir, Julia Wall, Elizabeth Wheeler, Caroline Williams, Hildegard Willmann, *Alice Winchester*, Annette Wiss, *Mary Louise Young.*

Students printed in italics are granddaughters of Smith. See page 61 for mothers' names.

ATHLETICS.—Fall Field Day was held Oct. 2 in the Scott Gymnasium. Inclement weather prevented the usual outdoor games. The Even team was victorious in the Odd-Even basket ball game, the score being 26–25.

The big new Brook Cabin of the Outing Club was introduced to the College on Oct. 9 with an old-fashioned house warming. The cabin was built with $600 appropriated by the Athletic Association and a gift of $500 from an alumna. It is situated on New Brook Hill and is less than two miles from the old Chestnut Mountain Cabin.

DEBATING UNION.—A debate with Cambridge University has been scheduled for Nov. 5. Several informal and interclass debates have been arranged to stimulate interest in debating at Smith.

DRAMATICS.—"The Marriage of Convenience," a farce by Alexander Dumas, was presented by Workshop on Oct. 20. Elsie Anderson '27 was the producer.

S. C. A. C. W.—The speakers since the opening of college have been Mary Clark '27, president of the Association, George Stewart of the Union Theological Seminary, and Rev. Arthur L. Kinsolving of Amherst.

Thirty members of the class of 1930 came to Northampton a week before the opening of college as members of the Christian Association Conference for freshmen. See article in front of magazine.

ELECTIONS.—1927: Marjorie Woodman, vice-president; Lucia Jordan, secretary; Leslie Winslow, treasurer; Harriet Mitchell, Council representative. The senior president is Ella-Bolling James.

1928: Polly Bullard, president; Laura Gundlach, vice-president; Ruth De Young, secretary; Margaret Haley, treasurer.

House of Representatives: Harriet Mitchell '27, president; Alice Himmelsbach '27, vice-president; Ruth Hazen '27, secretary.

OTHER NEWS.—The thirty-four juniors who

sailed for France late in August have been working at the University of Grenoble since Sept. 1. They have elected the following officers: Harriet Neithercut, president; Katherine Owsley, vice-president; Mary-Lois Ketcham, secretary; Lucy Mason, treasurer.

For the first semester of 1926–27 there are on the Dean's List 209 students: seniors, 102 (22.56% of the class); juniors, 52 (10.87%); sophomores, 55 (9.98%). A comparison with former years shows that the list varies but slightly in numbers: for the first semester of 1924–25 there were 203 students on the list and for 1925–26, 229.

Freshman Frolic was held Oct. 2.

Mountain Day was held on Oct. 11. This year, for the first time, Mountain Day was not announced in advance. The administration decided to wait for a pleasant day and to announce the holiday to the college by ringing the chapel bell and the bell on Martha Wilson Tower at 7 A.M.

RESIDENCE REGULATIONS

In view of the fact that so many phases of college life this year are influenced by the new residence regulations we are printing them in full.—EDITOR'S NOTE.

THE minimum residence requirement for undergraduates for a college year shall be two full semesters in college less seven nights of absence in each semester. The administration of this rule and the granting of exceptions for such reasons as illness shall lie with the Administrative Board. Every night spent outside of a college house whether in or out of Northampton, will be included as one of the seven nights. Saturday nights spent at the cabins by members of the Outing Club will not count as nights of absence. All other nights at the cabins will be included in the seven nights.

The Thanksgiving holiday shall be regarded as lasting for twenty-four hours, so that a student may be absent either for the night preceding Thanksgiving Day or for the night following Thanksgiving Day, but not for both, without having that absence count as one of the seven permissible nights of absence from college.

Registration will be required on the first day of each semester according to instructions issued by the Registrar's Office. The semester will close officially for the individual student at the end of her last examination.

All inquiries concerning these regulations should be made at the Warden's Office.

APPOINTMENTS TO FULL PROFESSORSHIPS

ALEXANDER J. D. PORTEOUS, M.A. in Classics 1921, in Philosophy 1924, Edinburgh University, B.A. in Literae Humaniores 1923 Oxford University, Professor in the Department of Philosophy. Professor Porteous holds from 1924–29 the Rhind Classical Scholarship, the Guthrie Fellowship in Classical Literature, the Ferguson Scholarship in Classics, and the Shaw Fellowship in Mental Philosophy. From 1924–26 Mr. Porteous was Assistant Lecturer in the Department

ALEXANDER PORTEOUS

WILLIAM TAYLOR

of Logic and Metaphysics at the University of Edinburgh.

William Sentman Taylor, B.S. 1916 Gettysburg College, M.S. 1923 University of Wisconsin, A.M. 1920 and Ph.D. 1921 Harvard, Professor in the Department of Psychology. Professor Taylor was an Assistant in Philosophy and Psychology at Gettysburg 1916–17, and Assistant in Philosophy at Harvard in 1919–20. He held the James Walker Fellowship at Harvard in 1920. He was a Lecturer in Psychology at Bryn Mawr in 1921–22, Instructor of Philosophy, University of Wisconsin, 1922–23, and Professor of Philosophy at the University of Maine 1923-26.

THE SMITH COLLEGE SCHOOL FOR SOCIAL WORK

THE ninth summer session of the Smith College School for Social Work was held in Northampton from July 2 to August 28. For this session, 94 students were enrolled and 89 completed the work. Twenty-eight seniors returned for their final session, and, in accordance with the vote of the Trustees, the degree of Master of Social Science was awarded to 23 who were holders of the Bachelor's degree from recognized institutions and who completed the work to the satisfaction of the staff. Nineteen students, all experienced social workers, attended the summer session not expecting to complete the full course. Eight were registered in the course for deans, and 34 were registered for the full course, have completed the first session, and have entered upon their field experience of the second session.

The attendance, 89, the largest the School has had since its foundation, was drawn from 25 different states. Canada (4) and Switzerland, Washington, California, Texas, and Mississippi, as well as the middle states and New England, were represented, Massachusetts, New York, and Pennsylvania leading the list with 10 each. The School contained graduates from 39 universities and colleges, Vassar leading with 6, followed by Smith and the University of Wisconsin with 4 each.

An experiment was attempted, which proved to be very successful, in having the course in psychiatry given as a coöperative course by three distinguished psychiatrists from various fields—Dr. Frankwood E. Williams, Medical Director of the National Committee for Mental Hygiene, Dr. Lawson G. Lowrey, Director of the Cleveland Child Guidance Clinic, and Dr. David M. Levy, Director of the Mental Hygiene Clinic for Children at the Michael Reese Dispensary in Chicago. In addition to these resident lecturers, the School was visited by nineteen visiting lecturers.

The second session opened September 1 with 34 students obtaining their field experience in various clinics and hospitals, Minneapolis, St. Paul, Chicago, Cleveland, Philadelphia, New York, Newark, New Haven, Worcester, Boston, Foxborough, and Taunton. These students are placed in seven groups under instructors appointed by the School, and gain their field experience under the direction of the supervisors of their various agencies. Fifteen of the class are attached to hospitals for mental diseases, one to a state committee for mental hygiene which is doing clinical work in child guidance, one to the Family Society of Philadelphia which is coöperating with the Child Guidance Clinic, and the rest in child guidance clinics. Contact is kept with these students by the School through frequent reports and visits by Miss Bertha C. Reynolds (Smith 1908), Associate Director, and the Director.

EVERETT KIMBALL, *Director*

THE METAMORPHOSIS OF HATFIELD AND SOME REMINISCENCES

IT was not easy for the Trustees to decide to turn Hatfield House, one of our original and hence best-beloved dwelling houses, into Hatfield Hall. There were traditions in Hatfield, memories which filled every nook and cranny; there were personalities that had made the very walls alive; and at first thought it seemed nothing less than sacrilege to substitute classrooms and offices for the parlors and student bedrooms which had outlived so many college generations. And the Trustees considered the matter with solicitous care. The College has grown to 2000 students and the faculty numbers more than two hundred. We have a new gymnasium, to be sure, and a new music building, but our recitation rooms have remained about the same and the faculty have fairly sat upon each other's laps when it came to office space. Hatfield House had always run on a deficit—because it did not accommodate enough students to make the revenue overbalance the overhead. The College simply couldn't afford *not* to make the change. And it was done.

And, as so often happens in this world wherein we take so many forward steps with fear and misgiving, the experiment has proved a great success, and Hatfield Hall bids fair to be the most desired of all our academic buildings. There are housed therein "all the Romans and most of the Greeks," as one of our classicist friends told us proudly, and, to continue her nomenclature, there are also many of the Franks and some of the Spaniards. There are an Economics and Sociology seminar room and two other seminar rooms in which are classes for Bible, English, and Government. There are nine spick and span new classrooms with new chairs and velvety blackboards; there is a large light room for the Latin museum, and there are offices for twenty-five members of the faculty. Many of these are on the third floor, to reach which the broad main stairway was continued from the second floor. The whole interior shines with fresh paint and refinished wood work, and the walls are a soft warm tan. Those who have loved Hatfield House these many years need never fear that it will no longer be an integral part of the College—indeed, considering the Romans and the Franks alone, it is easy to see that more Smith College students will enter its doors and travel up and down its stairs in

just one year than have lived within its portals in all its long and honorable career. E. N. H.

Some Reminiscences

We publish with delight Mary Breese Fuller's remembrances of the days when Miss Hesse ruled over Hatfield and Miss Jordan's salon was in full sway.

SO Hatfield House is to become Hatfield Hall. In undergraduate language, it is no longer a "dorm," but has been elevated into the ranks of an academic building. I am sure it will live up to this spiritual change as well as it did to its enlargement in 1894 and its moving in 1908. But I suppose that single room of mine which always made me think of "Man wants but little here below and wants that little long" is blotted out. And the echoes of N. B. reciting French poetry in the bath tub have vanished with the back stairs. So has gone the shadow of the distinguished alumna visitor who gave up afresh every day the task of finding her room in the intricacies of the third floor and leaned patiently against the wall until someone should lead her home.

I believe the piazza will be left where our one freshman gave her party to the nineteen seniors. But what about those dormer windows from which we hung out and chirruped to the Washburn House at the first Smith College celebration of Columbus Day? On the morning of October 12, 1892, President Seelye recalled to us the anniversary of Columbus's landing on the next day. He pictured vividly the probable scene at two o'clock in the morning, the moon shining over the water, the consummation of faith, and so forth, and wound up in ringing tones: "I have no sympathy with this tendency to belittle Columbus."

We, too, decided not only to refuse to belittle Columbus, but to enlarge him. So at one A.M. each of three houses staged a silent party of some sort with shrouded windows and muffled lights. Our party in the Hatfield House was a feast, graced only by pure American products, pop corn, chocolate cigars, large cookies with the head of Columbus. At five minutes of two, at a toot from a horn, the girls of Hubbard, Washburn, and Hatfield turned on their lights full blaze, threw open their windows; at the second toot at exactly two o'clock we all burst out into "America." The first verse went with fair harmony but the second and third! Of course firecrackers and other types of noise followed the singing. In the midst of the mêlée Miss Hesse, the lady in charge, suddenly appeared in our room: "Young ladies, I do not mind the singing, but this hanging out of windows and hollering I consider *extremely vulgar.*" In chapel the next morning the President remarked with a twinkle: "Tell it not in Gath, lest the Philistines turn and mock us."

Miss Hesse was an exquisite lady of the old school, whose strongest word of condemnation was "extremely vulgar." She, as well as Miss Jordan, had a group of literary friends, including her brilliant young nephews, the "Hapgood boys," so that the social life of that period made the house a place of special privileges for the students of the nineties.

Miss Jordan's stimulating personality and generous hospitality brought to us a long procession of interesting people who sat at the Hatfield House table, told stories by the parlor fire, or exchanged quips with Miss Jordan in her room, while especially privileged seniors sat by with happily cocked ears. Charles Dudley Warner, Mark Twain, and Richard Burton were frequent visitors. Of course Mr. Warner's geniality and charm made him a great favorite. He always insisted that he was a "Hatfield House girl" and was to be greeted as such by the other members of the household wherever they saw him. The antics of Mr. Clemens, sometimes of the sort which led Mrs. Aldrich to refuse him a seat at her dinner table, were joyfully welcomed by us.

Thomas Davidson, the Adirondack philosopher, after a profound lecture on Aristotle, sat on the floor by the fire with the girls around him, insisted on the lights being turned out, and recited "Bairnies Cuddle Doon" and other Scotch ballads to his entranced audience. Agnes Repplier's poignant wit awed a dinner table and set more than one future essayist on her path. Ruth McEnery Stuart told how she came to write "Sonny," and Henry James wove for us some of his marvelous tapestry.

Miss Jordan herself was a constant stimulus. Her mental alertness and catholic recognition of literature in any guise led her to choose a great variety of books for her evening readings to us. Her enjoyment at the reactions of the students to every book seemed to be always fresh. And how her magic tongue and presence wove townspeople, faculty, and students together on her Tuesday afternoons!

Good luck go with Hatfield Hall as it always dwelt in Hatfield House.

MARY BREESE FULLER 1894

THE SCHOOL OF POLITICS

AS we go to press we are presented with the program for the School of Politics to be held in Sage Hall Oct. 29 and 30. It is conducted with the coöperation of Smith College by the Massachusetts League of Women Voters and the subject is "Current Political Issues." The program follows:

FRIDAY, OCTOBER 29

The State's Part in an Election.
Frederick W. Cook,
Secretary of the Commonwealth.
Larger Phases of Present Party History.
Phillips Bradley, A.B.,
Professor of Political Science, Amherst College.
Symposium: Party Platforms of 1926.
Republican—Hon. John C. Hull,
Speaker of the House of Representatives.
Democrat—Mr. Joseph Ely.
The Workers Party of America, the Socialist, and the Socialist-Labor Parties have been invited to take part in the discussion.
Citizenship in a Republic.
William Allan Neilson, Ph.D., LL.D., L.H.D.,
President of Smith College.
State Versus Nation or State in Coöperation with Nation.
Robert D. Leigh, Ph.D.,
A. Barton Hepburn Professor of Government, Williams College.

SATURDAY, OCTOBER 30

Government Responsibility for Material Prosperity.
Esther Lowenthal, Ph.D.,
Professor of Economics and Sociology, Robert A. Woods Foundation, Smith College.
Some Economic Issues that will Face the Next Congress.
William Orton, M.A., M.Sc.,
Professor of Economics and Sociology, Smith College.
The Plight of Agriculture.
Dorothy Wolff Douglas, Ph.D.,
Instructor in Economics and Sociology, Smith College.
The People as Legislators.
Everett Kimball, Ph.D.,
Professor of Government, Smith College.

FROM THE MINUTES OF THE TRUSTEES' MEETING

A SPECIAL meeting of the Board of Trustees was held on Friday evening, October 15, at the President's House, at which the President outlined the policies and tendencies of the college, and a general discussion followed.

Saturday morning, October 16, was occupied

by the Trustees in visiting the physical equipment of the college and in committee meetings.

. The regular annual meeting was held Saturday afternoon at two o'clock in the President's Office.

The annual Report of the President was presented and was accepted and ordered printed as usual.

It was voted that the action taken in June authorizing the conferring of the degree of Master of Social Science on graduates of the School for Social Work be made retroactive.

The following officers of the Board were elected:

> President, William Allan Neilson
> Vice-President, John A. Houston
> Treasurer, George P. Hyde
> Secretary, Annetta I. Clark

It was voted that the Secretary be instructed to acknowledge to Mrs. Gallagher her gifts to the Browsing Room in the Library, and to accept in behalf of the Board the gift of four pictures presented by Miss Mary Stevens of Northampton.

It was voted that the President be authorized to bring before the Board at its next meeting suggestions for the personnel of a Visiting Committee of the Art Department.

Meeting adjourned.

ANNETTA I. CLARK, *Secretary*

THE BLAZED TRAIL AND AFTER

MLLE. CATTANÈS has brought her junior group home again, and we are figuratively flying the flag in her honor. Not that it was a hard group to shepherd; it was not. Indeed if this second group for whom the trail is blazed is half so good Smith College will be proud of it. Nonetheless the race that Mlle. Cattanès ran is a good race and no one

COLLEGE CAL

Nov. 3. . . . . The Flonzaley Quartet
Nov. 4. . . . . Dr. E. A. Lowe (lecture)
Nov. 5. . . . . Cambridge-Smith Debate
Nov. 6. . . . . Miss Crook (address)
Nov. 7. . . . . John Duke (recital)
Nov. 10. . . . . Field Day
Nov. 10. . . . . Workshop
Nov. 14. . . . . Faculty Recital
Nov. 17. . . . . Elshuco Trio
Nov. 24. . . . . Richard Crooks (tenor)
Nov. 25. . . . . Thanksgiving Day
Nov. 25. . . . . Wilson T. Moog (recital)
Dec. 1. . . . . Christmas Sale
Dec. 3 and 4. . . . Dramatics Association

THE NOTE ROOM

Written by Elizabeth M. Bacon '28, Drawings by Priscilla Paine '28 *

I WONDER how much you who are reading this remember about October at college? Do you know that sweep of maples gloriously red across Paradise and the golden, slow-dropping elms in front of chapel? Do you remember how the air feels when the sky is piercingly blue and how new books smell, and the exhilaration of a new pencil? Did you feel sad at leaving summer behind you? Did you feel a flash of rebellion at the thought of work and weren't you agreeably surprised to find that you still had a mind and it could function? Didn't you get a little excited about the things you might discover, the people you might find? It is the same now and, reluctantly eager, we are shaking ourselves free of mental moth balls and preparing for tremendous encounters.

While the "esprit" is the same there are outward and visible changes which the returning student will notice as she toils up Main Street, sagging with second-hand chairs, pillows, curtains, picture-wire, and a bulb; changes which the freshman will accept as she rushes to the station in a futile attempt to excavate her trunk. There is a convention, in Northampton, by which all trunks must rest three days before undertaking the arduous trip from the station to a campus house.

In the first place the new quadrangle is triumphantly completed. Martha Wilson sits in splendid self-satisfaction with Morrow on one side and Gardiner on the other — a glorious trio! If you are impressed with the outside wait till you go in! Such chintz, such furniture—they look all of them like the

very nicest covers of *Country Life*. It is a privilege to live with three such gracious personalities as these houses have become, although of course there are always some weak and slothful souls who feel they are a long, long way from chapel; and the sound of the bicycle bell is heard in the land as a veritable flotilla of wheels starts through the archway as the bell in Martha Wilson chimes at eight twenty-five.

There is another new personality, The Tryon Art Gallery, which was inaugurated with a "Reception and Formal Opening" on October 8, to which the grown-ups were invited but we were not. We got a peek inside, however—a peek at gay lights, festive evening dresses of ladies, sober dress clothes of gentlemen, and lucky, lucky students darting about with food. It is a delightful place. Outside it has bushes with red berries; inside there is a glorious bronze cat, who came up from New York in an exhibition sent up from the Ferargil Galleries. It is dignified and beautiful, and stays open on Sunday afternoons, which gives the uninitiated a chance to go in and marvel. There is still another change: Hatfield House, having graduated as a student has, this year come back to teach and has been changed from a dormitory into classrooms. Although inexperienced, she seems to be holding her own with the older and more conservative pedagogues like Seelye, Pierce, and even Lilly. Being of a curious turn of mind we made a special trip to Miss Leonard one day to find out what had become of all the dwelling-house furniture in Hatfield. We came away

* "Girls may come and girls may go but I go on forever," sighed the QUARTERLY as it watched Eleanor Hard and Dorothy Rand graduate last June. For two years Eleanor had taken care of the Note Room and had done it with so much color that we wondered what we should ever do without her. And now we know. Her mantle has fallen on Elizabeth Bacon '28, a junior granddaughter whose mother was Caroline Mitchell '97. She makes her bow in this issue. Eleanor, by the way, writes from Washington, "How I should like to be in the Connecticut Valley with Mt. Tom all hazy in the distance and the autumn leaves on Green St.," and we think she's going to be a bit homesick when she reads a Note Room in which she has had no part. We introduce also Priscilla Paine '28. She, too, is a granddaughter, daughter of Mary Tillinghast '99, and we hope that she will continue to wield the clever drawing pen that Dorothy dropped for her diploma. Good hunting to us all!—EDITOR'S NOTE.

convinced that she is as Scotch as the President for there seems to be a bit of Hatfield House everywhere. The beds are in the employees' rooms in the new dormitories, the gas range over on Henshaw, and many a parlor is the dressier for Hatfield. Miss Leonard told us also about the Browsing room. During the summer Mr. and Mrs. Gallagher, who gave the room as a memorial to their daughter, have generously redecorated it, made the curtains and rugs fresh, and the room is as beautiful as when it was new, and a delight to us all. Perhaps the greatest shock, the difference that we feel most keenly, is the population of the erstwhile grindroom with stacks. Those round little tables, with nice green shaded lights hanging over them, have gone, and gone with them is the gayest place in the Library. At chapel one day the President remarked that "Seelye has been redecorated." It does seem very clean, but we are still looking for the decorations! The strangest thing, however, is the unnatural quiet of Arnold and Belmont this year, and the appearance of certain well known "Belmontese" on campus.

However, before we had seen all these things college began in real earnest. It began on Tuesday, September 28, at eight-thirty, when we heard the chime greeting us who were coming back and ringing an enthusiastic welcome to six hundred and thirty freshmen who were hearing it for the first time. Can you remember the breathlessness that came with your first chapel? The Faculty, remote and superior in their caps and gowns; people in swarms around you, subdued, very attentive; the thousands of faces all unfamiliar; the sudden hush; the music; the singing; and then the President? Always at first chapel he welcomes the latest amazing gallery of freshmen and all of us on the ground floor and tells us what has been going on through the summer. This year the changes were easy to see but the President told us that Mr. King, the genius of the campus, had been ill the entire summer. "For 35 years," the President said, "Mr. King has spent his summers in getting the college ready to open. This year the work has fallen to his son, and of him Mr. King has reason to be proud." And then he talked to us a little sadly, a little sternly, about the advantages of living a college life at college, or, to be more specific, of living our college lives at this college. We wish we had space to quote all his words.

You will observe [he said] that the number of returning students is smaller than usual. This fact is due in part to their desires and in part to ours. A good many wore away in the course of last winter; some more have disappeared this summer. . . . As I announced to you last spring, we rather hoped that a number of those then with us would find other interests in the course of the summer and we thought they might be led to a decision on that point by the requirement the faculty had introduced in regard to residence, and we told those students, on the whole, that their not liking that requirement was a sign that this was not the place for them. . . .

While we believe in other forms of activity, of entertainment, of education, we are, nevertheless, determined that this shall be primarily an institution of learning. . . . We in the academic profession realize that the proportion of born students, of potential scholars in so large a number cannot be so great as it was when college was attended by a small number of people who felt distinctly a scholastic calling. Our purpose then is to revise our training to make it available and really useful to this new constituency without sacrificing the essential character of scholarship. It would be very easy to turn this institution into a center of engaging social life with a few duties to give a kind of relish to a perpetual holiday. It isn't what we are here for. We should be false to the trust imposed in us. We are not going to yield to that; we are going to insist that the intellectual life here shall be the main life, even if we have to dispense with large numbers of admirable and effective persons.

And then the President said something about the system of government under which we find ourselves living at college. The "creation of a self-respecting, self-conducting, self-directing individual is mainly what we are after," and he explained the relations between the faculty, students, and trustees as clearly as he explains everything. And in conclusion said:

The new students are welcome here to co-operate in a hard and important task. We do not desire that any of you should leave, in fact, we have elaborate machinery devised for keeping you here. We want to preserve our tradition and improve our tradition, and all those students who enter this college today are welcome to join us in that duty.

Last June it seemed as though the new restriction, seven nights a semester away from college, would cause a great deal of kicking at the traces, and occasional ruptures thereof. Now that we are here, with last year's problem of deciding how often one could leave college and get away with it, rather generously settled for us, things are going on very much as usual. There are differences of course: one doesn't waste a night on the midnight, and one takes the 8:15 on Saturday morning instead of the 4 o'clock Friday. Seven nights doesn't sound like much but Smith seems to be making the most of them, and we don't forget that one night at Thanksgiving doesn't count.

The Administration is hard put to it, at present, to think of some new privilege which can be attached to the Dean's List. As year by year the privileges formerly enjoyed by that exclusive body have been granted to the common herd or abrogated for everybody, the Administration has, with extraordinary alacrity, substituted some new honor. Now they are all exhausted, and the Dean's List has become purely honorary—an announcement which was received in dubious silence one morning in chapel. Perhaps they'll think of something soon; unaccompanied honor seems just a little intangible for a B average. Student Government has started out with high hopes for a good year. The freshmen have been properly and seriously coached on the rules and the new House Councils bid fair to maintain the coöperation and morale of the houses in a highly satisfactory way. "The proof of the pudding—" and there will be more to say of that later. Meantime read what Tatty Bingham says on pages 32 and 128.

Besides the absorbing routine of everyday life, with days that begin with a scramble to make breakfast and end, officially, at ten when one hurries home from the Library laden with books to be returned before chapel next morning—besides these days there have been extras. Of course the first and outstanding extra was Mountain Day. All that we knew about Mountain Day was that it was "to be announced." On a Monday morning the President told us that we might expect Mountain Day sometime the next week. "When you hear the chapel bell ringing between seven and seven-thirty it means that there will be no school on that day." No one knew, everyone guessed, and there was great excitement and speculation. Monday was cloudy, Monday night it got colder, and Tuesday dawned supremely clear. It dawned to the tune of the chapel bell calling at the top of its (what does a bell have instead of lungs?) calling at the top of its clapper that there'd be "no school to-day." It was a glorious day—a red and gold and amber day, a laughing, blue day. It was warm enough to wear a sweater and just cold enough to need one. The leaves

had been polished over night and vaunted themselves against the sky, like triumphant banners of a marching army. People did all sorts of things. There were buggies, filled with hay, picnic luncheons, and girls; there were swarms and swarms of bicycles; there

were Fords bursting with fur coats and berets. There were people on horseback; people in trucks, overflowing, with only room left to bring back cider! People walked to the cabin; people walked the Range; people ran over Mount Tom; people had delightful picnics in the woods, by the river, under a tree. Everyone was everywhere except at home. All day long it was a nice day, and when it got dark it was a bewitching night. Honesty forces me to admit that there wasn't very much of a moon, but we felt as though it were full, very large, and extremely moonlighty! The next day there were classes and we were stiff and unprepared, but our rooms were brilliant with leaves and our eyes shining with the wind that had blown in them all day.

Before Mountain Day, though, there was Freshman Frolic, a bewildering and jovial affair to which one takes a supposedly shy freshman and finds she knows—EVERYONE! The Class of 1930 looked very large and very nice, and the rest of the college beamed at them from the floor, while the Administration sat in the gallery and approved. At least it looked as if it did. And, incidentally, it is just as well we have a huge gym if freshman candidates for Smith are going to prove themselves so amazingly clever at passing exams. Speaking of which I forgot to mention the day in chapel when the President announced the freshmen prize winners. He made each one stand up to the admiring gaze of all her envious peers and older sisters. On two other occasions the freshmen were featured in John M. Greene—and both occasions were musical. I refer to Freshman Song Trials, when the assembled college sings, to a variety of gyrations graceful and otherwise, "Just One College for Us" and the "Purple in Triumph Waving" until it is faint with repetition and laughter, and to the morning when the freshman choir, full to the last inch of seat in the back row, burst upon our gaze and sang with such precision and vigor that last year's champions had best put their best voices forward.

Another extra was the Philharmonic which came and played Tchaikovsky's Fifth Symphony to us. They played it superbly and we all felt very happy. Mary Lewis sang and we came to listen. The Hampton Quartet entertained us delightfully both at Sage Hall in the evening and at chapel the morning after. The Faculty played to us one Sunday evening. They gave us a concert of eighteenth century music played on the harpsichord and clavichord. The Faculty are really very clever and the music they played, all brittle, delicate things, was enchanting. Nice things are going to happen, too, for the Flonzaley Quartet is coming, and the Elshuco Trio; the Boston and Cleveland Symphonies, the English Singers, Kreisler—we are saving up for that already —and all sorts of other exciting people. The Repertory Company is back again, with some familiar faces, some new. They have amused us hilariously for the last two weeks, and we hope they'll stay a long time. Elsie Anderson gave Mr. Hansell a run for his money when she produced "A Marriage of Convenience" for the benefit of the stage fund. It was done beautifully and ran three nights. The stage fund, however, is quite undernourished and needs a good deal of benefiting. Mr. Sherwood Eddy talked to us, in an exciting meeting on "Russia, a Warning and a Challenge." Hugh Walpole, under the auspices of the Hampshire Bookshop, gave two brilliant and most amusing talks and Professor S. Radnakrishnan, of the University of Calcutta, spoke on "Philosophy and Civilization." And the School of Politics, held at Smith under the auspices of the League of Women Voters, educated us on all sorts of problems about which as actual or potential voters we ought to inform ourselves. More shame to us that we didn't go in larger numbers! How shall we acquit ourselves in the Cambridge-Smith debate so soon to come, we wonder!

"The world is so full of a number of things . . ." and, while we jerk our minds to higher levels, we are getting "Charley Horse" and black and blue spots from hockey and soccer, we are learning about basket ball, we are shooting bows and arrows, we are swimming, and dancing and hoping it's making us thin, and we are taking the shells up Paradise (Paradise no longer being in the "shy and retreating mood" in which we found it when college opened). It poured on Field Day, so instead of hockey there was a basket ball game. Field Day brings to mind the Outing Club which has just been presented with a new cabin. It is a beautiful cabin with two rooms and an enormous fireplace; and the Outing Club is so proud of it that every time they hear the word "cabin" they beam and look self-conscious.

At the instigation of Mr. Orton, the Carnegie Institute, and others a new and very popular organization has come into being, the International Club. Limited to fifty members it has meetings every two weeks to discuss problems, national and international. Members who are absent for more than three meetings, without an academic excuse, are dropped, and way is made for one of the patient, prospective internationalists on the waiting list.

Speaking of Internationalists, word has come to us of the juniors in Grenoble through Mrs. Morrow, who saw them there soon after they had arrived. I quote only bits of what she said one morning in chapel:

Usually when I sit on this platform, although I realize it is a great honor to sit on a level with the President, the Dean, and the Faculty, usually I wish that I were sitting down there with the undergraduates. . . . But I hope that to-day you notice an indifference in me, a serenely beautiful indifference. You are just as keen and good-looking and bright as the last time I stood here, but I can look at you perfectly calmly and without envy. All the envy that I have is centered on those thirty-four juniors in France!

I went there and saw them starting work at the beginning of September. Classes begin at eight and last until four. There are recitations in the afternoon, but there are none on Saturday. If you are a very good girl, you go on some little excursion to the mountains, and if you are not so good a student, as some I know, you labor on a theme or translation. The university where the girls are studying is in part of an old church. They listen with almost breathless attention. You know, when you are trying to take down a new language it is like being slightly deaf. There is also a certain stirring of pride when you work with people of other nationalities. It is a trifle hard to find that a Roumanian can speak French better than you can; that an English girl can translate better than you can, and most annoying to see two Dutch boys who can do your work in half the time it takes you. You want to come up to the Roumanian, you want to do as well as the English, and you certainly want to beat the Dutch. They are spurred on by the fine record of the juniors who were over there last year and who did so well.

One of the girls said she liked all the mountains around Grenoble, but she wished that one of them were Mount Tom. That is an appreciation of Massachusetts in terms of French geography, and that is my entire point, all the point that I am trying to make this morning. Some of us never know our homes, our college, until we go away. I think there are many people who can explain to you better than I can what our juniors are doing at Grenoble. But the course that interested me most was one that was not written, not scheduled—a course in the appreciation of Smith College. I suppose that no one in this room needs that course, but if any of you want it, won't you meet me at the White Star dock, for I should love to chaperon you.

While the college applauded Mrs. Morrow and the juniors in France, it turned about and craned its neck to welcome back the seniors who had been in France last year. It is particularly nice to see them in the homely haunts of Green Street and Elm Street, because they wear about them a certain air, a faint and tantalizing whiff of "cosmopolitaness." We think that they are glad to be back—we hope they are, because we are very proud of them and very glad to see them; but all the same, there is something about them that sets them apart from us, a certain "je ne sais quoi"—which they can pronounce, and we cannot!

The air is full of November now, and already there have been flurries of snow. The wind howls around the Library, whipping the last yellow leaves off the trees and whirling them spitefully into the gray clouds. Fur coats scuttle between classes, and the astronomy observers swear gently at the stars with icy breath. The football games are getting important now—and blue or red hats go New Haven or Bostonward each week-end as long as the precious seven nights permit! The college has collected itself and us and has settled down to business. Around it there is an atmosphere of coming winter. The trees are getting bare down by Paradise so that the President's House stands out in lovely relief as we walk or bicycle up from Allen Field, around the edge of the pond, and so to our new quadrangle homes. The nights are clear and very cold. The dead leaves in front of the Library crackle when we step on them and are whirled into eddies on windy days. Inside the Library, it is warm and light and very quiet. Perhaps it is because we want good marks that we are working hard, perhaps it is because we realize that four years are not very long, and there are a great many things we should like to know—but perhaps it is that in some vague, half-understanding way, we feel that on our shoulders has fallen the burden and the privilege of bringing to fruition those seeds of trust and generosity which have been sown here by our families, the college, and the alumnae.

" The last long mile "

THE ALUMNAE ASSOCIATION

OUR NEW PRESIDENT, MARY FROST SAWYER 1894

We are very glad to introduce Mrs. Sawyer formally to her constituency. She is the wife of James Cowan Sawyer who for twenty-five years has been treasurer of Phillips Academy, Andover. She has two sons of whom the elder is Yale '24, Harvard School of Business Administration '26, and the younger is still in Yale. She was the senior president of her class and was vice-president of the Board of Directors of the Alumnae Association from 1900–03. During our $4,000,000 campaign she was chairman of her district. One of her friends tells us that the dreamy look in her eyes in this picture is most deceptive, but of the friendliness of her greeting there is no mistake.

GREETINGS to all the members of the Smith College family, scattered far and wide but bound together by the ties of loyalty to our Alma Mater.

This year brings a new executive to our Association; but the average member will not be conscious of the change. Due to the time and thought which preceding officers have put into the machinery of the organization and also to the very able permanent force with which its office in Northampton is manned, the Association could function quite satisfactorily without a President. However, there is a pleasant provision of the Constitution which bestows on some fortunate mortal the title with the emoluments appertaining thereto: said emoluments consisting of a renewal of that happy undergraduate feeling of proprietorship, and the opportunity for service to the College.

The present incumbent enters the office at a time when we seem to be resting on our oars a bit. We have not laid them down; we are merely letting them lie in the rowlocks while we gather strength and courage for the next stroke— the Alumnae Fund. "New occasions teach new duties." What we have accomplished in the past indicates what we shall hope to do in the future. Always the College has needs; may our Alumnae Association ever be ready to meet them!

MARY FROST SAWYER 1894

DATA FROM THE OFFICE

The Alumnae Council will convene in North-ampton, February 17, 18, and 19.

The Parade Chairman for June 1927 is Catharine Weiser 1917. Chairmen of costume committees in classes holding reunions next June are asked to submit designs for costumes to the Parade Chairman at the earliest moment. Address, 226 Pine St., Holyoke, Mass.

The Alumnae Office was "at home" to the 46 freshman granddaughters on Oct. 21. An informal reception was held in the offices, and refreshments were served. Several of the Association officers and directors who were in Northampton for the fall meeting were also present.

The fall meeting of the Executive and Finance Committees was held in Northampton, Oct. 22. There was also a meeting of the Alumnae Fund Committee which is recorded under a separate caption.

NEWS OF THE ALUMNAE FUND

The Executive Committee has appointed the following members of the Alumnae Fund Committee: Harriet (Bliss) Ford '99, chairman, to serve for three years, Alice (Wright) Teagle '04, five years, Elizabeth (Cutter) Morrow '96, four years, Anne Coburn '21, two years, and Stella Tuthill '07, one year. The President and Treasurer of the Alumnae Association, the General Secretary, and the Alumnae Fund Secretary are also members of the Committee ex-officio.

After the discussions of the Committee it was decided that the Alumnae Fund should stand aside until June in order to leave the field free for the Juniper Lodge Committee and the Burton Memorial Fund Committee. The position of the Alumnae Fund Committee was outlined by its Chairman to the chairmen of these two committees in the following letter, which we quote here because of its interest to the alumnae in general:

October 23, 1926

The new Alumnae Fund Committee held its first meeting yesterday, with the Executive Committee of the Alumnae Association, and talked over its general set-up and the various splendid projects which are awaiting its sponsorship.

As Acting Chairman, I had supposed that we would start at once on the preparation of material so as to be able to go into effective

action as soon as the February Council should have passed upon our suggestions, and that we would then have our first alumnae offering to present at the 1927 Commencement. I think that this supposition was also pretty generally shared by the various individual members before the meeting.

However, when the group mind got to work, especially after it had been brought up to date on the status of the Juniper Lodge and Burton Memorial Funds, it was decided unanimously that we ought to postpone actual adoption of a project until June, in order to leave the field free in the interim for the Juniper Lodge Committee, working through the clubs and special donors, and the Burton Memorial Committee, working through the classes.*

The Fund Committee, though eager and ready to begin its work, realizes what an unhappy and confusing situation would result if alumnae giving were in any way diverted from these two objectives which are still in process.

For your further information I should add that at the February Council meeting the Fund Committee plans merely to confer with the class representatives and the Council on various projects, the better to prepare for its proposals to be made in June; but it will be made perfectly clear at that time that the Committee considers that until June the Juniper Lodge and Burton Memorial Funds have right of way. This decision will also be published in the November QUARTERLY.

Please accept our united wishes for a success even beyond your dreams in your work during these coming months.

Most cordially yours,
(signed) HARRIET C. BLISS FORD, *Chairman*

JUNIPER LODGE FINANCES

The Juniper Lodge Endowment Fund, on Oct. 20, amounted to $18,385.93. Miss Caverno has given further data about Juniper Lodge on page 38. The Boston Association is to give a Juniper Lodge Bridge Party at the new University Club, Nov. 15.

LOCAL CLUBS

ALBANY.—Professor Bixler (Biblical Literature) will speak at a meeting of the Albany Club on Nov. 6.

ATLANTA.—The Club will be addressed by President Neilson, Nov. 15.

BOSTON.—The Boston Association will give a reception to 1926 on Nov. 5, at which Professor Kimball (Government) will be the speaker.

BROOKLYN.—An interesting program for the year has been outlined by the Brooklyn

---

*As the alumnae already know, these two projects, while they have received the endorsement of the Alumnae Association, are in no sense under its direction. In the interim between the Birthday Gift and the first project of the Alumnae Fund Committee they have been proposed and are being carried on by independent committees of loyal alumnae.—ED.

Club, starting with a bridge party on Oct. 4. At the November meeting the speaker was Professor Orton (Economics), on "The Purpose of a College Education."

CLEVELAND.—President Neilson will be in Cleveland Nov. 12-13, and will address a meeting of the Cleveland Club.

FITCHBURG.—Miss Caverno addressed the Club, Oct. 23.

JAPAN.—A letter received from Clara Loomis '00, written from Yokohama Sept. 24, assures the Association that each member of the Club is back at her post after a good summer. It was impossible to hold a meeting last year because the members were located so far apart. Miss Loomis writes: "Pray send more of your number to live in Japan, for there is plenty to do and we can then report some rousing Smith Club meetings."

MIAMI.—There has been no meeting of the Club this fall, as the members have been devoting all their time to recuperating from the hurricane. The president, Mrs. Arthur L. Yarborough (Katherine Wood '14) has a new address: 276 N. E. 22 St., Miami, Fla.

NEW HAVEN.—The Club will hold its first meeting of the season Nov. 6, with President Neilson as the speaker.

NEW YORK.—A series of talks by members of the faculty and other people from Smith has been arranged for the winter. The first was given on Oct. 23 by Miss Farrand, Director of the Press Board and Assistant Professor of English. Mrs. Scales will speak at the November meeting of her connection with the undergraduates.

. There has been so much dissatisfaction with the present location of the Clubhouse, because of its inaccessibility, that it has been put on the market. This was done with the idea that if a worthwhile offer is received the committee in charge will locate possible new sites. In the meantime, the Clubhouse is open at the old location, 233 E. 17 St.

ST. PAUL.—A rummage sale was held by the St. Paul Club, Oct. 21, 22, and 23. They also met for luncheon on Oct. 30.

UTICA.—Plans have been completed by the Utica Club to present Mordkin and his Russian Ballet, Nov. 17, at the Colonial Theater.

A. A. U. W. NOTES

National Headquarters and Clubhouse, 1634 Eye St. N. W., Washington, D. C.

THE INTERNATIONAL FEDERATION MEETS AT AMSTERDAM

In the October issue of the *A. A. U. W. Journal*, under this very caption, is the official account of the Conference. As it happens it was written by a Smith woman, Florence Angell 1911, secretary of the Committee on International Relations, and we commend it to your attention for the more formal recital and many details which we do not publish here. This summer the QUARTERLY had its own special correspondent in Amsterdam, namely, Florence Homer Snow 1904, General Secretary of the Alumnae Association of Smith College, and for news of the Conference we quote from her travelog.

THE 400 odd delegates and visitors to the "Fourth Conference of the International Federation of University Women" arrived in relays at Amster*dam* (accent on the last syllable, with the a's very broad) on July 27 and 28, while the organization gathered headway in meetings of the administrative Council and various committees. Six of us were lucky enough to be lodged with Florence (Plaut) Hartog 1911 in a beautiful Dutch house at Emmalaan 7, near a park in the new section of the town: Caro Swett '95, Dr. Agnes Rogers, now at Bryn Mawr but formerly on our faculty, a Miss Reynolds and Miss

Janney from Seattle and Michigan, and Dr. Lüders, a brilliant and very likeable woman from Berlin, a member of the German Reichstag. Between meetings and into the night we held informal and most friendly discussions on politics and education and social affairs and such like meaty subjects, and as usual they were quite as profitable as the formal sessions. Mrs. Hartog gave a reception one afternoon to the 125 American delegates and we assisted in presentations to the receiving line and in dispensing the magnificent Dutch refreshments.

Dean Gildersleeve of Barnard, President of the International Federation, presided over the Conference with great charm and distinction. In her opening speech she urged a greater use of the opportunities now open to women—a higher quality of work, so that the world shall say, not "how excellent for a woman," but "how excellent." Dr. Simons, the president of the Dutch federation, on the other hand, plead for greater energy and activity in opening further opportunities, a difference in emphasis in key with the varying status of European and western women. And yet it is not fair to say that a country which has universal suffrage and imposes a fine of five dollars or so upon those who fail to cast their vote at the polls and have not presented a valid excuse beforehand —is less advanced than we!

The municipality greeted us in the person of Mr. Wibaut, "Member of the First Chamber of the States-General, Alderman for Finance and Municipal Services, Amsterdam, President of the Union Internationale des Villes," and opened the theater for us with dramatic readings in English, a German and a French one-act play, displaying thus the language versatility of their repertory actors.

The reports of activities by delegates from the 27 national associations, including the four newly admitted: Germany, Hungary, Poland, and Esthonia, resembled a roll call of the League of Nations. English and French are the official languages of the Federation, but English was used more than French, except for those presiding officers who used both with great facility. We were given at the Registration Desk large-headed colored pins showing which languages we could speak, the fluency being indicated by the size of the pin. Some delegates were veritable pincushions.

At the session on careers and home life for women, the honors were borne off by a Mrs. Gilbreth, of New Jersey, the mother of eleven children, and one time partner and now president (since her husband's death) of Gilbreth Inc., a well known efficiency engineering firm. And those who know her home and children testified enthusiastically to her unqualified success in that field of her life.

There was a session on secondary education, another on What University Women do in Holland and the Colonies, a marvel of condensed and vivid presentation of interesting statistics, another on The Promotion of Intellectual Coöperation, which included a report of the Institute on Intellectual Coöperation, two speeches on an international language (Esperanto) as an educational instrument (one of them by Mr. Sarnoff, vice-president of the Radio Corporation of America), and a final meeting on international fellowships for travel and research.

The Dutch Federation took us to tea at the Women's Club, escorted us to the museums and around the harbor and canals on boats, arranged for a whole day excursion by canal to the cheese market at Alkmaar, gay with the round yellow cheeses and the white suits and bright colored straw hats of the cheese

weighers from the various companies, and took us on an afternoon and evening trip to Monnikendam, Vollendam, Edam, and Marken, dining us royally at Vollendam amid a picturesque crowd of baggy trousered sailors home with the fleet on Saturday night and women and girls in striped skirts, chintz trimmed aprons, and wide lace bonnets.

There was a Smith luncheon which was a red letter day for us all. It was Miss Comstock's idea, and we put it into action at once, regretting only that nine out of the 24 we knew were present at the Conference could not be with us. The fifteen who gathered at the

board were: Ada Comstock '97, Olive Kirkby and Grace Neill '12, Florence Angell '11, Isabel Norton '03, Anna Cutler '85, Mina Kerr '00, Maude Miner Haddon '01, Julia Bolster Lewis '01, Amy Ferris '01, Carolyn Swett '95, Florence Plaut Hartog '11, Florence Snow '04, and Dr. Gilman, and of the former faculty, Edith Ware now at Russell Sage College. The other nine were: Ruth Bowles Baldwin '87, Frances Pellett '82, Louisa Fast '98, Frances Priddy '26, Eleanor Lord '87, Dr. Gleditsch (holder of an honorary degree), Dr. Agnes Rogers, now at Bryn Mawr, Mlle. LeDuc, now at Barnard, and Margaret Cameron formerly of the French Department.

Dr. Ellen Gleditsch, Docent of Physical Chemistry at the University of Oslo, Norway, was elected as the new president. Smith alumnae will be glad to recall that Dr. Gleditsch was given an honorary degree at Smith in 1914. The next Conference is to be at Geneva in 1929.

THE A. A. U. W. IN HOLYOKE

On Oct. 3 the Hampshire County Branch had a notable luncheon at which a number of distinguished guests spoke on various aspects of the International Conference. The Smith alumnae who spoke were President Ada Comstock '97, Anna Cutler '85, Florence Snow '04, and Helen McAfee '03,

NEWS OF OTHER COLLEGES

REGISTRATION AT OTHER COLLEGES

THE registration at Smith College is 2033 undergraduates and 34 in France, 64 graduate students and 1 in France, and 4 non-collegiate students, as given in detail on page 58. Grand total, 2101 and 35 in France. The total *last* year, including graduate students, was 2127 and 32 in France.

BRYN MAWR COLLEGE.—Seniors, 82; juniors, 84; sophomores, 85; freshmen, 128; graduate students, 94; hearers, 2; advanced standing, 2. Total, 477. (Total for last year, 519.) There are 11 foreign students enrolled, representing Canada, China, Cuba, England, Esthonia, Finland, France, Germany, and Japan.

CONNECTICUT COLLEGE.—Seniors, 104; juniors, 126; sophomores, 145; freshmen, 154. Total, 529. (Total for last year, 516.) Connecticut has also 5 special students, but no graduate or foreign students.

MOUNT HOLYOKE COLLEGE.—Seniors, 252; juniors, 250; sophomores, 268; freshmen, 223. Total, 993. (Total undergraduates for last year, 992.) In addition there are 11 special students, of whom 9 are foreign students who are not yet classified. There are 5 students registered as regular graduate students, and in addition 21 assistants who are taking graduate courses. Of the latter, 15 are working for an M.A. Mount Holyoke has this fall accepted 29 advanced standing students. There are in all 14 foreign students, representing Armenia, Chile, China, France, Holland, Hungary, Korea, Palestine, Russia, Turkey.

PENNSYLVANIA COLLEGE FOR WOMEN.—Seniors, 68; juniors, 71; sophomores, 83; freshmen, 114; special students, 2; graduate students, 4. Total, 342. Of these students 18 were received on advanced standing, representing 15 colleges and universities. There are no foreign students this year.

RADCLIFFE COLLEGE.—Seniors, 123; juniors, 184; sophomores, 197; freshmen, 227; graduate students, 262; special students, 37. Total, 1030. (Total for last year, 937.) Radcliffe has 3 students from England, 1 from China, 1 from Denmark, 1 from Japan, and 1 from Russia.

VASSAR COLLEGE.—Seniors, 247; juniors, 255; sophomores, 305; freshmen, 340. Total, 1147. (Total at the opening of college last year, 1149.) Vassar has 10 foreign students, 5 admitted this year and 5 last year, coming from Austria, Czecho-Slovakia, Greece, Hungary, India, Japan, Nassau, and Poland. Eleven students were admitted to advanced standing. There are no graduate students except those connected with some department.

WELLESLEY COLLEGE.—Seniors, 321; juniors, 320; sophomores, 407; freshmen, 421; advanced standing, 37; specials 8; graduate students, 49; graduates (hygiene), 24. Total, 1587. (Total for last year, 1600.) The foreign students number 12 (not including Canada). There is 1 each from Austria, China, France, Germany, India, Ireland, and Poland, and 2 each from Japan and Russia.

UNIVERSITY OF WISCONSIN.—An experimental form of college is being tried at the University of Wisconsin this fall, in order to test new curricula and teaching methods. 125 men students are to be enrolled the first year, all voluntary. The college has been approved by President Glenn Frank and will embrace the liberal arts. Dr. Alexander Meiklejohn, formerly president of Amherst College, will be its leader. One of the principal aims of this experimental college is to emphasize the individuality of the student. The tutorial method will be used, while the elective system is to be abolished. This new method of teaching is to be brought to bear primarily upon the first and second years of the college curriculum. The first year will be devoted to the study of one period of civilization, such as that of the ancient Greeks, while the second may take up certain problems in English history.

YALE UNIVERSITY.—The much discussed test of voluntary services instead of compulsory chapel is to be tested this year. It is thought that the building of a beautiful chapel and the strengthening of the religious work of various student organizations may promote a finer religious attitude on the part of the undergraduates as well as dignifying the religious services of the University.

ALUMNAE NOTES

CLASS NEWS

Please send all news for the February QUARTERLY *to your class secretary by January 3. The editors reserve the right to omit all items which in their judgment are not submitted in legible form.*

All changes of address are included in the new *Alumnae Register*, to be published in December, therefore they are not included in these items.

A list of Smith Granddaughters will be found on page 59, therefore their names are not included in notes of their mothers' classes.

1879
Class secretary—Mrs. Charles M. Cone (Kate Morris), Hartford, Vt.

1880
Class secretary—Mrs. Edwin Higbee (Netta Wetherbee), 8 West St., Northampton, Mass.

1881
Class secretary—Eliza P. Huntington, 88 Harvard St., Newtonville, Mass.

William Jewett Tucker, president emeritus of Dartmouth, husband of Charlotte (Cheever) Tucker, died Sept. 29.

1882
Class secretary—Nina E. Browne, 44 Pinckney St., Boston, Mass.

1882 will celebrate its 45th next June. Everyone plan to come.

The editor, quite on her own responsibility, is inserting the following extracts from a newspaper clipping which was received in the QUARTERLY office: "Miss Nina Browne of Pinckney St., Boston, will be a special guest at the Sesqui-Centennial exhibit of the American Library Association on 'Philadelphia Day,' Oct. 6. . . . Miss Browne was for twenty years the able registrar of the association and for thirteen of those years was secretary of the publishing board. She resigned in 1909, when the headquarters were moved to Chicago. In the many years of her service, all office work of the association and editorial labors passed through Miss Browne's hands and she has an exceptional knowledge of the history of the association and library work generally."

1883
Class secretary—Charlotte C. Gulliver, 30 Huntington Lane, Norwich, Conn.

Eveline Dickinson has taken an apartment for the winter at 535 Quince St., San Diego, Calif., but the Wilmington address, printed in the *Register*, will always reach her.

Elizabeth (Lawrence) Clarke is to spend the winter, as last year, at Tryon, N. C.

Clara Palmer is at home again and able to walk about the house.

Julia (Parker) Sawin was well enough to visit her summer home in Storrs (Conn.) for a few days this summer.

Ex-1883
Jane Robbins is at home again in Wethersfield (Conn.) after interesting months in Greece, Turkey, Italy, France, and England.

1884
Class secretary—Helen M. Sheldon, Fort Ann, N. Y.

Fanny Allis and Abby Mead are still teaching—the former at Fairfax (Vt.) and the latter at Miss Spence's School, New York City.

Anne Brooks spent July and August at "The Hawthorne," Jackson (N. H.), her summer home for some years past.

Betsey Merriam has been at her beloved Sky Farm, Woodstock (N. H.), since May 1, and this summer more than the usual number of friends have enjoyed the lovely spot with her. She expects to divide November between Providence and New York City. Betsey and Helen Sheldon were so delighted with North Carolina last spring that they are starting off again in Betsey's car about Dec 1. They plan to take an apartment in Raleigh for three months, with various side trips meanwhile. In March and April they intend to drive about in South Carolina, and go wherever else the spirit calls. Home again May 1.

Ida (Skilton) Cornish has had an eventful summer. In June, her daughter Margaret was married to Bradley Gray Bissell. In August, her daughter Ruth presented her with another grandchild, Barbara Atwater Smith, and just to round off the excitement, in September Ida moved to a new home.

1885
Class secretary—Ruth B. Franklin, 23 Sherman St., Newport, R. I.

1886
Class secretary—M. Adèle Allen, 144 Lincoln St., Holyoke, Mass.

Margaret (Atwater) Jones returned to her home in Wellesley Hills in August from her year in Europe.

Alice (Bradbury) Lewis and others of the San Fernando Valley chapter of the D. A. R. have published a most charming and valuable

book, "The Valley of the San Fernando."
It preserves the story of pioneer life and gives
an intimate view of the way Southern California was developed.

Marion (Bradbury) Hovey has followed in
her mother's footsteps in D. A. R. work and as
regent of a D. A. R. chapter has done distinguished work.

Garret H. Demarest, husband of Margaretta (Duncan) Demarest, died at his home
in Ridgewood (N. J.), Mar. 17. His long and
useful life was identified with church and welfare work. For 53 years he had been a deacon
in the First Baptist Church at Fairlawn and
all this time he had been vitally concerned
with Sabbath School development. He was
the first president of the Y. M. C. A. in Fairlawn, furthering every Christian movement in
the community. Margaretta spent the summer with Daisy (Carter) Duncan at Monrovia
(Calif.), returning through the Panama
Canal to New York. Daisy Duncan will
remain in Monrovia, 729 Valley View Av.,
several months longer.

Edith Gooding visited Kate Hurlburt in
July at her cottage on Lake Placid.

Annie (Russell) Marble has selected the
best passages in the "Leatherstocking Tales"
and has combined them in one volume attractive to young readers, "The Story of the
Leatherstocking," published by Appleton Co.

Harriett (Risley) Foote's rose garden has
made her a national character and has won
recognition for her beyond the limits of the
United States. She has been engaged by
Henry Ford to lay out a great rose garden of
10,000 bushes at his home in Dearborn, Mich.

Ex-1886

Hattie Cushman's niece, Carolyn Cushman
'27, is engaged to Frank E. Bailey, Dartmouth
'26, of Messena, N. Y. The engagement was
announced Oct. 2 at a dinner at the Manse,
given by Carolyn to a number of her classmates.

1887

Class secretary—Mrs. Alden P. White
(Jessie Carter), 3 Federal Court, Salem, Mass.

Ruth (Bowles) Baldwin has returned to her
home in Springfield after five months abroad.

Eleanor Lord and Alice Walton returned
from Europe on the same steamer and Belle
(Clark) Powell was due Oct. 2.

See Smith Granddaughters in Northampton
News.

Ex-1887

Nettie (Bancroft) Pierce's daughter Catharine has spent the summer abroad, but will
be at home this winter in Chicago.

1888

Class secretary—Florence K. Bailey, 174
Broad St., Claremont, N. H.

Lizzie (Parker) McCollester and her husband, Dean Lee S. McCollester of Tufts College, expect to spend Nov. and Dec. in Paris
with their daughter, Catharine (McCollester)
Gallaher '14.

Ex-1888

Harriet (Duguid) Amerman's husband died
Aug. 22 after a double operation at the
Syracuse Hospital.

Danube, a great river like the Mississippi where one had imagined only barren mountains. Hungary. from the car window was a vast sweep of fields of Indian corn. It might have been Iowa or Illinois.

"I am back at work again, teaching classes, correcting papers, and doing some sketchy housekeeping on the side. A Saturday morning in September I set out tulips, and picked and preserved plums, one jar of which I overturned on the floor. How would the Coördination of Women's Interests deal with such a situation?"

Ex-1890

DIED.—At Leonia, N. J., July 14, Irene (Gill) Keyser, widow of George W. Keyser and youngest daughter of the late Elisha Gill and Huldah Capen.

1891

Class secretary—Mrs. H. B. Boardman (Carolyn Peck), 27 Lowell Rd., Schenectady, N. Y.

Marion Hinkley writes that she has had a perfect summer in Maine with five Hinkley sisters and eight nephews and nieces, after a hectic year of moving and settling in Philadelphia.

Eva Lamprey is teaching Latin at the Mary Lyon School, Swarthmore, Pa.

Grace Weston is lecturing before clubs and other organizations on antiques, Early America, and the history of furniture. She has studied and collected antiques for years and the lantern slides that she uses in connection with her lectures are made from pictures of her own as well as other fine collections.

Lilian Skinner is on the missionary staff of the Bishop of Wyoming, and is stationed at Granger, Wyo.

See Northampton News for Freshman Granddaughters.

Ex-1891

Carrie Sayles's husband, Robert P. Heron of Utica (N. Y.), died suddenly in August, leaving four children, Donald, Dorothy, Robert, and Joseph.

1892

Class secretary—Mrs. Irving H. Upton (Katherine Haven), 20 Park View St., Boston 21, Mass.

Cora Coolidge's mother was very ill during last spring; she is more comfortable now and Cora writes that this fall's work is starting in very propitiously. From another source we learn that since Cora has been president, the college has raised $1,000,000, doubled its student body, and is now starting on an extensive building program.

Martha (Folsom) Marple's oldest son, Warren, graduated from Harvard last June.

Last year, the Perkins Institution for the Blind established a normal department to train teachers to teach the blind and Jessica Langworthy became the head of this department. She had been principal of the boys' section of this Institution for seven years and resigned this position to take up the normal work.

Florence (May) Rice's older son, William Foster Jr., was married July 7 to Edith Hauer of New York City. Her younger son, Winthrop, was married Mar. 19 to Esther Johnson of De Kalb, Ill. Winthrop is this year instructor in Romance languages in Syracuse Univ. and at the same time is doing graduate work toward an M.A.

While Anne Safford was spending a week at the College Club, seven of our Boston group had the pleasure of meeting her at luncheon on Sept. 24. She brought us word of Edith Brown, Mary Jordan, and Beth (Learoyd) Ewing whom she had seen during the summer. A similar group met with Clara Gilbert for luncheon at the College Club on Oct. 5 as she was returning from Europe.

Mary Chute, daughter of Leila (Swift) Chute, Smith '26, is studying architecture at M. I. T. Leila's older son, Richard, is in his last year at Harvard Medical and Oliver is entering Harvard this fall.

Helen Williams's mother died in July.

Ex-1892

DIED.—Elizabeth Ingram, Sept. 29, in the Winchester Hospital. For several years she had been a teacher in the Wakefield (Mass.) High School.

1893

Class secretary—Mrs. John E. Oldham (Harriet Holden), 16 Livermore Rd., Wellesley Hills, Mass.

DIED.—Bertha M. Shepard, July 23, at Hartford. Her mother, 91 years old, survives her, also a brother. For several years Bertha was a teacher at the American School for the Deaf, West Hartford. She had been ill for a year with arthritis but the school was holding her position for her. Before that she had taught in the Connecticut School for the Blind. She found work for the physically handicapped very interesting. Occasionally she wrote little stories for the magazines and pamphlets published by the Woman's Home Missionary Federation. Shy and retiring though she was, she will be much missed in her special line of work, and by her friends and classmates.

OTHER NEWS.—Jennie Campbell and Mary DuBois had a month together in Randolph (Vt.) this summer. Jennie is still interested in genealogical research in her vacations from teaching in Kansas.

Susan (Kelly) Babcock spent two weeks in Corey Hill Hospital last spring having treatment for her knee. Thanks to that and a summer's rest she is able to be about again.

Charlotte (Stone) MacDougall's daughter Charlotte (Smith '22) is engaged to Henrik de Kauffman, minister from Denmark to China and Japan. The wedding will be held in Portsmouth this fall.

Agnes Williston has taken a position in Springfield and her address for the winter is 126 Clarendon St.

Ex-1893

"Flora Calhoun," writes Jennie Campbell, "has taken 1150 different people to ride. Some are sick, some old, others shut in. One woman was 105 years old. Since her mother died in 1914, Flora has driven 70,000 miles in her four cars on her errands of kindness."

Maud (Emerson) Fitts's son Osmer was graduated from Tuck School, Dartmouth, last June, *cum laude.* He had a six weeks' Students' Tour in Europe and is entering Harvard Law School this fall.

1894
Class secretary—Mrs. John J. Healy (Katharine Andrews), 1104 Greenwood St., Evanston, Ill.

See Northampton News for Freshman Granddaughters.

1895
Class secretary—Carolyn P. Swett, Hudson View Gardens, 183 St. and Pinehurst Av., New York City.

Rose (Fairbank) Beals and Dr. Beals are spending their sabbatical leave in the United States. Rose writes: "We shall be glad to see the Home Land again, and our boy, who has grown from 12 to 19 since we saw him last, and many of you who have done so much for us and this work. ('95 may be included in this.) Our two girls, Annette and Charlotte, continue to thrive splendidly. They too are looking forward eagerly to the year ahead. When the college year opens we are to settle for the winter at Ann Arbor (Mich.), where our son Albert will be a senior in the University."

Edith (Mott) Davis has moved to Bermuda where Mr. Davis is in business. They sold their house in Glen Ridge, N. J.

Nan (Harrington) Green's oldest son, Thomas, is engaged to Natalie Rogers, Smith '24, of Kennebunk, Me. Tom graduated from M. I. T. this year, having completed the electrical engineering course in three years since his graduation from Yale in 1923. John is in Washington Univ., Seattle.

Carolyn Swett, after a delightful Mediterranean cruise during February and March, spent the spring and summer in Europe. She cannot begin to tell of all the Smith encounters she had. Traveling in Europe is much like crossing the campus during the Fiftieth reunion. She attended the Congress of the I. F. U. W. in Amsterdam, July 27 to Aug. 2. One noon a Smith luncheon, planned hurriedly, collected fifteen Smith alumnae and then there were nine who could not attend. Her last ten days were spent in Geneva and it seemed an appropriate ending to her Sabbatical leave which began in marveling at the remains of civilizations thousands of years in the past and ended in contemplating the efforts of those who are looking far ahead into the future.

Amy (Whittington) Eggleston writes that their address in San Diego is likely to remain permanent as they have built a house there and settled down.

See Northampton News for Freshman Granddaughters.

1896
Class secretary—Frances E. Jones, Hotel Chelsea, W. 23 St., New York City.

Emily (Betts) Strayer's father died in Brooklyn in July. He was Yale '66.

Margaret (Coe) Ninde spent part of the summer in Nantucket.

Mabel (Durand) Pine's son James gradu-

"Ladies and Hussars," a comedy by Fredro, was published last winter and another, "Iridian" by Krasinaki, has been accepted by the Oxford University Press.

Sarah (Tappan) Coe writes that her daughter Serena is being educated under "good Smith influences." She attends the Brimmer School in Boston which is manned in part by Minnie Pickering '94, Constance Williston and Mabel Cummings '95, and Julie Arnold '97.

1897

Class secretary—Lucy O. Hunt, 185 Beacon St., Hartford, Conn.

Mark our Thirtieth Reunion dates on your calendar, and let nothing interfere with that engagement. Plans will be under way soon, and we hope everyone will be eager to respond when called on for help.

Lois (Barnard) Vickers reports a visit from Catherine (Warnick) Hall "who, for a mother of a graduated granddaughter of Sophia Smith, looks very fine!"

Eleanor Bissell returned from France in September, and will remain East till after Thanksgiving.

Lucy Blake is beginning her twentieth year of teaching in Sanborn Seminary, Kingston, N. H.

Edith (Breckenridge) Fisk writes of hearing Ada Comstock at Clarissa's school graduation in June.

Ruth (Brown) Page has a famous daughter. Dorothy won the Women's Western Golf Championship last summer. She is a freshman at the Univ. of Wisconsin.

Alice (Gates) Hubbard will spend the winter at Triangle L Ranch, Oracle, Ariz. She recommends this life to all '97ers who are looking for health and freedom.

Gertrude (Hammerslough) Alexander writes that there was a large Smith delegation on board the S. S. Lancastria on her Mediterranean and Norway cruise this summer. The group met several times to discuss topics of current interest in the collegiate world, and once they met with representatives of other colleges. Besides Gertrude, the Smith group included Frances (Young) Allen ex-'96, Elizabeth (Thompson) Weller '09, Mae Patterson '11, Jeanne (Pushee) Thayer '12, Vera Cole '13, Katherine Ranson '17, Nell Russell ex-'25, Clara Allen '29.

Ruth (Jenkins) Jenkins is publicity director for the Community Chest in Madison (Wis.) and also continues her regular work of writing.

Jessie Judd was chosen last June to receive the American teacher's award as a tribute of honor for outstanding achievement in the State of Vermont. The award included a visit to the Sesqui-Centennial, and a gold medal presented by President Coolidge.

Climena Judd will return from China in December and in January will come to Northampton to take up her new duties as associate principal of the Burnham School.

Grace (Kelley) Tenney's daughter Martena is finishing her course at the Academy of Speech Arts, Boston. Eileen is at The Misses Stone's School, Washington. Grace

will be in Boston during the fall, and in Washington later.

Jessie Lockett spent the summer in Paris, going to the Sorbonne for three lecture courses. She met Bertha (Bogue) Bennett.

Florence (Low) Kelsey has taken a house in Cambridge for the winter, 11 Francis Av. Harlan and Seth are in Harvard, Katherine is a senior at the Buckingham School, and Jane a freshman there. Harlan has been a ranger in the Yellowstone Park for two summers.

Mary (Rockwell) Cole's son Shaw is a freshman at Dartmouth.

Louie (Rogers) Nichols's niece, Sally Rogers, is a freshman at Smith.

See Northampton News for Freshman Granddaughters.

Ex-1897

Emma Harrington is at the Central Square Branch Library in Cambridge.

Grace (Lockett) Brown has been in N. H. this summer, where her husband was painting. Mr. Brown was made an M.A. in June.

Edith (McChesney) Pennock's son is a sophomore in Amherst.

Harriette (Smith) Le Sauvage is writing music in her new home in California.

1898

Class secretary—Ethel M. Gower, 29 Mather St., New Haven, Conn.

Alma Baumgarten came home in September after a fourteen months' trip around the world. She will spend the winter with a friend at 130 Elgin St., Newton Centre, Mass.

Marion (Chapman) Jacobus has announced the engagement of her daughter Margaret to Lovell Hewitt Cook, Dartmouth '21. Margaret is a senior at Smith.

Gertrude (Cochrane) Smith ('10) writes: "I spend my days housekeeping, gardening, earning my living by making reproductions of old colonial candlewicking embroidery and netted bed canopies. I motor to Boston every month for Board meetings of the Massachusetts League of Women Voters, as Franklin County Director, and am also President of the Deerfield League besides doing legislative work for the Massachusetts Civic League. Georgia (Coyle) Hall and family visited me during Deerfield Academy commencement when son Louis graduated, carrying off the French prize—so I was proud of my guests. On Aug. 10, fifteen of the old houses of Deerfield were open to the public and about 3000 people walked through mine. I'm always glad to welcome '98ers and hope to have you all come here for a picnic with me at our next reunion."

Louise Hazen's father died Aug. 8 in Hartford, Vt.

Maud (Jackson) Hulst is still on the school board of Englewood and has been made associate principal of Dwight School, thus being able to look at schools from both the public and private viewpoint.

Edith (Kimball) Metcalf writes that having no youngsters at home now she is having an interesting time doing part-time work, tutoring in French, and giving lessons in French conversation.

Winifred (Knight) Thornton spends most of her winter in Tulsa, Okla. Her older son, James, is at the Univ. of Rochester and Knight is at the Choate School. She and Grace Kellam ex-'98 and Ethel Gower had a '98 luncheon together in Wallingford in Oct. She saw many '98ers when she went on to Boston for the wedding of Bab (Allen) Eaton's ('99) daughter.

Julia MacAlister furnished the Hostess Room in the Pennsylvania State building at the Sesqui-Centennial.

Mabel Rice had a busy summer as in addition to a month in Maine she took her examination at Columbia for the Doctor's degree and then attended the International Congress of Plant Sciences in Ithaca. She is now back at Wheaton College in charge of the botany department.

Stella Streeter reports several interesting trips in the far West and in Iceland, Norway, and Sweden.

Alice Todd writes that she is still enjoying her English teaching in Somerville, looking out for the girls' glee club and taking an interest in their athletic work.

Ethel Woodberry's cousin, Eleanor Dodge, 1908's class baby, is a Smith freshman. Ethel reports that the third payment of our 25th reunion pledge for the Library fund in honor of President Seelye was made last summer and amounted to $2306, bringing the total paid in to the College to $7267. The Library has already benefited from the fund to the extent of several hundred dollars as it has received interest from the money paid in in 1924 and 1925. Many class dues are still unpaid and would be most welcome, so this is a reminder that $3.00 should be sent to E. Woodberry, 56 Parsons St., West Newton, Mass.

Christina Wright is teaching in Central High School, Washington, and "still enjoys the work though the years are speeding on." See Northampton News for Freshman Granddaughters.

Ex–1898

Charlotte (Sherrill) Kernan's two daughters are at boarding school and her three boys go to a day school in N. Y.

Georgena (Smith) Hammond is president of the Women's Union of her church, a vice-regent of the D. A. R. Chapter, and a member of several boards. Her daughter is at Cornell and her son Payson, who recently returned from South America where he served on the Tacna Arica commission, is connected with the Goodyear Rubber Co. in Akron, O.

1899

Class secretary—Miriam Drury, 334 Franklin St., Newton, Mass.

Janet Eaton, Smith '26, daughter of Abby (Allen) Eaton, was married Oct. 2 to Charles Clark Macomber.

Edith (Hall) Dohan is to lecture again at Bryn Mawr during the present academic year. She contributes an article to the current issue of the *American Journal of Archaeology.*

Edith Tiemann and Eloise Santee motored through New England together in August,

stopping in Exeter (N. H.) to see Elizabeth (Bedell) Zeiger whose husband is pastor of the Unitarian church.

See Northampton News for Freshman Granddaughters.

1900

Class secretary—Gertrude E. Gladwin, 2323 Orrington Av., Evanston, Ill.

Florence (Brooks) Cobb's son Edward, Amherst '29, received the William C. Collar prize of $25 at Commencement.

Nan Hincks sailed on Sept. 7 with Ruth Huntington '97 for a three months' trip in Europe.

Mabel (Milham) Roys and her daughter Betty sailed on the *President Pierce* from San Francisco, on Aug. 7. In company with two other women, they are to be gone for six months, visiting mission stations in Japan, Korea, China, Philippine Islands, Siam, Singapore, and Northern India. They return by way of the Persian Gulf through Syria and Palestine, Constantinople and Paris.

Helen (Ward) Ward's son Theodore was one of nine Amherst juniors elected to Phi Beta Kappa. He also was one of five debaters who divided the Rodgers prize of $70 for public debating.

Mary (Wilder) Kent is one of the new corporate members-at-large of the American Board of Commissioners for Foreign Missions and has been made a member of the prudential committee of that body.

See Northampton News for Freshman Granddaughters.

1901

Class secretary—Mrs. Sanford Stoddard (Hannah Johnson), 499 Washington Av., Bridgeport, Conn.

Charlotte DeForest spent August at Wonalancet, N. H. She is now in Auburndale (Mass.) and has a tentative sailing date, Dec. 25, for her return to Japan.

Sarah (DeForest) Pettus's oldest son, John, entered Yale this fall.

Amy Ferris, Isabel Norton, and Julia (Bolster) Ferris attended the I. F. U. W. Conference at Amsterdam this summer, where they were delightfully entertained by many Dutch hostesses. They met Caroline (Saunders) Lindeke there, traveling with her mother and children.

Martha Howey spent the summer visiting in New England but has gone back to Ross (Calif.) to teach and to keep house for her young nephew. She says, "You have no idea what distinction even an eight-year-old husband gives one!"

Hannah (Johnson) Stoddard's second son, Goodwin, is a member of the "University Cruise" going around the world and preparing for college. His eldest son, Johnson, is at Harvard Law School, after graduating from Yale in June.

Rosamond Lent, who teaches Latin in the Calhoun School in New York, was in Rome this summer for six weeks at the fourth summer session of the School of Classical Studies in the American Academy there. Seventy students from all over the United States tracked Romulus and Remus to their lair, heard Caesar and Cicero reverberate, and basked with Horace on his Sabine Farm under the guidance of Professor Grant Showerman of the Univ. of Wisconsin.

May Lewis's niece, Elizabeth Lewis, is a freshman at college this year.

Alison Locke visited Northampton early in September bringing her niece, who she hopes will come to Smith soon.

Mabel Mead motored in Europe this summer and starts from New York in November for a six months' trip to India, China, and Japan.

Methyl (Oakes) Palfrey's daughters, Mianne and Sarah, have won for the third time the National Girls' Tennis Doubles.

Helen (Parsons) Cleveland has started a "College Preparatory Workshop" in Cambridge (Mass.), "the idea of which is based on the conviction that much of the difficulty in preparing for college is due to the failure to get a proper start in the subjects required." Mothers of college aspirants will sympathize and take notice!

Mary (Sayles) Moore and family spent the summer near Deauville, France, in a villa that belonged to F. Hopkinson Smith.

Jennie Shipman has returned to her work in Crane Junior College, Chicago, after spending the summer in Europe.

One of Irene (Smith) Compton's twin daughters, Josephine Lathrop, was married Oct. 6 in St. Louis to Willoughby Williams Jr.

Ethel (Stetson) Bingham's daughter Katharine has been abroad this summer motoring in Ireland, England, and France, and is now back at Smith heading Student Government with Amanda Bryan, chairman of Judicial Board. They live in Dewey House.

Marian (Sutton) Berry has established a very successful public stenography business in Los Angeles. She sees a great deal of Martha Criley.

Lena (Swasey) Parson has gone with her husband, who is National Secretary for Foreign Missions, in the Episcopal Church, on a four months' trip to visit missions in Liberia, West Africa.

Miriam Titcomb has just sailed for Europe to be gone until the last of December. She had a farewell party given her by the trustees of the Bancroft School, when she was presented with a beautiful ring as a token of esteem.

See Northampton News for Freshman Granddaughters.

1902

Class secretary—Mrs. L. F. Gates (Josephine Lamson), 723 Eighth St., Wilmette, Ill.

MARRIED.—Bertha Prentiss to Frederick S. Webber, Oct. 2. New address, 27 Sycamore St., Holyoke, Mass.

OTHER NEWS.—The Knox School in Cooperstown, of which Mary (Bancroft) Phinney is associate principal, sent three girls to Smith this fall.

Ruth Benedict is studying at the University in Vienna, Austria. Address, c/o U. S. Consulate.

Helen Chesnutt took her M.A. at Columbia in 1925.

Adeline Davidson is back in East Orange as librarian of the Free Public Library.

Edith Ely received an M.A. at Pennsylvania College for Women in 1926, in recognition of work done at Berlin Univ. in Germany and at P.C.U. Edith's three months' vacation was spent in France, Italy, Switzerland, and the British Isles. One of her experiences was in having the auto dug out of a snowdrift and almost freezing her feet, July 29! Nevertheless she recommends the trip from Cortina to Bolzano as most enjoyable for its wonderful mountain scenery.

Marion (Gaillard) Brackett and her husband have returned from their seven months' trip abroad.

Ethel (Green) Stamm sends greetings from her ranch in California, "La Favorita," where she raises fourteen kinds of fruit, besides nuts and melons.

Lu (Hayes) Sherry's husband died of heart failure, Sept. 17. The mothers of Ella (Van Tuyl) Kempton and Louise Irving have both died within the last year.

Emily (Huntington) Harwood's son Ernest is Clark Univ. '30.

Constance Jones helps in Americanization by teaching English to foreign women.

Jean (Jouett) Blackburn's oldest son is Harvard '28, the younger Haverford '30. Jean enjoyed a summer course in secondary education at Harvard this year.

Helen (Manning) Riggs is at present working at Columbia for an M.A. in institution management.

In addition to her teaching and position as dean of girls in West Springfield High School, Bess Neal is finishing her fourth year as precinct representative in the Town Meeting Assembly. Last February she made a trip to Washington to attend the Convention of Deans, and again in April with twenty high school youngsters on a sight-seeing tour.

Ellen Osgood took her M.A. at the School of Education in N. Y. Univ., June 1926.

Edith Spencer is studying abroad this year. Mail addressed to Mrs. J. P. Gilbert, Bolton, Mass., will be forwarded.

Louise (Vibberts) Pelton's son Henry is at Deerfield Academy preparing for Amherst.

Eunice Wead was abroad for seven months, part of the time working in the British Museum and the Public Record Office in London. She now is one of the faculty members of the newly organized Department of Library Science at the Univ. of Michigan.

See Northampton News for Freshman Granddaughters.

Ex-1902

DIED.—Ada (Hilt) Street, July 30. Her last work was in collaboration with her husband on the novel "Tides" to be published in November.

OTHER NEWS.—Lulie (Keith) Keith's sons are in Amherst, 1927 and 1930.

Juliet Patten at present is attorney for National Banks.

Can anyone send in news of the following,

88   THE SMITH ALUMNAE QUARTERLY

from whom mail has been returned from the addresses given in the *Catalog:* Mrs. Arthur Harlow (Grace Backwell), Mrs. J. H. Rapp (Marguerite Chambers), Mrs. Harris Masters (Fannie Elliott), Baroness von Urff (Elizabeth Geer), Mrs. Albert Bates (Carolyn Green), Mrs. A. F. Thompson (Olive Mowat), Guida Richey, Elizabeth Temple?

1903

Class secretary—Mrs. Francis W. Tully (Susan Kennedy), 3 Alwington Rd., Chestnut Hill, Mass.

MARRIED.—Edith (St. John) Smith to Louis John Esty, in Dec. 1925. They are living at 2545 Wellington Rd., Cleveland, O.

OTHER NEWS.—Marcia (Bailey) Marsh's older son, Bob, is a freshman at the Univ. of Maine, where he is taking the course in forestry for which the college is noted. Marcia's plans for the winter remain uncertain until they know more definitely about conditions in Miami. They have not heard any report about their bungalow, but think it was blown away.

Marion (Conant) Damon's son Roger won scholarship honors for his first year's work at Yale.

One of the most interesting of the very many things Emily Drew did in connection with the celebration of the 200th anniversary of the town of Kingston was that she restored and opened an old store that was built in 1797, closed in 1865, and had been almost untouched since that time. Having access to many treasure-filled attics in Kingston, she was able to make the old shop a really remarkable historic exhibit, with its ginger jars, tea chests, snuff scales, India calicoes, etc.

At the American Legion Carnival in Wellesley this fall, Marion (Evans) Stanwood took a twenty-five cent chance on a six-cylinder Essex sedan, latest 1927 model—and won it! Marion has hired a farm in Wonalancet (N. H.) and hopes to raise trout there next summer, and also to experiment a bit, perhaps, with the idea of raising muskrats for their fur.

Lucy (Hastings) Horsfall, her husband and three children, arrived from Australia in August to visit Fanny (Hastings) Plimpton. On account of Dr. Horsfall's illness they have given up their home in Sydney and will spend the winter at "Soncy," Bermuda.

We are glad to report that Anna Kitchel, who was seriously ill in the spring, is recovering her health after a successful operation. There is even a possibility that she may be able to resume her work at Vassar in February. She is staying with her sister, Helen (Kitchel) Daniells, in Toledo, O.

Helen McAfee was one of the speakers at the luncheon of the A.A.U.W. in Holyoke in October. "Mac" had an encounter with a burglar recently and succeeded in frightening him away most efficiently.

Alice Page sailed in October for a trip around the world—our third 1903 representative this year!

Clara Phillips's business address is the Hadley Book Shop, South Hadley, Mass.

Eleanor (Putnam) Bodell's son Jack won one of the best scholarships at Wesleyan last year.

Margaret Thacher is touring around the world with the "Floating University," as they call the liner *Ryndam* which sailed from New York Sept. 18, carrying 500 students, a faculty of 50 members, and a large additional staff. Dr. Charles F. Thwing, president emeritus of Western Reserve Univ., is in charge of the cruise. Margaret, who studied the problems of women in industry in South America, hopes to be able to carry on further study along those lines. She is again accompanying her friend, Miss Amy Woods, the well-known lecturer. Address until Apr. 15, c/o Univ. World Travel Cruise, Phelps Bros., 17 Battery Pl., N. Y. C.

Elizabeth (Viles) McBride writes from India: "Our school sale was a great success. We made nearly $3000. Our five-and-ten-cent-store table brought in over $200. I have not been able to get a list of the 1903 girls who sent money to Mrs. Moulton so I wonder if you will put a line in the QUARTERLY to thank them. We are to have the same kind of table next year and I should be most grateful for another donation. The money should be sent to Mr. Harvey Meeken, 14 Beacon St., Boston, marked very plainly for the Marathi Mission Table of the Kodaikanal School Sale, and the sooner it is sent the better. Waxed paper, which we can not get out here, percolator tops, and measuring cups were our most popular items. The school has a new principal who is full of modern ideas . . . I shall go back to Ahmadnagar in a few weeks, leaving three of my girls. Mr. McBride has gone already to open school. He reports that it is about 105° on our front verandah so I am glad I'm not there, but we should have rain soon to cool things off a bit."

Alice (Webber) Scofield, her husband, and five children (aged 7, 11, 14, 16, and 19) went on a camping trip to California and back this summer, a nice little jaunt of about 9000 miles in a Ford station wagon! They went out by way of the Grand Canyon of Arizona and back by way of Yellowstone Park. They camped out all but four nights out of the fifty-four. Twice they tipped over in the mud, once the gasoline stove set fire to the tail-board of the car, and once a terrific thundershower drenched their blankets in the night, but otherwise all was well.

All the 1903 husbands and sons are probably enjoying the series of articles by Marie (Weeden) Langford's husband, now appearing in many newspapers all over the country. He calls them "Between the Sidelines" and they tell the story of his 30 years' experience as player and referee in hundreds of championship games—thrills, big game secrets, critical decisions, the greatest players, the coaches, and everything that interests football enthusiasts. Perhaps many of the class have heard "Billy" broadcast some of the big games or will hear him this year from WBZ.

See Northampton News for Freshman Granddaughters.

Ex-1903

DIED.—Helen (Howell) Windsor, at Des Moines (Ia.) in June, after a long illness. She leaves one son, James, a senior at Yale. None of us can ever forget our dear freshman class president, nor did she ever cease to have a keen and loving interest in the class. Her death is a real loss to 1903.

OTHER NEWS.—Yettie (Du Bois) Ballantine was critically ill in Paris last summer with double mastoid, but she is now very much better.

Margaret (French) Baldwin's mother died in September, after a long illness.

Florence (Ross) Bell's son Dudley has been playing on the Harvard football team.

1904

Class secretary—Eleanor Garrison, 99 Marion St., Brookline, Mass.

BORN.—To Edna (Cushing) Weathers a second daughter and seventh child, Edna Esther, Aug. 11.

OTHER NEWS.—Mabel Barkley is managing the Means Weave Shop in Lowell, Mass. Basket-weave blankets made on hand looms are a specialty.

Annetta Clark took a flying trip to Augusta (Me.) in September, accompanied by Flörie (Bannard) Adams. "We went up to Muriel's to get the Adams pup which has been living there while the Adams-Snows were abroad. We had one day in Augusta and enjoyed Muriel and her babies immensely." Annetta reports eighteen 1904 daughters in College this year.

Leslie (Crawford) Hun's daughter Leslie completed her freshman year at Smith and is studying abroad this year. She will return to Smith next fall when her sister Betsy expects to enter.

Florence Snow found 1904 painted in large figures on the rocks at Torghatten Island, Norway, almost in the Arctic Circle. She kindly sent us her photograph taken beside the decoration. Florence was one of the speakers at the A.A.U.W. meeting in Holyoke in October.

Rita Souther was among the foreign travelers this summer. She motored herself about England, alighting for a time at the Lee Abbey Hotel in Lynton, where her society was greatly enjoyed by five of Eleanor Garrison's nieces and nephews and their mother.

Dorothy (Upham) Vaughan sailed on Sept. 28 from San Francisco for Yokohama, stopping one day at Honolulu. "Wayland is going to a scientific congress and Caroline and I are delighted to tag along. We have only six weeks in Japan but we hope to see a lot as the Japanese are planning many delightful excursions. We shall be back before Christmas."

Mary Van Kleeck sailed for Cherbourg Sept. 17 to attend an international committee meeting in Paris. From there she was going to visit some Canadian friends who have a house in Brussels. She expected to be back in about five weeks.

Alice (Wright) Teagle says: "My daughter Helen is entering Smith this fall. My son John Teagle III, sailed Sept. 18 on a university cruise around the world. Last year he was a freshman at Cornell."

Alice Morgan Wright, according to Edith Goode, has found a studio in Woodstock, Vt. She has procured 500 lbs. of clay and Edith says the results are very promising!

See Northampton News for Freshman Granddaughters.

Ex-1904

Grace (Buck) Stevens spent a week in London this summer, followed by a week of motoring. At the hotel in Edinburgh she fell in with Florence Snow and Flörie Adams. The next day Grace left for Norway from which Florence had just returned.

Florence (Covel) Avitabile went to Forte dei Marmi, Italy, again this summer. She writes: "We love it here at our seashore cottage. My boy, 14, is quite a sailor. He ventures out in a 'patino' when there is nobody else on the sea and you may be sure I am very thankful when he returns safely." Florence sent beguiling pictures of Raffaelo, Grazia, and little Florence for the class album.

Elsa (Longyear) Roberts and Elisabeth Telling went to an open-air buffet luncheon at Bess (Boynton) Millard's (Highland Park, Ill.). "It was a beautiful early summer day. The place is exquisite: iris, mandrake, and lilac everywhere around the unusual and very effective 'Log House' that gives the place its name." Elsa spent the summer at Vinalhaven (Me.), where she has a cottage. She said: "Last week I had the National Commander of the American Legion and the Headquarters Staff and the France Travel Committee, some seventeen men, highly thrilled at salt air and lobsters. I hung the family up on casual coat hooks, so to speak, and turned the house over to the Legion for four days."

Edna (Richolson) Sollitt's father, Mr. Benjamin F. Richolson, died this summer. He was one of the oldest members of the Chicago Bar Association. On Oct. 5 the Chickering Company presented Edna in recital in their own hall in New York. She has been reëngaged as soloist for the Barrère orchestra tour next spring.

Mabel (Sanders) Howell had a happy summer in a bungalow at Boothbay Harbor, Me. Mabel helped her husband celebrate his 25th reunion at Princeton and says, "I shall surely come to our 25th, so put me down now."

Marjorie Sinclair, who has recently emerged from the "Hide and Seek" column, says that after leaving college she went on a seven months' cruise in the South Seas. She has lived in Pasadena since 1904 with music and drama as her principal interests. For five years she was a member of three church choirs and a church quartet. In 1915 she became club and music reporter for the Pasadena Star News. During 1916–17 she was second character woman and "general utility" for the Savoy Stock Co. That summer Marjorie joined the reportorial forces of the Star News and after a brief return to the stage came back to review professional concerts and handle the weekly fine arts page. She says: "In addition to my experience with the Savoy Stock Co. I have worked with the Smith-King Players in Pasadena and Long Beach. During a summer art session under the auspices of the Pasadena Community Playhouse, I taught 'make-up' as I had done when in Portland (Ore.) three years ago, at which time I edited an issue of the Oregon State Parent-Teacher Association's magazine. I have had one play presented by professionals in California and by the Ypsilanti Players, 'As Ye Sow.'" Marjorie is at present assistant director of the Alhambra-San Gabriel Community Players.

1905

Class secretary—Mrs. Frank Mansfield (Alice Curtis), 9 Salisbury Rd., Brookline, Mass.

DIED.—Abigail Ferrell, Aug. 4, after a few days' illness. To those of us who had seen Abbie recently her death seemed almost unbelievable. Loyalty and unselfishness were two of Abbie's outstanding characteristics. She gave of her time and strength unsparingly for her family and friends. By old people and children, as well as by those of her own age, she was well beloved. We who are left behind and never expected to grow old without Abbie will miss her ready sympathy and thoughtfulness.

MARRIED.—Marietta Hyde to Samuel Hardman West, Aug. 10.

OTHER NEWS.—Florence (Bannard) Adams returned from Europe early in August, spent some time in Chicago, and now is at her home in Northampton.

Mary Campbell has been ill this summer, but is now back in her office.

Evelyn (Catlin) Groezinger's daughter Marion entered Bates College this fall.

Hilda Clark and her brother Schofield took a motor trip to Nova Scotia and the White Mountains this fall, visiting Helen Norwell on the way home.

Alice (Curtis) Mansfield and Marie Donohoe returned in August from a trip abroad, which included a motor trip through the Pyrenees, a week in Switzerland, another in Belgium, and a short stay in Paris.

Ella Emerson received the degree of M.Ed. from the Harvard Graduate School of Education in June. This year Ella will have charge of the psychological tests at the Winsor School, Boston.

Kate (Fairchild) Arnold and her family visited in Oregon and California this summer.

Mildred (Jenks) Whipple is president of the Worcester Woman's Club which has a membership of 1000. Mildred is also serving on the board of trustees of the public library in Worcester.

Elsie (Laughney) Carr welcomed most hospitably 15 of the Boston 1905-ers at her home in Bridgewater, Oct. 1. We enjoyed a delicious luncheon, a visit in Elsie's charming garden (let me say that Elsie is no amateur gardener, as she belongs to the Massachusetts Horticultural Society, reads much literature on the subject, and buys her seeds only from

pedigreed stock), and also had the pleasure of meeting her husband, a very busy physician, her daughter Nancy, who is to enter Abbot Academy next year on her way to Smith, and her son John, who is in the first grade at school.

Nancy (Lincoln) Newell's mother died in September.

Marion (Pooke) Duits, with her husband and son Sammy, aged 11 months (our youngest child, by the way), has been in Natick since June. They plan to return to Paris in November.

Marion Rice was ill most of the spring and summer, but after a sojourn in the hospital, a rest, and a visit with Mary (Hastings) Bradley, she reports that she is feeling fit again, and very much on the job in the department of Public Health Nursing at Simmons College.

Sue (Tower) Leete is now settled in her charming old house which she bought and renovated this summer in South Hingham.

See Northampton News for Freshman Granddaughters.

1906

Class secretary—Mrs. Eben Atwood (Edith Moore), 2732 Irving Av. S., Minneapolis, Minn.

Betty (Amerman) Haasis spent the summer with the children in the mountains fifty miles west of Asheville, where Barbara attended the practice school of the State Normal. Mr. Haasis is to study forest ecology at Johns Hopkins this winter, and assist Dr. Burton Livingston.

Lillian Barrett neglected her writing this summer to go in for a new project, the Actor's Festival, of which she is secretary. The beautiful old Newport Theater is being put in repair for them. The object is to produce good plays in protest against the organized immorality of the present day theater. Lillian speaks of missing quiet lunches with Helen Larmonth in N. Y.

Nettie Baumann and a friend sailed on Aug. 25 for Cherbourg, Tours, Spain, and the Riviera, returning from Naples Nov. 19.

Virginia (Cox) Brank hopes touring members of the class will stop off at her summer cottage in Castine (Me.) next summer. Her sixteen-year-old daughter plans to enter Smith in 1928. She has two boys of eleven and eight.

Ruth (Fletcher) Common says their main interest this past year has been in building a new house. She camped in the mountains this summer and gardened at home. She is now studying Spanish.

Alice (Foster) Mullins's daughter, Betty McCulloch, our class baby, was married on Sept. 28.

Charlotte (Gardner) McCall, with her husband and four daughters, spent four weeks in Massachusetts on the Cape, returning home by way of Boston, N. Y., and Washington. In Boston she visited Ruth McCall.

Ethel (Gleason) McGeorge and family spent the summer at Cuba (N. Y.) on a farm. She plans to go to Hamp in February as councillor.

Margaret Hutchins spent her vacation in

New York City and in Chautauqua, where she taught eighteen hours a week in the Library School, also in New Hampshire, and in Northampton with Margaret Norton. In October she went to Atlantic City to attend the American Library Association meeting, and help summarize and discuss papers on inter-library loans in the College and Reference Section.

Lucia (Johnson) Bing did some extension work for Ohio State Univ. in their experiment with summer camps for farm women.

Barbara (Kauffmann) Murray motored to her father's camp, Camp Percy, in the White Mts. with her husband and two-year-old daughter.

Mabel Kent was at Eagle Camp on Grand Isle, Lake Champlain, for two weeks, living in a tent.

Amy Maher was in Paris in June for the Congress of the International Women's Suffrage Alliance; then in Normandy, Brittany, and England.

Florence (Mann) Spoehr's husband, in charge of the Coastal Laboratory of the Carnegie Institution at Carmel, according to a newspaper clipping, "is making significant progress in his experiments with photosynthesis, or the process by which green plants utilize solar energy in the manufacture of sugars."

Janet (Mason) Slauson's family lived and entertained this summer on a large houseboat, anchored on the Canadian side of the Thousand Islands. She says, "The full beauty of the St. Lawrence River is never so striking as when one lives right on it."

Agnes (McCord) Brindley spent the summer in a shack in the woods with two-year-old James, while John, aged 16, an Eagle Scout, camped and canoed 300 miles in northern Wisconsin with his father. Elizabeth, aged 13, also camped. Agnes is active in the College Club, in social service, and in her church.

Blanche (Millard) Parkin plans to be in Pasadena again this winter at the Hotel Vista Del Arroyo. She saw Fannie (Furman) Potter's mother, husband, and little boy there last winter.

Edith (Moore) Atwood left her family of fourteen for a ten days' trip through the Yellowstone.

Helen (Moore) Bagg was on her way to Nova Scotia when news of her father's death called her home.

Margaret Norton spent July in Holderness, N. H. She and her mother have moved into an apartment where they will welcome classmates at tea.

Alice (Raymond) Biram is chairman of a committee on establishing a summer camp for the Hartford Y. W. C. A. For three years she has been head of the Girl Reserve Camp Committee. She is on the West Hartford Library Board.

Bertha Reed, according to a newspaper clipping, "took part in the celebration of the 200th anniversary of the founding of Kingston (Mass.), the birthplace of her parents. The Reeds have given the town a recreation building on the athletic field and Miss Reed acted

as hostess." The secretary understands that Bertha keeps up her painting.

Florence Root, Dean of Women of the College of Wooster (O.), was abroad this summer with her mother and sister. She plans to go again next year.

Alice Smythe visited Ruth (Fletcher) Common this summer.

See Alumnae Publications for note about Jessie (Vallentine) Thayer.

Genevieve Waters returned from Honolulu where she was living with Charlotte Dodge. She visited Ruth (Flather) MacBriar and Edna (MacRobert) Morse on the way home.

See Northampton News for Freshman Granddaughters.

Ex-1906

Gertrude (Fiedler) Mewborn's address is c/o Pittsburgh Press, Pittsburgh, Pa.

1907

Class secretary—Mrs. James L. Goodwin (Dorothy Davis), 10 Woodside Circle, Hartford, Conn.

Isabella Rhodes was appointed on July 1 assistant professor in the newly established School of Library Service at Columbia. Her address now is 126 Claremont Av., New York.

Ruth (Cowing) Scott sends the following notice: "There are no other items for the QUARTERLY this time because Dorothy is still in Europe. But as soon as she returns we will send out our first reunion letter with full news of the girls and all of our plans for June."

See Northampton News for Freshman Granddaughters.

1908

Class secretary—Mrs. James M. Hills (Helen Hills), 876 Carroll St., Brooklyn, N. Y.

Flora Burton gave a series of lectures at the summer session of the Hyannis Normal School.

Katharine Dauchy has returned from her long stay in Europe and is in Charleston, R. I. For the winter she and her mother expect to have an apartment in New York.

Bella Coale and Gladys Gilmore spent the summer in Europe.

May Kissock is taking a sabbatical year in New York and is living at the Smith Club.

See Northampton News for Freshman Granddaughters.

1909

Class secretary—Mrs. Donald Pirnie (Jean MacDuffie), 138 Milbank Av., Greenwich, Conn.

MARRIED.—Helen Wing to Arthur Hammond Graves, Sept. 1, at Brielle, N. J. New address, 1 University Pl., N. Y. C. Helen had an out-of-door wedding in the garden of her mother's summer home, with the members of the two families as the only guests. Mr. Graves is a Yale graduate and was at one time professor of botany at Yale. He is at present curator of public instruction in the Brooklyn Botanic Garden. Helen has been director of the School Nature League in New York City and is keeping on with it from her new quarters.

DIED.—Elizabeth Allison, Oct. 19, after a short illness.

OTHER NEWS.—There will be a class

luncheon in New York early in November—just for the fun of it. Mrs. William McCarroll (alias Genevra Gubbins) is in charge of the arrangements. It is hoped that there will be a speaker from the college as an additional *pièce de résistance*. Postal cards will be sent to all living near New York. If you would like to come, but do not receive a card, please write to Genevra.

Elizabeth (Alsop) Shepard, who had a house in Neuilly last winter, is still in France but is planning to return this fall.

Julia (Dole) Baird and her four children spent the summer at Spring Lake (Mich.), where they have bought a 26-acre farm. It is called "Orchard Point," and has horses, a cow, and a big vegetable garden. A snapshot of the two girls has been added to the class records.

Gertrude (Gerrans) Pooley and Eleanor (Mann) Blakeslee were at Thunder Bay, on the Canadian shore of Lake Erie, for the summer. Harriet (Byers) Deans was near-by, at Crescent Beach.

Florence (Hague) Becker is vice-chairman of the Constitution Hall finance committee of the D. A. R., with Edith (Scott) Magna as her commanding officer.

Henrietta Harris is president of the Business Women's Club of Massachusetts, having been national vice-president for her state for the last two years. She is also on the board of managers of the Old Ladies' Home, secretary of the advisory committee of the Family Welfare Association, and membership chairman of the Western Massachusetts Branch of the American Association of Social Workers. She is at present a private financial secretary in Springfield.

Grace (Hazeltine) Caughey's mother died in May.

Nan (Linton) Clark had a busy summer in Woods Hole. Her husband and daughter share her ability in dramatics, and were all active in giving a group of one-act plays at the Marine Biological Laboratories. There was a committee of about 100 to help, and the newspaper account says it was a great success.

Alice (Pierce) Barry spent the summer in Jaffrey (N. H.), with her son and mother. By maintaining a discreet silence she remained incognito until just before her return to Texas, when she spent a week in Northampton with Carol Brewster '96·

Jean (Richardson) Chase and her husband took a western trip this summer, stopping at Banff, Lake Louise, Vancouver, and the Yellowstone.

Edith (Scott) Magna has been appointed national chairman of the Constitutional Hall finance committee to secure funds for the new D. A. R. Hall in Washington (D. C.) and will visit as many states as possible this winter.

Ethel (Updike) Magna has built a new house in Cherry Circle, West, just outside of Memphis.

Delight Weston sailed in April for six months in England and France.

Jane (Wheeler) O'Brian was at Windmill Point (Ont.) this summer.

Come to the fall luncheon if you possibly can!

1910

Class secretary—Alice O'Meara, 12 Keswick St., Boston, Mass.

BORN.—To Louise (Marden) Wild a fourth daughter, Joan, Feb. 8.

To Loraine (Washburn) Hall a daughter, Anne Cuthbert, Aug. 30.

OTHER NEWS.—Helen Allen went back to what she called essentially a "Greek" Commencement. "I continue to revel yearly in the pleasure due to work with Professor Tyler, Miss Caverno, and Miss Barbour."

Helen (Hemphill) Parry writes: "To my surprise I find that Gladys Russell has a cottage at Croton Heights where we have just bought an acre. Hers is a very attractive one-room shack for week-ends. This is a small group of literary and professional people in what I think is the most beautiful spot in Westchester." Helen was planning to take the Vassar course in euthenics last summer.

Of the Minneapolis group, Katharine (King) Covey spent the summer in Europe; Mary Geesaman has returned from two years in California; they both, with Gertrude (Chandler) Fisher, had luncheon with Bernice (Barber) Dalrymple last September in the new house that she has just been settling.

Ruby Litchfield is back at Smith as Associate Personnel Director. She lives at Dawes House.

Louise (Marden) Wild wrote last June: "Believe me, these are strenuous days. Just now I am sewing on names for *four* camp outfits! The rest of the Wild family is staying in Winchester this summer as our farmhouse on the Cape burned to the ground last spring."

Mary Ann (Staples) Kirkpatrick and her husband spent three weeks of the summer in Canada with Phoebe (Parry) Reed and her husband. Do read in the October *Woman's Home Companion* Mary Ann's article on Budgets. She says that it all came about through a letter that she wrote last winter in a "Hobby Contest." Her hobby seems to be slowly but surely turning into a profession. She has also done a Budget Booklet for the *Companion*.

Loraine (Washburn) Hall's husband is now pastor of a church in Florence, Mass. Loraine is enjoying its proximity to Smith.

1911

Class secretary—Mrs. J. P. O'Brien (Margaret Townsend), 614 Madison Av., Albany, N. Y.

MARRIED.—Laura Wilber to Sydney Philip Noe, Sept. 11.

BORN.—To Edna (Hodgman) Carlaw a daughter, Mary Adelaide, July 22.

To Frederica (Mead) Hiltner a son, John Rutherford, Aug. 18.

To Ruth (Weber) Schaefer a daughter, Florence Louise, Aug. 17.

OTHER NEWS.—Carol Brown spent the summer in Europe.

Jo (Dormitzer) Abbott wrote at length this summer from Megansett, Mass. Her stepson,

Satin Linings That WEAR!

A LONG TRIP is a searching test of quality in clothing — and particularly of the linings. The inside of your coat gets more wear than the outside — constant friction, standing, walking or sitting.

Good style requires satin linings and good sense requires satin with *wearing quality*. It is annoying when far from home to have a lining go to pieces.

Skinner's Satin adds distinction to any garment and outwears other silk linings. For three-quarters of a century it has been the overwhelming choice of tailors and clothing manufacturers who use only the best materials.

In buying a suit or overcoat ready-to-wear it pays to look for the Skinner label. In ordering from a merchant tailor, *"Look for the Name in the Selvage."*

WILLIAM SKINNER & SONS · *Established* 1848

NEW YORK, CHICAGO, BOSTON, PHILADELPHIA. *Mills:* HOLYOKE, MASS.

"Look for the Name in the Selvage"

Linings for men's suits and topcoats · Linings for women's coats, suits and furs · Dress Satins, Millinery Satins, Shoe Satins

Skinner's Satins

Capen, graduated last June from Amherst. He was a member of the Chi Psi Fraternity and the Glee and Mandolin Clubs. He expects to go into business out west for a few years and then go in with his father in the D. R. Emerson Co. of Boston. Jo has spent the last year studying at Radcliffe and Harvard for her M.A. in psychology which she hopes to have by next February. She also works twenty hours a week at the Judge Baker Foundation (the Juvenile Court Clinic) as psychologist. (See page 39.) She says she hopes later to go into clinical work professionally. Her son Walter, aged 13, was at camp this summer but the other five were with her at Megansett.

Margaret (Foss) Thomas's father died this summer. Many of us have very happy memories of Mr. Foss and his friendliness to all of Peg's friends, and our sympathy goes to all her family.

Mira Poler spent August in Bermuda.

Charlotte (Rankin) Aiken visited in Saratoga this summer and in passing through Albany telephoned ye secretary and gave out much news. May her tribe increase! Why do not all 1911-ers do the same when passing within telephoning distance? Her four boys are now 9, 7, 3½, and 2 years old. The oldest now goes to a military school. When at home she sees a great deal of Marguerite (Butterfield) Ervin who also lives in New Orleans and who is busy putting music into the public schools there. She has two little girls. Two years ago she took the oldest child to Europe with her.

Marian (Yeaw) Biglow sends a picture of young Lucius in a bathing suit—which gives promise for the future of football at Yale. They are permanently settled now in Old Lyme, having bought a little stone house there (which is to be remodeled) and several acres of land, from which there are glimpses of the Connecticut River. She saw Jo Thomas this summer at the Art Association in Lyme.

1912

Class secretary—Mary A. Clapp, Galloupe's Point, Swampscott, Mass.

Helen (Bartholomew) Prizer writes that her entire family has just returned from four months in St. Jean de Luz, where they all studied French with great diligence and became captivated with the charms of the place.

Frankie (Carpenter) Huntington writes: "Much has happened to the Huntington family since your visit to the Villa Marie Amelie. We have traversed the ocean with no casualties, acquired a dog, and are established here on the Blue Ridge for the summer. But the chief item of importance to us is that we have acquired a permanent home. I should like it stated that I am never going to move again, only I fear that if you do we shall find ourselves pulling up stakes and changing the next month. So I will just cross my fingers and hope that our wanderings have ceased. Our address is 1906 23 St. N. W., Washington."

Mildred (Scott) Olmsted attended the Institute of Politics at Williams this summer

and reported it simply teeming with Smithites.

Carolyn (Sheldon) Jones writes from Cajeme, Sonora, Mexico: "I am sending you my new address. I left Tampico, where I have spent the past five winters, in March, stayed two months in Arizona to get the benefit of that glorious climate for the children, and came to Cajeme last week. Cajeme itself is nothing but a collection of warehouses, a few stores, and Mexican adobe huts, but it is the business center of the Yaqui Valley, which is fast developing into an important farming district rivaling the Imperial Valley in California. I am spending the summer at Hacienda Realidad, the ranch of one of my neighbors-to-be, while we build our house. There are some twenty American women scattered throughout the valley, living anywhere from one to twenty-five miles apart. We meet for lunch and bridge once a week, but except for that day, life is limited to one's own ranch. I am engrossed in building our own house, and in adapting myself to keeping house in a place where everything not produced on the ranch must be ordered from Nogales two weeks ahead of the time when it is needed."

Elizabeth (Tucker) Cushwa's father, William Jewett Tucker, president emeritus of Dartmouth, died Sept. 29.

1913

Class secretary—Mrs. Alexander Craig Jr. (Helen Hodgman), 314 E. 17 St., Brooklyn, N. Y.

MARRIED.—Eleanore Holmes to Willard E. Everett, June 27. Maude Barton was maid of honor and Clara Williamson and Edith Downes were two of the bridesmaids. Madeleine (Thompson) Edmonds, Irene (Overly) Cowan, Naomi (Kaltenbach) Lancaster, and Gladys (Wyman) Pride were there also.

Gladys McCain to Paul Weathers.

Helen Plumer to Charles Henry Clement, Sept. 1.

Meron Taylor to Christopher Kassenbrock.

BORN.—To Helen (Donovan) Craven her first son and third child, Donovan, May 27.

To Eleanor (Ford) Stelling a daughter, Janet, July 24.

To Margaret (Moore) Cobb her second daughter and third child, Margery Moore, June 14.

OTHER NEWS.—Marjorie Anderson has received her Ph.D. in English at the Univ. of Chicago. She is now an instructor in the English department at Smith.

Mary Arrowsmith has gone to Budapest.

Annie Dunlop returned in August from a four months' trip abroad, on the same steamer as Anna (Bailey) Smith. She writes, "Two weeks I spent with Lucile Atcherson in Berne where she was acting as Minister of the United States, since the Minister and the first Secretary had gone to the Disarmament Conference, leaving her in charge of the Legation."

Helen (Hodgman) Craig is keeping house for her father this winter. See above address.

Marion Parker writes: "Same job and same address. For extra activities I am serving as chairman of the program committee of the

New England Home Economics Association and director of the Massachusetts Home Economics Association; visited College last week and went through the new dormitories; very fine."

Clara (Savage) Littledale is managing editor for a new magazine, *Children*, a magazine for parents.

Emily (Smith) Pollet is teaching three classes in history at the Smead School for Girls in Toledo.

Olive Tomlin is teaching in Columbus School for Girls, Columbus, O.

Ex-1913

BORN.—To Marjorie (Boardman) Kinter a son, William Boardman, Mar. 25.

1914

Class secretary—Mrs. Herbert R. Miller (Dorothy Spencer), 120 Haven Av., N. Y. C. Telephone: Billings 2414.

MARRIED.—Ruth Lydia Brown to John Godfrey Harvey, July 22, in Portland, Ore. "We are now living at the above address (355 12th St., Portland, Ore.)."

Louise Howe to John Harry Marshall of 108 Everett Av., Providence, R. I., Oct. 2. Louise wrote: "The marriage will be a church one and my sister Harriet will be my only attendant. . . . Harry has an established home already as his sister has been keeping house for him and bringing up his little boy, Alden, who is now about eight and a half."

Florence Franklin to Charles Kinsley Ferry, Aug. 19, at the N. Y. Smith Club. Mr. Ferry is in the lumber business.

BORN.—To Mabel (Kirley) Robinson her first child and son, William Kirley, Apr. 1, 1925.

To Jenny (Luntz) Rabinoff her second child and daughter, Miriam Etta, May 8.

To Laura (Rice) Deming her sixth child and fifth daughter, Linda, July 1.

OTHER NEWS.—Jean Paton writes that the Burton Memorial Committee has decided to raise $10,000 for scholarships, each class which was in college under President Burton to be responsible for $1000. That seems a modest goal and we should make it very simple for our members, Jean as general chairman and Zimmie Zimmerman, class chairman. More anon.

Louisa Baker spent the summer in Europe.

Ora Belden writes from Paris, "I have at last ventured away from the beaten track of Rosemary [where she has taught since '19] by taking a year's leave of absence for work at the Sorbonne, if my courage holds out, at any rate for a stay of several months, teaching in an American School."

Anna Colman visited Betty (McMillan) Howard in June at East Hampton.

Marion (Corey) Koughan spent the summer with her two boys in her cottage on Peaks Island, Me. Her husband was connected with the Cobbs' camps for boys at Denmark, Me.

Marguerite Daniell writes that the only mountains she has climbed on foot have been in this country. She has climbed ninety-six, many of them as often as four times. This summer she was in Colorado and climbed to the summits of Twin Sisters, Taylor Peak, Hallett, Flat Top, Long's Peak, as well as to the Chasm and Blue Lakes and the Crater on Specimen Mountain. All of these range from over 11,000 to over 14,000 feet. To quote the newspaper, she "made the ascent on foot from Sprague's Hotel in the Glacier Basin over the north side of the peak to the Boulder Field. Part of the way there is no trail. Not more than six people a season make the ascent this way and few women have ever made it. The entire trip was made in eleven hours and a half including two hours on the summit. A new record for women was established."

Blanche (Darling) Bergeson writes that her husband has been elected president of Fargo College, N. D. "The campus borders on our home and we both taught there when we were first married. . . . It is an old college for this section, forty years, but three years ago, due to mismanagement and to our peculiar state financial situation, it closed its doors. Now my husband is assuming the big burden of clearing debts, raising money, etc., to reopen it, at the same time remaining head of his law firm. I often wish Fargo were nearer the main routes of travel. The latch string is always out for 1914 immigrants."

There was an interesting article in the *Meriden Record* about Anna Doyle. In 1925 she took the course for Deans at the summer session at Smith. She was then made dean of girls at the Meriden High School where she is also head of the Latin department. She is the first dean in the history of the school, and she has been highly successful. She helps the students with the problems which arise in connection with their studies and acts as a vocational guide both by personal interviews and by talks arranged for them. In the same way she coöperates with the school physician in matters of health and hygiene.

Amy Fargo was in Europe this summer.

Norma Kastl motored all through Maine this summer. She is still busy "publicizing" Mr. Filene in Boston.

Roberta King spent last summer motoring through Scotland and traveling extensively in England and on the Continent.

Sophie (Marks) Krauss broke ground for her new house in Seattle this summer.

Marguerite (Krusen) Williams will be in Orange from Oct. 20 to Apr. 15, as her husband needs to be near N. Y. for business reasons.

Catharine (McCollester) Gallaher spent last summer at Beg Meil on the coast of Brittany. She writes: "We have an apartment at 47 boulevard Péreire, Paris, and I do hope many '14ers will ring my bell before the year is over. . . . My husband's business takes him traveling and I have gone along on several trips—to Spain, Italy, Holland, Belgium, Switzerland, and the untouristed byways of France."

Dorothy Ochtman is a member of the Painters' and Sculptors' Gallery Association and of the National Association of Women Painters and Sculptors.

Helen O'Malley is dean of St. Mary's Hall and supervisor of secondary English of the Manila high schools.

Nellie Parker helped her mother run her inn near Bath (Me.) this summer.

Many will be interested to know of Gertrude Posner's work. She has been connected with the Retail Research Association for eight years, which is concerned with research in retail stores. The organization is made up of sixteen stores in different parts of the country, all working to distribute merchandise to the consumer as economically as possible. This means keeping the expense of operating as low as is consistent with good service. All the problems that arise in connection with operating expense are Gertrude's field: keeping the store clean, purchasing and consumption of supplies, wrapping and delivery, receiving and marking of merchandise, employment, payment, and training of employees, labor and time saving equipment. In addition to these major problems, her work has led her into studies of selling departments that have been operating at a loss. She has found her work very satisfying and recommends the field. She does a good deal of traveling.

Laura (Rice) Deming writes that Patsy went to a summer camp, that Elizabeth and Catherine spent August with their grandmother, and that she and Kenneth stayed at home with Linda and the workmen who were adding several rooms to their house.

Nelle (Robie) Eaton, besides bringing up two boys and being a farmer's wife, is trying to keep up her music (she sings at church and at the Woman's Club). She also earns pin money sewing and putting up canned fruits, vegetables, and jams, and drilling children's pageants.

Dot Seamans spent July at her brother-in-law's ranch at Hood River.

Dorothy (Upjohn) DeLano has gone to France for six months with her three children.

Elizabeth Zimmerman has moved to the New York Smith Club, 233 E. 17 St.

Ex-1914

BORN.—To Helen (Adams) Keig a second child and son, Edward Quincy Adams, Oct. 1, 1925.

OTHER NEWS.—Helen (Adams) Keig is prominent musically in Silsbee, Tex.

Elizabeth Barnes is a registered nurse, having graduated from the Nurses' Training School of the Northampton State Hospital in Sept. 1925.

See note about Martha (Watts) Frey in the Alumnae Publications.

Mardie (White) Webbe took her family to a camp in Colorado for August.

1915

Class secretary—Mrs. Dudley T. Humphrey (Marian Park), Loudonville, Albany Co., N. Y.

MARRIED.—Ruth Bartholomew to Oliver B. Judson, June 18.

Loretta Burns to William S. Kearns.

Mildred Hutchinson to Paul Eugene Gropp, Aug. 16. Mr. Gropp is an instructor in German at George Washington Univ. and their temporary address is 1878 Phelps Pl. N. W., Washington, D. C.

BORN.—To Louise (Becker) Benedict a third child and first son, Robert Anthony, Apr. 5.

To Elizabeth (Collinge) Holden a nine-pound son, Lyman Sanford, Sept. 23.

To Ethel (Dikeman) Trask a fourth child and second daughter, Elizabeth Mary, Jan. 1.

To Margaret (Francis) Ellis a third child and second son, William Rogers, Apr. 10.

To Elizabeth (Jennison) Christie three children, hitherto unrecorded: Janette Elizabeth, June 6, 1917; Anne Katherine, Oct. 15, 1918; Robert Christie III, Feb. 15, 1920.

To Bessie (Whaley) Pflaum two children, hitherto unrecorded: Charles, June 10, 1921; Harriet Marie, Mar. 13, 1925.

OTHER NEWS.—Katharine Boutelle spent seven weeks abroad this summer traveling with her father and step-grandfather and her sister Elizabeth '21, "the former very lively companions both in body and spirit despite their age." They were in the British Isles all the time, except two weeks in Paris and Tours. Her description of Galway and Connemara in Ireland make one long to go there. Briefly: "You go a long way through stunning mountain country, coming upon the sea in regular fjords, running eleven miles inland and deep enough for big yachts. Riding in a bus between hedgerows of fuchsia and past fairy glens, all a lovely yellow-green, with sunlight coming through the trees and a very light moss on everything."

Ada (Baker) Fellows has just returned from a grand spree in New York "to the ever busying and thrilling experience of building a house."

Betty Carpenter obtained a ten weeks' leave this summer and went to Europe with Marian Thompson '13. They visited England and the Continent. In Heidelberg, they saw a performance of "A Midsummer Night's Dream" given mostly by torchlight in the courtyard of the castle. Devon, the Rhine, and the Black Forest were what they enjoyed the most.

Anne (Cooper) Ferris has survived a sinus and tonsil operation on herself, an appendicitis operation on Jane, as well as calamities in their respective families, and is preparing for a festive winter, in spite of their apparent "jinx." She spent two weeks in Maine visiting Olive (Gauntt) Mahan, who had a cottage for the summer.

Ethel (Dikeman) Trask says, "A new baby, a new house, and a new Studebaker give a pretty lucid description of my daily news."

After having taught in Pittsburgh at a private school, Violet Franz went to the Eastern High School in Washington (D. C.) until last December, when her family moved to Los Angeles on account of her mother's health. At a Smith luncheon in June in Altadena, to which she went with Frances (Fitzsimmons) Waldron and Audrey (Haskell) Mallen ex-'15, she met K. Barnard and her sister and Florence Eis '16. When Violet wrote she was thinking of attending summer school.

Mildred Fraser is head of the English department in the Needham High School, or-

When writing to advertisers be sure to mention
THE SMITH ALUMNAE QUARTERLY

ganizing a hitherto "headless" department; she has also registered for an evening course in the Graduate School of Education at Harvard.

Angeline (Freeman) Kitson spent part of the summer in Wisconsin visiting her parents and part of it taking a course in "statistical drafting" in Columbia Summer School.

Elizabeth (Jennison) Christie spent a few weeks this summer visiting Natalie Murphy, President Burton's secretary when he was at Michigan, and brings us the following news of his family. Theodosia, who is married and living in Ann Arbor, spends part of the day taking care of her child, the rest, in a position in the Ann Arbor Hospital. Jane has grown into an attractive young person about to enter the University and Paul is also in college. Mrs. Burton intends to take some courses this winter in Columbia.

Clarise (Judd) Dake lists her occupation as "trying to be a good wife, mother, and housekeeper." Most of the day is spent with her two lively boys but she adds that she hasn't grown too old to enjoy dancing, tennis, swimming, and a bridge game.

Frances (Michael) Olmsted is selling a lovely line of silk underwear. She will be glad to write particulars to anyone interested. (I, as one of her satisfied customers, heartily recommend it.)

Margaret (Munsie) Hathaway is a regular substitute in the high school. Her mother has been desperately ill all summer, having had two very serious operations, but she is now convalescing at Margaret's house.

Elizabeth Page is now Sister Elizabeth of the Blessed Trinity. Address, Monasterio de Carmelitas Descalyas, Sancti Spiritus, Cuba.

Evelyn (Odlin) Attwood's father died at her home, June 7.

Marian (Park) Humphrey is the anxious grandmother of eight pedigreed Irish Setter pups.

Beatrice (Pierce) Lench has moved to 70 Morningside Dr., N. Y. C.

Nell (Ryan) Daniel writes that she and her husband were rusticating in the woods of Vermont this summer while he wrote. Mr. Daniel gave up his editorial work a year ago and has been "free-lancing" since. He has had several books published. Nell does research work for him, types many of his manuscripts, and is his business manager generally. They are starting the first week in October to drive out to Nebraska as Mr. Daniel has a book to do out west. "In the Favour of the King," a romance, "Ships of the Seven Seas," a history of shipping, and the beginning of a juvenile series of which "The Gauntlet of Dunmore" is the first, are among his published works.

Eleanor (Sackett) Cowles was granted a divorce from her husband, Russell Cowles, in Paris last May.

Mary (Spencer) Nimick moved into her new country house, July 1. All the family immediately gained at least five pounds apiece and she recommends the country for ease in handling children. After her house and children are attended to Mary teaches

pre-school age children for two hours every morning.

Besides two previous trips abroad, and a trip around the world last year, Agnes Taylor spent three months on the Continent this summer. Agnes went over on the Cunard Line in the Tourist Cabin to try it out. She motored through the Chateaux country and Brittany before going to Paris, saw the Prince of the Asturias at a bull fight in Segovia but left after the finish of one bull and three horses, motored over the Pyrenees from Biarritz to Carcassonne where they saw Comédie Française give "Othello" outdoors, besides doing many other fascinating things.

All the class seem to be "tripping." Marguerite (Tweedy) Biggs went to Colorado and California this spring for a month with a glorious week at La Jolla.

Leaky (Welles) English lives in Putnam, a small manufacturing town. The life sounds very pleasant. Her husband has a splendid church and a chance to do a big piece of work; there are some very congenial young married people with whom they dance and play bridge, tennis, and golf, and there is also her daughter Janet, a very wide-awake companion.

Ellen Williams wonders whether the fact that she taught one year in Madrid and two years at Penn Hall in Chambersburg (Pa.) should come under travels or occupation.

Jane Wilson says she feels like a permanent fixture in the same old job as serologist in the Newark City Hospital. By the card in the catalog she is Head Technician there. We are proud to claim her.

Ex-1915

BORN.—To Margaret (Jones) Jackson a second child, Jarvis Willis, Feb. 14.

To Minnie (Kroll) Berkowitz a second child and first daughter, Aug. 11.

OTHER NEWS.—Rhea (Grems) Inglehart moved Oct. 1 into a new home in Watertown that they have just bought.

After working in the same place for nine years, Guida Hopkins pulled up stakes and left with her sister for California to see their parents who are living there. They made many stops on the way out, the Grand Canyon, the Yosemite, and home by the Canadian Pacific and the Great Lakes. Guida is with the General Factory Manager of the Heywood-Wakefield Co. in Boston.

"Bonnie" (Jenkins) Daniels took both her children and spent five months abroad last year.

Madeleine (Rochester) Duffield says they spent the summer rusticating in Eden and that all they have to show for it is "a good brown healthy family and 300 jars of vegetables and preserves." She went on a camping trip with her husband for two weeks.

Florence (Taber) Allison had the privilege of singing last winter with a small orchestra composed of twenty members of the Boston Symphony.

Anne (Terhune) Eddy, after a ten-year interlude, is again taking up piano lessons and the morning practice which takes her back to the "good old days."

Barbara (Woodruff) Rukenbrod is living in Princeton and is president of the Provinceline Community Club. Her daughters, aged 11 and 8, are attending Miss Fine's School for Girls. Four years ago Barbara's house burned to the ground with a loss of everything, antiques, heirlooms, and her Smith book.

1916
Class secretary—Dorothy Ainsworth, 11 Barrett Pl., Northampton, Mass.

Because the class letter has gone out later than usual this fall and returns have not yet come in, our news is somewhat brief. In February, however, we hope to have so many items that we shall have to pay for extra space.

MARRIED.—Katherine Hasbrouck to William Muhlenberg Hiester Jones, Aug. 31. New address, 1554 Powell St., Norristown, Pa.

Dorothy Rose to Harry Wise Jr., July 8.

BORN.—To Emily (Clapp) Gleason a third child and second son, Edward Hollis II, Aug. 31.

To Elsie (Fisk) Phelps a third child and second daughter, Naomi Mary, July 11.

To Frances (Fleming) Winslow a first child and daughter, July 4.

To Miriam (Wood) Haseltine a first child and son, David Wood, July 11.

OTHER NEWS.—Louise (Bird) Ralston is moving in the near future to Pontiac, Mich.

Ruth (Blodgett) Shedden covered herself and the class with honor in various tennis tournaments this summer.

Louise (Brown) Hollister has just been in New York on a buying trip for her store in Pasadena.

Helen Cobb has returned to the U. S. A. after spending five years in Europe. She has been employed the last part of this time by the Associated Merchandising Corporation in Paris and in helping various members of her class to "see Paris."

Frances (Hall) Perrins's sister Barbara entered College this year. She played in the first Odd-Even basket ball game and led the freshman song at Freshman Frolic.

Ex-1916
MARRIED.—Helen (Hobbs) Cobb to Dr. Thomas William Harvey Jr., Sept. 7. Address after Dec. 1, 273 Tremont Av., Orange, N. J.

BORN.—To Ethel (Ellis) Foster a second child and son, Philip Alvin, June 17. Ethel's address is 23 Belair Rd., Wellesley, Mass.

To Mary (Robbins) Edgarton a son, Gardner, June 24.

1917
Class secretary—Florence C. Smith, 501 S. University St., Normal, Ill.

MARRIED.—Charlotte Ellis to Stanley William Fenton, Sept. 3.

BORN.—To Helen (Brown) Wells a daughter, Mary Kleber, July 17.

To Eunice (Clark) Schmidt a daughter, Anne Clark, Aug. 17. June's father died in July.

To Dorothy (Cole) Sturtevant a fourth

child and second daughter, Marion Brooks, July 8.

To Marie (Genung) Bryan a second son, William Joseph, July 16.

To Mary (Hudnut) Lockwood twins: a daughter, Mary Whiting, and a third son, Edward Whiting, Aug. 25.

To Alice (Hueston) King a daughter, Mary Elizabeth, Apr. 23.

To Chrystine (Wagner) Williams a third child and first son, Clayton Wagner, Aug. 13.

OTHER NEWS.—During the summer, Helen (Kingsley) McNamara and her husband spent three weeks in England and Scotland and three on the Continent—one each in Germany, Switzerland, and Paris.

Isabel (Platt) McClumpha, with her husband and daughter, sailed Sept. 18 for Paris where they expect to live for an indefinite length of time.

Margery Swett during the past year has contributed prose and verse to *Writers Monthly*, *Poetry*, *New Republic*, and *Stepladder*.

On Oct. 5, in New York City, Crosby Gaige presented "The Good Fellow," a comedy by George S. Kaufman and Herman Mankiewicz, with Ethel Taylor in the leading woman's rôle.

Harriet (Warner) Hoadley has returned to this country after a year in Europe where her husband has been doing research work in biology at university laboratories. This year Mr. Hoadley is to be at Brown Univ.

1918
Class secretary—Margaret Perkins, 3 Banks St., Chicago, Ill.

MARRIED.—Helen Ames to Paul Lameyer, Sept. 25. Eddie, Sue (Walker) Hamill, Himmie, and K. Delabarre ex-'18 were Amesie's bridesmaids. Helen and her husband are to live abroad.

Mary Guerin to Eldred Dewey Wilson, July 20. They will live in Tucson, Ariz.

Henrietta Opper to Frederick Stern, June 28. Henrietta wrote that she and her husband were taking a Midnight Sun Cruise, after which they would live in Newburgh, N. Y.

Rowena Stuckslager ('19) to Raymond Barragay McConlogue, June 7. Rowdy was married at her home, and she and her husband motored to California where they are living at 1942 Cheremoya Av., Hollywood. Mr. McConlogue is a lawyer.

Edna Wood to Dr. William Henry Turner, Aug. 18.

BORN.—To Katharine (Coe) Butzer a second child and first daughter, Betty, June 20.

To Dorothy (Erskine) Roberts a daughter, Dorothy Erskine, in 1924; a son, John Christopher, in 1925, who died at the age of three months; and a second daughter, Katharine, June 27.

To Frances (Hastings) Wilmeth a second child and first daughter, Frances Hastings, Aug. 14.

To Helen (Himmelsbach) Potter a son, Milton Grosvenor Jr., Oct. 13, 1925.

To Helen (Perkins) Knight a third child and second daughter, Margaret, Oct. 2.

To Eleanor (Tayler) Smith a son, Keenan Tayler, July 17.

To Isabelle (Wolfe) Harris a son, James Pardon Jr., Mar. 29.

OTHER NEWS.—Adah Attwood writes that she is still a rover—Florida in the winter, Asheville (N. C.) in the spring, and home in between times. The N. Y. Smith Club will always reach her.

Marion (Bancker) Vernon and her husband during the summer months for the last two years have been proprietors of "The Studio Tavern," situated on the main road five miles south of Manchester, Vt. From personal experience the secretary vouches that all who are motoring by and are lured in by the attractive road signs will find "The Tavern" most charming and picturesque with the additional asset of having comfortable beds and delicious food!

Elizabeth (Boyd) Beach writes that she and her husband and small daughter are deserting their beloved Oregon for Detroit where her husband returns to the Burroughs Adding Machine Co. Elizabeth expects to remain in Portland a few months longer to close up her remaining real estate business.

Ashley Burton is now doing institutional nursing instead of traveling as heretofore.

Elizabeth Clarke is in Virginia doing survey work with the Child Welfare League of America—adventurous work in the mountains and in a Ford.

Dorothea (Dann) Stevens is the proud possessor of a house of her own.

Elinor Edgar spent most of the summer and expects to spend the winter at Columbia taking pre-medical courses preparatory to entering medical school next fall.

Molly (Gazzam) Earling arrived in Seattle in September after a solid year in Nome, Alaska. Molly writes that by now they are all pretty good sour-doughs, and Nancy, her three-year-old, much prefers canned milk to fresh! In November they expect to return to Boston.

The name of Helen (Horton) Schofield's daughter, born last January, is Helen Elizabeth.

Frances Knapp is back at Smith in the Personnel Department as Placement Secretary.

Sarah Lippincott is now advertising manager in the department store of George Wyman and Co. in South Bend, Ind.

Bernardine Lufkin writes from her home in St. Paul of being on the up-grade after a long illness which has kept her in bed since February 1925.

Nancy McCreary spent last winter doing graduate work at Radcliffe and received an M.A. in English literature in June.

Mary Mensel has been made assistant warden at College.

Helen Otis and Hazel Sadler are still with the *Woman's Home Companion*.

Margaret Perkins returned in September from a wonderful four months' trip abroad.

On the same ship with her going over was Annie Kyle who was on her way to Palestine to gather material for a book she is writing. Mrs. Houghton of 26 Green was also among those present, and Miss Pinkerton of Haven House was on the returning ship, so Perki says she was well chaperoned.

Beulah Powers, having been for some time inaccessible by mail, has turned up at the N. Y. Smith Club where she boasts that she is the oldest living single member. Besides this position she is getting out a bulletin for a trade association of the oil industry.

Katherine Schultz attended the Institute for Instructors in Library Science at the Univ. of Chicago this summer, and has now returned to Skidmore for another year.

Bernice Wheeler is at home taking care of her mother who is an invalid.

Thelma Woodsome says that though she spent four years at art school she can't boast of any degree or of any illustrious work of art. She has been at home finding out what a series of repetitions housekeeping seems to be.

Grace Woods returned in June from two and a half years in India, teaching.

Ex-1918

BORN.—To Helen (Justis) Dunn a second daughter, Nancy King, Sept. 7, 1925.

1919

Class secretary—Julia Florance, 161 Livingston Av., New Brunswick, N. J.

DIED.—Alice Monica McCarthy, July 27, in Lawrence, Mass., after an operation for appendicitis.

In Memoriam

In the death of Alice McCarthy our class has lost a most loyal member and her intimate friends a true and adored companion. Alice was a brilliant student, valedictorian in high school and Phi Beta Kappa in college; along with this intense scholarly mind she had a most pleasing personality, making and retaining friends easily, and doing everything exceptionally well. She was held in the highest esteem in her community, where she taught in the high school and was active in club work. F. S. H.

ENGAGED.—Ambia Harris to Raymond Alastair MacDonald of New York.

MARRIED.—Martha Aldrich to Dr. Jackson Kenneth Holloway, June 5. Address, 217 Seventh Av. S. W., Rochester, Minn. Dr. Holloway is an assistant surgeon at the Mayo Clinic, where Martha is still working. They expect to be in Rochester about a year longer.

Elizabeth Willard to John Weller Brown, Feb. 16. Marion (Smith) Stoneman was a bridesmaid and Frances (Steele) Holden's husband an usher. Fran and Elizabeth (Wheeler) Richardson '16 attended the wedding. Address, Bexley, Columbus, O.

Margaret Woodwell to Franklin D. Johnston, June 10. Hazel Prentice was her maid of honor. Margaret is continuing her work as research assistant in internal medicine at the Univ. of Michigan and her husband is studying medicine there. Address, 2121 Highland Rd., Ann Arbor, Mich.

BORN.—To Carolyn (Case) Cook a second son, Jeffrey Wilcox, Apr. 24.

To Harriet (Chatfield) Vinkemulder a daughter and second child, Dorothy Chatfield, May 26.

To Frances (Cowles) Spaulding a son, Richard Cowles, July 7.

To Annette (Crystal) Lang a daughter and second child, Barbara, July 6.

To Catharine (Marsh) Bull a son, Thomas de Forest, June 24.

To Janet (Pennoyer) Little a second son, George Rockafellow, July 24.

To Irene (Shepherd) Parry a daughter, Anne Irene, Dec. 25, 1925.

OTHER NEWS.—Elizabeth Brown was buyer of misses' dresses for Hamilton and Co. in New Haven (Conn.) in the early summer and is now buyer of girls' ready to wear for W. M. Whitney and Co. in Albany, N. Y. She is living at the City Club, 1 Elk St.

Laura Carr spent two months in California this past summer. She saw Edith (Dohrman) Alexander when in San Francisco.

Marion (Craig) Keene was active in preschool-age committee work for the Indianapolis A. A. U. W. last winter. They had an interesting exhibit of toys and books for children in the fall and another of pictures for children in the spring.

Agnes (Decker) Eveleth writes from Via Randaccio 8, Milan, Italy: "Our plans to return to China were changed because of unsettled conditions there. During the winter we were traveling in the United States and in April we left for Milan. We are located for about six months in Milan in the apartment of Ezu Pinza, the bass opera singer. He is filling an engagement in Buenos Aires and later will go to New York for a twenty-four weeks' program with the Metropolitan Opera Co. We are enjoying Italy very much, especially the trips we take into the Alps and the Lake region."

Elizabeth (Hunt) Lockard is president of The Oranges (N. J.) Smith Club.

Elizabeth (Merz) Butterfield had the pleasure of seeing her chorus, "Spring," published by the Danielson Music House in Jamestown (N. Y.) in June. The Washington Heights Musical Club of New York sang it in May.

1920

Class secretary—Mrs. Arthur R. Hoch (Marian Hill), 312 N. Euclid Av., Oak Park, Ill. Assistant secretary—Josephine Taylor, 137 S. Scoville Av., Oak Park, Ill.

SECRETARY'S NOTE.—According to the promise in the fall letter, the following survey of the class records is being given. There are 422 living graduates; deceased 3; engaged 4; married 239 (an increase of 10, making 56.6% of the class married); children 205, of whom 111 are girls and 94 boys; mothers of 1, 95; of 2, 49; of 3, 6; of 4, 1 [Mabel (Lyman) Tapley]; Occupations: teachers 76; secretaries and related office workers 38; social service (including Y. W. C. A. etc.) 21; editorial and writing 10; laboratory technicians 18; selling 7; banking and insurance 5; architecture 2;

libraries 7; nurses 2; in business for themselves, 10. The Degrees are: M.A. 16; M.D. (and studying) 3; M.Ed. 1; D.Q. 1; LL.B. 2; M.Sc. 1; Ph.D. 3. A few additional figures that may be of interest are from the Ex Records. Of the 257 once listed as members of the class, 21 are now affiliated with other schools and colleges and wish to be dropped from 1920; 8 have died; 118 are married, 1 engaged, and there are 126 children, 58 girls and 68 boys.

A request has come to publish a short statement in regard to the status of the insurance policies. In 1920 four members of the class were insured for $10,000 apiece for 25 years, the $40,000 at maturity to be 1920's 25th Reunion gift to the College. The Class was to pay the premiums, which decrease slightly each year as the dividends accrue, the original individual share of $4.50 being cut as rapidly as possible. There has already been one decrease to $4.00 and the officers hope to be able to make another cut within a year or so. As yet no definite arrangement has been made with regard to the share that the insurance classes will have in the newly voted Alumnae Fund. You will be notified as soon as anything definite is decided.

ENGAGED.—Agnes Dowd to Osborne E. Brown, advertising manager of Gladding's in Providence, R. I. They have no definite plans as yet. Agnes is at present advertising writer for William Filene's Sons Co.

Helen Osborne to Robert Barton Strahan, Yale '20, of Newark, N. J. For the past three years Helen has been teaching biology and physiology in the high school in Newark.

MARRIED.—Katharine Bryan to Lowell H. Milligan, Dec. 28, 1925. Address, 5 Harvard St., Worcester, Mass. Katharine is a member of the Department of Education, working in the Worcester Art Museum. She gives story hours to children at the Museum, also talks and guidances to school classes and other groups.

Lucile Donmoyer to James R. Walter, Oct. 17, 1925. Address, 74 Kenilworth Pl., Brooklyn, N. Y. Mr. Walter is in the insurance business.

Emily Knight to Hugh John MacWilliams, June 5. Address, 400 James St., Syracuse, N. Y. Their honeymoon was spent at Banff and Lake Louise. Emily writes that her maid of honor was Margaret Mann '22 and that Dorothy (Clark) Eldred '20, Tat Saunders '19, Mary Merrell ex-'23, and Dorothy (Crouse) Witherill ex-'25 were at the wedding.

Marion Kron to Clyde H. Smith, May 18. Mr. Smith is sales manager of the Asheville School Estates and they are hoping to move into a home of their own there soon. Mr. Smith is from St. Louis. He is a Phi Delt, and was a Captain of Aviation in the War. Address, 34 Tacoma St., Asheville, N. C.

Marjory Lee to William H. Osborne Jr., Jan. 29. Helen Osborne (Marjory writes, "No relation to Bill") was a bridesmaid. Address, 279 Mt. Prospect Av., Newark, N. J. Mr. Osborne is a lawyer in Newark and was Princeton '20.

THE NEW YORK SCHOOL OF SECRETARIES

A Secretarial School Marked by Distinctive Features

It accepts only the best of student material.

It trains and equips through short intensive methods.

It seeks the individual development rather than a uniform result from all students.

It prepares men and women for active newspaper and magazine work; for special feature and publicity articles; for social and organization Secretarial responsibilities.

It emphasizes a three months' course.

It places its graduates in positions.

Students may enter on any date.

Special course in Short-story writing.

CANADIAN PACIFIC BUILDING, 342 MADISON AVENUE, NEW YORK, N. Y.

Vanderbilt 4039　　　　　　　　　V. M. WHEAT, *Director*

Secretarial Course

College women who aim for leadership in the business world find our Secretarial Course a solid foundation for future success.

Send for Bulletin

Ballard School, Central Branch, Y. W. C. A.

Established 54 years

610 Lexington Avenue　·　-　New York City

OLD COLONY SCHOOL

Secretarial and Business Training

For Young Women Graduates of
Private School, High School or College

One Year Course prepares for Executive Positions or the Management of Personal Property

Resident and day pupils

For Booklet or Information Write the Principals

Florence B. LaMoreaux, A.B.
Mrs. Margaret Vail Fowler

315-317 Beacon Street, Boston, Massachusetts

Miss Conklin's Secretarial School

THOROUGH professional training for secretaryships and executive positions.

The school occupies the studios of the Tilden Building; classrooms opening upon a roof garden have abundance of light and air.

The Bureau of Placement is a recognized feature of the School. Graduates are sought for varied and responsible positions.

Successive entrance dates.

Illustrated booklet

105 West 40th Street, New York

Telephone, Penna. 3758

Mary Lincoln to Herbert W. Porter, in 1926. Address, 11217 Bellflower Rd., Cleveland, O.

Marjory Lord to Artemas Packard, June 28.

Margaret Manning to Alexander Duff, Sept. 1. Mr. Duff is a public accountant. Address, 503 Beacon St., Boston, Mass.

Margaret Marsh to Charles Northrup Dailey, Aug. 9. Address after Dec. 1, 3506 Lincoln Av., Detroit, Mich.

Marian Myers to J. Harold Walton, Oct. 23. Mr. Walton is in the hardware and sporting goods business. Virginia Musk '21 was one of the bridesmaids. Address after Dec. 15, Homestead Av., Haddonfield, N. J. Last year Marian was a stenographer in her brother's real estate office.

The following announcement has come from Lisbeth (Urban) Beers's mother: "Last fall Lisbeth divorced her husband, Henry S. Beers, and on May 26 was married to Alin Howard Clark Jr. of New York. After Oct. 1 address 39 Grove St., N. Y. City."

BORN.—To Barbara (Arnold) Hutchins a second child and first daughter, Barbara Ann, Apr. 12.

To Louise (Atwater) Munson a second child and first daughter, Marjory Jeanne, Nov. 14, 1925.

To Cecily (Blackford) Jones ('21) a first son, June 5. The baby died on June 6.

To Mary Louise (Chandler) Eagleton a second son, William Lester Jr., Aug. 17.

To Barbara (Frantz) Russell a first daughter, Mary Katherine Gibson, Apr. 3, 1925.

To Sophie (Goldberg) Reiner a first daughter, Anne, July 8.

To Marion (Hancock) Munsell a first daughter, Mary F., in 1924.

To Ina (Hughes) Johnston a first daughter, Harriet Ballinger, Aug. 20.

To Rachael (Keeney) Thompson a first daughter, Ann Borodell, Aug. 1.

To Katharine (Kimball) Whitney a second child and first son, Wheelock Jr., July 30. Kay spent the summer in Maine and the baby was born there.

To Isabel (Kron) Patterson a first daughter, Alice Kron, July 23.

To Mabel (Lyman) Tapley a fourth daughter, Ruth, July 6.

To Madeline (Murphey) Marshall a first daughter, Virginia, Jan. 19, 1925.

To Mary (Radel) Keating a first daughter, Mary, Nov. 24, 1925.

To Alice (Rathbun) Sweet a first son, Sept. 1.

To Jessica (Raymond) Darlington a second daughter, in July.

To Marian (Rubins) Davis a first son, Horace Chandler, Aug. 12. She is to do research work in economics this year and her temporary address will be c/o American Express Co., London, Eng. Her husband has an Amherst Memorial Fellowship.

To Amy (Sheffield) Jaffrey a second child and first daughter, Madeleine Palmer, Dec. 5, 1925. Her little boy, announced rather vaguely a while ago, is named Walter Sheffield and was born on May 22, 1923.

To Hilda (Shepard) Coonse a first son, George Kenneth Jr., Dec. 18, 1925.

To Helen (Walker) Weyerhaeuser a third child and second son, George Hunt, July 8. Helen spent three months in Seattle this summer. They are moving into their new home soon.

To Mary (Howgate) Howgate a first daughter, Cynthia Ross, May 18.

To Virginia (Wiley) Price a third child and second daughter, Virginia.

To Elizabeth (Wyandt) Wood a first daughter, Sarah Wyandt, Sept. 8. The baby died the same day.

OTHER NEWS.—Mary (Acuff) Greey is moving into a new home, Ridgeview Rd., Princeton, N. J.

Jean Archibold will be at the Pennsylvania Hospital, 4409 Market St., Philadelphia, until July 1, 1927. She has been doing some amateur dramatics on the side, both acting and coaching.

Elizabeth Bates is still teaching piano at the Cincinnati Conservatory of Music. She received a diploma in pianoforte there in June 1923.

Josephine Battle landed in New York Sept. 5 after a two years' trip abroad.

Helen (Benjamin) Brown and her husband are to be in the middle west for a year or two. Temporary address, 130 Washington Blvd., Oak Park, Ill.

Marion Benjamin has been coaching and directing local dramatic productions in the high school and other places, besides her teaching.

Mary Bennett attended the Univ. of Pennsylvania from the fall of 1921 to the spring of 1926. In Feb. 1923 she received her M.A. in physiological chemistry and in June 1926 her Ph.D. in the same subject. She is now chemist in the Lankenau Research Institute which is connected with the Lankenau Hospital. The Institute was given by Mr. Rodman Wanamaker, son of Mr. John Wanamaker. She had her thesis published in the Aug. 1926 number of the *Journal of Biological Chemistry*.

Leah Brown has left Florida. She went abroad this summer.

Agnes Burnham writes: "I left Brockton in June 1925. This year I have been across the continent in my Ford and spent the winter in Calif. This summer I began work at Columbia for my M.A. in political science and in September I shall begin teaching in the Calhoun Private School for Girls." Address, 423 W. 118 St., N. Y. C.

Ellen Callahan is teaching history in the high school in Holyoke, Mass. She went to Europe in 1922.

Edith (Cohen) Wollison has taken four lecture courses under the Division of University Extension in the following subjects: music appreciation, applied psychology for teachers, teaching English to junior high school, and to adult immigrants. As a piano accompanist her work has been broadcast.

Ann (Corlett) Ford writes, "Still in Hammond, commuting to Cleveland as often as possible."

Mildred Cover is assistant to the dean in the College of Liberal Arts at the Univ. of Illinois. She went abroad this summer with Nora Kelley and they met Carol Rice in Scotland.

Anna Crane was a stenographer with the American Library Association in Chicago until April. Since then she has had no job.

Ruth Cushman is still teaching biology in the Norwich High School. She is also captain of a Girl Scout troop and assisted in the organization of the Girl Scouts there in Norwich.

Mary (Dangler) Dodd writes: "I spend most of my time with Billy now. He won an award of honor last year in a baby contest of several thousand. He is now on the waiting list for the nursery school in connection with the Univ. of California education and psychology departments. If he gets in by Feb. I hope to take some work there too."

The following address has been sent in for Bernice Davidson who has been lost for 4 years: 2326 Nella Vista, Hollywood, Calif. Although she doesn't answer repeated requests for news it is hoped that some one of you may be able to get her to do so.

Laura (Donnell) Hazard and her husband have been in some local dramatics in Flushing during the past year.

Hilda (Driscoll) Albee has been elected treasurer of the Free Library and a trustee as well. She is also on the book choosing committee.

Alice (Finger) Wilcox went on a cruise of the West Indies with her husband and mother this past winter. She expects to stay at home this winter to enjoy their new home.

Barbara (Foster) Sessions has been awarded a Carnegie Corporation grant of $1200 for study of art in Europe.

Dorothy (Gates) Allyn is to spend the winter in Arkansas with her father. Her husband will join them at Christmas time for a month or two. Dottie has been secretary of the District School Board.

Helen (Gill) Viljoen has a Ph.D. pending from the Univ. of Wisconsin for her work there in art and philosophy. She is teaching again at the Martha Washington Seminary and was hostess there during the past summer.

Dorothy (Gorton) Smucker writes again after a three years' silence. Neither she nor her husband has been very well during that time but both seem much improved now. Dorothy has been working for the Junior League and Smith Club and has been east several times but has never been back to College.

Virginia Heinlein hoped to be in Hamp this year but she is nursing a sick mother and is also entering upon her third year teaching at the Wheeling (W. Va.) High School. For two years she has had charge of the journalism department but this year is to do college preparatory work in English with the seniors.

Siloma (Hunt) Andrews writes that she is still keeping up her importing business and trying out an interesting experiment with her fast growing son. "A friend of mine who has a boy a few months older than mine coöper-

ates with me and we are experimenting in child play and giving each other a rest. We take turns taking care of the two boys while the other does just as she pleases (tennis, reading, sweeping, or what not, but totally uninterrupted and knowing that the child is in competent hands and at play). So far it has worked beautifully."

Helen Jack is still secretary at Milton Academy. She went to California this summer via New Orleans and the Grand Canyon.

Elizabeth (Kambour) Bedell is just recovering from a very serious siege of sleeping sickness. One of her close friends writes that she would be glad of letters provided you expect no answers as her doctor wishes her to use all her strength in recuperating. Her address temporarily is 80 Market St., Rockland, Mass.

Mary (Winton) Kimball has been enrolled in the Northwestern Univ. Commercial School as an auditor in a class in "investments" and "Europe since 1914." She has just returned from motoring out west.

Marguerite (Livingston) Eglinton went to Columbia for two or three summers and listened in at Cornell as a "visitor" last year.

Marion Lundagen is now technician in the laboratory of the Youngstown (O.) City Hospital.

Marguerite McKee has been assistant editor of the *American Historical Review*, living in Washington (D. C.) at 2314 Nineteenth St. N. W.

Cordelia (Merriam) Crabb is located near Boston now where her husband is working as a certified public accountant.

Grace (Merrill) Emery is about to move into a new home in Lincoln, Mass. At present she is back at the Library Bureau on a temporary job consolidating six different files into one central file for the statistical department.

Mary (Peck) Robinson writes: "Besides taking care of my family I have been doing some outside things: in 1921 was secretary of the day nursery and since 1922 have been active in the Everygirl's Club for Working Girls. Have been corresponding secretary of that for last two years, was a member of the Dunkirk Literary Club in 1922–23, and was elected a member of the Dunkirk Art Club in 1925."

Margaret Peoples is again teaching French at Smith.

Constance Reed is a laboratory technician at the Newark City Hospital.

Helen Rights went to the Pacific Coast this summer with Margaret Culberson '19. She went to Rutgers Summer School in 1925. She received no degree but completed requirements for a life certificate in New Jersey. She is teaching English in Roselle High School again.

Jessie Roberson has just returned from a summer abroad with her father.

Esther Roy is still teaching French in the Junior High School in Springfield.

Mary Seymour has just returned from nine months in Europe.

Darthea (Sharples) Lewis writes after two and a half years of silence: "We are still in Seattle living a very ordinary existence with an occasional high spot here and there. I was in charge of the Junior League show in May and also took part. We cleared $4600 which for our first experience along such lines was not considered bad."

Edith (Stein) Keim sends The Seneca Hotel, Chestnut and Seneca St., Chicago, as her address until June 1927.

Josephine Taylor is now director of the Emergency Bureau of the Y. W. C. A. of Chicago.

Ida Teller writes: "I have attended no college but have been doing voluntary and paid research work in bio-chemistry at the Pepper Clinical Laboratory of Research Medicine which is connected with the hospital of the Univ. of Pennsylvania. In 1924 I was made an associate member of Sigma Xi. In 1925 and 1926 I had Fellowships at the University Hospital. I collaborated in writing two papers with F. S. Hammett (published in the *Journal of Biological Chemistry*, Jan. 1922) and with Leon Jones M.D. and T. Grier Miller M.D. (published in the Archives of Internal Medicine, Mar. 1925). The latter was discussed in an editorial in the *Journal of the American Medical Association*. I am still at the Hospital."

Elizabeth Upton is Head of the Latin department in the Norwood (Mass.) High School.

Elsa Vieh is working for her Ph.D. at Harvard in Romance languages and literatures.

Olive Wall has returned from a two-year trip around the world. She expects to be in California all winter with her sister, at 1025 Roxbury Dr., Beverly Hills.

Isabelle Ward has been on Scribner's editorial staff for three years.

Dorothy Wells is a stenographer in the American Print Works in Fall River, Mass.

Fannye (Wieder) Blumenthal has been substituting occasionally for the secretary in the Corporation Counsel's Office in Hartford. She went to Florida last winter.

A newspaper clipping from the *Providence* (R. I.) *Tribune* announces that Iris Williams has gone to Florida as a volunteer for service in the devastated areas.

The *Weekly* announced that Ruth Willian had been promoted from instructor to assistant professor of music.

Henrietta (Zollman) Freud received her M.Sc. in 1922 and her Ph.D. in 1924 from the Univ. of Chicago.

Ex-1920

MARRIED.—Frances Fleming to Wingate Bixby, in St. George's in London, this last summer. Mr. Bixby, now of Kansas City, was formerly of Boston. Their address is 4644 Wornell Rd., Kansas City, Mo. Frances is president of the Junior League there.

Rey (Funk) Ewart to William G. Braid, in May 1924. Address, Box 1021, Santa Fe, N. M.

BORN.—To Clara (Azérad) Boizis a first daughter, Janine, June 19, 1925. Clara writes of her life in Algeria: "My life here is not very interesting. I live in a small village. There are many 'Kabyls' and very few French people. I have a nice little house with a pretty garden. I don't go very often to the town of Bougie. Algiers is four hours away. I am happy. My husband is very nice for me—but I'll never forget the 'good time' I had at Smith with you all, good friends! I am glad to know you don't forget me though I don't write much. I send you all my best regards."

To Katherine (Burrill) Field a second daughter, Burrill Field, Jan. 23. They call her Patsy. Address, 2728 Upton Av. S., Minneapolis.

To Clara (Guggenheimer) Binswanger a first daughter, Martha Ann, Aug. 16, 1923. Also a second daughter, Ida, Sept. 11, 1925. Address, 6623 N. 8 St., Philadelphia, Pa.

To Ruth (Laylin) MacDonald a first son, last spring. They are building a new home.

To Frances (Newhall) Wright a first son, July 21.

To Gladys (Nyman) Markward a second child and first son, John Sargent, Jan. 4.

To Margaret (Ranney) Stafford a fourth child and second daughter, Margaret Ranney, Apr. 4, 1927.

To Adele (Volk) Lombardi two sons, but she fails to give any dates or names. They have been living in Longview (Wash.) recently but expect to be transferred to Kansas City (Mo.) this winter. A permanent address for her is c/o L. W. Volk, Volk Bros. Co., Dallas, Tex.

To Dorothy (Jackson) Walker a first daughter, Dorothy Gale, July 14, 1925. Dorothy writes, "We call her Gale." Dorothy's husband graduated from Yale in 1917 and is now vice-president of Curtice Bros. Co. in Rochester (N. Y.), where their address is 5 Argyle St.

To Elma (Weichsel) Allen a second child and first son, Robert B. III, Apr. 14, 1925.

To Viola (Woodruff) Fletcher a daughter, in Nov. 1920. Viola wishes to be dropped from the class.

OTHER NEWS.—Katharine (Agler) Pope writes for the first time. They have been living in Waukesha (Wis.) for the past two years where Mr. Pope is an engineer in the experimental department of the Waukesha Motor Co. They have just bought an old stone house with an acre of ground five miles out from the town and Katharine says, "We are enjoying suburban life with our brood." Address, General Delivery, Waukesha, Wis.

Marjorie Dobbins graduated from the Univ. of California in 1925. She also studied landscape architecture. She wishes to be dropped from the class.

Ruth Ferguson wishes to be dropped from the class as she was only at college one month and knows none of the girls.

Grace (Fischer) Kribs's son William died as a result of a flu attack when he was nineteen months old.

Dorothy (Grant) Suydam writes after a long silence but says: "No news. The only scope my art now has is at home."

Helen Lynch used to work in Filene's in the "advertising." She has been quite ill recently. At present she is at the Nyack Club, Nyack, N. Y.

Frances McLallen writes after three years' silence: "I have spent the last six months in Panama getting tropicalized. I found a lure to the life there and hope to return one of these days. I was with the United Fruit Co. —in the banana department—helping to get the bananas from the plantations to the breakfast nooks of these United States. Before that I was in Hollywood, helping the Will Hays organization purify the movies for a while, then with the Hollywood Chamber of Commerce, and at other jobs of more or less consequence until they ceased to hold interest. At present I am visiting at home. Where I shall go from here no one knows." Address, Columbia City, Ind.

Ruth Shire answers her first class letter. She is district superintendent of the Kansas City Provident Association—the local charity organization there. Permanent address, c/o Kansas City Provident Association, 1115 Charlotte St., Kansas City, Mo. Temporary address, 205 Brush Creek Blvd., Kansas City.

Elizabeth Tuttle ('22) sailed on the *Paris* June 12 to spend the summer in France. She was to study at Dijon through July and spend Aug. in Paris and in traveling.

LOST.—Can anyone send the secretary news or addresses of the following: Mary Elizabeth (Clark) Roulet, Susie Farmer, Mildred Mather, Edith Thompson, Phebe Hyatt, Mary Elizabeth Huston, Helen (Tebbetts) Parker?

1921

Class secretary—Mrs. E. Graham Bates (Dorothy Sawyer), 8 Maple St., Auburndale, Mass.

ENGAGED.—Dorothy Burr to Frank Davis Halsey of Princeton, N. J.

Elsie Dey to W. Kenneth Wilson. Elsie expects to be married in the spring.

Ottilie Meiner to Paul James Fogel, Muhlenberg '19, of Morristown, N. J.

Marjorie Moulton to Donald Benner Hopkins of Montclair, N. J.

MARRIED.—Mary Betty Dietrich to W. Scott Hill of Schenectady, June 19.

Louise McLaren to Henry Houghton Cone Jr. of New York, May 3.

Madeleine Manley to John M. Lyle of Los Angeles, Oct. 31, 1925.

Florence Newell to L. Elliott Fitch of Rochester, N. Y., Sept. 11.

Elsie Orrell to Edward Richardson of Brookline, Sept. 11.

Rose Tomasi to Vincent Sassone of Boston, Aug. 30.

BORN.—To Elizabeth (Buckley) Buell a daughter, Nancy Maude, July 15, 1925.

To Anne (Collyer) Keck a second son, Charles, Dec. 28, 1925.

To Betty (Dafter) Belnap a second daughter, Nancy, Apr. 29, 1925.

To Polly (Dowden) McKinley a daughter, Pauline de Launay, May 10.

To Mildreth (Godfrey) Sutcliffe a second daughter, Barbara, Nov. 30, 1925.

To Ruth (Green) Wishart a second daughter, Lois Beckwith, May 25.

To Alice (Heebner) Williamson a son and second child, William Joseph Jr., Aug. 18.

To Helen (Hookway) Gallagher a second daughter and third child, Barbara, July 11, 1925.

To Catharine (Joralmon) Snow a daughter, Ann, June 27.

To Carlota (Lane) Peet a son, John Lehman, July 15.

To Margaret (Morison) Taylor a daughter and second child, Margaret Ann, May 9.

To Henrietta (Robinson) Herndon a son and second child, Richard Fleetwood, July 15.

To Rosa (Rosenthal) Kohn a daughter, Eleanor C., Aug. 15.

To Elsa (Schmidt) Janssen a son and second child, Werner Jr., June 4, 1924.

To Mary (Sears) Hough a son, Garry de Neuville III, Apr. 30.

To Hannah (Shipley) Goodyear a second daughter, Jane Lucia, Mar. 1.

To Priscilla (Silver) Luke a second son, John Anderson, Nov. 30, 1925.

To Emma (Smith) MacNichol a second son, Roland Smith, Oct. 30, 1925.

To Lois (Snow) Bowen a daughter, Gloria Lois, June 21.

To Hazel (Winans) Coe a daughter and second child, Jean Winans, July 10.

OTHER NEWS.—Alice Abbott is doing graduate work in Spanish and French at the Univ. of Illinois.

Helen Anthony ('22) writes, "Just home after 'doing' western Europe, meeting Smith graduates and undergraduates everywhere."

Helen Borneman is assistant cataloger at the Bryn Mawr College Library.

Katharine Brand traveled in England and Scotland last summer.

Helen Butler is in the woman's department of the National City Bank in New York.

To Anne (Clark) Fischer goes the sincere sympathy of the class. Her brother-in-law died on June 27, her father on July 17, and her father-in-law on Aug. 11. Anne and her family have now gone to live with her mother-in-law, who was left alone. Address, 234 S. Tremont St., Kewanee, Ill.

Margaret Cotton's mother has been ill for the past year. With an operation for appendicitis herself, Margaret has had an anxious year.

Marguerite Currier is cataloger at the Vermont State Library.

Winifred Davies writes of a "nice visit with Paulette Pélissier (Smith M.A. '21) in Paris."

Myrtle Doppmann is teaching Latin and English in the Northampton High School.

Miriam Dunn has received her Ph.D. from the Catholic Univ. of America at Washington.

Margaret (Goldthwait) Bennett's husband has just finished two years at St. Paul's, New Haven. He and Margaret are going to rusticate for a year on her family's farm.

Micket Gould is field captain of the Eastern Division of the Massachusetts Girl Scouts.

Rachel Harlem, besides her kindergarten teaching, is enjoying Little Theatre and Play-shop activities.

Marion LaMontagne studied last summer at the Sorbonne.

Louise Loewenstein writes, "After a glorious winter and spring spent in the Near East and Europe, I am planning to spend a year at home, keeping up my Italian and French and possibly doing some translation work in the latter."

Edith (McEwen) Dorian's husband has just joined her in the English department at the New Jersey College for Women. "We're having the time of our lives."

Caroline (Newburger) Berkowitz moved into a new home in Dec. Her brother died in Aug.

Ethel Phillips ('22) has had a long illness but hopes to be working soon.

Gertrude (Sehm) McIntire is building a new home.

Marjorie (Spring) Moore's husband has finished his medical training and has opened an office in Danville, Ill. Marjorie is still hoping to come East some day—"surely for our Tenth!"

Wolcott Stuart is taking a business course in La Fayette, Ind.

Florence Taylor is attending a school in Washington for three months to prepare for the Foreign Service exams. She is aiming for Diplomatic Service.

Charlotte Truitt is teaching in the Weston High School.

Kay Walker is off on a vacation trip to Italy.

Ella Louise Waterbury is at home resting after three strenuous years in New York.

Barbara Winchester is at home for a while.

Ex-1921

MARRIED.—Josephine Fellows to Lewis H. Van Billiard, Aug. 21.

Lavinia Strange to Dr. Leslie Bert Marshall, Oct. 19, 1925.

Gertrude Walther to Foster Holmes, June 17.

BORN.—To Mary (Brinkerhoff) Gilbert a second son, Henry Wilbur, Apr. 13.

To Florence (Dunn) Leonard a daughter, Barbara Jean, Apr. 5.

To Elizabeth (Ellison) Smith a son and second child, Ellison, July 12.

To Doris (Janes) Wilson a third son, Bradford Janes, Aug. 2.

To Claudia (Kellogg) Haines a daughter, Claudia Elizabeth, Feb. 16, 1924.

To Ruth (McClelland) Hanks a daughter, Ruth, Oct. 14, 1925.

To Albertine (Osius) Cosgrove a second daughter, Elise, Dec. 11, 1925.

To Pauline (Stoughton) Atwood a second son and third child, Theodore, Nov. 9, 1925.

To Elizabeth (Sykes) Michaels a daughter, Shirley Ellen, May 27.

To Alice (Wilson) Estey a second daughter, Joan, in Feb. 1925.

OTHER NEWS.—Rosamond Allen is off for Hawaii, Japan, and China this winter.

Elizabeth (Hatheway) Sachs recently took a six months' trip by auto across the continent and thence to Honolulu.

1922

Class secretaries—A–K, Mrs. Francis T. P. Plimpton (Pauline Ames), 1165 Fifth Av., New York City. L–Z, Mrs. George F. Hughes (Frona Brooks), 5 Cedar Pl., Garden City, N. Y.

ENGAGED.—Ruth Barnes to Frank Waldo Lathrop. He is a graduate of Yale and received his M.A. and Ph.D. from Cornell. He is now a member of the faculty of education department at the Univ. of Minnesota. They expect to be married during the Christmas holidays, and will live in Minneapolis.

Katharine Houghton to David Kelly. Mr. Kelly graduated from Rutgers in 1920, and was a member of Chi Psi. He also graduated from Harvard Law School last June, and is now practicing law in New York City.

Madeline Leonard to Paul Russell Plant, an electrical engineer and graduate of M. I. T.

Cathrine Marx to M. E. Koeppel of Bavaria. Cathrine spent the last year studying at the Univ. of Munich. Her wedding was to have taken place this fall but has been postponed because of the illness of her mother. She expects to live over there not far from Nuremberg.

MARRIED.—Mary Hale Harts to Robert Earl Jr., Sept. 11. Marian Thorndike '22 was a bridesmaid. They are living at 2233 Douglas Crescent, Utica, N. Y.

Mae Ingalls to Ralph Painter Howe, June 30. New address, 75 Haddon St., Bridgeport, Conn.

Margaret Murray Jones to Russell Bontecon, Apr. 21. They spent two months motoring in England and France and are now living at 20 Grotto Av., Providence, R. I.

Catherine Knowles to A. Elmo Cole, June 25. They were married in the First Presbyterian Church of Northville (Mich.) by her father, the Rev. Frank P. Knowles. Her husband comes from Constantia (N. Y.) and they will live at 101 Ostrom Av., Syracuse, N. Y.

Esther Moss to Dr. Forrest William Barry, Aug. 11. He has started his medical practice in Lockport, N. Y.

Gertrude Schwartz to Joseph William Ress, Nov. 11, 1925. Last winter they lived in Miami where Mr. Ress was practicing law, and in the summer they ran a boys' camp in Hendersonville, N. C.

Harriet Smith to Dr. Archibald H. Watt, Sept. 18. They are living in New York after a motor trip through the Green Mts. and Adirondacks.

BORN.—To Dorothy Florence (Clark) Albergotti a son, Robert P. Jr., Sept. 24.

To Constance (Boyer) Anderson a daughter, Ruth Conant, May 27.

To Evelyn (Gray) Cameron a second daughter, Isabelle, Aug. 22.

To Elizabeth (Bridgers) Daniels ('23) a daughter, Adelaide Anne, July 17.

To Dorothy Lee (Bryan) Firestone a son, Russell Allen Jr., July 29.

To Constance (Kline) Hamann a son, William Augustus III, May 11.

To Elizabeth (Barry) Johnson a daughter, Kate Eleanor, Mar. 5.

To Dorothy Curtis (Bourne) King a son, Starr M. Jr., Apr. 25.

To Barbara (Lufkin) Davis a son, Kenneth Newton Jr., Mar. 26. They have bought a little white Dutch Colonial house in Greenfield.

To Kathryn (Lyman) Bond a son, Kenneth Lyman, Sept. 4.

To Katharine (Peek) Zapf a daughter, Katharine Peek, July 7.

To Lillian (Potter) Dodd a second son, Frank Potter, July 12.

To Dorothea (Sanjiyan) Conard a daughter, Dorothy May, July 30. In September they came east for a visit.

To Paula (Schlegel) Frenzel a son, Robert Paul, June 15. They have bought their own home and moved in this September.

To Mary Ann (Whittemore) Sprague a daughter, Rosemary, July 8.

To Constance (Zonne) Shuman a daughter and second child, Mary Louise, July 28.

OTHER NEWS.—Marjorie Adams is teaching in the Iowa State Teachers College—tennis, hockey, and a variety of other things. She reports four gym floors and multitudinous physical exams.

Katherine Aldridge spent July voyaging in and about Calgary, Banff, and other parts of Alberta. She had a grand time at numerous rodeos.

Ruth Bemis has now ventured into the professional world and is studying landscape architecture in Cambridge. She reports it a "fascinating subject."

Joanna Beyer is still executive secretary of the Woman's General Study Club of Rome, N. Y., "which means responsibility for all activities from the janitors up and the keeping of 700 members interested and active—the last the hardest of all."

Frona (Brooks) Hughes has moved into a new apartment. She spent part of the summer in Connecticut with her family.

Vera Call spent the summer abroad with Beryl Hobson. They saw B. Walton at Stratford-on-Avon and had an opera date with Olivia Rogers in Paris, besides staying at the same hotel in Rome with Florence Williams '20.

Evelyn Clarke came to New York on June 1 and was immediately rewarded with a job at Macy's. She is now an assistant to the head of the interior decorating department, and is "quite enjoying life and the job."

Dorothy (Crydenwise) Lindsay has embarked on the writing game and is gaining "much valuable experience" as editor of the "Women in Sports" column in the Boston Herald.

Gladys (Dingledine) Diggs is now postmistress of the State Teachers College at Harrisonburg, Va. She has charge of a switchboard of 30 phones and is head of a supply room which fills the needs of 800 girls.

Jane (Dinsmore) Comey has been an invalid for almost two years as a result of a nervous breakdown, but is now on the up-grade.

Huldah Doron is still teaching music in Bangor (Me.) and reports that she adores her work.

Betty Gaylord is "still working at Yale and still enjoying it."

Elsye (Geisenberger) Le Vino has moved to a new apartment, and has given up her banking job until they are settled.

Adelaide (Guion) Webber took a motor trip east with her husband in August, and managed to run across several '22ers.

Isabel Harper spent the summer walking with her brother in Norway and Scotland. This year she will continue to dispense zoölogy at Smith.

Grace Havey has been traveling in Europe for three months and returns to Worcester this fall as kindergartner at the Bancroft School.

Marion Himmelsbach is just back from four months abroad with her sister Julie, and now has a new job as secretary of the evening session of the Univ. of Buffalo.

Margaret Hitchcock is teaching geology at Barnard, and is taking laboratory work and field trips in her work at Columbia.

Beryl Hobson had a most delightful summer in England and is teaching this year at the Bulkeley High School in Hartford.

Pat (Hoyt) Witte held a reunion of old Tylerites inspired by the arrival of Nance (Johnston) Weissblatt and her husband in New York.

Ibba (Hubbard) Cooper is taking music lessons and is interested in the League of Women Voters and political discussion groups.

Dorothy (Jenks) Gilson finds herself very busy with her household and her work for the Girl's Friendly Society, being on the Board of Directors.

Ellen Lane went to Columbia Summer School again this year and at International House. She is back for another year as director of religious education at Edwards Church, and as her family have moved to Northampton to be with her, she hopes all of '22 will let her know when they come back.

Star (Lawrence) Cornelius finds her young son disproving all new theories about discipline of the pre-school child. She does play and book reviewing (also camphor ball designing, whatever that is) for the Public Ledger.

Mildred Lovejoy spent ten weeks as assistant director of a Girl Scout camp this summer. This winter she will be doing some Scout work.

Rae (Lowenthal) Berolzheimer is in a small apartment in the South Shore district of Chicago. She finds time for a little golf and tennis besides cooking for two.

Katharine Macomber writes: "Am doing secretarial work for the business manager of the 'Save the Surface' campaign, which is doing educational advertising for the paint and varnish industry. I also am very much excited over having bought a week-end camp with my sister, at Croton Lake, Westchester Co."

Jean (MacDonald) Strong and her husband are running the Brooklyn Boys' School in New York.

Eleanor (Miller) Webb went back to Hampton to finish out her year after a six weeks' wedding trip abroad. Her husband meanwhile had to be in New York, but they are now settled in an apartment in Montclair.

Elvira Miller expects to take a course at the Ohio Mechanics' Institute this winter.

Louise Miller is beginning her usual fall musical activities "with the interesting addition of being accompanist in the vocal studio of Frederic Freemantle, noted Beethoven authority, tenor, and teacher in Steinway Hall, New York."

Ruth-Alice Norman has been roaming Europe again, Gibraltar to the North Cape and a lot on each side, this time.

Elizabeth (Patek) Laskin and her husband spent a second honeymoon in Europe, renting a little French car and driving it themselves through France.

Mildred Purdy is working at Columbia towards a Ph.D. and teaching psychology at the Bennett School.

Jane Quinby is doing interesting work with E. P. Dutton and Co.

Anna Ryan is acting as head of the French department in the Franklin High School after a most interesting summer in New York at Columbia.

Olivia Rogers is trying to settle down to teaching French in the New Haven High School after a wonderful summer abroad.

Carolyn Stewart has returned from an extensive European trip.

Louise Silber is sailing for Paris to spend the winter at the Institut Moderne de Violon and hopes to be ready for teaching on her return.

Isabel Stabler is secretary for a Quaker meeting in Washington.

Marion Stacey is back at work again "after a trip to the North Pole—that is, within fifty miles of the Arctic."

Louise Taggart was abroad for two months this summer.

Gertrude Windisch spent a "long, wonderful" summer riding horseback in Colorado and Wyoming and is sailing on a Mediterranean cruise Feb. 8.

Katharine (Winchester) Wakeman is doing substitute work in a private grade school.

Frances Upham spent two delightful weeks at Juniper Lodge and is back for her third year as social service worker at the Homeopathic Hospital, Boston.

Ex-1922

BORN.—To Margaret (Begg) Tenney a son, Charles M. Jr., Apr. 23.

1923

Class secretary—Mrs. Roswell C. Josephs (Frances Sheffield), Longfellow Court, Massachusetts Av., Cambridge, Mass.

ENGAGED.—Carolyn Colby to Dwight Chellis. They expect to be married next spring.

Elisabeth Johnston to Richard B. Cross of London.

Dorothy Woods to Dr. Paul L. Cleaver, a dentist in Springfield. Dorothy is going

abroad for a year, spending nine months in India teaching music in a school for American children in Kodaikanal. Her work will consist of teaching piano, singing, and producing operettas.

MARRIED.—Barbara Boyer to Norman S. Chadwick of Springfield, May 5. They are living in North Brookfield, Mass. She stopped teaching school in 1925 and last winter was at home in Winchester after being abroad with Frankie Arnold.

Marion Healy to Elbridge Alden Minard, Apr. 5. Margaret Gould '21 and Dorothy Treadwell '23 were in the bridal party. Mr. Minard is with Ginn and Co., and they are living at 61 Garfield St., Cambridge, Mass.

Bernice Hirschman to Dr. Henry Joseph Tumen of Philadelphia, in Salt Lake City, Aug. 3. After Nov. 1, they will live in Philadelphia.

Eleanor Holt to Donald Soule DeWitt, Aug. 14. They are living at 432 Madison St., Oconto, Wis.

Lois Kane to Clifton Wishart. They are living at 219 Fisher Av., White Plains, N. Y.

Grace Tripp to George Mack Jr., Sept. 25. Florence Tripp '26 was maid of honor. Helen Tripp '29, Grace Meyercord '23, and Dorothy (Page) Dole '23 were bridesmaids. Their address will be Rose Marie Apts., Chestnut St., Roselle, N. J.

Page Williams to Lieutenant Frank M. Albrecht U. S. A. They are sailing in November for three years in the Hawaiian Is.

Mildred Woodward to John Paul Jones, Sept. 18. They have taken a seven room house at 8 Allen St., Amherst, and hope to see '23 there.

BORN.—To Adeline (Eveleth) Cabot a daughter, Lucia Lee, May 16.

To Alice (Quayle) Osborne a son, James Morris Jr., Mar. 8.

OTHER NEWS.—Marion Bissell took her M.A. at Radcliffe in June, then went to France to spend some time in Normandy. She is spending the winter in Paris and Florence.

Josephine Hopkins plans to enter P. and S. medical school this fall.

Dorothy Treadwell has been sent to Norfolk (Va.) by Stone and Webster for six weeks.

1924

Class secretary—Beatrice H. Marsh, 9 Willard St. or 721 Main St., Hartford, Conn.

ENGAGED.—Natalie Rogers to Thomas Green, Yale '23 and M.I.T. '26.

MARRIED.—Elizabeth Babb to Richard Strong Foxwell, Sept. 15. New address, 2612 E. 33 St., Kansas City, Mo.

Janet Bannard to Robert Dudley West, Oct. 23.

Henrietta Clunet to Robert Light, Aug. 17. They are living on Far Hills Av., Dayton, O.

Lucile Howard to Lemuel Showell.

Hope Iseman to Leslie H. Prince, Oct. 30. They are to live at 145 Highland Av., Middletown, N. Y.

Esther Nast to Theodore Stone, July 21.

Millicent Possner to William Marsdon Brinkman, May 4, in Brooklyn. Mary Elizabeth (Reid) Oakley was a bridesmaid.

Millicent writes, "We had a lazy honeymoon in Marsdon's home at Southport (N. C.) with an energetic ending, driving north to Waterbury (Conn.) in a Ford roadster."

BORN.—To Etta (Anderson) Tuttle a son, Richard Sherman, May 7.

To Mary (Evans) Harrell a son, Aug. 20. They have a new home at 3221 N. Pennsylvania St., Indianapolis.

OTHER NEWS.—Dot Ambler is studying again this winter at the Central School of Hygiene and Physical Education in New York. During July and August she was councillor at Camp Merrie-Woode, Sapphire, N. C.

Fran Burnham and Hartwell Wyse have gone to Paris with Hartwell's mother to study art for nine months or more.

Jean Clifton is an instructor in Latin and history of art at the Univ. of Pittsburgh.

Mary Cullinan is studying household management and arts at the Garland School in Boston.

Betty Helmer was taking some courses in Geneva this summer. She gets her Ph.D. next June from the Univ. of London.

Katherine Hunt is finding that teaching subnormal children takes considerable preparation each day but she still has time left over for music.

Mildred Johnson is working for an M.A. in English at Cornell.

Helen Mandlebaum has been connected with the Rockefeller Institute for Medical Research (N. Y.) since Sept. 1925.

Alice Manley is doing secretarial work for Professor Jacobs, head of the education department of Brown Univ. In her spare time she is studying for an M.A. and working on shorthand.

Grace Pierpont is teaching Latin and French and coaching a girls' basket ball team in Saugerties, N. Y.

Moselle Smallhurst is secretary to Professor Steinkard of the biology department of N. Y. U. She and her mother have taken an apartment at 604 W. 115 St.

Helen Stucklen writes that she is taking an "M.Ed. at the Harvard Graduate School, and working hard to do it."

Florence Young has become Dean Bernard's secretary at Smith.

Alma Zubrod has returned from Europe to a new home at 115 Ocean Av., Brooklyn, N. Y.

Ex-1924

Secretary—Mrs. Edward I. Cooper (Laura Jones), 1070 Whitney Av., New Haven, Conn.

BORN.—To Laura (Jones) Cooper a daughter, Eveleth Irving, Aug. 20.

1925

Class secretary—Frances S. French, 165 E. 33 St., New York City.

BORN.—CLASS BABY.—To Louise (Featherstone) Ingraham a daughter, Suzanne, Aug. 13, in Sioux City, Ia. Suzanne is the first daughter born to a graduate of the class, and is therefore the Class Baby.

To Abby (Hooker) Willard a son, Henry Kellogg II, Aug. 11.

To Babette (Kafka) Mendleson a son, Jerome II, Aug. 12.

ENGAGED.—Marie Louise Barstow to Robert Lathrop Sharp. Mr. Sharp graduated from Dartmouth in 1925, and is now taking his second year of graduate work in English literature at Harvard. They expect to be married in June.

Mildred Buffington to Francis Rich of Chicago. They expect to be married Oct. 16, and will live in Chicago.

Constance Davidge to Daniel Morgan Brigham. They expect to be married in January.

Kathleen Grant to Philip Van Wyck of Summit, N. J.

Martha Jennings to Cooper Smith.

Eleanor Lawther to John Denson Adams. They will be married in February.

Elinor Robinson to Harvey P. Hood II, Dartmouth '18·

Lillian Silver to George Schwolsky, Yale '22 and Yale Law School '24· Mr. Schwolsky also lives in Hartford, Conn.

MARRIED.—Eunice Clapp to Robert Wallace Bostwick, Sept. 16, in New Haven, Conn. Mr. Bostwick is a graduate of Yale, 1923, and will graduate from the Yale Medical School in 1927.

Virginia Folsom to G. Gordon Forshay, Sept. 4, at Manchester, N. H. Betty Williams was one of the bridesmaids.

Kathryn James to F. Brittain Kennedy, June 12.

Edna Laurin to Ebbert Hughes of Springfield, Mass., June 26. Mr. Hughes is a graduate of Ohio Wesleyan. Marion Bond was one of the bridesmaids.

Esther Page to Neil H. Borden, Sept. 11. Josephine Benz, Beth Gould, Mary Joslin, and Elizabeth Kennedy were among the bridesmaids.

Marjorie Rankin to Spencer Franklin Smith, Sept. 18, in Ashmont, Mass. Helen Booth was maid of honor, and Caroline Jenkins was a bridesmaid.

Mary Rhodes to J. Sydney Stone, June 19, in Paris. Miss Cook was among those present at the wedding.

Olive Sharrett to Thomas Edward de Shazo, June 12, in Highland Falls, N. Y.

Beatrice Stuart to Hugh White Andes, Sept. 11.

OTHER NEWS.—Dorothy Albeck has just completed a secretarial course in Orange (N. J.) and on Feb. 1 she will start work with the Farmers' Loan and Trust Co. in New York City.

Vera Baker is with the American Optical Co. in Southbridge (Mass.), as Spanish correspondent. She says her work is very interesting.

Betty Beadle spent the winter and spring in the vicinity of the Mediterranean—Egypt, Italy, and Sicily. She spent the summer studying counterpoint and will return to the Peabody Conservatory this winter.

Catherine Blake spent the summer at the Westboro State Hospital, as physical director for women. This winter she will be back at

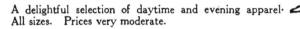

CLASSIFIED LIST OF ADVERTISERS

(See page 121)

Wellesley, finishing her physical education courses.

Leila Brady is teaching Latin and French in the Central High School, Lonaconing, Md.

Doris Burke taught last winter in Swanton, Vt.

Margery Cary will be at the Cathedral School in Garden City (L. I.) this winter. Her job will cover everything from tutoring to chaperoning.

Betty Coates will attend the N. Y. School of Social Work this winter and will live at the McLean Club, 94 Macdougal St.

Alice Curwen spent the summer in Europe, and is now an instructor in the zoölogy department at Smith and living at the Burnham School.

Frances French is working in Brentano's 47th St. store, in charge of the Small Book section.

Clarace Galt completed her training course at the Smith College School for Social Work in August, receiving the degree of Master of Social Science. She is now a social worker at the Medford State Hospital, near Framingham, Mass. She "scours the country for information about patients, in a Ford sedan, with the seal of the Commonwealth on the door."

Alice Garlichs is teaching Latin and social science in the Lyman School at Ardmore near Philadelphia.

Grace Gibson motored to Florida and back with her mother last winter and is going to Mandeville, Jamaica, this winter for four months. She expects to be at the Hotel Judson, New York, from Nov. 15 to Dec. 15.

Frieda Goodenough is now teaching on the staff of the Junior High in Amsterdam, N. Y. Her subjects are English and biology. She is living with Becky Beeman, who teaches at the same school.

Julia Himmelsbach has returned to Buffalo after four months in Europe, and has a position as secretary to the Episcopal minister.

Martha Hooker and her fiancé are building a house in the mountains of North Carolina, and are their own architects. Martha also has a position in the personnel department of the First National Bank in Boston.

Caroline Jenkins is taking a librarian's course at Columbia, and is living at 606 W. 116 St., N. Y. C.

Alice Judson writes that the Evanston Smith Club is giving a ball to raise money for a Smith scholarship. Alice is in charge of the tickets and Margaret Scott is chairman of the refreshments committee.

Grania Knott is still with Walter Hampden's company, which opened early in October in "The Immortal Thief."

Helen Low is working in the International Health Board of the Rockefeller Foundation. She loves the work and cannot praise the Foundation enough.

Louise McGregor traveled last winter in Egypt, Palestine, Italy, and India, where she met Miss Cook. This year she will stay at home and go on with her music studies.

Mary Sebring is teaching at the Beaver Country Day School in Chestnut Hill (Mass.), which is a school of progressive education and very interesting. Mary is staying at 272 Walnut St., Brookline, and her telephone is Regent 2166. She wants everyone who comes to Boston, to call her up.

Ethel Sherman spent last year in getting her M.A. in European history at Cornell.

Clara Smith spent two months abroad this summer with a Smith party of nine. Last winter she took the college graduate secretarial course at the Katherine Gibbs School.

Janet Wilcox is teaching English and dramatics in the Framingham High School and loves being so near Boston.

Mildred Williams is with the Rockefeller Foundation, 91 Broadway, N. Y. C.

Frances Wilson had a wonderful time in Europe this summer. She will be at Macy's again this year.

Dorothy Winslow is a social case worker at the Girls' Service League, 138 E. 19 St., N. Y. C.

Ex-1925

BORN.—To Helen (Redding) Carter a daughter, Betty Lee, Sept. 4.

OTHER NEWS.—Ruth Tester is playing in "The Ramblers" in New York and has received some excellent press notices.

1926

Class secretary—Gertrude E. Benedict, 8 Cabrillo Dr., Stanford Univ., Calif.

ENGAGED.—Evelyn Dupee to Lieut. George Louis Castera U. S. N. They expect to be married Oct. 16 and will live at 464 "B" Av., Coronado, Calif.

Marion Morse to James Calvert, Univ. of North Carolina '19.

Lucy Taylor to Thorvald F. Hammer, Yale 1918 S. They expect to be married in March.

Harriet Wolcott to John Works. They expect to be married Oct. 16.

MARRIED.—Mary Beecher to William Coxe, July 4. They spent their honeymoon abroad and will live in Asheville, N. C.

Elsa Brendel to Buell G. Tallman, July 7, at Lake View, N. Y.

Winifred Cozzens to Stephen Little, at Huntington, L. I., Sept. 25. They will live at 39 Wiggin St., Princeton, N. J. Helen Chapman, Charlotte Kudlich, and Laura Kimball were bridesmaids. They went to Bermuda on their wedding trip.

Dorothy Curtis to Ralph I. Hoyt, Sept. 13. Address, 1625 East Av., Rochester, N. Y.

Janet Eaton to Charles Clark Macomber, at West Newton, Oct. 2. New address, 68 Jameson Pl., Newton, Mass. Among the bridesmaids were Margaret Stearns, Henrietta Rhees, Laura Kimball, and Katharine Bingham '27. Alice Eaton '29 was maid of honor.

Elinore Eldridge to R. M. Goetchins, Sept. 24. New address, 167 N. Grove St., East Orange, N. J.

Marjorie Gaines to John Burchard, Sept. 7. They are living in Cambridge, Mass. The maid of honor was Ruth Hunter.

Laura Kramer to a Mr. Pollak, Sept. 22. New address, 5337 University Av., Chicago.

Jean Mack to Roy M. Greenthal, Sept. 15.

SERENITY

What is it worth?

IF you have known serenity of the mind, even once for a short time only, you will know that it is priceless.

But there are those who can sell you for a small part of your income one of the most direct steps to this serenity — they can sell you security, material security for the future.

They are life insurance agents.

They sell a priceless commodity at low cost. When a John Hancock Agent calls on you, remember this. It is worth while seeing him. Better still, it is worth your while to send for him and set your mind at rest on this score at once.

John Hancock

LIFE INSURANCE COMPANY
OF BOSTON, MASSACHUSETTS

A STRONG COMPANY, Over Sixty Years
in Business.   Liberal as to Contract,
Safe and Secure in Every Way.

Always Sold in a Yellow Box

Pro-phy-lac-tic

Tooth Brush

The *Pro-phy-lac-tic* really cleans between the teeth

The ordinary tooth brush merely brushes the surfaces

New address, 325 Prospect Av., Milwaukee, Wis.

Dorothy Norton to Myles J. Keating. Address, 37 William St., Portland, Me.

Dorothy Regensburg to Leon N. Stern. Address, 288 Fourth Av., New York City.

Marian Saunders to John Cheeseborough, in New York, Sept. 25. They are to live in Asheville, N. C. Mary (Beecher) Coxe and Helen Roberts were bridesmaids.

Isabel Urban to Stephen Chase Jr. Address, Box 295, Dunedin, Fla.

OTHER NEWS.—Betty Beam has a position in the office of a school in Maplewood, N. J.

Elizabeth Blacking is at Smith as an assistant in the psychology department. She is living in Capen Annex.

Rose Bullock is studying at Radcliffe.

Halo Chadwick is industrial secretary at the Y. W. C. A. in Springfield, Mass.

Elizabeth Chandler expects to study at Cambridge, England, this year.

Constance Chilton is spending the winter abroad with Betty Morrow '25. She attended an international conference last summer in Geneva.

Mary Chute is studying architecture at M. I. T.

Louise Cronin and Alice Curley took summer courses at Oxford.

Eleanor Fourtin is studying music in Paris for a year.

Dorothy Garland and La Tourette Stockwell are studying at Radcliffe.

Marion Guptill will continue her studies in Latin at the American Academy in Rome.

Marian Keiley is traveling abroad for the fall and winter.

Katharine Landon is spending a few months in France.

Jane Lockwood is studying for an M.D. at the College of Physicians and Surgeons, N. Y.

Eliza Morton is learning department store work with Jordan Marsh Co. in Boston.

Isabel Porter is studying architecture in Boston.

Dorothy Rand is studying art at Harvard.

Henrietta Rhees is working in a bacteriology laboratory in Rochester, N. Y.

Louise Rhodes is back at Smith as assistant in the music department. She is living at 84 Elm St.

Elizabeth Sanders has a position in a New York office.

Genevieve Shepherd is studying music and psychology in New York.

Caroline Walker is working for her M.A. at Bryn Mawr this year.

Elinor Woodward has a new address, 685 Ardsley Rd., Winnetka, Ill.

The following from '26 toured Europe this summer: Harriet Adams and Shorey Miller, Betty Beam and Peg Bates with Peg's family, Martha Botsford with her family, Peggy Glover, Mary Gordon, Helen McNair, Betty Shedd with her family, Hester Smith, Virginia Traphagen. Charlotte Kudlich, Kay Landon, Isabel Porter, and Dorothy Rand toured England together for two months.

Ex-1926

MARRIED.—Anne Gilbreth to Dr. Robert E. Barney, Sept. 18, in Montclair, N. J. Address, 2871 Hampton Rd., Cleveland, O.

Owing to 1926's excessive modesty on this its first appearance in the QUARTERLY, we are including the following items which arrived too late to be included in alphabetical order:

Eleanor Clark is studying at the Julius Hart School of Music in Hartford.

Laurestein Foster is on the staff of the Breath of the Avenue, a New York trade paper.

Eleanor French is teaching in the Masters School, Dobbs Ferry, N. Y.

Marguerite Juterbock is studying for her M.A. at Columbia.

Frances McGuire is teaching in the Hartford (Conn.) High School.

Dorothy McKay is doing social service work in Rochester.

Constance Mahoney is working in the Hampshire Bookshop.

Ruby Neal is studying at the Bryant and Stratton Commercial School in Boston.

Elizabeth Parnell is teaching in Indiana, Pa.

Mary Peirce is studying at the Sorbonne.

Frances Ryman is studying at Teachers College.

Dorothy Winterbottom is teaching history at her home in Rockville Center, N. Y.

NOTICES

ALL editorial mail should be sent to Edith Hill, College Hall, Northampton, Mass. Material for the February QUARTERLY should be typewritten and should reach College Hall by January 4. Please send subscriptions to Miss Snow at Rumford Bldg., 10 Ferry St., Concord, N. H., or College Hall, Northampton. Correspondence concerning advertising should be sent to College Hall. The dates of publication are November 20, February 20, May 20, and July 30, and subscribers failing to receive their copies within ten days after those dates should notify the business manager, as otherwise she cannot furnish free duplicate copies. The subscription price for one year is $1.50. Single copies 40 cents. Note the Gift Subscription QUARTERLY card explained on page 121.

Please send all news items for the February QUARTERLY to the class secretaries by January 3.

1927 COMMENCEMENT 1927

Ivy Day will be Saturday, June 18 and Commencement Day, Monday, June 20.

As usual, the available rooms in the college houses will be open to the alumnae at Commencement. *Members of the classes holding reunions should make applications for these rooms through their class secretaries*, through whom also payment should be made. Rooms will be assigned to

Man-power

The laboratories and shops of industry are the sources of many of the enduring attainments of our times. In the General Electric organization is an army of 75,000 persons, co-operating to make electricity do more and better work for you.

Four millions of the best man-power of Europe perished in the Napoleonic conquests. Military conquest is non-creative, while industry is always creative.

In the last ten years one American manufacturer—the General Electric Company—has created machines having a man-power forty times as great as that of all the lives lost in the Napoleonic wars.

GENERAL ELECTRIC

the reunion classes in the order of their seniority.   Members of classes not holding reunions should make applications directly to the Alumnae Office.
For a minimum of five days, the price of board and room will be $10.   Alumnae to whom assignments are made will be held responsible for the full payment unless notice of withdrawal is sent to the class secretary before June 1.   After June 1, notices of withdrawal and requests for rooms should be sent directly to the Alumnae Office.   At this time any vacancies left by the reunion classes will be assigned to members of the classes not holding reunions, in the order in which the applications have been received.
The campus rooms will be open after luncheon on Thursday before Commencement.

COLLEGE PINS

Alumnae desiring to procure college pins may send to Miss Jean Cahoon, Registrar, College Hall, for an order upon Tiffany and Co.   *Do not send money with this request*, but mail check direct to Tiffany upon receipt of the order from Miss Cahoon.   The price of the pin is $3.50, with initials, class, and safety clasp.   The full name will be engraved, if preferred, at a cost of 6 cents for each extra letter.

GRADUATE FELLOWSHIPS AND SCHOLARSHIPS

Information in regard to Fellowships and Scholarships for Graduate Study in this country and abroad may be obtained through the Chairman of the Committee on Graduate Instruction, College Hall 12.   Such aid for graduate study and research work is offered by a large number of Educational Institutions and Organizations.   As applications for some of these Fellowships and Scholarships must be submitted with credentials before January 1 and for the majority before March 1, it is essential that alumnae who are interested in applying for them should make inquiries as early as possible.   In inquiring state field of specialization.
A. A. U. W. FELLOWSHIPS.—This year the stipends for some of the fellowships offered by the American Association of University Women have been increased.   Eleven fellowships are offered ranging in amount from $500 to $1500.   For details regarding the terms of award for these fellowships and the procedure for application for them, consult the A. A. U. W. Fellowship Announcement for 1927, copies of which can be obtained in the office of the Committee on Graduate Instruction or from Professor Agnes L. Rogers, Chairman of the Committee on Fellowships, Bryn Mawr College, Bryn Mawr, Pa.

A REQUEST FROM JORDAN MARSH

A request for information has come from Jordan Marsh to the Institute for the Coördination of Women's Interests, which in turn has appealed to the QUARTERLY.   Briefly it is this: Jordan Marsh is eager to find college women who must either supplement the family income, or who for their own development need definite and regular outside interests.   The store is developing short hour selling positions from 12 to 4 o'clock.   College women who are interested are asked to communicate with Dorothy Weeks, Hiring Supervisor.

SHIPS THAT PASS IN THE NIGHT

There is a lady in England who this summer met a lady from America who "has some connection with Smith college either as teacher or alumna."   They traveled from Canterbury to Victoria on Monday, August 23.   Their ways parted, and the lady from England, whose name is Mrs. Thomas, "five feet three and slight," was so favorably impressed with her traveling companion that she is eager to find her.   They forgot to ask each other's names but Mrs. Thomas wrote to Smith College and asked for help.   Hence this notice in the QUARTERLY. Mrs. Thomas sends a memory drawing of her American friend which we have in the Alumnae Office.   If the American traveler sees this notice and will communicate with Mrs Emma O. Thomas, St. Bernads, 149, Tulse Hill, London S. W. 2, she will, in the good old agony column style, "learn something to her advantage."

A NOTICE FROM THE PHI BETA KAPPA FOUNDATION

"It is peculiarly fitting that the honorary society of Phi Beta Kappa, in commemoration of its 150th anniversary, should undertake a nation-wide campaign to restore respect for scholarship and to promote more inspirational teaching.   The Society seeks to establish an endowment fund providing annual awards for distinction in teaching as well as attainment in scholarship, and is now asking her 50,000 members to reach the goal of $1,000,000 by her birthday— December 5.   It is a call which every wearer of the golden Key should be prompt to heed."

AN ANNOUNCEMENT REGARDING SMOKING

Katharine Bingham, President of Student Council, has written for the QUARTERLY the following statement of the action announced in chapel on Nov. 5:

"Because of the carelessness of students in smoking in the college houses, the Council has felt it necessary to suspend smoking until Christmas.   A plan for smoking in the future will be announced before Christmas and will go into effect immediately after.   This suspension is due entirely to our realization of the tremendous fire risk involved in smoking in dormitories, and is to act as an effective reminder of our thoughtlessness in the immediate past."

INTERCOLLEGIATE ALUMNI HOTELS

Introducing an international effort sponsored by the alumni organizations or magazines of more than eighty colleges and universities to coordinate alumni interests and activities in a selected group of hotels, each of which is specifically prepared to cooperate with alumni organizations and the individual alumnus.

ROOSEVELT

MOUNT ROYAL

RADISSON

SENECA

BLACKSTONE

WILLARD

MAIN FEATURES OF THE INTERCOLLEGIAT
ALUMNI HOTEL MOVEMENT

CORONADO

Interested alumni can secure from a clerk at the desk of each Inte
collegiate Alumni Hotel an information leaflet which describes i
detail the Intercollegiate Alumni Hotel movement.

At each Intercollegiate Alumni Hotel there will be maintained a car
index of the names of all the resident alumni of all the participatin
institutions. This will be of especial benefit to traveling alumni i
locating classmates and friends.

OAKLAND

The current issues of the alumni publications of all the participatin
institutions will be on file at each Intercollegiate Alumni Hotel.

Reservation cards will be available at the clerk's desk in each de
ignated hotel and at the alumni office in each college or university
These reservation cards will serve as a great convenience to trave
lers in securing advance accommodations.

CLAREMONT

The managers of all Intercollegiate Alumni Hotels are prepared t
cooperate with individual alumni to the fullest extent and are als
prepared to assist in the creation of new local alumni associatior
and in the development and extension of the activities of those alread
formed.

URBANA-LINCOLN

SCHENLEY

CALIFORNIAN

SAINT PAUL

MULTNOMAH

PALACE

WALDORF-ASTORIA

ONONDAGA

WOLVERINE

LOS ANGELES-BILTMORE

BENJAMIN FRANKLIN

The alumni organizations or magazines of the following colleges and universities are participants in the Intercollegiate Alumni Hotel movement:*

COPLEY PLAZA

Akron
Alabama
Amherst
Bates
Beloit
Brown
Bucknell
Bryn Mawr
California
Carnegie Institute
Case School
Chicago
City College of New York
Colgate
Colorado School of Mines
Colorado
Columbia
Cornell
Cumberland
Duke
Emory
Georgia
Goucher
Harvard
Illinois
Indiana
Iowa State College
James Milliken

Kansas Teachers' College
Kansas
Lake Erie
Lehigh
Louisiana
Maine
M. I. T.
Michigan State
Michigan
Mills
Minnesota
Missouri
Montana
Mount Holyoke
Nebraska
New York University
North Carolina
North Dakota
Northwestern
Oberlin
Occidental
Ohio State
Ohio Wesleyan
Oklahoma
Oregon
Oregon A.
Penn State
Pennsylvania

Radcliffe
Rollins
Rutgers
Purdue
Smith
South Dakota
Southern California
Stanford
Stevens Institute
Texas A. and M. College
Texas
Union
Vanderbilt
Vassar
Vermont
Virginia
Washington and Lee
Washington State College
Washington
Wellesley
Wesleyan
Western Reserve
Whitman
Williams
Wisconsin
Wooster
Yale

LINCOLN

*In most instances both the alumni organization and the alumni magazine are participating as a unit.

WINDERMERE

INTERCOLLEGIATE ALUMNI HOTELS:

Roosevelt, New York City
Waldorf-Astoria, New York City
University Center*, New York City
Copley Plaza, Boston
University Center*, Boston
Blackstone, Chicago
Windermere, Chicago
University Center*, Chicago
Benjamin Franklin, Philadelphia
Willard, Washington
Radisson, Minneapolis

*To be built in 1926-27

Los Angeles Biltmore, Los Angeles
Palace, San Francisco
Olympic, Seattle
Seneca, Rochester
Claremont, Berkeley
Onondaga, Syracuse
Sinton, Cincinnati
Wolverine, Detroit
Multnomah, Portland, Ore.
Sacramento, Sacramento
Californian, Fresno

Lincoln, Lincoln, Nebr.
Oakland, Oakland, Cal.
Lycoming, Williamsport, Pa.
Mount Royal, Montreal
King Edward, Toronto
Coronado, St. Louis
Bethlehem, Bethlehem, Pa.
Urbana-Lincoln, Urbana-Champaign, Ill.
Saint Paul, St. Paul
Savannah, Savannah, Ga.
Schenley, Pittsburgh

SINTON

KING EDWARD

BETHLEHEM

LYCOMING

SAVANNAH

OLYMPIC

SACRAMENTO

The Intercollegiate Alumni Hotel movement is the result of a year's effort on the part of a Committee, the members of which have long been identified with alumni work.

The funds necessary to insure the success of the Intercollegiate Alumni Hotel movement are being advanced by the designated hotels, all of which have been selected after a careful study of their fitness for participation.

The committee on organization, the activities of which are controlled by a special group of the members of the Alumni Magazines Associated, has incorporated a non-profit corporation known as the Intercollegiate Alumni Extension Service, Inc. which will direct the polices of the Intercollegiate Alumni Hotel movement and serve as a coordinating unit between the alumni organizations and the designated hotels

OFFICERS AND DIRECTORS OF THE INTERCOLLEGIATE ALUMNI EXTENSION SERVICE, INC.

18 East 41st Street
New York City

LEVERING TYSON, *President*   W. R. OKESON, *Director at Large*   J. O BAXENDALE, *Treasurer*
            R. W. SAILOR, *Vice President*   E N SULLIVAN, *Secretary*

DIRECTORS

J O. BAXENDALE
Alumni Secretary
University of Vermont

DANIEL L. GRANT
Alumni Secretary
University of North Carolina

MARION E. GRAVES
Acting Alumni Secretary
Smith College

R. W. HARWOOD
Harvard Alumni Bulletin
Harvard University

ERIC F HODGINS
The Technology Review
Massachusetts Institute of
Technology

JOHN D McKEE
Wooster Alumni Bulletin
Wooster College

HELEN F. McMILLIN
Wellesley Alumni Magazine
Wellesley College

J. L. MORRILL
Alumni Secretary
Ohio State University .

W R. OKESON
Treasurer of
Lehigh University

R. W. SAILOR
Cornell Alumni News
Cornell University

W. B. SHAW
Alumni Secretary
University of Michigan

ROBERT SIBLEY
Alumni Association
University of California

E. N. SULLIVAN
Alumni Secretary
Penn State College

LEVERING TYSON
Alumni Federation
Columbia University

Smith College

NORTHAMPTON, MASSACHUSETTS

WILLIAM ALLAN NEILSON, PH.D., LL.D., L.H.D., *President*

SMITH COLLEGE was founded by Sophia Smith of Hatfield, Massachusetts, who bequeathed for its establishment and maintenance $393,105.60, a sum which in 1875, when the last payment was received and the institution was opened, amounted to nearly if not quite a half million of dollars. The College is Christian, seeking to realize the ideals of character inspired by the Christian religion, but is entirely non-sectarian in its management and instruction. It was incorporated and chartered by the State in March, 1871. In September 1875 it opened with 14 students, and granted 11 degrees in June 1879. In June 1926 the College conferred 460 A.B. degrees, and 17 A.M. degrees.

L. CLARK SEELYE, D. D., was the first president. He accepted the presidency in July 1873, and served until June 1910. He lived in Northampton as President Emeritus until his death on October 12, 1924. Marion LeRoy Burton, Ph.D., LL.D., was installed as president in October 1910 and served until June 1917. He left Smith College to be president of the University of Minnesota and later was president of the University of Michigan. He died on February 18, 1925. William Allan Neilson, Ph.D., LL.D., L.H.D., came in September 1917 to be president of the College.

THE College opens its fifty-second year with an undergraduate enrollment of 2033 besides 34 juniors who are spending the year at the Sorbonne, 65 graduate students, a resident faculty of 203, and 9 chief administrative officers. There are 10,334 living alumnae.

THE property owned by the College comprises 87.25 acres on which there are over a hundred buildings. There are botanical gardens and athletic fields, also a pond which provides boating and skating. There are 31 houses of residence owned or operated by the College besides 11 houses closely affiliated but privately owned. It is the policy of the College to give all four classes approximately equal representation in each house.

THE College fee for board and room is $500 per year and for tuition $400 for all students entering after 1925. Further details are published in the annual catalogs. The Trustees set aside approximately $100,000 for scholarships annually, besides which many special prizes have been established.

AMONG the distinctive features of the College are: (1) Junior year in France. A selected group of students majoring in French are allowed to spend their junior year at the Sorbonne under the personal direction of a member of the Department of French. (2) Special Honors. Selected students are allowed to pursue their studies individually during the junior and senior years in a special field under the guidance of special instructors. They are relieved of the routine of class attendance and course examinations during these two years. (3) The Experimental Schools: a. School for Exceptional Children. For public school children with special educational disabilities and retarded mental development. Conducted by the Department of Education in coöperation with the Northampton Board of Education. b. The Day School, an experimental school of the progressive type, also conducted by the Department of Education, offers instruction to children from five years of age through the work of the Junior High School. c. Nursery School, conducted by the Institute for the Coördination of Women's Interests in coöperation with the Department of Education. (4) School for Social Work. A professional graduate school leading to the degree of M.S.S. The course is fifteen months and comprises theoretical work in Northampton and practical work in the field.

FOR any further information about Smith College address the President's office, College Hall, Northampton, Mass.

The Smith Alumnae Quarterly

Published by the
Alumnae Association of Smith College

February, 1927

THE SMITH ALUMNAE QUARTERLY

February, 1927

TABLE OF CONTENTS

Published by the Alumnae Association of Smith College
at Rumford Building, 10 Ferry St., Concord, N. H.
Member of Alumni Magazines Associated

Florence Homer Snow 1904, Business Manager...... { Rumford Building, 10 Ferry St., Concord, N. H., or
Marion E. Graves 1915, Advertising Manager........ { College Hall, Northampton, Mass.

BOARD OF EDITORS

Edith Naomi Hill 1903.................College Hall, Northampton....................Editor-in-Chief
Elizabeth H. Kingsley 1919..Assistant to the Editor
Ethel Puffer Howes 1891   Anna T. Kitchel 1903
Jean Fine Spahr 1883   Marie E. Gilchrist 1916
Elizabeth Lewis Day 1895   Clara Savage Littledale 1913
Bernice Sanborn 1918

Price $1.50 per year (four numbers) in advance

Volume XVIII...No. 2

*Entered as second-class matter at the post office at Concord, N. H., under the act of March 3, 1879:
Copyright, 1927, by the Alumnae Association of Smith College.*

Smith College Fiftieth Anniversary Publications

The following volumes are being issued under the auspices of the College as part of the Anniversary celebration

THE STUDY OF MUSIC IN THE AMERICAN COLLEGE
By Roy Dickinson Welch, A.B.   *Price* $2.00 · *Postage* 15c

BEN JONSON'S ART: ELIZABETHAN LIFE AND LITERATURE AS REFLECTED THEREIN
By Esther Cloudman Dunn, Ph.D.   *Price* $3.00 · *Postage* 15c

SOPHIA SMITH, AND THE BEGINNINGS OF SMITH COLLEGE
By Elizabeth Deering Hanscom, Ph.D. *and*
Helen French Greene, M.A.   *Price* $2.00 · *Postage* 15c

A BIBLIOGRAPHY OF THE NORTH AMERICAN HEMIPTERA-HETEROPTERA
By Howard Madison Parshley, Sc.D.   *Price* $3.50 · *Postage* 15c

THE PLANTATION OVERSEER AS REVEALED IN HIS LETTERS
By John Spencer Bassett, Ph.D., LL.D.   *Price* $3.50 · *Postage* 15c

THE MORPHOLOGY OF AMPHIBIAN METAMORPHOSIS
By Inez Whipple Wilder, A.M.   *Price* $3.00 · *Postage* 15c

THE SALAMANDERS OF THE FAMILY PLETHODONTIDAE
By Emmett Reid Dunn, Ph.D.   *Price* $6.00 · *Postage* 15c

THE SHORT STORY IN SPAIN IN THE XVII CENTURY
By Caroline Brown Bourland, Ph.D.   *In Press*

JEAN-JACQUES ROUSSEAU, ESSAI D'INTERPRETATION NOUVELLE
By Albert Schinz, Ph.D., O.A.   *In Preparation*

←—————————————————————————→

On Sale at the President's Office, *College Hall, Northampton, Mass.*

Eric Stahlberg

*"To Smith College, Fall or Springtime
Or in Midst of Winter Drear"*

The Smith Alumnae Quarterly

Vol. XVIII   FEBRUARY, 1927   No. 2

Entered as second class matter at the Post Office at Concord, New Hampshire, under the Act of March 3, 1879.

The Tryon Gallery

Alfred Vance Churchill

Professor of the History and Interpretation of Art, and Director of the Smith Museum of Art since 1920

"ISN'T this beautiful!" "Is it for Mr. Tryon's paintings?" "Surely these are not *all* by Tryon?" "Are these pictures new?" Such are the first questions of Mme. or Mlle. Alumna as she steps through the door of the new Gallery and catches a first quick impression of the building and its contents. No, No! The answer to all these inquiries (except the first, on which Madame must form her own opinion) is a decided negative. Indeed not! Mr. Tryon's ideal from the very beginning was a building fitted to house choice works of many kinds—of every kind; beautiful enough not to disgrace them; spacious enough to give them a chance to speak; perfectly lighted, too, by night or day; and last of all secure (as far as human ingenuity can make it so) against fire, that priceless and irreplaceable treasures might not perish from the earth. One room, and only one, is devoted to his own paintings. The rest are for the works of others. And this was Tryon's desire.

We have brought together here as many as we could of the original works belonging to our permanent collection. The pictures and statuary you see before you are not "new." You have seen them all, or most of them, before. They are renewed through the beauty of the setting, and above all, perhaps, by the perfect light.

It has for some years been evident that we must have a new building. The unwonted emphasis laid on art education at Smith, the enlargement of our offering of courses and of the number of instructors in art, as well as the development of our plans for graduate work at home and abroad, all indicate the necessity of an important collection of original works, and of a safe and suitable home for them. The number of students majoring in art has increased, and many of these turn to museum work or teaching or other activities in which art of some kind has a share. Interest is constantly growing among the student body also, and we now have 967 pupils in art courses of one kind or another.

If our situation demanded a richer and more extended equipment, it called not less insistently for new rooms—lecture and conference rooms, library and study rooms. Now every room at present occupied by works of art in the new building releases a corresponding space in the old. Thus the Tryon Gallery has already proved a double blessing.

Those who knew and loved the old Gallery will naturally view these changes with regret, as do all of us who realize the debt we owe to Winthrop Hillyer, the original donor, and to the members of his family.   We may take comfort in the thought that this arrangement is in a sense temporary.   We have funds already in hand for a new Hillyer Wing, connected with the Hillyer Gallery, as soon as the need for such a structure arises.   When that time comes the Hillyer Building will be the permanent home of many beautiful works of art purchased from the Hillyer Fund.   Meantime we have established the practice of setting forth the names of donors, or of the purchase funds as the case may be, on tablets affixed to each original work in the collection. . . .   I might call attention here to the fact that this part of the institution is to be known in future, by vote of the Trustees, as the Smith College Museum of Art.   We have now, as you know, three galleries—the Hillyer Gallery, Graham Hall, and the Tryon Gallery.

The architect's plans for the new Gallery were brought to completion not long after Mr. Tryon announced his intention of renewing the project for building, conceived long before but interrupted by the war.   It is good now to remember that Mr. Tryon was in close consultation with the architect, Mr. Frederick Ackerman, who was his friend, with President Neilson, and with Mr. Churchill, for months preceding his final illness and death, and that all the essential ideas connected with the building were well known to him, and approved by him.

Ground was broken in June 1925.   We had hoped to occupy our new quarters by the following Easter, but were prevented by that series of petty accidents and delays that are the common lot of builders.   However, in September the work was completed, and at last we were ready to move.

Mrs. Tryon, whose interest in the Gallery has been identical from the beginning with that of her husband, was at once informed of the fact.   She made the long journey from South Dartmouth without hesitation, and for several days gave us the benefit of her taste and advice.   She supervised the entire arrangement of the Tryon Memorial Room, the hanging of her husband's pictures, even the placing of the furniture.   Indeed, she spared no pains, offering every counsel and assistance in her power in all parts of the building.

I might say here that if we have had no formal dedication or public opening (a fact that has seemed strange to some) it is chiefly that Mrs. Tryon seemed to have no interest in such a ceremony, seemed, in fact, not to desire anything of the kind, and informed us that she would not in any case be present.

By hard work on the part of the Museum staff during the latter part of the summer recess, installation was finally completed, and on September 27, when College began, the place was ready, and as this goes to print the Tryon Gallery is just finishing the First Semester of its Freshman Year.

As the new building has already been fully described in an essay known to many of my readers,* it remains for me to give you an idea of the structure as it now appears—complete, warmed, lighted, and in active use.

* *Bulletin of Smith College Museum of Art,* June 15, 1926.   This number of the *Bulletin* is devoted to the Tryon Art Gallery.   It contains an article on the building by Talbot Faulkner Hamlin, together with the architect's drawing and plans, and includes, also, a Tryon Bibliography and other material.   We shall take pleasure in mailing a copy to alumnae and friends of the College, together with a certificate of Annual Membership in the Museum, on receipt of $2.50.   Address the Secretary of the Smith College Museum of Art, Northampton, Mass.

Approaching the building, with its decorous proportions and pleasant Georgian air, one is perhaps inclined to wonder a little at something peculiar in its placing—so close on the street. That was done with intention, and I believe that the idea originated with President Neilson. With its doors standing open, except in the coldest weather, the hospitable little structure offers

THE TRYON GALLERY

a constant and cordial invitation to all. Students would have used it with the same freedom, back among the elm trees; but citizens and strangers feel the friendliness of its welcome as they could not have done in any other location.

We mount a handsome flight of steps and pass through the unpretentious vestibule in which is shortly to be placed a marble tablet, telling the visitor "in marble's language, pure, discreet" who gave the building and what their purpose was:

THAT THE STUDENTS OF THIS COLLEGE
MAY KNOW IN THEIR YOUTH
THE SOLACE AND INSPIRATION OF ART
DWIGHT WILLIAM TRYON AND ALICE BELDEN TRYON
HAVE DEDICATED TO THEM THIS BUILDING
MCMXXV

Another step and we find ourselves in the Main Hall, and see, to right and left and before us, the open doors of three galleries. The simple logic of the plan unfolds itself at once, and in the same moment we are aware of the unusual

color scheme.   One has seen gray rooms in museums before, but perhaps not a
gray museum.   Here the whole place is gray—warm, quiet, sober, silvery gray.
Just at first we might think all the rooms were alike, but we soon perceive that
they are subtly varied: the Hall a bit stately with its warm blonde coloring and
classic marbles; the Tryon Room delicate and refined; the Main Gallery somewhat darker and stronger in effect.

The Tryon Memorial Room is devoted to the work of the artist whose name
it bears.   All these paintings—everything in the room except two small
bronzes by Manship which the artist admired—came from Tryon's hand, even
to the portrait which stands on the easel.   As to these landscapes—some were

THE TRYON MEMORIAL ROOM, SHOWING MR. TRYON'S LAST WORK ON THE EXTREME LEFT

purchased years ago by President Seelye, when they could be had for small out-
lays.   Others were gifts from the artist.   One, the last to which he put his
hand, was sent by his widow to be hung here with the rest.

The arrangement of the room is in a sense temporary, for the College will
eventually come into possession of other paintings by Tryon, and many
beautiful things besides—tapestries, books, bronzes, and pottery.   Mrs.
Tryon would gladly have spared many of these things to us at this time, but
President Neilson urged her not to disrupt her home, so she was at last persuaded to keep her most cherished treasures about her.

The central gallery, on the main floor, is the largest room in the building,
measuring about 26 x 36 feet.   Its walls hold paintings by Brandegee, Thayer,
Dewing, Eakins, Wyant, Fuller, Inness, Ryder, Blakelock, Brush, Hassam, and
other Americans; and of the French School there are works by Michel, Gros,
Géricault, Delacroix, Courbet, Corot, Monticelli, Renoir, and Rodin.

The Special Exhibition Room (seen at the right as we enter the building)
represents one of the most necessary aspects of our work.   No matter how good

LOOKING INTO THE MAIN GALLERY

THE MAIN GALLERY

our permanent collection is, or may become, it will always be necessary, in order to keep the interest of students, faculty, and public as well as for the special demands of art instruction in various fields, to have recourse to borrowed works. We did what we could in the past to supply this need. For many years we have given loan exhibitions, usually from seven to ten during the col-

lege year, borrowing the exhibits from art dealers, from private collections, or from other museums. But these activities have been attended with anxiety and inconvenience, simply because it was impossible to request the loan of works of art of the quality which we wanted; not so much that the owners refused to lend their treasures (we have been treated with wonderful generosity and courtesy), but we could not, in good faith and conscience, ask that works of high monetary and aesthetic value be sent to a building that was not perfectly safe from fire. Of course, in an exceptional case, some devoted member of the Faculty might leave the bosom of his family and go to bed on a drawing table in the old building, mounting

LOOKING INTO THE SPECIAL EXHIBITION ROOM SHOWING THE OIESEN COLLECTION FROM KOREA AND CHINA

guard over the borrowed treasures. But this could hardly become our usual practice. (And besides, undermanned as we were, we should have risked losing the man with the works!) In brief, the old loan exhibitions were useful, but we did not often succeed in making them all that we desired them to be. But this Special Exhibition Room, designed specifically for its use, has helped us to solve the problem.

Would you like to visit the lower floor? "Why," responds Mme. Alumna, "is there anything down there?" Madame has already been astonished at the size of the place. She thought the building small; it turns out to be spacious.

She thought it had but one floor, and behold, it has two! At the foot of the staircase the Print Room first claims attention. Our collection of original prints is well started. We hope, before many years, to be able to offer a course in prints. Here farther on is a second large room, almost as large as the Main Room above, and full of paintings. And here is still another, but not so large, with the beginning of our Italian collection. *Despise not the day of small things.*

So you see we have, instead of the single great stately gallery originally projected, no less than six available rooms, sufficiently commodious, but not too large for a certain intimacy, and each adapted to its own special use. On the whole you will perhaps incline to agree with me that few museum buildings are as pleasantly inviting, and you will be able to recall none (or possibly just one?) built so simply and directly to its purpose. Much praise is due to architect Ackerman, to his able representatives and assistants, and to the many excellent and faithful artisans who worked together to build it.

The last few years have brought about a change in our ideals for the Museum of Art. Our collection was begun in 1880 as a group of American paintings. No attempt was made to represent, by original works, the art of other times and countries. Casts and photographs were the sole resources of the Museum in these fields. Although the College had done much to encourage studio work in drawing and painting, under the leadership of Mr. Tryon, it had made almost no effort to develop the fields of art history and criticism. The present writer was, indeed, the first resident teacher of these subjects. When he entered upon his duties, in September 1906, he found practically no precedent, and no provision for his work. There were neither photographs, lantern slides, nor lecture room. He was obliged to use the Chemical Lecture Hall, and the atmosphere of the place was in no sense the "atmosphere of art."

The gradual growth in the number of students electing courses in art, and the development of intensive work in various fields, brought on a rapid expansion in illustrative material. It also made the insufficiency of the original policy of the Museum increasingly apparent. The collection of American paintings which constituted our sole aesthetic asset was very well in its way, and we had good cause to be proud of it. But it would be more reasonable to ask a teacher to give a course in English literature, with nothing to read but American books of the end of the 19th century, than to compel him to teach Greek and Gothic and Renaissance art, with nothing to look at but American paintings of our own time.

The year 1920 marks the beginning of a more liberal policy, through which our collections are gradually coming to respond to the larger need. With three or four exceptions all the original works of art in the Museum (aside from the American paintings) have been acquired within seven years. These works have been purchased from funds belonging to the Museum, or have been presented to us by alumnae, or by undergraduates, or friends of the College. The first etching we ever owned, the Rembrandt that is the corner stone of our collection, was given by undergraduate members of the Studio Club. The only specimen of Egyptian painting we owned for many years was given by a former student, after the death of her father who had picked it up long ago while traveling in Egypt.

When the new policy went into effect, we were in need of almost everything. Our state was that of those who are savage with hunger. But as time goes on this condition passes, and we are beginning to look forward to a period of tranquillity and peaceful expansion.

As we come into the possession of the Hillyer and the Tryon bequests, we shall be in position to aspire to works of more ambitious price, if not of higher aesthetic importance, than those we have at present. And there is surely no reason to assume that these bequests are the last and only funds we shall have to depend on. The experience of institutions of our type is rather the contrary. The more funds they have the easier it is to increase them. *To him that hath shall be given, and he shall have more abundantly*, provided always that there is conviction on the part of the donor that a serious effort has been made, and that serious results are already accomplished. In these circumstances we are encouraged to hope that the Museum of Art has a large future before it, and that we shall be able, through the Department of Art and the Museum working in close conjunction, to accomplish a worthy and perhaps an exceptional work in the field of art education.

The desire to help things along is so truly a part of the tradition of Smith College alumnae that readers of the QUARTERLY would probably think my talk incomplete if I failed to tell them what they can do for us: Well, in the first place, then, I suggest that you join the Museum Association as an Annual Member. From this action, besides the satisfaction of helping to strengthen our work and enrich our collections, you will receive a Certificate of Membership conferring *all the rights and privileges thereunto appertaining*. And you will get the annual copy of the *Bulletin*, telling what the Museum is doing, giving you a list of accessions during the year with the names of the donors, and containing pictures of the more important gifts and purchases, with brief but scholarly essays describing them. After that I would remind you alumnae of your privilege and duty as purveyors in ordinary—or members of a Committee of the Whole, you might call it, for the College Museum—to let the Director of the Museum know whenever you discover a masterpiece of art that Smith College ought to possess. Keep watch, also, for works of art, single specimens or collections, owned by your relatives, friends, and acquaintances. Talk with them about art education at Smith. Send for printed matter, which can be had on application to the Secretary of the Museum, and place it in their hands. Owners of choice works are not seldom on the watch to see where they can place them to the best advantage when they themselves can no longer enjoy them (being quite aware that they cannot take them to Heaven). I may add that such owners are deeply interested in helping young women to earn their living in teaching or museum work, or some other form of art work. They are *not* interested, usually, in making painters or sculptors of them. They are immensely impressed with the thought of bringing the refining and inspiring influences of art into the lives of the people. And they like to give to an institution which has serious purposes in this regard, and especially to one that has buildings and funds and a good collection to begin with. Such, it seems, is human nature.

A Note on Scholarships

W. A. NEILSON

THE proposal to establish a memorial to the memory of President Burton, and the suggestion that this should take the form of an endowment for scholarships or fellowships make it appropriate to inform the alumnae of the situation of the College with regard to resources of this kind now at our disposal. It is clear from the comments on the suggestion which have come to the committee in charge of the proposed memorial that our constituency is far from realizing how we stand both in relation to our needs and in comparison with colleges of our class.

For some reason not easily explained, Smith has received much less in gifts and bequests for this purpose than her sister institutions. The total endowment for the purposes of scholarship aid now held by Smith College is $186,131, yielding an annual income of less than $9500. Vassar, with an enrollment slightly over half of ours, has now an endowment for scholarships of about $700,000 yielding an income of $35,000, nearly six times as much per student. Wellesley, with an enrollment about three-fourths of ours, has an endowment of $412,425 yielding an income of $17,528, nearly two and a half times as much per student.

There are now on the rolls over 250 students who have satisfied us that they need financial help in order to get through college, so that our income from funds given for this purpose would allow them an average of less than $40 a year. As a matter of fact we dispensed last year $78,627, over $69,000 of which was drawn from our current income. This is made possible by the increase in tuition, the Trustees having decided at the time the fees were raised that many more scholarships should be given in order to prevent the higher tuition from resulting in the loss, through lack of means, of a highly valued part of our student body.

The women's colleges of our type are running a greater risk than is generally recognized of becoming class institutions. Two of them already draw about 85% of their students from expensive preparatory schools. In spite of our efforts to check the tendency, our own proportion of high school students is diminishing. To hold this class, and to preserve the representative and democratic quality of the College, we shall have to increase rather than diminish the amount offered in scholarships. But obviously if a great part of the increased tuition has to be returned to the poorer students, there will be little left over for the increase in salaries and the other purposes which we had hoped to accomplish.

It is manifest, therefore, that both in relation to our needs and in comparison with our sister institutions, we are justified in seeking for a large increase in our funds for reducing the college expenses of that group of students who come to us well endowed with brains but poor in worldly goods.

The New Curriculum for Freshmen and Sophomores

FRANCES FENTON BERNARD

In the November QUARTERLY Professor Orton discussed the question of curricula in colleges similar to Smith but made no attempt to deal with our specific problems because at that time the Committee on the Course of Study was working on a plan for the revision of our curriculum. The Committee has now submitted its report; action has been taken; and Dean Bernard, as chairman of the Committee, here presents the plan to the alumnae. In order that it may be seen how representative the Committee was, we append their names. The original Committee on the Course of Study consisted of seven persons, as follows: Dean Bernard, chairman, the President, Professor Edna Shearer (Philosophy), Professor Caroline Bourland (Spanish), Professor Seth Wakeman (Education), Professor Howard Parshley (Zoölogy), Professor Sidney Fay (History). For this special piece of work this Committee was augmented by three persons: Professor Roy Welch (Music), Professor Grace Smith (Botany), and Professor William Orton (Economics and Sociology).

ON December 8, 1926, the Faculty adopted by a large majority a new curriculum for the Freshman and Sophomore years, to go into effect for the Freshmen entering next year and for each succeeding Freshman class.

Our present curriculum is now ten years old. During that time the courses given by the Faculty have changed and methods of instruction have been greatly modified, but the general plan has remained what it was ten years ago. Ten years, as progress in Education now goes, is a long time, a long life for the best curriculum in the world. In those years there have been surprising advances in educational theory. This period has seen a marked alteration in the lives of women, in the standards set for them, in the social and mental life open to them. It was natural then that some readjustment and revision should be needed. And, in fact, there has been considerable dissatisfaction with the general layout of studies which has apparently increased in recent years. Criticism has been heard from school principals, alumnae, and parents. Students too, in the first two years, have felt that college is too much like preparatory school. They have felt the number and burden of the requirements. Freshmen have lost interest in intellectual life and the zest of intellectual curiosity under a curriculum which presented some aspects of compulsion and routine.

Last spring, then, the Faculty commissioned the Committee on the Course of Study to prepare a revision of the curriculum for the Freshman and Sophomore years. The Committee has been working steadily on the plan. It was the final plan proposed by this Committee, after months of work, with constant consultation and conference with the Faculty, that the Faculty approved on December 8. The final plan represented a coöperative undertaking on the part of the Faculty and the Committee.

The chief features of the new curriculum are: a reduction of the groups from ten to four, the requiring of a minimum number of hours in each group in place of requiring specific courses, and a plan for fulfilling the language requirement by examinations on a reading knowledge of two foreign languages.

The present group system has grown up, apparently. It has no special basis in logic or in educational theory. The number of groups is accidental. There is no special magic in ten. And the distribution of departments within the groups is equally a matter of growth rather than principle. The new curriculum replaces the ten groups with four groups which rest, so far as logic is possible in these things, on clearly marked divisions of knowledge. The language group is distinct from the others in aim and method. Literature and the arts, placed together, are set off from the others by their emphasis on expression. In the third group, the sciences, the principle is obvious, and the fourth, the social sciences, are as naturally connected. These four groups are four recognized divisions of knowledge, four types of discipline. There is in three of these groups a time requirement. Particular courses which the student shall take are no longer specified. This arrangement still insures a reasonable distribution of work in the Freshman and Sophomore years, and some acquaintance with the various divisions of knowledge. Yet this time requirement is an elastic requirement. It leaves the student free in the various fields to choose her specific subjects, and this opportunity to choose should bring, we believe, added incentive to good work and added interest. This should be true even if the courses elected are those formerly prescribed. Now they will tend to be taken by those who need them, by those whose previous training, interest, experience, and abilities have created a background and stimulated a need.

In Group I, *The Languages*, there is no time requirement. The requirement is to be fulfilled in this group by passing a test on the attainment of a reading knowledge of two foreign languages.

The requirements in English and Spoken English and Hygiene must be fulfilled either by the passing of an examination or by taking specified courses.

Under the new plan the number of hours of work in the four years has been made equal, thirty in each year in place of the heavier burden of hours now required of Freshmen and Sophomores.

The values as well as the defects of this new curriculum will appear only in its actual operation. It can be modified and improved as experience shows need of change. We do not know as yet what students will do if left to themselves. We can only speculate as to their choices until we have actual evidence. The new plan gives us our first opportunity to experiment, to gather evidence of this sort. It is of tremendous educational value for that reason if for no other. But we expect it also to stimulate a better morale among students and a keener zest for work.

On the following pages the two curricula are presented for contrast; the present curriculum with its ten groups and its definite subject requirements for Freshman and Sophomore years, and the revised curriculum with four groups, elastic time requirements in three of these and the language test in Group I. Students now in college will continue under the old curriculum. Each incoming Freshman class will enter under the new curriculum.

The Present Curriculum

GROUPS

I. *English Language and Literature*
II. *Greek, Latin*
III. *French, German, Italian, Spanish*
IV. *Astronomy, Physics, Chemistry*
V. *Geology, Botany, Zoölogy*
VI. *Art, Music, Spoken English*
VII. *History, Government, Economics and Sociology*
VIII. *Philosophy, Psychology, Education, Biblical Literature and Comparative
　　 Religion*
IX. *Hygiene and Physical Education*
X. *Mathematics*

Freshman Year

1. GROUP I, English	2 hours
2. GROUP II or X, Greek, Latin, or Mathematics	3 hours
3. GROUP III, French or German or Italian or Spanish	3 hours
4. GROUP IV or V, Astronomy or Botany or Chemistry or Geology or Physics or Zoölogy	3 hours
5. GROUP IX, Hygiene and Physical Education	1½ hours
6. Elective	3 hours
	15½ hours

Sophomore Year

1. GROUP IV or V, Science	3 hours
2. GROUP VII, History	3 hours
3. GROUP VIII, Philosophy and Psychology or Biblical Literature and Comparative Religion	{ 3 hours { 2 hours 2 or 3 hours
4. GROUP IX, Hygiene and Physical Education	½ hour
5. Elective	7 or 8 hours
	15½ hours

Junior Year

1. A Major Subject	5 or 6 hours
2. A Distribution Subject	2 or 3 hours
3. Biblical Literature and Comparative Religion or Philosophy and Psychology	2 or 3 hours
4. Elective	2 to 5 hours
	14 hours

Senior Year

1. The Major Subject (continued)	7 to 9 hours
2. A Distribution Subject	2 to 3 hours
3. Elective	2 to 5 hours
	14 hours

The Revised Curriculum

General Requirement: Of the 120 hours required for the degree, 30 must be taken each year.

GROUPS	REQUIREMENTS
GROUP I—*Languages* English French German Spanish Italian Latin Greek [Hebrew] [Scandinavian]	All students must pass examinations on reading ability in two foreign languages, whether or not they have taken courses in Group I. Such examinations must be passed not earlier than the beginning of Sophomore year and not later than the beginning of Senior year.
GROUP II—*Literature and Fine Arts* Art Music Spoken English English Greek Latin French German Italian Spanish Biblical Literature	Twelve hours in Freshman and Sophomore years.
GROUP III—*Sciences* Mathematics Astronomy Physics Botany Geology Chemistry Zoölogy Psychology Hygiene	Twelve hours in Freshman and Sophomore years, six of which must be in a laboratory science.
GROUP IV—*Social Sciences* History [Government] Economics Sociology [Religion] Education Philosophy	Twelve hours in Freshman and Sophomore years.

1. Students not exempt by examination are required to pass English 11 and either Spoken English 11 or the Spoken English clinic.
2. Bracketed departments do not now offer courses to Freshmen and Sophomores. New courses proposed for Freshmen and Sophomores will be submitted to the Faculty in the usual way.
3. Students not exempt by examination are required to take Hygiene 11 or Hygiene 12b.

A War Baby Grown Up

Everett Kimball

Mr. Kimball, Professor of Government at Smith College, has been associated with The School for Social Work since 1919 and since 1921 has been the Director.

THE Smith College School for Social Work began as a war industry. In 1918 many colleges sought to establish courses or engage in activities which might be of service to the country in the World War. Some established courses for nurses, some for "farmerettes." As a result of a conference between President Neilson and the late Dr. Southard of the Boston Psychopathic Hospital, Smith College became the pioneer in a new field, and the experimenter in new methods. The first and avowed object of the course established at Smith in 1918 was to train "psychiatric social workers for shell-shocked soldiers," as we then hesitatingly stuttered out. The experience of the Allies in the War showed the prevalence of "shell-shock," and it was feared that the United States would be called upon to care for a similar proportion of soldiers so disabled.

Before the first class was graduated, the armistice came. Although only a small proportion of our armies saw actual service on the front, cases of "shell-shock" were unexpectedly numerous. The name "shell-shock" was soon abandoned, but the number of soldiers who were suffering from some mental, nervous, or personality handicap instead of decreasing, increased, and the problem which the Government faced was the care of these handicapped soldiers who outnumbered those who were suffering from wounds or disease. Thus psychiatric social workers, in steadily increasing numbers, were called upon to help in the rehabilitation of these unfortunates. Institutions for the mentally diseased demanded social workers who were equipped to understand their patients and to aid in their readjustment in the community. The psychiatrists saw that many of the cases which came for relief to social agencies were suffering from the beginnings of mental disease, from nervous breakdowns, from mental deficiency, or from personality flaws. Indeed, the late Dr. Southard estimated that at least 75% of the clients of social work agencies might be considered as needing advice or treatment from psychiatrists and the sympathetic adjustment by psychiatric social workers. Thus psychiatric social work, not dealing solely with the "insane" but as a technique in making social adjustments, came into being.

The group of psychiatrists with whom the Smith School was most closely associated were interested in the work of the National Committee for Mental Hygiene. This Committee, originally concerned with the improvement in the care and treatment of the mentally diseased, soon stressed the possibility of the prevention of such disease, and entered on a campaign of mental hygiene. The Commonwealth Fund of New York, in planning its program for the prevention of delinquency, was closely associated with the National Committee for Mental Hygiene, and from this association began the establishment of child guidance clinics which dealt with children who were suffering not so much from mental disease as from personality difficulties and unfortunate traits which might develop into mental disease and delinquency in the future. In dealing with these children, the psychiatric social worker was eagerly sought and became a most useful instrument in the adjustment. The first child guidance clinics were in connection with juvenile courts, and dealt with children who had shown open delinquency. But clinics are now established for the non-delinquent class, and are found in schools and colleges, and some deal with the preschool child. In all of these are psychiatric social workers, and in most of them graduates of the Smith School are found.

General agencies for social work very early saw the advantages of psychiatric social work in dealing with some of their cases, and many cases were transferred from general social work agencies to the more special ones, or the general agencies and the psychiatric agencies treated the case in common. Some of the larger social work agencies established mental hygiene clinics within their organizations, while an increasing number of agencies are employing psychiatric social workers to coöperate with the psychiatric agency in handling certain types of cases.

In other respects, the Smith College School for Social Work is a pioneer. It approached the problems of social adjustment from a new angle. It believed that social work was primarily the adjustment of personality to environment or to other personalities. It laid more stress upon the personality factors of the client than the immediate reason or precipitating factor which brought the client to the agency. It was more interested in why one person met financial reverses or domestic difficulties without assistance while another person needed assistance to adjust to the same difficulties. The School felt that the psychiatric approach or the understanding of the mental or emotional life of the unadjusted was the fundamental factor in social work. It believed that the success of relief, or of child placement, or of rehabilitation or readjustment of the socially maladjusted was largely conditioned by a sympathetic understanding of the mental and emotional life and the personalities of the unadjusted. It believed that the psychiatrist, in making a psychiatric study of the maladjusted, brought to social work new light and deeper understanding. It recognized that from the beginning, social workers had realized this and were attempting to achieve the same results. But it felt that modern psychiatry furnished an instrument of greater precision and that the psychiatric social worker acquired a technique more exact than that which was employed by social workers who either depended upon their intuitive understanding or had learned from long experience by trial and error how to handle certain personalities. The School did not depreciate the work of social workers, but believed that psychiatric social work and mental hygiene had a great contribution to make. Like true pioneers and enthusiasts, the staff and graduates of the School, in their enthusiasm, perhaps gave some offense by their insistence that psychiatric social work and the psychiatric approach were the fundamental basis and technique of all social work. It is a belief, however, which characterized and still characterizes the School, and a belief which, perhaps phrased a little differently, is being acted upon, if not formally stated, by an increasing number of welfare agencies.

In another way, the School is a pioneer. Holding the belief that psychiatric social work was fundamental, it held as a corollary that a rather long experience in field work in a psychiatric agency was a better preparation for social work than briefer periods in different types of agencies. This was contrary to the practice of all the established schools for social work and still is a point of criticism or a mark of distinction of the Smith School. Experience during the last eight years has shown us that the psychiatric social worker, while primarily attached to a hospital or a clinic, meets and handles either as a worker in her own agency or in coöperation with workers in the specialized agencies of family welfare, child placement and relief, pretty nearly all problems that these agencies handle themselves. The psychiatric social worker begins with the study of the personality and then attempts the necessary special adjustment, whether it be of relief, family welfare, or child placement. Theoretically, if possible, all social workers should have long experience in all types of agencies. This, however, is impossible. As the authorities of the School feel now, after surveying the work of eight years, it is still believed that a long experience in a psychiatric agency is of greater practical value to our graduates than briefer periods of experience in different types of agencies. It is freely conceded that the graduates of the School are lacking in variety of experience, but it is believed that their experience, concentrated as it is in the type of agencies with which the School is affiliated, is of greater value to them than briefer periods of experience in a wider variety of agencies.

In a third way, the School is a pioneer. At the time of the establishment of the School, instruction in field work and theory were carried on together. The weeks or the days of the week were divided between instruction given in theory at the schools and practical work in agencies. Partly because of the war emergency, and partly because Northampton was a small rural city, the orthodox method of instruction was impossible. The result has been that from the first instruction in theory was given at Northampton, while the field experience was obtained during the winter in agencies scattered throughout the country. From the first, the authorities of the School did not see how case work of a professional character could synchronize with an academic hour plan. The authorities wished their students to become integral parts of the agencies in which they were working to gain, even while they were students, the professional attitude and point of view. They believed that this was best accomplished by placing a few students in a comparatively large number of agencies, and by requiring the students to devote substantially all their time to learning the method and technique of the agency. The agencies have proved more than willing to coöperate. They have found that students giving their full time for nine months presented fewer problems than students who gave two or three days a week or a half day during the full week. The students themselves, placed in such conditions, generally very quickly lose their collegiate attitude of mind and return to the School for the third session, not experienced social workers, but with professional points of view, ideals, and the beginning of a technique which experience develops. It is interesting to note that this method of instruction, while sharply criticized at first, is being adopted with various modifications by an increasing number of schools.

The application and development of the Smith method is interesting to trace. Originally, the School coöperated with the Boston Psychopathic Hospital and with the state hospitals in Massachusetts and New York. Those were the days in which the demand for psychiatric social workers came chiefly from hospitals for mental diseases. With the development of mental hygiene, as applied to child guidance, the School began to coöperate with clinics. In 1922, the School began its connection with the Institute for Juvenile Research, of which Dr. Herman Adler was Director and Cornelia D. Hopkins (Smith 1919) Chief of Social Service. This connection has proved most helpful to both because it was a new center for field work, and because Dr. Adler most generously offers ten scholarships. In 1922, two students were sent to the demonstration clinics founded by the Commonwealth Fund, and a new connection was established which has led to an increasing number of students being trained in child guidance clinics, and on graduation undertaking that type of work. A little later, the School began to coöperate with the clinics for pre-school children established by Dr. Thom in Boston, and still later with the schools for feeble-minded in Massachusetts and with clinics in the public schools.

During the coming winter session, the 34 members of the class are distributed among 18 agencies from Boston to Minneapolis, from Philadelphia to Chicago, as follows: Child Habit Clinic, State House, Boston, 1 student; Michael Reese Dispensary, Chicago, 1; Connecticut Society for Mental Hygiene, New Haven, 1; Manhattan State Hospital, New York, 1; Institute for Juvenile Research, Chicago, 6; Essex County Juvenile Clinic, Newark, 3; Child Habit Clinic, 502 Park Square Building, Boston, 2; St. Paul Child Guidance Clinic, 2; Foxborough State Hospital, 2; Taunton State Hospital, 2; Boston Psychopathic Hospital, 2; Boston State Hospital, 2; Department of Child Guidance, Board of Education, Newark, 1; Cleveland Child Guidance Clinic, 2; Worcester State Hospital, 2; Minneapolis Child Guidance Clinic, 1; All-Philadelphia Child Guidance Clinic, 2; Family Society of Philadelphia, 1. The value of this distribution is remarkable. The students return for their third session bringing the class varied points of view and varied experiences. Such distribution, moreover, is invaluable to the School in extending its influence and in subjecting its methods and procedure to criticism not confined to one type of work or to one locality.

That there is little danger of the School becoming provincial or parochial may be seen from the fact that among the 89 students who attended the session last summer, 25 states and Canada and Switzerland were represented. Nor are the states confined to any one section of the country, for California and Texas, Washington and Mississippi, the middle west and the Atlantic seaboard were represented, as well as New England. Of the 34 in the entering class, all but 2 are college graduates—3 from Vassar, 3 from the University of Wisconsin, and 20 other colleges and universities, but none from Smith. Perhaps a prophet is not without honor, save in his own country. Since the School has been founded, about 200 have been graduated from the full course, most of whom are practicing their profession in agencies seeking for the technique they acquired at the School. The agencies with which they are working are distributed almost as widely as the sources from which our students come. Canada, Finland, Japan, Paris, and 26 states of the Union all contain one or more of our graduates.

Although the School was primarily founded to educate social workers, it was believed that such education should include, in addition to the field experience and instruction in theory, a piece of research. This research was primarily an academic requirement and is still emphasized as such. Experience, however, has shown that these pieces of research as developed in the thesis which is required for graduation, not infrequently contain valuable contributions to professional social work. Not infrequently, the agencies with which the students were associated desired some problem investigated, or some technique studied —in other words, a bit of research along some line which would be profitable to the agency. A rather large number of these theses have been deemed worthy of publication. It is hoped that this feature of the School, which is of great value, will never be neglected but that funds may be forthcoming for the publication of even more of these theses in some form of Studies.

For several years, the staff of the School has felt that the course of fourteen months was at least equivalent to the nine months of the academic year during which time a college graduate might obtain a Master's degree from Smith College. In order to get the point of view of the Faculty of Smith College, their opinion was asked, and it was unanimously voted, as an expression of opinion of the academic Faculty, that the Trustees were justified in granting the Master's degree to the graduates of the School. At the meeting of the Trustees in June 1926 it was decided that graduates of the School for Social Work who possessed the Bachelor's degree on entrance to the School might, on the completion of the course to the satisfaction of the staff of the School, be recommended for the degree of Master of Social Science. This vote of the Trustees was applied to the class which was graduated in 1926.*

The School is on the threshold of a new extension and development. For the past five years the Commonwealth Fund of New York has been studying the problem of the prevention of delinquency. Originally, it began in juvenile courts with court clinics and in schools with visiting teachers. From the first, it has financed the Bureau of Children's Guidance in connection with the New York School of Social Work, and has been responsible for the founding of child guidance clinics in many cities in the south, middle, and far west. Since the inception of the work, the graduates of the Smith School have found places on the staffs of these clinics and a number of students have been trained in them each year. With the close of its program, the Commonwealth Fund decided to concentrate its work and to establish in New York City an Institute for Child Guidance. This Institute is to be operated by a director in coöperation with an administrative board for the purpose of making possible study and research in the field of mental hygiene for children, to provide facilities for the training of psychiatrists and graduate psychologists, and field experience in child guidance for students in psychiatric social work at the New York School of Social Work and the Smith College School for Social Work, and to afford adequate clinical facilities for the thorough study and treatment of children presenting problems in behavior and mental hygiene. To represent the schools for social work, the directors of the New York School and the Smith College School were elected to

* At a meeting on Oct. 16, 1926, the Board of Trustees voted to make the degree retroactive, on recommendation of the staff of the School.

the administrative board.   To each of these Schools the Commonwealth Fund grants generous fellowships for the education of their students.

As has been said, the School has been fortunate in its associations.   The National Committee for Mental Hygiene has given its advice and criticism most generously, and Dr. Frankwood E. Williams, Medical Director of the Committee, has for years not only given the course in Social Psychiatry during the summer session, but has always been available for counsel.   The Commonwealth Fund of New York has granted to the School maintenance allowances and fellowships.   During the present year, the grant amounts to $12,000. With the New York School of Social Work, although it employs somewhat different methods from the Smith School, the association has always been most cordial.   It is to be expected that in the operation of the new Institute, these associations will be strengthened and the coöperation will be even closer.   The field of mental hygiene in child guidance is but at the beginning of most interesting and, it is hoped, helpful developments.   It is therefore extremely fortunate that the Smith School should be chosen as one of the two schools to coöperate in the newest and, from some points of view, the most untrammeled attempt in this direction.

Allan Neilson

October 31, 1909—December 1, 1926

Allan, only son of President and Mrs. Neilson,
died on December 1, 1926, after an
illness of many months during
which his gallantry and
courage were a constant
source of strength to
all who knew him.

The Nursery School on Kensington Avenue

Dorothy D. Williams

The Nursery School is a coöperative venture conducted for the parents by the Institute for the Coördination of Women's Interests. Miss Dorothea Beach, Demonstration Manager of the Institute, is Principal, and Miss Williams is assistant at the School. She has her B.S. from Teachers College, Columbia, and is a graduate of the Merrill Palmer School in Detroit, the famous prototype of so many nursery schools. At the close of Miss Williams's article Mrs. Ethel Puffer Howes, Director of the Institute, appends a few paragraphs explaining the meaning of the School as an experiment of the Institute.

THE Institute's first child is three months old, and has startled its parents a little in growing so swiftly from babyhood. Its first tooth, in fact, is coming several months ahead of time—the Nursery School is growing a sizable waiting list, and the original plan of enrollment of twenty children has been increased to twenty-five. The youngest child is two years and two months old and the oldest five years and eight months.

The children have established themselves very surely. Bobby comes in the morning with his mother, and after going to the nurse for nose and throat inspection, putting his wraps away, and taking his drink of water, he leans over the banister on his way upstairs to throw his mother a kiss and to say: "Goodbye, Mother, I'm going upstairs to build a train. You can go home and [a thoughtful pause] get the dinner."

The group is rather markedly divided, there being eight or ten two-year-olds and about the same number of fours, with but a few threes. There is therefore a somewhat different plan of work for the older and the younger children. In Bobby's playroom, that of the older children, the free play or work period is going on—block-building, painting, clay modeling, sewing, and so forth. A carpenter bench, which stands on the upper porch when weather permits, is a favorite piece of equipment. The children work alone or in twos and threes, and there is a good deal of conversation going on. At ten o'clock work is put away for a mid-morning lunch of orange juice and cod-liver oil, and graham crackers, a very popular repast. After a period of songs, rhythms, games, or stories, the children go outdoors to spend the rest of the morning.

Downstairs, with the two-year-olds, there is a good deal less talking. Cynthia, in carrying a cup of water from the tray to the table where she sits to drink it, has spilled a little. She has gone to get the pail and cloth from the bathroom and is wiping the floor with evident concentration and enjoyment. Perhaps the spill wasn't quite accidental. But there are very few of them. Elizabeth is turning color cubes over and over to find the red side. Jay builds cages for bears in the bay window, with Dorothea sitting on a bench near him stringing beads and giving advice in her own very intense but undecipherable language. Betsy and Barbara have chosen dolls, of course.

Virginia and Melinda are within a week of each other—two years and a few months. Both are only children. This week they have discovered that they can talk to each other and have things understood—or at least enjoyed—the delicate shadings of which are evidently lost to uncomprehending adults. There has been great joy and much exercise of this discovery. Virginia talks in

t's, l's, and soft a's, and Melinda in explosive sounds of many consonants and vowels. To-day they are enjoying a joke which seems to consist in turning the head sideways and looking up. They are sitting on the floor carrying on a voluble conversation punctuated with squeals of delight.

Music, the news period, and lunch follow. One of the observing students has given the news period the very academic title of "current events." These

THE YOUNGEST GENERATION

All but one of the children in the above pictures are "faculty children." Elizabeth Bixler is peeking out from behind Kitty Welch at the luncheon table and Jay Duke is draining his last drop of milk. In the circle, starting at the left with little Guthrie Darr, son of the pastor of the First Church, are Betsy Shedd, Jackie Guilloton, Dorothea Douglas, Janet Guiet, Jay Duke, Kitty Welch, and Elizabeth Bixler.

events are of great variety—new clothes, what the sun looked like on a foggy morning, a snow shovel, a visit to the aquarium, and so forth. The rest of the morning is spent outdoors. The children are encouraged toward self-reliance, and the wraps, as well as everything else in the child's day, are a part of the educational program. The youngest ones can manage with interest hats and mittens and half-started sweaters and leggings. Snaps on galoshes are a great triumph, and with much labor on everyone's part all are finally in the yard for play or out for a walk.

Packing boxes and the sandpile are the greatest delight out of doors, and here again, along with the other value of vigorous and imaginative play with raw material, important social contacts are made. Jane learns that children can't be whined and willed into acquiescence nearly so easily as adults. Florence learns that Bobby gives only a passing glance to an injured finger. Billy teaches manners in a very effective and natural way:

Jim in coming down the slide too fast bumped into Kitty, Billy's little sister. Kitty is crying with personal and very slight physical injuries when Billy comes to her assistance. "Just put your arm around her and she'll stop crying," is his frequent advice on such occasions. This time the case demands further action. He encircles her shoulders with his arm and turns to Jimmy.

"Jimmy, say 'Excuse me.'"

Jim sits on the bottom of the slide and hangs his head.

Billy repeats his request: "Jimmy, you hurt my sister. Say 'Excuse me.'"

A crowd is gathering. Billy continues his emphasis, never losing his temper and never relinquishing his goal. After the fifth repetition under the firmly fixed eye, Jimmy complies, smiles, and everyone is off for the slide again.

At noon half of the children go home for the day and the other half remain for midday dinner, afternoon nap, and another period of play.

The Institute believed in two things when it selected the Nursery School for its first experiment in coöperation: It believed in the value of group training under trained people for children of the pre-school age, and in the fact that the mother who has no release from the twenty-four hour job of child-care and home-care has not her best self to give to either. Certain things such as special equipment, contact with other children of his own age, the undivided attention of those interested in child-care, have been found possible in nursery schools when not possible in most homes, and the two institutions, the school and the home, can be made to supplement each other in a very helpful way.

The school is working continually for right habit training in the mental, physical, social, and character trends of the children's development. As can be seen, the best aids here are the children themselves. These habits sometimes are very firmly fixed. To get Elizabeth to wash her face before washing her hands or to lie down for her nap before putting her shoes together under the bed is next to impossible. Public opinion is very strong and a great help, especially at lunch. One eats what one may not like because everybody does. There have not been many feeding difficulties in this group, however. One instance is interesting.

Barbara, a newcomer to lunch, was being very slow about eating and had gone to her nap one day without dessert. A day later, when she came down to dinner and was served her dinner by one of the children, she said, "I don't like beans," to which the teacher replied, "But you're going to eat them anyway, aren't you?" Toward the middle of the meal one of the very responsible older girls looked over to Barbara's table, and said, "Is Barbara eating better to-day, Miss Beach?"

"Yes, I think so, Anne."

A moment or two later Anne called, "O Barbara, I just love beans, don't you?" and from Barbara came the heartfelt reply, "Yes, I do. I love beans."

The children are a great help, and together they and the teachers have accomplished certain things. A little girl has graduated from diapers and a bottle to bloomer dresses and two helpings of everything, feeding herself. A little boy has gained much in concentration, and another one is being released from the burden of intense self-consciousness and the concentrated focussing of two nervous parents. Many of the children have gained much in self-reliance and ability to take up a piece of work and carry it to a satisfactory conclusion.

The school is so organized that one of the mothers is present every day to be the assisting teacher. Their turns come every two weeks. This is of great service in cutting down the expense of the school and also in keeping a close connection between the home and the school and so keeping the training consistent. The mothers find it helpful to themselves in various ways. They have the opportunity of observing their own children in a social group and of observing other children and so getting a fairer estimate of their own. They see some advantages in watching trained teachers work with the children. With a co-operative group such as this one, there is opportunity to discuss problems with one another.

In some minds a school like this is a source of consternation, of fear that the little children are being trained into automatons and that mothers are losing all sense of responsibility for their children. This is quite the opposite of the aims of pre-school education, and we are glad to see that most of the opinion in Northampton is on the order of a conversation overheard on Paradise Road. Two women were walking and talking together. One: "You must visit the Nursery School. I am sure you will see something quite rare. All the parents are crazy about it."

Note by Mrs. Howes:

Miss Williams has given a vivid expression to the educational side of our Nursery School, and this is well, for it is our workers' entire concern with the children themselves which has given the School its unique and lovely character. Of its meaning as an experiment of the Institute something more may be said.

Our purpose, in brief, was to find out whether a group of parents could effectively coöperate to start a school which would be not only educationally valuable to parent and child, but also a help toward the time budget of the household, particularly for the mother. With this in view, we held in the Gateway House, during the academic year 1925-6, an extended series of parents' discussion meetings. Meanwhile we were ourselves making detailed budget studies of a possible nursery school at the Demonstration House, 58 Kensington Avenue; and it was for us an instructive experience to find that the spring meeting at which we covered three blackboards with this budget information was the one at which the parents finally voted to stand behind a school, and appointed a committee to draw up a plan of organization.   From this time on the enterprise proceeded under its own steam.   The committee issued its own admirable prospectus, called a meeting at which officers of the Parents' Organization were elected as follows: president, Mrs. Seelye Bixler (Mary Thayer '17); secretary, Mrs. Roy D. Welch; treasurer, Mrs. Frank E. Dow.   The Parents' Organization takes entire financial responsibility for the School; its budget, met by fees for tuition, covers rent to the College for the six rooms it uses at Demonstration House, equipment, food, service, and part-salary for Miss Williams (the Institute assumes part for the present as part of the "cost of research").   In the same way the Institute gives the time of Miss Beach, as Principal of the School.

A very important rôle is played by the "assisting mothers," who follow a carefully worked out routine, and are outspoken in their appreciation of what they are gaining in method and insight.   One mother, who is a trained nurse, assumes the morning inspection; another is regularly employed to prepare the school luncheon and supervise in the afternoon.

The Parents' Organization continues to take the initiative: it has called a meeting with the school physician, Dr. Jane D. Armstrong '10, and has organized an active study group, with a complete year's program.   The first meeting, addressed by a nose and throat specialist on "Common Colds," was large and enthusiastic.

On the side of time relief, it is interesting to note that five of the mothers are doing full-time professional work, while seven others are carrying at least part-time professional interests—in all, more than half our constituency.

The Institute's experiment, therefore, we may say is in so far forth successful. It would seem to have demonstrated that a group of parents can agree on a plan, establish a budget, and "carry on," in this particular field of coöperative self-help, and that the help is actually effective.

We have always carefully distinguished between our "Institute" and our "college" activities.   Our relations with the Department of Education have been happy; we have had from them freely counsel and coöperation.   Two fellowships, a generous gift to the Institute from Mrs. J. Stanley Resor of New York, have been administered by the Education Department, and the Fellows, Miss Beatrix Tudor-Hart, a B.A. of Newnham College, Cambridge, and Miss Emma Flinn, a B.S. of Teachers College, Columbia, and kindergarten supervisor in State Teachers College, North Dakota, have been delightful co-workers in the school.   A limited number of graduate students in education have also been "observers"; but the question so often put to us by alumnae, "Aren't you doing anything with the undergraduates?" must be answered negatively.   Our present mandate covers no such activities.

A Trip to the Dutch East Indies

EMMETT R. DUNN

Assistant Professor of Zoölogy

In the spring of 1926 Professor Dunn was zoölogist of an expedition to the Dutch East Indies in search of giant lizards. The two specimens brought back and placed in the New York Zoölogical Gardens were reputed to be the only living ones in captivity. Professor Dunn's book, "The Salamanders of the Family Plethodontidae," issued under the auspices of the College as one of the Anniversary Volumes, has just been published.

IN 1912 a new lizard was described from the tiny island of Komodo, 500 miles east of Java. Comparatively few people saw the brief description, published in the East Indies, which told of a specimen nine feet six inches long, and said that the animal was known to reach a length of twenty-three feet. But *Varanus komodoensis*, for such was the name given to the beast, gradually became a topic of conversation among people interested in reptiles, and finally, after rumors of several different expeditions had proven to be merely rumors, an actual outfit took the field.

This expedition was financed and led by Mr. Douglas Burden of New York. He was accompanied by his wife. I was appointed zoölogist. Mr. F. J. Defosse of Indo-China, a noted big game hunter, completed the white personnel.

At the outset our information consisted of the matter contained in the original description of 1912; of the rumor that the Duke of Mecklenburg had obtained a thirteen-footer in 1923, and had shot a thirty-footer which had escaped. The animal was said to occur on Komodo and on the western end of Flores, which is a much larger island. It should be expected on Padar and on Rinja, which lie between Komodo and Flores.

I arrived in Batavia May 1, coming from New York. The Burdens and Defosse came later. During the interval I went into the mountains in Western Java and collected frogs and small lizards. I also met many of the scientists stationed at the Botanical Gardens in Buitenzorg. There I saw a paper by Mr. Horst, a government official in western Flores, which gave an account of the country in which the big lizards lived and which cast grave doubt on their exceeding thirteen feet in length. Furthermore I found that the Duke of Mecklenburg's largest specimen was about eight feet six inches long, and that what we had previously heard was pure fiction. This was somewhat of a wet blanket, but still left us the hope of obtaining record specimens, although we must needs exercise care, since they were protected by law and we were allowed only fifteen.

When the Burdens and Defosse arrived they had with them Lee Fai, the Pathé man in Singapore. Thanks to the kindness of the Colonial Government we were allowed the use of the *S. S. Dog*, a small but seaworthy boat, which had been previously in use for Fish Commission work.

We set sail from Batavia June second and for some days passed along the north coasts of Java, Bali, Lombok, and Sumbawa, with their ever shifting panorama of tremendous volcanoes, Tengger, Idjen, Batoer, Rinjani, Tamboro. Late in the afternoon of the sixth we entered a narrow bay and dropped anchor in Bima Roads. Here resided the Sultan who owned Komodo and here we were to hire natives for the trip; and here the next morning we saw two captive lizards brought by natives from Komodo. There had been poaching on the island and certain men had been arrested and two live lizards taken from a trap. One of them was said to have attacked and seriously injured a horse which approached too closely. The larger was somewhat over eight feet long. (These were the same two which Cobham, the British aviator, saw at Bima in August, and concerning which he cabled the *Times* that he had seen "two live dragons.")

We made our arrangements, and on the eighth went to Sape, at the east end of Sumbawa, to pick up our natives. On this day we saw Komodo, dim to the east, for the first time.

On the ninth we went through the ten knot tides of the Linta Straits and landed on the east coast of Komodo at one in the afternoon. There was a very ramshackle and poverty-stricken fishing village on the shore of a small bay. We talked a bit with the natives and then walked around the bay and saw a few wild pig. Next day we went exploring for water and camp sites. The woods were fairly open and most of the lower slopes and ridges were grass-covered, but heavy forest filled the narrower valleys and seemed to cover much of the higher country. Defosse and I went north in the low country, and found a spring near a deserted village. We also followed up creek beds which, in the dry season, when the southeast Monsoon was blowing steadily from off the vast deserts of interior Australia, made open sandy roads into the interior. Here we saw many tracks, obviously made by lizards, which used these natural paths just as we would. We came on a box trap, made by poaching natives and abandoned. Two lizards had been caught there and had died and been reduced to skeletons. The larger would have been somewhat over eight feet long. We saw numerous deer and pig. Burden had gone west into the higher hills of the interior. He saw no immediate sign of lizards, but many deer and a few buffalo, and a great deal of water in rocky basins in the stream bed. We decided to camp first at the old village site and later to try the hills.

The first two days were taken up in exploring the neighborhood, shooting pig for bait, putting up three blinds and setting baits at them along the various draws or dried up stream beds. In the course of these excursions we saw our first lizard, a very small one of which we got merely a glimpse, and we made the unwelcome discovery that there were cobras on Komodo. Of these we saw plenty—"more," said Defosse, "in the days on Komodo than I have seen in as many years in Indo-China." But they were small and not very aggressive and no one was bitten. Besides these there were green tree vipers, plenty of them, and a few thick-set spotted ground vipers. Harmless snakes were few in species and in individuals. A few kinds of small lizards scurried about in the woods.

Once the blinds and baits were set most of the time was spent in watching at them. We arranged one of them so that the movie camera could be set up there, and at all three in turn snare traps were set, a noose of rope being attached to a bent over tree so that a lizard coming to feed at the bait would release a trigger and the tree springing straight would hoist him into the air where he could easily be tied to a pole and brought into camp. The same procedure was followed later in the hills, where we camped at about two thousand feet elevation.

My own work was not connected with the trapping or with the photography. I did a good deal of the watching at the blinds in order to shoot, I attended to the skinning of all the specimens, and incidentally I would pick up small lizards and snakes of the various species, and occasionally wander out at night with a light to find nocturnal creatures. In the course of these performances I managed to see over fifty individuals of the big *Varanus*, and to see them carrying on a number of activities.

One day in the low country I spent the morning skinning and in the afternoon I went with one native to a blind. On the way I disturbed three medium sized *Varanus* at a dismantled trap. At the blind two came around but were rather too small to shoot. As the lizards observed rather strict hours, coming out at 8.30 and going home at about 4.30, I knocked off at the latter time and wandered further into the interior, collecting some of the smaller species. On my way home I decided to visit the trap once more, and, taking a rifle and leaving the boy in the draw, went to the place. There I saw a monstrous looking creature whose shoulders seemed to fill the door of the trap. He was absorbed in feeding and did not see me, and as they are quite deaf he had not heard me. I watched him for awhile, then called the boy to look. As the boy came up, the lizard drew back his head and stared at me, and at that I let him have it. He plunged forward into the trap and collapsed. Luckily for the specimen I had shot him directly in the eye so that the skin bore no mark. This was a very old male, and measured nine feet and one inch. Two others the same general size were seen—one with a blunt tail which was taken alive and later escaped, and one Defosse shot which had a tail shorter by three inches. The latter had swallowed the whole hind half of a deer at once, and was shot two days afterwards looking for more food. All the larger specimens were males, and as we stayed on the island until July fifth, and saw many other specimens, we feel fairly certain that they never grow over ten feet long.

The second largest we got alive was eight feet and three inches, and survived the trip to the States. This one was rather amusing, for Defosse and I went to the trap late one afternoon with some natives only to find everything gone, tree and all, the tree broken off close to the ground. Then we began to look about and found the beast, still tied to the tree and tangled up on a hillside some fifty yards off. Some little maneuvering was necessary to get ropes around him and get him down hill and trussed up.

In the hills Defosse shot one on a wooded hillside and tore it so badly that it was not brought into camp. I, wishing to measure and sex it, went there only to find it gone and a bloody trail leading downhill. There ensued an argument —I claiming it had not been killed and had gone under its own steam; and Defosse, justly proud of his own marksmanship, that it was certainly dead and something else had dragged it off. We followed the trail down to a bamboo thicket where Defosse began to consider the climb back. I went on and promptly lost the trail without Defosse's keenness to aid me. But a few yards more and I heard a loud hiss and something moving. Certain that I was right

I went on a bit on hands and knees and finally caught sight of a patch of lizard the size of my hand and fired. The noises stopped and I went up to find that Defosse was right and I had killed another whose teeth were still clinched in death in the body of the one he had been dragging away to eat.

After Komodo we went to Padar, and found a tiny desolate island with lizard tracks in two places on the beach. Then on five hundred miles east to Wetar, where the natives, according to the American sailing directions, were head-hunters. They came down to the coast to meet our boat, a procession of school children waving two Dutch flags and singing the Dutch national anthem.

Then we went back and I went off alone on to Lombok, while the rest went to Bali. On Lombok I headed for the great volcano Rinjani which I had seen from the sea both going out and coming back. Over twelve thousand feet high, it had been a splendid and fascinating sight. Much walking and a pleasant time alone with the natives got me to a cool camping spot at the upper edge of the pine forest at nine thousand feet. Rinjani has a crater five miles by four, and it is over a mile from the edge of the crater down to the lake which occupies it. In the center of the lake rises a secondary cone thirteen hundred feet high. The inner drop is straight down; the outer slope of two miles is so steep that a stone set rolling seems never to stop. And there is a wind coming irregularly, right and left, like a boxer, so that a good bit of my time I was on my hands and knees. But I never hope for a more marvelous view.

Down from the mountain I was guest at a native dance in a small village. A full moon rising to the east, Rinjani towering to the west, many torches flaring in the narrow streets of the kampong, long silver fingernails on the hands of the superbly graceful dancing girl, and the friendly Malays in their colored cloths made a final and a memorable picture.

Lines in Lieu of Lineaments

*In the "Woman Citizen" for November appeared an article entitled "Baird Leonard, Merrymaker." Now Baird Leonard is Smith 1909 and the lines which appear with her signature as a sop to the editor for declining to have her photograph published with the article are so delectable that we have received permission from the "Woman Citizen" and from Miss Leonard to reprint them here.—*THE EDITOR.

I will not let my photograph
  Appear upon the printed page,
No Savage Reader then can laugh
  And murmer, "Lady, act your age!"

For if the public cannot trace
  My eyes and forehead, nose and lips,
I MAY get credit for a face
  That threatens thrones and launches ships.

What College Means to Two Hundred Girls

MARY E. MENSEL

From time to time it is the privilege of the QUARTERLY to devote some space to the girls who by their own efforts are paying in whole or in part for their education, and we welcome this article which the Assistant Warden, Mary Mensel, Smith 1918, has prepared from the data of the Self-Help Bureau. It will be remembered that the Smith Students' Aid Society is another agency available to students needing assistance, and that the Scholarship Funds of the College care for still other emergencies.

IF the college students of to-day were asked the question, "Why have you come to college?", the answers received would be varied and numerous, ranging all the way from "to get an education" and "to be better able to support myself later on," to "I came to college to have a good time" or "to pass four years in a pleasant way." There is one group of students at Smith, however, whose answers to this question would not be so varied, for these girls have come here with a very definite purpose. They are the girls who are entirely or partially earning their expenses by the work they do in the summer and during the college year, and no girl bent on just having a good time would elect to earn her board and perhaps to borrow money to meet her other expenses. In the Self-Help Bureau, which is part of the Office of the Warden, we come to know these girls well and we consider it one of our greatest privileges and joys to work with them.

We have registered with us this year approximately 200 students of whom 35 are earning their board in campus and off-campus houses, by waiting on table, setting tables, or doing watch duty, which is answering bells. The rest are girls who supplement their reserve funds or their pin-money by doing odd jobs which we may be able to give them from time to time. Last winter the students registered with us earned about $5000 in amounts ranging from 70 cents to $200. The work we can give them is of various sorts and the remuneration varies from 20 cents an hour for watch duty to $1.00 to $1.50 an hour for tutoring. They care for children, copy music, run errands, dust books, deliver posters advertising exhibits held by outside firms, wash dishes, wait on table, typewrite, and, in short, do practically anything that is asked of them. Some 15 students work regularly in the College Library or the Art Department; certain others deliver the College *Bulletin* each week, still others the College *Weekly* and the *Monthly*. We have one student who as custodian of Students' Building receives $100; the girl in charge of the Seelye Hall Note Room is paid $15; one other acts as Loan Librarian and is paid $45. These three and the students on the Furniture Exchange and the Business Manager of the Freshman Handbook are appointed either by us or after consultation with us in order that they may be girls who deserve and need the financial aid these positions bring. The Business Manager of *Weekly*, while not appointed in any way by us, is also invariably some one on our list.

Some of the most interesting information we get is in regard to the summer earnings of our students. To some girls, their summer work is of vital importance, since their cash resources for the winter may be entirely dependent on what they can save in the summer. From the statistics we have been able to gather, we have learned that last summer 151 girls, holding 153 positions in 30 different kinds of work, earned $17,548.15. This is a general average amount earned of $116.21, though when taken by classes the average for the seniors was $162.25, for the juniors $111.34, sophomores $93.23, and for the freshmen $132.77.

The girls did office work of all kinds, worked on playgrounds as supervisors or assistants, were counselors at camps, where they sometimes received a salary or in some cases received their living only, acted as governesses, tutored, read for publishing houses, taught music, did public library work, waited on table in summer hotels, did housework in private homes, worked in various capacities in stores, and so forth. One student, as an officer of a state industrial school, earned $70 besides gaining experience that will be most helpful later on, two were in hospital laboratories getting training for future positions, another earned $90 being in charge of the children's clinic in a large New York hospital, taking case histories of children from 4 to 12 years of age, one was hostess at a tea room on the Cape and came back with $275 to her credit and a rich fund of experience. Think what it means to a girl who works hard all year, perhaps wondering how she can meet expenses, to come back in September with $350 actual cash as the result of reading for a publishing house; or consider the actual results to the peace of mind and academic work of a student who says that because of her summer earnings of $200 she can face the year with equanimity, knowing that that amount, with what she can earn during the year, will be sufficient for college expenses. One student doing a little tutoring and besides that acting as supervisor of a group of grammar school children stringing tobacco on one of the farms of the American Sumatra Tobacco Co., earned $100 and got untold profit from the experience.

We could go on and on, citing one interesting case after another, but these few culled from the group will give an idea of what a girl will and can do when bent on a college education which she herself must finance.

PARADISE SNOW-BOUND

How I Do It

GERTRUDE BLATCHFORD STEARNS

Mrs. Stearns graduated in 1922 and was married in 1923. The title to the paper that she sends us is her own; if we were writing one we should be tempted to call it, "Exhibit A and also Q. E. D. for the Institute for the Coördination of Women's Interests."

WHEN I wrote my reply to the questionnaire sent out by the Institute for the Coördination of Women's Interests, I realized all of a sudden that I was a perfectly good example of the thing the Institute is trying to accomplish. That is, I am a college graduate (Smith 1922); I have a home (a six-room flat); a family (a husband and three small children, the oldest, two and a half); an income too small to permit engaging trained help (my husband is Assistant Principal of the High School, and you know what teachers' salaries are!); and I live in a small town where you can't get good help if you can afford it. As for my "intellectual and professional occupations," they are numerous. I am the only substitute for the high school. In the summer time I tutor. Last summer I had from three to five pupils daily, besides being organist in one of the local churches. I helped to organize a Dramatic Club last winter and took part in the first play. I also helped to organize a University Extension Course and attended its lectures. I am on the program committee of the Study Club, and I take lessons and practice on the cello. Besides this, I find time to read half a dozen books a week and review some of them for the public library.

The preceding paragraph seems to be "chockful" of I's. But this is a record of one person's experience, after all, and a good deal of it will not and could not apply to everyone. As I try to stand off and look at my affairs impersonally, I realize that having the time and the opportunity to do these things is largely a question of wanting to do them. Naturally, my days are full to the brim, but that is the way I like them. My housekeeping would certainly shock some of my New England ancestresses, but, to my mind, being "houseproud" is a fault rather than a virtue. I cannot spend every moment of the day and night with my children, but I am not at all convinced that that is either necessary or desirable. My husband has to help me with the housework, the children, and the meals, but he is the kind of a man who cannot endure sitting down and watching his wife work, so he would give me assistance under any circumstances. Accordingly, if you are the sort of a person who can't have half a dozen irons in the fire at the same time without feeling rushed to death; if to you dusting comes before practicing; if you feel it your duty to take entire personal care of your children; and if your husband can't or won't help you, then you won't sympathize with me at all, and my ideas will have very little interest for you.

Of course, the one thing that is absolutely essential to enable one to do anything outside the home, is help of some sort. No matter how incompetent she may be as far as housework is concerned, if I can find someone who will simply stay with the children while I am out of the house, I can get along. My husband has his lunch at the school cafeteria, so I have no noon meal for grown-ups to prepare. My children have always been perfectly healthy and accustomed to amusing themselves, so they require very little care except to have their meals prepared. These are very simple and almost any girl can easily be trained to get them ready and to give the baby her bottle. Except when I am teaching school, I am rarely away at noon, and practically never at the evening meal, so that I can attend to them personally if it is necessary. However, there are few girls, no matter how inexperienced, who cannot be taught to do a few things. I have never had any very expert or skilled help, but this is the way I manage: I teach the girl to do what things are absolutely necessary for the continuous operation of the household. That includes dishwashing, washing children's and baby's clothes, feeding children and preparing their meals, dressing and undressing and putting them to bed. Sometimes I do not even include the dishwashing. This, you will see, provides for the essential points in caring for the children during the hours when I might possibly be away. If I am teaching school, for instance, I know that the children will have their dinners and their naps, and that the baby will be fed at the proper time, that they will have clean clothes for the next day, and we shall have clean plates for our dinner. Or, if I am at a meeting that keeps me late in the afternoon, I know that they will have their suppers and be put to bed. These things must be done at a certain time, whether I am there or not. Everything else *can* be done at any time of day or night when I have the opportunity. So after teaching the girl to do these absolutely necessary things, I have her do as many more as she is able to, and I do the rest. Cooking, ironing, and housework are the things which are most likely to be left for me to do. I suppose that some people would not like to do their work at unconventional times, but I would much rather teach school in the morning and cook in the afternoon (school is over at quarter past one), than to cook in the morning and not teach at all. The same is true of ironing. As for housework, that opens up another line of thought on which I have most decided convictions.

Too many women's lives have been made dreary and empty by the burden of housework. Nowadays we hear a great deal of rejoicing because of the many conveniences and labor-saving devices of modern living conditions. It is true that we no longer have to scrub acres of soft wood floors, struggle with wood fires, heat all our water on a kitchen range, do the washing in a wooden tub with a board to scrub on, and iron with ponderous devices heated on a stove.

Housework is no longer the physical effort that it used to be, but in a great many cases it is drudgery still, in that it is everlasting and never ceases. I know women who have every modern labor saving device imaginable, who still find enough to do to keep them busy all day long. They don't have time, so they say, to read, to practice, to go to lectures or belong to clubs, and would be simply horrified at the thought of any work outside their homes. These are the women for whom life is unbearable if the whole house is not dusted daily, the kitchen floor washed, a fresh pie or cake baked, and once a week the whole house turned upside down in a frenzy of cleaning. To be sure, they like to do it, but that does not alter the fact that it leaves them no time for anything else.

I am a firm believer in order and neatness, but, like all good things, I think it is possible to have too much of them. In the first place, whether she has a profession or not, there should be things in life that seem more valuable to a woman than a continual round of sweeping and dusting. And in the second place, too great a passion for neatness is not conducive to a happy family life. Husbands do not enjoy it when the home is so painfully neat that they feel unnecessary themselves, and children cannot be happy unless they are allowed to scatter their playthings around to a certain extent.

My home gets a good general cleaning once a week. That is, the floors are swept and dry-mopped, rugs vacuum-cleaned, woodwork and furniture dusted. Things like polishing furniture, cleaning silver, washing woodwork, dusting books, and so forth, are done often enough to keep things looking well, but as seldom as possible. In my six-room flat, this weekly cleaning takes two or three hours. When I do not have a capable girl (which is most of the time), I do it on Saturday mornings. Then if I am busy nothing more of this sort is done until the next Saturday. When time is limited, it is much better spent in putting things away and keeping rooms in order, than in dusting and sweeping. A cluttered room, even though it is clean, makes an untidy impression, but a little dust under the radiator or on top of the piano on Friday makes no vital difference to anyone, especially when it is going to be removed on Saturday. Things really can't get so very dusty in a week, you know, and if the rooms are orderly, the dust is scarcely noticed. In proof of this, I offer the fact that I am considered a good housekeeper. I am so little impressed with the importance of the "daily dusting" type of housekeeping that I don't do it even when I am at home. To me it is much more important to practice, or to read. And I would not think of working in the evenings. Those are always left free to spend with my husband in any way that we choose.

My husband has a very important place in my scheme. First of all, he likes to have me do all these outside things, and encourages me in them. He feels that I am a more interesting companion because of them. And so, if he arrives at home at five-thirty in the afternoon, and I don't get here until six, and as a result we don't have supper until six-thirty, it doesn't occur to him to suggest that I should come home earlier for the purpose of getting his supper. He would be much more likely to start getting it himself! I help him correct papers and make out averages and report cards, and he sees no reason why he should not help me with the sweeping on Saturdays, or dressing the children in the morning, or washing the dinner dishes.

There is one other matter that has a bearing on this business of making free time, and that is the question of cooking. My system is what I have seen expressed as "cooking once and eating twice." That is, I practically never cook only enough of anything for one meal. Meats, cake, pies, cold desserts are all just as good the second day as the first. This way of planning one's cooking is a great time saver. I prepare a roast of meat, make a couple of pies and a cake or some cookies, and then for several days all that is necessary for a meal is to cook the vegetables. By doing this on the days when I am at home, I can be away most of the time for several days, if necessary, and still have a good dinner in a short time when I come home at night. I avoid monotony by repeating my menus as seldom as possible. If we have not had a roast of beef for four or five weeks, we do not mind having roast beef three days in succession.

This is how I manage when it is necessary. Last year I carried on all the activities I have mentioned, with my only help a high school girl from three to six in the afternoon, and sometimes in the evenings. She did nothing but care for the children and I did the rest. The days that I taught, I had an older girl take care of them in her own home until three, when the other girl would bring them home. Last summer when I was tutoring three to five hours a day, I had no help at all. By planning my housework and cooking as I have described, I can always have as much time as I want to do things at home. It is only the question of caring for the children during one's absence that makes help necessary at all. Aside from that, I have found that it is quite possible for one woman to maintain a home in comfort by her own efforts, and at the same time carry on a considerable amount of outside activities.

As the servant problem is becoming more and more acute, we shall apparently have to do a great deal of our housekeeping ourselves, and I feel that the sooner we get away from some of the old ideas, the better off we shall all be. The care of young children will always be a difficult problem for a mother who does things outside the home. Living as I do in a small town with no trained help, nursery schools, kindergartens, and so forth, but with a certain amount of inexperienced help available, I have found this solution, which is to me quite satisfactory. If my work were permanent and regular, I should not want to have my children cared for entirely by a young inexperienced girl, but since I am here a great many mornings and afternoons at different times, I can give them a good deal of personal attention. The evenings, when my husband is at home, are always free. I should not spend any more time on housework if I never stirred from my doorstep. Since my children, my husband, and my home are none of them slighted, I feel that as far as I am personally concerned, I have solved quite well the question of Coördinating Women's Interests.

Radium at Close Range

CONSTANCE LINCOLN TORREY

Miss Torrey disclaims any data for the making of an editorial note, but the fact that she has been with the Bureau of Standards in Washington almost continuously since her graduation in 1920 speaks for itself. We had not realized how interesting and significant her work was (she herself called it "routine testing of radium") until we saw her picture and a page interview in the *American Magazine* last fall. The account she has written for the QUARTERLY is even more complete than was that interview. She lives in a Y. W. C. A. residence in Washington and last winter captained a team of business women during the drive for $700,000 for a new Y. W. C. A. in that city.

WORK at the Bureau of Standards is extremely interesting, as the Bureau has many different lines of work, and many projects in research fields. The work can almost be divided into two classes, routine testing and research work. It would take books to describe the many problems worked out at the Bureau which are of interest not only to the skilled scientist but to the layman as well. Here is the only place in the United States where optical glass is made. Researches in paper manufacture have increased by 50% the life of one dollar bills. Work is done on problems relating to the use of concrete and brick. Fire tests are made on building materials and on insulated safes. Radio broadcasting and receiving have been standardized. The standards of mass on which all weighings in this country depend are here. Investigation is being made which will yield a more exact value for the constant of gravitation. Electric telemeters which permit the direct reading and recording of stresses in inaccessible places have been devised. Methods are being standardized for testing the color fastness of dyed materials. Liquid air, liquid hydrogen, and similar liquids are produced here. Many thousand clinical thermometers are tested here each year. Work is done on the fine structural analysis of spectral lines. The green auroral line of oxygen has been produced. One could go on, for pages; and one can realize the magnitude of the Bureau's work when one realizes that only last December the Bureau celebrated its twenty-fifth anniversary. It is not an old Bureau, yet it has accomplished wonders.

My own work with the testing of radium is practically routine testing with very little or really no research work. There is a wide field for research in the subject of radioactivity, but we usually have too much testing which needs to be done and which cannot be laid aside for other work.

In America radium comes all the way from the mountain tops of western Colorado and eastern Utah, from flat surfaced rocks 8000 feet above sea level and more than fifty miles from a railroad station. It is found in such small quantities in an ore called carnotite that from two to five tons of ore are necessary to yield one gram, or one twenty-eighth of an ounce of radium. This is the main reason for the very high price of radium, although in the last three years the price has dropped from $120 to $70 a milligram, owing to a very rich deposit of pitchblende which was discovered in the Belgian Congo in Africa. Other reasons for the high price are the reducing and refining processes, for each ton of ore requires two tons of coal, one ton of chemicals, and fifty tons of water.

We are not in the business of refining the crude ore. When the material is received by us it is in the form of a salt, usually radium bromide or sulphate, and is hermetically sealed in a glass tube, metal needle, or glazed plaque, ready for use by the doctor or hospital. The needles are usually of a steel alloy or of platinum, and look like an ordinary sewing needle except that they are slightly shorter and a little larger in diameter. These seem to be the common form for therapeutic use, the reason being that there is no danger of breaking the needle, and it may be placed in any portion of the body with minimum pain and effort. In hospitals where radium treatment is the principal object, such as the Howard Kelly Hospital in Baltimore, the radium salt is put into solution, and the gas from it, radium emanation or niton, is pumped off and then put into glass tubes. This gas has all the necessary qualities for treatment, although it decays very rapidly so that it loses half its value in about four days. Use of this gas eliminates any danger of loss of the actual radium. In some hospitals, the emanation is put into minute glass tubes, called "seeds," and these are left in the body of the patient and are disposed of by the natural functioning of the body. For surface applications and for tonsil operations, the flat plaque is used. This can be placed directly upon the malignant growth, and covers a fairly large surface, two or four square centimeters, at one time.

But the application of radium in treatment of diseases is entirely apart from the work of the Bureau. We do not attempt to do any therapeutic work. Our testing is for the actual value of the radium content of an applicator, so that the physician will know that when he pays out ten, twenty, or even one hundred thousand dollars, he is getting something worth that, and not common table salt.

The packages containing the radium sent here for test come usually by registered mail. Every package is carefully opened and every preparation carefully examined and washed in soap and water, this latter being done to avoid any contamination of the surface of the applicator which may have been acquired during the process of manufacture. The preparations are put into glass tubes marked for identification, and are placed in lead lined boxes. These are kept locked securely in a safe which is also lead lined. During the above process and during the testing process we never touch the radium with our hands, always using six-inch forceps. Our unpacking is done behind a heavy cast iron screen for protection from the dangerous rays.

The actual testing is done not by weight, although our results are in milligrams, but by the power of the potent rays from radium to ionize the air around a charged gold leaf electroscope and thus discharge it. Radium emits three kinds of rays, called alpha, beta, and gamma rays, all three of which will discharge an electroscope, but our instruments are constructed so that we test only for gamma rays. We have one standard made up by Mme. Curie and several others of various sizes which we have standardized from this one. We first find the rate of discharge of an electroscope with one of our standards as a source, and then with a preparation sent in for test. This rate is timed in seconds and tenths of a second with an ordinary stop watch.

When first sealed, radium has no active rays, and it requires thirty days for a preparation to reach its equilibrium value, as it is called. Our readings are always taken over an extended period of days, in order that we may be sure that the applicators have attained equilibrium. If they are growing, and if the concern submitting them for test requests an immediate test, we are able to take readings and, by a carefully worked out formula, extrapolate our values. Six years ago when Mme. Curie visited this country, the women of America presented her with a gram of radium worth at that time $100,000. The gram was put up in ten sealed glass tubes and was measured and certified by our laboratory, using the method described.

This same method in principle is used in finding radium that has been lost. Some years ago we lost a needle worth about a thousand dollars. We searched every crack and crevice of the laboratory but the needle was nowhere to be found. Then we went to the incinerator with a portable electroscope, and soon discovered by the action of the instrument that the needle was present in a can of rubbish. It took patience to divide the trash again and again until the small object was found, but patience is generally rewarded, and the needle was recovered, much to the joy of all of us. An electroscope can be made so sensitive that when radium was accidentally thrown out with bandages into the furnace of a hospital, a careful search showed that it had been incorporated with the ashes in the making of a concrete sidewalk.

When I first came to the Bureau and was appointed to the radium section, we had a large number of workers. At that time there seemed to be a greater demand for radium and we tested and certified approximately four million dollars worth each year. But the demand has decreased as well as the price and we now handle only about one million dollars worth a year. Also there are only two of us handling the tests, a girl from Goucher College and I. We share the responsibility practically equally, for we both have been at the Bureau the same number of years.

Our greatest care and danger is in the fact that the rays from radium are detrimental to one's health, when one is continually exposed to them. But, as I said before, we use forceps for all handling of the preparations, and, as far as possible, work with a lead screen between us and the radium for protection to our bodies. The very penetrating rays from radium tend to weaken the worker. They will burn the skin, lower the red corpuscles in one's blood, lower the blood pressure, and tend to make one subject to pernicious anemia. But we are very careful, and the Public Health Service is interested in our well-being, takes our blood count frequently, gives us a thorough physical examination each year, and looks after us in a general way. The first effects of lowered vitality would show in the blood count, and as long as this is within normal range, we can feel quite sure that all is well with us.

We also do a small amount of photometric work in the testing of radium luminous materials such as are used on the dials of watches and clocks. This work was very important during the war, but has dropped to a minimum at present.

At one time we made emanation tests of various devices used to make water radioactive, and also of water from springs supposed to be of great healing power. We stopped these tests primarily because the producers used our reports in such a way as to make the consumer think that we were endorsing the therapeutic value of this weakly radioactive material. Also, when it became known that the Bureau made such tests, we soon became swamped with samples of ore, specimens of water from mineral springs, and various pads, belts, gloves, powders, and tablets, all supposed to be radioactive. Some were and more were not, but we had to stop the tests because we had more important work to do. The producers of all these devices claim that they will cure any ailment that has a name and some that haven't. Doctors have proved that water containing a prescribed amount of radium is beneficial, but most of the devices advertised contain such a minute quantity that there is no benefit from them. To the layman, though, the word "radium" has a magic sound, and if he sees advertised pads, lotions, pills, and other "radium" devices for a comparatively small sum, he immediately invests in some one of them, much to his loss. He does not know that radium treatment should be given only by physicians skilled in the use of the material.

The work, although routine, requires a considerable amount of accuracy and skill, but it is interesting, and, as I said at the start, the Bureau of Standards is a very interesting and educational place with its numerous laboratories for highly specialized work and its large staff of skilled scientists.

A DRY POINT OF QUEEN MARIE OF ROUMANIA
BY ELISABETH TELLING 1904

The drawing was made in an hour's time while Her Majesty ate luncheon at the Union League Club in Chicago. The date on the drawing should be November 16.

A Servant of the People

AGNES C. JONES

Miss Jones graduated in 1916. During the World War she was a unit chairman of the Council of National Defense in Maplewood, N. J., and captain of the Motor Division of the Newark Branch of the National League for Women's Service. She was the choice of the League as its representative to lay a wreath on the bier of the Unknown Soldier and marched in the procession to Arlington. In the fall of 1925 she won in the primaries on the Republican ticket and subsequently was elected to the Assembly—the lower house of the New Jersey Legislature. She was reëlected this fall and is now serving her second term in the Assembly. In addition to her political work she is still continuing as Supervisor of Visual Education in the South Orange and Maplewood schools. This means that she has charge of securing educational films and stereopticon slides for the schools. She goes to each of the ten schools in the district one day every other week to explain the various films and slides.

I BELIEVE that there is great opportunity for women in politics, and women all over the country are proving this. Within the next few days 122 women will take their places in 34 State Legislatures—eleven as State Senators. In my own state of New Jersey, nine Assemblywomen will take the oath of office. In addition to these members of the State Legislature, New Jersey boasts of one of the three women members of the present Congress, two members of the County Boards of Freeholders, and many other women who are serving in important elective and appointive offices.

In outlining what to me seem the most important qualifications for the aspirant to public office, I hope that my readers will appreciate that I realize my own limitations and am merely picturing for them my ideal woman politician.

The first and most important qualification is a real desire for some public service. This desire must be so strong that the potential candidate is willing to give up much of her social and personal life, for public office is a hard taskmaster. This is particularly true of the new entrant into public life, for besides having to devote a great deal of time to her office, she must of necessity attend many meetings and social functions. One's constituents wish to know personally for whom they are voting. During the last campaign, I made about 125 speeches, sometimes covering as many as ten meetings in one night. In some counties, naturally, the candidates are called on for less campaigning, but the county which I represent as one of twelve Assemblymen has a population of over 650,000 people. Right here let me say that a stomach of cast iron is an invaluable aid in any campaign. One day before the last election, I went to two afternoon teas, then spoke at a dinner, where everything was served from soup to nuts, and had refreshments served at four evening meetings. I must have had a starved look, for everyone insisted that I partake of various delicacies ranging from hot dogs and coffee to pickles and ice cream.

The real joy in my public career so far has been the contact with so many interesting people, with their divergent viewpoints. Anyone holding public office as the gift of the people must be tolerant of other people's religious, political, and other affiliations. Unless a woman has a real love for humanity there is no place for her in an elective office.   Being what is called "a good mixer" is an absolute essential.   Besides serving the public in the office one holds, there is rarely a day goes by that the politician is not asked for help in some direction. It may be to get information about someone in an institution or merely a request for copies of a bill, or for any one of a hundred different things, but each request must be taken care of promptly and cheerfully.

Many women entering public life optimistically believe that they are going to accomplish great reforms in our body politic.   They are apt to become embittered when they find out that they cannot change the world overnight. Any real reform takes years and years of constant drudging, and it is a wise maxim for the embryo politician to remember that "Rome wasn't built in a day."

In the Legislature, it is particularly important that one see issues above personalities.   Here one is required to answer yes or nay about a thousand times during a session.   Very often a good measure is defeated because of the lobbyists working for its passage, and likewise some poor measures are passed.

I can say truthfully that the men in politics are exceedingly courteous to all of the women even when they disagree with us on issues.   Of course, I can speak only for New Jersey, but I am sure that the women all over the States who are actively engaged in public life will agree with me.   One very important thing for the women to learn is not to take things personally.   I have seen men on the floor of the Senate or the House opposing each other's measures and apparently only waiting to get outside to have a "Dempsey-Tunney."   Fifteen minutes later, I have seen these same men eating luncheon together—apparently the reincarnation of David and Jonathan.   As for the men giving the women credit for having any brains, I believe that the men are very quick to recognize and reward ability, but only after the women are seen to have that elusive something called "political judgment."

A woman—or man, for that matter—who holds public office must have the courage to stand or fall by his or her convictions.   No one who is not well acquainted with legislative work can imagine the tremendous pressure brought to bear on any law-making group.   Selfish ambition has been the rock on which many politicians have grounded.   Politics is the one profession where ambition for higher office is apt to mar an otherwise brilliant career.   When the office-holder votes with one eye on the effect his vote may have on his personal advancement, the other eye may easily become blinded to public interests.

There are few fields outside of politics where the old system of apprenticeship still remains.   Men work their way up from the Ward and County Committees, and women must do likewise.   The whole structure of our political life is built on the Ward and County Committees of our two big parties.   It is here that the women can do real constructive work.   They soon learn the ropes and become invaluable not only to their parties but to their state.

If the women could only realize the tremendous power for good or evil of the average politician, they would see that not only they themselves but their families vote and vote intelligently at every election.   It is the politicians who decide how much money is to be raised by taxation and how this money is to be spent.   Is it to be spent wisely for good schools, good roads, and well staffed, up-to-date institutions to care for the unfortunate wards of the state, or is it to be spent foolishly and extravagantly? The public, through their votes, can determine how their money is to be appropriated.

I should like to appeal to Smith graduates all over this wonderful country of ours to exercise their franchise and to take an active interest in the management of the government in the locality in which they live. Theodore Roosevelt Jr. said recently that there are two classes of people in America, the governed and the governing. Those who vote are the governing. The product of Smith College should certainly always be among the governing.

Current Alumnae Publications

COMPILED BY NINA E. BROWNE

ALLEN, MARJORIE S. 1906 (Mrs. Seiffert). Ballad of a Man-made Woman; Ballad of a Wistful Lady; Black Kitchen; Thread for a Needle, in Braithwaite's Anthology of Magazine Verse, 1926.—The Hidden Door, in Outlook, Dec. 29.

APPLETON, HELEN L. 1908 (Mrs. Read). The Exhibition Idea in Germany, in The Arts, Oct.

BARBOUR, ELLEN G. 1903 (Mrs. Glines). No Roses, in Braithwaite's Anthology of Magazine Verse, 1926.

†BARNARD, FLORENCE, 1893–96. Outlook in Thrift Education. Boston, Savings Banks Assoc. of Mass. [Prize of $500.]

BEAUPRÉ, OLIVE K. 1904 (Mrs. Miller). Science and Art, in Christian Sci. Jour., Dec.

CARTER, OLIVE, 1911. (In collaboration with Stella Boothe.) The Mary Gay Stories. World Book Co.

†CHRYSLER, JOSEPHINE L. 1901. Pleasantville, Play Village for Blind Children, in Outlook for the Blind, Sept.

COIT, ELEANOR G. 1916. The Summer Industrial Conferences of the Y. W. C. A., in Workers' Education, Nov.

CONDÉ, BERTHA, 1895. Spiritual Adventuring. Studies in Jesus' Way of Life. Nashville, Tenn. Cokesbury Press.

CUTTER, ELIZABETH R. 1896 (Mrs. Morrow). Cheek of June; Lot's Wife; An Old Map, in Braithwaite's Anthology of Mag. Verse, 1926.—This Pine-tree, in Scribner's, Dec.

DEFOREST, CHARLOTTE B. 1901. An Interview, in Missionary Herald, June.—A Song of Ascents, in Christian Century, Nov. 25. —Thanksgiving, an Aspiration, in Congregationalist, Nov. 18.

DUTTON, MAUDE B. 1903 (Mrs. Lynch). From Door to Door, in Commonweal, June 16.—Five-Mile Book Shelf. Forum Reprint.—†The Magic Clothes-pins. Boston. Houghton.

† Already in collection.

EASTMAN, LUCY H. 1901–Dec. 1902 (Mrs. Reynolds). Lose not your Reward, in Christian Sci. Jour.—Spreading the Good News, in Christian Sci. Sentinel, July 24.

†FOSTER, M. LOUISE, 1891. Water as the Basis for a Study of Chemistry, in Jour. of Chemical Education, Oct.

GILCHRIST, MARIE E. 1916. Chance-fallen Seed, in Braithwaite's Anthology of Mag. Verse, 1926.

GILCHRIST, MARTHA D. 1900 (Mrs. Bayard). Reviews, in Commonweal, Aug. 11, Sept. 8. —Mr. Drinkwater puts Byron under a Microscope, in Internat. Book Review, Nov.

GRUENING, MARTHA, 1909. Learning by Living, in New Republic, Nov. 10.

HALL, EDITH H. 1899 (Mrs. Dohan). New Inscriptions from Cyprus, in Amer. Jour. of Archaeology, July–Sept.

HARTE, MAY A. J. 1901–03 (Mrs. Bosman). Woman's Place in Babylon, in Rosary Mag., Sept.—Cookery, Ancient and Modern, in R. M., Nov.

HASTINGS, MARY W. 1905 (Mrs. Bradley). Caravans and Cannibals. N. Y. Appleton.

†HAWKINS, ETHEL W. 1901. Review, in Atlantic, Dec.

HAZARD, GRACE W. 1899 (Mrs. Conkling). Brahms, No. 2 D Major, Op. 73, in Braithwaite's Anthology of Mag. Verse, 1926.— A Sonnet Letter, in North Amer. Rev., Dec.–Feb.—West Indies, in Commonweal, Sept. 22.—Porto Rico, in C., Dec. 1.

†HERMAN, MAIDA, 1912 (Mrs. Solomon). The Relation of Psychiatric Social Work to Mental Hygiene, in Mass. Soc. for Mental Hygiene, Monthly Bulletin, Oct.

IRWIN, ELISABETH A. 1903. The Youngest Intellectuals, in New Republic, Nov. 10.

†JENKINS, RUTH D. 1897 (Mrs. Jenkins). Tea-Wagon Suppers for the Holidays, in McCall's, Dec.

JUDSON, ALICE C. 1925. C. L. Sewing Circle, in Child Life, Dec.–Jan.

LEONARD, BAIRD, 1909 (Mrs. Zogbaum).
†Lines in Lieu of Lineaments, in Woman
Citizen, Nov.—Read These Books, in
Harper's Bazar, Jan.
LEWIS, MARY S. 1893-Apr. 1895 (Mrs.
Leitch). He Who Knows a River; On
Reading the Poetry of a Mystic; My Neigh-
bor Compares Her House with Mine; Webs,
in Braithwaite's Anthology of Mag. Verse,
1926.—The Unrisen Morrow. Phila Dor-
rance Co.
MAXSON, RUTH P. 1905 (Mrs. Aughiltree).
The Cruise of the Watermelon, in Motor
Camper and Tourist, Aug.—Four Sketches,
in L'Alouette, Spring.—Ghost, in Braith-
waite's Anthology of Mag. Verse, 1926.—
Of Quiet Things, in Christian Sci. Monitor,
Sept.—Round his Neck, in Detective
Story Mag., Sept.—The Wag of Wigs, in
D. S. M., Nov.—Wanderfoot to his Wife, in
Interludes, Apr.-May.—Will Shakespeare's
Widow, in Stepladder, July.
NICHOLL, LOUISE T. 1913. Encounter;
Glacier, in Braithwaite's Anthology of Mag.
Verse, 1926.—Pediment, in Commonweal,
Sept. 8.—Refraction, in Saturday Review
of Books, Nov. 13.—Terminal, in New
Masses, Aug.
OPPENHEIMER, EFFIE K. 1914 (Mrs. Vac-
tor). The Atheist, in The American
Israelite.
†PERRY, JENNETTE B. 1886 (Mrs. Lee). I
Enter the Kitchen at Fifty, in Pictorial
Rev., Jan.
PETHERBRIDGE, MARGARET, 1919 (Mrs. Far-
rar). The Cross Word Puzzle Book, Series
6. N. Y. Simon and Schuster.
PHILLIPS, JEANNETTE C. 1913 (Mrs. Gibbs).
Portia Marries. Boston. Little, Brown.
RICHARDSON, BERTHA J. 1901 (Mrs. Lucas).
Public Women in Married Life, in Book-
man, Nov.—†Women's Clubs, New Style,
in Woman Citizen, Nov.
†RUSSELL, ANNIE M. 1886 (Mrs. Marble).
Book Comrades in the Home, in Congrega-
tionalist, Dec. 2.—Mabel Osgood Wright,

† Already in collection.

in Boston Transcript, Dec. 11.—The Story
of Leatherstocking. N. Y. Appleton.
†SAVAGE, CLARA 1913 (Mrs. Littledale).
Two's Company. What's Three?, in Chil-
dren, Oct.
†SCUDDER, VIDA D. 1884. Review, in At-
lantic, Dec.—Social Ideals in English Let-
ters, a Reading Course, in Wellesley
Alumnae Mag., Oct.
SHERMAN, ELLEN B. 1891. Poems, in Bos-
ton Herald, Oct. 5, 7.—The Inner and
Outer Law [of Writing], in The Editor,
Sept. 25.
STOREY, VIOLET A. 1920. Grapes, in Good
Housekeeping, Nov.—A Prayer for the
New Year, in G. H., Jan.—A Little Girl
Comes to Visit [and] To Lucy, in Common-
weal, Nov. 10.—Neighborly, in Child Life,
Dec.
STORM, MARIAN, 1913. The Cuernavaca
Road, in N. Y. Herald Tribune, Sept. 22.—
†Discovery, in Forum, Nov.
SWETT, MARGERY, 1917. Corpus Christi, in
Braithwaite's Anthology of Mag. Verse,
1926.—More or Less Esoteric, in Bookman,
Oct.—Advice Before Rouging, in B., Nov.
and in N. Y. World, Nov. 14.—Confessions
of a Contributor, in Writer's Monthly, Nov.
—Troublesome Geese, in W. M., Jan.—
The Dull Sweet Pain of Nothingness, in
Poetry, Dec.—Whimsical Wisdom, in P.,
Jan.—Easy Cooking, in Progress, Nov.—
Furry Folks' Christmas, in Good Council,
Dec.—Why Women Fail in Business, in
North Amer. Rev., Dec.-Feb.
TRENT, LUCIA, 1919. Consolation, in Con-
temporary Verse, Aug.-Sept.—Dawn Stars.
N. Y. Harrison.—Gray Aftermath; Un-
revealed, in Braithwaite's Anthology of
Mag. Verse, 1926.—†Poems; Review, in
Greenwich Village Quill, Nov.
TUNNELL, BARBARA M. 1912-13. At the
Poetry Contest, in Century, Dec.
WHITCOMB, MARY S. 1900 (Mrs. Clark).
Letter, in Missionary Herald, June.
WYETH, HAZEL, 1916 (Mrs. Williams). Two
Back Yards, in Ladies Home Journal, Jan

Notes on Publications

WE note with pride that Smith alumnae are represented by ten authors contributing
twenty poems to Braithwaite's Anthology of Magazine Verse for 1926.

WE acknowledge with great appreciation the receipt from Little, Brown and Co. of an
autographed copy of "Portia Marries," by Jeannette Phillips Gibbs. Mrs. Gibbs,
Smith 1913, is the wife of A. Hamilton Gibbs. She was admitted to the Massachusetts Bar
in 1918, married in 1919, and practiced law for two years in a Boston office, and so the theme of
her novel—a law career after marriage—is one on which she is well-qualified to write. Mr.
and Mrs. Gibbs are spending the winter in Italy where they are working on two new novels.

Hide and Seek

Name	*First Class Mail returned from*
Helen Ames 11	c/o National City Bank, Kansas City, Mo.
Mrs. W. Howard Bailey 10 (Marion Richards)	Conway, N. H.
Marion Barnhart 16	1160 Gaylord St., Denver, Colo.
Dorothy Bartlett 21	8 Belleview St., Dorchester, Mass.
Mrs. Sheldon Booth 11 (Corinne Barbour)	87 Grand View Av., Wollaston, Mass.
Mrs. York Brennan 17 (Hilda Berry)	18 Gramercy Park, N. Y. C.
Pauline Breustedt 21	471 Park Av., N. Y. C.
Mrs. William W. Carr 92 (Margaret MacDougall)	43112 9th Av. N. E., Seattle, Wash.
Mary Dupee 24	5221 Cornell Av., Chicago.
Mrs. William E. Eaton 09 (Fanny Fiske)	c/o Naval Hospital, Chelsea, Mass.
Frances Eisner 24	174 Main St., Poughkeepsie, N. Y.
Zena Freedman 22	1040 Bryant Av., N. Y. C.
Hazel Gibbs 17	238 York St., New Haven, Conn.
Clara Hallock 06	259 S. Cherry St., Galesburg, Ill.
Edith Harkness 94	Evanshire Hotel, Evanston, Ill.
Mary Judson 99	604 W. 146 St., N. Y. C.
Marion Kohlrausch 17	129 W. 13 St., N. Y. C.
Mrs. Joseph A. McLinley 18 (Adeline Moore)	Virginia Court Apts., Vallejo, Calif.
Virginia Moore 24	122 E. 77 St., N. Y. C.
Edda Morgan 16	54 Scott St., Chicago.
Mrs. Myrl S. Myers 11 (Alice Brown)	2184 Glenwood Av., Toledo, O.
Edith Nicholls 19	94 Haine St., New Haven, Conn.
Alice O'Malley 98	467 Hudson St., Oakland, Calif.
Sybil Pease 13	44 Martin St., Cambridge, Mass.
Mrs. Henry L. Potter 12 (Doris Dow)	2856 W. 100 St., Chicago.
Mrs. Joseph H. Raney 02 (Hope Dill)	5514½ Lexington Av., Los Angeles, Calif.
Mrs. Joseph W. Ress 22 (Gertrude Schwartz)	2464 Geneva Ter., Chicago.
Mrs. Thomas L. Robinson 12 (Elizabeth Wilson)	Alamosa, Colo.
Mrs. James O. Safford 12 (Amy Waterbury)	South Dartmouth, Mass.
Martha Sims 14	Spartanburg, S. C.
A. Louise Smyth 10	141 Bigelow St., Newark, N. J.
Mrs. Bertha S. Stanford 00 (Bertha Sanford)	3509 5th Av., Pittsburgh, Pa.
Mabel Taylor 90	4 Arlington St., Boston, Mass.
Mrs. John J. Teal 16 (Isabelle O'Sullivan)	Ocean Drive W., Stamford, Conn.
Mrs. Philip W. Whitcomb 10 (Gertrude McClintock)	Osborn Rd., Walton-on-Thames, England.

LET US TALK OF MANY THINGS

OUR WIDOW'S CRUSE

THERE is one article in this issue which certainly does take us back! It is Professor Kimball's "A War Baby Grown Up," and just for our own amusement we searched into the archives of the QUARTERLY—make no mistake, even a publication only eighteen years old has its archives—for the number in which we timidly and letter by letter wrastled with that horrible word p-s-y-c-h-i-a-t-r-y. Nobody dared pronounce it above a whisper because nobody really knew where the accent fell and was fearful of herself falling too hard on the wrong syllable (although in all probability no one would have known that it was the wrong syllable!). Nobody except the very elect had the dreamiest idea what it was all about, and even the elect couldn't extract enough Anglo-Saxon words from the maze of scientific terms to make the matter crystal clear. But at all events a summer session in "Psychiatric Social Training"—a war emergency measure pure and simple—was launched at Smith in the forty-third year of the College and the first of the administration of President Neilson.

In fact, in the very same issue which bandied "psychiatry" and "psychiatric" from column to column appeared President Neilson's Inaugural Address and the Story of the Unit after the Great Retreat in March. Those were the days when our columns were filled to the last em with war news from at home and abroad, and well we remember wondering what on earth we should find to fill a QUARTERLY when those direful but thrilling days were done. And then the war ended; and the QUARTERLIES have been filled and filled and filled again like a veritable widow's cruse. We simply must resist the temptation (and, by the way, did you ever hear of the man who said he could resist anything but temptation?) of running through the tables of contents of these post-war years, for there is much editing

to be done and the Alumnae Council will soon be demanding its money's worth of QUARTERLY. But if anyone is under the delusion that an educational institution is a static place that gets a bit ingrowing in the midst of a changing world let her sit down with her back numbers of the QUARTERLY (no, that is too much to ask; they have gone the way of all flesh long since of course)—let her think of the college before those soul-inspiring, purse-emptying campaign days of the $4,000,000 Fund; before we had the Capen School; before the Quadrangle was started, let alone finished; before the New Gymnasium and Sage Hall were anything but castles too high in the air to belong to our world; before there were special honors; before the Juniors went to France and foreign students came to our campus and every wave of the Atlantic bore its hundreds of alumnae to European shores (which means of course before the war wrote Internationalism into our dictionaries and taught us that all the world is just next door); before, long before we planned a Birthday Gift or the thoughts of our Golden Jubilee filled every waking hour; before—well before there were any bobbed heads on the campus, and she will understand what a deal of musing the editor has done since reading Professor Kimball's article about the War Baby Grown Up and considering the college of only nine years ago.

Verily there isn't an issue in which some new educational adventure or beautiful addition to our physical equipment does not clamor for recognition, and this time there are three: the new curriculum, the Nursery School, and the Tryon Gallery. A word to the wise—and indeed we have no time to discuss them if we would for the alumnae notes have led us such a pace that we are simply breathless with our vain endeavor to make them stay put long enough to corrall them between covers. Never in all the experience of the QUARTERLY have those items bombarded it so insistently as now—over 1400 intelligent gentlewomen who once walked more or less decorously in our campus ways are sailing and steaming and flying all over the created universe.

Oh no, we need never fear that the cruse which supplies our QUARTERLIES will fail so long as President Neilson and the alumnae of Smith College go marching on.

E. N. H. 1903

"THE FAITH THAT IS IN YOU" IN a publication which goes to the alumnae at this time it seems impossible to ignore a question which is arousing in the press much unfavorable comment concerning the College which we love: namely, smoking in the college community. If we were to believe all we read— and it would appear from some of the letters which have come to our attention that many do believe all they read however ill-informed the source may be—we should conclude that Smith College has gone to the dogs and that every girl in it is under a cloud of smoke day and night and is conducting herself in a more or less rowdy manner in the tea rooms of the town.

This of course is perfectly unthinkable and on the face of it utterly absurd. We have only to go back to the college of our own day to realize that now as then at least four-fifths, and probably a larger proportion, of the student body are quietly going their ways as good citizens, ordering their lives in harmony with the high ideals for which the College stands and has stood since it opened its doors in 1875, and that it is the other unthinking fraction which in all college generations causes the problems that must be met.

This particular problem happens to be more conspicuous and puzzling than most problems, and it has been made conspicuous and puzzling not by the colleges but by society in general. The colleges did not introduce smoking into their communities, it was brought to them from the homes and communities from which the students come. In other words, the same society which is now so keenly and sincerely deploring the present situation is quite directly responsible for that situation, and, in so far forth, should prove itself most patient and sympathetic with the colleges in their attempts to reach a reasonable solution of the matter.

This problem is not peculiar to Smith College. All colleges for women are confronted with it; all colleges for women are praying for grace to say with St. Paul, "We are perplexed, but not unto despair." Some colleges may have found a solution which has really solved it to the satisfaction of students, administration, and alumnae. In some colleges the letter of the law may lie down with the spirit like the lion and the lamb. If this is anywhere true, we congratulate such colleges from our hearts, and confess that that happy day has not yet arrived at Smith.

Why is this so? The reasons that come to our mind most compellingly are that the student affairs at Smith are in the hands of Student Government; that the administration is playing fair with Student Government and keeping hands off; and that the unthinking fraction of the student body previously mentioned has failed to establish any connection between the letter and the spirit of the law. President Neilson made a very fine address at Last Chapel last June in which he explained to parents and friends the attitude of Student Government and of the administration at the time the smoking question intruded itself so insistently. He said:

More and more it was impossible for the Student Council to treat this as a moral issue without reflecting on the moral standards of a large number of the families of our students. The administration did not feel that this was a happy time for it to step in and remove from the student body jurisdiction in this matter. Clearly a system of student government which was subject to having taken out of its hands at any moment any matter on which the administration had a different opinion would soon collapse. If the administration trusts the Student Government Association to make decisions on these matters, it must be prepared to stand by what it does—its mistakes as well as its wisdom. It has done so in this case at the cost of many protests, at the cost of much offense to good people and the friends of the College because it believed that keeping faith with the students in this matter of self-government was of more importance than those matters of manners and health which seemed to some extent to be compromised. So the students this spring decided that they would smoke in college, and they have, . . . Meantime, the present situation must be frankly acknowledged to be the outcome of the principle of education on which we are proceeding.

In the letter which Mrs. Scales and the President sent in the summer to the parents of Smith students, they said:

It is a fundamental principle at Smith College that we seek to develop in the students the power of self-direction. The freedom necessary for such development inevitably involves the possibility of mistakes and a certain amount of waste, but without such a risk character cannot grow. . . .

There are, of course, limits to the Grant of Powers given to Student Government. For instance, the attendance system operative last year was modified by the Faculty this year because the College found itself unable to fulfill its academic responsibilities when students absented themselves in such numbers from class exercises. In chapel this morning (January 17) the President spoke of the clause in the Grant of Powers which stipulates that the administration shall have jurisdiction in matters pertaining to the relationship between the college and the community; he emphasized the importance of a right attitude towards student government if it is to be a workable system of government for a college community; he once more reminded them of their tendency to formulate rules suitable for adults and then to live under them like little children whose joy it is to try to beat the game. He stated clearly the unenviable position in which the unthinking fraction of the college was putting the administration and the rest of the student body, and he reiterated the desire of the administration still to believe that the students are capable of conducting their affairs wisely and without interference.

We may or we may not believe in student government, but certainly the President pays no empty compliment to the students, for to give a reason for the faith that is in him in the face of so much criticism takes a kind of courage that we must hope will be rewarded. Surely it is the part of the alumnae to demonstrate their faith in their college by remembering that the administrative officers and a very large majority of Smith College students have the smoking problem very much at heart and are seeking patiently and zealously for its solution.

EDITH N. HILL 1903

PLEASE KEEP OFF THE GRASS WHILE agreeing with Mr. Eliot* that it would be both interesting and profitable to have a model theater at Smith (sometime in that dim Utopia when we have enough dormitories and classrooms and

* November QUARTERLY. "A College Theatre."

office space) I rise to protest at his choice of location. If there is one part of the campus that is dear to alumnae tradition it is the stretch of green between the Alumnae Gymnasium and Students' Building. It means spring nights, and step sings, and all those delightful and intangible sensations that the thought of undergraduate days brings to mind. For the good of the College we come back to Northampton and gladly lose our way in a maze of new buildings and unfamiliar faces, but for the good of our alumnae souls leave us intact this one cherished reminder of the days when we too "were only seventeen."   1919

RESPONSES TO ANTI-OBITUARY JUDGING from various personal letters which have come to the editor since printing the letter by Anti-Obituary in the November QUARTERLY and making comments on the problem of In Memoriams in our publication, the editor did not make herself entirely clear. Neither she nor her board has "decided to give up publishing tributes to alumnae," as one alumna understood. They simply present the whole problem as a most difficult and important question and beg that the subscribers to the QUARTERLY and the class secretaries consider it seriously and help the editorial board in its solution. We print below two perfectly definite and helpful reactions from two class secretaries, and also a clear statement from another alumna, who we hoped would elaborate her reasons for her opinion. We shall be glad of further comment in the May issue.

1 *Dear Editor:* In response to the question in the last QUARTERLY by Anti-Obituary, I emphatically say by all means omit In Memoriams.

If there are those who still like them, or if a member is unusually prominent in her class, could not the obituary be included in a class letter?

I only regret that I was not the one to propose this, for I have talked about it so much to my family. To be personal, I will cite the Dartmouth magazine, which dwells at such length on the finest qualities of those who have gone on that I find the class news columns most depressing.

Soon after I became secretary a year ago, a classmate wrote the following: "Much as I love to read about my old pals in the QUARTERLY, I would rather find a scanty column than such as I read awhile ago. I happened to glance through the notes of a class some years ahead of ours, and it seemed to me that every member was either recovering from an operation or about to undergo one! It sounded like a hospital ward, or the front porch of a sanitarium."

Having the same feeling about this, I omitted the news of an accident to a classmate recently, which was sent to me by another classmate, especially because the girl was all right at the time the clippings reached me. I wrote to the thoughtful classmate and explained my idea of happier news, and inserted one bit of livelier interest I found concerning this unfortunate girl. Yours most sincerely, E. M. A.

2 The suggestion made in the last QUARTERLY to omit In Memoriams of deceased graduates appeals to me as eminently desirable. "Anti-Obituary" in her letter covers the objections tersely and completely.

In the interest of good taste and of good sense, let us confine our eulogies to our class letters.   F. E. J.

3 I have some remembrance that such tributes were to be eliminated from the QUARTERLY in the future. I think the action is drastic but I accept your good judgment if you still think it seems best. I am sorry for the Judgment. . . . * * *

A GESTURE OF PROTEST THERE is a tiny mote in the interesting compilation of data about Smith Women on School Boards in the November QUARTERLY * which led me to consult the dictionary definitions of dogmatism. But it befell that the dictionary terms were too violent to suit my purpose. I could not without giving justifiable offense say that this mote is "unduly or presumptuously positive or authoritative in manner of utterance," that it is written "with bold and undue confidence or arrogance," or that it asserts "a matter of opinion as if it were fact" or asserts "a matter of fact without due evidence." Such terms might be germane to a learned assault upon The Dogmatic Pedagogy of 1926 versus Intellectual Rights of Conscience. But it happens that it is only a gentle, ladylike gesture of protest that I would make against the coupling of an anti-vaccination attitude to the "inconceivable ignorance and prejudice' of using an end of rubber hose for corporal punishment. It is quite probable that the rural school board with which the Smith woman struggled in vain had not been moved to its attitude by a

"Smith Women on School Boards."

searching and scientific investigation into the inefficacy of vaccination, but may we not admit that it might have been, along with many good doctors and true, who are as ready to write the dictionarial "obs. or archaic" against this term as against the rubber hose?

* * *

MIDYEARS FOR ALUMNAE NEXT week the shadow of Midyears falls on the College, and somehow it seems as though for the sake of Auld Lang Syne we alumnae should put ourselves through a bit of an examination also. And so we reprint the sixty-seven questions of the Smith Quiz which the Alumnae Office has revised for the Smith clubs.* True to the form of all midyears we do *not* publish the answers, but we know where they are to be had if any of them have slipped your minds!

1. When did Smith open its doors to students?
2. How many were in the first graduating class?
3. Who was the chief adviser of Sophia Smith?
4. Where was Sophia born?
5. Which is the oldest dormitory?
6. What was the original endowment of Smith?
7. What is the present endowment?
8. What was the original acreage of the campus?
9. What is the present acreage?
10. What is the motto of the college?
11. In what county of Massachusetts is Smith?
12. Where is the President's house?
13. Where and what is the Browsing Room?
14. Name one head of house and tell which house
15. Name the 6 dormitories in the quadrangle.
16. What is the residence requirement at college?
17. How many times may a student change her campus assignment during the 4 years?
18. Name 3 distinguished members of the Faculty
19. Name any published work of any member of the Faculty, past or present
20. Has there ever been one of your classmates on the Faculty, and, if so, who?
21. What are the minimum and maximum salaries paid to members of the teaching faculty?
22. Who is the Warden of the college?
23. What are her duties?
24. Who is the Dean of the college?
25. What are her duties?
26. Who is the Treasurer of the college?
27. Name one class dean

* Originated by the Rhode Island Club.
Revised by the Alumnae Office, 1926.

28. Who is the College Physician?
29. In whose memory was the college chime given?
30. In whose memory was the college organ given?
31. Who wrote "Fair Smith"?
32. Who wrote "Alma Mater"?
33. Name 3 departmental societies or clubs
34. What degrees are given in course by Smith?
35. In what month does Mountain Day occur?
36. Name 3 social events of the year
37. Name the 4 class colors and in proper order beginning with the freshman class
38. Name one literary organization in college
39. Name one student publication
40. What is the tuition at Smith per year?
41. What is the regular price of room and board in a dormitory per year?
42. What are the 3 houses in which living expenses are less?
43. How do they differ?
44. Name 4 ways in which the students help themselves financially through college
45. Name 2 portraits owned by the college
46. What kind of a School conducts a summer session at Smith?
47. What is the largest building in the Smith College group?
48. Where and what is Graham Hall?

49. State within 50 the number of under-graduate students in college this year
50. State within 25 the number of graduate students in college this year
51. What is the name of the religious organization of the college?
52. From what institution of learning did President Neilson come to Smith?
53. How many trustees are there?
54. What is the length of term of those elected by the board?
55. How many trustees are elected by the alumnae?
56. What is the length of their term?
57. Name 2 men and 2 women trustees of the college
58. State within 500 the number of alumnae
59. Name 3 distinguished living graduates
60. Name one officer of the Alumnae Association and tell what office she holds
61. What is the "Institute for the Coördination of Women's Interests"?
62. What is the first practical experiment of the Institute?
63. What does the Students' Aid Society do?
64. How must a girl qualify to join the group of Juniors in France?
65. What is meant by "Special Honors"?
66. What are the qualifications for "Special Honors"?
67. What are the Experimental Schools?

The President Burton Memorial Fund

THE President Burton Memorial Committee, after its appointment in the spring, consulted with those who were most familiar with President Burton and with Smith, and agreed that a Scholarship Fund was the most fitting memorial to one who had devoted much of his time and energy to give others an opportunity for study under favorable conditions. The President Burton Memorial Fund is, therefore, to be a scholarship fund, administered by the Trustees of the College, in units sufficiently large to defray most of the expenses of the recipients, thus being distinctive among scholarships at Smith. President Neilson said of it: "None of the suggestions so far made seems to me to combine so well the double purpose of benefit to the scholarship of the College and a living memorial to President Burton," and President Comstock writes: "I am delighted to hear that the memorial to President Burton is to be a scholarship fund. Nothing, I feel sure, would please him better and nothing could be more useful to the College."

There seems to be a mistaken notion that Smith is comparatively well endowed with Scholarship Funds. On the contrary, the deficiency in that line has to be met from current funds. President Neilson's article [page 141], will explain our status and show that not only to do honor to President Burton but also to serve our Alma Mater, we may well make the fund a large one.

Though a Scholarship Fund is useful, obviously, in proportion to its size, the spirit of gifts to this memorial is more important than their amounts. No goal has, therefore, been set for the fund. The $10,000 already contributed or pledged, comes from over a thousand alumnae of 28 classes in amounts varying up to $250, and is both representative and generous. This will yield, however, only $500 annually. A small amount from everyone reading this article will double our fund, while large amounts will help to give Smith a scholarship endowment equal to those of her sister institutions. Ten girls in Tenney House in 1917 bought a Liberty Bond. They have just sent it with the accumulated interest to the President Burton Memorial Fund.

Pledge cards will be enclosed in the March notices from the Alumnae Association for the convenience of those who have not already contributed to the fund.

JEAN A. PATON 1914, *Chairman*

NEWS FROM NORTHAMPTON

BULLETIN BOARD

VESPERS.—The vesper speakers since Nov. 1 have been: President Bernard I. Bell, S.T.B., of St. Stephens College; President Irving Maurer, D.D., LL.D., of Beloit College; Rev. J. Edgar Park, D.D., of West Newton; Rev. Ralph W. Sockman, D.D., of New York City; Rev. Robert Seneca Smith of Yale; Rev. Henry H. Tweedy, D.D., of Yale Divinity School; President Neilson; Rev. Samuel V. V. Holmes, D.D., of Buffalo; Dean Charles R. Brown, D.D., LL.D., of Yale Divinity School; Rev. Gaius Glenn Atkins, D.D., L.H.D., of Detroit; Rev. William P. Merrill of New York City.

CONCERTS.—The second concert of the Smith College Concert Course was given Nov. 24 by Richard Crooks, tenor; and the third was given Dec. 15 by the English Singers. Walter Gieseking, pianist, appeared Jan. 25 as the fourth number of the Course.

The Flonzaley Quartet gave a concert in Sage Hall, Nov. 3. The first Elshuco concert was given by the Elshuco Trio on Nov. 17, and the second by the South Mountain Quartet, Jan. 19.

A joint concert by the Dartmouth and Smith Glee Clubs was given Dec. 8.

There have been six faculty recitals: a piano recital by Professor Duke; a recital by the orchestra, accompanied by violin and piano; a recital by Professors Donovan, Duke, Marie Milliette, and Ruth Willian; a two-piano recital by Professors Hall and Locke; a song recital by Professor Sinclair; and a piano recital by Professor Robinson.

A student recital was given on Dec. 14, and on Dec. 15 there was a concert by the Mandolin Club.

Organ recitals were given daily during midyears.

LECTURES.—The following lectures have been given: "How the Classics Came Down to Us" by Dr. E. A. Lowe of the University of Oxford; "University Life in Oxford and Cambridge" by Professor Margaret Crook (Biblical Literature); "University Life in France" by Professor Hélène Cattanès (French); "University Life in London and Other British Cities" by Miss Clarke (Philosophy)—these last three under the auspices of the Committee on Exchange of Students; "The Centenary of St. Francis of Assisi" (in Italian) by Professor Anacleta Vezzetti (Italian); "The New Era in Palestinian Archaeology" (illustrated) by Dr. W. F. Albright, Director of the American School of Archaeology at Jerusalem (auspices of the Department of Biblical Literature); "Anatole France intime" (documents inédits) by Edouard Champion of Paris (auspices of the Department of French); "Undergraduate Study in France" by Professor Cattanès; "The Scientific Attitude" by President George E. Vincent of the Rockefeller Foundation; "Ancient Utopias" by Professor Gilbert Murray; "The Frontier Woman" and "The Life of Pasteur" (motion pictures); "The Birth of Art in the Caves of France and Spain" (illustrated) by Miss Mary E. Boyle (auspices of the Departments of Art and History); "The Economic, Political, and Moral Results of Fascism" by Professor Gaetano Salvemini, formerly of the University of Florence; "Evolution and Contemporary Philosophy" by Professor R. F. A. Hoernlé of the University of the Witwatersrand, Johannesburg; "The Human Talking Machine" and "The Nature and Development of Human Speech" by Sir Richard Paget of London; "The Distinctive Function of Woman in Creating a New Type of Civilization " by Dr. Felix Adler of the Society for Ethical Culture (William H. Baldwin Jr. Memorial Lectureship).

A lecture was given Nov. 5 by Richard Curle under the auspices of the Hampshire Bookshop on "Conrad's Voyages in the Nations in His Books."

At the meetings of the International Relations Club the following questions have been discussed: "The War Debts: Germany's Reparation, Anglo-American Settlement"; "Discussion on the Best Policy for the United States Regarding War Debts: The French Debt"; "New Europe" by Dr. Ernst Jäckh of the Institute of Political Science in Berlin; "Present-Day China."

THE LIBRARY.—Two gifts have been received by the Library. One of them, given by Professor Elizabeth Hanscom, consists of two books given her in 1895 by Mrs. Martha Smith Tenney, former owner of Tenney House. They are "The Improvement of the Mind" by Isaac Watts, D.D., published by James Loring's Sabbath School Book-Store of Boston in 1829; and "An Abridgement of Lectures on Rhetoric" by Hugh Blair, D.D., published in Northampton in 1818.

The second gift, from Mrs. Alice (Peloubet) Norton '82, consists of nine volumes of the S. Converse edition of the works of Jonathan Edwards. The third volume of the complete ten is missing, but fortunately was already owned by the Library, having been presented by Olive Rumsey from an early edition of the same set.

LYMAN PLANT HOUSE.—The annual exhibition of chrysanthemums by the class in horticulture was held at the Plant House, Nov. 11–13.

THE SMITH COLLEGE MUSEUM OF ART.— The second special exhibition of the year, on view in November, consisted of a group of landscapes and figure pieces by a number of the best known American painters of the last half-century. It was loaned through the courtesy of the Macbeth Galleries of New York and the Vose Galleries of Boston.

The third special exhibition consisted of a group of French Landscapes of the 19th Century, loaned by the Boston Museum of Fine Arts.

The fourth special exhibition consisted of Chinese and Korean works of art from the collection of His Excellency J. S. Oiesen.

Fifty-nine drawings of antique statuary by

Ingres were on view in the Tryon Gallery for one week in January. They were loaned by DeHauke and Co. of New York.

OTHER NEWS.—The Children's Home Association presented Ruth Draper, monologuist, in a performance in John M. Greene Hall, Dec. 3.

Jacques Copeau, Director of the Théâtre du Vieux Colombier, read in French, Jan. 17, the play "L'annonce faite à Marie" by Paul Claudel. On Jan. 18, he read Racine's "Andromaque."

Departmental Notes

President Neilson attended the meeting of the Board of Directors of the Coöperative Bureau for Women Teachers on Nov. 6. On that date, he also addressed the meeting of the New Haven Smith Club. On Nov. 9, he broadcast from station WEEI, having accepted their invitation, with twenty-six other New England college presidents, to join in an educational program. He presided at a luncheon of the Foreign Policy Association in Springfield, Dec. 11, a meeting which Mrs. Bernard also attended.

Mrs. Scales spoke before the New York Smith Club on Nov. 19 and will address the Bridgeport Smith Club in February.

Dean Bernard addressed a meeting of the Holyoke Smith Club, Dec. 6.

Miss Blake spoke before the Philadelphia Smith Club on Dec. 11, and addressed the Cambridge Smith Club on Jan. 24.

Mrs. Ethel (Puffer) Howes told the Smith Club of Lynn of the work of the Institute for the Coördination of Women's Interests at its meeting Nov. 29.

ART.—Professor Churchill was recently elected vice-president of the College Art Association of America.

BIBLE.—Professor Harlow attended a two-day conference, called by Sherwood Eddy, of those interested in social and religious problems. It was held at International House, New York City.

Professor Wood read a paper before the Society of Biblical Literature and Exegesis in New York, Dec. 28 and 29, on "Borrowing in Religion." He was elected president of the Society for 1927. Mr. Wood was president for 1926 of the National Association of Biblical Instructors which met at Columbia, Dec. 29–30. He gave the presidential address on "Religious Values and Academic Teaching."

Professor Margaret Crook attended the meetings of both these societies and Professor Bixler attended the second. Miss Crook spoke in Montreal on Sunday, Nov. 28, preaching at the Church of the Messiah in the morning and at the People's Forum in the evening, broadcasting the address.

BOTANY.—Professor Elizabeth Genung spoke on "Teaching Bacteriology in a College of Liberal Arts" at the 28th annual meeting of the Society of American Bacteriologists held in Philadelphia, Dec. 28–30.

ECONOMICS AND SOCIOLOGY.—Professor Barnes addressed the annual conference on the teaching of history, held at Philadelphia, Dec. 4, and on Dec. 6 he addressed the Freethinker's Society of New York. He spoke before the Detroit Labor Forum on Dec. 12. Professor Barnes was elected one of the vice-presidents of the American Association for the Advancement of Science. On Dec. 28 he was one of the opening day speakers of the 41st annual meeting of the American Historical Association held in Rochester. His subject was "The Essentials and Non-Essentials of the New History." At the 21st annual meeting of the American Sociological Society held at St. Louis, Dec. 28–31, he read a paper on "English Sociology," and also presided over the division on Historical Sociology. The Roll of Honor for 1926 in *The Nation* contains his name, listed under literature "for his efforts to discover and set forth the truth as to the origin of the World War."

Professor Hankins will go to New York every week-end the second semester where he will conduct a course of graduate work in sociology at Columbia.

ENGLISH.—Professor Grace Hazard Conkling's sonnet sequence in the December issue of the *North American Review* has been awarded a first prize by the Poetry Society of America. "Poetry In and Out of School" was the subject of a lecture given by Mrs. Conkling at the meeting of the Teachers' Association of New York State, held at Rochester, Nov. 4. She has begun a series of lectures to continue throughout the year at Bradford Academy.

Professor Katharine Woodward gave a report at the meeting of the Mount Holyoke and Amherst College Chapters of the Phi Beta Kappa Association in New York, Dec. 9. The meeting commemorated the sesquicentennial of the Society.

FRENCH.—Professors Schinz, Guilloton, Grant, Louise Bourgoin, Yvonne Imbault-Huart, Guiet, Marthe Sturm, and Miss Titchener attended a meeting of the Modern Language Association, held at Harvard, Dec. 29, 30, and 31. Professor Schinz presided, and Professor Grant served as secretary of a group meeting on the subject of French Literature of the 19th Century. Professor Guilloton read a paper on "La Querelle de la Poésie Pure."

Professor Robert has been chosen one of the five examiners in French for the College Examination Board. On Nov. 11 and 12 he attended a meeting of the New Jersey Modern Language Teachers' Association at Atlantic City, where he presented a paper on "Intensive Reading as a Means of Modern Language Learning."

GOVERNMENT.—Professor Kimball toured the middle west, Dec. 16–22, speaking before Smith Clubs and visiting clinics in connection with his work as director of the Smith College School for Social Work.

HISTORY.—Professor Bassett has been elected secretary of the American Historical Association.

Professor Fay presided at the general session on Modern European History which ended the recent conference of the American Historical Association, held at Rochester.

HYGIENE AND PHYSICAL EDUCATION.—Professor Abby Belden spoke on "The Outing Club as a Part of the College Sports Program" at Skidmore, Dec. 9.

An eight weeks' course in Girl Scout leadership, sponsored by the department, is being given by Miss Elsa Becker of the National Girl Scout Headquarters in New York. It began Nov. 8.

MUSIC.—Professor Welch was one of the speakers at the semicentennial celebration of the Music Teachers' National Association, held in Rochester, Dec. 28, 29, and 30.

FACULTY SCIENCE CLUB.—The meetings of the Club have been addressed by Professor Frances Grace Smith on "The Biological Laboratory at Barro Colorado Island, Panama"; by Professor Dunn on "The Trip to the East Indies"; by Paul F. Kerr, Ph.D., of Columbia, on "X-Ray Crystal Methods Applied to Mineral Study"; and by Dr. Robert H. Galt on "The Tactual Sense in Relation to the Reception of Sounds of Speech."

SABBATICAL ABSENCES have been granted

as follows: for the year, Professors John Spencer Bassett, Howard R. Patch, Harris H. Wilder, Inez W. Wilder, Associate Professor Eleanor S. Duckett, Mary A. Dunham, Librarian. For the second semester, Professors Caroline B. Bourland, Edna A. Shearer, H. Edward Wells.

LEAVE OF ABSENCE for the second semester has been granted to Assistant Professor Margaret G. Scott.

OTHER NEWS.—A daughter was born to Professor and Mrs. Robert Withington on Nov. 20.

PUBLICATIONS.—Barnes, Harry Elmer. "The Repression of Crime." N. Y. George H. Doran.

Blake, Mabelle Babcock. "Guidance for College Women, a Survey and a Program for Personnel Work in Higher Education." D. Appleton and Co.

Foster, Mary Louise. "Life of Lavoisier." Smith College Monographs.

Hankins, Frank H. "The Racial Basis of Civilization." A. A. Knopf.

Hicks, Granville. "Eight Ways of Looking at Christianity." Macmillan.

Lieder, Paul R. and Lovett, R. M. (Univ. of Chicago) and Root, R. K. (Princeton). Editors "Readings in English Literature." Houghton, Mifflin Co.

Patch, Howard R. and Withington, Robert. Contributors to the new book, "Essays in Memory of Barrett Wendell," published by the Harvard University Press, Oct. 1926.

Undergraduate News

ATHLETICS.—The Annual Fall Field Day which was to have taken place on Nov. 24 had to be cancelled because of the weather.

Fall Crew competition for form was held Nov. 17.

The Outing Club took its fifth annual winter trip this year under the leadership of Professor Abby Belden. The party left Boston Dec. 30, spent a week exploring Waterville Valley, New Hampshire, and returned to Northampton.

During the Christmas vacation both the Chestnut Hill cabin and the new Brook cabin were robbed and almost everything of value taken. The loss was about $150.

The Athletic Association has reopened the Allen Field Club House as a tea room. The two upper floors are devoted to attractive bedrooms where guests of students may stay while in Northampton, and in which students themselves may stay without losing one of the "seven nights" allowed them by the new residence rule.

The juniors won the interclass hockey tournament, defeating the sophomores in the final game with a score of 3–2. The All-Smith hockey team is: Janet Olmsted and Leslie Winslow '27, Frances Galt, Elizabeth Hilleary, Virginia Marshall, Emily Pettee, Caroline Schauffler, and Elizabeth Waidner '28, Marion Neilson, Agnes Rodgers, and Louise Veo '29. Senior: Catherine Cole, Ruth Sears, Theodora Wagner, Rives Stuart, Kathryn Patterson, Wilhelmina Luten, Leslie Winslow, Dorothea Breed, Janet Olmsted, Marjorie Dow, Selma Erving. Junior: Margaret Lee, Virginia Marshall, Elizabeth Waidner, Julia Hafner, Emily Pettee, Edith Sedgwick, Frances Galt, Elizabeth Hilleary, Caroline Schauffler, Barbara Ellis, Polly Bullard. Sophomore: Margaret Palfrey, Agnes Rodgers, Jeanie Kerns, Mary Hollister, Marion Neilson, Virginia Veach, Eleanor Langdon, Mary Nisbet, Sarah Shurtleff, Elizabeth Edwards, Louise Veo. Freshman: Sarah Furst, Lucie Bedford, Haideen Henderson, Florence Meeker, Cordelia Dumaine, Frances Furst, Fanny Curtis, Janet Mahony, Barbara Hall, Priscilla Fairchild, Emeline Shaffer.

The seniors won the interclass soccer tournament, defeating the sophomores in the final game. The All-Smith soccer team is: Mary Arnold, Helen Ferguson, Pearl Hathaway, Elizabeth Hawkins, Alice Ripley '27, Mary V. Mills, Evelyn Niemann, Marion Smith '28, Mary McClintock, Janet MacInnes, Frances Ranney, and Sally Redman '29. Senior: Alice Ripley, Helen Ferguson, Doris Pinkham, Katharine Bannon, Elizabeth Walling, Pearl Hathaway, Elizabeth Hawkins, Marjorie Madden, Mary Arnold, Margaret Hebard, Elinor Chaplin. Junior: Mary Gaylord, Elizabeth Taylor, Alice Blodgett, Katherine Campbell, Margaret Stone, Evelyn Niemann, Elizabeth Newman, Marion Smith, Nell Hirschberg, Victoria Pederson, Mary V. Mills. Sophomore: Elizabeth Buechner, Frances Ranney, Carolyn Bixler, Sally Redman, Mary McClintock, Janet MacInnes, Hilma Peterson, Mary Steele, Priscilla Feeley, Eugenie Paterson, Sally J. Hill. Freshman: Elizabeth Babcock, Arline Genthner, Margaret Goodlatte, Antoinette Ockert, Eileen Selkirk, Adelaide Hall, Ruth Belden, Martha Shaeffer, Ruth Watrous, Naomi Bruce, Edda Renouf.

The advanced classes in swimming have been playing water polo, and have had informal teams, with competitions. Classes in swimming for members of the faculty are held on Tuesday nights. There are also classes in swimming and gymnastics for children of the faculty.

CONFERENCES.—Katharine Bingham '27, president of Student Council, attended the conference of the Women's Intercollegiate Association for Self-Government held at Trinity College, Washington, D. C. The members of the conference represented 55 eastern colleges.

Caroline Roberts '27 represented Smith at the second annual conference of the National Federation of Colleges, held at the Univ. of Michigan, Dec. 4, 5, 6. The general subject for discussion was "The Students' Part in Education."

Sarah Morrow '27, business manager of Weekly, attended the conference of Business and Advertising Managers of Eastern Women's College Newspapers held in New York. They visited the offices and inspected the plant of the New York World.

A Women's Intercollegiate News Conference was held at Vassar, Nov. 12, 13, 14, to discuss newspaper problems and receive expert advice. Alene Smith, editor of Weekly, and Sarah Morrow '27 represented Smith.

The annual conference of fifteen eastern college Press Boards was held Dec. 4 and 5 at Mount Holyoke College. Miss Margaret Farrand, director of Press Board, Theodora Wagner '27, president, and Hilda Pfeiffer '27, news editor, went from Smith.

Fifteen delegates from Smith attended the Milwaukee Students' Conference from Dec. 28–Jan. 1. They discussed various aspects of the theme "What Resources Has Jesus for Life in Our World?" The conference included several large meetings at which speakers of eminence gave their views: Henry Sloane Coffin, Reinhold Niebuhr, Charles W. Gilkey, Glen Clark, Richard Roberts, Harry Emerson Fosdick, and others. Besides these there were smaller, more personal gatherings under the guidance of discussion leaders. Florence Lyon '28 headed the Smith delegation. Two foreign students, Harano Kiyo of Japan and Louise Goepfert of Germany, were members of the group. The others were: Mary Clark, Doheny Hackett, Clementine Miller, Doris Russell, Charleta Taylor, Josephine Woolfolk '27, Beatrice Edwards,

Elizabeth Fleming, Jane Harding, Helen Sage, Constance Stockwell, and Agnes Woodhull '28. Miss Mary Mensel '18, Assistant Warden, accompanied the delegation.

DEBATING.—A Cambridge-Smith debate was held Nov. 5, on the subject: "Resolved that this house deplores the policy of the University of Cambridge respecting women." The speakers for the affirmative were Caroline Roberts and Harriet Jones '27, Charlotte Drummond '28. The speakers for the negative were H. B. Herklots of Trinity College, A. L. Hutchinson of Christ's College, and Wilfred Gurney Fordham of Magdalene College.

DRAMATICS.—The Workshop presented three experimental plays on Nov. 10, at Students' Building: Hartley Alexander's "Earth-Trapped," produced by Hansen Currier '27; "Silver Spangles," a Hallowe'en fantasy by Patrick Scarlet, produced by Margaret Grout '28; and Alfred Kreymborg's "People Who Die," produced by Doris Russell '27.

"Sappho and Phaon," by Percy MacKaye, was the fall production of D. A. on Dec. 6.

ELECTIONS.—College song leader, Bertha Kirk '27.

1928: chairman of Junior Prom, Aletta Freile; fire captain, Barbara Mettler.

1929: president, Dorothy Harger; vice-president, Effie Manson; secretary, Frances Adams; treasurer, Elizabeth Baker; song leader, Esther Beard. Effie Manson is the daughter of Effie (Comey) Manson '98 and Frances Adams is the daughter of Margaret (Potter) Adams ex-'04.

1930: president, Helen Teagle; vice-president, Priscilla Fairchild; secretary, Katharine Adams; treasurer, Susan Albright; song leader, Helen Hebbard; choir leader, Lois Hoover. Helen Teagle is the daughter of Alice (Wright) Teagle '04 and Susan Albright is the daughter of Susan (Fuller) Albright '91.

S. C. A. C. W.—The speakers at the Tuesday evening meetings have been: Mrs. Scales; Barrett Rich of Louisville, Ky.; Ernest V. Stires of Alexandria, Va.; Mr. Zero of New York City. On Dec. 14, the meeting was held in the Browsing Room, and consisted of readings by President Neilson.

STUDENT GOVERNMENT.—A new smoking rule went into effect after the Christmas holidays. The action was taken by a vote of the student body in recognition of the fire risk involved in smoking in the dormitories. Students may smoke along the path around Paradise Pond, in the Boat House, and in the tea rooms in Northampton. (Certain tea rooms have decided not to allow smoking: namely, the Mary Marguerite and the Manse. In Beckmann's smoking is allowed only on the second floor.)

OTHER NEWS.—Dr. Harry Emerson Fosdick, pastor of the Park Avenue Baptist Church of New York, and one of the Trustees of the College, will be the 1927 Commencement speaker.

Dr. Henry H. Tweedy of Yale Divinity School is to be the speaker at the Week of Prayer services, Feb. 13–18.

Mr. Kenneth Lindsay of London, who is now making a speaking tour of this country under the auspices of the League for Industrial Democracy, addressed the undergraduates in chapel, Nov. 9.

Mr. Frederick J. Libby, of the National Council for the Prevention of War, one of the most effective organizations in the country working for the preservation of the peace of the world, spoke in chapel, Nov. 23.

Smith College is planning to enter a candidate in the second annual Intercollegiate Current Events Contest which is being sponsored by the *New York Times*. The local prize is $250 and a medal, the winner of which competes with the students of other colleges for a prize of $500.

Golden Rule Sunday was observed at the College, Dec. 12. All the campus houses had soup, stew, and prunes for dinner, the typical dinner of a Near East orphan—instead of the usual soup, chicken, vegetables, and ice cream.

Spring Dance is scheduled for March 5.

After a long silence, the *Campus Cat* appeared early in January in a New Year's issue.

As a part of the vocational guidance program under Miss Knapp, frequent meetings are being held for all seniors. They are addressed by speakers who are qualified to give advice on some particular occupation open to college women. On Nov. 11 the speaker was Mr. Beatley of Harvard, whose subject was "Education"; Miss Mary Tolman '14, of the Women's Educational and Industrial Union, spoke Dec. 8 on "Business";

Professor Wakeman also discussed "Education" on Dec. 15; and "Social Work" was Professor Kimball's topic, Jan. 19. There have also been several discussion meetings, and many other subjects will be presented by various authorities at future meetings.

Arrangements were made by Press Board to present the radio announcements of the Princeton-Yale and the Harvard-Yale football games in Sage Hall. The cheering was led by some of the men of the faculty.

A party for the employees of the College was given in the Crew House, Nov. 11, the primary object being to stimulate interest in the formation of employee athletic, dramatic, and glee clubs under student supervision. About 150 maids attended this first meeting and showed much enthusiasm over the proposed plans. They appointed four of their members to confer with a student committee and to start the organization of the various group activities. It is hoped that such entertainments may be held frequently, and the QUARTERLY will publish further data about the new venture in the May issue. Similar clubs have been in existence at Bryn Mawr, Vassar, and Wellesley for some time.

KATHERINE PHELPS 1928

JOHN G. SHEDD
July 20, 1850–October 22, 1926

WHEN Smith College was engaged in the campaign for a million dollars in the first year of President Burton's administration, Mr. John G. Shedd of Chicago generously gave to that fund the sum of $50,000. This gift was used to endow the Helen and Laura Shedd Foundation and Professor Schinz of the Department of French holds that chair. The College since that time has held Mr. Shedd in grateful remembrance and learns with sorrow of his death on October 22, 1926. Since 1872 Mr. Shedd had been in Chicago with Field, Leiter, and Company and its successor, Marshall Field and Company, of which concern he was president for many years. His two daughters, Laura (Mrs. Charles Schweppe) and Helen (Mrs. Kersey Reed), are graduates of Smith in the classes of 1900 and 1905 respectively.

The article on the opposite page is reprinted from the *Weekly* in the hope that the alumnae will contribute to the discussion. THE EDITOR.

MR. ELIOT SUGGESTS PLAN FOR SENIOR DRAMATICS *

The weakness of our recent plays from the box-office standpoint—notably "Ruy Blas," "The Taming of the Shrew," and "Sappho and Phaon"—has been disquieting. Art in the theater requires much money, and dramatic work without art, without means of doing everything necessary to create a theatric illusion above all disharmonies or amateurishness, should be confined to an experimental Workshop and never offered to an audience that is charged money to suffer it. In the case of the D. A., there is still money, although fewer and fewer students are paying for season-memberships; but in the case of Senior Dramatics, since the change of Ivy Day from Monday to Saturday, there is little hope of money enough to produce plays on the traditional scale. Commencement always used to be the time, and the only time, when one could aim at art, sure of an income well above $3000. Now, lacking financial security, there is grave danger that the art side of our productions will be lastingly impaired.

The tradition of Senior Dramatics is long and rather splendid. They started very tentatively with modest "stunts," but the sixth production was suddenly famous: the "Electra" of Sophocles, in the Greek, when practically no Greek plays had ever been given in America except the great "Oedipus" at Harvard which no doubt inspired Smith to the experiment. A few years later Racine's "Athalie" was given—again, I think, in the original tongue. In 1895 began the succession of Shakespearian plays that continued until the war with but two brilliant breaks: 1904's production of Kalidasa's "Sakuntala" in a version made by one of its members, the sculptress Alice Morgan Wright, and 1908's valiant but less praiseworthy "Pretenders" of Ibsen, coached by the same director who had just made the first American production of the play at Yale. About the Shakespeare plays there grew up a formality and solemnity almost unthinkable to-day. . . . Two of these elaborate and long-prepared productions may perhaps be specially mentioned: 1906's "Hamlet," which was given again by the Smith Club in New York in April 1907 and is vividly remembered for the beautiful acting of its protagonist, Elsie Hearndon Kearns, and 1915's "Romeo and Juliet," when "modern" scenery was first used. . . .

* Reprinted in part from *Smith College Weekly*, Jan. 12.

In the outburst of enthusiasm for dramatics that followed the war, the classes ran their own plays with less faculty or professional supervision. When there was practical unanimity in choosing the vehicle, as was the happy fortune of 1919 and 1921, excellent productions resulted. There was a general desire to shun Shakespeare, and in "The Yellow Jacket" (an ideal "show" for the occasion) and Brieux's "False Gods" (for the first time in America), these two classes succeeded in finding superlative alternatives. . . . In 1920, "Sappho and Phaon" was first chosen, and then rejected because it offered parts to too few actors; in 1922 Sheldon's "Garden of Paradise" was first choice, but had to be abandoned when estimates of its cost went mounting toward $5000. In both cases, hackneyed Shakespearian plays were substituted. In 1923, the contest was long and furious, but the original choice, Andreiev's "Black Maskers" (again, first time in America) was sustained. . . .

But of late, interest both in Senior Dramatics and in D. A. seems to have slackened. Trials are casual, rehearsals unpunctual, audiences supercilious. Classes no longer attempt to choose their own Senior Play: they let a committee do it. And after the $1100 deficit in 1923 and 58 cents profit in 1924, experimentation is feared and financial worries limit enthusiasm. It is known, further, that the Administration disapproves of so many seniors giving up so much of their time and effort at the close of their course, and would prefer that the Commencement Play be a revival of something already once produced. Is there a way to arrange this, to be sure of sufficient money for a worthy production, and to keep up the best traditions of Senior Dramatics as well?

I think there is, and to inject fresh life into the D. A. at the same time. In October or at latest in November (except of course this year) let a Joint Committee of seniors and juniors be empowered to choose a big play that will be equally suitable for Commencement and for Prom. Let it be understood that when given at Prom, the play will be as thoroughly prepared and scene-rehearsed at the Academy as Senior Dramatics have always been. Then let this two-class committee ask the Council of D. A. (seniors, of course) to put the play on at Prom time with the formality, sense of responsibility, experienced direction, long rehearsal, and loving pains that Senior

Dramatics were so blessed with—the juniors guaranteeing to the D. A. 30% of the cost, and the seniors 70%. This division of the burden I arrive at by estimating that 1000 seats can be sold for the one May performance and well over 2000 in June, at two evenings and a matinée between them, on the afternoon before Ivy Day. The matinée *three* afternoons before Ivy Day that was tried last year cost more than it took in, and that time is needed anyway for rehearsal (being the one free day between final exams and first performance); but there *must* be a third performance and it seems agreed that the afternoon of Friday, when the alumnae arrive, is most auspicious. . . .

The work of the D. A. Council on this biggest of its productions would begin immediately after the Fall Production, for music must often be composed, scenes and costumes planned, long before trials for parts are held in February. At these trials all four classes would compete, and the coach have four times as many possibilities of finding the ideal actress for each part as she would with seniors only. Next, a fortnight after midyears, the Council would proceed to select their own successors, as at present; but (unless acting) they would remain in authority all the spring, with the Junior Council working under them, learning from them. An augmented and refreshed staff of this character could have all preparations for the production well started before spring vacation, and the play ready to give in May with the same professional thoroughness as formerly in June, provided the workers in it were allowed three days for rehearsal at the Academy. . . .

Now someone will surely rise up in her mind and shout "Gruach!" in complete devastation of my idea. "Gruach" was done in May 1925 by the Senior D. A. Council, and in spite of proving ill-prepared and in every way unsuitable, was revived for four performances in June. But how was "Gruach" chosen? By a single strong-willed director, not a committee representative of the dramatic personnel of two classes. And how did it come to be revived (instead of, say, a shortened version of "The Faithful") in the face of general disfavor? Again, a single forceful personality! It is most unlikely that by my plan here suggested any play could be chosen that did not fit the tastes and the occasions of its sponsors; but if one did fail in May, drastic things could yet be done to it before Commencement; its cast shifted, its scenery rebuilt, even its text altered or rewritten. The opportunity to see it tested before the Prom audience would be invaluable to the producer about to readjust it for Commencement showing. . . .

I have outlined this scheme to the 1927 Committee To Choose A Play, and they approve. I think, however, that they should not fix upon any play without calling in, to deliberate, the Junior Prom Chairman and other representatives of 1928, and of course the D. A. Council. And a very important point is the guaranteeing by the two classes of their respective shares of the expense, for of course the D. A. cannot produce anything upon the traditional Senior Dramatics scale without such guarantee. Livingston Platt's sumptuous production of "Much Ado" in 1924 cost, I am told, about $3600; last year's skimped and penurious "Shrew" cost almost $2800. Somewhere between them, say $3200, is the least that a good show, given four times, should be expected to cost. With but two evenings and a problematical afternoon to perform on, the seniors alone cannot now hope to take in $3200 (though receipts from three evenings were over $3700 in 1923 and $3600 in 1924), but 70% or 75% of $3200 they surely will take in, and have the artistic advantage of a May performance as well, if 1928 and D. A. are agreeable. . . . SAMUEL A. ELIOT Jr.

COLLEGE CALENDAR IN BRIEF

Feb. 14–18	Week of Prayer
Feb. 17–19	Meeting of Alumnae Council
Feb. 18	Meeting of the Trustees
Feb. 20	Katharine Gorin (recital)
Feb. 21	Pablo Casals (recital)
Feb. 22	Washington's Birthday
Feb. 25	Workshop Production
Feb. 27	Faculty Recital
Mar. 1	Boston Symphony Orchestra
Mar. 2	Prof. E. de Sélincourt (lecture)
Mar. 5	Spring Dance
Mar. 6	Miss Willian (recital)
Mar. 10	Dr. Arthur Haas (lecture)
Mar. 16	London String Quartet
Mar. 18	Workshop Production
Mar. 19	Intercollegiate Debate
Mar. 20	Beethoven Commemoration Recital
Mar. 21	Fritz Kreisler (recital)
Mar. 23–Apr. 7	Spring Recess
Apr. 15–16	Faculty Opera
Apr. 17	College Symphony Orchestra
Apr. 20	Choir Competition
Apr. 24	Mr. Donovan (recital)
Apr. 27	Workshop Production
Apr. 30	Cleveland Symphony Orchestra
May 7	Choral Concert
May 14	Dramatics Association Production
May 20	Junior Promenade

The Note Room

Written by Elizabeth M. Bacon '28· Drawings by Priscilla Paine '28

CTOBER, with a howl, blew itself into November which settled down, sniffling grimly, to be disagreeable. The college caught its first cold, and bought galoshes. People hurried between classes looking cold, unattractive, and abused, and everyone reminded everyone else that someone had said this was to be the coldest winter since eighteen-something. We shivered and wrote home for more blankets. The trees all at once seemed indecently naked and the brown, frozen ground had little ponds of ice in the morning.

The temperature of the college, however, was neither so cold nor so settled as the outdoors, for with November came new struggles with the smoking question. To begin at the beginning of a question that is still far from being solved: we were allowed to smoke after the Easter vacation last year. At that time we could smoke downstairs in those dormitories which voted in favor of it, but not on the campus, or the streets, or in the tea houses. We smoked, but we "smoked like fools." This September we picked up our cigarettes with the added fervor of the summer. The consequences were rather humiliating. Between the last week in October and the first five days of November, four houses were endangered by fire. We smoked like children and there was only one thing to do. On November 5 the Council President made the following announcement in chapel:

Because of the carelessness of the students in smoking in the college houses, the Council has felt it necessary to suspend smoking until Christmas. This suspension is due entirely to our realization of the tremendous fire risk involved in smoking in the dormitories, and is to act as an effective reminder of our thoughtlessness in the past.

Immediately before the Christmas vacation, a general vote was taken on the three alternatives:

1. No smoking in Northampton.
2. Smoking in the Crew House and Boat House.
3. Smoking in the Crew House, Boat House, and those Tea Rooms which will permit smoking.

The last was selected and went into effect immediately after the Christmas holidays.

Unless there is further legislation by the tea rooms, the problem seems solved for the immediate future.* The majority of the college seems pleased with this arrangement, as it keeps the dormitories free from the haze of smoke that hung in them before, and yet provides an agreeable place for even the most incessant smokers. Of course there are still the Easts and Wests of the question "and never the twain shall meet." There are those who deplore the fact that the student body feels it must have its smoke—and who wish

As the Press Sees Us

that part of it might be taught a little of the art of smoking. By this it does not mean rings and spirals—but common neatness, cleanness, and the fact that fire burns. Opposed to them are those who feel that no council should restrict their "personal liberty"; that "in men's colleges they can smoke in *their* rooms, so why can't we"; and that anyway smoking is a very vital part of a student's happiness. Between these two extremes stands the majority of the college. It likes to smoke. It doesn't want to burn

* At present there is no smoking in the Manse, the Mary Marguerite, and downstairs in Beckmann's.

things or to be offensive—it doesn't feel that smoking is at all necessary. It merely wants to be allowed to smoke when it likes and where the rules permit. Moderate smoking is general. But it is due to a small group of people who seem to be unaware of the reputation they are giving the college, that the stories of "thick blue haze" and "piles of ashes" are being circulated. It is this small industrious group that we must blame for any impressions of a feverishly smoking college. In general, however, smoking now is less than it was when we smoked in our dormitories. The problem of smoking, although it is serious, is for us very simple. We see nothing wrong about our smoking if we knew how, but we don't. Until the college has been educated to the refinements of smoking there will always be a problem—the old, old problem of putting lighted matches into the hands of careless children.

It was on the day the Council "suspended smoking until Christmas" that Cambridge arrived to debate. The subject was: Resolved, That this house deplores the policy of Cambridge University respecting women." To quote from the *Weekly:*

The skill with which this question was met by both teams showed a marked improvement over last year's memorable Oxford-Smith debate.

Although the Cambridge humor was not so rampant as that of Oxford had been, still Smith is learning gradually that the English regard their debating—with us at least—more as an exhibition of interpretative dancing than a solemn game of soccer—speaking in terms of "intellectual exercise." We felt a little heavy, trudging through the subject in conscientious galoshes instead of those delightful English winged slippers. However, the galoshes won by a popular vote—the populace being, of course, Smith.

And, speaking of voting, it was at about this time—Election Day, indeed—that Smith College woke up to the fact that it is located in the old home town of the President of these United States. It was noised abroad that President and Mrs. Coolidge were coming home to vote and that they would drive up Elm Street in an open machine at nine o'clock in the morning or thereabouts. Chapel accordingly spilled out on to Elm Street and stood in two lines in the pouring rain, umbrellas bobbing, and red, yellow, and green rain coats glistening. True to their promise,

the presidential pair did weather the elements in an open car and bowed and waved their way to their modest home up on Massasoit Street. Later in the morning there was a reception at the High School and many of us went down between classes to pay our respects. Somehow it does liven up a dull Tuesday morning to have the President and the first lady of the land in your very midst, no matter what your politics may be.

To return to the campus—Workshop gave its fall production soon after this. These plays always have an experimental tone, both on account of the producers and the choice of plays. This year they experimented too far. They put on an Indian masque, a Hallowe'en fantasy, and "People Who Die" by Alfred Kreymborg, none of which was very successful.

Then suddenly everything was eclipsed in Big Games, and the seven nights that had been so carefully cherished against the time of need began to check themselves off one by one and two by two as the college gathered its fur coats and week-end bags together and dashed off week after week. Not that we all went, O dear no. Enough of us stayed at home to crowd Sage Hall on the afternoons of the Yale-Harvard and Yale-Princeton games to hear them by radio. This was surely one new thing under the Smith sun and added a feather to Press Board's cap; for Press Board it was who arranged for the broadcast, sold lollipops and gum and sandwiches to the bleachers and, by the same token, added many shekels to its dwindling coffers thereby. The *Weekly* tells of one of the occasions thus:

Sitting in the Yale or Princeton cheering section, decorated by blue and orange ribbons respectively, the audience managed to restrain its enthusiasm in an effort to catch every word of the announcer. However, in the more exciting periods, applause and shrieks of delight were uncontrollable. . . .

Besides football there were the finals of the hockey, which we played off in two very close and thrilling games that left the class of 1928 hot and dirty, tired and victorious! And there was, of course, a regular orgy of taking in the hockey and soccer teams. Somebody or other was always sitting in the front rows of chapel bedecked with a flower of the proper hue, and although we did hear great tales of the terrible casualties which the November freshman warnings caused, for all we could see the teams came up smiling. Down in the swimming pool there has been great fun with water polo with informal teams and many events promised for next semester. Happily the swimming pool can snap its fingers even at New England weather and boldly say what it will do without that damning phrase "weather permitting," with which announcements of field days and crew days have to bolster up their hopes. This fall the former was postponed and postponed and finally thrown off the calendar altogether and the fall crew competition was held so late in November that Paradise was in complete darkness before the last shell had passed the judges.

During November there were a great many tempting extras—the Elshuco Trio and the Flonzaley Quartet and Mr. Richard Crooks, who sang delightfully, were among the outstanding attractions. Then came Thanksgiving! This year, by our new residence rule, we were allowed to go away at Thanksgiving for as long as we liked, within the confines of our seven nights. Naturally there was an exodus. Tuesday night they began to go; Wednesday they kept on going; Thursday they were gone! They began coming back Thursday night, but the college was not itself again until the following Monday. Everyone was delighted with the new arrangement, instead of the old required attendance before and after Thanksgiving Day, and we all echoed heartily the President's booming "God save the Commonwealth of Massachusetts!"

On Monday we were all back—at midnight on Tuesday, November sneezed itself out of existence, and December, the month of snow, of clear still nights, of holidays and open fires and Christmas carols began.

But it began sadly, for at noon on the first day of December, Allan Neilson died. The college as a whole did not know Allan, but in this place of many loyalties, the one in which we all share and which, more than anything else, binds us into a unit is our loyalty and great affection for the President. His sorrow was, in some small measure, ours. Until Christmas time the college was a little quieter, a little more thoughtful, realizing suddenly what the President meant, admiring his tremendous courage, and longing inexpressibly to help. From Wednesday the first until the following Sunday most of the extra-curricular activities were postponed, and in little ways we tried to express our sympathy to the President and Mrs. Neilson. On Sunday morning, a soft, white morning,

there was a very simple, poignant memorial service for Allan. That was all; but when the college went back again to its crowded, self-absorbed days, it went back quietly, graver, and perhaps a little older.

On Friday, the first real snow came. It began snowing in the afternoon and came down softly, silently, mysteriously, like a Christmas carol, until all the trees were heavy with it. Ruth Draper came and gave some of her inimitable character sketches that night. She made us scream and ache with laughter over the class in Greek poise, and then suddenly feel dangerously teary at her characterization of the French woman waiting in vain for her soldier husband's return. The two weeks before the holidays are always very crowded, but this year kept us so busy that vacation seemed almost a relaxation.

The annual Christmas Sale cannily put itself first of the month so it caught us before we had become too deeply involved and cleared nearly a thousand dollars in one day. Where on earth the magic wand that suddenly transforms Studes into a veritable block of Fifth Avenue gift shops keeps itself the rest of the year we can't imagine, but it certainly does simplify the Christmas problem for many a puzzled shopper.

The Mandolin Club gave its annual entertainment at about this time. It's not a highbrow afternoon that, but if you are looking for some good clogging, a few excellent monologues, and some tunes that will set your feet to jigging, we recommend it.

Next came the Dramatic Association's beautifully staged production of "Sappho and Phaon" by Percy MacKaye, and directly after that the Smith and Dartmouth Glee Clubs gave their Christmas concert. It is a pleasant change to hear men singing in John M. Greene, but this year, contrary to the usual precedent, Smith sang better than Dartmouth, who seemed rather to explode with their superb voices. They ended gloriously with Handel's "Messiah" sung by both clubs.

The next night, M. Edouard Champion of Paris gave us a brilliant and amusing talk on Anatole France. M. Champion had known him well and his stories about him had that delightful "inside information" air that makes stories so pleasant to repeat.

That same night, Dr. Jäckh of Berlin spoke under the auspices of the International Relations Club on "New Europe"—talking of the interdependence of the European countries and summing up Germany's mission as "the stone which the builders rejected, the same has become the chief corner stone." The next night President George Vincent of the Rockefeller Foundation spoke on "The Scientific Attitude." What he said had enough sound value and common sense to make a very dull instructive lecture, and the way he said it was so witty, so brilliant, that we swallowed a great many informational pills without knowing it until they began to work. After that came the climax toward which this rich, crowded week had been working—Professor Gilbert Murray! To have him lecture here is a tribute both to the College and the President—and the college crowded to hear him. He spoke on the "Origin of Greek Poetry": "Love, strife, death, and that which is beyond death, in a combination of dance and song that soars like a singing bird inspired by a worship of nature, is the fountain head of classical poetry." And he went on to tell about the first choruses and their leaders who danced on the village threshing floors—often reading bits in the original Greek which were enchanting for their music and beauty of sound, although probably quite unintelligible to most of the audience.

Tumbling off the honeyed heights of Hybla and Hymettus the college found itself in the busy rut of "things-to-be-done-before-Vacation." The same rule that did not apply to Thanksgiving vacation did not apply to Christmas, so that we could leave as soon before and come back as late after the vacation as our seven-night limit would allow. However, before classes began to thin out and morning chapel was attended only by those who have a distinct leaning toward Christmas hymns, the President read. That reading is one of the nicest things that happens all year and makes such a Christmasy, holiday air that we forget this is the college we were so anxious to leave when we reserved our seats to go home, weeks ago. Everything always comes in lumps here and the same night that the President read, the English Singers sang. They sang, without accompaniment, some of the most bewitching old English songs—Elizabethan, most of them, but some even earlier. There was so much lilt, so much laughter and melody in them that the audience laughed, and tapped its foot, and nodded

its head and behaved exactly as though it had forgotten it was an audience.

The Bookshop had a Christmas party to which we went. We sat about among the books and listened to Hugh Walpole scintillate for an enchanting and swiftly flying evening. Then there were Christmas Vespers, and the sparkling outdoor Christmas trees—two this year, for besides the usual one in front of Wallace there was one in the very center of the Quadrangle.

Then came Vacation. The exodus was not so explosive as in other years, as half the college had gone before the appointed day. Vacations are so funny to watch. One sees a tall, slim person wound with tortuous ropes of pearls, wrapped in a fur coat and bonneted in a black pill box that rests on the bridge of her nose, and one thinks, "I never saw *that* before!" until with a shock one recognizes the fat, dumpy girl who always wore that horrible pink jersey dress and purple béret; and one reflects on the benefits of vacation. Those students on the registrar's list had to attend their last classes, and consequently left on the last train, which was most appropriately called "The Cahoon Caboose!" The last shiny suitcase was jammed onto the "Caboose" and, puffing with its load, it bumped out of sight, leaving a trail of white smoke behind it—

    Vacation
        had
            come
                and gone—
"My dear, I had the most *divine* time—" "Lord, it's cold here—" "Really, he's too sweet—" "No, the ring hasn't come yet, and of course it's a secret, but I just wanted you to know—" "Wreck, my dear, simply dead—" "Not a wink of sleep—on my honor, didn't close my eyes *once* the whole time" were heard, screamed above the babel of taxis, trunks, suitcases, friends, and remarks, mostly impolite, about the weather. Vacation was over. It can't honestly be said that opening chapel was crowded, and the President remarked with a twinkle—but with an undertone of warning under the twinkle, so to speak—that he congratulated those who were there on having got there at the time the calendar said the college began!

There is nothing in the world more uncomfortable than the consciousness of coming

Three of the pictures on the opposite page were taken for the *Weekly* by Mildred Cole '27 and are reprinted by permission. The Outing Club picture was taken by Walter Merryman. Professor Withington very kindly printed the captions. THE EDITOR.

The Back Campus
in January

Ten Minutes Before the Hour

Commuting from the New Dorms

Bertha Kirk '27
College Song Leader

The Winter Trip of the Outing Club

exams and the holidays gone. We can think
of ten thousand things we don't know that
we'll be sure to be asked—we know we should
learn them, but something has slipped out of
place, and it takes a week of sharpening pencils,
buying pads, unpacking, and clearing up
before we can bring ourselves to work.
Another trouble is that there are too many
lectures to go to—people we must not miss—
and so we trot off with a pleasant, but decep-
tive, feeling of doing the larger duty. One
of the most interesting, and certainly the most
exciting, people who have spoken here is
Professor Gaetano Salvemini, formerly of
the University of Florence and now an exile.
"It is not true," he exploded, "that Mussolini and the Fascists saved Italy from the
Bolshevists; Mussolini did all he could to help
the prevalent interest in Italy after the war,
he did all he could to have a republic." It is
impossible for anyone to imagine the dramatic possibilities, the range of sound and
gesture contained in that sentence, unless she
heard Professor Salvemini. His point of
view, which was violently, gloriously anti-
Fascist, anti-Mussolini, was extremely interesting and very enlightening. One so
rarely hears the other side. Professor Salvemini treated the whole problem in a more
or less historical light, showing that so many
of the innovations claimed as the work and
genius of Mussolini are merely the natural
reactions and developments of a nation recovering from the war.

M. Jacques Copeau, the famous French
actor, read "L'annonce faite à Marie."
He reads beautifully and with enormous
variety of tone. It seemed unbelievable that
such a soft, pleading girl's voice could come
from a man. The next day he read "Andromaque" to a *most* enthusiastic audience.
And speaking of enthusiastic audiences
reminds us of Sir Richard Paget's lectures
on the Human Talking Machine. The
amazing things in the talking line that he
did with his fingers and a few stage properties
left his audiences gasping. And then Dr.
Felix Adler finished up our lecture orgy with
two evenings of absorbing discussion on the
distinctive function of women in the new
civilization. And as if the lectures on our
own campus weren't enough to lure us from
our desks almost any evening, the Progressive
Club of Hampshire County has offered at least
five that it was hard to resist.

Among the pleasantest things that happen

on a Sunday in Northampton are the contributions which our art and music faculty make
to the day. Every Sunday afternoon the
Tryon Gallery is open and some member of
the department talks about whatever special
exhibition is on view—just lately the drawings
of antique statuary by Ingres have been a
great treat—and nearly every Sunday evening
there have been faculty music recitals in
Sage Hall—lovely programs all of them.

By the way, before we reach the end of our
tale—and Sophomore Carnival is so late that
it doesn't get into this issue at all—we should
mention one sad and one cheering bit of news:
during the vacation the Outing Club cabins
were broken into and everything taken; and
the Allen Field Clubhouse is open once more
as a tea house *and* student guest house.

The time for exams draws oppressively
near—there are dismal "summings up" in
classes, the library is horribly crowded.
People hurry past with a preoccupied air and
their arms full of books. People drink coffee
at midnight; people get into little bunches
and mix each other up about the things they
haven't learned. Very bad, all this; very
discouraging for the faculty, very discouraging for us. Nobody enjoys it, but everyone
does it. It seems to be the necessary "attendant circumstance" of examinations.

It does seem ironic that at this particular
time the weather should choose to be warm
and puddly, with spring in the air. Of course
there is snow—not very nice snow either—all
over everything and of course it is "January
and February," and of course any fool knows
that there is no use getting spring fever before
March 21, *but* there is a certain something in
the air that smells like Spring. Nature always
does that in January and it isn't fair. There
is no use jumping in a mud-puddle—it is
winter, and it's exam time, and we'll get a
cold if we aren't careful. So on a day that
smells like Spring we have to walk around
the puddles, and that is depressing too.

It is about this time that we begin to look
like a college, and from steady wear and close
association our clothes begin to look alike.
The college, reading from bottom to top,
starts with galoshes—last year they were open
and flapped with assertive little noises, but this
year they are fastened by the top clasp and
bulge at the bottom. The stockings defy
description! They are as gorgeous as oriental
birds, as strident as jazz, and they cavort
from the ankle up to the knee in a bewilder-

AROUND CAMPUS

ON A WEEK-END

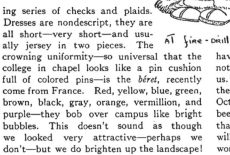

AT fire-DRILL

ing series of checks and plaids. Dresses are nondescript, they are all short—very short—and usually jersey in two pieces. The crowning uniformity—so universal that the college in chapel looks like a pin cushion full of colored pins—is the *béret*, recently come from France. Red, yellow, blue, green, brown, black, gray, orange, vermillion, and purple—they bob over campus like bright bubbles. This doesn't sound as though we looked very attractive—perhaps we don't—but we do brighten up the landscape!

As this goes to press the ponderous jaws of Midyears are closing on us. Thank goodness the weather has cheered up enormously and is crisp and sunshiny again— just made for skating! Chapel has dwindled to a cozy few which will be cozier yet since the President remarked only to-day with a look at the lonely few in the gallery, "I think it would be more friendly if the remote members of 1930 would join the rest of us in

LIBRARY

MID-YEARS

the lower regions during this period." It is a time when we are not at our best. We have "left undone those things which we ought to have done and done those things we ought not to have done and there is no health in us." The good resolutions, the ambitions, the enthusiasms with which we watched October whirl into November seem to have been lost. Those happy innocents who feel that Herculean cups of coffee and no sleep will teach them what three months of class work has failed to are finding relief in cramming; but there are others, perhaps a little blasé, who look regretfully back and wonder why they thought that "anything is better than work." Anyhow, exams are here and there is very little we can do about it. When they are over, we shall wonder why we got so excited, and say complacently, "We might have known he (she or it) wouldn't flunk us."

There is one thing about examinations. The novelty never seems to wear off.

THE ALUMNAE ASSOCIATION

PRESIDENT, Mary (Frost) Sawyer '94.....................210 S. Main St., Andover, Mass.
VICE-PRESIDENT, Alida (Leese) Milliken '00.............951 Madison Av., New York City.
SECRETARY, Mabel (Chick) Foss '05....................226 Bay State Rd., Boston, Mass.
TREASURER, Sara (Evans) Kent '11.....................44 Virginia Ter., Kingston, Pa.

DIRECTORS

Edith (Angell) Cranshaw '11   Grace (Middleton) Roberts '14
Harriet (Bliss) Ford '99   Mary Smith '08
Nellie Joan Oiesen '13   Mary Tolman '14
Amy Ferris '01   Mary Goodman '96
Mary Raymond '91   Eunice Wead '02
                   Dorothy (Olcott) Gates '13

NOTES FROM THE OFFICE

The Alumnae Council convenes in Northampton February 17 (Thursday), 18, and 19. On Thursday after a business session, the Council will be addressed by Mrs. Scales, Professor Mensel, chairman of the Board of Admission, Dr. Gilman, and Florence Angell '11, Secretary of the International Committee of the A. A. U. W. In the afternoon there will be a conference with the Faculty, and, after inspection of the quadrangle, tea with the Faculty at Martha Wilson House. In the evening, the Workshop will present a miracle play. On Friday, there will be an opportunity to visit classes and the Smith College Schools; meetings of class and club representatives, and a conference and tea with the Student Council in the Crew House. In the evening the councillors will be received by President and Mrs. Neilson and the Art Department in the new Tryon Gallery. Saturday morning will be devoted to the final business session, to an important question hour with the alumnae trustees, and a conference with President Neilson.

The councillors-at-large will be Miss Angell and Alice (Wright) Teagle '04, of the Alumnae Fund Committee.

The annual conference of the Education Committee will be held in Northampton on Saturday, February 19, at the close of the Council Meetings. There will be addresses by alumnae engaged in educational work and open discussion of educational experiments. The conference is in charge of Mary Raymond '91, chairman of the Education Committee, and principal of the Hathaway-Brown School in Cleveland.

Nellie Joan Oiesen '13 has been appointed chairman of the Local Clubs Committee in the place of Dorothy (Olcott) Gates '13, resigned. Miss Oiesen and her committee are at work upon a new series of Club Bulletins and a handbook for clubs, which will contain suggestions for club programs and a revision of the model constitution.

During the Christmas holidays three of the foreign students at Smith, Miss Nora Edmed of England, Miss Louise Goepfert of Germany, Miss Clara Fetter of Hungary, were entertained at clubs and in homes by the Smith Clubs of Boston, Buffalo, Chicago, and New York. The friendly hospitality of the alumnae was enthusiastically appreciated by these members of the Smith family so far away from their own homes.

The Parade Chairman for June 1927 is Catharine Weiser '17. Chairmen of costume committees in classes holding reunions in June are asked to submit designs for costumes to the Parade Chairman at the earliest moment. Address, 1023 7th St., E. LasVegas, N. M.

Florence Snow '04 as alumnae secretary, Edith Hill '03 as editor of the QUARTERLY, and Marion Graves '15 as advertising manager will attend the conference of the Association of Alumni Secretaries and Magazines at the University of North Carolina at Chapel Hill, N. C., the last week in April.

JUNIPER LODGE

The cash gifts received for the Juniper Lodge Endowment Fund, on Jan. 17 amounted to $22,864.73. Many of the Clubs have reported various activities in behalf of the fund, and it is hoped that when returns from these come in, they will complete the $30,000.

LOCAL CLUBS

The BOSTON Association inaugurated the New University Club building with a successful bridge party of 100 tables for the Juniper Lodge Fund. At its January meeting Dr. Douglas Thom, Consulting Psychiatrist at College, spoke on Mental Hygiene and the College Student. Edith (Elmer) Wood '90 of the Institute for the Coördination of Women's Interests was the speaker at the February meeting. At the meeting on Mar. 2, the alumnae councillors will report and also the President of the Student Council, with a musical program by Marion Clapp '04· The annual luncheon with President Neilson as the guest of honor will be held at the new Hotel Statler, Apr. 16. Helen Greene '91 will speak on Antioch, and Florence Snow '04 on alumnae affairs.

Laura (Lord) Scales '01· the Warden, is scheduled to speak to the BRIDGEPORT Club in February.

The BROOKLYN Club secured funds for a scholarship for a Brooklyn girl at Smith from its annual bridge party and cake and candy sale in December. Dorothy Kenyon '08· doctor of law from New York Univ. Law School and chairman of legislation of the New York League of Women Voters, addressed the January meeting.

President Comstock of Radcliffe and of Smith '97 talked to the CHICAGO Club at its Christmas meeting at the Women's Athletic Club on Smith from the trustee point of view. The Club is planning a series of public lectures by a member of the Smith faculty.

The CLEVELAND Club gave a gay and colorful Pirate Ball during the holidays for the scholarship-fellowship fund. Prof. Kimball (Government) spoke on the Smith of To-Day at the December meeting. Prof. Kimball spoke also to the DETROIT Club on the same trip.

The EASTERN NEW YORK Club entertained the Albany branch of the A. A. U. W. at luncheon at the Albany Country Club in November.

The FITCHBURG Club presented Mary Lewis of the Metropolitan and Charles Naegele, pianist, in a joint concert for its scholarship fund in December. The Club has established a reputation for providing the community with concerts of the very highest standard.

At the December supper meeting of the HAMPSHIRE COUNTY Club two seniors described their experience in France as juniors.

At the luncheon of the HARTFORD Club, Feb. 12, Florence Snow '04 and Miss Mabelle Blake, Personnel Director, are scheduled to speak.

At the INDIANA Association's Christmas luncheon news of College activities was brought by Ruth Burford of the freshman class.

The LYNN Club held one of the ever successful rummage sales in the fall.

The MAINE Club gave one of the equally popular bridge parties in Portland in November.

The flourishing new club in MIAMI invites alumnae visiting in Florida to its fortnightly meetings on Wednesdays. Communications should be sent to Mrs. D. Richard Mead (Catharine Chadbourn '21), 2234 N. Bay Rd., Miami Beach.

The MINNEAPOLIS Club conducted a Smith College Week at the Donaldson store during November for its scholarship fund.

The MONTCLAIR Club gave a benefit bridge in December at the Colonial Tea room.

The annual bridge and fair of the NEW HAVEN Club was held at the Lawn Club in December.

The most ambitious event in club annals this year has been the benefit matinée of "Aida" at the Metropolitan, Dec. 30, by the NEW YORK Club. The Juniper Lodge Endowment Fund was the gainer by some $3000 as the result of this performance and the annual dance at the Plaza, Dec. 29. [See next page.]

The Club of the ORANGES (N. J.) at its first meeting of the season staged a fashion show, featuring costumes from 1893 to the present day owned and worn by club members. Margaret Farrand '14· director of the College Press Board and Assistant Professor of English, spoke on college affairs at the November meeting. At the January meeting the speaker was Dr. James Plant, Director of the Essex County Juvenile Clinic in Newark, and guests at the meeting were several former students of the Smith School for Social Work who are working with Dr. Plant.

The ROCHESTER Club held a library luncheon in November, with addresses by members of the Rochester Public Library staff. The speaker at the holiday luncheon was Prof. Welch (Music). Prof. Barnes (Economics and Sociology) and Prof. Fay (History) were also guests.

The ST. LOUIS Club was addressed by Prof.

Meyerhoff (Geology) at its January meeting.

The joint luncheon of the MINNEAPOLIS and ST. PAUL Clubs was held in St. Paul, Jan. 3.

Prof. Welch gave the first of a series of lectures arranged by the SPRINGFIELD Club, Dec. 8. At the December meeting of the Club students from College spoke on student government and junior year in France.

Prof. Kimball spoke at the December meeting of the TOLEDO Club.

The UTICA Club presented Mordkin and his Russian ballet for the benefit of the Juniper Lodge Fund.

Dr. Dennis, vice-chairman of the U. S. Tariff Commission, formerly of the Smith Faculty, addressed a fall meeting of the WASHINGTON (D. C.) Club.

The WISCONSIN Club entertained at luncheon the Smith delegates to the Student Conference during the Christmas holidays. Prof. Meyerhoff spoke at the Christmas meeting of the Madison Branch.

Miss Jordan spoke at the November meeting of the WORCESTER Club.

SMITH COLLEGE CLUB OF NEW YORK

The Club of New York is suffering from growing pains. The Clubhouse is now six years old and has met successfully one of the purposes for which it was organized—*i.e.*, the housing of the younger alumnae. Whether it has been meeting the requirements of the majority of Smith graduates in and near New York is the question which the Club is going to study this spring.

There are several suggestions to be considered by the Club Members:

1. To sell and build further up town in a more central location.
2. To reconstruct the present building, greatly increasing its capacity and efficiency.
3. To reconstruct the present building and maintain some general club rooms in a more central location.
4. To unite with the other colleges in a coöperative building in which we would own our club floors.

The financial question seems unfortunately the leveler of our fondest ambitions, but we hope to evolve a plan that will be enthusiastically endorsed by the majority of our membership.

GINLING NOTES

In spite of troublous times in China, Ginling seems to be going on its way undisturbed. It opened this fall with an increased registration and a particularly good corps of teachers and staff. There are about 150 students now in the three dormitories.

Last year alumnae clubs and individuals contributed the substantial sum of $2583, and we hope to make a good showing again this year. Clubs are urged to send in their contributions before June 1 as the report must be ready for the meeting at Commencement. The treasurer is Mrs. Teresina Peck Rowell, 2045 Garfield St., Hinsdale, Ill.

Ruth Chester '14 hopes to go back to China soon and will take up her old work in chemistry at Ginling. She is the sole representative of Smith there this year—quite an unusual state of things—as Edna Wood '18 came back last August to be married.

The need of new teachers is an ever present one and we should like to get more Smith alumnae. Send the name of anyone whom you think might like to consider such a position to Prof. Irving Wood or Miss Ellen Cook. College teaching experience is desirable, and some graduate work is almost a necessity, but ability to teach and the power to adapt oneself to new conditions are absolute essentials. With these qualities an extremely interesting experience is assured.

INTERCOLLEGIATE ALUMNI HOTELS

Since writing for the November QUARTERLY (page 56) the story of the Intercollegiate Alumni Hotels advertising movement, twelve new hotels have been added to the list of hotels which are serving throughout the country as headquarters for alumni activities. There are now 45 of these hotels and Smith alumnae are requested to note the list on pages 254 and 255 of this issue and to use the hotels on every possible occasion. Card indexes containing the names of resident Smith alumnae are on file at every designated hotel and also the ALUMNAE QUARTERLY.

ALUMNAE NOTES

CLASS NEWS

Please send all news for the May QUARTERLY *to your class secretary by April 3. The editors reserve the right to omit all items which in their judgment are not submitted in legible form.*

1879

Class secretary—Mrs. Charles M. Cone (Kate Morris), Hartford, Vt.

1880

Class secretary—Mrs. Edwin Higbee (Netta Wetherbee), 8 West St., Northampton, Mass.

1881

Class secretary—Eliza P. Huntington, 88 Harvard St., Newtonville, Mass.

1882

Class secretary—Nina E. Browne, 44 Pinckney St., Boston, Mass.

At our forty-fifth reunion in June, we expect to be housed in the Wallace House, with the Washburn as an annex, if it is needed. The class supper will be held on Friday evening, June 17, at the Sophia Smith Homestead in Hatfield. On Saturday, Alice Peloubet would like to have us take supper with her in her new home in Northampton, at 66 West St.

The Reunion Committee is: Alice (Peloubet) Norton, chairman, Caroline (Hungerford) Mills, Grace Blanchard.

1883

Class secretary—Charlotte C. Gulliver, 30 Huntington Lane, Norwich, Conn.

The Settlement House at 38 Lawrence St., Hartford, Conn., is known as Mitchell House, in honor of Mary (Clark) Mitchell, who started the settlement and interested members of the Hartford College Club in the project. At the December meeting of the Club a play was given by children from Mitchell House.

Susan Daniels is at the Hotel Gregorian, 42 W. 35 St., N. Y. C., for the winter.

In the fall, Henrietta (Harris) Harris with Anna Morse, her guest, called on ten or twelve classmates within motoring distance of Springfield. Henrietta, with her husband and daughter, is to sail Jan. 15 on the *S. S. Asturias*, Royal Mail Line, for South Africa via South America and the Mediterranean. They expect to return in the early summer.

·A recent book of poetry, "Lines and Lyrics," by Cora Williams, may be ordered for the benefit of the College. For details consult the author or the class secretary.

Ex-1883

Mabel (Allen) Sleeper has moved to 12 Upland Rd., Wellesley, Mass. Her husband's ill health prevents his preaching.

Jane Robbins will spend the next few months at the College Settlement, 84 First St., N. Y. C.

1884

Class secretary—Helen M. Sheldon, Fort Ann, N. Y.

DIED.—Alice Gladden, Dec. 3, 1926, at her home in Columbus (O.) after a second stroke of paralysis on Dec. 2. ·

In Memoriam

In our senior year our class prophet, Clara French, very appropriately applied to Alice Gladden Mrs. Browning's words: "'Tis her thinking of others makes you think of her." Certainly never did anyone ask less for herself, and give more abundantly to others.

Alice's real life work may be said to have begun in 1904, when she and Miss Grace Jones (Bryn Mawr) took over and became headmistresses of the Columbus School for Girls—a school which, under their wise leadership, has become one of the best preparatory schools in the country, widely known and respected. The co-headmistress writes of Alice, "She made an enormous contribution to any work she undertook." And one of her former teachers adds, "I doubt whether any person ever gave herself more fully to an institution than did Miss Gladden." A member of '84, who knew Alice intimately for many years in Columbus, was impressed by the serenity with which she met all the many claims upon her time and thought, and by her great personal joy in her work.

A memory so delightful to the writer that she wishes to share it with '84, is that of the Sunday evening, after church, spent in the Gladden home with Alice and her father, at a time when they were the only members of the family left there, and Alice was the best and closest of companions to him. Together they softly sang the hymn written by Dr. Gladden and, many years later, sung at Alice's funeral:

In hope that sends a shining ray
Far down the future's broadening way,
In peace that only Thou canst give,—
With Thee, O Master, let me live.

OTHER NEWS.—Clara Clark is again in the old Elm St., Northampton, home of college days. She and Harriet Hillman had a delightful trip to Porto Rico last April. Clara enjoys being able to walk about freely, after many years of illness.

Florence (Heywood) Holden spent a week at the Richardsons' home in Ilion (N. Y.) last summer.

Lou Kelsey writes, "My only news is that I have at last resigned from teaching, and that I expect to be at home more now."

Betsey Merriam and Helen Sheldon are to be at 1201 Hillsboro St., Raleigh, N. C., until March 1. Martha (Cox) Bryant came to lunch with them as they passed through New York, and they hope to see Kate (Dunn) Spalding in Pinehurst (N. C.) if she comes there as usual for Feb. and March.

Helen (Rand) Thayer rejoices in her grandson, Thayer Ainsworth Greene, now nearly a year old. Helen's son Sherman graduated from Amherst last June and is now a student in the Harvard Graduate School of Business Administration.

Elsie Tiemann and her sister have gone to Europe for at least a year. Address, c/o Morgan and Co., Paris.

1885

Class secretary—Ruth B. Franklin, 23 Sherman St., Newport, R. I.

1886

Class secretary—M. Adèle Allen, 144 Lincoln St., Holyoke, Mass.

Ginevra (Fuller) Duncan and her husband, Rev. James C. Duncan, have the distinction of serving one church for forty years, their only pastorate. The event was quietly celebrated last June.

Kate (Haggett) Warren's sister Winifred is Dean of Women at the Univ. of Washington in Seattle.

Harriet (Parsons) Wells is making her home with her son in Philadelphia since Dr. Wells's death.

Harriett (Risley) Foote has been deeply bereaved in the death of her friend and coworker, Emma Schumacher, who for nearly thirty years had been associated with her in all the garden work in Marblehead, and whose vivid personality had touched many lives and extended the spirit of hospitality and good will so widely that she seemed as much a part of the Rose Garden as the roses themselves.

Annie (Russell) Marble was one of the authors who spoke at the Women's University Club in New York, on the evening of Dec. 5, when the book exhibit of the year was at the Club. Cosmo Hamilton, Ford Madox Ford, Margaret Widdemer, Josephine (Daskam) Bacon were the other well-known authors.

Ex-1886

Charlotte (Burleigh) Boyer and Mr. Boyer are at home in Tavares (Fla.) for the winter.

Esther Fowler of Sholapur, who has been identified with Missionary School work in India for thirty years, is to be in this country for several months. She visited Hattie Cushman in Monson in November. She and Ellen (Davis) Wood were the guests of honor at a luncheon given by Annie (Russell) Marble in November when the Woman's Board of Missions met in Worcester.

Grace (Gallaudet) Closson is occupied in preparing the work of her late husband for exhibition.

1887

Class secretary—Mrs. Alden P. White (Jessie Carter), 3 Federal Court, Salem, Mass.

Jessie (Carter) White's daughter Barbara, Smith '21, was married in Salem, Nov. 27, 1926, to Richard K. Baker of Boston, Harvard '19. They are spending two months in France and on their return will live in Boston.

Ex-1887

Nettie (Bancroft) Pierce's husband, Wilson H. Pierce, died on Dec. 27, 1926, in Chicago, where they have lately made their home. The burial was in Waterbury (Conn.), where they lived until the last two years. Mr. Pierce was a prominent lawyer. He had been for many years an invalid. His effort to keep on with his business and his heroism during a most trying and prolonged illness and Nettie's long years of cheerful devotion and care have filled the hearts of their many friends with sympathy and admiration.

1888

Class secretary—Florence K. Bailey, 174 Broad St., Claremont, N. H.

After a year spent in study at Rome and in delightful wanderings through Italy, Switzerland, Germany, and France, Daisy Blaisdell has returned to her work in the German department of the Univ. of Illinois.

Dr. Adelaide Brown, with her niece, Phoebe Brown, is enjoying a trip around the world. She sailed from San Francisco Sept. 4, and expects to reach home June 29.

Mary (DeVol) Wilcox's second grandchild, Eleanor, was born Oct. 29, 1925.

Martha (Everett) St. John's mother died in Boston, Nov. 11, 1926, in her 89th year.

Louise (Husted) Church's new address is 3012 N. 20 St., Tacoma, Wash. Louise conducts, with great success, a current events class of 150 members.

Frances (Lyman) Burt's son Stanley had a trying experience with the recent terrible storm in Cuba, but fortunately escaped unharmed.

Lizzie (Parker) McCollester has a second granddaughter, Mary, born in Paris, Nov. 23, 1926, to her daughter, Catharine (McCollester) Gallaher '14.

Martha (Plack) Fisher's address for the present is c/o Dr. Andres, 4019 Grosman Av., Long Island City, N. Y.

Ex-1888

Susie (Bosworth) Munn's grandchild, Leslie Searle Munn Jr., was born June 16, 1926, in Somerville, N. J.

1889

Class secretary—Lucy E. Allen, 35 Webster St., West Newton, Mass.

Alice (Buswell) Towle's second daughter, Caroline, was married in Trinity Church, Boston, June 26, 1926, to Henry Sturgis Russell, and is now living on a lemon and walnut ranch at Carpinteria, near Santa Barbara, Calif. Alice hopes to visit her in March. The third daughter, Alison, is at Dobbs Ferry, under Jane Cushing's wing.

May (Goodwin) Avirett won special honors (95% or over) in practical nursing from the Department of Education of the Brooklyn Y. W. C. A. last summer.

Florence (Seaver) Slocomb has been elected to the Massachusetts Legislature, as Republican representative from Worcester, and is now one of three women members of the "Great and General Court."

NEW ADDRESS.—Mrs. W. A. Clark (Alice Johnson), 5 Winchester St., Brookline, Mass.

Ex-1889

Mabel (Fiske) Johnson's second son, Charles, died Nov. 28, 1926, at Middletown (O.), after a year's illness. His beautiful character and his successful social work, especially for children, make the loss a great one.

1890

Class secretary—Annie S. Wyckoff, 95 Clinton Av., Jamaica, N. Y.

Louisa Cheever was abroad last summer with her niece, Eunice Wheeler, Smith '25, traveling in southern France, Switzerland, the Austrian and Italian Tyrol, and northern Italy. Especially interesting to her were a passion play given by the peasants in a small village near Kufstein once in ten years; the gathering of peasants in native costume at Botzen to greet the King of Italy on his first visit to the Irredenta since it became Italian; the famous Palio at Sienna, and the glory of the flowers in the Engadine.

Virginia (Forrest) Lucia writes: "My work outside housekeeping has included some writing for the new school, opened in Northampton by Miss Whitaker and Dorothy Bement '12, formerly of the Capen School. I try to help them out when they find themselves crowded with letters to be answered. I have served as secretary and treasurer of various organizations in Hampshire County, particularly the Hampshire County Branch of the Woman's Board of Missions."

Susan (Homans) Woodruff went to Florida the latter part of November for six weeks. She returns to her farm in February.

Nancy (Rogers) Perkins announces the marriage of her son, Albert, Nov. 4, 1926, to Myrell Armstrong, at Trinity Chapel, N. Y.

DIED.—Jan. 13, at Monson (Mass.), Louise Capen ('90 Art), daughter of Elijah Capen and Harriet Gill.

1891

Class secretary—Mrs. H. B. Boardman (Carolyn Peck), 1307 Lowell Rd., Schenectady, N. Y.

May Booth is spending the winter in Florida.

Alice (Clute) Ely's youngest son, Robert, has a position in Newark with the Public Service Commission of New Jersey.

Eunice Gulliver writes that not nearly enough was said in the last QUARTERLY about Grace Weston's lectures. She heard Grace talk in Norwich and said it was delightful, pleased all who heard her, and that her slides were beautiful.

Carolyn (Peck) Boardman is spending the winter in Chandler (Ariz.) with her husband, who is convalescing from a recent illness.

1892

Class secretary—Mrs. Irving H. Upton (Katherine Haven), 20 Park View St., Boston 21, Mass.

Helena Woodbridge ex-'27, daughter of Belle (Adams) Woodbridge, was married Oct. 30, 1926, in the chapel of Columbia Univ., to Paul Austin Wolfe. President Henry Sloane Coffin of Union Theological Seminary and Rev. Austin Wolfe of Kansas City, father of the groom, officiated. The bride wore her mother's wedding dress and her godmother's lace veil. They are living in Keene Valley, N. Y.

Lyn Bridges's brother-in-law, Abbott Rice, in whose family she made a second home and who was a member of the Massachusetts legislature for several years, died on Oct. 10, 1926.

Florence (May) Rice has a grandson, Winthrop Huntington Rice Jr., born Dec. 25, 1926.

The Boston Smith Club held a bridge party in November at the new University Club (men's), making $405. This sum was sent to Juniper Lodge as a memorial to Mary (Rankin) Wardner, who was president of the club at the time of her death.

At a business meeting of the College Club in Boston in October it was voted that a memorial to Mary (Rankin) Wardner be made to take the form of library improvement, either in room facility or additional books, as a special committee shall determine. '92 will be interested in this as Molly's services to this Club were especially valuable; she gave here liberally of her time, strength, and sane judgment, and each one of us may desire to help toward this splendid tribute when the plans are more definite.

1893

Class secretary—Mrs. John E. Oldham (Harriet Holden), 16 Livermore Rd., Wellesley Hills, Mass.

Virginia Lyman is general chairman for our next reunion in June 1928. Already she is busy with plans and she hopes to announce all her committees in the spring Class Letter. Be prepared to help her if she calls on you. Virginia is another of our '93 Braillers. She is chairman of Braille in the Englewood Red Cross Chapter. She says that copying a book is slow and exacting work but interesting.

Margarita May came East this fall from her home in San Francisco, visiting New York, Boston, and Northampton.

Mabel (Short) Vincent's mother died recently and she has gone home to settle the estate. They have given up their apartment in Brookline and for the present her address is c/o Dr. E. T. Vincent, 93 Massachusetts Av., Boston.

Charlotte MacDougall '22, daughter of Charlotte (Stone) MacDougall, was married Nov. 18, 1926, to Hendrik de Kauffmann, minister from Denmark to China and Japan. They were married by the Rev. Roland Cotton Smith, at the Portsmouth Navy Yard, where Rear Admiral MacDougall is Commandant.

1894

Class secretary—Mrs. John J. Healy (Katharine Andrews), 1104 Greenwood St., Evanston, Ill.

Elizabeth (Balch) Jackson's daughter Harriet is engaged to Henry Newbegin of Cambridge. He is a graduate of Williams.

Mary (Clark) Putnam's daughter Martha is to be married to James Lusk Holman of St. Paul. He graduated from Harvard in 1917.

Bertha (Noyes) Stevens, her husband, and daughter Marcia have returned from six months abroad. Marcia studied part of the time at the Sorbonne. She is now at Boston Univ. Secretarial School.

Anne Paul has returned from another of her numerous trips to Europe. This time she drove her motor car from the door of her Boston house onto the steamer, motored about Europe in it, and, returning, drove off the ship back to her home.

Teresina (Peck) Rowell went to New York in November to attend the executive committee of the National Council of the Congregational Church. She writes: "In Stamford I saw Fanny (Bancroft) Long who is just back from a happy visit in England with her brother and sister. In Northampton I had luncheon with our faculty members, Molly Richardson and Mary Lewis." Teresina's daughter Teresina is now a sophomore at Smith, having transferred from Beloit College.

Minnie Pickering will spend her sabbatical year abroad. Leaving in February, she will spend part of her time in northern Africa, Palestine, and Greece.

Lillian (Rice) Brigham's son Daniel is to be married on Jan. 12 to Constance Davidge of Binghamton, N. Y., Smith '25.

Grace (Smith) Jones's daughter Catharine is with our Professor Powers in the University Travel Bureau.

Kate (Ware) Smith's son Milton is studying at Harvard Theological School.

1895

Class secretary—Carolyn P. Swett, Hudson View Gardens, 183 St. and Pinehurst Av., New York City.

Nan (Harrington) Green and Dr. Green are traveling again in California and Arizona. She writes: "When you can, just say in the QUARTERLY that I am still treasurer. We need the interest on the $5.00 dues."

DIED.—Lucy D. Heald, July 14, 1926, in Westboro, Mass.

1896

Class secretary—Frances E. Jones, Hotel Chelsea, W. 23 St., New York City.

DIED.—Elisabeth Stone, suddenly, Jan. 2, in Hartford, Conn.

In Memoriam

The members of '96 will receive with sorrow and a sense of personal bereavement the news of Elisabeth Stone's sudden death on the second day of the New Year. No one more than she could have wished for the opportunity of continuous service to the end, such as she was able to render, even though her health had been somewhat impaired of late. Her fine work and influence as a teacher and faculty adviser in the Hartford Public High School had been continuous since her graduation from Smith. Her recent associations with the College were through her visits there as alumnae councillor and through the

presence of her niece, Mary Todd, in the class of 1926. Just as in college her character and friendship were valued, so in the later years of her busy life her clear judgments, kindly ways, and strong personality were a benefaction to the institution she served so loyally. Those who have known her and loved her from girlhood feel keenly the loss of a very rare friend.

J. G. C.

OTHER NEWS.—Mabel (Bacon) Ripley has tried an innovation in education in her family. She has kept the girls at home a year before they entered high school. They spent their time performing home duties, learning how best to use their allowances, and how to buy sensibly. They also had plenty of music and outdoor life. Mabel's son and his father have planned a trip to Europe together "unhampered by females."

Marian (Baker) Lloyd's daughter Janet is at Skidmore, her son Marshall at Ann Arbor.

Charlotte (Boone) Slade's two older sons are taking the engineering course at Harvard. Benjamin is a senior and John Milton a junior.

Anna (Curr) Woodward's husband is a member of the New York State Board of Regents of the department of education.

Alice (Day) Gardner's oldest son, Harris, is at Hamilton College. Her daughter Sarah will be ready for Smith next fall. She writes that she is at the same old jobs—attorney-at-law, housekeeper, and chauffeur.

Alice Dike writes of the fun as well as the hard work involved in equipping a Home Management House for practical work in connection with the household economics course at Simmons College.

Nancy Hoisington is living with her brother in Rye, N. Y.

Harriet (Learned) Taussig's son Joseph is studying medicine at Washington Univ., St. Louis.

Eliza (Lord) Jaquith's plans for the year have been somewhat changed. Under the auspices of the American Home Missionary Association, she is a visiting teacher in the 23 negro schools which they help to support. She was chosen to carry out a new project whose aim is—through a study of the masterpieces of the world—to help the negroes to see and enjoy beauty in their own surroundings.

Nan Myrick gave up her hospital work some years ago to be with her mother. She is now able to combine her home duties with medical work for Schrafft and Sons, which she finds very interesting.

Georgia (Pope) Sawyer's eldest son, Henry Jr., is a sophomore at Harvard.

Sophie (Washburn) Bateman's son Leon was married June 12, 1926, to Hilda Rantilla.

Ex-1896

Mary Carpenter has been a semi-invalid since her breakdown in college her junior year. She writes that she feels in better health now than ever before.

Emeline Smith's days are very full as she has the sole care of her invalid mother.

Gertrude (Porter) Hall's husband died Jan. 10 in Beirut.

1897

Class secretary—Lucy O. Hunt, 185 Beacon St., Hartford, Conn.

DIED.—Dec. 16, 1926, at Gloucester, Florence (Dustin) Burnham, wife of Dr. Allen Burnham, after an illness of many years. The girlhood friends of Florence remember her for her loyalty, hospitality, and a fine quality of responsive understanding. She was an active and enthusiastic member of the Gloucester Smith Club, a prominent participant in church, Sunday school, and civic affairs, as long as her health permitted, and a devoted mother to three stepsons and two daughters.

H. P. W.

OTHER NEWS.—The Boston Group enjoyed lunch together in the fall, and then gathered at Louise Peloubet's and had a most delightful afternoon talking of class doings. They plan to have "drop-in" luncheons the third Tuesday of the coming months, so if you are in Boston call up Edith (Taylor) Kellogg, 20 Craigie St., Cambridge, and join the group.

Helen Atwater brings honor to '97 in being chairman of the Woman's Joint Congressional Committee, which consists of representatives of 22 organizations of national scope, interested in furthering legislation of special importance to women.

Rachel Baldwin is again in Pasadena for the winter. Any "touring '97-ers" will be most welcome at 995 Elizabeth St.

Eleanor Bissell returned to Pasadena in January, after four months in the East.

Helen (Boss) Cummings writes that Carolyn has made Glee Club this year, as well as the College Orchestra.

Edith (Breckenridge) Fisk's daughter Clarissa is in Chapin, and is a member of the Freshman Choir. Edith and she will spend next summer in Europe.

Anna Carhart is at 56 W. 75 St., returning in Dec., after building a cottage at Dorset, Vt.

Isabelle (Cutler) Blanke has returned after two years abroad, and is in N. Y. C.

Elizabeth (Cole) Fleming had a charming '97 tea at her home, Nov. 30. Fifteen were there, and reunion plans were discussed. Elizabeth was on the general committee for the Milwaukee Student Conference, and attended it with her son, who was in the Yale delegation.

Ida (Darling) Engelke and her family have a fruit farm at Neoga, Ill. It was bought by "unanimous vote" of the four Engelkes, and they all "love" it.

Grace (Dustan) Rawson is wintering at North Craftsbury, Vt.

Albertine (Flershem) Valentine writes that horseback riding is her chief diversion. Her son John is a sophomore at Harvard.

Mae (Fuller) Curran's son David is at Princeton, and Rita graduates from Smith in June.

Elizabeth Hobbs is in Lakeville (Conn.) after a long time in France. She actually lived in the Louvre, part of the time, with a French family. Her room was directly under the Mona Lisa, and undoubtedly Bessie hob-nobbed with the ghosts of Catherine de Medici and her victims.

Climena Judd writes most entertainingly of her experiences in China. She returned via Suez—her third trip around the world. In London she was with Edith (Howe) Sawbridge, and had a Smith "reunion" with Susan Titsworth, who is teaching at Smethwick this winter. Clem's new address is 6 Bedford Ter., Northampton. She is Associate Principal of the Burnham School.

Alice (Lord) Parsons attended the Washington Conference on the Cause and Cure of War. She met Anne (McWilliams) Gans, Anna (Casler) Chesebrough, Alice (Maynard) Madeira, and Emma (Lootz) Erving.

Caroline (Mitchell) Bacon's mother died on Thanksgiving Day, 1926.

Edith Noble was in Northampton recently, and saw several '97-ers and their daughters.

Mary (Shepard) Clough tells a thrilling tale of the arrest of her son Shepard and his wife as Belgian "spies!"—because they had attended the meetings of the Nationalists in Antwerp, where Shepard is working on his Ph.D. thesis, "Nationalism in Belgium."

Louise Smith's mother passed away Dec. 1, 1926.

Elsie Tallant spent several weeks in Kentucky, speaking as a specialist in maternal and infant hygiene, for the Children's Bureau.

Edith (Taylor) Kellogg is studying French and attending all the French lectures possible in preparation for her year abroad. She sails June 16, and so will miss reunion, alas!

Rina (Townsend) Barnard sailed in January with Edna Mason '98 for Constantinople, then to Italy via Egypt, to meet Townsend who is with the University Cruise. Lucy is in Scribner's advertising department.

Lil (Ware) Knight's daughter Peg is a freshman at Northwestern Univ., and is in the French class with Grace (Mathews) Philbrick's son Schuyler. Richard Knight was married last year and lives in Florida.

Florence (White) Talcott writes enthusiastically of her garden and the wonderful display of spring bulbs she is looking forward to.

Ex-1897

Margaret (Miller) Cooper has had two pictures, 25 x 30, in the winter Academy of Design in the Fine Arts Building on 57 St., N. Y. C.

Beulah (Greenough) Hardy spent the summer in England with her daughter, who is engaged to an Englishman. Beulah's new home is at 336 Meehan Av., Mt. Airy, Philadelphia, Pa.

1898

Class secretary—Ethel M. Gower, 29 Mather St., New Haven, Conn.

Annie Brooks is teaching at Athol and has just completed her second term of three years as a member of the school committee; she is also a library trustee.

Mattie (Brown) Fincke wrote in December: "My school where I was director of music, the Ely School, Greenwich, Conn., has just burned down, destroying a goodly part of my wardrobe, books, and music. I have had a most interesting experience there and love the teaching. My four children spent Christmas with me and are very happy, so let clothes and music go!"

Gertrude Chase worked at the Harvard Summer School and in addition to her other degrees has acquired a Φ B K.

Georgia (Coyle) Hall writes: "Big Louis got smashed in an automobile accident last summer and that made half our New Canaan house burn up because I left an oil heater burning while I dashed down to Stamford to watch him suffer. The heater set fire to the house which being some 150 years old in spots took to fire like a duck to water, and if a chemical engine and a lot of V. F. D. hadn't come along our home would now be a part of one of the great wide open spaces. At present both Louis and the house are restored. Virginia and Adelaide are enjoying college and manage to get several A's in their work in spite of many extra-curricular activities. Louis Jr. went back to Deerfield for another year although he has all his points for college, has a D in football, and is on the school orchestra. Next fall he goes to Amherst, my Alma Mater-in-law."

Josephine (Daskam) Bacon's daughter Deborah is working in the Henry Street Settlement in N. Y.

Della (Finch) Sammis says: "I am doing the same old things but *not* in the same old way, teaching, housekeeping, etc. My stepdaughter is teaching in Mass. this year and my 10-year-old son goes to high school soon."

Ethel Gower was registrar for the Second Conference on the Cause and Cure of War which was held in Washington in Dec.

Ex-1898

Jessie (Bingham) Kimball writes, "No special news except we have a *fine* granddaughter and a *fine* grandson and have bought a home in West Newton where we hope to 'live happily ever after.'" Address, 212 Chestnut St., West Newton, Mass.

Lucy (Cable) Biklé ('01) is editing her father's letters which she hopes to bring out in book form before very long.

Lavinia Clark is now making her home at St. George's, Palm Harbor, Fla.

Florence (Fowler) Bradley was chairman of the New Haven Smith Club Fair and Bridge that raised $900 for Juniper Lodge and the Club's scholarship fund.

1899

Class secretary—Miriam Drury, 334 Franklin St., Newton, Mass.

The secretary regrets that she has no news, but there is reason to believe that the class book will soon be published and in the hands of those members who signified a desire to possess a copy.

1900

Class secretary—Gertrude E. Gladwin, 2323 Orrington Av., Evanston, Ill.

Aloysia (Hoye) Davis was the chief speaker at the October meeting of the Holyoke Woman's Club. She spoke of her six years' experience as chairman of the legislative de-

partment of the Federation of Women's Clubs which involved many trips to Washington in the attempt to promote measures that had been approved by the Federation. She emphasized the point that despite those who have opposed woman suffrage, women's influence in politics has always been beneficial to the community at large.

Lucy (Lord) Barrangon's daughter Eloise has been taken into Alpha.

Leonora (Paxton) Miller is spending the winter at The Boulevard, Miami Beach (Fla.), and hopes that any of her friends who come south will look her up.

Laura (Shedd) Schweppe's father, John Graves Shedd, died in Chicago on Oct. 28, 1926, after a brief illness. [See page 186.]

Ex-1900

Katharine Darrin has been giving a series of six current events talks in the Twentieth Century Club of Buffalo this fall and winter. Since 1913 she has been giving talks of this sort in many eastern states, before women's clubs and schools.

DIED.—Ethel (Sayles) Rice, June 18, 1926.

1901

Class secretary—Mrs. Sanford Stoddard (Hannah Johnson), 499 Washington Av., Bridgeport, Conn.

Agnes (Childs) Hinckley has recently acquired a charming home at Manset, near Mt. Desert, Me.

Emma Durkee's father died on Dec. 9, 1926.

Agnes (Gilchrist) Watterson's second son, David, won a four year scholarship at Western Reserve Univ., Cleveland, for citizenship and high standing.

Laura (Lord) Scales and Agnes (Childs) Hinckley gave a wonderful granddaughter dinner party in December where 22 guests were entertained, two of whom were class nieces—Buffy's and May's. Evidently they liked the sample for they are hereby broadcasting for names of all 1901 nieces. Great pride and satisfaction in the entire group have been expressed by both hostesses.

Jean Morron was in Paris last summer studying French.

Ona (Winants) Haverkamp and her husband, the Rev. Frederick Haverkamp, will spend Christmas and the rest of the winter in the Holy Land, touring Persia, Egypt, Greece, and Czecho-Slovakia before returning home Sept. first.

1902

Class secretary—Mrs. L. F. Gates (Josephine Lamson), 723 Eighth St., Wilmette, Ill.

Helen (Durkee) Mileham's father died on Dec. 9, 1926.

Alice (Egbert) Howell, with five lively youngsters, spent considerable time last summer vagabonding in Europe, having vastly amusing experiences over the peasant's reception of the girls, tramping in knickers and bérets—like boys.

Ruth French has been made Field Secretary for the Boston League of Women Voters.

Grace Macdougall was elected a member of the Smith chapter of Phi Beta Kappa in 1925.

Martha (Riggs) Griffith and her husband are taking a trip around the world on the *Empress of Scotland*. They are scheduled to reach their home (Palmyra, N. Y.) about Apr. 15.

Virginia (Tolar) Henry's oldest son is Yale '27.

NEW ADDRESS.—Mrs. R. Werner Marchand (Grace Watkinson), 106 Alexander St., Princeton, N. J.

1903

Class secretary—Mrs. Francis W. Tully (Susan Kennedy), 3 Alwington Rd, Chestnut Hill, Mass.

NEW ADDRESS.—Mrs. Frederic A. Pfeil (Virginia Bartle), 439 W. 24 St., N. Y. C. Virginia's husband had a very serious accident about two years ago. He was badly burned in an explosion and for a time was not expected to live. Now he has recovered his health and was able to accept a position offered him in New York. Virginia, who has never liked to be idle, is also enjoying a new position. She is a section manager at Macy's.

Lewis Ward, Alice (Bookwalter) Ward's son, is in the freshman class at Yale and won one of the DuPuy Memorial Scholarships. Doesn't that speak well for the school where Lewis prepared—at Kodaikanal, India—the one for which Elizabeth (Viles) McBride and Alice work so hard?

Marcia (Bailey) Marsh is with her mother in her old home at Machias (Me.) this winter.

The January calendar of the College Club of Boston had a decided 1903 flavor, for Hayes (Breckenridge) Brigham was the director for the month, Florence Howe one of the two ushers, while Laura (Post) Breed was hostess at one of the teas.

Rodericka (Canfield) Baker's mother died in October after a long illness. Rodericka's daughter Anne is preparing for Smith at the Northampton School for Girls.

Marion (Conant) Damon's son Roger has been elected to the Yale fraternity of Alpha Delta Phi.

Annie Dunn reports a delightful trip through the British Isles. Mr. and Mrs. Ray Stannard Baker (he is "David Grayson," the author) were in the same party. Annie is now regaining her health after a serious operation. The sudden death of one of her brothers retarded her recovery.

Helen Goodspeed is at home now and is making an efficient Smith Club secretary.

Mabel (Griffith) Edwards writes: "Mr. Edwards accepted a position here (Gettysburg, Pa.) as head of the department of physics in Gettysburg College last Sept. We like it very much. Surely some 1903ers will come through here and I hope they will look us up."

As our Class Treasurer arrives in Europe from one direction, our Class President will be getting there from this side of the world! May Hammond writes that she is to have a three months' leave of absence from the Alumnae Office and that she and Maud will start on Feb. 23 for a tour abroad, mainly in France and Italy.

Ethel Hutchinson finishes her semester's work at the Boston Normal School on Feb. 7 and plans to be married on Mar. 5. A 1903 luncheon with the bride as the guest of honor was being arranged for some Saturday in February. Ethel will become Mrs. C. Madison Chilton and her address will be 917 Faraon St., St. Joseph, Mo.

Isabel Norton reports that she will be in the office of the Near East Colleges this year.

Almeda (Reed) Hardy's son William graduated from Exeter last June and is now at Dartmouth.

Fannie Stewart's mother died in November of pneumonia, a great loss to Fan as they had been constant companions. Fan writes that she will go on with her teaching, about which she has always been enthusiastic. She says, "This year my classes are very interesting—chemistry, botany, physiology, and general science." Fan has spent many interesting summers. Now she reports one in New Mexico, another in Alaska, and last year she was in Wyoming.

The Class Treasurer before long will be coming into view on the eastern horizon. Margaret Thacher, off on the "University Afloat," spent Christmas on the Pacific; early in January was in India—Bombay, Agra, and Aden—and was to reach Egypt Jan. 19.

Ex-1903

Eleanor (Dick) Swan's husband has been appointed a United States Circuit Judge. During his administration as Dean of the Yale Law School it has taken its place in the front ranks among American law schools and the *Yale Alumni Weekly* says the loss of Dean Swan is "a matter of sincere regret mixed with congratulations."

Alice (Jones) Lewis dashes back and forth between Honolulu and Boston. This fall she came on with Dudley, who was entering Harvard; saw Marion, who graduated from Dobbs Ferry last June, safely ensconced at Pine Manor, Wellesley; then spent some time in visiting; made a stay at Pinehurst—and got back to Honolulu for Christmas!

1904

Class secretary—Eleanor Garrison, 99 Marion St., Brookline, Mass.

BORN.—To Elizabeth (Barnard) Stewart a third son and fifth child, Hamilton, Oct. 4, 1925.

To Harriet (Butler) Crittenden a fourth son and fifth child, Lyman Butler, May 27, 1926.

OTHER NEWS.—Florence Alden writes: "I have been here (Eugene, Ore.) six years and gone east every summer but last summer. I had a glorious time exploring this wonderful country, sleeping under the stars on a pneumatic mattress."

Mary Bancroft is back at Abbot Academy after eight weeks in England last summer.

Mabel Barkley has opened a tea room in Lowell, Mass., "The Open Door," 8 Carpet Lane.

Elizabeth (Barnard) Stewart writes: "The Stewart family spent three delightful months at East Setauket, L. I. Then we came to Augusta (Ga.) where Col. Stewart is in command of the Arsenal. I have a freshman daughter at Smith and I doubt if any others in her class of 630 could write more enthusiastic letters home."

Olive (Beaupré) Miller's daughter Virginia, now at school in Winnetka, will be ready for college in 1929. Olive says: "At present she has an eye turned toward Wellesley. I am trying to keep my hands off and let her decide for herself. Our new books this year are: 'Nursery Friends from France' and 'Tales Told in Holland.'"

Mildred Bennett is spending the winter in California.

Heloise Brainerd attended the second annual congress of the National Student Federation of U. S. A. held at Ann Arbor in December. She spent two days in Pittsburgh visiting higher educational institutions for the Pan-American Union.

Mabel Brown is secretary and registrar of the Normal School in Keene, N. H. "Although this is the youngest of the New England normal schools it has grown to be one of the largest with 550 students."

Maude (Brown) Mazeine's son Graham, one of Brooke (van Dyke) Gibson's Gunnery School boys, is a freshman at Colgate.

Sophie (Burnham) Westcott is spending the winter: in Cambridge, at 7 Craigie Circle. "Sophie and Sallie are preparing for college at the Buckingham School and Bill is at Browne and Nichols."

Edith Camp spent three months abroad last summer, visiting Ireland. She spent an evening in Paris with Mary (Humstone) Fox.

Mary (Chambers) Folwell says: "Some years ago I inherited, in direct line from William Penn's grant in 1713, 350 acres of rich farm land. Happily my husband shared my hobby and we have now developed a fine Jersey dairy farm. I have a manager and twelve men and a growing herd, now about 60, and an increasing organization. Because of my husband's business and the children's school we can't live in any of the three beautiful old houses but make frequent trips there. We are delighted to show our model farm to anyone interested." Chambers' Rocks Farms, Inc., is at Newark, Del. In Merion (Pa.) where they moved last spring, a house had to be built large enough for Mary's family of six children, a ward, a father-in-law, and a nurse. Her oldest boy is at Haverford and the youngest girl at a French kindergarten. Billy will be three in August.

Anne Chapin is at Johnson Hall, 411 W. 116 St., N. Y. C. "I am living in this big dormitory for postgraduate women students as assistant to Miss Butler who is the head of the house."

Helen (Cilley) Alder writes: "In June my husband resigned as headmaster at Adelphi Academy, Brooklyn, where he had been seventeen years, to accept a similar position at the Blake School, a country day school in Minneapolis. Address, 2304 Aldrich Av. S. Bradbury is a freshman at Princeton, John is

in high school at Blake, and Lavinia is at Northrop School."

Marion Clapp is preparing musical and dramatic programs for women's clubs. She is chairman of the Drama Committee of the Women's City Club of Boston.

An astute citizen of Northampton wrote the following inspired paragraph to the Gazette this fall: "Though the largest woman's college in the world is situated here, we have never had a woman mayor. There is, perhaps, no one who so efficiently links town and college as the one I would name; her executive ability is well known both to Northampton and to Smith; her interest in everything municipal and collegiate is keen; she is a native of the city and the product of its schools; she has served so well for twenty years; an ardent worker in the community, widely known throughout the city, and popular wherever known. Capable, enthusiastic, honest, tactful, indefatigable, and intelligent, who would make a better mayor than Miss Annetta Isabel Clark?"

Marie (Conant) Faxon's son Conant entered Harvard this fall. Bill is at Loomis.

Nellie (Cuseck) Connolly will represent the Merrimac Valley Club at the Alumnae Council meetings in February. Nellie spent some time in Chocorua (N. H.) this summer, making two visits to Juniper Lodge.

Elizabeth Dana is dispensing delicacies at the Sea Venture Tea Room, North Shore, Pembroke, Bermuda, from January till May.

Marguerite Emerson is spending the winter at Pine Mountain, Ky. She is housemother at Ethel (deLong) Zande's ('01) school in the Model Home, a primitive four-room cottage where three girls at a time do housework for six weeks in addition to their regular school work. Last summer Marguerite was matron of the Y. W. C. A. camp at Ashburnham, Mass.

Eleanor Garrison had visitations with Adèle (Keys) Hull, Dorothea (Wells) Holt, Margaret (Leatherbee) Kendal, and Helen Mabie in Summit (N. J.) this fall. She saw Edna (Cushing) Weathers and her diminutive, brown-eyed baby—our youngest child!

Pauline (Geballe) Newlin is teaching general science and chemistry in the high school in Portland, Ore.

Annie Gilligan has gone to Hartford (Conn.) to teach in the Bulkeley High School. Address, 143 Jefferson St.

Laura Glazier has been teaching in the Hartford Public High School since 1909.

Elsie (Harris) Durbin's son Gilbert is at the Case School of Applied Science in Cleveland. Dorothy is in Burnham preparing for Smith.

Flora Keeney has moved from Portland (Ore.) to 1697 Euclid Av., Detroit, Mich. At present Flora is in Manila. She is general secretary of the Y. W. C. A. which has just been organized there, a new departure in the Philippines.

Georgina (Kellogg) Reynolds, besides keeping house for her two boys, teaches in the Anniston (Ala.) High School, and the day it closes steps into the State Normal School, where she teaches till August.

Adèle (Keys) Hull wrote, "We are having a belated vacation trip in Margaret (Leatherbee) Kendal's attractive summer home on Peconic Bay." Adèle's son Cameron is spending the winter in California with his aunt.

Marie Ketcham has moved to 1769 Columbia Rd., Washington, D. C. She is an enthusiastic osteopath, specializing in finger surgery. Marie says, "I feel that I am needed in this work as I have the small fingers essential to reconstructing the Eustachian tubes." She is particularly successful in helping deaf people.

Bob (Kimberly) Shirk spent the summer in Redlands (Calif.), helping to remodel the Contemporary Club House.

Frances Lockey is Dean of Girls and head of the Latin department in the Leominster (Mass.) High School. Last February she received her Ed.M. from Harvard.

Katherine (McKelvey) Owsley's Katherine wrote from Grenoble, "We have had such varied experiences, all delightful, that the thought of leaving this country for the sidewalks of Paris is almost heart-rending."

Helen Marble went around the world last winter with her sisters. This year she is sharing an apartment with Elizabeth Biddlecome at 74 Fenway, Boston.

Jane (Mitchell) Olds's son Edward is at Exeter, David is at school in Haverford, Pa.

Marion (Paige) Leake's daughter Constance graduated from Miss Porter's School last June and came out this winter. Eugene is at the Hill School and John at Hotchkiss.

Helen (Peabody) Downing has sold her New Canaan house, "Driftway," to Marion (Prouty) Bensen and moved further into the country. New Canaan (Conn.) is still her address.

Mary and Mrs. Pusey visited Betty in England last summer. They took Betty to Paris with them "for two heavenly weeks" and then went to Switzerland.

For over a year Ellen (Quigley) Sawin has been "making a real home for the children of professional or business people. At present there are thirteen of them varying in age from three years to seventeen. It is just one big happy family." Ellen's attractive house is in Delaware, six miles from Wilmington (Box 293), on a hill, facing the sunset and overlooking twenty acres of playground. Babies are particularly welcome. The older children have gardens and revel in consuming the fruit of their hands. A descriptive booklet can be had for the asking.

Cathleen Sherman had a successful summer with her tea house at Castleton, Vt. She is spending the winter with her sister Louise, in Ripon, Wis.

Elisabeth Telling has been etching royalty. No other than Queen Marie herself. While Her Majesty partook of lunch at a Chicago club, Elisabeth was given an hour to finish her portrait. The Queen signed it cheerfully and expressed her approval. It has been adorning Ackermann's window on Michigan Av. [See page 170.]

Evelyn (Trull) Bates is president of the Montclair Smith Club.

Dorothy (Upham) Vaughan writes: 'My husband, daughter, and I are just returning from the third meeting of the Pan-Pacific Science Congress held in Tokyo. I have never been so glad of any good thing that has come to me as this very interesting and delightful trip. Words are inadequate to express our appreciation of the rare beauty and charm of things seen there, both material and spiritual, and the almost overwhelming hospitality and kindness that was showered upon us by our Japanese friends."

Edith (Vaille) Weeks's son Frederick, an enthusiastic Harvard freshman, is a member of the Pierian Sodality. She has been nursing Philip successfully through scarlet fever.

Olive (Ware) Bridgman is back in Cambridge after a year abroad.

Una (Winchester) Warnock's son Winchester is a Bowdoin freshman.

Alice (Wright) Teagle has been appointed to serve five years on the Alumnae Fund Committee. Her son John has gone on a University Cruise around the world. Helen is president of the freshman class at Smith.

NEW ADDRESSES.—Mrs. William H. Adamson (Ernestine Fowler), 37 Coolidge Av., Glens Falls, N. Y.

Mrs. Harvey D. Bailey (Florence Lovett), 140 Post Rd., Darien, Conn., Box 142.

Gertrude J. Comey, 807 Hickman Rd., Augusta, Ga.

Abby Merchant, 35 Grand St., White Plains, N. Y. (temporary).

Mrs. Newcomb (Ruby Hendrick), 181 Summit Av., Upper Montclair, N. J.

Ex-1904

Grace (Buck) Stevens returned to Boston after a summer in Europe. In addition to her regular law course at Boston Univ. she is taking four electives.

Alice Carlisle, with her parents, is spending the winter in Charleston, S. C.

Alice (Hatch) Nelson has moved from Pasadena to 36 Fairmont Av., Newton, Mass.

Hazel (King) Bakewell spent the Christmas holidays skiing with her husband in the Sierras.

Margretta Kinne took two courses in kindergarten methods at Columbia last summer. She is teaching in the Ramapo Valley Country Day School in Suffern, N. Y.

K. C. (McConnell) Ludlow's daughter Kathryn is preparing for Smith at Kent Place School in Summit, N. J. While entering her daughter at school, K. C. visited Edna (Cushing) Weathers at Short Hills.

Winifred (Newberry) Hooker says: "My older son, Richard, and younger daughter, Mary, had infantile paralysis this fall on our Berkshire hilltop. They are very lucky, Mary recovering entirely while Richard is promised complete recovery within a year."

Although Helen Robinson migrated to 1905 she seems like a sister. She is a running mate of Mary Bancroft at Abbot Academy. In

August she spent ten days in Pelham with Daisy (Gamage) Specht.

Jessamine Rockwell writes from Carmel, Calif., "My activities are confined to two children and a gift shop, 'The Jasmine Bush.'"

Sallie Tannahill received her M.A. from Columbia in October.

Florence (Wells) Ireys's son Calvin is at Deerfield Academy. She has a fourteen-year-old son John and her Marguerite is in the third grade at school.

1905

Class secretary—Mrs. Frank Mansfield (Alice Curtis), 9 Salisbury Rd., Brookline, Mass.

Your class officers are very anxious to check up on all addresses, so will you please send in the return postals at once, whether your address has changed or not, and don't forget to add news of yourselves and families.

MARRIED.—Helen Colby to W. Emery Horton, Apr. 17, 1926. Address, 265 Winter St., Norwood, Mass.

BORN.—To Fannie (Smith) Powers a third child and first daughter, Helen Janet, Nov. 5, 1925.

OTHER NEWS.—Helen (Abbot) Lapham writes that Edna (Capen) Lapham with her entire family took a house very near her in Menlo Park (Calif.) last summer, so their eight children were together for the first time.

Alice Brimson is president of the Baptist Missionary Training School in Chicago. In the course of a month's trip in the east in the interests of the school she addressed the congregation of the Baptist Church in Northampton, visited College, and stayed two days at the Sophia Smith Homestead in Hatfield.

Alice Evans, who is on sabbatical leave from Pomona, is studying at Teachers College. After February she plans to be in Europe for six months.

Ruth Cook and Josephine Webster sailed Oct. 16 for a six months' holiday in England, Southern France, and Italy. Josephine has a leave of absence for that period from her position as executive secretary of the Vermont Children's Aid Society.

Bess (Freeman) Peirce is chairman of the physical education department of the Y. W. C. A. in Worcester this year. Her oldest daughter, Betty, has entered the Misses Kirk's School, Bryn Mawr.

Marion Gary is now one of the two representatives from Vermont on the regional committee of Girl Scouts for New England.

Mary (Hastings) Bradley writes: "My book, 'Caravans and Cannibals,' is just published (D. Appleton and Co.). It is the record of our expedition of 1924 and 1925 in the Belgian Congo. I am very busy with lectures, articles, and my lively family."

Alice Hopkins, representing the library department at Simmons, attended the 50th Anniversary of the American Library Association, held this winter in Atlantic City and Philadelphia. Alice is secretary-treasurer of the Cambridge Smith Club.

Louise Kingsley is president of the Washington Smith Club. Alfred Dennis was the speaker at their opening meeting.

Bertha Lovell is case supervisor and assistant field director, American Red Cross, Letterman General Hospital, Presidio, San Francisco. Address, 1955 Leavenworth St., San Francisco.

Elsie (Mason) Powell's oldest son, Mason, was married Oct. 26, 1926, to Rita Sebring of Spencer, Mass. They are living in Columbia (S. C.), where he has a position with the American Agricultural Chemical Co. Elsie's next son, Townsend, is a sophomore in high school. Alger Jr. is in the sixth grade and small John is still at home. They have had an unusually busy season on the fruit farm this year.

Bertha (Page) Smith's little daughter, Claire, died Oct. 31, 1926.

Marjorie Perry writes that she hasn't done anything but ride horseback, and then she adds: "Last spring I took my brother's little boy, eight years old, with me to camp, two hundred miles on horseback over two ranges of mountains. There all summer I taught girls to ride, and led them into the high country where we slept out, and traveled with pack horses. Often there were forty-five in our line, and we always sought the big country that was too rough for civilization. Eleanor Bliss '24 helped me and together we stayed a month after camp closed, to roam the country and hunt new trails. We lived alone on the hill, three miles from town, and found our own food of mushrooms and whatever game we got on our rides. Coming home in the fall we had to cross a 1200-foot pass in a blizzard."

Helen (Shedd) Reed's father, John G. Shedd, died Oct. 22, 1926, at St. Luke's Hospital, Chicago, following an emergency operation for appendicitis. [See page 186.]

Martha Smith writes: "I have taken a job at the Y. M. C. A. in New Haven, where my work is both secretarial and social. I am assistant to the membership secretary, and also take charge of all suppers etc. put on by the various clubs. This means the buying and planning, and even working for several affairs each week. My new address is 1220 Chapel St., New Haven, Conn."

Anne Streator's father, Rev. Martin L. Streator, died July 22, 1926, after a long illness.

NEW ADDRESSES.—Mrs. C. T. Brimson (Julia Childs), 1042 Avenue Catalonia, Coral Gables, Fla.

Mrs. K. C. Reed (Helen Shedd), 1550 N. State Parkway, Chicago.

Ex-1905

The Orlando (Fla.) *Sunday Reporter-Star,* of Nov. 28, 1926, contained a half-page article telling of the real work Ruth (Brown) Godfrey is doing for school and civic interests. She has been the prime factor in establishing standardized lunchrooms in every school in the city and also has undertaken to see that teachers coming to Orlando have suitable living quarters at low cost. Her work has resulted in the opening of two "teacherages," real homes, conducted by the school board, and run at minimum cost, so that no profit is made and the teachers get the maximum of comfort and pleasure.

Helen (Dill) Heald writes, "We have bought a farm in Morristown, and hope soon to be living on it."

Eleanor (Marshall) Thurman since her husband's death in 1923 has been associate secretary for the Federated Societies on Planning and Parks, and of the American Civic Association, in Washington, D. C.

Isabel (Salsich) Conway's daughter Janet made her début Dec. 21 at a dance given at the Hotel Somerset, Boston. Isabel's older daughter, Virginia, announced her engagement that same evening to a Mr. Sherbrook of Boston.

1906

Class secretary—Mrs. Eben Atwood (Edith Moore), 2732 Irving Av. S., Minneapolis, Minn.

If anyone wishes to add to the class letter, please let the secretary know before Mar. 1.

BORN.—To Alice (Raymond) Biram a son, James Raymond, Dec. 15, 1926.

OTHER NEWS.—Marjorie (Allen) Seiffert expects to be in Calif. in Feb.

Sarah Bartlett attended the American Library Association meeting at Atlantic City in the fall.

Eleanor (Fox) De Caro returned from Panama about a year ago. Her husband is a captain in the army, stationed at Fort Howard, Md.

Lucy Melcher is vice-president of the Rhode Island Smith Club, also of the A. A. U. W. there. She is teaching.

Ethel Moore wrote a delightfully friendly letter of some length to the secretary. She lives alone with her eighty-seven-year-old father on a farm, with no near neighbors. She gets away very little, but teaches her mother's Sunday school class of women older than herself.

Florence Root's mother died Jan. 17.

Mary Smith is still in the out-patient department of the Minnesota Univ. Hospital. She had a six months' leave from April to Oct. and spent it abroad. In Scotland and especially in England, her traveling companion had relatives, so their visit was unusually pleasant.

Jessie (Vallentine) Thayer reports that she is doing more writing.

Margaret (Richardson) Gallagher is too busy to take more than short vacation trips to the outlying hills, and to Long Island Sound in the summer. She is president of the women's club of her church.

1907

Class secretary—Mrs. James L. Goodwin (Dorothy Davis), 10 Woodside Circle, Hartford, Conn.

MARRIED.—Mildred Haire to Hugh Tyler, Aug. 28, 1926. Address, 247 W. Fourth St., N. Y. C.

Hope Sherman to Harold Elno Smith, Apr. 4, 1925. Hope received her M.D. at Johns Hopkins in 1925 and since then has been "part-time wife" and part-time research fellow at Western Reserve, working with Dr. Gerstenberger at the Babies' and Children's Hospital. She is still Dr. Hope Sherman, *not* Mrs. Smith.

Stella Tuthill to George Albert Whipple, Dec. 29, 1926. Address, 2020 Orrington Av., Evanston, Ill.

BORN.—To Frances (Morrill) Luby a daughter, Miriam Frances, Feb. 16, 1926.

To Marion (Niles) James a son, Richard Hills, Jan. 6, 1926.

To Louise (Peters) Duboc a daughter, Suzanne, June 23, 1926.

OTHER NEWS.—Eva (Baker) Lewis has adopted a baby boy, George Fenn Jr., and appears to be an ideal modern mother.

Gladys Duffee has returned from Japan to her home in Marshfield. She has taken up her magazine subscription agency again.

Dorothy (Evans) Noble is just back from three months in Japan where her husband was delegate to the Pan-Pacific Science Congress in Tokyo, and they were royally entertained by the Japanese Government.

Katharine Frankenstein is doing research work for Barton, Durstine and Osborn, an advertising agency in New York.

Kate Huntley is in New Haven doing investigating for the National Bureau of Economic Research.

Ethel (Kenyon) Loomis is president of the Woman's Club of New Britain, Conn. Her oldest son is at Amherst, class of 1930.

Lilian (Major) Bare says she has found Huntington (N. Y.) virgin soil for organization purposes and she has started a Parent-Teacher Association, a Community Center, and a League of Women Voters.

Mason (Montgomery) Condict, who for six years has been studying and working in landscape architects' offices in Boston, has gone into an office in Washington where she can take care of her own work. Last year she edited "The House Beautiful Gardening Manual."

Julie (Park) Vanderbilt is teaching and supervising in the Dwight School, Englewood, N. J., one of her own daughters being among her pupils.

Stella (Tuthill) Whipple, Edna True '09, and Catharine Hooper '11 have formed the North Shore Travel Service. They are ready to help anyone who is going abroad at any time with advice and itineraries.

May (Welsh) Sewell ('08) with her husband and little daughter returned from Australia in June. She had many interesting experiences including an appendicitis operation two weeks previous to sailing for home.

NEW ADDRESSES.—Mrs. Thomas E. Van Winkle (Eleanor Dickson), 28 Clinton Av., Maplewood, N. J.

Mrs. Horatio E. Smith (Ernestine Failing), 168 Irving Av., Providence, R. I.

Mrs. John R. Milligan (Beatrice Humphrey), New Canaan, Conn.

Mrs. J. Carleton Loomis (Ethel Kenyon), 565 Lincoln St., New Britain, Conn.

Mrs. Charles D. Baker Jr. (Eleanor Little), 27 Browning St., Baldwin, N. Y.

Mrs. Burt H. Leonard (Mabel Norris), 13 Pennoyer St., Rowayton, Conn.

Mrs. Raymond A. Linton (Morley Sanborn), Fairhope, Ala. (until spring).

Mrs. George B. Neumann (Louisa Stockwell), 55 Ketchum Pl., Buffalo, N. Y.

Mrs. Frederick H. Cone (Ethel Woolverton), 439 E. 51 St., N. Y. C.

Ex-1907

Elisabeth (Ford) Bacon is managing a large apartment house in New York.

Lucy (Pinkham) Burnham's daughter Jennie was married Sept. 27, 1926, to Donald Ewen Cameron and lives in Leicester, England.

Edith (Wilson) Bruen has continued her studies since leaving college, taking a major sequence in French and a secondary sequence in home economics by correspondence in the Univ. of Chicago, and hopes eventually by establishing three months' residence at the University, to receive a degree. Her older daughter is nearly ready for college.

NEW ADDRESS.—Mary Pettengill, 462 Chestnut Hill Av., Brookline, Mass.

1908

Class secretary—Mrs. James M. Hills (Helen Hills), 876 Carroll St., Brooklyn, N. Y.

MARRIED.—Sarah Simpson to Talbot Faulkner Hamlin, Nov. 17, 1926. Address, 325 E. 72 St., N. Y. C.

BORN.—To Lucile (Parker) Mersereau a fourth child and first daughter, June, June 21, 1926.

To Alice (Walton) Wheeler a fifth child and third son, Daniel Gould, July 19, 1926.

To Amy (Everett) Wing a fifth child and first daughter, Amy Webster, May 12, 1926.

ADOPTED.—By Helen (Barr) Smith, in April 1925, a year-old boy who is named Barr Smith.

OTHER NEWS.—The May School in Boston, where Harriette Abbott teaches history, has purchased a fine building, formerly occupied by the University Club on the water street side of Beacon St., into which they expect to move in February.

As part of her job as Research Assistant at Yale Observatory, Ida Barney has just published with Frank Schlesinger, Director of Yale Observatory, volume 4 of the Transactions of the Astronomical Observatory of Yale Univ. It is entitled, "Catalogue of the Positions and Proper Motions of 8359 Stars."

Jane (Thomson) Bausman writes that she is busy with her work at the Henry St. Visiting Nurse Service.

Florence Boyle is part owner of "The Black Sheep Tea Room" at 54 Tamalpais Rd., Berkeley, Calif.

Hazel (Joerder) Brown has transcribed into Braille Stevenson's "Prince Otto." She has also learned to typewrite.

Louise (Stevens) Bryant has just completed editorial work on a book entitled, "Clinics, Hospitals and Health Centers" which is being published by Harper Bros. She is also completing a monograph, "Clinics and Non-Medical Social Agencies."

Bella Coale writes, "On the steamer going over, Gladys Gilmore announced a tea for Smith people and drew sixteen, including Mr. Wells and Mr. Robinson of the faculty."

Ruth Eliot is taking a year off and studying at Columbia. Her address is 438 W. 116 St., N. Y. C.

Marjorie Henry returns to Paris again this winter for further study.

Helen Hyndman is manager of a Doubleday, Page book shop at 38 Wall St., N. Y. C.

Clara (Meier) Schevill is a professional singer and vocal teacher. She gave a public recital in October of a program which sounded more than interesting. For the past two years she has been contralto soloist at the Fourth Presbyterian Church, Lakeshore Drive, Chicago.

Lucy Shaffer has a year's leave of absence from work in this country and is assisting in Miss Moxley's School for American Girls, Villa Helene, Via P. Stanislao Mancini, Rome.

NEW ADDRESSES.—Mrs. Robert E. Blakeslee (Caroline Brackett), 43 Garden Rd., Wellesley Hills, Mass.

Mrs. Wallace F. Thompson (Bessie Cary), 258 High St., Lockport, N. Y., c/o Mrs. Howard Daggett.

Mrs. Arthur P. Hosford (Amy French), 13 Florence St., Natick, Mass.

Mrs. Seymour Barnard (Eunice Fuller), 98 Joralemon St., Brooklyn, N. Y.

Adalene Hill, 1055 Wilshire Blvd., Los Angeles, Calif.

Mrs. Samuel F. Monroe (Edith James), 911 Carteret Av., Trenton, N. J.

Mrs. M. Dison Griffith (Grace Kellogg), 218 Shelley Av., Elizabeth, N. J.

Mrs. Henry E. Comings (Marjory Lewis), "Shore Hill," Manhasset, N. Y.

Mrs. Charles W. Atwater (Alice Merriam), Middletown, Conn.

Mrs. Frederick W. Lehmann Jr. (Margaret A. Mills), 3220 John Lynde Rd., Des Moines, Ia.

Mrs. Eugene L. Mersereau (Lucile Parker), 1012 Gasco Bldg., Portland, Ore.

Mrs. Whitney H. Joyce (Ada Reeve), 24 University Rd., Brookline, Mass.

Mrs. John Pullman (Helen Ribbel), 4659 Castellar St., Ocean Beach, Calif.

Mrs. Philip M. Rodgers (Myrtle Smith), 35 Wood St., Honolulu, T. H.

Mrs. Roswell Davis (Helena Stone), 91 Cross St., Middletown, Conn.

Mrs. Arthur D. Ralston (Mildred Varney), 5136 Bloomington Av., Minneapolis, Minn.

1909

Class secretary—Mrs. Donald Pirnie (Jean MacDuffie), 138 Milbank Av., Greenwich, Conn.

BORN.—To Marjorie (Carr) Jamison a third daughter, Marjorie, in Sept. 1926.

To Jessie (Haver) Butler a son and second child, Richard H., Aug. 26, 1926.

To Edith (Merritt) Lane a third child and first daughter, Edith M., July 13, 1926.

To Dorothy (Ringwalt) Hartley a second child and first daughter, Mary Clarkson.

To Dorothy (Woodruff) Hillman a fourth child and second daughter, Hermione, June 22, 1926.

DIED.—Elizabeth Allison, Oct. 19, 1926.

In Memoriam

In thinking of Elizabeth, Wordsworth's poem about Lucy has always seemed very appropriate. Of a rare and fine nature, Elizabeth, too, lived along an untrodden way. The spiritual facts of her life are the most significant—her devotion to her family, her church, and her college, an interest that was both responsive and unfailing. The college and her class filled a large share of her life: since graduation she had been in the Registrar's Office, and later in the Hillyer Art Gallery as curator. Much loved by the class, she will be greatly missed.

NEW ADDRESSES.—Mrs. F. M. Orndorff (Jean Alexander), 2737 Eastwood Av., Evanston, Ill.

Mrs. John T. Metcalf (Ruth Clark), 161 S. Prospect St., Burlington, Vt.

Mrs. S. D. Killam (Florence Forbes), 31 Alvin Av., Toronto, Can.

Mrs. G. J. Schmucki (Vivien Forbes), 27 St. John's Wood Rd., London N. W. 8, Eng.

Winifred Kaltenbach, The American Hospital, 63 blvd. Victor Hugo, Neuilly-sur-Seine, France.

Mrs. Ronald Lee (Louise Putnam), "The Driftway," Hook Rd., Bedford, N. Y.

Mrs. W. W. Young (Helen Seymour), 446 Ridgewood Rd., East Orange, N. J.

OTHER NEWS.—An unofficial luncheon of the Class, with Genevra (Gubbins) McCarroll and Gertrude (Bussard) McCarthy as luncheon committee, took place on Nov. 19 at the Smith College Club in New York. Prof. Everett Kimball was guest of honor, giving in his talk a stimulating picture of the present-day ideals of the college. Seventeen members of the class and Helen (Hills) Hills '08 were present. The whole affair was a great success; and we are looking forward eagerly to another reunion at the Club.

Eleanor (Burch) Jackson says: "We drove up from Miami about two weeks before the hurricane but were there for a mild one in July. We expect to locate permanently in Chicago."

Lucy Cole, with her father and mother, sailed on Jan. 29 on the Clark Tour of the Mediterranean. Towards the end of the trip they plan to leave the party and have a few weeks to themselves, returning home in April.

Elaine Croston is having a leave of absence this year. The first half she spent studying at Columbia, and in February went abroad for six months. She was at Winifred (Williams) Hildebrant's for Thanksgiving.

Lincoln (Dunbar) Holmes was in Paris last summer and passes on the news of Win Kaltenbach's new work.

Florence (Forbes) Killam writes that Toronto is her permanent address.

Vivien (Forbes) Schmucki moved to London last June, where her husband is European sales manager of the Monroe Calculating Machine Co. She had a wonderful summer in Switzerland, and was back in New York with her husband for two weeks at Christmas.

Mary Gleason found the work with the Near East Relief too harrowing and now has quieter quarters at Columbia as secretary to Dr. Paul Munroe, director of the International Institute of Teachers College. Mrs. Marion LeRoy Burton has an office next to hers.

Winifred Kaltenbach in June was asked to become Superintendent of the American Hospital at Neuilly, France, and Director of the Nurses' Training School. She finally accepted, and is enjoying it immensely. Beth MacDuffie '20 happened to visit the hospital on the day when Mr. and Mrs. Douglas Fairbanks were making an official inspection. She reports Win as very impressive. A letter from Winifred, dated Yonkers, Jan. 4, says she is here for the holidays. The hospital is fifteen minutes out of Paris and if any 1909-ers want help, "socially, shoppingly, or medically while in Paris, I'll be delighted to dispense advice. There are 120 beds in the hospital and about 75 pupils of many nationalities, but all instruction is in English. We are trying to graft American nursing on to many nations where nursing is not yet on a high plane. The hospital is for Americans and their wives or husbands. Elizabeth (Alsop) Shepard has just bought an apartment from the hospital.

Henrietta Harris is giving valuable aid to the Old Ladies' Home of Springfield, of which she is a director. She is making a special study of the practical housekeeping details, with interesting menus for the 60 inmates as her chief objective.

Emilie (Martin) Lewin drove to Asheville (N. C.) last summer and recommends that every one read "The Test" in the October issue of the *Atlantic*.

San Si Di, Marion Mead's Chinese Shop, is very successful. Marion has doubled the size of her quarters and increased her sales force.

Anne Mitchell says that only an operation for tonsilitis prevented her from coming to the November luncheon.

Gertrude (Schwarz) McClurg had double pneumonia last August and spent the fall recuperating in Denver. She plans to spend the winter in Chicago.

Katharine (Sewall) Austin writes that her husband has temporarily abandoned the law, hoping to improve his health by less confining work. He is traveling through the East, representing a Barre (Vt.) Granite Co. Katharine herself is very busy as director of the Junior Aid of her church and with her work in the Music Study Club.

Ros (Underwood) Perry is president of the Junior League of Denver.

Louise (Winthrop) Ellis and family are in New Orleans for the winter, returning to Des Moines in April.

Dorothy (Woodruff) Hillman's father died Oct. 3, 1926, in Auburn, N. Y.

Willie Young is with Mabel Stone at the Chatham (Va.) Episcopal Institute. Mabel writes that Willie is a wonderful help there.

Ex-1909

MARRIED.—Marion Miller to a Mr. Fernald, Oct. 9, 1926.

1910

Class secretary—Alice O'Meara, 12 Keswick St., Boston, Mass.

BORN.—To Josephine (Frawley) Yantis a son, John Frawley, Feb. 19, 1926. The baby died Feb. 25.

To Edna (Gibson) Taylor a daughter, Leila Martha, Oct. 30, 1924, and a son, Daniel David, July 23, 1926.

To Laurel (Sullivan) Ely a son, Frederick DeForest, Dec. 7, 1926.

To Dorothy (Waterman) Waldron a daughter, Jessica, Oct. 10, 1926.

NEW ADDRESS.—Mrs. Jesse V. Perry (Wilma Ridgway), 1705 Dorchester Rd., Brooklyn, N. Y.

OTHER NEWS.—Jane Armstrong, M.D., opened an office last fall in Plymouth Inn and already has a flourishing practice in Northampton.

From Ward Baker comes a highly interesting letter telling of her new home in California: "I've not done a thing I'd planned, except buy the ranch. I wanted a new Spanish stucco bungalow and I bought a Minnesota-type house with yellow clapboards and red roof. I planned to settle in the San Fernando Valley, 25 miles from Los Angeles, so that I could do Ph.D. work and here I am 52 miles from Los Angeles and in the San Bernardino Valley, 8 miles from San Bernardino itself and too far for university commuting at present. But Pomona is near and I may be able to do some work later. We have a 2½-acre grapefruit and poultry ranch —225 trees, more than half of which are bearing; two 250-bird units and poultry storehouses and 500 five-months' pullets. Mother stood the trip out splendidly. We drove 4300 miles in 16 days' actual running time, going via the northern route, and within six weeks of the time we left Painesville (O.) were settled in our new home! This will be my hard week (Sept. 27) for irrigation comes Thursday, and chicken-house cleaning and spraying the next two days, and between times I'm weeding and fertilizing and getting ready to put in a winter vegetable garden." Ward encloses a snapshot of herself which makes us think that she is quite equal to the demands made on her by this pioneering existence.

In *Arts and Decoration* for Oct. 1926 a full page was devoted to pictures and text describing Adiene (Bergen) Hart's new house, which was designed by Mr. Hart, who is an architect. "It is constructed of stone with unusually placed and picturesque high casement windows."

Beth (Blodgett) Tirrell went to Europe the summer following reunion primarily for the study of French. Most of the time was spent at the Univ. of Grenoble, where her group was assigned a special professor. "We returned to Paris via Mont Blanc, which always means 'Monsieur Perrichon' to me. During our two weeks of lectures at the Sorbonne I must confess that I cut many of them, as I wanted to see Paris. My final tour took me to Nancy, Strassburg, Brussels, and London.

The past year, since my return, I have really been living again [Beth has to watch her health] and have been doing some extras such as faculty advisership and coaching a play."

Mary Brewster has a year's leave of absence from the Albany State Library and is spending it in Paris, teaching cataloging to women of all nations at the American Library.

Edna (Gibson) Taylor is living for awhile at Bellows Falls (Vt.) but will be glad to get back again to the beautiful Black Hills country in South Dakota. She likes the West immensely.

Elizabeth (Jameson) McCreery lost her younger brother last June, following a painful accident. Her father is far from well and so she has been doing the detail work of his business, administering her brother's estate, and helping out her mother, as well as running her own household. Recently her father has given the city of New Castle (Pa.) a fund for the erection of a new hospital and her mother and she are among the trustees who are to build it. Elizabeth reports that the class treasury is once more in very healthy condition. She also says: "I note that several of our classmates are breaking into print, the *Woman's Home Companion* being the medium. I have read articles by Henrietta (Sperry) Ripperger and by Mary Anne (Staples) Kirkpatrick. And not long ago I heard Esther M. Smith over the radio speaking in the interest of the Parent-Teachers Association in Pittsburgh."

Mildred Perry writes, "I am buried under the crudest attempts at journalism most of the time (apropos of Alice O'Meara's taking a course in technique of essay and editorial writing this winter) for I've five classes (in Milwaukee) this year and at times wonder whether I can write a sentence that's complete in thought!" Mildred is also studying French.

Marjorie (Valentine) Seidel is spending the winter in Toulon, France, with her small daughter so that she can be near her husband, who is a naval officer attached to the U. S. fleet in the Mediterranean.

Louise (Van Wagenen) Anson's husband, the Hon. William Anson, died of pneumonia in London, June 22, 1926. Louise is again in this country, staying at Head of the River Ranch, Christoval (Tex.), with her little girl. Her plans for the future are as yet undecided.

Gladys (Van Deventer) Baxter had two flying visits to "Hamp" last summer. She says that Dr. Gilman, back for the year and living at Tenney House, misses her gay neighbors of sixteen years ago in Albright and wishes that they were back. Gladys sent on a letter from Laura Lenhart '08 who is doing valiant work at St. Luke's Hospital in Shanghai, China, because it contained news of three of 1910-in-China. She writes: "I went to Japan for my summer vacation and found Azalia Peet upon the same mountain. She struck me as the happiest missionary I have known. She lives in a big Japanese house and uses it for social work among college and factory girls. Last month Betty Wright arrived and

I had a short visit with her. It was quite a surprise to find little Betty so fat—otherwise she was just like herself. Marjorie (Browning) Leavens stayed with me several days at different times. She is held up by the war from going back home and the last I heard of her was from Nanking where she was staying in a family near enough to Ginling for her to do some work there. Marjorie is interested in astronomy and is reading in French on the subject."

Martha (Washburn) Allin writes: "My boys are old enough (5 and 9) and my house running smoothly enough so that I can continue with the work in fine arts I've been doing for the last two years at the Univ. of Minnesota. I have three, sometimes four, half-days a week in sculpture and water color classes. My first attempt at exhibiting met with success, for last fall a water color was accepted for the Twin City Artists' exhibition at the Art Institute. There was I, hung along with the professionals, and it quite took my breath away. I'm wondering whether I could do it again. In the meanwhile club work has fallen by the wayside and music is just stumbling along. Painting is better than music for my old age anyway—it doesn't require so much physical dexterity!"

1911

Class secretary—Mrs. J. P. O'Brien (Margaret Townsend), 614 Madison Av., Albany, N. Y.

ENGAGED.—Eleanore Ide to Richard H. McIntyre of Bayside, N. Y.

DIED.—Marian (Keith) Gray, late in Sept., 1926, following a long illness.

BORN.—To Eleanor (Barrows) Gregg a daughter, Nancy Barrows, May 16, 1926.

To Marion (Beardsley) Aberdeen a son, Robert Beardsley, July 12, 1926.

To Margery (Brady) Mitchell a second daughter and fourth child, Anne Hubbard, Apr. 27, 1926.

To Madeline (Burns) Wilson a daughter, Eleanor Burns, Jan. 7, 1926.

To Gladys (Burlingame) Barlow a son (her sixth child), Thomas, July 29, 1926. The baby died Oct. 5.

To Annah (Butler) Richardson a son hitherto unreported, Charles Arthur, Apr. 20, 1923.

To Anne (Doyle) Flaherty a son, Edmund, July 3, 1925.

To Chloe (Gillis) Terry fourth and fifth daughters, Barbara, Mar. 31, 1925, and Suzanne, Apr. 20, 1926.

To Mary Esther (Ely) Simmons a son, William Westerman, June 4, 1925.

To Emilie (Heffron) Sisson her fourth son, Alexander, Sept. 14, 1925.

To Adelaide (Peterson) Love a daughter, Esther Gloria, Oct. 6, 1926.

To Dorothy (Rogers) Barstow a third son, Paul Rogers, Oct. 22, 1925.

To Helen (Rose) Kahn a daughter, Grace Helen, May 25, 1926.

To Mary (Stevens) Colwell a second daughter and fourth child, Eleanor Howard, Oct. 19, 1925.

To Mary (Tweedy) Davis a daughter, Mary Edrienne, June 29, 1926.

To Bertha (Ward) Thompson a daughter, Jane, in 1925.

To Katherine (Wilbar) Utter a daughter, Jean Chilton, Sept. 28, 1926.

NEW ADDRESSES.—Mrs. Howard D. Williams (Margaret Clark), c/o Mrs. Z. L. Potter, 103 Lincoln Park Dr., Syracuse, N. Y. Mr. Williams has just been appointed foreign representative of the National Cash Register Co. and they expect to start around the world next summer, going first to Australia. When they reach Europe Margaret's mother is to meet them with the children and they will live in Paris for a while.

Mrs. George H. Rupp (Zita Johnston), Imperial Mine, Michigamme, Mich. Mr. Rupp is the mine superintendent.

Mrs. John P. Farnsworth (Audrey Mallett), 247 Wayland Av., Providence, R. I.

Elizabeth Nye, 68 Montague St., Brooklyn, N. Y.

Mrs. James L. Hutchison (Dwight Power), 3 Oneida St., Rye, N. Y.

Persis Putnam, c/o Mrs. E. V. Platt, Newcastle, Del.

Mrs. Francis H. Bird (Harriet Smith), 342 Thrall St., Clifton, Cincinnati, O., where her husband is professor of commerce at the University.

Mrs. Fernando Lavenás (Margaret Sullivan), 3199 Juramento, Buenos Aires, Argentina.

Mrs. Joseph J. Reilly (Anna May Walsh), 106 19th St., Jackson Heights, N. Y. Her husband is now professor of English at Hunter College, N. Y. C. They spent the summer of 1925 in Europe.

Mrs. Joseph R. Thompson (Bertha Ward), 2699 Fairmount Blvd., Cleveland, O.

Mrs. Walter A. Schaefer (Ruth Weber), 385 Passaic Av., Nutley, N. J.

Mrs. Edgar Toll Glass (Carolyn Woolley), Sunset Farm, West Hartford, Conn.

OTHER NEWS.—Katharine (Ames) George's work in Providence as Y. W. C. A. president ceased last summer but she is still deeply interested in it. They have bought an old New Hampshire home, vintage of 1777, and spend their summers restoring it.

Ethel Bailey is spending the winter in La Jolla, Calif.

Florence Baker conducts a tour to Europe each summer.

Corinne (Barbour) Booth has been traced as far as Cohasset (Mass.) three years ago, where she was seen in the act of buying out a gift shop, accompanied by a daughter, a pet poodle, and her mother. The plot thickens. Where did she go from there?

Ruth (Barnes) Gorman is president of Friendly House Board (Mansfield, O.), president of Visiting Nurses' Association, and member of the Community Chest Board. She and her husband are building a new home of the early American farmhouse type in a large wooded tract at the edge of Mansfield.

Florence Barrows is on leave of absence from Connecticut College and is doing graduate work in genetics under Dr. Sinnott. She is trying for an M.A.

Elsie (Baskin) Adams is back again in Greenwich, Conn.

Florence (Blodgett) McClelland is spending the winter with her family in Florida.

Olive Carter is an editor with the Macmillan Co., N. Y. C. See Alumnae Publications.

Virginia Coyle is director of health at the Bennett School, Millbrook, N. Y.

Henry R. Johnston, husband of Helen (Earle) Johnston, has been made a trustee of Williams College.

Harriet Ellis is teaching at the Cambridge-Haskell School.

Alice (Godwin) Denney has been president and organizer of the Y. W. C. A. for rural Delaware and a member of the Child Welfare Commission of that state, but had to give up these activities on account of her health. She is teaching her little girl at home, the Calvert School course.

Miriam Gould spent last summer at Smith (at Gillett House) as professor of social and applied psychology at the Smith School for Social Work.

Emily (Hix) Faber is bringing up two little nieces. She has had them since babyhood and they are now 8 and 10 years old.

Catharine Hooper has started a Travel Bureau (The North Shore Travel Service) with Edna True and Stella (Tuthill) Whipple in Evanston. They book anyone anywhere, furnishing tickets, itinerary, hotels, motors, and everything necessary or desired with no service charge. This does not mean she has moved to Chicago or that they are not also having their usual summer trips abroad. She is the N. Y. representative and will be glad to take care of anyone in the East planning to travel.

Margaret Howison is assistant in the Nashua (N. H.) Public Library.

Lenore Little is assistant secretary of the Church Pension Fund, N. Y. C.

Gertrude (Lyford) Boyd and her husband came from Scotland last fall with her mother and father on a month's visit to Chicago, Hot Springs (Va.), and New York. She managed to see most of her old friends in that short time. In Nov. 1925 she was elected a parish councillor for the first ward in the Parish of Ayr, standing as a Moderate as opposed to the Socialists, not as a Unionist or Liberal.

Dicky (McCrary) Boutwell spent several weeks in the East last fall, dividing her time between Albany and N. Y. C. They built a cabin in the mountains near Estes Park last summer.

Gertrude (McKelvey) Jones's mother died last November.

Winifred (Notman) Prince has been elected vice-president of the N. Y. State A. A. U. W.

Mae Patterson is agent and organizer for the Frank C. Clark Cruises. On the cruises of the last two summers she writes that they have had Smith teas with 12–15 attending. She expects to organize a party for the 1928 World Cruise and see Smith graduates everywhere.

Of the Best Class Baby, Flora writes that she is a big girl. In three years she will be in college if all goes well. She is very athletic, rides and swims well, and plays everything.

Sophronia Roberts, having spent a month in Johns Hopkins last spring, claims now to be a 1927 model. She spent the summer in Brittany with Ruo Joslin '12 and saw Smith people in all sorts of out-of-the-way places. She is now back at her job as special agent for the Equitable Life in Pittsburgh.

Margaret (Townsend) O'Brien's mother died in December.

Mabel (Ward) Fraser is living in Swarthmore (Pa.), where her husband is associate professor of economics. They are trying out the British Honors idea in advanced work, much the same as at Smith. Mr. Fraser did Honors work himself at Aberdeen Univ. He has just published a book through Alfred A. Knopf, "Foreign Trade and World Politics."

Betty (Wilber) Noe and her archeologist-husband are at home in New Brunswick after a two months' trip through most of the cities east of Chicago. She saw and reported on most of 1911.

Adine (Williams) Lambie hopes to be in the East next year as her husband will have a year's leave of absence from his work as professor at the Univ. of Minnesota.

Ex-1911

BORN.—To Dorothy (Tew) Johnson a daughter, Mary Lucia, Mar. 20, 1926.

NEW ADDRESSES.—Mrs. Edward S. Freedman (Rosina Mandelberg), 36 Warren Ter., Longmeadow, Mass.

Mrs. Walter H. Cassebeer (Kathryn Sabey), 252 Edgemere Dr., Charlotte P. O., Rochester, N. Y.

1912

Class secretary—Mary A. Clapp, Galloupe's Point, Swampscott, Mass.

MARRIED.—Betty Rudolph to William Asher Crane, of West Caldwell, N. J., Oct. 12, 1926. Frances Espy was one of the bridesmaids and there were numerous Smithereens among the guests.

BORN.—To Leila (Allyn) Schelly a son, Cyrus Young, Dec. 29, 1925. Leila's husband died on June 29, 1925.

To Mildred (Carey) Vennema a second son, John Hamilton, Nov. 23, 1926.

To Eleanora (Chesley) Nutter a first son and second child, Edward Harvey, Aug. 10, 1926. Eleanora has been chairman of the school board of Epsom (N. H.) for four years.

To Isabelle (Cook) Smith a daughter, Elizabeth Bailey, Aug. 31, 1926.

To Jinnie (Fink) Whipple a first daughter and third child, Janice Marr, Oct. 25, 1926.

To Helen (Garfield) Buckley a first daughter and second child, Janet Porter, Mar. 29, 1925.

To Helen (Gates) Fitchet a first daughter and third child, Sarah Ellen, in May 1926.

To Annie (Goddard) Dellenbaugh a first daughter and third child, Adèle, Oct. 12, 1926.

To Margaret (Gould) Elder a son, Henry Knox Jr., Mar. 10, 1926.

To Gertrude (Lake) Merrick a daughter,

Margaret. "Toots" has four other children —two girls and two boys.

To Josephine (McKey) Stock a first son and third child, Douglas McKey, Mar. 28, 1926.

To Marguerite (Osborne) Ham twins, Wallace Osborne and Winifred Osborne, July 26, 1926.

To Elfride (Siegel) Durrett a son, Davis Wertenbaker, Aug. 1, 1926.

To Mildred (Spring) Case a third son and fourth child, Douglas Ackerly, Feb. 25, 1925.

OTHER NEWS.—Ruth (Baldwin) Folinsbee and her family are back in New Hope after six months in England and France. The young ladies celebrated their sojourn in Oxford by sprouting the measles.

Beth Battles ('15) commutes between Natick (Mass.), where she teaches French at the Walnut Hill School, and Europe, where she voyages of a summer.

Louise (Benjamin) Kendall writes that she is busy as a bee, transporting her children to institutions of learning, and being president of the Sunnyside Mothers' Club—all this in Sunnyside Gardens, Long Island City.

"Lel" Brower has bought an old place in the country—Knox, Albany Co., N. Y.—and plans to celebrate the Fourth of July, 1927, by opening the "Merrymen's Tea House" therein. A warm welcome is promised—but no reductions!

Helen Brown is still acting as secretary to Miss Helen Frick and living with Helen Denman '10·

Ellen Caverno is active in the campaign for farm relief in the West.

Jessie (Churchill) Thompson resigned her position as assistant secretary to the Governor of Maine, after the death of her mother and father, and is spending the winter in California. Address, 2614 Lincoln Av., Alameda.

The Univ. of Chicago well may boast that its assistant professor of art in interior decorating and costume design is Miss Marion Clark, Smith College 1912.

Uarda (Clum) Fisher wrote in the autumn that she was busily campaigning for Mills and Wadsworth.

We were recently much impressed with a newspaper article—all pictures and reading—describing Alice Comstock's work on her apple farm near Providence, R. I.

Martha Dennison has succumbed to the lure of the Orient again and is back in Bombay as general secretary of the Y. W. C. A.

Ruth Elliott hopes to finish her work for a Ph.D. at Columbia this June. Last year she received a graduate fellowship from the University. As recreation she reports a marvelous summer in the British Isles in a Ford.

Mildred (Evans) Emerson is still head accountant in the Boston Insurance Co.

Mildred Fogel has a part-time stenographic position at Teachers College.

Helen (Forbes) Orwig wrote in the summer that she was recuperating from an operation in an old farmhouse which they had just purchased, and which they were enjoying renovating.

Edith (Gray) Ferguson and Jeanne (Pushee)

Thayer are rapidly becoming professional travelers. Edith, after a visit to South America with her father last winter, junketed all over England and Scotland with her little Jean last summer. Jeanne, with her son Philip, cruised with Raymond and Whitcomb from Tunis to the North Cape last summer; and has just spent the Christmas holidays with her entire family on a tour of the West Indies.

Hazel (Hanchett) Harvey is deep in the remodeling of a new house in Lowell.

Ruth (Harper) Andersson wrote from La Jolla (Calif.) where she was convalescing from an operation.

Dotty Hawkins is librarian at the Univ. of Delaware and also has a finger in the plays produced by the Aircastle Players —their local "Little Theatre."

Maida (Herman) Solomon is a living example of the Coördination of Women's Interests. She swings her family of three children and husband, as well as maintaining her active interest in medical social work—she is just now president of the American Association of Psychiatric Social Workers.

Ruth Joslin, just returned from Europe, is living at 146 E. 49 St., N. Y. C.

Two poems of Maisie (Koues) Sachs are to appear in "London Poetry of Today" during the coming winter.

Sue (Phelps) Zimmermann writes that she has embarked in a gift box business and that she is finding the venture most interesting.

Margaret Plumley is still with the committee on dispensary development in New York.

Marion Scharr is director of Women's activities at the Young Men's and Women's Hebrew Association in Pittsburgh.

The Seamans twins are once more living near each other, Ethel having moved to Santa Monica (Calif.) about a year ago. They both hope to come to reunion.

The First National Bank of Boston still remains safe in the hands of Ruth Mildred Smith, who is in the commercial letter of credit department. Almost all of her spare time she is directing toward the destinies of the Old Powder House Club, a business women's club of about 200 members of which she is the president.

Louisa (Spear) Wilson's daughter, Phoebe, died in Dec. after a long illness.

Margaret Upton forsook the bacteria at Washington Univ. last summer long enough to frisk through England, Scotland, Scandinavia, Holland, and Belgium.

Matilda Vanderbeek is back in New York after a sojourn in California.

"Bill" (Williams) Haynes has moved up from the wilds of Greenwich Village and is living at 150 E. 73 St., N. Y. C.

Olive Williams's mother died while she was in England last summer. Olive is now back in Buffalo teaching at the Franklin School.

Genevieve (Wilson) Imlach's husband died in May 1926.

DIED.—Margaret (Koehler) Ingersoll on December 2, 1926, after the birth of a baby daughter.

Ex-1912

MARRIED.—Harriet Bucknam to Dr. Thomas Albert Foster, Sept. 9, 1926. Address, 105 Pine St., Portland, Me.

OTHER NEWS.—Margery Bedinger, after several months in Europe—(who of the class except me *was* home last summer? M. A. C.)—has forsaken her position of issuing literary rations to the U. S. Army (*i.e.*, librarian at West Point), and is now in command at the State College of New Mexico. She seems to have forgotten her early Salem background when she says that Pauline (Gardner) Donnell, whom she has recently seen, lives *only* 200 miles away! When not charging books she is charging all over the countryside on horseback. She says that it is all very wonderful, and that she rejoices in the change.

Evelyn (Coulter) Bonner is living in Buchanan, Mich.

1913

Class secretary—Mrs. Alexander Craig Jr. (Helen Hodgman), 314 E. 17 St., Brooklyn, N. Y.

MARRIED.—Ruth Bache-Wiig to Theodore Mitchell Pease, Yale '14, July 9, 1926. New address, 40 Summit St., Springfield, Mass.

BORN.—To Susan (Raymond) King a second daughter, Nancy, June 16, 1926.

To Mercy (Stock) Buge a third daughter, Janet Elizabeth, Jan. 16, 1926.

To Inez (Tiedeman) Chapin a third son and fifth child, Daniel, Nov. 14, 1926.

Ex-1913

NEW ADDRESS.—Mrs. Wright Clark (Marjorie Perry), 14 Blackthorne St., Chevy Chase, Md.

1914

Class secretary—Mrs. Herbert R. Miller (Dorothy Spencer), 120 Haven Av., New York City. Telephone: Billings 2414.

BORN.—To Helen (Choate) Barrow her third child and son, Denwood Hicks, Nov. 2, 1926.

To Blanche (Darling) Bergesen her second child and daughter, in the summer of 1926.

To Ruth (Hellekson) Lindley her second child and daughter, Laura Jane, Dec. 10, 1926.

To Catharine (McCollester) Gallaher her second child and daughter, Mary, Nov. 23, 1926, in Paris.

To Marie (Pierce) Kimball her first child and son, John Ritchie Jr., Nov. 17, 1926.

To Helen (Rounds) Moody her first child and daughter, Dorothy Haile, Sept. 14, 1926.

To Ruth (Stinchfield) Leavitt her second, third, and fourth children, Rosilla Foss, Oct. 2, 1920, Helen Ruth Elizabeth, Jan. 28, 1923, and her second son, Harold Otis Shattuck, Aug. 23, 1925.

NEW ADDRESSES.—Barbara Addis, 40 Park Pl., New Rochelle, N. Y.

Mrs. H. K. Norton (Edith Egbert), Glenwood Lodge, Yonkers, N. Y.

Harriet Hitchcock, 250 E. 105 St., N. Y. C.

Mrs. J. J. Waygood (Emma Miller), 653 Ferne Av., Drexel Hill, Pa.

Helen R. Moore, Scarsdale Lodge, Scarsdale, N. Y.

Elizabeth Roby, 7 or 8 E. 87 St., N. Y. C.

Eleanor H. Saladine, 54 Vernon St., Brookline, Mass.

Mary H. Tolman, 80A Cedar St., Boston, Mass.

OTHER NEWS.—Margaret (Beckley) Converse says that last year she was asked to report for the newspapers a lecture that Miss Jordan gave to the New Haven Smith Club on "The Modern Drama." You can imagine her delight when, fascinating and brilliant as the lecture was, there was not one word about the drama, modern or ancient!

Just to show whoever else may read these notes what an outstanding class we really are, we reprint from our class letter: "Edith Bennett sang at the opening of the Sesqui-Centennial on July 5 before thousands."

Louise (Breier) Sundermann left for the West in December.

Ruth (Brown) Harvey is continuing her library work since her marriage as she was under contract. She enjoys the work.

Anna Colman expects to go back into business again at the Queen Anne Shop near Boston.

Gertrude Cranston, after six years of teaching at the George School (Pa.), taught last year in a Philadelphia school. She took one unit of work at the Univ. of Pennsylvania and planned to take two more last summer for courses in education.

Marguerite Daniell expects to spend two weeks in N. Y. in January.

Frances Hooper sails for Italy about Feb. 10. She will be in New York a few days before she sails.

Marjorie Jones and her mother spent the summer in Central America. They may go to Cuba this winter.

November brought Sophie (Marks) Krauss on her annual visit to New York. There were many gatherings in her honor—the largest at lunch with Misses and *nées*, Knight, Mayer, McConnell, Middleton, Moore, Roby, Seamans, and White.

Helen O'Malley was in California last April for a vacation with her family, some of whom live in Oakland. She did not get East.

See Alumnae Publications for note about Effie (Oppenheimer) Vactor. She has also had many poems published in the Ohio newspapers.

Portia Pratt sailed for Italy Dec. 11. She expects to spend the winter abroad and to continue her study of bookbinding in Paris.

Ruth Ralston spent two months in France and England last summer, studying the decorative art of the 17th and 18th centuries. She made trips to numbers of houses furnished in the period, among them the Tudor Manor House at Bradford-on-Avon.

Gwendolen Reed passed the Paul Passy phonetics examination last July in Paris. It has been a great help in her work.

Betty Roby has been working part time and studying the rest at Columbia. She expects to take a full-time job early in 1927.

Verra (Thomas) Griffith in addition to helping her husband in his work as editor of the magazine, *Boating*, has been interested in dramatics of the little theatre type and, we hear through those who have seen her, has become very clever in her impersonations.

Mollie Tolman addressed the students at College in Dec. on Business Opportunities.

Carolyn (Welles) Ellis and her family landed in Bombay in June. They went straight to Islampur. After busy days of settling, getting a proper milk and water supply, etc., they began on their outside work. Dr. Ellis gained permission to use the church building to treat patients. When the rain came, it came heavily and brought much sickness with it. Much of the work is teaching the natives what they need. Carolyn and her husband make many friends in different castes and there is a good deal of visiting to do among their village friends, who are most gracious. Carolyn has had sewing and homemaking classes at her bungalow for the little girls. Dr. Ellis's sister is there visiting and they were expecting Carolyn's sister Margaret for Christmas.

Dorothy (Whitehead) Conklin has moved back to Buffalo. She has had Roz's little boy with her since Sept. 1 and he will stay with her until Lieut. Phillips can make a home for his children. As he is an aviator that is not possible at present.

Jeanne Woods took a short trip to Chicago this fall to see Phyllis (Fergus) Hoyt '13 who has written music for many of her poems (the most recent being "Rosamond"), some of which Phyllis has broadcast.

About 20 attended the N. Y. 1914 tea, Dec. 11, at Madeleine (Mayer) Low's.

Mrs. Burton is giving a course in religious education at Teachers College. Her address is 20 Austin St., Kew Gardens, N. Y.

Mrs. Middleton (Grace Roberts's mother) has seen a good deal of "Bunny" and Mrs. Abbott this fall in Florence. She says that Prof. Abbott seems well, although he is not strong.

K. Knight, D. Seamans, E. Roby, E. Edson, M. Spahr, H. Moore, and G. (Middleton) Roberts were at the New York Smith Club in Nov. to hear M. Farrand speak on her Press Board work.

Grace (Middleton) Roberts and Mollie Tolman (as Alumnae Association directors), and the secretary plan to go to the Alumnae Council meeting in Feb.

Ex-1914

BORN.—To Virginia (Flad) Deane her second child and daughter, Elisabeth Towner (named for E. Bancroft and E. McMillan), July 17, 1926.

NEW ADDRESS.—Lillian Jones, 831 Laurel Av., Bridgeport, Conn.

1915

Class secretary—Mrs. Dudley T. Humphrey (Marian Park), Loudonville, Albany Co., N. Y.

MARRIED.—Mary Anne Cornelius to Thomas King Whipple, Dec. 11, 1926. Address, 1416 Scenic Av., Berkeley, Calif.

Madeleine Weeks to Ralph Lawrence Erickson, Aug. 17, 1926, in Los Angeles.

BORN.—To Guendolen (Reed) Stuart a third child and second daughter, Carol Marden, Oct. 11, 1926.

To Esther Root (Mrs. Franklin P. Adams) a son, Anthony, Nov. 19, 1926.

To Jennette (Sargent) Drake a third daughter, Marilyn Aiken, Oct. 2, 1926.

To Janet (Van Sickle) Hartwell a daughter, Janet Dickson, Nov. 28, 1926.

DIED.—Ellen (Fertig) Cross, Nov. 17, 1926. It is with great sadness that we record Ellen's death. Mr. Cross wrote the Chicago Smith Club asking that the information be sent on for the alumnae records, but it was too late to learn any details. Knowing that one of Ellen's most intimate friends should write the notice it will be omitted until the next QUARTERLY. Dorothy is writing to her husband to express the Class's sympathy.

NEW ADDRESSES.—Mrs. George B. McClary (Adelaide Caldwell), 840 S. Grand Av., Pasadena, Calif.

Dorothy Carman, 435 W. 119 St., N. Y. C.

Mildred Hutchinson (Mrs. Paul E. Gropp), Apt. 51, 1830 R St. N. W., Washington, D. C. Mildred is keeping her own name both socially and professionally.

Mrs. J. J. Dale (Helen Pearce), 109 Monticello Pl., Buffalo, N. Y.

A. Lilian Peters, Huletts Landing, Lake George, N. Y. Temporary, c/o Equitable Trust Co., 23 rue de la Paix, Paris, France.

Mrs. Eleanor S. Cowles (E. Sackett), 131 boulevard Raspail, Paris VI, France.

Mrs. Harvey C. Rextrew (Dorothy Saxton), 36 Edgewood Av., Albany, N. Y.

Daisy Shaw, 284 Federal St., Greenfield, Mass.

Mrs. Lester L. Riley (Eleanor Sibley), c/o Zion Episcopal Church, Douglaston, N. Y.

OTHER NEWS.—Bessie Bailey is still teaching French in Arlington Senior High and spent last summer studying at the Univ. of Toulouse and traveling in France and Switzerland.

Anne Bohning has just finished four years in Rush Medical School of the Univ. of Chicago, spent a year abroad in study, and a year in Presbyterian Hospital (Chicago), and is now looking around for a practice. Her permanent address is Box 124, Ranger, Tex.

Anne Bridgers has sold a play, "Coquette," written with George Abbott, which Jed Harris expects to produce this winter.

Bunnie (Burns) Jones spent a month last fall on a beautiful inlet in B. C. near Vancouver while her son was on a real man's camping trip with his father.

Marian Chase has written an article entitled "The Importance of Shop Arrangement" to appear in an early number of *Gift and Art Shop*.

Lorraine Comly is taking a course in international relations at Syracuse Univ., working in the Boy's Club and other Syracuse charities.

In September, Dorothy (Cooke) Sihler wrote: "We have just had the joy of bringing seven-weeks-old Billie into our home so that Frances could have a brother."

Eleanor (Gibbons) Olcott writes from India: "We have just been home to America and back in the last six months—an interesting route, through the Red Sea, Canal, and Mediterranean and across Europe, the stops coming so close together that there's always excitement. A taste of flying from London to Paris. Wonderful to be home—though I felt alien often. America is so rich and so smug often, that when one has seen the other side of life, the other countries and their terrible need, America's careless wealth is often shocking. Now we're settled down again to our village school visiting, trying to raise the standard of our pitiful needy schools." Eleanor has classes and meetings for the women in the city so that they can come in contact with the Christian women and their ideals.

Fannie Jourdan is secretary in the department of education of Yale Univ. She is keeping house in a little apartment furnished with antiques.

Mary Alice Kelsey is teaching in the Piedmont Schools, five miles from Berkeley. Her father, Rev. Henry H. Kelsey, died last July after an illness of over a year.

Jeannette (Mack) Breed is still greatly interested in the University Coöperative Nursery School but has taken on the house management of the Orthogenic School of Chicago, of which Dr. Josephine E. Young is acting head. Some day she hopes to study for a degree in institutional economics and management. Last spring her eldest child, Mary Jane, died the day after her ninth birthday. Jeannette's little son died six years ago.

Florence Meng is still head of Latin-French in Pottstown High School, working hard, enjoying it, and beginning to be serious about providing for a comfortable old age.

Katharine Pearce is librarian in the Woman's College of Constantinople.

Lilian Peters expects to travel in Europe all winter and to be gone eight months.

Helen (Pratt) Rose is the president of the Woman's College Club of Passaic, a thriving, growing club of 200 members. That and her two daughters and her home keep her busy.

Lee Ramsdell says: "Nothing much to tell. Went abroad this spring; came back in May; housecleaned; Girl's Club, you know small town life. House full all the time, small nephews and nieces, old ladies and friends of my own vintage. Expect to study in N. Y. this winter at the Art Student's League."

Leonora Reno is keeping house for her father and has a full-time position in the secretary's office at the California Institute of Technology, besides keeping up her music and going to an evening gym class. At a wedding she met Theodosia Burton, who told her that Jane is at Emma Willard and going to Smith in two years and that Paul is engaged to a Detroit girl, a niece of Jessie Bonstelle.

Christine (Ruth) Grier's husband is professor of biology at Des Moines Univ., Ia.

Dorothy (Saxton) Rextrew has just had the sixth holiday season of her own business, designing and manufacturing the "Dorothy" line of baby goods, including dresses and Tiny Tad Bibs, "The Little Shavers' Clothing Savers." Dorothy has a little girl of her own

OTHER NEWS.—Martha Abbott's mother died Sept. 27, 1926.

Baltimore has a group of very active '16ers: Emily (Ames) Pickett, who is president of the Smith Club while Helen (Higbie) Mower ex-'16 is secretary; and Justina Hill is president of the Baltimore College Club. Eunice Stebbins is working for a Ph.D. at Johns Hopkins.

Frances (Bradshaw) Blanshard spent the summer in England and France. She is back at Swarthmore acting as dean of women for the year.

Helen Browning expects to go to Washington in April to the D. A. R. Congress.

Irene (Copps) Crowley spent six weeks at Cornell last summer.

Marjorie Darr is with the Main Line of Federation of Churches at Bryn Mawr, Pa.

Margaret Donaldson is teaching English in a high school in Concord, N. C.

Helen (Dunn) Gillespie expects to be in New York City to follow up some courses in salesmanship.

Frances Eaton was called to Miami for Red Cross relief in September to stay several months.

Marie Gilchrist is living at home, working in the Cleveland Public Library.

Gwendolen Glendenning is teaching in Shore School Inc., Beverly Farms, and living at home. She has a class of five little girls and teaches all subjects of the seventh and eighth grades. She says, "It is fine to know how to do percentage once more and know all the countries of Asia."

Lucy (Goodwin) Leach left Wyoming to be in Cleveland with the class baby and her family in time for Thanksgiving. They sail on the S. S. Homeric for the Mediterranean cruise on Jan. 22.

Helen (Gulick) King writes, "I hope 1916 will respond with real enthusiasm to the President Burton Memorial Fund, for I feel sure he meant more to 1916 than to any other class."

Emma (Hartford) Nelson and husband are contemplating a South American trip after the holidays.

Margaret (Henry) Graver, with son and husband, went to Europe last summer. They took an aeroplane from London to Amsterdam.

Margaret (Jones) Little and her husband have bought a house a mile from Andover Station with two acres of land.

Margaret (Leighton) Wallace acted as camp mother at a small boys' camp in Moosehead Lake region last summer.

We were glad to hear from Marion (Phelps) Burnett. She writes, "My side line is my fiddle which I use occasionally."

Rosamond Praeger went to Sweden last summer and was bridesmaid in a wedding there which took place at midnight under the midnight sun. (We are going to give a full account of this in the next issue of Snappy Stories.) She is now with the department of health in Syracuse, N. Y.

Adelaide (Rawls) Taggart and her husband and three daughters are spending the winter in France. They are at present in Cannes at the Hotel Alsace Lorraine.

Angela (Richmond) Cooke is vice-president of a division for a Community Chest drive and is very busy doing all the other things "that get wished on a weak-minded woman who has nothing to do but all her own housework." (That purple smock is earning its keep in the home.)

Hope Stone is assistant head of the translation department in the Guaranty Trust Co., N. Y. C. She did extra work last winter in the Cherry Lane Theatre in N. Y. She was assistant to the manager and general utility man. At present (on the side) she is manager of the foreign department for a N. Y. Theatrical Agency, securing rights on outstanding European plays and translating them. Her address is 22 Willow Rd., Brooklyn, N. Y.

Marie (von Horn) Charlton when last heard from was en route to Brazil where she expects to be for two years in Rio de Janeiro. Her address is U. S. Naval Mission to Brazil, c/o Postmaster, N. Y. C.

Isabel (Wardner) Rollins and her husband took a trip to Panama this fall.

Marjorie (Wellman) Freeman has taken Dot (Attwill) Oates's job as president of the Rhode Island Smith Club.

Emily Williams sailed for England last April and spent reunion time in Norway. She returned in September.

Anna (Young) Whiting just had her tonsils removed "under the most excellent chaperonage of Dr. Faith Meserve." Anna is to be in the next edition of "American Men of Science" and may spend her second semester in Russia.

NEW ADDRESSES.—Mrs. W. M. Smith (Virginia Andrews), Ho Ho Kus, N. J.

Mrs. Ernest Davis (Mabel Austin), 205 W. 57 St., N. Y. C. Mabel visited Northampton this fall for the first time in several years and is most enthusiastic.

Mrs. C. E. Reed Jr. (Gladys Doyen), 412 Wesley Av., Oak Park, Ill.

Muriel Kennedy, 45 Linden St., Hackensack, N. J.

Mrs. John Babbitt (Edith Wells), 812 E. Main St., Washington, Ind.

Mrs. M. S. Mumford (Helen Whitman), 1314 Greenwood Blvd., Evanston, Ill.

Ex-1916

MARRIED.—Margaret Jensen to Leiba Smith, Apr. 4, 1922.

Maidie Wellington to Oliver Marble Gale.

BORN.—To Edith (Dodd) Culver a third child and second son, Aug. 17, 1926.

To Frances (Dunn) Bush a son, William Ralph, May 20, 1926.

To Margaret (Jensen) Smith two daughters, Mary Margaret, Sept. 13, 1923, and Jean Elizabeth, Apr. 5, 1926.

To Florence (MacMillan) McDonald a son, Carlton August Klump, Feb. 25, 1926.

NEW ADDRESSES.—Mrs. J. K. T. Philips (Janet Freeman), Captain's Walk, Woodmere, N. Y.

Mrs. Clifford Lane (Florence Hibbs), 2700 Broadway Av., Pittsburgh, Pa.

1917

Class secretary—Florence C. Smith, 501 S. University St., Normal, Ill.

MARRIED.—Ruth Baragwanath to Dr. George W. Cramp, Oct. 1, 1926. Dr. Cramp is a graduate of Colgate, 1918. Address, 921 President St., Brooklyn, N. Y.

Josephine Cameron to Barnard Sawyer Bronson. Address, 372 Hudson Av., Albany, N. Y.

Margaret Comey to Robert G. Pingry, July 4, 1926. They are living in Millbrook, N. Y. Margaret is continuing in her position as financial secretary of the Bennett School.

Percie Hopkins to Albert Morton Turner, Aug. 25, 1926. Mr. Turner has received degrees of A.B. and Ph.D. from Harvard, and is at present associate professor of English at the Univ. of Maine. Percie is also teaching at the Univ. Address, 13 Pond St., Orono, Me.

Selina Whitla to William W. Braham, Jan. 18. Mr. Braham is a graduate of Westminster College '15 and the Univ. of Pittsburgh Law School. New address, 226 Fairfield Av., New Castle, Pa.

BORN.—To Jeannette (Abbott) Kitchell a fourth son, Jonathan Webster, July 11, 1926. The baby died on Nov. 26, 1926.

To Sara (Alcus) Schornstein a daughter, Felicia, July 11, 1926.

To Tounette (Atkinson) Bacon a second daughter, Bettina, Oct. 23, 1926.

To Katherine (Baker) Kennedy a son, Hugh Richard Jr., Oct. 3, 1926.

To Lois (Brantly) Hazelbaker a daughter, Lois Brantly, Nov. 8, 1926.

To Winifred (Chase) Hazelwood a fourth child and third son, James Lyman, Nov. 21, 1926.

To Lois (Clark) Sullivan a third son, Richard Acheson, Apr. 10, 1926.

To Greta (Conklin) Bridgman a second child and first daughter, Joan Elizabeth, June 9, 1926.

To Sybil (Davis) McNamara a daughter, Sybil Lea, July 25, 1926.

To Florence (Hatch) Perry a son, Bertel Jr., Nov. 18, 1926.

To Beulah (House) Mitchell a daughter, Sara Catherine, Oct. 9, 1926.

To Katharine (Johnson) Johnson a son, Frederick Harrison Jr., Aug. 3, 1926.

To Maude (Leach) Martin a second child and first son, J. Carlisle, Jan. 1925; and a third child and second son, Arthur Leach, Nov. 20, 1926.

To May (Libbey) Hewes a second son, Richard David, Aug. 16, 1926.

To Katharine (Nissley) Arnold a second child and first son, Samuel Paul, June 28, 1926.

To Ruth (Shepard) Fast a daughter, Martha Louise, Oct. 29, 1926.

To Marguerite (Swift) Clark a second child and first daughter, Margaret Elizabeth, Aug. 6, 1926.

To Elizabeth (Wilson) Lynch a third child and second daughter, Emily Fenimore, June 22, 1926.

OTHER NEWS.—Dorothy Anderson is teaching in Poughkeepsie (N. Y.) and studying at Columbia.

Margaret Arndt returned in November from seven months in Africa and Europe.

Elizabeth (Beaver) Bill writes from Singapore: "We are very comfortably settled in a fairly large compound house and big garden. The house is on a knoll and besides is built up high—bungalow style with a big verandah all around so there is seldom a time when we do not have a breeze. There are nineteen doors from the house to the verandahs and these, with five windows, have to be closed at night or at least we have to see that the 'boy' closes and locks them. At the moment my husband is in Sumatra on a three weeks' business trip and at night I'm afraid I don't appreciate the doors as much as I should. I should have a great deal of leisure. I have seven servants; but sometimes it's harder work to get other people to do what you like than to do it yourself. There are three Malays, three Chinese, one Indian. Our common language is Malay. My cook (he says he went to cooking school in England) speaks English; but it is an open question which is better—his English or my Malay. We have over thirty rubber trees, dozens of palms, banana trees, other native fruit trees, orchids, shrubbery of all kinds, and a tennis lawn." Betty hopes any 1917ers journeying around the world will look her up.

Althea Behrens is an auditor of income tax returns of Rhode Island.

After two years in California, Elizabeth Brooks is again teaching at the Kimberley School, Montclair, N. J.

Ann (Campbell) Duncan is doing part-time social work.

Martha Chandler holds a half-time job as dramatic director at South End House, 40 W. Newton St., Boston. With the other half time she is studying pre-school education at the Ruggles St. Nursery School, and taking courses at Harvard and Boston Univ. On Sundays she has a Sunday school class and a story group in connection with the church of which her father is pastor.

Helen Clarke took graduate work at the Univ. of Chicago last year. At present she is doing social work at the State School, Sparta (Wis.), by way of valuable experience before she returns to her teaching next year.

Claire Cowgill has charge of advertising and fashion analysis at Buffums Department Store, Long Beach, Calif.

For six months, Margaret Devereaux has a position as Red Cross Weld County school nurse with headquarters at Greeley, Colo.

Edith (Dexter) Johnson studies child psychology three days a week at Columbia and is doing museum extension work in Norwichtown, Conn.

Eleanor (Eustis) Farrington is building architectural models.

Bessie (Fisk) Lake is resuming her harp study for the first time since graduation.

Helen Grant is, like the Smith College juniors, spending the year in France, at Grenoble and the Sorbonne. Address, American Express Co., Paris.

Marion Gude started work toward an M.A. at Columbia last summer. This winter

she is teaching again—Englewood, N. J.
Dorothy (Hamilton) Brush's mother died
in July.
Katharine Hawxhurst teaches college pre-
paratory Latin at the Roland Park Country
Day School, Baltimore, and is praying the
College Board exams and Tenth Reunion do
not conflict in June.
Marjory Herrick is secretary to the editor
of the magazine *Antiques*.
Marjorie Inman spent the spring of 1926 in
Europe. This winter it is to be California.
Helen (Jones) Farrar is captain of a Troop
of Hawaiian Girl Scouts and chairman of the
camp committee. In addition she makes
landscape gardening drawings for her sister
Catherine, ex-'19.
Marie Knowles is assistant supervisor with
the Boston Community Health Association.
Marion Lathrop is in the office of the Fam-
ily Welfare Dept. of the United Workers,
Norwich, Conn.
While Raelene Leavitt teaches at the
Passaic (N. J.) High School she is studying
secondary education at Teachers College.
Dorothy Lorentz is in the professional
candy-making business using "Lor-Entz" as
the trade name for her home-made candies.
Mathilde Loth is practicing pediatrics in
New York City. Three afternoons a week
she has a dispensary appointment at the
Babies Hospital.
Martha MacGuire is attending the Grace
Hickox Studio of Dramatic Art and studying
voice at the Sherwood Music School in Chi-
cago.
Margaret (Ney) Tucker's father died in
July.
Margery Swett has made a permanent
change of her personal and professional name
to Margery Swett Mansfield.
Adah (Richard) Judd is deputy commis-
sioner of Girl Scouts and Brown Owl to a
Brownie Pack (her small son is mascot) in
Holyoke.
Margaret (Riley) Bresnahan and her hus-
band were travelers in the Mediterranean and
Europe last winter and spring.
Sarah Scott is social service nurse in the
Bethlehem Day Nursery, N. Y. C. Her work
is concentrated health work on the all-im-
portant pre-school child with a little social
case work on the side.
Marion Sherwood is aiming toward a Ph.D.
from Yale this June in the department of
bacteriology, pathology, and public health.
At the same time she is technician in the New
Haven Hospital where she is busily engaged in
isolating and typing tubercle bacilli from
children under two years of age. This is
correlated with the X-ray work, tuberculin
work, and follow-up work.
Deborah (Simmons) Meader is finding
much of interest and help in working under
Mrs. Edwin Weeks, president of the Children's
Bureau, with groups of mothers of pre-school
children in Kansas City.
Eleanor Spencer besides teaching history of
art at the Pine Manor School pursues her
hobbies—lettering and illuminating, trans-

lating and copying medieval manuscripts, as
well as a little sketching.
Marian Stark's official title is "instructor in
clinical chemistry, Univ. of Wisconsin Medical School." She teaches a class in metabo-
lism to third year "medics." She helps with
research work, mainly metabolic.
Dorritt Stumberg is "gaining ground in her
pursuit of a Ph.D. at the Univ. of Chicago."
Gertrude (Syverson) Fladeland is in Florida
for two months this winter.
Rachel (Talbott) Beaty occupies herself
with choir work, Parent-Teachers, Woman's
Club, and College Club interests. She was in
Florida in Oct. at the time of the third hurricane, sufficiently bad, she thinks. In Feb.
she returns to Pompano (Fla.) for the rest of
the winter.
Dorothy (Thomson) Abbe's father died in
June.
Florence (Ward) Kane has a kindergarten
of twelve children every morning from 9–12
at her house. The faculty consists of three—
one kindergartner, one French mademoiselle,
and Florence who is the music and rhythm
department.
Catharine Weiser from Nov. to Mar. is at
1023 7th St., East LasVegas, New Mexico,
where she is loafing in an attempt to have
nothing whatever to do with sinus in the
future.
Margaret Witter spends her mornings as
medical director of the Schrafft stores, New
York City, and her afternoons at clinics and a
private practice, small but growing.
Ella Wood received a degree of Ed.M. from
Harvard in Feb. 1926. At present she is
teacher of English and dean of girls at Abington High School, North Abington, Mass.
Ruth Woodrow has been with the San
Francisco Visiting Nurse Association since its
organization a year ago.
Lucile (Woodruff) Carlo journeyed in the
summer with her mother and year-old daugh-
ter to Vienna, where she joined her husband
who was studying pediatrics. They are now
at home in Fort Wayne.
NEW ADDRESSES.—Martha Chandler, 18
Rockland St., Taunton, Mass.
Helen I. Clarke, State School, Sparta, Wis.
Mrs. Norman P. Cubberly (Wilhelmina
Wright), 55 Elwood Rd., South Manchester,
Conn.
Margaret Devereaux, c/o Y. W. C. A.,
Denver, Colo.
Mrs. Kenneth F. Duncan (Ann Campbell),
215 W. 13 St., N. Y. C.
Mrs. Z. Seamon Fogelman (Emily Finck),
48 Grandview Av., North Plainfield, N. J.
Selma Gulick, 251 W. 89 St., N. Y. C.
Mrs. Oliver M. Hayden (Dorothy Clark),
617 W. 27 St., Wilmington, Del.
Mrs. Leigh Hoadley (Harriet Warner), 32
Overhill Rd., Providence, R. I.
Carrie E. S. Lee, 1116 P St. N. W., Wash-
ington, D. C.
Mrs. Charles A. MacLeod (Frances Butler),
1045 Ocean Av., Brooklyn, N. Y.
Mrs. Charles McClumpha (Isabel Platt), 3
rue Taitbout, Paris, France.

Mrs. T. Edward McNamara (Sybil Davis), 2189 Mars Av., Lakewood, O.

Mrs. Arthur S. Maris (Daisy Holst), Charleston, W. Va.

Mrs. Juan Mendoza (Imogen Abbott), Peruvian Legation, Berlin, Germany.

Mrs. Robert S. Morris (Helen Springborn), 2284 Bellfield Rd., Cleveland Heights, O.

Mrs. Richard Schornstein (Sara Alcus), 6045 Hurst St., New Orleans, La.

Marion Sherwood, Sterling Apts. (707), 350 Congress Av., New Haven, Conn.

Mrs. Robert Shoemaker (Elizabeth Wells), 132 Essex Av., Glen Ridge, N. J.

Margaret Witter, 438 W. 116 St., N. Y. C.

Ella F. Wood, 8 Wolcott Rd., Brookline, Mass.

1918

Class secretary—Margaret Perkins, 3 Banks St., Chicago, Ill.

MARRIED.—Helen Eddy to Emery C. Resch, Sept. 11, 1926. Helen writes that she announced her engagement in July, and was married at her summer home in the Adirondacks. Sandy McConnell was one of the bridesmaids. Mr. Resch is a graduate of Penn State, and is doing boys' club work in Syracuse. Helen is director of religious education in one of the churches there. Their address is 505 University Pl.

Helen Sammis to Newton Bruce Ashby of Des Moines (Ia.) and New York City, Aug. 25, 1926. Address for the winter, 146 Willow St., Brooklyn, N. Y.

BORN.—To Katharine (Bradley) White a second child and first daughter, Janet, Sept. 13, 1926.

To Dorothea (Dann) Stevens a second son, Edward Webster Dann, Oct. 19, 1926.

To Elisabeth (Hilles) Reynolds a daughter, Elisabeth Lee, Sept. 15, 1926.

To Martha (Lawrence) Read a second son, William Lawrence, July 8, 1926. Martha and her family have moved to 810 Ocean Parkway, Brooklyn, N. Y.

To Adelaide (Libby) Levassor a first son and second child, Alain Yves Alexis, Oct. 9, 1926.

To Margaret (Matthews) Otte a second son and third child, Corwin Robert, Oct. 17, 1926.

To Katharine (Rice) Mollison a son, Oliver Spencer, July 23, 1926.

To Catherine (Woodworth) Watkins a third child and first daughter, Catherine Woodworth, Apr. 14, 1926.

OTHER NEWS.—Helen (Ames) Lameyer writes from Florence, Italy, that buying furniture for her apartment, interviewing servants, etc. in Italian is increasing her vocabulary immensely. Address, Via Palestro 1.

Elsie Briggs is at the Univ. of Wisconsin studying for her M.A.

Fran (Coates) MacPherson writes that Margaret (Button) Hand, who has been very uncommunicative for some time, is living at 1181 West Blvd., Los Angeles, and has a baby girl, Nancy, about eight months old. She also says that Elizabeth (Boyd) Beach has been visiting in Los Angeles, and that she,

Louise (Hunt) Kilpatrick, Peg (Button) Hand, to say nothing of Fran herself, are all pledged to return to Northampton for their tenth.

Bernice Henderson has been .d to the mental hygiene department of the Community Health Association of Boston. She is assistant to the head of the department and advises and trains the nursing staff in mental hygiene and also makes personal visits to problem patients.

Esther (Lovett) Barraclough and her husband have moved to Durham (N. H.) where Mr. Barraclough is state extension forester in the extension department of the State Univ. Address, Durham, N. H.

Katharine (Mosser) Pediconi and her husband were in the U. S. A. for a month this fall. Dr. Pediconi was official Italian delegate to the Anti-Tuberculosis Conference in Washington.

Cadzie (Reed) Molthan and her husband took their three little daughters abroad last summer where they had a villa at Le Toucquet from May until November.

Mary Sleeper is instructor in music at Mills College (Calif.) and finds her work most interesting. There are about 600 students there, and Mills has the distinction of being the only woman's college west of the Mississippi. Sleepy is delighted that her new job has taken her to a place where she won't get snowed on this winter!

Marion (Taylor) Lyndon, who kept up her personnel work for three months after her marriage, has discovered her "ready-made" family, Roger, 8, and Ann, 6, her husband, the housekeeping, and a dog make a very satisfying full-time job, so has given up her business career. Marion lives in Westfield, Mass., 52 Broad St., and likes it very much.

Mildred (Willcox) Belknap and family moved to 188 Montross Av., Rutherford, N. J., this fall, where they have bought a home. Mildred's young hopeful, now aged 5, entered kindergarten and wanted to know how many days it would be before she could go to Smith!

The secretary would be glad of any definite information regarding Clara Hart. Mail sent in care of her father, Mr. C. M. Hart, Union Depot Ticket Office, Toledo, O., has not been returned but the secretary doesn't know whether this reaches Clara herself as she has had no response to her urgent pleas for news.

Florence Cochran falls into the same category. Mail sent to her latest address, according to the Postmaster, Mundelein, Ill., is not returned, but evokes no reply.

Ex-1918

MARRIED.—Marion Bailey to Frank Donald Brigham, Sept. 18, 1926. Marion writes that for five years she has been assistant kindergartner in the Norwich schools. Last summer she went abroad with her sister, after which she was married. Address, 181 Washington St., Norwich, Conn.

OTHER NEWS.—Helen (Blanchard) Swett writes that she and her army husband have been in Honolulu since 1923 and find it increasingly difficult to break away. Last year

PURE SILK has great strength and elasticity —
and *incomparable beauty*. That is why Fashion
prescribes Skinner linings — because America's
best wearing Satin is also the richest in appearance.
In ready-to-wear garments look for the Skinner
label. In ordering from a merchant tailor

"Look for the Name in the Selvage"

WILLIAM SKINNER & SONS · *Established* 1848

NEW YORK, CHICAGO, BOSTON, PHILADELPHIA. *Mills:* HOLYOKE, MASS.

*Linings for men's suits and topcoats and women's coats, suits and
furs   ·   Crepes, Dress Satins, Millinery Satins, Shoe Satins*

Skinner's Satins

Helen taught English to 120 Japanese children, and this year she is at school herself and enjoying it greatly.

1919

Class secretary—Julia Florance, 161 Livingston Av., New Brunswick, N. J.

DIED.—Lufrerry (Low) Inwood, Nov. 1, 1926..

ENGAGED.—Ruth Goldsmith to Sidney T. H. Northcott, Harvard '09· This is Ruth's second year of teaching at the Coolidge School in Watertown, Mass.

MARRIED.—May Bartlett to Dr. Edward W. Griffey, New Year's Eve. Dr. Griffey is connected with the Houston Clinic. Address, 1921 Norfolk St., Houston, Tex. May attended the Chicago Smith Club luncheon at noon on her wedding day.

Dorothy Merchant to Porter Gale Perrin, Sept. 20, 1926, in Northampton. Mr. Perrin graduated from Dartmouth in 1917 and is teaching English and working for his Ph.D. at the Univ. of Chicago. Address, 5519 Kimbark Av., Chicago.

Julia Treat to Stanley Benjamin Wright, Sept. 25, 1926. Mr. Wright graduated from Andover in 1915 and Yale in 1919. Mildred (Beals) Darling and Lois (Hodges) Clark '21 were bridesmaids.

BORN.—To Laura (Bisbee) Deane a second daughter, Martha, Oct. 11, 1926.

To Elizabeth (Hunt) Lockard a son and second child, Arthur Hunt, Dec. 30, 1926.

To Dorothy (Marquis) Johnson a second son, Marquis Seller, Oct. 4, 1926.

To Jean (Sinclair) Winton a son, on June 27, 1926.

To Helen (Small) Withington a daughter, Elizabeth, Nov. 20, 1926.

To Grace (Valentine) Wiss a fourth daughter, Grace, May 17, 1926.

OTHER NEWS.—Helen Davis and Margaret (Petherbridge) Farrar were on the committee that arranged for the special matinée performance of "Aida" at the Metropolitan Opera House, Dec. 29, 1926, under the auspices of the New York Smith Club for the benefit of the Juniper Lodge Endowment Fund.

Elsie (Finch) McKeogh was abroad for six weeks in Aug. and Sept., joining her mother in Paris.

Leslie Gates is enjoying a winter at home after seven years of social welfare work. Address, 107 South St., Auburn, N. Y.

Barbara Johnson returned in September after a delightful year of travel abroad. In Vienna she had the pleasure of meeting Prof. Kimball. One of her most interesting experiences was assisting in the inventory and appraisal of an estate, which included the Villa Palmvari in Florence and the Castle Lenzburg in Switzerland. She is now sales manager for the *Woman Citizen* and was in Hartford for a while, organizing a force of representatives to solicit three-year subscriptions at $5.

Dorothy Kinne is most enthusiastic about her job as director of athletics and teacher of the first grade of the Ramapo Valley Country Day School in Suffern, N. Y.

Eunice Lilly is at home after spending the past four years as secretary at Centenary Collegiate Institute in Hackettstown, N. J.

Beatrice (Marion) Ackerman visited her parents in France last summer.

On the committee for the Christmas Dance of the New York Smith Club at the Plaza, Dec. 29, 1926, were Catharine (Marsh) Bull, chairman, Elizabeth Atterbury, Margaret (Petherbridge) Farrar, and Margaret Sherwood.

Hazel Prentice became an interne on July 1, 1926, in the Woman's Hospital, 2137 N. College Av., Philadelphia.

Dorothy (Speare) Christmas made her début in "Lucia di Lammermoor" at Asti, Italy, Sept. 14, 1926, with such success that a gala performance was planned in her honor in Milan. She has written about her début in an article soon to appear in *Pictorial Review*. Her fourth novel, "The Virgin of Yesterday," is scheduled for publication by George H. Doran Co. in the near future.

Tat Saunders has opened a new shop at 21 W. 50 St., N. Y. C., which is most attractive and conducive both to purchases and relaxation with its inviting davenport and easy chairs. Margaret Mann '22 will have charge of the shop at Palm Beach during the winter season, assisted by Margaret MacLeod.

Margaret Winchester is director of Religious Education of the First Congregational Church of Manchester (N. H.) and also has a club of Syrian girls at the Y. W. International Institute.

NEW ADDRESSES.—Mrs. Millard S. Darling (Mildred Beals), 134 Oakland Ter., Hartford, Conn.

Mrs. Donald G. Graham (Juanita Fisher), 907 Eleventh Av. N., Seattle, Wash.

Mrs. C. Lester Seaman (Janet Mitchell), 30 S. Munn Av., East Orange, N. J.

Mrs. Edward Griggs (Margaret Stephenson) 200 N. Main St., West Hartford, Conn.

'Ex-1919

Catherine (Jones) Richards is planning to take her two sons to England in the near future and study landscape gardening in Kew Gardens.

NEW ADDRESSES.—Mrs. Euclid W. McBride (Elizabeth Clapp), 5 Westmoreland Pl., Pasadena, Calif.

Mrs. Howard H. Tomlinson (Frances Ford), 133 Union St., Montclair, N. J.

1920

Class secretary—Mrs. Arthur R. Hoch (Marian Hill), 312 N. Euclid Av., Oak Park, Ill. Assistant secretary—Josephine Taylor, 137 S. Scoville Av., Oak Park, Ill.

ENGAGED.—Carol McBurney to Francis Storm of New York. She is giving up her job as American representative of the Wayfarers Travel Agency and expects to be married in June. She writes, "I met my beau in Montreux this summer."

MARRIED.—Edna Stewart to A. Meredith MacColl, Nov. 10, 1925. Mr. MacColl is a Presbyterian minister. Address, Bellewood Av., Dobbs Ferry, N. Y.

Virginia Thompson to Reginald Brock

Nora Kelley is principal of the I. N. Bloom School in Louisville. She was in England and Scotland last summer with Carol Rice and Mildred Cover.

Francisca (King) Thomas is still secretary to Dr. J. H. Means at the Massachusetts General Hospital.

Lucile Larson's father, who disappeared suddenly in 1923, was found in Texas and has returned to Chicago to be with the family.

Olive Lawrence has been writing several plays lately that have been used on the programs of the school where she teaches.

Elisabeth Liffler is at home this year. Address, 36 Edgeline Rd., Brookline, Mass.

Marjory (Lord) Packard's husband is a teacher at Dartmouth. She is still running the book department of the College Bookstore there. Address, 52 College St., Hanover, N. H.

Marjory (MacKay) Lansdale writes, "Spent last summer in the Italian Tyrol to get the children away from the Salonika heat and dust."

Judith Matlack is an instructor at Simmons again this year. She received her M.A. in 1926 from Boston Univ.

Glenna Newhall is working for a large manufacturing concern, the Crouse-Hinds Co. in Syracuse.

Vera (Prentice) Clark sends this address, River Edge, N. J.

Antoinette Price is a student nurse in the Philadelphia General Hospital.

Helen (Reece) Peterson is playing in the Franklin Trio (violin, cello, and piano) which gives concerts and recitals in Franklin County and vicinity. She also does some solo work. This fall she has been giving lecture recitals on the "Sonata from Bach to Grieg" in conjunction with Miss Mina L. Day, pianist.

Carol Rice is still teaching at the Univ. of Wisconsin. She was abroad last summer studying in a gym school in Denmark and also traveling.

Olive Rockwell is doing psychiatric social work in the Child Guidance Clinic, Cleveland. This clinic is under the National Committee for Mental Hygiene and the Commonwealth Fund.

Augusta Rubin is a graduate student at Radcliffe and is taking some courses in the social ethics department at Harvard. She spent eight months last year traveling in Europe. Temporary address, 11 Shepard St., Cambridge, Mass.

Vesta (Sawyer) Amidon writes that her baby girl is almost well now after a long siege of illnesses. Temporary address, 1219 Trinidad Av. N. E., Washington, D. C.

Elisabeth Schneider received her M.A. from the Univ. of Pennsylvania in English literature in 1926 and is now an instructor in English at Temple Univ., Philadelphia.

Marion Selden was secretary last year at Radcliffe. This year she is secretary of the young people's department of Trinity Church, Boston, and writes, "My present job is absorbingly interesting."

Helene Smith studied educational and vocational guidance at Harvard last summer.

She is now teaching English in the South Orange High School and writes: "I am now working into the Guidance Field with class sponsoring, directing the schedule selection of pupils, assisting in the college selection field and also in the character problem cases. I worked out differentiated courses of study for use in ability sections in English (segregated on the basis of A. Q. and I. Q.) and talked on this before the principals' assembly of the State of N. J. in New Brunswick last spring."

Jane Stafford is on the editorial staff of Hygeia, the health magazine published by the American Medical Association. She had two signed articles in Hygeia, one on the "Work of Henry Rose Carter" and the other "Safety First of July Fourth."

Helen Tappen is teaching piano at a residence studio in her home. She taught school until 1924.

Charlotte Thomas is at home this year but is to go to Florida for the winter, though not to teach as she usually has.

Ruth (Thompson) Drisko's address is 27 Heckle St., Wellesley Hills, Mass.

Harriet van Zelm is secretary to a high school principal this year.

Julia (Warner) Herdic writes, "My travels —Hot Springs (Va.) in the fall and California in the winter."

Florence (Williams) Smith is teaching again this year. Her husband received his Ph.D. in economics and is now an assistant professor at the Harvard School of Business Administration. Address, 66 Warner St., Hudson, Mass.

Ruth Willian is teaching again at Smith. She is also on the faculty of the Julius Hartt School of Music at Hartford, Conn. This year she is giving a series of public sonata recitals; she has already played in about two hundred concerts. She spent part of the summer in Europe and also went to California.

Ruth Worcester did private tutoring and lived at home in 1924; in 1925 she was business manager at the Waltham School for Girls; and this year is again doing private tutoring.

Arva (Yeagley) Bergan is an officer and committeewoman of the Federated Woman's Club in Tampico, Mexico. She is now chairman of the American School Endowment Fund Com. of the Club and writes, "We are trying to raise 3000 pesos for the work before Christmas."

Marion (Zimmerman) Sprague now has a U. S. address, 136 College Av., Annville, Pa.

Ex-1920

LOST.—Marion Whittaker. Until 1922 Marion corresponded regularly with the secretary and her mail since then, until Aug. 1926, always was delivered. Since then her mail is returned unclaimed. Old address, 910 S. Lincoln St., Urbana, Ill. Please help find her.

MARRIED.—Clarice White to Theodore H. Thomas, Aug. 14, 1926. Address, 204 Crafts St., Newtonville, Mass.

BORN.—To Eva (Rettenmeyer) Hartman twin sons, Philip Emil and Paul Arthur, Nov. 23, 1926. She has one other son living and lost another at birth. She writes: "We

came to Baltimore a year ago when my husband accepted a position as research associate at the Carnegie Laboratory of Embryology, Johns Hopkins. Dr. Carl has transferred his attentions from the Texas opossum to the monkeys in the new colony being formed here. Between monkeys and twins we are having an interesting time of it.' Address, 19 Merrymount Rd., Roland Park, Md.

To Alice (James) Blaine a second son, Darwin James, July 14, 1926. Address, 275 Clinton Av., Brooklyn, N. Y.

To Jessamine (Jones) Wilder a first son, Walter Llewellyn, May 23, 1926, at Ann Arbor, Mich. She has moved back to Minneapolis to be there for several years "at least." Address, 4925 Drew Av. S.

To Dolly (Powers) Hixon a third child and first daughter, Shirley, July 15, 1926. Address, 2471 Robinwood Av., Toledo, O.

To Dorothy (Morgans) Havener a second daughter, Lillian Morgans, Sept. 7, 1924. Address, 112 W. Main St., Middletown, N. Y.

1921

Class secretary—Mrs. E. Graham Bates (Dorothy Sawyer), 8 Maple St., Auburndale, Mass.

MARRIED.—Barbara White to Richard Kimball Baker of Boston, Nov. 27, 1926. France was their choice for a wedding journey.

Ruth O'Hanlon to Olcott Mitchell Brown of Salem, Oct. 30, 1926.

BORN.—To Alida (Bigelow) Butler a son, Allison, Oct. 19, 1925.

To Ruth (Chovey) Lushear a daughter, Caroline Finch, Nov. 17, 1926.

To Harriet (Snyder) McCaw a second daughter, Mary Lamar, Sept. 23, 1925.

To Jane (Wilder) Prest a son, Samuel Wilder, Feb. 15, 1925.

To Marjorie (Winslow) Briggs a daughter, Mary DeQuedville, July 4, 1926.

OTHER NEWS.—Marion Bayer writes: "Met Frances Holden at Chitina, Alaska, last summer. Alaska is certainly a wonderful country."

Since her mother's death a year ago in May, Helen Begley has been living at home in Holyoke and continuing her teaching there. She would be glad to hear from any of the girls who come back to visit.

Alavene (Brown) Barlow writes from Dania, Fla., "We are just twenty miles north of Miami, where we have a fine Smith College Club."

Margaret Cobb is society editor of the *Cleveland News*.

Alice Cook is teaching English at the Calhoun School in N. Y. C. and working toward her Ph.D. at Columbia. Her present address is 423 W. 118 St.

Since graduation Sophie Gerson has traveled in the western part of this country for two summers, one summer in Canada, and the past one in Europe. She is secretary of the local branch of the A. A. U. W. and the League of Women Voters.

Adelia Hallock, our representative in China, writes as follows on Sept. 26, 1926: "I have just opened the Girls' School for the

fall term with an enrollment of a little over a hundred. Thirty-one of the girls are in the Junior Middle School, the rest in the Primary School. So far this year, all is peaceful. We hope the war will not strike us. There is still anti-foreign and anti-Christian feeling, but the work is continuing and growing."

Ruth Hensle is teaching in Mt. Vernon, N. Y.

Harriet (Howe) Greene is working in the chemical laboratory of the Evans Memorial in Boston.

Julia (Howell) Hatheway is spending the winter at Belleair, Clearwater, Fla.

Alfhild (Kalijarvi) Wuorinen is research assistant in chemistry in the pathology department of Columbia Medical School.

Edith (Ketcham) Brinton acts as secretary to her husband who is a physician.

Martha Kirsten is "still clerking in the Times Square Bookshop and hopes to stay there indefinitely."

Mildred (Louer) Bird took a semester's work at Northwestern last year.

Harriet O'Brien took courses in advertising at Boston Univ. the year following graduation, with Selma Pelonsky '19. For a time she was assistant advertising manager of Chandler and Co., Boston. For the past three years she has been writing for a Boston advertising agency. She is the author of a recently published book entitled "Smith College Today."

Elinor (Palmer) Vroman has returned to Portland to live.

At the age of 27, the husband of Marie (Poland) Fish has been appointed director of the new $1,000,000 Museum of Sciences in Buffalo.

Catherine Sammis reports that her long desired wish for travel has been granted; first, Europe last summer with Beatrice Walton '22, and two Vassar girls, and then across the continent with her father on the Bankers' Convention trip in the fall. She has now started a position with a Y. W. C. A. in New York. Cath saw May Bossi in Paris and Alison Bowie in Edinburgh.

Lois Slocum is an instructor of astronomy at Wellesley.

Dorothy Weed is again teaching music at the Diller-Quaile School and studying music with Miss Diller and Miss Quaile.

Marjorie (Winslow) Briggs gives music lessons in odd moments.

During the past year, Wynna Wright has done illustrations for *The American Girl Magazine*, *Every Girl's*, *The Youth's Companion*, and *House Beautiful*.

NEW ADDRESSES.—Mrs. W. B. Stimson (Florence Chester), 1920 Panama St., Philadelphia.

Florence N. Gary, 1058 Browning St., Los Angeles, Calif.

Mrs. Henry Eckhardt (Athalie Rowe), Pinecrest Rd., Sherbrooke Park, Scarsdale, N. Y.

Ex-1921

ENGAGED.—Ethel Phillips ('22) to Lindsley Noble.

MARRIED.—Kwe Pau Huang to George

Hwang of Peking, in Oct. 1925. Kwe Pau is still dietitian at the Union Medical College at Peking.

Miriam McHugh to Clifford A. Taney Jr. of Minneapolis, Aug. 14, 1926.

BORN.—To Grace (Loomis) Shaver a son, Charles Leslie, Jan. 11, 1926.

To Helen (Totten) Warfield a second son, Totten, July 25, 1924.

OTHER NEWS.—Louise (Burrell) Shevlin writes: "We returned to Bend (Ore.) in April after three and a half years in Omaha. We had a very active Smith Club in Omaha and I am going to miss it."

Margaret Kent is working in the neurological clinic at the Massachusetts General Hospital.

Louise (Powe) Hoyt recently traveled in France and Holland.

1922

Class secretaries—A–K, Mrs. Francis T. P. Plimpton (Pauline Ames), 1165 Fifth Av., N. Y. C. L–Z, Mrs. George F. Hughes (Frona Brooks), Box 393, Garden City, N. Y.

DIED.—Gladys (Fee) Hodgman, Dec. 31, 1926, after the birth of a son, Thomas Fee, Dec. 20.

MARRIED.—Virginia Conklin to Richard Armit Wood, Nov. 8, 1926. New address, 4432 Mill Creek Parkway, Kansas City, Mo.

Margaret Ford to Lawrence M. Handley, Apr. 16, 1926. They are living at 475 N. E. 32 St., Miami, Fla.

Eleanor Evans to Erwin Cory Stout, Nov. 10, 1926. Mr. Stout is in the real estate business in Indianapolis and is a brother of Schatzie Stout '21, who with Mary (Evans) Harrell '24, Margaret (White) Loomis ex-'22, and Elizabeth (Marmon) Hoke took part in the wedding.

Dorothy Johnson to Leonard S. Poor. Address, 5332 Delmar Blvd., St. Louis, Mo.

Charlotte MacDougall to Hendrik de Kauffmann, Nov. 18, 1926. He is minister from Denmark to China and Japan. They are going to China by way of Denmark, then the Suez Canal and India. Address, c/o Foreign Office, Copenhagen, Denmark.

Jane Massie to Fendall Marbury, Dec. 11, 1926.

Ann Scroggie to O. Pomeroy Robinson Jr., Sept. 4, 1926. Address, 10 Alger Pl., New London, Conn.

Eleanor Steele to Charles William Belmer, Oct. 2, 1926. Address, 123 Waverly Pl., N.Y.C.

Una Whitehurst to John Kenneth Mickle, Oct. 23, 1926. Frances (deValin) Haigh was one of her attendants. Address, 26 E. 10 St., N. Y. C.

BORN.—To Hannah (Abraham) Muhlfelder a daughter, Helen, Oct. 1, 1926.

To Katharine (Adam) Byrne a daughter, Barbara Dana, May 16, 1926.

To Gertrude (Blatchford) Stearns a third child and second daughter, Janet Cynthia, Oct. 14, 1926.

To Frona (Brooks) Hughes a daughter, Octavia, Oct. 1, 1926.

To Dorothy (Chapple) Soper a son, E. B. Soper IV, July 21, 1926.

To Ruth (Ferguson) Vanderburgh a daughter, Louise, Oct. 14, 1926.

To Willa (Orr) Swaney a daughter, Nancy Orr, July 31, 1926. Willa spent the summer with her family in Saginaw (Mich.) as her husband was transferred from Boston to Chicago.

To Sadye (Stone) Green a son, Robert Stone, Oct. 29, 1925.

To Greta (Wood) Snider a daughter, Gratia Lowell, Oct. 29, 1926.

To Esther (Ziskind) Weltman a daughter, Elienne Ruth, Oct. 28, 1926.

OTHER NEWS.—Eleanor Bachman is assistant to the editor of *The New Yorker* with an office at W. 45 St., N. Y. C.

Dorothy (Benson) Davis is enjoying the luxury of a real home for the first time in years at the Naval Academy, Annapolis, where her husband is aide to the Commandant of Midshipmen. She is living in the Yard which makes her feel almost as if she were back on campus.

Elizabeth Brooke is still doing private duty at the Presbyterian Hospital, where Jessie Wilson is on the interne staff.

Dorris (Bryant) Baldridge had a month's vacation with her husband in Alabama and North Carolina, leaving the baby in New York.

Miriam Buncher is enjoying her experience in the social service department of a hospital in Honolulu but regrets that she won't be back for reunion.

Isabel Conklin spent part of the summer being a waitress at the Middlebury College School of French, where one speaks nothing but "le doux parler de France" for seven weeks, amidst a most interesting group of French professors and writers. Among many other activities she has been working on a school course in modern European history and is going to teach another year at the Baldwin School.

Elizabeth Crain worked for ten months in the stock department of the Southern California Edison Co. Then she spent March, April, and May in Honolulu where she had the luck to see a volcano in action.

Marion (Crozier) Keeler finds that the California sunshine agrees with her two babies. She hopes to get back for reunion.

Florence (Denison) Bullard reports the loss of her 18-months-old son, Norwood, who died on Nov. 7, 1926.

Edith Donnell is still teaching dancing and occasionally giving recitals with the Marsh Dancers.

Phyllis (Creasey) Straight's husband has fully recovered from sleeping sickness and has taken a position in New York.

Nell Driggs is having a most interesting time in one of the newest departments of the Los Angeles city school system, the hearing conservation department. They teach lipreading to the hard-of-hearing children in the public schools. She would be glad to hear of anyone interested as they are looking for new teachers.

Betty Durrell did a "Marathon" in Europe

last summer, France, Italy, Switzerland, Germany, Belgium, Holland, England, Scotland in less than three months. She is now teaching at Highland Hall, Hollidaysburg, Pa.

Charlotte Gower has achieved an M.A. at the Univ. of Chicago and is now going in pursuit of a Ph.D. She helped excavate American aborigines in northern Illinois this summer, by which she acquired a heavy coat of tan and some publicity.

Catherine Grigsby is head of the French and Latin department at Virginia Normal and Industrial Institute.

Margaret (Hays) Baum, in conjunction with a Radcliffe girl, organized a summer group of "supervised play" for children from two to five years. She also has a winter nursery school for children from two to four.

Dorothy (Higbie) Tracey and her husband have moved into a new home at Hemlock Rd., Short Hills, N. J.

Dorothy (Hogan) Guider spent the whole summer in New Hampshire where Thelma Ledbetter, Emma (Lincoln) Weaver, and Georgiana (Morrison) Ely '21 visited her.

Katherine Howland is psychiatric social worker and research assistant in a mobile mental hygiene clinic which is held in various communities throughout the state of Iowa.

Esther (Irving) Francis, having moved four times in three years, is now happily settled in her own home town where her husband is teaching in his old high "Tech." Her address is 164 W. Alvord St., Springfield, Mass.

Ruth Irwin is back at Yale to complete her work for an M.A. in religious education, writing her thesis under Seneca Smith. She expects to be married shortly after Commencement.

Anne (Johnston) Weissblatt is in New York for the winter; her address is 124 W. 72 St.

Ruth Joshel spent a fascinating summer chaperoning twelve Smith undergraduates abroad where they were entertained by European students. As a result she finds another year of teaching drab in comparison.

Evelyn Lawley is Assistant Principal, Dean of Girls, and teacher of mathematics and science at the Northfield (Mass.) High School.

Barbara McKay is living with Harriet Wolverton in New York for a few months. "A hard and heavy working winter is anticipated by both."

Margaret Mann has opened a shop at 21 W. 50 St., New York, in partnership with Tat Saunders, operating under the name of Tat Saunders—dresses, hats, French novelties, accessories.

Elisabeth (Marshall) Perkins writes: "Have just built a new house and spent the summer putting the family through whooping cough. Am teaching Bible at Bradford Academy, doing church work, and arranging 'intercollegiate broadcasts' on the radio."

Estelle Moulton is studying business administration at Boston Univ. after having worked in an accountant's office for two years.

Rhoda Orme took graduate work at the Univ. of Pennsylvania last summer and is teaching Latin at Summit (N. J.) High School.

Dorothy Prescott has been for the past two years private secretary to Mary L. Jobe (Mrs. Carl Akeley, widow of the African explorer). Last summer she "practically" ran Camp Mystic, Conn. Her New York address is 607 Fifth Av., c/o Miss Jobe.

Katharine Prickett is still teaching biology in Riverhead (N. Y.) and going to "the city" for excitement. She has "seventy darling freshmen" under her wing.

Emily Reed taught for two years at Hindman (Ky.) Settlement School, went to Recreation Training School in Chicago one year, and last year did community work at the Stearns School Center, Newton, Mass.

Dean Roberts is working at etching this winter.

Louise (Robertson) Schmid is employed as research assistant in the Institute of Child Welfare at the Univ. of Minnesota. They are doing interesting psychological experiments on infants.

Katharine Sanford is doing laboratory work in a doctor's office in Cleveland, after two years as a technician in a hospital on Long Island.

Ruth Robeson has been working in the Rochester (N. Y.) Public Library (circulating department) since returning from Europe two years ago.

Ruth Scheibler spent the summer in California where she went to be maid of honor for Agnes Wilson '23 at Santa Monica.

Margaret Schneider is instructor in the department of biology at the Univ. of Maine. She got her M.A. in zoölogy at Columbia last June.

Eleanor Scofield is still working for Arnold Joens Co., Chicago—"advertising and enjoying business." She is living at the College Club.

Blanche Shaw spent part of Sept. in Atlantic City. She is back in Indianapolis for the winter.

Pearl Smith is again at North Easton (Mass.), teaching history.

Anna Trott is staying with a French family in New Brunswick (N. J.), ' hoping to attain some fluency in speaking their language."

Margaret Ward stopped at Northampton on her way home for Christmas to see Herr Muser and Frau Muser, Mrs. Neilson's father and mother. She is studying at the Robert Brookings Graduate School, Washington (D. C.), in the field of political science. Address, 127 Centre St., Milton, Mass.

Aileen (Woodman) Robinson has moved to Pittsburgh where her husband is teaching at The Arnold School, a boys' private day school.

Elizabeth Woodson is again in New York with The Ronald Press Co., after a four months' vacation in Kentucky.

NEW ADDRESSES.—Mrs. Raymond B. White (Helen Carroll), 1230 W. 58 St., Kansas City, Mo.

Hilda Couch, River Rd., Grand View, N. Y.

Margaret Hinckley, The Tea Farm, Summerville, S. C.

Mrs. William H. Crawford (Elizabeth Ives), 350 Wade St., Bridgeport, Conn.

Mrs. John O. Holmes (Anne Lochhead), 129 W. 13 St., Anderson, Ind.

Estelle Moulton, 7 Keswick St., Boston.

Mrs. R. A. J. Morrison (Dorothy Peirce), 611 Cowen St., Garrett, Ind.

Katharine Sanford, 3226 Euclid Av., Cleveland, O.

Mrs. Sylvester H. Bingham (Vivian Savacool), The Taft School, Watertown, Conn.

Margaret Schneider, Box 193, Orono, Me.

Mrs. Philip E. Green (Sadye Stone), 284 Moraine St., Brockton, Mass.

Mrs. George A. Trowbridge (Jean Whiting), 148 Everit St., New Haven, Conn.

Ex-1922

MARRIED.—Eleanor Kimball to Edward W. Eames, June 23, 1926. They spent the summer in France, and are now at Deerfield Academy, Deerfield, Mass.

BORN.—To Irene (Richardson) Flagg a son, John Hamilton Jr., May 22, 1926.

DIED.—Lorna (Wolfenden) Parker, Aug. 28, 1926. She was drowned in Lake George when her canoe upset.

OTHER NEWS.—Dorothy (Buttolph) Clarke writes: "Warren Jr. (aged 2 years) was sent to his grandparents in Chicago early in the summer when Mr. Clarke and I decided to leave Miami. We filled the Chrysler and started on our long journey north, so fortunately for us we missed the terrible disaster." Address, c/o Mr. W. A. Buttolph, 5429 Cornell Av., Chicago.

Dorothy Dudley has reopened her kindergarten in her own home for the fourth year. She is doing settlement playground work at the Dobbs School Day Nursery in New York three afternoons a week.

Jeanne (Geiger) Shons's fifteen-months-old son, Charles H. Jr., died Feb. 27, 1926.

Polly (Haskins) Williams went on a cruise of the West Indies last spring. She has been busy carrying on the work in a Methodist parsonage, but this month expects to start on a trip around the world with her mother and husband. They will visit her sister in Shanghai.

Eleanore Kapff is teaching sixth grade in Boston.

NEW ADDRESSES.—Mrs. Burton G. Tremaine Jr. (Dorothy Chapman), 2704 Derbyshire Rd., Cleveland Heights, O.

Mrs. Alvah G. Strong (Marjorie Hall), Allen Creek Rd., Brighton Sta., Rochester, N. Y.

1923

Class secretary—Mrs. Roswell C. Josephs (Frances Sheffield), Longfellow Court, Massachusetts Av., Cambridge, Mass.

NOTE.—Everybody *must* pay her class insurance premium or the class will be unable to keep up this form of collecting our 25th anniversary gift. Also Frances Arnold writes that only one-third of the class has paid its class tax. If more do not pay, it will mean an increased tax next year.

ENGAGED.—Oriana Bailey to Herbert H. Lank, a graduate of the Univ. of Delaware.

They became acquainted in France where they were both studying in 1923–24. There were ten Smith girls at the announcement party. They are planning to be married next fall.

Katherine Howk to John McMymn Williams, a graduate of the Univ. of Wisconsin. He is now with the Bucher Advertising Co. of Chicago. They expect to be married sometime in May.

MARRIED.—Anne-Gilbert Bell to Robert Shedd Noble, Dartmouth '14, Dec. 19, 1926.

Alice Eggleston to Henry Pratt of Milwaukee, Nov. 16, 1926. They are going to live at 246 Prospect Av., Milwaukee, Wis.

Helen France to George Rainer Lyons, Sept. 6, 1926. Dorothy Smith ex-'23 was maid of honor. Muriel Clarke '23 and Leola Benninghoff ex-'22 were two of the bridesmaids.

Eleanor Frost to John Hurd Jr., June 29, 1926. Mr. Hurd is reading English literature at Oxford and will teach at Dartmouth next year. Eleanor is teaching singing at the National Park Seminary in Forest Glen, Md. She was in Paris last year studying and singing. They spent their honeymoon in Switzerland and Normandy.

Margaretha Geisel to Floyd C. Dahmen, Gettysburg College '23, Harvard Law School '26, Nov. 11, 1926. They are living at 13 Alton Pl., Jamestown, N. Y.

Helen Gottschaldt to James Douglas McClintock. They left Arizona and in touring through California, they fell in love with it and decided to settle there. Their address is 6770 Milner Rd., Hollywood, Calif.

Isadore Luce to Archibald William Smith, Dec. 16, 1926. Address, 9 Wallace St., Bombay, India.

Katheryn Maley to Eli Cole Smith, July 17, 1926. They are living at 711 S. Palmetto, Daytona Beach, Fla.

Charlotte Phillips to Emerson Francis Haslam. Charlotte writes: "I finished my training as a nurse at the Presbyterian Hospital in New York in Dec. 1925. I went back to Worcester and did district work for awhile and was married the first of June. Because I had previously promised to take a former patient and her two children to England, I deserted my husband for a flying trip across. My husband has a baby chick farm in Westwood (Mass.) and I am learning how much cod liver oil and powdered milk go in their formulae. After the rather narrow, hectic existence of training, it is fun to teach Sunday school and belong to the Dorcas Society."

Dorothy Strasser to Harold Beenhower. She is getting used to living in Europe. They will probably spend the winter months in Rome and return to Amsterdam in the early spring. Address, Roemer Vesscherstraat 40, Amsterdam.

Eleonore Taylor to Richard M. Ross. Address, Pelham Court, Pelham, N. Y.

BORN.—To Julienne (Dumortier) Peck a son, Milton Gregory Jr., June 6, 1926.

To Minerva (Ellis) McCracken a son, Thomas Everett Jr., Oct. 5, 1926.

To Esther (Emery) Steiger a second child and first daughter, Elisabeth Ann, May 13, 1926.

To Mildred (Frost) Eaton a second child and first son, James H. Jr., June 30, 1926.

To Lucy (Joseph) Bing a son, Allan Joseph, Feb. 27, 1926.

To Henrietta (Kilborn) Raymond a daughter, Bettie King, May 26, 1926.

To Dorothy (Morgan) Austin a daughter, Jeanne, Feb. 8, 1926.

To Florence (Munsie) Woodward a daughter, Ruth, Aug. 28, 1926.

To Dorothy (Smith) Copeland a son, William Abbott, Sept. 9, 1926.

To Sally (Spahr) Chapman a son, S. Hudson III, January 13, 1926. Sally's husband is an instructor in the French department at Yale, and she likes living in New Haven.

NEW ADDRESSES.—Mrs. Francis Callery (Virginia Annan), 940 Park Av., N. Y. C.

Mrs. C. A. Steiger (Esther Emery), 163 Pleasant St., Holyoke, Mass.

Mrs. J. H. Eaton (Mildred Frost), 5 Morton St., Andover, Mass.

Mrs. Carl V. Heron (Rosalind Hubbell), 446 E. 66 St., N. Y. C.

Mrs. Herman Heyman (Josephine Joel), 1046 North Av. N. E., Atlanta, Ga.

Mrs. Clifton Wishart (Lois Kane), 9 Davis Av., White Plains, N. Y.

Mrs. Roger Cutting (Florence Lufkin), 26 Ward St., Woburn, Mass.

Mrs. J. A. Austin (Dorothy Morgan), Grasdon Hall, Larchmont, N. Y.

Mrs. J. E. Woodward (Florence Munsie), 599 Highland Av., Malden, Mass.

Mrs. Paul D. White (Ina Reid), 43 Linnaean St., Cambridge, Mass.

Martha Schaible, 38 W. 10 St., N. Y. C.

Mrs. Harold Hood (Frances Smith), 624 Woodlawn St., Fall River, Mass.

Mrs. R. N. Brainerd (Agnes Wilson), 1290 S. Highland Av., Los Angeles. Agnes hopes any of the class who come to Los Angeles will look her up.

OTHER NEWS.—Frances Arnold is doing volunteer church work of all kinds, that keeps every minute full. She has just been elected Girls' Friendly Society president for the diocese of Maine.

Lillian Baker is private secretary to the business promotion manager of the new Statler Hotel in Boston.

Caroline Bancroft spent last summer visiting in England and France. She expects next summer to conduct a party, so far composed of girls below the age of twenty, on a motor tour through Europe. She will be glad to furnish details to any one writing her at New Canaan, Conn.

Mary-Louise Bates is a new member of the Dayton (O.) Westminster Choir. It is hard work—the classes start at 7.30 A.M.—but very interesting. On Nov. 8 they started on a six weeks' concert tour.

Christine Berger is teaching 6th and 7th grade arithmetic. She had a summer in Europe.

Peg Blake came back in July from California, visiting a friend on a "real honest-to-goodness stock ranch" on the way back. This winter she is working with the United Fruit Co. as secretary-stenographer. She will be glad to send anyone interested new recipes for "Meloripe" or ordinary bananas.

Alice Blood is director of the Health Education Department of the Kalamazoo Y. W. C. A. It is hard work, much of it at night, but most satisfying. She spent the summer attending conferences and visiting. She met Margaret Davenport in Baraboo, Wis.

Jo Bree is studying at Yale after three years of teaching.

Elizabeth Buck is registrar of the Social Service Exchange in Fall River.

Priscilla Capps is director of the industrial work for refugees in Athens under the American Friends of Greece, a bureau of the Near East Relief. They employ from 400–500 women in embroidery and weaving and sell their products both there and here in America. Most of Priscilla's time is spent in studying the old Greek embroideries and adapting them to modern work, and in trying to restore their dying art. She says Athens is a fascinating place to live, with enough revolutions to make life interesting, and a pleasant social life.

Madeline Cary, after working a year in Seattle, started home via Honolulu, Panama, Cuba, and Florida. She is now working in New York as private secretary to a junior partner in a life insurance agency.

Margaret Clough has a most interesting job with the New York Board of Underwriters, taking charge of the female personnel. She was in England and France from May to Sept. Her address is 340 Montrose Av., South Orange, N. J.

Mary Coley is studying at Union Theological Seminary and living at International House. She says it is hard to tell which is more interesting.

Miriam Conklin is scenario editor for Life Cartoon Comedies in New York. She works in the same office as Eleanor De Lamater. On her way east this fall she visited Alice (Quayle) Osborne.

Katherine Debevoise is educational interne at the Lincoln School of Teachers College.

Olive Dougherty is now an interior decorator, only taking time off for a vocal lesson now and then.

Veera Engle is doing secretarial work now but is looking for something interesting in the small circulating library line.

Amy Erlandsen is keeping house, working in her father's office, and has just finished running the Red Cross drive in her district. Her new address is 175–19 Devonshire Rd., Jamaica, N. Y.

Nerissa Fitzsimmons is an assistant in the psychology laboratory at Detroit Teachers' College.

Frances Ford is doing club work and keeping on with her music.

Janet Frantz has the same job in the Index of Christian Art in the art department at Princeton. She motored through France last summer.

Camp Marienfeld ·· Chesham, N. H.

32nd Year (*Mt. Monadnock in the background.*) July and August

For Boys, ages 8–17. Address the Headmaster, Raphael J. Shortlidge, The Choate School, Wallingford, Conn., or: Mrs. Shortlidge, — Helen Wetmore Houghton, Smith, 1912.

Athletics:
Swimming
Water sports
Tennis
Horseback Riding
Baseball
Hiking
Wrestling
Boxing

Music:
Violin, Vocal,
Piano
Group Singing
Orchestra
Summer Study:
Make-up work,
for promotion, or
methods and habits of
study

Occupations: Camp craft, nature study, clay modeling, metal and wood work, radio construction, photography, dramatics.

Large staff of mature and experienced masters, a master to five boys.

The Swimming Cove

Peggy Gantt is enjoying her last year at medical school, and living with four other medical students. She spent the summer as an interne in various hospitals.

Alice (Gould) Edman's husband is a correspondent for out-of-town newspapers in Pittsfield, Mass.

Matilda Gross is teaching high school English in the Gilbert School in Winsted, Conn.

Katherine Hannon is taking an intensive business course at Gregg Shorthand School in Phoenix. She spent part of the summer in Boston and New York.

Margaret (Hannon) Walsh is secretary to A. B. McIntrie, manager of the Boston office of an advertising agency, and is very busy with a job and housekeeping.

Margery Hawley is teaching physical education in St. Joseph, Mich.

Ethel Henin is now acting in the Sam H. Harris production of "We Americans."

Lucy Hodge received her M.A. from Radcliffe last June, and is going on "in fear and trembling" towards her Ph.D. exams.

Helene (Hodgkins) Kellogg has just moved back to Springfield, her home town. She is planning to go into Girl Scout work again there. Her address is 115 Knollwood St., Springfield, Mass.

Elizabeth Hotchkiss is doing secretarial work in Chicago.

Betty Johnston sailed Nov. 17 for England to be married there in December. Her address is c/o R. B. Cross, Bush House, Aldwych, London, W. C. 2, Eng.

Eleanor Kohn is doing case work for the Charity Organization Society in New York.

Laura (Lane) Johanson is very busy, running frantically from meeting to meeting. She is a Girl Scout captain, president of the Ladies' Society, preaches every once in a while, works with the religious education side of their job, and keeps house in a little white home. Their church has just been redecorated.

Mary Lange is teaching history at Newtown High School in New York City. She is taking some history at Columbia, and looks forward to seeing Professor Fay there in spring term.

Margaret Lawler is instructor in English in the Junior High School at Greenfield.

Sarah Lingle is teaching French in Converse College in Spartanburg (S. C.), a most attractive college. She visited Peg Landon '24 and Jane Baker '25 in New England last summer, but seldom sees any Smith people of our generation in the South, so she hopes to see any of '23 who go that way to Florida.

Josephina Lucchina is still head of the Italian department in the Classical High School in Waterbury (Conn.) and is studying at Yale, preparatory to studying in Italy.

Dorothy Lutz is a stenographer in an advertising agency. Her address is 84 Euston Rd., Garden City, N. Y.

Kay Lynch is a special class teacher in Demarest, N. J. She is trying to bring the class up to state standards and make out a course of study for a special class.

Onnolee (Mann) Gould is fixing up their new house in Lincoln, Neb. She expects to be kept busy this winter with Junior League work.

"K" Mason is just back from three and a half months in England and France.

Jeannette Mathers spent last summer in Norway and saw a little of Sweden and Denmark on side trips to Stockholm and Copenhagen.

Grace Meyercord is a librarian at the Hotel Shelton, New York.

Harriet Montross writes, "I am studying French and taking vocal lessons, begging for the local charities, and making myself generally useful in the activities of the village." The village is Peekskill, N. Y.

Crucita Moore is instructor of music in the Barrington School, Great Barrington, Mass.

Edith Morris spent a restful summer in Sewanee (Tenn.) where they now have a summer home. She is back teaching English at St. Mary's School in Memphis.

Martha Morse writes that she is a "home girl" this winter, doing Girl Scout work and learning stenography and typewriting.

A clipping from the Worcester Post says that Gertrude Mullaney is teaching English and history in the Walpole (Mass.) High School.

Dorothy Myers returned from Germany and is now doing a very interesting survey for the National Consumers' League. She and Margie Heath '25 have an apartment together.

Dorothy Neff has been working at Brentano's, New York, after a trip abroad.

Rosie Nelson is back in Alabama for her second year of teaching in a school for colored children. Mary Bohn '26 is with her this year. She felt like a real Southerner the other day carrying home a stick of sugar cane which one of the children had brought her.

Helen Nowels spent eight weeks last summer in Europe and is now doing graduate work at the Univ. of Wisconsin.

Dorothy Patten is teaching six forms in English in the York (Pa.) Collegiate Institute, and standing up on the platform every morning to lead the chapel singing. She is most enthusiastic over everything connected with her job.

Annie Porter is assistant social worker at the State Hospital in Howard, R. I.

Ruth (Purvis) Lawrence is a reader in the statistics department of Harvard School of Business Administration.

Eloise Reder is a children's librarian.

Esther Rhodes is teaching piano at Mary Baldwin College in Staunton, Va.

Sarah Riggs is working for an M.A. in English at the Yale Graduate School, and living with her parents, who are having a sabbatical year in America. Next year she goes back to her school in Constantinople.

Jane Robinson is very busy studying piano and working afternoons on a part-time job at the Lenox School in New York.

Helen (Schulze) Burch is president of the Chicago Field Hockey Assn., captain of the North Side hockey team, treasurer of Arden

Shore Assn. (a philanthropic organization), chairman of the publicity committee of the Chicago Public School Arts Society, on the house committee of the Chicago College Club and the auxiliary board of the School of Domestic Arts and Sciences!

Henrietta Sebring works in odd moments for Olive (Beaupré) Miller '04 and her Book House for Children. She spent the summer at *Life's* camp for girls, and has since joined her family in an attack of "motoritis" over 2500 miles of three states.

Constance Siegel is a substitute school teacher in New York.

Harriet Sleeper is a teacher in the third grade in the Brooklyn Ethical Culture School.

Lillian Smith is a bacteriologist at the Henry Ford Hospital in Detroit.

Ermina Stimson is in Paris studying art and doing fashion illustrating for an American buyer. She writes, "The first is ART and the second pot-boiling,—both interesting enough to keep me here for a third winter, with traveling in odd times." Her address is 190 boul. St. Germain, Paris VII.

Lillian Taylor has taught English in the Fitchburg High School since Sept. 1924. She is faculty adviser for the girls' debating club.

Marian (Watts) DeWolf writes: "I am following my husband's ship from Reval, Esthonia, and other Baltic ports to Gibraltar and the Mediterranean. We shall be home next June."

Helen Welch is girls' work secretary in the Pawtucket-Central Falls Y. W. C. A.

Betsy Wheeler is taking a nurse's training course at the Pasadena (Calif.) Hospital.

Katharine Whitlock is continuing her secretarial course at Miss Conklin's School in New York. She has just returned from a trip all over the Continent with a month at the University Club in Paris with Ann Broad, who is still there.

Katharine Wilder is a music teacher in the high school at Catonsville, Md. She went to Harvard Summer School last summer, and is planning to study piano this winter at the Peabody Conservatory in Baltimore.

Ellen Williams is sailing Jan. 1 for her fourth winter in Europe. She expects to study in Paris and to be in Italy and England until summer.

Ex-1923

ENGAGED.—Esther Babbitt to George Frederick Howe of Burlington, Vt. Esther is an associate editor of *The Youth's Companion*.

Beatrice Schurman to Holbrook B. Cushman of New York, Princeton '18.

MARRIED.—Mildred McConnell to Raymond L. Hamilton, Princeton '20, Oct. 8, 1926, in Montclair, N. J.

Helen Prickitt to William Franklin Buchanan, Oct. 16, 1926.

BORN.—To Laura (Bowyer) Meeker a second son, Walter Bowyer, Sept. 30, 1926.

To Alice (Dean) Livingston a daughter, Susan Philida, Feb. 23, 1926.

To Beatrice (Fellows) Eckberg a daughter, Joan Alline, June 21, 1926.

To Sue (Noble) Coe a son, Benjamin Noble, Nov. 25, 1926.

To Helen (Read) Robinson a second son, Shepard Douglass, Apr. 15, 1925.

To Eleanor (Perkins) Parker a second child and first son, Franklin Eddy III, Aug. 22, 1925.

OTHER NEWS.—Isabel (Barton) Morse is taking a correspondence course in secretarial correspondence from Columbia, as well as taking care of her two small sons.

Helen (Deiches) Oppenheim did some work on the plans for a big national conference of the Child Study Assn., held in Baltimore in November.

Lillian Kennedy is a medical illustrator in Atlanta (Ga.), having taken a special course in medical illustrating at Johns Hopkins last year.

Phyllis Stanley is research technician in the zoölogy department in the State Univ. of Iowa.

Isabelle Sweetser is training for personnel work and is at present with E. T. Slattery and Co., Boston.

Solveig (Winslow) Wenzel is instructor in the speech and dramatic department at Hunter College, New York City, and also coach of the Lenox School's yearly school play.

1924

Class secretary—Beatrice H. Marsh, 9 Willard St. or 721 Main St., Hartford, Conn.

ENGAGED.—Carol Waterbury to Stuart Clay Campbell of Whittier, Calif.

MARRIED.—Isabel Aloe to Howard F. Baer, June 16, 1926. Mr. Baer is Princeton '24 and a Cloister Club man. Address, Virginia Apts., Charleston, W. Va.

Eleanor Bailey to Earl H. Eacker. They are at home at 4 Ayer Rd., Boston, Mass.

Dorothy Hopkins to Isaac H. Curtis of Chicago.

BORN.—To Barbara (Farnham) Seamans a son, David Manning, Oct. 17, 1926.

To Agnes (Matzinger) Cattell a daughter, Mary Virginia, Aug. 26, 1926.

To Miriam (Montelius) Clapp a daughter, Joan, July 19, 1926.

To Elizabeth (Thomson) Fricke a daughter, Jeanne Kepner, Oct. 6, 1926.

To Mabel (Wilson) Davenport a son, Walter, Mar. 14, 1926.

OTHER NEWS.—Catherine (Condict) Yates is now in Buenos Aires, where her husband is in the diplomatic service. Address, c/o American Consulate General, Buenos Aires, Argentina.

Catherine Cullinan is teaching freshman English in the Bridgeport (Conn.) High School.

Edith Fitton is back at Miami Univ., Oxford, O., after a summer spent motoring with another girl from the Univ. through Estes Park, Yellowstone, and then East to Boston and Cape Cod, camping in tourist camps most of the way.

Barbara (Frost) MacCracken is doing some advertising for McKennee and Taylor Real Estate Co.

Virginia Gardiner is studying singing with

Mrs. Dudley Fitts of Boston. Last year she studied French diction with Elsa Vieh '20.

Mildred Gertzen is now assistant credit manager for Prentice Hall Inc., publishers, 70 Fifth Av., N. Y. C. She and Serena Pendleton are singing with the Women's Univ. Glee Club.

Pemala Harrison has enrolled for a year's study at the Sorbonne.

Gwendolyn Heyworth is taking courses in municipal government and immigrant education at Columbia, and teaching night school two evenings a week.

Helen Hopkins is "wandering slowly around Europe—Italy for the winter and perhaps Spain for Easter." Address, c/o American Express Co., Athens, Greece.

Margaret Idleman is teaching chemistry and physics at the Ethical Culture School, N. Y. C.

Bee Marsh is editing the weekly *Legislative Bulletin* of the Connecticut League of Women Voters. (Prepare to elect a new class secretary in June!)

Betty Noyes, being struck by the scarcity of news from our class, contributes this about herself, "I spent the summer abroad, making a hurried tour with stops at London, Bruges, Cologne, Madrid, Seville, San Sebastian, Paris, and other places." She is now assistant in corrective gymnastics at the Univ. of Illinois. Follow her example and send in your contribution!

Marion (Knickerbocker) Palmer has a new home at 6 Bloomfield St., Lexington, Mass.

Bessie Romansky is teaching seventh and eighth grade science in Hartford, Conn. Her avocation is organizing junior clubs and other such activities.

Marguerite Sowers is secretary to Dean Pegram, executive head of the physics department at Columbia. She is living with Agnes (Matzinger) Cattell and family at 183 Pinehurst Av., N. Y. C.

Gwendolen Washington is taking a secretarial course in Evanston and tutoring a girl in French.

Who sent unsigned letters from these addresses: Raleigh, N. C.; 218 E. 48 St., N. Y. C.; and the Arden School, Lakewood, N.J.?

Ex-1924
Secretary—Mrs. Edward I. Cooper (Laura Jones), 1070 Whitney Av., New Haven, Conn.

1925
Class secretary—Frances S. French, 165 E. 33 St., New York City.

BORN.—To Anna (Dallinger) Turner a daughter, Ann Elizabeth, Dec. 4, 1926, in Buffalo, N. Y.

ENGAGED.—Marion Bond to C. Stuart Avery, of Milton, Mass.

MARRIED.—Constance Davidge to Daniel Morgan Brigham, Jan. 12, in Binghamton, N. Y.

Mary Gerould to Troyer S. Anderson, in Sept. 1926. Mr. Anderson is a Dartmouth graduate, has a Harvard M.A., and has been a Rhodes scholar at Oxford for the last three years. At present, he is teaching history at

Mary Gardner to Foster Robertson, Univ. of Toronto '22· They expect to be married in June.

Kathleen Heile to Reginald Stebbins, Yale '23· Mr. Stebbins is a brother of Katharine Stebbins.

Lorraine Le Huray to William Walter Commons, Williams '25· Mr. Commons is with the Open Road, Inc., in New York.

Florence Marmorstein to Samuel Rosenfeld of Akron. They expect to be married in the early spring.

Dorothy Recht to Roy Plant. Dorothy is now teaching.

Helen Sanderson to Lieut. Edward C. Craig, U. S. A. They expect to be married in the spring.

Esther Smith to Midshipman Martin Lawrence. They expect to be married in June. Esther is now secretary of recreation at the Boston Girls' City Club and says that it is very interesting with hours like a night watchman's.

Alberta Thompson to W. Kenneth Eaton. The engagement was announced at a tea Nov. 20, at which Elizabeth Sherwood received. They expect to be married about Easter time.

Virginia Traphagen to Cecil Bernard Richardson, an Englishman and author. Trap says she would ask the class to the wedding but they're planning to elope. She is studying at Columbia for her M.A. in psychology.

MARRIED.—Dorothy Albright to Dr. Philip Newman, Jan. 8. New address, 110 N. 8 St., Allentown, Pa.

Margaret Buell to Donald Wilder, Amherst '26, Nov. 20, 1926. Address, 9034 148th St., Jamaica, N. Y. Mr. Wilder is on the editorial staff of the Brooklyn Eagle.

Lillian Davis to Frederick C. Davis, Dec. 25, 1926. Address, 9 S. Park St., Hanover, N. H.

Margaret Ley to Eric Kent. New address, 64 Sagamore Rd., Bronxville, N. Y.

Margaret Lloyd to Albert Aiken, Dec. 17, 1926. They are living at 9 Prospect Av., Mamaroneck, N. Y. Peggy is teaching music in the Rye Country Day School.

Minerva Ramsdell to John B. Russell, Nov. 20, 1926. Address, 31 Sewell St., Wollaston, Mass.

Judith Scheinberg to Abbe Epstein. They went to Europe on their wedding trip.

Ethel Stretch to William O. Andrews, Nov. 18, 1926. Address, 733 Springfield Av., East Orange, N. J.

Helen Wright to F. H. Hovey Jr., Harvard '22, Dec. 16, 1926.

OTHER NEWS.—Ruth Abbott is taking a secretarial course in N. Y. C.

Elizabeth Allen is learning buying at Miss Prince's in Boston.

Alice Bailey is studying stenography in Rochester, N. Y.

Vera Bane is to be married in June to Robert Alcorn and meanwhile spends much time sewing and cooking.

Hélène Basquin is doing Girl Scout work in Gary (Ind.) and I should judge it is all fine

except for a slightly heavy atmosphere due to Sinclair and Standard Oil Refineries, Grasselli Chemical Works, Dutch Cleanser and cement and glue factories!

Cathleen Bell, Lib Creighton, and Evelyn Olsen are taking the training course at Lord and Taylor's.

Gladys Beach is studying the psychology of religion at Yale Divinity School.

Louise Billstein is taking the librarian course offered by the N. Y. Public Library and is living with Midge Hessler and Kay Van Hoesen.

Mary Bohn is teaching in Calhoun, Ala.

Elizabeth Bridges is teaching gym at The Misses Allen School in West Newton.

Christine Burgess is attending the School of the Museum of Fine Arts in Boston.

Caryll Burhenn is editorial secretary at Ginn and Co., publishing house, Boston.

Terry Caperton is able to typewrite (slowly) and occupies herself in a publishing house and with housekeeping.

Carolyn Case made her début in Chicago this winter and is having a social whirl.

Patricia Cassidy is taking a business course.

Betty Chandler wrote from Oxford to a friend, "I'm having the most thrilling time learning everything from Anglo-Saxon to how to keep warm over a diminutive coal grate fire—I bicycle through priceless little medieval streets called Logic Lane, The Turl, etc., in my short sleeveless black gown and squashable cap, and go to fascinating teas where conversation is thoroughly cosmopolitan and crumpets keep hot on trivets."

Catherine Chipman is resident psychologist at the Walter E. Fernald State School and says that the only disadvantage is a tendency to classify people in subways according to probable I. Q.

Marion Christie attended the N. Y. School of Secretaries and now has a fine position with a New York architect.

Betty Church is at the Theatre Guild in N. Y.

Anna Clark has a position in the editorial department of the Survey.

Claire Cremins has a position in the office of the East African Government in New York.

Frances Cowles is in the Hispanic Society Museum, N. Y. C.

Alice Curley is studying for an M.A. at Yale.

Violetta Curtis is secretary to Dean Cross of the Yale Graduate School.

Peg De Lay is taking courses in education at Northwestern. She is on the All-Chicago hockey team.

Rachel Derby is working at interior decorating in Macy's.

Lucile Donelson, Effa Maroney, and Janet Perry are at the Katharine Gibbs School, N. Y. C.

Gertrude Doniger is a secretary at the Crown Point Spar Co., N. Y., but is looking forward finally to a literary career and is now writing a sociological treatise.

Kay Dowling has a position with the Manufacturers Trust Co. in N. Y. and attends art school evenings.

Hortense Fair has a position selling in Gilchrist Co., Boston.

Celia Fisher is assistant psychologist at the Cleveland Child Guidance Clinic.

Edith Foshee is studying voice and taking cooking lessons. She is going to Cuba in the spring.

Peg Foster is studying for her M.A. in geology at Boulder College (Colo.) and has joined the Kappa Kappa Gamma Sorority.

Marian Frauenthal is studying medicine at the Bellevue Hospital and New York Univ. Medical College.

Katherine Frederic was leader of the Open Road Tour from college last summer—they were guests of foreign students and succeeded in strengthening international relations at various dances. Kay is now learning to be a buyer at C. Crawford Hollidge, Boston.

Dorothy French is in the actuary department of the Berkshire Life Insurance Co.

Marjorie French is teaching math. at St. Mary's Cathedral School, Garden City, N. Y.

Susie Friedlander is abroad for several months seeing France, Italy, Sicily, Egypt, and England.

Mary Louise Gasser is teaching modern European history and community civics at the Owensboro (Ky.) High School, and her sister Elizabeth is doing substitute teaching there also.

Marcia Gehring is doing a little of all kinds of work in the Portland Public Library and says that one day a week in the children's room is worse than three finals on the same day.

Eleanor Golden is at the Gallic School in N. Y.

Katharine Gould is at the New York School of Secretaries.

Dorothy Grauer is an assistant teacher in the Park Country Day School near Buffalo.

Jane Greenough plans to go abroad in March for six months.

Agnes Griffin is at the New York School of Secretaries.

Gwen Guthrie is taking courses at the Univ. at Seattle.

Eleanor Gutman is studying medicine at Yale.

Margaret Hammond is taking a secretarial course at Columbia.

Shirley Harris is studying at the Cambridge School of Landscape Architecture.

Sidney Hartly has a position in a bookshop in Chicago.

Martha Hazen is in newspaper publicity work, assisting a professional publicity director who has charge of the Y. W. C. A., Near East colleges, etc.

Jean Henderson is working in the N. Y. State Public Health Laboratories.

Ruth Hunter is doing library work and filing at the Laura Spelman Rockefeller Memorial.

Vivian Iob has a position in the Massachusetts General Hospital.

Lois Ittner is studying at the Sorbonne and before this took an extensive trip through Europe.

Dorothy Jones is studying for her M.A. in history at the Univ. of Pennsylvania.

Ruby Jordan is secretary to the director of standards and supplies of the Y. M. C. A. of New York.

Mary-Jane Judson has almost completely recovered from a serious operation performed last summer.

Katherine Keeler is a news editor of the *South-West Telegram Weekly* in Chicago.

Marjorie Krantz is doing graduate work at Yale preparatory to going into Mr. Baker's department of the drama.

Mary Lane has a fine position as secretary at St. Paul's Church, Washington, D. C.

Harriet Leach is laboratory technician at Massachusetts State Infirmary, Tewksbury.

Olga Leary is studying medicine in Boston.

Dorothy Leger is studying at Russell Sage in Troy, N. Y.

Betty Lewis is teaching at the Union (N. J.) High School.

Sana Long is taking a secretarial course in Boston.

Carol Lord has returned from a four months' tour abroad and has also visited Margaret Oliver in Cleveland.

Alma Lubin is studying piano at the Cincinnati Conservatory with Marcian Thalberg.

Louise McCabe is working with the Laura Spelman Rockefeller Memorial.

Margaret McCready has a position at the Society of Arts and Crafts in N. Y. and is taking a business course evenings.

Mary McGregor is studying landscape gardening in N. Y.

Josephine Mann has been in the book department of Jordan Marsh for the holidays.

Janet Marks is attending the Univ. of Cincinnati and doing graduate work in history and education.

Ruth Martin is assistant hostess at the Brick Church Neighborhood House, N. Y. C.

Elizabeth Marting is at the New York School of Social Work.

Ruth Montgomery and Marian Wilson are studying for their M.A.'s in psychology at Columbia.

Ruth Murkland is teaching in Orange, N. J.

Eleanor Mussey is taking courses at the Art Institute of Chicago.

Winifred Murfin is studying at the Corcoran School of Art in Washington. This summer she did social work in the children's surgical ward of the New Haven Hospital.

Dorothy Norris is teaching in Ashby (Mass.) where they still have quilting parties.

Marian Olley is an associate editor at the Pilgrim Press in Boston and has an apartment with Caryll Burhenn.

Kathleen O'Neil is an interpreter of French and Italian in the Division of Immigration and Americanization in Springfield.

Janice Paine is teaching at Emma Willard School, Troy, N. Y.

Hope Palmer has a position at Scribner's, N. Y. C.

Mildred Parsons is substitute teacher of Latin and math. at the Northampton High School.

Mary Perkins is studying law at Yale.

Jane Pither is teaching at Kemper Hall.

Maroe Pratt is studying at Pierce Secretarial School, Boston.

Frances Proskauer is at business school.

Betty Purdum is training to be a nurse at the Presbyterian Hospital in Chicago.

Margaret Rejebian is doing social work at the International Immigration Bureau, N. Y.

Bella Ress is doing social work with the Associated Charities of Pittsburgh.

Elizabeth Saunders and Katherine Van Hoesen are at R. H. Macy's Training School.

Freda Seidensticker has a position in the library of the Princeton Theological School.

Betty Shedd and Hester Smith are together in Paris and studying at the Sorbonne. They spent their vacation at St. Moritz after practicing this fall at the Palais de Glace.

Dorothy Sloan is at the Massachusetts General Hospital Laboratory School, Boston.

Helen Smith is studying at the Boston School of Interior Decoration. This fall she and Flora Macdonald were in Havana and had an exciting experience in the cyclone.

Sara-Henri Solomon is studying at the Prince School, Boston.

Dottie Spaeth has gone West for the winter, acting as secretary for her father.

Helen Spaidal and Marcia Wadhams are going abroad in March for six months with Helen's family.

Marion Spicer is teaching European history and English in the Rockville (Conn.) High School.

Ruth Stanford is at Moser Business College in Chicago.

Margaret Stearns is taking a business course in N. Y.

Katharine Stebbins and Betty Alcorn were among those going abroad in January.

Eleanor Stevens is assistant secretary at Roycemore School in Evanston, Ill.

Alice Stevenson is studying public health at Yale.

Catherine Sullivan is studying for an M.A. in psychology at Clark Univ., Worcester.

Katharine Thayer is teaching French and Latin at the high school in Charlemont, Mass.

Harriett Todd has a position at the Strong Memorial Hospital, Rochester, N. Y.

Mona Towsom is abroad for several months.

Florence Tripp has a position with Rothschilds, Bankers, in N. Y. C.

Eleanor Walton is teaching in Charleston, S. C.

Margaret Ward is reader for Professor Hankins and studying for her M.A. at College.

Phyllis Watts has a position with a financial house on Wall St. and is living with Janet Studholme in N. Y. C.

Janet Wickham is supervisor of personnel activities in the New Jersey Division of the N. Y. Telephone Co.

Katharine Wiggin is taking a course at Miss Farmer's School of Cookery.

Helen Williams is studying at the Sorbonne for the winter.

Ruth Williamson has been giving mental tests at the Children's Home in Duluth and to State problem cases. She is taking a Mediterranean cruise in February.

Pauline Winchester is teaching at the Rye (N. Y.) Country Day School.

Marion Windisch is studying art at the Cincinnati Academy and expects to go abroad in the spring.

Catharine Witherell is teaching elocution at the George School, Bucks Co., Pa.

Elinor Woodward and Miriam Beede are studying at Simmons Secretarial School.

Mary Yarborough is convalescing from a serious operation and is at home.

Louise Zschiesche is research assistant in the heart laboratory of the Boston City Hospital, where she has been so successful as to discover a new stain which is to be named for her.

Ex-1926

MARRIED.—Irma Cedar to Jesse Dann. Address, 1450 50th St., Brooklyn, N. Y.

Mary Alice Murray to Harry Oard, a student at Yale Medical School.

BORN.—To Virginia (Adams) Early a daughter, Virginia Alice.

To Sally Knight (Hill) Kroll a daughter, Sally Mayo, Nov. 17, 1926.

DIED.—Elizabeth (Henry) Manning, in Honolulu, in Dec. 1926, as the result of an automobile accident.

OTHER NEWS.—Priscilla Beach is studying piano and organ.

Mina (Dessez) Cassard has gone to Brazil with her husband, Lieut. Commander Paul Cassard, who is aviation member of the U. S. Naval Commission to Brazil.

Virginia Lee is nursing in New York, having graduated last spring from the training school of the Post Graduate Hospital.

Sally (McAll) Childs is doing special work in Newton. Mr. Childs is studying for his M.A. at Harvard.

Betty Williams is studying art in New York.

NOTICES

ALL editorial mail should be sent to Edith Hill, College Hall, Northampton, Mass. Material for the May QUARTERLY should be typewritten and should reach College Hall by April 1. Please send subscriptions to Miss Snow at Rumford Bldg., 10 Ferry St., Concord, N. H., or College Hall, Northampton. Correspondence concerning advertising should be sent to College Hall. The dates of publication are November 20, February 20, May 20, and August 1, and subscribers failing to receive their copies within ten days after those dates should notify the business manager, as otherwise she cannot furnish free duplicate copies. The subscription price for one year is $1.50. Single copies 40 cents. Please send all news items for the May QUARTERLY to the class secretaries by April 3.
(over)

1927 COMMENCEMENT 1927

Ivy Day will be Saturday, June 18, and Commencement Day, Monday, June 20.

As usual, the available rooms in the college houses will be open to the alumnae at Commencement. *Members of the classes holding reunions should make applications for these rooms through their class secretaries,* through whom also payment should be made.   Rooms will be assigned to the reunion classes in the order of their seniority.   Members of classes not holding reunions should make applications directly to the Alumnae Office.   '
For a minimum of five days, the price of board and room will be $10.   Alumnae to whom assignments are made will be held responsible for the full payment unless notice of withdrawal is sent to the class secretary before June 1.   After June 1, notices of withdrawal and requests for rooms should be sent directly to the Alumnae Office.   At this time any vacancies left by the reunion classes will be assigned to members of the classes not holding reunions, in the order in which the applications have been received.
The campus rooms will be open after luncheon on Thursday before Commencement.

COLLEGE PINS

Alumnae desiring to procure college pins may send to Miss Jean Cahoon, Registrar, College Hall, for an order upon Tiffany and Co.   *Do not send money with this request,* but mail check direct to Tiffany upon receipt of the order from Miss Cahoon.   The price of the pin is $3.50, with initials, class, and safety clasp.   The full name will be engraved, if preferred, at a cost of 6 cents for each extra letter.

AMERICAN ASSOCIATION OF UNIVERSITY WOMEN

The biennial convention of the A. A. U. W. will be in Washington, D. C., March 31, April 1 and 2.

SMITH COLLEGE FELLOWSHIPS AND GRADUATE SCHOLARSHIPS

Address, Chairman of the Committee on Fellowships, College Hall, Northampton.

SMITH COLLEGE FELLOWSHIPS. — Six fellowships. $600 each and tuition. For graduate study at Smith College, unrestricted as to subject. Open to graduates of Smith College and to women graduates of other colleges and universities of high standing. (In the case of graduates and faculty of Smith College a fellowship may be awarded for study elsewhere in this country or abroad.)
SMITH COLLEGE FELLOWSHIPS IN EDUCATION.—Six fellowships in Education. $500 each and tuition. Open to graduates of Smith College and to women graduates of other colleges and universities of high standing.
INTERCOLLEGIATE COMMUNITY SERVICE ASSOCIATION FELLOWSHIP.—One fellowship of $600. Open to graduates of Smith College only. For study, in Boston, New York, or Philadelphia, consisting of practical work and academic work. Offered by the Smith College Alumnae Association and by the I. C. S. A.
ALUMNAE FELLOWSHIP.—One fellowship of $600. Open to members of the graduating class of Smith College only for study at Smith College or elsewhere in this country or abroad. Offered by the Alumnae Association of the College.
SMITH STUDENTS' AID SOCIETY FELLOWSHIP.—One fellowship of not less than $500 for training in vocational work. Open to members of the graduating class and to alumnae of not more than two years' standing. Offered by the Smith Students' Aid Society.
SOPHIA SMITH HONORARY FELLOWSHIPS.—Fellowships without stipend awarded to members of the graduating class and to graduates of the College of fellowship grade who do not require financial assistance.
THE ANNA D. KYLE SCHOLARSHIP.—One scholarship of $1000 to be used for study in the American School of Oriental Research in Jerusalem. Open to graduates of Smith College only. Given by Miss Anna D. Kyle of the class of 1918.
THE HARRIET BOYD HAWES SCHOLARSHIP.—One scholarship, the income of a fund of $3000 established by the class of 1892 in honor of Harriet Boyd Hawes, and tuition. For graduates of Smith College or women graduates of other colleges or universities of high rank.
SMITH COLLEGE TUITION SCHOLARSHIPS.—Four scholarships covering the cost of tuition, unrestricted as to subject. Open to graduates of Smith College or to women graduates of other colleges and universities of high standing.
SMITH COLLEGE SCHOLARSHIPS IN EDUCATION.—Three scholarships in the department of Education covering the cost of tuition, open to graduates of Smith College and to women graduates of colleges and universities of high standing.

Roosevelt New York　　Mount Royal Montreal　　Radison Minneapolis　　Seneca Rochester　　Blackstone Chicago　　O'Henry Greensboro, N. C.　　Pere Marquet Peoria

Willard Washington

Coronado St. Louis

Oakland Oakland, Calif.

Wolford Danville, Ill.

Neil House Columbus

Claremont Berkeley, Calif.

Urbana-Lincoln Urbana, Ill.

MAIN FEATURES OF THE INTERCOLLEGIATE ALUMNI HOTEL MOVEMENT

Interested alumni can secure from a clerk at the desk of each Intercollegiate Alumni Hotel an information leaflet which describes in detail the Intercollegiate Alumni Hotel movement.

At each Intercollegiate Alumni Hotel there will be maintained a card index of the names of all the resident alumni of all the participating institutions. This will be of especial benefit to traveling alumni in locating classmates and friends.

The current issues of the alumni publications of all the participating institutions will be on file at each Intercollegiate Alumni Hotel.

Reservation cards will be available at the clerk's desk in each designated hotel and at the alumni office in each college or university. These reservation cards will serve as a great convenience to travellers in securing advance accommodations.

The managers of all Intercollegiate Alumni Hotels are prepared to cooperate with individual alumni to the fullest extent and are also prepared to assist in the creation of new local alumni associations and in the development and extension of the activities of those already formed.

Schenley Pittsburgh　　Californian Fresno　　Saint Paul St. Paul　　Multnomah Portland, Ore.　　Palace San Francisco　　Ponce de Leon Miami　　Francis Marion Charleston, S. C.

George Vanderbilt, Asheville, N. C. — St. James, San Diego — Waldorf-Astoria, New York — Onondaga, Syracuse — Wolverine, Detroit — Biltmore, Los Angeles — Benjamin Franklin, Philadelphia

THE PARTICIPATING COLLEGES:

The alumni organizations of the following colleges and universities are participants in the Intercollegiate Alumni Hotel movement:

Copley-Plaza, Boston

Lincoln, Lincoln, Neb.

Akron, Alabama, Amherst, Bates, Beloit, Brown, Bucknell, Bryn Mawr, California, Carnegie Institute, Case School, Chicago, City College New York, Colgate, Colorado School Mines, Colorado, Columbia, Cornell, Cumberland, Emory, Georgia

Goucher, Harvard, Illinois, Indiana, Iowa State College, James Milliken, Kansas Teachers' Coll., Kansas, Lake Erie, Lehigh, Louisiana, Maine, M. I. T., Michigan State, Michigan, Mills, Minnesota, Missouri, Montana, Mount Holyoke, Nebraska

New York University, North Carolina, North Dakota, Northwestern, Oberlin, Occidental, Ohio State, Ohio Wesleyan, Oklahoma, Oregon, Oregon State, Penn State, Pennsylvania, Purdue, Radcliffe, Rollins, Rutgers, Smith, South Dakota, Southern California, Stanford

Stevens Institute, Texas A. and M., Texas, Union, Vanderbilt, Vassar, Vermont, Virginia, Washington and Lee, Washington State, Washington, Wellesley, Wesleyan College, Wesleyan University, Western Reserve, Whitman, Williams, Wisconsin, Wooster, Worcester Poly. Inst., Yale

 Windermere, Chicago

 Olympic, Seattle

INTERCOLLEGIATE ALUMNI HOTELS:

Roosevelt, New York; Waldorf-Astoria, New York; University Center,* New York; Copley-Plaza, Boston; University Center,* Boston; Blackstone, Chicago; Windermere, Chicago; University Center,* Chicago; Benjamin Franklin, Philadelphia; Willard, Washington; Radisson, Minneapolis; Biltmore, Los Angeles; Palace, San Francisco; Olympic, Seattle; Seneca, Rochester; Claremont, Berkeley

Onondaga, Syracuse; Sinton, Cincinnati; Wolverine, Detroit; Multnomah, Portland, Ore.; Sacramento, Sacramento; Californian, Fresno; Lincoln, Lincoln, Nebr.; Oakland, Oakland, Cal.; Lycoming, Williamsport, Pa.; Mount Royal, Montreal; King Edward, Toronto; Coronado, St. Louis; Bethlehem, Bethlehem, Pa.; Urbana-Lincoln, Urbana, Ill.; Saint Paul, St. Paul; Savannah, Savannah, Ga.

Schenley, Pittsburgh; Wolford, Danville, Ill.; Neil House, Columbus; Pere Marquette, Peoria; Southern, Baltimore; St. James, San Diego; Park, Madison; O'Henry, Greensboro, N. C.; Sheraton, High Point, N. C.; Charlotte, Charlotte, N. C.; George Vanderbilt, Asheville, N. C.; Francis Marion, Charleston, S. C.; Ponce de Leon, Miami

*To be built in 1926-27

 Sacramento, Sacramento
 Park, Madison

 Southern, Baltimore

Charlotte, Charlotte, N. C. — Sheraton, High Point, N. C. — Sinton, Cincinnati — King Edward, Toronto — Bethlehem, Bethlehem, Pa. — Lycoming, Williamsport, Pa. — Savannah, Savannah, Ga.

THE RUMFORD PRESS

CONCORD, NEW HAMPSHIRE

[*One of the* MOST COMPLETE
Printing & Binding Plants
in the EASTERN STATES]

¶ MAGAZINES, school and college catalogues, town histories, genealogies, scientific books, annual reports, color work and all classes of high grade printing receive our expert services.

¶ THIS great institution has been built up by giving the most careful attention to the wants of individual customers, by keeping delivery promises, and by charging fair and reasonable prices.

PRINTERS *of* MANY MAGAZINES *of* NATIONAL CIRCULATION

Rumford Press Product Means Quality

CLASSIFIED LIST OF ADVERTISERS

When writing to advertisers be sure to mention
THE SMITH ALUMNAE QUARTERLY

𝔖𝔪𝔦𝔱𝔥 ℭ𝔬𝔩𝔩𝔢𝔤𝔢

NORTHAMPTON, MASSACHUSETTS

WILLIAM ALLAN NEILSON, PH.D., LL.D., L.H.D., *President*

SMITH COLLEGE was founded by Sophia Smith of Hatfield, Massachusetts, who bequeathed for its establishment and maintenance $393,105.60, a sum which in 1875, when the last payment was received and the institution was opened, amounted to nearly if not quite a half million of dollars. The College is Christian, seeking to realize the ideals of character inspired by the Christian religion, but is entirely non-sectarian in its management and instruction. It was incorporated and chartered by the State in March 1871. In September 1875 it opened with 14 students, and granted 11 degrees in June 1879. In June 1926 the College conferred 460 A.B. degrees, and 17 A.M. degrees.

L. CLARK SEELYE, D.D., was the first president. He accepted the presidency in July 1873, and served until June 1910. He lived in Northampton as President Emeritus until his death on October 12, 1924. Marion LeRoy Burton, Ph.D., D.D., LL.D., was installed as president in October 1910 and served until June 1917. He left Smith College to be president of the University of Minnesota and later was president of the University of Michigan. He died on February 18, 1925. William Allan Neilson, Ph.D., LL.D., L.H.D., came in September 1917 to be president of the College.

THE College opened its fifty-second year with an undergraduate enrollment of 2033 besides 34 juniors who are spending the year at the Sorbonne, 65 graduate students, a resident faculty of 203, and 9 chief administrative officers. There are 10,822 alumnae, of whom 10,325 are living.

THE property owned by the College comprises 87.25 acres on which there are over a hundred buildings. There are botanical gardens and athletic fields, also a pond which provides boating and skating. There are 33 houses of residence owned or operated by the College besides 11 houses closely affiliated but privately owned. It is the policy of the College to give all four classes approximately equal representation in each house.

THE College fee for board and room is $500 per year and for tuition $400 for all students entering after 1925. Further details are published in the annual catalogs. The Trustees set aside approximately $100,000 for scholarships annually, besides which many special prizes have been established.

AMONG the distinctive features of the College are: (1) Junior year in France. A selected group of students majoring in French are allowed to spend their junior year at the Sorbonne under the personal direction of a member of the Department of French. (2) Special Honors. Selected students are allowed to pursue their studies individually during the junior and senior years in a special field under the guidance of special instructors. They are relieved of the routine of class attendance and course examinations during these two years. (3) The Experimental Schools: a. School for Exceptional Children. For public school children with special educational disabilities and retarded mental development. Conducted by the Department of Education in coöperation with the Northampton Board of Education. b. The Day School, an experimental school of the progressive type, also conducted by the Department of Education, offers instruction to children from five years of age through the work of the Junior High School. c. Nursery School, conducted by the Institute for the Coördination of Women's Interests in coöperation with the Department of Education. (4) School for Social Work. A professional graduate school leading to the degree of M.S.S. The course is fifteen months and comprises theoretical work in Northampton and practical work in the field. (5) Special facilities for the study of Music and Art. (6) Personnel Bureau. A trained staff dealing with the problems of the individual student.

FOR any further information about Smith College address the President's office, College Hall, Northampton, Mass.

Announcing the Opening

(ABOUT MARCH 1st, 1927)

The Hotel Northampton

A modern Guest-House founded
and built by the Community of
Northampton and Smith College

A WIGGINS HOTEL

LEWIS N. WIGGINS, *Managing Director*

The Smith Alumnae Quarterly

Published by the
Alumnae Association of Smith College
• • •
May, 1927

THE SMITH ALUMNAE QUARTERLY

May, 1927

TABLE OF CONTENTS

Published by the Alumnae Association of Smith College
at Rumford Building, 10 Ferry St., Concord, N. H.

Member of Alumni Magazines Associated

Florence Homer Snow 1904, Business Manager...... { Rumford Building, 10 Ferry St., Concord, N. H., or
Marion E. Graves 1915, Advertising Manager........ { College Hall, Northampton, Mass.

BOARD OF EDITORS

Edith Naomi Hill 1903.................College Hall, Northampton...................Editor-in-Chief
Elizabeth H. Kingsley 1919..Assistant to the Editor

Ethel Puffer Howes 1891   Anna T. Kitchel 1903
Jean Fine Spahr 1883   Marie E. Gilchrist 1916
Elizabeth Lewis Day 1895   Clara Savage Littledale 1913
Bernice Sanborn 1918.

Price $1.50 per year (four numbers) in advance

Volume XVIII...No. 3

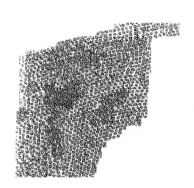

By courtesy of the Weekly

The Dewey House Reception

Margaret Sprowl '27 and Helen Teagle '30 in the soft silks and flowered muslins of fifty years ago

The Smith Alumnae Quarterly

VOL. XVIII   MAY, 1927   NO. 3

Entered as second class matter at the Post Office at Concord, New Hampshire, under the Act of March 3, 1879.

Dewey House Rounds Out a Century

IN THE DAYS OF '79

The site for Smith Judge Dewey and it was that those fourteen val- "neighboring counties 1827 and so had already of distinguished service dent Seelye himself told noted jurists and states- were entertained within have been, if not so varied and colorful, and, unsentimental as the now supposed to be, the to-day resolved to cele- birthday with pomp and College was bought from to his stately residence iant '79ers came from round." It was built in seen nearly fifty years —years in which, Presi- us, some of the most men of Massachusetts its walls. Its second fifty stately, at least more forward-looking and younger generation is Dewey House girls of brate its hundredth ceremony. And so, to- gether with Miss Kingsley, the head of the house, they issued their invitations for a reception; they scoured their grandmothers' attics for costumes of yesteryear; and on the evening of February 26 they lighted the windows of the old house with glowing candles, they filled the hospitable rooms with flowers, and in the soft silks and flowered muslins of fifty years ago they entertained their company. By a happy circumstance Mrs. Mary Gorham Bush of the Class of 1879 was one of their most honored guests, and by another happy circumstance we have persuaded Kate Morris Cone, another member of that pioneer class, to reminisce a little in the following paragraphs of those days when

> "*Parents awoke, ambitious girls were found,*
> *Fourteen arrived from neighboring counties round*
> *And the new college stood on solid ground.*"

THE Dewey House made a perfect setting for the Intelligent Gentlewoman of whom we were to hear so much. She was actually there to welcome us that September day so long ago. The wheels crunched on the gravel, the ardent young President ran out to greet me, and behind him in the doorway stood the Lovely Lady with blue eyes and light curls, tall and graceful, with sweeping skirts, a fichu and lace, and the most delightful, gracious manners in the world. It was Miss Sarah Humphrey, daughter of a college president, long mistress of his house, and to the manner born of curving staircases and stately rooms. She was the brightest spot of that first term. We went to bed the first night lighted by candles stuck in potatoes, and she made it seem a joke. The furnace proved inadequate to the heating of the house, and she built cheerful fires on the hearth in the back parlor on chilly evenings and Sundays and holidays. She had us into her sitting-room for an hour after supper

to sew on our gymnasium
to us "Alec Forbes" by
dispensed the inadequate
and grace. Here is a
House which she told us.
J. G. Holland, author of
trina," worked for Judge
back hall bedroom which
meadow where grew a
tree he wrote his first
log from the window.
Hopkins, perfect lady
who never let us be cold
created the position of
dered unnecessary that
was what Miss Hum-
at the head of the long
and capable women who

KATE MORRIS CONE

"While fathers yielded, jeer-
ing more or less,
Fond mothers racked their
brains to find a dress
Girlish and graceful, simple
and yet fine,
To deck the youthful forms
of '79."

suits while she read aloud
George Macdonald. She
food with cheerfulness
story about the Dewey
When he was a boy Dr.
"Bittersweet" and "Ka-
Dewey and occupied the
looked out on the
willow tree. About that
poem. We could see the
Then there was Mrs.
and perfect housekeeper,
or go hungry again. She
Lady in Charge, and ren-
of Lady Principal which
phrey was. She stands
procession of delightful
these fifty years have

been heads of houses. She dressed handsomely, always a little real lace cap for
one thing, was of middle height and a little stout, moved slowly, and had great
gentleness and dignity of manner.   Her rooms were furnished with things of her
own, much more becoming to the house than the red plush suite which long stood
in the drawing-room—let me call it drawing-room! From the first Miss Cushing
and she dearly loved one another, and no one thought of being jealous—they
were so plainly kindred spirits. When Mrs. Hopkins retired from the Dewey
House she built a little house where Miss Cushing and she lived together, and

she willed it and all
Cushing at the time of
How old were these
Dewey House on its
young things in our
perhaps as much as
probably what they

KATHARINE BINGHAM AND AMANDA
BRYAN '27 AT THE DEWEY HOUSE
RECEPTION

there was in it to Miss
her death.
ladies who started the
new career? To us
teens they seemed old,
forty, and that is
were.

The William Allan Neilson Chair of Research

At the chapel exercises on Monday, April 25, an announcement was made and a gift presented which brought the full assemblage of students and faculty to their feet in spontaneous and prolonged applause. The announcement was made by Mr. George McCallum for the Board of Trustees and is of profound importance to Smith College; but the true significance of the extreme enthusiasm was not because the gift presented by Mr. McCallum was to enhance the academic reputation of the College but because it was made by the Trustees to our President in honor of the completion of his ten years as President of Smith College and as a testimonial of their "great admiration, affection, and esteem" for him. In the July issue we shall publish further details and a picture of the first incumbent of the William Allan Neilson Chair of Research, but in this place we simply quote Mr. McCallum's speech and President Neilson's response.

Mr. McCallum said:

MR. PRESIDENT, Members of the Faculty, Students of Smith College:

I am here this morning as a representative of the Board of Trustees of Smith College.

You are so accustomed to hear a text as a preface to the statements from this platform that I quote as a preamble to my remarks the words of a Scotchman, "And what shall we gie this dear wee small man of ours for his tenth birthday?"

You all know that this June will see the completion of ten years of valuable and constructive work by William Allan Neilson as President of Smith College. It seemed to a number of the friends of the College that this period should not pass without some definite recognition of this accomplishment.

Knowing President Neilson, we realized that a personal gift would be distasteful to him. However, we did know, because of his well-known interest in scholarship and research, that if we could find some scholarly activity which would be of advantage to education in general and especially to Smith College and incorporate this into our college activities, such an action would be pleasing to him.

We all know that women's colleges have so far had little opportunity to develop along the lines of research and scholarship, solely because teaching has been their paramount activity and money has been lacking to encourage those other activities which are almost universally a part of the work in men's colleges and universities.

It seemed, therefore, that the best testimony we could give at this time of our appreciation of our President would be to establish a Chair of Research, bearing his name.

Of course, the next question was, in what field shall the holder of this Chair make his research? There seemed to be at the moment an outstanding need in American colleges for a thorough-going scientific experimental approach to psychology as a basis for the social sciences. We decided, first, to found a chair of research and, secondly, that the investigations undertaken should be in experimental psychology.

A number of people were found who were willing to pledge the money needed, friends who have frequently shown their interest in the needs and welfare of Smith College. Their action at this time was partially dictated by their interest in the College, partly because of their interest in psychology, but mainly because of their admiration for President Neilson and their enthusiastic approval of what he has accomplished here in ten years.

Enough money has been secured to establish a Research Chair for a five-year period. It is the hope of the original donors to this Fund that the published results made by the holder of this Chair in the coming five years will prove so valuable to education and Smith College that other friends will come forward to make the Chair permanent, the idea being that each succeeding incumbent shall also be here for a five-year period, and that during each period specialization of scientific investigation be made in different fields.

The donors of the Fund felt that the first incumbent of this Chair of Research should be an outstanding international figure, a man distinguished and recognized in the world as an experimental psychologist. For this reason they have called a graduate and Doctor of Philosophy of the University of Berlin, Dr. Kurt Koffka. . . .

Dr. Koffka's position in the world of experimental psychology is second to none, and in our minds he is a most satisfactory first incumbent for Smith College's Memorial Chair of Research, the first such Chair in any woman's college in America.

You members of the student body must in the main content yourselves with the knowledge that the fame and position of Smith College in the academic world are greatly increased by Dr. Koffka's presence here. He will have no classroom work, which will thus make it impossible for you to come into the constant pleasant intimate contact with him that you do with the other members of the Faculty.

For the members of the Faculty, the Trustees are hoping that Professor Koffka will prove an interesting, companionable, and stimulating personality, and that you will gain much of pleasure and profit from this new co-worker.

We feel that it will be impossible for the reputation of President Neilson to be increased by Dr. Koffka's work, when in later years the splendid results from his years as President of the College will upon review be found sufficiently noteworthy, but some slight additional luster may be reflected upon his term as President by the fact that this Memorial Chair of Research was established and continued during his term of office.

The Trustees have established this William Allan Neilson Chair of Research because of their great admiration, affection, and esteem for President Neilson. It is not only a memorial of this tenth anniversary but an expression of their unqualified approval of the President of Smith College, for himself as a man with his broad human interests and sympathies, his fair-mindedness and his insight, and their appreciation of his splendid administrative and constructive work during the past ten years for Smith College.

I take pleasure, Mr. President, in the name of the Trustees of Smith College, in announcing and presenting to you this William Allan Neilson Chair of Research.

President Neilson responded:

Mr. McCallum, my colleagues, members of Smith College: I have the distressing feeling of being present at my own funeral, for in my own country at least, that is the only occasion on which people say things like that. Mr. McCallum is a Scotchman too, and possibly it was very hard for him to look a living man in the eye and tell him such things even if he believes them.

It is quite true that when I came to Smith College ten years ago, my main interest and hope was to further the intellectual life of the College, both among the Faculty and the students. It is also true that circumstances have turned a very large part of my time and energy to problems of building plans, finance, and affairs dealing with the physical and social life of the College, so that only a fractional remainder has gone to what I believe I was primarily brought here to do. Not that that remainder is contemptible. A good deal has happened here in these ten years, though I by no means claim exclusive credit for it, in the matter of education and scholarship. In this matter of scholarship, we have increased very extensively the means by which the members of the Faculty and some of the more advanced students might present their results to the learned public. And from time to time the Trustees have given appropriations of money for scholarships and fellowships to aid individuals in research and have made additions to the library to increase its resources. We realize that this is only a beginning. It is my opinion that the effectiveness of teaching, which I believe is our first interest here, is dependent upon the intellectual activity of the teacher. I do not believe that you will find a college teacher accomplishing the best results, who is not interested in the progress in his or her particular field, and is not following the research at the frontier. Nor do I believe that it is possible to follow research at the frontier without an impulse to take part in the pioneer work there—to experiment and find out for oneself.

The antithesis between teaching and research which is reflected in many educational journals and on many platforms, is a false antithesis. So far from having an institution making up its mind whether it will teach or seek new truth, I do not think it can teach effectively unless a large part of its Faculty is interested in new truth and is participating in the search for it.

It is therefore an extremely gratifying choice which my friends have made in seeking to do me this honor—the choice of the establishment in our midst of a Chair and laboratory which will be devoted to pure research, and which is, I am led to understand, quite likely to engage in a form of research particularly closely akin to teaching, namely, problems in the psychology of learning. We are all engaged in research in these problems. We are all of us very much aware of their difficulty in theory and practice. So it seems to me that at this very important juncture we are taking hold of what is for us the most important subdivision of the field. So far as I know there is no purely undergraduate college in America which has a chair devoted entirely to research. No college I know of has had the courage, the resources, the insight to do what this group of friends have done for Smith. It may be a landmark in the intellectual life of the undergraduate college in this country.

I don't need to tell you how grateful I am for the recognition of what I have tried to do in Smith College, which is symbolized in this action of the Board of Trustees, Faculty, and Alumnae. Through you, I wish to express my thanks which I assure you are very deeply felt. Nothing could have given me more appropriate pleasure—hardly anything I think a deeper pleasure—than this gift. It is a recognition not only of momentary value, not only of reflective value on the past, but of future value, and it is in the future that I shall hope to deserve it.

Again the Freshman Curriculum

FRANCES FENTON BERNARD

The interest in the new freshman curriculum announced in the February QUARTERLY has been so great that Dean Bernard has written a more detailed article for our further enlightenment. It is important to keep in mind that the term "hour" as used in the discussion of the curriculum signifies the attendance of one hour a week at class (or its equivalent laboratory period) throughout the year. The *Pamphlet of Information for Entering Freshmen*, which will contain all necessary data about the curriculum, will be sent to successful candidates with their certificate of admission in July.

The Revised Curriculum for the Class of 1931 and Later Classes
FRESHMAN AND SOPHOMORE YEARS
(15 hours to be taken in each year)

GROUP I. Languages.
> English, French, German, Greek, Hebrew, Italian, Latin, Scandinavian, Spanish, Spoken English.
> All students must pass examinations on reading ability in two foreign languages, whether or not they have taken courses in Group I. Such examinations must be passed not earlier than the beginning of Sophomore year and not later than the beginning of Senior year.

GROUP II. Literature and Fine Arts.
> Biblical Literature, English, French, German, Greek, Italian, Latin, Spanish, Art, Music, Spoken English.   6 hours

GROUP III. Sciences.
> Astronomy, Botany, Chemistry, Geology, Hygiene, Mathematics, Physics, Psychology, Zoölogy.   6 hours
> Three hours must be taken in a laboratory science.

GROUP IV. Philosophical-Historical Studies.
> Economics, Education, Government, History, Philosophy, Religion, Sociology.   6 hours

ELECTIVE   12 hours

Students not exempt by examination are required to pass English 11, Hygiene 11, and Spoken English 11, 13a or b, or the Spoken English clinic.

Courses in Economics, Education, and Sociology are not as yet open to Freshmen.

THE Freshmen who enter College next year will face a very different curriculum from that demanded of entering students in the preceding years. The Greek-Latin-Mathematics requirement will no longer exist. The modern language requirement, French, German, Italian, or Spanish, is dropped. The History, Philosophy-Psychology, and Bible requirements are gone. In the case of English 11 and Spoken English and Hygiene, exemption by examination is provided. In other words, no specific courses are required except English 11, Spoken English 11, and Hygiene. English 11 may be passed off by examination instead of taken, Spoken English 11 may be passed off, or the clinic substituted for it, and in the case of Hygiene 11 an alternative course, Hygiene 12b, is provided as well as exemption by examination. The Freshman who is well prepared for college in these subjects, then, may pass them off.

Under the new curriculum, the Freshman must then decide in what two foreign languages she wishes to be examined. She is required to take examinations on reading ability in two foreign languages. These examinations must be taken not earlier than the beginning of Sophomore year and not later than the beginning of Senior year. A student may come to college prepared to take these examinations or she may prepare for them by taking courses in the language departments in college, or she may prepare for the examinations during one or two of her summer vacations. The rest of her course is elective. But she must distribute her choices among three groups of departments. She must take six hours in Freshman and Sophomore years in Group II from among the following subjects: Art, Music, Spoken English, English, Greek, Latin, French, German, Italian, Spanish, Biblical Literature—a wide variety of possibilities. She must take six hours in Freshman and Sophomore years from the group of sciences. And she must take six hours in Freshman and Sophomore years in the fourth group, which includes History, Government, Economics, Sociology, Religion, Education, Philosophy. Her choices in these groups are limited by the fact that only certain departments in each group offer courses to Freshmen and Sophomores. The new *Course of Study Bulletin* shows which these are.

Suppose that a Freshman when she enters is prepared to pass the language requirement, and to pass off English 11, Spoken English 11, and Hygiene 11. In the first year she will take three hours in each of the three groups, Literature and Fine Arts, Sciences, Social Sciences. Out of the courses open to Freshmen in these groups she may choose what she wants. These will constitute nine hours of the fifteen which each student must take each year. The other six are completely free. Courses open to Freshmen may be elected in any or all of the four groups. They may be scattered, or a Freshman may have already a special interest in a particular field, and decide to take all of her elective hours in the subject in which she intends to major. The majors have not been changed, nor the requirements and prerequisites for the majors. They must still be based upon a course taken in Freshman or Sophomore year. It is still important and necessary for the student to have the choice of her major on her mind from the beginning and to select her courses in Freshman and Sophomore years with some view to the major later.

In other words, the Freshman must have fifteen hours of work in the year. The present regulation that each student must carry three 3-hour courses at one time still holds. Although the curriculum is so elastic that if a student desires she may fulfil the time requirement in each of the groups in either year, in general nine of the fifteen hours in each year would be distributed between Groups II, III, and IV, three hours in each. The Freshman would be taking a course in Literature, Art, or Music (Group II), a course in Science (Group III), and a course in History or Philosophy or Religion or Government, the only departments open to her at present in Group IV. Six hours of completely free electives are left, to be chosen in any group. But if English 11 were not passed off, two of these six hours would go for that in Group II; if Spoken English 11 had to be taken, part of the hour requirement in Group I could thus be fulfilled. The remaining four hours would in many cases probably be given to a foreign language in preparation for the examinations on reading ability.

The time requirements in three groups insure a distribution of work for the first two years in the various fields of knowledge. The language requirement provides for the acquisition of certain necessary tools. The opportunity for the choice of actual courses under the time requirement and the complete freedom of election in two-fifths of the student's schedule make possible a wide sampling, or a certain degree of specialization. But the responsibility for choices is laid on the student.

When the Council Came to College

February 17–19, 1927

IT was a quarter of a year ago that the Council came to College, and all the copy that it made has been edited, printed, and sent to Smith far and wide long ago by that indefatigable Alumnae Office of ours. Why then should the QUARTERLY go back and back and pick up the threads of those busy, inspiring days and fill more pages with an account of its doings? Well, just because we have a feeling that there is a stray alumna somewhere or other who will be glad to refresh her mind again concerning many of the significant and important words that were spoken and also because the Council was so full of the spirit of Smith College that it simply isn't possible to cover the winter term without at least touching the high spots, albeit ever so briefly.

Come to think of it, however, that last phrase may evoke painful memories, for the things that the weather did to the Council in those three short days included glazing every inch on which their neatly galoshed feet trod so smoothly with A 1 ice that "touching the high spots" was about all any of them did in their hazardous tiptoeings to Sage Hall. In fact one of our most idealistic trustees was heard to say in public that it was all very well to talk about raising money for salaries and dormitories but she thought the thing the College needed most was Ashes!—and everyone applauded, you may be sure. With which introductory remarks we begin.

THURSDAY, FEBRUARY 17, 1927

9.15 A. M. *Business Session:* Sage Hall, called to order by a gracious word of greeting from Mrs. Sawyer, the President of the Association. Committee reports: Virginia Mellen Hutchinson '00 for the Juniper Lodge Endowment Committee, Jean Paton '14 for the Burton Memorial Committee, Harriet Ford '99, chairman, for the Alumnae Fund. Mrs. Hutchinson reported a total of about $28,000 and Miss Paton a total of about $11,000 for these two very important funds. See pages 312 and 335 for later news. Mrs. Ford had organized various members of her committee into a troupe of speakers and with herself as impresario we were regaled with data grave and gay about our Alumnae Fund since its birth in 1912. Stella Tuthill Whipple '07 told of the ups and downs of its childhood when some special emergency or other was always pushing it out of the way. However, it did manage to collect (and give away) between 1912 and 1925, $104,000.

May Hammond '03 gave interesting statistics on alumnae funds in other colleges. After three years, at Mount Holyoke 57% of the alumnae are contributing. Bryn Mawr reports a 51% increase in the number of donors by the third year. Amherst in four years has nearly doubled the amount received in the first year and more than doubled the number of contributors.

The second project, scholarships, is a very pressing need and has been carefully outlined in the report of the President Burton Memorial Fund Committee.

As for the first choice of the President and Committee: "No one," declared Mrs. Morrow, "who has sat for even a short time on the Board of Trustees can fail to have been impressed with the terrible pressure that is on us all the time, pressure from outside, the feeling that we are not going to be able to hold at Smith the best type of teacher. I think there is not a trustee who would not answer unhesitatingly that the greatest need of the College to-day is an increased endowment for the salaries of its professors."

See President Neilson's article about salaries on page 283, and Fund material on page 337.

10.30 A. M. *Conference with Laura Lord Scales '01, Warden.* See page 273.

11.00 A. M. *Conference with Mrs. Ethel Puffer Howes '91' Director of the Institute for the Coördination of Women's Interests.*

11.15 A. M. *Conference with the Alumnae Trustees.*

Mrs. Scales's talk is always most eagerly enjoyed and we have persuaded her to revise the stenographer's report and let us print most of it on page 273.

Mrs. Howes reported great progress for the Institute. The proof of this year's pudding was found in the Nursery School to which we trouped on Friday morning; and she told us also of the surveys now finished or under way. The survey of Smith College graduates, 500 of them who are combining professional and domestic interests, has been completed. A second survey has been made of unselected graduates with the help of the Detroit Smith Club. A third survey is now being made in China for the American and foreign Chinese college graduates in and around Peking. Several studies are now in progress, such as a study on the profession of landscape architecture for women, a study on the possibilities of free lance journalism in and around New York, and a subsidiary study of a very interesting coöperative community in Iowa. The Institute has already taken the first steps in a cooked food supply experiment. This is being worked out through the coöperation of one of the tea rooms in Northampton. The Institute is also working towards a home assistants experiment.

The conference with the alumnae trustees was, as Mrs. Sawyer said, a regular Ask Me Another game with Mrs. Morrow, Miss Van Kleeck, and Mrs. Emerson, in which they scored 100%. They answered all sorts of questions about the duties of the Trustees and the policy of the College regarding buildings, salaries, and teaching, and we were glad to have Mrs. Emerson quote in the latter connection the President's remarks to them on the principle of freedom of teaching at Smith. We quote it here:

Our tradition is in favor of complete freedom, and our experience seems to show that such freedom produces loyalty to the College and consideration for its interests. With the writing and speaking of the faculty outside, the College has not concerned itself at all. The question as it has arisen during the present administration has always seemed to me to be not, "Are the views of Professor X as proclaimed in his lectures or his books in all respects correct?" but, "Assuming that Professor X's views may be in part erroneous and to some people offensive, can the College afford to suppress him or his views at the cost of creating an atmosphere of censorship and hampering free thought and free discussion by fear of dismissal?" The history of attempts to limit academic freedom leaves no doubt as to the answer. The greatest universities have been the most tolerant.

2.30 P. M. *Conference with the Faculty, Professor Gladys Anslow '14' presiding:* Mlle. Cattanès, "The First Group of Juniors in France"; Miss Sampson, "Why Smith has Graduate Students"; Mr. Kennedy, "An Experiment in Graduate Study in the History and Criticism of Art"; Miss Ainsworth, "Physical Education at Smith."

The QUARTERLY says with all the pride of a newspaper that has scooped a good story that the first three of these talks have been written up in detail in previous QUARTERLIES, so we make no comments here except to repeat the figures for graduate degrees which may have been forgotten. At the present time 279 students (206 Smith alumnae and 73 graduates of 57 other colleges) have received the degree of M.A. Three graduates of Smith and one of Bryn Mawr hold the degree of Ph.D. from Smith.

Dorothy Ainsworth '16' in charge of Physical Education, outlined the general tendencies in physical education and how the problem is being met at Smith:

We no longer think of health as simply keeping the muscles and organs of the body in perfect condition. The individual is not divided into separate parts, mind and body. You cannot exercise one and leave the other out as was thought possible according to the methods formerly used. The idea now is to try to build up the whole person, a person who can act well in any situation— not to take separate parts and fit them together. One tendency is to stress the participation of a larger group in sports. There is also a tendency to shift from team games to individual sports such as tennis, riding, swimming, which the student can continue after college. . . .

Just supposing you were an entering freshman, this is what would happen to you. You would have, first of all, a physical examination, and would be given a sports rating which would place you definitely in a certain group of sports. If you were put in the first group, you would have your choice of any sport, soccer, hockey, archery, cricket, tennis. No freshman may take swimming until the physical examinations, which are very strict, are completed, but the first group may take swimming in the spring. Students who are not quite so strong, and whom lighter work would suit better, may not play baseball, but may choose archery or tennis. If you are in the group which needs special attention, archery would be the only sport you could elect, or you may need special gymnastics under the care of Miss Thomas. Then when you come inside for indoor work, you would have a winter term of body mechanics which is based upon the principle of forming habits of good posture which we have thought extremely essential. This continues with gymnasium work throughout the term. In the spring you could take baseball, hockey, rhythms, swimming, tennis, or track.

Sophomore year your sports would be the same as freshman year. There are, of course, advanced sections. All of sophomore year is free elective work if you have passed your freshman year. The choice lies between basket ball, indoor baseball, Danish gymnastics, dancing and rhythms, and winter sports for which the girls will have to furnish skates, skiis, or snowshoes. The instructors will go out with them, and the weather will decide what the sport for the day will be.

The required work for the first two years is three hours per week, but we are trying to build up in these two years an attitude of interest in the work offered so that the upperclassmen may be interested to continue the work with us.

We went from these conferences to a very gala tea with the faculty in the newest new dormitories. It is well that the tower of Martha Wilson stood out like a beacon of hope, for the ground under our feet was a veritable slough of slippery mud and perhaps it was by reason of this that, the dormitories once gained, they and the faculty seemed peculiarly friendly and delightful, and, to say the very least, adequate. In the evening the directors and alumnae trustees gathered for a feast of reason and flow of soul in the very delightful trustees' dining-room. It was cut short by the clock—that disturber of many an interesting conference—for at eight everybody splashed down to the Students' Building to see "Noah," the Miracle Play presented, in collaboration with the weather, by the Smith College Theatre Workshop. It was worth a good wetting just to see those animals go in two by two, the elephant and the kangaroo!

FRIDAY, FEBRUARY 18

8.30 A. M.   *Chapel.*
9.00 A. M.–1.00 P. M.   *Opportunity to visit classes,* including the Nursery School and the schools in Gill Hall.
2.15 P. M.   *Meetings of Class and Club Representatives.*
4.00 P. M.   *Tea and conference with the Student Council at Crew House.*
8.30 P. M.   *Reception. The Tryon Gallery.*

Truly we of the Alumnae Council would all have been Phi Beta Kappas had we followed the gleam in our undergraduate days with the avidity with which we hunted up classes and professors on this morning! The meetings of the Clubs and Classes were so profitable and spirited that there are rumors that next year there will have to be more than one of each.

And then came the frosting on the cake in the guise of the tea and conference with the Student Council. We who have slipped and slided down that stairway to the Crew House year after year always love to watch the delight with which the newcomers partake of the chocolate and cakes and listen to all that the girls have to tell of the College that belongs equally to them and to us. This year even a seasoned listener thought that there was something particularly reassuring in the attitude with which the student officers are approaching the problems that are so much more confusing than those of our day; and it is good to note that various alumnae who had come to Council very genuinely worried about certain aspects of college life as they had been interpreted by the daily papers and insidious rumors had their faith once more renewed. "With such girls as these at the head the students can't go very wrong," was the comment of more than one. We do not need to quote very much of what the various speakers said because student government and student activities are the meat and drink of every QUARTERLY and therefore you know it all—or ought to! We do note, however, that Polly Bullard, then president of the junior class and now the new president of Student Government, said that actual figures—much to the amazement of everyone—showed that out of 2000 students only 780 took their full quota of seven nights last semester. Moreover, of the relation of marks to class attendance she gave the following illuminating figures: girls absent 2 times or less had no D's; the marks of those absent 5 times or more contained all the D's. Two students who had cut 5 times got an A or a B, but these seem to be two cases out of 2000. Amanda Bryan, chairman of Judicial Board, gave such a clear presentation of the problems that come to the Board and the methods of solution that we quote her here.

Statistics are disagreeable things so I am going to give you mine first and then see what conclusions can be drawn from them:

Last spring there were 73 cases of infraction, this October there were 18, and in November 62, divided as follows: smoking, 16; blue cards, 24; motoring, 12; ten o'clock rule, 5; technical, 5; total, 62. In December: smoking, 35; blue cards, 7; motoring, 6; ten o'clock rule, 4; technical, 1; total, 53. The cases were divided as follows: seniors, 11; juniors, 9; sophomores, 15; freshmen, 18. In January: blue cards, 7; motoring, 5; ten o'clock rule, 1; total, 13. There were 3 seniors; 2 juniors; 2 sophomores; 6 freshmen.

I do not know how to explain the large number of cases brought to Judicial Board in November. Of course, the greatest number of cases had to do with errors in blue cards and these were made mostly by freshmen, who in spite of the work of the Freshman Commission had not been sufficiently impressed with the necessity of putting P. M. for afternoon and not A. M., and so forth. In December and the latter part of November, the most important and largest number of cases concerned smoking. Mrs. Scales has I know told you a great deal about smoking and I do not want to burden you with a repetition. For our part, we are all glad that smoking has ceased at last to be the main subject of conversation. I think it was Macaulay who said: "You cannot expect a man to swim until you have first thrown him into the water." And that is what the administration has done to us in respect to smoking. We have gone down twice now, but we are hoping that we are now with our heads above water for good. Perhaps you noticed from the statistics that in January we had no cases of infringement of the smoking rule after the new system went into effect. On the whole, we feel that the new arrangement is working well. In visiting the different tea rooms in town, perhaps you have seen one or two girls smoking as they shouldn't, but you may not have noticed the much larger number smoking properly, or the rest of the college which isn't smoking at all—which we think is even more proper.

December was a very difficult month in respect to smoking. Council, aware that public opinion was not behind the old rule as it stood, could only give penalties to the best of its discretion. Now we know that public opinion is back of our new regulation and the whole attitude of the college has changed. Those people who were penalized in November were looked upon as martyrs to the cause of personal liberty; now those girls who smoke in an unladylike fashion, bringing criticism upon the college, are regarded by their classmates with disfavor, as incapable of utilizing their new freedom. If we have succeeded in settling this difficult question of smoking in such a way that the student body can give its whole-hearted support to the rule, we feel that we have done a great deal, and that all the stress and strain of last fall was worth while.

Blue card cases are usually merely technical errors, although we sometimes find that there is a premeditated plan behind the apparently technical error.

The ten o'clock rule is on the whole extremely well kept and most infractions of it grow out of something more serious, as motoring after dark and being delayed through some accident. This is of course a double misdemeanor, and the student usually pays a double penalty.

I suppose you want most to hear about the type of penalty we inflict and about the way in which a case comes to our attention. We work in close contact with Mrs. Scales's office, and we cannot thank Mrs. Scales and Miss Mensel enough for their help and advice in cases that demand more experience and discretion than we have.

We try to think of the students who come before our Board as individuals and not as mere "blue-card cases," and we are hoping next year to institute a plan whereby this personal contact will be further stimulated. The members of Judicial Board, all officers of their classes, are among the busiest girls in college, and they regret exceedingly that they have no time to follow up the cases that come before the Board for their action. Next year, therefore, we are hoping to have Judicial Board representatives, elected from each class, who will be responsible for keeping in touch with the students in their classes who come before Judicial Board.

As to penalties, the most serious is a demerit. A student having a demerit can cut no classes; she is technically on the Registrar's list, she cannot leave town, she cannot go motoring. She can do practically nothing but go to classes and see her friends. Penalties of any sort, however, seem a crude sort of thing when working with people. Penalties do not seem to reach the heart of the

matter. By degrees we hope we may eliminate penalties altogether. It seems
to me that of the hundred or more people to whom we have given penalties,
only a few have really benefited from them; but under the present system, in-
fliction of penalties is the only thing to do. What I should like to do in each
case is to change the person's point of view so that the girls coming before
Judicial Board, after talking over their mistakes, will want to go out and start
on a new track. We feel repaid if in the course of a year we succeed in changing the attitude of even three or four girls. We want to make the students·
understand why we have to live under rules.

One of the reasons, it seems to me, for the large number of cases this year is
the fact that more people have voluntarily reported themselves, and this is
very encouraging. I should like to have one hundred cases a week if I could
think that all infringements were coming to me. Of course, there is always a
great deal going on that we do not know about, but we do feel that the percentage has been reduced. On the whole, I believe that having a larger number
of cases brought before the Judical Board means that students are beginning to
understand more clearly the reason behind the rules and are feeling more
keenly their responsibility for observing them.

Miss Blake of the Personnel Department has been extremely helpful in co-
operating with us in cases that are obviously due to maladjustment. Through
her, students are put in touch with a trained psychiatrist who can give students
expert individual attention.

I am looking forward to the time when punishments will be eliminated
under a system of rules which will make infraction improbable: a set of rules so
simple, so obvious, and so necessary that it will be scarcely necessary to write
them down.

In the February QUARTERLY was an illustrated article on the Tryon Gallery
and so it is quite unnecessary to emphasize the fact that the reception held
there Friday evening was a very beautiful and rare treat to us all. The
exhibition of Mr. Kennedy's photographs was not the least delightful of its
features.

SATURDAY, FEBRUARY 19

8.30 A. M. *Chapel.*

9.00 A. M. *Business Session.* Marguerite Page Hersey '01 was nominated for member of
the Nominating Committee of the Alumnae Association. Miss Wolfs's report for the War
Service Board was read. Contracts for the building of the new dispensary have been assigned
and work is to be begun. Our problem now centers about the expiration of our five-year agreement with the commune and of our annual subsidy of 10,000 francs towards the nursing service,
and the wise disposal of our balance. Miss Raymond '91 for the Education Committee reported
that the Committee is keeping itself informed about new experiments in education, and about
curricula. She mentioned the reading lists for which there were 1400 requests this year, and
urged the importance of scholarships and fellowships, particularly for foreign students. Miss
Oiesen '13 spoke of the fine coöperation received from clubs in entertaining foreign students
during the Christmas vacation. Stella Tuthill Whipple reported that 33 clubs had contributed
to Ginling a total of $3000 in 1925. Forty-nine clubs have Ginling correspondents.

9.30 A. M. *Remarks by Florence Angell '11, International Secretary of the A. A. U. W. and
Councillor-at-large.*

9.45 A. M. *Conference with Dr. Florence Gilman, College Physician. See page 272.*

10.15 A. M. *Conference with Professor Ernst Mensel, Chairman of the Board of Admission.*

10.45 A. M. *Conference with President Neilson and adjournment.*

There is not adequate space even to name all the activities of Miss Angell as
secretary of the International Relations Committee. The Committee has
charge of the selection of American women students for Oxford, is concerned
with the interchange of secondary school teachers (this year Susan Titsworth

'97 is exchange professor), is supposed to be a reservoir of information on all questions of national and international education, and so forth.   Last summer her Committee had a most interesting summer school for American women teachers in Oxford.   Eminent speakers gave lectures on English literature and history.   The school was held for three weeks and 250 representatives of almost every state in the union attended.

The plan for work of the Hygiene and Physical Education Department has undergone a number of such important changes that we have asked Dr. Gilman to give her account of them in some detail.   See page 272.

Every November for some years Professor Mensel has been good enough to keep the QUARTERLY up to date on matters of admission to college.   We do not therefore reprint him here.   Certain facts seem to be emerging which tend to prove that although candidates from high schools are decreasing in number and those from private schools increasing, the college records of high school students are on the whole higher than those of private schools.   It is impossible to draw conclusions or to foresee the end, but we shall look eagerly for further utterances from the Board.   The question of whether Smith will continue to admit under both the old and new plan is much discussed.   Vassar admits now only under the new plan.   Professor Mensel feels that one absolute test for all students would mean an improvement in teaching in the schools and would be better for the student body.

It is always a great temptation to quote the President in full, but we were born and bred in New England where economy in expenditure of space is as sacred a principle as economy in expenditure of money and we simply cannot repeat subjects which he has already covered in other QUARTERLIES.   These include the experimental schools, our physical equipment, comment on the juniors in France, and Mr. Kennedy's graduate group in art.   For his explanation of the salary situation see page 283.   Last summer new stacks to accommodate about 50,000 volumes were set up in the Library.   This addition will take care of the increase for the next five years only.   We quote his remarks on married women teachers, preference to alumnae daughters, the proposed plan of the Music Department, and his concluding paragraph, which is perhaps the most important of all.

Some institutions have a rule against a husband and wife both teaching on their faculties, and others regard a woman teacher's marriage as equivalent to a resignation.   A college for women would hardly be expected to favor such an attitude; yet few realize how far Smith College has gone in the opposite direction.   We have had this last year six married couples in regular academic positions, six other married women whose husbands are not on the staff, and six wives of professors who do occasional work as assistants or readers.   There are many advantages in this situation and I have observed only trifling disadvantages.

When a student is a candidate for admission to Smith College, and in the light of all the information in the hands of the admission committee is rejected, that is not a misfortune to that student, but a happy escape.   I wish you would get this point very clearly and use it with all your friends whose daughters are not admitted.   It is no favor to a girl to admit her to a college for which she is not prepared, and I do not think that very many students are excluded who are thoroughly prepared.

In the second place, if you admit daughters of alumnae who are definitely below the level of preparation at the bottom of our present list, they would be admitted, if our machinery works properly, only to be rejected the next February. If you think that is a favor to alumnae, I do not.

This privilege would be of no use unless it was continued all the way through college, and it was understood that the degree of the daughters of alumnae was a cheap degree, meaning a certain percentage less than the degrees given to daughters of outsiders. Is that what you want? Now that is not a figure of speech; it is not any use letting in poorer girls than we let in unless we treat them easier all the time they are in college, and our drawing a line in the fall is really an attempt to prevent students from embarking upon a career for which they are not equipped. . . .

The study of music and a mastery of musical literature is at a disadvantage as compared with literature and the fine arts. The Music Department here uses our numerous and excellent concerts, and supplements those by faculty recitals which are often historical in their choice of programs. A great addition to these opportunities would be made if we could obtain the services, say twenty times a year, of a competent quartet to play chamber music, the programs to be selected by our teachers, and the performances to be not concerts but demonstrations, with possibility of repetition of passages, and so forth, to increase their value as material for study.

In closing the President said:

If I had not chosen the subject I did, I probably should have talked to you about the real perplexity of a number of the alumnae in regard to the religious life of the College. A little wider view would extend these perplexities to the religious life of America, and a little wider still to the religious life of the world. There is a very strong tendency in regard to all criticisms on religion, morals, and manners to regard the College as an isolated group in a vacuum. There is also a tendency to unload on the College responsibilities that were formerly regarded as parental. I could talk at great length on this whole matter, but I wanted to tell you that the administration of the College, all of us College officers, are very much interested in this, and are watching it with great care. The Trustees took one action yesterday which is indicative of their interest. The students tried this year to run their Association for Christian Work without even secretarial help from the outside, but they had not tried it for more than three or four months before they regretted it, and came back and said they wanted a secretary again. Instead, Miss Mira Wilson, dean of the class of 1927, who finishes her deanship for that class this year, is going to be asked to become director of religious work and social service. [See page 323.]

And then there were all sorts of votes of thanks and tying up bits of business and the Council was adjourned, much wiser and even more loyal than when it had convened three days before. Somehow those words of the President about the "strong tendency in regard to all criticisms on religion, morals, and manners to regard the College as an isolated group in a vacuum" struck home, and we left Northampton resolved that we would be more patient and more consistent in our endeavors to coöperate with the Student Council and the Administration in helping Smith College to realize its high ideals.

Our Health Department

FLORENCE GILMAN

College Physician and Chairman of the Department of Hygiene and Physical Education

WE are trying this year to review our whole plan of teaching, training, and supervising health, to abolish some of the outgrown and cumbersome details, and to bring it more into the real life of students and their needs. Our problem is to keep in touch with the actual health of individual students, to get their ideas regarding health clear, and to make them do some training that will build up a more sturdy and vigorous vitality. Each member of our department must realize the whole task and see that her particular share—whether it be coaching hockey, giving a health examination, or directing a class discussion in hygiene—contributes to this constructive health program.

There is to be some change in each of the three parts of the work, and our plan under the new curriculum is as follows: A one hour course in hygiene is required of all freshmen unless they can pass an examination at entrance. Examination for exemption will be given and schools will be encouraged to prepare their students for it as we believe this subject should be so well taught throughout the grades that it need not be carried as a college requirement. So far, however, it is not so. The course will be taught as a recitation-discussion in groups and will count for credit as a regular one hour course. An elective course in Hygiene, going into the subject more deeply, may be taken instead of the required short one. Lectures to the class as a whole will be given up except as an occasional addition, for we have found this method of teaching hygiene unsatisfactory.

Physical education is no longer to carry academic credit but is to be put more frankly on a basis of health training. It is to be required of all students, as now, during the first two years and, in addition to that, any student who shows during the third and fourth year that she is falling below her own individual best must take up whatever program her Health Adviser maps out to fit her needs. This program shall become a requirement for her and the Administration promises full support in insisting that students shall give physical fitness true consideration.

The Health Adviser is a member of the Department of Hygiene and Physical Education—either a doctor or trained teacher. There will be ten or twelve of them, and each freshman is to be given into the care of her Health Adviser as soon as she has had her entrance physical examination. This adviser will follow her all through college—not with frequent nagging and bolstering up, for we have no intention of supplying nursemaids—but to check her up at least twice a year, watch her progress in training, development, and adjustment from the health standpoint, and be ready not only to suggest but to insist upon some change in program when it is needed.

In this way we hope to have a better knowledge of the physical condition of all students in college. At present we keep sending for those in whom we have found defects to come for reëxamination, but we see little or nothing of many others who really need direction. With the twice yearly checking up of weight, height, body mechanics, muscle tone, color of the blood, response to exercise, endurance, nervous and emotional stability, and health habits, we should be able to teach each student to go ahead all the time in her health building instead of standing still or lagging behind or getting in a bad hole. We aim to make her see what positive health is for her, how to acquire it for herself, and to train her body as a tool to use with the most power possible to cope with the world effectively, continuously, and happily.

In addition to these required consultations, the doctors will continue, of course, to see any students who wish advice or help at any time. There will always be some convalescent or temporarily debilitated or handicapped students who must be kept more closely under the supervision of the doctors. We also keep in close touch with those who are really ill, although town physicians are treating them. It is our part to be sure and to be able to convince parents that everything possible is done for complete and rapid recovery.

The Health Adviser will simply know about any of these intercurrent troubles in order to help the girl to readjust her living in accordance with them. She is always to keep in mind that although we must consider health and give it the best possible chance, we do it only in order to go ahead with our lives most happily and satisfactorily—never as an end in itself.

Some Theories and Methods of Handling Undergraduate Life

Laura W. L. Scales

The conference which the Council had with Mrs. Scales was unquestionably one of the most valuable of the entire session and we reprint her talk almost in full. Mrs. Scales asks us particularly to say that it is most informal, as it appears here, that it is in fact simply the stenographic report slightly revised, and that she is conscious that it is far more adaptable to the spoken than the written word. As for us—the subjects that she discusses are far too important for us to quibble about form.

I WANT, at the risk of a great deal of repetition, to talk about some theories and methods of handling the undergraduate life of the College. Before we talk about that I think there are certain generalizations and truths that we probably would all admit. One is that the College is a part of the world, not a thing set aside and out of the stream of events, and that no one can talk about college or think about college except as a part of the total atmosphere of the life of the time. Another generalization is that college is a training place, not a final place and not an end in itself, but a training for their life of the people who are here. The third generalization is that it is a mobile organization, that of all places in the world it is not a static place, that you cannot have generations of young people constantly going through and keep things fixed.

There are a few theories under which we are working which are by no means new but which, perhaps, have different accents from time to time, and the first one of which I shall speak is the tremendous importance of intellectual activity and interest. This would seem to lead me, of course, to a discussion of the curriculum, but I am not going to discuss that. I want to speak of the life of the students as a whole. Because of the feeling that intellectual activity and interest are of paramount importance, it is part of the method of the College that all shades and kinds of truths and ideas should be presented to the undergraduates. I remember hearing Mr. Hopkins, President of Dartmouth, say that when he left the industrial world where he had been at work for a few years, and came back to be President of Dartmouth, he was impressed with the inferiority of discrimination among college students as compared with the men whom he had seen in the factories; that the latter were better able to pick out the salient points in the presentation of a subject than college students; and he decided that the college students had had set ideas spoon fed to them, that the men in the factories had found on the corner a soap box orator who presented them with every kind of truth and untruth, rational statement and irrational statement, and the men had to pick from here and there what was true. As he reflected on that he decided that that opportunity had seldom been allowed adequately to the college student. The response at Dartmouth was to establish what is called the Forum and the Round Table.

Presentation of all sides of a question at college is something that has been going on here. We carry it out in our lectures. We have had Pacifism presented by Norman Thomas and Major General Ryan. We have had every kind of speaker here representing all sorts of subjects. In vespers we have had people who range from Doctor Bell, who represents, perhaps, the most conservative wing of the Episcopal Church, on to John Haynes Holmes of the Community Church.

Another method of fostering intellectual activity is through the new residence regulation. Some of you who have heard undergraduates talk may think that the residence regulations were passed as a punitive measure to keep a lot of girls at home on Sunday. That may be incidental, but it is not the primary reason. The residence regulation is this, that a student who is to receive a degree at Smith College must be in residence during each semester minus seven nights. That was voted by the Faculty as a requirement primarily, I think, because of the intellectual needs of the College. In America, as you know, the vogue for culture is not so widespread and so intense that you can count on your undergraduates thinking of that as their first interest, if they have the opportunity of having Palm Beach and Broadway compete with it. Now students have to stay here where intellectual interests are part of their environment.

You may ask, "Why have a residence regulation and not an attendance requirement?" There exactly is the point. There is a great difference between compulsory attendance at classes if you are trying to stimulate intellectual interest, and having the people on hand where they may get it. Probably most of you have read in the last year the continual opposition that there has been in colleges where compulsory attendance was required at chapel. You know what goes with the idea of compulsion in the minds of most young people to-day. If attendance was required at classes, it would probably increase study to some extent, but you would also run the risk of having students who did the greatest amount of work considered as grinds, people who did not use their own minds, but who got caught in the system. Give the students an opportunity of considering their intellectual lives their own to make, keep them on hand where they must inevitably get intellectual stimulus, then they may find a really joyous piece of work that they themselves can go into. I think this different way of handling classroom work is giving the better student a chance to develop a personal interest and show herself a much more vital person than one who merely does what the system makes her do. Also if the student is here and feels herself free to take part in the intellectual life of the College she may even go beyond the strict routine of the classroom into some side interest that is brought up through her study there. She may have time to do it if she is here. She may have the interest to do it if she goes about it of her own accord.

I was very much entertained the other day. A freshman was in my office and she said to me that she had hated the place during the fall. Then she said: "I am working now. Isn't it funny how much better you like a place when you work?" That was a very vital experience that had come to her, which she had discovered all for herself!

The second theory that we have always worked on at Smith, of course is the importance of environment. We are a residence college and the surroundings that go with it are our own. Probably all of you who come back each time are impressed with one aspect of our environment, which we have, I rejoice to say, stressed more and more, and that is the aspect of beauty. . . .

We have stressed all along, and I hope we shall never depart from it, the necessity of simple living as a part of the College. We have it in the ordering of our houses, in the arrangement of rooms, in the planning of the daily life, in the table, and we have it in such things as the hours which the College keeps. A girl said to me the other day, "Why, of course, ten o'clock is perfectly absurd when you are used to Broadway and the theater and so on," and it is. But we are not New York. It seems to me absolutely essential to keep that ideal of plain living and high thinking in our College as we have had it. Of course, the housing of the College is centered about the idea of democracy. The many kinds of people of vastly different classes are brought together into a compact group. That, of course, has been one of the great accomplishments that has been brought to pass through the Fiftieth Birthday Gift, which has given us an opportunity to get some common standard of housing. We haven't the houses for the richer and the houses for the poorer girls that we had before and we haven't the separation so much as we had into invitation houses and other houses. This year will end the senior invitation houses. That leads to great loss in some ways to the girls who have had the pleasure of living in that way. The girls themselves have been very fine in realizing that it was part of the ideal that we are working toward, of a unified and more democratic standard of living.

Again the residence regulation plays its part in the environment and influence of the College. It was the idea also, I think, in passing the residence regulation, that if the students were personally here they would find a great many things in their environment which otherwise they would lose.

It is our hope that they will also find their pleasures here a little more.   These presumably will be along the line of deepened friendships, of wider interests in the intellectual things.   One wishes that it might be possible in a place like Northampton to learn that there is a delight in very simple pleasures.   One does not have to have speed or excitement or great display to enjoy one's self for the four years of college life.   If that ideal could possibly come to a person, I don't know that the College could do any one thing more important for an American girl.

Further, we emphasize the importance of responsibility.   That, of course, is the whole background of the theory of student government.   To bring a person up to be a self-sustaining person must be done by means of responsibility. I remember that at one time one of the people who visit colleges to investigate and criticize, came into my office and asked me what I thought of student government, and I said to her, "It depends on what you are talking about. If you are talking about it as a means of getting things done, it is very imperfect, but if you are talking about it as an opportunity in education to teach people how to do things, I think it is the only way possible."   She looked at me and said, "You are the first person who has said that to me."   I do not suppose she had been around very much or she would have heard it before, because it is the whole background of student government.   I am presenting that theory to you because that has brought the college perhaps as much criticism as any other issue, as it has worked out in relation to smoking.

Personally, I am excessively weary of talking about smoking, but I want to show you how it works out by the method of delegating responsibility.   Up to almost a year ago, we had no smoking at Smith under the regulations of the college.   It was handled by the student government group, and it was their stand that there should be no smoking.   A year ago in November a meeting was called by some of the other women's colleges of all the women's colleges to discuss the question of smoking.   Our students were asked to join, of course, which they did.   Vassar had a form of smoking; Bryn Mawr was about to introduce it, and, of course, our students were asked to consider it.   They came back with the feeling that something must be done about this question, since all the colleges were talking about it.   One thing that was asked of them by the administration was that they should not be influenced by outside pressure, that if it was something that should be considered at Smith, it could be considered, but it was not to be done for anybody else's sake.   It was left in the hands of the students, with the risk, of course, that there might be a change. The students went slowly about it.   They took four months, which is an excessively long time in the life of an undergraduate, but at the end of four months they brought up the question to be voted upon by the undergraduates, and a year ago in March it was voted that there should be smoking in the houses. A tremendous change was wrought by that vote.

Now, of course, if people think that smoking is a moral issue, they think that the administration had no right to leave it in the hands of the students. If it is not a moral question, it then becomes a question of fair play: Let the students govern as long as their action agrees with your opinion; take the power from them the minute they do something of which you do not approve.

In the interest of fair play it was not right for the administration to take smoking out of the students' hands. Smoking went into effect in the dormitories, and, of course, it was badly overdone. The manner of smoking was one that most of us had not looked forward to. It was done unattractively and badly; in fact, nothing could prove that the girls didn't know how to smoke so much as the way they have smoked here.

Manners became bad and houses disorderly in comparison with what they had been. We all of us kept hands off, and smoking was allowed to take its course. Through the spring term it went its way. We came back in the fall and the administration then stepped in to the extent of saying that in houses where there is more than one room, one room must be kept orderly, with no smoking in it, for the people who are non-smokers. The students themselves took a vote, as they are pledged to do each year, and five houses voted against any smoking, a decided change from the spring.

Obviously the situation had quieted down appreciably, but by one of those strange combinations of events it happened that four fires were started by smoking. The understanding was that the question was in the hands of the Student Council, with this statement from the President, that the property of the College could never be turned over to the students and that he had to make sure of ways of safeguarding the life and property of the College. The Council at once suspended smoking in the houses. As no way was presented by Christmas time for safeguarding smoking in the houses, the question of a return to the practice of the fall never came up to the students. It was dropped, and a vote was taken at Christmas time as to whether there should be any smoking. There was a very considerable vote that there should be no smoking at all. The majority, however, voted for smoking in the Allen Field Club House, in the Crew House, and in tea rooms permitting it.

Now the thing that happened was this: the enormous change from smoking very easily in the houses to smoking under difficulties was accepted by the College with scarcely a murmur. We have had since the beginning of this winter term no smoking in the houses. I think literally the student body has accepted and acted on the fact that they cannot smoke in their houses.

We are still in an unpleasant phase of smoking. In the town two of the tea rooms do not allow it, one of them because it is obviously a bad business investment. The logic of the fact is driven home to the students. It is not because someone in authority has said to them, "You cannot smoke," but the facts speak to them. "If you cannot smoke and smoke well, people are not going to put up with it, because it is not good business or good conduct." There is a very decided difference now in the attitude of the students towards smoking. It is now by no means accepted as the best form at Smith.

We are sure that this is not the end of the thing, but I wanted to say to you that by this training in responsibility facts which they recognize have been brought home to our students, when the word of mere authority would have taught them little. If we had students who before they came here were disciplined by necessity and fact, it might be possible to do differently. It is simply amazing how few students know that if you touch fire you will be burned! They have lived always under protection. The gas stove is not in the part of the house where they are, the radiator is covered over—they hardly know that fire will burn them.   Now, it is very hard to teach people facts when they have had no basis to build on beforehand.   I think inevitably we are not in an ideal position in our student government, but I think the method we are using is an extremely valuable method; whether it is hurting us too much in inviting criticism of course I cannot tell.

Another theory is the importance of the individual.   That is not a very easy theory to work out in any community life.   It is the theory, of course, that the individual is important rather than the mass or the group, and that is back of a great deal of administrative change in college.   It came first in the building up of the Class Deans' offices, the introduction of the Warden's office, and the Personnel Director's office.   It is the attempt to find out the needs and capacities of the individual rather than to put her into a class.

Another way of meeting the need of the individual, of course, is in the housing of the College in small groups; also in teaching in smaller sections.   I was interested the other day when I happened to be at the house of one of the professors who taught us when I was in college, to hear her say: "It is so different. In those days we were teaching classes of forty.   Nobody would think it was the same place now."   So that with the increasing size of the College has come the decreasing size of the unit for work.

I think one of the problems most constantly before the student to-day is the huge problem of society at large: the rights of the individual as against those of the community.   It is over and over again brought up in all the regulations of the College, and it is one of the problems that is most frequently at the root of the cases of discipline that come up.   The reasoning that goes on is always extremely interesting to me, as I hear the students discuss whether the individual can override the community.

Now, what are the results of this way of handling the College?   Of course, at any given moment it is very much easier to see the defects than to see the good results; the victories are more apt to be hidden victories than obvious ones, I think.   It is a more difficult way of dealing with the college problem and probably a way which brings upon the College greater criticism.   The method should never be judged by the freshmen in the College or by what the freshmen in college say, which is one of the chief sources of information to some! It should be judged by the seniors or by the graduates, and if we succeed in sending young women out into a world where standards are by no means fixed with a capacity for self-direction, discrimination, and wide vision the College will, let us hope, be fully justified.

Gargamellian Housekeeping

MARGARET L. FARRAND

We hasten to quote Miss Farrand's note to the editor when submitting this fearsome title: "In case you have forgotten your Rabelais, Gargamelle was the mother of Gargantua." That helps a little! And, moreover, thus enlightened we claim that the title is none too high sounding for Housekeeping at Smith College, which of course is what this article is about. Miss Farrand '14, Director of the Press Board and, in QUARTERLY circles, newsgetter extraordinaire, has procured all her material from Miss Leonard, purchasing agent, Mr. King, superintendent of grounds and buildings, and Mr. Hyde, treasurer of the College, and has worked it up into a story of great interest and significance to everyone concerned in Smith College.

THE Elizabethan writer who wished to give his contemporaries a sense of the infinite length of eternity—usually in connection with a salutary description of the pains of hell—used to attempt an impression by some such image as this:

Though all the men that ever God made, were hundred handed like Briareus, and shoulde all at once take pennes in their hundred handes, and doe nothing in a whole age together, but sette downe in Figures and characters, as many myllions or thousands as they could, so many myllions or thousands they could never set down, as this worde of three syllables *Eternall*, includeth: an Ocean of yncke would it draw dry to describe it.

A picture of the housekeeping problem of Smith College must be drawn in much the same terms.

Have you any conception of what that housekeeping problem is? If, for instance, it takes one man x hours to shovel the path from your house to your garage, how many hours will it take how many men to shovel all the walks on the college campus after a snow storm? Perhaps you think that because you, as an alumna, have x children and Smith has 2000 the answer may be found by solving a not too difficult equation. But the process is not so simple; consider only that the 2000 children live in 44 houses scattered over 87.25 acres of ground and that they all go to chapel in John M. Greene, and you will begin to conceive the dimensions of the problem.

We are accustomed to think of the financial needs of a college in terms of dormitories and art galleries, of faculty salaries and scholarships. There is something about $5000 for a chair of philosophy that touches the imagination differently from $5000 for eggs (as a matter of fact we spend $11,000), yet if the student is to take advantage of the classroom and the library, she must be nourished, lighted, heated, shoveled, and all these things require an enormous steady outlay not only of brains and energy but of dollars. We pride ourselves that our college training teaches us to face facts whether we like them or not, and it is therefore imperative for us to realize on how huge a base of homely expenditure that college training rests.

We should never be able to face these facts if it were not for Miss Leonard, Mr. Hyde, Mr. King, and their respective assistants. The offices of the Purchasing Agent, the Treasurer, and the Superintendent have an extraordinary faculty not only of accomplishing staggering quantities of work and of stretching every hundred dollars further than any ordinary mortal could ever make it go, but also of knowing to a penny how much each job they do costs, in a way which is little short of miraculous to the average housekeeper who never can make her accounts quite balance. The facts and figures in which we shall now begin to talk run for the Treasurer and the Purchasing Agent through the current college year, for the Superintendent from January 1926 to January 1927. We are not trying to give you a balanced budget but rather some conception of the routine housekeeping expenditures of Smith College. Remember only that such routine expenditures increase yearly with increases of any kind in the college plant.

Let us begin with that eternal problem, cleanliness. Once, on a mountain lake remote from libraries, I had a violent argument with a friend as to whether the Walrus had said "seven maids with seven mops" or "forty maids with forty mops." His contention was that it must have been seven because the mind refused to visualize forty mopping maids. He was right, but it merely goes to prove the inferiority of the masculine mind, and likewise that truth is stranger than fiction, for forty maids would scarcely be noticed in Northampton where— and remember that we are a simple democratic college where everyone makes her own bed—the maids' payroll runs to $82,000 a year. The mops cost $3800, that is if you add brooms, brushes, soap, and general cleaning supplies. Dish towels, 2220 of them, run to $737. The College Laundry pays for itself and when it begins to make a profit it reduces the rates to the dormitories but, in order that it may be self-supporting, the dormitories must pay it for the washing of their bed and table linen, and that comes to $21,000 a year.

Even with the best of laundering, sheets and towels will wear out. Of course when one opens three brand new dormitories one expects an expenditure for equipment, but remember that, in addition to the new ones, we have twenty-nine campus houses all going full blast. This is what it requires to keep them stocked:

Bed Linen, $2600	Table Linen, $2640	Towels, Hand and Bath, $437
(5000 pieces)	*(2356 pieces)*	*(1632 pieces)*
2500 sheets	1920 napkins	
1800 pillow cases	346 squares	
700 spreads	90 cloths	

Add to this, please, a miscellaneous item of $1067 for doilies, table scarves, and so on, and remember that bed linen does not include blankets of which we must have 200 a year at a cost of $1000.

Three other large expenditures are necessary in the dormitories every year: for floor coverings $3000; for glass, china, and silver $3200; and for furniture $25,000. We need annually 9000 new pieces of china; 4000 of glass; 500 of silver. The expense for furniture includes not only new articles for dormitory rooms but furniture repairs, dry cleaning, and the repairing of mattresses.

And the student must be not only lodged but boarded. Food figures we have published occasionally before but their fascination never ceases even though the average mind reels at the thought of 14,000 quarts of cream and 80,000 loaves of bread. We want to keep you sane for a page or two more so we shall simply present a table without comment. These figures are approximate only, based upon supplies and current expenses to date.

Compilation of Expenditures for College Houses

1926–27—FOODS

BREADSTUFFS	BUTTER AND EGGS	CANNED GOODS	COFFEE	FRESH FRUIT AND VEGETABLES
$16,000— bread and rolls, $12,000; crackers and cookies, $4,000	$29,720— butter, 40,000 lbs., $18,720; eggs, 25,000 dz., $11,000	$24,000 for both fruit and vegetables, soup and fish	$4,850— 10,000 lbs.	$19,500
Note: 80,000 loaves of bread, 30,000 dz. rolls				*Note:* The above amount does not include potatoes and apples.

ICE CREAM	MEAT, FISH, AND POULTRY	MILK AND CREAM	POTATOES AND APPLES	SUGAR
$10,000— 29,000 qts.	$45,000	$32,000— milk, 200,000 qts.; cream, 14,000 qts.	$8,500— potatoes, 4000 bu., $7,500; apples, 350 bbls., $1,000	$3,600— 56,000 lbs.

Certainly the undergraduate is not undernourished.

To turn from the inner to the outer woman, there is the little matter of dormitories. We accept, of course, although we regret it, the hard fact that it costs money to build dormitories; but we forget too often that it also costs money to keep them built. Mr. King's annual report to the President contains, for instance, the quiet little item of ten thousand dollars for painters and a terse but colorful statement—or would it be more accurate to say that it is set down in black and white?—reads: "The exteriors of 54, 58, 62 Kensington Avenue, 7, 16, 65 Paradise Road, 76, 91 Elm Street, 8 College Lane, 22 Belmont Avenue, Haven and Dawes Houses were painted. Porch floors and steps on *all* dormitories were painted. For the above work these supplies were used: 4700 lbs. of white lead, 65 gallons of shellac, 320 gallons of turpentine, 258 gallons of linseed oil, 80 gallons of outside floor paint, 160 gallons of inside paint, 40 gallons of inside varnish."

In addition to this the roofs of 7 houses and 21 porch roofs were painted with 35 gallons of paint. And floors: 512 were varnished with 300 gallons of varnish, and 3200 lbs. of wax were spread on about 2185 others. The slight hairbell does not, alas, raise its head elastic from the fairy tread of our healthy student body, and even though they do not walk on the ceilings five hundred of those had to be done over last summer. It took 2300 lbs. of kalsomine.

Roofs must of course be kept over the heads of the young, not to mention the faculty, and do you consider wall papers a luxury? The lowest terms to which repapering can be reduced is 3000 rolls, hung on 225 rooms.

And now, Maud, please come out into the garden, though I fear it may lose for you some of its romantic charm when you learn that we spent last year

$1352.91 for grading.   The little matter of lawn mowing comes to $1493.33—and that accounts only for the electric mowers.   Keeping the athletic fields in condition costs $1265.53.

Closely connected with this business of lawns and walks is that matter of snow shoveling which seems to have such perennial fascination for the alumnae. It is, I fancy, the gambling element in that item which makes it a source of perpetual interest.   Even President Seelye could not, in a hard winter, economize on snow.   Mr. King's figure, which covers parts of two winters, is perhaps fairly typical.   It reads: equipment $98.82; labor $1686.85.

When you consider that we have not given you here by any means every item and detail, merely some of the most striking, doesn't Mr. King's payroll of $155,916.60 seem remarkably low?

Other people, of course, besides Mr. King and Miss Leonard spend money. It would be an endless task to list them all, but perhaps two items, telephones and pianos, will serve to suggest the others.   Dormitory telephones, as you remember only too well, are self-supporting nickel-in-the-slot machines, but administrative telephones—and we don't begin to have as many as the faculty and staff would like—cost $6500 a year.   And pianos—we have been told that a college should have ideally one instructor to every ten students but so far no one seems to have worked out the exact proportions between students and pianos.   Whatever it may be Smith comes, I fancy, fairly near it, for we have, in Sage Hall and the college houses, 116 of them.   These pianos must be tuned and, even on a very advantageous contract rate, that costs the Music Department $1160 a year.

The figures scattered through this paper can perhaps be brought into a significant series if they are considered in connection with three simple but suggestive statements:

Gas		$9,000
Electricity		
Dormitories	$16,000	
Academic buildings	9,000	$25,000
Coal:		
Dormitories	$60,000	
Academic buildings	30,000	$90,000

That trio symbolizes what this article has been attempting to do: to move through talk to illumination in order to generate—but symbols should not be driven home; we will leave the rest to your imagination.

Yet imagination is not the right word on which to end.   The statements you have been reading are not, alas, romance; they are facts of a very solid nature, facts which must be taken into consideration whenever an alumna would think constructively on the problems of collegiate education.

The Alumnae Fund and Salaries

W. A. NEILSON

THE $1,000,000 Fund raised under President Burton was for salaries. The teachers were not then paid enough even by pre-war standards, and there were not enough of them. Money for salaries was the most urgent need, and the income from this fund made possible a twenty per cent improvement.

Scarcely was it raised when the war came, and when that was over we discovered that it had taken about forty cents off all the dollars of our endowment and our income. So the alumnae raised the $4,000,000 Fund and devoted half of it to salary endowment, thus adding $100,000 a year to the annual income for this purpose. By increasing fees we have succeeded in supplementing this addition to a point at which the salaries of the faculty buy almost as much as they did before the war.

Meantime, two things have happened: first, there has been an enormous increase in the numbers of students all over the country, with a corresponding increase in the demand for teachers; and, secondly, the other colleges have also raised their fees and their endowments, and are bidding higher for the services of desirable teachers.

As the men's colleges are able to raise more money than we can, and as our sister colleges like Wellesley, Vassar, and Bryn Mawr have larger proportionate endowments than we have, it is becoming increasingly difficult to hold our more distinguished professors, or to get our fair share of the more promising younger scholars, in the face of the larger salaries that are being offered elsewhere. Our announced maximum is $5000, and only eleven of our faculty of over 200 have reached that. Several men's colleges (not universities) in our neighborhood have a maximum of $6000; about forty colleges and universities in the United States have a maximum greater than ours, according to figures just published by the American Council of Education. Our fees are among the highest in the country and cannot safely go higher. We have had to devote half of the last increase to scholarships in order to prevent limiting our constituency to the well-to-do and wealthy.

We are facing the prospect of having to use a part of current income for pensions. No teacher joining the profession after 1915 is eligible for a pension under the Carnegie Foundation. For those entering later, annuities may be secured through the Teachers' Annuity and Insurance Association, and the College agrees to pay half the premium up to five per cent of the salary. This contribution so far has come from the interest on $75,000 set aside for the purpose in 1920. But the number of teachers in this group increases annually as do their salaries, and after this year the interest on our pension fund will not be adequate. This means drawing on current income, and so reducing the amount available for salaries. Hence another reason for increasing the salary fund, merely to hold our own.

The alumnae need no argument to be convinced that the quality of our teaching staff is the most important consideration affecting the welfare of the

College. After all, the College exists to give good teaching, and, good teaching means good teachers. Good teachers cannot be engaged, and having been engaged, cannot be held, if our salary scale falls notably below that of our competitors. We can and do overcome a certain handicap by giving reasonable schedules of hours, by keeping down administrative work and affording some leisure for research, by availing ourselves of local conditions to provide moderately priced living accommodations, and by the assurance of greater academic freedom than is customary in some institutions. But the financial odds against us are growing, and it is easy to see how in a few years we may begin to lose ground if we are to continue to be at a disadvantage in the salaries we can offer. The general rise in the level of teachers' salaries throughout the country is in itself to be welcomed, both because it is deserved and because it will tend to draw good material into the profession. But it will work against Smith College unless we can keep pace with it.

In June the disposition to be made of the first year's contribution to the Alumnae Fund is to be decided. There is no purpose to which it can be devoted of more vital importance to the College than that of enabling the administration to maintain and improve the quality of our teachers.

Educational Ventures in Other Colleges

WE read with great interest in the last number of the *Wellesley Alumnae Magazine* that Wellesley has adopted for the completion of the work for the B.A. degree a general examination at the close of the senior year on a major subject of three or four courses in a department. This requirement goes into effect with the class of 1928. Dean Alice Waite in describing the plan says:

We hope and believe that we are taking a step in the right direction and that the Wellesley B.A. will stand for a higher degree of intellectual attainment, greater intellectual and moral vigor, for it may well take character as well as mentality to win through to success under this new plan.

Three years ago Mount Holyoke introduced the general examination in the major subject as a requirement for graduation and believes that its standards have been greatly advanced thereby.

The Institute of Euthenics at Vassar, which has been described in previous QUARTERLIES, is to hold its annual session this summer from June 22–July 22. There is an interesting advertisement of the session on page 383.

Beginning in February, the Women's College in Brown University is requiring of all freshmen a new course in Knowing and Thinking. The purpose of the course is explained by Dean Margaret Morris as follows:

In recent years the women's colleges as a group have become increasingly conscious of the need of relating their students to their future adjustments as women in the world outside the college walls. . . . The Women's College in Brown University proposes, therefore . . . to offer to its freshman students a new course in knowing and thinking with the primary purpose, not of introducing them to the college world, but of opening to them glimpses of the larger world in which they live and in which they will have to play their parts, and also of putting before them the problems of the modern educated woman. . . .

Smith, Internationally Speaking

DOHENY HACKETT

Miss Hackett, who graduates from Smith this year, is herself one of the students who have spoken internationally, for last summer she held the S. I. U. Scholarship of the Students' International Union in Geneva, of which Maude Miner Hadden 1901 is founder and now vice-president. Any alumnae who are given to regard the college girls as "an isolated group in a vacuum," with no interests beyond their own, will be gratified and amazed to learn what an active leavening of international consciousness has been developed on the campus with the undergraduates themselves as the motive power.

THERE is a great deal of interest these days in developing an international mind, but at Smith that process has been going on for so long that it is amazing to realize the great number of international activities on the campus. This is a brief glimpse of the ways in which undergraduates are internationally occupied.

In the fall the foreign students are eagerly sought by their American sisters as friends and informants. They are asked innumerable questions on their native land and customs. In classes and out of classes the questioning goes on. At the meetings of Cosmopolitan Club, which the foreign students manage and preside over, talks are given by each girl on her country. These contacts with girls our own age, who have similar interests in life no matter where they come from, do a great deal to create an international spirit and understanding in college, and so keenly is this appreciated that the undergraduates have expressed a desire to have the number of foreign students increased.

Last spring the organization called Round Table was absorbed by the International Club, which was formed to deal with problems of political and social interest arising in our own and other countries. There are about fifty enthusiastic members and a large, clamoring waiting list. This year such topics as the Debt Settlement and the Chinese Situation have been discussed. At a recent meeting a referendum was taken on Nicaragua, and whether or not America should arbitrate with Mexico. The National Student Federation of America will send the result of this vote in all colleges to President Coolidge.

At International Club the members do not rely on books and newspapers for material and information. The foreign students are anxious to give as accurate information as they can—and those students who have traveled either during the term, or during vacations, are eager to clear the issues for discussion. I mention midterm travel because of two important conferences which were held this year.

The National Student Federation of America organized a conference at Ann Arbor specifically for national problems and those connected with the colleges, but the Smith representative, Caroline Roberts '27, says, "There was a sincere feeling of international goodwill." The two official foreign representatives, one from the C. I. E. (Confédération Internationale des Étudiants), the other from Der Deutsche Studentschaft, addressed the Conference and told of the interest with which European students were watching the work of the Federation. Similarly at the Y. M. C. A.–Y. W. C. A. Conference at Milwaukee the feeling of common interest and coöperation, tolerance and friendship was widespread.   There were 241 foreign delegates representing 35 nations.   These joined in a general resolution, unanimously adopted, that, "conscious of the limitations of their knowledge upon the great questions of this conference they asked their colleges and universities to provide better opportunities to learn the facts concerning their international relations, the causes and cure of war, the human factor in industry, the causes of discontent, and the problems of religion in the modern world."   Smith sent fifteen delegates to Milwaukee.   Reports of both conferences were given to the undergraduates in chapel and great interest was manifest by all classes.

During the summer many undergraduates travel and study abroad.   The International Student Hospitality Association and the C. I. E. have arranged for certain groups visiting Europe to be met at the border of each country by two students of that country who are equipped to promote international understanding by their explanation of the facts and circumstances of their country.   It is expected that this summer a group of fourteen Smith students chosen by Student Council from applications will go under the chaperonage of Mrs. Helen Pratt, head of Morris House.   The National Student Federation of America is entertaining in this way a group of European students coming to this country for one month this summer.

Last summer the Y. W. C. A. organized a Women's Student Pilgrimage to Europe to investigate the work accomplished by the International Student Service, formerly the European Student Friendship Fund to which Smith College has been the largest single contributor in the U. S.   They visited student coöperative and self-help enterprises in London, Paris, Vienna, Prague, Berlin, Geneva, Budapest, Belgrade, and Bucharest.   They also attended the I. S. S. Conference in Jugoslavia where there were representatives of thirty-one other nations.   Adeline Taylor '28, our delegate, worked on the self-help questions with representatives from the other countries, who were enormously interested in the great difference between our schemes and theirs.   Some other topics of discussion were the problems of the intellectual surplus in Europe, and the economic questions touching upon these problems.   The College has listened with great interest to Adeline's report and benefited by her sympathetic understanding of the European economic and political problems and the way in which the different student groups meet them.   So important do the students consider this opportunity that this coming summer they are sending Margaret Ogden '28 as a representative of Smith, and Student Council and S. C. A. C. W. have each contributed $200 towards her expenses.

This insight and sympathy is gained by living in student groups of such heterogeneous membership that one may really come into direct contact with individuals.   The Sorbonnites discovered this at Grenoble.   Internationally speaking, they had a wider field there than at Paris.   Many European students attend that University and the bonds of friendship are soon established regardless of nationality, race, or creed.   I saw it happening in Geneva.   Smith students at the University of Geneva and at Mr. Zimmern's School of International Studies talked excitedly with Indians on their problems with far greater comprehension than they would have if another American had explained the situation to them.

The Students' International Union, in Geneva, was founded to serve as student headquarters where members of all colleges and universities, young men and women of every nation, may meet and become friends. The American students who hold scholarships which enable them to study in Geneva and work at the Union have a privilege indeed. Last summer I realized the value in having such a club center where students meet informally, study, read, write letters, and gather for afternoon tea, lectures, conversation, evening entertainments, and musicales when I watched Russians and Poles, Britons and Hindus, French and Germans—and Americans—exchanging ideas together, and being friends. It is expected that the holder of one of the scholarships this summer will be from Smith. The office of the Union is 522 Fifth Av., N. Y. C.

The group of undergraduates who have had any of these opportunities to appreciate the international influences at work in colleges all over the world have a strong sense of the unity of the student movement. Formally and informally this international circle is widening and the undergraduates at Smith are sturdy and vigorous members in the movement for understanding and fellowship among the young people of the world for the health and happiness of the nations.

The Second Group of Juniors in France

ALICE A. WOODARD 1928

"The circling years roll on"— It seems only à few brief months since that first group of juniors set forth eagerly and timorously for France, and now the second group is almost at the end of its wonderful year, and the third group is poised for flight. Miss Woodard, now in France, is quite right in saying that the second group also is making history for Smith College, and we are glad of her charming story. We have invited a member of the first group, which is now finishing its senior year on the campus, to round out the tale of the whole experiment in the July QUARTERLY.

TO last year's group of juniors in France belongs the honor of being the first to try out the new and courageous plan of Mlle. Cattanès. Had they not made such a glorious success of their year there never would have been a second group. Hence we of the second group owe everything, even our mere presence here, to them. We realize that, thanks to them, we are making a reality out of what last year was just an experiment. Our claim to fame is quieter and more prosaic than theirs, but still we like to think that we are establishing a new tradition, and that we are in a sense making college history. Our ideal is not only to follow the example that they set for us but to raise the standard just a bit higher.

It is now just about six months since we arrived in Grenoble. Even four months of Parisian influence cannot develop in us the proper contempt of life in the provinces. For me the memories of those two months will always hold a particular charm. In Grenoble, as in Paris, we lived in private families. Some of us were outside the city at La Tronche, in charming villas. Others of us lived in fifth story apartments of buildings where elevators were unheard of. But the climb to these dizzy heights (French influence showing up!) was always rewarded by the fact that from every window of the apartment could be had a magnificent view of the snow-capped mountains which encircle the town. I lived in one of these apartments with two charming old ladies, so quaint and amusing that you felt Daudet must have known them. Think of having as a house-mother someone who could hold you breathless with the tales of what happened to her grandmother during the Revolution, or be telling you in the next minute what it feels like to be trapped in the wreck of your home which had just been bombarded by the Germans. Think of going to market with Maria, the maid, not because you had heard that market places were picturesque and interesting to see, but because you really wanted to buy the vegetables for luncheon. Think of going alone with Maria, instead of being one of a straggling party of fifty shunted about by a be-megaphoned American Express guide. Think of taking a foolish little tram that looks just like the Toonerville Trolley out to Pont Claix and there seeing the old Roman bridge and having tea on the terrace overlooking the river. You are so enchanted that while you've been lingering there over your tea the shadows have grown longer and longer, the sun has set, and the moon is coming up over the other side of the blue mountains. Think of all these things and you will have only the faintest notion of what our life in Grenoble was.

Our work consisted of drill in phonetics, vocabulary, grammar, composition, and translation. It seemed at the time more or less dry and uninteresting work. But since our arrival in Paris it has proved to be the groundwork and foundation of all our work at the Sorbonne. At first it was all we could do to make out what the professors were saying to us, to say nothing of trying to take notes and assimilate any intelligent information from the lectures. But from mere force of habit we soon got over that difficulty. We had regular classes from eight until twelve every morning, and one or two lectures on subjects of general interest in the afternoon. We had written work to do for all of our classes and one composition a week. This written work was a great help to us when it came to our examinations, for the French professors lay a great deal of emphasis on the form in which you give the information you know. At home any signs of intelligence about a question are greeted with shouts of glee by the professor, whereas here an intelligent notion of the subject is taken for granted by the professor beforehand, and your merit lies in giving some individual thought to the question and presenting the result in a clear and interesting fashion.

Our lectures were given in the chapel of an old monastery, and our classes were given in the tiny rooms, cells, I believe, of the monastery itself. Painted saints still looked down upon us from the chapel walls in mild surprise, and listened with sympathetic smile to our lectures on the uses of the verb "to be." In the courtyard an old sundial was painted on the whitewashed walls, and fig trees made black and white patterns on the wall. And once in the late fall we had a class by moonlight! and no one thought anything of it!

So it was in this quaint old-world atmosphere that our two months in Grenoble were spent. On the week-ends we went on trips to any number of fascinating places. To Chamonix to set foot on the famous Mer de glace, or to Avignon to see the palace of the popes, to "Les Charmettes," the home of Mme. de

Warens, or to Lamartine's famous Lac de Bourget. So, with such places to visit, it is easy to understand that even in France week-ends played an important part in our lives.

Meanwhile in our "families," faced with the alternative of being either dumb or unintelligible, we were forced to speak French daily; although I shudder now to think what kind of French it must have been.

As the time went on our examinations loomed up more and more terrifyingly. Examinations written in French and corrected by exacting French professors are bad enough, but the thought of oral examinations upset us completely. After all, in a written examination you can spend fifteen minutes thinking up the answer to a question that you may not know anything about, whereas in an oral examination your confusion is quite obvious. Then, too, there is the cheerful thought that once face to face with that kind-hearted ogre known as a professor, from sheer nervous tension your mind may just cease to function. Of course, the examinations and even the "orals" were not so terrific as we had imagined them. Still, one thing we had not counted on was their utter and perfect lack of any system whatsoever. In presenting yourself for an oral examination it was merely a question of who could push the hardest to get up to the professor's desk. Consequently, if you were a timid soul and never had taken gym in college, after standing for at least two hours in a crushing jam in front of the professor's desk you finally got the coveted place and took your examination. But you were so exhausted that anything you did know about the course was in a dim, vague fog, and what was more you didn't seem to care, by that time, whether you passed the examination or not. In spite of the more technical difficulties of the situation, twenty-nine out of thirty-five of us passed the examination.

And so we arrived in Paris to begin our real year's work. The first few days were spent in getting acquainted with our new "families," and in trying to find our way about the Sorbonne and around Paris. Never having known the subways of New York or Boston, riding in the metro here has become one of my favorite sports. There is an element of mystery about it that is quite delightful. You just go down into a little hole in the ground, run up and down numerous staircases, take the first train that comes along, and get off when you feel like it. If you're not where you wanted to be, why then you just pick another staircase. The metro has the added charm of being one of the few places in Paris not overrun by Americans. Here at last you can discover that elusive Parisian phenomenon known as a Frenchman. You can study him in all forms and varieties, and I really think that our course at the Sorbonne on "French Life" should be supplemented at frequent intervals by an hour's ride on the metro. Of course busses are fun too, and when you can ride to school, up through the market places, past Saint Sulpice all rose and grey, and the gardens of the Luxembourg all blue and misty in the early morning light, it is no wonder that we envy those juniors of next year and all the years after.

In our work at the Sorbonne we follow a division of courses known as the "Cours de Civilisation française." This consists of nine different courses. We usually take eight only—four each semester. The choice of courses depends largely upon what we have taken at Smith. But in general the first semester we take 19th century literature, history of art, contemporary history, and French life (its structure and social makeup). The second semester we take Renaissance literature, general history of France, geography, and philosophy. We have outside reading to do for each of the courses and on the average of one composition a week. These compositions are corrected and returned to us. Mlle. Delpit goes over these copies with us, explaining the corrections, pointing out our particular faults, and suggesting ways of correcting them. These compositions are of the greatest value to us, for we learn by mere force of habit to put our ideas down in French and in the required form. In this respect, I think, we all feel we have made a great deal of progress. Personally, I can remember that in Grenoble a two-page composition meant at least five or six hours of work. I began by assembling all the grammars, dictionaries, books of synonyms and idioms that I could find, and hidden behind these I would moil and toil for hours over every phrase and sentence. Whereas now a French dictionary is usually sufficient, and once in a while a whole sentence even comes to me in French!

There are so many and varied opportunities to be found here that you can make your life what you want it to be. You may devote all your time to work, or you may illustrate and supplement your work by visits to the cathedrals and museums. If you are interested in art all the Louvre is yours. If you are interested in music you have the opera, and if you're just interested in people and psychology you may try to define the French mentality as you see it in your "family" and the French people that you meet. In any case there is no dearth of things to do; our life is rich in opportunities. It is up to us to choose between them and to realize that there is no use dissipating our energy in trying to do everything.

As Christmas time drew near we began to make plans for our vacation. For this one year what troubled us was not whether we should go to the New Year's Eve party with "Bob" or with "Dick," but it was whether we should go south for Christmas and save Italy or England for spring, or vice versa. For those of us who stayed in Paris, Christmas will always bring delightful memories of midnight mass at Notre Dame, the gay "réveillon," and week-end trips to old cathedral towns. For those of us who, tired of Paris's rain and fog, went to Switzerland, there will be memories of winter sports at their best, and for those who went south to Nice and Cannes there will be the triumphant memory that for once this winter they were warm!

But vacation was soon over, and we settled down to the usual preëxamination grind. Of course we had survived the examinations in Grenoble, but examinations at the Sorbonne were an entirely different matter. Here you are given one question on each of the four subjects you have taken. You choose one question and write a composition on the subject it treats; you are given three hours for this. You are graded not only on the information given, but the grammatical errors made and the form and style of your composition. The afternoon of the same day you have two questions on each course except that course which was the subject of your morning's dissertation. You are given fifteen minutes' time in which to answer each group of questions. The following day the results of the examinations are announced and those who have passed the written examination are admitted to the oral—a sort of "from the frying pan into the fire" arrangement. This year only five of the thirty-five of us who took the examination failed the written and only two of us failed the oral; which is a record of which we are rather proud.

There is a good deal of talk going on about unfriendly relations existing between the French and the Americans in Paris. We see very little of it. Most of the stories told are grossly exaggerated, and when this is not the case my first impulse is to blame the Americans. The situation arises, I believe, from the fact that there is very little actual contact between the two peoples. It is perfectly possible to live in Paris without knowing any French at all—in fact, it has been said of one Frenchman that he knew enough English to get about Paris in the summer time. In most of the bars, restaurants, and night clubs, dear to the hearts of some, but fortunately not all Americans, no Frenchman has ever been known to set foot. So each nationality only knows the other by reputation, and that reputation is usually highly colored, false, and quite deplorable. There is an organization which is doing a great deal to prevent this state of affairs. It is the "Accueil aux Etudiants des Etats-Unis," which is admirably directed by Mme. Seligman-Lui. Through this organization we and other American students in Paris are invited to receptions and teas given by French women in their own homes. Here we meet other French people, and we see them afterwards for tea, bridge, or a morning's walk in the Bois. So in a quite natural fashion we come to know and understand them as well as any of our own friends. Anyone who has done this will neither listen to, nor help to spread, some of the ridiculous notions one hears so often about the French people in general.

Spring has just now come to Paris. We had always heard of how lovely Paris was in the springtime, but we had never realized just how enchanting it could and would be. The fountains are playing in the Tuilleries, the passenger boats are again plying busily up and down the river, little children are sailing boats in the pools of the Luxembourg gardens, the lilac beneath my window is in bloom, and moonlight in our garden is magic pure and simple. But with the arrival of spring comes the realization that our year is nearly over. We can't help envying just a little those juniors who will follow us. In spite of the fact that we shall be glad to be back home and in college, we know that our year will leave with us an impression and memory never to be forgotten.

The Second Year in the Personnel Office

MABELLE BABCOCK BLAKE
Personnel Director

THE past two years have shown us very clearly that when help in adjustment to college life is offered to college women they accept it voluntarily, and the majority coöperate in an effort to find out the cause of maladjustment and to discover the remedy for improvement. The Personnel Office began its work at Smith College last year. Much of the time was spent in determining the form of organization that would best meet our individual needs. We are still learning from our experiences but we can report progress.

Freshman Interviews. What have been our chief interests this year? The one that perhaps stands out as the most important is the effort that has been made to have an hour's conference with every freshman as soon as possible. With our large entering class we were not able to complete the list during the first semester, but surely by the first of May all will have been seen. And what has been the purpose of this first interview?

To discover first needs.
To put the student in touch with the person who can best help.
To urge each to find her own interests and potentialities.
To get at the student's own point of view in order that she may get the most out of college and put the most in.

Problems of Upper Classmen. Upper classmen have come in increasing numbers for help in academic, social, vocational, and emotional adjustment. If it is true that many students have in the past graduated from colleges without any understanding of what the world is all about or without a knowledge of their own powers, surely given an opportunity to counsel with individual students we should be able to help some in self-discovery, in securing emotional balance, in getting a knowledge of occupational opportunities after college, and thereby lessen the number of misfits within college and outside in the community.

Classes in How to Study. Another interesting phase of the work this year has been the classes in how to study. In coöperation with the Class Dean, we gave an opportunity to some of the students who had received official warnings at the middle of the first semester to meet in small groups in order that we could make an attempt to find out the cause of failure and to suggest the remedy.

A description of one of these classes will give some idea of the method used. In this group there were 23. A letter was written to each student stating that we were aware of the fact that she was not doing so well as she was capable of doing in her academic work, and inviting her to meet with others for a general discussion concerning the cause of her difficulty and consideration of methods for improvement. Twenty-one of the 23 came to the first meeting. Two were prevented because of illness. The following questions were discussed:

REASONS FOR DIFFICULTIES: those which were most apparent were:
Lack of preparation. This did not mean a general lack but in specific

subjects. Some students, for instance, who were doing poorly in Latin had had no experience in sight translation. Others who were doing unsatisfactory work in French had never had any conversation.

Lack of objective.

Lack of interest in subjects.

No idea of how to balance time.

Two were in college against their wishes; one of these was tolerant of the situation because she believed every girl ought to have an education; the other was most antagonistic.

But the chief difficulty that was offered was the fact that they did not know how to study. This led to a general outline as to how to approach subjects and how one could use one's mind to the best advantage. A very simple textbook was suggested on this general subject and the class was asked to meet again within two weeks after there had been an opportunity to follow some of the suggestions made. At this second meeting there was 100% attendance and there was no question but that the students felt they were making progress. At the end of the first semester practically all the students in this group completed the work satisfactorily. It would be too much to claim that the study class was the cause of the improvement but if we could have similar classes over a period of years and then make comparisons, we possibly could judge their value. All the students were given an opportunity for personal interviews and many of them came to the office to discuss their individual problems.

The study classes were conducted by the personnel director and her associate, Miss Ruby Litchfield 1910, who was added to the staff in September.

Special Help Given. Dr. Thom, our psychiatrist, who began his work here last year, has continued to come two days a month. There has been an increasing interest shown on the part of the students as well as faculty, and a number of the students themselves have asked to have appointments with him. "Mental Hygiene in the college means the search for increasing efficiency and therefore increasing happiness of students."

Vocational Work. At the beginning of the year the work of the Appointment Bureau became one of the divisions of the Personnel Office, and Miss Frances Knapp 1918 was added to our staff as vocational secretary. We have attempted to give our seniors as much vocational advice as possible and to discover how best this division could serve the alumnae. At the opening of college the senior class president appointed a student vocational committee from the class of 1927, to work with Miss Knapp in finding out what the students wanted to know about occupational opportunities. The committee in turn appointed a student in each college house as a vocational representative. This group was to help in registering at the Personnel Office students who were looking for jobs and to pass on to the committee any suggestions for further guidance. Many of the plans that have been put in operation have been initiated by this student group.

The seniors were invited to attend a general meeting in October, at which a survey of the field of opportunities was given. Later they each wrote down three occupations which held the greatest interest for them and about which they wanted to know more. These were given in the following order: Education, Writing, Social Work, Science, Library Work, Art, Museum Work, Landscape Architecture, Dramatic Work. Meetings followed at which these different occupations were discussed, two days being given to each. An expert on the subject came to the first meeting, and on the second day those who were particularly interested in the occupation met for further discussion. The students have also been urged to search for information themselves and to bring to our vocational files articles which might be helpful to other students. On the whole these meetings have been well attended and there has been a great demand on the part of undergraduates for the privilege of meeting with these occupational groups. Some have already stepped in unawares and the committee agrees that there should be a general invitation given to them next year.

At this writing 448 seniors have registered, and 236 credentials have already been sent out.

Returns from the Class of 1926. The returns from the questionnaire which was sent to the members of the class of 1926 have been most interesting. Space will not permit us to summarize these completely, but a few facts will be of interest:

The total number of registrants was 445. About 53% answered the questionnaire. The number employed is 108. Of this number, 70 secured work by their own efforts, 18 through commercial or other agencies, 20 through the Appointment Bureau or other departments of the College. Sixty-one of those not employed are doing graduate study.

Follow-up of the Alumnae. Follow-up cards have been sent to the alumnae. As a result approximately 525 have asked to be considered for a change in position next year, and since September nearly 500 credentials for the alumnae have been sent out. From July 1, 1925, to July 1, 1926, 54 alumnae were placed by the Appointment Bureau. This would seem to indicate that the chief function of the vocational division of the Personnel Office to alumnae is to send out credentials and to keep them well informed as to the best opportunities in the occupational field. One can readily see that it is essential that information be kept up-to-date. We therefore make a plea to the alumnae to keep us informed of any change of address, any change in plans, or any facts about themselves which will be of worth in suggesting new positions.

Dean Hawkes of Columbia University has described the function of student personnel work as "that of making conditions under which educational work is done as favorable as possible, so that the real purpose of the institution can be fulfilled." This we believe to be the chief aim of the Personnel Office. "It is an attempt to recognize the needs of students as individuals and to help them more effectively in achieving the development best for themselves and for their relation to society."

WHAT ALUMNAE ARE DOING

Homestead Orchards

ALICE MAY COMSTOCK

Miss Comstock graduated in 1912, but according to her biographical card it was not until 1923 that she went "back to the land." The issue of the *Providence Journal* of which she speaks is responsible for this article, which will appear at just about the time her orchard is in bloom.

IF any of you are subscribers to the *Providence Journal* you must know that you are hearing from "one of the most successful women apple-growers in Rhode Island." The paper said so last fall in a glowing write-up with pictures and everything, so of course it must be so. We told the Windsors, our neighbors and the apple kings of the state, that they must-be relieved to have orchardists so near them to whom they could run for advice on important matters! They got the point and grinned in appreciation.

My partner, Maude Chace, and I acquired Homestead Orchards on September 16, 1925. The farm contains eighty-five acres of which twenty are planted to apple trees. Of these there are around seven hundred, all bearing, and including perhaps twenty varieties. A full half of the trees are Baldwins; the other three main varieties are Greening, Gravenstein, and McIntosh.

We bought the place from Albert J. Mowry, whose family had lived on it for five generations. That is why we named it Homestead Orchards. Mr. Mowry was anxious to have someone buy it who would not cut it up into lots, but who would keep it an orchard. He had planted all the trees himself; but he was no longer able to do the work which the place required, and he preferred to sell rather than to hire the necessary help.

The house is in very good condition—an attractive white farmhouse, a story and a half high. The country around is wild and hilly. It seems somehow remote and far from civilization, but it really is not, for Providence is only eleven miles away, and the small town of Greenville only three. The veterinary who recently visited one of our horses said that those three miles were the worst in the state—but we have lived on a far more bumpy road, and know better.

The house and out buildings are set in quite a distance from the main road on a lane lined with apple trees. People often enter our lane and think they are going somewhere. "Where does this road lead?" they inquire, and are surprised to learn that it leads directly into our cranberry bog. We sold fifty bushels of cranberries out of that bog a year ago, and besides that it is a lovely, sheltered skating pond in winter. If we can cut ice from it, and arrange some way of getting a swimming pool, we shall be satisfied with the number of crops it gives us. Back of the bog is Wionkhiege Hill on which we own some acres of gray boulders and dead timber—not very valuable land perhaps, but full of caves and fascinating surprises. Also our farmer sent more than a winter's supply of fuel crashing down over those boulders this year, so it is useful as well as delightful.

My partner has been growing apples for seven years. She was always interested and was delighted with the chance of helping a friend renovate an old orchard on her father's country place. They took a ten weeks' course at Massachusetts Agricultural and went hard at it pruning the old trees and planting young ones. When the friend married, two years later, I took her place in the orchard. We soon, however, began to wish for trees of our own on which to expend our energies, and hence the adventure of Homestead Orchards. I did not take any course at Amherst and acquired most of what I have learned from my partner, which is convenient, because I can blame her if I make mistakes.

We are asked very often, "What are you doing now in the orchard?" This is natural perhaps in January or April, for to most people an orchard exists only when it is in blossom, or when the fruit is ripe. Once, however, I was a little startled when my brother-in-law, who is quite an orchardist himself, inquired absent-mindedly in the middle of October: "Let me see, what is it you are doing now up there?" "Doing?" I cried, "*Now?* Well—I wish you'd come and help us do it!"

Our picking season began rather dramatically this fall by the departure of our hired man. He had been coming by the day for nearly a year and he announced one Saturday night that he was "through." This with the prospect of a huge apple crop gave us a moment's pause. We knew we could not pick five thousand bushels of apples by ourselves. However, we need not have worried. Pickers walked on to our place without our stirring a finger. In a short time we had a corps of young, energetic, and highly entertaining boys of eighteen or twenty, who considerably enlivened the place during the autumn months. At eight o'clock the excitement began with the arrival of one worker on his motorcycle—great noise and speed! Two others came bringing a small police puppy, and a fourth brought a very good singing voice, which often made the tops of the trees resound pleasantly to "Bye, Bye, Blackbird." To the question asked us, "Do you feed your pickers?" the answer was, "No, they bring their luncheons, and feed our dogs."

Somehow or other our apples were picked, and then the cellar was piled high with Baldwins—over two thousand bushels of them—four feet high. How delicious they smelled! But they had to be sorted and it looked like rather a hopeless task. With our farmer, who came with his wife in November and has made life for us a much less strenuous affair, we worked through the winter in a cold dark cellar, ploughing our way through this wall of apples, sorting them into their various grades—selling the poorer ones and storing the best. We gave ourselves a stint—so many bushels a day. We stuck to it and, lo and behold, early in February it was done.

Our next job was pruning, which I think is more interesting than any other orchard work except grafting. When you have opened a tree to the sun and air, shaped its top, scraped the loose, rough bark off its trunk, you feel how much better it can breathe. We have grafted a little this spring, changing our Yellow Transparent which are practically worthless to Gravenstein. It never ceases to amaze me how a little shoot or scion made into a wedge and fitted under the bark of a fresh cut stub, so that the cambium layers of the shoot and the old tree are touching, can determine the kind of apples while the whole system of the tree you are changing has nothing to say. My partner is trying to graft a silver moon rose on one tree, but this is an experiment.

We are hurrying with our pruning for the spring is early and soon it will be time to spray. We spray five times: when the green tips are about a quarter of an inch long, when the blossoms first show pink, when the blossoms are almost all fallen (this is the most important spray for it gets the coddling moth which makes wormy apples), and two summer sprays for the fruit. In between sprays there is always pruning and cultivating and in July thinning out the poor, diseased apples and spacing the good ones so they can grow to the proper size. We haven't so much time for this as we should like to find, for we know it pays. Two bushels of large perfect apples take less time to pick and bring in more money than six bushels of small mediocre fruit. The seasons rush by in an orchard—soon it will be August again with more apples to pick!

Of course the question of financial success must be considered, though we have not had our orchard long enough to tell much about that. We think we have a good commercial proposition on our hands, but this has been a very bad year to test it out. Apples have been very plentiful and horribly cheap. It cost a great deal to pick them and they were hard to sell at an advantage. However, we are not in the least discouraged. An orchardist from Virginia said: "I think you two are lucky—you bought your orchard at the time of the very worst depression. Things will have to be better." Our poorest apples we send to wholesale, paying ten cents a bushel for cartage. They are sold on commission and bring in very little. Luckily for us—else we might be discouraged—we have a good private trade in Providence, and we sell to one large market as well as to seven or eight smaller ones. We deliver these apples or hire a boy to deliver them in our half-ton truck, which has weathered five winters of rough roads and heavy loads, and which the Ford doctor says has three more years of life in it.

We had the amusing experience this winter of being paid ten cents a bushel for having our barn and cellar cleaned out. There were some miserable cider apples, which had been frozen and thawed and frozen again innumerable times, piled up in the barn. An Italian coming up to buy asked how much these poor ones were. We would almost have paid him to take them, but my partner said, "Ten cents a bushel." That was all that was said. We did not appear eager, in fact we acted a little reluctant—as though those apples were somehow dear to us and we rather hated to part with them. To our amazed joy he came back later and bought ten dollars worth of this waste. What a feeling it gave us to see them roll out of the lane. As the farmer remarked gleefully, that ten dollars was just like a Christmas present.

We think that is a good omen for the future, and meanwhile there are other things which console us for not being millionaires after one year. It is not inconsiderable, for instance, in May or early June, to step out of your own doorway into heaven. I do not know how else to describe our orchards in bloom. Then, too, there is always something happening on a farm, even if it is only Old Maude, the horse, literally sitting down on the job and refusing to back the load of apples into the cellar way. We lead a highly varied life, at times—helping spread manure in the morning perhaps, then dashing madly to town in the afternoon and attending a tea, returning to a late dinner and spending the night out in the barn awaiting the birth of a calf. "So young—it totters when she licks it with her tongue." It is interesting to do things which you never expected to do. I felt like a child with a wonderful new toy when after many struggles I found that I could swing the lever on our sulky plough and really make it go. Not that I ever could or would do much ploughing, but just—conquering the thing! It gives me a thrill to "chew" down a tree—not very large, and very badly chopped, but *down*.

We are often in real touch with the elements. It is an experience to be snowed in and have to dig your way to the horse barn; or to walk a mile on snowshoes in a driving blizzard to bring home the milk—we had no cow a year ago. Last spring while I was digging a hole for a peach tree I looked up to see that the smoke, which we had been anxiously watching beyond the hills, had become fire—the fire was on our land, our hill. We collected pails and bags and hurried to fight it. There were several men already on the scene—the fire had spread from quite a distance. We were all day fighting it—beating out the edges with wet bags, guarding now this place and now that. All our neighbors were at work. The fire threatened several farms, but was finally controlled by the fire department and all the volunteer workers. In the afternoon the Red Cross served coffee in our orchard. It was very excellent coffee too!

That night my partner and I noticed two smouldering eyes in the woods beyond our orchard of young trees. We thought it safer to go and put them out. Afterwards we sat on a knoll overlooking the bog. There was such serenity in the still evening. We love it here. It is wonderful never to be bored, to be outdoors, to be well, to be closely in touch with fundamental things. We love our animals and we really love our trees. I think I love them almost best before they have acquired any concealing foliage and you can see their shapes, for the shape of an apple tree is very lovely.

> I love the wind-blown apple trees
>   That watch us passing by;
> Crooked, and bare, and fearless,
>   Against the winter sky.
>
> They top the lonely hillsides,
>   The fierce snows wrap them white;
> And through their barren branches
>   The great stars shine at night.

ONE TO THREE

"Others, Why Not I?"

Dorothy Saxton Rextrew

In 1920, Dorothy Saxton, Smith 1915, started on her business career in a very small way. Now she has seventeen people working for her and a showroom in New York for the

ONE TO THREE

wholesale trade. She was married in 1922, but is still "coördinating," with her office in her own home and her own little daughter (the "tiny-tad" on the left) as her very particular inspiration. The little girl on the right, Mrs. Rextrew tells us, is herself at the age of three, long, long before Smith College or a career entered her head. The two pictures appear on her letterhead, and we hope you will look up her advertisement on page 389 of this issue.

WHILE in college, like every other classmate, I faithfully attended the prescribed number of sermons, lectures, and talks. In 1915 I graduated filled with the same amount of determination that my 316 colleagues had. It was not a determination to do well what everyone else was doing, but to do something that no one else had ever done. If I am not mistaken, this is the same self-delusion that absorbs every other young graduate the first few months after her Alma Mater has presented her to the world and she is declared to be a full-fledged and accepted alumna.

As we all know, however, this first blush of inspiration dwindles in a steady process, and not long after graduation I found myself out of the clouds at the bottom of a hill along with the rest of the world of real men and women. After my awakening, I looked about me to find that other folks were really doing things—things that meant a great deal to the world or meant a great deal to them, either financially or otherwise; and for a few years I alternately contented myself and tormented myself with listening with an increasing amount of envy to their stories of success and accomplishment. I invariably came away putting to myself the question, "Others do it, why not I?"

In December, 1920, I was resolved to know the answer. I created the first production of business which now requires some seventeen workers to supply the demand. I felt convinced that in spite of what seemed to be a flooded market in infants' wear, there was still room for something that was unique and well done to the last detail. I chose as my first article a child's bib, made it entirely by hand, and appliquéd on it in colors objects taken directly from children's storybooks, such as ' Reddy' Squirrel," "Benjamin Bunny," "Peter Rabbit," "Red Riding Hood," and " Little Boy Blue."

My first sources of consternation were the questions, "Could I create a demand? Would anyone buy them? Where would I find my buyers?" I knew that if they lived at all they could be found in New York City, so I mustered my courage and sent my first consignment to New York for approval or rejection. I can never forget my excitement when I received in return an order from one of the largest concerns there catering to the infant trade, which gave me the added courage I needed to continue in the development of my idea.

I gradually worked out an assortment covering over sixty subjects well known and loved by all children—naming the bib "The Tiny-Tad Bib," with the added slogan, "Little Shavers' Clothing Savers." Although I have made them for over six years I have never ceased personally to be fascinated by them and still get a thrill thinking how cunning they will look on the "Little Shavers" and how much fun some "Tiny-Tad" will get wearing his storybook friends.

Within a very short time I added the "Dorothy" line of handkerchiefs for ladies and men. These were added because I wanted some article to reach and please grown-ups. In designing ladies' handkerchiefs, I tried to make them just a little different from those novelties then on the market. This applied also to the men's. Men are indeed particular shoppers and seem to insist upon the gayest of combinations.

The need for helpers grew. With some difficulty I was able to secure from time to time additional workers who appreciated and could carry out the details of fine handwork.

As I received a few more orders, the fascination of business grew upon me, and I found myself absorbed more and more in it. The game of selling thrilled me although every interview or letter did not mean an order. I did occasional advertising in trade magazines and through college publications offered a percentage to college funds. After furnishing "Tiny-Tad" bibs for a children's party as favors, and handkerchiefs for a couple of large benefit bridge parties, I decided that if properly pursued these outlets would develop real sales. Results have confirmed this.

Within a year after starting my business, I set out on a real adventure, a selling trip of several days through New York State. A day or two of this proved that undoubtedly this method of selling was by far the best. There followed trips through Massachusetts and Pennsylvania and summer trips through the mountain resorts, with repeated visits at fairly regular intervals. Increasing business and the coming of my little girl, Ruth, two years ago, brought about permanent representation in New York and Chicago.

Of course it is only natural that inspirations have come for additional items. Last year, baby dresses from one to three were brought out in response to repeated requests from buyers for a certain style in these sizes. Nursery laundry bags, made to resemble a cunning yellow duck, are also manufactured. A varied line of unusual infant or slumber pillow slips was designed. Again these were introduced with the feeling that there was a field for the unique.

I will not bore you with a detailed recital of my progress, except to say that since my first timid step in 1920, my staff of workers has increased from one to seventeen and my monthly output from five dozen to sixty dozen pieces. Orders have been shipped to practically every state.

You will no doubt be interested to know that I have the office in my own house. All the handwork is done in the homes of the workers and I manipulate the shipping and all of the executive detail from my "Home Office." This leaves me free for designing and selling.

After being in business two years I was married.   I was told by many that a business career along with marriage could not be.   Though it means hard work I have been able by being systematic in my day's work, by having help in my home, and with the constant interest and enthusiasm of my understanding husband to find the greatest happiness and enjoyment in my daily life.

In conclusion I add that I would not trade my business and all it means for any of the tales I used to hear about before I made my attempt, or for any of the dreams. I had before I started to work.   I enjoy every bit of it and am more than gratified with the returns that it gives me, feeling that I have answered to my own satisfaction the question: "Others, Why Not I?"

In Memoriam

CHARLOTTE CHESTER GULLIVER

Born, September 11, 1860   Died, March 31, 1927

OUT of the midst of a full and radiant life, there has passed one of the most loyal of Smith alumnae, Charlotte Chester Gulliver, of the class of '83.   Although her intimate friends knew that for about eight years she had a slight heart trouble, her death came without warning, after a day of normal and happy activity.

Since her graduation from college, she has continued an active interest in its affairs.   From 1887 to 1891 she was the President of the Alumnae Association.   As an Alumnae Trustee, she served a term from 1895 to 1901.   After the first reunion of her class she was appointed its secretary for life.   At the time of her death, she was the President of the Eastern Connecticut Smith College Club.

In all her relations with other people she was not only adequate but gifted.   Many persons try sincerely to meet requirements.   She did not have to try, she met them.   She was not compelled to do this or that in order to bring out the best in others; she was just herself, and they reacted to her stimulating personality.

Hers was a rare combination of natural disposition, heart and mind.   It would seem that her clear and legal intellect might easily absorb so much power that less would be left for the emotional side of her nature.   But her force seemed to have no limitations.   None who knew her failed to realize her greatness of heart, her sympathy to the point of quick tears, her self-sacrifice that went even to the point of self-effacement.   Add to that sympathy her quickness of mind in apprehending need, and the result was a help to others that was instant, wise, and effective.

Her life-work was that of an educator.   With the exception of one year, when she was teaching in The Porter School at Farmington, Connecticut, she has given to The Norwich Free Academy—a school founded by her uncle at Norwich, Connecticut—her finest powers in a service of forty years of teaching.   It is not possible to measure the results of her stimulating contact with the minds and characters of young people at the most receptive period of their lives.   The universal admiration and affection of all her students show how significant was her far-reaching influence.

'83

Green Mountain Goodies

KATHARINE SEWALL AUSTIN

Every now and then there is an advertisement of Green Mountain Goodies in the QUARTERLY and so delicious are they that we are glad to know more about them. It seems that the business as carried on by Mrs. Austin (Smith 1909) and Florence Merritt (Smith 1907) is—at least as far as Mrs. Austin is concerned—a kind of coördination of women's interests undertaking with no particular problems involved. Watch for the advertisement again next fall!

I COULD write of the "sugar bush"—hundreds of maple trees with shiny buckets hanging on them; of men in hip boots tramping through the snow and slush, collecting the sap; of a little sugar house perched on a Vermont hillside, cords of wood piled close by to keep the sap a'boiling; of a blue, blue sky above, and glimpses to the west of blue Lake Champlain and snow-covered Adirondacks beyond; of the unmistakable tang of spring in the crisp air, and that good smell of boiling sap! I could write of it all, for it is all a part of the maple sugar business—but alas, contrary to common belief among our customers, it is not *our* part of the business.

It was in February, 1920, that the few Smith alumnae in our neck of the woods met at a luncheon at my home for a Smith rally. Though we numbered only five, we were inspired with enthusiasm enough for a score, by the leader of our district, Lura Bugbee Cummings 1907, of Burlington. In a moment of great optimism the three St. Albans alumnae ventured to pledge jointly $700 and individually $50 each, to the $4,000,000 Fund. We hit upon the sale of maple products as being a distinctively Vermont way to raise the money, and one most likely to be successful. In less than a month's time our number was reduced to two by the death of Mary Read Brooks 1900; and Florence Merritt 1907 and I were left to carry the thing through: $800 to raise, and four years in which to do it.

Neither of us owned a sugar orchard, nor had we a cent of capital, but we managed without either, as it turned out. We set to work at once to find out who in our immediate vicinity made the very best maple sugar and maple syrup. It may be interesting to note that we buy our sugar from a woman. She makes literally tons of sugar each spring and fall. The syrup we get from different sources, because it is not always possible to secure a sufficient amount of the highest grade from one man. We have two or three men who save for us their finest product, and we have learned to test by taste, weight, color, and consistency to distinguish good syrup from that of inferior quality. There are as many grades as there are of apples, for instance. We have sold only first quality products, a policy that surely pays, for the satisfaction expressed by our customers is general and the number of instances where we have had to replace orders because of spoilage is very few, considering that our commodity is a perishable one. We did not stop at sugar and syrup, for we knew of a Mr. Story in a neighboring village who has a secret process for making most delicious maple cream, a comparatively little known product, which we were sure would be popular (as it has proved to be) if we could only give our prospective customers a taste. We induced Mr. Story to make up some tiny sample cups of his cream, which we sent to alumnae, choosing names at random from the *Alumnae Register*—at the same time advertising our maple sugar and syrup too, all under the name of "Green Mountain Goodies." It worked, and orders poured in. Also we found a market in Northampton, where my aunt, then in charge of 12 Green, sold quantities of the products for us to college and town folk. At the end of our first spring season, in July 1920, when all bills were paid, we sent Mr. McCallum a check for $150 toward our pledge. We were at least "on our way." In July 1923 we paid off the last $40, and indulged in a small dividend ourselves, feeling very jubilant at having met our obligations in less than the allotted time.

Two things doubtless helped us mightily. In the first place we felt justified in asking top-notch prices, since it was for the Fund, and our customers were all interested. Secondly, we were fortunate in having very good sugar years, those first three. The maple sugar business depends entirely upon the weather, a most uncertain quantity. Days must be sunny and warm enough for sap to run, and nights cold enough to freeze, to insure the best run. Sometimes warm days do not come until so late in the spring that the buds have started on the trees before sap will run—then it will be bitter. Storm and other variations of weather affect the "run," and consequently some years, like the last two or three, have been very poor sugar years, and the supply of high-grade syrup has been limited.

It sounds simple enough, just buying from the makers and selling to fellow alumnae, but there were many problems at first. For instance—how were we to pack and crate syrup for shipping? Some one told us of a heavy corrugated cardboard container made expressly for that purpose. That would be so easy. Just slip a can inside, tie it up, and send it on its way. We invested about $50 in said containers, only to find when they arrived that some of the syrup cans would not fit—some having square bases, others oblong! The next blow was that the Post Office would not accept them, fearing leakage. The express office has always been less fussy, but we soon decided that wooden crates were the thing, and we became fairly good carpenters. We had the boards cut to size and nailed them together ourselves. (I should hate to say how many cans I punctured at first!) Now we buy the crates for syrup and pails of sugar, all assembled except for the last strip of wood, which is quickly and easily nailed on. Our cardboard boxes, by the way, were by no means a total loss, for they were most useful for packing other orders. Other problems have arisen through the succeeding years, and each year we learn something new about our business. But we have gradually worked things out so that it runs along about as smoothly as any business can.

We have two busy seasons: in the spring, of course, which is the *real* sugar season, when sap runs and new syrup is made, and at Christmas time. The syrup for fall and winter use is sealed hot in big steel barrels, containing from 50 to 60 gallons. When properly barreled and stored it will retain its flavor for months, some even say for years. It is from this syrup that our fall and winter sugar and cream are made. We order in small quantities to insure a supply freshly made, and the products are just as delectable as those of the spring. In fact, we have been surprised to find that we do a larger business at

Christmas time than in the spring, partly, no doubt, because so many people use our products for Christmas gifts.

By the time our pledge was paid, the business was such a "going concern" that it seemed like wasting opportunities to drop it.   So we revised our price-list downward—our New England consciences not allowing us to profiteer for anything but the Fund—and kept on.   Each spring and fall we send our price-lists to all our customers, and once a year samples to a hundred or so new names from the *Alumnae Register*.   This task takes more consecutive time than the rest of the work, but a few evenings are usually sufficient to accomplish it. Booking and acknowledging orders, packing and shipping, can be done at odd moments, filling in chinks of time without becoming burdensome.   It can all be done at home, and with a little planning fits very comfortably into the general scheme of home life.   The correspondence has been a most pleasant part of the business, renewing old acquaintances and making new ones, all in a most friendly spirit.   Two friends in particular I have acquired through these channels for whom I have come to have a real affection, albeit I have never seen them.   We have had almost no trouble collecting bills.   I believe in the seven years only two alumnae accounts are uncollected.   That, of course, is due to our Smith clientele!   We have not become bloated bondholders.   Some years have been lean and some fat (ter), but the extra five and ten and twenty-five dollar dividends that occasionally fall to our lot are very useful.   Each year we think perhaps will be our last, but there is a certain fascination about the thing that keeps us going and that I presume will continue to keep us going as long as we live in the Green Mountain State.

Dancing from Coast to Coast

Charlotte Perry

Ever since 1912 Portia Mansfield (1910) and Charlotte Perry (1911) have been dancing through the alumnae records via their dancing camp or their concert and vaudeville troupe. Miss Perry writes us that last fall they brought eleven girls to New York to be the ballet in Rachel Crothers's new musical comedy, "Spring Magic," which was taken off to be rewritten eight days after its opening.   It left the ballet and producers penniless.   "We had to produce a vaudeville act," she writes, "with the little means left.   This act, the 'Perry Mansfield Dancers,' is now booked for a year on Loeb's circuit.   On the strength of this we sent for our concert company, the 'Portia Mansfield Dancers,' and they are booked for a whole year."

TO land on one's feet, professionally speaking, after such a fall, takes apprenticeship.   We served ours in three long winters of continuous travel, covering the country from Cleveland and Buffalo to the West Coast.   The Middle West, overpopulated with towns like Lima, Ohio, and Fort Wayne, Indiana, where no cooked food is available except pork and mashed potatoes, we usually did in the blizzard season.   Nebraska, Colorado, Utah, and Wyoming all had glorious bits of color and scenery.   But the part we loved most of all was spring in the Washington lumber towns.   There we drove in a huge auto bus with our baggage on a trailer and followed the windings of the Hood Canal through great green forests.   For three years we worked steadily from September to June, spent summers at camp and didn't even take a day off Christmas.

Parts of trouping are much nicer than other parts. We never could decide whether we preferred concert tours to vaudeville bookings. The concert tours are much harder, but we felt so much more stylish and had so much more class when we arrived in a town than we did when we were a unit on a vaudeville circuit.

In order to make a concert tour pay we had to play even the little towns, and our arrival always created a sensation. In Rexburg, Idaho, they actually met us with a sleigh and four horses and we swarmed all over it, and felt we wouldn't be doing it justice if we did not sing all the way down the street.

Hotels are of two types: the ones that boast of ancient grandeur and the ones that boast of new plumbing and a barber shop off the lobby. As a concert troupe we leave almost no room for anyone else in the lobby, and until we are stowed away upstairs the town congregates in the front entrance of the hotel and outside the plate glass window that usually frames the feet of the town's leading traveling men.

There is a routine usually followed on these tours, which allows part of the company to go immediately to sleep upon arrival, while the other part goes to the theater and unpacks baggage, costumes, and scenery. In the small towns there is a naïve lack of equipment that calls forth all of our ingenuity. Once we had to hang our back drop on the wall of the building with large nails. A man with a borrowed ladder did this. Then when at twelve-thirty we got around to taking down the back drop—the rest of the trunks being packed and strapped, the big stage doors open to the two-below-zero night, and the town's one drayman waiting to get things on the wagon for the 1.06 train—there was no ladder and no man to take down the back drop! It was twenty-two feet off the floor and even our acrobats were too tired to function helpfully. But the manager had a little boy—the kind that I am sure will develop into a Shubert or a Frohman, so quickly does he react to emergencies. He asked for a baton from the flies, and when they lowered it for him he sat on it as you would on a swing, holding one rope, and they pulled him up again until he was on a level with the nails and curtain. Then he just swung himself horizontally sideways parallel to the back wall of the theater and with each swing he pulled the curtain farther, jerking out a nail. This may not sound dangerous to a layman, but it was positively heroic and yet very simple. We made the 1.06 and didn't even send the little boy a box of chewing gum, for the life of a trouper is just one long giving up of companionships that might have proved pleasant.

But to continue with the differences. In vaudeville, there is less of that jumping about in day coaches, catching trains at dawn or worse, unpacking and packing the same night, and always facing new problems back stage in the way of lighting equipment, space for hanging drops, and dressing-rooms that require fur coats hung over the cracks to keep out the wind.

In Hoquiam, Washington, we went down after our first performance with our arms full of silver balloons, gilded swords, wooden shoes, and other evidences of our heroic struggle to please, and found our dressing-rooms under two feet of water. All thirteen of us rushed back up the narrow stairs, shouting to the stage crew that a terrible accident had happened and that somehow we had struck water. The stage crew didn't even bother to stop hauling up the ropes and sweeping off the stage, but answered in the tone of those forced always to explain natural phenomena to the uninitiated: "That is just the tide. It don't come much higher than it is now and it will go down again about nine o'clock." Of course, the fact that they had not mentioned this to us and that our shoes were floating gaily around, in and out of the dressing-rooms, meant nothing to the stage hands. The company, being well seasoned by this time, was greatly enamored of the scenery below stage. It got funnier and funnier as the tide got higher and more things appeared on the surface of the waves.

Now in vaudeville we are much less spectacular. We enter a town much less conspicuously than the undertakers' convention would, go to a hotel, and get mistaken for a traveling basket ball team or a group of school teachers. At the theater, only two are needed to hang and unpack and rehearse the music with the orchestra.

You may be garrulous and boasting to others on the bill if you happen to have met them before, or be of a garrulous, boasting type that greets his fellow workers with a complete history of his former triumphs in other and bigger cities than this and bigger and richer circuits than this. The true vaudevillian sets up a defense immediately against being associated with anything but the biggest cities and the best "houses." Our group had no class at all in vaudeville, for in some miraculous way they retained their sense of humor and had the bad taste to mention openly their pleasure in unimportant towns and cheap circuits. One apprentice month we spent on the "Circuit of Broken Hearts."

Once we took a boat all day in the sunshine in February on Lake Coeur d'Alene, which runs its clear blue fingers up among the green hills of Idaho. Just at dusk we met the town—a clean little white one scattered through a forest of lovely evergreens that came straight to the shore of the lake. A charming white-haired Catholic priest met us at the wharf. He said the whole town had seen our pictures on the tiny theater and couldn't wait to get a glimpse of beauty and hear a little music. We couldn't believe our eyes when we walked into the funny little theater, the size of a very small town movie, and found a little lattice fence built around the orchestra pit and covered with roses, to greet us. The stage was so small that we had to cut our movements in half, but we loved those people so that we tried to put everything into the face that there wasn't room to put in the feet. The applause was worth the effort. And yet a description of the Coeur d'Alene booking was what lost us our prestige when we played Columbus on the Keith circuit.

For three years we followed the profession and the baggage across the country. But that life is over for us and seems rosy and carefree and rich in freedom and distinction compared to our present one. We now are producers, and live, so to speak, on Broadway, and our only friends are Bookers. They drug us in the morning with promises of a booking or of five or six bookings, but by the time it is dusk on Broadway and the lights are making a yellow dust across the sky above the buildings the drug has worn off. Another day of patient waiting in offices is before us. Even that has its cheerful side, however, for life in the outer office of a booker is not dull and never lonely. The charms of that and the vicissitudes of giving birth to an act that will be acceptable in the eyes of the Chosen—that is *another* story.

Children and Poetry

MARJORIE COMSTOCK HART

"Begging the question as to whether it is possible to teach poetry at all," writes Mrs. Hart, Smith 1907, "I do feel that some aspects of poetry can be communicated and that is what I am trying to do in two of the private schools of Providence." She herself has taken several courses in poetry, one with Professor Robert Gay at Boston University and one with Professor Benjamin Clough at Brown, and a course in writing with Dr. Tanner of Boston University. She has had a number of poems published. It was, however, through her constant reading of poetry to her three children that her ideas crystalized, and she found an absorbing avocation. She is, incidentally, a sister of Alice Comstock, who writes the delightful article on apple raising elsewhere in this issue.

"Tiger, tiger burning bright
In the forests of the night"

WHENEVER I hear these lines I always thrill to them, not only on account of their intrinsic beauty, but also for the fact that they were the first lines of poetry that I ever heard my son Henry repeat of his own initiative. Then too, they are the verses that I hold responsible for the birth of my desire to give children some of the poetry to which they are not so commonly exposed.

I remember that I was singing to my three-year-old boy Henry some of the lyrics from "A Child's Garden of Verses," and that these lines of Blake slipped in half unconsciously, but it was these lines and not "The Friendly Cow" that my baby repeated to me of his own accord some days later. It was this fact that made me wonder why children were not given more often, along with the charming poems especially written for them, some of those other poems which stir the imagination of all who feel beauty through poetry's medium. For it is not necessary to understand a poem with the mind in order to be moved by it.

In the October *Atlantic* for 1925 there is a most stimulating essay on Science and Poetry by I. A. Richards, a fellow of Magdalen College, Cambridge. Mr. Richards divides poetry into two streams, the intellectual and the emotional or instinctive. The intellectual stream points to or reflects things, the instinctive stream deals with the things that thoughts reflect or point to, though of course these two streams have "innumerable intercommunications and affect each other intimately." Mr. Richards maintains that, though both are important in the appreciation of poetry, it is the instinctive quality, which comes more through the senses than through the mind, which is essential.

The schools have not emphasized this point in the past, and although there has been a change for the better lately, we still find children denied the inspiration of poetry that has always been considered too old for them, or we discover them learning merely well written verse like "Warren's Address to the Soldiers" or "The Village Blacksmith." Now there is no objection to using these verses for the purpose of instilling patriotism, or of teaching the beauty of honest labor, but there is a distinct objection to giving them to children as poetry. We must remember that children are poets, and if we give them the real thing, some of them at least will respond and will get that delight which

cannot be defined but which is immeasurable. If we give them merely pleasant verse, they will either find us out, or have their taste dulled at the outset.

Begging the question as to whether it is possible to teach poetry at all, I do
feel that some aspects of poetry can be communicated, and that is what I am
trying to do in two of the private schools in Providence, Rhode Island, the
Lincoln School and the Gordon School, for these two schools decided to try my
proposed poetry talks. As this is the first year of the work, and as the last term
is yet to come, it is hard to say just what has been accomplished.

During last summer I made an outline of what I wanted to say, and also an
anthology of poems for illustrations. These poems were taken for the most
part from other anthologies such as "This Singing World," "Silver Pennies,"
"Rainbow Gold," and "Golden Numbers." Most of the recent anthologies for
children are admirable because they include so much real poetry that before was
supposed to appeal only to adults. I especially like Mr. Untermeyer's "This
Singing World" and Mr. de la Mare's "Come Hither." I did not confine myself, however, to anthologies for children. Many of the poems used are to be
found in adult collections like "Verse of our Day" or "The Oxford Book of
English Verse," and in many cases I choose poems without recourse to any
anthology.

The talks were divided, like Gaul, into three parts. From October until the
Christmas vacation, we studied the technique of poetry, although I did not
frighten the children by that name. Then, until the spring vacation, the children were occupied in choosing poems to form an anthology that they themselves would like, and during the last term I hope to review the first term's
work and to give more time to the memorizing of poems which the children and
I will choose together.

As I go to the Lincoln School every week and to the Gordon School every
other week, I have arranged my talks a little differently for the two schools, but
I have used the same poems as material. I have the fourth, fifth, and sixth
grades at the Lincoln School each for twenty minutes, and at the Gordon School
I have the fourth and fifth grades each for the same length of time, and the
sixth and seventh grades together for twenty minutes also. The fourth and
fifth grades at the Gordon School comprise both boys and girls. In the other
grades at both schools my pupils are girls.

During the first term, devoted to poetry's technique, we talked of story
poetry, singing poetry, and acting poetry; of rhymed and unrhymed verse; of
poems with and without stanza form; of the different length stanzas; of rising
and falling rhythm; of accent and stress; of 1, 2, 3, 4, and 5 stress verse; and of
the use of words in poetry. I read poems to illustrate the different points, at
first telling the children what each poem illustrated, and then reading other
poems and asking the children to tell me what type of a poem it was, how many
stresses the verse had, how many stanzas there were, what was the effect of the
words or of the rhythm, or what picture flashed before them as I read, as the
case might be. Sometimes the children would get quite excited in discussing
these different points, and I felt that they enjoyed the poem more because they
were playing with it, and that they were using their ears as well as their minds.
Of course the important point is, not that the children recognize the different

elements of technique, but that by this means their interest is stimulated in the instinctive stream of poetry, which deals with the thoughts reflected, and that they are not forever occupied with the "poet's message."

The children were asked to bring poems to school to show these different points. Of course there were many mistakes, but the surprising thing was that there were so many children who got the idea and seemed to enjoy doing the work. I am sure that the hearty coöperation of the grade teachers brought about some of the results.

In the second term the children have been choosing the poems for their anthologies, under different classifications. One week they were asked to find unrhymed poems, the next a poem of a certain number of stresses in each verse, then a poem of so many verses to a stanza, a fairy poem, a lullaby, a patriotic or hero poem, a poem about a place, a humorous poem, and finally any poems that they loved the best. From these poems I am making my choice, so every poem in the anthology has been chosen by a child, and yet the teacher has had a say also. If five or more in a class choose the same poem, it will be included automatically.

In every grade, "Barbara Frietchie," "Paul Revere's Ride," or a similar type of poem was chosen, but I think that it is mainly because these poems tell a story, and because the children are so familiar with them. It delighted me to find that every grade responded to Walter de la Mare's "Isle of Lone," to "The Ancient Mariner," and to Matthew Arnold's "The Deserted Merman." Indeed one grade chose this long poem to learn by heart to recite on Poetry Day.

Of course I am suggesting to the children that they write poetry, but only if they have something to say and want to say it in verse. If they keep eyes, ears, and spirit awake and if they read a great deal of poetry this desire is likely to come. Already some of the children have written good original verse.

I feel that the only excuse I have for doing this work is that I love both children and the poetry which I read to them. I can but hope that our talks may help each child to regard poetry as a part of his life, for if a child lives in the atmosphere of poetic beauty, he will seek poetry for joy and consolation as he grows older. He will have something which the world cannot take away. Perhaps in times of disillusionment he may turn to Hamlet's words:

> "If thou didst ever hold me in thy heart
> Absent thee from felicity a while
> And in this harsh world draw thy breath in pain
> To tell my story."

If he does, his spirit will be healed, for words like these always bring peace.

Hide and Seek

Name	First Class Mail returned from
Christine Adams 20	5525 Center Av., Pittsburgh, Pa.
Helen Ames 11	c/o National City Bank, Kansas City, Mo.
Mrs. W. Howard Bailey 10 (Marion Richards)	Conway, N. H.
Marion Barnhart 16	1160 Gaylord St., Denver, Colo.
Mrs. Sheldon Booth 11 (Corinne Barbour)	87 Grand View Av., Wollaston, Mass.
Pauline Breustedt 21	471 Park Av., N. Y. C.
Clarinda Buck 21	5609 Kenwood Av., Chicago.
Mrs. William W. Carr 92 (Margaret MacDougall)	43112 9th Av. N. E., Seattle, Wash.
Mrs. W. Paxton Cary 07 (Jeannette Welch)	300 San Fernando St., San Diego, Calif.
Edna Donnell 16	520 E. 77 St., N. Y. C.
Mary Dupee 24	5221 Cornell Av., Chicago.
Frances Eisner 24	174 Main St., Poughkeepsie, N. Y.
Zena Freedman 22	1040 Bryant Av., N. Y. C.
Mrs. Glen H. Gardner 21 (Dorothy Butts)	18805 Jordan Av., Hollis, N. Y.
Alletta Gillette 07	305 Bellevue Av. N., Seattle, Wash.
Marion Howe 24	4 Grove St., N. Y. C.
Mary Judson 99	604 W. 146 St., N. Y. C.
Mrs. Harry Keeler Jr. 22 (Marion Crozier)	407 A Av., Coronado, Calif.
Mrs. Walter Keplinger 00 (Henrietta Brown)	814 N. Wallace St., Indianapolis, Ind.
Marion Kohlrausch 17	129 W. 13 St., N. Y. C.
Mrs. Joseph A. McLinley 18 (Adeline Moore)	Virginia Court Apts., Vallejo, Calif.
Edda Morgan 16	54 Scott St., Chicago.
Mrs. Carl J. Norton 07 (Edna Higgins)	R. D. 2, Box 139, Yakima, Wash.
Mrs. Henry L. Potter 12 (Doris Dow)	2856 W. 100 St., Chicago.
Mrs. Joseph W. Ress 22 (Gertrude Schwartz)	2464 Geneva Ter., Chicago.
Helen Richards 00	310 W. 95 St., N. Y. C.
Mrs. George Roehrig 07 (Gertrude Cruden)	324½ Husband St., Stillwater, Okla.
Mrs. Thomas L. Robinson 12 (Elizabeth Wilson)	Alamosa, Colo.
Louise Rowley 23	837 W. Center St., Rochester, Minn.
Martha Sims 14	Spartanburg, S. C.
Mrs. Bertha S. Stanford 00 (Bertha Sanford)	1841 University Av., N. Y. C.
Mrs. Martin Tevlin 14 (Dorothy Hannigan)	233 River St., Braintree, Mass.
Anna Wallace 13	138 Center St., West Haven, Conn.
Jessie Williams 18	130 E. 57 St., N. Y. C.
L. Ethel Woolf 07	176 Capitol Av., Atlanta, Ga.

Current Alumnae Publications

COMPILED BY NINA E. BROWNE

ALLEN, MARJORIE S. 1906 (Mrs. Seiffert). Ballad of a Queen [and] Ballad of the Dolphin's Daughter, in Poetry, Feb.— Ballad of a Scarlet Shawl, in Saturday Rev. of Lit., Jan. 22.—†Thistle and Thorn, in Outlook, Feb. 9.—Ballads of the Singing Bowl. N. Y. Scribner.

APPLETON, HELEN L. 1908 (Mrs. Read). The Transformations of a Museum, in Arts, Mar.

BARBOUR, ELLEN G. 1903 (Mrs. Glines). Five poems, in Palms, Feb.—Three poems, in Poetry, Apr.—Law, in Writer's Monthly, Feb.

†BEAUPRÉ, OLIVE K. 1904 (Mrs. Miller). Tales Told in Holland. Chicago. Book House for Children.

BRANCH, ANNA H. 1897. A Charmed Life. Review, in Yale Rev., Jan.

CHILTON, ELEANOR C. 1922. Shadows Waiting. N. Y. John Day Co.

COMSTOCK, MARJORIE S. 1907 (Mrs. Hart). A Boy Reads, in Lyric, Mar.

CONDÉ, BERTHA, 1895. A Way to Peace, Health and Power. N. Y. Scribner.

CUTTER, ELIZABETH R. 1896 (Mrs. Morrow). Youth Passes, in Contemporary Verse, Feb.–Mar.

DAMON, INEZ F. Music 1900–03. Teaching the Unity of Art, in Jour. of N. E. A., Feb.

DEFOREST, CHARLOTTE B. 1901. Kobe College in Perspective, in Congregationalist, Mar. 17.

DUNBAR, OLIVIA H. 1894 (Mrs. Torrance). Feminism Plus Single Tax, in New Republic, Jan. 12.—Reformers, in Yale Rev., Apr.

†DUNTON, EDITH K. 1897 (Margaret Warde, Pseud.). Sparrow, in Youth's Companion, Sept. 16.—Left or Right, in Y. C., Sept. 23. —The Wrong Ticket, in Y. C., Oct. 14.— Puck of Pendleton, in Y. C., Nov. 4.— Turnips and Platinum, in Y. C., Nov. 11.—The Outsider, in Y. C., Feb. 3.

FALLOWS, ALICE K. 1897. Everybody's Bishop: the Life of Rt. Rev. Samuel Fallows, D.D. N. Y. J. H. Sears.—Bishop's Beer, in Century, Feb.

†FOSTER, M. LOUISE, 1891. Life of Lavoisier. Smith College Monograph, 1.

FULLER, CAROLINE M. 1895. Kitten Whiskers. N. Y. Duffield.

†GOODALE, DORA R. Art 1890. The Test of the Sky Phila. Dorrance Co.

HART, ELIZABETH H. 1924. The Heaven of Virgins, in Modern Language Notes, Feb.

HAWKINS, ETHEL W. 1901. Introduced by Mr. Housman, in Atlantic, Mar.

HERMAN, MAIDA, 1912 (Mrs. Solomon). The Dissatisfied Married Woman. Radio Talk. Station WEEI, Nov. 29. Reported in

† Already in collection.

†Boston Herald, Feb. 21, as All Groups Among Women Show Discontent.

HOPKINS, ALICE L. 1905. The College Library, in Simmons College Rev., Nov.

HUMPHREY, ZEPHINE, 1896 (Mrs. Fahnestock). Winterwise. N. Y. Dutton.

JENCKES, ALICE C. 1922. St. Jerome, in Boston Museum of Fine Arts, Oct.— Adoration of the Magi, in Dec.—Two paintings by El Greco, in Apr.

†LYNCH, CAROLINE V. 1894. The Housing of Women Students in Boston, in Our Boston, Aug.

MCAFEE, HELEN, 1903. Ancient and Modern Legends, in Yale Rev., Apr.—In Kemalist Turkey, in Saturday Rev. of Lit., Feb. 26.—On Not Keeping a Diary, in Bookman, Feb.

†MAHER, AMY G. 1906. Are Women's Wages a Special Problem? Toledo. Information Bureau on Women's Work— Trend of Women's Wages, Ohio, 1924. Toledo. Inform. Bureau.

MAXSON, RUTH P. 1905 (Mrs. Aughiltree). †Just Where to Strike, in Detective Story Mag., Jan. 29.—Lord of the Changing Seasons, in Country Bard, Winter no.

†MERRILL, GEORGIANA, 1890–92 (Mrs. Root). Local Federation the Next Step. Boston. Pilgrim Press.

†MERZ, ELIZABETH L. 1919 (Mrs. Butterfield). Meeting Waters, Anthem. Jamestown, N. Y. Danielson Music House.

ORMSBEE, MARY R. 1907 (Mrs. Whitten). The New Servant. N. Y. Doubleday, Page.

†PEASE, DOROTHY, 1911. Actinobacillus Meningitis, in Amer. Jour. of Diseases of Children, Dec.

PETHERBRIDGE, MARGARET, 1919 (Mrs. Farrar). The Cross Word Puzzle Book. 7th Ser. N. Y. Simon and Schuster.

†PUFFER, ETHEL D. 1890 (Mrs. Howes). Coöperating Mothers, in Woman Citizen, Feb.

REED, CLARA E. 1901. More Notes on Cliff Swallows, in Auk, Jan.

ROBERTSON, WINIFRED, 1911. Mexico, in Mexico, Autumn no.

SCUDDER, VIDA D. 1884. Brother John. Boston. Little, Brown.—†The Bishop's Crusade to Stir our Wills to Action, in The Witness, Jan. 20.—†Review of Galahad, in Atlantic Bookshelf, Feb.—International Value of Christian Ethics, by William Younger, in Anglican Theol. Rev., Jan.— †The Problems of Socialism—from a College Window, in New Leader, Jan. 29. —†The Social Conscience in American Churches, in Commonwealth (London), Feb.—†Sons of Francis, in Churchman, Mar. 5.

SHERMAN, ELLEN B. 1891. A Book of Enchantments, in Roundabout, May.—Kipling's Attitude, in Saturday Rev. of Lit., Mar. 19.

SPEARE, DOROTHY, 1919 (Mrs. Christmas). A Virgin of Yesterday. N. Y. Doran.—Sweet but Dumb, in Pictorial Rev., Apr.

†STOCKS, ESTHER H. 1924. Coöperating Mothers, in Woman Citizen, Feb.—A Nursery School for Mothers, in Amer. Children, Mar.

STOREY, VIOLET A. 1920. A Certain Little Girl, in N. Y. Sun, Feb. 28.—Discovery, in N. Y. Telegram, Mar. 21.—Sleep, in N. Y. Tel., Mar. 22.—Pitch Lake, Trinidad, in

† Already in collection.

N. Y. Tel., Mar. 29.—Frontispiece, in Commonweal, Jan. 19.—Gothic, in London Spectator, Feb. 26.—Pumpkins, in College Humor, Jan.—Remnant, in N. Y. Times, Jan. 17.—A Butterfly Wing Pin, in N. Y. T., Feb. 11.—In February, in N. Y. T., Feb. 21.—To an Old Lady, Dead, in Churchman, Feb. 19.—Woman's Exchange. Barbadoes, Christian Sci. Monitor, Jan. 18.

SWETT, MARGERY, 1917. An Educational Experiment, in North Amer. Rev., Mar.—Yaddo, in Poetry, Mar.

WARE, KATHARINE, 1894 (Mrs. Smith). Another Chance to Help Atlanta University, in Congregationalist, Jan. 20.

The President Burton Memorial Fund

The President Burton Memorial Fund cannot be an adequate memorial to the second president of Smith College, but in proportion to its size it will render the service he was so eager for. The willing and glad response to this proposed memorial is in itself a tribute which he would have appreciated.

The figures for the classes are listed below, giving those of 1911–1920 separately as they started through their committees in the fall. Their total is $13,549.32.

1911	$703.00	1916	$1,485.00
1912	1,330.25	1917	1,556.00
1913	1,568.50	1918	1,300.57
1914	2,907.50	1919	889.50
1915	1,234.50	1920	573.50

Almost all the other classes are represented in the Fund and it is hoped before June that every class will have contributed. The total from the classes who were not in college during President Burton's administration is $4,277.20.

There have been a few gifts from other sources. An extra of $5.24 from the Alumnae Association, Faculty gifts of $101, and gifts from six clubs as follows:

Eastern Connecticut	$50.00
Montclair	100.00
Brooklyn	200.00
Grand Rapids	100.00
Cincinnati	100.00
New York	250.00

The grand total to date is $18,732.76.

Although the pledge cards in the Alumnae Association mailing were for those who had not been informed of the Fund, some who had already responded sent in additional contributions. The Committee hopes that there will be many more gifts before June so that the Fund may be a fuller expression of our devotion to President Burton, our loyalty to Smith, and our desire to make further education possible for those who should have it. Contributions, with name, class and address, may be sent to Jean Paton, 56 Avon St., New Haven, Conn. Payment of pledges should be marked as such, and checks made payable to the President Burton Memorial Fund.

JEAN PATON, *Chairman, for the Committee*

LET US TALK OF MANY THINGS

THE TIME HAS COME

THE Time Has Come to talk of so many things that the editor is desperate and is sorely tempted to throw up her pencil and say, "Do read this QUARTERLY through. Everything that anybody knows about Smith College past, present, and future is packed in somewhere, and it is all important and tremendously interesting." That is what we really feel like saying even after putting together page after page and page after page of copy, but we are afraid to risk it because we suspect that some busy people after running quickly over their class notes (and everybody else's perhaps) and dipping into the News from Northampton (we have nearly drowned in campus news there is so much of it) will—we hope, reluctantly—put the magazine down with the optimistic remark, "I'll leave the rest until I can really sit down to it." And, knowing life as she is lived, that is a state of affairs that we simply cannot bear.

The Time Has Come. Sit down to it now! Read the thrilling news about the establishment of the William Allan Neilson Chair of Research on page 259. That is not only honoring President Neilson in a perfectly stunning way but is also advancing the academic prestige of Smith very signally. Note also on page 324 the honorary degree which the University of Edinburgh is conferring on him. Gaze on the amazing figures about housekeeping at Smith (we are sure no Ask Me Another is needed to tell you who Gargantua is, and for a real honest to goodness Ask Me Another we refer you to page 321). Gaze on our illustrious contributors, not forgetting a particularly delightful group in What Alumnae Are Doing. In fact, don't stop reading until—well, have you by any chance noticed that the inside of the back cover is filled with information about Smith College?

The Time Has Come for the Alumnae Association department to bristle with hints of Commencement, and the time has come to offer the keys of the College once more to all its far-faring daughters. We know one who is coming from India, because a card came only yesterday saying, in effect, "I've read my February QUARTERLY to-day from cover to cover; do hold the May one for me in America for I am coming back to Northampton in June." No need to wonder whether she can shut her eyes and see the "happy river meadows" and catch the lacy shadows of the great New England elms on the soft green of the campus on an evening in spring!

The Time Has Come this year for another thing as well. President Neilson is rounding out his tenth year as President of Smith College, and although a tenth birthday party may not be as pretentious as a fiftieth it is a joyous and significant occasion for us all and one that we shall delight to celebrate, for there are thousands of us alumnae who appreciate what great things he has done as our chief executive and who are eager to join in the song the undergraduates sing to him so affectionately:

"There's a bonny Scotch laddie we've loved from the start,
We pledge our allegiance; he's won all our heart—
And we'll follow his guiding beyond and away
For we love him forever and ever and aye."

Yes, we certainly do suggest that you begin right now to make your plans, as the Lady from India has made hers, to come back to Northampton in June for

The Time Has Come.

E. N. H. 1903

HOW CAN SHE DO IT?

GERTRUDE BLATCHFORD STEARNS'S article in the February QUARTERLY has caused a ripple that has gone even beyond Smith circles, and we wish there were space to quote all the comments, written and spoken, that have come to our editorial ears. Those ears, let us say at the outset, listen sympathetically alike to those who applaud Mrs. Stearns's achievements, to the doubting Thomases who need more proof, and to those who neatly and succinctly say, "It can't be done." We mention this fact because one communication sent to the administration by a Gentleman from Philadelphia remarks pleasantly:

As this article appears in your magazine it must have the sponsoring of your magazine. The editor sponsors the fundamentals held down in Mrs. Stearns's article. These fundamentals are that we are privileged to get married, bring offsprings into the world, and neglect them while we go off tutoring, instructing, and educating others, fondly relying on the fact that we are so highly intellectual; that we are so highly intelligent, our offsprings will be marvelous prodigies, tutored by a high school student.

Help! Help! The editor is a poor lorn bachelor maid with no "offsprings" at all, but if she were a married lady with a dozen she would not sponsor anybody's fundamentals *so long as she was editor.* All she is concerned with is that the opinions voiced in the articles she publishes are honest opinions of the authors; and in this particular instance she not only has Mrs. Stearns's written word, but she has had a long interview with Mrs. Stearns herself and is sure that she does all the things she says she does and that she is honestly convinced that neither her babies, her husband, nor her home is neglected. We have seen pictures of the two oldest children and they look as though they were brought up line upon line, precept upon precept on Holt (if Holt is still the Milton Works on baby feeding!). Further than that we dare not go, but after passing on Mrs. Stearns's blanket invitation to all sceptical mother-housewives to "come and spend the week-end or longer with me and observe the conditions you find here" we proceed to a few quotations from letters.

One mother of one writes:

It is probably only a notion of mine that children are copyists, and that they become as much as possible like the grown-ups with whom they associate. Are my four years at Smith a pleasant dream, or do I recall words of wisdom faithfully transcribed to my notebook, in effect: "What price heredity? Environment is the thing." Untrained help! I've had plenty of it when engagements away from home made it necessary. . . . Having just been to a lecture by Dr. Adler I am impressed anew with a child's infinite complexities and the thought and patience that are necessary to see and comprehend its reactions. Dr. Adler said very little about untrained help in dealing with them, as I recall.

Do not think for a moment that I am completely satisfied with housekeeping and child-raising as a métier. The fascination of faring forth in the morning to struggle in the wide, wide world of which we used to sing so lustily has me in its grip at times, I confess, and when my child is past pre-school age and I can afford trained help to assist in keeping my small house a pleasant place to live in, perhaps I too can have an Activity. At present the price would be too high.

Finally, as I sit back smugly with 'How I Do It" down in black and white before me, I confront myself with a question that has graced many a tea table discussion of late. Was our college education intended to fit us for filling every minute of our time with activity or was it designed to enable us to perform the necessary tasks that confront us thoroughly and intelligently, and to enjoy profitably the leisure that remained? E.L.W.

And a mother of two writes:

. . . Mrs. Stearns is so perfectly satisfied with her system it seems useless to challenge her. True, there is much in her article to commend. I agree with and practice her theory of "cooking once and eating twice." Neither am I a daily duster, but I must admit that were my house dusted only once a week it would not be a very comfortable place to live in, even if things were in place. I have only two children, aged three and six, and instead of an inexperienced girl every day I have an experienced one every other day who washes, irons, cooks, and cleans on those days. In accordance with Gertrude Stearns's premise that someone to stay with the children is the first requisite, it will be seen at a glance that I usually stay home three days a week and on the other three fare forth to college club, lectures, charity and community work, bridge (I must admit), and other activities that make up the average busy life. This is merely to show that my duties both inside and outside the home are quite comparable with those of Gertrude Stearns. . . . Her situation, I think, is rather unique, for she must have no nerves, perfect children, and an angelic husband.

But the pronouncement that should really strike terror into the soul not only of Mrs. Stearns but of all college graduates whether or not they are the mothers of "offsprings" comes from that same Gentleman from Philadelphia. (He by the way saw the article as it was reprinted in a Philadelphia daily paper.) He goes on, from the paragraph previously quoted:

I sincerely believe that it would be a good thing if an article such as this was placed in the hands of every college-hoping family; it might be brought about that the American people could begin to see what collegiate education was leading us to.

The QUARTERLY rests the case!

BULLETIN BOARD

VESPERS.—The vesper speakers since Feb. 1 have been: Rev. Paul Jones of New York City; Dean Shailer Mathews, D.D., LL.D., of the University of Chicago; Canon Harold A. Prichard, M.A., of Mount Kisco, N. Y.; Rev. Arthur L. Kinsolving of Amherst; Rev. Henry Sloane Coffin, D.D., of New York City; Bishop Francis J. McConnell, D.D., LL.D., of Pittsburgh; President Neilson; President J. Edgar Park, D.D., of Wheaton College; Mr. S. K. Ratcliffe of England.

CONCERTS.—The fifth concert of the Smith College Concert Course was given Feb. 21 by Pablo Casals, violoncellist; and the sixth was given Mar. 8 by the Boston Symphony Orchestra. Fritz Kreisler, violinist, appeared Mar. 21 as the seventh number of the course, and the Cleveland Symphony, Apr. 30, gave the eighth concert.

The second concert in the Chamber Music Series was given by the Paul Shirley Ensemble in Sage Hall, Feb. 9. The third in this series was given Mar. 16 by the London String Quartet.

An organ recital was given Feb. 20 by Louis Vierne of the Notre Dame Cathedral, Paris.

Besides these concerts of the regular courses, the college musical program has included a piano recital by Katharine Gorin 1915; a musical vesper service by the Smith College Glee Club, Professors Marie Milliette, Ruth Willian, and Postley Sinclair; a concert by the Smith College Symphony Orchestra; a faculty recital by members of the Department of Music; a recital by Professor Ruth Willian, violin, and Professor Hall, piano; a Beethoven Commemoration Recital by members of the Department of Music; and an organ recital.

LECTURES.—The following lectures have been given: "The Nationalist Movement in China" by Mr. Grover Clark, editor of the *Peking Daily Leader;* "Lincoln Likenesses" (illustrated) by Miss Helen Nicolay of Washington; "The International House" by Mrs. Harry E. Edmonds of New York; "Dorothy Wordsworth" by Professor Ernest de Sélincourt, D.Litt., of the University of Birmingham (auspices of the Department of English); "Man and the Universe" by Professor Michael I. Pupin, Ph.D., LL.D., Sc.D., of Columbia University; "The Atom as a Source of Energy" by Professor Arthur Haas of the University of Vienna (auspices of the Department of Physics); "Les Voyages d'Autrefois sur les routes de France" (illustrated) by Professor Hélène Cattanès (French); "The Outlook in Europe" by Mr. G. P. Gooch (auspices of the Department of History); "The Genius and the Criminal in the Light of Biology" by Professor Jon Mjoen of the Winderen Laboratory at Oslo (auspices of the Departments of Sociology and Zoölogy); "Summer Schools Abroad" (brief addresses by members of the Committee on Exchange of Students, Doheny Hackett '27, and others); "Amsterdam in the Seventeenth Century" (illustrated) by Professor Adriaan J. Barnouw, Ph.D., of Columbia University; "Some Ancient Theatres, Mostly Roman" (illustrated) by Professor Wright (Latin); "The Relation of Roumanian to Other Romance Languages" by Mr. Léon Feraru of the Department of Romance Languages, Columbia University (auspices of the Department of Italian); "Rasgos esencials de la fonética española" by Dr. Tomás Narvarro Tomas of Madrid (auspices of the Department of Spanish); "The International Aspects of Immigration" by Professor Donald R. Taft of Wells College.

A lecture was given Mar. 15 by Francis Brett Young under the auspices of the

Hampshire Bookshop on ' The Writing of
Novels," and one by Richard Halliburton
on Apr. 26.

At the meetings of the International Rela-
tions Club the following subjects have been
discussed: "Foreign Influence in China";
"The United States in Mexico and Nicaragua.
Is It Intervention or Protection?"; "Mexican
Problems and the Policy of the United States."

A series of three lectures on Poetry was held
at the People's Institute in February and
March. The first lecture, on "Ballads," was
given by President Neilson, the second and
third being conducted by Professors Rice and
Grace Hazard Conkling.

WASHINGTON'S BIRTHDAY.—The speaker at
the morning exercises was Professor William
Ernest Hocking, Ph.D., Litt.D., of Harvard
University. His subject was "Imitation and
Its Cure."

COMMENCEMENT SPEAKER.—The Commencement speaker for June 1927 will be Dr.
Harry Emerson Fosdick of the Park Avenue
Baptist Church, New York, and a Trustee of
the College.

THE LIBRARY.—A bibliography of Na-
thaniel Hawthorne, compiled by Miss Nina
Browne, the college archivist, has been given
by her to the Library. The bibliography is
one of a series of literary bibliography by
Houghton Mifflin Co. It is the second of
Miss Browne's gifts this year, the first being
volumes five through thirteen of the *Library
Journal*, which were needed to complete a
series already in the possession of the Library.

Miss Marion E. Dodd 1906, of the Hampshire Bookshop, has presented the Library
with a facsimile of the manuscript of Milton's
minor poems. The original of the manuscript
is in the Library of Trinity College, Cambridge.

Another gift to the Library, a book entitled "Ancient Furniture, A History of Greek,
Etruscan and Roman Furniture," was made
by Mrs. Gisela M. A. Richter, Litt.D., of the
Metropolitan Museum of Art in New York.

LYMAN PLANT HOUSE.—The annual exhibition of spring-flowering bulbs by the class in
Horticulture was held Mar. 10–13.

THE SMITH COLLEGE MUSEUM OF ART.—
The first of the exhibitions since Feb. 1 consisted of examples of painting and sculpture of
the Italian Renaissance, loaned through the
courtesy of Sir Joseph Duveen, Bart.

Photographs taken by Professor Kennedy
during the summers of 1925 and 1926 made up
the next exhibit. These photographs were

23–26. A one-term course in educational and vocational guidance is being given this semester by Miss Blake.

ART.—Professor Kennedy gave a series of eight lectures, beginning Jan. 31, on "Some Painters and Sculptors of Florence in the Renaissance," at the Central High School in Springfield.

BIBLE.—Professor Harlow gave the first of two talks on "Sure Guideposts in Your Life Work Choice" at the Central Congregational Church, Worcester, Mass., Jan. 8. Professor and Mrs. Harlow will conduct a European tour this summer, providing unusual sight-seeing opportunities and a series of conferences with important religious and political leaders of European affairs.

The Bible class in Christianity and the Present Social Order left Apr. 22 for a three-day visit to the New York slums and labor headquarters, to study the problems about which they have been theorizing. The experiment was carried out under the direction of Professor Harlow.

CHEMISTRY.—Professor Mary Louise Foster has been invited to return next year to the School of Pharmacy of the University of Madrid, where she taught seven years ago, to equip their new chemical laboratory and organize a major in chemistry. Further details will be given in the July QUARTERLY.

ECONOMICS AND SOCIOLOGY.—Professor Barnes addressed the Brooklyn Jewish Center, Jan. 17, on "The Implications of Living in the Twentieth Century." He took part in a debate on the Volstead Act held at the First Presbyterian Church, Jamaica, N. Y., Jan. 25. On Feb. 5 he spoke before the City Club of Baltimore and on Feb. 9 addressed the fiftieth annual convention of the North Carolina Conference for Social Service held in Raleigh, N. C. He addressed the Pennsylvania Conference on Social Welfare, Feb. 12. Mr. Barnes was the speaker at the Women's City Club of Cleveland, Feb. 21. His topic was "The Responsibility for the World War."

Professor Hankins debated with Dr. Shailer Mathews of Chicago at the Brooklyn Institute of Arts and Sciences on Mar. 23, upholding the negative side of the subject "Resolved, that a belief in immortality is essential to a preservation of morality." Mr. Hankins conducted a visit to Welfare Island, Mar. 26. More than 75 Smith students took advantage of this opportunity to observe well-conducted charitable and reformatory institutions.

Professor Orton gave two lectures in Chicago upon invitation of the Chicago Smith Club, Mar. 31 and Apr. 2.

ENGLISH.—Professor Grace Hazard Conkling read selections from her own poetical works and those of her daughter at the Century Club of Rochester, Feb. 3. "Contemporary Poetry" was the subject of her lecture at the Knox School, Cooperstown, N. Y., Feb. 25. Mrs. Conkling spoke at the luncheon given by Harriet Monroe, editor of *Poetry*, at the Henry Jewett Repertory Theatre, Boston, Mar. 10.

Professor Rice gave a lecture on "The Intellectual Front of H. G. Wells" at the opening meeting of the Traveler's Club of Springfield, Feb. 23.

FRENCH.—Professor Schinz made a lecture tour in the Middle West, in March, stopping at Bloomington, Ind., Cleveland, O., and Oberlin, O. His subjects were "The Modernity of J. J. Rousseau" and "The Centenary of Romanticism."

Professor Guilloton gave a lecture on "The Island of Dread" before the Alliance Française, in Portland, Me., Feb. 7.

Professor Robert has received the Palmes Académiques from the French Government and is now an officer d'Académie. This honor is awarded to those who have done exceptional work along educational lines and was given to Professor Robert by the Minister of Public Instructions, M. Herriot.

Professor Guiet was elected Vice-president of the Association of Professors of Romance Languages at its meeting in Holyoke, Apr. 8.

GOVERNMENT.—Professor Kimball discussed the Mexican-Nicaraguan disturbance before the Women's Republican Club of Rhode Island, Jan. 14. He spoke before the same club Feb. 11 on the McNary-Haugen bill.

GREEK.—Professor Julia Caverno presided as President of the Classical Association at its meetings at Holy Cross College, Worcester, in April.

HISTORY.—Professor Fay is conducting three courses for graduate students at Columbia during the second semester. The courses are: "German History from 1871–1914"; "The General Causes of the World War"; and a seminar on "German Policy before the War."

MATHEMATICS.—Professor Harriet Cobb spoke before the Culture Club of Springfield, Mass., concerning the social conditions in China.

MUSIC.—Professor Duke and Mme. Cora Claiborne, a Springfield contralto, gave a joint recital in Springfield on Mar. 23.

Professor Gorokhoff is conducting an Easthampton (Mass.) Choral Club.

Professor Welch gave a series of four lectures concerning music before the Westfield Women's Club during January and February.

PHYSICS.—Professor Jones returned this semester after a half-year leave of absence, which he spent at Yale. He read a paper on "The Nodal Lines in Bells" at the meeting of the Physics Association held in New York, Feb. 25 and 26. Mr. Jones has done much experimenting with the Carlile chime at Smith and during his sabbatical absence he worked with the chime in the Harkness Tower at Yale.

Professor Waterman gave an address on "The College Entrance Examination in Physics" at a meeting of the Eastern Association of Physics Teachers held at Harvard University on Mar. 11.

ZOÖLOGY.—Professor Parshley will teach during the summer at the University of Chicago.

FACULTY SCIENCE CLUB.—At the meeting held on Mar. 4, Professor Priscilla Fairfield spoke on "Modern Theories about the Evolution of Stars." Professor Elizabeth Genung spoke Apr. 22 on "Some Problems in Standardizing Biological Stains."

PUBLICATIONS.—Bassett, John S. "Expansion and Reform."

Neilson, William Allan. "Charles W. Eliot, the Man and His Beliefs."

See Trustee Minutes for Sabbatical absences, leaves of absence, and promotions.

———

OTHER NEWS.—Professors Margaret Scott (History), Edna Shearer (Philosophy), and Caroline Bourland (Spanish) sailed Feb. 10 for Genoa. They plan to return to this country in September, after studying and traveling in Europe.

In order to help pay for equipment, the parents' organization of the Nursery School gave a skit Apr. 25 in the Alumnae Gymnasium, entitled "A Typical Morning at the Nursery School," the leading parts being played by various faculty parents.

In March a daughter was born to Professor Curti (History) and Mrs. Margaret Curti (Psychology); and a son to Professor and Mrs. Guilloton (French).

A son was born Apr. 6 to Mrs. Henry Chandler (Florence McArdle) of Westfield, Mass.

ceive an official certificate must have spent two week-ends at the Outing Club Cabins.

Classes in horseback riding are being conducted by Professor Abby Belden during spring term. This is the first time such a course has been offered as an organized sport.

Smith took first place with 24½ points in the telegraphic swimming meet with Michigan, Wisconsin, and Iowa Universities which was held on Mar. 3. The girls swam in their own pools, the results being telegraphed to the other colleges. The other scores were Wisconsin 13½, Michigan 11½, Iowa 1½.

The regular swimming teams have been announced as follows: *Senior:* Mary Arbenz, Elinor Chaplin, Margaret Day, Clarice Goldstein, Elizabeth Lovell, Wilhelmina Luten, Kathryn Levy, Priscilla Page, Doris Pinkham, Edith Rau, Edith Tyler, Leslie Winslow. *Junior:* Kathryn Brickner, Lucille Flank, Marian Field, Mary Gaylord, Bettina Griebel, Margaret Lee, Caroline Schauffler, Marion Smith, Sylvia Ward. *Sophomore:* Mary Couch, Mary Crafts, Beulah Greenburgh, Mary Hollister, Cordelia Job, Catherine Jones, Janet Kauffman, Yvonne Kopetzky, Jeanie Kerns, Claire Levin, Caroline Mowry, Rosa Mitchell, Jessica Scott, Elizabeth Warren, Hildegard Willmann. *Freshman:* Helen Black, Sylvia Goldman, Adelaide Hall, Mary Howell, Ruth Hunt, Edith Hess, Rachel Perry, Katharine Prichard, Ethel Strock, Jane Stewart.

The results of the interclass competition which included three separate meets are as follows: Seniors 54½, juniors 137, sophomores 37½, freshmen 12.

Water polo began this fall as an experiment and was carried on informally for a time without any regularly selected teams. But as the season wore on, teams were selected, and water polo took its place among the other sports at Smith. The juniors won the final game in the Odd-Even Competition.

The annual demonstration of the work done in the classes in Physical Education took place on Mar. 12. The department presented classes in rhythms, clogging, Danish and Swedish gymnastics, besides the final game of the basket ball tournament.

AWARDS.—"S" pins were awarded Apr. 13 to the six upperclassmen best exemplifying the highest ideal of a Smith student. See page 331.

Prizes and fellowships will be announced in the July issue when the list is complete.

CONFERENCES.—The annual intercollegiate literary magazine conference was held at Smith, Feb. 11 and 12, to edit the second edition of *Young Pegasus,* which is an anthology of the college verse and prose selected by undergraduates from material drawn from college publications and published by the Dial Press. The colleges represented were Columbia, Goucher, Barnard, Wilson, Harvard, Vassar, Mount Holyoke, Williams, Yale, Bryn Mawr, Smith.

Smith sent several delegates to the Drama conference held at Yale University the weekend of Feb. 11.

Twenty delegates attended the Western New England division of the "Christian Way of Life Conference" which met for the fourth time at Northfield, Mass., Feb. 11–14.

. DEBATING UNION.—The Dartmouth-Smith debate took place Feb. 25 on the subject: "Resolved, that Great Britain should abandon the Stevenson plan for the limitation on the export of rubber." Gertrude Perelmutter and Elizabeth Stoffregen '28 supported the negative and were defeated by a majority of 39 votes.

Radcliffe and Connecticut College met Smith in the Intercollegiate Debate, Mar. 19, on the question: "Resolved, that the Philippine Islands shall be granted complete independence within five years." The negative team of each college traveled and the affirmative debated at home. The Smith negative team was composed of Jane Harding and Elizabeth Stoffregen '28; the affirmative of Gertrude Perelmutter and Gertrude Smith '28· Smith defeated Radcliffe in Northampton and Connecticut defeated Smith at New London.

DRAMATICS.—On Feb. 10 Workshop produced the miracle play "Noah," written by Professor Eliot. On Feb. 25 it presented four adaptations made in English 317. They were "Miscegenation" from Edna Ferber's "Show Boat," by Catherine Groff '27; "The Mock Beggar" from Sheila Kaye-Smith's "The Mock Beggar," by Dorothy Ettelson '27; "The Sire de Malétroit's Door" from Stevenson's work of the same name, by Henrietta Wells '27; "Bliss," adapted from Katherine Mansfield's "Bliss" by Beatrice Plumer '27·

On Apr. 19, Workshop presented four modern plays written by members of the senior class in English 31. The plays were: "New Year's Call," produced by Mary Blackford '27 and written by Elsie Anderson '27; "Moon Madness," written by a Holyoke graduate and produced by Elizabeth Lovell '27; "The Marplot," written by Henrietta Wells '27 and produced by Hansen Currier '27; "A Bargain for Two," written by Agnes O'Shea '27 and produced by Doris Russell '27·

Spring play and senior dramatics will be one and the same thing this year, "The Beaux' Stratagem." The play will have as faculty adviser Professor Samuel Eliot Jr., and will be produced by the 1927 Dramatic Council with the new D. A. Council chosen this spring. See further notice in this department.

On Mar. 17 and 18, Workshop presented a comedy of college life written by Eleanor Golden '26, of Washington, D. C., and entitled "Extra Curriculum."

Mrs. Dorothea Spinney of New York City read Euripides's "Medea" in Sage Hall, Feb. 28, under the auspices of D. A.

ELECTIONS.—President of Student Council, Polly Bullard '28 of Elmira, N. Y.; chairman of Judicial Board, Ruth De Young '28 of Chicago; president of Athletic Association, Caroline Mowry '29 of Englewood, N. J.; president of S. C. A. C. W., Florence Lyon '28 of Buffalo, N. Y.

Martha Kellogg '28, editor-in-chief of the *Weekly;* Sarah Taylor '28, editor-in-chief of the *Monthly;* Constance Stockwell '28, president of Press Board.

Producing director of Dramatics Association, Helen Huberth '28; stage manager, Margaret Grout '28; business manager, Eleanor Ball '28·

1927: Toastmistress for Class Supper, George Pearson.

1928: Council members, Julia Hafner and Mary Mills.

Thirty-six members of the Class of 1927 and two from the Class of 1928 were elected to the Zeta of Massachusetts Chapter of Phi Beta Kappa.

From 1927: Pauline Alper, Grace Asserson, Phyllis Bache, Ruth Champlin, Rita Curran, Margaret Day, Eleanor Deland, Caroline Doane, Mary Doran, Charlotte Eisenberg, Selma Erving, Constance Harvey, Margaret Little, Lucella Lunt, Ada Mattraw, Eleanor Miller, Hélène Millet, Helen Moore, Janet Olmsted, Katharine Pillsbury, Mary Pillsbury, Edith Reid, Caroline Roberts, Ruth Sears, Anna Sharon, Anne Smith, Helen Smith, M. Virginia Smith, Margaret Sprowl, Dorothy Tebbetts, Theodora Wagner, Annie Weaver, Flora Webb, Clarice Webber, Geraldine Whiting, Gertrude Woelfle.

Spring Dance was held on Mar. 5.

The class choir competition for the Morrow Cup was held Apr. 20. The judges were Fräulein Margarete Dessoff, Conductor of the Madrigal Choir of the Institute of Musical Art and Guest-Conductor of the Schola Cantorum; Professor William C. Hammond of Mount Holyoke College; and Professor E. Harold Geer of Vassar. The trophy cup, won last year by 1929, was won this year by 1930, with 1927 a very close second.

Fifty-four members of 1929 are eligible to work under the Special Honors system.

There are 266 undergraduates on the Dean's List this semester. From 1927, 130; from 1928, 69; from 1929, 46; from 1930, 21. Last semester there were 209 on the Dean's List.

At the vocational meetings for seniors the following talks have been given: "Social Work" by Professor Kimball (Government); "Personnel Work" by Miss Kneeland of the University of Pittsburgh; "Library Work" by Miss Eunice Wead '02· of the School of Library Science, University of Michigan; "Opportunities in R. H. Macy and Co." by Miss Jane Tildsley '18 of R. H. Macy and Co.; "Writing" by Mrs. Josephine Daskam Bacon '98·

Under the auspices of the Department of Zoölogy three alumnae were invited back to College on Apr. 20 to talk to the undergraduates about opportunities in scientific fields. The alumnae were: Mina Winslow '13· who came from the Museum of Zoölogy at the University of Michigan; Mary Dailey '22· who came from the Massachusetts General Hospital to talk on hospital laboratory work; and Annie Minot '15· who came from Vanderbilt University and spoke on medical research.

A lecture on "Greenwich House" was given Apr. 22 by Mrs. V. G. Simkhovitch, director of Greenwich House in New York.

The *New York Times* Intercollegiate Current Events Contest was held at Smith on Apr. 16 and the local prize of $250 was won by Wilhelmina Luten '27· See examination and data printed elsewhere in this department.

Of general interest to the alumnae is the opening of the new Hotel Northampton, which is now fully completed. The former Alumnae House, having been leased by Miss James, is now open under new management and is called Jewett Inn. See advertisements of both these hotels in this issue.

DOROTHY DUDLEY 1929

THE NEW YORK TIMES INTERCOLLEGIATE CURRENT EVENTS CONTEST

THE *New York Times* organized this year an Intercollegiate Current Events Contest, a kind of super "Ask Me Another" in which it invited eighteen colleges and universities, including Smith, to participate. A local contest was first held in each of the colleges, and the *Times* presented the winner of each local contest with a prize of $250 and a bronze commemorative medal. The winners of the local contests are to participate in an Intercollegiate Contest on May 14 for a prize of $500. We print below the local examination given at Smith on April 16, and won by Wilhelmina Luten '27· who will go to New York on May 14 to enter the intercollegiate examination. Professor Fay, Professor Orton, and Professor Rogers set the examination for Smith.

PART I. (One and a half hours)

A. Each name in the left-hand column is associated with activity at a place in the right-hand column. Indicate the appropriate association by marking figures from the left-hand column in the blank spaces in the right-hand column:

1. W. E. Borah	—— Chicago
2. Georg Brandes	—— Thoiry
3. Esme Howard	—— Denmark
4. Ahmed Zogu	—— Mecca
5. Carlos Ibanez	—— Bucharest
6. W. Cuno	—— Zagreb
7. N. Jorga	—— Albania
8. S. Raditch	—— Chile
9. General Carmona	—— Denver
10. J. V. A. MacMurray	—— Oporto
11. Eugene Chen	—— Ottawa
12. W. L. Mackenzie-King	—— Idaho
13. G. Stresemann	—— Peking
14. Ibn Saud	—— Warsaw
15. E. W. Kemmerer	—— Washington, D. C.
16. W. E. Dever	—— Hankow
17. Ben B. Lindsey	—— Hamburg

B. Indicate the appropriate definition in the right-hand column of the subject in the left-hand
   column by marking corresponding figures in the blank spaces in the right-hand column:

1. G. P. Gooch —— A President of the United Mine Workers
2. Vivian Phillips —— A Chinese philosopher
3. William Phillips —— A monetary unit worth about 14 cents
4. Belga —— A Nicaraguan politician
5. William Green —— A British Liberal Party organizer
6. Leon Blum —— Editor of *L'Action Française*
7. Reichswehr —— A leading critic of Fascism
8. Otto Gessler —— A Legislative body
9. General Hertzog —— President of the American Federation of Labor
10. Podestá —— A Bolshevist newspaper
11. G. Salvemini —— A monetary unit nominally worth about 19 cents
12. Storthing —— A German Minister of Defence
13. Hu Shihl —— An agent provocateur
14. R. Garibaldi —— A Japanese political party
15. Dinar —— A French socialist leader
16. J. B. Sacasa —— A delegate to the British Imperial Conference
17. Pravda —— A British historian
18. Ryndam —— A former British Premier
19. Léon Daudet —— A special correspondent of the *N. Y. Times*
20. Walter Duranty —— United States Minister to Canada
21. Seiyukai —— A military defense organization
22. Vilna —— A municipal official
23. Macao —— A floating university group
24. J. Stalin —— A large island off the coast of Siberia
25. Sakhalin —— A communist leader
26. John L. Lewis —— Former capital of Lithuania
27. J. R. MacDonald —— A Portuguese port

C. Indicate the appropriate definition in the right-hand column of the subject in the left-hand
   column by marking corresponding figures in the blank spaces in the right-hand column:

1. Emil Ludwig —— A New England college president
2. L. Stokowski —— Agent General for Reparations
3. Sinclair Lewis —— Editor of *Foreign Affairs*
4. H. A. L. Fisher —— Author of a biography of Lord Bryce
5. Count Herman Keyserling —— An organizer of farmers' coöperatives
6. Gilbert S. Parker —— An orchestral conductor
7. Ellery Sedgwick —— Editor of the *Atlantic Monthly*
8. Anne Douglas Sedgwick —— Author of "The Old Countess"
9. A. Conan Doyle —— An electrical inventor
10. Kurt Koffka —— A director of the General Electric Company
11. E. M. Hopkins —— A young operatic singer
12. Marion Talley —— A noted aviator
13. Roy Chapman Andrews —— A practical exponent of ethics in business
14. R. E. Byrd —— A Paris newspaper correspondent
15. A. Sapiro —— A judge of the U. S. Supreme Court
16. Louis Brandeis —— An exponent of the Gestalt theory
17. Owen D. Young —— A German philosopher
18. Sisley Huddleston —— Director of the Metropolitan Museum of Art
19. Edward Robinson —— A biographer of Napoleon and of Wilhelm II
20. E. A. Filene —— Author of "Elmer Gantry"
21. William D. Coolidge —— A leader of scientific expeditions
22. Archibald C. Coolidge —— A student of psychic phenomena

PART II. (One hour)

Discuss as fully as possible within an hour the truth or falsity of two of the following quotations; illustrate your answers by reference to events of the past year:

1. "Good government is no substitute for self-government."
2. ' Intellectual propaganda is a necessary prerequisite for successful revolution."
3. ' International finance is a force making for peace."
4. ' Nationalism in a country is strengthened when the country is subjected to intervention by
   foreign armed forces."
5. ' The limitation of preparations for chemical warfare is more important than the limitation
   of naval armaments."
6. ' President Coolidge's proposal for a conference on the limitation of naval armaments will
   weaken the League of Nations."
7. "The Mellon-Berenger Debt Agreement ought to be revised."
8. ' The Coolidge administration has unduly neglected the American farmer."

THE DIRECTOR OF RELIGIOUS WORK AND SOCIAL SERVICE

At the February meeting of the Board of Trustees Miss Mira Wilson '14 was appointed to this office. This action of the Trustees crystallized the great interest of the administration in the religious life of the college. We quote President Neilson's remarks to the Council concerning the real perplexity of a number of the alumnae as to this aspect of college life:

"A little wider view would extend these perplexities to the religious life of America and a little wider still to the religious life of the world. There is a very strong tendency in regard to all criticisms on religion, morals, and manners to regard the college as an isolated group in a vacuum. There is also a tendency to unload on the college responsibilities that were formerly regarded as parental. I could talk at great length on this whole matter, but I wanted to tell you that the administration of the college, all of us college officers, are very much interested in this, and are watching it with great care. The Trustees took one action yesterday which is indicative of their interest. The students tried this year to run their Association for Christian Work without even secretarial help from the outside, but they had not tried it for more than three or four months before they regretted it, and came back and said they wanted a secretary again. Instead, Miss Mira Wilson, dean of the class of 1927, who finishes her deanship for that class this year, has been asked to become director of religious work and social service."

Miss Wilson throughout her undergraduate days was very active in the work of the S. C. A. C. W., and in 1919 came back to serve as its executive secretary. In 1921 she became a member of the department of Biblical Literature in which she carried full-time teaching until she became dean of the class of 1927, from which time she has done part-time teaching. She will this June usher her class into the wide, wide world and next year will still retain her place in the department and take up this new and very important position.

THE FEBRUARY TRUSTEES' MEETING

AT THE meeting of the Board of Trustees held on February 18, 1927, the following votes were passed:

That the President be authorized to purchase the Drury property at 66 Paradise Road, and the Brewer property at 138 Elm Street.

That the recommendation of the Department of Art that the College again undertake to provide graduate instruction in art abroad during the year 1927–28 under the directorship of Professor Clarence Kennedy be approved.

To approve the budget for 1927–28 presented by President Neilson including the following promotions:

From Associate Professor to Professor: Esther Dunn (English) and Elizabeth Avery (Spoken English). From Assistant Professor to Associate Professor: Catharine Koch (Botany), Yvonne Imbault-Huart (French), Vera L. Brown (History), and Emmett Dunn (Zoölogy). From Instructor to Assistant Professor: A. P. A. Vorenkamp (Art), Sara Bache-Wiig and P. Alice Evans (Botany), Mildred Hartsough (Economics and Sociology), Margaret Peoples (French), Gertrude Goss (Hygiene and Physical Education), and Mary E. Clarke (Philosophy). From Assistant to Instructor: Keren Gilmore (Chemistry), Edmée de Pombarat (French), and Phebe Ferris (Geology).

That the appointments to the rank of Associate Professor shall in the future be for a term of years only, and that the function of the Committee on Tenure and Promotion shall be extended to include reappointments in that rank.

That the following sabbatical absences and leaves of absence be granted:

For the year, Associate Professor Jessie Y. Cann, Associate Professor Mary Louise Foster, and Assistant Professor Anna A. Chenot.

For the first semester, Professor Suzan R. Benedict, Professor Albert Schinz, Associate Professor Grace H. Conkling, and Associate Professor Samuel A. Eliot.

For the second semester, Professor Harriet R. Cobb, Associate Professor Sidney R. Packard, and Assistant Professor Mary L. Richardson.

Leaves of absence for the year, Associate Professor Chase Going Woodhouse, Assistant Professor Solon Robinson, Alice O. Curwen, and E. Frances Stilwell.

That the title of the Department of Biblical Literature and Comparative Religion be changed to the Department of Religion and Biblical Literature, and that the title of the Geology Department be changed to the Department of Geology and Geography.

That Miss Mira Wilson be appointed Director of Religious Work and Social Service.

That President Neilson express the gratitude of the Board of Trustees to Sir Joseph Duveen for his gift to the Smith College Art Museum of two Rosselini panels.

ANNETTA I. CLARK, *Secretary*

COMMENCEMENT DRAMATICS

"THE Beaux' Stratagem," by George Farquhar, is the play that the Senior Class and the Dramatic Association will produce together this spring to serve as both Spring Production of D. A. and Commencement Play. It will be presented as the regular May entertainment, then will be reworked

under the direct supervision of the Senior Class for graduation week. This new arrangement permits a more perfect result and saves both time and money. The alumnae and guests will see a play which has been presented once and improved in the weak points that appeared in actual performance. "The Beaux' Stratagem" will be developed from the original choice of cast with the idea of being given as a Commencement event. The cast contains all available material from the Senior Class and supplements this talent by drawing from the rest of the college. Rehearsals began after spring vacation to prepare for the first presentation in May. If staging, costuming, or casting needs changing after this production, improvements will be made by intensive work just before Commencement. Seniors' responsibilities that have formerly begun in February with the start of Senior Dramatics rehearsals will be reduced. The Dramatic Association and the class will share expenses. Instead of spending months of practice and an extravagant sum of money on two plays that are produced independently, each organization will profit by throwing its energy into a common cause. Furthermore, Senior talent is free for the Spring Production and Commencement Dramatics contain the choice of talent from the whole college.

The choice of this play, "The Beaux'

e Room

Drawings by Priscilla Paine '28

hunting for the North Pole, and finding it was a lovely lady in disguise (to wit, Helen Teagle, freshman president); someone in the "correct skating costume for females" taken from Godey's "Ladies Book"; hot coffee and doughnuts; excellent music, and lots of exercise for the freshmen—all combined to make it so successful that the sophomores were as inflated with pride as the robins are now (with worms).

On Sunday, the 13th, the traditional "Week of Prayer" began with Dr. Henry Tweedy of Yale as the speaker. Dr. Tweedy is regarded with great admiration and affection by the college, to such an extent, in fact, that one young enthusiast was heard to remark, "Gosh, but he'd make a wonderful father!"

The following Sunday, Louis Vierne, the blind organist of Notre Dame de Paris, played to a house crowded and standing on tiptoe. He played beautifully, so beautifully that we counted the evening as one of the richest of the entire year. ..

On the 22d came what the *Bulletin* pompously announced as the "Washington's Birthday Commemoration Exercises"—but what we call "Rally Day." All sorts of splendid things happen then, but for sheer, downright impressiveness, nothing can touch the parade of the Faculty in their brilliant hoods and gowns, as they march into John M. Greene Hall for the morning exercises. Blue and purple and yellow and green and red and black; the extravagant, ermine-trimmed hoods of the French Universities; the scarlet gown of the University of London—the glorious procession marched down the aisle to the thundering of the organ, and, at the end, covered with hoods of every color, symbolizing every degree, came the President, looking, in the fantastic brilliance of his yellows and blues and reds like a learned doctor of the Black Arts who ruled the court of the Borgias and did mysterious things. The student body, "brave in ribbons" and dressed in white, made an excellent background. If the Faculty knew what those caps and gowns and mysterious hoods did to their prestige, they'd never be seen without them. The freshmen and sophomores in red and yellow ribbons

peered down from the balcony on the junior
and seniors in purple and green, and they
wished they knew as many of the faculty
names as their older sisters seemed to. It
was a wise organist who filled John M. Greene
with a torrent of sound in order to drown out
such excited whispers as: "Look at M.
Guilloton's cap! Look at the ermine on that
one. What a pretty color blue Mr. Bixler
has—Do all M.D.'s wear green? The Dean
has a new gold tassel on her cap. That's Miss
Dunn in red—I wonder what those things the
President has are!!!" The music stopped,
and the whispers were suppressed, and then
came the services, with an address by the
Reverend Ernest Hocking on "Imitation and
its Cure." It was splendid. There really
should be space to quote it in full.

We are [he said] a most imitative people.
In our thinking as well as in our actions we
lead a life of competition which is one of the
most imitative relationships. In business,
in athletics, and in social life, we are watching
those about us, looking for every item of advantage that could give us a step ahead. Yet
imitation is not what everyone wants. It
undermines energy, it is a form of self-aliena-
tion, of repression, a failure of self-confidence
—whoever makes much use of it is bound to
rebel; the rebellion may take the form of trying to be different at all cost. What we need
is not imitation, but appropriation—imitation
takes over the external qualities of the thing
imitated, plagiarizing it: appropriation probes
into the inner meaning and penetrates into the
fundamental idea, which it adopts or renews.
Outwardly imitation and appropriation seem
so much alike that it is hard to differentiate
between them, but appropriation can be de-
tected in that part of life in which it is impossible to be imitative—in one's real pleasures.

The phrase "not imitation but appropriation"
has become a popular one at college—where it
has vast opportunities for application. There
was a roar of music, and all the gorgeous hoods
filed out. Then came the seniors and the
juniors and the sophomores and the freshmen
stampeding and racing toward the new gym,
dragging bewildered and terrified guests in
their wake. The Rally in the Gym, to one of
the still trembling guests, must have seemed
like a particularly tempestuous sea of faces,
from which, at intervals, came explosions of
song and storms of laughter or applause.
The most outstanding feature, besides the
gaudy and grotesque class animals, and the
general riot of decoration and sound and song,
was the Senior Stunt. A front porch (Hatfield, we hear) was adorned with fair ladies of
the gay nineties filling an affable row of rock-

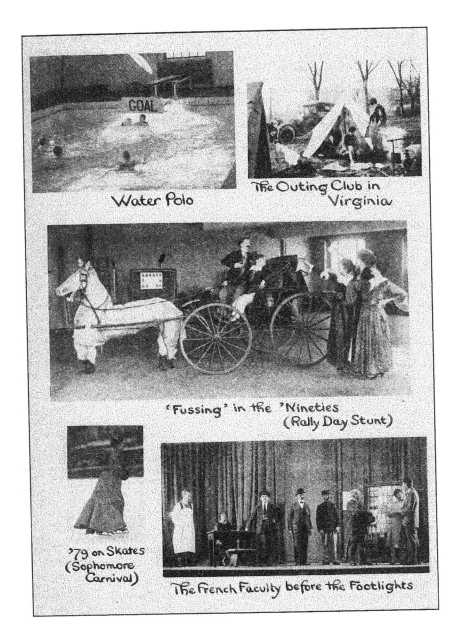

Water Polo

The Outing Club in Virginia

'Fussing' in the 'Nineties (Rally Day Stunt)

'79 on Skates (Sophomore Carnival)

The French Faculty before the Footlights

sation on the theory of Evolution between "Harry Elmer" and "Proffy Wood." Then came the Faculty Show as a rowdy climax to the evening. One of the most outstanding features of the faculty shows is that the performers enjoy it almost as much—no, I'm not going to say "if not more" than the audience. The scene was laid in the house of a professor who was trying, amid domestic and foreign distractions, to correct examination papers. The proceeding offered an interesting explanation of some of our marks! Then the whole ensemble tripped the boards to the lively strains of "Where do you work-a John?" "I work at the Smith-a Col." The cast included an odd yellow dog, two plumbers, two superb fruit venders, Cupid, a Rubenesque chorus girl, two small boys, a kiddie car, the Professor, a small and timid student, and, last and largest, Mr. Parshley in the shape of an enormous and vociferous colored woman. After that we had to go to bed and rest!

That the Workshop plays were successful reflects even greater glory on them than they would otherwise enjoy, in that they were not in the least an anticlimax after Rally Day. Workshop gave four adaptations from modern short stories that were cleverly staged and well acted.

March came in with the smell of wet earth —fat buds and the first robins: a vague general excitement and a stir of spring in the air. March is the Peter Rabbit among months— mischievous, unexpected, always appearing suddenly around corners; and this March was exceptionally surprising. There were warm delicious days when you ran outdoors with your sleeves rolled up and began to hunt excitedly for peach blossoms and arbutus and lilacs and all sorts of impossible things. There were other raw, snowy, miserable days when you shivered under your fur coat, and swore, and swore, and wondered if spring would never come.

March is always punctuated with an exclamation point in the middle called "Spring Dance." All the houses have dances and orchestras and real men and we all stay up until eleven! To be sure, Spring in New England on the first of March is really only the substance of things hoped for, but nobody seems to think the name a misnomer and a wonderful time is had by all. Mr. Parshley wrote an account of part of it which is full of atmosphere in the nonesuch Faculty issue of the *Weekly*:

The most extraordinary feature of this year's Dance was the interior decoration of the Crew House, the work of White Lodge and 30 Green and evidently inspired by the Junior year in France. The windows were completely concealed by large posters, done in the manner of some Parisian night club, perhaps Le Lapin Agile; and the walls and rafters bore post-impressionist and even vorticist works of art set off by appropriate mottoes in a sort of French, none of which seemed to mean "Home is Where the Heart Is" or anything of the sort. Over the entrance, downstairs, was a tasteful—sheaf, shall we say?—of vegetables, and the name of the resort "Au bal de musette des grosses legumes." All this, combined with a rotund and serious accordion player in the orchestra, gave an exotic atmosphere to the place, in spite of the railroad station stove and the evident 100% Americanism of the men.

March is so full of "a number of things" that we are distracted. The athletics have been particularly virulent. There was an exciting basket ball game in which the freshmen put the sophomores to shame. The intercollegiate swimming meets, when the records of the other teams come over the radio, and our records are sent back as they are made, provide some of the busiest moments that are lived in the gym. Once Smith swam against Michigan, Iowa, and Wisconsin all at once! and won, we are proud to say. There was also an interclass swimming meet—and all the gymnastics culminated in an impressive orgy known no longer as the "Gym Drill" but as the "Demonstration." In speaking of it, Miss Ainsworth said: "The program will include not only a regular day's work in both Danish and modified Swedish gymnastics, but also clogging, rhythms, and the final game of the basket ball tournament. The aim of the demonstration is to show all types of work carried on daily through the winter term in the gymnasium." The affair was a great success, especially from the viewpoint of 1928 —who got the greatest number of points in the tournament and who won the Inez Chapin cup for the first team. The freshmen were runners up and the seniors came in on the caboose with the third prize. The All Smith basket ball team was chosen and everyone went away feeling happy and vigorous.

The March musical program has been extraordinarily rich and varied. It started with a faculty recital by the Department of Music, followed by the Boston Symphony. This concert is always an event—when we put on our evening clothes (if we have seats) and pretend we are in the Paris Opera House.

The London String Quartet played delightfully—and made us wish that the English Singers could come again soon. There was a Beethoven Commemoration Recital given by the Department of Music, with a particularly well-chosen program. Mme. Schumann-Heink sang in John M. Greene on her farewell tour. She was tremendous and superb. We looked at her with our mouths open. She was charming, and talked to us between songs, calling herself grandmamma. We loved her, and clapped and clapped until she protested that she couldn't sing any more. Two nights before vacation, we crowded to hear Fritz Kreisler. His triumph is in a large degree a personal one, as his programs seem to get more and more uninteresting each year, although his playing is, of course, magnificent, and he is capable of transforming the stupidest composition by his rendering of it.

The last Saturday of February, Dewey House celebrated its hundredth anniversary with a reception. It has the place of honor in this magazine, we are told. Candle light and flowers were everywhere. Instinctively voices softened and the dignity of the nineteenth century was infused into a twentieth century reception. What a delightful change!

The lectures have been so many and varied that there is only room to mention a few: A reading of the "Medea" by Mrs. Dorothea Spinney; a lecture on Dorothy Wordsworth by Ernest de Sélincourt; a very interesting talk by Mr. Arthur Haas of Vienna on the "Atom as a Source of Energy," and one by S. P. Gooch on "The Outlook in Europe." Mr. Jon Mjoen gave one of the most illuminating talks this year on "The Genius and the Criminal in the Light of Biology."

Usually two of the most exciting chapels of the year come in March, and this year they arrived and "went off" true to form. On the first the Phi Betes were announced and we—of the lower strata—sat breathless and admiring and clapped, and clapped, and clapped; at the second the new officers of Student Government were named. This year Katharine Bingham and Amanda Bryan announced their successors: Polly Bullard, president of Council, and Ruth de Young, chairman of Judicial Board. We thundered applause, and everyone looked at everyone else with a pleased "I told you so" expression. There was a third impressive chapel in spring term and a fourth that topped them all of which we shall tell you presently.

And so March melted and froze and blew and shined itself straight to vacation time. Trunks came down from the attic, and up from the cellar—and with a rush and a tumble and a final slam to our books we were off. "In the spring a young man's fancy . . . "

. . . But two weeks isn't really long enough —so we all came back, and only a few of us had diamond rings sparkling self-consciously on our left hands.

Since we have been back many things have happened—lectures on interesting subjects—but the weather has been too enthralling. Even so soon we have forgotten those raw, unsympathetic April days when we longed for the fur coats that we trustingly left home to be done up in moth balls! and the lectures haven't seemed important at all.

Then there was the Annual Choir Competition for the Morrow Cup, which, quite aside from the big silver cup, is itself one of the most delightful events of our musical year. The four choirs all in white look impressive enough to constitute the whole student body without any help from the less tuneful of us, and this year the contest was so close that the announcement that for the third time the freshmen had won—maybe with a wee bit of irritating cockiness—was received with more suspense than usual. The seniors came in as a very close second, the President said, which was no more than right. And speaking of music we should have noted with pride that in March the Glee Club went down to New Haven and sang before an audience that would have done the Boston Symphony proud.

And now for the third and fourth exciting chapels mentioned long ago in the winter. First was the announcement of the "S" pin

b. Good health; *i.e.*, taking good care of oneself, 5 points.

c. Taste and neatness, 5 points

4. Personal attributes, 15 points

Here an attempt is made to judge the student's charm and personality, and such things are considered as poise (true

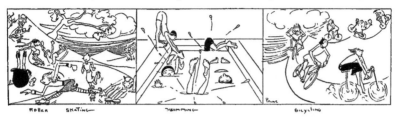

ROLLER SKATING   SWIMMING   BICYCLING

awards. To win an "S" a girl must be representative of the highest ideals of the College, and it is easy to imagine with what applause we greeted the super six who blushingly found their way to the platform. Their names and pictures are on page 331. Lest you fail to realize just how important an award is have won glance through the summary of the system by which the committee grades the students.

1. Ability in sports, 15 points
   a. For best sport, 9 points
   b. For second best sport, 6 points
2. Attitude toward sports and toward college life in general, 30 points
   a. Toward sports, 5 points; *i.e.*, good sportsmanship, interest, and helpfulness toward other players.
   b. Toward college life in general, 20 points; this attitude to be qualified by such words as dynamic, coöperative, unselfish, law-abiding, dignified, courteous, tactful, friendly, not antagonistic or domineering, and with initiative.

self mastery, not social poise only), ability to meet and command unembarrassed any situation in which she may find herself, dignity, unself-consciousness, resourcefulness, originality, responsibility, sincerity, and genuineness of character.

You have already read of the fourth great chapel, and it is sufficient to say that when "The Chair" was presented to President Neilson we all shouted with pride and enthusiasm and wondered to ourselves just what it was, and what it meant, and whether we would ever see the shadowy, famous occupant —or incumbent, to speak academically.

Twice this spring term have the faculty stepped before the footlights. Once it was in a double bill with the students in the French Club. The students gave "Celui qui épousa une femme muette."—and gave it brilliantly— and the faculty, "L'Anglais tel qu'on le parle" —and gave it ditto. The second time the faculty-parents of the Nursery School children —and other parents as well—gave a demon-

ARCHERY   HURDLING   RIDING

c. Development in college life, 5 points; *i.e.*, a girl who develops into "S" pin quality while in college receives a slightly higher grading in these 5 points than one who has made no progress in college.

3. Carriage and appearance, 15 points
   a. Good posture at all times, 5 points

stration of a morning in the school. The old gym was transformed into a sweet little kindergarten and Mr. Welch and Mr. Bixler, and Mr. Guilloton and Mr. Kennedy *et al.* as their respective small sons and daughters drank orange juice and played games and took naps until the audience begged for mercy.

"Here's To You"

Top: "S" PIN AWARDS. Caroline Schauffler '28, Ella Bolling-James, Leslie Winslow, Janet Olmsted, Ruth Sears, Catherine Cole, '27.

Center: Polly Bullard '28, President of Student Government, Ruth De Young '28, Chairman of Judicial Board.

Bottom: PHI BETA KAPPA GRANDDAUGHTERS. Caroline Doane (Lucy Daniels '96), Janet Olmsted (Marguerite Prescott '03), Rita Curran (Mae Fuller '97), Dorothy Tebbetts (Frances Ayer '93), Selma Erving (Emma Lootz '97), Mary Pangborn (Georgia Wood ex-'96), Elizabeth Hamburger (Amy Stein '04), Eleanor Deland (Isabel Adams '96), Margaret Day (Elizabeth Lewis '95).

Speaking of President Neilson reminds us that we have not mentioned our Easter vespers. We all went in spite of the warm, delicious afternoon and we shall long be grateful for the President's talk. The *Weekly* made no attempt to quote him verbatim but summarized as follows:

When some students come here and learn that the teachings of the intellectual world may no longer harmonize with the doctrines taught in childhood, they experience a violent reaction against their former beliefs. "They think they have lost their faith, but they know not where their faith lies." They have not carefully considered and defined what their religion actually is.

Underlying the stories of Jesus' life and teachings are a series of facts which do not depend on the historical authenticity of the records. The spirit of the Master's work lives on and is "constantly being betrayed and crucified and buried in the tomb" until, in the despair after grief, it is found to be immortal.

Antiquarians, when they find the events of the New Testament do not coincide with history, and anthropologists, when they say the records are only legends, believe they have thus buried Christ. Astronomers, who preach a new doctrine of the creation of the universe, and biologists, who uphold another theory of the origin of man, believe they have disproved the validity of Jesus' power. But sooner or later it is discovered that Christ is risen and is only waiting to be "identified" again.

Finally, the theologians in their disputes over creeds and dogmas seem to have lost sight of the Teacher, but when they refer to the Lord's own words, He is again resurrected to them with all the purity, justice, honesty, and self-denial of a noble life.

Spring has come. The bank by the Observatory is covered with golden daffodils and bright tulips and blue and purple and small pink hyacinths. The willows are no longer yellow, but the softest, blowyest green—the elms have new leaves, and in the grass are tiny bluets. The apple trees have pink buds; the cherry trees are cloudy and white. The magnolias have full, ivory blossoms—and everywhere there are golden splashes of forsythia. On sunshiny afternoons the air is fragrant with spring smells, and lazy canoes float across Paradise and disappear down the stream between the maple trees. The fountains have started and the evenings are full of the twitterings of birds.

The seniors are piling clouds of dust over the countryside in their new cars—and their friends are all being very nice to them in the hope of getting a ride. (Meantime without waiting for invitations they swirl dizzyingly about on roller skates, bowl swiftly on bicycles, or just plain hike over the hills and dales with or without the paraphernalia of the Outing Club, which by the way is doing itself very well with its new cabins and the memory of its spring vacation trip through the south. The new class in horseback riding is tremendously popular. In fact, everyone is very happy. To stay indoors is quite impossible—there are picnics everywhere, and right here at home wonderful things are happening on Allen Field and Paradise, not just because Field Day and Float Night are just around the corner but because it's Spring.

Next week is first step sing—and you are to be told a secret about how the seniors will be all dressed in blue with berets on their heads, singing a song about being "blue berries."

We have forgotten there was ever a Spring before—perhaps there wasn't—I can't remember—anyhow it *is* Spring now!

THE BANK BY THE OBSERVATORY

THE ALUMNAE ASSOCIATION

THE FOUR COMPETITIVE CUPS

Attendance (non-reunion)	Costume	Reunion Song	Attendance (reunion)

HAVE YOU VOTED YET?

Proxies with names and qualifications of the candidates for officers and directors, plus two amendments to the By-laws, were mailed to members of the Association the first of May. The Polling Committee pleads for 8300 votes from the 8300 members, and argues that a 100% use of the franchise is not too much to expect from our intelligent Smith constituency. If you have not already returned your ballot, mail it to-day!

The Board of Directors of the Association is proposing an amendment to the By-laws which would do away with the provision for the payment of the life membership fee in seven installments of five dollars. The interest on these small annual sums (which are invested as principal) is not sufficiently large to atone for the loss in annual dues which is resulting from the flocking of members to this bargain, and the treasury finds itself the poorer by some $600 of annual income.

The other proposed amendment is only a matter of clearness of definition of the Council membership.

STOP! LOOK! LISTEN!

1776 will hold its annual reunion amid "the green foliage and bright sunshine of Commencement."

The guidance of this distinguished group has been placed in the hands of the Class of 1918, and the following information is now available (more later):

Seelye Hall 11 will welcome all and provide fun, sociability, and information.

The "Neilson uniform" will be shaken out and pressed and ready for one and all; there will be a heavenly Bat on the banks of Paradise, near the Crew House, at 5.30 on June 18, with inexpensive but filling nectar.

One of the oldest batting societies (now not in existence) will present the original tin cup to the class returning with the most numbers who can show "that they are dignified, but sociable."

Write at once to the Alumnae Office for rooms on campus, and send in your reservations for a place at the Crew House.

APPOINTMENTS

Chairman of the Alumnae Assembly Program Committee: Dorothy Hawkins '12; *Polling Committee for ballots for officers and directors:* Ruby Litchfield '10, Katharine (Dickson) King '20, and Dorothy Ainsworth '16; *Chairman of 1776 for Commencement 1927:* Florence Bliss '18; *Chairman of Costume Cup Committee:* Amy Ferris '01; *Committee to award Reunion Song Cup:* Professor Welch of the Music Department, Dean Bernard, and Josephine (Sewall) Emerson '97.

COMMENCEMENT 1927

Wednesday, June 15

P. M.
7.00	Step Sing

Thursday, June 16

8.15	Dramatics, "The Beaux' Stratagem"

Friday, June 17

A. M.
9.00	Chapel Service, the last of the year
9.45	Alumnae Song Practice
10.00	Conference of the Institute for the Coördination of Women's Interests. Sage Hall. Subject: "Problems of the Nursery School as a Social Experiment." Round Table Subscription Luncheon at 1 P. M. The Manse
12.00	Luncheon Meeting of the Board of Directors

P. M.
2.30	Dramatics
2.30	Meeting of the Alumnae Council. Seelye Hall 10
3.45	Meeting of the Class Secretaries and Presidents. Seelye Hall 10
8.15	Dramatics (preference at this performance is given to seniors and their guests)

Saturday, June 18

A. M.
9.15	Alumnae Parade
10.00	Ivy Procession. (The indoor Ivy Exercises are open to alumnae only when guests of seniors.)
10.30	Annual Meeting of the Alumnae Association. Sage Hall
12.00	Colloquium Reunion. Stoddard Hall

P. M.
12.30	Luncheon Meeting of Alumnae Fund class representatives. Crew House
2.00	Annual Meeting of the Board of Trustees of Smith College. The President's Office
2.15	Meeting of the Students' Aid Society College Hall 7
4.00	Concert by the Glee Club and Students of the Department of Music. John M. Greene Hall
4.00–6	Society and Departmental Club Reunions
6.30–10	Illumination of the campus
7.30	College Sing
8.30	Song Competition for Reunion Classes
9.15	Concert by the Glee Club. The Island

Sunday, June 19

A. M.
9.30	S. C. A. C. W. and Ginling Meeting. Students' Building
11.00	Baccalaureate Service. For seniors.

P. M.
3.00	Concert by the Symphony Orchestra and students of the Department of Music. John M. Greene Hall

4.30–6	Reception for the seniors and their guests and alumnae: President and Mrs. Neilson, 8 Paradise Road Dean Bernard and the Faculty, The Quadrangle
8.00	Organ Vespers.

Monday, June 20

A. M.
10.30	Commencement Exercises. John M. Greene Hall

P. M.
2.30	Alumnae Assembly. Sage Hall
3.45	Meeting of the Board of Directors. Sage Hall
6.00	1927 Class Supper. Alumnae Gymnasium

Class officers who are to attend Commencement will be glad of the opportunity on the program to continue the discussion of class affairs for which there never seems to be sufficient time at the February Council. This additional meeting of class representatives is called for Friday afternoon, June 17, at 3.30.

NOTES FROM THE OFFICE

The Finance and Executive Committees of the Alumnae Association broke away from the established custom and held their spring meeting at the Alumnae House at Poughkeepsie, through the courtesy of the Vassar Alumnae Association. Budgets and programs became matters of rare vitality, when formulated amidst surroundings of carved oak, flowers, and embroidered hangings. For an evening and a morning the committees held themselves sternly to their agenda, and not until the delectable luncheon with Vassar officials and Smith members of the Vassar faculty, in the Elizabethan dining-room, did they yield to leisurely and outspoken coveting of this splendid center of hospitality and educational activity. Something Georgian, perhaps, would be more suitable for our simple red brick and white pillars of the Connecticut Valley. But even if the Trustees are reluctant to turn Dewey House over to the alumnae for a campus headquarters (the suggestion has been made to this effect!) we might well be mindful of our need for an Alumnae Building and contemplate devices for its greatest usefulness. Stranger dreams *have* come true!

Five of the foreign students at Smith, Miss Edmed and Miss Tudor-Hart of England, Miss Klumpp and Miss Goepfert of Germany, and Miss Fetter of Hungary, were entertained during the spring vacation by members of the Smith clubs of Philadelphia, Baltimore, and Washington.

OVER THE TOP FOR JUNIPER

The Juniper Lodge Endowment Fund Committee is happy to report that it has reached its goal. In fact, it has passed far enough beyond the $30,000 mark to be assured of a sufficient sum to cover the amount lost through the inheritance tax on the $20,000 left by Mr. Reynolds. Juniper Lodge now has its full $50,000 Endowment Fund, can snap its fingers at poverty, and add to its other charms the serenity and assurance that come from financial competence.

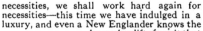

The committee appreciates not alone the generous response to its appeal but the cordial, ungrudging spirit in which gifts have been made. Comparatively few of the alumnae may ever actually be guests at Juniper Lodge, but if the words in letters accompanying contributions are to be trusted, many have experienced a vicarious joy from that alluring home in the hillside with its neighbors of mountain and lake. We as alumnae have worked hard in the past for necessities, we shall work hard again for necessities—this time we have indulged in a luxury, and even a New Englander knows the joy and uplift of spirit that comes from an occasional excursion into the world of the unnecessary.

The committee's debts of gratitude are many. Before the Endowment Fund Committee was appointed, Miss Cutler had begun collecting funds, Miss Caverno and the general Juniper Lodge Committee have worked steadily with the special committee, the Alumnae Office has contributed of its skill in keeping records, and club presidents and committees in clubs have done their part. To all these and to the many individual contributors the committee wishes at this time to express its heartfelt thanks.

Respectfully submitted,
ADELE ADAMS BACHMAN
RUTH FRENCH
VIRGINIA MELLEN HUTCHINSON

JUNIPER LODGE ENDOWMENT FUND

Report of Cash Receipts Credited to Clubs February 1, 1926–April 21, 1927

Atlanta	$10.00	Montclair	$756.60
Baltimore	250.00	New Hampshire	910.00
Berkshire County	25.00	New Haven	653.00
Boston (Greater)	5,624.95	New York and Brooklyn	8,359.20
Cambridge		Northern California	25.00
Lexington		Oranges	320.75
Lynn		Philadelphia	397.00
Salem		Pittsburgh	190.00
Winchester		Portland (Oregon)	5.00
Bridgeport	215.00	Rhode Island	116.00
Brooklyn (see New York)		Rochester	186.00
Buffalo	110.00	St. Louis	5.00
Central Illinois	95.75	St. Paul	125.00
Chicago	1,138.00	Southeastern Massachusetts	139.50
China	15.00	Southern California	395.00
Cincinnati	100.00	Springfield	480.00
Cleveland	1,040.00	Syracuse	285.00 }
Colorado	10.00	Cortland	60.00 }
Columbus	20.00	Toledo (see pledge)	
Detroit (Club contribution)	50.00 }	Vermont	140.00
(Individual gifts raised by a member)	200.00 }	Washington, D. C.	113.60
Eastern Connecticut	184.00	Wisconsin	200.00
Eastern New York	125.50	Worcester	485.00
Fitchburg	100.00		
Franklin County	30.00	Unspecified	341.00
Gloucester	58.00	Amount secured before February 1926	
Grand Rapids	75.00	from various sources	3,549.78
Hampshire County	480.00	Interest	581.04
Hartford	932.00		
Holyoke	117.00	Total cash received	$31,567.67
Indiana	816.00		
Kansas City	100.00		
Maine	269.00	Pledged in addition:	
Merrimac Valley	169.00	Syracuse	$459.00
Minneapolis	390.00	Toledo	95.00

Memorial Gifts

The gift from Greater Boston is in memory of Mary (Rankin) Wardner '92; from New Hampshire, in memory of Agnes Hunt '97; from the Syracuse Club, in memory of Harriet (Dey) Barnum '16; from Bertha (Allen) Logan '95 in memory of her mother, Harriet C. Allen; and from Florence (Gates) Judd '10, in memory of her father, Frank P. Hopwood.

ALUMNAE FELLOWSHIP

The Alumnae Fund Fellowship has been awarded for 1927–28 to Mary Pangborn '27, daughter of Georgia (Wood) Pangborn ex-'96. Miss Pangborn will study physiological chemistry at Yale.

THE CONVENTION OF ALUMNI SECRETARIES AND EDITORS

On April 27–30 the annual convention of this august body is held at the University of North Carolina in Chapel Hill. Miss Snow, Miss Collin, and Miss Hill will attend.

LOCAL CLUBS

The BALTIMORE CLUB has held its annual rummage sale and cafeteria supper to secure its scholarship fund. The Club entertained Florence Angell '11, A. A. U. W. International Secretary, and Nora Edmed, graduate student at Smith.

A series of afternoon lectures by Professor Welch (Music), Professor Kennedy (Art), and Professor Rice (English) was arranged by the BERKSHIRE CLUB for the benefit of its scholarship fund.

At the annual luncheon of the BOSTON CLUB at the new Hotel Statler, Apr. 16, the speakers were President Park of Wheaton, President Neilson, Florence Snow '04, Virginia (Mellen) Hutchinson '00, and Josephine (Sewall) Emerson '97. The completion of the Juniper Lodge Endowment Fund, achieved that week, was announced.

The annual business meeting of the BROOKLYN CLUB, Apr. 4, concluded with a stunt party by the younger members. Alice (Barrett) Heeran '04 was elected president.

On Mar. 5 at the meeting of the BUFFALO CLUB, Marie (Poland) Fish '21 spoke on the Sargasso Sea expedition.

At the spring luncheon of the CHICAGO CLUB, Apr. 2, reports were given by the councillors and a graduate of Ginling studying at the University of Chicago spoke. Professor Orton gave two lectures on economics in April under the auspices of the Club.

The CENTRAL ILLINOIS CLUB met in Peoria Feb. 5. Teresina (Peck) Rowell '94 spoke on a recent visit to College.

Members of the CLEVELAND CLUB and of the Maison Française were entertained at the Hathaway-Brown School Mar. 8 to meet Professor Schinz (French). The Club gave a series of bridge parties at private homes in

March for its scholarship fund, ending with a luncheon at which Bertha (Groesbeck) Haskell '00 talked on the Juniors in France.

The DETROIT CLUB has set an excellent precedent by holding a joint meeting with other college clubs at the official Intercollegiate Alumnae Hotel. (See page 398 of this number!)

At the March meeting of the EASTERN CONNECTICUT CLUB held for the report of the Council, the Smith Quiz was used for an old-fashioned spelling match. The Club made the first contribution (unsolicited) to the Burton Memorial Fund.

The FRANKLIN COUNTY CLUB plans to attend the Faculty Opera at College, May 14.

Students at Smith who were at home for the spring vacation were entertained at tea by the GRAND RAPIDS CLUB, Mar. 23.

Special to the *Herald Tribune* from Miami, Fla.: "Members of the Smith College Club met at the Royal Palm Hotel this morning (Mar. 10) and motored to Hollywood for the day, having as their guests a number of visiting Smith alumnae."

The MINNEAPOLIS CLUB was addressed in March by Professor Chapin of the University of Minnesota, formerly of Smith, and in April by Lincoln Colcord.

The NEW HAVEN CLUB broke all records for local concert attendance when the Smith College Glee Club packed Woolsey Hall on Mar. 12 and made a substantial sum for the Club's scholarship fund. It is said that not even the Boston Symphony has ever drawn out a larger audience.

President Neilson, Dr. Fosdick, and Professor Harry Overstreet were the speakers at the annual luncheon of the NEW YORK CLUB on Apr. 23 at the Hotel Pennsylvania.

At the luncheon of the CLUB OF THE ORANGES on Apr. 1 about 20 undergraduates were guests. The Smith Quiz furnished the entertainment.

Amanda Bryan '27, retiring chairman of the student Judicial Board, is scheduled to speak at the May meeting of the RHODE ISLAND CLUB.

In March the ROCHESTER CLUB renewed its agreement with a dry cleaning establishment whereby the Club receives 15% from all the orders given by members and friends of the Club.

Florence Snow '04 talked on "An Alumna's Day at Smith" at the March meeting of the SPRINGFIELD CLUB. A card party of 50 tables was given on Apr. 26 for Juniper Lodge. On May 14 the Club plans to go to Northampton by motor for a day's visit of the College, lunching together with an address by one of the College officers, and having tea in Gardiner House, one of the new quadrangle dormitories.

The SYRACUSE CLUB gave a concert by the Amherst Musical Clubs, Apr. 3, followed by its annual spring dance.

Josephine (Dormitzer) Abbott '11 spoke to the WINCHESTER CLUB Apr. 26 of her work at the Judge Baker Foundation. The Club has again, for the sixth year, arranged a series of ten current events lectures by Miss Eunice Avery, the proceeds going to a graduate of the Winchester High School for a scholarship at Smith.

In February the Milwaukee Branch of the WISCONSIN CLUB presented the Flonzaley Quartet in a benefit concert for Juniper Lodge. The Madison Branch raised its share by a joint rummage sale with the Wellesley Club.

The WORCESTER CLUB held a "white elephant" sale for Juniper Lodge in February. In April a tea was given for the Worcester undergraduates, at which the Smith Quiz was used as an "Ask Me Another" stunt, and Louise Whitney '27 spoke of her experiences in France with the juniors last year.

The QUARTERLY notes with pleasure that many of the clubs held meetings directly after the February Council, when reports from the club councillors were given.

THE ALUMNAE FUND

The Alumnae Fund doesn't intend to shoot until it "sees the whites of their eyes," but it will easily be seen that the Committee is marshaling its forces in a superb manner. Mrs. Ford (Harriet Bliss '99) says in the most cryptic tone in the world, "Tell them that there will be the gayest kind of a Fund stunt at Alumnae Assembly," and her letter recently sent to the Class Presidents, asking for the appointment of Class Representatives to form the auxiliary body of the Alumnae Fund, is a masterpiece, dramatic and irresistible. One can see these "super-women," with "much energy, imagination, a sense of adventure, and a real desire to serve the College and their classes in this ideally practical way," rushing to enlist in time to attend the first momentous meeting of Class Representatives at Commencement, on Ivy Day.

The seven classes of 1918, 1919, 1920, 1921, 1922, 1923, and 1924, which have insurance policies or equivalent plans for reunion gifts, in existence prior to the adoption of the Alumnae Fund, received a special memorandum. Two courses of action were set forth: the first, "to abandon the existent plans by class vote, contribute the accumulated amount to the Fund, and join the new project. Presumably the nature of the insurance policies would make this difficult if not impossible in some cases." The second course, which the Central Committee feels would be "a happy solution of relationships," would be for the classes "to continue to function independently," sending "to the Alumnae Fund Committee an annual statement of the total paid into the class fund and the names of the contributors. This statement would be included in the general report with an annotation to indicate that actual cash has not been contributed."

The charter of the Alumnae Fund provides that the purpose to which each annual gift is to be devoted "shall be determined by the Fund Committee in consultation with College Trustees and the Alumnae Council." In preparation for Commencement and the Council meeting read the President's article on "The Alumnae Fund and Salaries."

A. A. U. W.

The program of the A. A. U. W. Biennial Convention at Washington, March 30 to April 2, analyzed through a college spectrum, revealed the following Smith rays: Chairman of the Committee on Educational Policies and speaker on "An Interpretation of the Educational Program," Ada Comstock '97; contributor to the Discussion Group on Preschool Education, chairman of the Committee on the Coördination of Women's Interests, and speaker on "The Woman's Orientation Course: What Shall Be Its Basic Concept?", Ethel (Puffer) Howes '91; speaker on the "Influence of College Women on Rural Education," Marion Gary '05; chairman of the Conference of Presidents, Deans, and other Representatives of Corporate Members, and speaker on "Mental Hygiene as an Integral Part of the College Course," Cora Coolidge '92; speaker on "Values in Education," Dean Bernard; leader of the discussion at the Legislative Breakfast, Laura (Puffer) Morgan '95; vice-chairman of the Program Committee, Alice (Lord) Parsons '97; vice-chairman of the Washington Committee on Convention, Helen

(Woodward) Wilson '97; chairman of the Committee on the Economic and Legal Status of Women, Professor Chase (Going) Woodhouse; chairman of the Committee on Housing, Edith (Elmer) Wood '90; chairman of the Committee on Place of Next Convention, Helen Atwater '97; member of the Committee of International Fellowships Appeal and speaker at the Conference on International Fellowships, Maude (Miner) Hadden '01; secretary of the Committee on International Relations, Florence Angell '11; delegates from the Alumnae Association of Smith College, Alida (Leese) Milliken '00, Agnes (Childs) Hinckley '01, Florence Snow '04, Louise Kingsley '05, Helen Atwater '97, Elizabeth Bryan '09, Hazel (O'Neil) Fenning '11 (who was also chairman of the Washington Branch Committee), Laura (Puffer) Morgan '95, Isabel Stabler '22, Dorothy (Mack) Nichols '16.

During the four crowded days of the Convention, a most stimulating array of speeches, conferences, reports, and business sessions held the devoted attention of the more than 500 attendants, from the first day's visit to the public schools of the District up to the reception which closed the Convention,

after Dr. Meiklejohn's prospectus of the Wisconsin Experimental College. At the International Dinner, 1000 delegates and visitors were addressed in the brilliant ballroom of the Hotel Mayflower by the Undersecretary of State, the ambassadors of Great Britain, Italy, and France, the ministers of Czecho-Slovakia and the Irish Free State, Mrs. Wicksell of Sweden and the Mandates Commission of the League of Nations, and Dean Gildersleeve of Barnard. The Association was received by President Coolidge in the White House Grounds, and by Mrs. Herbert Hoover at her home. The National Clubhouse, magnificently solvent now, was the center of part of the Convention activity, and with all the matters of administrative finance in a healthy condition, the Association launched a campaign for a million dollars for fellowships, national and international. The baskets of pralines distributed by the Louisiana delegation were a happy variation of lobbying practices—and exceedingly successful, for the Association will convene at its next meeting in 1929 in New Orleans, under the chairmanship of President Woolley of Mount Holyoke.

F. H. S.

A LETTER FROM CHINA

Just before going to press, a letter was received from Ruth Chester '14, written from Shanghai, April 1, describing the taking of Nanking by the Nationalist forces. She says in part:

"When it became evident that the looting soldiers were attacking foreigners and their property, our Chinese faculty and students insisted on our staying in our faculty residence, out of sight. They met the different groups who came to our campus, talked with them, fed them, led them through the buildings and did everything possible to shield us. They kept us all morning entirely free of any contact with the soldiers until we were convoyed in safety to a larger group of foreigners in one of the buildings of the University of Nanking where we were protected for over 24 hours by Nationalist soldiers under a responsible officer. While we were there, we were visited many times by both faculty and students, who did everything possible for our comfort and brought many of our things to us. When the very sudden order came the next day for immediate departure we were all very loathe to go, but there seemed no other way. It was especially hard to leave the little group who had done so much for us to face alone the difficulties and possible dangers ahead, but it seemed clear that our remaining would only have added to their problems. After several days of suspense, good news has come through and we know they are safe. For the time being they are carrying on as many classes as the much reduced faculty will allow. . . . There are many difficult problems of adjustment ahead, and the new Ginling which will emerge from this chaos will certainly be different in many ways from the old Ginling. . . . No one quite knows just where to lay the responsibility for this most unfortunate outbreak, but one thing is clear: it is in no sense representative of the vast majority of the people of China. They deplore it as much as we, and are as ready as ever to welcome us and our help. Ginling therefore still needs your sympathy and interest and support as she faces a future that is now very uncertain, but in which she still hopes to continue her contribution to the women of China."

ALUMNAE NOTES

CLASS NEWS

Please send all news for the July QUARTERLY *to your class secretary by June 15. The editors reserve the right to omit all items which in their judgment are not submitted in legible form.*

1879
Class secretary—Mrs. Charles M. Cone (Kate Morris), Hartford, Vt.

Mrs. Cone writes to the editor: 'About the only newsy thing that can happen to '79 is to die, and I think we have all lived through the winter—old ladies, round about 70, settled for life as to income, home, and adventures, not a thing worth printing. I have had four appeals for money for the college this winter—won't I please organize my class for its part in the Alumnae Fund, the Burton Memorial, Juniper Lodge, and Phi Beta Kappa. Bless everybody's soul, there isn't any organizing in us, and since the Four Million Dollar Fund and the Birthday Gift not a cent to be had! We can only look on with surprise at the versatility of the younger alumnae in thinking up causes, and their energy in pushing them."

1880
Class secretary—Mrs. Edwin Higbee (Netta Wetherbee), 8 West St., Northampton, Mass.

Mary Locke's mother, Anne Lincoln Locke, died the middle of December in Westwood (Mass.), after celebrating her hundredth birthday on Nov. 26, 1926. Her remarkable character was described by her pastor at the time of the birthday celebration, when he spoke in the highest terms of her alert mind, her interest in community affairs, and her constant concern for the welfare of others. Her home was considered a veritable "Community House," where hospitality and goodwill were dispensed for more than fifty years.

1881
Class secretary—Eliza P. Huntington, 88 Harvard St., Newtonville, Mass.

1882
Class secretary—Nina E. Browne, 44 Pinckney St., Boston, Mass.

Haideé (Soule) Bothfeld reports the birth on Dec. 22, 1926, of her ninth grandchild, Walter, son of Theodore Jr.

Ex-1882
Mary (Huggins) Gamble reports eight grandchildren, all of whom she has seen this winter. Her sons Sidney and Clarence were members of Dr. Sherwood Eddy's party in Russia. Mrs. Clarence Gamble spoke at the Women's City Club, Boston, in April on Personal Impressions of Soviet Russia.

1883
Class secretary—Mrs. Charles H. Haskell (Louise Woodward), 6 Huntington Pl., Norwich, Conn.

DIED.—Charlotte C. Gulliver, of heart failure, Mar. 31.

Word has already reached each of you, through the kindness of Louise Haskell, of the terrible loss that has come to us in the death of our beloved secretary. For forty-three years she served us most faithfully and loyally and was the one tie that kept us all together. Now we must draw together in her memory.

Louise Haskell has consented to act as secretary for a time—and at our next reunion we must elect one to carry on. As soon as details are arranged, plans for a memorial for Charlotte will be sent to you.

An In Memoriam to Charlotte will be found in the front of the magazine. E. L. C.

1884
Class secretary—Helen M. Sheldon, Fort Ann, N. Y.

Anne Brooks has spent a quiet but enjoyable winter in Malden, doing a little tutoring, and thus keeping up her zest for Latin cross word puzzles. Anne had a pleasant little visit with Alice Mills not long ago.

Who says the world is wide! Sarah Delano, Abbie Mead, and Ida (Skilton) Cornish are living in the same block in New York City.

Alice Gladden left her home to her beloved Columbus School. The little pre-school, which had claimed Alice's chief interest for some time, will still carry on there.

The southern motor trip of Bessie Merriam and Helen Sheldon was interrupted early in March by Helen's illness. She came back to New York and Bessie continued with her cousin, Mrs. Olive Weeden of Providence, R. I. They went through the mountain region of North Carolina, visited South Carolina in azalea and magnolia time, and attended the wonderful Easter celebration of the Moravians at Winston-Salem, N. C.

In June Vida Scudder ends her long service as professor of English literature at Wellesley. She will probably spend next year in Europe, but will retain her home on Leighton Rd., Wellesley.

Early in February, William Spalding, husband of Kate (Dunn) Spalding, died of pneumonia at their home in Syracuse. Of him the *Syracuse Journal* says: "In the death of William Spalding, Syracuse loses a citizen who throughout his years of useful service had been an advocate and an exemplar of clean living and honest healthful sports. He was a firm believer in the value of religion to youth in following a normal life."

Elsie Tiemann and her sister have been having a delightful winter in Sicily, Naples, Rome, and on the Riviera.

1885

. Class secretary—Ruth B. Franklin, 23 Sherman St., Newport, R. I.

DIED.—Mabel Fletcher, at Exeter, N. H., Mar. 7.

OTHER NEWS.—Elizabeth (Cheever) Wheeler's eldest son, Bancroft (M.D. Harvard Medical School '24), is taking a special course at Roosevelt Hospital, N. Y. C.

Mabel (Haines) Martin spent the winter in San Diego, Calif. She writes that she is making good progress toward being quite well again.

Virgie (O'Brion) Merrill also spent the winter in California.

Clara (McFarland) Hobbs and her husband have been in New York for the winter. In May they go to their summer camp, Sagawatha Lodge, which opens this season for its seventh year.

Ex-1885

Helen Bartley, who never fails to send a class letter, writes that she often sees Ellen Clarke, another former member, also living in Burlington, Vt.

Nellie (Elliot) Freeman announces the birth of her first granddaughter, Audrey, last November.

1886

Class secretary—M. Adèle Allen, 144 Lincoln St., Holyoke, Mass.

DIED.—Kate (Haggett) Warren, Feb. 24, at her home in Spencer, Mass. Kate was one of the best known and most beloved women in Spencer, having been actively connected with the church, the literary and the social life there for more than 25 years. Her daughter Helena, wife of Theodore Reuman of Stamford, Conn., graduated from Smith in 1917.

OTHER NEWS.—On Apr. 9 Frances Goodwin entertained the College Club in Boston members of her class within reach.

Ex-1886

A Memorial Exhibition of the works of the late William Baxter Closson, husband of Grace (Gallaudet) Closson, is to be held May 9–21 by Robert C. Vose of Boston, in his galleries. Oils, pastels, watercolors, and wood engravings will be shown.

1887

Class secretary—Mrs. Alden P. White (Jessie Carter), 3 Federal Court, Salem, Mass.

1888

Class secretary—Florence K. Bailey, 174 Broad St., Claremont, N. H.

1889

Class secretary—Lucy E. Allen, 35 Webster St., West Newton, Mass.

The class president and secretary arranged an '89 "Get-together Luncheon" at the Boston

College Club on Mar. 15. There were present: Margaret (Lovejoy) Butters, Lucy Allen, Ella (Abbot) Wilder, Mabel Fletcher, Alice (Johnson) Clark, Annie (Thompson) Lambert, and Grace White.

Ella (Abbot) Wilder's son Frank is teaching at the Mount Hermon School.

Lucy Allen entertained the Boston A. A. U. W. at her home on Apr. 9. Lucy is sending ten of her 1927 graduates to eight colleges. Another graduate of the Allen School, Sarah Taylor, has been chosen editor-in-chief of the *Smith College Monthly*.

Mabel Fletcher has resigned her position in the Yale Nurses' Home, and has been recuperating in and near Boston.

Ex-1889

Julia (Crouse) Houser has returned from a year in Europe and has been in Boston for the winter.

Dr. Harriet (Parker) Vaughan and her husband came to America on furlough last July, and have been living at 135 Pine St., Fitchburg, Mass. They expect to return to India in the fall.

Abigail (Seelye) Scudder and Dr. Scudder recently spent a few months abroad.

1890

Class secretary—Annie S. Wyckoff, 95 Clinton Av., Jamaica, N. Y.

May Brown's husband, Frederick A. Killmer, died at his home in Glens Falls (N. Y.), Dec. 4, 1926.

Carrie Dodge writes: "I spend my winters in New Hyde Park, Mass.; my springs in Washington, D. C.; my summers in Europe or Maine; and my autumns in Omaha, Neb. My permanent address is Women's University Club, 106 E. 52 St., N. Y. C. I am well and happy and am starting for Europe May 12."

Susan (Homans) Woodruff was senior member on Mar. 31 at a Smith College luncheon in Huntington, L. I., for which twenty-five invitations were sent to alumnae and undergraduates, all living in the vicinity of Huntington. How we do grow! That is enough for a new club! Among the guests was Carolyn (Sprague) Wright '15, Leonora Sprague's niece.

Nan (Lathrop) Greene went to Italy with her husband in February for a four months' trip.

Elizabeth (Sherrill) Kent's address is 41 W. 10 St., N. Y. C., where she is living with her two sons, both of whom are in business in New York.

Leonora Sprague writes: "I had a bad breakdown three years ago through overwork for many years, carrying all sorts of things besides teaching. It was my thirty-sixth year of teaching, having taught two years before going to college. I got in an immense amount of work of all kinds and had much fun out of it too. My record never sounded distinguished, because I gave up chances at big jobs for the sake of the family, running the house and so on, and for the sake of work with individual children whom I cared about. Last year I had a wonderful trip abroad.

Among other things I motored over a thousand miles in Scotland and England in luxurious cars, kept house in Oxford in a marvelous 17th century house, stayed five weeks on the coast of Devon—all this after a fairy story cruise on the Mediterranean. My sister and I are all that are left of my family, and I do the housework, dig in the garden, and obey the behests of a very lordly cat. I am now able to see one or two people at a time, and enjoy them, for my specialty has always been ' people'; and some day I hope to teach again.''

Your secretary represented the class at the Alumnae Council in February, and had a most delightful and illuminating time. The college is a vast and complex machine, and one does not realize its complexity till one goes to the Council, and hears something of the inside of things.

1891

Class secretary—Mrs. H. B. Boardman (Carolyn Peck), 1307 Lowell Rd., Schenectady, N. Y.

Susan (Fuller) Albright and Carol (Peck) Boardman spent several months in Arizona and California this winter. They were in Chandler (Ariz.) at the same time.

Charles Woolsey Cole, son of Bertha (Dwight) Cole, received in October the award of the Addison Brown scholarship at Amherst. The award is made annually to "that member of the Senior class who, being already on the scholarship list, shall have attained the highest standing in the studies of the Freshman, Sophomore, and Junior years.''

Edith (Granger) Hawkes of Fulton (Calif.) is greatly interested in Parent-Teacher work and is editor of the new district paper, *The Parent Teacher Messenger*. Her daughter Eleanor graduates from the high school in Santa Rosa in June.

Eunice Gulliver's sister Charlotte, Smith '83, died suddenly Mar. 31.

Mary Louise Foster has been granted a sabbatical year to return to Spain to carry on the work she began seven years ago. The Junta has built a new chemical laboratory and has invited her to come back and equip it and organize the new courses. The Spanish girls were very keen about American laboratory methods and she looks forward with pleasure to returning to Madrid to build there a miniature course in chemistry as taught at Smith College. She has written a small book on "Lavoisier, His Life and Work" which has been published by Smith College as No. 1 of the Smith College Monographs.

Fannie (Ordway) Kastler's son Arthur is doing research work in blood chemistry at Columbia while studying for his Ph.D. Two of her sons are attending Tulane Univ., New Orleans, and her daughter Ruth is teaching.

Pleasant letters have been received from Marion Hinkley, Mary Sabin, Alice Sherwood, May Smith, and Laura (Sawin) Tilley.

Ex-1891

Lucia Cary spent last summer in Europe and is now at home again in Fredonia, N. Y.

1892

Class secretary—Mrs. Irving H. Upton

(Katherine Haven), 20 Park View St., Boston 21, Mass.

Edith Brown sails June 16 for Europe to be away until the spring of 1928; she will be accompanied by Alice Mundt. Miss Kimball, Edith's aunt and last near relative, who lived with her, died last December.

Lena (Tyler) Chase's son, Cornelius Jr., was married to Lucille Hildreth Keep, Mar. 5, in N. Y. C. They will be at home at Peekskill (N. Y.) Military Academy.

Eleanor (Cutler) Daggett writes: "I have been elected to membership in the National Committee for Mental Hygiene and for many years have been recording secretary of the Connecticut Society of Mental Hygiene. Also for two years I have been registered in the Graduate School of Yale Univ. for advanced study in the Department of Italian.''

Blanche Morse is in Europe but will be back in time for our reunion.

Florence (May) Rice and husband sail on July 1 for a year's travel in Europe. Mr. Rice is having a leave of absence from his Boston school position. Florence has a granddaughter born Mar. 20, the daughter of William Foster Rice Jr. of Baltimore.

Those interested in the Phi Kappa Psi Society are helping to raise a memorial to Molly Wardner who was one of its founders.

The reunion plans are full of promise: already (early April) we have heard from 21 who expect to be present. Do not fail to return in June to the Fountain of Youth.

1893

Class secretary—Mrs. John E. Oldham (Harriet Holden), 16 Livermore Rd., Wellesley Hills, Mass.

Caroline Bourland has been granted a sabbatical absence for this semester. She published a book on the Spanish novel this spring.

Stella Bradford has been giving a course of lectures in the Central School of Hygiene and Physical Education, N. Y. C., this past winter, besides carrying on her office work and giving instruction in corrective exercise.

Florence (Corliss) Lamont has a second grandson, Edward Miner Lamont. Florence went on a cruise to the West Indies in February.

Florence Jackson has returned from her annual tour of southern colleges and schools where she has lectured on "Occupations for Women" and done advisory work. Among other things, she attended the meeting of the National Association of Deans of Women at Dallas, Tex.

Sue Knox has been confined rather closely to her home this winter by illness but says her health is improving now. [On the eve of going to press, word came of Sue's death on Apr. 21, at her home in New Brunswick, N. J.]

Virginia Lyman and her sister sailed Mar. 26 on Panama Mail *S. S. Columbia* for Los Angeles. They are to spend a month in Pasadena and go to the Yosemite in June and to Alaska in July, back by Canadian Rockies, home by Aug. 1, and up to Islesford (Me.) for a month or so.

Grace (Stevens) Wright's mother died Mar. 29. She was 85 years old and had lived with Grace at Wellesley Farms the last few years.

Mary (Vanderbeek) Giles represented the class at Council this winter. Her daughter Marian was on the Freshman Honor Roll from the class of '29·

Ex-1893

Mary Copeland's husband, John Kemater, died Feb. 10 after an illness of two months.

Nan (Sigsbee) Kittelle sent a New Year's card from Cavité where Admiral Kittelle is Commandant, showing the charming entrance to the Comandancia, once the residence of the Spanish admirals, and now the quarters of the Kittelles. She writes that they saw China and Japan en route to the Philippines and that she finds life at Cavité perfectly fascinating.

Evelyn Hatch, daughter of Elisabeth (Smith) Hatch, is one of the girls who has been chosen to go with the College's third group to France next year.

1894

Class secretary—Mrs. John J. Healy (Katharine Andrews), 1104 Greenwood St., Evanston, Ill.

Ethel Devin is in California visiting May Willard. On her return she will stop in Cleveland to visit our president, Jeanne (Lockwood) Thompson.

Mary (Frost) Sawyer and her husband, who is treasurer of Phillips Academy at Andover, are in England visiting and studying the great English schools. She will return before Commencement.

Gertrude Gane wishes to remind all classmates who will be in the vicinity of Juniper Lodge during the summer that Wonalancet is very near and she will be delighted to see them.

Edith Harkness is keeping house for her brother who is studying at the Univ. of Chicago. Her new address is 6033 Kimbark Av., Chicago.

1895

Class secretary—Carolyn P. Swett, Hudson View Gardens, 183 St. and Pinehurst Av., New York City.

Bertha Bardeen spent March in Daytona (Fla.) and then came home to begin her new work in the editorial department of the Iroquois Publishing Co. of Syracuse.

Ruth (Conro) Elkins's husband died in Jan. 1926. Her two sons are in Harvard, '27 and '28· Ruth is serving a second term on the School Board of Andover, N. H.

Caroline Fuller is writing a series of songs for children, "circus songs" she calls them. Those of you who have radios may hear them before long. Her new child's book, "Kitten Whiskers," will be published this spring.

Adeline Hinckley writes of a busy, happy life keeping house in her own pleasant "flat" in Worcester, devoting her afternoons to an invalid sister in a sanitarium.

Mabel (Hurd) Willett's youngest son, Herbert, a student in a Washington (D. C.) high school, died last month.

Lydia (Kendall) Foster's son was married in Sept. 1926 to Pauline Hitchcock.

Eva (Cook) Rudd, Julie (Gilman) Clark, Mary Goodman, and Anne (Young) Copeland are all living in the same part of Hartford.

Laura (Crane) Burgess is now a saleswoman for Angell, Van Schaick, and Co. If you contemplate buying a home or building in Scarsdale or Westchester County, Laura will be glad to help you.

Elizabeth (Cutter) Morrow read from her own poems at a benefit for the Camp Fire Girls given at the Repertory Theatre in Boston. We hope that you have read some of Bess's charming poems in *Scribner's* and in other magazines.

Mary Goodman visited Miriam Webb in February on her way south to spend a month with her sister in Florida. Mary sailed for Europe in April. She plans a leisurely wandering through Sicily, Dalmatia, Italy, and France.

Eva (Hills) Eastman and her husband have just returned from a flying visit to France to see their younger son who is at school in Neuilly.

Margaret (Manson) Holcomb's son Harry has graduated from Yale.

Polly (Poland) Cushman had charge of the decorating of the Women's Republican Club of Boston for its fall opening. Her work was widely commented on and admired.

Mary Smith has returned from her year in China where she had many unusual and thrilling experiences.

Sophie (Washburn) Bateman has a new granddaughter, Eleanor Preble Jones, daughter of Lois (Bateman) Jones.

Anne (Young) Copeland served as your official representative at the Alumnae Council owing to the absence of your president and the disability of your secretary. Attendance at the Student Council meeting seemed to her as well as to other delegates whose opinions we have heard expressed to be one of the most interesting and heartening experiences of the session.

Ex-1896

Sara (Perkins) Sturgis's son, Milton Jr., spent part of the Christmas holidays with Ellen (Duckworth) Trull. He is taking the mining engineering course at Harvard. His sister Isabel is specializing in geology at Washington State Univ.

1897

Class secretary—Lucy O. Hunt, 185 Beacon St., Hartford, Conn.

The replies for reunion have been most gratifying, but we hope many more will come. We have to get that Cup, you know! Write Jane Vermilye (110 Lydecker St., Englewood, N. J.) that you'll be there. And don't forget that you have the privilege of sharing in the reunion gift. Do it now!

The secretary wishes there was room to report the 30 or more delightful letters she has received from our loyal exes. We expect to see many at reunion.

The New York and Boston Groups had splendid get-togethers in March, and they helped arouse enthusiasm for June.

Wanted! Pictures of our college days, and of our present homes and of our families. Send to D. R. Caverno, 6 West St., Northampton, by June 1. Mark plainly.

———

Mary (Barrows) Irwin's daughter Charlotte is an "ecstatic freshman" at Gill, John is studying at Univ. of California, and Eleanor is back from seven months in Paris.

Ruth (Brown) Page's son Gilman was married in March to Mary Kury of Madison.

Grace (Browne) Broomell writes that her husband is president of the Colorado Ski Assn. and vice-president of the National Assn. Myron, a junior at the Univ. of Colorado, is interested in writing and hopes to be a college professor; Doris is literary editor of her school paper; Beatrice is the state champion ski jumper of her class; while Rachel is the domestic one of the family.

Anna Carhart is teaching at the Scoville School, 1006 Fifth Av., N. Y. C.

Florence (Day) Stevenson will attend the General Assembly of the Presbyterian Church in San Francisco in May. Elizabeth (Cole) Fleming will be one of the speakers there.

Gertrude (Dyar) ter Meulen is president of the Greenwich College Club.

Albertine (Flershem) Valentine plans to bring her 14-year-old Jane to Hamp. She is a "candidate in preparation" for Smith.

Alice (Goodwin) Schirmer reports a trip to Porto Rico, made especially enjoyable by meeting several Smith graduates.

Mary (Hewitt) Mitchell expects to go abroad with her husband in June. They will be in London most of the winter, where Mr. Mitchell will be studying.

Ella (Hurtt) Barnes sailed in April for a Mediterranean cruise. She hopes to be back in time for reunion. Ella entertained the N. Y. group at tea, Mar. 5.

Florence (Keith) Hyde will be at the head of a Vacation Bible School this summer, where she hopes to demonstrate her ideas of child development by dramatic activities.

Agnes (Jeffrey) Shedd has a grandson, Frederick Jeffrey Blodgett, born Feb. 7 to her daughter Marion, Smith '21·

Ruth (Jenkins) Jenkins recently sponsored a White Elephant sale for Juniper Lodge.

Marian Jones is making her home with a friend at 116 Hope St., Providence, R. I. She is very busy with community and Americanization work in connection with her church.

Katherine (Lahm) Parker has recently returned from Europe, but plans to go over again early in the summer to bring back her daughter, who is studying there. Her address is Billswood, Forest Av., Lakewood, N. J.

Ellen (Lormore) Guion has finished a university extension course in appreciation of music, and is the proud possessor of a certificate therefor. She recently took the part of Fagin in "Pictures and Readings from Dickens," at the Newton Community Club.

Florence (Low) Kelsey's son Harlan has announced his engagement to Ruth Driesbach of Duluth. Florence will take her two girls abroad in August for the winter.

Edith (Melluish) Davis's oldest son has

the interesting government job of overseeing the beacons on the airway for mail pilots from Chicago to St. Louis. David is a junior at Williams.

Perley (Merrill) Macfarland has been elected president of the N. J. Branch of the A. A. U. W.

Louise Peloubet is working on a project of the Newton Council relative to boy and girl life in Newton, especially the use of leisure time in connection with juvenile delinquency.

Katherine (Perkins) Clark writes of a delightful trip to the Coast with her husband and Anne Rust. They tried all the H. Morrises in the telephone directory in Los Angeles, but didn't find our Harriet.

Clara (Phillips) Rogers writes that Carol is studying art and French in Paris, and hopes to enter Smith in the fall. Dorothy will take up interior decorating at Miss Sacker's school. Clara herself is much interested in the Foreign Policy Assn., and often meets Ada and Jdy there.

Margaret Rand took work in vocational training at Harvard Summer School in 1925, and spent last summer with Edith Williams on Pine Lake, Mich.

Fairfax Strong sends a message to '97 to stop and see her at the Baldwin School, or during the summer at her cottage at St. Hubert's, three miles from Keene Valley in the Adirondacks.

Edith (Taylor) Kellogg's husband has been made full professor of mathematics at Harvard.

May (Ward) Dunning has moved to 31 Glen Rd., Wellesley Farms, Mass.

Grace (Wiard) Young's son graduates from Wesleyan this June.

Florence (Whiting) Grover is engaged in the organization of a Woman's Board of the Boston City Missionary Society. As a trustee of the Avon Home for Destitute Children, she is busy visiting the children in their boarding homes.

Anna Woodruff returns from California in June and hopes to come to reunion.

Ex-1897

Florence Barnard sends a copy of *Common Ground*, containing an introduction given by her at a meeting of the Economic Committee of the Massachusetts Teachers Federation. The four objectives she suggested were adopted as a basis for the work of the Committee.

Margaret (Miller) Cooper spent the winter in California. She reports having pictures in four recent exhibits—at the Winter Academy in the Fine Arts Building, at the Pennsylvania Academy of Fine Arts, at the National Arts Club (N. Y.), and at the Lyme Summer Exhibit.

Katherine (Garland) Vilas is doing some ensemble work with a cellist, is an active member of the Woman's Club, and is on the board of the Society for the Blind.

Alice (Pearl) Whittemore has charge of the real estate department in her father's office in Bangor, and also keeps up her shop in her home.

Caroline Rice is dean of women at Colorado Woman's College.

Ellen (Rushmore) McKeon writes of her varied interests: psychology, women's clubs, Parent-Teachers Assn., and best of all her daughter Ellen, who is headed for Smith.

Rozel Trull has moved to 50 Commonwealth Av., Boston.

1898

Class secretary—Ethel M. Gower, 29 Mather St., New Haven, Conn.

Emma (Byles) Cowperthwait came home from Europe in February, lunched with Edith (Ames) Crosby and other '98ers in Boston, and went on to Northampton to see her senior daughter, Marian. She left her younger daughter, Eleanor, in Paris where she is studying the violin. Emma expects to spend the summer abroad again.

Rejoyce (Collins) Booth has left her ranch and lives near her sister in Hollywood. Her father was instantly killed by an automobile Feb. 19.

Ruth (Duncan) Duff reports a busy winter's work: "Have completed two copies of Gilbert Stuart portraits, commissions for a Washington lady whose ancestors they were, and am now finishing the second portrait from photographs of the grandparents of a Boston woman."

Louisa Fast has been in Florence (Italy) "personally conducting" several young Americans on vacations from their European schools.

Mary Joslin writes: "I am living with my aunt and we travel a good deal. Of late our annual trips have largely been around the Caribbean. Porto Rico, Guatemala, Havana have been some of our ports of call. One of our trips took in California where I saw Rejoyce Collins, who gave a Smith luncheon and garden party for us."

Julia (Morris) Foster has been in Europe for two months with her husband.

E. Thacher has spent the winter abroad and writes enthusiastically of Greece.

Ex-1898

Nora (Barnhart) Fermier writes: "I am an extremely busy mother of four—Florence and George about to graduate from the Campus High School in May, Emilie (nearly fourteen) already making a record as a real poet, and little Bertha. With all these cares I have managed to publish a few poems and have won several prizes. My poem, 'The Ladder,' won the national prize offered by the General Federation of Women's Clubs. My husband is vice-dean of the Engineering School of the Agricultural and Mechanical College of Texas, one of the largest military schools in the country."

Ethel (Boynton) Meikle's son is in Cornell Medical School. Her address is now 128 Pleasant St., Arlington, Mass.

Grace (Child) Bevan's address is 71 Munroe St., Hartford, Conn. She is librarian for the Phoenix Mutual Life Insurance Co. "Besides the routine work of buying books and giving them out to our employees and salesmen all over the country, I conduct reading courses, look up scores of interesting questions, and give talks on the use of books to our training classes for salesmen—a busy life.".

Grace Kellam, while still connected with the Yale Publishing Association, is manager of the Book and Quill, a book shop and lending library which has been recently opened in New Haven.

1899

Class secretary—Miriam Drury, 334 Franklin St., Newton, Mass.

The following '99ers met for luncheon at the new University Club in Boston on Feb. 25—13 at the table! Abby (Allen) Eaton, Helen (Andrew) Patch, Clara (Austin) Winslow, Mary Bell, Edith Burrage, Gertrude (Churchill) Whitney, Florence (Dow) Estes, Miriam Drury, Alice (Foster) Blodgett, Ethel (Gilman) Braman, Alice (Moore) Nutter, Harriette Patterson, Annah (Porter) Hawes. Molly Keyes sent the galley proof of the classbook which we examined with interest. She says with regard to it: "Anyone who has not ordered a copy and wants one should send her order to Miriam (Choate) Hobart (Mrs. Newton B.), Taft School, Watertown, Conn., accompanied by check for $2.50. Something has been written by all but 18 of the graduates, and about 6 more have been written up by friends, while 42 non-graduates have written."

Clara (Austin) Winslow gives the following interesting account of her family: Richard, the oldest son, is a freshman at Tufts College, of which his father is a graduate and trustee; Marjorie, Lasell '29, will after graduation either enter some college as a junior, or specialize in music; Donald is a sophomore in the Newton High School; Priscilla is in the seventh grade in the junior department of Lasell. Just for home practice and pleasure they have a "family orchestra" of six pieces. The family spend the summers on their farm in Turner, Me.

Elizabeth Beane is completing her second year as librarian of the Plymouth (N. H.) Normal School. She writes, "I enjoy the work, a new field for me, but often wish I were nearer Boston."

Gertrude (Churchill) Whitney recently took a leading part in the comedy, "The Whiteheaded Boy," by Lennox Robinson, given by the College Club of Lawrence, Mass. Her son George has been awarded the Lincoln medal given by the Illinois Watch Co. for writing the best essay on Lincoln. He is also a member of the executive committee of the Methuen High School debating club.

Gertrude Hasbrouck sends greetings from Pasadena (Calif.), where she and her mother are spending March and April.

Lucy (Tufts) Bascom and her oldest daughter, Sally, are spending several months in Albuquerque, N. M.

Martha (Vance) Drabble writes: "My address is now 365 Appleton St., Holyoke, and I am in the Public Library here with Elizabeth Ray. We are almost living college days over again."

Elsie (Warner) Voorhees says: "Of course I am a member of the Hartford Smith Club. The last meeting I attended was held in Eleanor (Goldthwait) Graves's lovely new home in West Hartford." Her own home she describes as "the little old farmhouse we have been hoping for years to find. A fascinating path through two meadows back of our lot leads to the rose garden of Elizabeth Park."

NEW ADDRESS.—Mrs. Charles T. Malcolmson (Margaret Wilkinson), Ethel Walker School, Simsbury, Conn. Permanent address, c/o Chicago College Club, 196 E. Delaware Pl., Chicago. Margaret's son Charles is a freshman at Kenyon College where Mary (Southworth) Williams also has a son.

Ex-1899

NEW ADDRESS.—Mrs. Thomas W. Wilby (Agnes Andrews), 51 Vernon St., Brookline, Mass.

1900

Class secretary—Gertrude E. Gladwin, 2323 Orrington Av., Evanston, Ill.

The secretary has had most gratifying results from the class letter sent out in March. The personal letters which have come in have been a delightful surprise and make one feel that we should never return to the formal card questionnaire. Thanks to those who have written, our budget of news is increased and each mail is hopefully searched for more of the friendly letters. A great deal is too personal for these notes, but much enjoyed.

Ruth (Albright) Hollister's daughter, a sophomore at Smith, made the hockey and swimming teams. Her son Evan Jr. also excels in athletics. Ruth's summer home on the Canadian shore of Lake Ontario is the happy gathering place of all her own and her children's friends. During two months 325 extra meals were served there! By publishing this she may be even more swamped by traveling classmates.

Jennie Edgcomb is personnel director for the fifth floor of R. H. Stearns in Boston.

Annie (Foster) Murray has a daughter in the sophomore class at Mount Holyoke.

Helen (Gager) Brown has given up the work of probation officer in Columbus, and has bought out a candy factory and store. Her daughter is a freshman at Lake Erie College, and is on the glee club, swimming team, and is assistant editor of the Lake Erie Record. Her boy is going to Ohio State Univ. next fall. Helen is much interested in the Players' Club which Agnes (Jeffrey) Shedd '97 founded, and which is housed in an old barn.

Mabel (Hartsuff) Trowbridge is kept busy visiting schools in which are her own three and three foster children. Lately she saw one boy at Hotchkiss and a girl at Abbot, and visited Harriet (Huffman) Miller who has a sophomore son at Harvard. Mabel says she is building a week-end cottage on their farm near Detroit, a forerunner of a house they intend to have later where she plans to spend her old age raising dogs, flowers, and apples.

Gertrude (Henry) Mead's daughter Eleanor (our class baby) recently accepted a position in Santa Rosa (Calif.) to organize recreational work for women and girls in a community center. Ruth Mead is a sophomore at Mills.

Edith (Hollis) Curtiss has a senior son at Harvard.

Helen (Kerruish) Buffum will spend another year in Switzerland with her daughter. Her address is Petit Beaumont, au de Beaumont, Bethusy, Lausanne.

Emily (Locke) Ward has two daughters who teach and one engaged in secretarial work. Two daughters live at home and her son is a freshman at Harvard. Her letter contained such a fine extract from a sermon that I am quoting a part of it, "Young people to-day are better than they have ever been, but they sorely .need to be better, for the simple reason that they are facing greater hazards, meeting severer temptations, struggling with more complexity than we, the older generation, ever have known." Emily voices her own belief in the young people of to-day, and she has ample opportunity to judge for she lives on the campus of Milton Academy.

Ruth Perkins rounds up all the 1900 people in and near Boston every now and then for a luncheon at the Woman's City Club. A good idea to follow in other centers.

Nelle (Quirk) Kline recommends the climate of San Diego for summer vacations and hopes some classmates will try it. Her son Quirk is six and a half. She often sees Stella (Barse) Cole, who lives near and who has two daughters.

Helen Richards is going abroad this June for a sabbatical year.

Mary Sayles has published a book, "The Problem Child in School," which has had most favorable notice in various quarters. Her new book is in process of writing. Her work is under the Joint Committee on Methods of Preventing Delinquency.

Fanny (Scott) Rumely writes: "I am getting a thorough education at last, at Columbia Univ. In other words, I have a daughter in Horace Mann kindergarten, a boy in elementary at Lincoln School, a girl in junior high, and another in senior high—contemporaries of Sally (Sanderson) Vanderbilt's boys at Lincoln. I am undergoing parental education at Lincoln, gymnastics at college, and scientific management of the home in postgraduate conferences. I like my job a lot, but it is strenuous from kindergarten to P.G." It certainly sounds so to a maiden aunt of a single niece and nephew!

Florence (Whitin) Parsons and family are leaving for an indefinite stay in France. Her husband, Theophilus Parsons, and a collaborator, Cameron Burnside, "have a new and scientific theory of color which results in perfectly beautiful, rich, and real effects, not queer, because their construction and drawing is sound." Lorraine goes for a year abroad and returns for her last year at Miss Madeira's to prepare for Smith. Chauncey, after a summer with his family, comes back for junior year at Brown; Paul, Harvard '24, is finishing a business course there; Theophilus Jr., Cornell '24, is working in a research laboratory in the Anaconda Copper Co. in Montana. From another source I learn that Mr. Parsons has had pictures exhibited several times at the Corcoran Gallery.

Mary (Wilder) Kent writes of a wonderful trip the family had to the Pacific Coast last summer, camping, riding, climbing, and flying; and the two children who were with them learned that their parents could keep up with them. Mary says her big job is still on the American Board of Foreign Missions which has recently been reorganized. She represented the W. B. M. in turning over the resources of her own Board to the new organization, but the work is not finished yet.

Mary (Whitcomb) Clark and her husband have returned to their former field at Ahmadnagar after the death of the head of that mission. Mary expects to come over for her daughter Mary's graduation from Smith in June.

Ex-1900

Alice (Barrows) Fowler has recently returned from a three months' vacation in Europe. Her daughter graduated from Connecticut College last June.

Edith (Barry) Withington's son Herman graduated from Dartmouth in 1926. He is a salesman for the Armstrong Cork Co.

Martha (Leach) Fisk's husband is carrying out the program for new buildings at the State Univ. of Iowa. Her daughter graduated there and did postgraduate work at Bryn Mawr, and is now assistant to the Dean of Women at the Univ. of Wisconsin. Her son is studying architecture at the Univ. of Pennsylvania. She herself is taking a course in the history and appreciation of music at the Univ. of Iowa.

Rachel Studley, after another winter in Sebring (Fla.), is about to open Loch Haddin Inn, in Lorain, O. Her address is 2905 E. Erie Av.

Cornelia (Tearse) Miller's oldest son graduated at Cornell in 1925, her daughter is studying music in Minneapolis, and the youngest son is a freshman at the Univ. of Minnesota.

1901

Class secretary—Mrs. Sanford Stoddard (Hannah Johnson), 499 Washington Av., Bridgeport, Conn.

Alice (Cummings) Hudson is conducting her husband's coal business in Fitchburg since his death last spring.

Amy Ferris has been invited by the Metropolitan Museum of Art in New York to give one of its Sunday afternoon lectures this spring.

Ethel Hawkins, who has an article in the March *Atlantic*, is leaving Miss Hall's School in Pittsfield this June to go to Schenectady to live with her brother and his family.

Methyl (Oakes) Palfrey's daughters, Mianne and Sarah, are known as "Sister Lenglens in the Making." They have recently won the national girls' indoor doubles championship in tennis.

Agnes (Patton) Woodhull has been visiting her daughter "Patsy" at Smith and is planning to send her daughter Caroline later.

Lena (Swasey) Parson writes: "My husband and I have just returned from seven months in Europe and West Africa—the four months in Liberia, the Gold Coast, and Sierra Leone were full of adventure and interest every moment. We traveled some 1600 miles by coast cargo boats, surf boats, kinoos, ox carts, hammocks, and on foot and were in native villages in the bush where a white woman had never been seen before and among the most primitive of Western African tribes."

1902

Class secretary—Mrs. L. F. Gates (Josephine Lamson), 723 Eighth St., Wilmette, Ill.

Hello, 1902! Everybody ready for the grand reunion? Did everyone receive her copy of the reunion notice I sent two weeks ago? I have extra copies for any who did not. The most important thing is to notify Ella Van Tuyl immediately as to how many reservations you wish, so take pity on her and do not delay. Twenty-fifth reunion is a momentous occasion: paralysis or small pox the only legitimate excuses for non-appearance. So let's all be there with bells on. Jo.

1903

Class secretary—Mrs. Francis W. Tully (Susan Kennedy), 3 Alwington Rd., Chestnut Hill, Mass.

MARRIED.—Ethel Hutchinson to Rev. Cleo Madison Chilton, D.D., Mar. 5. Pleasant items of news drift in about Ethel: a wedding present of $4000 from the church; moving into and furnishing a new apartment; joining the College Club and Women's Club of "St. Jo"; and many social activities in honor of the bride. Address, 917 Faraon St., St. Joseph, Mo.

Blanche (Lauriat) Chandler to Daniel Edgar Manson, Jan. 28, in New York. The following day they sailed on a two months' trip to Egypt and the Mediterranean ports. Their home will be at 292 Clinton Rd., Brookline, Mass.

NEW ADDRESSES.—Mrs. George M. Sabin (Mary Hickok), 217 S. Union St., Burlington, Vt.

Mrs. Frank D. Layton (Ethel Keep), 4 Walbridge Rd., West Hartford, Conn. For the past sixteen years Ethel has been connected with the social service department of the Hartford Dispensary. She has worked in the children's clinic, orthopedic clinic, and for the last six years has been in charge of the special clinic for venereal diseases, working more especially on children and family problems in this connection. In addition, she has been secretary of the Dispensary for ten years and she organized and supervised a Convalescent Home to which children are sent direct from the institution. Ethel's husband is now vice-president of the National Fire Insurance Co.

Mrs. Warren S. Hayden (Elizabeth Strong), 3035 Monmouth Rd., Cleveland Heights, O. Elizabeth's son Sherman is a sophomore at Williams.

OTHER NEWS.—Our Class Baby, Ella Belle Bliss, became a graduate nurse last November. She is now an anaesthetist at the Worcester City Hospital, so her mother, Lucia (Bailey) Bliss, writes. Lucia's son Albert, a senior at Dartmouth, has scored

many points for the gym team and set a new Dartmouth record for the rope climb in one meet. Arthur is a senior at high school and won a medal for a Lincoln essay recently.

Alice (Bookwalter) Ward writes: "We are enjoying a visit from my father. He started out on a world trip in 1924 to visit his three daughters and came on to Ceylon in December, after a stay of two years in Peking with my youngest sister. He seems quite delighted with our island home and finds our Ceylonese friends very congenial."

Margaret (Buchwalter) Martin writes: "Oscar is a sophomore at Princeton, Morris is at 'The Hill,' and Margaret is hoping to enter Smith in a few years."

Another Princeton sophomore is Dorothea (Burnham) Pond's "Billy," who is an honor student. Dot's daughter Mary graduates from the Burnham School in June and the two younger boys are freshmen in high school, "bound for Princeton some day."

Roma (Carpenter) Goodhue's husband, Dr. Ned Dunham Goodhue, died very suddenly last September. His death is a great loss to Dayton and to the medical profession, for he had done extensive and important pathological work.

Helen (Carter) Hewitt's son Carter is at Princeton and her daughter Gillette at the Emma Willard School, headed for Smith.

Harriet Clark and May (Bates) Appelt report a week together in New York, doing the town for May's two little girls, even visiting the Statue of Liberty—more unusual than-trips abroad nowadays!

Jean (Cochrane) Armstrong writes from Nassau in the Bahamas, where she spent the winter, that Jean, her older daughter, is to enter the Masters School at Dobbs Ferry this fall to prepare for Smith and that her boy Frank is now at the Berkshire School en route for Yale.

Esther Conant continues her delightful meanderings over the map of Europe. Latest reports are a month in Vienna, long stays in Budapest and Prague, painting along the Riviera, with Florence for the springtime. She will probably return next fall—for a while at least.

Aside from her work as director of music at the State Normal School, Inez Damon B.M. has for the past two years been director of the Choral Club of the Middlesex Women's Club. The *Lowell Courier-Gazette* of Mar. 29 contains a long and complimentary account of a concert given before the members of the Club. It says: "Under Miss Damon's musical guidance the chorus of about 45 voices has made steady progress since its début a year ago. . . . For a climax there is ample volume, but under Miss Damon the chorus has learned to use it with discretion. Quality of tone after all is the end the director seeks and attains in more than the ordinary degree."

Maude (Dutton) Lynch writes: "I have been trying, now that my youngsters are all in school all day, to take up a little writing again. . . . I gave a talk this fall before the

Parent-Teachers Association of one of the Yonkers Public Schools on 'Reading to My Children.' . . . This winter I have been working on three readers that one of the large publishing houses of school books expects to bring out shortly. I find the writing job has to be quite secondary to the main job that I am doing, namely, raising a family. Sam, my oldest boy, is hoping to go to Dartmouth or Yale after one year more in Lincoln School, and Elizabeth, a year after that, to Swarthmore, and Paul the following year to Yale, so perhaps four years from now I can do some serious writing."

On Apr. 5, the report from the A. B. C. F. M. headquarters in Boston was that Dr. Lora Genevieve Dyer was "carrying on" well, and in comparative safety, at her hospital at Foochow, China. She had a thrilling experience when the Cantonese army passed through the town and did for a time have to close the hospital and go to Pagoda Anchorage, near the harbor and the American battleship. Some of the missionaries went to Manila but Genevieve stuck to her job, and now that the raiding and looting soldiers have gone farther north has been able to open the hospital again, the attitude of the Chinese in Foochow being very friendly.

Edith Everett is now associate director of the White Williams Foundation, an organization which is doing social work in the schools of Philadelphia. She writes, "I hope Elisabeth Irwin is coming down sometime soon to talk to our staff." Edith has been for the past two years president of the National Association of Visiting Teachers and is a lecturer in education at Swarthmore.

Klara (Frank) Kempton writes: "Husband is head football coach and instructor in French in the Hill School. George is Yale Sheff '29, and out for crew, elected to St. Anthony (Delta Psi) last fall. David is Hill '29, preparing for Stevens Tech. Janet is at the Holmquist School, New Hope, Pa., en route to Smith, we hope!" [Doing wonderful things at the piano, we hear.] The family spent a month last summer in the wilds of Ontario and expect to begin a new camp near North Bay, Ontario, this summer.

Carolyn (Fuller) Wheeler reports that she has a troop of 40 "Cubs," a local movement, preparatory to the Boy Scouts, taking in boys from 8 to 12, one her younger son.

Theodora Gerould writes: "My sister and I are enjoying our 'sabbatical year'—no chickens! All our attention goes to gardens, hers to flowers and mine to vegetables."

Grace (Gilbert) Graff and her husband have been spending the winter on their first trip abroad, landing at Naples and working up to England.

Isabel (Grier) Jack and her husband took the Caribbean cruise in February. Isabel's daughter Eleanor is preparing for Smith.

Mabel (Haberstroh) Hargraves's son Julian, now twenty years old, will graduate from Williams in June and expects to enter Harvard Law School next fall. He has been on the honor list, winning a desirable scholarship, has played on the golf team, and belongs to Delta Gamma.

Fannie (Hastings) Plimpton has been spending the winter with her two children in Arizona.

Lucy (Hastings) Horsfall, her husband, and three children are now living in Bermuda where they expect to build a home near "Soncy."

Helen Hill is on the nominating committee of the Classical Association of New England and presented the report of the committee at the annual meeting in Worcester in April. She will again be a reader of Latin for the College Board in June.

After an illness of many months, Mabel Hill's father died last October.

Florence Howe sailed Mar. 2 for a two months' trip in France and England. She hoped to meet Margaret Thacher for part of the tour.

Elizabeth Jack writes on letter paper headed "Little Valley Nursery, Parkside Drive and Overland Street, Elizabeth Jack, Peoria, Ill.," and rumor reaches us that she owns and manages it herself.

Bertha (Johnson) Campbell writes: "My hobby is gardening—just enough market gardening to pay the expenses of my flowers. We are planning to take the children to Halifax this summer while my husband attends the convention of Maritime Optometrists. There is a beautiful motor trip along the St. John River (the 'Rhine of America'—minus the castles) with excellent roads, and we plan to investigate some of the fishing camps. If anyone is interested, I'd be glad to send details, and more than glad to have a call or a visit from anyone of 1903."

Katherine (Knox) Covey writes: "John is a junior at Lehigh, in the band and Musical Clubs. They go on a tour in May and broadcast from WJZ. My daughter Betty is at Mechanics in Rochester, taking costume designing and crafts. Jim is a sophomore in high school and senior patrol leader of his Scout Troop. Dick is just an active, athletic boy in the sixth grade."

Margaret (Lunt) Bulfinch is serving her sixth year as a member of the school board of Dover, Mass. She was secretary of the board for three years and has been chairman ever since. Last winter she wrote several articles for a health magazine on the School Lunch, Posture, Mental Health, and similar subjects. Margaret is also president of the Dover Women's Club, clerk of the First Parish Unitarian Church, and vice-chairman of the Visiting Nurse Association of Dover, Medfield, and Millis. Her husband, like his famous ancestor, is a successful architect, his firm having just completed the new Fogg Art Museum at Harvard among other things. Margaret writes: "For the past five years we have spent our summers on the water, first on a houseboat in Marblehead Harbor while the children were small, and now on a motor boat. We cruise all along the coast from Buzzards Bay to Maine and make our home port off the Boston Yacht Club at City Point."

Have you read "Ancient and Modern Legends" by Helen McAfee in the April *Yale Review?*

Frances (McCarroll) Edwards sends a charming and happy letter about her daughter Beatrice's engagement. "Bee's" fiancé is David Fall, the son of Mr. and Mrs. J. Horton Fall Jr. of Evanston, Ill. He will graduate from Williams in 1928, at the same time that Bee will graduate from Smith. He was a Hill School boy, prominent in the life of the school, played quarterback on the school team and is now quarterback of the Williams football team. Frances and her husband recently made a three weeks' visit to Hill School alumni centers which included Minneapolis, St. Paul, Pittsburgh, Chicago, Detroit, and New York.

Anna (Marsh) Suter writes that she is busy hatching chickens. She says: "My infant has been going to kindergarten this year. Carrie's [Carrie (Marsh) Jenkins] children are in junior high. We had a joyous but all too brief glimpse of Eleanor (Putnam) Bodel recently."

Emma Miller writes that she is still first assistant of the headworkers at the College Settlement of Philadelphia.

Annie May Murray and her sister with their two adopted children had a cottage in Tryon (N. C.), where they spent the greater part of the winter.

Loella Newhall writes: "Still teaching languages (any kind, French, German, Spanish, and Latin) in the Lynn English High School. Spent last summer remodeling my house, which I am now enjoying very much. Expect to sail June 29 for a trip to Europe."

Maybelle (Packard) Newcomb is vice-chairman of the Greenfield Hospital Organization Branch and chairman of the Ways and Means Committee. She has been president of the Franklin County Smith Club and represented the Club at the Alumnae Council. For the past six years she has been on the Executive Board of the Woman's Club of 350 members and for two years its president.

Carlotta (Parker) Honeyman is planning to send her daughter Barbara to Smith in a year or two and will come east to enter her at college—a pleasant anticipation for her many friends who have not seen Carlotta in many years, as Ilwaco is so far away.

Eva Porter last summer completed her work at Columbia for a Master's degree in English and was awarded the M.A. in October. She writes with enthusiasm of the Emma Willard School. She hopes to go abroad this summer.

1903 is very proud that our "Class Daughter," Marguerite (Prescott) Olmsted's Janet, is one of the "Phi Betes." See page 331.

Beatrice Putnam's two nephews have been, since her brother's death, her legal wards. Their mother died many years ago and Beatrice has always cared for the boys. Robert graduated from Exeter last year and is now at Yale, and Mitchell will graduate from Exeter in June and hopes to enter Yale in the fall.

Helen (Robinson) Riker has been made manager of the women's department of the Binghamton Agency of the Security Mutual Life Insurance Co. Her daughter Louise plans to take a secretarial course when she graduates from high school. John is just entering high school.

Ruth Stevens's mother died very suddenly and peacefully Mar. 29 and Fannie Stewart's father, who had failed steadily since the death of Fan's mother in November, died in March in Florida, where he had gone to try to regain his health.

Katherine Bolman, Florence (Tullock) Bolman's daughter, will be one of the "Juniors in France" next year.

Alice (Warner) Hamilton writes, "Erskine is at Antioch, same class as Teddy Stanwood" —Marion (Evans) Stanwood's son.

Edith (Wyman) Rolfe with her husband and the three boys is to spend the summer motoring through Italy, Switzerland, and France. Maurice is an honor student at Dartmouth. Charles enters Andover in the fall.

Alta (Zens) Vineyard's son "Jimmie" completed his high school course in three years and a half and they are in France for the spring and summer. They may go to Africa later.

Ex-1903

Does anyone know the present address of Maude (Douglas) Hopkins, Mrs. James Hopkins or Mrs. Douglas Hopkins? She has, in the past, always answered class notices so we are very anxious to find her, but mail is returned from the Chicago Beach Hotel, Chicago, Ill., which she last gave as her permanent address.

A letter from Sara (Crawford) Dana tells of the death of both her parents, her mother in Oct. 1925 and her father less than three months later. Sara's son Crawford is a freshman at Yale. She writes, "We still keep our house in Cooperstown, but it was impossible for me to live there alone so my address now is Miller Apts., Franklin, Pa."

Julia (Edson) Davis's daughter Mary is at Bradford Academy, headed for Wellesley.

Grace (Scofield) Sawin's son George, incidentally Alice (Webber) Scofield's nephew, is a sophomore in the Harvard Engineering School.

Luella Stewart writes: "Haven't done a thing since July 1922 except live in the same apartment, work at the same job, take a few trips, go to a lot of shows, and have 28 short prose pieces and 53 alleged poems published in the *Sun*, the *Evening Post*, the *American Legion Weekly*, and the *New Yorker*. Oh, yes, and go to the Brooklyn Smith Club!"

1904

Class secretary—Eleanor Garrison, 99 Marion St., Brookline, Mass.

Bertha Davenport sends a charming picture of her "Red Farm House," Westminster, Vt. It is on the Connecticut River Highway to the White Mountains. Guests are accommodated overnight or by the week. Bertha says the view is wonderful.

Gertrude Douglas will be with the Conservation Commission in the Biological Survey of the Finger Lakes district this summer. She says: "The native fish are getting very scarce. Fish eat plants, and my job will be to identify water plants." Ithaca will be her base of operations.

Margaret Estabrook continues her office of secretary to the Dean of St. Paul's Cathedral in Boston under Dean Sturges, successor to the late Dean Rousmaniere. Margaret's father died Mar. 10.

Helen Hall lost her father in November. Helen visited Marie (Conant) Faxon in Rochester (N.Y.) last March.

Olive (Higgins) Prouty sailed for Bermuda Mar. 25.

Ellen Hildreth started for Italy the middle of March, returning in June.

Lois James has leased the Alumnae House, which is now being managed under the name "Jewett Inn." Lois continues to offer luxurious accommodations at The Whale Inn, Goshen.

Phila (Johnson) Burck's daughter Barbara is to be married on June 25 to Harry Rae Callender Jr. of Los Angeles.

Bee (Kingsbury) Watson's son Frederick is a Dartmouth freshman. Ethel Hazen has a boy in the same class.

Lucie (London) Moore writes: "My Robert is working hard at Thacher School where he is very happy. Budge (Hotchkiss) Streit has just been here, a treat for us all." Belle (Lupton) Pike and her three children also saw Lucie in Los Angeles, en route to Honolulu.

Mary Pusey's mother died suddenly at Atlantic City, Mar. 6.

Edith (Vaille) Weeks and her husband made a flying trip to Boston in March, visiting Northampton on their way home. "It was a heavenly evening, mild and moonlit. There is an undeniable charm about the place."

Alice M. Wright spent the first week-end in March with Helen Mabie in Summit, N. J.

Spring visits were made by Marion Clapp to Montclair (N. J.), by Evelyn (Trull) Bates to Boston, and by Alice Robson to Montreal.

The daughters of Nellie (Cuseck) Connolly and Dorothea (Wells) Holt have been chosen to spend their junior year in France.

1904 had had two luncheons; one during the Alumnae Council meetings in Northampton, Feb. 17, at The Manse. Present: Helen Choate, Florence Cook, Nellie Cuseck, Louise Fuller, Eleanor Garrison, Anne Mead, Evelyn Trull, Una Winchester, also class daughters belonging to Elizabeth Barnard, Mary Comer, Florence Cook, Nellie Cuseck, Lilian Ehrich, Helen Lincoln, Amy Stein, Dorothea Wells, Una Winchester, and Alice B. Wright.

The second luncheon was held at the Boston College Club, Mar. 25. The guests of honor were Annetta Clark and Florence Snow. Present: Emma Armstrong, Marion Clapp, Ruth Crossett, Marion Doane, Eleanor Garrison, Helen Hall, Margaret Hamlin, Alice Hatch, Priscilla Jouett, Bertha Keyes, Helen Marble, Rita Souther, Bertha Thresher, and Olive Ware.

Ex-1904

Elsa (Longyear) Roberts says her Mary is among the first violins in the Dana Hall orchestra. Horace is at Harvard and John at Exeter. For the Easter holidays Elsa was planning to transport Mary, with a flock of her school friends, to their cottage at Vinalhaven, Me. This winter Elsa has been active on the concert stage. A newspaper account of her Jenny Lind performance says, "She appeared in a duplicate of the costume worn by the famous artist and interpreted her songs with dramatic ability, distinction, and charm."

Blanca Will is on the staff of the educational department at the Memorial Art Gallery in Rochester, N. Y.

NEW ADDRESSES.—Gertrude Douglas, 149 Chestnut St., Albany, N. Y. (after May 1).

Priscilla Jouett, 15 Grozier Rd., Cambridge, Mass.

LOST.—Mail has been returned from: Emma Gray (Mrs. Louis S. Caswell), Yonkers, N. Y. Laura E. Smith, 542 School St., Athol,Mass. Clara T. Waterman, Oak Park, Ill.

1905

Class secretary—Mrs. Frank Mansfield (Alice Curtis), 9 Salisbury Rd., Brookline, Mass.

Eleanor (Brown) Whitney accompanied her husband on a business trip to Germany, Switzerland, France, and England. They sailed Feb. 22, and expect to return in May.

Ella (Burnham) May tells us that after a glorious fall in the Adirondacks she has been strenuously housekeeping this winter and also has substituted as superintendent in a Sunday school of 180. In their more frivolous moments Ella and her husband have reveled in amateur dramatics.

Charlotte (Chase) Fairley's family are moving to New Canaan (Conn.) where her husband has been made assistant headmaster of the Mott School for Boys.

Clara (Clark) Brown is enjoying her new work. At present she is putting a new card index system in one of the big insurance companies in Boston.

Louise Collin is planning a six weeks' trip to France this summer, sailing from New York July 16.

Clara Davidson was obliged to resign last spring from her position in the department of Biblical literature at Smith, on account of her mother's ill health. With her mother she spent the winter months in Eustis (Fla.), is spending April in Augusta (Ga.), and plans to return to Pleasantville (Pa.) early in May.

Dr. George H. Blakeslee, husband of Edna (Day) Blakeslee, was selected to deliver the Dr. James Schouler lectures at Johns Hopkins Univ., from Mar. 23 to Apr. 8.

Louise (Dodge) Whitaker is working actively in the interests of the Boy Scout organization in Medford.

Emma Hirth is executive secretary of the Personnel Bureau of the National Board of the Y. W. C. A., 600 Lexington Av., New York.

Alice Holden sails early in June for recreation and study in France and England.

Marcia Johnson writes: "I am now engaged

as assistant at the Owl Book Shop, a new and very popular enterprise in Orlando, Fla. It is the only thing of its kind here."

Nancy (Lincoln) Newell is doing most interesting and artistic decorative painting in restoring antique furniture and trays.

Ruth (Maxson) Aughiltree writes that her father, Dr. Henry M. Maxson, known to many 1905ers, retired this last year from the superintendency of the public schools of Plainfield (N. J.) after 34 years of active service—not because of ill health, but because he had reached the age limit. Ruth, herself, had a year's struggle with pneumonia and its after effects, but is in "Braithwaite's Anthology" again this year, and still turning out mystery yarns. Recently she was awarded the Torch Press Prize for poetry for her poem, "Will Shakespeare's Widow."

Bertha (Page) Smith is president of the Baby Hygiene Society of Portland, Me.

Ruth (Redington) Griswold has written the music for Grace Hazard Conkling's "The Scissors Grinder." Ruth has had many of her songs broadcast and used in public concerts in Chicago this year.

Harriette (Shadd) Butcher is building superintendent at the Russell Sage Foundation in New York. Her home address is Hotel Seville, 28 St. and Madison Av., N. Y. C.

Sue (Starr) Kelso's daughter Jean, who expects to enter college in the fall, is to be a junior counsellor and tennis instructor at Lin-E-Kin Bay Camp in Maine this summer.

Ethel Young, with her sister, spent the winter in the South. They will be home in Huntington (N. Y.), May 1, after a month in Washington and Greenwich.

Ex–1905

Lucy Clark's temporary address for this year is c/o Equitable Trust Co., 23 rue de la Paix, Paris, France.

1906

Class secretary—Mrs. Eben Atwood (Edith Moore), 2732 Irving Av. S., Minneapolis, Minn.

May I use space here to thank the other secretaries for sending me copies of their class appeals for news? We secretaries can at least stimulate each other! The secretary's life is a constant search for tempting bait to bring even a nibble.   E. M. A.

See Alumnae Publications for note about Marjorie (Allen) Seiffert.

Betty (Amerman) Haasis has temporarily changed her address to Cullowhee, N. C. Following the episode mentioned in the class letter of her home being unwittingly rented to bootleggers, Betty says: "Then from a nearby blasting operation came a large rock, crashing down through the roof and ceiling, just missing my baby and a friend. During Jan. the house was empty, and was broken into by a very polite bandit who simply mixed himself some pancakes and melted up some sugar to eat on them. He neatly swept up the glass he broke in the kitchen door and departed, not touching another thing in the house, locked the door after him, and left the key in the bread box on the back porch. We are now trying to rent or sell." Betty helped with the examination of 250 children in the graded school in Cullowhee, and is running a nutrition class for the underweights.

Margaret (Bridges) Blakeslee, our vice-president, leaves for California in April on a business trip with her husband.

Bernice Dearborn is a member of the scholarship committee in her high school. She finds it a constant strain on her sympathies, for there is much more need than supply. Here is a case of demands for help in tuition at her very door.

Ruth (Fletcher) Common is doing private tutoring. After Easter she is to teach Latin at the Santa Barbara Girls' School to fill a vacancy.

Caroline Hinman will conduct her horseback and camping trip in the Canadian Rockies, June 27 to Aug. 31. Her address is 80 Prospect St., Summit, N. J. I give this address without her solicitation. Her circulars are most alluring.

Catharine Mitchell spent three months on Sanibel Island (Fla.), returning home in April after having satisfied a bewildered mother that Smith should be her daughter's Alma Mater.

Lucy Melcher was councillor from Providence (R. I.) at the Alumnae Council in February.

Edith (Moore) Atwood and family spent over two months in California, mostly in La Jolla. They are certain that they have found the satisfactory place to live where informality and not too great a sense of permanence exist. We admired Hazel (Goes) Cook's lovely home at Chula Vista, set in the midst of a citrus grove, and overlooking valley and mountain. Elizabeth (Roberts) Browne dropped in for a call.

Agnes (McCord) Brindley is deep in College Club work. She belongs to a group studying pre-school education, another on foreign relations, and attends lecture courses in connection with the club. There are only a half-dozen Smith girls in the town. Her other big interest is social service work. Agnes has a boy preparing for West Point and a daughter who hopes to enter Smith in 1930.

Melinda (Prince) Smith is at 427 N. New St., Bethlehem, Pa., during her father's illness.

Helen (Putnam) Kingsbury's youngest child, Philip, has passed away, leaving two older boys and one girl.

Mary Smith gave an enlightening talk on her University Hospital work before the Minneapolis Smith Club at one of its monthly luncheons.

Ex–1906

Olive (Harrison) Whitney also has a "lovely home in the midst of a citrus grove" in Upland, Calif. The family plans to go abroad soon for an extended stay.

1907

Class secretary—Mrs. James L. Goodwin (Dorothy Davis), 10 Woodside Circle, Hartford, Conn.

BORN.—To Violet (Stocks) Proctor a second child and first daughter, Ruth Ramsdell, Mar. 16.

OTHER NEWS.—Marguerite Barrows has spent three strenuous years working with the N. Y. Charity Organization Society. After a delightful nine weeks' trip abroad last summer she is now general secretary of the Family Welfare Department of the Visiting Nurse and Family Welfare Association in Bristol, Conn. She writes that she has enjoyed the snow and being in the country. Address, 120 Judd St., Bristol, Conn.

Gertrude Blanchard has taught school for two years in California but has decided to give it up. With her parents she has bought five acres of "what looks like desert land" near San Fernando. They are clearing it and expect to have a chicken and goat ranch there some day. Present address, Box 448, R. 1, Pacoima, Calif.

Louise (De Forest) Veryard writes from Kobe College, Japan, where she is with her sister Charlotte: "We were ordered to evacuate Changsha on Jan. 12. I was out of our home 30 hours after the notice came with all our trunks and one packing case. My husband was in Shanghai on Y. M. C. A. affairs, so friends helped me off. It is incredible how courteous the common people have been —just exactly as usual—and yet how the communist group have finally interfered with everything in everyday life. Changsha is called 'Little Russia'."

An exhibition of V. J. Smith's paintings was held in Rochester in March. They received much favorable comment and a number of canvases were sold.

Nettie Strobhar is back in New York doing part-time private secretary work and living at the Smith Club.

NEW ADDRESS.—Mrs. Ethel (Willard) Eddy, 364 Main St., South Manchester, Conn.

Ex-1907
NEW ADDRESS.—Ruth Olyphant, 268 Starling Rd., Englewood, N. J.

1908
Class secretary—Mrs. James M. Hills (Helen Hills), 876 Carroll St., Brooklyn, N. Y.

A 1908 luncheon was held at Town Hall Club, N. Y., Saturday, Mar. 12, in honor of May Kissock. Those who attended were Aline (Coursen) Ward, Bella Coale, Edna Newton, Kate (Bradley) Lacy, Gladys Wood, Alma Bliven, Betty Seeber, Sallie (Simpson) Hamlin, Ruth Eliot, Orlena (Zabriskie) Scoville, Helen Ufford, Margaret (Rice) Wemple, Edith (Cowperthwaite) Egbert, Helen (Appleton) Read, Eva (Price) Hobson, Helen (Hills) Hills.

Edna (Schell) Burgess has had a difficult winter with much illness in her family. She is moving this spring to 512 Beacon St., Boston. The summer she will spend in a cottage at North Scituate Beach.

Louise (Stevens) Bryant is executive secretary for the Committee on Maternal Health which is a research group of physicians. Her job is to keep track of some dozen experiments, laboratory and clinical, in the field. Her work includes study, laboratory, and languages

with a considerable amount of administrative detail, a difficult combination. Her business address is 370 Seventh Av., N. Y. C.

Jane Thuman is likewise enjoying a new job. She is librarian of the Roosevelt Junior High School, a pioneer work which she finds most interesting. Her address is 109 Chestnut St., New Bedford, Mass. This summer she expects to be at 1231 S. Wilton Pl., Los Angeles, Calif.

MARRIED.—Irene Fitzgerald to William Thompson Hawthorne, Mar. 1926. Address, c/o The American Red Cross, Sacramento, Calif.

BORN.—To Margaret (Kingsley) Long a third child and second son, Robert Kingsley, June 6, 1925.

To Mabel (Rue) Frederick a second child and first daughter, Catherine Ray, Jan. 28. Address, S. 2707 Rhyolite Rd., Spokane, Wash.

Myrtle (Smith) Rodgers's older child, Joan, aged three, is in kindergarten. Her son, James Philip, was born May 2, 1926.

Ex-1908
Grace Grimshaw is high school librarian in Paterson, N. J.

Edna Macdonald is head of the violin department, James Millikin Univ. Conservatory, her address being 209 N. Fairview Av., Decatur, Ill. Her orchestra numbers 25 and she has a student string quartet. Both organizations have given public concerts and have done broadcasting.

NEW ADDRESSES.—Mrs. Lawrence Allen (Helen Abbott), 24 Bridge St., Manchester, Mass.

Mrs. Harper Silliman (Gertrude Cookman), 1103 Franklin St., Wilmington, Del.

Mrs. Edward H. Lorenz (Grace Norton), 56 W. Hill Dr., West Hartford, Conn.

1909
Class secretary—Mrs. Donald Pirnie (Jean MacDuffie), 138 Milbank Av., Greenwich, Conn.

BORN.—To Charlotte (Draper) Hall a daughter and first child, Eleanor D., Jan. 30.

DIED.—The mother of Grace (Miller) Piper and Marion (Miller) Fernald ex-'09, Jan. 6, of pneumonia.

NEW ADDRESSES.—Mrs. L. H. Shepard (Elizabeth Alsop), c/o Dr. G. F. Alsop, 282 W. 4 St., N. Y. C.

Lieut.-Commander W. E. Eaton, Medical Corps, U. S. N., U. S. S. Florida, c/o Postmaster, N. Y. C. [husband of Fanny (Fiske) Eaton].

Mrs. W. H. Stevens (Pearl Parsons), 210 W. Lockport St., Sayre, Pa.

Mrs. J. S. Thomson (Lois Robinson), 5 Clarendon Pl., Buffalo, N. Y.

Commander Reuben S. Coffey, U. S. N., Bureau of Navigation, Navy Dept., Washington, D. C. [husband of Elinor (Scollay) Coffey].

The two gentlemen from the Navy have entered our lists, as the Navy Department has no record of the addresses of the wives, and Elinor and Fanny are at present among our Lost Ladies.

OTHER NEWS.—Elizabeth (Alsop) Shepard arrived in New York in March and will be at her father's until the middle of May.

Helen (Andrews) Minkler is president of the Women's Club of her church, "trying to catch up with the possibilities for service offered by our new plant, dedicated this October. My husband says I live there! Besides this I have done a little work in other lines—being chairman of one of the nominating committees for the Evanston Women's Club (Social Service Dept.), and going up to Rock Island as delegate to the State D. A. R. Conference. Edith (Scott) Magna was one of the most effective speakers there."

Elizabeth Bryan is with Miss Madeira again. Hilda (Stedman) Cross had planned to visit her in cherry-blossom time, but her son Henry broke his nose and she had to give up the trip.

Hazel (Douglass) Allison and her 12-year-old son are partners in many enterprises, raising everything from peanuts and cantaloupes to chickens. Both nearly burst with pride when their peanut crop won first prize at the Pinehurst Fair. One day a week she runs the school cafeteria; she says she is not teaching now, but just loafing!

Louise Elmendorf is studying at Columbia this year for an M.A. She spent her spring vacation with Hazel (Douglass) Allison.

Florence (Forbes) Killam writes from her Canadian igloo that Peter adores kindergarten and that they are both happy in their new home.

Louise (French) Buckley writes that her 5-year-old Mary climbs every tree in sight and is eagerly anticipating school next year. Florence Paine's mother wrote her that Florence has had a trip abroad recently and is studying at Harvard this year.

Caroline (Garrett) Tuthill has been in Bermuda lately, stopping in Montclair to see Sheila (Bryant) Swenson on her way home.

Bertha Goldthwaite, in addition to her labors as headworker of the East End Union in Cambridge, which serves 400, has brought up her brother's two motherless children. Irene is now a florist and designer, Clarence is preparing for Technology. Bertha is industrial chairman of the Boston League of Women Voters, legislative chairman of the Boston Federation of Women's Clubs, legislative chairman of the Settlements of Boston, and secretary of the Massachusetts Council on Women and Children in Industry. This last group is unofficially connected with the State Department of Labor and Industry.

Margaret Hatfield writes of her school: "Eighteen children, hours, 9–12.30; 3 group teachers; 4 specialists (carpentry, basketry, carving; modeling and painting; science; and French). E. Moos has dancing and I have music. Next year an all-day program."

Louise (Hennion) Fisher for next year serves in the following ways: vice-president, Hartford League of Women Voters; vice-president, Women's Republican Club; deputy-commissioner, Girl Scouts; director of the Hartford Tuberculosis Society; member of Community Chest Budget Committee; house chairman of the Town and Country Club; president of the Parent-Teachers Association. The Boys' and Girls' Trades School, for which she has been working for some time, will be decided upon this spring.

Annie (Lane) Dodge and her husband have recently inherited a furniture manufacturing plant, reproducing Colonial mahogany furniture and making special pieces to order. The firm of Whidden and Harris (E. Whidden ex-'09) is one of their customers. They visited Northampton this fall and were much impressed with the new buildings.

Nan (Linton) Clark has taken a sabbatical year from dramatics, as she has been too busy getting her own family settled in new quarters and incidentally helping a number of other families in her department get settled. The University is planning a new Anatomy Building and she says: "The family eats and drinks blue prints. However, we have a comfortable house and we have met charming people and when tadpole season begins we shall feel really at home!"

Jean (MacDuffie) Pirnie has been teaching this year and is a part-time impresario.

Anne Coe Mitchell spent part of the spring in Bermuda.

Marcia (Reed) Binford was delegate to the State D. A. R. Conference in Orono (Me.) this year.

Dorothy (Smith) Abbott has been visiting Sheila (Bryant) Swenson this spring.

Jane (Wheeler) O'Brian has been in New York lately to have her portrait painted. Eleanor (Mann) Blakeslee came with her, and they both spent a day in Montclair with Esther and Sheila.

Anne Wiggin writes: "My job is not primarily money-raising, but I am secretary for Friendly Relations with Foreign Students who are in the United States, trying to help them make the necessary adjustments to life in this country and at the same time to educate American students to the point of appreciation of the cultures and backgrounds which these students represent. The 1500 who are in this country represent 73 of the countries of the world and since most of them are unusually fine people my task is about the most thrilling mortal can imagine! Incidentally, I do work for the raising of money for the Student Friendship Fund and for that cause I have visited about 40 schools this year. My territory extends from Maine to Ohio and south to Florida, and in the south as far west as Mississippi, but of course I do not cover all of it every month! This summer I am going to Europe with a group of American students and professors and deans of women and student secretaries. We are going to visit the students of Europe and try to represent to them some of the good of America and not all of its bad."

Ex-1909

MARRIED.—Marion Miller to Harold Edward Fernald, Oct. 9, 1926, at the Union Church in Waban. They have been living in Marion's old home, and since Mrs. Miller's death Marion has been keeping house for her father and husband. She has given up her work as office manager for her father.

1910

Class secretary—Alice O'Meara, 12 Keswick St., Boston, Mass.

BORN.—To Esther Ann (Smith) Wherry a son, in Mar. 1926.

OTHER NEWS.—Katherine (Bennett) Brehm has returned from Europe. She studied piano over there and now is playing accompaniments "with distinction," they say. She could not play more musically than she did in college!

Adiene (Bergen) Hart courageously took her four children to Europe last summer.

Marion (Booth) Trask, once more in this country, has had interesting experiences the past four years in her search for authentic antiques in France. "Our recreation," her husband writes, "consisted in nursing Marion (Pooke '05) Duits's Dutch-American baby, of short and long trips to Cathedral cities, of a sojourn at Menton where Florence Snow '04, Florence (Bannard) Adams '05 and Jane, Mary Clapp '12, and Professor and Mrs. Abbott dropped in. There Marion kept house, climbed, and played on the beach with Louise Van Wagenen and her little Edith." Marion now has an interesting studio-salesroom at 37 E. 57 St., New York, filled with beautiful and to-be-coveted objects—pewter and dower chests and 16th century fabrics.

Marjorie (Browning) Leavens, whose husband is treasurer of Yale-in-China, decided that it was best to leave China for a while and so arrived in this country early in March. She expects to settle down with her parents for some months and can be reached c/o F. W. Browning, R. D. 7, Norwich, Conn.

In her trip around the world last year, Harriet Crozier-of-the-adventurous-spirit (for she went alone) spent a few days with Eva (Jenison) Pruyn at San Diego; played in Honolulu with Helen (Allmond) Wanamaker '08 and her family. Her letter tells nonchalantly of experiences in Japan and China, in Manila and Port Said, in Genoa and the Italian Riviera. And now she is once more in Havana, working for the Royal Bank of Canada.

Margaret (Dauchy) Migel and her husband dashed off to the South for a few weeks last winter. Peg is much interested this year in F. F. Noyes rhythm and in the study of child psychology. She is blessed with a splendid laboratory containing five little personalities, in which to work out her problems!

Elizabeth (Jameson) McCreery's father, Mr. David Jameson, died Mar. 20.

From on board *S. S. Sabaudo* comes a letter from Helen Jones, telling of six weeks of gay and interesting travel in Europe with Helen (Hills) Hills '08 as an appreciative companion. "We saw friends, opera, clothes, and sights in Paris, visited antiquity in and around Avignon, wild modern gardens and finally historic gardens in and about Genoa. It has been a glorious trip and all the better for having been made in winter!" Helen is back in New York planning lovely gardens and grounds for her clients, with the added inspiration of those six weeks to draw upon.

Helen King is on her annual tour—this time to the Mediterranean for several months.

Margaret (Means) Payne's husband died in March.

From Estelle (Valentine) Newman comes the news that on Mar. 31 a Smith luncheon for graduates, exes, and undergraduates living in Huntington Township (L. I.) was held and well attended. Estelle was one of the committee in charge and they hope that from this meeting may develop a North Shore of Long Island Club covering other nearby towns. Estelle's time is more or less her own now that her ' only child " is a second-grader, and so she serves on all kinds of forward-looking committees, such as that of Public Health Nursing, Service League, and Parent-Teachers Association. She also substitutes in the high school and tutors occasionally. On the side she and her husband have a young farm, two dogs, and many chickens. By now 100 baby chicks will have been delivered from Marjorie Talbot's Naacook Farm stock to her tender care.

Your secretary saw Norma (Anderson) Hyde not long ago, with little Norma. Norma reports that Ethel (Wilson) Nichols has been on a business trip with her husband to Holland, staying for some time in Amsterdam.

These are exciting times and often dangerous ones! Marjorie Smith sent a newspaper clipping from Bridgeport (Conn.), which reports the wounding of Betty Wright by Chinese burglars last November at the Presbyterian Mission in Nanhsuchow. She was operated upon twice before the bullet was found, but is now restored to health and back at work as principal of the Mission School.

1910 had a successful luncheon at The Manse during the Council meetings in February in Northampton. Jane Armstrong, busy M. D., was there; also Betty (Gregory) Perkins, our patient and efficient room committee of last reunion; Helen (Evans) Chilson, most prosperous assistant purchasing agent for the McCallum Hosiery Mills; Loraine (Washburn) Hall, enjoying so much her new baby; Evelyn (Canning) Keyes, with fine pictures of her good-looking boys and with plans for a garden of perennials; Leslie Leland, who had just blown in to Northampton; Norma (Hoblit) Woods, and Alice O'Meara, representatives at the Council. We missed Ruby Litchfield. She had been called away by the sudden death of her father.

Ex-1910

June Stone's father died Mar. 19.

1911

Class secretary—Mrs. J. P. O'Brien (Margaret Townsend), 614 Madison Av., Albany, N. Y.

DIED.—Marie Zulich, Apr. 4.

BORN.—To Marguerite (Butterfield) Ervin twin daughters, Lavinia Millsaps (Pat) and Marylouise Butterfield (Polly), Mar. 11. Marguerite has had five children, four of whom are living.

To Mary (Dickinson) Bogardus a daughter, Mary Constance, Dec. 6, 1925.

To Florence (Masterman) Sullivan a daughter, Elizabeth M., Dec. 9, 1926.

To Mary (Patten) Coleman a daughter, Frances Page, Apr. 5, 1926.

To Charlotte (Phelps) Dodge a son (sixth child), David Walbridge, July 24, 1925.

OTHER NEWS.—Elizabeth Abbe is studying at Miss Conklin's Secretarial School. Temporary address, 233 E. 17 St., N. Y. C.

Florence Angell, international secretary for the A. A. U. W., spoke last January in Burlington (Vt.) to a gathering of Vermont women representing various branches of the A. A. U. W.

Alice (Brown) Myers wrote in Feb. that she and her husband were trying to return to China in spite of the conditions there.

Jo (Dormitzer) Abbott spoke at the Educational Conference after Alumnae Council in Northampton in Feb. on the Treatment of Problem Children. She has been asked to write a book on Children's Behavior Problems, to be published in about a year by the Judge Baker Foundation.

Margaret (Foss) Thomas and her husband have left Rochester, and are now back once more in Boston. Temporary address, 30 Bay State Rd.

Sarah (Johnston) Hitchcock writes that they are beginning their fifth year in Nagasaki, Japan. Althea Marks spent two days with her last July when Althea was making a tour of Japan, China, and Manila aboard the *Empress of Russia*.

Edith (Lobdell) Reed has just won a prize of $100 from the National Federation of Musical Clubs for a song, "Swans," (words by Sara Teasdale) which will be sung at their convention in Chicago this April. A book of first grade piano pieces is also being published which will be ready in May. She wrote both words and music (with the help of her children). The title is "Sing-Along." Her 7½-year-old Dorothy has a poem coming out in the May *Child Life*.

Winifred Robertson is still teaching Bible and English at Sara Keen College, Mexico City. See note in Alumnae Publications.

All of 1911 will be sorry to learn of the death of Dottie White's mother in February. Dottie and her father and sister took a sea trip to California immediately after, stopping at Havana and Balboa. She expects to return to Ridgewood in April.

Ex-1911

BORN.—To Marjorie (Fuller) Emerson a son, Franklin Pierce, Feb. 9, 1926. This is her fifth child. One son, Henry, died at birth in 1922.

Rhoda (Moore) Haskell is clerk of the State Mutual Life Assurance Co. in Worcester, Mass.

1912

Class secretary—Mary A. Clapp, Galloupe's Point, Swampscott, Mass.

MARRIED.—Margaret Brearley to Dion Kanouse Dean, Lehigh '06, Sept. 12, 1925. Margaret writes that they are living at 16

Pierpont St., Rahway, N. J., and also reports two stepchildren, Ruth Orr, born in 1914, Robert Aaron, born in 1917, and one daughter of her own, Margaret Ann, born Aug. 29, 1926.

BORN.—To Frances (Davis) Landry a third daughter, Priscilla Frances, Jan. 26.

To Cyrena (Martin) Toll a son, Giles Darwin, Jan. 16.

To Arline (Rorke) Hill a son, Greer Bennett, Oct. 1, 1926.

To Rosamond (Starin) Hyman a daughter, Alice Louise, Feb. 7.

OTHER NEWS.—Mildred (Ashley) Gould has turned to histrionic activities, reporting that she has participated in two plays during the winter.

Martha Dennison has put on her seven league boots again and gone back to India, this time as general secretary of the Bombay Y. W. C. A.

Hilda (Edwards) Hamlin with her three boys is wintering in Paris. She hopes that all 1912ers will look her up in her apartment at 144bis Boulevard du Montparnasse, and see whether her French accent is as good as she thinks it is, or whether it is as quaint as her sons would have her think!

Also among our French residents is Rachel (McKnight) Simons, who has been hibernating on the Riviera. She hopes to make the grade to reunion, but fears that ten days after landing in which to open up and start running her home in Sewickley may interfere.

Ruth Mellor has a job with the Children's Aid Society and a habitation with Mildred (Scott) Olmsted and family in Rose Valley, Moylan, Pa.

Louise Michael is helping to bring the Paris fashions to Buffalo through the medium of the Hickson Shop, which she manages.

Helen (Northup) Jackes's mother died on Jan. 1 at Helen's home in Toronto.

Ex-1912

Margery Bedinger, who is tireless in her labors as secretary of the ex-members, has sent in the following gossip:

Miriam (Howard) Challice is still enthusiastic about her hospital library work.

Helen (Norris) Smith won the New Jersey State golf championship last year, and was semi-finalist in the National, all this in addition to caring for her four children.

Isabelle (Noyes) Brugler lives at Belle Haven, Greenwich, Conn. She reports her occupation as that of housewife and gardener.

1913

Class secretary—Mrs. Alexander Craig Jr. (Helen Hodgman), 314 E. 17 St., Brooklyn, N. Y.

MARRIED.—Isabel La Monte to Edmund Byrne Hackett, Feb. 12, in London, England. Address, 164 E. 72 St., N. Y. C.

BORN.—To Jane (Garey) Barus a second son and fourth child, Oct. 25, 1926. Jane writes, "That makes two boys and two girls, the boys on the ends and the girls in the middle."

To Helen (Gillette) Wright her third son, Harold Burns, Sept. 28, 1926.

To Dorothy (Jones) Heath a son, Fenno Follansbee Jr.

To Virginia (Martin) Meyer her first son and second child, Henry Lewis II, Mar. 3, 1926. "We have just come back from Havana—life is rosy and busy."

To Dorothy (Olcott) Gates her third daughter and fifth child, Deborah, Mar. 27.

To Anna (Pelonsky) Weissblatt a son, Richard Willard, Aug. 31, 1926. "I guess sociology would class me with the Floating Population. My present address is 36 Concolor Av., Newton, Mass."

To Dorothy (Usher) Wilson her fourth son, Leonard Usher, Jan. 1.

OTHER NEWS.—Mary Arrowsmith writes: "This familiar looking little card arrived the other day and I'm sending it back chiefly to wish you a Happy New Year, and to lament that I'll be back in time just to miss Commencement. However, our 15th isn't far off now—doesn't it seem incredible! For the rest, I am here as a fellow under the Hungarian Department of Education, going to classes at the University and trying to look as if I knew what was being said. I'm also collecting bits of one thing and another, which may eventually turn into a dissertation. I'm billeted in a government boarding school so that I get glimpses of the Hungarian educational system, in which I am greatly interested. Budapest is quite the loveliest city I know as far as situation is concerned, with the Danube flowing through the center of the city and wooded hills rising behind the old town of Buda, and there is much of interest to see and do. But quite the nicest thing about Budapest and Hungary generally is the wonderfully gracious, generous hospitality that one finds everywhere."

Lucile Atcherson writes from Berne, Switzerland, Feb. 12: "This is my last message to 1913 from Switzerland, for I have just received word of my transfer to the legation in Panama City, to which post I shall proceed Mar. 15. Remember that there will always be a warm welcome for visiting 1913ers there." Lucile was third secretary at Berne, but will be second secretary at Panama.

Catharine (Chapin) Blake says: "I'm on the same job—two very lively boys and a busy husband. (He is now manager of the Travelers Insurance Co. branch office at New Haven.)"

Sarah (Cheney) Despard writes: "We've just come back from our second trip to England with the children and had another successful venture. My husband and I went to Egypt leaving the boys in England, and found them thriving on our return."

Vera Cole writes: "Last summer my sister and I had a wonderful cruise to the Mediterranean. We visited Portugal where a revolution is in process, Spain, Morocco, Gibraltar, Algeria, Italy, Switzerland, France, Norway, Sweden, Scotland, and England. We went from London to Paris by airplane. I have given several lectures on my trip since my return. There were a dozen Smith girls on the cruise. I am enjoying my classes in the City High School and am taking a Saturday course at Columbia. Have just become a member of the Society of Mayflower Descendants."

Beatrice (Darling) Day is "still living in the country and loving it. Very busy, but nothing to bring forth any headlines! Looking forward to 1928."

Winifred (Durham) Potter's husband died Aug. 15, 1926, in France. Her new address is 3232 Clarendon Rd., Cleveland Heights, O.

Ruth (Gardner) See writes: "I've developed into the Great American traveler. Three months last spring in Italy and France and now sailing Jan. 15 for Buenos Aires, home Apr. 5 after 'doing' South America. Last year and the year before I went to the School of Commerce at Northwestern and patched up a few of the holes in my education."

Rosamond Grant's mother returned her card, saying: "I am sending this card just to let you know that Rosamond is still up in the mountains of New Mexico, where she has been for two years hoping to get back to her normal state of good health. She hasn't been well since her return from France with the Unit. My daughter Helen, Smith '22, is with her at present. We all loved President Burton and I shall hope to send on a check to swell the Memorial. Rosamond loves the Southwest and will stay on indefinitely."

Elizabeth Greene went to Florida with the Red Cross hurricane relief. "We've had a great time and what we don't know about building houses and mortgages!"

Margaret (Hawley) Ely sends "congratulations to the girls who wrote our friendly bell for 1927. The only news I can think of is that I have a new job this year which I find particularly enjoyable. It is teaching in the secretarial department of Carnegie Tech. After the hustle and bustle of a large high school I feel quite calm and collected with a maximum of four classes a day. Three of the four are composed of college graduates who are taking our one-year intensive course in secretarial work. Wellesley, Wilson, Trinity Univ. of Edinburgh, and Pennsylvania College for Women are all represented in the group."

Helen (Hodgman) Craig: "On New Year's eve my brother's wife, Gladys Fee '22, died, leaving her tiny son Tommy so that the Craigs with my brother and his baby have gone back to my father's home to prove that three families can live under one roof."

Through Gertrude (Van Buskirk) Prescott your secretary heard that Alice (Kent) Roder lost her little daughter who was about three.

Mary (Larkin) Foran says: "Recently I found Helen (Readio) Lowe living a few blocks away and it has been fine to get together with a 1913er. Her Barbara and my triumvirate, Ellen, Thomas, and Grace, are fast friends (most of the time)."

Merle (McVeigh) Chamberlain was in Florida this winter. She and her daughter Anne live with Merle's father and mother. They usually plan to reach North Adams by May 1.

Clara (Murphy) Tead writes, "My chief but humble news is that I've taken on more work at the Women's City Club and am the executive secretary this winter."

Hildur Osterberg: "Same school but new job—counselor—that means no classes to teach, but all the new students to meet, the standardized testing to do, and numerous other related and intensely interesting jobs to plunge into."

Irene (Overly) Cowan: "What's wrong with 1913? Not a class has such a poverty-stricken report on members' activities. Twice in recent years I sent news of trippings to and fro and I failed to get into print." (Secretary's note: Irene went to the coast, I remember, and I fear I kept this to myself. I apologize and promise to do better in the future.)

Mathilde Parlett: "I am living in western North Carolina—teaching, keeping house for my brother, raising chickens, busy every minute. Expect to spend the summer studying at the Univ. of North Carolina."

Gertrude (Patterson) Swinney: "We have traded our other home for a new and nicer one. Incidentally, it is near the golf course, where I spend most of my time in summer."

Caroline (Paulman) Beers: "I believe I need some help from the Institute for the Coördination of Women's Interests, for since last October I've been trying to help my husband in his business, run a home, and bring up an active two-year-old—all with no help but a nursemaid. My husband had a serious operation in October and I'm trying to help him through the winter so he may conserve his strength for the summer which is his busy season."

Madeline Pfeiffer: "As head of the English department at Pittsfield High School I spend my winter supervising Young America's effort to master the mother tongue. My summers are spent at Columbia in mad pursuit of a Master's degree."

Marian Thompson: "Having spent the past summer in Europe with Betty Carpenter '15 I can think and talk of nothing but going again, which we are already planning! In the meantime I'm working for my M.A. at Columbia."

Lucy Titcomb: "It was a nice sight to see a 1913 envelope when I got back from a very sudden and lovely trip. My sister decided to take a year off and go abroad and I went along. We had a thrilling trip by motor across northern Africa amid veiled ladies and turbaned gentlemen, then up through Sicily, Italy, and three weeks of opera in Paris at Christmas time. We had such a pleasant tea party with Mr. and Mrs. 'Bunny' Abbott in Florence."

Emily (Van Order) Clarke writes from Belgium: "Another year passed and still I am on this side of the Atlantic, but am counting the months now until our return; sixteen more to go. Hope to be back in Hamp for the fifteenth, although it coincides with my husband's receiving his M. B., Ch. B. from Edinburgh. My voice lessons with Desire Demest continue to give me great joy. It is a satisfaction to be accomplishing something more than the usual nursery and home duties of a mother of four. We migrate to the shore as usual after Easter for the summer."

Anna Wallace is still in New York with the American Eugenics Society. "This fall I was in Philadelphia a good deal of the time as I was in charge of the society's booth at the Sesqui. I had a wild time trying to get all our exhibits in running order and keep them so, but it was good fun just the same in spite of the folks who would tamper with the machinery at night."

Edith (Warner) Patton: "We have just returned from a wonderful trip to La Jolla (Calif.) and Pasadena. Met Helen McBurnie's mother in Pasadena."

Ruth Whaley: "At present I am living in Chicago and doing my best to conduct the high school girls at the Faulkner School through the mazes of College Board math and physics."

Clara Williamson: "Nothing new to report. In my third year at the Library of Congress trying to keep the periodicals of the world catalogued."

Ruth (Wilson) Borst: "I am very much interested in the 'new' child psychology and am chairman of the Child Study Committee of our Branch of the A. A. U. W. I have helped to secure subscriptions to Clara Savage's new magazine, *Children*, and recommend it to all 1913 mothers!"

Margaret (Woodbridge) Price: "I'm back at legal stenography and enjoying it and both Mr. Price and I are studying with Mr. Olmsted who is connected with our new Miami Univ."

Sara (Wyeth) Floyd: 'Have been busy raising airedales and two boys for several years, but am planning to get back to Hamp if they will let me."

NEW ADDRESSES.—Mrs. Francis L. Foran (Mary Larkin), 1652 N. Long Av., Chicago.

Mrs. John B. Reid (Harriet Moodey), 141 Maple St., Springfield, Mass.

Ex-1913

BORN.—To Beatrice (Griffith) Smith a son, July 14, 1926.

OTHER NEWS.—Helen (McBurnie) Bumpus writes, "Still doing nothing startling but have learned to skate with my three kiddies and as we have a rink on our place it is great fun."

Helen Orr: "The 1913 New Year's greetings reached me in Paris. I shall show them to Ernestine (Chase) Bradley who lives here. We looked at the pictures of freshman year. What awful clothes we did wear! I'm here in Paris for nine months of hard work with a violin professor and trying to absorb general culture incidentally. Those years of French classes at college help some, but I'm quite rusty after twelve years out."

Eleanor (Smith) Collada: "Because my business since leaving college has been mostly travel I have been negligent about dues, information, etc. However, now that I am in N. Y. C. (I was married recently) I hope to keep in closer touch with Smith doings. I am leaving on my fifth cruise to the Mediterranean as hostess on the *Homeric*, returning in April. My husband is with the Knoll Hotels."

1914

Class secretary—Mrs. Herbert R. Miller (Dorothy Spencer), 120 Haven Av., New York City. Telephone: Billings 2414.

BORN.—To Elson (Barnes) Norbury her third child and first son, Frank Barnes, June 5, 1925.

To Christine (Becker) Anderson her first child and son, Willa Jean, Mar. 28.

To Mary (Broughton) Kleinstuck her second child and daughter, Caroline, Apr. 8, 1925.

To Dorothy (Conrad) Silberman her first child and son, David, Conrad, or Henry, Mar. 21.

To Amy (Ellis) Shaw her second child and first daughter, Elizabeth Amy, Mar. 2.

To Bertha (Goff) Scoville her first son, John Harris Jr., Oct. 26, 1925.

To Almeda (Johnson) Baumann her second child and daughter, Virginia Anne, Oct. 3, 1926. Her first little daughter died soon after birth in 1923.

To Sara (Loth) Bach her second child and first daughter, Alice, Jan. 8.

To Virginia (Mollenhauer) Maynard her second child and first son, Edwin Post III, July 28, 1926.

To Katherine (Wood) Yarbrough her third child and second son, Douglas Grimes, Jan. 23.

To Margaret (Woodward) Cumings her third child and son, William Francis, Feb. 12, 1925. She went through measles, whooping cough, chicken pox, scarlet fever, infantile paralysis, and pneumonia in 1926 so the announcement of William was delayed!

NEW ADDRESSES.—Louisa Baker (temp.), 188 Minerva Av., Derby, Conn.

Mrs. J. G. Harvey (Ruth Brown), 812 Skidmore St., Portland, Ore. ("Until further notice. We live under constant possibility of a transfer to some other northwestern city.")

Ruth Cleaver, 10 Smith St., Paterson, N. J.

Mrs. C. P. Ross (Ruth Cobb), 410 High St., Clarendon, Va.

Mrs. ·C. C. Baldwin (Esther Cutter), 163 Harris Av., Freeport, N. Y.

Carolyn E. Dean (temp.), 39 Arroyico Lane, Santa Barbara, Calif. She writes that she is "avoiding the Minnesota winter" and plans a trip east in June.

Mrs. H. K. Norton (Edith Egbert), 420 W. 119 St., N. Y. C.

Mrs. J. H. Scoville (Bertha Goff), 44 N. Quaker Lane, Hartford, Conn. "I have moved seven times in three years." She has hopes of being settled now.

Mrs. L. E. Crowther (Julia Hamblett), 430 E. 185 St., Cleveland, O. "We are pleasantly located in the cottage of an estate right on Lake Erie shore front." The big house is used as a clubhouse catering to special parties. They act as caretakers for the grounds. Mr. Crowther is also working for the Willard Storage Battery Co.

Mrs. E. F. Robinson (Mabel Kirley), 2156

S. Geddes St., Syracuse, N. Y. "Have just bought a new home and am enjoying equipping and settling it."

Mrs. E. P. Maynard Jr. (Virginia Mollenhauer), 128 Willow St., Brooklyn, N. Y.

Mrs. Lon C. Hill Jr. (Georgiana Owsley), 720 Prospect Av., Winnetka, Ill. Since Georgiana's father's death she has been living with her mother. She writes in Jan. that she is "interested in transplanting one native Texan (her husband) to Chicago's sunny clime—it now being five below zero."

Mrs. J. C. Bostelmann Jr. (Sophie Pratt), Hewlett, N. Y. "I am making some special teaching rolls for the Duo Art and my business address is Aeolian Hall, Fifth Av. and 54 St., N. Y. C."

Mrs. Dorothy (Upjohn) DeLano (temp.), 11 rue Scribe, Paris, France.

Mrs. F. W. Boye (Beatrice Wentworth), (perm.) c/o Adjutant General, Washington, D. C.; (temp.) Cavalry School, Fort Riley, Kans.

Mrs. H. A. Schubart (Pauline Werner), c/o Equitable Trust Co., 23 rue de la Paix, Paris, France (temp.).

Mrs. A. L. Yarbrough (Katharine Wood), 4250 Ingraham Highway, Coconut Grove, Miami, Fla. Also Stratford, Conn.

OTHER NEWS.—A snappy '14 lunch took place in N. Y. C. on Jan. 29 with our trusty Agnes (Morgenthau) Newborg as generalissimo. Twenty-three of us heard the interesting tale of Alice Darrow's adventures in the Orient. She taught English and music in Japan, psychology at Ginling, developed a deep interest in Kipling's works, met the living Buddha, and came home via Manila, India, and France. Edith (Egbert) Norton gave us a graphic picture of China, saying that the unrest was very real (the unrest having since become upheaval), that the smattering of western education was in the hands of a tiny number and that China was waking up to the fact that the foreign concessions were not necessary. Russian influence, being crowded out of Europe, naturally turns to the East and it is strong in China.

The '14 lunch in Northampton· on Feb. 19 was nothing short of amazing. 19 members broke bread together at the Alumnae House under the wing of Ruth McKenney. Rain and slush did not daunt us—we came from Springfield, Holyoke, and farther. On the Council were Grace (Middleton) Roberts and Mollie Tolman as directors, Dorothy Seamans and Emma (Miller) Waygood representing the New York and Philadelphia Clubs, Jean Paton as Burton Memorial chairman, and Dorothy (Spencer) Miller as class representative. Gladys Anslow was the chairman of the Faculty Committee for consultation with and entertainment of the Council. Gladys spoke and presided with great charm and dignity and Mollie and Jean in turn fired the Council to new efforts in behalf of the Burton Fund.

Margaret (Alexander) Marsh is writing a book on Bolivia.

Louisa Baker is teaching English in Derby

(Conn.) and planning to continue graduate work in education at Harvard next summer.

Elson (Barnes) Norbury is acting and directing in the Centennial Theatre in Jacksonville, Ill.

Helen (Bell) Priester was in N. Y. C. and Boston in March. She is considering opening a gift shop in Davenport next winter.

From *The Tennessean* (Nashville), we have news of our long silent Edith Brodie. In a series of articles written at the instance of the vocational guidance department of the Altrusa Club to help young "Miss Nashville" to choose her way in the world, Edith is Exhibit A. She is director of the School of Nursing at Vanderbilt Hospital. The paper says: "Perhaps in no other one woman in Nashville is the epitome of professional success, both personal and financial as well as to the community as a whole, reached so well as in Miss Brodie. She came to do one of the biggest pieces of executive work in the field of nursing that her profession knows. Incidentally Miss Brodie is one of the highest salaried women in Nashville." After college Edith taught in high school for four years; she went to the Vassar Training Camp for Nurses in 1917, assisting in the influenza epidemic after the Armistice. She completed her nurse's training at the N. Y. City Hospital and then took six months of graduate work at the N. Y. Tuberculosis Hospital. For two and a half years she was assistant superintendent of nurses at the Buffalo City Hospital, following which she was theoretical instructor at Washington Univ. School of Nursing in St. Louis, where she completed work for her M.A. prior to going to Nashville in Feb. She is quoted in the paper: "'Although the V. T. S. for Nurses has been in existence since 1912, mine was the task of reorganizing its curriculum and of making it a department of the Univ . . . Under the plan adopted here a girl high school graduate may attend the school for a year and a half and while she continues her requirements for a B.S., may be using this training not only as a part of her college units, but may use it to earn her way in the Univ. . . .' Miss Brodie believes that the old traditional prejudice in this section against nursing will pass. . . . For the southern woman, she believes, is eminently better fitted to teach, serve, and help the South to higher health standards."

Ruth (Brown) Harvey writes, "I resigned my job as head of the order department in the Portland Public Library Dec. 24, and we moved into this bungalow." She is enthusiastic about the job of getting settled.

Betty Case finished being general chairman of the Junior League of Trenton's show which netted about $9000 just before she sailed Jan. 15 for a Mediterranean cruise.

Ruth Chester got to China the latter part of Feb. and was in Nanking Mar. 7 when the ruction came. At first they (the Ginling group) were protected by an officer of the Cantonese army who had a sister in the colony. When this protection was withdrawn they went to Nanking and were with the group that was besieged there. After the threat of the U. S. Navy to bombard the town they were allowed to leave for Shanghai on the *Preston*. Her family had a cable Apr. 3 that she is safe and well. She was uncertain as to her plans. Three hundred missionaries are coming back on a ship which has been chartered for Apr. 9. Ruth was not certain whether or not she would be among them.

Helen (Choate) Barrow's father died Jan. 3. Her mother, who has been quite sick, has gone to make her home with Helen.

Bertha (Conn) Bien has been made a life member of the Council of the Mothers' Club which she started about five years ago. They now have 136 members.

Edith (Egbert) Norton's husband, Henry Kittredge Norton, has just had his book, "China and the Powers," published by John Day Co.

Helen Ellis expects to take an automobile tour through Great Britain and Europe this summer with her family.

Margaret L. Farrand is director of publicity for Smith, the Women's College at Brown, and the Assn. of University Professors.

Mary (Fay) Hamilton is contemplating the organization of a small private school in Portland. Plans are in progress.

Marion (Freeman) Wakeman is moving to Ham in June.

Helen (Gaylord) Tiffany moved into her new home in March. They have enjoyed the planning and building.

Since the death of her mother in December, Sarah (Hoadley) Abbott has been living with her father in New Haven at 1574 Chapel St.

A letter from Rosamond (Holmes) Phillips's father in appreciation of Jean's poem tells us that her son is still with Dot (Whitehead) Conklin and her little girl is with Rosamond's brother near Pittsburgh.

Marjorie (Jacobson) Henle is doing part-time work for a newspaper syndicate.

Mabel (Kirley) Robinson's husband is a civil engineer and he is to give two lectures a semester in the College of Applied Science at Syracuse Univ.

February brought Grace (Kramer) Wachman to N. Y. for a short visit.

Orange (N. J.) will from now on be the permanent home of Marguerite (Krusen) Williams and family.

The summer plans of Madeleine (Mayer) Low center about Lake Placid.

Grace (Middleton) Roberts and family will spend part of May and all of June in England.

Agnes (Morgenthau) Newborg's new summer home in Putnam Co. (N. Y.) is engaging her time and interest. She has been taking courses in gardening at Teachers College.

Rebecca (Newcomb) Gardner is taking care of her invalid mother.

Dorothy Ochtman has been teaching this winter at Rosemary Hall. She was awarded Honorable Mention for a picture "Garden Flowers" at the Exposition of Women's Arts and Industries in N. Y. in Sept. She had a portrait of her father in the last exhibition of the National Academy of Design. She expects to go to Europe early this summer, having been awarded one of the John Simon Guggenheim Memorial Fellowships for study in the art galleries in Europe and for creative work in painting. She was one of the judges for the Garden Club at the International Flower Show in March.

Nellie Parker has been managing her mother's college annex at 8 Belmont this winter. She hopes to spend May and June in Scotland. In the summer she and her mother will run "Eamesholm Inn" (former home of Emma Eames) at Bath (Me.), which opens July 1 (see Blue Book and the A. C. A.). She is hoping for much 1914 patronage.

Helen (Peters) Wilson was in Pasadena to visit her family in Feb. She visited in Portland (Ore.) before she returned.

Marion (Rawson) Gillies and Marcia spent the winter in California. She planned to visit Dorothy (Schofield) Shapleigh in St. Louis on her way home in April.

Evelyn (Rheinstrom) Hirsch, whose husband died in 1923, spends six months a year traveling with a very congenial widow from Chicago. Last summer they went to Norway, this spring they go to the Mediterranean, concentrating on Greece.

Ernestine (Robbins) Sharkey's Sammy Jr., 1914's first child, passed to Junior High School last June with the highest marks in the school and the highest intelligence test. Ernestine collaborated on the writing of a play, "Christmas in the Court of Venice," which was given Dec. 21 in Trenton. She spends her summers in Maine and plans to take her two oldest boys abroad in two years. She hopes some of us will come to see her in her remodeled farmhouse. She would love visitors, particularly in the spring and on Princeton game days.

Florence Root went to Korea last fall under the Southern Presbyterian Mission Board. Grace (Wells) Whitney visited her in Cooperstown just before she left.

After a winter and summer of illness, Eleanor Saladine is feeling much better. "I have my old job back again (in the Boston Psychopathic Hospital) but under the auspices of the Veterans' Bureau instead of the Red Cross and in many ways it is much more interesting. I am working under my beloved Dr. Thom."

Marion Scott writes that anyone in '14 ordering or securing orders for her candies will help the Burton Fund, as she will give 25% of such orders to it (the money, not the candy!). Kobi Candies, 1684 Beacon St., Brookline, chocolates $1 the pound.

On the side, Ruth Seabury is president of the Alumnae Assn. of the Boston Students' Union. Any Smith alumna who in P. G. days was at the B. S. U. is hereby urged to join and help her in a stiff job of student aid. Only $1 a year to join. The A. B. C. F. M. of which Ruth is educational secretary has just gone through a merger with three boards which has given her a new national department.

Dorothea Simmons, having returned from a visit to the Adirondacks, in March was on her way to Florida.

Ruth (Taylor) Hills's husband had a serious operation in December. He is recovering slowly.

Evelyn (Thompson) Jones and her family enjoyed a winter in Bermuda free from snow and housekeeping. They returned in March.

Ruth Tomlinson will be a counselor at Camp Wyonegonic, Denmark, Me., this summer.

Margaret Torrison is in New Mexico for the winter.

Narka and Zoe Ward will spend the summer in France.

"We survived the hurricane," writes Katherine (Wood) Yarbrough, "without any great loss, except inasmuch as it affected business conditions in general here. . . . Like most of our friends we made a lot of money, but have lost a good part of it. However, we are just as enthusiastic as ever about Miami and believe absolutely in its future growth and prosperity. It has already 'come back' to a large extent and there is really a much more normal and healthier atmosphere here than in the boom days. Coconut Grove is very charming. It is quite old and established and I suppose that appeals to the New England in me." Katherine was president of the flourishing Miami Smith Club until last November.

Helen Worstell and Elizabeth Zimmerman will be counselors next summer at Camp Accomac, Sandy Creek, Me.

Ex-1914

DIED.—Florence Englander, of influenza, in 1918.

Mabel (Veeder) Karow, Nov. 30, 1926. Her husband writes: "Mabel always took such an interest in the activities of the Smith alumnae that I know you will be shocked to hear of her death. She had been losing strength for almost two years and while she looked well, she was really never in good health during that time. Finally an operation was necessary and she did not rally properly from the shock. We thought that she was getting over the crisis but complications came along and she did not have the strength to overcome them. We have one child living, Louise. . . . I am keeping up my home for her sake with an excellent nurse for her. Some day I hope that she will go to Smith. The girls in the local Smith Club gave Louise a silver drinking cup."

MARRIED.—Olga Poulsen to Henry Harrison Nelson. Address, 627 S. Lorraine Blvd., Los Angeles, Calif.

BORN.—To Elizabeth (Adams) Ferguson her third son and fourth child, William D., Dec. 21, 1926.

To Mary (Ferguson) Young her first son and third child, Edward William Jr., in 1922.

To Marie (Hedrick) Stigers her first son and child, in Feb. 1926.

NEW ADDRESSES.—Mrs. T. George Yaxis (Anastasia Alexandrakis), 2804 Brightwood Av., Nashville, Tenn.

Mrs. W. T. Burns (Marjery Beckett), Ralston, Neb. She has three children, Bobby, five, Billy, three, and Nancy, two.

The Smartest New Colors

in the Smartest Fabric .. Skinner's Crepes

THE spring's a blaze of color — the blues, the reds, the greens, the beiges, and white, with brilliant relief, for the country . . . . . .

If you're wise you'll use Skinner's Crepes — no fabric better from the mode's standpoint — and they have wonderful wearing quality.

The white dress shown above has pleated skirt, long, slender coat on cardigan lines, and sleeveless blouse with the smartest of trimming in lipstick red to match the brim of your hat. White used to be an extravagance. Now that it washes and doesn't turn yellow, every woman may have it.

Ask for Skinner's Crepes — and "Look for the Name in the Selvage."

WILLIAM SKINNER & SONS, Established 1848
New York, Chicago, Boston, Philadelphia — Mills, HOLYOKE, Mass.

"LOOK FOR THE NAME   IN THE SELVAGE"

Mrs. Cecil I. Cady (Paula Cady), 6 Archer Pl., Tarrytown, N. Y.

Mrs. M. S. Williams (Marion Deings), Plumtrees, Bethel, Conn.

Mrs. E. W. Young (Mary Ferguson), 721 E. Alton St., Appleton, Wis.

Mrs. Stigers (Marie Hedrick), 12 Fargo St., Baldwin, N. Y. Marie is connected with the N. Y. Public Library.

Mrs. O. J. Caron (Marietta Higman), 1427 Astor St., Chicago.

Mrs. W. J. Ehrichs (Ida Grace Holcomb), 170 N. Oak St., Ridgewood, N. J.

Mrs. J. P. H. Perry (Augustine Lloyd), 830 Mt. Pleasant Court, Winnetka, Ill. (temp.). "Trying to adjust myself to the middle west and wondering whether it is to be my permanent home."

Barbara Tunnell, 101 The Puritan, Louisville, Ky.

OTHER NEWS.—Anastasia (Alexandrakis) Yaxis is "renewing my youth and falling in love with this charming southern city [Nashville]. . . . I make fruit cake at holiday time and sell it and put the income on my daughter's Smith College fund."

Elizabeth Barnes, whose profession is nursing, is doing some book collecting, reading, and writing in her spare time. She expects to have two poems published in the "American Anthology" (Unicorn Publishing Co.) and there is a prize of $100 offered for the most popular poem. So please advertise the sale of the "Anthology."

Dorothy (Dewey) Blake is absorbing Kunst, Kultur, Wurst, and beer in Munchen, Germany. She expects to shop in Paris and London and come home next summer.

Margaret Easton's medical career has been interrupted by a breakdown caused by overwork. Her enthusiasm was greater than her strength.

Mary (Ferguson) Young has been ill most of the time for the last six years but she feels sure that she is on the high road to recovery.

Ida Grace (Holcomb) Ehrichs's husband was killed by an automobile last summer. She is now doing saleswork at Franklin Simons's, N. Y. C.

Barbara Tunnell during the past six months has had articles and poems accepted by *Scribner's*, *Century* (two, there is a poem in the Dec. 1926 number), *House Beautiful* (two), and an article in the Dec. 1926 *Arts and Decoration*. She has been recommended to write the Georgis volume for the series on Early American Architecture being published by the American Institute of Architects. She wrote the Georgis Chapter for the book on Historic Gardens being published by the Garden Club of America. She is kept at home by her mother's health.

Martha (Watts) Frey's father writes that she has been in a sanitarium since September.

Mardie (White) Webbe hopes to go to a ranch in New Mexico for the summer.

1915

Class secretary—Mrs. Dudley T. Humphrey (Marian Park), Loudonville, Albany Co., N. Y.

ENGAGED.—Marion Graves to John Francis Duffey of Northampton.

MARRIED.—Ellen Williams to Gustave Menderson Weil, Dec. 27, 1926, at Albuquerque, N. M. New address, Castle Apts., 1412 W. Central Av., Albuquerque, N. M.

BORN.—To Alice (Cragin) Lewis a third child and second daughter, Alice Williams, Mar. 3.

To Mildred (Foster) Covell a third child and first son, Otis Dexter Jr., Jan. 14.

To Madge (Hovey) Spencer a fourth child and third son, Richard Winslow, Mar. 6.

To Margaret (Munsie) Hathaway a daughter, Caroline, Mar. 17.

To Esther (Paine) La Croix a fourth child and third daughter, Susanne, Feb. 18.

To Katharine (Pratt) Dewey a fourth child and second son, Edward, July 1926.

To Ruth (Waterman) Ritch a second daughter, Marian, May 1, 1926.

To Alice (Welles) English a third child and first son, James Fairfield Jr., Feb. 15.

NEW ADDRESSES.—Mrs. William R. Dewey Jr. (Katharine Pratt), Pigeon Hill Rd., Weston, Mass.

Mrs. C. Edward Bell (Dorrice Robinson), Hancock Point, Me. Temporary address, 4312 Osage Av., Philadelphia, Pa.

OTHER NEWS.—K. Boutelle, Adèle Glogau, S. E. Foster, Mary Stevens, Eleanor Park, and K. (Vermilye) Alford lunched together when Kato was in N. Y. in February. She is writing the ex-members about the Burton Memorial Fund.

Sally (Bryant) Lyon writes, "Not much news except that I am practically well again and almost as fat as ever."

Maudita (Clement) Bowen's address should be Old Army Rd., Scarsdale, N. Y. She lives in the same house but they have renamed the street.

Dorothy (Dulles) Bourne has been organizing Leagues of Women Voters in Dutchess County.

May (Day) Gardner is keeping house and working in the garden.

Helen (Frey) Taylor's mother died at Helen's home last November.

Katharine Gorin gave a piano recital Feb. 13 at College and one on Mar. 1 at the Town Hall, N. Y. C. Her program included Franck's prelude, chorale, and fugue; groups by Brahms, Chopin, and Medtner, and single pieces by Rachmaninoff, Stravinsky, and Dohnanyi. Quoting from the *N. Y. Times* of Mar. 2: "Miss Gorin made much of the broad style and bell-toned sonorities of the beautiful work of César Franck, and where she missed some lesser niceties of detail the same vigor marked her Brahms playing and the same lively imagination that of the Russian composers. Having an individual talent, she was said to have received her training at Smith College and later in Chicago, besides two years' scholarship with Lhevinne and work in composition with Adolf Weidig." Esther Root, Adelaide Heilbron, and Maudita (Clement) Bowen were among her audience in N. Y.

Camp Marienfeld   ⸴ ⸴   Chesham, N. H.

32nd Year   (*Mt. Monadnock in the background.*)   July and August

For Boys, ages 8–17. Address the Headmaster, Raphael J. Shortlidge, The Choate School, Wallingford, Conn., or: Mrs. Shortlidge, — Helen Wetmore Houghton, Smith, 1912.

Athletics:
Swimming
Water sports
Tennis
Horseback Riding
Baseball
Hiking
Wrestling
Boxing

Music:
Violin, Vocal,
Piano
Group Singing
Orchestra
Summer Study:
Make-up work,
for promotion, or
methods and habits of
study

Occupations: Camp craft, nature study, clay modeling, metal and wood work, radio construction, photography, dramatics.

Large staff of mature and experienced masters, a master to five boys.

The Swimming Cove

Catherine (Okey) Geiger's husband is the associate manager of the Foreign Bond Dept. of the Equitable Trust Co. of N. Y.

Guendolen (Reed) Stuart taught a class and managed the orchestra until three weeks before the arrival of Carol last October, and resumed teaching after Christmas. Fortunately they have escaped earthquakes, typhoons, and tidal waves that devastated some parts of the Philippines last year.

Dorrice (Robinson) Bell's husband and a friend have started a chemical bacteriological laboratory in Philadelphia, of which Dorrice is the secretary. She says it looks as if they were settled there now, although they will have to move again as they can have their present house only for a year.

Alice (Welles) English's home had a diphtheria quarantine when the baby was two weeks old. All's well with them now, however.

Ex-1915

DIED.—Elizabeth Doolittle Smith, July 14, 1925, after being ill twelve years with tuberculosis.

WANTED.—The married name and address of Elizabeth Richardson, formerly at 70 John St., Ilion, N. Y.

1916

Class secretary—Dorothy Ainsworth, 11 Barrett Pl., Northampton, Mass.

ENGAGED.—Marjorie Miller to Louie Holmes Robertson of Elizabeth, N. J., formerly of Texas. Mr. Robertson is a graduate of Harvard and served in France during the war. He is at present a chemical engineer with the Standard Oil Co.

MARRIED.—Alice Huber to Abijah Charles Fox, Mar. 19. Mr. Fox is a graduate of Rutgers Univ. New address, 367 N. Mountain Av., Upper Montclair, N. J.

BORN.—To Hawley (Rodgers) Willson a first child and daughter, Mary Ann, Jan. 26. New address, 5 Cedar St., Clinton, Mass.

BEG YOUR PARDON.—Beverly Noel Williams, second child of Hazel (Wyeth) Williams, is a young lady, not a second son as reported in the last QUARTERLY.

NEW ADDRESSES.—Mrs. Earle S. Burnett (Marion Phelps), 4005 Oakland St., Fort Worth, Tex.

Mrs. Thomas Laine (Mary Corbet), 307 E. 4 St., Mt. Vernon, N. Y.

Mrs. H. George Reinecke (Esther Stewart), Highview Av., Sound Beach, Conn.

Mrs. Harold Staples (Margaret Smith), 52 Paterson St., Providence, R. I.

OTHER NEWS.—Adelaide Arms is with the Stuyvesant Square Bookshop in New York.

Agnes (Betts) McCulloch and her husband have just returned from a cruise to the West Indies.

Edna Donnell, when last heard from, was in Göttingen (Germany), perfecting her knowledge of the German language.

Emma Helen (Hartford) Nelson sailed Feb. 5 for two months in South America.

Headlines in the *New York Evening Post* state, 'Agnes C. Jones, N. J. Lawmaker, is author of bills on sale of Firearms." Three cheers for our politician!

Katharine Kendig is still head of the general literature department of the main Los Angeles Library. She had a poem, "Burnt Offering," in the August 1926 number of *Lyric West*. In addition she is raising wirehaired fox terriers.

Jean (Tait) Robertson and her husband took a trip to Bermuda last summer.

Caroline (Bruner) Sharpless is teaching this year in the Shippen School for Girls in Lancaster, Pa.

Lora Varney ('17) writes, "Still trying to show eugenists that two foster female parents can bring up 2000 feathered children better than 200 natural parents."

Ex-1916

MARRIED.—Dorothy Norton to Collier Whittemore Baird, June 7, 1923.

Louise Thomas to Horace W. Pote, Dec. 30, 1925. Louise is taking a course in short story writing and French, preparatory to a trip abroad. Her husband is getting his Master's degree in statistics and economics analysis.

BORN.—To Dorothy (Benton) Wood a fourth child and third daughter, Nancy, in 1925.

To Hester (Newhall) Brown a fourth child and second daughter, Elizabeth Newhall, July 1, 1925.

To Dorothy (Norton) Baird two sons, Collier Whittemore Jr., Mar. 21, 1924, and John Torrey, Oct. 2, 1925.

To Mary (Robbins) Edgarton a first and a second son, Charles Frederick II, June 17, 1920, and Henry Robbins, Mar. 11, 1924. Mary's third son has already appeared in the QUARTERLY.

OTHER NEWS.—Hortense (Hart) Pomeroy has been president of the Worcester College Club for two years.

Tess (Martin) Daniels has a new address, 575 Salisbury St., Worcester, Mass.

Ethel (Sparks) Sparks is vice-president of the Women's Council of her county.

Gladys (Stearn) McKeever spent last summer camping in the Berkshires with a three weeks' trip in the Laurentian Mts. in Canada.

1917

Class secretary—Florence C. Smith, 501 S. University St., Normal, Ill.

MARRIED.—Tessa Schmidt to Dr. Hans H. Reese, Apr. 19.

BORN.—To Marjory (Bates) Pratt a son, Dana Joseph, Dec. 9, 1926.

To Miriam (Cooke) Barnes a second daughter, Patricia Jameson, Apr. 6, 1926.

OTHER NEWS.—Elizabeth (Boswell) Cheadle lists as her activities, "President, Norman (Okla.) Branch A. A. U. W; chairman, Christmas Health Seal Campaign; active in Garden Club, Bridge Club, Drama Club, D. A. R."

Marjorie (Chalmers) Carleton announces the completion of her third novel which is to appear in book form in the late summer.

Dorothy (Cole) Sturtevant's two-year-old son, Alan, died Jan. 12.

Dorothy Gibling is working for an M.A. at Columbia and teaching physical education at the Carroll Club.

Dorothy (Hamilton) Brush is on the boards

of the Women's Protective Association, Child
Guidance Clinic, Institute of Music, Girls'
Council, Y. W. C. A.

Helen Slaughter has been doing graduate
work in medicine in Vienna. Although she
studied for a while in Paris, London, and
Berlin, she is finding more that she wants in
Vienna and will be busy there until summer.

Eleanor (Stearns) Towns is director of
religious education in the Woodhaven (N. Y.)
First Presbyterian Church. "The job includes case work, helping with building plans,
coaching basket ball, and 'selling' modern
methods and ideas to church and community."

Helena (Warren) Reuman's mother died
Feb. 24.

NEW ADDRESSES.—Dorothy Gibling, 160
Claremont Av., N. Y. C. (until Aug.).

Mrs. Angereau Heinsohn (Margaret Lylburn), Gramatan Court, Bronxville, N. Y.

Eleanor Humphreys, 1373 E. 57 St.,
Chicago.

Mrs. Carroll C. Pratt (Marjory Bates), 12
Howland St., Cambridge, Mass.

Mrs. Carlos A. Rogers (Caroline Hosford),
800 True St., Amarillo, Tex.

Ruth M. Woodrow, 1080 Broadway, San
Francisco, Calif.

Ex-1917

MARRIED.—Margaret Bacon to Edward
Vassar Ambler, Sept. 29, 1926. Address, 224
Washington St., Gloucester, Mass.

Adelaide Cook to Arlington E. Smith, Oct.
16, 1926. Mr. Smith is Cornell '16· They
are living at Cornada Hotel, 5212 Cornell Av.,
Chicago.

Marian Fuller to Norman H. S. Vincent.
Address, 206 Riverway, Boston, Mass.

Marian Hamilton to Frederick Edwards,
May 12, 1926. Address, Speculator, N. Y.

Beatrice Weil to Winfred W. Hawkins,
July 19, 1923. Address, 245 Wood Court,
Wilmette, Ill. She has a son, Donald Win-
fred, born in 1925.

BORN.—To Fay (Pierce) Beij a second child
and first daughter, Barbara Elizabeth, Mar.
29, 1926.

OTHER NEWS.—Carolyn Harris is a substitute teacher in the White Plains (N. Y.)
schools.

Madeleine (McDowell) Greene is a director
of the Women's Club, is absorbed in parental
education work of the P. T. A, and is rounding
out her seventh year of private tutoring.

Fay (Pierce) Beij received an M.A. from
George Washington Univ. in 1925. She is
now an instructor in zoölogy there.

A message was received from Edith (Proctor) Fletcher as she was enjoying a motor trip
through Italy during the winter.

Frances (Starrett) Crawford has been made
special correspondent for the Seattle Post-
Intelligencer at Olympia, Wash. Her work
ranges from State House routine to Supreme
Court decisions.

Beatrice (Weil) Hawkins took her M.D.
from Rush Medical College, Chicago, in 1923.
She is now practicing as a children's specialist.

NEW ADDRESSES.—Edith Mereen, 2440 Hillside Av., Berkeley, Calif.

Mrs. Joseph Lawton (Mary Norton), 411
Belgravia Court, Louisville, Ky.

Mrs. Thomas D. Moore (Ruth Brown),
1780 Autumn Av., Memphis, Tenn.

Mrs. Nestor S. Rowland (Emma Lane), 115
Grove St., Bristol, Conn.

Mrs. Winthrop H. Smith (Gertrude Ingram), Robin Rd., Englewood, N. J.

1918

Class secretary—Margaret Perkins, 3 Banks
St., Chicago, Ill.

Answers to the February class letter have
been coming in quite satisfactorily, and the
secretary wishes to thank all those who have
sent their replies so promptly. To date, 86
members have paid back dues, 137 questionnaires have been returned from 1918 proper,
and 24 from ex members. Of course there
are many still out, but the secretary eagerly
looks for them in each mail, and prays that
they haven't been pigeonholed. Send them
in, and have a free conscience as well as an
up-to-date record!

DIED.—M. Gertrude Anderson, Apr. 8, after
an illness of several months.

MARRIED.—Marion Lane to Harold Bright-
man Thomas, Oct. 9, 1926. Mr. Thomas is
production manager of the Kolynos Co., and
he and Marion are living in New Haven.
Marion writes that housekeeping and odd
jobs fill her time. She has been studying
Braille, but hasn't yet mastered the 50-page
manuscript required by the A. R. C. for a
certificate. Address, 33 Livingston St., New
Haven, Conn.

Edna Rosenfield to Si Bekenstein, Nov.
30, 1926.

Elizabeth Spencer to Arthur A. Blue, Feb.
16.

BORN.—To Elisabeth (Bartlett) Jenks a
daughter, Anne Lavinia, Dec. 23, 1926.

To Hazel (Dise) Adams a second child and
first daughter, Cynthia Ann, July 18, 1926.

To Esther (Fanning) Francis a fourth
child and third daughter, Mary, July 6, 1925.

To Augusta (Forker) Reid a son, Horace
Withers Jr., July 2, 1926.

To Stella (Garrett) Lee a daughter, Julia
Rensselaer, Feb. 20.

To Margaret (Gustetter) Neeld a third
child and first daughter, Margaret Anne,
May 21, 1926.

To Anne (Howell) Condit, in India, a son,
Daniel Dale Jr., Feb. 20.

To Marguerite (Jewell) Loomis a second
son, Richard Scudder, Nov. 17, 1926.

To Cecilia (Matthews) Anderson a second
child and first daughter, in Sept. 1926.

To Sylvia (Smith) Shepard a second son,
Charles Robinson Smith, Feb. 22.

To Elizabeth (Wiley) Dunlap a second
child and first daughter, Helen Wiley, Nov.
6, 1926.

OTHER NEWS.—Margery Alden, who has
been service-aide for the last eight years
with Cheney Bros. in South Manchester
(Conn.), is now attending the Prince School
of Education for Store Service in Boston.

Sara Bache-Wiig has been made assistant
professor of botany at Smith.

THE SANTA BARBARA GIRLS' SCHOOL

Resident and Day Pupils. Eleven acres. Country life and sports. Sleeping Porches. Open-air rooms. Riding. Swimming.

Basis of work: **Clear Thinking.**

MARION L. CHAMBERLAIN, A.M., *Principal*

Post Office Box 548   Santa Barbara, Calif.

ILLSIDE

A School for Girls
NORWALK, CONNECTICUT

In a beautiful New England town, one hour from New York. Girls from all parts of the country. Four residences, schoolhouse, gymnasium. Extensive grounds. Preparation for all colleges. Special courses. Outdoor life. Catalog.

Margaret R. Brendlinger, A.B. (Vassar)
Vida Hunt Francis, A.B. (Smith)
Principals

GRAY COURT
A School *for* Girls

Gray Court, beautifully situated at Stamford, Connecticut, fifty-two minutes from the Grand Central Station, New York, offers the unusual advantages of country and seashore.

Primary, Intermediate, College Preparatory, Secretarial and Cultural Courses, with opportunity for special work in Music, Arts and Crafts and Spoken English. Horseback Riding. All Athletics.

WRITE FOR ILLUSTRATED CATALOGUE

Jessie Callam Gray, A.B., Smith
Principal
STAMFORD · CONNECTICUT

HOWE-MAROT
COUNTRY BOARDING SCHOOL
College Preparation

Marot Junior College
Two-Year College Course

For Catalog address

MARY L. MAROT, Principal
THOMPSON, CONNECTICUT

The Low and Heywood School

A country School for Girls one hour from New York City. Thorough college preparation, also general and postgraduate courses. Separate cottages for younger girls. Sixty-second year begins Sept. 28, 1928.

SHIPPAN POINT, STAMFORD, CONN.

MISS MADEIRA'S SCHOOL

1330 19th Street, N. W.
Washington, D. C.

A resident and day school for girls

LUCY MADEIRA WING, A. B.,
VASSAR

Mrs. David Laforest Wing
Head Mistress

Saint Margaret's School

1875   1927

A New England School for girls

Thorough Preparation for the Leading Colleges for Women.
Art, Music, and Special Courses.
New 20-acre country estate for recreation.
Well-organized athletic program.
Conveniently situated. Two and one half hours from New York City.
Catalog on request. Box C.
Alberta C. Edell, A. M., Principal, Waterbury, Conn.

Dorcas Brigham received her M. A. from Smith last June.

Gladys (Chace) Kinkead's small daughter, born in 1925, is named Ruth Elizabeth instead of Barbara as previously reported.

Gladys David is taking a course in public speaking at Plymouth Institute, Brooklyn.

Anna Fessenden is teaching mathematics in the high school at Needham, Mass.

Eleanor (Grant) Rigby and a friend are owners of The Little Tavern, Cheshire, Conn.

Margaret (Hepburn) Snyder writes that she is continuing her education in the electric washing machine, a new Steinway grand, the art of flying kites, roller skating, and other chores in the day's run. Besides this she is a director and chairman of the general education department of the Y. W. C. A.

Frances Jackson has been architectural draughtsman with May and Hillard, Architects, since July 1926.

Dorothy-Kate (Johnston) Dent writes that she and her husband have been moved from place to place ever since their marriage in July 1925. They are now back in Boston, however, where Dorothy is continuing her work with the Massachusetts Labor Department.

Doris Kendrick is 1918's third doctor. She received her M. D. from the Univ. of Michigan in 1926, and is now interning in the Memorial Hospital, Worcester, Mass.

Annie Kyle is still busy writing. She has had a poem in *Scribner's* and stories in several issues of *St. Nicholas* and in *The Portal*.

Barbara Lincoln, beginning Apr. 1, is to be director of personnel and education with the Sage Allen Co. in Hartford.

Dorothy (Martin) Foster expects to spend April and May in Europe.

Edna (Miller) Lamb is teaching English in the Belmont High School in Los Angeles.

Helen (Neill) McMaster is studying English at the Univ. of Buffalo, hoping for an M.A. in 1928.

Martha Phelps has been spending the last 4½ years in the Orient, according to a note which the secretary received from Martha's mother, and at present is in Tokyo. Mrs. Phelps writes that she expects Martha home in the spring, but as yet her plans are indefinite.

Margaret Perkins was one of nine eighteeners to lunch together at Hamp at Council in February. There were present Mary Mensel, Sara Bache-Wiig, Dorcas Brigham, Abby Belden, Frances Knapp, Gertrude Wolff, Kay (Redway) Brown, and Florence Bliss, and a jolly time was had by all. Council proved to be more interesting than ever, if such a thing can be imagined, and your secretary came home silently blessing the class for giving her the opportunity to attend, and all reënthused and newly educated as to the wonderful place Smith is and will continue to be.

Gertrude Philbrick is head of the French department in the high school where she has taught for the last five years.

Julia Pressey is cataloging in the Univ. of Illinois library.

Caroline (Reed) Molthan, who spent six months abroad last year with her three small daughters, writes that she is about to go again without them.

Dorothy Simpson feels the urge of foreign shores so she is departing on her third trip abroad this spring.

Marjory Stimson, who is nursing field representative for the A. R. C. in Mass. and R. I., hopes to get a three months' leave and go with the Bureau of University Travel this summer to England, France, and Italy.

Meredyth Wetherell is assistant secretary to the Animal Rescue League of Fall River, active in Junior League work, and on the music committee of the Woman's Club.

Anna White is teaching Latin in the New Haven High School and is still studying at Yale for an M.A. in education.

Lucille Wilson is girl reserve secretary at the Y. W. C. A. in Troy, N. Y.

Edna (Wood) Turner and her husband expect to return to China sometime this spring.

Martha (Wright) Mitchell and her doctor husband and their two children have gone to Vienna for a few months where Dr. Mitchell expects to study.

NEW ADDRESSES.—Mrs. Frank L. Beach (Elizabeth Boyd), c/o Burroughs Adding Machine Co., Detroit, Mich.

Mabel Buckner, 300 Putnam Av., Whitneyville, Conn.

Mrs. Carl N. Rexroad (May Buckner), 444 Clinton St., Columbus, O.

Mrs. Wynkoop Kiersted Jr. (Janet Cook), 6820 The Paseo, Kansas City, Mo.

Mrs. Frederick Stevens (Dorothea Dann), 95 St. James Pl., Buffalo, N. Y.

Mrs. Charles McM. Noble (Jeannette Duncan), 524 Brookside Dr., Birmingham, Mich.

Mrs. Rensselaer W. Lee (Stella Garrett), 36 Edwards Pl., Princeton, N. J.

Mrs. Henry B. Rigby (Eleanor Grant), Cheshire, Conn.

Mrs. Milton G. Potter (Helen Himmelsbach), 191 Hodge Av., Buffalo, N. Y. (after June 1).

Mrs. William S. Kilpatrick (Louise Hunt), 1204 S. Ogden Dr., Los Angeles, Calif.

Mrs. William E. Dent (Dorothy-Kate Johnston), 1203 Boylston St, Boston, Mass.

Mrs. Kirkland W. Todd (Kathryn Kerr), 1227 Wightman St., Pittsburgh, Pa.

Annie Kyle, 1 Grace Court, Brooklyn, N.Y.

Barbara Lincoln, 117 Sigourney St., Hartford, Conn.

Mrs. George E. Anderson (Cecilia Matthews), 2647 Sedgwick Av., N. Y. C.

Mrs. Harold S. Lamb (Edna Miller), 137 S. Witmer St., Los Angeles, Calif.

Esther Nichols, 43 rue Galilée, Paris, France.

Mrs. Howard K. Walter (Alison McEldowney), 5256 Wilkens Av., Pittsburgh, Pa.

Julia Pressey, 1207 W. Oregon St., Urbana, Ill.

Mrs. George E. Longstaff (Marene Richards), 22 Tams Apts., Huron, S. D.

Mrs. Otto W. Kracht (Marion Underwood), Grasdon Hall, Larchmont, N. Y.

Mrs. Simon B. Kleiner (Regina Wendel), 671 Orange St., New Haven, Conn.

Mrs. H. D. Dunlap (Elizabeth Wiley), 1722 Cornell Av., Knoxville, Tenn.

Helen Witte, 57 Hillside Av., Glen Ridge, N. J.

Ex-1918

MARRIED.—Virginia Miner to W. W. Harryman, in 1920. Address, 507 Alter Rd., Detroit, Mich. Virginia's husband is a nerve specialist.

Helen Tawney to George F. Bokum, May 28, 1926. New address, 18 E. Elm St., Chicago, Ill.

BORN.—To Margaret (Ambrose) Ramsay a son, David Jr., Aug. 14, 1925.

To Florence (Breckenridge) Sperry a second child and first son, Peter Breckenridge, Sept. 19, 1926.

To Mary (Lilly) Fisher two sons who have never been reported: Robert Lilly, Mar. 3, 1923, and William Lilly, May 15, 1924.

To June (Love) Stratton a son, Walter Love, Sept. 21, 1926.

To Emily (Welsh) Myers a third child and second daughter, Anne Welsh, in Jan. 1925.

OTHER NEWS.—Ruth Hitchcock reports that besides being church organist, she is teaching piano and organ.

Anna Nagle is secretary to a managing and designing engineer of the General Electric Co. in Pittsfield.

Dorothy (Rand) Whitaker has been taking a three-year art course at Pratt Institute, and expects to finish this June. She says it seems very strange to be back at school again after all these years, and that she is the only married member of the class.

NEW ADDRESSES.—Mrs. David Ramsay (Margaret Ambrose), 23 Dudley Pl., Yonkers, N. Y.

Mrs. Burton C. Bovard (Alice Buckman), 333 Elm Pl., Leonia, N. J.

Mrs. Edward G. Redfield (Eveleth Derby), 7 Chester Pl., Englewood, N. J.

Mrs. Edward R. Schauffler (Doris Howes), 6008 Cherry St., Kansas City, Mo.

Mrs. Whitaker (Dorothy Rand), 365 Lincoln Pl., Brooklyn, N. Y.

Mrs. E. K. Carver (Ruth Ripley), 215 Flower City Park, Rochester, N. Y.

Mrs. Stuart C. McLean (Marie Sanderson), Sunrise Bay, Glengary, Idaho.

Mrs. Edwin C. Fager (Mary Sponsler), 419 N. Oakhurst Dr., Beverly Hills, Calif.

1919

Class secretary—Julia Florance, 161 Livingston Av., New Brunswick, N. J. Assistant secretary—Eleanor Fitzpatrick, 141 E. Gorgas Lane, Germantown, Pa.

ENGAGED.—Mae Haskins to Gilbert A. Starr of Beverly, Mass. She expects to be married in May and to live in Worcester, where her husband is interested in advertising.

Frances Halsted to Dr. Gerald Reid Jamei-
son. She will probably be married in June but is still planning to receive an M.D. of her own in June 1928.

MARRIED.—Ruth Goldsmith to Sidney T. H. Northcott, Feb. 19. Address, 394 School St., Watertown, Mass.

Lucia Trent to E. Ralph Cheyney, who is an advertising man, a writer, poet, and author of "Touch and Go." Lucia and her husband together edit Contemporary Verse. Her latest collection of poems is called "Dawn Stars." Address, The Civic Club, 18 E. 10 St., N. Y. C.

BORN.—To Dorothy (Bartlett) Canfield a son and second child, William Chase, Nov. 23, 1926.

To Katherine (Brosnihan) Flanagan a second son, Jack, Nov. 22, 1926.

To Eleanor (Clark) Bean a daughter, Elizabeth Anne, Nov. 7, 1926.

To Sally (Clement) Pease a third son, William, Sept. 11, 1926.

To Helen (Comey) Putnam a daughter, Caroline, Dec. 6, 1926.

To Margaret (Corcoran) Sullivan a daughter, Joan, June 5, 1925, and a son, Richard, Oct. 19, 1926.

To Caroline (Crouter) White a son, John Edgerton Hunter, Jan. 31.

To Elizabeth (Demarest) Greenhalgh a daughter, Elizabeth Ann, Jan. 26.

To Grace (De Veber) Little twin daughters, Patricia and Grace, Mar. 17. Grace will be busy this summer for Sylvia and George are only three and two years old respectively.

To Martha (Fowler) Gordon a son, Charles Fowler, May 16, 1926.

To Florence (Houchin) Skinner a first daughter and second child, Grace Evelyn, June 30, 1926.

To Florence (Kelman) McCandless a first son and second child, John Kelman, June 16, 1926.

To Lucy (Kingsbury) Piper a second daughter and third child, Nancy Nims, Mar. 13.

To Mary (MacArthur) Bryan a first daughter and second child, Mary Catherine, Sept. 19, 1925. Mary's husband is a visiting lecturer on physiography in the department of geology at Harvard this year.

To Grace (Nelson) Fischer a first son and second child, Chester Owen Jr., Feb. 8.

To Margaret (Petherbridge) Farrar a son, John Chipman Jr., Mar. 22. The Seventh Cross Word Puzzle Book has been published this spring.

To Marion (Post) Hidden a son, William Post, July 19, 1925.

To Jessie (Reidpath) Ludlum a second daughter, Cordelia Branch, Mar. 7.

To Doris (Smith) Bowlus a second son, John Magruder, Aug. 7, 1926.

To Alberta (Smith) Wells a daughter, Jean Louisa, Apr. 12, 1926.

OTHER NEWS.—Katherine (Adams) Haskell moved into a new house on a 8000-acre ranch just before Christmas and is most enthusiastic about its location among the foothills in Arizona.

Lois Allison spent six weeks in Bermuda this winter.

Frances Anderson is head of the English department of St. Mary's School in Peekskill, N. Y.

Elizabeth Atterbury is planning to sail Sept. 24 on the *S. S. Paris* in order to complete her course at the New York School of Fine and Applied Art at the Paris branch, Place des Vosges.

Lilian Ball is supervising the study of English in the Hudson (N. Y.) High School. She received an M.A. from Columbia last October.

Eleanor (Bedell) Burt is helping her husband, who is starting in business as a consulting physicist and maker of scientific instruments.

Helen (Bingham) Miller, Margaret (Stowe) Gillmore, and Isabel (Knowles) Rust arranged to be in Chicago at the same time in March.

Elizabeth Brown is assistant buyer of the Misses' Dress department of B. Altman and Co. in New York and is living at home.

Mary Clark is preparing to take her final examination for an M.A. from Columbia, while teaching college English in the Westfield (Mass.) High School.

Edith Coit is teaching the 4th and 6th grades in "Le Cours Français," a small private school in Philadelphia, and spending the other half of her time at "The Twickenham Bookshop."

Alice Cronan teaches general science and mathematics in the Chicopee (Mass.) Junior High School.

Rose Daly is librarian of the Shelton Hotel Library in New York City.

Dorothea Dower teaches English in the Easthampton (Mass.) High School.

Irene Drury is connected with the Houghton Mifflin Publishing Co. in Cambridge, Mass.

Laura Ellis is looking forward to a three months' motor trip through the British Isles and Europe with her family this summer.

Ethel Emery is doing secretarial work for the National Committee on Visiting Teachers and is living at the New York Smith Club.

Katharine Fleming is taking postgraduate courses in history at Columbia.

Julia Florance sailed Apr. 2 on the *S. S. Colombo* for four months of travel in Sicily, Italy, Switzerland, and France.

Jean (Fyke) Gerould's husband died very suddenly Jan. 31 of acute nephritis.

Margaret Faunce, Ruth (Perry) Neff, Mae Haskins, and Rebecca (Mathis) Gershon have lost their mothers recently.

Rosa Hodgkins is teaching mathematics and history in Douglass (Mass.) and expects to go into the antique business in Ellsworth (Me.) during her vacation.

Gladys Holmes attended the summer school for American graduates at Oxford last year.

Marjorie Hopper is practicing medicine in Nyack (N. Y.) where she has an office on the main street. She is on the staff of the local hospital. She works in the gynecology department of the Cornell Clinic in New York City three afternoons each week.

Helen (Hotchkin) Means returned to Chicago from Peru in October and expects to go to Newfoundland for the summer.

Elizabeth (Hunt) Lockard was chairman of a most successful 1919 Class Supper at the New York Smith Club on Mar. 21. Twenty classmates gathered and were pleasantly surprised when Nora (Hamlen) Robinson arrived unexpectedly.

Barbara Johnson is doing editorial work for *Charm*, which is published by L. Bamberger and Co. in Newark, N. J. Europe is to be on her program again this summer.

Rebecca (Jones) Butler is enjoying teaching music and accompanying.

Elizabeth Kingsley and Dorothy Kinne are planning to sail July 15 on the *S. S. Rochambeau* for two months in Europe.

Katharine (Lamont) O'Donoghue is an ideal hostess in Malta, according to the personal experience of the secretary's parents.

Frances Lowe was connected with *Politics* for two months and is now secretary to the manager of The Northfield in East Northfield, Mass.

Gladys Kern is teaching English in the Bayonne (N. J.) High School.

Leila Knapp has charge of the Ladies' and Savings Departments of the Vermont People's National Bank of Brattleboro.

Frances McLeod has a unique shop in Milwaukee (Wis.) in which she deals in books, art, and advertising.

Frances Maher is teaching in Brooklyn (N. Y.) and living at the New York Smith Club.

Muriel (Mertens) Townley is building a summer home on the edge of the Knollwood golf course in Lake Forest, Ill.

Margaret (Osborn) Emery is corresponding secretary of the Boston Smith Club. She ran a Juniper Lodge bridge party in Brookline, and raised $400.

Ruth (Perry) Neff expects to move into a new house, "English Tudor period," about the first of May.

Eleanor Ripley is interested in old French furniture and is connected with Isabella Barclay, 16 E. 53 St., N. Y. C. She has an apartment at 184 Waverly Pl.

Eleanor (Ritchie) Alexander is secretary of the Lynn (Mass.) Smith Club.

Edith Schwarzenberg is studying mental hygiene at the New York School of Social Work.

Mary Shea is teaching mathematics in the Holyoke (Mass.) High School.

Eunice Sims is secretary to the chief of the Claims Division in the U. S. Veterans' Bureau in Little Rock, Ark.

Eleanor Smith received an M.A. from Columbia and a Teachers College diploma last fall. She is enjoying her duties as dean of girls as well as her classes in mathematics in Agawam, Mass.

Genevieve Smith is a member of the teaching staff in the Miami (Fla.) High School.

Dorothea Thomas expects to spend part of the summer in New York City studying professional theaters. Her course in Acting and Play Production at Rollins College is a huge success.

Jessie Thorp is doing secretarial work for Dr. Baker of the Carnegie Institute of Technology.

Ruth (Walcott) MacKenzie is directing the first school for parents ever introduced in Rochester (N. Y.), under the auspices of the Women's City Club.

Eleanor (Ward) Cornelius enjoyed a two and one half months' trip to Havana and Jamaica the first part of the year.

Peggy (Zinsser) Douglas's husband has been elected to Congress and Peggy came up to Washington for two weeks with him when he took the oath of office.

NEW ADDRESS.—Mrs. Alfred M. Jonap (Henriette Bloom), 20 Burton Woods Lane, Avondale, Cincinnati, O.

Ex-1919

MARRIED.—Sarah Coburn to Schuyler L. Hoff, June 7, 1926. Address, 4924 Center Av., Pittsburgh, Pa.

Elizabeth Wickes to Irving Marshall, June 1925. Address, 76 Chedell Pl., Auburn, N. Y.

BORN.—To Ethelind (Cary) Litle a son and third child, William Jr., Oct. 12, 1925.

To Maurine (Mitchell) Fite a second daughter and fourth child, Frances, Nov. 24, 1926.

To Bonnie (Taylor) Reed a son and second child, David, in February. Her daughter Marcia is two years old.

1920

Class secretary—Mrs. Arthur R. Hoch (Marian Hill), 312 N. Euclid Av., Oak Park, Ill. Assistant secretary—Josephine Taylor, 137 S. Scoville Av., Oak Park, Ill.

NOTICE.—In the spring letter sent to the delinquent members of the class a request was made for help in locating those (6 in number) who have never answered a class letter and several others who are notably lax in news and dues. That list is quoted here with a few additions and it is especially requested that you all aid in the search. At least three years have passed since a letter has come from any one on the list and they will be permanently lost unless a great effort is made to get them to write headquarters. If one of these girls lives in your city, though you may not know her, call her on the phone and impress upon her the importance of keeping in communication with the class. The list is: Rosalind (Apple) Weise, Helen Barry, Jane (Caldwell) Lobdell, Mary Frances (Cathcart) Stevens, Helen (Cole) Downey, Harriet (Cook) French, Mary Cooper, Louise Crowley, Bernice Davidson, Nyok Zoe (Dong) Tsiang, Achsah Dorsey, Ruth (Dowell) Svihla, Margaret (Fitzgibbon) Carey, Frances Flint, Henrietta Fort, Ruth Freeman, Dorothy (Gale) Hamilton, Belle Gruskin, Mildred Mae (Johnson) Hawkins, Lucile Larson, Alice McClary, Mary Marley, Norma (Mueller) Lorenzer, Florence Penfold, Charlotte Ress, Inez (Sharman) Moran, Adaline (Shick)

Dyer, Edna Soule, Edith Sullivan, Mary (Tilson) Garrett, Lisbeth (Urban) Clark.

It may be of interest to note that this is the first issue of the QUARTERLY since our graduation that has contained no notice of a marriage!

ENGAGED.—Christine Adams to Ralph Davis Jones of Pittsburgh, nephew of Secretary of Labor James J. Davis.

Elizabeth Upton to Rev. Herbert H. Knight, minister of the Congregational Church of Claremont, N. H.

BORN.—To Harriet (Broughton) Bishop a second son, John Broughton, Feb. 11. Address, 271 Cornell Rd., Portland, Ore.

To Annie (Breuer) Reynolds a first son, in Apr. 1926. She gives no name.

To Dorothy (Clark) Eldred a first son, Dwight Beardsley Jr., Jan. 14. This announcement comes in Dorothy's very first letter. She writes that her husband is business manager for the Fox-Case Corp. in N. Y. C. and that their address is 45 Wallbrook Rd., Scarsdale, N. Y.

To Harriet (Cook) French a first daughter, Mary Ann, Sept. 5, 1926. Address, 158 Stanford Av., Elyria, O.

To Ann (Corlett) Ford a first daughter, Ann Amanda, Oct. 22, 1926. They have moved back to Cleveland and are living with Ann's parents temporarily. Address, 11015 East Blvd.

To Helen (Hadley) Gander a second son, James Thomas, Dec. 12, 1926. Address, 2557 11th Av. W., Seattle, Wash.

To Frances (Smith) Johnson a third child and second daughter, Joy Frances, Mar. 16.

To Priscilla (Stetson) Alger a first son, Stanley Francis Jr., Oct. 29, 1926. Priscilla's husband is a shoe salesman with Leonard, Shaw, and Deane, Inc. She was captain of the Girl Scouts and a member of the Executive Board of the Woman's Club in 1924, a lieutenant of the Girl Scouts and corresponding secretary of the Woman's Club in 1925, and in 1926 she was president of the Ladies' Aid Society of the church and a member of the Legislative Committee of the Woman's Club.

OTHER NEWS.—Margaret Andrus is secretary of the Committee on Formal Education of the American Eugenics Society, Inc. Permanent address, 1325 Minerva Rd., Ann Arbor, Mich. Temporary address, 3502 New Medical Bldg., Univ. of Michigan, Ann Arbor, Mich.

Lillias (Armour) Painter took a three weeks' cruise to Alaska last July. Her husband has been trainer and surgeon to the Pasadena High School football teams since 1924. They have bought "a lovely corner lot in Altadena near our wonderful mountains and just north of Pasadena and hope to build within a year."

Margaret Broad writes: "Have traveled around the Mediterranean, through Egypt and Europe, and am now spending the winter with my family in Switzerland. Expect to stay in Europe another year and then return to California via India, Australia, and the South Seas."

Leah Brown is a publicity writer for the Coral Gables (Fla.) Publicity Dept.

Helen Cass has an advertising business of her own. She also teaches six hours a week advertising and business management at Rutgers. Address, 528 Riverside Dr., N. Y. C.

Frances (Chick) Peabody is living in New York this year. She confirms the birth of her third child, giving his name, Arthur William, and the date, Dec. 5, 1925, and writes, "Still pursuing my M.A." Address, 514 W. 114 St., N. Y. C.

Katharine (Cornwell) Draper's husband is treasurer of the Bankers Trust Co., Hartford, and their address is 15 Case St.

Geneva Croxford is doing research work in cardiology with the N. Y. Heart Assn. Address, 233 Fulton Av., Hempstead, N. Y.

Jeannette (Croxford) Johnson is teaching this year. She also does public reading (and has for ten years). Her husband does oral surgery. Address, 34 Oak St., Augusta, Me.

Louise DeGaris is teaching girls' physical training at the Illinois Woman's College in Jacksonville.

Gertrude (Fitzgerald) Wilcox's address is 1980 Lake Dr., Grand Rapids, Mich. Her husband does investment banking.

Elinor Fears is personnel director in B. H. Dyas Co., Los Angeles.

Valeria Foot came home from Europe in time for Christmas after six months abroad. She will be in Pinehurst (N. C.) till May.

Agnes Grant is working with the Women's Educational and Industrial Union in Boston. At present she is helping with the Third Annual Exhibit of Craftsmen-at-Work. Address, 124 Babcock St., Brookline, Mass.

Christine (Hubbard) Lindsley's address is 1538 Grand Av., Seattle, Wash.

Virginia (Noel) Long has a new home, 715 Thomas St., Oak Park, Ill.

Marjorie (Lord) Packard and her husband have just left for Europe to be gone about six months in study and travel. They will be back in Hanover by the first of September.

Vera (MacKen) Friend's husband is a doctor specializing in eye, ear, nose, and throat work. Address, 88 Church St., South Manchester, Conn.

Elisabeth Perkins has left the Low and Heywood School and taken a position in the President's office at Hunter College. New address, 142 W. 70 St., N. Y. C.

Harriet (Pratt) Lattin received her M.A. last June from Ohio State Univ. She is now working on her Ph.D. in history.

Carol Rice has a new address, 1438 Mound St., Madison, Wis.

Emily Sellstrom is at home this year and writes: "Am president of the Y. W. C. A. and College Club, recording secretary of Crèche (day nursery), on the Executive Committee of the Fortnightly (a literary club), and in Mozart Club, Players Club, Saddle Club, doing work for the blind, and church work. Leaving for Florida Mar. 9 and will attend as a delegate the A. A. U. W. National Convention in Washington, Mar. 31 to Apr. 2."

Violet Storey lost her father the last of March. She writes: "I have written verse for many English and American periodicals. Have been reading my own poems before various clubs and societies and also over the radio."

Ex-1920

DIED.—Beatrice (Tyler) Flood. The following very brief announcement was received from her husband: "Died, June 9, 1926, at the birth of our second boy."

Eleven of the items below have been culled from the first letters the secretary has ever received from these girls.

MARRIED.—Anna Baker to A. Parker Barnaskey, Aug. 30, 1920. She writes: "I went to Syracuse Univ. 1917–18 after Smith, taking special courses in journalism, and spent 1918–19 at the U. S. Secretarial School in N. Y. I am doing a little newspaper work now locally. My husband is general manager of the Westcott Chuck Co. and our address is 569 Broad St., Oneida, N. Y."

Jessie Burns to Harvey Edward Frye, May 1, 1926. Her husband is a representative of the American Cable Co. Permanent address, 1320 N. Lawrence Av., Wichita, Kan. Temporary address, The Shirkmere, Wichita.

Edith Emmons to Raymond Palmer Pennoyer, June 19, 1926. Her husband is with the Carnegie Steel Co. Address, Roland Park Apts., Baltimore, Md.

Grace Hart to William J. Marlowe, Oct. 20, 1926. Grace's husband is an electrical engineer. Permanent address, Jefferson, Mass. Temporary address, Suite 12, The Columbia, Leominster, Mass.

Annie Laurie Hoard to Frank Miner Brewer, Apr. 28, 1921. Her husband is in the advertising business. They have two children, Laurie Ann, May 4, 1922, and Barbara, Aug. 10, 1923. Address, 57 Crescent Dr., Glencoe, Ill.

Frances Humphrey to George D. Williams, June 15, 1925. Her husband is an accountant. Address, Poultney, Vt.

Kathryn Liebmann to W. J. Clark Brannion, Oct. 12, 1926. They are now living at the Château Frontenac, E. Jefferson Av., Detroit, Mich. Kathryn's husband is in the advertising business and she was on the N. Y. American in 1924 and had several signed articles. Kathryn writes, "I am a newspaper woman though not active at the moment."

Elizabeth McAllaster to Thomas Fairbanks Remington, Sept. 1, 1921. They have two girls, Josephine McAllaster, Jan. 3, 1923, and Anne, Aug. 4, 1926. Address, 23 Ashton Rd., Bronxville, N. Y.

Anna Mary McCarthy to Wilbur Fiske Gordy, Aug. 4, 1921. She took a secretarial course at Columbia in 1918–20. Her husband is in the rubber industry. They have one daughter, Jane Niles, Oct. 17, 1924. Address, 21 Schuyler St., Rockville Center, N. Y.

Anne Oldham to Captain Henry W. Borntraeger, Oct. 10, 1925. Her husband is a Captain in the U. S. Army stationed at Miller Field, Staten Island, N. Y. They

have a daughter, Anne, born Sept. 4, 1926.

Helen Painter to Ken G. Fraser, June 20, 1925. Helen's husband is a logging superintendent. They have a daughter, Phyllis Jean, Mar. 28, 1926. Address, Sultan, Wash.

Helen Mary Smith to Harry J. Abrams, June 26, 1923. Helen Mary attended Russell Sage College 1919-21 and received a B.S. Her husband is in the automobile business. Address, Chatham, N. Y.

Vitula Van Dyne to John Dent McCutcheon, June 2, 1926. Vitula received her B.A. from the Univ. of Missouri in 1921. Her husband is a bond salesman. Address, 6829 Kingsbury Blvd., St. Louis, Mo.

Irene Wallace to Leslie W. Page, Nov. 26, 1921. Her husband is in the real estate business. They have a daughter, Ruth Irene, Dec. 29, 1922. Address, 7811 East End Av., Chicago.

BORN.—To Sue (Alexander) Butterfield a first son, Alexander Porter, Apr. 6, 1926, in Pensacola, Fla. Sue's husband is a naval aviator, attached to the Aircraft Squadron, Scouting Fleet, Norfolk, Va.

To Margaret (Boyle) LeBrun a second child and first daughter, Eleanor Carey, Sept. 14, 1926. Margaret's husband is a bank cashier.

To Kathleen (Connolly) Yager a first son, Barret G., July 5, 1925. Kathleen's husband is an advertising director and style writer. Address, Spring Av., Troy, N. Y.

To Dorothy (Greenhalgh) Delemarre a second daughter, Margaret F., Nov. 28, 1925.

To Faith (Hall) Appleby a second daughter, Joan, July 11, 1926. Faith attended the Univ. of Minnesota. Her husband is manager of P. W. Chapman and Co., Bonds. Address, 2704 34th Av. S., Seattle, Wash.

To Frances (Heile) Pike a first daughter, Joan Frances, Aug. 18, 1926. Address, 46 W. 15 St., Chicago Heights, Ill.

To Ruth (Hill) Paige a third child and first daughter, Jean, Mar. 5. Ruth writes: "No more shop. Have been here at the Mare Island Navy Yard since October." Address, 426 Wilson Av., Vallejo, Calif.

To Dorothy (Hitchings) Stockton a first daughter, Harriet Bond, Apr. 7, 1925. Also a second child and first son, George A. Jr., Aug. 30, 1926. Dorothy's husband is a grain broker. Address, 120 Abingdon Av., Kenilworth, Ill.

To Elinor (McClure) Funk a second son, Robert Donald, Aug. 18, 1926. Elinor writes: "My travels include Panama, Jamaica, most of the European countries, as well as Northern Africa and Asia Minor and from the Atlantic to the Pacific. My only approach to being in the public eye is to be the sister of a rising young novelist, Robert E. McClure. My husband is part owner of the *Glendale Evening News.*" Address, 1550 Cleveland Rd., Glendale, Calif.

To Julia (Martin) Anthony a second son, David Martin, Nov. 20, 1926.

To Hilda (Morse) Howarth a second child, May 12, 1925, but Hilda fails to divulge the name. Her husband is manager of the knife department of the Simonds Saw and Steel Co. and Hilda is secretary of the Fitchburg Visiting Nurse Assn.

To Sylvia (Taylor) Chandler a first daughter, Phyllis, Oct. 3, 1926. Sylvia graduated from the Univ. of Chicago in 1921, receiving a Ph.B. Her husband is a bond salesman. Address, 475 Belleview Pl., Milwaukee, Wis.

To Viola (vonDeesten) Kuhlen a first daughter, Lois Marie, Sept. 17, 1926. Viola's husband is a teacher.

OTHER NEWS.—Alice (Best) Rogers writes that her husband is a lumberman. She adds that she imports English antiques in addition to her other occupations.

Marguerite (Boucher) Wickwire graduated from Barnard. She is trained to be a library assistant but is not active now.

Angelyn (Brown) Goetzman's address is Clover Rd., Brighton, Rochester, N. Y. Her husband is in an interior woodworking mill.

Jessie (Canning) Young's address is c/o Union Tank Car Co., Port Tampa City, Fla.

Mary Eleanor Chapman received her B.A. from Elmira College in 1921. She is now secretary to the *American Architect*, 243 W. 39 St., N. Y. C.

Miriam Cummings is now research secretary to the American Child Health Assn., 370 Seventh Av., N. Y. C.

Rhoda (Dean) Milligan's address is 21 Theron St., Johnson City, N. Y. Her husband is a bed-laster in a shoe factory. Rhoda graduated from the Univ. of Maine in 1920 and from Farmington Normal in 1921.

Susan (Emison) Gee's husband is a banker and is president of the Farmers State Bank.

Grace (Fischer) Kribs's address is 2531 26th Av. N., Seattle, Wash. Her husband is assistant sales manager of the Builders Brick Co. Grace attended the Univ. of Washington in 1918.

Frances (Fleming) Bixby writes that she has been in Europe for the last three summers. She is president of the Junior League again this year. Address, 810 W. 52 St., Kansas City, Mo.

Pearl Gridley writes: "A student this year. Have gone to Northwestern to finish my interrupted college career. Get my B.A. in June."

Helen (Grimes) VanWeventer is doing advertising for L. Bamberger and Co., Newark, N. J. She received her B.A. from the Univ. of Minnesota in 1920. Address, 215 W. 13 St., N. Y. C.

Helen (Hanley) Moore's address is 19 Kensington Av., Jersey City, N. J. Her husband is a mechanical engineer.

Mary Hollingshead is an art teacher. She graduated from the Univ. of California in 1921, attended the Univ. of Washington in the summer of 1924, and the Ashland School of Art in 1925.

Marie Long asks that a special plea be published asking for the donation of books to her for her work in the Hospital of Joint Diseases in N. Y. C. She organized an ambulatory library several years ago and the work has proved of great benefit to many of the pa-

THE NEW YORK SCHOOL OF SECRETARIES

A Secretarial School Marked by Distinctive Features

It accepts only the best of student material.

It trains and equips through short intensive methods.

It seeks the individual development rather than a uniform result from all students.

It prepares men and women for active newspaper and magazine work; for special feature and publicity articles; for social and organization Secretarial responsibilities.

It emphasizes a three months' course.

It places its graduates in positions.

Students may enter on any date.

Reduced rates for summer courses.

Special course in Short-story writing.

CANADIAN PACIFIC BUILDING, 342 MADISON AVENUE, NEW YORK, N. Y.

Vanderbilt 4039 V. M. WHEAT, *Director*

BALLARD SCHOOL
Central Branch, Y.W.C.A.

College women who aim for leadership in the business world find our Secretarial Course a solid foundation for future success.

Send for Bulletin

Ballard School graduates always in demand.

610 Lexington Avenue ⸱ New York City

OLD COLONY SCHOOL
Secretarial and Business Training

For Young Women Graduates of Private School, High School or College

One Year Course prepares for Executive Positions or the Management of Personal Property.
Resident and day pupils.

For Booklet or Information Write the Principals

**Florence B. LaMoreaux, A.B.
Mrs. Margaret Vail Fowler**

315-317 Beacon Street, Boston, Massachusetts

Miss Conklin's
Secretarial School

THOROUGH professional training for secretaryships and executive positions.

The school occupies the studios of the Tilden Building; classrooms opening upon a roof garden have abundance of light and air.

The Bureau of Placement is a recognized feature of the School. Graduates are sought for varied and responsible positions.

Enrollment for October 4th and successive entrance dates.

Illustrated booklet

105 West 40th Street, New York

Telephone, Penna. 3758

tients in the hospital. Home address, 71 Central Park W., N. Y. C.

The following Exes are still lost: Violet Alderman, Leta Adams, Ida Anderson, Alice Beckett, Solene Benjamin, May Benoit, Barbara (Seelye) Bottome, Jeannette Bruce, Nancy Calder, Bettie (Cary) Fox, Shirley (Choate) Peters, Mary Elizabeth (Clark) Roulet, Elizabeth Clarke, Dorothy (Moore) Congdon, Lillian Cramer, Emma Louise (Davis) Cross, Margaret Crowley, Flora Eaton, Lillian (Godchaux) Feibleman, Mary (Forker) Goodall, Ruth Forsythe, Susie Farmer, Margaret Fisk, Evelyn Hamburg, Elizabeth Huston, Phebe Hyatt, Carol (Smith) Lane, Emma Leary, Ruth Lee, Sara Lewis, Virgene Maltby, Miriam Martinez, Mildred Mather, Mary Morrow, Hélène Mus, Winifred Mackay, Dorothy Nauss, Elizabeth Odell, Helen (Tebbetts) Parker, Anne (Perkins) Phillips, Gertrude Smith, Susan (Stephenson) Walker, Margaret Stambaugh, Mary Sullivan, Edith Thompson, Anne May Weldon, Mary (Wells) Zick, Marion Whittaker, Helen Wiener, Pauline (Lewin) Williams, Abbie Anne Wilson.

1921

Class secretary—Mrs. E. Graham Bates (Dorothy Sawyer), 8 Maple St., Auburndale, Mass.

ENGAGED.—Madelaine Gile to Dr. John Pollard Bowler, Dartmouth '15. Dr. Bowler is practicing medicine in Hanover.

Roberta Saunders to Curtis Saunders, Yale '13.

Frances Treadway to Lee Wallace.

MARRIED.—Ida Louise Dohme to Felix Agnus Leser, Jan. 8. Address, 115 E. Eager St., Baltimore, Md.

Frances Helmick to Harold Hobart Buell, June 19, 1926. Temporary address, Box 27, Mobile, Ala.

Katrina Jameson to John H. Jack, Dec. 27, 1926, in Washington, D. C. Address, Central Agencies Ltd., Valparaiso, Chile.

Sallie Kline to Howard G. Myers. Address, 51 Riverside Dr., N. Y. C.

Olive Lyman to Marshall A. Webb, Sept. 11, 1926. Address, 222 Otis Av., St. Paul.

Anna O'Connor to Dr. Frank Knope, Oct. 4, 1926. Address, 154 Rockingham St., Rochester, N. Y.

Marjory Porritt to Harry K. Nield, in July 1926. Marjory left immediately for England where she and her husband were furnishing a 16th century house. Word has come of Mr. Nield's sudden death on Oct. 23, 1926, after four days' illness. Marjory is to remain in England until summer. Address, The Old College, Barnet, Herts, England.

Helena Smith to Henry Pringle. Address, 364 W. 26 St., N. Y. C.

Josephine Smith to Alton Davis Bryant, June 26, 1926. Address, 91 Osgood St., North Andover, Mass.

BORN.—To Eleanor (Armstrong) Smith a second child and first daughter, Cara Elizabeth, Feb. 2.

To Margaret (Bardwell) Woodworth a second child and first son, Robert Cushman Jr., June 17, 1926.

To Virginia (Downes) Addis a daughter, Joan Virginia, Nov. 20, 1926.

To Ernestine (Fay) Scott a second son, William, Feb. 3.

To Elizabeth (Graves) Hill a second son, William Norbert Jr., Dec. 13, 1926.

To Helen (Gutman) Sternau a second child and first daughter, Virginia Anne, Feb. 15.

To Mary (Holyoke) Marsh a daughter, Molly, Nov. 9, 1926.

To Eunice (Hunton) Carter a son, Lisle Jr., Nov. 18, 1925.

To Charlotte (Kunzig) Maurer a second daughter, Charlotte Anne, Dec. 3, 1926. Charlotte's first child, June, died a few days after her birth in June 1925.

To Charlotte (Lindley) Wurtele a daughter, Ann Lindley, Nov. 14, 1926.

To Elizabeth (Rintels) Bernkopf a son, Michael, Jan. 11.

To Marion (Shedd) Blodgett a son, Frederick Jeffrey, Feb. 7.

To Elizabeth (Somerville) Woodbridge a son, James Ormond, July 17, 1926.

To Hazel (Sprague) Moore a second son, Joseph Wyman, Nov. 6, 1926.

To Catherine (Stickney) Relf a son, John Lawrence, Mar. 12.

To Virginia (Wenner) Gaskill a daughter, Emily Jane, Feb. 23.

To Cora (Wyman) Richardson a third child and second daughter, Virginia, Mar. 8.

OTHER NEWS.—Eleanor (Armstrong) Smith has moved back to Cleveland and is living temporarily with her family at 2520 Stratford Rd.

Lynda (Billings) Mitchell writes that she has been working on a historical prologue and movie of the Revolution from the Yale University Press. She and her husband are both in it.

May Bossi is connected with the Holland American Line in Paris, telling everyone how, when, and where to shop. Her father died in Italy last summer. May spent Christmas with her mother and sister in Milan.

Kathryn (Caine) Marvin sailed Feb. 17 for a Mediterranean cruise with her father and mother. Mr. Marvin will join her the first of April in Florence and they will travel for two months in France and England.

Ariel Carstens is teaching in Townsend this winter. She spends her summers as subdirector of Camp Allegro at Silver Lake, N. H.

Minnie-Brown Clare graduated from the Smith College School for Social Work last September and is now the psychiatric social worker for the San Diego County Juvenile Court.

Margaret Cotton has recently been in California, going out by way of the Canal.

Dorothy Davis is doing interior decorating from her apartment at 186 Sullivan St., New York.

Bridget Fitzgerald taught for two years at the Burnham School in Northampton. For the last four years she has been teaching history and English in the Holyoke High School.

Frances Holden received her Ph.D. from Columbia last year and is now teaching in the psychology department at New York Univ.

Alice (Jaretzki) Cooper has purchased a home in Westport (Conn.) which she is furnishing with early American antiques.

India Johnson is on an eight months' European trip as companion and tutor for a twelve-year-old girl.

Grace King spent the winter in Florida with her mother and sister.

Mildred (King) Sangree is teaching science and mathematics in the State Normal School at Glassboro (N. J.) and keeping house.

Sallie (Kline) Myers is writing publicity, besides doing her housework.

Camilla Loyall and Dorothy Schuyler sailed for Italy in March 1926. After a marvelous trip through Italy, Camilla spent the summer studying in Geneva, returning home in September, while Dorothy got a job with the Bankers Trust in Paris and lived at the American University Club. She returned in January.

Ruth Lyman took a trip to California with her father in the winter.

Harriet Murdock is marking time in New Haven—and out—until she returns to Europe.

Georgiana Palmer is teaching Greek for the second semester at Mount Holyoke during the absence of one of the department. She plans to continue her study of Greek at the Univ. of Chicago next fall.

Helen Pillsbury is doing publicity work for William H. Baldwin, 299 Madison Av., New York.

Marie (Poland) Fish, according to an article in the *New Bedford Sunday Standard*, "will go down in scientific history as the discoverer of the long-sought egg of the common American eel." Marie found four freshly spawned eel's eggs when she was a member of Dr. Beebe's expedition to the Sargasso Sea, and the find is considered one of the triumphs of the expedition. By careful incubation, Marie managed to hatch one of the eggs. The baby eel, together with one of the unhatched eggs, has been preserved and will be sent to the National Museum in Washington. "Thus," continues the article, "a secret that has eluded the researches of scientists and the speculations of philosophers for more than 2000 years has been unriddled at last."

Adela Pond received her M.A. from Smith last June. She is studying at Columbia this winter and finds it interesting to live at International House.

Lelia Thompson wrote an article entitled "Beneficiaries under Modern Life Insurance Policies" which appeared in *The Annals of the American Academy of Political and Social Science* for March 1927. Lelia has the distinction of being one of the two women members of the Association of Life Insurance Counsel.

Katharine Walker toured through the Middle West in March, interviewing campers for Camp Serrana.

Helen Watts is assistant professor of English at Fisk Univ. She finds college teaching fascinating work, though exacting. She writes, "I am glad to be back, because Fisk under a new president is looking towards a great future." Address, Box 196, Fisk Univ., Nashville, Tenn.

NEW ADDRESSES.—Mrs. R. T. Addis (Virginia Downes), Lancaster Av. and Garret Rd., Rosemont, Pa.

Ruth Duncan, 2102 Roosevelt St., Clinton, Ia.

Mrs. H. F. Dean (Margaret Hannum), 279 Walnut St., Brookline, Mass.

Mrs. C. M. Peck (Eunice Hovey), 35 Hudson St., Oneonta, N. Y.

Mrs. L. C. Carter (Eunice Hunton), 2307 Seventh Av., N. Y. C.

India Johnson, 147 E. 50 St., N. Y. C.

Mrs. R. A. Thompson (Lorna Mason), Box 25, Saranac Lake, N. Y.

Mrs. Olcott Brown (Ruth O'Hanlon), 40 Chestnut St., Salem, Mass.

Mrs. C. J. Fish (Marie Poland), 400 Elmwood Av., Buffalo, N. Y.

Mrs. F. C. Furlow Jr. (Geraldine Silver), 31 E. 79 St., N. Y. C.

Mrs. L. E. Thayer (Virginia Speare), 48 Warren St., Newton Center, Mass.

Mrs. W. G. Avirett (Helen Weiser), Deerfield, Mass.

Ex-1921

BORN.—To Lavinia (Strange) Marshall a daughter, Pamela, Jan. 23.

OTHER NEWS.—Ruth Brooks makes six cross word puzzles a week for a syndicate including the *Boston Herald, Newark Evening News,* and the *Utica Daily Press.*

1922

Class secretaries—A–K, Mrs. Francis T. P. Plimpton (Pauline Ames), 1165 Fifth Av., N. Y. C. L–Z, Mrs. George F. Hughes (Frona Brooks), Box 393, Garden City, N. Y.

See Notices for Commencement announcements. Dorothy (Crydenwise) Lindsay, 4 Walnut St., Boston, is Chairman of Reunion.

To the Friends of Peggy Franks

Last November, just a year after her tragic death, a movement was started to raise a memorial to Margaret (Franks) Gordon. Because of her interest during undergraduate years in stage design, it seemed appropriate to raise a Fund for Experimentation in Stage Design, using the income each year under the direction of the College Art Department for making stage and costume models, or putting on a play in which the Department might wish to experiment with special ideas in staging. Letters sent to the members of 1922 have brought many responses which the Committee wishes to acknowledge with thanks. Friends from her home in Rockville Center and some members of other classes have also sent gifts. An invitation is herewith extended to any others who wish to join in perpetuating Peggy's memory through the advancement of art. There has been received to date $316 with a promise of $100 additional. Perhaps it is too much to hope for, but $500 would make a splendid gift worthy of the devotion of her friends. The

The QUARTERLY is co-operating with the Intercollegiate Alumni Extension Service, Inc., in the endeavor to gather information about our alumnae.

Will you help us by answering the questions below, and sending your reply to the Alumnae Office, College Hall?

All information will be considered strictly confidential.

Annual income.................................

Annual income from investments.................

Life insurance carried..........................

Other insurance carried.........................

Number of automobiles owned..........Make......

Married.......................................

Children...................Age........Sex......

What interests me most in the QUARTERLY..........

....

gift will be presented to the College at the Fifth Reunion of 1922.

DIED.—Virginia Reed, at Annapolis, Md., Feb. 4. She was taken ill during a visit to Dorothy (Benson) Davis, and died after a very short and severe illness in the hospital.

In Memoriam

Virginia found life full of friends, full of sunlight and happiness; because it was so radiant with possibilities for her, it became so for all who knew her. It is hard to realize that she, who had so much the gift of living, has relinquished it. Even those who knew her during her short illness loved her and did everything in their power for her. We to whom she has been a loyal and constant friend will always keep the memory of her sunny nature, her generous loving spirit, that she may still reveal to us the true gift of living.
D. B. D.

MARRIED.—Ruth Scheibler to Clarence Lyman Rice, Nov. 16, 1926. Address, 10 Lancaster St., Cambridge, Mass.

BORN.—To Marjory (Lewis) Schoonmaker a son, Lewis, Nov. 27, 1926.

To Celia (Silberman) Sonnenfeld a daughter, Marcia Caryl, Jan. 26. Her new address is 750 Western Av., Albany, N. Y.

To Helen Amy (Smith) Mellor a second son, Charles Richard, Nov. 25, 1926.

OTHER NEWS.—Dorothy (Benson) Davis is enjoying this country once more. Her husband is stationed at the U. S. Naval Academy this year, teaching.

Frona (Brooks) Hughes with her six-months-old daughter has been enjoying the early spring in Urbana (Ill.), visiting her parents.

Eleanor Chilton has just published her first book, "Shadows Waiting."

Carita (Clark) Ackerly sailed with her doctor husband in April for five or six months of study in England—preparing for research work to be done at Worcester on their return. He has been having a year of "medical work from a physical rather than the mental viewpoint" on psychiatric patients at the Worcester State Hospital.

Isabel Conklin is giving up her teaching position at Baldwin School (Bryn Mawr, Pa.) to study next year.

Frances (deValin) Haigh is a private secretary in the Wall Street district.

Margaret (Hays) Baum is active in Rochester (N. Y.) civic affairs.

Helen (Lawton) Hathaway gives her new address. They are starting housekeeping in Apt. 31-B, 3412 Spring Garden St., Philadelphia, Pa.

Dixie (Miller) Webb represented the Class at Alumnae Council in February.

Janice (Ozias) Collins is living in the suburbs of Durham, N. C. Her husband is on the faculty of Duke Univ. Her daughter, Eleanor Peers, is now "life sized" and charming. They are to be in Princeton again for the summer.

Ruth Robeson has just been spending some time in Florida and Camden, N. C.

Mathilde (Rugé) Huse's mother and father are living with her.

Dorothea (Sanjiyan) Conard says that life in N. D. seems to be full of Church, Eastern Star, Rainbow, Delphian, and Masonic Societies.

Helen Stenger is working in the wholesale clothing business in New York, and living in an apartment nearby.

Thalia (Stetson) Kennedy has moved. Address, 7001 McCallum St., Germantown, Pa.

Margaret Storrs is to be an instructor in English at Bryn Mawr next year, working for her Ph.D. She and a friend have a little "addition to a house" with "a newly acquired genie of a black Alice who takes the weight of the practical world off our shoulders." They are going abroad the first of July, taking Peggy's brother and three others to walk, boat, and drive about the British Isles.

Eleanore Thorp has been spending the winter in New York. She was in Jenks Bardwell's wedding party.

Margaret Ward is to do part-time teaching at Barnard, studying for her Doctor's degree over a period of years.

June (Wilson) Brainerd and her husband went abroad in February to stay till May—"a horse show in Dublin and a steeplechase in England."

1923

Class secretary—Mrs. Roswell C. Josephs (Frances Sheffield), Longfellow Court, Massachusetts Av., Cambridge, Mass.

DIED.—Carolyn (Colby) Chellis, Apr. 1, in Claremont, N. H., three days after her marriage to Dwight F. Chellis.

ENGAGED.—Adeline Boyden to Clyde A. Horn of Evanston, Ill. They expect to be married this spring.

Virginia Forbes to Merwin William Swenson, Dartmouth '23. They will be married next fall. She is assistant office manager of Harcourt Brace and Co.'s branch office in Chicago. Her address is 911 Michigan Av., Evanston, Ill.

Grace Kelsey to Elbert C. Weaver, Wesleyan '22, Sept. 1, 1926. Paula Thomas and Dorothy Williams '24 were in the wedding party. Their address is 171 Washington St., Hartford, Conn.

Isabelle McLaughlin to Rockwell Rittenhouse Stephens of Chicago. She is executive secretary of the Chicago Council on Foreign Relations, mostly organizing meetings for discussion of foreign affairs.

MARRIED.—Oriana Bailey to Herbert H. Lank, Mar. 19, in Newton Center. Oriana and her sister had a double wedding. They will live in New York.

BORN.—To Marion (Healy) Minard a son, Richard Alden, Jan. 12.

To Beatrice (Jaques) Coghlin a daughter, Jacqueline, Mar. 11.

OTHER NEWS.—Lucy Carr is running a bookshop with her sister, Laura '19. Address, 102 Ashland Av., East Orange, N. J.

Mary (Frazier) Meade writes from Anking, China: "We resigned last Oct., and are sail-

ing in May, via Suez, for the States, unless obliged to leave earlier. Our ultimate destination is unknown. I teach a little and do a little anthropometry and spend a great deal of time wondering what is going to happen next." Her permanent address is 913 Floyd Av., Richmond, Va.

Eleanor (Frost) Hurd gave a song recital in Hanover on Mar. 22.

Helen Hazen has been traveling in Europe and the U. S. national parks.

Louise Leland, after two years in Marshall Field's, is trying the "great post-college profession of home-girl" and finds "it's a gift." She has been bicycling through Holland and Ireland and hunting in Wyoming. Her address is c/o J. A. Leland, Springfield, Ill.

Margaret (Macleay) Leavitt and her husband are at St. Simon's Island near Brunswick (Ga.), where Mr. Leavitt is doing engineering work on a large development. Their stay is indefinite.

Charlotte Moore is secretary to the Child Study Department of the Erie (Pa.) schools.

Alice (Parker) Fisher is advertising manager for a radio house. New address, 5 Goodwin Pl., Boston.

Isabelle Pease is teaching English in the Deering High School, Portland, Me., after attending Harvard Summer School.

Edith Yereance is in the Tat Saunders Shop with Tat Saunders '19 and Margaret Mann '22. She is keeping the New York shop open while the others are at the Palm Beach end.

Ex-1923

ENGAGED.—Ruth Burt to Lieut. Robert Tappam Chaplin, Coast Artillery Corps, U. S. Army.

MARRIED.—Gertrude Smith to Kenneth James Merford. She taught in high school for two years and has been married nearly two years. They are living at 1226 39th Av. N., Seattle, Wash.

BORN.—To Margaret (Barber) des Cognets a second child and first daughter, Elizabeth Barber, Sept. 22, 1926.

To Esther (Pugsley) Burt a third child and second son, Chester Avery III, Feb. 12.

OTHER NEWS.—Elinor Lagerman was going to visit "Sallie" (Smith) Brown and try to market some short stories while in New York.

1924

Class secretary—Beatrice H. Marsh, 9 Willard St. or 721 Main St., Hartford, Conn.

ENGAGED.—Dorothy Biggs to Harlow Herbert Curtice of Flint, Mich. They expect to be married May 5, and to spend their honeymoon in Europe.

Emily Green to Robert B. Sherman of Columbus, O.

Lida Lochhead to Neil C. Estabrook, Univ. of Pennsylvania '24.

Alice Roos to Louis Ehrenfell. They expect to be married in June after Mr. Ehrenfell gets his Ph.D. in chemistry at Northwestern.

Lena Whittle to Dick Elam Smartt of Manchester, Tenn. They are to be married in June.

MARRIED.—Margaret Cooley to Mahlon

Pitney of Morristown, N. J., Oct. 23, 1926. They are living at 22 Franklin Pl., Morristown, N. J.

Betty Derby to Ralph Edward Gibson, Apr. 4. After finishing her teaching year at Smith, Betty and her husband are going abroad for the summer, planning to spend a couple of weeks with Mr. Gibson's family in Edinburgh.

Isabel Geisenberger to Monroe Benjamin Englund, Mar. 24. They are at home at 19 Bartlett Av., Pittsfield, Mass.

Lois Haskell to Charles O. Wilson, Dec. 30, 1926. Their address is 30 Southgate Park, West Newton, Mass.

Mary Elizabeth Mackey to F. Jordan McCarthy, Dartmouth '26, in June 1926. Their address is 2914 Cortelyou Rd., Brooklyn, N. Y.

Mary Elizabeth Phenix to Donald Stuart Laughlin, Mar. 30. Their wedding trip includes Paris and London.

Marjorie Pinkham to Wallace L. Trumper, M. I. T. '24, Sept. 10, 1926. They have recently moved from Columbus (Ga.) to 680 Forrest St., Beaumont, Tex. Mr. Trumper is connected with Stone and Webster of Boston.

Evelyn Sample to Clarence Fleet. New address, Cutchogue, N. Y.

Katharine Woodruff to Rupert Barnes. Address, Apt. 1A, 4248 Lawson Av., Chicago.

BORN.—To Margaret (Adams) Drukker a daughter, Joan, Jan. 27.

To Josephine (Eicher) Barclay a daughter, Feb. 28.

To Isabel (Beggs) Harvey a son, Kenneth A. Jr., Sept. 15, 1926.

To Alice (Beyer) Vosburgh a daughter, Leonie de Milhan, Jan. 3.

To Helen (Blanchard) Mitchell a daughter, Mar. 27.

To Ruth (Breen) McGrath a daughter, Anne Marie, Sept. 8, 1926.

To Carlotta (Creevey) Harrison a son, Dirck Rey, Mar. 10. Carlotta also has a daughter, Barbara.

To Rebekah (Evans) Sellers a son, Stephen Wentworth, Oct. 6, 1926, named for his maternal great-great-grandfather who founded the Wentworth Military Academy.

To Caroline (Eshman) Liebig a daughter, Charlotte, Nov. 19, 1926.

To Virginia (Hunter) Kimball a son, Lewis Everett Jr., Mar. 21.

To Florence (Wattis) Lane a son, Frederick Henry Jr., Mar. 20.

NEW ADDRESSES.—Mrs. W. Marsdon Brinkman (Millicent Possner), 2102 E. 15 St., Brooklyn, N. Y.

Mrs. H. S. Marcus (Myra Schwab), 105 W. 73 St., N. Y. C.

Mrs. Charles H. Mosher (Doris Sherman), 2921 High St., Des Moines, Ia.

OTHER NEWS.—Mary Bailey has been working this past year for Pitkin and Mott, landscape architects in Cleveland.

Eleanor Bell has been teaching at the Crallé Winter School in Fort Myers (Fla.) this winter, a small private school with grades from kindergarten to high school and three teach-

When writing to advertisers be sure to mention
THE SMITH ALUMNAE QUARTERLY

ers. Eleanor finds it "something in the way of experience!" Isabel Wisner '25 is also a teacher there.

Elizabeth Benton is teaching Latin, English, and history in Castleton on Hudson, N. Y.

Grace Brown is studying for an M.A. at Columbia.

Frances Burnham has been studying in Paris this year and plans to travel next year in China and Japan, spending several months in Peking.

Clara (Colton) Vaughan finds that housekeeping and being "reader" for her husband keep her busy.

Anna de Lancey is living in 'an orange-and-green-and-white attic" at 28 Fayette St., Boston, and studying at the Pierce Secretarial School.

Virginia Dorlon received an M.A. from Columbia in February. This summer she is conducting a tour to Europe.

Edith-May Fitton is touring Europe this summer, staying in France next winter to assist in a study of social conditions in Europe.

Katharine Gauss is still finding Smith Press Board training useful in the publicity bureau at Princeton.

Margaret Goldsmith has been working since December in the chart department of the National Industrial Conference Board in New York.

Elizabeth Hart, "after a laborious winter at Radcliffe, anticipates with glee a summer in Europe."

Lois Healy is still family case worker and dramatic leader at the Chicago Commons.

Grace Harrison is teaching business methods and business English in the Junior High School in Livingston, N. J.

Margaret Hill is learning about rare books in her father's shop in Chicago. She will join the throng going abroad this summer.

Virginia (Jones) Kitzmiller is now with the Grenfell School, St. Anthony, Newfoundland.

Mildred Lower is doing case work with the Vermont Children's Aid Society in Burlington.

Elizabeth Mackintosh is teaching biology at the Senior High School, New Britain, Conn.

Victoria Manoukian is helping families of ex-soldiers through the Red Cross. Last summer she took a walking tour through Switzerland.

Florence Mitchell is secretary in the J. Walter Thompson Co. of New York.

Constance Moody is studying at the American Academy of Dramatic Art, N. Y. C., and living at 32 Washington Sq.

Margaret Moir expects to go abroad in May. This winter she has been studying theory at the Institute of Musical Art of New York.

Esther (Nast) Stone has been busy furnishing a new apartment at 1720 E. 56 St., Chicago.

Charlotte (Nelson) Murphy and her husband are at present stationed in Muscat, Arabia. Major Murphy is in the Foreign and Political Department of the Government of India.

Helen (Nelson) Englund expects to complete by June the required work at the Univ. of Minnesota for an M.A. in English.

Serena Pendleton has been with the Chase Secretarial Corporation of New York (not the Chase National Bank as previously reported), since Nov. 1925.

Dorothy Perry has taken a position as a bank stenographer and reports it much easier than teaching.

Julia Pierson and Pauline Hayden started out to attend summer school at the Univ. of Wisconsin last summer but after a week of school were injured in a bus accident and spent July in a hospital. They are both teaching this year, Julia in Carrollton (Ill.) and Pauline in Westfield, Mass.

Grace Proffitt has been studying at the New York School of Social Work this winter and doing family case work.

Mary (Reid) Oakley, besides her housekeeping, is substituting and tutoring in English, Latin, and trigonometry in Freehold, N. J.

Therese (Rosenstein) Marks deserted her bookshop for three weeks this spring to go to Charleston, S. C.

Catherine Ryan gives her address for the spring months as Paris, France.

Marguerite Schauweker was in Italy in March. Mail reaches her c/o the American Express, Paris.

Moselle Smallhurst is secretary to the editor of Town and Country and in charge of the art and social calendars. There are three other Smith girls in the office, Florence Baker '24, Marion Turner '25, and Peggy Van Kirk '26.

Eleanor Smith is teaching in a private school in Pittsfield, Mass. She is going to England for the summer.

Evelyn Smith is going abroad this summer after reunion and staying over next winter to study music.

Constance Stanley is head of the Spanish department at the Univ. of Maryland. She leaves in June for a three months' tour of Europe with special study in Spain.

Elizabeth (Stephens) Bigelow's husband has been made executive head of a new bank in Greenwich, Conn. "Until fall when we expect to build a house, write me at 'Homestead Hall,'" says "Steve."

Clare Wait is teaching English in the Cambridge (Mass.) High and has an unofficial interest in musical activities there.

Gwendolen Washington visited Elizabeth Meyer in California this spring.

Ex-1924

ENGAGED.—Mary Hall to Bryson Frederick Thompson, Yale '21.

MARRIED.—Eleanor Arnold to Walter T. Sorg. Address, 514 Prospect St., Massillon, O.

Margaret Bullock to Edward Carrington Thayer, Oct. 17, 1925. They have a daughter, Margaret Bullock, born Sept. 2, 1926. Address, 43 Linnaean St., Cambridge, Mass.

Mary Button to Charles F. Allen Jr., Sept. 25, 1926. Since leaving Smith, Mary has spent her time studying music, one year at

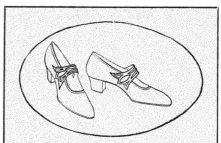

Oberlin Conservatory and three years in Boston. Her address now is 17 Beckford St., Salem, Mass.

Dorothy Challis to Eugene LeMoyne Biddle, Nov. 5, 1925. Their address is 7422 17th Av., Brooklyn, N. Y.

Margaret Fitch to Thomas Stevens Van Alyea, June 24, 1925. Her daughter, Harriet Fitch, was born Aug. 28, 1926. Address, 1467 Downer Av., Milwaukee, Wis.

Mary Gable to Thomas Weir Norton, last May.

Anita Haven to Harris Frozier, Feb. 19. Anita finished college at the Univ. of Wisconsin and has been in Chicago as employment manager of the firm which publishes *System Magazine.*

Jeannette Scott ('25) to Vincent Vandervoort, Oct. 1, 1925. They have a son, Robert Scott, born Sept. 3, 1926.

BORN.—To Olive (Abeel) Wyker a daughter, Alice Abeel, Apr. 17, 1926.

To Margaret (McKee) Damon a son, Russell Howe, Sept. 13, 1926.

To Martha (Sommerville) Williams a son, William Fischer Williams Jr., Jan. 10. Her latest address is 1264 Park Av., Rochester, N. Y.

To Evelyn (Woodward) Richards a daughter, Eleanor Woodward, Mar. 2. Eleanor has a sister, Marian Soule, born June 21, 1925.

NEW ADDRESS.—Mrs. James H. van Buren (Florence Bell), 530 Linden St., Ann Arbor, Mich.

OTHER NEWS.—Elizabeth (Blanchard) Faber expects to spend a second long summer at Nippersink Lodge, Wis.

Elizabeth Blandford went to Miss Wheelock's Kindergarten School in Boston after leaving Smith, and is now in her third year of teaching first grade in the Saugus (Mass.) public schools.

Lucetta Brehm worked for the Corman Advertising Co. for a time, but is now secretary to the owner of the Brown Bulb Ranch in Capitola, Calif.

Mavis (Kydd) Fenner was a member of the committee of the "Dollars and Sense Ball" held in New York this spring for the benefit of the Society for the Control of Cancer.

Barbara (Lane) Partridge has been at 25 Appleton St., Salem, Mass., for the last year, but she expects soon to be back in Hingham and would welcome there any of '24·

Lida Raymond has taken two trips abroad since she left Smith. She graduated from Northwestern in 1925. After Sept. 15, her address will be 874 Hill Rd., Winnetka, Ill. Her present address is 37 Indian Hill Rd.

Ruth Redfield is teaching high school Latin, French, and world history in Sabetha, Kan. Next year she expects to live at Johnson Hall, N. Y. C., and study for a Master's degree in philosophy at Columbia.

Janet Sturm writes of occasional trips to New York, visits with Grace Brown, Frances Brown, and Mary (Wynne) MacDonell, and a summer spent with Frances and her two sisters, both Smith, on a ranch near Cody, Wyo. She has also been doing charity work at home.

1925

Class secretary—Frances S. French, 165 E. 33 St., New York City.

ENGAGED.—Elizabeth Barrett to John L. Young. They expect to be married in May.

Helen-Forbes to Neil Williams of Chicago. Mr. Williams is Dartmouth '25, and is now studying law at Northwestern Univ. They expect to be married on June 29, in Buffalo.

Martha McAvoy to Ensign Shane Hastings King. Ensign King graduated from Annapolis in 1925 and is now stationed at Newport, R. I. Martha is working at the Curtis Publishing Co. in the Commercial Research Division.

MARRIED.—Mildred Buffington to Francis Marion Rich, Univ. of Illinois '25· Christine Baumann was maid of honor, and Helen Carpenter ex-'25 was a bridesmaid. New address, 7754 Essex Av., Chicago.

Josephine Cannon to Richard H. Watt, Jan. 24. They went to Europe on their wedding trip.

Marjorie Hedwall to Raymond B. Munger, Feb. 24, in New York. Nancy (Templeton) Munger was the only attendant. They will live at 41 Prospect St., Waterbury, Conn.

Elizabeth Judkins to Hermon Spencer Pinkham, Feb. 28, in Cleveland Heights, O.

Arline Knight to Lloyd L. Parker, June 4, 1926. They moved into their brand-new house last September, and their address is now 76 Washington St., Hudson, Mass.

Harriet Kuhn to Richard Stix of Cincinnati, in Aug. 1926. Her address is 4520 Paddock Rd., Cincinnati, O.

Eleanor Lawther to John Denson Adams, Jan. 11. Virginia Hart, Dorothy Ordway, and Virginia Robinson were among the bridesmaids. Eleanor says that they were all in Dubuque for a while before the wedding, and had quite a reunion.

Dorothy Ordway to Vincent Farnsworth Jr., Apr. 9.

Marie Rose to Arthur M. Rosenbloom, Dec. 23, 1926, in New York. Their permanent address after May 1 will be Schenley Apts., Pittsburgh, Pa.

Lillian Silver to George Schwolsky, Jan. 19. They spent their honeymoon in California, and are now at home at 132 Mansfield St., Hartford, Conn.

Lois Smith to A. Leland Lusty.

Catherine Spencer to John M. Goodnow, M. I. T., '22, Sept. 18, 1926. They are living at 34 Allston St., Boston, Mass.

Virginia Thieme to William Samuel Morris, Feb. 19, in Fort Wayne, Ind. New address, 1621 Ridge Av., Evanston, Ill.

OTHER NEWS.—Frances Bolton is librarian of the Yale Forestry School, and she is also studying at the Yale Graduate School for a future Ph.D. in English. She describes the Smith Glee Club concert at New Haven, followed by a dance given by the New Haven Smith Club, at which "Dean Bernard and '27 and '28 looked very familiar."

Lydia Brigham and a friend from Skidmore are in charge of our old college favorite, the "Arm Chair," and love it. Lydia is also

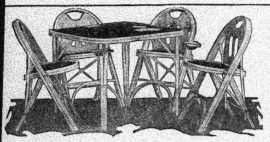

recording secretary of the Springfield Smith Club.

Priscilla Brown is working in Scribner's in New York and is living with Adelaide Avery in an apartment, address unknown.

Ida (Burgess) Gray is now living in Louisville, Ky., at 305 Hillcrest Av.

Elsie Butler is in charge of the *New Republic's* one and only bookshop on 34 St., just east of Park Av., where she may be found at all hours of the day.

Gladys Clark is teaching French in a junior high school in West Medford (Mass.), and living at 115 Boston Av.

Betty Fitzgerald and Jean Wise are living together in Paris at the Amer. University Club. Betty is studying bookbinding and Jean is working at the Alliance Française. Address, 4 rue de Chevreuse, Paris.

Ruth Gordon took a secretarial course at Simmons last year and received her B.S. last spring. She is now back at Simmons as secretary to the director of the School of Secretarial Studies, which is the largest of the five departments of the college. She also manages the Appointment Bureau.

Ruth Hamilton is teaching in Taunton (Mass.) High School.

Helen (Hartzell) Roberts and her husband are moving to Denver where their address will be 667 Downing St.

Katherine (Humphries) Browning has a new hobby, stamp collecting, and she begs that anyone who has U. S. stamps before 1875 in their old collections will communicate with her. She adds, "If you have any stamps on envelopes, *please* do *not* take them off."

Eustis Hundley has had a job as assistant in Miss Houston's kindergarten in Kansas City, all winter. She expects to come east this summer.

Virginia Hunt tutored Latin in Decatur High School in the fall, and is now on a Mediterranean tour.

Judelle (Huston) Hunting reports that she has covered most of the United States and part of Canada since her wedding. She has just returned to Rochester after a trip to Florida.

Alice Judson was a bridesmaid in Ginny Thieme's wedding. She is on the Chicago board of the A. A. U. W., along with a prep school president, two college deans, and several others.

Anne Kohler is on the *Empress of France*, taking a Mediterranean cruise, and will return the end of May.

Louise Marion has been in Paris all winter, living at the Amer. University Club, and studying at the Ecole de Science Politique.

Ruth McKeown has taken a secretarial course, and had two jobs: one in an attorney's office and the second with a new company in Utica. She is also active in the Smith Club and A. A. U. W. work there and does considerable typing for the Wellesley Club.

Elisabeth Morrow returns from France in June. Next year she will teach at the Dwight School for Girls in Englewood. We suppose her subjects will be English and French.

Dorothy Pickard is still teaching at Smith. She has three sections of Spoken English 11, and also does office work. She went to France last summer and there joined Mr. Eliot's party for a tour of inspection of the European theater. Among other interesting happenings, they were entertained at tea in Max Rheinhardt's castle.

Katharine Sears has returned from France, England, Scotland, and Belgium, and three months of Italy. Now she is working at the Children's Art Center in Boston.

Mary Sloan is back from Europe, and has a position in St. Louis.

Josephine Tompkins's father, who was a captain in the Navy, died suddenly in Panama a short while ago.

Betty Wales has been taking extension courses at Columbia, and the course in Problems of Juvenile Employment. Now she is at the Commonwealth School. She says she is trying to learn the art of dressmaking.

Elizabeth Ward is secretary to the principal of Milton Academy at present, but she hopes to be in New York next year with the rest of the class.

Frances West spent last summer in England, Switzerland, and Germany. Now she is at home, keeping house, and carrying a part-time job as head of the volunteers at a social work agency. She is also president of the St. Paul Smith Club.

Clara Williams has gone to Rome to do some translating and to continue her studies over there.

Ex-1925

Josephine Benz is treasurer of the Smith Club in St. Paul.

Isabel (Munroe) O'Brien has a son.

Helen (Page) Berlage and her husband live at 570 Jackson Av., Glencoe, Ill. They have one son.

1926

Class secretary—Gertrude E. Benedict, 8 Cabrillo Dr., Stanford University, Calif.

ENGAGED.—Eleanor Alcorn to Courtney C. Bishop. She is now teaching at Garrison Forest School, Garrison, Md.

Barbara Beadle to Thomas Walker of Manchester, England.

Mary Bohn to Thomas H. Tyler, Princeton '26.

Marjory Connor to Lawrence Stanley.

Louise Cronin to Frank L. Harrington, a graduate of Dartmouth and now a senior at Harvard Law School.

Aurelia Graeser to Lawrence B. Murphy. They expect to be married in the fall.

Drucilla Griffiths to A. Davis Morse. She is now teaching English and history in Waterport, N. Y.

Elizabeth Howland to Stowe Wilder, Amherst '26. They expect to be married in June and live in Hartford, Conn.

Sally Lovell to Alexander Bush of Louisville, Ky.

Winifred Ray to Franklin King Jr. of Northampton.

Sara-henri Solomon to Lawrence T. Mayer, Syracuse '20.

THE RUMFORD PRESS

CONCORD, NEW HAMPSHIRE

One of the MOST COMPLETE
Printing & Binding Plants
in the EASTERN STATES

Ruth Strong to Maurice A. Commings of Cambridge, Mass.

MARRIED.—Jean Boyce to Paul M. Courtney. Address, 9 Platt St., Poughkeepsie, N. Y.

Ruth Chandler to William Wilson Holden, Mar. 25. Mr. Holden was Yale '22·

Evelyn Dupee to Lieut. George Louis Castera, U. S. N., Oct. 16, 1926.

Helen Ferguson to Dr. Howard Zulech. They are living at 738 St. Marks Av., Brooklyn, N. Y.

Frances Mandelbaum to Milton K. Arenberg, Feb. 17. Address, 1540 Lake Shore Dr., Chicago.

Ruth McGuire to Wilbur G. Steinbright, Feb. 26. Peggy Pfeiffer was her maid of honor.

Pauline Ormsbee to Howard A. Casey, Jan. 15. They went to Bermuda on their wedding trip.

Elizabeth Symons to William B. Meloney V, Mar. 5. New address, 457 W. 24 St., N. Y. C.

Deborah Ware to Adrian F. Head of California. They were married in England in the middle of February and are spending their honeymoon in Denmark.

Katherine Weidler to Joseph S. Roberts.

OTHER NEWS.—Alice Bailey writes that she is working as stenographer for her father.

Helen Bray is proof reading and says she finds book work fascinating.

Marion Davidson is teaching in Manchester, Vt.

Maxine Decker is at home studying vocal music and a little art. She adds that she is helping "entertain" the town by telling stories and coaching plays and pageants.

Ruth Fielden is teaching Latin and French in New Haven, Vt., "a typical Vermont town."

Helen Green is working at Scribner's.

Agnes Griffin is secretary at the American Institute of Applied Music, 212 W. 57 St., N. Y. C. Her new address is 75 Chestnut Av., Bogota, N. J.

Marian Guptill expects to travel and study in Greece this month and plans to return to U. S. about June 20.

Dorothy Halpert is taking the department store training course at Jordan Marsh's, Boston.

Evelyn Harding is teaching in Oxford, Mass.

Helen Hay has charge of an advertising column in her town paper called "TownTalk." She signs herself "Ellenay" in this new and "subtle" form of advertising which she inaugurated herself.

Mary Jane Heath is studying at Purdue.

Katharine Hill returned from Bermuda in April, and plans to go to Nantucket for the summer.

Lois Jacoby is writing free-lance articles for newspapers, and is living in N. Y. C. with Gertrude Doniger and Louise Riteman.

Doreine Jones teaches English, physics, and civics at the high school in Utica.

Laura Kimball, Charlotte Kudlich, Margaret Davidson, and Mildred Whitman left in March for a Mediterranean cruise. Laura and Charlotte expect to be gone until June, visiting France and England after the cruise.

Alice Lufkin is town supervisor of physical education in Dover-Foxcroft (Me.), and is teaching physical education, history, and English in the high school, which position she says guarantees a speaking acquaintance with every child in town.

Estelle McDermott is doing interior decorating under Rose Cumming in New York.

Marian McFadden is assistant librarian in the Shelbyville Public Library where she supervises the children's room six days and two nights.

Frances McGuire is teaching history at the Terryville (Conn.) High School, where she has the titles of head of the history department and dean of girls.

Shorey Miller finds secretarial work in a large bank in Chicago very interesting.

Charlotte Murray is assistant librarian in the Flushing Branch Library.

Arloine Neufeld is working in the laboratories of the Pillsbury Flour Co. in Minneapolis.

Margaret Oliver is abroad with her parents.

Katharine Phelan is studying with the Theatre Guild in New York and has an apartment with Christine Gibbs, who is working in the Frick Art Library.

Julia Lynn Pitner teaches in a girls' preparatory school in Chattanooga, Tenn.

Helen Rackett, Josephine Wood, and Margaret Burrows are living at the Windsor Club, Boston. Jo is at the Massachusetts General Hospital, and Barbara and Margaret are taking the training course at Jordan Marsh's.

Dorothy Recht expects to be married in May.

Elisabeth Rice has just returned from a two months' tour of the West Indies and Florida. She is filling the time between now and reunion with housekeeping and "spring cleaning."

Polly Robertson is assistant in chemistry at the Univ. of Illinois.

Elizabeth Ryan is taking the merchandise course at Jordan Marsh's.

Frannie Ryman is studying at the Sorbonne and writes of having seen Eleanor Fourtin and Mary deConingh there.

"Poss" Sanders is doing landscape architecture work near San Francisco.

Ruth Stanford has a stenographic position with Henri, Hurst, and McDonald, an advertising agency in Chicago.

Laura Stiehl is studying for an M.A. at Columbia.

Olive Stull is a "teaching fellow" at Syracuse Univ.

Bertha Vogel is teaching French, German, and English in Clinton, Conn.

Elizabeth Voit is working in the office of Susan M. Rebhan, Attorney-at-law. Her new address is 4209 Euclid Av., Cleveland, O.

Irma Wegener is taking a graduate course in library service at Columbia.

Peggy West has just begun a course in applied art in Washington, D. C.

Jessie Willever is teaching history in the high school in Easton, Pa.

·NO·
I Am Busy

WHY do you say that when a life insurance agent calls on you?

It may be true, but why are you busy? It is largely because you wish to make the future secure for yourself and your family.

But the John Hancock agent wishes to do the same thing for you. He does not come to add to your troubles but to lessen them. He has for his commodity the security of your future.

Perhaps the next John Hancock agent who calls on you can answer some of your problems. He has the training and deals in policies to fit the needs of yourself and your business.

Why Not See Him?

John Hancock
MUTUAL
LIFE INSURANCE COMPANY
OF BOSTON, MASSACHUSETTS

A STRONG COMPANY, Over Sixty Years in Business. Liberal as to Contract, Safe and Secure in Every Way.

Always Sold in a Yellow Box

Prophylactic Tooth Brush

THE WORLD'S STANDARD TOOTH BRUSH PRESERVES THE TEETH.

The Prophylactic really cleans between the teeth

The ordinary tooth brush merely brushes the surfaces

NEW ADDRESSES.—Vera Bane, 407 S. Underhill, Peoria, Ill.

Helen Bray, 23 Longwood Av., Augusta, Me.

Anna Clark, 157 E. 72 St., N. Y. C.

Marjorie French, Cathedral School of Saint Mary, Garden City, N. Y.

Marjorie Krantz, 45 Trumbull St., New Haven, Conn.

Winifred Murfin, 3618 Ordway St., Washington, D. C.

Ex-1926

ENGAGED.—Elinor Angell to Christian J. Litscher Jr. She is now working as a private secretary.

MARRIED.—Isabel Foulkrod to William D. Sherrerd Jr. They are traveling in Egypt with Mr. Sherrerd's parents and expect to return about May first.

Margaret Hawkins to S. Clark Seelye, June 12, 1926. Address, 14 Arnold Park, Rochester, N. Y.

BORN.—To Emmy (Clason) Hayes a daughter, Larrier, Nov. 9, 1926.

OTHER NEWS.—Frances Flood is in charge of the Montessori teaching at Brimmer School, Boston.

Katherine Garrison is studying art in Paris.

Peggy (Pond) Church writes that her occupation is "cook, chauffeur, gardener, nursemaid all in turn with a bit of writing in between." She has just returned from a trip to the Carlsbad Caverns. Peggy hopes that she may hear from anyone who comes to Santa Fe.

NOTICES

All editorial mail should be sent to Edith Hill, College Hall, Northampton, Mass. Material for the July QUARTERLY should be typewritten and should reach College Hall by June 1. Please send subscriptions to Miss Snow at Rumford Bldg., 10 Ferry St., Concord, N. H., or College Hall, Northampton. Correspondence concerning advertising should be sent to College Hall. The dates of publication are November 20, February 20, May 20, and July 30, and subscribers failing to receive their copies within ten days after those dates should notify the business manager, as otherwise she cannot furnish free duplicate copies. The subscription price for one year is $1.50. Single copies 40 cents.

Alumnae are urged to memorize the list of Intercollegiate Alumni Hotels on the double spread advertisement on pages 398 and 399 and make every possible use of the hotels designated.

1927 COMMENCEMENT 1927

See page 334 for Commencement Program

As usual, the available rooms in the college houses will be open to the alumnae at Commencement. *Members of the classes holding reunions should make applications for these rooms through their class secretaries,* through whom also payment should be made. Rooms will be assigned to the reunion classes in the order of their seniority. Members of classes not holding reunions should make applications directly to the Alumnae Office.

For a minimum of five days, the price of board and room will be $10. Alumnae to whom assignments are made will be held responsible for the full payment unless notice of withdrawal is sent to the class secretary before June 1. After June 1, notices of withdrawal and requests for rooms should be sent directly to the Alumnae Office. At this time any vacancies left by the reunion classes will be assigned to members of the classes not holding reunions, in the order in which the applications have been received.

The campus rooms will be open after luncheon on Thursday before Commencement.

SENIOR DRAMATICS TICKETS

Tickets for Dramatics will be on sale at Alumnae Headquarters in Seelye Hall, Thursday, June 16, from 2 to 5, and Friday, June 17, from 9 to 1, and at the Academy of Music box office after that time. See page 324 for further data.

BOOKS FOR CUSHING HOUSE

Suzan Benedict '95 and Susan Rambo '05 wish to acknowledge gratefully the many gifts of books for the library of Cushing House which friends of Miss Cushing have sent them.

THE QUESTION OF IN MEMORIAMS

At the meeting of Class Secretaries during Alumnae Council, the question of In Memoriams for the QUARTERLY was discussed. It was the sense of the meeting that in the future the class secretaries should try to have such material more biographical in nature than has hitherto been the custom.

UNIVERSITY OF VIRGINIA SUMMER QUARTER

Upon going to press we are notified that the catalogue for the summer quarter, in session June 20–July 30 and Aug. 1–Sept. 3, is issued. For all information address Secretary of Summer Quarter, Box 149, University, Va.

Smith College Fiftieth Anniversary Publications

The following volumes are being issued under the auspices of the College as part of the Anniversary celebration

THE STUDY OF MUSIC IN THE AMERICAN COLLEGE ·
By Roy Dickinson Welch, A.B.   *Price* $2.00 · *Postage* 15c

BEN JONSON'S ART: ELIZABETHAN LIFE AND LITERATURE AS REFLECTED THEREIN
By Esther Cloudman Dunn, Ph.D.   *Price* $3.00 · *Postage* 15c

SOPHIA SMITH, AND THE BEGINNINGS OF SMITH COLLEGE
By Elizabeth Deering Hanscom, Ph.D. *and*
HELEN French Greene, M.A.   *Price* $2.00 · *Postage* 15c

A BIBLIOGRAPHY OF THE NORTH AMERICAN HEMIPTERA-HETEROPTERA
By Howard Madison Parshley, Sc.D.   *Price* $3.50 · *Postage* 15c

THE PLANTATION OVERSEER AS REVEALED IN HIS LETTERS
By John Spencer Bassett, Ph.D., LL.D.   *Price* $3.50 · *Postage* 15c

THE MORPHOLOGY OF AMPHIBIAN METAMORPHOSIS
By Inez Whipple Wilder, A.M.   *Price* $3.00 · *Postage* 15c

THE SALAMANDERS OF THE FAMILY PLETHODONTIDAE
By Emmett Reid Dunn, Ph.D.   *Price* $6.00 · *Postage* 15c

THE SHORT STORY IN SPAIN IN THE XVII CENTURY
By Caroline Brown Bourland, Ph.D.   *Price* $3.00 · *Postage* 15c

JEAN-JACQUES ROUSSEAU, ESSAI D'INTERPRETATION NOUVELLE
By Albert Schinz, Ph.D., O.A.   *In Preparation*

←——————————————————————————→

On Sale at the President's Office, *College Hall, Northampton, Mass.*

When writing to advertisers be sure to mention
THE SMITH ALUMNAE QUARTERLY

VANDERBILT, N.C. | ST. JAMES San Diego, Calif. | WALDORF-ASTORIA New York, N.Y. | ONONDAGA Syracuse, N.Y. | WOLVERINE Detroit, Mich. | BILTMORE Los Angeles, Calif. | BENJAMIN FRANKLIN Philadelphia, Pa.

Intercollegiate Alumni Hotels

COPLEY-PLAZA
Boston, Mass.

LINCOLN
Lincoln, Neb.

WINDERMERE
Chicago, Ill.

Every Dot Marks an Intercollegiate Alumni Hotel

Asheville, N.C., *George Vanderbilt*
Baltimore, Md., *Southern*
Berkeley, Cal., *Claremont*
Bethlehem, Pa., *Bethlehem*
Birmingham, Ala., *Bankhead*
Boston, Mass., *Copley-Plaza*
Charleston, S.C., *Francis Marion*
Charlotte, N.C., *Charlotte*
Chicago, Ill., *Blackstone*
Chicago, Ill., *Windermere*
Cincinnati, Ohio, *Sinton*
Columbus, Ohio, *Neil House*
Danville, Ill., *Wolford*
Detroit, Mich., *Wolverine*
Fresno, Cal., *Californian*

Greensboro, N.C., *O'Henry*
High Point, N.C., *Sheraton*
Kansas City, Mo., *Muehlebach*
Lincoln, Nebr., *Lincoln*
Los Angeles, Calif., *Biltmore*
Madison, Wis., *Park*
Miami, Fla., *Ponce de Leon*
Minneapolis, Minn., *Radisson*
Montreal, Canada, *Mount Royal*
New York, N.Y., *Roosevelt*
New York, N.Y., *Waldorf-Astoria*
Northampton, Mass., *Northampton*
Oakland, Cal., *Oakland*
Peoria, Ill., *Pere Marquette*
Philadelphia, Pa., *Benjamin Franklin*

Pittsburgh, Pa., *Schenley*
Portland, Oreg., *Multnomah*
Rochester, N.Y., *Seneca*
Sacramento, Cal., *Sacramento*
St. Louis, Mo., *Coronado*
St. Paul, Minn., *Saint Paul*
San Diego, Cal., *St. James*
San Francisco, Cal., *Palace*
Savannah, Ga., *Savannah*
Seattle, Wash., *Olympic*
Syracuse, N.Y., *Onondaga*
Toronto, Canada, *King Edward*
Urbana, Ill., *Urbana-Lincoln*
Washington, D.C., *Willard*
Williamsport, Pa., *Lycoming*

OLYMPIC
Seattle, Wash.

SACRAMENTO
Sacramento, Calif.

The Intercollegiate Alumni Hotel movement is sponsored by the Alumni Secretaries
and Editors of the participating colleges and directed by

INTERCOLLEGIATE ALUMNI EXTENSION SERVICE, 18 E. 41st St., New York, N.Y.

PARK
Madison, Wis.

———————————— DIRECTORS ————————————

O. BAXENDALE
Alumni Secretary
University of Vermont

MARION E. GRAVES
Smith Alumnae Quarterly
Smith College

HELEN F. McMILLIN
Wellesley Alumnae Magazine
Wellesley College

R. W. SAILOR
Cornell Alumni News
Cornell University

L. C. BUSCH
Alumni Secretary
Rutgers College

R. W. HARWOOD
Harvard Alumni Bulletin
Harvard University

J. L. MORRILL
Alumni Secretary
Ohio State University

W. B. SHAW
Alumni Secretary
University of Michigan

DANIEL L. GRANT
Alumni Secretary
University of N. Carolina

JOHN D. McKEE
Wooster Alumni Bulletin
Wooster College

W. R. OKESON
Treasurer of
Lehigh University

ROBERT SIBLEY
Alumni Secretary
University of California

E. N. SULLIVAN
Alumni Secretary
Penn State College

LEVERING TYSON
Alumni Federation
Columbia University

E. T. T. WILLIAMS
Brown University

SOUTHERN
Baltimore, Md.

NORTHAMPTON
Northampton, Mass.

CHARLOTTE, N.C. | SHERATON High Point, N.C. | SINTON Cincinnati, O. | KING EDWARD Toronto, Can. | BETHLEHEM Bethlehem, Pa. | LYCOMING Williamsport, Pa. | SAVANNAH Savannah, Ga. | MUEHLEBACH Kansas City, Mo.

When writing to advertisers be sure to mention
THE SMITH ALUMNAE QUARTERLY

CLASSIFIED LIST

See pag

𝔖𝔪𝔦𝔱𝔥 ℭ𝔬𝔩𝔩𝔢𝔤𝔢

NORTHAMPTON, MASSACHUSETTS

WILLIAM ALLAN NEILSON, PH.D., LL.D., L.H.D., *President*

SMITH COLLEGE was founded by Sophia Smith of Hatfield, Massachusetts, who bequeathed for its establishment and maintenance $393,105.60, a sum which in 1875, when the last payment was received and the institution was opened, amounted to nearly if not quite a half million of dollars. The College is Christian, seeking to realize the ideals of character inspired by the Christian religion, but is entirely non-sectarian in its management and instruction. It was incorporated and chartered by the State in March 1871. In September 1875 it opened with 14 students, and granted 11 degrees in June 1879. In June 1926 the College conferred 460 A.B. degrees, and 17 A.M. degrees.

L. CLARK SEELYE, D.D., was the first president. He accepted the presidency in July 1873, and served until June 1910. He lived in Northampton as President Emeritus until his death on October 12, 1924. Marion LeRoy Burton, Ph.D., D.D., LL.D., was installed as president in October 1910 and served until June 1917. He left Smith College to be president of the University of Minnesota and later was president of the University of Michigan. He died on February 18, 1925. William Allan Neilson, Ph.D., LL.D., L.H.D., came in September 1917 to be president of the College.

THE College opened its fifty-second year with an undergraduate enrollment of 2033 besides 34 juniors who are spending the year at the Sorbonne, 65 graduate students, a resident faculty of 203, and 9 chief administrative officers. There are 10,318 living alumnae.

THE property owned by the College comprises 87.25 acres on which there are over a hundred buildings. There are botanical gardens and athletic fields, also a pond which provides boating and skating. There are 33 houses of residence owned or operated by the College besides 11 houses closely affiliated but privately owned. It is the policy of the College to give all four classes approximately equal representation in each house.

THE College fee for board and room is $500 per year and for tuition $400 for all students entering after 1925. Further details are published in the annual catalogs. The Trustees set aside approximately $100,000 for scholarships annually, besides which many special prizes have been established.

AMONG the distinctive features of the College are: (1) Junior year in France. A selected group of students majoring in French are allowed to spend their junior year at the Sorbonne under the personal direction of a member of the Department of French. (2) Special Honors. Selected students are allowed to pursue their studies individually during the junior and senior years in a special field under the guidance of special instructors. They are relieved of the routine of class attendance and course examinations during these two years. (3) The Experimental Schools: a. School for Exceptional Children. For public school children with special educational disabilities and retarded mental development. Conducted by the Department of Education in coöperation with the Northampton Board of Education. b. The Day School, an experimental school of the progressive type, also conducted by the Department of Education, offers instruction to children from five years of age through the work of the Junior High School. c. Nursery School, conducted by the Institute for the Coördination of Women's Interests in coöperation with the Department of Education. (4) School for Social Work. A professional graduate school leading to the degree of M.S.S. The course is fifteen months and comprises theoretical work in Northampton and practical work in the field.

FOR any further information about Smith College address the President's Office, College Hall, Northampton, Mass.

RUMFORD PRESS
CONCORD

Announcing the *Opening*

(APRIL, 1927)

The Hotel Northampton

A modern Guest-House founded
and built by the Community of
Northampton and Smith College

A WIGGINS HOTEL

LEWIS N. WIGGINS, *Managing Director*

The Smith Alumnae Quarterly

Published by the
Alumnae Association of Smith College

• • •

July, 1927

THE SMITH ALUMNAE QUARTERLY

July, 1927

TABLE OF CONTENTS

Published by the Alumnae Association of Smith College
at Rumford Building, 10 Ferry St., Concord, N. H.
Member of Alumni Magazines Associated

Florence Homer Snow 1904, Business Manager ..... { Rumford Building, 10 Ferry St., Concord, N. H., or
Marion E. Graves 1915, Advertising Manager....... { College Hall, Northampton, Mass.

Volume XVIII..No. 4

Smith College Fiftieth Anniversary Publications

The following volumes are being issued under the auspices of the College as part of the Anniversary celebration

1. SOPHIA SMITH, AND THE BEGINNINGS OF SMITH COLLEGE
   By ELIZABETH DEERING HANSCOM, PH.D., *and*
   HELEN FRENCH GREENE, M.A.   *Price* $2.00 · *Postage* 15c

2. THE STUDY OF MUSIC IN THE AMERICAN COLLEGE
   By ROY DICKINSON WELCH, A.B.   *Price* $2.00 · *Postage* 15c

3. BEN JONSON'S ART: ELIZABETHAN LIFE AND LITERATURE AS REFLECTED THEREIN
   By ESTHER CLOUDMAN DUNN, PH.D.   *Price* $3.00 · *Postage* 15c

4. A BIBLIOGRAPHY OF THE NORTH AMERICAN HEMIPTERA-HETEROPTERA
   By HOWARD MADISON PARSHLEY, Sc.D.   *Price* $3.50 · *Postage* 15c

5. THE SALAMANDERS OF THE FAMILY PLETHODONTIDAE
   By EMMETT REID DUNN, PH.D.   *Price* $6.00 · *Postage* 15c

6. THE PLANTATION OVERSEER AS REVEALED IN HIS LETTERS
   By JOHN SPENCER BASSETT, PH.D., LL.D.   *Price* $3.50 · *Postage* 15c

7. THE MORPHOLOGY OF AMPHIBIAN METAMORPHOSIS
   By INEZ WHIPPLE WILDER, A.M.   *Price* $3.00 · *Postage* 15c

8. THE SHORT STORY IN SPAIN IN THE XVII CENTURY
   By CAROLINE BROWN BOURLAND, PH.D.   *Price* $3.00 · *Postage* 15c

9. JEAN-JACQUES ROUSSEAU, ESSAI D'INTERPRETATION NOUVELLE
   By ALBERT SCHINZ, PH.D., O.A.   *In Preparation*

On Sale at the PRESIDENT'S OFFICE, *College Hall, Northampton, Mass.*

WILLIAM ALLAN NEILSON

"We congratulate President Neilson on his distinguished record.
We are proud of what he has done for the College in the past ten
years. That of itself is a memorial worthy of the life-work of
any president. May he have a long continuance of happy life
and successful effort for the College! To this end we pledge him
our loyal support and unfeigned affection."

(*See opposite page*)

The Smith Alumnae Quarterly

VOL. XVIII   JULY, 1927   No. 4

Entered as second class matter at the Post Office at Concord, New Hampshire, under the Act of March 3, 1879.

The Alumnae Resolutions for President Neilson

The Commencement of 1927 was preëminently the tenth birthday party of President Neilson. Throughout the week there were many expressions of affection and esteem which will be noted elsewhere, but we are proud to open the QUARTERLY *with the resolutions passed by the alumnae and read to the President at the Alumnae Assembly.*

WE, the alumnae of Smith College, take the completion of the first decade of President Neilson's administration as a fitting occasion for celebrating its achievements and for expressing to him as our President our confidence, loyalty, and esteem.

We record with gratitude his wholehearted devotion to the interests of this College, as well as the fidelity and resourcefulness with which he has met the great and varied responsibilities of his office. He has spared neither time nor strength in the service of this institution; alike amid encouraging successes, and anxious, burdening cares of administration, in term time and vacation, at home and abroad, even under the shadow of personal sorrow, with resolute and cheerful courage he has labored unremittingly for its welfare.

We note with pride the conspicuous fruits of these labors, resulting in an impressive increase in the physical equipment of the College during the past decade. We recall also the notable additions to the Library and other departments, the enlargement of the Faculty, and the development of the newer offices of administration.

We note with particular satisfaction the measures that have been taken to encourage scholarship in the College, and to enhance its educational prestige. We hail as eminently fitting the signal recognition which has recently been given to this side of his administration by the founding of the William Allan Neilson Chair of Research.

We watch with sympathetic interest the working out of the policies by which the administration is seeking to develop in the student body capacity for self-direction through the discipline of freedom, and to train them by the exercise of enlightened personal judgment and considered independence of action to face their responsibilities as members of the community. No one knows better than the President the difficulties and dangers attending the experiment, or the need of modifying from time to time the application of its conditions. Our confidence is in his intelligence and his integrity. He himself is the shining example to the students of the union of the uutrammeled mind and rigid devotion to duty. His conduct of the religious exercises of the College, his illuminating talks at chapel on public affairs, his incisive comments on student standards of behavior, and the sane touch of his humor seem to us rare contributions to undergraduate life. We, as alumnae, appreciate especially the friendliness and spirit of comradeship with which he has admitted us to the counsels of the College.

We congratulate President Neilson on his distinguished record. We are proud of what he has done for the College in the past ten years. That of itself is a memorial worthy of the lifework of any president. May he have

a long continuance of happy life and successful effort for the College! To this end we pledge him our loyal support and unfeigned affection.

SARAH GOODWIN 1892, *Chairman*
HARRY NORMAN GARDINER L.H.D. 1924
MARY CLAPP 1912
ANNA WILSON DICKINSON 1906
ELLEN HOLT 1890
MARTHA HOOKER 1925
MARY COMER LANE 1904
HARRIET SEELYE RHEES 1888
EMMA SEBRING 1889
ANNE BARROWS SEELYE 1897

An Honorary Degree from Yale

ONE of the highest honors that can be bestowed upon a Harvard man is a Yale degree. The giving of the degree of Doctor of Letters to President Neilson at Yale Commencement is a signal recognition of his distinction, and also of the increasing importance of the institution he so nobly serves. The occasion was a brilliant one. The list of honorary degrees had been kept as usual a profound secret, and the President's appearance on the platform was a surprise to the audience, which included many alumnae and other friends of Smith College. In presenting Mr. Neilson to President Angell and the corporation Professor William Lyon Phelps spoke as follows:

In the academic trinity—teaching, scholarship, administration—Dr. Neilson has attained the first rank. As a teacher at Harvard, he was universally beloved; he satisfied the thirst of the most advanced students, and raised a thirst in others. He inspired young men, and whatever signs of honor can be given to a professor by undergraduates were bestowed upon him. During these years of success, he won a high reputation among his peers in other institutions by his contributions to scholarship. Then came the call to leave the life of a teacher and a scholar for the life of an administrator and executive, to leave the world of men for the world of women. He did not want to do this; but, being a Scotsman, he found the call to duty and to a great task an irresistible temptation. He had not been long in his new work before it was clear that a vital force was enlivening the whole college. The President was idolized by the students, and even beloved by the Faculty. He maintained the social integrity of the largest of our women's colleges; he introduced radical innovations in honors courses, the junior year in France, and other experiments. This year marks the close of the first decade of his administration, and friends of Smith have celebrated it by establishing at the institution the William Allan Neilson Chair of Research, by which a distinguished scholar will live at the college for five years, with his time entirely free for original work. Dr. Neilson is known to Smith undergraduates and graduates for his scholarly enthusiasm, his personal friendliness, and his appalling frankness. He combines the sincerity of Scotland with the amenity of America.

President Angell conferred the degree in these words:

In appreciative acknowledgment of an unusual sweep of solid scholarship, of a fine and discriminating taste in letters, and of a lasting service to the highest ideals of liberal education, Yale confers upon you the degree of Doctor of Letters and admits you to all its rights and privileges.

The Commencement Address

HARRY EMERSON FOSDICK, D.D.

(Delivered June 20, 1927)

PRESIDENT NEILSON, Members of the Board of Trustees and of the Faculty, Young Women of the Graduating Class, and Friends: I frankly presume this morning upon the fact that I am a member of the Smith College family and do not come here as a stranger. You will allow me then to forego any attempt to be formally academic, even on this academic occasion, and will permit me to do the only thing I am interested in doing—speak directly and practically to you, the members of the graduating class.

If it did not sound so dreadfully old-fashioned, I should call the subject of my remarks Good Taste. George Eliot in her poem on Stradivarius, maker of beautiful violins, says,

"Antonio Stradivari has an eye
That winces at false work and loves the true."

That is good taste—an eye that winces at false work and loves the true. John Ruskin even went so far as to say that in the last analysis good taste is the only morality. This subject is chosen because of two aspects of the generation's life that you are now going out to share and to influence. On the one side old codes, conventions, and traditions of behavior are obviously breaking down. They used to guide our fathers and in their time did valuable service, but their influence plainly is waning and in some realms is almost defunct; and on the other side we face new situations where there never have been any codes, conventions, and traditions of behavior. Old codes of behavior gone; new situations where there never have been codes of be-havior, that is the condition which the new generation faces, and the upshot is obvious—if we are going to live well ourselves and get the world well on, we must possess our own inward standards, have our own effective and creative good taste, possess an "eye that winces at false work and loves the true."

You are going out into a generation one of whose characteristics is the breakdown of old codes about right and wrong. Personally I am persuaded that this new generation is much more hopeful than its predecessor but it certainly is different, and in no point is the difference more obvious than in the present attitude toward time-honored codes of right and wrong. The gist of the difference lies in the fact that once right and wrong had a well defined content. People knew what was right and what was wrong. The social code, supported by family, church, and school was clear. The words right and wrong conjured up in the imagination pictures of well defined types of behavior that the community in general commonly recognized. But now—I need not elaborate the obvious—the situation is rapidly shifting. What is right is the question. What is right in family life, in sex relationship, in personal habits, in economic practices, in international dealing? Nothing is a foregone conclusion now in any of those realms, and the sign manual of a *bona fide* member of the new generation is that he refuses unquestioning acquiescence to any conventional code of conduct.

To be sure, there are plenty of

families, schools, and churches that propose still to enforce the old codes. Here, for example, is a household in which across the generations from faithful sire to faithful son, in spite of black sheep who refused to run with the flock, has been handed down the family code. Such and such things were forbidden and such and such things were allowed in that household, and now the proposal is to take a growing youth and run him into the mold of that well defined convention. Well, if you can get away with that in your family you are unusually fortunate. A father recently said to me with mingled amusement and consternation that his thirteen-year-old daughter had just informed him that he was hopelessly mid-Victorian.

The fact is that the new generation has no respect for artificial conventions. The new generation disallows the authority of an external code, and the futility of talking to it in such terms is obvious when one takes account of families, churches, and schools that thereby are losing their grip as moral guides upon the consciences of youth.

This morning, therefore, I suggest a fresh approach to the ethical problem. I commend it to you who now go out to face the teasing questions of behavior in this modern age. Frequently youths come to me saying in effect, "I am through with conventional codes of conduct; I do not know what is right and what is wrong, but I will not trust any ancient code to tell me, and I have no aspiration to be a saint and according to the standards of the elder generation live a righteous life." To whom habitually I say, "Very well, we will not talk about codes of conduct, and we will say nothing about being a saint and living a righteous life, but what about being an artist and living a beautiful life? Can you so easily escape that appeal? To have a very fine opinion of yourself, so fine that you would hate to live an ugly life, to exercise good taste about living, instinctively to feel the difference between fair and foul as a skilled bank teller by the very touch can discriminate between true money and counterfeit—that is not appealing to a code. That is appealing to something very deep in us, that ranges high, and reaches far."

Of course I am aware that a thoroughbred authoritarian who has been accustomed to stake everything on a well defined conventional code will think that appeal shallow. I am certain it is not shallow. I am convinced that it is the end and goal of true education and true religion.

Consider, for example, two children coming from two different types of home. One child has been drilled and disciplined in a code. Docile of temperament, let us say, dominated by aggressive parents, timid perhaps, and timorously preferring the peace of obedience to the fury of family disfavor, the child has accepted the code. Now, however well behaved the deportment of that child at the beginning, anybody who understands this new generation will pray for mercy on him when he escapes the dominance of the family and faces situations demanding independent judgment and taste. A mother of my acquaintance said recently that she proposed to make her daughter think what she wanted her to think until she was eighteen years old and then she could begin to think for herself. The Lord have mercy on that girl!

Here, on the other hand, is another kind of child coming from another type of home, where the primary endeavor has been to develop within the child a very high opinion of his life. Here the habitual appeal has been not to a conventional code but to the child's own developing sense of good taste. Here the method has been not to say that this or that book is forbidden, but to make so positively attractive the books that are worth reading that the low cannot allure a palate accustomed to a nobler fare. Here the idea has been not to slam doors around the child's life on things taboo and therefore alluring, but to open so many doors on aspects of life thrilling and lovely that there may grow within the child what the New Testament calls "discernment to approve the things that are excellent." When now you consider a child going out from such a home with something in him akin to a musician's ear that rejoices in fine harmony when it is heard and winces at discord, you see what John Ruskin meant when he said that good taste—what you do positively like—is the only morality.

At any rate that is the only kind of youth whom I would trust in this modern time. Standing in the presence of vulgarity, he may not like it; walking where vice walks, he may hate it; seeing futility, selfishness, and purposelessness, he may shrink from them. The finest ethical gift that any home can give a child or any institution help a growing youth to achieve, mightier by far than all codes and conventions, is such effective and creative good taste.

I well recall the man who first introduced me to the English classics. He used to take me up into his room and quietly read to me the loveliest things in English speech. He made a quite incalculable contribution to my life. He did for me the finest service that

one person can do for another. He changed my taste.

If now the major truth with which we are dealing is fairly clear, let us trace out some of its ramifications. Consider the commonly mooted question of obedience. Multitudes of modern youth are in rebellion against obedience. The very word is obnoxious to them. Why should they subject their personalities to something alien to themselves? Now, I deeply sympathize with such youths, but there is one thing that may be said to them. Whenever they use the word obey they seem to be thinking of something outside themselves. They say, "We will not obey," and imply an external convention, but what about obeying something inside yourself? What about obeying an imperious eye that "winces at false work and loves the true"? Some time ago I heard one of the leading educators of the United States make an address on education. He talked about obedience in a typically modern way. He tore it into shreds, jumped up and down on the remnants, and what was left he threw out of the window. As I listened I fell to wondering why it was that as I recall my early youth, while obedience undoubtedly was there, it did not seem to have done the harm which this man thought it should do. Then the crux of the matter became plain. Whenever he mentioned obedience he was thinking of an external and authoritative code imposed dogmatically upon a growing youth, and he was right in what he said. But as I recall my early education that is not what obedience meant. Some of us were so fortunate that from the beginning we were trained to obey something inside ourselves, so that when we left home we took it with us.

You mid-Victorians here, the last frazzled remnants of a once mighty race, will recall that Tennyson in one memorable passage pays a high tribute to England's queen, and in particular you will recall that ringing phrase, "Oh! loyal to the royal in thyself." When you are all through with your modern talk about obedience and toss codes out of the window you have not yet touched the nub of the question. "Oh! loyal to the royal in thyself."

Again, let us apply our truth to that realm where moral problems always take fire, the love side of life. Everybody else is talking about sex. It were a pity if in this high and cleansing place we could not speak of it. The attitude which many of the younger generation are taking toward this question is obvious. They have thrown over old conventions of right and wrong; that is to say, they refuse to define those terms in the ancient ways. "Cannot the old codes of sex relationship be changed?" they ask. To which, of course, the answer is obvious: Surely they can be changed. Anybody who knows history knows that codes of sex relationship have been in constant process of modification. There was plenty that was rotten and hypocritical in the old codes of sex relationship that some of the elder generation honor too highly. They would better be changed. "Why then," says youth, "talk to me about your old rights and wrongs?" to which I say, "Who is talking to you about old rights and wrongs?"

Of course, you will never permanently get rid of those words, right and wrong. Whatever debases personality is wrong; whatever elevates personality is right. There will be no supercession of that stubborn fact.

But if, for the time being, the words right and wrong connote to you chiefly an external, artificial convention in sex relationship, I am quite willing to discuss that problem without mentioning right and wrong. When you have dropped right and wrong you still have left two other words quite as searching—beautiful and ugly. The love side of life can be the most beautiful thing in human experience, or it can be the ugliest. Which shall we have it?

You do not need from me any description of the attitudes that make love beautiful. You must have seen some high and alluring exhibitions of it. I often wonder, from the man's point of view, whether if he were honest with himself he would find much difference between his ideal of a beautiful love and the old standard

"To love one maiden only, cleave to her,
And worship her by years of noble deeds,
Until they won her . . ."

You do not need from me any description of the attitudes that make love ugly. You must have seen and read enough of it. Mark it, when you drop right and wrong, when you smash up the old codes in rebellion, you have not yet touched the problem. Love can be very beautiful or it can be very ugly.

If the necessity of an inward taste is clear in realms where codes are losing their influence, surely it is clear in those realms where there never have been any codes. Lindbergh could not base his exploit on a convention. There were no conventions. He was dealing with a new medium; he was handling a new situation. To be sure, I do not mean that in these new realms there is nothing old to guide us—of course there is. Every successful thing that man does is a combination of the old and the new. Reading recently that fascinating book by Professor Lowes, "Convention and Revolt in Poetry," I was struck by the fact that in passage after passage one could take out the word poetry and substitute religion or education or human life in general and have the critic's words hold true. For poetry like human life has its florescent periods, its Elizabethan epochs, when it pours forth a creative flood that bursts over old boundaries and channels new thoroughfares of the spirit. Then there comes a time of conventionality. Old forms of rhythm are left into which lesser spirits put words, from which the fire and fury of creative genius has departed. You have then formalism, frigid conceits instead of fortunate eloquence, and empty forms of poetry move abroad as though suits of clothes walked down the street with nobody in them.

Out of such an age of conventionality Professor Lowes is right in saying that there are two ways of escape. Some become rebels against the old forms. They write free verse, new rhythms, no rhythms, and some turn to the old forms, revivify them, pour genius and passion into them. So in our time we have had on one side writers of free verse; on the other side spirits like Rupert Brooke, dead in the great war, who took an old sonnet form and poured passion into it—

"If I should die, think only this of me:
That there's some corner of a foreign field
That is for ever England."

Is not Professor Lowes right in remarking that both these ways have worth? Is not free verse valuable? Yes, says he, "Fresh beginnings are excellent stimulants to a jaded world." And are there not values in the old? Yes, says he, "Cut the connection

with the great reservoir of past achievement and the stream runs shallow and the substance of poetry becomes tenuous and thin."

So all progress is a combination of the old and the new. That is true even of Lindbergh's flight. Something new was there, an amazing machine that our fathers could not have dreamed, and something old, personal courage, very ancient, associated with the sublimest hours of human history from the beginning. Nevertheless, as with Lindbergh so with us. We have to carry the old out into new situations where there never have been any codes and conventions.

In 1774 a scientist named Scheele first discovered chlorine. It is a very powerful chemical, by the use of which billions upon billions of gallons of water are annually purified in the United States so that the population can safely drink it. But alas! that is not the whole story. The same chemical is also the substantial basis of chlorine gas, that sinister abomination of the war. There in a nutshell you have the problem of our western civilization. Modern science puts into our hands tremendous new powers with which we can help or destroy, save or damn mankind, and whether we will save or damn mankind with the new powers that science gives is not a problem of science. It is a problem of character, of spiritual quality, of the faiths, motives, and ideals that inwardly dominate mankind. It is a question of taste, of the things we do so powerfully like that we will bend all our energies to their achievement.

If ever there was a generation that needed inward spiritual gyroscopes, inward spiritual quality, fine judgment, high tastes, great faiths in the midst of a situation where old codes have gone and new codes have not yet come, it is this generation into which you go.

Finally, it would not be fair to our truth if we represented it merely as negative and prohibitive, keeping us from going wrong. Good taste, largely conceived, is one of the creative forces in human life. That is why some of you young people are so fine. For you are fine. This new generation of yours is more frank, more candid, cleaner and wholesomer, healthier, more promising than the generation in which I was brought up. For when a youth, facing the waning influence of old codes and meeting new situations where there are no codes, in lieu of them builds up within himself a fine high taste that like a musician's ear loves harmony and winces at discord, you have spiritual quality begotten which no code can produce.

The finest things in human history have never been wrought by codes anyhow. When Handel wrote the "Hallelujah Chorus," thinking that he saw the heavens opened and heard the angels sing, that was not a matter of code but of passionate love for something that was lovely. When Paul in the thirteenth chapter of First Corinthians caught sight of a society founded not on greed but on coöperation and good will, that was not the product of a code but of vision and taste. Even in large social questions taste is creative. Think of an ancient and inveterate institution like slavery, long established, apparently inexpugnable, turning the hearts of the righteous to water within them. At first our fathers liked it; then they were complacent about it; then they felt it ugly, hated it, shrank when they thought of it, until it went to pieces. There you have a profound transformation of public taste whose issues were revolutionary. To-day we are living through a similar transformation of taste about war, that ancient and immedicable evil of human life. Once our fathers liked it. "If war fail thee in thine own country, get thee swiftly into another," said a knight errant of the fourteenth century to a boy chevalier. But now multitudes of people are beginning to think the processes of war, its motives, its methods, its results, intolerable. What once our fathers liked we now abhor.

Change of public taste is not a small matter. You can measure the progress of humanity by it: from loving mud huts to loving Gothic cathedrals, from beating tom-toms to appreciating Bach, from glorifying war to believing in brotherhood. They are the great world changers who change public taste. To that high task you young women of privilege are summoned—in yourselves to maintain a fine standard amid the prevailing vulgarity and lowmindedness and so to change the likes of your generation that you may make a more decent world in which God may rear his family.

Kurt Koffka

IN the May QUARTERLY was announced the establishment by the Trustees of the William Allan Neilson Chair of Research in honor of the completion of the first ten years of the presidency of President Neilson and as a testimonial of their "great admiration, affection, and esteem for him." The terms on which the Chair was established were given and the name of Kurt Koffka as the incumbent for the first five years. We publish here further details of Dr. Koffka's distinguished scholarship and career.

Kurt Koffka was born in Berlin in 1886. He went through the Gymnasium in Berlin and was at the University of Berlin in 1903–4 and 1905–8. He studied at the University of Edinburgh 1904–5. He took his Ph.D. at the University of Berlin in 1908, was at the University of Würzburg 1909–10, and 1910–11 he was assistant at the Academy of Frankfort-on-Main. From 1911–18 he was Privatdozent at the University of Giessen where, since 1918, he has been Professor. In 1924–5 he was Schiff Professor at Cornell. In the summer of 1925 he taught at the University of Chicago and this past year has been Visiting Professor of Psychology at the University of Wisconsin. Professor Koffka has published: "Zur Analyse der Vorstellungen und ihrer Gesetze" and "Die Grundlagen der Psychischen Entwicklung," which has been translated into English and Spanish. He is the editor of a series of publications, "Beiträge zur Psychologie der Gestalt," and co-editor of "Psychologische Forschung." He is also a contributor to German, French, Spanish, and English journals.

Professor Koffka, together with Professor Wolfgang Köhler and Professor

KURT KOFFKA

Wertheimer of the University of Berlin, is responsible for the experiments which have led to the development of the Gestalt theory in psychology.

He will have at Smith a fully equipped laboratory for his research and is not expected to teach, but will be absolutely free to study and experiment, publishing or not as he prefers.

Americans Once More

LAURA L. BRANDT

The march of the calendar turned the Juniors-who-were-in-France into the Seniors-who-are-in-Northampton when the chapel bell rang last September. It was by no means the simple process by which the juniors who remained on the campus assume seniorhood when they tunefully take the steps on that night in June, and Laura Brandt's account of the metamorphosis (she was of course a member of that pioneer French group) will be read with sympathetic interest and, we believe, a sense of congratulation that we may count that experiment in education a decided success.

A METAMORPHOSIS is a very strange occurrence indeed. Only the wood nymphs of Old Greece have ever actually mastered the art of remaining charming despite the fact that some wilful god with a taste for novelty has turned them into a frog or a reed without a moment's notice. What marvelous powers of adaptability they must have had! Would that we (who have become Americans after having been French) had been equally endowed.

I awoke one October morning to a jangling seven o'clock rising bell, wondering at the early hour while waiting impatiently for Lucie's knock and the sweet aroma of hot chocolate that would greet my nostrils after a sleepily murmured "entrez." Nothing happened. After a while I heard a strange sound of heels flopping loose-jointedly down the hall outside accompanied by the familiar unmistakable tinkle of a tooth brush in a glass. I suddenly realized that this was not Paris, and groaned. If bestirring myself meant making up into the semblance of a couch this uncomfortable piece of furniture upon which I lay, I might as well stay in it. My roommate returned before I had come to any decision, however, and, rudely bursting in upon my distress, waved a wet washcloth unsympathetically above my head. Some moments later I found myself in her room inflicting corporal punishment with the blunter extremity of what is commonly known as a mule.

Breakfast—not a delicate, esthetic, subtle "petit déjeuner," but a plain uncompromising toast-and-cereal-breakfast—awaited me downstairs and I drank my Stygian pool of coffee with a very wry face indeed. No one could possibly have been more aggressive and unpleasant. The campus was very beautiful and I tried to find a compensation for my disagreeable temper by strolling to recitations across the grass and saying to myself at intervals: "Ha! I couldn't do *this* in Paris. I'd have to go underground and take the stuffy 'métro'."

Sour grapes! At this point somebody with a lordly whistle hustled me and my temper off the greensward but we remained inseparable all day. Not even once was I allowed the pleasure of exhibiting a French accent or mangling French verbs. The habit of a year being too strong for me, I once attempted to take a taxi down town— in memory of those overgrown red ones—but when a taxi actually came along I let it go because of its plush and wicker trimmings and its driver with the prosaic felt hat and the air of a man-about-town. The only spark of sympathy during all that bleak day came from the Bible professor who comfortingly suggested replacing the junior year in France by a graduate year in Palestine. At ten o'clock, the time when all good children should be in bed in Northampton, I stole downstairs to try the door. I was prepared to argue in seven different ways that two nights off per week had been allotted me last year and that I must have my two nights this year as well. But my house mother pointed out lucidly that Mrs. Scales would not be likely to take the same point of view. When, with undeniable logic, she insisted that the Draper was an unworthy substitute for the Café de la Paix, I turned sadly away and went upstairs to a room with windows that opened up and down instead of in and out. I had a last fleeting vision of my room in Paris with its fireplace, its quaint green wall paper and its two old prints—one of François I. with an enormously large nose and a larger self-conscious smile.

How often during the year just past the juniors-who-were have said: "A year ago to-day." How often we have relived that year with a: "Te rappelles-tu, mon cher?" Work here began in October, a month which meant to us the invigorating autumn of Grenoble set in orange and golden-brown mountain slopes. A raw plodding November brought regretful longings for Paris and street vendors selling warm brown chestnuts, overflowing their paper cornucopias. On November 11, our thoughts flew back to Verdun and we relived two days of mud and rain-flavored sight-seeing in a bleak land of trenches. Christmas vacation reminded us of Holland or Italy or Spain. With midyears came pictures of long walks to and from the Sorbonne through a Paris wrapped in the gray cloak of cloud and rain that we had learned to find so becoming. March brought an early windy vaca-

tion as well as the memory of a thrilling and paternal visit to which the words, "Where have you been, Billy boy, Billy boy," so boldly refer. On Easter we were once more in Northampton, and on a blowy Sunday morning we relived those warm sunshiny hours spent on the green slopes of Fiesole when the great bells of the Duomo sent a challenge out through the iridescent air. Spring came, bringing memories of the flower vendors whose baskets had spilled out to us so charitably the lavish gold and the sweet perfume of mimosa blossoms. And June?—we were buried under exams and Commencement, and Paris became for the moment beckoning but remote—a city belonging only to our past and our future.

This year of ours, then, became a very beautiful jewel of many facets. When we suddenly found ourselves seniors we felt like strangers in a strange land and, having not yet learned that our jewel was an Open Sesame to many things of great value, we left it unset and forgot to make it useful as well as ornamental. In other words, it has taken a whole year for us to learn where to place our values and how to gain a sense of proportion. We have often been asked, "How does it feel to be back?" Well—life has not been all beer and skittles!

In October we were plunged ruthlessly into the very middle of the old routine and with bewildered feelings we attended our three or four classes a day. Everything seemed new yet strangely familiar. Since our taste for novelty had been sharpened we set out to enjoy our senior year with a will, sure that it would be "easy compared to France." This was our first mistake born, perhaps, of a slightly superior attitude towards things American. College grew daily harder. Work seemed far more difficult than when we had left. We attended to class assignments impatiently, and criticized too easily American methods of teaching. We must have been a reversed sample of those Americans one is forever meeting abroad who take such pride in intolerantly magnifying into national misdemeanors the national customs of foreign countries. Americans, we said, were overbearing, arrogant, and thoughtless besides being superficial and self-satisfied. Once one tries, it is easy to find such damning catch-word adjectives that overlook both sides of the question. Our year was obviously too near. We could not seem to find the right focus for it. We lacked perspective. We longed to take notes in French again, to enjoy more leisurely and apparently more thorough study, or to walk down the Boul' Mich' feeling hopefully certain that the tall youth in front with the wide brimmed black hat and the air of a nonchalant Mephistopheles had cast a backward glance upon our ankles!

After Christmas vacation we returned to make more unjust comparisons. The year dragged as it neared the end. What seems to have characterized most of us from that time on was a certain detached attitude. A year away does make a surprising difference in the things one considers important at college. We no longer worried about "popularity." We were like onlookers at a game in which we took part only occasionally but which we thoroughly enjoyed. This was when we began, yes, actually began to think. At this crucial moment the seed planted in France commenced to grow. The senior year,

then, became the necessary and supplementary part of our junior year and we discovered why the experiment, without it, would have been incomplete.

Nothing could have been better for us after such a year of great activity in France than this return to a comparatively quiet place—an unassuming, familiar, lovely spot. We began to learn how indispensable college had become to us and we also had time to assimilate all the facts we had gathered so indiscriminately last year. Once having sifted the good from the bad and having learned to place values properly we could dare to play more successfully at being tolerant judges. We could hope to be more constructive in the future and less destructive in the present.

A tea was given by the Dean during the semester just past for Mademoiselle Carrière, a French girl who came as a delegate from France to study student life in America. As is usually the case in such gatherings the point that came up for discussion was the immaturity of American students as compared to the foreign ones. This word, it seems to me, lies at the basis of any tolerant comparison that is to be made between the French and the Americans. But in France it is used too often in the derogatory tone of one who pronounces judgment unsparingly. America's youthfulness does often lack humility. It is, however, an older wisdom which, while advancing French educational methods on the road to scholarly work, has caused them to sink, now and then, into a somewhat unprogressive rut. It is lack of it which has made our preparatory schools such weak foundations for college work. Since we *are* young we have more recently been trying to discover our faults by experimenting with new educational methods. Our youthful outlook may, perhaps, be interpreted by the fact that we still have a large amount to learn and that we must not waste this precious gift by hours of uncreative reading or desiccating study. Our colleges do often teach us misconceptions and that superficial half-knowledge which is sometimes worse than ignorance. Yet in France students search out the whys and wherefores of a subject until they cannot see the forest for the trees! I think the year in France made great advances in teaching us how to relegate facts to their proper places and to pay more attention to larger realities.

Yet would we have discovered all this had we not had the vantage point of a senior year given to us, in which to observe last year from the proper point of view? I doubt it. It has of course seemed at times interminably long. We were spoiled by the stimulating presence of that greatest of all cosmopolites—Paris. A dormitory and campus life deprived us of contact with the actual world. But as each day brought us farther away from our adventure its full significance began slowly to dawn upon us. Inevitably we began to say: "What a pity—we never realized how great an opportunity that was!" When reading of the exploits of those juniors replacing us in France we said regretfully: "Oh, if they only knew how lucky they are!"

Most of us, upon our return, were required to take a French grammar course with Mademoiselle Cattanès, who will never cease to groan at the way we murder her mother tongue. She struggled bravely with us all year

but there were many times when she had to wrestle with our wandering attention as well. The map of Paris in the corner of the classroom was greatly responsible for this! It was one of those delightful maps that one finds in front of all "métro" entrances. One can waste hours in front of them trying to untangle a blue line that will take one to one's destination. During classes, then, we traveled north to St. Denis or walked all the way out the Champs Elysées to the Bois. We followed imaginary artists with flowing hair up the Boul' Mich' to the busy Place Denfert and we called upon the swans in the beautiful Parc Montsouris. We ferreted out our friends on the Ile St. Louis and took them to tea "chez Pons." We dropped into the Sorbonne to call for a corrected theme and then we went to the Luxembourg to watch the entrancing bare-legged French children climb on to ponies or sail boats in the pond. We were about to climb on a pony ourselves— since there are no S. P. C. A.'s in France—when a gentle tap on the desk brought us off the pony's back with a thud. Mademoiselle's gentle remonstrance, "Eh-bien, mes enfants," saved us from a dangerous moment.

Last chapel is now over and as an experiment we must make our bow and retire. Our hearts belong once more wholly to our Alma Mater. President Neilson has given us his blessing with the assurance that we fitted back gracefully into the thirty-two places we left behind. Furthermore he has dubbed us "friendly souls" and for what more could we possibly ask? Surely our experiment has been a success.

A College for Women in Spain

MARY LOUISE FOSTER

Miss Foster 1891 has her Ph.D. from the University of Chicago and is associate professor of chemistry at Smith. In the fall of 1920 she went as exchange professor to the Junta which supplies residences and supplementary facilities for the students of the University of Madrid, where she organized a chemical laboratory and taught American laboratory methods. She was the first woman to teach science to women students from the University and nothing can more clearly testify to her success than the fact that the University has now asked her to equip new and larger laboratories built with Government funds. Miss Foster sailed for Spain in June.

SEVEN years ago I went to Spain to teach American laboratory methods to a group of women students from the School of Pharmacy, University of Madrid. Two courses in qualitative and quantitative chemistry were given in two small rooms which had once been a stable. There were twenty-five students in the two classes the first year, working four hours a week without credit from the University, merely for the sake of improving their technique and advancing in their chosen profession. From the time when Santa Teresa cultivated her garden of herbs and ministered to the sick in her parish, pharmacy has offered opportunities to Spanish women not open to them in any other profession. It is, therefore, a favorite course with them in the University.

My methods followed closely those in use in Smith College and set up standards of initiative, independence, and clear thinking based on experimental and documentary evidence, *i.e.* on the student's notebook record. It is in these methods that we differ very much from the ordinary Spanish system. At the end of the year, the students did receive credit at the University for their work with me. One of the seniors was granted a fellowship which brought her to New York to live in Brooks Hall while she studied in the School of Pharmacy of Columbia University and learned the routine of a hospital laboratory in one of the big hospitals of the city. She is now head of a very successful laboratory-pharmacy in Malaga. Another holds a similar position in Sevilla.

The second year of my stay, there was added to our general equipment a small balance room, made out of a lean-to where the gardener had been keeping his tools. The number of students was doubled with representatives from nineteen provinces. At the request of the seniors a short course in organic chemistry was introduced. The total inadequacy of the University equipment made this laboratory work very profitable for those who could successfully carry the hours in addition to their already heavy schedule, and the opportunity for this extra experimental work was highly appreciated. One of those who had the course for two years has recently finished two years of research study at the Sorbonne, the award for which she won in a national competition. Another is assistant to the professor of chemistry in the University.

Two years ago this little building was torn down and another more spacious has been put up in its place at the end of the garden of the Residencia para Señoritas. It is these new laboratories that I am now invited to equip. Some new courses will also be introduced and a major in chemistry organized. It is my intention to use Smith College as my model and to set up a miniature Stoddard Hall in Madrid. With the establishment of other science courses in the Gulick Memorial Hall in 1928, two long-dreamed-of "castles in Spain" will become a reality in the shape of a women's college.

The foundation of this "beautiful castle" is due to two people, one a Spanish professor in the University of Madrid in the last quarter of the nineteenth century and the other the wife of an American missionary in the last decade of the same period. The former was Don Francisco Giner de los Rios and the latter Alice Gordon Gulick. The present achievement in the reform of Spanish education is the result of the coming together of the forces set in motion by these two idealists who cared so much for liberal culture.

Don Francisco was an eminent, much loved teacher who developed his ideas of what a liberal education should be in the "Institución libre de Enseñanza." Here originated all the plans later incorporated by royal decree in the "Junta para ampliación de los estudios científicos e históricos" (Board for the development of scientific and historical studies) under the direction of his friends, Menendez Pidal and Manuel Cossío and his devoted disciple José Castillejo. Under the energetic leadership of the latter, college halls, libraries, research laboratories, traveling fellowships, and finally a big preparatory school for boys and girls have developed since 1901. The directors of these activities still draw their inspiration from Don Francisco by weekly meetings in his former home and by the reading of his letters on the anniversary of his birth.

In 1892, as the result of a country-wide appeal by Alice Gordon Gulick, "The International Institute for Girls in Spain" was chartered in Massachusetts. It was empowered to establish and maintain a school for the education of Spanish women. The hope of the founder was that eventually there would be in Madrid a college like Mount Holyoke, Vassar, Smith, or Wellesley. Many schools from all over the United States contributed to this enterprise and their names honorably decorate the doors of the different rooms in the Gulick Memorial Hall in Madrid.

Until 1915, the teachers and directors of the International Institute went from the United States, establishing American methods of education and physical development. At that time the war made it difficult for the Boston Board to carry on and the Junta, whose methods and standards were similar to ours and whose need of more ample quarters for their secondary school was very great, was very glad to hire the building for themselves. When the war was over, the Institute coöperated with them by sending over teachers of English and of physical education. After twenty-five years the Spanish Government has become convinced of the worthwhileness of the work done by the Junta and last year gave sufficient money for them to build their own schoolhouse, which will be completed next year. This sets free once more the Gulick Memorial Hall. It is the plan to fit it up as a science building with laboratories for botany, physics, and zoölogy. Then the women's college under the direction of Señorita de Maeztu will become a reality.

Tireless energy and unfailing enthusiasm on the part of both Spaniards and Americans have won this hard fight against antiquated method and strongly entrenched conservatism. Among the latter have been many college women. Conspicuous for her zeal and devotion is Susan Huntington Vernon, whose home is a center for Spanish culture. Many Smith women have acted as teachers or directors in the International Institute, namely, Caroline Bourland '93, Louisa Cheever '90, Marian Selden '20, Helen Peirce '21, Beatrice Newhall '17, and Ellen Williams '15. In return we have had two Spanish women on the faculty of Smith and one student. Contributions from the Student Community Chest go each year to promote the liberalizing of education for Spanish women. And the end is not yet, for, to celebrate the twenty-fifth anniversary of Alfonso's reign, his people are giving him instead of a monument an American University to be modeled after Harvard and to be built in one of the parks of Madrid. Work will begin next year, and soon Madrid will have a splendid modern university.

Scholastic Aptitude at Smith College

David Camp Rogers

It is apparent that the scholastic aptitude tests used in connection with the Board Examinations for admission to college have been given too short a time to be subjected to final judgment, but in this paper Professor Rogers suggests very interesting correlations between academic grades and the intelligence tests given at Smith to college freshmen. It is fair to assume that the scholastic aptitude tests will prove just as valuable in the near future.

IN the rapidly widening use of psychological tests which has developed since the World War, the colleges and universities have taken an active part, and experience has appeared to indicate that the tests can be applied to a number of college problems. The connection in which they have been most extensively studied by the colleges is that of the selection of students for admission. In this matter the evidence of their probable usefulness was adequate to induce the College Entrance Examination Board to adopt, in April 1925, a resolution providing for the organization of a committee for adding a psychological examination to its program.

For this committee Professor Carl C. Brigham of Princeton University has been appointed chairman, and additional members have been taken from Brown University, Dartmouth College, Yale University, and Smith College. Upon its organization the committee promptly began the collecting and testing of examination material to be used in the examination period of June 1926. All of the colleges represented in the committee had been experimenting with psychological tests. At Princeton in particular a large amount of work had been done, and a particularly valuable mass of test material and statistical findings has been brought to the disposal of the committee from this source.

A problem which the committee

took up for early and serious consideration was the selection of a title for its examination which might be expected to diminish rather than increase the prevalent exaggerations and other misunderstandings in regard to the significance of such procedures. The title Scholastic Aptitude Test, based on phraseology already in use at Princeton, was the solution found for this question.

The first Scholastic Aptitude Test was given on June 23, 1926, at the various centers of College Board Examinations, 8040 candidates participating in it. The majority of the test papers reached the New York office promptly and 7000 had been scored by the end of the third day. Within two weeks all necessary computations and records had been made and reports had been mailed covering all examination centers except five (four of these in foreign countries).

The committee in its Manual, published early in 1926, described the different ways in which intelligence examinations had been used by colleges. It avoided any specific recommendation as to uses to be made of the scores from the Scholastic Aptitude Test except the suggestion that they be treated as supplementary to records from other examinations and from academic work. The Board of Admission of Smith College adopted a policy quite in accordance with the views of the committee, accepting all students whose examinations in academic subjects were high and whose records were otherwise clear, and using the Scholastic Aptitude Test scores as supplementary evidence for cases of students whose records otherwise were near the border-line.

From the beginning, experiments bearing on the permanent as well as the temporary needs of the committee have been under way, and since the completion of the scoring of the first Scholastic Aptitude Test the committee has maintained an office at Princeton, under the direction of the chairman, in which statistical studies bearing upon its work are being vigorously carried forward.

The statistical correlations of the scholastic aptitude scores and other entrance criteria with first semester grades at Smith College have been computed. One outcome is the fact that in general the correlations are lower than in other recent years. The query is suggested whether there is some special factor of unreliability in this set of college grades. Are there, for instance, among our new instructors, a few who with the earnestness of reformers are applying somewhat different standards in their marking - than prevail with other teachers? Statistics bearing upon this question have not yet been obtained.

The correlation for last year's Scholastic Aptitude Test indicates that the test has significant predictive value. It appears to be a little lower than the average of the correlations for the academic entrance examinations and lower than our own intelligence examinations have given in former years. The Scholastic Aptitude Test of the present year should be decidedly superior to that of last, and since the measures under way for experimental preparation of test material for later years are more extensive and thorough than the individual psychologists and institutions that have worked in this field hitherto have generally been able to afford, a considerable improvement for later years may be confidently anticipated.

For a number of years the so-called

intelligence examination has been regarded in this college not only as a possible means toward the selection of candidates for admission, but, with fully as much emphasis, as a basis for advice during the period of the college course. We have been interested, therefore, in attempting to combine such features in a single examination that while carrying out the purpose of a general scholastic aptitude test it can also be used for indications of certain more specific capacities such as speed, accuracy, memory, reasoning, and general information.

Since many of the forms that would properly be used in such an examination are already present in the Board test, it was considered at Smith, in planning our college test for the past year, that it would be unnecessary to repeat these in our own examination. Our own test, consequently, was made largely out of types of material which appeared significant as indications of specific traits but which had not come yet to be recognized as dependable for the testing of general intelligence. In the record sheet for each freshman, which has gone this year from the psychology office to the administration offices, an attempt has been made to combine the scores from both examinations in a single convenient summary. Prepared under the plan just described, our Smith College Examination has given a somewhat better correlation with college studies than either the Scholastic Aptitude Test or the Board Entrance Examinations. This evidence, combined with the recommendation of the members of the Personnel Department and other officers of administration that have used the test, appears to justify the continuation of the experiment.

Statistical studies based upon the examinations of earlier years have been carried on more or less regularly in the Psychology Department. It is hoped that in the fairly near future the results will be published in some detail. In the meantime some of the conclusions which our data appear to indicate may be of interest. They are in part as follows:

The students who meet the requirements for admission to college at early ages are, in the average, brighter than those who enter later (with marked individual exceptions, of course) and they do better college work.

Some of the traits which the intelligence examination measures improve little if at all during college ages. Simple memory is a notable example. In the main the traits tested by the different parts of the examination do improve during the college period; they continue to do so throughout the range of ages represented by any considerable number in the college group; this improvement is at a slower rate in the higher ages.

The girls who enter young improve more in intelligence during the four years than do those who are older. Those who work hard at studies do not improve in the tested traits at a measurably different rate from those who spend more time in the other interesting things with which college girls keep busy.

Compared with the average improvement in these traits during the four college years, the differences within any single class (brought to college from heredity and previous environment) are relatively large—something like eight times as great. In general information such as our questions have tested, the differences within the class at any time are about four times the amount of the average four-year gain.

Reflections on the Eve of Commencement

GEORGE PEARSON

 "From the moment that each one of you changed the tassel from the right side and draped it over the left ear you became alumnae of Smith College," said Mrs. Sawyer in welcoming the seniors to the alumnae ranks; but the QUARTERLY did not wait until then to invite 1927 to make its début into alumnae circles, and these reflections were written by George Pearson—toastmistress at class supper—while they were still "dot svell senior class" with the diploma just enough beyond reach to be alluring but not so alluring as "this campus of ours in the spring."

WE are grown up now, and to our intense surprise we find we do not like it nearly so much as we thought we should. We had looked forward to graduation, jubilantly ticking off the things that were over and done with: "We'll never go home for another Christmas vacation"— "The last midyears we'll ever take"— "Thank heaven this is the last time I'll ever have to see about having furniture transferred." As we come nearer and nearer to the fatal day, however, we do not find relish in the doing of last things; in fact, we have a sneaking suspicion that this uprooting is not to be a celebration at all, but a time for wailing and sorrow. After all, it will be rather a wrench to leave the friends of four years' standing and try life in the big city, or the open country, or whatever the case may be.

These four years have gone so swiftly that it hardly seems possible for so much to have happened. Buildings have sprung up before we have had time to realize that ground was broken. We have a new Music Hall, with a medium-sized auditorium, fitting in between John M. Greene and Graham Hall; we have a Gymnasium, with a white tiled shower-room and the most elegant swimming pool in the country—a genuine museum piece. Best of all, the Dormitory Quadrangle between Paradise Road and Kensington Avenue is now complete. We have had qualms about that Quadrangle. When we left in June of 1926 we rather thought that Ellen Emerson and Cushing and Jordan would forever look out upon a distressing vista of ragged doorways and gentlemen in overalls. Imagine our surprise then, to find, upon returning in September, that the roofs were on, the curtains hung, and Gardiner, Morrow, and Martha Wilson bristling with activity.

We have witnessed the passing of old landmarks as well as the welcoming of the new. Hatfield House is no longer a dormitory. It has been made over into classrooms and instead of witnessing the nightly prayers and morning ablutions of some thirty youthful occupants, its walls echo to voices raised in scholarly answers to stern quizzings.

One by one off-campus houses are being abolished. In the fall of 1926 we found 21 and 17 Belmont boarding houses, 24 Belmont an apartment, 20 Belmont in a transitional stage, and 22 and 13 Belmont and 36 Green regular campus houses. Next year 16 Belmont will be an apartment and 30 Green an off-campus house for all classes instead of the sacred precinct of the graduating class. We mourn this passing of off-campus invitation houses, but we are open to conviction and will watch with unbiased interest to see how the new housing plan works.

We are amused and puzzled at the way in which cutting and residence rules have been tried out on us. In our freshman year we could leave town only for three week-ends a semester, while our older sisters had perfect freedom to leave town whenever the spirit moved them. We were allowed 27 cuts a year, with 18 as maximum for one semester. Sophomore year things were slightly changed; we still had 27 cuts, but the number of cuts in each class each semester was limited to double the number of hours for the class; 2 cuts in a one-hour course, 4 in a two-hour course, and so on. Junior year inaugurated a brief period of riotous freedom. Cuts were unlimited and all but freshmen could leave at any time for as long as they wanted. We commuted between New York and Northampton; we dashed out to Chicago or down to Florida on week-ends; we saw our best friends married in California. The freshmen, in order to make their three week-ends go as far as possible, stayed away from college for weeks at a time. Senior year has seen yet another change. Our absence from town has been limited to seven nights a semester, and it seems ironic that our class cuts have not been limited to agree with this putting of a fence about the town. And how we have hoarded those precious seven nights! Invitations are weighed in the balance and no feeling of politeness can move us if we think our second blessed opportunity is better than the first. The "Midnight" from New York, upon which one used to see all one's friends of a Sunday night, now has practically no business at all. Who wants to spend a night on a train with nothing to look forward to but a bleak and blear-eyed descent upon the platform of the Northampton station in the cold gray light of early morning?

The class of 1927 is the first one to be deprived of the opportunity to fall from the rafters of the Gymnasium or to take long and possibly dangerous rides into the country in a vain attempt to make their Frolic as uncomfortable as possible for the juniors. It was decided that the class of 1926 should not have a Junior Frolic, and we are glad, for we might have felt in honor bound to break their bones and our own into the bargain.

After Easter vacation in 1926 smoking was allowed in the living-rooms of all houses which voted to permit it. We indulged furiously for a time, but the next fall, after two or three minor accidents, we began to realize that the thing was being done to death and the student body imposed a new and more severe ruling. It is now permissible to smoke in tea rooms which allow it, in the Crew House, and in a restricted area around Paradise. Smoking at present seems not to affect either town or college to any extent.

One of the most amusing changes which has taken place is in our clothing. In our freshman year our skirts practically touched the ground. We did not think we looked really well unless the distance from waist to hem was at least twice the distance from waist to neck. We wore our hair sticking out from our heads like box hedges and to show our ears was very daring. If a girl's hair was cut like a boy's we mourned with her the toll which scarlet fever exacts. But now all is changed. We are considered ultra-conservative if our skirts are sixteen inches from the ground. Hardly an ear but shows, and no surprise is registered when we see a feminine head completely shorn. It gives us a strange feeling to realize that when we come back to our tenth reunion we shall shriek with laughter over our senior snapshots.

Just a month or so ago something wonderful happened. It was announced in chapel that the Trustees had presented us with a gift: the William Allan Neilson Chair of Research. Nothing could be more fitting than to name thus the chair of which Professor Koffka is the first incumbent. President Neilson has brought to us unfailing enthusiasm, deep interest, and a splendid inspiration. We were only sophomores when President Seelye died and we never knew President Burton at all. We cannot but regret these facts but President Neilson has given us so much that we feel no want. His ability to meet a difficult situation, combined with his sympathetic understanding, will be an influence for good during our whole lives. Our feeling of respect and affection for him is the chief thing which will hold the Class of 1927 together when we have gone our separate ways and life in Northampton seems to grow very vague indeed.

As for what these "separate ways" will be—who can tell? Certain it is that although we may be "highbrow alumnae" we have no idea of sitting around just "lookin' for a lovin' man." Four hundred and forty-nine of us, or 94% of our 464 A.B.'s, have registered with the Vocational Bureau and 376 of these have asked to be placed on the active list. Seventy-four have indicated their preference for teaching, but business is a close second, scientific work comes next, then architecture, and, surely as a testimony of our appreciation of our Art Department, 11 of us want art work and 6 work in art museums. We've been wearing our caps and gowns for the past month and singing

A.B., A.B., almost an M.A. or Ph.D.

but somehow we are less confident than we were a month ago. The wide, wide world is assuming rather alarming proportions and just what does it mean to be an alumna of Smith College? Our hope is in our new officers, for with Amanda Bryan for president, Harriet Mitchell for vice-president, Ruth Sears for treasurer, and Catherine Cole for secretary surely the Class of 1927 can't go far wrong.

THE NEW OFFICERS
RUTH SEARS, CATHERINE COLE, HARRIET MITCHELL, AMANDA BRYAN

Current Alumnae Publications

COMPILED BY NINA E. BROWNE

THE QUARTERLY acknowledges with appreciation the receipt from the publishers of two exceptionally interesting books written by Smith women.

Little, Brown, and Co. sends "Brother John" by Vida D. Scudder 1884. "The purpose of the book," writes the author, "is to depict the ardent and disturbed life of the sons of St. Francis in the period immediately following the death of the saint. It centres in that struggle between the more conventional element in the Order, and the Spirituals or Zealots, which ended in the deposition of Brother Elias. . . . It is an episode of spiritual biography through which is rendered vivid to the imagination one of the most intense social experiments in Christian history. The modern parallel to this struggle of social idealists has been made implicit throughout." The book is an Atlantic Monthly Press publication.

From Doubleday, Page, and Co. comes "The New Servant" by Mary Ormsbee Whitton 1907. It is a fascinating account of the new era in home mechanics in which electricity in the home comes into its own. We quote from an extensive review in the *New York Times:*
"How electrical devices save human wear and tear, with facts about cost of operation and maintenance, are some of the things the book tells in detail. The author shows the widest familiarity with scores of electrical appliances, as well as with the wider technical aspects of the electrical industry. For the benefit of the housewife she reduces to simplified language many of the technical terms which have mystified the layman. She even includes a brief electrical dictionary. In the book is a chapter devoted to wiring the new home and another to wiring an old home that is being modernized. Both include suggestions as to the location of electric switches and outlets. The author points out that wiring of old residences has been developed to a point where it is an art, that owners of old residences have hesitated in the past to have their houses wired because of the great inconvenience and patchwork involved, but that now expert electricians have developed methods of wiring old houses with a minimum of inconvenience to the occupants of the building and with a minimum of repairs to walls and ceilings."

APPLETON, HELEN L. 1908 (Mrs. Read). The Pioneer Woman, in The Arts, Apr.

BARBOUR, ELLEN G. 1903 (Mrs. Glines). Grapes. Challenge. Vampire, in Poetry, Apr.

BARROWS, MARY E. 1897 (Mrs. Irwin). Aids to Prayer, in Christian Century, Mar. 17.—First Love. True Love. The Beacon, in Univ. of Calif. Chronicle, Apr.

BOURLAND, CAROLINE B. 1893. The Short Story in Spain in the Seventeenth Century. Smith College Fiftieth Anniversary Publications.

†CLARKE, ELIZABETH L. 1916. What Vermont is doing with Potatoes, in Home Acres, Apr.

CUTTER, ELIZABETH R. 1896 (Mrs. Morrow). St. Francis of Assisi, in Voices, Apr.–May.

DASKAM, JOSEPHINE D. 1898 (Mrs. Bacon). Wanted: a Rural Epidemic of Education for Health, in Red Cross Courier, June 1.

†DAVIS, FANNIE S. 1904 (Mrs. Gifford). The Last Dream, in Atlantic, June.

FARRAND, MARGARET L. 1914. The Americans in South Devon, in Landmark, May.—How College Freshman Math. Became 'The Thing' to Enjoy, in Christian Sci. Monitor, May 6.—The Matthew Arnold Troupe Plays America, in Book Notes, Feb.–Mar.

HAWKINS, ETHEL W. 1901. [Reviews] in Atlantic Bookshelf, Apr., May.

HOUGH, MARY E. 1897. Himself took our Infirmities, in Congregationalist, Apr. 7.

† Already in Collection

†JENKINS, RUTH D. 1897 (Mrs. Jenkins). There are Joys in Maidless Homemaking, in McCall's, June.

KYLE, ANNIE D. 1918. Santa Claus Sahib, in St. Nicholas, Jan.

LEWIS, MARY S. 1893–Apr. 1895 (Mrs. Leitch). The Road to London, in Literary Digest, May 28.

LOOMIS, CLARA D. 1900. How Christ came into one Life, in Missionary Link, Apr.

†McAFEE, HELEN, 1903. The Menace of Leisure, in Century, May.

†MAHER, AMY G. 1906. Littlebrook. [Toronto.]

MAXSON, RUTH P. 1905 (Mrs. Aughiltree). Gypsy Wife, in Commonweal, Apr. 27.—An Old Quarrel, in The Circle, Apr.–May.—Mrs. Samuel Pepys Spends an Evening at Home, in Lyric West, Mar.—†Spruce Tree House, in Country Bard, Spring.

†MERCHANT, HELEN B. 1899. An Investment Complex of which Women, More than Men, are Guilty, in Woman Citizen, May.

MERRILL, GEORGIANA, Art 90–92 (Mrs. Root). My Host Divine, in Congregationalist, June 2.

MILHAM, MABEL, 1900 (Mrs. Roys). Traveling through a Mission, in Women and Missions, June.

†PAINE, FLORENCE A. 1893–Oct. 1895 (Mrs. Noyes). Translation of Iridion, by Z. Krasiński. London.—Ladies and Hussars, by A. Fredro. N. Y. S. French, 1925.

NICHOLL, LOUISE T. 1913. Light, in Sat. Rev. of Lit., May 28.

†ORMSBEE, MARY R. 1907 (Mrs. Whitton). The New Housekeeping Based on Friendly Coöperation, in Woman's Home Comp., June.—†The New Servant. Doubleday, Page, and Co.

†PUFFER, ETHEL D. 1891 (Mrs. Howes). The Foundations of Aesthetics, in Proceedings of 6th Internat. Cong. of Philosophy.

†RICE, MABEL A. 1898. The Haustoria of Certain Rusts . . . , in Bulletin of Torrey Botanical Club, Apr. 14.

†RUSSELL, ANNIE M. 1886 (Mrs. Marble). Grace Hazard Conkling, in Boston Transcript, May 7.

†SAFFIAN, SADIE, 1920. Mentally Retarded Children of Jewish Dependents, in Jewish Social Service Quarterly, Mar.

†SCUDDER, VIDA D. 1884. [Reviews] in Atlantic Bookshelf, May, June.—Why Utopias Never Come: Forever Arriving, in Adult Bible Class Mag., June.

†SHERMAN, ELLEN B. 1891. Our Cooler Martyrdoms, in Open Court, Mar.

SPEARE, DOROTHY, 1919 (Mrs. Christmas). A Virgin of Yesterday. N. Y. Doran.

†SPERRY, PAULINE, 1906. Plane Trigonometry. Richmond, Va. Johnson Pub. Co.

STEVENS, LOUISE F. 1908 (Mrs. Bryant). †Better Doctoring, Less Dependency. Committee on Dispensary Development of the United Hospital Fund of N. Y.—From the Outside Looking in, in Modern Hospital, May.—Medical Social Service and Outside Agencies, in Jour. of Hospital Social Service, June.

†STOREY, VIOLET A. 1920. Her Garden. Miss Ruby's Daffodils, in Churchman, Apr. 23.—One of the Professors, in Boston Transcript, May 9.

SWETT, MARGERY, 1917. Many Voices, in Bookman, June.—Mystic on Wheels, in Commonweal, May 18.—Warnings, in Poetry, June.

†SYMMES, FRANCES, 1885–86 (Mrs. Allen). A Voice on the Air just now [Pres. Seelye's], in Holyoke Transcript, June 10.

THOMPSON, LEILA E. 1921. Beneficiaries under Modern Life Insurance Policies, in Annals of Amer. Acad. of Pol. and Soc. Sci., Mar.

TINKER, GRACE T. 1884–86 (Mrs. Davis). Lights of Kobe, in Missionary Herald, May.

†TOLMAN, MARY, 1914. The Young Home Economics Graduate and Her Career, in News Letter of the New England Home Economics Assoc., May.

TOOKER, HELEN V. 1915. A Close-up of Porto Rico, in St. Nicholas, Mar.

TRENT, LUCIA, 1919. Labels and Libels, in Contemporary Verse, Apr.–May.

†TUBBY, GERTRUDE O. 1902. Telepathy, A Laboratory Label, in The Quest, Apr.

†TUNNELL, BARBARA M. 1912–13. A Young Portrait-painter Exhibits, in Century, May.

WILD, LAURA H. 1892. A Better Index of Faith, in Congregationalist, May 12.

WHITTINGTON, AMY, 1895. (Mrs. Eggleston). Fairy Airships, in Child Play, Mar.

†YOUNG, ETHEL F. 1905. Old Lace, in Country Bard, Spring.

W. A. N.

Scholar   Administrator   Citizen   Teacher

Wise with a wizard's wisdom: well of knowledge!
Inspiring leader, loved by all the College;
Liberal, he drives the shallow-minded mad;
Life is his interest—not a passing fad;
Inflexible opponent of the wrong,
Alive and sympathetic, human, strong,
May he be with us long!

Above all petty factions, he holds sway;
Loving a laugh, he can be carefree, gay;
Loathing a lie, a look of his can flay;
At Duty's call, he never knows dismay,
Nor seeks another way.

No meanness blinds him: broad his view, and wide.
Examining ideas from every side,
Interpreting the treasures of the Past,
Lessons he gives us, which will always last.
Sincere, yet tolerant, he guides the school,
"Owre blate to seek, owre proud to snool,"
Nor would we change his rule.

At the request of the author this poem is published anonymously.—THE EDITOR.

The Story of The Week

Starting and a-parting
From our husband and our child,
Starting and a-parting is a process
rather wild;
But when college calls us back
There is naught to do but pack—
Oh, it's joyful starting and a-parting!

YES, we may as well confess at the very outset that we just plain stole that idea for a starting from 1902's Roamin' in the Gloamin' song. Our version may not be so good as theirs—anyway we aren't going to enter any song competition with it—but if there are any highbrow alumnae who think that it's unethical to plagiarize the work of 1902's hard-working song committee, all we can say is that we wager that if they had sat themselves down for seventeen years and tried to start the Story of the Week for seventeen Commencements they would vote with their hands on their hearts that all is fair in love, war, and Commencements. Try it and see! And when it comes to the "parting"—well, there is a long, long trail to travel before we get there but we announce right now that it's highly probable that we shall keep right on plagiarizing for "starting and a-parting are the hardest things we do." And that's a real honest-to-goodness 1902 line with no plagiarizing about it.

As a matter of fact we might have started out with any number of other songs for somehow everybody seemed to have a particularly hard time get-

ting away from homes and babies and jobs this year; but instead of sitting down and crying about it and deciding that it was just more than they could do to get the baby parked with any lady relative or to tell their boss that thousands and yet thousands strong they wanted to raise a song to their Alma Mater, they lightly tossed a few things (not forgetting their coats and rubbers if they happened to belong to '76) into a suitcase, and—well, let them speak for themselves:

We drew out all our money
And we started off with glee,
We said to those who were staying home,
"I wish you could come with me."

At least that's the way 1907 decided to coördinate women's interests in this particular month of June when the years had circled full twenty times since they had gone out from their Alma Mater to that "world so bright and free" of which they had sung in their Ivy Song. Twenty-four, mere infants as the Smith family goes, of course, wrote a very fancy ditty about

Taking one consideration with another, with another,
An Alumna's lot is not a happy one
BUT when
You get a notice that it's your reunion, your reunion
And an invitation to come back to Hamp, back to Hamp

You decide to leave your husband and your
young one, and your young one
You get out your writing paper and your
stamp, and your stamp—

And that, as far as the Alumnae Office
was concerned, has been the important
thing in all these pre-Commencement
weeks, for to contemplate another
Commencement of calm leisure such as
last year's would have been more than
we could have borne. Oh yes, it was
thoroughly nice, 1901, and '16, and
the rest of you cozy little reuners of
yesteryear, "but," said the Alumnae
Office, "if we are going to *sing* thousands and yet thousands strong, let's *be*
thousands and yet thousands strong."
(Goodness knows we need to be to
get any volume at all into our singing!
And if that's a slam, take warning all
you threes and eights who will be
coming back next year.) And speaking
of threes and eights reminds us that
we could have adapted (somehow
that's a nicer word than "plagiarized")
one of '97's songs for a starting, to wit:

East, west, north, south,
All aboard for Hamp,
See the Big Parade that streams
To fair Sophia's camp.
When we get together
Watch each two and seven—
Aren't we still beyond a doubt
The finest under heaven?

For the benefit of the *very* young, we
mention that the tune is a classic
called "The Sidewalks of New York,"
and, we submit, that and that alone
hints at the vintage of "the girls that
made the nineties gay."

Well, to return to the Alumnae
Office and the size of this Commencement. Gone are the days when the
Office is hard put to it to squeeze
returning alumnae into space enough
to hold a cot because, forsooth, our
magnificent new Quadrangle stands
four square with single room after
single room at the disposal of
reuners and, besides, in this year of

grace Northampton's elegant new hotel
opened welcoming doors to additional
scores. Sing a paean of thanksgiving,
somebody, for that comfortable hos-
telry. We should think that not only
alumnae but Commencement families,
particularly the fathers, would now be
willing to send yet another daughter to
Smith College and think with com-
placency of still another Commencement season.

We can't seem to get on with this
running commentary—but what we
were trying to say when that last song
so rudely interrupted our train of
thought was that it looked for a while
as though this might be a small Commencement, as last year's was, and
reunion chairmen and the Alumnae
Office felt very solemn, and then
everybody got to coördinating and got
out their writing paper and a stamp
and the result was that while it
couldn't hold a candle to the Birthday
Party—dear me, that isn't a pun, for
as a matter of fact it did of course add
two candles to that party—and it
wasn't so big as the year just preceding
the Golden Anniversary, still it *was*
much, much larger than last year,
and, as '76 at least would testify,
there wasn't anything particularly
"leisurely" about it. It was preëminently a celebration for President
Neilson. It was, as Miss Comstock
said in the most thrilling speech we
have ever felt go down our spinal
column and of which you shall hear
more anon, the "tenth year of our
devotion to him as our president,"
and that was enough to make any
alumna pack herself and eleven classmates and countless suitcases and
maybe a husband or two into a Rolls
Royce or a Ford or the good old Boston
and Maine (we suspect the husbands
weren't invited if it was the Boston

and Maine, for one of the chief functions of a reuning husband is that of chauffeur, we are led to believe) and come bowling, or chugging, or honking back to Hamp, "where the campus grass is green," as early in that block of days which we cheerfully call Commencement Week as circumstances permitted. And right here we want to warn all Commencement automobiles to watch out for those new traffic signals down on Main St. If you think you can come honking and waving up Elm St. and straight through the Grécourt Gates without giving a look to the right or left you are very much mistaken. Indeed no. "Stop on the red, get ready on the yellow, go on the green, *If* you please." And while you are stopping on the red, glance in at the shop windows and see the bright yellow "We welcome Smith alumnae" stickers by which Northampton greets us reuners. If you happened to get here on Wednesday all the better, for that meant the Last Step Sing when the seniors were all in their caps and gowns and looking at least as old and dignified as alumnae who have been out—Heavens, what are we thinking of: we must consider our subscription list and skirt lightly around this question of age, although for the matter of that after watching '82 tramp dauntlessly up and down these old familiar ways day after day we think anyone whose family name is Smith can snap her fingers at Father Time. The seniors *felt* mighty old anyway, and we don't blame them for we remember that night in June when we sang our own version of their

Sun is sinking in the west, shadows longer
   grow,
O'er the campus that we love, clouds are
   drifting slow;

You will see the scenes we love still in future
   Mays,
But the sun is setting fast on our college
   days.

Twenty-six was there in large numbers, "unashamedly collegiate," as they themselves admitted, and '26 could have told them that no sooner did the sun set on "college days" than it rose on *alumnae* days, and any of the rest of us could have told them that the sun will set sooner on the British Empire than it will on the alumnae days of Smith College. Be it distinctly understood that we are not speaking of *Commencement* days for any such spread eagle assertion about the Commencement sun, especially at this the very beginning of Commencement, would be highly dangerous. In fact we simply mention in passing that the weather at this stage of the game was fair, but not warmer—well, not much warmer than a cool day in December, shall we say?

And on Thursday the Alumnae Office gathered itself together and repaired to headquarters in Seelye Hall as advertised, and to it came all the day long alumnae of Smith College eager to get their names down in black and white and to flip over the leaves of the great book wherein were inscribed names and Commencement addresses of pals they had not seen since Commencement days long past. And, incidentally, they managed to acquire a goodly packet of parti-colored tickets to see them through various delectable events; and if so be they were members of the Association in good and regular standing (and a person could hardly be that without being a subscriber to the QUARTERLY also, now could she?) they were recipients of the chicest of white crêpe paper under-arm bags bound in gold wherein all reunion impedimenta could be neatly dropped; and we may mention that if anyone was seen going away from Headquarters without said bag it was as good as getting her name posted in her favorite club! And that's that.

Thursday of Commencement Week is a kind of setting the stage day for everybody: seniors are still marching and countermarching for some procession or other—poor things, we wager that no senior class that ever graduated yearns to repeat *that* part of its college days—the Sophomore Push Committee is getting all pepped up for its business of bossing the rich and the great; advance reunion committees are flinging their purple and red and yellow and green banners out of the windows of Seelye Hall; and, this year at least, even the sun was doing a bit of rehearsing of its own. First it

peramental of operatic stars. And if anyone minds having the sun called a star it shows she is entirely ignorant of the tremendous part he plays in a Smith College Commencement. But the greatest rehearsing of all was going on down at the Academy where Dorinda and Lady Bountiful *et al* were preening themselves for

DRAMATICS that very evening. We were sorry that the trains and reuning automobiles (actually the shining creatures do seem to be as crazy about the excitement as their respective owners!) couldn't hustle a bigger audience of alumnae over the hills and valleys in time for "The Beaux' Stratagem." For the matter of that, however, perhaps it isn't fair to blame them entirely, for alumnae don't seem to flock to Dramatics as they did in the old days. Maybe it's

"The Beaux' Stratagem"

came out of a great fleecy white cloud and threw long beams of vivid light across the velvet grass, then it danced in all sorts of gay patterns under the great lacy elms, and then, just as the whole dress rehearsal audience of alumnae was ecstatic in applause, it scurried under an ugly-looking monster and mumped like the most tem-

because they can't get back so early as Thursday night; maybe it's because they can't bear to use so much of this saved daylight within doors with a comparative—only comparative!—seal upon their lips; and maybe (and here we may be speaking as one of those "frazzled members of a once mighty race" of which we were later to hear) just *maybe* they long for the good old days when Will Shakespeare was the presiding genius of the play. For, say what you will, "the play's the thing," and while it may be interesting historically to restore the drama of the early 18th century we did hear the opinion voiced that perhaps this particular play wasn't a type to restore for a Commencement audience. The really fine introduction on the first page of the program, however, did much to put the Commencement audience *en rapport* with the times. We quote in part:

"The Beaux' Stratagem" was, from its initial triumph in 1707 until well into the nineteenth century, one of the most popular of English plays. . . . Its continuous success was due to its happy intermediateness between the satiric, unmoral comedy of the Restoration and the sentimental, coyingly moral comedy of Steele and Cumberland. It is the true fore-runner of Goldsmith and Sheridan: it shares their gaiety, while preserving something of the dash and fire of Congreve. . . . We cannot believe that anyone will take it as expressing our own ideas or tastes, but rather as an attempt by earnest students of the theatre's arts and letters to recreate the charm of a bygone dramatic era.

Certainly when it comes to lovely lines—well, there just weren't any! and of lovely situations there certainly were none. But, and here we can wax enthusiastic, there were lovely costumes, sweet billowy silks and satins, and the ladies who wore them were dainty and twittery and maintained the "light frivolous spirit of this gay and careless comedy" throughout the play. And there were lovely settings and charming lighting effects achieved by Mr. Larkin and his students; and there was much good acting. We couldn't always hear the words, perhaps because most of us mid-Victorians still wear our ears discreetly covered, and, to tell the honest truth, in this particular instance perhaps it was just as well for one of the young reuning classes—much too young to

have caught our conservatism—was heard to murmur as she sped across the street to Trebla's, "I trust that when parents see it to-morrow night they will realize that it is pure comedy." And we feel sure they did. And, speaking of Trebla's, there was a deal of "meeting and a-eating with the pals of 1902" and with the pals of everybody else before, during, and after Dramatics; and our classmates' bobbed heads and permanent waves and convex- or concave-mirror figures, as the case might be and the years decree, so absorbed our attention that if visions of Dramatics went through our heads at all as we at last "dropped off" in those old familiar cots in our tidy campus rooms we are inclined to think that we saw once more the swaying, charming Mrs. Sullen and the winsome Dorinda and did no philosophizing at all about the stratagems of the beaux of the early 18th century. And when we awoke to the dulcet sound of a campus rising bell we had just two thoughts in our heads: first, to get into the dining-room before the fatal hour of eight, for we yearned to be polite to our most courteous campus hostesses, and to get down to

LAST CHAPEL before the fatal hour of nine, because that particular event of Commencement is the one we cherish in our memories year after year. We may say that we had more trouble doing the first than the second for John M. Greene Hall is a hospitable place and, moreover, there was plenty of room, for we state with regret that this pushing the Commencement calendar ahead (or is it back?) a day makes it increasingly hard for school-teaching alumnae to get to Last Chapel at all. It's a great pity, but there never was a column of assets that didn't have the joy taken out of it by a flanking column of liabilities, and maybe more people can stay through Monday once they do get here than used to be able to stay through Tuesday. And anyway this is a digression and we shall be late to chapel after all our boasting if we aren't careful. What an impressive service it is! The Faculty are all in cap and gown and so too are the seniors. Undergraduates, fathers and mothers, uncles and aunts, and alumnae were assembled there—and we aren't saying that an alumna couldn't be several kinds of these lady relatives as well—and the service began as we rose at the entrance of the President. You who have gone out from Smith College know well the order of exercises for Last Chapel: There is the chant, "Arise, shine, for thy light is come"; there is that reading from the Scriptures that, whatever be our race or our creed, has been our guide to things spiritual since we, as seniors too, heard them read on our own Last Chapel morning: "Finally, be strong in the Lord and in the strength of His might." The reading went on and on—"work out your own salvation with fear and trembling"—"Rejoice in the Lord always: again I will say, Rejoice"—to its triumphant close: "Finally, brethren, whatsoever things are true, whatsoever things are honorable, whatsoever things are just. . . ; if there be any virtue, and if there be any praise, think on these things." To thousands of the daughters of Smith College those ringing phrases bring thronging memories of our great first president: memories immortalized in that lovely poem of the anniversary year:

Once more we bow our heads and hear his wise
Wingèd, triumphant voice assail God's throne,

Sweeping our childish prayers up with his own.
We catch the steady fire of his face:—
"If there be virtue—if there still be praise—
Think on these things—"

To thousands more they recall with deepest affection and admiration that young, virile second president of ours whose voice resounded in eloquent tones as he sent the seniors forth; but no one of us will ever forget the extraordinary beauty and sincerity of President Neilson's reading, no one of us will fail to rejoice that things that are just, things that are pure, things that are honorable are cherished in Smith College as in the days when '79 rose to sing the same Last Chapel hymn with which we closed the service on this the fifty-second year of the College— "Hark, hark, my soul, angelic songs are swelling."

The service over we settled ourselves down to hear the review of the year which the President always gives at this time and which we consider one of the folksiest times of the week. This year he was better than ever for it was a review not only of this year but of the decade that he has been our President. First he made a bow to 1927 and said that when he came to the platform he found on the desk a handsome new Bible, the gift of the Class to the College. "The need of one," said he, "is evidenced by the condition of the old one which has been in use so many years, and I want to thank them for it."

We are always in an editorial quandary when it comes to writing up the President's speech at Last Chapel. It is always so good we want to quote it all, but—what about the printer's bill? So we as always shall just do the best we can.

For the last ten years [he began] I have been hoping to come to Last Chapel and announce that we have had a normal academic year. Never before has it been my fortune to have this wish fulfilled. There has been war and influenza, a coal strike and a $4,000,-000 drive, and once the dean left us, and once there was no dean, and once there was a new dean, and then there was the Fiftieth Anniversary,—always something to trouble the monotony of our days. But this year, we have had a normal year. We have sent away the usual number of naughty girls; we have sacrificed the usual number of stupid or lazy girls. We have had slight thrills of excitement, however. We have entered upon the completed Quadrangle of the new dormitories, and have gathered in the pledges which were made at the Fiftieth Anniversary for the Birthday Gift, and have collected $619,059.60 for that fund. We have entered on the new Tryon Gallery which was almost finished this time last year, and I suppose we may regard ourselves as almost at the end of our building era for the time. For some years something has been in the course of erection here. To-day, there are no holes in the ground, and there is no sum of money to spend for that purpose.

We have added during the year two small buildings: the Brewer house on Elm St., which will give us, with the exception of the two churches and the Tucker and Bartley houses, possession of all the property on the west side of Elm St. from Kensington Av. to West St. We have bought on Paradise Road the Drury house next to Sunnyside, which will be put in order this summer as the first unit of houses for graduate students.

The new residence rule, which seemed exciting when it was announced, has had rather a calming than a disturbing influence. This time last year we were discussing some legislation of the students in regard to smoking, and it needed all the strength of the administration to enable it to keep to its principles and keep its hands off. The students had the usual experience of young smokers and got sick of their indiscretions. By the middle of the year this had settled down, not to the satisfaction of everybody, but to a point where this habit was no longer dangerous to college property, and no longer obtrusive on the college campus. I am not going to repeat the discussion of our principles of a year ago. On the whole the undergraduates seem more worthy of our confidence than they did a year ago.

He spoke of the fact that next year's freshman class is going to enjoy a new curriculum. Poor darlings, they were even then getting ready to take those fearsome examinations that will prove (d. v., or Board-of-Admission-v) an open sesame to that new curriculum of which they do not now even dream! The Institute for the Coördination of Women's Interests came in for a good

word, and we were to hear more about it later so do not repeat here. It has justified even its high-sounding title and what higher praise is there?

The President then spoke with a twinkle in his eye about those one-time juniors in France, now seniors in cap and gown sitting before him.

This year [said he] we had a thrill receiving back into our ranks those juniors who had spent last year in France. We awaited their return with interest and not without apprehension. Their colleagues in the class of 1927 didn't know what might have happened to them, whether they would find them the same friendly souls they were when they left, or whether they would be so exalted and sharpened intellectually that they would have risen above all college activities and not want to play with us any more. On the first Sunday of the term, as I was coming into this hall to conduct Vespers, I met one of these students. She told me that she was so delighted with college activities, not having had any for a whole year, that she was even coming to Vespers. I might say she was even coming to Vespers when I was going to conduct them. I can conceive of no greater proof of the juniors being reabsorbed in the college. [Appreciative laughter from the college.] The second group is now in France, and the third group of some 43 students is already selected and will go to France in August and be under the direction of the Professors Guilloton.

The College has been the recipient of several fine gifts: We have received installments of the Tryon and Hillyer gifts, the Hillyer gift to date amounting to $416,000 and the Tryon $205,000, and there is more to come. The Commonwealth Fund of New York has given us $12,000 for scholarships in the Smith College School for Social Work. The alumnae, more especially those who were here when Mr. Burton was president, have collected as the Burton Memorial Fund $21,000.* The students present and past who have lived at White Lodge, which this year will close its 26 years of existence as an off-campus house, have given $2500 as capital to be used for residence scholarships.

* By Monday the Fund had reached $27,600. THE EDITOR.

The President then spoke of the Chair of Research, but, characteristically, he didn't mention the fact that the Trustees established this William Allan Neilson Chair of Research because of their "great admiration, affection, and esteem for President Neilson."

The most exciting announcement which has been made in the year in academic matters is the establishment of the chair of research in psychology to be occupied for the next five years by Professor Koffka. This chair has not been unconnected with the length of time I have been coming here and speaking at Last Chapel. It indicates as striking an innovation as anything that has happened in these ten years and mention of it will serve as a transition to some comparisons.

As I said at the time the announcement was made, I am not aware of any undergraduate college having a chair of this kind, a chair having the purpose of adding to knowledge with no teaching function attached to it. It will be of value to the world at large, to the faculty and the whole college community here in Northampton, and it will increase the intellectual life and prestige of this institution.

The thing we care most about in changes in the college is the matter of standard of work actually accomplished by the students. Everything else is machinery. Our object is the quickening of the lives of the students who pass through this college, training them in sound thinking, strengthening their intellectual fiber. Now it is very difficult for anyone in the college or outside of it to gauge our success in this matter. There are some considerations, however, which seem to have significance.

Let me compare some things about the class of 1920, that came in the year Mr. Burton retired, and the class of 1930 that came in last September. When the class of 1920 came in, it had 614 students. Of these, 26 came in solely by examination. Out of the 614, 125 entered with conditions.* Of the class of 1930, which came in with 629 students, all were admitted by examination, and only 13 entered with conditions. We started therefore with a much more highly selected group of students than we did ten years ago, and I feel free to say that if the academic work accomplished by the class of 1930 is not better, with all apologies to those of the class of 1920 who may be here, it will be a reflection upon the administration of this institution. There has been a great deal of misunderstanding with regard to the exclusion of students. Very few of the students in the past few years who have passed all of their examinations clear have been kept out of the group of colleges to which we belong. What has happened is rather the reduction of the number of conditions. In the case of these 13 students there were good reasons for sup-

*The figures given here are figures corrected from those actually quoted at Last Chapel.—THE EDITOR.

posing that, though not complete in their records, they were able to do good college work. The number of students dropped in the course of the college year has remained about the same, consequently one can only infer that the demands made upon the undergraduates have been gradually rising during these past ten years. There are some qualifications that statisticians would make regarding the conclusions I am pointing to, but I believe there is excellent ground for the opinion that the standards of scholarship have risen during these years.

Meantime, a large number of changes have occurred financially and physically. Ten years ago the total possessions of the College amounted to $4,750,000. To-day, they amount to $11,754,000. Ten years ago the money spent upon instruction for a college of 1917 students was $270,000. To-day, with only a hundred more students, the budget for instruction is rather more than double— 5% increase in students, 100% in cost of instruction. Ten years ago, we gave scholarships amounting to $20,000. This year, $86,000 was given, that being largely necessitated by the increase in charges. The money spent upon the library has just about doubled. The money spent upon maintenance of buildings and grounds is nearly three times as large, because the number of buildings and extent of grounds have increased as well as the scale of wages. Ten years ago, leaving out the cost of board, the current expenses were half a million, now they are $1,300,000, and with the dormitories, almost two million dollars a year. We are a fairly large business concern, you see.

The things that have been done that are concerned with attention to the student as an individual are various. When I came in contact with the college first, the most usual remark made to me by outsiders about the work here was that, of course, with so many students it was impossible that they could be as well looked after as in a smaller college, and impossible that they could see as much of their teachers. Obviously this was a danger which was shared by a great many other institutions. So, in common with other institutions, this college has been working toward an elimination of that danger by increasing the number of devices by which individual students should not be lost. We remember that, during President Burton's time, through the Fund of $1,000,000 he had decreased the number of students per instructor from 16 or 17 down to 10 or 11, and that is where we are to-day. That being the case, I do not see why students should find instructors difficult of access. The ratio of ten students to one instructor is regarded as a very fair ratio, is improved upon by hardly any institution, and is reached by only a minority in this country.

The establishment of class deans and of the Personnel Bureau are efforts on the part of the administration to break up the mass and bring direct advice to the individual students. Problems in connection with this are still being studied and a great deal of progress is being made.

Special Honors apply to the student at the top. A very large part of the machinery of looking after individual students in colleges is concerned with the student at the bottom. Now while the student at the bottom is often a very worthy person, she is receiving more than her share of interest and attention here as well as elsewhere. Special Honors was an attempt to strike a balance. The student in the middle should be the next to receive attention.

The President next spoke about the limitation of the enrollment. We implore every intelligent gentlewoman to read his words and learn them by heart for we are weary of repeating over and over again the simple sentence, "No, there is nothing in Sophia's will to prevent the trustees from limiting our enrollment."

Perhaps one of the most important questions is the limitation of enrollment. This seems a simple fact, but I never saw a fact spread among those concerned so slowly. We decided seven years ago that the college should not grow in numbers, but I still meet persons who ask me questions which show that they do not understand this decision. Had we still continued to receive students as we did in 1917, the college would have been double its size, and where the students would have lived and read and been taught, I don't know. There was nothing for the trustees to do but to set a limit, and we set that limit at the point which would permit the whole college to come into this building—approximately 2000. This was an important consideration, because while class deans and the Personnel Bureau attend to the individual, meeting in this building keeps the college together as one body.

Abolition of compulsory chapel here was accomplished without any disturbance. You know what a fuss is made about it in men's colleges. They dispute and discuss, and they carry it to the student body, the faculty, the trustees, and the newspapers. As far as I remember, the announcement was made, and voluntary chapel went into existence. The attendance in chapel has not fallen far. I do not know of any college where they have as large a voluntary chapel as we have here. It serves the purpose of maintaining the esprit de corps of the college, and helps us to realize our common interest.

The graduate school was started in the college long ago, but it continues to grow, and in ten years has doubled, now numbering about 70. Among women's colleges of our kind it is third largest. The largest is Radcliffe, the second Bryn Mawr.

We listen almost complacently when anyone talks of our housing problem, for lo, as the President said, it isn't any more a really pressing problem.

The outstanding problem from the physical point of view ten years ago [he said], was the housing of the students, and there again we have more than doubled the houses. Next year we shall have 1750 students in campus houses. Ten years ago it was 850. This is one of the great accomplishments made possible by the liberality of the alumnae.

Another change has occurred in regard to the number of students who come here from the various states. Formerly Massachusetts sent the largest number. Now it is New York. Massachusetts and New York each send us approximately one-fourth of our students, and the rest are scattered over the United States, with from 7 to 10 students from foreign countries. By our statistics we find that this college, when I first came here, had a plurality of Congregationalists. Now for several years the Episcopalians have been the largest body.

Part of the development of the college with which I myself have had anything to do, and from which I have received great pleasure, has been the development of the grounds and the removal of eyesores. Mr. King and I have had this as our reward for less pleasant tasks. We receive more universal commendation for this than for anything we have attempted along academic lines. Perhaps the cleaning out of College Lane has been the one act of this administration against which I have heard no protest.

At this point we interrupt to say that the fact that the class of 1927 appreciates the beautifying of College Lane was fully demonstrated by the dedication of their Class Book which reads as follows:

To
FRANKLIN KING

Who for forty years has devoted himself to the development and preservation of the tangible beauties of our college, and who, through the setting he has given us for work and play, has indelibly imprinted his personality in our memories and endeared himself to our hearts

The President continued:

I am expected at this time to tell you what we still want. We want more money for salaries to pay our good professors better, and get more of them. We want funds for educational experiments; some very promising ones are held up because of lack of funds. We want money to buy the field across the pond to extend athletic activities. [This began to sound like the "stunt" with which we were regaled later in Commencement!] We still have need for five more houses for students.

"This Campus of Ours in the Spring"

We want more funds for the library. We would like to have funds for the publications of the faculty so that the expense of publication will not come out of current funds. We have, as many of you know, a singularly small endowment in scholarships here so that the sum of $100,000 which will have to be given back to students next year must come out of current income! We need a gift to enlarge the stage of Students' Building, and one to build the missing steps on the east side of the Quadrangle.

Mercy, hurry along with that Alumnae Fund for the land of plenty seems to be still a long way from the Smith campus!

And then came the announcement of the prizes: English prizes and French prizes, Bible prizes and Music prizes; never in our day were there so many bright girls who excelled in so many different things and we were all out of breath when the President finished. You are referred to page 493 for details.

At this point the President sat down and the whole audience applauded him loud and long. He bore it patiently for a while and then signalled for Mr. Moog to strike up the organ. Mr. Moog, however, being wise in his own generation, did no such thing. The President looked a bit puzzled, and then Mr. Deane rose, doffed his mortar board, made the President a deep bow, and proceeded to read some very fine resolutions from the Faculty to congratulate President Neilson on his tenth anniversary as President of Smith College. It certainly was exciting and the longer we listened the more excited we got. The first paragraphs of the resolutions reviewed the remarkable progress of the College during the ten years of President Neilson's administration. The full text will be found on page 488, but we repeat the last paragraphs here:

This material and intellectual progress is preëminently the work of President Neilson. But the Faculty would also acknowledge his sympathetic coöperation in the problems of their work, the eagerness with which he has welcomed suggestions looking toward increased vitality of teaching, the pleasure and inspiration they have received from direct contact with his distinguished scholarship, his penetrating criticism, and his humane and genial personality.

Be it therefore resolved: that the Faculty of Smith College recognizing not only the distinction, but the unflagging devotion which President Neilson has given to the College, congratulates him on this tenth anniversary of his administration, and expresses the cordial hope that he may long continue as our Head, "reaping," like the Greek prophet of old, "the harvest of the mind's deep furrow, whence goodly counsels grow."

And then how we did clap. In fact we rose perfectly spontaneously and kept right on applauding, until it hardly seemed polite to keep the President waiting any longer to respond to Mr. Deane. And how he can think on his feet no matter what the occasion may be! He said:

Mr. Deane, and my other colleagues of the Faculty:—Had I been aware of your intention of reading these resolutions, I should have spared this audience the enumeration of details of the progress in the College during the past ten years.

I realize the generosity of Mr. Deane and his colleagues in attributing to me these accomplishments. As a matter of fact, that kind of credit comes to the administrative officer of a college as a matter of compensation for the criticism. He deserves the credit as much as he deserves the abuse, and since he must take the one, he is fain to accept the other. My part has been a small part. I do not think I have often got in the way, but all this increase in money is due to my predecessors' efforts, and to the alumnae. By my own unaided efforts, I have not brought in one per cent of that money. I have never undertaken to ask for money, and not much has come to me unasked. Others have done it.

The changes in the academic part of the work have arisen from suggestions from a group. Very few have originated with any one person. Very few of them have come into operation in the form in which they occurred to any one person. My function has been backing up suggestions and handing them to the faculty and administrative officers, and taking part in the discussion.

Some of the operations in the School for Social Work, which I did not refer to this morning, I have had nothing to do with at all. Dr. Southard and Dr. Jarrett, Professor Chapin and Professor Kimball have made the school. I did one thing. I had a chance given me in 1918 and I decided in the absence of the trustees to start. I hardly knew what it meant. That is the most rash thing I have ever done in Smith College, the biggest gamble I ever took, and it came out right. The work and credit of keeping it up belongs to these people I have mentioned.

I could have said a lot more about what has happened in the Music Department and in the Art Department. I didn't mean to enumerate these accomplishments as mine, but they were changes which I had observed, and of which I was proud. They have been possible because of the most exemplary Board of Trustees that ever college president worked under—interested and coöperative, and knowing their place! [we were quick to give him the appreciative smile he asked for here]—and because of a faculty which has worked with a great variety of opinion, with great energy in expressing their opinion, but with the interest of the College at heart, and without malice. A great deal of it has been the result of compromise, compromise which often seemed to be disappointing, but which often turned out to be wise. Much of the progress has been possible because of a body of alumnae who have, as I have already indicated, kept our wealth from being halved by economic conditions. The alumnae, by their occasional visits through the year, and by their correspondence, give one the sense that the College is not merely here on this spot, but contains a large body throughout the country, keeping its interests at heart. I have had an undergraduate body whose relations to me have been even more satisfactory, if such a thing were possible, than those of the trustees. No one ever got from a student body such support as I have had. We never have student revolts—I scold them more than they have ever been scolded in their lives, and they seem to enjoy it. It has been a very interesting ten years, the richest ten years of my life, and I thank Mr. Deane for what he has said on behalf of the Faculty, and I thank the representatives of all these other bodies for having given me the chances that I have had.

Once more we applauded, and this time there was a catch in our throats which wasn't to go entirely away until all Commencement was over, for this was only the beginning of the thrills we had telling the President that

We'll follow his guiding beyond and away
For we love him forever and ever and aye.

And once again he sat down, and once again he signalled to Mr. Moog to sound the organ, and once again Mr. Moog turned a deaf ear; and this time Mr. Wright, the College Marshal, rose, doffed *his* mortar board and said, "We are not through, Mr. President, the undergraduates have something to say." The poor President looked absolutely dazed but we clapped on and on as Amanda Bryan, who has this year been chairman of Judicial Board, stepped up to the platform and addressed him in one of the most charming and affectionate little speeches it has ever been our good fortune to hear. She said quite simply that the undergraduates had no resolutions to read to him but that if he would just sit down a few mo-

ments she wanted to talk to him. And then she went on:

President Neilson, first of all I think I shall thank you for what you have just said about us. I didn't know that we would be returning a compliment so soon.

When we first came here, you told us, as you usually tell the freshman class, that the sophomores would tell us some things that were not true. And they did. They told us an awful thing for they said, "Of course you realize that when your senior year comes, President Neilson will be taking a leave of absence. You didn't! And now it seems hardly fair to thank you for that by making you listen to another address, but we just had to make it, especially after we heard that the faculty had the same idea, although we have nothing tangible like the Koffka chair of research to offer, nor, as I said, any set of resolutions. There are a great many things that I had planned to say about the changes we have seen covering four years, but that part has already been said, so we will leave it out.

Last night in looking over a series of addresses made at the time of President Neilson's inauguration, I found one by President Eliot which contained the following statement:

I think it must be an abundant source of satisfaction in working for Smith College as President, trustee, or teacher that the College sends year by year into American society a stream of young women well-fitted to be the equal mates and effective comrades of pure, vigorous, courageous, reasoning, and aspiring young men.

The gaps in our ranks will testify to your success along this line.

We feel grateful for the mistakes we have been allowed to make. One thing which President Neilson and the faculty did not speak about is the close personal touch he has maintained with all of us. Very seldom is he "in conference." We meet him on campus, some of us are fortunate enough to have him in class, and we hear him in chapel. He gives us all a chance to meet him in person. We appreciate and profit by his discussions of current events. We also have his reading of the Bible. You see he has worn out one on us. We asked him whether he would be able to cross-index the new one as he had the old. You see we thought the old one was cross-indexed because there was always a passage to fit every occasion, no matter how unexpected that occasion was, but to our surprise he said he had no system of cross-indexing.

We realize now what President Seelye and President Burton mean to the alumnae when they come back, because of our kindred feeling for President Neilson. We feel that he has advanced along lines which these two men, who did so much toward the founding and establishing of the College, would have followed if they were here. When we go out into the world, we shall try to remember the things we have learned from President Neilson. We learned, first of all, the saving grace of a sense of humor, and yet how to be serious when necessary. We learned important lessons in tolerance, in sound thinking. And when we come back, we shall offer him our heartiest, sincerest, and most affectionate congratulations.

Surely to have won devotion like that from hundreds, nay thousands of young women among whom he lives in daily contact must not only have gladdened the heart of President Neilson, but also must have repaid him a thousand fold for his own "unflagging devotion" to this college. It was some moments before he could answer Amanda Bryan at all and then it was only his "saving grace of humor" which relieved the tension of the occasion. He simply said:

If there is any secret in keeping an undergraduate body from having a sense of grievance, it lies in the art of keeping one step ahead, saying it first, proposing it first, granting it before it is demanded, and I am very glad to have illustrated this on one occasion by having replied to this very gracious and charming speech before it was made.

And *then* Mr. Moog didn't have to be told to strike up

To you, O Alma Mater

and we sang it—even we alumnae who thought we knew "Fair Smith" better—without a falter to the end.

We clapped the senior class down the middle aisle and then, presto, the real three-ringed circus of a good old-fashioned normal Smith Commencement began sure enough. Mary Dixon vainly endeavored to corral everybody down to the front rows to practice the Alumnae Parade song; but goodness gracious, most of the reuners were so worried about rehearsals for their own songs for the song cup competition that they couldn't wait to be put through the paces of "Thousands and yet thousands strong." However, there was a small, a very small, remnant saved and we did our best to hold up our

heads and squint only surreptitiously at the words, and we may say there was one elegant tenor that, lost though she be to the Metropolitan Opera Company, certainly did carry us over the "we thy daughters, gather once again to thee" in fine style.

Eighty-seven, back for its fortuitous fortieth, says in its own reunion report—and by the way if it weren't for all those reunion reports this particular chronicler of Commencement would be even crazier than she is, for be it known to all and sundry that she is *not* a centipede and no one with less legs than a centipede (with the possible exception of the combined legs of '76) could live to make the entire rounds of the whirl of these next days—well, '87 says that after Last Chapel "the pace of everyone quickened." Eighty-seven is dead right. It quickened. In other words everyone dashed somewhere! Maybe down to the station to hail in some late arrivals and bring them triumphantly into the arena in a banner-bedecked machine; maybe to Bicknell's to lay in a still larger assortment of stout Commencement footgear—there will be a song about that later!—maybe, if you were 1902, back to those stylish new dorms where the 25-year reuners were splurging around in single rooms and almost a bath tub apiece. But eventually it is safe to say everybody panted breathlessly into class headquarters in Seelye Hall—unless of course they were as affluent as '17 and boasted a whole building of their own at the Burnham. For the matter of that of course *they* needed a lot of room for their whoo—goodness, we nearly let the cat out of the bag!

Well, to return to headquarters. Just as you were nicely occupied in Oh-ing and Ah-ing over the magnificent lot of handsome husbands and babies there modestly displayed, as like as not some hard-hearted but desperate costume chairman put you to work on something or other that was designed to draw the costume cup into your laps on Monday—unless like '24 you didn't have any laps—with no argument at all, and while you were fashioning—well, never mind that, it's too early to talk about costumes anyway—a regular slave-driver of a song leader insisted on practicing new songs and old songs over and over again with a canny ear out for the most successful song-competition song, until it was a wonder anyone was able to utter a word of simple prose for the rest of Commencement. And, moreover, if you didn't get involved in a class meeting at the same time you were lucky, for class meetings are the easiest things that any reuning class ever does. For instance, we saw the backs of 1907 shutting out the sunshine for two mortal hours one afternoon. Heaven knows what goes on in them but we suspect search for the super-superwoman in each class was pretty engrossing this year. At all events they certainly do seem to be one of the most popular of indoor sports. And, speaking of indoor sports, what a plunging into the swimming pool there was! Any time anybody lost anybody for as much as half an hour (and really there ought to be a radio set up on campus for broadcasting the lost classmates) it was safe to make tracks for the pool; not that you could pick your bosom friend out from any of the other sleek gray seals but you could sit on the edge and rest your poor tired footies for a space.

And the footies reference brings us logically to the "Class of '76, the class that by the college sticks." We may

say that they were in fine fettle this year (thanks to the unobtrusively efficient leadership of 1918) and we can prove it by the simple statement that in sublime defiance of their footies, they elected to have headquarters on the *second* floor of Seelye Hall; not, be it understood, that they were getting highbrow or above their betters but as a further demonstration of their desire to get out of the way and be inconspicuous. Their great plaid banner flung itself out to the breezes as proudly as any "red, green, yellow, or purple" and every now and again they bounded up the stairs singing, "And we ain't got weary yet," and their Neilson plaids were as chic and up to date as any of the red hats and green stockings and purple—well, in simple English, purple trousers that began to dart stealthily about even as early as Friday. More of '76 anon. They are, we submit—evidence of the Alumnae Fund Chairman who is soon to take the center stage notwithstanding—the true "superwomen" of Commencement and they are on in nearly every act, and when it comes to raising money for a *really important* gift—well, nuff said!

So much for the general busyness of this Friday morning, but lest anyone think that no one came back to these haunts in a really serious mood we shall now try to make our feet keep still long enough to take a look in at the Institute for the Coördination of Women's Interests which was having a conference down in Sage Hall. And the fact that perfectly normal reunion-minded alumnae sat there all morning long was proof enough that there is something in this business of coördinating sure enough. The general topic was "Problems of the Nursery School as a Social Experiment" and certainly every phase of those problems was discussed forwards and backwards. Mrs. Ethel Puffer Howes, the Director, presided of course, and the speakers were Mrs. Erwin Schell of the Cambridge Nursery School, on the "Independent Nursery School"; Winifred Notman Prince '11 of the Schenectady Play School, on the "Mothers Play School"; Eleanor Hope Johnson '94 of the Department of Psychology, Hartford School of Religious Pedagogy, on a "Nursery School Experiment in a Day Nursery"; Mary Thayer Bixler '17 of the Northampton Cooperative Nursery School, on the "Affiliated Nursery School"; Dorothea Beach, principal of the School, and Dorothy Williams, head teacher. Now we don't know in the least how it feels to be a mother but it is perfectly clear to us that if we *were* a mother and had had the chance to come to this conference and hadn't taken that chance we should regret it exceedingly for it was A number 1, even a maiden aunt could tell that. It was followed by a most delicious luncheon at The Manse and that was followed by more talks. This time the subject was "Continuity for Women" and it is perfectly evident that that subject was not covered in its entirety in one hour and a half! Mrs. Howes discussed briefly the preliminary steps which the Institute has taken in its two other experiments: the cooked food supply kitchen and the home assistants group; Miss Eleanor Lord spoke of the results of a most interesting survey, conducted under the auspices of the American College Woman's Club of North China, of the Chinese and foreign women who are coördinating in any way. She called attention to the fact that in spite of the war there was a far

larger per cent of replies to the questionnaire than we had been able to elicit from any group in this country and also to the fact that the problems in China seemed to be about the same as those here; "coöperation of husbands" and "a sense of frustration" seemed to be phrases common to both groups. The President was there and of course he spoke. Poor man, we mean only to compliment him but it does sometimes seem as though the very thought of food with always the few words to speak after the meal would be almost too much for him. However, we know of no meeting at Commencement time which would be content to do without him. This time he said very little, but that little hit the nail on the head as always. He said that he wondered what sort of people those were who complained of a sense of frustration. Hadn't they perhaps suffered from the same sense while they were children and when they were in college? How about frustrated lives anyway; what kind of people cannot combine home and intellectual activity, and, before tabulating results from any set of questions, isn't it necessary to know more about the people who are answering them? He spoke perhaps three minutes—we wished it had been an hour.

All the time that this luncheon was going on, the Board of Directors of the Alumnae Association was gathered round a luncheon table in the very next room, hashing and rehashing material for the Council meeting that very afternoon and for the Association meeting the next day. That Board of Directors and that Alumnae Fund Committee do very little idle twirling of the thumbs at Commencement time and it's just as well to pause a moment and offer up a word of thanksgiving for their very self-forgetting services. They swallowed their last strawberry a bit hastily on this particular occasion and fairly ran for the aforementioned COUNCIL. You can read all the minutes on page 502, minutes being the one thing that we absolutely refuse to include in this running commentary because *they* are intended for leisurely perusal. As we look back on that meeting the high spots seem to be Dean Bernard's little talk about the William Allan Neilson Chair of Research and of how happy the College was on the day on which it was announced, and Harriet Bliss Ford's tantalizing hint of the fun we were going to have with the Alumnae Fund at Assembly. She only hinted and far be it from us to do any more, but don't stop reading now or you'll regret it. By the way, if you are interested in reading more about the Chair than you got in the May QUARTERLY—and of course you are—turn back to page 409 and see a picture of the gentleman himself.

We have a funny twist in our minds, for every time we went out on the campus and saw those white-coated satellites of Mr. King who sat at their ease in real chairs all day (and we do believe all night) to guard the campus drives from sacrilegious tires we thought of that Chair, and every time we thought of that Chair we sang wearily to ourselves the senior song in which they are begging for a chair:

We'd rather not use it for research
We'd be glad of a place just to sit—

Anyone might think '76 had written that song and, believe you me, it was only by exercising our Christian fortitude overtime that we refrained from tipping one or two of those guardians of the gates out of those chairs and acquiring "a place just to sit."

Don't for a moment think that Council meeting was the only thing on the Friday afternoon program. Not at all. There was Dramatics again, but there is no use in a senior class thinking that alumnae will spend a whole reunion afternoon within doors for anything whatsoever, because they won't: the lure of the out-of-doors is too strong, and this particular day every machine with an inch of gasoline gathered unto itself its hundreds and fled away and away into the hills and happy river meadows where the daisies and buttercups were tossing their white and gold and where all through the woods and carpeting every hillside the laurel was pinker than anything that anybody could think of except the sunset sky itself.

And Friday night the class supper orgy began! Verily to an onlooker or to a '76er it doth appear that "Meeting and a-eating are the easiest things we do," and we will say that 1902 frankly admitted it. They simply said, "We had a class supper every night," and let it go at that. Anyway, '76 gathered itself together behind College Hall, threw its plaidies nonchalantly over its shoulders, went through a spirited rehearsal of all its latest successes with just enough new songs to

suggest that it was still capable of learning a thing or two, and started on its round of serenades. It told us pathetically that it would do almost anything on earth to please the reuners because it felt it would be so dependent on them another year but that it didn't really feel that it *could*

> Eepha sopha leepha sopha
> Seepha sopha sil

all the way up Mount Holyoke to where 1902 was, and who are we to blame them? They did tramp gaily over to '92 at the Episcopal Church, however, and rendered, "We are the Class of '76, Parlez-vous," and at the urgent request of the very dressy ladies gathered there they gave, after much searching about for the right note to start on,

> Gone are the days when we bore all rules a grudge.

The sopranos and altos seemed to range from Mount Holyoke with 1902 to the basement of the Baptist Church with 1912, but finally they compromised and went pleasantly on:

> Gone are the days when we stuffed ourselves with fudge,
> Gone are the days when we scoffed at dew and damp,
> We're coming with our coats and rubbers back to Hamp!

It certainly did make a hit and '92 returned "To-whit, to-whoo, we're '92," which ends up with the modest but we doubt not the true statement:

> Our motto to the world we'll tell
> We do, and have done, all things well.

Then '76 pranced down to 1907 at the Edwards Church (it's just as well to take *those* stairs when Commencement feet are fairly rested). They were well received and did a turn or two with Hinky-dinky parlez-vous, noted the amazing headdresses which adorned the heads of that class which has at last "tottered over the ghastly brink of 40" (no, they don't look it), and then proceeded down to 1912, and just as they got in and got the "Gone"

well pitched in came the President, and before him even '76 backs out backwards. They hung around outside, however, and when he came out chuckling at 1912's

Right then the college lost its high moral tone

they escorted him up to Dramatics and then slid down the hill to '17 in the Crew House and called it a day as far as their official duties were concerned. To be sure they dropped in at Beckmann's and Trebla's later and consumed gallons of pink ice cream and "straw" drinks the while they swapped yarns with every other alumna in Hamp; lent a sympathetic ear to the serenading over at the Academy when Dramatics had for the third time dropped the curtain on "The Beaux' Stratagem" and the whole college gathered there to tell the cast that it was the finest cast that ever stood before the footlights of the old Academy, as the college has done ever since the circling years began, and then everybody—What! "went to bed?" We dunno, did they? All we know is that just as we were dropping off we heard a voice outside our window say: "It certainly looks like it!" and quicker than a wink that fear that lurks underneath all our Commencement jollity until Ivy Day is past leaped to the fore and we said to ourselves, "It's going to rain!" But we were wrong, for when we fearsomely opened our eyes the next morning— Behold the Sun! A perfectly resplendent, Golden Anniversary, Hallelujah Chorus Sun and without further ado we hasten to say that the weather on this   .

IVY DAY was Heavenly. Brilliant blue of the sky with here and there just enough of a white cloud to give the blue perspective, a soft June wind that wouldn't for the world have disarranged a senior's careful coiffure, let alone an alumna's gay apparel, bright shifting lights in the arching elms and emerald grass, and color everywhere. Great splashes of color, red and green and yellow and purple, filling the campus with gayety and beauty! Who can tell of the pageantry of an ivy morning such as that? Surely not this scribe whose pen has faltered just here time and time again. Once more we lived through the ordeal (and here we speak as the editor) of corralling the presidents of the reuning classes long enough to get their pictures taken. Look well, O classmates, for it represents great self-control on the part of many! Once more we waited for the marshals to line up their motley array, once more we saw the laurel-wreathed standards lifted high and the band poised for the first blare, and then we scurried for a point of vantage near the Library steps—for it was there that the President and Mrs. Bernard reviewed the Parade—

and waited with all the parents who didn't in the least know what all this excitement on the back campus was about. All they knew was that their Marys and Susies had told them that the Ivy Procession was to come up the canvas-laid walk, and everybody could see that that had nothing whatever to do with the kaleidoscopic crowd over where the band was. Well, well, ivy day morning is one time when Commencement parents get even more than their money's worth! And then came the martial strains of the band, the Push Committee gave a final and most emphatic punch to their orders, and the Big Parade which had gathered from "east, west, north, south to fair Sophia's camp" swung into line and over the campus green from Chapin with the great white and gold banner of Smith at the head. O dear, O Dear, thought we, as we got the merest birdseye glimpse of the costumes *en masse*, whatever will the Costume Committee do? After the Officers came the Class of 1882, and we certainly are going to write them in capital letters whenever we get the chance for they were the queen

Forty-five Circling Years

ELLA-BOLLING JAMES
PRESIDENT 1927

KATHERINE McCLELLAN
PRESIDENT 1882

" *Style Plus on the Campus* "

bees of this Commencement (and more than that as you shall later hear), perky and charming in their parasols and scarfs of "mulberry and conch shell." We learned just what to call those colors long, long ago when they came back for their thirtieth or thereabouts and never shall we insult them by calling them bromidic red and pink. They had comfortable camp stools tucked beneath their arms but as for subscribing to their "We're called the old ladies, decrepit old ladies"— don't you believe it! Hard after them was sweet '87 in yellow "himations" (we learned our lesson here too) and dainty white parasols; and then to-whit, to-whoo, here's '92 with narrow brown fillets and ribbons and their big Greek banner, all very classic we do assure you, and with the cutest, softest little brown owl perched daintily on the left shoulder. You are not to think that '76 was leaving all the gaps between reunion classes unfilled. Not a bit of it. Every '76er had flocked to her own standard and there were almost no classes unaccounted for, and the more plaidies there were in the procession the better the Scotch laddie on the reviewing stand liked it, ye ken. Ninety-seven have waxed very demure since their sheik days of only five years ago for this year they were in simple white with only the yellow ribbons and gold and black pins of that wonderful Golden Anniversary Parade to proclaim them the "finest under heaven." No, we are wrong there: we *think* that anyone reading the signs which they carried proudly aloft would have suspected their weight in gold and their illustrious history! All of a sudden in the midst of their very up-to-date ranks appeared a maiden in a muslin that swept the ground and sleeves

that filled the universe. She looked older and a little sadder than her companions and the sign above her said, "As we were in '97." *O tempora, O mores!* Presently came one of the handsome dashing sheiks before mentioned and that sign said, "As we were in '22," and then the yellow band gave way to a bobbing line of red— well, we couldn't make out whether they were lanterns or roses but as they got closer we decided that we would choose roses as the simile for the scarlet hats of 1902, for the faces under them were so young and blooming! They were walking and a-talking with their pals in 1902 with all the dash of college days, and they certainly did look "Style Plus" to us. Around their necks were academic red hoods denoting, as their sign said, that they had taken "100-plus degrees of satisfaction" and the *tout ensemble* was thrilling; then came the natty green turbans of 1907 bobbing along so close to the red of 1902 that the result was a kind of Merry Christmas effect that did much to add to the gayety of nations. They had stylish green shopping bags and stockings as green as the Emerald Isle and—well, their 1⅔ child per graduate may think they are "middle-aged" but to us they looked like up-to-the-minute débutantes. We learned later that their crisp skirts were 15 inches from the ground while 1902's were only 14 —which is one way to mark the passing of the years! As a matter of fact, however, it was 1912 who got the vote of the sidelines as being the "youngest looking of all the bunch." And that was a compliment worth having for they were just in the simple white of any summer day plus the purple ribbon that testifies beyond the shadow of a doubt to their royal

lineage. They weren't all dressed up but just 1912 as is. Almost we could hear them singing their song of five years ago:

If that's 1912 then the calendar lies, I'll say.

We are putting them in a picture all by themselves because they really deserve a *summa cum laude* for not blazing forth in their royal purple as they yearned to do, but their costume committee understood that it was the wish of the Board of Directors that classes beginning with the fifteenth dispense with costumes and, "loyal to the royal in themselves," they obeyed. They were mistaken and we all regret the mistake but it does cheer our hearts to have such a demonstration of the spirit of coöperation.* They had signs too, good peppy signs as did all the classes, but we shall never in the world get this colorful lengthy line of alumnae in front of the President if we linger over them. "Whoops the gay Nineties" fairly shouted the striking white-head-dressed, black and yellow hooped ladies of 1917, and here we balk at describing all the 57 varieties of costumes. There was a rube band, the last horse and buggy in Northampton driven by the comic strip characters in *The New Yorker* to the life (the picture is a bit small but you get the idea "as the saying is"); there were the aforementioned ladies plus à la mode black mitts, and there was a very elegant, silver planed Lindy. How he happened to drop back into the gay nineties it did not appear, but he was superb even to the tiny wheels on his feet. 1922 brought us news of the world beyond Smith College also for they paraded more than a hundred

* We regret to state that we are not putting them in a picture. The fact is we can't find a picture of them. Such royalty evidently dazzled the eyes of the official photographer, and no camera fiend 1912er can be found this side of the Atlantic! THE EDITOR.

strong in red Chinese coolie coats with mysterious and mighty clever signs on their backs and in their hands. The wee but oldest of their "108 Little Celestials" had her own little ricksha and So Fi Ah herself carried their scroll. (You really must read their own description, our fingers are all tangled up!) Good gracious, what have we here?—scores of rakish 1924 "modern maids piratical" stealthily approaching in red neckerchiefs and sashes, hoop earrings, *and* purple trousers (shades of '97's trailing-skirted lady). We hate to confess how becoming we thought they were; and now, bringing up the rear (miles and miles of rear, it seemed) was '26, the youngest of all, and, still feeling that college was the place to ask and answer questions, they had decked themselves with big red "Ask me Another" question marks, dainty red ruffs, pointed hats, and scarlet canes. We liked them a lot and we do hope that somebody answered their pathetic plea, "Who was Rosetta Stone?" before they got discouraged asking.

Well, at long last we have called the roll and all the time they were marching, marching, marching to all sorts of stirring tunes, but now as the last question mark came into the alumnae magic circle Mary Dixon waved her baton and everybody tried to sing thousands and yet thousands strong. We can't boast of the result, we really can't, but the spirit was there and anyway we sang to the President and Mrs. Neilson and Dean Bernard and, swinging off in fine style, lined our handsome selves up to review the seniors. And we certainly did agree with 1907 when they remarked pseudo-indignantly that they didn't see why on earth the band thought "O Mother Dear Jerusalem" was a suitable tune

with which to hail us off the center of the stage! We had only a few minutes to wait this year and we spent them in loudly rejoicing at the weather. There was still brilliant sun; there was no wind at all; and there was practically no temperature that anybody could put her finger on, so absolutely did it melt into the soft June landscape! It was the Golden Anniversary weather all over again. And then came the Ivy Procession and it certainly was the very loveliest that anybody ever saw. There wasn't a dissenting voice about that and if anyone had come to Commencement wax sentimental over their appearance on this their Ivy Day, but we beg to say that if we had been the proud alumnae mothers who watched them pass we should have nearly burst with pride. As a matter of fact they did, and we entirely forgive them their supercilious air as they sailed past us in the proud glory of their motherhood, Indoor Ivy ticket in hand. Oh well, we had a class daughter of our own, and we too went in and looked down from the gallery of John M. Greene on those acres and acres of roses swaying gently above the background of their delicate green leaves

"THE SENIORS PASS"

(perhaps one of those frazzled remnants we heard about) a bit skeptical as to the younger generation, the beauty and poise and sweetness of this particular cross section of it certainly put her fears to rest. First came the juniors in ravishing pastel gowns and big garden hats bearing the lovely loops of laurel and then

The seniors pass, each with a rose in hand.

We are well aware that we shall lose all caste with our newest alumnae if we and pure white dresses of the seniors. The sun flooded the hall; there were laurel and palms on the platform, and suddenly that line from the Ivy Song of two years ago came to us with vivid meaning:

We have touched the hem of beauty
In this place.

Indoor Ivy is really the seniors' private entertainment with and for their families and they certainly do have a good time, and seeing as how so many alumnae in these days since the college is going on fifty-three *are* families it is only fair to quote a bit of the proceedings in this their QUARTERLY, and this year we choose Annie Vaughan Weaver's humorous speech— and that's rather good of us for she isn't what you could call really enthusiastic about us alumnae (poor dear, she forgot how soon her diploma would push her into our arms). She said:

The orator's highest privilege is to address an audience which believes that his cause is the world's supreme cause. That is my privilege to-day. For we know that you believe we are the greatest of all classes of all time—that it was left for us to set all forms, to crown and glorify all traditions, to cross the T in Smith. We are the class Smith has been waiting for all these years, and now that she has fulfilled her great mission she may relax her tension, slumber pleasantly, and for the future produce classes just from force of habit.

We do apologize for the three under classes whom you have seen sporting about campus, trying to be useful but really serving as admirable foils for our grace and attributes. If you have mistaken one of such persons for a Senior, it is due to the spirit of imitation which our presence compels, and is, therefore, pardonable. We do apologize also for those strange creatures, the alumnae, our forerunners and pioneer sisters. Forgive them, for they made us possible. Without them to experiment on, our faculty could never have disciplined themselves for us.

We are glad you are here for three whole days. You will see us in white, in rainbow scheme, and in scholastic dusk. You will hear us musically and oratorically. But you cannot feel us—for we are not of this world. You always suspected that we were angels, ever since at the age of two we spoke that first mystic word which no one except yourselves understood. Now to-day as you see us you can say, "I told you so." You are the audience of all times. For four long years even we have been waiting for you. Those dark days freshman year before the President and faculty realized that we were the appointed, the anointed class, when deans and wardens advised and even verged upon scolding us, we thought of you and carried on. Sophomore year when jealous upperclassmen, chagrined over their eclipse, sneered at us we bit our teeth and thought of home. Last June when 1926 snatched away the honors, and only grudgingly, prickingly, gave us their senior pins, we smiled the smile magnanimous, for you were at that moment made the parents of Seniors. During these past months, when all have bowed down

before us, we have held high our heads, saving the acknowledging bow for you. To you, our parents, we, like all the great, attribute our greatness, our brains, our allowance, our shoes. We know that you are moved, grateful, proud, and all the other paternal-maternal adjectives. But we hope still more that you will remain thus moved in the months to come. For though we have been angels for twenty-one years, which is a long while for angels to tarry on this earth, still we too are forced at last to the choice of all celestial beings, of either flopping off to our own celestial sphere, or of unwinging ourselves and stepping down among men. We have chosen the latter, nobler course.

And now, we beg you, please swing on to those good parental emotions while our unearthly hands accustom themselves to bread and butter and typewriters. That job may not turn up before September, and even then the boss may some day say, "Go, and do not return!" And then, fathers, may you remember this day and understand. And, Mother, when we burn the toast, when we bake bricks instead of bread, when we confuse salt and baking powder, think of roses, and ivy, and Commencement, and remember that for four years our thoughts have been on honey. Knowledge may be power, but it is neither men nor money. We may be single for months and months. Our business activities may at first receive no pecuniary recognition. But sooner or later our efforts will be, must be, crowned, for we are the inevitables.

Smith College thanks you for choosing her as the scene and machine of our blooming. We could not help blooming, but she believes that nowhere else could we have bloomed such a bloom.

Ah ha, now we know why this particular senior class seemed so especially enchanting: we have, forsooth, been entertaining angels unawares! and with this belated acknowledgment to the appointed and anointed class we tiptoed from the gallery with the applause of those heaven-kissed Parents of Seniors ringing in our ears and sped down to our own

ALUMNAE ASSOCIATION meeting in Sage Hall. It was well under way and looked as gay as a garden party with all the little blobs of color scattered about the hall. One particular group over on the extreme left immediately caught our eye: we had no idea just why excepting that they looked particularly intelligent even in the midst of all the intelligent gentlewomen but we were soon to learn that they were—nuff said! There were committee reports and election results of course and you will find them all over in the Alumnae Association department where we had time to see that there was a predicate for every subject instead of leaping from high spot to high spot as we do in these crowded pages. There were resolutions read on the passing of Charlotte Gulliver, beloved member of '83 and one time devoted Trustee of the College and President of the Association. The resolutions are printed on page 503. We heard with shouts of joy (metaphorically speaking) that the Juniper Lodge Endowment Fund had gone over the top at $33,607.12; Jean Paton reported for the Burton Memorial Fund and gave us all a chance to add to our contributions so that when the sum was announced at Assembly Monday it might be really worthy of the man for whom it was named. Mrs. Sawyer announced that the Board of Directors had appropriated $1000 from the treasury and there was a round of applause for that. There was another announcement which Mrs. Sawyer made anent the tenth birthday of President Neilson that caused great excitement and there were some resolutions, but wild horses couldn't drag any more information from us because we refuse to steal the thunder from an Alumnae Assembly that will go down in history hand in hand with that of the Fiftieth Birthday Party, and it's the greatest pity in the world that all 10,000 of you couldn't have been present.

And then at the request of Mrs. Sawyer, Harriet Bliss Ford leaped to her feet and, as chairman of the Alumnae Fund, gave us a—well, you can call it a report or a speech or an address if you want to but we call it an education that we shan't forget for many a day. Would that we could quote it in full but you will find the gist here and in the aforementioned Alumnae Association pages, and on your honor as an alumna of Smith College we charge you to read it all. Never, never, never from this time forward skip anything that has for a caption Alumnae Fund. Of course Mrs. Ford's main points were to get the Association to adopt two recommendations, to wit,

(1) To amend the charter of the Alumnae Fund so that payments shall be made payable to the Alumnae Fund of Smith College instead of to the Alumnae Association.
(2) To ratify the project for the coming year: salaries for the faculty to be applied in whatever way the trustees may deem advisable

and we may as well say now that both these recommendations were adopted literally with our left hand on our heart and our right hand upraised. It was, as you may imagine, an unusual sight for a supposedly formal meeting! but Mrs. Ford isn't formal, thank heaven. Of course there was a third point that didn't have to be voted on, and that was that 100% of givers is the really important thing.

She promptly reminded us that already about 80 of the leading colleges and universities have alumnae-i funds and that we voted last year to resurrect the one that we started in 1912— that one that Mrs. Morrow claimed she had treated as a kind of stepchild when all the drives were on.

She then with many prideful gestures and graceful phrases which tripped from her tongue like so many pearls introduced her Central Executive Committee to us (their names are over in the A. A. pages and will later be written "up yonder" in letters of gold, we trust) and then she went on to say that the Committee was making its real début at that present moment for there for the first time was the General Committee (with a superb gesture to the right), these blushing débutantes sitting in the seats of honor. "Ah ha," said we for the second time that morning, "we knew we could tell appointed and anointed ones when we saw them" for it was the very group we had remarked upon entering.

Look well and admiringly upon this magnificent band of Smith's superwomen. [She went on.] There are 48 representatives of the classes that have graduated the 48 United States of Alumnae, plus 4 who haven't yet. The Plus Fours call themselves undergraduates. They are really Alumnae in the Egg. They think Smith is a college for them. We know it's just an incubator for good alumnae! and these prove that they are getting better all the time. They are all one extraordinary breed, with a strain of bulldog, a dash of the wily serpent, with more than a dash of the gentle dove, and possessing the better qualities of pickpockets and safe-crackers! They are just our little Girl Scouts, doing a good deed every day of their lives for Smith, for years and years, for it is a life work. See to it that you never make them bow their heads in shame when the roll of honor is called. Note especially the class of '80. It may well look proud. Two or three weeks ago, without a hint from us, entirely unsolicited, without our spending even 2 cents for postage, two gifts of $5 each came rolling in from that class. * * *

Who wouldn't be a blushing débutante after such a début as that and who wouldn't be proud to be super-women privileged to work under such a super-superwoman as Harriet Bliss Ford and who would be so mean as to let her or them down? Answer me that, O you whose family name is Smith! She then proceeded to review the education in giving which all the 48 states of alumnae have had, and then to nail down reason after reason why it was appropriate to give the money raised this coming year for faculty

salaries; and all that you will find under its proper caption and with a surprise initial—you'll recognize it fast enough at this stage of your education. The meeting adjourned on what we think we might call a distinctly high note.

And then everybody thought about eating again and some of the elect went to Colloquium, and some went foraging for themselves in a regular "bun and banana" mood, and some, and these were the real elect, went down to the Crew House for the Fund luncheon.

And how about that Fund luncheon? Well, a good time was certainly had by all. First there was satisfying food served by the ladies of one of the many churches in Northampton. Those churches without which there just couldn't be any Commencement at all! Then there was a feast of reason and flow of soul (to say nothing of wit) the like of which we have seldom heard. The stock for the privilege of being an Alumnae Fund superwoman went up about 100% after Harriet Ford and Bess Morrow got through winding us around their fingers. Mrs. Ford explained that the meeting was a kind of service school for learning the technique for acquiring those "better qualities of the pick-pocket and safe-cracker," and that obviously Bess Cutter Morrow, magically transformed from the cutter of Birthday Cake fame to our "revenue cutter"—groans from the super-women—was the one to tell us how it was done.

We can't give you her speech, more's the pity, because she didn't write it, and while she most promptly handed us a few pencilled notes from which sprang her inspired words we are still far enough removed from the yellow variety of journalist to be delicate about putting quotation marks around pencilled notes. She spoke of course to the superwomen but it won't hurt the rest of us to listen in for she told them that this business of raising money had to be backed by strong personal conviction. She said they must cultivate the Alumnae Fund habit just as a child's habits are cultivated; they must incorporate their belief in the Alumnae Fund into all their creeds. She said that, whereas as a child she had been taught to say, "I brush my teeth and say my prayers," she now said, "I brush my teeth, I say my prayers, and give to the Alumnae Fund." To our delight she went through other of her pronouncements:

I believe in my church, in my country, and in the Alumnae Fund!
I give to foreign missions, to hospitals, and to the Alumnae Fund!
I admire George Washington, Abraham Lincoln, and the Alumnae Fund!
I pay my income tax and I give to the Alumnae Fund!

and so forth until she had us all on fire to go out and proclaim our own particular credo. She gave the superwomen a few points as to how to be good pickpockets and we shan't give her recipes away, but her last point we emphasize because it's a good text for all good alumnae:

It is important to stress the point that we are joining ourselves to a great and splendid movement of our own times. Perhaps none of us will ever fly across the Atlantic, but by allying ourselves with the Alumnae Fund we can be connected with a great work, the education of women.

Then after some discussion about business details for the superwomen (later we shall print the calendar which is to be their Bible) there was a rehearsal for the Assembly Stunt, and here we drop the curtain. It was terribly exciting and all the little Plus Fours who were present certainly must have had a few of their fears about

being "highbrow alumnae" put to flight.

Saturday afternoon was really so full of a number of things that it simply wasn't possible to do everything. For instance, everyone should have gone to the Students' Aid meeting and put their minds on helping the Society solve some very puzzling problems. In tabloid form the report is as follows:

Annual dues amount to $1360.45, or $15.65 less than last year. The Fellowship Fund, however, has increased by 32 life members. Gifts for the year total $3636.48, less by $181.39 than for last year. This year there were heavy demands for loans. Forty-nine girls have taken 73 loans to the amount of $8527.50. This was divided among 33 seniors, 21 juniors, and 19 sophomores. We have received $4247 in returned loans, or $875.05 less than last year. Overdue loans amount to $15,399.65 or $1544 more than last year.

It was this matter of overdue loans that particularly depressed the Society and the treasurer's report ended with the following pessimistic paragraph:

Why do not the borrowers of to-day assume more responsibility about paying back their loans? In the spring we sent out over 60 letters to graduates of from five to fifteen years' standing, asking them if they could make some payment on their loans, or at least send a word of explanation. We had 5 or 6 replies in answer to these letters; 3 checks only came in. Is it fair to the present undergraduate to withhold from her sums which would be easily available if her older sisters had met their obligations?

Everybody did not go to this meeting, as we said, because there were class meetings here and class sings there and down on Allen Field the alumnae and students were playing a most absorbing game of hockey. Goodness only knows who won, but we saw three of those fierce-looking pirates of '24 with their earrings bobbing and their purple trousers turned up to knicker length (we should hardly have thought those trousers would have cramped their style!), and we have a good deal of respect for the undergraduates who tackled them. Of course there were society reunions but the real "ticket" event of this afternoon was the Glee Club concert. We do hope there weren't many who missed it for they sing like—well, not wishing to be sentimental we simply state that we hope you'll remember that a senior herself admitted that they were "angels" and there were many, many seniors in the Glee Club, and that's that!

Something must be said sometime in this story about the feverish epidemic of ivy planting that went on in season and out up around the new dormitories. It will be no time at all before we can go up to any one of them and sing "Ivy round thy towers growing." Saturday, Sunday, Monday the rites went on. Sometimes it was a mere unsentimental dropping of the ivy into the ground but usually, ah, usually there were ceremonials! Ninety-seven had very lovely exercises in which a lovely poem by Nan Branch was read. We quote in part:

For centuries upon these gracious walls
Our vines shall hold eternal festivals
And sometimes that old magic in the air
Shall sweep upon the passer-by a sense
Of color and of music and delight—
Then some mysterious glee shall shake the
    night
With romance old and glory so intense
That he will say—feeling such passion near—
The God of Immortality is here.
How many a girl shall one day lightly pass
And say—this ivy was my mother's class—
And centuries from now, in its rich state,
Its leaves shall hear some casual voice say,
That ivy was my mother's great, great, great,
    great—
Then shall the mystic presence laugh and
    play—
And the God step forth with leaves all ashine
And bless that little daughter of the vine.

Ninety-two planted its ivy on Cushing House and read a sweet tribute to Miss Cushing which is included in their own report; and 1902!—somehow even this chronicler who ruthlessly skips from grave to gay and back

again with such unliterary abandon hesitates a wee bit to expatiate on 1902's ivy planting in the very next sentence, as the saying is, to Nan Branch's poem. Anyway, they didn't do it until Sunday and we believe we'll tell about it in its proper order. We shan't forget it—Oh no, we shan't forget it.

Along about 5.30 another whole set of class suppers took the center of the stage and among them was little old '76· She appreciates beauty as well as the next one and tramped as fast as her footies would carry her down to the greensward between the boathouses on the edge of Paradise, and there she collected her red, green, yellow, and purple selves into as tight a little bunch as possible and gave herself a good time over her buns and bananas and bottled drinks at 15 cents per. So peppy were the leading spirits, however, that the last sandwich was hardly down before they made us go through our repertoire preparatory to the strenuous evening (two nights of class suppers are awfully hard on '76 and on the President too for he is as gracious as they about making the rounds). We carolled forth, "We're going back to our home in Hamp"; we put our plaidies on as turbans à la the undergraduates, and all too soon had a really dress rehearsal of our *pièce de résistance* to "Bonnie Dundee":

You poor old reuners, we're sorry for you;
You've no time to play you have so much to
    do;
We know what it's like, we were once in your
    fix
Till we struck out for freedom and '76·

Chorus:

So gaze at our costumes and list to our song;
We know they will fill you with jealousy
    strong.
A year from this June all your troubles will
    pass
And we'll let you bat round with our wonderful class.

It's something to hear '76 come out strong on that päss and cläss. They may be modern but they certainly do know their Back Bay! Somehow the classes didn't urge us to linger as long as usual but as a matter of fact they didn't linger themselves, for an Ivy Night schedule is a fearsome, albeit enchanting, thing to live through in this pinched up Commencement; and long, long before all the toasts were given the college was singing down on the steps of Studes and

IVY NIGHT had begun. We could "hear their voices ringing, across the twilight shadowed grass" as we alumnae gathered—quietly lest the fathers and mothers grouped closely in those few treasured seats miss a word of the new songs and old songs that the college loves so well. Seventy-six dashed in for one hilarious minute with its Spirit of '76 drum and fife corps at the head, but there was much less singing by other classes than usual. Perhaps the seniors did not know that we too loved to share in that last college sing.

Earth in its beauty has no fairer spot
Than this campus of ours in the spring

they sang, and then, just as the setting sun was touching the clouds with rose and the laurel and azalias over by the Observatory were glowing more and more pink, they simply had to stop because the schedule of events pressed hard on their heels. And so after the Alma Mater—and you could hear echoes of that way up the campus—they gave up the steps and the Alumnae Song Competition was on. There was a big audience for that too for the parents very properly held on to those seats although they hadn't an idea what kind of animals alumnae were anyway and looked all evening

long as though they were glad that Annie Vaughan Weaver had apologized for us. The prize award committee sat importantly in the very front and that inimitable pair of 1917 comic strips mounted the steps and announced the classes. One after the other they got themselves on to the steps as best they could and with all the éclat of Rally Day songsters rendered their chosen ditties. And maybe you think that only the younger classes competed! Not a bit of it. The Class of '82 stepped jauntily forth in its mulberry and conch shell and gave us:

We're called the old ladies,
Decrepit old ladies,
And perhaps we should grant it as true;
But list to our plea, now
When you may agree now
To judge from a fresh point of view.

We're coeval with Pinafore,
Perennial Pinafore,
And Pinafore's still going strong;
As juniors we gave it
And now we would brave it
To furnish the tune for our song.

Then consider our claim now,
And award us no blame, now
That still youthful in spirit we feel.
May such spirit attend you
And happiness lend you
Through all that time has to reveal—

and they sang as snappily as a chorus of Gilbert and Sullivan stars, bless their hearts. Everybody was in costume of course, in fact, Chinese '22 had added unto itself gorgeous red lanterns to add to the gayety of nations. And speaking of lanterns, just as the daylight savings at last got spent a long line of lanterns popped on over the heads of the singers—shall we call them head lights instead of foot lights for our opera stage? It was a gay sight and never again shall we who heard '17 declare

And S-M-I-T-H is the only place
Such illustrious girls should go

or '07 with its "Funny things we do," or—no, we simply can't get involved with all those ivy night lyrics, but what we mean is, heaven be praised that we weren't on the Song Committee!

All this time, as we said, it had been getting darker and darker; lanterns were glimmering in the gardens; lanterns were luring us all the way up College Lane, and there we heard the first soft strains of the harp in the "Song of the Volga Boatmen" and saw the white-clad Glee Club float gently from behind the Island, singing. An Island all glowing with colored

LOOKING DOWN PARADISE TOWARDS THE
ISLAND

lights with just above it Venus casting her shimmering reflection in the water! You who were here last year or for the Fiftieth know the beauty of that island interlude; you who have not seen it have still a lovely thing to look forward to on some ivy night in June. Song after song floated over the banks of Paradise—"Santa Lucia" seems still to haunt our memories—and not until "Fair Smith" came over the water did we once more turn towards

campus where the swaying lanterns beckoned us here, there, and everywhere. There was no President's reception in the Library this year and we alumnae selfishly regretted that for we love to stand without in our reunion clothes and watch the rich and great in evening gown and dinner coat go in and out the lighted way. However, we were quite busy enough surging around the campus in our "orthopedic shoes" or singing on some convenient steps to crowds of admiring parents and junior ushers and push committees (here, we were not entirely sure whether we or they were doing the admiring!). And speaking of sitting, we saw one class calmly requisition a few of its husbands and get them to heave a Turkish rug out of their headquarters, and there they sat in haughty disregard of the "damp and dirty ground." Every now and again the Spirit of '76 charged through in a non-stop flight that would have made anything but the Spirit of St. Louis look like an accommodation. They hinky-dinky parlez-voused in great style and Georgia Coyle got away from a reuning Amherst husband long enough to lead the footies. Ninety-seven (who by the way hadn't competed for the cup because one of her own number had contributed it) sat under a finest under heaven banner and sang about themselves thirty years ago. One verse went:

Our picture hats were wobbly and our skirts
      were wide and long—
No sleeves were ever larger and our petticoats
      were strong
And Mennen's Talcum Powder box was not
      considered wrong
By the girls who made the nineties gay.

The Brown Owls of course were very much awake and feeling reminiscent but a bit cocky about their contribution to the styles of the day, as witness the "Bowery" song:

When first we stepped on the campus grass
A shawl was worn by every lass;
A tam on her head, a bustle behind,
No such sights any more you'll find,
But soon was started a fashion new
And who was leader, but Ninety-two.
Shirtwaists neat, with neckties too.
They've never gone out any more!

and 1919 suddenly emerged as a large and joyous unit and told the world that there was life in the old girl yet. It seems that they were having the time of their lives in an informal eighth which seems to be a kind of glorified regular and '76 all rolled in one. Eighty-seven was abroad looking quite too young to be out and '82 in a solid mass sat on Washburn House steps till the last lantern was out and said to all and sundry

We have Smith and we have heaven.
    Lucky women we.

Lucky women were we all, and when at last Ivy Night was officially over (meaning when the lanterns were out, and we plead for a little more time next year) we wished that we could tell the seniors and sophomores singing sadly and lingeringly on and on down at Studes that the loveliest word in "O Fairest Alma Mater" is the last word of all—

    O Fairest Alma Mater,
    You hold and claim us—*still*.

"Officially over" means eleven, and campus houses didn't close until midnight. Where, Oh where are the gay young—everybody? Well, it had been a strenuous day; the ubiquitous strawberry and chicken salad had done their best, but food was indicated; and at the risk of an anti-climax to this day of radiant joy truth compels us to state that at the witching hour of 11.45 we saw various green hats, and red ruffs, and plaidies consuming sausages and the humble scrambled egg at Beckmann's. Worse than that! When we squeezed ourselves into the last crack in the door at 11° 59' 59" we felt

a splash of rain on our shoulder! And when we got up on a Commencement SUNDAY morning if we were a senior we looked like this. Again

truth urges us to a confession. This is the very same cut that we used in this very same place five years ago, and 1927 is probably the only one who doesn't recognize it! But 1922 will, Oh, 1922 will, because she is the lady in cap and gown looking out on her Baccalaureate day, and '97, and '12, and all the rest of you reuners will for you were all here then hopping over the puddles and dodging the cloudbursts, and we do hereby implore you to speak to the weather man on your next reunion for a sunny Sunday as well as a heavenly ivy day. We have one more cut that we could put in here too. It's of a poor disgusted father standing out in the rain disconsolately trying to read the Sunday paper the while he balances an umbrella in his arms. There were many just like him hereabouts and we were even sorrier for them than for the seniors. As for the alumnae—they all belong at least potentially to the class of '76 which comes back "with its coats and rubbers" and they keep right on visiting with their pals rain or shine. On this particular Sunday they went to the S. C. A. C. W. meeting down in Students' Building. Some people think that is just a prayer meeting but it isn't at all; it is a very thrilling experience meeting and it's worth going out in the rain for. Harriet Taylor '23 spoke of work at Hampton Institute; Alice Chapman '22 spoke simply and convincingly of some of the problems and rewards of social work in a big city; Mira Wilson '14, senior dean and the new leader of religious work at College next year, reassured us—if we needed reassuring—about the spiritual life here on the campus and suggested the possibilities of her new position, and Mabel Milham Roys '00 told us the story of Ginling in these last grilling months. Her narrative was quite the most thrilling thing we have heard since the Great War. On second thoughts we *are* putting that cut in for the campus was dotted with fathers and if we weren't so honest you would think it a new picture, for overcoats haven't "gone up" in five years!

The seniors have their Baccalaureate at eleven in Sage Hall, and it is

their own private meeting with the President. We envy them that, but we do not begrudge them, and we always go down to see them enter. This year as the last one in cap and gown made a flying leap over the puddles we saw a lone figure under an umbrella. Poor soul, thought we, she must have thought she could get in. Not at all. She was simply an extra special loyal alumna of Smith College who knew perfectly well that she would not be admitted but had slopped all the way down from the new dorms to see the seniors just because she thought they were such a "beautiful class." And if that isn't a Simon pure compliment, O '27, we give up.

And it rained and it rained, but class bats were in order just the same. Nineteen-twelve betook themselves to the Crew House, and '02 went to the Whale, so water was nothing in their lives, and somebody went out to Sophia's. Indeed the little house under the elms had its doors wide open through these reuning days, with a welcome for all the eating and meeting parties. If the fathers had, so to speak, weathered the morning their lives were saved, for the afternoon was full of things to do. There was the very interesting exhibition of students' art work in the lovely Tryon Gallery, for instance, and, well, we don't know about fathers but certainly the alumnae mothers and a goodly number of aunts paddled down to the Plant House and even sauntered through the gardens. But they came back for the Orchestra concert. And such a concert! We always love to go with someone who hasn't known quite how fine our music is and consequently has her breath taken away by the lovely things she hears. It wasn't raining much when we took that heavenly path near Paradise, where the old laundry and the dump heap used to be, and went to the receptions.

Frances Valentine in their reunion report gives the delicious details but, being the author of their ivy song, she was too modest to quote it, and, although goodness knows we ought not to afford the space, a magazine like the QUARTERLY which caters

THE GARDENS AND A PEEP AT THE PRESIDENT'S HOUSE FROM PARADISE

First to the President's, where all the fathers and mothers in their Sunday best were Oh-ing and Ah-ing at the lovely view down the glade (we almost wept because the rain had beaten down that yellow rose which is our special joy), and then into the newest dormitories to greet the Dean and our faculty friends and to do some Oh-ing and Ah-ing on our own account at the lovely "signs following" of our Birthday Gift. And now that we are in the Quadrangle we may as well tell about that planting of the ivy by 1902, although it didn't happen until later when the ground was just mucky enough to make the footsteps of the class a bit squggy as they marched from Cushing around to Gardiner with a handsome ivy chain of green string with here and there (mostly there) a few daisies bunched perkily.

only to the best poetic thought can't allow this gem to perish with that daisy chain. Here it is with only an occasional lament deleted:

Back in the days of 1902—
Listen to our tale of woe—
There grew a little vine on Seelye Hall
Planted by the very best class of all.
It grew and grew—
Listen to our tale of woe.

All people walking the campus through—
Listen to our tale of woe—
Admired that vine of emerald hue,
And praised the class of 1902 . . .

One day while crawling across the dew—
Listen to our tale of woe—
A strep-to-coc-cus of hideous hue
Spied the splendid vine of 1902 . . .

He bit that vine of emerald hue—
Listen to our tale of woe—
And then he gnawed it through and through,
Though it fought like a lion it no could do—
Eheu, eheu!
Listen to our tale of woe.

But the gay old gells of 1902—
Listen to our tale of woe—
Said we'll show that bug a thing or two
We'll plant another ivy bright and new—
Hurroo, Hurroo—
Let's forget our tale of woe.

So now we bust this sod right through—
Watch our little ivy grow—
It's a tough little plant and its wants are few.
All it needs is a drink or two—
Mon doo, mon doo—
Watch our little ivy grow.

Chorus:

No more trials for these two—
The tough little vine of emerald hue
And the gay old gells of 1902—
Hurroo, hurroo—
Finis to our tale of woe.

It was, as may be imagined, very nearly the *finis* of all the onlookers and it certainly did take the application of President Burton's definition of an educated person, "one who can make transitions easily," to get us in a proper frame of mind for Organ Vespers. It was all lovely but the "Seraphic Song" of Rubenstein's with the organ, two junior soloists, a violin obbligato, and the junior choir will sing forever in our memories. And it was COMMENCEMENT MORNING. Not a brilliant sunshiny morning, to be sure, but a hopeful-sun-almost-out, coolish morning, and as long as the seniors were to be in "scholastic dusk" as to costume and the gay hoods and appurtenances of the Faculty would brighten up any landscape it didn't so much matter whether the sun sulked or not. We alumnae had a harder time than usual deciding whether to go or not to go to Commencement—there was a lure on the campus and there was a lure in Harry Emerson Fosdick! Indeed so strong a lure that alumnae seats gave out too soon and some had to be content with viewing the senior and Faculty procession, but the rest of us went decorously into John M. Greene; stood up respectfully when the seniors entered, and with them formed an audience—if not a guard—of honor through which the academic procession marched to the platform. The Reverend John Whittier Darr of the First Church offered the invocation, and, as everybody knows, Dr. Fosdick gave the Address. The President's introduction was significant. He said:

The class of 1927 has had more than usual opportunities to exercise its own judgment in making decisions and the results of this privilege are demonstrated by their choice of a Commencement speaker. I have the honor to welcome Dr. Harry Emerson Fosdick of the Park Avenue Baptist Church of New York City.

Of course you have read the Address on page 403, and understand just how strongly it appealed to that great audience. Then came the conferring of degrees. We don't want to boast, but we heard one dignitary who has attended more Commencements than we can muster in all our circling years say that in his opinion Smith College had the technique of Commencements

PRESIDENT NEILSON AND DR. FOSDICK

DR. ALICE HAMILTON, MISS JEAN MACKENZIE, MRS. ELIZABETH COOLIDGE (see page 458)

THE SMITH ALUMNAE QUARTERLY

down to a finer point than any other institution he knew. The exercises were actually interesting, he said, as well as dignified. And so they are, and we aren't ashamed to confess that thrills went down our backs and lumps were in our throats from the very moment when the President said: "The candidates for the degree of Bachelor of Arts will present themselves at this time." This year 353 young women arose (there were 464 degrees awarded to 1927, curiously enough the identical number awarded 1926 last year) but the other 111 were very fancy kinds, as you shall hear. Dean Wilson, the senior dean, arose and said with evident pride:

I have the honor to present these candidates for the degree of Bachelor of Arts and to certify on behalf of the Faculty that they have fulfilled the regulations prescribed by the College for that degree,

and the march up to the platform began, the tassels were neatly shifted—we *think* from left to right but we were not tassel-wise in our day. As girl after girl came back up the aisle, diploma in hand, she somehow unerringly caught the eye of her parents, and their tender, prideful smile told us better than any words that these academic seniors of ours are the "anointed and appointed" in many homes. And then came the "degrees with a difference." "The candidates for the degree of Bachelor of Arts *cum laude, magna cum laude, summa cum laude* draw near," and 105 young women rose; the 84 *cum laudes*, then the 19 *magna cums* marched to ever more vigorous music until Mary Pangborn, a *summa cum* (Margaret Adams, the other one, was not present) mounted the platform to a regular hallelujah chorus volume of sound. Next Dean Bernard rose and presented the Special Honors group, of which 1 with

honors, 3 with high honors, and 2 with highest honors had "fulfilled the regulations prescribed by the College," and as these last two, Elizabeth Hamburger and Caroline Wagner, went down the aisle then indeed did the

. . . great organ almost burst his pipes
Groaning for power.

The names of the *magna cums, summa cums,* and Special Honors students are on page 493 and many of them are daughters of alumnae. Twenty candidates for the degree of Master of Arts were presented by Professor Myra Sampson, and then came the "surprise" degrees—academically known as Honorary Degrees! The President said:

Elizabeth Sprague Coolidge, musician and friend of musicians, best known to Smith College as founder of the Elshuco Trio, who by her intelligent enthusiasm and her generosity has with singular success encouraged the production of distinguished musical compositions, has established at the national capital a center for the cultivation of chamber music, and has contributed to the elevation of musical taste in Europe and America, by virtue of the authority of the Commonwealth of Massachusetts, vested in the Board of Trustees of Smith College, and by them delegated to me, I confer upon you the honorary degree of Master of Arts.

And once again we applauded appreciatively at the admission of so distinguished a person into the great Smith family. There were two more honorary degrees and with the conferring of them Smith College honored herself very signally. After Mrs. Coolidge, a slight little figure arose to the President's call:

Jean Kenyon Mackenzie, author in prose and poetry, missionary, traveler, fragile in body but dauntless in spirit, who has studied the natives of West Africa with sympathy and insight, has ministered to them without condescension, and in books abounding in humor and with great charm of style has made for them countless friends among her own people. . . . I confer upon you the honorary degree of Master of Arts . . .

The honorary degree of Doctor of Science was conferred upon the third candidate as follows:

Alice Hamilton, Doctor of Medicine and honorary Master of Arts of the University of Michigan, Assistant Professor of Industrial Medicine in the Medical School of Harvard University, Member of the Health Organization of the League of Nations, a pioneer in her field of science, a humanitarian whose interests and beneficent activities are limited by no boundaries of class, race, or nation. . . .

And so, "with greatest distinction," as Miss Wilson translated the *summa cum laude*, the exercises of the Forty-Ninth Commencement came to a close, and we poured out on to the campus and straight to the magic circle of the seniors where the diplomas were changing hands so fast that in an incredibly short time everyone had her own and the grass was dotted with proud seniors posing for pictures for fond parents—but we like ours of the unbroken circle best!

THE SENIORS' MAGIC CIRCLE

Next on the program was that delightful luncheon at the President's for distinguished guests, Boards of Directors, and a few others—and the yellow rose had raised its head hopefully towards a grudging but yielding sun. And then with high anticipation everybody hurried down College Lane and over the campus to Sage Hall for .

ALUMNAE ASSEMBLY. It was a real sure enough party this year, and while of course it's true that there is one glory for the fiftieth and another glory for the tenth, when the Smith family undertakes to give a tenth birthday party to its President it is some party! Everybody who

didn't have to take a train or one of those reuning automobiles the minute the festivities were over was in her reunion regalia and over on the left were all the Fund superwomen flaunting those very same red, green, yellow, and purple mortar boards with which the Fiftieth was so gay, and the four little "Alumnae in the Egg" wore berets, and everything was so gay that we knew even before Mrs. Sawyer told us that the serious part of Commencement was over and that we had come for an hour of play. In short we looked very much like what she told our newest playmates, the Class of 1927, that we were: "effervescent, rather blatantly loyal, rather pathetically enthusiastic alumnae of Smith College"; and although at the time she said it, '27, who filled nearly the whole right section of the hall, looked a little world weary, and more than a little doubtful as to whether they wanted to play in our alumnae yard, we noticed that before we were through with the party they had perked up considerably and were effervescing a good bit themselves, so we guess that they aren't so sorry that they flipped that tassel from the left side to the right after all. As a matter of fact all but 20 of them have already joined the Alumnae Association and that's more than—no, we won't make you older ones get out your check books in the very middle of the

party. When Mrs. Sawyer invited
'27 to sing us a song we certainly were
glad they chose the one about the
Chair. It goes in part:

Oh, I wish that the trustees would give me
A chair with my name placed on it.
Oh, I'd rather not use it for research
I'd be glad of a place just to sit.

Though I've not been in college for ten years
Still my four years have not been in vain,
To increase our importance in Cambridge
And at Yale I have worked under strain.

Now I could reap the fruits of my labors
But parlors are crowded it's true.
So please listen to my entreaty
And give me a chair that holds *two!*

How the President, up there on the
platform, did chuckle at that! As
long as this was a very special kind of
party we are going to reverse the order
of proceedings a little and give out the
prizes first. For instance, who got the
alumnae song competition cup? Why
1902, to be sure, with "honorable
mention for '82 and '12'." as Mrs.
Sawyer said, and added that there was
also "an official award for '82 not only
for their musical ability but for being
the best sports on the campus." And
"a right good āward too," say we,
paraphrasing their Pinafore a wee
bit. Nineteen-two, somewhat surprised
we thought, but no end pleased, got
all its red hats and voices together and
gave us the "Roamin' in the Gloamin'"
song and now we hope it's clear why
we burst out with it, or nearly it, at
our very starting!

Style Plus, on the Campus,
That's the Class of 1902;
Style Plus, on the Campus,
In our clothes and costumes too.
We're not old and feeble yet,
We've our hair and teeth, you bet;
Oh, it's lovely—Style Plus, on the Campus.

Meeting and a-eating
With our pals in 1902,
Meeting and a-eating
All day long and all night too,
And we never eat too much
Cause we all are going Dutch—
Oh, it's lovely meeting and a-eating.

Walking and a-talking
With all the 1902s,

Talking and a-walking
In our orthopedic shoes;
Though our days of youth are past
With our arch-preserver last,
It's still lovely walking and a-talking.

Starting and a-parting
From our pals in 1902,
Starting and a-parting
Is the hardest thing we do;
But we know we'll never lack
For a pull to draw us back
To another starting and a-parting.

Nearly everyone got some kind of a
plum this Commencement time for
Mrs. Sawyer now announced that the
Costume Cup had gone to the Whoops,
the gay nineties ladies of 1917, with
honorable mention to the smart green
and white ladies of 1907 and the
modest little ask-me-anothers of '26·
And the reunion attendance cup was
won by the brown owls of '92 (maybe
being on the job day and night counts
double!) and the non-reunion attendance cup by '86·

And now, all those little details being attended to, on with the program.
Mrs. Sawyer introduced Jean Paton's
report on the Burton Memorial Fund
—or rather her presentation of the
Fund—with a delectable Scotch story
which we shall not repeat because we
can't make our typewriter roll its r's
half so burringly as Mrs. Sawyer
made her tongue. Miss Paton said:

The tangible evidences of Marion Le Roy
Burton's presidency at Smith College are
many, and it is fitting that these contributions
should be symbolized by so important a building as Burton Hall. But President Burton
made many other contributions to the College, the intangible evidence of which is in the
atmosphere about us, and, still more, perhaps,
in the lives of those who sat as students under
him. It has seemed fitting to the alumnae,
then, that President Burton should be commemorated at Smith not only by bricks and
mortar, but by a memorial not precisely intangible, yet capable of producing results
beyond those which the outer eye can see.
It has been agreed that this memorial should
take the form of a scholarship endowment
fund, and that each Burton scholar should receive a sum sufficient to defray most of her
expenses through a college year.
The Fund originated, naturally, among
those classes who were undergraduates during
Doctor Burton's presidency, but it could not

be confined to this group, for those who were in college under President Seelye feel infinite gratitude to President Burton for the delicacy and skill with which he sensed the vision of the great first president of Smith College; while those who have been students under President Neilson feel infinite. gratitude to President Burton for laying the solid foundation of the structure which his successor is now building. Alumnae of all classes agree that the chief end of this College is to add to virtue, knowledge. Alumnae of all classes unite with the faculty and other friends therefore in presenting to the College the President Burton Memorial Fund that, as certain of our own poets have said, students yet to come may "touch the hem of beauty in this place." I, therefore, Mr. President, have the honor of presenting to you on behalf of the President Burton Memorial Fund Committee, $27,600.

The President accepted the gift in the following words:

I have great pleasure on behalf of the Board of Trustees in accepting this gift, the largest scholarship endowment that we have to be used for a single scholarship. I have naturally been in consultation with this committee during the process of raising the fund and they know that the trustees, all of us, feel that no more worthy purpose could be served by this memorial than the one to which the committee has finally devoted it. You have heard during the period when this fund has been in process of being raised of the need that the College has for it. The nearer we approach to demanding from regular students the cost of education here, the more imperative it is that we should provide funds for those who are not able to meet these charges. It is essential to the continued democracy of the College; it is I am sure a purpose that Mr. Burton would have approved very warmly, and the trustees are very grateful to those who have served to perpetuate the memory of the second president of the College in a way in which he would have been delighted to be honored. It is a substantial addition to our funds for this very important purpose.

Then we heard of the Juniper Lodge Endowment Fund. Miss Caverno had already sung her paean of thanksgiving in writing (?) but Ruth French 1902 now came to the platform, "Style Plus" personified, and added a P. S. which should have been sung to Lohengrin's "Wedding March"!

The beauty of Juniper Lodge [she said] is as the holiday beauty of a June bride. The endowment fund committee as a proper parent has gathered a dowry for this bride, a substantial dowry of $33,619 for Juniper Lodge. As a representative of the committee I present this dowry to the President and Trustees of Smith College, to have and to hold from this time forward, for richer, not poorer.

Whereupon with the plaudits of the audience she handed the President one of those little pink (or yellow or green) slips which make college presidents smile the world over. And smile our President did as he said that although sometimes at Commencement he had a grievance because he was called on so often without any notice at all he would like to assure the alumnae that as long as they cared to accompany their surprises with checks he was perfectly willing to be taken unawares. And then after thanking the committee and the alumnae who had contributed he gave a brief review of the circumstances under which the College acquired Juniper Lodge, the financial problems which the acceptance of the gift had entailed, and the extraordinary usefulness of the vacation home which these last summers had demonstrated. He concluded:

Now the whole problem of its maintenance has been solved by the generosity of those who have contributed to this fund. I think this is one of the things that Smith College can rejoice in as being their exclusive possession. No other institution so far as I know has anything like it. I congratulate the College on its attainment and the trustees on being thus financially secured and their consciences being put to rest for the supply of funds for its management without drawing upon the endowment of the institution.

Well, that's one more thing checked off the College's Christmas list! And that wasn't all, either, for Mrs. Sawyer now announced two other gifts: The class of '92 has added $2500 to the graduate scholarship fund of $3000 in honor of Harriet Boyd Hawes, established five years ago, and 1922 presents the Margaret Franks Gordon Memorial Fund of $525 for experimentation in stage design under the direction of the Department of Art.

Next, with a sweeping gesture towards the gay superwomen over whom Harriet Ford was hovering like a gentle dove, Mrs. Sawyer introduced her and them as the producer and cast for a stunt which she assured us might be hard on the ear drums but was bound to entertain. And it did! All the dignitaries, meaning the President, and Mrs. Sawyer, and two or three ladies whom we as yet do not name, hastily betook themselves off the platform; Mrs. Ford ascended and gave a brief recitative, or prologue, or what you will, to put us *en rapport* with the subtleties which were to follow. She said:

At the Annual Meeting on Saturday, among many other things I said that you just could not keep an alumna of Smith College from giving money to Smith College. She will do it! Now, what happens when this generous zeal is unrestrained, when the alumnae are on the loose, if they do not have an Alumnae Fund to direct them? Each alumna will have a crop of bright ideas of things that she thinks would be very nice for the College to have. Now multiply these bright ideas by 10,325, the tally of living alumnae yesterday, and add to this 464 new bright ideas from that very bright class of 1927, and you can see that the result for the administration would probably be something resembling a three-ringed circus, a menagerie, and a riot. In order to drive these truths home we thought that we would put on something that would visualize the effects of *not* having the Alumnae Fund. So the committee knocked together a little morality play, something like "The Beaux' Stratagem," except there are no male characters and the love motif does not enter! The performers are 52 of these superwomen. The leading ladies, some of them, have dropped by the wayside already and the generous young classes, such as '27 and '01 [and her fingers weren't crossed either!] and others have stepped into the ranks. The title of the play is "Bright Ideas, or Without Benefit of the Alumnae Fund and With Benefit of the Alumnae Fund." It is in two acts. Act I—without—is full of turmoil and terror. Act II, on the contrary, is dignified, majestic, and full of lofty endeavor.

Then the gaily bedecked superwomen marched to the platform and each one had a BIG MONEY BAG

in her hand. Alice Teagle '04, a star member of the Fund Committee, waved her baton and '79 (looking amazingly like '27) said:

I want some money for some library books—

and then one after another in loud and pleading, indignant and teasing tones we heard declaimed:

80—I want some money for some landscape garden nooks.
81—I want some money to pension campus cooks.
82—And I want some money to improve the freshmen's looks.
83—I want some money for a college kettle drum.
84—I want some money to suppress chewing gum.
85—I want some money to create a vacuum.
86—And I need some money, an enor-mous sum.
87—I want some money for a housewives' school.
88—And I want some money for another swimming pool.
89—And I want some for a vestibule.
90—And I want endowment for the ten o'clock rule.
91—I want some money for a chair of charm.
92—I want some money for a fire alarm.
93—I want a little money to keep the girls from harm.
94—Oh, I want a *million* for every last school-marm.
95—Fire is a menace, let's make the roofs of slate.
96—I want some money for a John M. Greene gate.
97—Our theater needs money. It's in an awful state.
98—I want *some* money,—if I'm not too late!
99—I want money for a handsome campus wall.
00—I want some money for a recreation hall.
01—*I* think the Students' Building much too small.
02—But *I* want a store-house before next fall.
03—I want some money for some pretty campus lamps.
04—I want some silver cups for all the College Champs.
05—I want some money for lots of Week-end camps.
06—And let's give the faculty some nice new rubber stamps!
07—I want some money for some traveling scholarships.
08—Let's endow some red caps to carry all our grips.
09—No, let's endow a series of those Junior Paris trips.
10—I want *your* money. Here, fill in all these slips.
11—I want about a million to buy a lot of land.
12—I want a kitchen garden. *All* their vegetables are canned!
13—I have a *lovely* project, but *no one* will understand.
14—Let's buy up all the cigarettes and make them contraband.
15—I want some money for a first class silver screen.
16—*I* want some money to paint the greenhouse green.
17—I want to subsidize the alumnae magazine.
18—Let's subsidize everything, if you know what I mean!
19—I want an awning for the Ivy Day Parade.
20—I think the sidewalks ought all to be relaid.
21—I want a tutor for each girl with a low grade.
22—*I* don't like *any* of the suggestions *you* have made.
23—I want an elegant Alumnae Club Hotel.
24—I think some statues on the campus would be swell.
25—I *want* to give the *President* an Italian garden well.
26—And I want some money, but what for I cannot tell!
27—I want some money to start a Prix de Rome.
28—I want to give each student a long-distance telephone.
29—I want to move the college to a town that's all its own.
30—*And I want some money to send Alumnae home!*

FIFTY-TWÒ SUPERWOMEN WITH MRS. FORD AND MRS. TEAGLE, THE SUPER-
SUPERWOMEN, AT THE RIGHT

We hope we were wrong in thinking that that last line spoken by the freshman in the red beret was the loudest of all! Anyway by that time every one of the 52 was worked up into a regular frenzy and they all began to mutter, "I want some money for—I want some money for" and it got louder and louder and more insistent and more insistent and faster and faster and goodness knows there might have been a real riot if the chairman hadn't suddenly shouted, "Curtain." In Act II all was "calm, majestic, dignified." There stood the superwomen, smiles of kindness and benignance on their brows. At a signal they stepped forward two by two and with "lovely grace and pleasing gestures" (we quote the stage business, but we think the words too mild by half) they placed their overflowing money bags on the table and swept off the platform. The chairman quickly grabbed a handy poster on which was a dollar sign and a figure one and more ciphers than even a Smith alumna ever saw, and declaimed in loud and ringing tones:

One hundred million dollars for what the College says the College wants!

After the tumult and the shouting had died she said, perhaps by way of an epilogue, that although that colossal sum was only a prophecy the class of '80 had already made a gift without being asked; the class of '86 had pledged 100% of the members present; an '87 member had given $100 and so had a member of '09 so "with $345 as a little pebble the avalanche has begun!"

Maybe we can call that stunt the "cake" part of the President's birthday cake, for to tell any president that his alumnae body proposes to supplement the bread and butter budget with additional funds must seem like promising a bit of cake on each Commencement, and it's up to us to see that it isn't a one-egg cake either! But as far as this particular Birthday Cake was concerned, what we were now looking for was the frosting! So everybody calmed down, the celebrities went back to the platform, and Mrs. Sawyer turned to one of those ladies who up to this time had taken no part in the celebration, and said:

I am not familiar with the popular college songs of the time when Miss Comstock was your Dean, but I feel fairly sure that one of them began, "Here's to our Ada, We would not trade 'er." Here she is, not as President of Radcliffe or even as Trustee or ex-Dean of Smith, but just as an alumna of Smith College.

And in the course of time Miss Comstock was able to make herself heard! We confess right here that entirely contrary to our editorial practice we did not send these words of hers for her O.K. And the reason we didn't is because we were in perfect terror lest she should change even one of them. What she said was so perfect, so satisfying to us all, that we simply refused to take a chance, and if she objects—but she won't, so why worry! She looked at the President (and she and the president are such friends that we are going to

commit another editorial crime and reprint a picture that we published just a few short years ago) and said:

Someone told me once about a college professor of one of our universities who was rebuked by his wife for gossiping about the president. "My dear," he said, "the president of this university is permitted to make speeches in public about education, about the way we teach young people, to point out our defects as well as our occasional successes. He talks to the public; he talks to the alumnae; and once a year at the expense of the university he is able to print a report in which he quite lets himself go. Our only redress is to get together occasionally in the club and talk about him." Now *we* have a president who takes all of the privileges mentioned. He prints a report every year; he makes speeches—good speeches, startling speeches. If I talk too long to-day it will

be because I am afraid of what he will say when I stop. He made a speech not long ago at the inauguration of the president of a woman's college. He tried to describe to this young president what she would probably have to endure from the various groups with which she would be associated. The students came off easily; the trustees "not so good"; the faculty and the alumnae—it may comfort you to know that he said positively he would not go so far as Will Rogers who says that college students are all very well, but they should be killed before they become alumnae.

Now, this is a family party. It is as private an occasion as we are ever likely to have, considering our numbers, and I propose that we get even to-day by talking about the President. I am going to ask Miss Goodwin, who has known Mr. Neilson a long time and who has associated with herself other people who have known him, to set the ball rolling.

Miss Goodwin, who was the second of the three hitherto unnamed ladies on the platform, rose and read to the President the resolutions printed on the first page, which we had passed at the Association meeting on Saturday. She read them very beautifully, bringing out so many things that we wanted him to know that when she came to the closing sentences, "May he have a long continuance of happy life and successful effort for the College! And to this end we pledge him our loyal support and unfeigned affection," we rose spontaneously and with great applause. Miss Comstock picked up the ball instantly and gave it another toss with

Those opposed? I think the ayes have it. I am reminded of something that happened after Mr. Neilson had been here about four years. There was a convention of student government officials at a neighboring college, and the president of our student government association went as a delegate. When she came back she came into my office to tell me about the affair, and during our conversation I asked her what she thought of the college where they had been entertained. "It is a funny college," she said. "Funny," I said, "funny in what way—funny buildings?" "No, it was beautifully equipped." "Funny students?" "No, very nice girls." "Were you entertained in a queer way?" "No, delightful hospitality." "Well, what was there funny about it?" I said. She thought a long while and then produced this reason: "It seemed to me," she said, "that they were not proud of their president." I may say that she belonged to a class that came back wearing Scotch caps and plaids and singing, "We love a laddie." Now Smith is not a funny college according to that definition.

At the risk of infringing upon those standards of good taste of which Mr. Fosdick spoke this morning, I think it would be pleasant to be a little more personal, to go over in some detail, in a thorough-going way, some of our reasons for being proud of our president. [She certainly was getting back at him.] Well, we are proud of his renown as a scholar. We all blush modestly when Shakesperean scholarship is mentioned. We know who is who in that field, and we know that other people know. We are very proud of his reputation as a teacher in six institutions—Bryn Mawr, Columbia, Barnard, Harvard, Radcliffe, and Smith. I had known that he was reputed to be a great teacher, but I never knew quite the extent of his reputation until this very spring. A candidate for a position in the Radcliffe Club of Boston, in the ballot which was gotten out in which there were the pedigrees of each candidate, alleged as one of her reasons for being elected to the office that she had been a member of Professor Neilson's class in the criticism of poetry in 1908. But quite seriously, one of the things for which we have to be most grateful to President Neilson is that somehow or other—and I cannot imagine how he has managed it—he has found time to use his teaching gift in Smith College.

We are proud of his reputation as an administrative officer. Every little while in the papers you see a list of great administrative officers in the colleges and universities of this country, and although the names in general are those of the presidents of the great universities, the name of the President of this College is almost never lacking. We have reason to be nervous when those chairs are vacant.

Most of us as presidents of colleges owe whatever distinction we have to the institutions with which we are connected, but in this case, fellow alumnae, it is our President who confers distinction on us. We like very much, I think I may say, his attitude toward women. Now I have thought a great deal about how to describe that attitude, and this is the nearest I can come to it—except for a slight flirtatiousness, he hasn't any! About that flirtatiousness I may remark that not long ago he said to President Woolley that he was really a very shy man. She replied, "Mr. Neilson, I should be afraid to meet you if you were any less shy."

But it is true that I have never seen the slightest reason to suppose that he thought the education of girls the least bit less important than the education of boys. He never discounts an idea because it is a woman's idea. He never has any of that uneasy desire to assert superiority which we sometimes meet. To come right down to the point— you see I have been getting on more and more dangerous ground all the time—I am afraid that our emotions as far as President Neilson is concerned are not Platonic. I do not know whether it is more creditable to Mrs. Neilson or to us that we can be so fond of her.

Mr. Terry says that when Miss Ellen Terry was in her prime every sensible young man proposed to his beloved in some such words as these: "Since I cannot have Miss Terry, may I have you?." It almost goes without saying that every intelligent gentlewoman who is a graduate of Smith College must respond to the beloved in some such words as these: "Since I cannot have President Neilson I suppose I can put up with you." There was the word "esteem" in those resolutions, but it is a cold word. I am *devoted* to this President. What about you?

Well, at this point she flung out her arms towards us, and we just naturally went quite wild with our enthusiastic assent to her declaration. And we may add that Mrs. Neilson sat in the front row and never gave the slightest quiver of jealousy!

On this tenth birthday of our devotion [Miss Comstock went on] it seems inevitable that there should be a present. We wanted to get something personal. Somebody thought of a locket with all our hair! [The President looked as though he were going to turn and run. It was almost worse than that moment at the Fiftieth Birthday Party when he suggested that he might have to kiss the whole family.] But I said, No, that is mid-Victorian. So we tried to think what a president would find most useful. Something for his desk? College presidents are never at their desks. Something for his home? College presidents are never at home. What article after all would be most useful to a thoroughly modern college president? Well, you will see.

And at this point somebody (we were too excited to see who it was) wheeled a baggage truck on to the platform and on it was a be-au-ti-ful suitcase, one of those revelation varieties which only the very great ought to carry. Talk about surprises! The President looked as though he had been suddenly stricken dumb, and before he could recover, Miss Comstock proceeded to say:

Mr. President, lest you should think that this is a going-away present I wish to remark that inside it is the price of a return trip ticket—a thousand dollars in gold, a hundred dollars for each year of your presidency, to indicate the 100% of happiness you have brought us—in gold because we think that is what you are. We hope you will use this bag for good times as well as in pursuit of your official duties, and the one thing we ask of you is that you will always come back.

If anyone can think of any new way in which to say that we applauded and that as we did so *both* our hands were on our heart we beg her to step to the typewriter. We are quite beyond words.

And as for the President—he, too, was more moved than we have ever seen him as he said:

Mrs. Sawyer, Miss Comstock, Miss Goodwin: It was a rash remark that I made a little while ago about being willing to be taken unawares. I have been put into many situations of emergency since I came to Smith College—worst of all at class suppers—and have spoken a vast deal of nonsense on these occasions when a college president was supposed to be on tap, but I don't think I have ever found a situation quite so difficult as I find it now. I cannot pretend that I am not deeply moved by what Miss Goodwin and Miss Comstock have said. I cannot pretend that their gracious goodwill hasn't carried them in their enthusiasm beyond that point of severe intellectual discrimination and exactitude which I have tried to impress upon the younger students of this institution. There is—you of the class of 1927 know—surrounding any profoundly felt fact a kind of aura of emotion that really does not falsify but only beautifies. I am anxious to believe that there is a foundation of fact in what you have been saying. I am glad that I know that there is something of emotion surrounding it, and I am even more grateful for the feeling than I am for the recall of the facts.

I don't think anybody could have been treated better by an institution than I have been treated by Smith College, and it is all nonsense to talk about who confers distinction on whom. Nine and a half years ago, during my first winter here, I went down to Cambridge, and crossing the Harvard yard I met Professor George Herbert Palmer whose advice I had disregarded in coming to Smith College. He met me and asked me, "Well, how is it going?" trying to be pleasant and forget that I was here against his will; and I said, "Suspiciously smoothly." He said, "Yes, it would be that way the first year, but the third year you will begin to have difficulties and by the tenth year you will be called elsewhere or fired." Professor Palmer was correct at every point. The first year was very smooth, thanks to Miss Comstock. The third year I had difficulties but survived. The tenth year of course both things couldn't easily happen, but one of them did, and I am still here!

The action of the trustees on Saturday in urging with what under other circumstances would have been suspicious warmth the taking of a longer vacation than usual, and the presentation of this glorious object here, would make a more suspicious man doubtful of your motives. I have, however, Miss Comstock's word as to what this actually means, and I always take Miss Comstock's word on anything. So even if I am late in the fall I am coming back. It is hardly any use to repeat what I tried to say at chapel with regard to giving me credit for things that you have done and the trustees have done and the faculty have done. I know more about you all than any one of these groups because I have received coöperation from all of you, and in this case my story is the true one. So you can thank the trustees and the faculty and the faculty and the trustees can thank you, and I am willing as a member of the trustees and as a member of the faculty and as an alumna or alumnus to take my share with each of these bodies. The only body I am really never a member of is the undergraduate body, and in some cases they have made amends as soon as they have become alumnae.

Your secretary suggested that I should say over again at this assembly some of the things, the high points, of the last chapel. I was doubtful about that advice and now I can see what it was that she mercifully meant. She meant really, "Do not trouble preparing a different speech for the alumnae assembly because you won't have a chance to make it."

I am perfectly incapable of matching the eloquence and wit of the previous speakers. I am equally incapable of telling you what I feel about the way you have all behaved to me at this the end of my tenth year here. I presume I have the same feeling as most people accustomed to speak in public who find that they can pretty well say what they want when the things they talk about do not matter to them, and they fall down completely when the things do matter; but I want to thank the alumnae and the faculty and the trustees—and I would the undergraduates if they were here—on behalf of my family as well as myself for the possibility of a life as interesting and as rich and surrounded by as much human warmth as anyone can hope to find on this earth.

And then we sang to him, but something in our throats interfered with the tune and anyway he knew what we meant. Something had to happen and happen quick to relieve the tension, and something did! in fact, two somethings. First, a boy (anyway she looked like a boy) rushed down the aisle with a great bunch of telegrams, honest to goodness, *bona fide* telegrams from the Smith clubs, and, second, the Class of '76 in the person of Florence Bliss '18 rose to the emergency. Take it from us, you can bank on '76 to put the finishing touch on any little party that Smith College wants to pull off, and, as we hinted some 20 pages back, when it comes to making presents, birthday presents in particular, she simply can't be beat. Listen:

On this memorable occasion—ten years of faithful duty—we 76ers wish to have an inconspicuous, but sincere, part in expressing our undying loyalty and good fellowship to President Neilson.

While for several good reasons: the Alumnae Fund, the unpaid pledges, taking daughters of friends and classmates to dinner, our gift is perhaps not so startling as it might be, nevertheless, it is filled with tradition, antique but not antiquated, astonishing but not loud. As Betsie Ross used various pieces of clothing to make the American flag, we have taken our oldest plaid shawl to fashion your gift. The shawl was worn by the original 76er herself, and therefore holds in its folds the traditions of that organization. We guarantee that when wearing this gift you can be spotted on any golf links, campus, or public thoroughfare. It is distinguishing but not marring.

President Neilson, behold our gift, together with our loyalty, sincerity, and good fellowship.

And with that she pulled out of her hand bag a gorgeous plaid necktie and a pair of plaid golf stockings that beyond a doubt were guaranteed to make the wearer's feet scream when they touched the ground. Never have we seen such plaid. Nay, more, never have we known there was such plaid, but '76 knew, and loyal to the plaidie in themselves they brought it to their President's feet.

What could the President say, when he could say anything at all?

I have found [said he] by the experience of many Commencements that in dealing with the Class of '76, the only safe repartee is silence.

And that was the end of the party; and we simply ask you, would you believe that any college, even Smith College, could have two such joyous, sparkling birthday parties as our fiftieth and our tenth in the space of two short years? Whatever we are going to do to maintain our present exalted level only the gods know, the gods and maybe the superwomen, for perhaps in the sweet bye and bye they will come bearing that $100,-000,000 for the College for what the College wants and then, Ah then, what a meeting there will be! We got their pictures—by dint of sheer bullying—as they left the party; poor dears, they wanted to put in a few last hours of this last reunion day, as did all the rest of us. But how few they were! Just another glimpse of Paradise where we could hear the "shallow water's tune" as it slipped over the dam, just one more little visit under the campus elms with friends from whom we hated to part; perhaps, if we were lucky, just a look at the lovely senior class sitting in "rainbow scheme" over their class supper; and then—well, then all those very new alumnae and all we older ones who have come back and back and back as the June days call went out through our college gates and through the happy river meadows; but as we went we all, from the oldest to the youngest, sang a little sadly and a little gladly:

STARTING and a-parting
From Smith College and from you,
Starting and a-parting
Is the hardest thing we do;
But we know we'll never lack
For a pull to draw us back
To another starting and a-parting.
                    E. N. H.

Reunion Reports

1882—THE FORTY-FIFTH

OUR forty-fifth reunion brought together a goodly number of '82' graduates and exes (we have forgotten any difference now) and three who graduated in other classes but spent much of their college life with us. One "ex" came who had never reuned with us before, and we hope she had such a good time that she'll come to our fiftieth, and as many more as we have.

Since we were fortunate enough to be the fourth class to graduate, we were the oldest reuning class and led the Alumnae Parade, next to the officers of the Association. We thought we bore the banner for devotion, with Gertrude Palmer McClanahan coming from the Pacific Coast, till we learned that one alumna came to her reunion from Hawaii. We didn't get the cup for attendance either, though we generally have it in non-reunion years. Our "conch shell" parasols and our stools (how even the younger alumnae envied us those) still served as our "costume."

Were we not a little audacious to enter the song competition? Annie Jackson's rhymes to the tune of "Little Buttercup" received much applause though the cup went to better singers than we, or a better song. We were rewarded at the Alumnae Assembly for our efforts by "honorable mention" and were called "the best sports on the campus." (Perhaps it's not best to analyze that compliment too closely; we'll take it at its face value.)

It was a pretty strenuous program, from the play Thursday to the serenade Monday night. Then add to the regular doings conferences on business matters, song practice, the planting of an ivy at Gardiner House, a tour of the Library with Nina Browne, an inspection of the new houses around the Quadrangle, a talk on her Constantinople experiences by Alice Norton, and our talk-fest Sunday night, of which more anon. Katherine McClellan proved a most firm and efficient manager—in fact something of a Mussolini. But what should we have done without her and our most helpful committee!

You can imagine the supper out at Mother Sophia's Friday night around tables beautified by the flowers of our class colors which were the gift of Ellen Cheever Rockwood, and the charming favors made by Edith Leach. President and Mrs. Neilson looked in on us (President Neilson, by the way, seems to be devotedly loved); we heard letters from the absentees and talked about them; we stood in silence thinking of those who had left us (our Treasures, Molly Gulliver called them); we had various toasts; in a brief business meeting reëlected our officers, and then took possession of our special "bus" for a not-too-quiet ride home.

Another occasion not to be forgotten was the cozy supper at Alice's pretty little apartment, with our "class baby" as waitress. Here we gathered around Professor Tyler, the only one of our teachers left in Northampton, and sang to him the songs that Isabel McKee Hidden and Annie Jackson and Grace Blanchard had written. (You'll find them in the Robin when it comes to you again.)

That was a brilliant idea of Katherine's, to have us form a circle around Mrs. Ingle's open fire Sunday night and "have a talk." Each one must in turn report on herself. If she shrank away and declared that her life was quite prosy and she had nothing to report, we cried "questionnaire" and proceeded to bombard her with such questions that the most incorrigible modesty had to give way under the pressure.

The hospitality of the Washburn House as dispensed by those two kind ladies, Mrs. Ingle and Professor Cobb, was all that heart could wish. Some of the "girls" were back in their own rooms or with the roommate of college days.

The weather—except on Sunday—was perfect, and the campus never lovelier, with its blossoming shrubs and ivied walls and lawns of vivid emerald. Perhaps next to the renewed friendships the memory of college we shall carry away will be that procession in the Saturday morning sunshine—the juniors in their pastel-colored gowns carrying the long ivy chain; the seniors in their simple white crêpe dresses, not too scant or short, each carrying her long-stemmed rose. Girlhood still spells idealism and we of '82 like to think that those roses symbolize high purposes such as were set before us by our own President Seelye and have always been upheld by his successors.   E. L.

1887's FORTIETH

TO 1927 the number is appalling of course, poor young things as they are, but to us it represents riches, the joys of the oft-repeated reunions, the accumulated jokes and laughter and tender memories, closer friendships, ever growing pride in our college. No, we don't envy the new alumnae. Their coffers are empty as yet, ours are full to bursting.

Some of us were wise and fortunate enough to come early, giving ourselves time to forget the work-a-day world outside and to become once more really at home in the "Happy Valley" before Commencement actually began. For us there were walks through the shady streets as well as about the campus, a visit to the flowers in Childs Park, a long morning in Paradise—lovelier always than we remember it—a pilgrimage to Sophia's home, and a memorable drive to the Pelham hills on a perfect afternoon. There was time too to enjoy quietly the dignity and charm of the Tryon Gallery and to see faculty friends.

With the Last Step Sing and the Last Chapel the Commencement program really began and the pace of everyone quickened. Eighty-sevens came one by one to headquarters in Park Annex where our sign was stretched between pillars. There were ten of us to attend Senior Dramatics, fifteen for the delectable and chatty supper at The Whale in Goshen to which "Little Grace" and Annie Van carried us Friday evening.

Earlier in the day some of us had tried to learn how women were coördinating their interests, the same being set forth at a luncheon given by the famous Institute. Eleanor Lord carried off the honors of that occasion by the fine form of her report.

Of course Saturday was the day of days, one long varied program that filled every minute. As everyone will report, the weather was all an ideal June day could be. We went gayly forth in the modest glory of our yellow tunics and white parasols and, marching almost at the head of the procession—only '82 and '86 ahead of us—felt no envy of the scarlet interrogation points, the airplanes, or the pirates behind us. Did we not stand for review directly in front of the President and Dean? Repetition never blurs the beauty of the Ivy Parade. Every year its picture seems fairer than the year before—and we go on to Alumnae Meeting glad to have seen it once more.

By mid-afternoon we started out again, first for the Symphony Concert, and then for the ceremonial planting of our second class ivy on Gardiner House. Bessie Gill as president performed the actual labor under the expert advice of our horticulturist, Helen Holmes, while one or two brought water in mugs to lave the roots and several willing feet firmed the earth about the plant, supposed to be an "ampelopsis"—though opinions differed. Mae Shute's Ivy Song was read, that being deemed more prudent than singing it, and as Alice Gale could not remember the text of her former oration the program was informally closed by the cheerful wish: "Here's hoping you may flourish as our first ivy has on College Hall!"

Class supper was appropriately held in The Manse where Martha Woodruff's great grandparents were married. Nineteen sat down around the yellow candles and roses, 15 graduates out of 34. We regretted the absence of the nineteen and sent our special greetings to those who were ill or had illness at home. Just as the program was to begin President Neilson looked in upon us long enough for a few cordial words and a few autographs, obtained under partially false pretences as admission tickets to the campus. "All's fair—" at reunions. After that President Gill introduced one of our travelers, Helen Gamwell, who with her husband, Major Budd, has been as she said "round the corner" from Sinn Fein excitements in Ireland, revolutions in Portugal, and strike mobs in Germany. Eleanor struck a less serious note in a "pome" which proved beyond doubt that '87, far from ever being mid-Victorian as dates might indicate, was always radically inclined, even in the matter of bobbed hair. Helen Holmes, for two years hostess at International House of the League for Peace and Freedom, in Geneva, shared with us in delightful fashion incidents of the life there, its many-sided contacts and its contributions to brotherhood. Elizabeth Mason performed the immemorial rite of reading '87's freshman list and Jessie Carter closed the program with some graceful verses looking backward and forward down the years.

The light was still clear in the west when we adjourned to the campus, but lanterns were lighted and the competitive sing was under way. You who have been at reunions know the beauty of the lights along the walks, among the trees, up and down the slopes. Some of you have seen the newer features: the lighting of the Island and the singing by the Glee Club on floats—a bit straight out of

Fairyland. You'll not wonder that at least two of '87 did not leave till the lanterns were nearly all down.

What an uncompromising rain that of Sunday was! How many times we put on raincoats and unfurled umbrellas going and coming to and from S. C. A. C. W. and Ginling meetings and the various receptions of the President and faculty we cannot count, but nobody minded a little dampness. '87 gathered around an open fire at headquarters in a vacant period between social functions and held a class meeting. We missed our president, Bessie Gill, called home by illness, but we approved a full treasury and the plan for the Alumnae Fund—one member giving $100 as a starter for it—and we took the bold step, considering our size, of deciding to establish a scholarship fund, hoping to do this in ten years. A memorial for Carrie Day from her sisters will form a nucleus. Lillian Fay will continue to guide the flight of our Robin. In the evening Eleanor gathered the out-of-towners in her pleasant rooms and there the classics were revived: "Gentle Jane" and the immortal tale of little Fanny and her skipping rope. Old stories and new were told and Jessie gave us a mirth-provoking monologue of the Christmas distractions of a young mother.

On Monday with diminished numbers but continued enthusiasm we sat in high places at Commencement, enjoying the reward of our years, and last of all we shared the thrills of a most spirited Alumnae Assembly. As the scribe dashed up the hill in pursuit of suitcase and hat box, the strains of "Alma Mater" followed her, and she sang in her heart:

Here's to '87
She's the best class under Heaven

—and the earliest to say so. Listen to the conclusion of the whole matter: Come back *early* to Commencement if possible, but Come Back! It will give you new vision, fresh courage, and joyful memories. H. B. C. P.

HIGH SPOTS OF THE '92 REUNION

TO begin at the end, we won the cup for attendance. Forty-one strong we were, including our long-lost Isabel—Strong as ever. As usual, we flaunted our good wood-brown, now personified in the beautiful little owls, miraculously created by our super-versatile president. They perched on our shoulders in the Alumnae Parade as we marched in classic costume carrying our owl banner and also our big and impressive motto: Πᾶσιν Καλῶς Χρῆσθαι. Unique is more than ever the word for '92.

A double-starred event was the class supper. Florence Barker Came, fresh from the circumnavigation of Africa, presided delightfully. "Wail me the woes" of a shackled historian not permitted to report the speeches of Elsie Jordan, Laura Wild, Elizabeth Underwood, Bertha Stone, May Stoddard Yeomans, Eleanor Daggett, Helen Nichols Smith, Isabel Strong, all of whom showed that '92 is tinglingly alive. In the general talk that followed Lena Chase gave glimpses of her Elizabeth's experiences as a Junior in France. There were also greetings from absentees, including Elizabeth Fisher Clay whom we had so hoped to see. And we stood with bowed heads to hear the list of those from whom there could be no message—now lengthened by the names of Mary Rankin Wardner and Grace Dennen. The table was beautiful with Harriet James's flowers and the surrounding faces made lovely by experience. We were disappointed not to have the greeting of President Neilson, who was unfortunately in Amherst, but we joyfully welcomed the songful '76.

Our class meeting was a triumph of parliamentary procedure. We dodged all reconsideration by skilfully-worded amendments and finally voted to add our new gift of $2500 to the $3000 already devoted to the Harriet Boyd Hawes Scholarship. For a moment Lyn lost her self-control in stating the motion that hereafter our reunion costume be "restricted to accessories." Who says we're not modern? Note: Do we really need a gavel? Lyn finds a shoetree so satisfactory! Good news! The present officers will serve again. May their responsibilities weigh as lightly as the owls upon their shoulders! Last of all we voted for a loose-leaf class book—not illustrated—to be compiled for our next reunion. So let everyone take account of stock!

At the Phi Kappa Psi meeting Saturday afternoon Elsie Pratt Jordan and Caroline Steele, in behalf of themselves and Mary Nixon (unavoidably absent) presented the Society with a Medici print as a memorial to Mary Rankin Wardner, one of the five '92 founders.

Other delights were a tea with Laura Wild and her dog at South Hadley, a so-called picnic supper—really a party—at Laura

Scoville's on Round Hill, and a Sunday morning breakfast together with seven daughters and a niece at the Hotel Northampton. Here Harriet James gave us a thrilling talk on the Y. W. C. A. for which she is an enthusiastic worker.

Monday morning we planted our ivy on the Cushing House. The ceremony began with near-hysterics led by Katherine Upton, who gasped out, as Lyn gingerly walked the edge of the cellar window and plunged out of sight behind an evergreen to dig the hole below our numerals on the wall, "It's so exactly like us!" When these preliminaries were safely over, we sang—surprised at remembering the words so well—"The ivy is a winsome thing." Then we gathered close for Cora's "oration" which in wisdom and humor exceeded even our expectations. Fortunately for us all it will be printed later. After the following "ivy poem" by Caroline Steele we sang "Fair Smith" and moved to headquarters to join the Commencement procession.

IVY POEM

Our memories cling to the past
Like ivy to the wall;
And lovingly we plant this vine
That we may here recall
The gracious charm, the quiet strength,
Of her whose honored name
Distinguishes this college house,
Reminder of her aim.
Who lived serene the scholar's life
Uncramped by pedantry,
Keeping true-poised her womanhood
In fine simplicity.
So let us plant an ivy here
To give this wall a grace
Of lovely light and shadow like
The beauty of her face.

Affectionate cheers for our three lovely daughters, Elizabeth Chase, Catherine Cole, and Lucia Jordan, whom we saw take their degrees. They are worthy of their mothers— "nuff sed."

Last of all the Alumnae Assembly crystallized every floating particle of our enthusiasm for Smith College with a conviction that we shall continue

Loyal and true
To '92
And to fair Smith for aye!   C. L. S.

THE THIRTIETH OF '97

"THE joy of comradeship" was ours as '97 gathered for her 30th. Headquarters at 9 Seelye were all that Mary Rockwell and Martha Cutler could make them. Silhouettes of the '97 girl and the 1927 woman, done by Martha, flanked the clock on which at least 75 were indicated as reuning. Everything for our guidance and comfort was there. At informal teas there on Thursday and Friday we greeted and visited.

We were impressed with our age when we marched among *early* classes in the Alumnae Parade on Saturday morning. But when the band began to play, we stepped forth in yellow and white feeling as young as ever. Grace Kelley in a '97 Ivy Day dress was lovely, and Florence Clarke wore majestically the Sheik's costume of our '22 reunion. Many yellow banners with reminiscent legends educated the onlookers. And weather this Ivy Day! It was honestly "a rare June day." Our throats ached with the beauty of it all as the sunshine played under the elms upon white-clad seniors and pastel-tinted junior ushers. How much more the girls of to-day adorn the campus than did we in our big-sleeved, much-ruffled "white muslins and serges," trailing over the ground!

Of course we attended en masse the Alumnae Association meeting Saturday morning (except mothers of seniors) and in groups many other gatherings that day. But none brought the joy that came with Class Meeting Saturday afternoon. With E. Cole in the chair and Lucy at her side, business went through with unusual finish. We voted our reunion gift to the Burton Fund. We stood in silence in memory of the dear ten who have left us in the last five years. Elsie Tallant, as general chairman for reunion, called for sub-chairmen's reports, though their works had spoken for them eloquently. New officers were elected, and old thanked in appropriate style.

The only flaw in class supper Saturday evening was its limited time. The daisies and buttercups, gathered by sons and daughters, made lovely the tables in Edwards Church parlors, and as we sat about them we did indeed look good to each other. "J. D.," as toastmistress, needs no comment, nor does the program planned by her and Anne Barrows. A reunion ode sent by Mary Barrows voiced the thoughts of us all. Selma Erving '27 gave us a lovely daughter's-greeting. Elsie Tallant, Genevieve Knapp, Clem Judd, and Nan Branch made delightful and characteristic contributions, and Mary Lewis Leitch read one of her recently published poems. Muriel Haynes '04 generously came to us with a short film of President Seelye, and Anne beautified it further by brief words, likening him to a river and quoting the line he loved—"the glory of still going on." Reassuring was Mrs. Scales's talk on administering the social life of the college in these days when girls really do go out into "the wide, wide world," and must learn to meet it. President Neilson's welcome visit was too hurried for our liking, for we always want to hear him talk.

Throughout our supper, the strains of ' Alma Mater" came to us from the chime. We would gladly have lingered, but we couldn't miss the beauty of the illuminated campus, nor the lovely singing of the Glee Club. The colored lights on the Island made a wonderful background for the girls, and Venus hung above them in perfect splendor. Later we took our part in song from the steps of Seelye. We had good songs and they say we performed better than usual. Why not, when a college daughter had directed our practice?

We had a family supper at The Manse Sunday night, with dear old faculty members, charming sons and daughters, and fine husbands as guests. And Jean Mackenzie joined us too (see Commencement write-up).

Monday morning we stood in the Quadrangle while E. Cole planted a new class ivy. We sang "Alma Mater"; Ada read Agnes Hunt's ivy song of '97, a beautiful thing, we know. And Nan read a poem written for this new planting. (Copies of both coming later.) An inexorable usher's wand separated the lucky from the unlucky in the Commencement parade, as we reached John M. Greene Hall, so only a few of us saw 1927 in cap and gown or heard Dr. Fosdick's splendid appeal.

It was all so wonderful—the physical beauty everywhere, the fineness of everything and everybody, the companionship—that we are certain our 30th was the finest ever. Don't miss the 35th!

A. C. C.

1902

"THE very best reunion ever" seemed to be the sentiment of every 1902er who came back for our 25th, and while the words of a disinterested male observer whom Maroe Sater picked up at Boyden's who said he had "never seen a better preserved group of middle-aged women," was not just the way

"us girls" would have put it, still it's evidence that we made a hit.

We lived in the new dormitories on the Quadrangle where (quite different from our day!) every floor abounded in bath tubs, showers, wash bowls, hair washing arrangements, and patent tooth-brushing bowls (which we never did exactly master in our short stay). Lots of members and former members of the class who had not been back for recent reunions turned up like prodigal daughters and you bet we were glad to see them all. We had, all told, nearly a hundred here. Fun started Thursday night with Senior Dramatics, which were good, but couldn't touch the famous first performance of "Romeo and Juliet" which lasted till 1 A.M.

Our magnificent appearance in the Ivy Parade was conclusive evidence that costumes should *not* be given up by the older classes. Our smart sport hats of red straw, our red hoods obviously indicating some high degree, and our red-covered song sheets with floating ribbons brought forth much well-deserved praise (see above).

We had class suppers every day, one on top of Mt. Holyoke, along with Amherst 1912, and two in basements, so our average was right on the level. We had a lot of grand husbands along—I've no doubt that Carol Childs, Helen Durkee, Eda Heinemann, Jessie Wadsworth, Bertha Prentiss, and Faith thought it much safer to keep them where they could watch over them. Even so, they were not too safe. Bertha, however, slipped up when she looked over the napkin rings and not being able to find one marked "Prentiss" thought she was left out till Maude pointed out one marked "Webber," which she took, blushing like a bride. One thing, however, struck sadness to the heart of our President and that was the alarming percentage of illiteracy in the class. Staggered by the multitude of dumb questions put to her every hour, she at last shrieked despairingly at everyone who approached with an inquiring look, "Can't *you* read?" Apparently we couldn't.

We had never thought we were so much on singing, but "practice makes perfect," and Ethel Bradley kept us at song rehearsal ignoring our groans and protests till the very hour of the cup competition, and our reward came in having the announcement made at the Alumnae Assembly that the cup for the best reunion song had been won by 1902,

Sunday night we had our own Ivy Parade and planting. We didn't advertise it too much for we didn't want to spoil the seniors' ivy exercises by comparison. Still, we had a good many spectators. Forming at Cushing House, the Ivy Procession, with a dandy daisy chain of green string and tufts of daisies (just to be different from the seniors) wound around the Quadrangle. To provide for the contingency of *no* audience we had a chorus of stout (voiced) singers to sing to the rest of the class our lovely and spirited ivy song. Half way round, Mary Woodbury, as the spirit of 1902, clad in a tight and trailing fawn-colored skirt and a bright purple velvet jacket (it was the coat to her "best suit" sophomore year) and picture hat met the procession and marched at the head. Katie Holmes, at the proper moment, thrust the ivy into the ground, christened and gave it its first drink with a strictly prohibition bottle of White Rock, and as our song concluded we marched back to Cushing to the songs of 1902 days. Long may we remember them!

Because successful celebrations are always the result of careful planning and because we could think of no one who would keep us together in the next five years as well as Maude has, we walked right over her protest and made her president again. And if you who didn't come back want a really good heart-warming three or four days, be here in 1932.

F. W. V.

1907–1927, OUR TWENTIETH

"AREN'T you proud that it's twenty years?" demanded one of those grand examples of the good old brand of class spirit, in the tone of one whose "head is bloody but unbobbed." As a matter of record, this historian cannot truthfully report that all of us in 1907 have arrived at this stage of spiritual triumph, but at least most of us have attained acceptance of the fact itself, for, accepting the universe along with Margaret Fuller, there's no use balking at the last twenty years of it. But even middle age brings its consolations. While one is 37, or 38, or even 39, one can still fool oneself into believing that she still retains some semblance of youth. However long we may hover on the ghastly brink of forty, once the dread plunge is taken one begins to discover that it isn't so frightfully awful to be middle-aged. Cheer up, then, O younger grad! If you can survive the first

fifteen years, you'll find that the 20th is rather jolly after all.

That of 1907 began auspiciously with a cheerful class supper on Friday night, attended by 97 of our venerable selves, showing that at 40 plus we still like something that we can put our teeth into. For the occasion, the class antiquarians produced treasured costumes of the vintage of 1907, and actually wore them, though in some instances a veil, as it were, had to be drawn over rear hooks and buttons. Surveying these proofs of what we must have looked like twenty years ago, we found ourselves in the position of the rustic who viewed the camel and announced that there ain't no such animal. One is led to the conclusion that in 1907 the brain seldom exceeded the waist in girth, a statement that readers may take any way that they like. Besides the costume parade, other intellectual features included a speech from Ethel (Woolverton) Cone, who brilliantly applied the analytics of modern pedagogy to the costume-mysteries of our college past, while Marion (Carr) Condit explained wittily how Phi Beta Kappa hadn't assisted her in bringing up her children. Of course, Ruth (Cowing) Scott presided, assisted ably by Marjorie (Comstock) Hart as chief stunt-master and Dorothy (Evans) Noble as toastmistress. An unexpected pleasure was an informal visit from President Neilson who furnished a tempting sample of the "damned charm" celebrated by his compatriot, Sir J. Barrie. It may be stated confidentially that President Neilson appeared to enjoy the costume parade. Also it may be mentioned privately that although nothing stronger than asparagus was consumed at this feast of reason, nevertheless several otherwise brilliant members of the class forgot to turn the lights on their cars, and later discovered them officially ticketed for having been left contrary to the Northampton traffic rules.

Saturday morning found us out bright and early, ready for the Alumnae Parade, in our class costume, which was by direction white dresses fifteen inches from the ground (count them), white shoes, and green stockings. Nifty green turbans and shopping bags completed an ensemble well adapted to conceal the ravages of time. The morning breezes caressed our elderly shoulders somewhat coolly at first, but later in broad sunshine we could read our parade mottoes, proclaiming among other things the fact that 1907 now averages 1⅗ child per graduate, ⅗ of a husband, and ⅛ of a bob. Nevertheless, in spite of green stockings draped coyly along fifteen inches of shank, it did give our middle-aged ears a shock to hear "O Mother Dear Jerusalem" rendered gaily by a brass band as a march for the amalgamated alumnae of Smith College.

A survey of the juniors and seniors in their Ivy Parade brings the conviction that the present generation is about 100% better looking than we were in the same time and place, or else there must have been a special parade of the less comely privately conducted in some uncharted corner of the campus. We also strongly suspect that the drain upon the paternal bank account for improved sartorial effect is about 500% higher than it was in the days when we were content to have our souls shine beautifully forth, if they could.

Of our own class singing that evening, the less said the better. We judge that 1907 is a bit off on lyric self-expression just at present, or that the two-hour class meeting previous to the sing may have affected our vocal chords. But in spite of damp and mosquitoes, we reposed our green limbs on the shores of Paradise and listened pleasurably to the more expert warblings of the Glee Club. We were also creditably informed that even later some of our more dashing members "gryphon-greened" it a bit about the campus, to prove the relativity of time and space, or something like that.

Sunday produced the first touch of real reunion weather, very wet, and of a temperature that demanded what Ethel Woolverton would describe as a five to ten piece mind. Nevertheless, we all fared forth to Sophia Smith's homestead in Hatfield, under our own gasoline power, with only one flat tire in the convoy, which shows that there is something to be said for a college education. Sunday and Monday brought the regular college graduation functions, reported elsewhere in the QUARTERLY, and also the breaking-up of our own various jolly houseparties, with tender regrets at parting somewhat tempered by the prospect of once more controlling our own breakfast food, and likewise (low be it spoken) our own bath tub.   M. O. W.

1912's FIFTEENTH

THE first real event of importance to 1912 reuners was Class Supper, a delectable affair in more ways than one. We should like to pass on to our absent members the real meat of this occasion, but we know our remarks would be blue-penciled by the editors as being of too intimate and personal a nature. We will merely say in passing that there was no evidence of self-consciousness or reticence on the part of the speakers, and none of those silent moments so frequent at large gatherings. In fact, our President, Ho-T, had great difficulty in keeping all of us from talking all the time. Jobs, with and without families, was the most popular subject of discussion, with education of the young as a close second. President Neilson honored us with his presence while he consumed a fruit cocktail and pronounced us more hospitable than a class which he had previously visited and from which he had obtained only an olive!

As Ivy Day approached, members of 1912 gathered together in groups to murmur protestingly about costumes. Recommendation had gone forth from alumnae headquarters that classes which had been out of college fifteen years or longer should wear *only* a modest ribbon fastened with a chaste numeral over virgin white. Why this discrimination? Why should not 1912 blaze forth in the royal purple? Nevertheless we conformed. Picture then our consternation on that bright Saturday morning to see 1907, 1902, and other older classes gather on the campus arrayed in gay caps, socks, bags, and sundry other decorations.

The best they could say of *us* was that we looked dignified, but anyway we *were* conspicuous for our numbers and our noise. We know this because we heard later that an absent 1912er asked a member of the graduating class, after reaching home, whether she had seen 1912 at Northampton. "See 1912?" she replied, "how could I help it?" Well, that's comforting, anyway.

On Saturday afternoon our class meeting was held in Seelye Hall, with Ho-T masterfully presiding and our Mary, tried and true, coaching from the side lines. Both of them modestly offered to resign their jobs in favor of new candidates, but it was unanimously voted to let them enjoy themselves for another term at least. Moreover, a particularly good reason for reëlecting these officers was that we couldn't think of any two people who could possibly fill their places. Several business matters were then discussed and a report of our prosperity given by the treasurer, Dorothy Marcus. Among other things we voted to donate a sum of money to the Students' Aid Society in memory of Lucia Houpt, and to increase our class contribution to the President Burton Memorial Fund. Many who had not yet contributed to this Fund promptly responded and we were able to bring the total of our class gift well over the $2000 mark. The Dix system of reunions was again brought up for discussion, and a request made for the publication of another Year Book to be brought out on the occasion of our Twentieth. Singing and general hilarity marked the closing moments of the meeting.

Our Sunday picnic, scheduled to take place at Ruth Cooper's summer residence in Plainfield, had to be held in the Crew House for rainy reasons, but the meal itself, provided by Helen Hulbert (who will ever forget her box lunches at the Fiftieth?) was a masterpiece, and after we had showed our appreciation by eating every crumb, we gathered about the open fire for a real family party and heard interesting things from and about our many illustrious members.

Alumnae Assembly on Monday afternoon was our last gathering and provided a most fitting climax to those four eventful days. In other pages of the QUARTERLY you will read of how the alumnae surprised President Neilson on his Tenth Anniversary and provided him with a suitable outfit for his vacation. Thus ended the four flawless days of 1912's Fifteenth.   H. P. C.

OUR TENTH

NOW that I have counted the laundry, watered the plants, and generally set things in the house to going again, I must sit down and recapture the glory that was '17's, both as a record for those who were at our tenth reunion and to tell others who were not all about it.

First of all, we won the cup for our costume which represented "the gay nineties." We will admit that we thought ourselves quite fetching in our yellow and black, ankle-length, sleeveless gowns beamed by those space-taking sticks, our parasols, and high white coiffures. Personally, I think it was the mits that did it. They were the frosting which capped the cake, so to speak. Hazel Toolan was responsible for our rig.

And then, there was Mary Dixon. I ask you now, was there ever a drum major like her? I, modestly, have always had a secret ambition to boom the bass drum in a band, but never could I hope to wave the baton at the head of the entire alumnae parade with quite the élan of our Mary! She was our song leader and stunt-concoctor too. And—well—likewise did she excel in making speeches and as a result we passed public resolutions of appreciation and made private ones concerning more songs and stunts for our 15th.

Our contingent in the parade was full of contrasts. Fran (Montgomery) Bowes, very dashingly dressed as Lindy and cavorting about in "The Spirit of St. Louis," was our mascot. We were led by a rube band, and the unforgettable Izzy Gardner and Theodate Soule dressed as the "Whoops" (comic strip characters in *The New Yorker*) rode in the last carriage drawn by the last horse in Northampton. We helped Mary Dixon, by the way, draw that wagon back to its livery stable home on Center St. at 11.45 Saturday night, to the confusion of Elm St. traffic. The horse, which was only human, had died on us!

Class supper Friday night at the Crew House helped us to mend the gaps in the ten years which our classic reunion books had left open. President Neilson came to see us and ate our chicken salad which we assured him was the best he could get at any of the reunion suppers that night. We had some stunts which contrasted courtships of then and now. Then we just sat around the table and talked, each contributing something, sometimes voluntarily, sometimes only upon Marion Cohn's, our toastmistress's, persuasion, of the experiences of the past ten years.

Sunday morning, we elected our new class officers. [See class notes.]. We made our contribution of $2000 to the Burton Memorial Fund, and $50 to the Students' Aid in memory of the class members who have died.

Just how many 1917ers were back is a matter of conjecture, as some did not register. There were 103 names in our class book, but more than that were back. Helen (Jones) Farrar came clear from Honolulu to be with us and we had several from California.

Our tenth was a milestone as earlier reunions weren't, we felt, as we stood on the sidelines and watched the seniors march and thought of all that had happened to us since our Ivy Day. It is the first real stopping place since we took to the road after Commencement. One year, three years, even five years do not give one much time in which to acquire husbands and babies and laurels.

But by ten years, it is high time to ask and answer the question, "Well, what have you done?" And the ivy, which we too planted by Martha Wilson at this reunion, was the stake driven in to mark our first allotment of achievement, of joy—and of sorrow too.

When we meet elsewhere we are the new persons we have become, but when we get together at Hamp, we seem "as we were," and I think it was the discovery that there is something about us as individuals and about our class that doesn't change, which made our tenth reunion so satisfactory to us all.

D. P.

1922's FIFTH REUNION

THE Four Winds Blew Us To Hamp! The veracity of said red and gold signboard could not be disputed as 151 of us from North, South, East, and Westerly saluted and officially registered. Nor did our winds once cease to serve us through four glorious days; for, though the gale did not waft numerous late arrivals into official registration, it swelled our ranks to a degree well worthy the name of Fifth. Our first hour was one of rediscovery. Long embracing campus glances en route to Seelye 17, our class headquarters, greetings everywhere, assigned a room with roommate, hasty shaking of clothes, a bell suddenly cutting the air, a rapid descent, around a dinner table with the old crowd, and lo!—the speaking of a happy delusion, "You have never been away!" We were content.

"The Beaux' Stratagem," the senior play, impressed us. "Never in our day were we so professional!" "Do have another peppermint, and do you notice how well they manoeuver their skirts?" "It takes real ability to get such subtle lines across, and they have it!" "I trust their parents understand this is pure comedy." And in the current of such sage observances we found ourselves at the new Trebla's, where with nourishment histrionic and stomatic we ended the day.

Friday morning found us early at the Last Chapel service. We liked the seniors in their caps and gowns, and were pleased that President Neilson considered it an unusually normal year. Next we turned our attention to those things which loomed most beguiling, for, despite the scheduled alumnae song practice, numerous of us faded away: to the Bookshop to peruse the etchings and remarkable book reductions; to hunt up friends; to the swimming pool; to meditate in the Note Room and Library. Herein we have it by her own confession, one of our smaller members curled up in the President's private chair, where she did sleep peacefully.

Three o'clock found us again at headquarters with "Pudge" Donnell to lead us in song. It was a highly social song meet, since some of the red coolie coat costumes being over-ample or -snug for the figures assigned them must needs be changed at that time; and incidentally our portrait gallery of beautiful babes reëxamined with prideful interest. "Pudge" as always was good natured and soon extracted a goodly singing of the old songs to prepare us for the events of the next day.

Ivy Day and harmonious weather go hand in hand. We forgot the clouds of our own in making this memorable. As our coolie coats were Chinese, our signs were the borne testimony of a similar state. "Bernie" did herself proud with them. Besides those same winds that blew us to Hamp, and the symbol of each, there was a group devoted to ancestor worship which was headed by "108 Little Celestials"—this the present number of our babies "Are Already Venerating These Illustrious Ancestors." The ancestors followed with So Fi Ah herself carrying a scroll; Ah Dam, of Wealth of Nation's fame, whose picture was accompanied by a picture of Chinese money; then the Smith Brothers, Tra De, Mar Kh. Our Two Illustrious Presidents, Sun Yat Sen and Neil Sen, made a noble accompaniment to the banners of our Lion and Alma Mater.

Our most enjoyable parade over, during which our class baby, Jean MacLeod, abandoned the dignity of her red chariot to trot beside it, we watched with admiring faces the procession of juniors, the bearers of the ivy chain, through which, in due course, came the white-clad seniors. They were lovely, very young, very serious. Someone said, "I should say none of us look a bit older, if anyone asked me." No one did, but we felt better.

Our class meeting briefly over, in which Alice Jenckes was unanimously reëlected president, we gathered once more, this time at the Plymouth Inn and the red lanterned and gaily laurel bedecked room of 1922's banquet. The head table was decorated by Mrs. Reed, in loving memory of Virginia. Our most beloved member and guest of honor, Dean Benedict, assured us though many changes had taken place, our college was upholding its ideals as strongly and as loyally in the present as it had ever done in the past. President Neilson looked in upon us with an unlighted cigar as Naomi was reminiscing in delightful fashion of the good old days. Our resourceful toastmistress, "Dixie" Miller, seeing a way to detain the President, beckoned Naomi to finish. The President then confided to us he could find no match at 1887's supper. Could we oblige him? A match walked out, triumphant! Surely we have not lost the capacity for adjustment. Professor Hildt, hovering within social proximity, paid us the delicate compliment that as yet we were not buxom. We thank him! "Dixie" informed us that 225 of our number are matrimonially embarked; the residue of us range in versatility from 56 teachers to 2 actresses.

"Kempie" topped the evening with a red lantern for each of us as we sallied forth to Students' Building to sing. At which point "Bernie" established a precedent, since with no little grace she distributed candy and nuts, the mementoes of our happy dinner, to our campus friends, who, once recovered from their surprise, did accept with avidity.

After drinking in Paradise, silhouetted by clouds, and songs of a shadowy Glee Club that echoed in our hearts, we found our way back quietly, for in the solemnity and beauty of that twilight we realized again what meaning our college had for us. Soon we were flickering ourselves and lights in and out, merrily giving and as gaily receiving many serenades.

Small wonder that we slept through the rain of a gray Sunday morn! We bestirred ourselves for dinner, and filled the remainder of the day with the President's reception, and that of the Dean and Faculty at The Quadrangle. At evening Vespers, we wondered why we had ever let one go by in our own college days.

Monday morning found some of us packing, some with tickets for Commencement, some with hopes. The latter rushed the doors and, although in a somewhat frayed condition upon so doing, considered Dr. Fosdick's address and the exercises well worth it. More of us packed; remnants appreciated the stunts of the Alumnae Assembly. At last we were all gone, carrying with us appreciation to Dorothy Lindsay, Catherine Murray, Bernadette Stack, and Margaret Kemp, and those others who contributed to the success of our Fifth, regretful only that the rest of our members could not have been with us.   G. L. R.

1924 REUNION

HAIL! Hail! The gang's all here!
We used to be respectable
But now we are disreputable

so, flippantly, did '24 take President Neilson's comment on its appearance. We were disreputable, and as he very well knew we gloried in our disgrace. Until Saturday morning we had been merely alumnae (or occasionally undergraduates to some near-sighted visitor who could not see how wrinkled and gray we were) prowling about looking for changes which we knew would be for the worse, and lending a critical ear to Senior Dramatics. But on Saturday morning we appeared to a startled world as Pirates! No one could mistake us for Push Committee now.

Our rakish purple caps, our curtain-ring earrings, our red neckerchiefs and sashes all were effective, and in themselves would have made us distinguished. And when one adds the trousers—those purple trousers with a numeral on each leg, those trousers that draped so voluminously about the thin girls and were so alarmingly tight for the less thin— no wonder we were the heroes of the urchins about town, the talk of the faculty, and the despair of the young men who were trying to view college ways with nonchalance. The costume was indeed striking, and we added to the universal interest in it by losing various parts of it in public places, until ultimately our battle cry became "All together now." Our song leader, in particular, felt a distinct need for "someone to watch over me." But it was comfortable, and with its two pockets which bulged with all our worldly goods was so eminently practical that a movement was on foot to make trousers a part of our costume each reunion until our fiftieth. (No vote was taken on this.)

We gathered, only seventy odd of us, about our piratical purple banner—a mere handful, but for noise (politely, enthusiasm) we outdistanced all the rest. Seeing '22's class baby in her chariot made us a bit jealous because we had no small pirate, Marion Clark's daughter being kept at home to help take care of a very new sister. We regained our usual amount of inflation, however, when we read our signs and knew that each member of the class could claim 84/1000 of a baby.

After we had passed with stealthy steps the President's reviewing stand, and had watched the Ivy Procession and so decided how all our summer clothes should be made, we disbanded, and in small groups went about important business, gossip (how we did gossip, in spite of weighty matters like jobs, husbands, and children to talk about!), having our tintypes taken, invoking the spirit of Mr. Gilbert to give us new words for Mr. Sullivan's music. Officially, we are ashamed to say, we were almost nonexistent. Our intentions were good, but even at so important a ceremony as planting the class ivy in front of Martha Wilson House only five or six of us were present.

Class meeting began in somewhat the same spirit as the ivy planting, but it had one great advantage: it was closely connected with class supper, and pirates must eat. It ended by being a very full meeting (if puns are permitted). See class notes for new officers. Grace Lowe had taken over her duties as song leader long before. Our most important decision of a financial nature was to turn over our class insurance policies when they matured to the Alumnae Fund.

Miss McElwain told us some lovely stories which we're sure she had been saving especially for us, and when the President came in, ostensibly to borrow a match, she expressed her pride in her non-smoking children. Pride came before a fall, we fear, if she went out to Paradise to listen to that most gorgeous Glee Club. However, *we're* very proud that she wasn't able to furnish the match herself!

When it comes to song contests, we really can't brag. Someone may have been on the tune, but that is not a proven fact. Our acting ability saved us from utter disgrace, but we do not feel at all offended that the cup was not held out to us on the spot. By the time our patter songs about our piratical selves had assumed some sort of shape, 1928, our very little sister, came around and diffidently serenaded us with the same airs. Any feeling of mortification we might have had at hearing so vast an improvement was dispelled by '28's charming manners, and we all sang with spirit to Gilbert and Sullivan. Of course we ended the evening singing with our oldest and best friends, '22 and '26; it was after twelve when we picked ourselves up from the concrete sidewalk and dashed for home.

We're coming back again. We felt sorry for the ones who stayed away. "Girls, don't ever be too blasé or too busy to come to reunion," one of us said, "no matter how many husbands you have!" If all our husbands break all their limbs they can't keep us away from our fifth! L. E. J. C.

After the Alumnae Parade we were able to forget ourselves sufficiently to enjoy watching Outdoor Ivy. It was planted this year on the north side of Seelye.

The Glee Club singing on Paradise was, we must admit, nearly as perfect as when we were there singing ourselves. The song contest of reunion classes was held just before this on the steps. Perhaps we are too young to make an impression on the judges, for we did not win the prize. Our contest song is quoted below:

Tune—"How Could Red Riding Hood"

Oh, when we graduated we all thought we knew a lot;
We had our A.B.'s in our hand, we thought that we
    were hot;
Then they started all these questionnaires
    And so our families
Said here's a chance to show
    How YOU got those swell degrees:

Chorus

Who is the King of Greece?
Does endive grow on trees?
And how does a steam engine run?
    Who wrote Evangeline, and how?
    And how many people ride bicycles now?
What's an incisor?
Where's the ex-Kaiser?
· And who is Rosetta Stone?
    Our former vanity's vanquished and dead;
    We know we haven't one fact in our head:—
    But you know and I know our color is red,
In hopes to learn, you see,
And true humility,
We've come back to college once more.

At midnight 1922, '24, and '26 all gathered on Seelye steps and sang, and sang, and sang, long after everyone else was worn out and gone.

Sunday it rained. And if it ever rained harder anywhere we hope never to see it. Many of us took the opportunity of a day free from too pressing engagements to inspect the Tryon Art Gallery and the new Hotel Northampton, both of which came off favorably in our estimation. The Sunday afternoon concert and organ vespers drew a large representation also, and we attended the President's reception and the faculty reception at the newest New Dorms. Dean Bernard received at Martha Wilson.

The Quadrangle is really very impressive, and we have confidence that it will very soon look less bare, for the reuning classes all planted ivy there. Laura Kimball planted a root for the class of 1926 at the corner of Morrow House. There were no special ceremonies connected with this. Inspection of the ivy we planted last year is encouraging, for it looks strong and aspiring, having now reached as high as the sixth brick on the Libe.

We felt more at home this year at the Alumnae Assembly meeting, and especially enjoyed seeing Miss Comstock, who came to make the presentation of the gift to President Neilson.

Having survived a 50th reunion of the College we thought the gathering of parents and admiring friends and alums rather small until we tried to get into John M. Greene for Indoor Ivy and Commencement, when we changed our mind, and to take a remark of Dr. Fosdick's quite out of its Commencement address context, after standing throughout the latter exercise and awaiting the privilege of being among the first to beam upon the newly-made alumnae we began to feel like the "last frazzled remnants of a once mighty race."

Class supper revived us, and though comparatively few of us remained, it was a very happy party who greeted Dean Benedict and Mrs. Sawyer, the president of the Alumnae Association, as our guests of honor. Dean Bernard and Mrs. Scales and President and Mrs. Neilson were also our very welcome guests though but for a short time. The roll call produced news of our recent accomplishments with several M.A.'s to our credit. We went over to the Gym to see 1927, and to give our stunt which was a take-off of course, and was called the "Smith Belle's Stratagem." After that we hurried back to Studes to see the movies taken of our activities last year, and eventually went reluctantly to packing and thoughts of time-tables, departure—and our third reunion.   L. L. F.

(See next page for Alumnae Registration)

REGISTRATION AT ALUMNAE HEAD-QUARTERS, COMMENCEMENT 1927

Many more persons were in Northampton but unfortunately did not register at Headquarters. We are sorry not to be able to include them here.

1882

Grace Blanchard, Nina Browne, Annie Jackson, Eleanor Larrison, Katherine McClellan, Isabel McKee Hidden, Alice Peloubet Norton, Maria Vinton, 8. *Ex-1882:* Lina Eppendorff, Louise Girdler, Mary Hidden, Annie Peirce Lougee, Gertrude Palmer McClanahan, Nella Phillips Shuart, Stella Shuart, 7.

1887

Jessie Carter White, Hannah Clark Powell, Lillian Fay, Alice Gale Jones, Helen Gamwell Budd, Bessie Gill, Helen Holmes, Celeste Hough Drury, Grace James Mirick, Eleanor Lord, Elizabeth Mason, Elizabeth Pinkerton Webster, Anne Van Kirk Geller, Alice Walton, Martha Woodruff, 15. *Ex-1887:* Antoinette Bancroft Pierce, Ellen Russel Houghton, Antoinette Smith Angle, 3.

1892

Abby Arnold, Winifred Ayres Hope, Florence Barker Came, Eliza Bridges, Marion Burritt, Cora Coolidge, Ruth Cushman Anthony, Eleanor Cutler Daggett, Jane Cutler, Sarah Goodwin, Katherine Haven Upton, Mary Henshaw, Mary Jordan, Katherine Keeler, Miriam Kerruish Stage, Martha Kimball, Jessica Langworthy, Emily Lathrop Calkins, Elizabeth Learoyd Ewing, Christine Mansfield Cole, Blanche Morse, Elsie Pratt Jordan, Anne Safford, Etta Seaver, Bertha Smith Stone, Caroline Steele, May Stoddard Yeomans, Eliza Swift Chute, Emma Tryon, Lena Tyler Chase, Elizabeth Underwood, Wilhelmina Walbridge Buffum, Laura Wild, Helen Wolcott, 34. *Ex-1892:* Mary Burnham Bowden, Laura McConway Scoville, Sara May Lawton, Helen Nichols Smith, Harriet Parsons James, Isabel Strong, 6.

1897

Belle Baldwin McColl, Rachel Baldwin, Anne Barrows Seelye, Lillias Blaikie Thomas, Helen Boss Cummings, Anna Branch, Grace Breckenridge Fisk, Helen Brown Coit, Anna Carhart, Anna Casier Chesebrough, Dorothea Caverno, Florence Clarke Boone, Margaret Coe, Elizabeth Cole Fleming, Ada Comstock, Isabelle Cutler Blanke, Martha Cutler, Albertine Flershem Valentine, Ethelwyn Foote Bennett, Mae Fuller Curran, Julia Goodrich, Alice Goodwin Schirmer, Mabel Hersom Jones, Ruth Hill Arnold, Elizabeth Hobbs, Jean Hough, Mary Hough, Lucy Hunt, Florence Johnson, Mary Johnson, Marcia Jones Taylor, Marian Jones, Climena Judd, Jessie Judd, Florence Keith Hyde, Grace Kelley Tenney, Bertha Kirkland Dakin, Genevieve Knapp McConnell, Ada Knowlton Chew, Jessie Lockett, Alice Lord Parsons, Ellen Lormore Guion, Grace Lyon Rickert, Edith Maltby Marshall, Alice Maynard Madeira, Mary Merrill Macfarland, Caroline Mitchell Bacon, Edith Montague White, Lucy Montague, Harriet Patch Woodbury, Louise Peloubet, Clara Phillips Rogers, Elisabeth Redfern Dennett, Frances Ripley Willard, Mary Rockwell Cole, Louise Rogers Nichols, Josephine Sewall Emerson, Mary Shepard Clough, Edith Sligh Miller, Mary Smith McKenney, Julia SturteVant Merriam, Alice Tallant, Therina Townsend Barnard, Helen Tredick, Jane Vermilye, Mary Ward Dunning, Mary Wells, Katharine Wilkinson, Helen Woodward Wilson, 69. *Ex-1897:* Alice Bell, Helen Kennard MacKenzie, Mary Lewis Leitch, Imogene Prindle, Catherine Warnick Hall, Stella Williams, 6.

1902

Marion Aldrich Allison, Clara Allen, Mary Allison, Mary Bancroft Phinney, Mildred Barber, Ethel Barnes Burns, May Barta Birdseye, Rachel Berenson Perry, Anna Bliss Phelps, Ethel Bliss Woodworth, Mary Bohannan Chubb, Jessie Brainerd, Helen Bryant, Carolyn Childs Haslam, Edith Claflin, Florence Clexton Little, Avis Coburn Churchill, Leona Crandall Hagen, Annie Cranska Hill, Julia Davis Richmond, Emily Dunton, Helen Durkee Mileham, Marjorie Elder Stevenson, Edith Fales, Catherine Fogarty, Ethel Freeman, Ruth French, Frances Gardiner Ford, Caroline Gleason Larkin, Mary Glover, Stella Goss Wohlgemuth, Eugenie Hadd, Edith Hancox, Katherine Harter Alexander, Nellie Henderson Carter, Madeleine Hewes, Lilian Holbrooke, Bertha Holden Olney, Katharine Holmes, Mary Howe, Louise Irving, Constance Jones, Jean Jouett Blackburn, Helen Kelley Marsh, Louise Knapp Baumgarten, Josephine Lamson Gates, Edith Lobdell Pusey, Mary MacDonnell, Helen Manning Riggs, Sabina Marshall, Grace Mason Young, Maude Mellen Nelson, Ursula Minor Burr, Elizabeth Neal, Edith Newcomb,

Constance Patton Hurst, Laura Paxton, Julia Peck Albee, Maida Peirce Stearns, Louise Perkins Batcheller, Hulda Pettengill Greene, Mary Phillips Harriman, Faith Potter Weed, Bertha Prentiss Webber, Sara Richards, Martha Riggs Griffith, Jane Ripley, Maroe Sater Scott, Sarah Schaff Carleton, Maude Shattuck, Mary Smith, Nann Smith Warner, Susan Smith, Edith Souther, Ethel Stratton Pettengill, Virginia Tolar Henry, Ethel Treat, Gertrude Tubby, Frances Valentine, Louise Vanderbilt, Ella Van Tuyl Kempton, Augusta Vibberts Pelton, Jessie Wadsworth Burns, Helen Walker, Elizabeth Warnick Phillips, Eunice Wead, Selma Weil Eiseman, Elizabeth Whitin Keeler, Lucy Wicker, Louise Woodbury, Mary Woodbury Howard, 91. *Ex-1902:* Helen Atherton Govier, Eliza Atwood Thompson, Ethel Bradley Carnell, Edith Church Mackay, Elizabeth Fish Campbell, Lavarah Fish Wheaton, Olive Foster Stengel, Ellen Gould, Marian Harris, Helen Pease Miller, Susie Skinner Raymond, Florence Sturdy Ross, 12.

1907

Jessie Allen Knapp, Elizabeth Ballard Crofut, Helen Barber, Leonora Bates, Gertrude Blanchard, Emma Bowden Proctor, Winifred Bradbury Moore, Ruth Broadhurst Baxter, Helen Bull, Mary Campbell Ford, Ada Carpenter, Marion Carr Condit, Hazel Catherwood Cameron, Bertha Christiansen, Anna Churchill, Margaret Coe Blake, Marjorie Comstock Hart, Ruth Cowing Scott, Ethel Curry Beach, Helen Curtis Taylor, Clara Dibble, Louie Dickson Van Winkle, Ethel Dow, Gladys Duffee, Cherrie Duffey Pierson, Mary Eddy, Marian Edmands, Virginia Elliott, Dorothy Evans Noble, Marion Felt Sargent, Ethel Felton, Mary Foot Lord, Katharine Frankenstein, Ernestine Friedmann, Alice Goodman Gilchrist, Mildred Haire Tyler, Mary Hardy Pemberton, Sophie Harris Nichols, Pauline Hayden, Mabel Holmes, Myra Hopson, Nathalie Howe, Olive Hurlbut, Eloise James Turner, Ethel Kenyon Loomis, Emily Kimball, Anna Kriegsmann Maxwell, Edna Lindsay, Eda Linthicum McNair, Eleanor Little Baker, Sophie Lytle Hatch, Lilian Major Bare, Harriette Mann, Alice Maxcy Bates, Hortense Mayer Hirsch, May Miller Haff, Helen Moodey Moog, Bessie Moorhead Reed, Frances Morrill Luby, Harriett Murphy Finucane, Mabel Norris Leonard, Mary Noyes Spelman, Jessie Oliver Smith, Mary Ormsbee Whitton, Julia Park Vanderbilt, Margaret Paton Filley, Edna Perry Yeomans, Margaret Pitman Chamberlain, Elsie Prichard Rice, Dora Reid Kimber, Anna Reynolds Morse, Muriel Robinson Burr, Dorothea Schauffler Higinbotham, Virginia Smith, Nettie Strobhar, Frances Taylor Whitney, Mildred Taylor Noyes, Myra Thorndike Tibbetts, Louise Thorne Fullerton, Olive Tolman, Helen Treadwell Wilkinson, Carolyn Tucker, Agnes Vaughan Latham, Edith Walters, Bessie White, Ethel Willard Eddy, Hope Willis Rathbun, Edna Wood Williamson, Marguerite Woodruff Fowler, Katharine Woods Lacey, Ethel Woolverton Cone, 91. *Ex-1907:* Cyrena Case Kellogg, Helen French, Edith Pendleton Norris, Mabel Worthen Wood, 4.

1912

Lena Anderson Dimond, Mildred Ashley Gould, Gladys Baily, Adrienne Baker Conybeare, Ruth Baldwin Folinsbee, Helen Bartholomew Prizer, Elsie Becker Oquist, Ruth Benjamin, Arline Biggs Gott, Ruth Binkerd Stott, Margaret Brearley Dean, Margaret Burling Kremers, Margaret Burt, Mary Butler Wright, Ada Carson Robbins, Elsie Cather, Mary Clapp, Anna Cliff, Uarda Clum Fisher, Harriet Codding Maxwell, Alice Comstock, Ruth Cooper, Gladys Copp, Emily Coye Wood, Miriam Cragin, Alberta Crespi, Elizabeth Curtiss, Gertrude Darling Benchley, Marion Denman Frankfurter, Dorothea de Schweinitz, Gertrude Dunham, Ruth Elliott, Ruth Emerson, Dorothy Faunce Helm, Edith Fitzgerald Dibble, Elaine Foster Cross, Sally Frankenstein, Elsie Frederiksen Williams, Helen Garfield Buckley, Helen Gates Fitchet, Annie Goddard Dellenbaugh, Edith Gray Ferguson, Hazel Hanchett Harney, Helen Hancock Hardy, Dorothy Hawkins, Florence Hedrick Miller, Maida Herman Solomon, Lillian Holland Smart, Helen Houghton Shortlidge, Amy Hubbard Abbott, Helen Hulbert Blague, Natalia Jobst Klotz, Ruth Johnson, Lydia Jones Burbank, Frances Krause, Florence Lange, Margaret Lockey Hayes, Rachel McKnight Simons, Sarah Marble, Dorothy Marcus, Eleanor Marine, Florence Martin, Ruth Mellor, Katharine Moakley, Louise Naylor, Grace Neill, Mary Nickerson Osgood, Mildred Norton, Lucy O'Meara, Priscilla Ordway, Henrietta Peabody Carlson, Nellie Pennell Simpson, Helen Perkins Hayes, Catharine Pierce, Margaret Plumley, Jeanne Pushee Thayer, Grace Redding, Carol Rix Stone, Edna Roach McClure,

Elizabeth Rudolph Crane, Alice Sawin Davis, Marion Scharr, Mildred Scott Olmsted, Ethel Seamans Gillette, Myrtle Seamans Seward, Charlotte Simmons Ormond, Ada Simpson Risley, Estelle Smith, Elizabeth Tucker Cushwa, Margaret Upton, Sarah Van Benschoten Darling, Helen Walker Waldron, Carolyn Ward Ingling, Margaret Washington Pfeiffer, Leslie Weatherston Haskell, Elizabeth Webster, Martha Westcott Davis, Gladys Wheelock Bogue, Louise White Dombrowski, Dorothy Whitley Goode, Edith Williams Haynes, Olive Williams, Louise Wood Tirrell, 103. *Ex-1912:* Miriam Howard Challice.

1917
Jeannette Abbott Kitchell, Eola Akers Hungerford, Marjorie Allen Cook, Margaret Ailing Sargent, Gladys Atwell, Katharine Baxter, Althea Behrens, Rachel Blair Bowers, Margaret Bonnell, Grace Brownell, Alice Bugbee, Helen Burnett Townsend, Ann Campbell Duncan, Martha Chandler, Winifred Chase Hazelwood, Eunice Clark Schmidt, Marion Cohn, Dorothy Cole Sturtevant, Eleanor Coolidge Wood, Donna Couch, Claire Cowgill, Ethel Davison Deming, Marguerite Deware Jacobs, Edith Dexter Johnson, Dorothy Doeller, Margaret Duff DeBevoise, Dorothy Emerson Morse, Eleanor Eustis Farrington, Bessie Fisk Lake, Harriette Fulton Bothwell, Doris Gardner Colson, Isabel Gardner Blake, Hazel Gibbs Neville, Frances Gibson, Augusta Gottfried, Martha Gray, Eunice Grover Carman, Elma Guest Balise, Dorothy Hamilton Brush, Helen Hastings, Helena Hawkins Bonynge, Katharine Hawxhurst, Marjory Herrick, Dorothy Hewitt Wilson, Mary Ann Hiss Emerson, Marion Hooper Augur, Alice Hueston King, Eleanor Hunsicker Ward, Marjorie Inman, Muriel Irving, Helen Jones Farrar, Nan Keenan Hartshorn, Helen Kingsley McNamara, Marie Knowles, Marion Lathrop, Maude Leach Martin, Esther Lippitt Haviland, Dorothy Lorentz, Margaret Lylburn Heinsohn, Margaret McClure Fisher, Anna McGrath Donnelly, Martha MacGuire, Esther Merritt Sisson, Lillian Miller, Florence Miner Farr, Frances Montgomery Bowes, Louise Morton, Lois O'Donnel, Agnes Peterson Hungerford, Dorothy Pratt, Jean Ramsay, Helen Rawson, Adah Richard Judd, Lucena Robinson, Marjorie Root Edsall, Marjorie Rossiter Troxell, Elizabeth Schmidt Turner, Ruth Shepard Fast, Marion Sherwood, Mary Smith, Theodate Soule, Eleanor Spencer, Eleanor Stearns Towns, Ethel Taylor, Ferne Taylor, Frances Terry, Mary Thayer Bixler, Mary Tomasi, Hazel Toolan, Doris Van Du Zee, Alice Watson Campbell, Catharine Weiser, Virginia Whitmore Kelly, Constance Wood, Eleanor Wood Thomsen, Ellen Wood Hicks, Constance Woodbury Dodge, 97. *Ex-1917:* Margaret Evens, Madeleine Harrington Peterson, Dorothea Page, Frances Tuteur Crilly, 4.

1922
Marjorie Adams, Betty Alexander, Mildred Alfred, Helen Anthony, Ann Axtell Morris, Elizabeth Bixler, Gertrude Blatchford Stearns, Eunice Blauvelt, Constance Boyer Anderson, Elizabeth Brooke, Charlotte Butler, Beatrice Byram, Laura Cabot, Alice Chapman, Catherine Clark Maxson, Dorothy Clark Albergotti, Mary Coolidge, Hilda Couch, Adelaide Cozzens Beatty, Phyllis Creasey Straight, Dorothy Crydenwise Lindsay, Helen Cunningham, Flora Davidson, Martha Davidson Kearsley, Helen DeGroat Bader, Edith Donnell, Elizabeth Donnell, Huldah Doran, Faith Dudgeon Taylor, Caroline Fisher, Elinor French, Margaret Gabel Conover, Helen Hall, Isabel Harper, Edith Harris, Doris Harrison White, Frances Haskell Luke, Virginia Hatfield, Grace Havey, Elizabeth Hilliard, Marion Himmelsbach, Margarette Hines, Arline Hobson, Dorothy Hogan Guider, Margaret Humphrey Windisch, Alice Jenckes, Dorothy Jenks Gilson, Dorothy Johnson, Ruth Johnson, Helen Johnston, Ruth Joshel, Mary Judson, Edna Keeler Dadirrian, Margaret Kemp, Mary Kerrigan, Madelyn Kingsbury, Ellen Lane, Naomi Lauchheimer Engelsman, Evelyn Lawley, Edna Lawrence Cornelius (Starr Lawrence), Mildred Leeper, Madeline Leonard, Marjorie Lewis Schoonmaker, Mildred Lovejoy, Nancy McCullough Rockefeller, Dorothy Mac-Donald, Elizabeth Marmon Hoke, Harriet Marsh Blanton, Mildred Mason, Eleanor Miller Webb, Elvira Miller, Marjorie Morrison, Catherine Murray, Ruth-Alice Norman Weil, Dorothea Nourse, Edith O'Neill, Helen O'Reilly, Rhoda Orme, Anna Pennypacker, Joyce Petterson Watson, Lillian Potter Dodd, Katherine Ranney Davenport, Eleanor Rau Leon, Irma Rich Gale, Ruth Robeson, Grace Rogers, Olivia Rogers, Mathilde Rugé Huse, Caroline Schofield, Elizabeth Scoville Horn, Ann Scroggie Robinson, Anna Sheedy, Catherine Smith Wilford, Harriet Smith Watt, Helen

Smith Mellor, Marion Stacey, Bernadette Stack, Carolyn Stewart, Margaret Storrs, Claire Strauss Arenberg, Mary Sullivan, Dorothy Taylor, Marian Thorndike, Eleanore Thorp, Elizabeth Tillinghast Gavitt, Louise Townsend Bethel, Frances Upham, Beatrice Walton, Marian Watkins, Una Whitehurst Mickle, Myrna Wilderson, Dorothy Williams Shaler, June Wilson Brainerd, Katharine Winchester Wakeman, Esther Ziskind Weltman, Viola Burgess Smith, 116. *Ex-1922:* Winifred Dodge Blood, Marion Stowell Southwick, Candace Thoman, Margaret Winton, 4.

1924
Esther Beckwith, Frances Blomfield, Dorothy Braley, Ruth Breen McGrath, Olivia Bridges, Dorothy Brown Dean, Jean Cochrane, Lois Cole, Margaret Davenport, Eleanor Deegan, Helen Ferguson Russell, Elizabeth Fogle, Dorothea Freeman, Mildred Gertzen, Martha Glenz, Helen Gordon Cate, Emily Green, Marion Hall, Dorothy Harris, Pauline Hayden, Marion Hendrickson, Edith Hill, Katharine Howard, Grace Lowe, Elizabeth Mackintosh, Beatrice Marsh, Elizabeth Meyer, Elizabeth Noyes, Frances Page, Serena Pendleton, Dorothy Perry, Grace Pierpont, Julia Pierson, Eva Prediger, Mary Remick, Bess Romansky, Marion Ropes, Moselle Smallhurst, Virginia Smith, Esther Stocks, Harriet Tyler, Ruth Tyler, Helen Walsh, Faith Ward, Gwendolen Washington, Helen Wheeler, Florence Young, 47. *Ex-1924:* Laura Jones Cooper.

1926
Eleanor Alcorn, Elizabeth Allen, Eloise Anderson, Adelaine Atherton, Vera Bane, Alice Banton, Gladys Beach, Betty Beam, Jean Boyce Courtney, Elizabeth Bridges, Helen Chapman, Harriett Child, Marion Christie, Elizabeth Church, Mary Chute, Eleanor Clark, Margaret Clarkson, Frances Collins, Constance Conary, Anne Connor, Claire Cremins, Louise Cronin, Alice Curley, Virginia Cuskley, Marion Davidson, Mary Deemer, Alice Dolan, Kathryn Dowling, Ruth Eiseman, Elizabeth Flavin, Laurestein Foster, Eleanor French, Marjorie French, Louise Fry, Marcia Gehring, Adele Goldmark, Mary Gordon, Aurelia Graeser, Dorothy Grauer, Helen Green, Agnes Griffin, Marion Griffin, Dorothy Halpert, Margaret Hammond, Helen Hay, Virginia Heffern, Vivian Iob, Lois Ittner, Emily Johnson, Laura Kimball, Helen King, Harriet Leach, Elizabeth Lewis, Margaret Lloyd Aiken, Carol Lord, Flora Macdonald, Janet McGee, Margaret McGlynn, Frances McGuire, Ruth McGuire Steinbright, Dorothy McKay, Janet Marks, Adeline Miller, Ruth Montgomery, Charlotte Murray, Ruby Neal, Arloine Neufeld, Margaret Oliver, Elizabeth Parnell, Mildred Parsons, Janet Perry, Isabel Porter, Laura ProVost, Barbara Rackett, Henrietta Rhees, Elisabeth Rice, Mary Robertson, Helen Roper, Elsie Rossmeisl, Sally Scott, Freda Seidensticker, Genevieve Shepherd, Elizabeth Sherwood, Dorothy Sloan, Helen Smith, Marion Spicer, Mary Stack, Ruth Stanford, Margaret Stearns, Alice Stevenson, Ruth Strong, Janet Studholme, Catherine Sullivan, Katharine Thayer, Bertha Vogel, Caroline Walker, Marion Ward, Phyllis Watts, Katherine Weidler Roberts, Margaret West, Mildred Whitman, Janet Wickham, Jessie Willever, Ruth Williamson, Janet Wise, Catharine Witherell, Harriet Wolcott, Josephine Wood, Elinor Woodward, Helen Wright Havey, 110. *Ex-1926:* Mary Fisher, Margaret Truax Hunter, 2.

"1776"
1879: Mary Gorham Bush. 1880: Netta Wetherbee Higbee. 1881: Alice Browne, Amelia Owen Sullivan. 1883: Mary Clark Mitchell, Elizabeth Lawrence Clarke, Edith Leach, Caroline Marsh. 1884: Mary Mason, Jane Morse Smith, Ex-1884: Mina Wood. 1885: Ruth Franklin. 1886: Adèle Allen, Mary Baker Fisher, Mary Eastman, Frances Goodwin, Abby Howes, Annie Russell Marble, Henrietta Seelye, Abby Slade. Ex-1886: Mabelle Clough, Hattie Cushman, Esther Fowler, Grace Gallaudet Closson. Ex-1888: Susie Bosworth Munn. 1889: Harriet Cobb, Margaret LoVejoy Butters. 1890: Jessie Burnham Downing, Virginia Forrest Lucia, Ellen Holt. Ex-1890: Cornelia Moodey, Grace Whiting Seaman. 1891: Nellie Comins Whitaker, Bertha Dwight Cole, Carolyn Peck Boardman, Mary Phillips Houghton. Ex-1891: Constance Waite Rouse. 1893: Frances Ayer Tebbetts, Harriet Bigelow, Ellen Cook, Gertrude Flagg, Harriet Holden Oldham, Frances Smith, Mary Vanderbeck Giles. 1894: Sarah Bawden, Mary Frost Sawyer, Eleanor Johnson, Florence King, Jeanne Lockwood Thompson, Mabel Moore White, Anne Paul, Ada Platt Benedict, Mary Richardson. Ex-1894: Kitty Lyall Merrill. 1895: Bertha Allen Logan, Suzan Benedict, Helen Goodrich DeGroat, Caroline Hamilton, Florence Lord King, Elizabeth Mann, Ella Shaver Phelps, Amelia Tyler, Leola Wright.

1896: Clara Burnham Platner, Elizabeth Cutter Morrow, Lucy Daniels Doane, Ellen Duckworth Trull, Edith Leeds Bannon, Grace Lillibridge Russell. Ex-1896: Anne Rust. 1898: Florence Anderson Gilbert, Emma Byles Cowperthwait, Georgia Coyle Hall, Ethel Gower, Maud Jackson Hulst, Myrtle Kimball Wilde, Elizabeth McFadden, Carol Morrow Connett, Elizabeth Mullally, Elisabeth Thacher. Ex-1898; Elizabeth Cochran Bliss, Cara Walker. 1899: Helen Andrew Patch, Harriet Bliss Ford, Miriam Choate Hobart, Helen Clark LeaVitt, Ethel Darling, Miriam Drury, Ethel Gilman Braman, Amanda Harter Fogle, Grace Mossman Sawyer, Elizabeth Ray, Mary Smith LiVermore, Ada Springer Weller, Martha Vance Drabble, Margaret Wilkinson Malcolmson, Ex-1899: Harriette Patterson. 1900: Alfa Barber Calkins, Edith Emerson, Lucy Lord Barrangon, Edith Monson, Mary Whitcomb Clark, Elizabeth Whitney, Mary Wiley Thayer. 1901: Julia Bolster Ferris, Helen Brown, Annie Buffum Williams, Agnes Childs Hinckley, Alice Cummings Hudson, Mildred Dewey Hay, Katherine Dillon, Amy Ferris, Florence Hinkley Dana, Grace Larmonth Snow, Antoinette Putman-Cramer, Alice Richardson Rawlinson. Ex-1901: Isabel Adams Dodge, Helen McIntosh Galbraith. 1903: May Hammond, Aida Heine, Edith Hill, Helen Hill, Alice Murphy, Loella Newhall, Maybelle Packard Newcomb, Marguerite Prescott Olmsted, Florence Ripley Willis, Margaret Thacher. Ex-1903: Sara Crawford Dana. 1904: Harriet Abbott, Miriam Clark, Nellie Cuseck Connolly, Louise Fuller, Eleanor Garrison, Carrie Gauthier, Helen Hall, Muriel Haynes, Annie Mead Hammond, Florence Snow, Mary van Kleeck, Alice Wright Teagle. 1905: Florence Bannard Adams, Ruth Bigelow Christie, Louisa Billings, Charlotte Chase Fairley, Mabel Chick Foss, Louise Collin, Alice Curtis Mansfield, Alice Danforth, Evelyn Hooker, Alice Lawlor Kirby, Susan Rambo. 1906: Alice Hildebrand, Ethel Monson Holcombe, Margaret Norton, Gladys Pierce, Helen Pomeroy Burtis, Melinda Prince Smith, Bertha Reed, Genevieve Waters, Edna Wells Root. Ex-1906: Sarah Walters Miller. 1908: Ida Barney, Ethel Bowne Keith, Carolyn Burpee, Harriet Childs, Helen Hills Hills, Lucy Raymond Gladwin, Ada ReeVe Joyce, Esther Stone. Ex-1908: Bertha Shepard. 1909: Louise Putnam Lee, Marion Smith Bidwell. 1910: Helen Bigelow Hooker, Evelyn Canning Keyes, Edith Carson, Breta Childs, Elizabeth Gregory Perkins, Eva Jenison Pruyn, Blanche LeGro, Ruby Litchfield, Elizabeth Nichols Chamberlin, Muriel Seeley Welles, Bertha Skinner Bartlett, Marjorie Smith, Mary Anne Staples Kirkpatrick, Elsie Sweeney, Helen Walters Eldred, Anna Washburn Hall, Helen Whiton. 1911: Amy Alvord Borst, Madeline Burns Wilson, Virginia Coyle, Josephine Dormitzer Abbott, Eleanor Fisher Grose, Gertrude Moodey, Winifred Notman Prince, Anne Parsons Hall, Dorothy Pearson Abbott, Anna Walsh Reilly, Katherine Wilbar Utter. 1913: Anne Donlan, Dorothy Douglas Zinsser, Marian Drury, Anne Dunphy, Agnes Folsom, Mabel Girard Mazzolini, Winifred Glasheen, Ruth Higgins, Grace Jordan, Ruth LeGro, Mary Libby Wilks, Agnes McGraw Brown, Harriet Moodey Reid, Sarah Porter, Lucy Titcomb.

1914: Gladys Anslow, Elizabeth Barney, Amy Fargo, Marion Freeman Wakeman, Hera Gallagher, Eleanor Halpin Stearns, Ruth McKenney, Nellie Parker, Jean Paton, Mary-Olive Phillips Bailey, Laura Rice Deming, Dorothy Spencer Miller, Dorothy Thorne, Mary Tolman. Ex-1914: Elizabeth Adams Ferguson. 1915: Charlotte Baum, Katharine Boutelle, Dorothy DaVis, Marion Fairchild, Marion GraVes, Florence Hanford, Jennie McLeod, Esther Mather Phelps, Marian Palmer Faulkner, Marian Park Humphrey, Helen Safford Reynolds, Jennette Sargent Drake, Amy Walker. 1916: Dorothy Ainsworth, Marion Bartlett, Dorothy Buhler, Helen Cobb, Dorothy Eaton Palmer, Marie Gilchrist, Priscilla McClellan Whelden, Mary McMillan, Vera Montville, Helen Strong Belknap, Marjorie Wellman Freeman, Marguerite White Stockwell. 1918: Sara Bache-Wiig, Florence Bliss, Dorcas Brigham, Alice Coon, Olive Copeland, Mary Elder, Eva GoVe Seely, Dorothy Knight Crone, Mary McMahon Sproesser, Mary Mensel, Margaret Oldham Green, Vera Rothberg Brown, Dorothy Stanley, Corinne Thompson, Alice Tower. Ex-1918: Myrtle DaVis Davis. 1919: Lois Allison, Elizabeth Atterbury, Grace Barker Smith, May Bartlett Griffey, Alice Bulkley, Laura Carr, Anna Comaskey, Helen Crittenden Robinson, Annette Crystal Lang, Dorothea Dower, Irene Drury, Eleanor Fitzpatrick, Katharine Fleming, Mary Foster, Antonia Gariépy Grant, Jane Griffin, Mae Haskins Starr, Elizabeth Hunt Lockard, Rebecca Jones Butler, Lucy Kingsbury Piper, Elizabeth Kingsley, Frances Lowe, Constance McLaughlin Green, Dorothy Martin, Frances Murphy, Edna Newman, Mary O'Neill, Marion Post Hidden, Eleanor Ripley, Esther Rugg, May Shaw Finn, Helen Small Withington, Doris Smith Bowlus, Mary Stephenson Griggs. Ex-1919: Evelyn HaViland. 1920: Ruth Bardwell Ladd, Helen Barry, Rosalind Bement Porter, Frances Chick Peabody, Marjorie Day, Katharine Dickson King, Hannah Goldberg Krauskopf, Elizabeth Humphrey, Helen McMillan Hendrickson, Helen Moriarty, Edith Sullivan, Elizabeth Upton, Iris Williams, Ruth Worcester. 1921: Helen Barker, Anne Coburn, Mabelle Hobbs, Helen Peirce, Ellen Perkins, Helen Pittman, Catherine Sammis, Dorothy Sawyer Bates, Elizabeth SomerVille Woodbridge. 1923: Mary Coley, Gertrude Humphrey, Katharine Jacobus, Hazel Kendrick, Marion Morris, Lillian Prediger, Sarah Riggs, Marion Smith Bell, Harriet Taylor, Elsa Wachter, Mildred Woodward Jones. Ex-1923: Edith LinVille Goldsmith. 1925: Priscilla Alden Anderson, Elizabeth Allen, Jane Angwalt, Helen Booth, Lydia Brigham, Mary Brower, Alice Curwen, Rose Dyson, Faith Ely, Barbara Estabrook, Clarace Galt, Grace Gibson, Lucelia Harrington, Ruth Hene, Julia Himmelsbach, Vieno Kajander, Leta Kirk, Doris Latimer, Mary Mangan, Helen Munz, Marjorie Peabody, Mary Rhodes Stone, Madeleine Rice, Elsie Riley, Sylvia Scaramelli, Louise Schmauk, Lillian Silver Schwolsky, Helen Smith, Josephine Tompkins, Anne Whyte, Dorothy Winslow. Graduates, 350; non-graduates, 23.

Attendance

Graduates, 1131; Non-Graduates, 73; Total, 1204.

TABLE SHOWING THE NUMBER OF SUBSCRIBERS TO THE QUARTERLY BY CLASSES *

Year	Total	Subscribers	Year	Total	Subscribers	Year	Total	Subscribers	Year	Total	Subscribers
1879	9	3	1892	75	42	1905	194	125	1918	402	288
1880	7	5	1893	97	52	1906	213	125	1919	385	249
1881	17	8	1894	98	51	1907	256	148 .	1920	424	288
1882	23	13	1895	138	84	1908	283	149	1921	431	292
1883	45	27	1896	131	76	1909	308	182	1922	499	362
1884	34	20	1897	163	119	1910	361	197	1923	353	248
1885	31	17	1898	131	66	1911	345	214	1924	425	316
1886	40	21	1899	178	98	1912	349	223	1925	454	350
1887	34	16	1900	202	107	1913	366	206	1926	469	401
1888	41	21	1901	229	135	1914	311	209	1927	464	342
1889	42	25	1902	215	120	1915	308	197	Non-graduates		486
1890	48	33	1903	217	124	1916	320	217	Non-alumnae		387
1891	63	33	1904	228	138	1917	324	212			

Totals: Graduates 6994
Non-graduates 486
Non-alumnae 387

7867

Total living graduates: 10780

* Compiled July 1, 1927

LET US TALK OF MANY THINGS

VICARIOUSLY SPEAKING! ONE thing we have discovered in these post-Commencement days, namely, that the *Springfield Republican* has a most discerning staff of editorial writers, and, as one editor to several others, we make them our deep salaams, and pay them the highest compliment we know by plucking an editorial bodily from the Sunday edition of June 26 and setting it down here where an editorial from the Commencement-beset editor of the QUARTERLY ought to go. And why not? We were about to take our pen in hand and inscribe a few words on exactly the same subject and it's just possible that we might not have been able to do any better, so why take a chance? The *Republican* says:

President Neilson's Administration

The alumnae gift of $1000 to President Neilson to commemorate the 10th anniversary of coming to Smith college is a fitting expression of gratitude for the work he has done there to develop a liberal college. A few days later came the honorary degree of Litt.D. from Yale which Dr. Neilson may rightly regard as a distinguished credential of success in his administration. . . .

By strenuous efforts—quite unpredicted in his previous record as a man of great scholarly attainments, but little administrative experience—he has brought Smith to the front rank of women's colleges. Its faculty is today considered to be of exceptionally high quality, while the physical growth of the college has also been taken care of, especially in the matter of building new dormitories to house almost the entire student population.

Of equal importance has been the spirit of inquiry and intellectual curiosity which he has striven to foster and which has borne tangible fruit in the establishment of the Institute for the Co-ordination of Women's Interests at Northampton. The various kinds of experimentation, such as that conducted by the psychology department in the school for children with individual differences, and in Prof. Wakeman's day school, indicate that Smith's president has been willing to encourage and support new ideas and new activities from the pure love of knowledge.

Perhaps Dr. Neilson's greatest contribution as an educator, however, has been his fearless insistence, in the face of bitter and thoughtless opposition, that the true object of learning is to free the human spirit from prejudice and fear and that to achieve this end complete freedom of expression must be accorded every point of view. This has brought on him much criticism which scarcely bore the light of logical inspection. But it would seem from the alumnae's action Monday, which may justly be deemed a mark of esteem and affection, that this criticism does not represent the sentiment of the great body of Smith students, whether past or present.

And that's that! Never has the QUARTERLY editor so enjoyed writing an editorial. Would that the *Springfield Republican* were also moved to compose that Hydra-headed Story of Commencement Week that rises before said editor whichever way she turns!

E. N. H.

MAGNA SED APTA AMID the groans of the returning alumnae anent the size of the college—the monstrum horrendum, cui lumen ademptum—rose the dissenting testimony of those who are alumnae mothers of granddaughters, and who have witnessed the mechanism of the college in action. It is a marvelous engine, and well adapted to its job. Where smaller colleges are content with a president and a dean, we boast a President (we do indeed!)—a Dean, four Class Deans, a Warden, two personnel directors, and many advisers. Instead of dealing with five hundred or a thousand students through two officers, we deal with two thousand students through ten or twelve officers. The simplest type of alumnae mathematics can arrange the proportions of that example. Each girl comes under the observation of at least six persons, and this does not include her housemother, who observes her daily, or her upper class adviser, who sees her off her guard. The mechanism is adequate, and lo, the College, for purposes of worry, has become four little colleges instead of one over-size one.

This fact I have seen illustrated repeatedly in the four years of a daughter's course. Perhaps the best proof of mechanic fitness is flexibility. Smith College students are individuals, and the laws are made to fit them, not they the laws. This human attitude begins with the committee on admissions—that terrifying board which seems to many an aspirant a committee on exclusions, but which is in reality human, conscientious, and reasonable to the last degree. Candidates who are in quarantine when they should take the examinations, candidates who are sick when they do take them, candidates who are given wrong information by persons they are justified in believing—have all been known to be admitted, in spite of technical deficiencies. I have no doubt at all that a properly recommended candidate plunged into sudden sorrow, or shocked or injured in an accident, would find her case considered. The committee wants the best girls in college, and under the blessed heading of "Any other evidence," listens to anything it can find out about its applicants.

The human and reasonable consideration of the individual girl goes on in connection with her studies, her health, her pleasures. I have known a class dean to say to a freshman who had exhausted her quota of week-ends, and many more, through exasperating slight illnesses, that she might have a week-end just for fun! This unexpected gift insured the loyalty to rules of that freshman and of many of her friends. I have known the college physician to get a girl interested in sleeping and eating as much as the twenty-four hours could hold for her, because she told her to watch her own weight, and regulate her athletic activities accordingly herself, instead of giving her a fixed rating. One student who left college of her own volition, to take up work she loved and could succeed at, was persuaded thereto by her class dean, who made her feel that she had done her best, and was not ignominious or cowardly to give up the effort. This girl would have been crushed and cringing for years if she had understood that she was dropped, and could not have continued her course in any case. The dean "saved her face," and perhaps saved her personality, by her humanity.

This kind of bending of rules does not imply breaking them in the least. Students do not stay in college when their stand is low. But they are helped to stay, and, if necessary, they are helped to leave. Warnings, tutors, hours consecrated by confidences, all beset the path of the erring scholar and make her way plain. In other colleges I have known of freshmen who flunked out almost unwittingly. Warnings had been misunderstood; marks had remained unexplained; notices had been mislaid, or not taken seriously. Perhaps at home "bills rendered" flip into the nearest wastebasket. How then can daughter realize that "this means you"? At Smith College, faculty, administration, students, all pursue, explain, warn. The freshman is asked repeatedly how the work is going now; how much her tutoring has cost; what she still has to do in the vacation. She understands; she wakes up; she is a brand saved.

Where such individual aid is always on tap, and even inundates the campus, the system—logical, flexible, humane—could be adapted to any number of students. Smith cuts her cap according to her cloth, and it fits!

E PLURIBUS UNA

HOW ONE HUSBAND DOES IT The worm will turn and we gladly make way for the outpourings of a very efficient husband of a very efficient Smith alumna on this matter of coördination. We don't think he is sarcastic! We think he is telling the exact truth, but are you going to let him have the last word on this controversy entitled, "What Price Coördination?"

ONE rarely crows over one's wife, but there are certain advantages we have which should not be allowed to go unadvertised. One of these is the opportunity to work all day in a quiet office uninterrupted by the myriad demands of a household.

An experience in writing a technical paper is in point. I get away from the bedlam at home, reach the office a little before eight, and get out a block of paper for a good early start. Jones is also there with the morning paper bought at the front gate. Many interesting things have happened over night, half a dozen ball games, a long distance airplane flight, and a murder or two. Eight-twenty and not a mark on paper.

The next ten minutes are spent feverishly blocking out the paper. Then the telephone bell rings.

"Is Adams there?"

"No, he is at home sick. Can I do anything for you?"

"Does a promise mean anything to him?"
"I guess we can make good on his promises as well as he can, what's the matter?"
"That R & L machine is due for shipment to-day. What about it?" . . .
. . . An hour shot. Fifteen more minutes on the paper. Telephone!
"Can you come down to my office for a few minutes to discuss a series of experiments we are about to start?"
Lunch time.
Back at work again. The original train of thought does not look quite satisfactory, I'll start another. Telephone.
"I have a man from the 'X' company, can I bring him over to see you a minute, I'll be right over." And just as they arrive one of the executives drops in to see what you are doing and one of the machinists does not understand a drawing, a hose line in the next room has sprung a leak. There is the thump of an unbalanced motor running on the floor overhead and the roar of a big blower in the next room.
I guess I'll go home and finish the job to the tune of "Bobby Shafto" and "What are you doing, Daddy?"

* * *

THE "PLACE" OF ALUMNAE THERE has been much discussion in the public press and elsewhere as to the exact duties of trustees in their relation to institutions of learning. As we well knew, before President Neilson referred to it in his talk at Last Chapel, Smith College has been fortunate above most colleges and universities in the personnel of her Board of Trustees and the attitude they have taken toward the teaching activities of the college. Any question as to their "place" has never needed discussion here. It is evident in the experience of many colleges that another and similar question needs a similar airing and that is the "place" of the alumnae in relation to questions of teaching and administration.

Some time ago when, it seemed to me, a department of the College in which I was most interested was not holding its own with other colleges (that time is long past), I met an alumnus of a large college who headed a department of teaching in another of our largest colleges for men. It seemed an opportunity to put to him the question, "Supposing you went back to your college, to which you are devoted, and found that the subject with which you are so familiar

was being taught in a way inferior to that in most of the colleges you know, is there anything you think you, as an alumnus versed in that subject, could do about it?" "Nothing whatever," he replied, "it would be quite outside any right I had as an alumnus." Since then examples of the effort "to do something about it" on the part of alumni in various places have come to my attention, but always these efforts seem to defeat their own best end and I have come entirely to the position of the man I have quoted. With one exception, however, and that is that the valuable relation which exists at Smith College between the alumnae and their representatives on the Board of Trustees presents an opportunity for discussing events in the College or qualities in its teaching which may be troubling the mind of any alumna. Full expression there seems allowable and, indeed, desirable, for how else can misunderstandings be cleared away or suggestions really valuable be made? I cannot see that we need any other outlet, any other source of information. Both because of regulations governing most colleges and universities and because of President Neilson's liberal policy which we all heartily subscribed to in the resolutions passed at the meeting of the Alumnae Association, no one person can decide any policy of moment at the College. The Alumnae Trustees are as much in touch as any individuals with the sort of questions which occasionally agitate the minds and feelings of the alumnae and they certainly feel their responsibility to the other alumnae who nominated them to such a degree that any question or suggestion brought to them would receive most earnest consideration. This has never been questioned; I do not believe it ever will be.

It is to be hoped that as we have been in the vanguard in the dignity, efficiency, and loyal service of our Trustees, so we may be in the understanding and poise with which we alumnae meet changes inherent in the changing times or incidents bound to occur in any progressive and experimentally-minded institution.

ELEANOR HOPE JOHNSON 1894

WE HAVE CHOSEN A GOOD PART TOO I HAVE been so busy these past few months, I've only just got around to setting down my reactions on paper to Mrs. Stearns's remarkable article in the February QUARTERLY. Such a piece as hers usually makes me feel very humble, which may account in part for my delay in saying anything about it. She is so obviously one of those super-women, who have been evolved by our modern process of education, as the Gentleman from Philadelphia has pointed out! In the presence of such as she I am abashed. You see, there is nothing super about me. In the first place, I like to cook, and keep house, and raise children, and I don't want to have to do anything else. By that I don't mean I don't want ever to have a vacation, or give a party, or go to church. I simply have no urge whatever to possess a Community Standing. I know any number of capable, energetic females who, like Mrs. Stearns, are extremely important in the fields of endeavor in which they function, but their ambitions leave me cold.

What does not leave me cold, however, is the combination of pity and scorn with which they regard such humble ones as I. Sometimes they make me feel as if they thought there was something positively disgraceful about the type of woman who refuses to serve on committees, and who shudders at dust on the piano. Dust on the piano in itself does not hurt anybody, but the urge to remove it is to my mind quite as commendable as the urge to organize, say, a high school orchestra. "Everyone to his own taste," said the old lady when she kissed the cow, and I am so glad there are energetic souls who can and do organize orchestras. More power to them! My particular urge is to stay at home and keep the piano dusted, metaphorically speaking, for my boys to practice on that they may presently qualify as members. Nobody can run orchestras without boys and girls to play in them, and I just wish that these people who are so smart in their fields of "outside activity" would be kinder to those of us who can't do much besides be the motive power for the rising generation. I really think we are a very important, if inconspicuous, part of the community. I certainly realize my limitations—six weeks without a maid have taken six pounds from a frame ill-designed to spare them. I know I can only do about so much, but I am certain that what I do do is extremely worth while, and I think I deserve at least a respectful attitude from those who can do more than I. I've never held with the usual mother-sacrifice point of view. I don't consider my life at all sacrificial. I like it, and I

believe in it. What I don't like is having people tell me that I am submerged, that my education and fine intellectual powers (sic!) are being wasted, that my "life is made dreary and empty by the burden of housework." I resent the implication that I am lazy because I will not work on committees, or join clubs, or undertake an outside job, besides fulfilling my normal destiny as wife and mother. There are lots of women who can successfully combine all these outside stunts with domesticity. I don't criticize them, partly because I don't dare, they resent it so keenly, but mostly because I admire their ability. I am proud to belong to the generation that has produced them. I wish they, in their turn, would come to feel that people like me, in spite of our limitations, had chosen a good part too, and were as worthy of their admiration and commendation.

ALICE CONE PERRY 1913

CARRYING ON AT GINLING — THE May QUARTERLY printed excerpts from a letter from Ruth Chester dated April 1. Since then several letters have come from her and from Chinese students or members of the staff. The QUARTERLY has space to quote only sparingly from these letters but gladly refers interested alumnae to the Women's Union Christian Colleges, 419 Fourth Av., N. Y. C., for all information about that heroic little group of Chinese who are daily proving what Ginling has done for the women of China and what her students intend that she shall do as they look forward into the future.

One letter in particular emphasizes that vision in the following sentences:

In the evenings we would all gather in one social room, under the light of a single kerosene lamp, for we no longer have electricity on account of the lack of oil. After hearing the reports from different delegates, we would discuss plans for the next day. Our single aim is that Ginling College must exist. China does not have many educational institutions for women. We must not lose what we have.

From another letter:

Since we came down here to Shanghai, where some of us are still waiting, we have been able to keep in fairly close touch with the little group of students and Chinese faculty who are still there, by letters and by reports from people who have gone up to Nanking, or from those who have come down here from the college. During the first two weeks or so after the "fall" of Nanking the people in power were the extremists—the "left wing" or Communist group—and the prospects for the future independence of such institutions as Ginling were dark. Later when Chiang Kai Shek arrived there this group was overthrown and for the present, at least, the moderates are in power and the group at Ginling has been more hopeful that they can continue to keep the buildings and equipment intact and that Ginling will be allowed to continue. It seems fairly clear that the attack on foreigners and their property in Nanking was a Communist plot, the chief purpose of which was to discredit Chiang Kai Shek. It certainly helped to precipitate the crisis within the party, resulting in the establishment in Nanking of another "Central Government" which is in open opposition to the one in Hankow which is dominated by the Communist element. Whether this is a permanent split or not, and which side will prove stronger if it is, no cautious person will attempt to predict at present, though I think it can be safely said that the very real danger which the Communist influence presents is much better understood by large numbers of Chinese—and foreigners too—than it was two months ago, which is one of the hopeful elements in the situation.

The spirit of the group still at Nanking has been splendid and they have been eager to be allowed to remain at college. . . .

From a letter dated May 10 written by Ellen Y. T. Koo, sister of T. Z. Koo, who is a member of the Chinese staff still carrying on at Ginling:

Now I will tell you something about Ginling after the incident. Soon after the foreign faculty members left Nanking, the Chinese faculty members and the students got busy and organized different committees dividing the various kinds of the work of the college. The sad thing is the number of the Chinese teachers is so small, nine in all; two took care of the finance, one took care of the high school (a class for practice teaching in the Education Department), one had to deal with the outsiders, and the rest took care of the academic work.

During the first week, we were so busy to attend meetings and lectures from the members of the new party, so no classes were going on at all. Every evening teachers and students would meet together and talk about the important things of how and what we were going to do with Ginling at this critical time. Students were leaving us every day on account of the tense strain and upset conditions, but all the students, teachers, and servants agreed that we must preserve Ginling in spite of danger. Then a joint committee was formed, consisting of the members of the Conference Committee and the heads of all student organizations. This committee was to act for the college at present. A telegram and an express letter were sent to Shanghai asking help from the members of the alumnae, who

sent two delegates immediately to help us.

During the second week classes began, of course, not regularly on account of the lack of many teachers, but all of us who are here began our work as best as we can. We had to stop classes whenever some members of the party would come here to give lectures on the three principles of Dr. Sun, and so forth.

These two weeks were memorable weeks. We could never forget them, because our hearts were full of empty feeling, darkness, apprehension, worry and anxiety, and also were burdened with heavy responsibilities which we were not used to before. During the first few days we had asked the new party to send over some soldiers to protect us and also large notices to be put up at our gate to prevent the soldiers to come in to stay, as some other schools and churches were occupied by many of them. The far distance of our college to the city, I mean to the real town, is also a protection. Those who came into Nanking first are mostly the extremes of the party, who were more or less Anti-Christian and Anti-Foreign.

About April 9, Commander-in-chief Chiang Kai Shek arrived in Nanking to the joy of everybody. Then the atmosphere gradually changed to better stage. . . .

The Inauguration of the new Central Government was taken place on April 18 and it was a big affair of Nanking. Our students were invited to attend and the party sent over two busses to take them back and forth. Also they are asked by the party to help in the National Women's Association, Students' Union, and other activities. . . .

We are having chapel every morning and services every Sunday. The student religious committee is taking charge of that and making out programs. The boys from the University came over to join us every Sunday. On Easter Day we had a service and a Scene at the Tomb in the early morning, and a song service at 11 o'clock, both were very beautiful, which brought us real peace of the heart and more strength to conquer evil.

Though the noise of cannonades at Pukow and Hsia Kwan, the bombs from the aeroplanes are still threatening us every day, yet we are very optimistic and still hope for the best, because we are more or less used to them now. Therefore, we are thinking of a summer school, not an ordinary one but just two months, June and July, to let our girls to make up their lost lessons, if the conditions will allow by that time.

A new Administrative Committee was formed about the middle of April consisting of seven alumnae, two Chinese faculty members, and two students. I am one of them (to the surprise of myself). This committee is to act as part of the Board of Control and the administrative duties of the college at present time.

Ginling will appeal to you for your patience, love, and sympathy at such a time more than ever before, because we are struggling very hard and trying our very best to preserve Ginling materially and spiritually. . . .

FACULTY RESOLUTIONS

The following resolutions on President Neilson were read by Professor Deane, acting as spokesman for the Faculty, at the Last Chapel service:

"UNDER President Neilson's administration the material resources of the College have been much increased. Land and buildings have been acquired; the new quadrangle has been built. The College has a new Gymnasium, a new Music Hall, a new Art Gallery; and the beauty of the campus has been greatly enhanced.

"The efficiency of the administration has been promoted by the institution of the Class Deans, the appointment of a Warden, and the organization of a Personnel Bureau. The teaching staff has been enlarged and strengthened. The School of Psychiatric Social Work, founded to meet a war emergency, has continued as a professional training school. The growth of graduate work is manifest in a greatly augmented number of candidates for the Master's degree. Research has been substantially advanced, and this phase of President Neilson's interest has already been recognized by the friends of the College in the foundation of a research professorship in his honor.

"In the undergraduate course of study, always the central interest of the College, significant changes have been made. The major courses have been strengthened; a system of study leading to special honors has been inaugurated; qualified students of French have been given the opportunity to study in France. In the last year a new course of study for freshman and sophomore years has been adopted.

"This material and intellectual progress is preëminently the work of President Neilson. But the Faculty would also acknowledge his sympathetic coöperation in the problems of their work, the eagerness with which he has welcomed suggestions looking toward increased vitality of teaching, the pleasure and inspiration they have received from direct contact with his distinguished scholarship, his penetrating criticism, and his humane and genial personality.

"Be it therefore resolved: that the Faculty of Smith College, recognizing not only the distinction, but the unflagging devotion which President Neilson has given to the College, congratulates him on this tenth anniversary of his administration, and expresses the cordial hope that he may long continue as our Head, 'reaping,' like the Greek prophet of old, 'the harvest of the mind's deep furrow, whence goodly counsels grow.'"   •

SMITH COLLEGE SCHOOL FOR SOCIAL WORK

THE tenth summer session of the School for Social Work opened July 2 with an entering class of 40 students, the largest since the establishment of the two-year course in 1919. There are 33 seniors, of whom 31 are candidates for the M.S.S. degree, 15 experienced social workers who have registered for the summer session in psychiatric social work, and six deans for the special course offered for school deans. All but three of the entering class hold the B.A. degree, one the M.A., and one the Ph.D. The 94 students at the School represent 36 colleges and universities and 24 states of the Union besides Canada, England, France, and Hungary. Seven of the entering students are Smith graduates of 1927: Priscilla Bache, Virginia Condie, Eleanor Crissey, Adelaide Hennion (holder of a fellowship from the Family Society of Philadelphia), Helen H. Smith, Dorothy Spear (holder of the fellowship of the Children's Aid Society of Philadelphia), and Emily Sutton.

The School is very fortunate in the fellowships which are offered to it by various agencies. Eight $1200 fellowships are offered to students in the School by the Commonwealth Fund of New York, ten $450 scholarships by the Institute for Juvenile Research, Chicago, two $450 scholarships by the Michael Reese Dispensary, Chicago, two $600 scholarships by the St. Paul Child Guidance Clinic, one $450 scholarship by the Minneapolis Child Guidance Clinic, one $720 scholarship by the Cleveland Child Guidance Clinic, two $1200 fellowships by the Family Society of Philadelphia, one $1200 fellowship by the Children's Aid Society of Philadelphia, and one $1200 fellowship by the Children's Bureau, Philadelphia. In addition there are ten internships in hospitals, which pay all maintenance expenses during the second session, from September to June, and the Baltimore and St. Louis Smith Clubs each support a scholarship at the School.

NOTE FROM THE PRESIDENT

The following note has been issued by President Neilson:

A QUESTIONNAIRE used in the winter of 1924–25 in a sociology class in Smith College is at present being circulated in various communities, particularly in New England, accompanied usually by misleading or ambiguous statements concerning the use which was made of it at Smith. Many of you were not in college at the time the questionnaire was used and most of you then in college never saw it, as it was used only by one advanced class, but it is possible that some of you will receive inquiries from your parents concerning the matter and it may be convenient for you to have the exact facts at your command.

The questionnaire was given to a class of about seventy students, members of the class of 1925, in their senior year. They were studying, in an elective course in sociology, the history of the institution of marriage. The questionnaire was composed by a committee chosen from their own members and was answered anonymously, the data obtained being solely for class discussion. It came to the notice of the administration several months after it was given, and assurance was received that it would not be repeated in any future class.

(*Signed*) W. A. NEILSON

BULLETIN BOARD

VESPERS.—The vesper speakers since May 1 have been: Rev. Harry Emerson Fosdick, D.D., LL.D., of New York City; Rev. Theodore G. Soares, D.D., of the University of Chicago; Rev. J. V. Moldenhawer of Albany.

CONCERTS.—A student organ recital was given on Apr. 25. A joint concert by the Yale and Smith Glee Clubs was given on May 7. An organ recital was given by Elizabeth Dresch '27, May 8, and there were also senior recitals by Isabelle Dahlberg and Jessie Downing. The students of the Department of Music gave a recital on May 17. A musical vesper service was given on May 15 by the freshman choir with Mrs. Richard Donovan as soloist and Dorothy Fay '27 as violinist.

LECTURES.—The following lectures have been given: "Timbuktu and the Niger" (*illustrated*) by Professor Leland Hall (Music); "Literatura contemporánea española: la novela" by Maria de Maeztu, Ph.D., LL.D., of the Residencia de Estudiantes, Madrid (auspices of the Department of Spanish); "Hearing through the Fingers" (*illustrated*) by Professor Robert H. Gault, Ph.D. [Postponed until fall.] "Utah, Its Scenery and Vegetation" (*illustrated*) by Professor Henry Chandler Cowles, Ph.D., Sc.D., of the University of Chicago (auspices of the Department of Botany); "Manufacture and Use of Antitoxins and Vaccines" by Dr. Benjamin White of the State Antitoxin and Vaccine Laboratories.

At a meeting of the Zeta of Massachusetts Chapter of the Phi Beta Kappa Society, held May 2, Edwin Grant Conklin, Ph.D., Sc.D., of Princeton University was the speaker.

At the meetings of the International Relations Club the following subjects have been discussed: "Present Outlook in Central Europe and the Balkans"; "The League of Nations: Its Limitations and Achievements."

THE SMITH COLLEGE MUSEUM OF ART.—The special exhibition from Apr. 24–May 8 consisted of Coptic textiles of the early Christian era. The collection included 121 specimens of embroidery, beautiful in color, texture, and design.

OTHER NEWS.—At a meeting of the Voice Club, held May 2 in the Browsing Room, Mr. Joseph Auslander, the poet, read from his own works.

A lecture by Mr. Will Rogers was given in John M. Greene Hall, May 9, under the auspices of the Dickinson Hospital Aid Association.

. Mr. Clarence Darrow spoke on "Newer Views of Crime and Punishment," in John M. Greene Hall, May 12, under the auspices of the Hampshire County Progressive Club.

Department Notes

President Neilson was a guest of honor and speaker at the luncheon of the Boston Smith Club, Apr. 16, and of the New York Smith Club, Apr. 23. On May 6 and 7 he attended the meetings of the New England Association of Colleges and Secondary Schools at Trinity College, Hartford, Conn. He represented the University of Edinburgh at the dedication of the new campus and buildings of Hartford Theological Seminary Foundation, May 14, and also attended the meeting of the Foreign Policy Association in Springfield. The President attended the Five College Conference at Wellesley, May 19–20, and the inauguration of President Park at Wheaton, May 21. He delivered the Commencement address at the Marot Junior College, Thompson, Conn., June 8, and at the Burnham School, June 14.

Dean Bernard, Professor Orton, and Professor Barnes (Economics and Sociology) also attended the meeting of the Foreign Policy Association held in Springfield, May 14.

Dean Bernard and Mrs. Scales also attended the Five College Conference at Wellesley, May 19–20. This group, consisting of Smith, Vassar, Mount Holyoke, Bryn Mawr, and Wellesley, meets for the purpose of enabling representatives of different colleges to discuss and compare their common problems.

Dean Bernard addressed the State Meeting of the Girl Scout Leaders, at Springfield, May 4.

ASTRONOMY.—Professor Priscilla Fairfield, Professor Vera Gushee, and Miss Guiler attended a meeting of the Bond Club at Harvard College Observatory, May 14.

Professor Harriet Bigelow attended the meeting of the American Association of Variable Star Observers at Yale Observatory, May 21, and at the invitation of Dr. Frank Schlesinger, director of the observatory.

BIBLE.—Professor Margaret Crook preached at the morning service at the Edwards Congregational Church, Northampton, Apr. 24.

ECONOMICS AND SOCIOLOGY.—Professor Barnes will continue his studies on the subject of the responsibility for the World War by

further travels in Europe this summer. He will devote most of his time to personal interviews with the leading diplomats now alive who presided over the crisis of 1914.

ENGLISH.—Mr. Arvin and Mr. Hicks will give a new course next year, "Literary Movements in the Twentieth Century."

Professor Grace Hazard Conkling entertained Miss Dorothy Lathrop during the latter part of April. Miss Lathrop illustrated Walter de la Mare's "The Three Mullah Mulgars" and "Down-a-down-Derry" and several books by W. H. Hudson and George MacDonald.

FRENCH.—Professor Schinz will offer a course on "The History of the French Novel" at Harvard Summer School. He will leave early in August for a sabbatical leave in Europe. He will spend most of the time in Paris doing research work and will return to Northampton in February for the second term.

Professor Robert will offer two courses in connection with Romance languages at the Columbia Summer School. He attended, as College Board Examiner, a meeting of a committee on College Entrance Examinations, held in New York City the third week in May. He went in June to correct French examinations for the Board. The other members of the Department who corrected College Entrance Examinations this year are: Professors Grant, Anna Chenot, Louise Bourgoin, Yvonne Imbault-Huart.

Professor Marthe Sturm will give a course in Phonetics this summer at the Institut de Phonétique of the Sorbonne. Prior to her trip abroad she will go to Canada to do further research in French Canadian Phonetics.

Professor Hélène Cattanès will spend the greater part of the summer in Northampton and will go to Nova Scotia later for a short vacation.

Professor Aline de Villèle will spend the summer in Paris and La République d'Andove in the Pyrenees.

Professor Grant will spend the summer at Harvard, preparing a book, "Selections of French Travellers in America," which will be published within a year.

GOVERNMENT.—Professor Kimball addressed the Republican Women's Club of Pennsylvania in Philadelphia, Apr. 28. His subject was "Parties, Politics, and the President."

ITALIAN.—Professor Margaret Rooke lectured at Yale on Mar. 24, under the auspices of the course on Pre-War Italy. The lecture was on Italian poetry 1865–1915. She spoke on Apr. 3 at a Polish meeting in Carnegie Hall for the benefit of the Kosciusko fund to facilitate exchange of students between Polish and American Universities.

MUSIC.—Professor Welch spoke at Wellesley, May 11, on "Modern Music." He will give a course in the Appreciation of Music at the Harvard Summer School.

Professor Duke gave a piano recital on May 7 in the Little Salon of the New Aeolian Hall, New York City.

Professor Hall plans to spend a part of the summer in Southern Morocco where he will study the Arabic language and then proceed into the Atlas Mountains if possible. In case the hostility of the African tribes proves too great Mr. Hall will go from Eastern Algeria through the desert by caravan to Mauretania. His purpose is to trace the infiltration of Arabic music into that of the Berbers and black people. He will be away from Smith during the next college year.

Professor Josten will travel abroad during the summer, attending the festivals of modern music at Frankfort and Baden-Baden, the Wagner festival at Bayreuth, and the Handel festival in Göttingen. He hopes to obtain material for an opera to be given at Smith.

Professor Robinson will spend his leave of absence studying in Paris. During the latter part of the summer he and Professor Hall will take a three weeks' walking trip through the Pyrenees.

Professor Marie Milliette will study voice with Louis Graveur in California this summer. She will teach voice during part of the summer in Cummington, Mass., at the Playhouse-in-the-Hills.

Professor Ruth Willian is to spend her summer studying violin under Carl Flesch in Germany. Two of her students will accompany her on this trip abroad.

PHILOSOPHY.—Professor Anna Cutler spoke at a meeting of the Smith College Club of New Bedford, May 21.

SPOKEN ENGLISH.—Professor Elizabeth Avery was elected president of the Eastern Conference of Public Speaking held in New York City on Apr. 22 and 23. Professor Jacob read a paper at the conference on "Rhythm in the Reading of Prose and Verse."

PUBLICATIONS.—Barnes, Harry Elmer. "Genesis of the World War." Third revised edition. . .

Barnes, Harry Elmer, and Davis, Jerome (Yale Univ). Vol. I, "An Introduction to Sociology: a Behavioristic Study of American Society"; Vol. II, "Readings in Sociology." Professor Hankins was one of the five experts who assisted in executing the volumes.

RESIGNATIONS of persons of permanent appointment.—Associate professor Edward J. Woodhouse (Government).

NEW APPOINTMENT.—Dr. Gilman, who returned to Smith last fall to act as College Physician for one year, has accepted an appointment at Radcliffe. Her place here will be taken by Dr. Anna M. Richardson of New York City. Further details and other appointments will be given in the November QUARTERLY.

OTHER NEWS.—The faculty opera, Handel's "Julius Caesar," was presented May 14 at the Academy of Music.

Professor Larkin (Art) gave his marionette show May 17 at the People's Institute for the benefit of the Mississippi Flood Relief Fund. The music accompanying the show was composed by Professor Duke (Music).

Smith College has received a grant from the Carnegie Foundation which makes possible employment of a professional string quartette and other artists to illustrate courses in the study of musical literature next year.

Undergraduate News

ATHLETICS.—Field Day, May 18. The largest number of points was won by 1929. The largest individual score, 31, was made by Agnes Rodgers '29. To the juniors was given the cup for the best athletic record throughout the year. 1928 won the junior-freshman baseball game.

The *All-Smith Tennis* team is: Margaret Palfrey '29, Elizabeth Waidner '28, Ella-Bolling James '27, Sara Cameron '27.

Float Night, May 27. The seniors carried off the honors and captured the crew trophy, awarded on rowing for form as well as for the races. The first senior crew made the best time score, 1 minute 10⅘ seconds. The floats in the Pageant this year were decorated to represent songs, the prize going to the float entitled "Sur le Pont d'Avignon," with second prize to "Lohengrin." The *All-Smith Crew* was announced as: Anna Sturgis, Eleanore Kratz, Margaret Patten, Barbara Barr, Marion Hubbell '27.

The student-faculty baseball game was

won by the faculty with a score of 22-14. The lineup for the faculty was: Mr. Barnes (Sociology), Mr. Parshley (Zoölogy), Mr. Hankins (Sociology), Mr. Bixler (Bible), Mr. Hyde (Treasurer), Mr. Fay (History), Mr. Guilloton (French), Mr. Meyerhoff (Geology).

Outing Club gave 16 certificates, recommending the students who completed the requirements of the Outing Club Councillors' Training Course for positions in camp work for the summer. The second annual convention of the Outing Clubs from the leading eastern women's colleges was held at Smith, May 13-15. The colleges represented were: Vassar, Wellesley, Wellesley Hygiene, Mount Holyoke, Skidmore, and Connecticut.

The members of the *All-Smith Swimming* team are: Wilhelmina Luten, Leslie Winslow, Edith Tyler '27, Mary Gaylord, Bettina Griebel, Margaret Lee, Caroline Schauffler, Marion Smith, Sylvia Ward '28.

The highest score in the annual individual swimming competition, held May 25, was made by Edith Tyler '27, with a record of 14 points. Second place was won by Margaret Grout '28 with a score of 10; Dorothy O'Leary '28 was a close third with 9 points.

CONFERENCES.—Helen Wallace '28 led the Smith delegation of 10 students attending the Eastern Student Conferences at Silver Bay, June 17-27.

DRAMATICS.—D. A. presented "The Beaux' Stratagem" by George Farquhar at the Academy of Music, May 11. The same performance was given for Commencement Dramatics, June 16 and 17.

At the open meeting of Alpha and Phi Kappa Psi, May 28, the play presented was "Belinda" by A. A. Milne.

On May 18, Workshop presented four plays: "Columbine in Business" by Edith L. Field, produced by Dorothy Wagner '28; "The Golden Doom," written by Lord Dunsany and produced by Eloise Barrangon '28; "Jael," written and produced by Dorothy Ettelson '27; "Everybody's Husband," written by Gilbert Cannon and produced by Constance Stockwell '28.

The Workshop and Faculty Performance for the Stage Fund was given on June 1. Workshop presented "The Scandal about the School," an historical comedy written by Mary Arbenz and Henrietta Wells '27. The faculty production was "Press Cuttings" by George Bernard Shaw.

ELECTIONS.—1928, senior president, Julia Hafner of St. Louis, Mo.; head usher, Nancy Barnett; editor of 1928 Year Book, Caroline Schauffler.

1929.—Council members: Margaret Palfrey, Ruth Houghton; Judicial Board member, Alice Eaton; class historian, Helen W. Smith.

STUDENT GOVERNMENT.—At a mass meeting of the student body held after chapel on May 18, the students voted to continue the present system of required chapel attendance. The rule reads: "Each student shall attend chapel on the average of at least four times a week in each semester."

The Residence Requirement for next year is as follows: The minimum residence requirement for undergraduates for a college year shall be two full semesters in college less seven nights of absence in each semester. Only those students may extend their winter or spring recesses (either at the beginning or at the end) who for all other purposes are absent less than three of the seven nights of the semester.

OTHER NEWS.—Florence Lyon '28 was chosen to represent Smith at Junior Month held annually in New York City by the New York Charity Organization Society, to enable students to study existing social conditions.

On the evening of May 25, Observatory Hill became the scene of a dance drama, "La Giara," given by the intermediate and advanced classes in Rhythms under the direction of Miss Edith Burnett.

At the vocational meetings for seniors the following talks have been given: "Occupational Therapy" by Miss Marjorie Greene of the Boston School of Occupational Therapy; "Museum Work" by Miss Edith Abbott of the Metropolitan Museum of Art; "Architecture" by Mr. Henry A. Frost, director of the Cambridge School of Domestic Architecture and Landscape Architecture.

Five more members of 1929 joined the Sorbonne group. They are: Virginia Bourne, Dorothy Clark, Elsie Pond, Louise Squibb, Vivian Zerbone. This increases the number of students who are eligible to spend their junior year in France to 43. They will spend the first days in Europe as guests of the Union Internationale des Etudiants at Geneva. Teresina Rowell, daughter of Teresina (Peck) Rowell '95, has decided to remain in No thampton and it is possible that several others will also remain.

Lucia Jordan '27 (daughter of Elsie Pratt

'92) was awarded honorable mention at an intercollegiate contest in poetry held this spring at Mount Holyoke. Five leading women's colleges were represented: Vassar, Bryn Mawr, Wellesley, Smith, and Mount Holyoke. The judges of the contest were: Witter Bynner, Jessie Rittenhouse, and Robert Greenwood.

Junior Prom was held on May 20. The Prom show was "You Never Can Tell," presented by the Cap and Bells Society of Williams.

Smith College is again opening the swimming pool to the women of Northampton with the coöperation of the Hampshire County Branch of the Red Cross. Lessons will be given during July and August under the direction of Dorothy Bruce, Red Cross Life Saver. Four hundred and forty course tickets have been sold.

· Awards

The Helen Kate Furness Prize for the best essay on a Shakespearean theme was awarded to Isobel Strong '27. The subject for this year was "The Tragic Hero in Shakespeare."

The Henry Lewis Foote Memorial Prize of $25 was awarded to Christina Lochman '29 for attaining the best grade in an examination given by the Department of Biblical Literature to the competing students taking the elementary course in Biblical Literature.

The Emogene Mahony Memorial Prize, consisting of the income from a fund of $500, was awarded to Elizabeth Dresch '27 for proficiency in organ.

The Emma Kingsley Smith Memorial Prize of $25, given by her husband, Robert Seneca Smith, to be awarded in the College year 1926–27 to the student in "Religion and Ethics of the Bible" who, having attained a grade of A or B for the first semester's work, submitted the best essay on a topic connected with the work of the Department, was awarded to Virginia Katherine Harrison '27.

. The Clara French Prize of the income of $5000 was divided between Elizabeth Hamburger and Doris Russell. This prize is given to that senior who has advanced farthest in the study of English language and literature. Elizabeth Hamburger is the daughter of Amy Stein '04.

The Hazel Edgerly Prize was awarded to Eleanor Miller '27, recommended by the Department of History for unusual ability in that subject.

The Trustee Fellowships, open to women graduates of Smith College or other colleges of equal rank for advanced work in various departments of study, were awarded to Madeleine de Blois of McGill University for the study of Physics; Barbara Palmer, Cambridge University '27, to study Philosophy; Joyce Horner, Oxford '27, to study English; Alice Roberts, University of Colorado '23, to study French; Margaret Wattie, Oxford '24, to study English. A fellowship for the study of Medicine at Johns Hopkins was awarded to Marian Ropes '24.

The Harriet Boyd Hawes Scholarship, established by the class of 1892 at its 30th reunion, for advanced work in various departments of study, was awarded to Mildred Moyer, Penn. State '26, for a second year of graduate work in the study of French at Smith.

The $1200 fellowship offered by the Children's Aid Society of Pennsylvania for study at the Smith College School for Social Work, has been awarded to Dorothy Spear '27.

The Alumnae Fellowship for 1927–28 was awarded to Mary Pangborn '27 for graduate study in physiological chemistry at Yale. Mary Pangborn is the daughter of Georgia Wood ex-'96.

The Frances A. Hause Memorial Prize was awarded to Mary Pangborn '27 for excellence in chemistry.

The John Everett Brady Prize for excellence in the sight translation of Latin prose and verse was divided between Lucy Kendrew '28 and Jean Ryan '28. This is the first year the prize has been awarded.

Marjorie Lawson was awarded the Arthur Ellis Hamm prize for the best midyear record in the freshman class.

A three months' summer training scholarship at the New York School for Secretaries offered to a Smith College senior by Mrs. Virginia Wheat, was awarded to Katherine Morris.

Elizabeth Stoffregen '27 is one of the six American students to whom the International Union has awarded scholarships to study at the Geneva School of International Studies this summer.

HONOR LIST OF 1927

Cum laude.—Eighty-four seniors were graduated *cum laude.*

Magna cum laude.—Degrees were conferred upon 19 candidates *magna cum laude.* They were: Pauline Alper, Ruth Champlin, *Eleanor Deland,** Mary Doran, Charlotte Eisenberg, *Selma Erving,* Margaret Hilferty, Lucella Lunt, Eleanor Miller, *Janet Olmsted,* Katharine Pillsbury, Caroline Roberts, Anne Clark Smith, Helen Houston Smith, *Dorothy Tebbetts,* Annie Vaughan Weaver, Clarice Webber, Anna Whiting, Gertrude Woelfle.

Summa cum laude.—Degrees were conferred upon two candidates *summa cum laude.* They were: Margaret Adams and *Mary Pangborn.*

The Special Honors students graduated as follows: Honors, *Antoinette Dodge* (English).

High Honors: Grace Asserson (History), Anna Sharon (Biblical Literature). Flora Webb (English).

* Girls whose names are in italics are daughters of the following alumnae respectively: Isabel (Adams) Deland '96. Emma (Lootz) Erving '97. Marguerite (Prescott) Olmsted '03. Frances (Ayer) Tebbetts '93. Georgia (Wood) Pangborn ex-'96, Isabel (Adams) Dodge ex-'01, Amy (Stein) Hamburger '04.

Highest Honors: *Elizabeth Hamburger* (English), Caroline Wagner (History).

Four hundred and sixty-four A.B.'s were conferred on 1927, and five as of the class of 1926, a total of 469. Twenty A.M.'s were conferred.
                                    DOROTHY DUDLEY 1929

FROM THE TRUSTEE MINUTES

AT the meeting of the Board of Trustees held on June 18 the following gifts were accepted:

The James Gardner Buttrick Fund of one thousand dollars given by Mrs. Buttrick in memory of her husband. The interest on this fund is to be used for a prize for an essay in the Department of Religion and Biblical Literature.

A collection of instrumental music given to the Department of Music by Judge Joseph R. Churchill and his daughter, Anna Churchill, of the Class of 1907.

A Revival of Handel's "Julius Caesar"—As Others Saw It

ROY DICKINSON WELCH

Chairman of the Department of Music

"IN the artistic annals of America May 14, 1927, is a date that will be remembered. On the evening of that day Handel's opera ' Julius Caesar' (London, 1724) was performed for the first time in the United States. The selected theater was the Academy of Music at Northampton, Mass.; the sponsoring body, the Department of Music at Smith College." These sentences stand at the head of Pitts Sanborn's column in the *New York Telegram* of May 16. The same article (which runs to two columns and a half) concludes with a statement which modesty would prevent a member of the College making unless he made it in quotation marks. "It is possible to say without exaggerating," concludes Mr. Sanborn, "that the production was a very long feather in the cap of the Music Department of Smith College, as well as a milestone that can't be disregarded in the musical history of the United States.'

This performance of " Julius Caesar" was produced with much the same resources as those that were used in last year's revival of another work, never previously heard in America. Last year's opera was Monteverdi's "Coronation of Poppaea." The fact

that neither had previously been given in America is, of course, only incidentally interesting. What is more important is that both are works of significant musical and historical importance. Both operas were exhumed from unmerited oblivion and set upon the stage by Professor Werner Josten. Professor Josten is an operatic conductor of much European experience and of seasoned discrimination. The singers and the orchestral players were chiefly members of the College community. Two of the leading rôles in "Julius Caesar" were sung by persons imported for the task. The staging was designed and carried out by Professor Oliver Larkin of the Department of Art.

This year's performance, like last's, attracted much attention from the authoritative critics in the East and from distinguished musicians. The audience was what the society column describes as brilliant. What the audience thought is to be reported most wisely in the words of the authentic critics who heard the performance. For those skeptical of journalistic criticism let it be said that the writers of these articles had no inducement to come save a complimentary

ticket! And, between ourselves, the fact may be circulated that even the undergraduates stayed through to the end.

"The colleges are one of our defences against the smug life, the dull life." Thus began Mr. H. T. Parker in the *Boston Transcript* for May 16. "They make new departures, they discover forgotten possessions —even to the operas of George Frederick Handel. . . . The faculty and the students of Smith College set on the stage Handel's 'Julius Caesar.' As a performance it exceeded all possible expectation. There was virtue in it and renown. The Metropolitan Opera House with the resources of New York at its disposal wonders whether an opera by Handel is possible in America. The outcome at a college in Northampton should allay its doubts."

Mr. Olin Downs in the *New York Times* of May 15 included in his column on this performance these statements: "Handel's opera was mounted with limited scenic resources and with singers of limited technique and stage experience, but with a spirit, a prevailing intelligence and coördination of effort that drove home the vitality and frequent dramatic significance of the music. Palpably an amateur performance, this one justified itself by its subject and by its devotion to its task."

The setting and the costuming which Professor Larkin ingeniously devised out of very limited resources were felicitously described by Oscar Thompson in *Musical America* for May 21. "One of the happy touches," Mr. Thompson writes, "of to-night's performance was its purposeful adherence to the costumic anachronisms of

Handel's day. Old prints, such as those in Streatfield's 'Handel,' as well as the Tiepolo painting which the producer was said to have taken as a model, show that artists and stage folk of the times had only the quaintest notion as to feminine attire in the preceding century. They had some idea as to what a Roman Emperor might be expected to wear; but a Cleopatra or a Dido was more than likely to appear in something like the mode of the Hanoverian ladies-in-waiting. To-night's stage pictures were given the benefit of this droll clash of periods; the Centurion of the Legions showed no surprise at the feminine frigates that sailed majestically his way, and Caesar was not amazed that his Queen of Egypt should be powdered and furbelowed as the courtliest of these high-sailing dames."

In all the reviews high commendation was liberally bestowed upon Professor Josten's capacities and enthusiasm. The soloists and the chorus seem, if the reviews are to be trusted, to have given an acceptable performance of the parts that fell to them. Miss Milliette and Mr. Sinclair of the Department of Music were, by several critics, singled out for especial commendation and the College itself which, through the administration, liberally guaranteed this undertaking was not overlooked by the chroniclers. "As Yale with its plays serves the spoken drama," says Mr. Parker in the *Boston Transcript* (May 16), "so Smith with its ancient operas nurtures the music of the theater. Sooner or later the Metropolitan or the Chicagoan Stage may find room for an opera by Handel. Its larger means will amplify and adorn the voyage of discovery. At Northampton, a college laid the course."

The Note Room

Written by Elizabeth Bacon '28·   Initial by Priscilla Paine '28

THE first of May was "a beautiful day to be glad in," warm and flooded with sunshine. The apple blossoms were in tight, pink bud and the lilacs hung fragrant with promise among their smooth green leaves. The senior class went "a-Maying," all in their summer dresses. They sang to Miss Wilson, their class dean, and left a May basket on her door; they sang to Mrs. Scales and left another there; then they hung a great big May basket on the handle of the President's door and sang and sang until he came out and made them a little speech. Perhaps he only said good-morning. I can't tell, because juniors weren't invited. May Day begins the series of festivities that lead up to Last Step Sing and Ivy Day and culminate in graduation. After having made such an auspicious start, the weather failed miserably to live up to itself. Perhaps it couldn't make another day as delicious as the first of May, but anyhow it didn't try very hard. There were lovely warm days—but they were separated by periods of cold and cheerless rain, and the college slopped around in slickers and thought seriously of going to the President about an Ark. On the nice days there were little bunches of two or three people in bright dresses studying under all the trees. A rather too enthusiastic alumna once remarked that to her college seemed like a "garden of flowers" —unfortunately she meant the girls, but had she referred to the campus on those days when the iris was blue under the willow and the azaleas in pink and golden blossom, and everywhere on the soft green grass there were girls in lavender and blue and yellow and poppy colored dresses, there might have been more veracity in her remark. Paradise is covered with canoes and row boats, and whenever the weather permits the tennis courts are alive with swinging rackets and flashes of balls.

This year Miss Ainsworth has made much more of the tennis than before. Besides the usual tournament, each girl has been graded carefully as to where she stands on the scale of players. The newest innovation this year, in sports, has been a riding ring for those equestriennes who are not able to take the road. (Horseback riding is actually a part of elective gym work and I hear.that alumnae from time immemorial are green with envy.) It is down on West Street, and although not pretentious fulfills the regulations. In archery there have been some new shoots which are most amusing—among them are balloons and a black cat. Swimming has been tremendously popular, and for the first time an All-Smith swimming team has been organized. Of course the usual baseball and track and dancing activities have prevailed, especially among the freshmen. Field Day is the culmination of the athletic year, and it was actually held on the specified date this spring. The field was a regular three-ringed circus with baseball, archery (the freshmen won here), tennis, and track all going on at once. No need for anybody to get bored. The juniors won the cup for the best athletic record during the year, but Agnes Rodgers '28 seemed to walk or run or jump away with most of the individual honors. She hurdled, and dashed, and threw a javelin and tossed a discus as to the manner born. The sophomores carried off the honors for jumping, the seniors made successful spectators, and everybody consumed ice cream cones enthusiastically.

One evening in May the dancing classes gave a ballet called "La Giara." It was a Sicilian peasant story by Pirandello set to music by Alfredo Casella and was given on Observatory Hill. Unhappily the weather had been unsympathetic to it night after night and it was cold and miserable when it was finally given. It was a pity too, for the beauty of a really lovely thing was marred thereby. Nothing marred the enthusiasm of the Outing Club conference held a bit earlier in the spring. Delegates came from Vassar, Wellesley, Holyoke, Skidmore, and Sweet Briar and the Smith hostesses tried not to act too proud when they showed off their cabins, in the building of which they really are the pioneers.

Float Night was clear—more than that can't be said of the weather, because it was raw and bleak and cold and never a picture could be taken. First there was exhibition rowing—then races which were won by the seniors. Then came the floats—a Japanese scene, a Spanish setting, an Old-Fashioned Garden, a vegetable barge, a float called

"Venetian Moon," all decorated with balloons. The prize-winner was called "Sur le Pont d'Avignon" and on it two gallant gentlemen and two deliciously French ladies danced to the music of a flute. Directly after the prize was awarded a large part of the audience repaired to the Gym to see an exhibition of Morris and Sword dances given by a team of twelve men and women from the American Branch of the Old English Folk Dance Society. It was the merriest sort of an evening they gave us and it ended up by their inviting us to learn a country dance. And so we did, lining up all down the gym: faculty, and faculty wives, students, and maybe a stray fusser or two, and stepping off as gaily as though we were really on the greensward of Merrie England itself.

There haven't been so many lectures this spring as usual and that is just as well perhaps. The college and, even more, the town turned out to hear Clarence Darrow speak on Crime and Punishment, and how we did argue pro and con for weeks afterwards! Mr. Joseph Auslander read some of his poems in the Browsing Room and Richard Halliburton spoke at the Bookshop on the "Glorious Adventure," but it was Will Rogers who won the heart of Smith College. For two hours and a half he drawled on about everything on earth and we rocked back and forth in ecstasy. He ended up with his amazing stunts with his lariat.

"The Pipes of Pan have piped the spring" —only here the pipes have been made manifest in solider forms such as the Smith-Harvard Glee Club concert and the Faculty Opera. The Glee Club concert was a superb finish to the concert course. The joint singing was well balanced, especially in the "Round About the Starry Throne" of Handel, where the combination of men's voices with the girls' made a glorious effect. The most impressive thing in the whole evening, however, was the "O Vos Omnes" by Vittoria which was perfectly done by the Harvard Glee Club. To quote from *Weekly:*

In view of the fact that the Harvard Glee Club is one of the best organizations of its kind it might seem an unwarranted bit of conceit for the Smith Glee Club to attempt anything so ambitious as a joint concert, were it not for the fact that our club has been steadily increasing in fame for a number of years, and their concert in New Haven marked for them a definite arrival in the choral world.

The faculty presented Handel's opera "Julius Caesar" for the first time in this country. The *Weekly* says:

. . . more of the outside world have gotten a march on us. It has been reserved for them to draw our attention to the accomplishments of our own department. Perhaps the slight hint from without will help us to appreciate more fully what is happening in our own midst.

Perhaps the slight hint from within helped too, because the Academy was full of interested and enthusiastic spectators. Of course in an opera the acting is always sacrificed to the music, but in this what there was of it was well done. The costumes and staging were excellent and of course the music is beyond a layman's criticism, and you are referred to the account of the opera on page 494.

Dramatically the college has had an active spring. "The Beaux' Stratagem," the Commencement play, was first given in May as the D. A. spring production. It was delicious! The acting was well sustained and the eighteenth century humor was thoroughly appreciated by the twentieth century audience, but, unfortunately, it wasn't a very large audience. D. A. is so very much more successful with comedy than tragedy that it is a pity it doesn't try it oftener.

The faculty and Workshop gave a joint performance for the benefit of the stage fund. Surely there never was a faculty so coöperative as ours. "Press Cuttings" by Bernard Shaw was delightfully done by a practically all star faculty cast and "The Scandal about the School," written after the eighteenth century manner by two seniors, was most successfully acted by Workshop. Also successfully acted were the four plays that Workshop presented independent of stage fund or faculty. Two of the plays were original and the other two were Dunsany's "Golden Doom" and "Columbine in Business" by Edith Field in Harvard 47.

Meantime the month of May held other things as well. The Phi Bete dinners were still going strong. House after house bedecked itself with flowers, loaded its table with the campus equivalents of nectar and ambrosia, dressed itself up in its company clothes, and invited the favored faculty and always the favored President to the festal board. They do say that the poor President got to the point when corned beef and cabbage would have been a welcome variant to the delicious but omnipresent fried chicken and strawberry. Then came the days when the Special Honors students who had gazed on the rest of us so pityingly at midyears went down into the depths of their final examinations, and we who lived neighbor to them went on tiptoes and wrung out towels and thanked whatever gods there be that we had stuck to the beaten if lowlier path of the straight A.B. And ·all the time were the step sings, when we swallowed our dinners at lightning speed and gathered around "dot svell senior class" to sing gay songs and sad songs and just plain humorous songs.

> When May time is over
> And gay June must pass,
> We will hear your voices ring still
> Across the twilight shadowed grass

sang the juniors. It is easy to be a bit sentimental at step sings and somehow it seems to be perfectly good form even in this unsentimental age.

One morning in May—the sixteenth, to be strictly accurate—the seniors burst forth in a thundercloud of caps and gowns at chapel. No one seemed to appreciate what an epochmaking morning that was, but I have since learned that never in the history of Smith seniors has such a thing been done before. At any rate the subsequent thunderclouds in the sky and hot weather in between and jeers of the underclassmen so discouraged them that only a very small handful of persistent scholars appeared in them all term. Cap and gown at chapel is one thing but it did look a bit odd to see an academic figure perched on a bicycle bowling swiftly from the new dorms, and is a mortar board the equivalent of a chauffeur's cap, I wonder? Mention of caps reminds me that gypsy turbans were all the rage for every conceivable occasion for us undergraduates whose heads were still untroubled by the thought of diplomas in June.

Of course the most interesting and exciting, and really important thing—always excepting Commencement week—that happens in the spring is Junior Prom, with all its attendant festivities. The weather was splendid. It took itself severely in hand and produced a beautiful blue and golden day and a cloudless, starry night—both of which were warm. Of course everyone looked astonishingly lovely— Garden Party in the new Quadrangle, with booths and grass and sunshine, was delightful. People in soft dresses and enormous floppy hats walked around with their escorts and looked just like grown up ladies and gentlemen. It was such a pleasant change! There was dancing in the big living-rooms for those who didn't realize that they should make the most of the sun. Prom itself was really so gratifying to the soaring hopes of the juniors in the beauty and good taste of the decorations that the chairman and her committee should have especial commendation. The lights in the green decorations around the balcony made a flattering *aura* to set off the beauty of people who did not, in the least, need it. There were swinging Japanese lanterns along the white canvas-covered walk that led to the Gymnasium; and more lanterns on the roof of the swimming pool,· throwing shadows on the people strolling up and down, gave an almost European touch of elegance to the party. The faculty were very much in evidence even in the crowd of feminine stags. The junior and senior stags stayed on to the glorious end but it was positively pathetic to watch the little sophomore "runners," who had worked like devoted slaves on the Committee, glance apprehensively at the clock and, sharp on the stroke of ten, flee from the ball like true modern Cinderellas. Mr. Hicks wrote in *Weekly*:

I must confess, however, that sometimes it required a rugged physique to make one's way through the congestion. When dancing became too difficult I usually singled out one of the more massive members of the faculty, Mr. Bixler or Mr. Barnes, if possible. By following in their wake and taking advantage of the havoc they wrought I could usually circle the hall with a minimum of collisions!

Mr. Fay and Mr. Bixler were among the particular beaux of the evening, although all their colleagues enjoyed a new kind of attention from their students, differing widely in form and intensity from that bestowed upon them in the classroom. It would be interesting to know which they enjoyed most. As a corollary to Prom I include the stern but effective instructions issued by the Committee. They are recommended *in toto* for the future:

To prevent all misunderstanding, Prom Committee wishes to make clear the duties and privileges of freshman and sophomore runners. In the first place, Prom is absolutely barred to all runners except those serving on sophomore committees. But they may go to Garden Party and the Saturday Club dances, not, however, for their own amusement, but to give the juniors' men a good time. Each runner is also expected to straighten her junior's room after she has gone to Prom and to leave something in the way of sustenance for her. Runners should not send flowers. Instead, this privilege belongs to the juniors or seniors who are expected to send them to their runners as a reward for their exertions.

Then came the warning shadow of exams. The college took its books—even the ones with the leaves uncut—sharpened its pencils, and sat down to hard work. Seniors became impossible. Those who had maintained a B average for four years now talked seriously and insanely of not graduating. They tried on their caps and gowns surreptitiously before their mirrors and practiced flipping the tassels with the left hand while grasping an imaginary diploma from the imaginary hand of the President with the right. They looked sentimentally at all the stones they had tripped over and sang part songs on their way home from the movies. The rest of the college took their exams with their usual pessimism and coffee, but the seniors talked so much about theirs that it left the underclassmen with an impression that each of them had ten! Exam week was distractingly warm, and one delicious day followed another. The campus looked tantalizingly lovely and the grass particularly green after the rain. There were enough sane people so that Paradise was covered with canoes, and every evening little or big bunches of people could be seen walking —if they had no senior friends, riding if they had—on their way to a picnic.

There was a dreadful period of rumors: were they flunking a large part of the senior class or only half—or perhaps less—? Then the freshmen all had their Latin exams and packed their trunks and left, and their rooms were cleaned for the alumnae. Then the sophomores, all except Push Committee, handed in their "27" papers to Miss Dunn and with a sigh of regret and relief left on the next train. The juniors stayed—to wear their big hats on Ivy Day and see their "just one step aheads" graduate. The seniors—but enough has been said about them already and, besides, their families began to come, or their fiancés, and in either case they were kept busy. The juniors looked at them jealously, and wished they were as grown up as a cap and gown and diamond ring seemed to indicate.

Then, suddenly and unexpectedly, the Last Step Sing had come. The weather was too irritating for words—all day it rained a little and then cleared a very little, and then just sulked and looked glum and gray. But just at sunset it recovered its sense of humor and the clouds all cleared and the sun came out, and it was a perfect evening. People walked across the lawn in front of Studes and watched the seniors, looking strange but rather nice in their caps and gowns, assemble on the steps. Mothers tried not to look proud or self-conscious. Fathers talked to other fathers and tried not to show how impressed they were. The faculty wandered around with their dogs or children, looking more human than ever before. The Push Committee—painfully true to its name—crowded us all behind ropes so that the hoops could be rolled from the Library. No one could have suspected anyone of preliminary practice!

Then the seniors began with:

> For now the spring is here
> The best time of the year. . . .
> Won't you come out and sing?

They expressed the ambitions that four years of instruction had nourished, to the tune of "Yankee Doodle":

> Every day in every way
> My family grows more worried,
> 'Cause no one has a job for me
> But I just won't be hurried;
> Daddy says, "Please get a job,
> You'll have to earn your keep, dear,"
> But next year doesn't worry me
> Because I know it's Leap Year.

The popular sentiments about caps and gowns were reflected in:

> Seniors here and there
> Seniors everywhere
> Dressed in cap and gown;
> In Trebla's yesterday
> I heard two of them say,
> Yours looks wonderful,
> Yours looks marvelous,
> Quite sets off your style,
> Everybody else looks cute
> But I look simply vile.

Then came the last—and when the seniors all stood up to sing their song of last year

> In joy but half in sorrow
> We take these steps from you—

we had a catch in our throats—and when they slowly marched off the steps singing "Our campus fair again is green and gay" we all felt miserably what they had sung so gaily:

> Oh, who will ever take our place? . . .
> Nobody Can, Nobody Can,
> NOBODY CAN, CAN, CAN.

THE ALUMNAE ASSOCIATION

THE NEW ELECTIONS

THE new officers are: vice-president, Helen (Gulick) King '16; secretary, Ruth Higgins '13; treasurer, Eleanor (Adams) Hopkins '16· The new directors are: Clara Porter '06, Elizabeth Hugus '16, and Miriam Titcomb '01·

REPORT OF THE PRESIDENT

IF you do not keep a cash account and balance your receipts and expenditures each night, you are morally certain at the end of the month that somehow and somewhere you have lost a substantial sum.

In much the same way the Alumnae Association, during what seems to be an uneventful year, might feel that nothing had been accomplished did we not pause to take account of stock in the form of an annual report. Such a survey reveals that the standing committees have been functioning as usual, with the Education Committee holding an interesting conference in connection with the February meeting of the Council, the Committees on Ginling and the War Service Board still carrying on, and the Committee on Class Organization and Records decidedly alive. The Homestead Committee has painted the Homestead and the Committee on Local Clubs has revived the *Bulletin* with two numbers full of valuable material, and has issued an interesting chart of Club activities.

Pleasant happenings have been the award of the Alumnae Fund Fellowship to a Smith granddaughter in the person of Mary Pangborn '27, daughter of Georgia (Wood) Pangborn ex-'96, and the recognition of our neighbor, the Burnham School, by flowers and a message of congratulation.

The outstanding accomplishment of the year has been the completion of the Fund for Juniper Lodge made possible by the efforts of a devoted committee and the hearty coöpera-

tion of the clubs. Last Commencement the goal seemed far distant—it is pleasant to record that now the endowment has been (quite characteristically for an alumnae enterprise) oversubscribed.

Much time and thought has been given by the Alumnae Fund Committee to perfecting the plans for the Fund which will begin to function soon after Commencement. This Fund is to serve as the visual and recognized channel for alumnae giving and we hope will become more and more valuable to the College as the years go on.

MARY (FROST) SAWYER 1894

ANNUAL REPORT OF THE "QUARTERLY"

ONCE again we stand before you and protest that there just "ain't no such animal" as an annual report of the QUARTERLY other than the QUARTERLIES themselves. That being the case, "as the saying is," 7502 of you—and we trust that the two has been increased at least a hundred fold since you have made the rounds of Alumnae Headquarters—have received a quarterly report of the QUARTERLY since this time last year, and we submit that if you will lump them all together—467 pages of text, 95 pictures, 4423 personal items, and 92 pages of advertising— you will have an annual report of everything in the world that the editors know not only about the QUARTERLY but about Smith College, about her 10,000 plus alumnae, about Education with a capital E, and, incidentally, about the printing business.

All these years we have felt a bit guilty about our reluctance to write formal annual reports, but this spring we went to a convention of alumni secretaries and editors at which a fellow sufferer, who is also called on perennially for a report, arose and patiently drawled out that as far as he was concerned annual reports were pretty much all alike except that one year you "hollered in one place and the next year you hollered in another," and that comforted us mightily.

Well, we have "hollered" about the fact that, although we are fortunate in having a larger per cent of paid subscribers than other college periodicals, our subscription list is still about 3000 smaller than our total alumnae body—Oh, yes, we know that there are alumnae mothers and daughters who naturally share one copy, to say nothing of a group of friends who do likewise, with less excuse—why don't you reunion classes do something about working up a 100% subscription list right now? We've hollered about the fact that it costs more than $9000 to produce four QUARTERLIES, we have hollered about our superb lot of advertisements, paying particular attention of late to the four impressive pages of each issue setting forth the magnificent number of intercollegiate hotels which are scattered all over the country and which specialize in service to the alumnae of all coöperating colleges, of which Smith is of course one. We have hollered, and this holler is perennial although muted because we realize how far short of our hopes is our achievement, about our great desire to make the QUARTERLY so reflect the spirit and the ideals of Smith College that no one whose family name is Smith can consider her budget complete without that modest item of a dollar fifty. And now this year we are going to holler in still another place.

We are going to holler about the privilege of being the editor of the QUARTERLY all through this first ten years of the administration of President Neilson. It has been and is a thrilling task, and no amount of blue Mondays, when the articles don't come and the engravers' bills make the business manager turn on us her reproachful eye, can more than temporarily dim the joy we feel in working so closely with a man as truly great as he. Since the day he came ten years ago he has been the QUARTERLY's greatest friend. He has made our task of interpreting the College sympathetically an easy one because he has honored us by discussing its problems and outlining its policies and its hopes in such a way as to make us feel that we too have a real part in a great enterprise. His utter devotion to Smith College is a constant challenge to do our best. Of the things which he has done in this decade you heard at Last Chapel. We have been privi-

leged to record them all. We have never in all these years been forced to make bricks without straw. These past ten years have been red letter years for the editor of the QUARTERLY, and although she has a guilty feeling now and then that she ought to resign and let someone share her good fortune she hangs tenaciously on.

This then is the end of our annual report. You may say as the Scotchman did when he too had listened to an annual report: "There are several reasons why I dinna like it. Furst, she read it; second, she dinna read it verra well"; but we are sure that this time at least you will not add as he did, "And thurd, it was no worth the readin'."

EDITH NAOMI HILL 1903

ALUMNAE OFFICE REPORT

A REALLY conscientious report of a year in a busy alumnae office would carefully parallel the items in the annual budget. It would draw upon your sympathetic imagination to picture an overworked office staff, frantically addressing and sealing $1445.33 worth of stamped envelopes containing $327.55 worth of miscellaneous printing—but not thus does my report this year conform to the Old Plan. It is rather New Plan and pseudo-comprehensive, and its few subjects offered for examination are all elective and little likely to pass any board of admission.

The reasons for this change are, first, because after 20 years of operation of this service bureau of ours, I take it for granted that you are sufficiently familiar with its procedure so that you do not need, for instance, to be urged to send us your new address when you move. I shall leave this hackneyed and favorite topic of mine to the Bureau of Education of the Department of the Interior, which has just published a treatise of 127 pages, bursting with tables and statistics, entitled "Residence and Migration of University and College Students." And yet, in passing, I cannot refrain from inquiring plaintively: What are we to do, when not only students and alumnae, but also *Universities* pick themselves up and float around the world? Someone has suggested that there should be added to the collection of college songs: "Where is my wandering Alma Mater to-night?"

And, second, because this alumnae secretary in person has just been blessed with a sabbatical year, a great innovation in alumnae annals. It was made all the more perfect by the efficiency and devotion to Smith interests of the staff at home, but understudying has had one disastrous effect. It has driven our first assistant, Marion Graves 1915, who has been with us for nearly ten years of invaluable service, to forsake us for a matrimonial position. Council and Commencement and all the round of days seem problematical without her, but happily she is not departing from Northampton, and she has rashly promised to come to our rescue in case of emergency.

To resume the argument. By means of this glorious sabbatical, I have achieved that detached point of view that a year's European holiday gives. I can look upon alumnae organization from afar, in rational perspective, and see the whole forest unobscured by nearby trees. Or rather I *could*, for the first fortnight after returning. During that first fortnight, like any United States congressman, I had conclusions about European affairs, too, though I kept them to myself. I knew perfectly well what was the matter with Italy and the Balkans and the franc and the dole—what else could you expect in a continent without a single organization of alumnae? How could you agree to any terms for any debt settlement, if the populace had never been trained to an alumnae fund?

Later in this "normal academic year," when I found I was losing the splendid isolation of a well-poised executive who never stoops to sharpen a pencil or seal a letter, I betook myself to the annual convention of the American Alumni Council at the University of North Carolina, and there, in the company of 150 other great minds, deliberated on many stirring topics, from "The Embryo State of an Alumnus, or how to develop alumni spirit before graduation" (you notice that the pre-school child is followed by the pre-Commencement alumnus) to Education as a continuing Process, for alumni who are starving for cultural opportunities.

Complacently flattered by the compliments of deans and college presidents who addressed us, we tried to act as if we believed we really were "determiners of public relationships," "interpreters of education," exponents of a new profession superior to that of the college presidents themselves. Our presidential host, however, relieved the exalted strain by comparing us to that infamous guild of this crooked and perverse generation, the bootleggers, who say that what counts in their profession isn't so much the money they make, as the people they meet!

In order to keep the office tools of our trade bright and shining, during this process of merging from trade into profession, and in order to avoid what our President calls "the limitations of professional thinking," we subscribe to certain trade journals. One of them, called *Sales Management*, is putting forth from its service department a unique summer sales campaign. Its announcement begins thus:

Dear Miss Snow:

In connection with the plans you are undoubtedly making to get the largest possible volume of business during July and August, we are submitting the enclosed proposal to the Alumnae Association of Smith.

And then follows this sample letter which is intended for our Smith salesmen:

Dear Bill:

In the brown envelope you will find an honest-to-goodness shark's tooth from Barbados. It was pulled from a jaw like the one on the envelope this letter came in.

I am sending you this curiosity because it symbolizes a point which has much to do with the success you will have selling boots, or buttons, or Smith QUARTERLIES, during the next eight weeks.

The oceans are full of fish, many of them bigger than the shark, but the tiger of the sea commands more respect and gets more attention than any other fish,—because he uses his teeth.

The sales world is full of salesmen, but those who are getting the business these days put TEETH into their sales presentation, and get BITE into their sales talk. . . . That is why I am sending you the tooth of a fighting fish— I want you to keep this thought in mind.

Yours for a Record Summer,

* * *

FLORENCE H. SNOW 1904,
General Secretary

ABRIDGED MINUTES OF THE ALUMNAE COUNCIL MEETING

THE Alumnae Council met on June 17 at 2.30 P.M. in Seelye 10, with the president, Mrs. Sawyer, presiding.

The by-laws were amended for the sake of clarifying the words of the provision for membership.

On recommendation of the Central Committee of the Alumnae Fund, approved by the President and Trustees of the College and the Executive Committee of the Alumnae Association, it was *Voted:* that the gift which the alumnae shall endeavor to secure for the College in 1927–28 through the agency of the Alumnae Fund shall be applied to faculty salaries in whatever way the Trustees may deem advisable.

Dean Bernard spoke of Dr. Koffka and the William Allan Neilson Chair of Research at College which he is to occupy next year.

The Alumnae Office was encouraged to continue the plan of having some of the foreign students entertained by the local clubs during the Christmas and spring holidays.

Gladys Anslow '14 outlined the history and content of the *Club Bulletin* and asked for criticism and suggestions for its further development.

A vote of thanks to the retiring secretary, Mrs. Foss, was passed.

MABEL (CHICK) FOSS 1905, *Secretary*

ABRIDGED MINUTES OF THE ANNUAL MEETING OF THE ASSOCIATION

THE Alumnae Association held its annual meeting in Sage Hall on Saturday morning, June 18, with the president, Mrs. Sawyer, in the chair.

Reports for the year were read by the president, general secretary, and the editor of the QUARTERLY. The audited treasurer's report, read by Eunice Wead '02, in the absence of the treasurer and the chairman of the finance committee, was adopted. The budget for the coming year, as submitted by mail, and amended to reduce the item for receipts from annual dues by $500, was also adopted.

Ruth French '02 reported the total of the Juniper Lodge Endowment Fund as $33,-607.12.

Jean Paton '14 announced that the Burton Memorial Fund had reached something over $23,000, which would yield an income sufficient for one full scholarship covering all expenses, and one partial scholarship. The committee hoped to have a larger sum in hand before the fund was presented to the College at the Assembly. Mrs. Sawyer announced the appropriation of $1000 by the Board of Directors as a gift to the Burton Fund from the Association.

The project of the Alumnae Fund for the coming year, namely, salaries for the faculty, to be applied in whatever way the Trustees may deem advisable, as adopted by the Alumnae Council, was ratified. Mrs. Ford, chairman of the Central Committee, in her report drew attention to the 48 class representatives of the Fund, seated together as a body at the meeting. On recommendation of the committee, it was

Voted: To amend the charter of the Alumnae Fund, so that payments shall be made payable to the Alumnae Fund of Smith College, instead of to the Alumnae Association.

Marguerite (Page) Hersey '01, nominated by the February Council, was elected a member of the Nominating Committee.

Two amendments to the by-laws, submitted by mail, were adopted: the first, corresponding to the amendment to the Council by-laws, for the sake of clearness in expression, struck out the words "every class" from Article VII, The Alumnae Council, Section 1, Paragraph f, second sentence, and inserted the words "all other classes"; the second struck out the words "or of thirty-five dollars in seven payments of five dollars each, provided that the entire sum is paid within seven years" from Article XI, Section 4, Life Membership. It was explained that these partial payment life memberships were a loss to the Association treasury, the income from interest on the investment being insufficient to atone for the decrease in annual dues.

The following resolutions in memory of Charlotte Gulliver '83, presented by Anna Cutler '85, were adopted:

Charlotte Chester Gulliver held the office of President of the Alumnae Association from 1887 to 1891, and that of Alumnae Trustee from 1895 to 1901. These were formative years for those offices; her undergraduate life also fell in the period critical for determining the general type of Smith College student. As an undergraduate and as an alumna she brought to the service of her Alma Mater an able, well-ordered, and inspiring mind, broad sympathies, unswerving loyalty, and sincerity. Her handling of executive business was systematic and forceful. Her grasp of administrative problems was profound, owing to her unusual ability to hear sympathetically and weigh judicially many differing points of view. Time ripened her mind and enriched her experience without robbing her of the gayety of youth. She not only represents the finest type of official service, but when we have figured to ourselves the kind of woman whom we liked to call the representative Smith graduate, she was personified for us in Charlotte Gulliver.

JULIA HARWOOD CAVERNO '87, *Chairman*
CLARA FRANCES PALMER '83
ANNA ALICE CUTLER '85

Resolutions as a tribute to President Neilson in honor of his tenth anniversary as president of the College were read by Anne (Barrows) Seelye '97 in the absence of the chairman of the committee, Sarah Goodwin '92, It was voted to adopt the resolutions and have them read by Miss Goodwin to President Neilson at the Assembly. [See opening page.]

Mrs. Sawyer entrusted the meeting with the confidential news that the Directors had appropriated $1000 from the treasury as a gift to President Neilson and that the gift in a "suitable receptacle" provided by the Directors would be presented at the Assembly.

Ruby Litchfield '10' chairman of the Polling Committee, read the names of the officers and directors elected to serve for 1927–28. [See department heading.]

Pamphlets containing annual reports of other committees were distributed at the meeting, and will be published in the *Alumnae Register* in the fall.

A vote of thanks was given to the retiring officers: Alida (Leese) Milliken '00' vice-president, Sara (Evans) Kent '11' treasurer, and Mabel (Chick) Foss '05' secretary.

MABEL (CHICK) FOSS 1905, *Secretary*

TELEGRAMS TO THE PRESIDENT

FIFTY-THREE of the local clubs sent telegrams of congratulation to President Neilson on his tenth "birthday." They were delivered to him at Alumnae Assembly and came from: Baltimore, Cincinnati, Gloucester, Hampshire County (letter), Hartford, Montclair, New Haven, The Oranges, Pittsburgh, Rhode Island, Winchester, Wisconsin, Berkshire County, Bridgeport, Cambridge, Columbus, Grand Rapids, Miami, Portland (Ore.), Utica, Worcester, Buffalo, Detroit, Eastern Connecticut, Indianapolis, Kansas City, Philadelphia, St. Paul, Syracuse, Vermont, Eastern New York, Fitchburg, Rochester, Salem, Seattle, Southern California, Franklin County, Minneapolis, Cleveland, Lexington, Lynn, Maine, Merrimac Valley, Nebraska, New Hampshire, Springfield (note), Chicago, New York, Southeastern Massachusetts, Washington, Boston, Brooklyn, Central Ill.

GINLING COMMITTEE REPORT

Some figures from the report of the Treasurer:

Reported at Annual Meeting, June 20, 1926	$2540.71
Received during summer	413.50
Total receipts 1925–26	$2954.21
Receipts for 1926–27	$2117.50
Immediate Relief Fund	30.00
Total	$2147.50

THE BURTON FUND

MISS PATON'S presentation of the Fund to President Neilson at Alumnae Assembly will be found on page 460. The members of the President Burton Memorial Committee are: Jean Paton '14' *chairman*, Marion (Yeaw) Biglow '11' Helen (Houghton) Shortlidge '12' Sophia (Smith) Birdsall '13' Elizabeth Zimmerman '14' Adèle Glogau '15' Augusta Patton '16' Esther (Lippitt) Haviland '17' Dorothy (Rose) Handerson '18' Ruth (Pierson) Churchill '19' Katharine (Dickson) King '20'

The total gift of $27,600.79 will yield almost enough income to make possible two Burton scholarships annually: one, if the Trustees deem it fitting, in the undergraduate body, and the other in the graduate body. The Fund is a foundation which can be increased at any time by individual subscription or legacy. The gifts by classes are:

CLASS	AMOUNT	CLASS	AMOUNT
79	......	03	$106.00
80	......	04	341.00
81	$30.00	05	147.00
82	80.00	06	110.00
83	60.00	07	400.00
84	297.00	08	691.00
85	5.00	09	34.00
86	25.00	10	110.00
87	70.00	11	657.00
88	153.00	12	1612.92
89	110.00	13	1616.50
90	155.00	14	3575.50
91	56.00	15	1362.50
92	10.00	16	2200.00
93	111.00	17	2043.60
94	272.00	18	1403.57
95	497.00	19	983.00
96	387.00	20	813.50
97	1769.00	21	130.00
98	34.00	22	100.00
99	95.20	23	80.00
00	681.00	24	104.00
01	257.00	25	72.50
02	600.00	26	122.00

The gifts by clubs are:

CLUB	AMOUNT
Eastern Connecticut	$50.00
Montclair	100.00
Brooklyn	200.00
Grand Rapids	100.00
Cincinnati	100.00
Rhode Island	50.00
Salem	10.00
Central Illinois	10.00
Cambridge	100.00
Hartford	75.00
Fitchburg	25.00
Maine	50.00
Berkshire County	50.00
Franklin County	50.00
Kansas City	75.00
Springfield	75.00
Vermont	20.00
New Hampshire	50.00
New York	250.00
Detroit	150.00
From Classes	$24,569.79
From Clubs	1,590.00
Faculty and Other Friends	441.00
Alumnae Association	1,000.00
Total	$27,600.79

MRS. FORD ON THE ALUMNAE FUND

Being quotations from her talk at the Annual Meeting. See also page 448

See also page 448

EVERAL days ago I came across this little gem in the *Times:*

Turkish President Prepares a speech two days long for delivery at the first General Congress of the People's Party. It reviews the whole history of the Turkish Nationalist movement and then touches lightly on later events.

Even if he touched heavily he would hardly awake the sleepers!! Now I could hold you spellbound without a doubt for at least two days talking about the history of the movement of the Alumnae Fund, but I shall confine myself to touching lightly on later events. . . .

Those of you who were here at the February Council meeting will recall that three projects had been named by the President for our consideration, Faculty Salaries, Scholarships, and a Storehouse,—with strong emphasis on Salaries. Since then the Trustees have recommended salaries. In April the Central Fund Committee voted to make salaries the sole objective and secured the approval in April of the Executive Committee, and yesterday the Council ratified the vote. Now it is not legally necessary to secure your ratification, but to-day we ask this meeting to ratify it, and not just with a rubber stamp but with your hands on your hearts.

In preparation for this, to me, great event to-day, I have been going through the musty files of the QUARTERLY, and many papers and pamphlets and pieces of publicity and have been tremendously impressed with the education we have had in two things. First, in the significance of faculty salaries, and second, a much longer education in giving, and the significance of giving.

We do not quote very much of what Mrs. Ford said on salaries, because as she admitted, nearly all her material came from utterances of President Burton, President Neilson, and Mrs. Morrow in QUARTERLIES of January 1911, November 1919, and May 1927. She clinched the matter with quotations from a *Times* editorial entitled, "What Price Teaching," the last sentences of which were: "Certain contrasts are too glaring. We read of millions upon millions poured into new college dormitories, stadiums, gymnasiums, assembly halls, but the professor too often remains the forgotten man of education. Happily, many colleges have moved within recent years to improve his financial status. But more ought to be done."

Concerning our education in the Significance of Giving, Mrs. Ford said:

Alumnae always have given from the very first; you can't keep them from giving. They gave in many ways in addition to the big amounts they gave to the original Alumnae Fund, to the million and four million dollar campaigns, with magnificent generosity, throughout the War, to the Birthday Gift, in countless other ways. They have the habit of giving already.

Another still more significant thing they have learned is that when they give money to Smith it is not just money. The money is a symbol of sacrificial loyalty. It is an outward and visible sign of their faith in the institution, in the people who are running it, in one another, in the place it can occupy in the world, and in the future.

So it seems to me that we have a splendid background from which to set forth upon this long road of annual giving. We cannot do it in parade step fashion, or in a hundred yard dash. We shall have to adopt the long route march stride of the soldier. Recently the regulation pack in the army has had its weight reduced by half so that they can march further. I think that our pack has been considerably lightened with the removal of drives, and that we ought to be able to march pretty far.

Quite a number of people have asked me how far we ought to march during this first year. Now it is not legal for us to set any goal, I believe. With the Fund we are not to have that sense of pressure, of drive. . . .

There is one Goal of which I may speak without breaking the law, and that is 100% giving. Not the size of gifts but the *number of givers* is to be our concern. And with the President's permission, I hereby appoint you all a flying squad to aid our Fund chairmen in making this possible. Let our ideal be, in the words of an Alumnae Fund chairman, "Something from everyone—gladly."

Now I have no misgivings about the sort of report that I shall be able to make as I stand here a year from to-day. Mrs. Morrow once said, "Anyone can begin a big job. It takes real people to finish it." And you look like real people to me.

So it is with real confidence, Madam President, that I read the following recommendation:

"The Central Committee of the Alumnae Fund, having consulted with and secured the approval of the President, the Board of Trustees, the Executive Committee of the Alumnae Association, and the Council for the project for the coming year,

"Recommends to the Alumnae Association: That the gift which the alumnae shall endeavor to secure for the College in 1927–28, through the agency of the Alumnae Fund, shall be applied to Faculty Salaries in whatever way the Trustees may deem advisable."

I move the adoption of this recommendation.

The recommendation was adopted and Mrs. Ford said:

In the bright lexicon of Smith there is no such word as *fail*.

CLASS NEWS

Please send all news for the November QUARTERLY *to your class secretary by September 29. The editors reserve the right to omit all items which in their judgment are not submitted in legible form.*

1879
Class secretary—Mrs. Charles M. Cone (Kate Morris), Hartford, Vt.

1880
Class secretary—Mrs. Edwin Higbee (Netta Wetherbee), 8 West St., Northampton, Mass.

1881
Class secretary—Eliza P. Huntington, 88 Harvard St., Newtonville, Mass.

Eighty-one gives cordial greetings to her youngest daughter, Martha Sullivan, of the class of 1927.

Alice Browne has consented to be our Class Representative for the Alumnae Fund. Now everybody to her support!

1882
Class secretary—Nina E. Browne, 44 Pinckney St., Boston, Mass.

For report of reunion see page 468.

1883
Class secretary—Mrs. Charles H. Haskell (Louise Woodward), 6 Huntington Pl., Norwich, Conn.

Mary Stuart Anthony and Miss Allen will spend the first two weeks in July at the Straits Mouth Inn, Rockport, Mass.

Sally Bush underwent a successful operation for cataracts in May.

Mrs. F. A. Dart, "Mother Dart" of the Hubbard House, died in New York, May 22.

Abby Gregory Willard is the newly elected president of the Eastern Connecticut Smith College Club.

1884
Class secretary—Helen M. Sheldon, Fort Ann, N. Y.

1885
Class secretary—Ruth B. Franklin, 23 Sherman St., Newport, R. I.

Ex-1885
Margaret (Soule) Hough's husband, Garry de Neuville Hough, died in Vineyard Haven, May 31, after a long illness.

1886
Class secretary—M. Adèle Allen, 144 Lincoln St., Holyoke, Mass.

The center of the get-together in June included Esther Fowler and Annie (Russell) Marble's daughter and Hattie Cushman's niece, both of whom graduated this year. The class made the two girls members of the Alumnae Association. This was the first time in Esther Fowler's missionary work that furlough and reunion have coincided. Sixteen were present at supper.

Adèle Allen is again reader in Latin of College Board entrance examinations at Columbia this June.

Margaret (Atwater) Jones had an exhibit of her water colors at Hathaway House, Wellesley Hills, in May and June, which aroused enthusiastic interest. The subjects ranged from the Maine coast to Italian shores.

Helen (Kyle) Platt returned in June from a long stay abroad.

Bertha (Ray) Harriman spends the summer in France. Her sister, Julia (Ray) Andrews ex-'87, was elected in May president of the National Society of Colonial Dames.

Harriett (Risley) Foote has given to the Art Department a suit of Japanese armor and rare old shawls.

Annie (Russell) Marble and family spend the summer in Europe.

Etta Seelye visited at Grove Park Inn in Asheville (N. C.) for the month of May, bracing up in the most beautiful spot in the world for her duties as class representative on the Alumnae Fund.

Lucy (Wright) Pearson and her husband sailed in June for a two months' sojourn in Europe as the guests of their daughter, Betty (Pearson) Gillum, Smith '14·

Ex-1886
Mabel (Kidder) Selden sailed for Europe June 10.

Elizabeth (Mellen) Hodge died on Jan. 13.

1887
Class secretary—Eleanor L. Lord, Box 50, Rosemont, Pa.

For report of reunion see page 469.

Our new president is Jessie (Carter) White.

OTHER NEWS.—Julia Caverno will be hostess at Juniper Lodge for the summer.

Grace Hubbard will spend the summer at Shirley Center, Mass.

Eleanor Lord is retiring from active educational work and will be for an indefinite period with friends in Rosemont, Pa.

Elizabeth Mason will visit Anne (Van Kirk) Geller in Dorset (Vt.) for a few days and later will be at Juniper Lodge.

Ex-1887
Nettie (Bancroft) Pierce with her daughter

Catharine will sail in September for Japan. Annie (Bliss) Perry with her husband and daughter Margaret will sail in July for a year abroad.

1888

Class secretary—Florence K. Bailey, 174 Broad St., Claremont, N. H.

Jennie (Chamberlain) Hosford's son Donald was married Jan. 29 to Helen Fye of Cleveland.

Marion Dwight's address is no longer 122 Newbury St. A little later she and her sister Julia will occupy an apartment on Beacon St., but until further notice her forwarding address is c/o Old Colony Trust Co., 222 Boylston St., Boston.

Martha (Everett) St. John has at present no permanent address, but letters will reach her if sent to 25 Beacon St., Boston. Eighty-eight rejoices with her in the arrival on Apr. 25 of another grandson, Robert Pierce, second son of Harold and Elizabeth St. John. Martha plans to sail about Aug. 1 as a delegate from the American Unitarian Assn. and the General Alliance to the International Congress of Religious Liberals to be held Sept. 4 to 8 at Prague.

Dr. Jane (Kelly) Sabine with her daughter Janet, who finished her course at Radcliffe in January, sailed in March on an extended trip to the East. Their address is c/o Hottinger and Co., 38 rue de Provence, Paris, France.

Ellen Wentworth and her aunt Nora Hatch sailed on the *George Washington* Apr. 20, to be gone until November. Their address is c/o Baring Brothers, London E. C. 2, England.

1889

Class secretary—Lucy E. Allen, 35 Webster St., West Newton, Mass.

Elsie Atwater has taken a Mediterranean cruise this spring.

Alice (Buswell) Towle has joined the ranks of grandmothers.

1890

Class secretary—Annie S. Wyckoff, 95 Clinton Av., Jamaica, N. Y.

Jessica (Burnham) Downing writes: "I speak with pride of a piano recital given by my daughter Jessie 1927, on the last Tuesday evening in May in the College Music Building. She played her entire program without notes, although she has not been majoring in music. This, with her junior year at the Sorbonne, is enough to thrill any mother, don't you think?" Jessica's chief outside interest is the library of the Kansas City Art Institute, to which she recently gave over a hundred books. She started it with contributions of time and money, and has been its godmother and chief provider ever since. She spent several weeks in New York last winter poking around in old bookshops and out-of-the-way places, collecting rare and unusual books.

Bessie (Cravath) Miller writes: "A year ago last winter we put the children in school in Geneva, and Mr. Miller and I traveled in many different countries. I rejoined the children in May but got sick, so that Mr. Miller had to return to Geneva from America where he had gone to resume work. Last winter we were in Columbus, and I spent the year trying to regain my usual pep. I have been most interested in the Foreign Policy Assn., the Liberal Club of the University, and international and interracial friendship groups—which are to me most worth while. This summer we shall visit my brother on Long Island."

Rose Hardwick talked over the radio May 3 on the "New Point of View on Children's Behavior." This was in connection with a woman's forum, conducted by the Mass. Dept. of Education. Rose is Dr. Rose S. Hardwick, Head Psychologist, Div. of Mental Hygiene, Mass. Dept. of Mental Diseases. This item comes via Lucy Thomson.

A letter from Florence (Kelsey) French tells of her two grandchildren, her daughter Helen's children, and says that her baby Dorothea graduated this last June from Oberlin, and plans to study landscape architecture.

Lucy Thomson writes: "I am doing just the same as when we last met—chief cook and bottlewasher at home and at the office. The latter offers constant variety which makes it interesting. My work this spring has included an ark for a synagogue, a golf club and caddy house, a garage for a jail, a parish house, a boys' club, Colonial and Italian ironwork, a photostat room, not to mention the houses we always have with us. I have been busy as usual at home with guests, seeing a small niece through graduation and collecting credentials for her next school."

Will someone please send the addresses of Frances B. Strickland and Mabel Taylor to the secretary? Frances's last address was 31 Joy St., Boston. Mabel's last address was 4 Arlington St., Boston.

At the annual luncheon of the New York Smith Club seven of 1890 were present: Maud Phillips, Susan Homans, Annie Wyckoff, Rose Lyman, Grace Royce, Gertrude James, and Jessica Burnham. The married ladies will please forgive the omission of their married names—they don't seem quite natural to our classmates.

Annie Wyckoff is spending July and August in France.

1891

Class secretary—Mrs. H. B. Boardman (Carolyn Peck), 1307 Lowell Rd., Schenectady, N. Y.

Amy Barbour sails July 2 to England where she will be until September.

Alice (Clute) Ely's husband, William G. Ely, recently retired from the General Electric Co. after 35 years of continuous service. Alice and her husband are planning to spend the next two years in travel.

Bertha (Dwight) Cole's son Charles graduated from Amherst in June.

Susan (Fuller) Albright's daughter Nancy was married in April to a Mr. Hurd of Buffalo.

Olive Rose Garland is spending the summer in California.

Carol (Peck) Boardman's son William graduated from Yale in June.

Twenty-six girls received diplomas and 15 girls received certificates for the college course at the Knox School in Cooperstown (N. Y.) of which Louise (Phillips) Houghton is principal.

1892

Class secretary—Mrs. Irving H. Upton (Katherine Haven), 20 Park View St., Boston 21, Mass.

For report of reunion see page 470. All class officers were reëlected.

A Pageant Play in the interest of international amity, entitled "Horizons," has been written by Winifred (Ayres) Hope. This was presented at the General Federation Meeting of Women's Clubs at Atlantic City in May 1926 and other presentations have been given in four different cities.

Just as we were going to Commencement word came of the death of Grace Dennen in Los Angeles. We have no particulars as yet.

Helen Rowley and sister go abroad this summer and will join Florence (May) Rice and husband for a motor trip in southern England.

Caroline Steele has retired from teaching and sails in August for Greece and Constantinople, where she will join her sister. Together they will travel in Egypt. Caroline returns to Philadelphia in November where she will make her home.

Helen Wolcott is first vice-president of the Hartford Smith Club which office carries with it the making of the program for the year.

Our class baby, Isabel (Wardner) Rollins '16, was elected president of the Boston Alumnae Association in May. With an interim of one year she succeeds her mother who died in office.

Three of our daughters graduated in the class of 1927: Elizabeth Chase (*cum laude*), Catherine Cole, and Lucia Jordan. Catherine Cole received the Smith S in the spring.

1893

Class secretary—Mrs. John E. Oldham (Harriet Holden), 16 Livermore.Rd., Wellesley Hills, Mass.

DIED.—Susan Varick Knox, at her home in New Brunswick, N. J., Apr. 21.

In Memoriam

In the days of long ago Sue Knox was one of those always studious, always interested, always serious, always merry girls who are prized in any college class. She was a friend-of-all-the-world, and without a clique. So she continued, even through a long period of ill health, even till her death, increasing her interests, increasing the number and variety of her friends, as was witnessed by the church full of people, of differing age, color, sex, and social position who were present at her funeral. There is no way of saying how much the class of '93 will miss its president. The first year after graduation Susan became our chosen leader, a place she held until her death. "The difference to me—", is what many have been saying since her busy, useful life came to an end.

She meant much in her home, to her aged parents, and also to the children of the next generation. In her church she taught a large class of young men and, with her rich equipment and quick response, must have been an untold help to youth in its conflict. To her

community she gave active social service as a worker in the Needlework Guild, in the Middlesex Hospital Aid Society, and as secretary of the Travelers' Club. She had much musical talent and this was devoted to everyday uses—her Sunday school orchestra, for instance. In her simple life, so full of radiant friendship, her classmates found an inspiration they counted on, increasingly, during the thirty and more years of her service.

"Her friends can best perpetuate her memory by letting her mantle of faith and service fall upon them."

Frances (Ayer) Tebbetts and Col. Tebbetts came on to Northampton from Fort McPherson (Ga.) for the graduation of their daughter Dorothy. '93 sent Dorothy the Friendship Brooch we give to our Smith senior daughters and congratulated her on being taken into Phi Beta Kappa. She graduated *magna cum laude*.

Stella Bradford and Grace (Field) Spottiswoode attended Susan Knox's funeral services and Stella sent daffodils from '93, our class flower. As Stella is vice-president, she is taking over Sue's duties.

Jennie Campbell's address for the summer is Mankato, Kans. She is sponsor for the big Girl Reserve Club in the high school of Abilene where she teaches, and sent in an interesting program of the banquet attended by 196 mothers and daughters. She will spend the summer in Vermont with Mary DuBois and in some of the cities where she can do genealogical research work.

Frances (Darling) Niles's address in the *Register* should be 83–21 Vietor Av., Elmhurst, N. Y.

Mary DuBois has been teaching at the Oxford School, 695 Prospect Av., Hartford (Conn.), this year and expects to return there in the fall.

Julia Dwight and her sister have taken an apartment in Richmond Court, 1213 Beacon St., Brookline, and move in July.

Mary (Hamilton) Marquis has been ill all winter but wrote that after a minor operation she expected to get well quickly. They will spend the summer at their beach cottage at East Newport (Calif.) as usual. Her daughter Virginia, aged 15, attends Mary Wilson's school at Berkeley.

Florence Jackson is on a trip to the Far West to speak at the Deans' Conference of the N. E. A. at Seattle. She will also lecture at the State Normal Schools in Ellensburg (Wash.) and Bellingham, and at the summer school of the Oregon Agricultural College at Corvallis. She will return by the Canadian Rockies and be home by Sept. 1.

Grace (Lane) Beardsley visited her brother in Milton in April and attended the Boston Smith luncheon. She plans to spend part of the summer at her brother's home on the Cape.

Anne (Morris) Stevens is to be chairman of our committee to collect our Reunion Gift to the College. She will also be '93's Alumnae Fund representative. As she was recovering from an operation she was not strong enough to be in Hamp in June so the secretary attended the Fund meetings in her place.

Helen (Putnam) Blake left in May to go to France to join her daughter Betty who is one of the juniors in France, and return with her in August.

Helen (Whitman) Walker's daughter Dorothy was married last July to Guerra Everett, a lawyer. He is practicing in New York and they are living in Kew Gardens.

Agnes Williston sailed June 12 on the *Laconia* for a trip abroad, returning via New York Sept. 6.

Elizabeth (Williston) Bullard and her husband spent most of last winter in Monrovia (Calif.), with a seven weeks' trip to Hawaii. They will spend the summer at Marblehead Neck and hope to be in Hartford next winter as Judge Bullard is much improved in health.

Ex-1893

Alice (Rich) Cate won the first prize of the press department for the best-written account of a club meeting, at the annual meeting of the Massachusetts State Federation of Women's Clubs in May.

Mabel (Warner) Metcalf, who has been ill some time, writes that she is gaining slowly and is able to enjoy much of life in a quiet way.

Grace Torr and Elisabeth (Smith) Hatch attended the Boston Smith luncheon for the first time, in May.

1894

Class secretary—Mrs. John J. Healy (Katharine Andrews), 1104 Greenwood St., Evanston, Ill.

As your secretary will be abroad during Sept. and Oct., please send class news for the next QUARTERLY to Teresina (Peck) Rowell (Mrs. Wilfrid), 204 S. Garfield St., Hinsdale, Ill.

Eleanor Hope Johnson was elected to Phi Beta Kappa this spring.

Jeanne (Lockwood) Thompson's daughter Ruth graduated from Smith in June.

Teresina (Peck) Rowell has been elected assistant moderator of the National Council of the Congregational Church to represent the women of the denomination.

Ada (Platt) Benedict's son Stuart was graduated from Williams in June.

Grace (Smith) Jones's daughter Catharine sails in August to spend two years of graduate study at Oxford.

Kate (Ware) Smith was called recently to California on account of the death of her brother, Edward Kitchell Ware, who was formerly the President of Atlanta Univ.

1895

Class secretary—Carolyn P. Swett, Hudson View Gardens, 183 St. and Pinehurst Av., New York City.

Marie (Bowers) Hall and her husband are going to work for a while at Woods Hole before going to Maine for the summer. Marie is much interested in the Eugenics Society, a society always full of interest to biologists.

Clara Burnett had a wonderful two months' trip to California last fall with her daughter (Smith '20) who is settled in Pittsburgh.

Dorothy Fulton's life after graduation was spent in close companionship with her father and she went with him on his various geological trips. She has given his fine collection in paleontology to Western College for Women, Oxford (O.), of which college her father was trustee for many years. She has never been back to a reunion since graduation, and it behooves us to write and tell her that we will accept no excuses in 1930 and that there will be a hearty welcome for her.

Pearl (Gunn) Winchester has moved to Darien, Conn. Margaret, our class baby, is religious education director in the Hanover Street Church, Manchester, N. H. Pearl's fourth and last daughter to go to Smith is to be one of the Sorbonne juniors next year.

Annette (Lowell) Thorndike is in Europe for a few months. Her husband was invited to give the annual lecture before the Shakespeare Society in London. They return to spend the rest of the summer on Cape Cod. In January Annette and Professor Thorndike leave again for Europe to enjoy their sabbatical leave.

Nan (Paret) Davis writes: "The vigor and power of these young ones who can run home and profession fill me with awe. Even with one maid-of-all-work and only one child to care for I can't do much more than take care of my home. There is always the question in the back of my mind: have we the right to take time to run a house fastidiously or is that a luxury denied to those who haven't much money and who could do public service? On the other hand, shouldn't children have the privilege of living in a home daintily cared for —isn't that a part of civilization? I adore life in a small city which is dominated by a big university. The smallness of the city gives the friendly feeling that one feels in a village, and the university makes it a cosmopolitan community. There is simplicity of life here, too, which makes the parents' problem somewhat easier."

Dorothy (Reed) Mendenhall, after spending last year in Europe educating her two boys and traveling with her husband to all the laboratories of physics on the Continent, has settled down in a new home in Madison (Wis.), in which house she hopes to live always.

Gertrude Simonds's father died in January after a long illness. Some of us remember with great pleasure the week-ends when Mr. Simonds came to Northampton. His cordial, genial, whole-hearted way of taking the whole house in and giving us a good time won us all. Gertrude is living in Haverhill with her mother.

Josephine Wilkin had sabbatical leave from Feb. to Sept. 1926 and spent the months in Italy ("the whole month of May in Florence"), Belgium, and France.

Mary Louise Williams teaches in the high school of Kenosha (Wis.) and is enjoying her work in a new building. She travels or attends Columbia during her summer vacations.

Ex-1895

Helen (Davis) Lamb has been successful as a portrait painter since college days. She is also an authority on Colonial furniture and lectures before clubs.

Alice Holdship's husband, Edward Twichell Ware, died in California, May 21, after a long illness.

1896

Class secretary—Frances E. Jones, Hotel Chelsea, W. 23 St., New York City.

DIED.—Claire (Hammond) Rand, June 3, in Cambridge.

In Memoriam

Ninety-six will miss Claire sorely, for her loyalty to class and college have been unswerving. Her life was devoted largely to her children and her joy in life came through them. She was especially happy in living to see her brilliant daughter Dorothy graduated from her beloved college. For some months Claire had known that her tenure of life was to be short, but with the courage with which she had met earlier crises, she maintained her usual cheer. In the last swift weeks she must have been comforted by the loyal comrades who rallied around her and who in her passing lose a friend of rare fidelity. E. W. R.

OTHER NEWS.—Isabel (Bartlett) Bunker's son George was graduated from the Univ. of Wisconsin in June 1926, and her daughter Isabel is entering her junior year there.

Bess (Cutter) Morrow and Mr. Morrow have returned from abroad where they went to join their daughter Elisabeth, Smith '25·

Ellen (Duckworth) Trull's daughter Eleanor was one of two to receive honorable mention this year for the Helen Kate Furness Shakespeare prize.

Mary Goodman as a result of an accident had to defer the European trip upon which she was to have sailed in April. She is at home in New Haven.

Eva (Hills) Eastman and her family are in Europe. She will be at her summer home in Sharon (Conn.) after the middle of August.

Harriet (Learned) Taussig's daughter Lucelia is one of the group selected to take the junior year in France.

Polly (Poland) Cushman spent six months of last year in Rome, detained by the illness of her son. She found residence in the Italian capital in these times both interesting and uneasy.

Harriet (Teasdale) Lingley writes that the two histories which she has been helping her husband to write are at last finished and they are looking forward to a lazy summer as a reward for their labors.

Caroline Wing and her family have remained abroad this year owing to the illness of her father.

Georgia (Wood) Pangborn's daughter Mary was one of two to graduate *summa cum laude*. She made Phi Beta Kappa in her junior year, and has been awarded the Alumnae Fund Fellowship for 1927-28 to study physiological chemistry at Yale.

NEW ADDRESS.—Mrs. William W. Harts (Martha Hale), American Embassy, Paris, France.

1897

Class secretary—Mrs. George W. Woodbury (Harriet Patch), 28 Eastern Point Rd., Gloucester, Mass.

For a report of the reunion see page 471.

The following officers were elected at class meeting: president, Mary Byrd Wells; vice-president, Alice Weld Tallant; secretary, Harriet (Patch) Woodbury; treasurer, Ella (Hurrt) Barnes.

1898

Class secretary—Ethel M. Gower, 29 Mather St., New Haven, Conn.

Alma Baumgarten has spent the winter in the West. When last heard from she was visiting her brother in California and had seen the Picketts and other '98ers.

Cellissa (Brown) Norcross celebrated her 25th wedding anniversary with a large reception and dance at the New Haven Lawn Club in May. Her son Arnold is now a sophomore at Yale.

Emma (Byles) Cowperthwait's daughter Marian graduated in June *cum laude.*

Frances (Comstock) Morton has bought a house in a suburb of Baltimore. Her new address is 1 St. Martin's Road, Guilford, Baltimore. She motored to Canada in July and expects to spend the rest of the summer at Sugar Hill, N. H. Her son Copeland Jr. enters Princeton in the fall.

Josephine (Daskam) Bacon spoke at the Boston College Club in April. She and her son Selden Jr., who goes to Yale this year, are spending the summer abroad.

Nellie (Fairchild) Wallace has sold her Providence house and is in Brooklyn (Conn.) for the summer.

Elizabeth McFadden has recently published "Product of the Mill," a play on child labor which took the Craig Prize and ran for 59 performances. It is now available for Little Theatres.

Elizabeth Mullally has resigned from the Burnham School and is going to teach Latin and Greek at the Franklin School in Buffalo.

Elizabeth Padgham, to the deep regret of her parishioners, has resigned from the Church of Our Father in Rutherford (N. J.) after a pastorate of 22 years, in order to be with her mother. She writes: "The church is out of debt, every organization working well, and the spirit is splendid. Someone else should come in now and carry on the greater things. Ties of work, friends, and home of 22 years are not easily broken but when I am ready I trust another field will open up for me." Her present address is 120 Shonnard St., Syracuse, N. Y.

Some dozen or more '98ers were back for Commencement and had several informal reunions including a supper at The Manse Sunday evening.

Ex-1898

Clara (Jepson) Beers went abroad in May for a short trip with her husband in connection with work of the Mental Hygiene Society.

1899

Class secretary—Miriam Drury, 334 Franklin St., Newton, Mass.

The following 99ers had supper together at The Manse, Northampton, June 18: Harriet (Bliss) Ford, Miriam (Choate) Hobart, Helen Clark, Ethel Darling, Miriam Drury, Ethel

(Gilman) Braman, Grace (Mossman) Sawyer, Harriette Patterson, Mary (Smith) Livermore, Ada (Springer) Weller, Margaret (Wilkinson) Malcolmson. Quite fair for a non-reunion year!

Helen (Andrew) Patch and Annah (Porter) Hawes were in Amherst over Commencement attending the 30th reunion of their husbands.

Gertrude (Churchill) Whitney recently took the part of an old lady in a one-act play produced in the Repertory Theatre of Boston by members of the Repertory Theatre Workshop.

Ethel (Gilman) Braman is the class representative on the Alumnae Fund Committee. Be prepared to receive a letter from her.

Molly Keyes is rapidly convalescing from a major operation performed at the Lowell General Hospital on May 31. She cannot say enough in praise of the skill of the surgeons and devoted care of the nurses which she has received.

Ada (Springer) Weller and her husband spent the winter in Florida on a house boat picturesquely named "Moonlight."

Margaret (Wilkinson) Malcolmson is to be one of the four assistant deans at the New Jersey College for Women, New Brunswick.

The secretary would be delighted to see any '99er who may be near Boothbay Harbor (Me.) this summer at her new bungalow at East Boothbay.

1900

Class secretary—Gertrude E. Gladwin, 2323 Orrington Av., Evanston, Ill.

Ruth (Albright) Hollister's husband, Evan Hollister, has been elected president of the Associated Harvard Clubs.

Helen (Ward) Ward's son Theodore is one of four prominent seniors at Amherst selected to compete for the Bond Prize for public speaking.

Meta Bentley's address for the summer will be Windham, N. Y.

Aneita Brown is motoring for six weeks in England, Wales, and Scotland with Ethel Wright, her sister Alice '01, and other friends. Her new address is 175 W. 72 St., N. Y. C.

Otelia Cromwell is supervisor of 75 teachers of English and history in five Washington high schools. She is about to publish the dissertation written for her Ph.D. at Yale in 1926, "Thomas Heywood: A Study in Elizabethan Drama of Everyday Life." The sympathy of the class will go out to her in the death of her youngest sister and her father within two months.

Cora (Delabarre) Hunter's daughter is a Phi Beta Kappa and graduated in June from Wellesley.

Grace (Dunham) Gould's daughter Elenor is finishing her freshman year at the Univ. of Minnesota.

Marguerite Gray is busy with her Garden Club, "The Diggers," and a class in current history in the College Women's Club of Pasadena. Her mother had one of her recent water colors hung in an exhibit by Pasadena artists this spring. "Pretty good for eighty-one," writes her daughter.

Gertrude Gladwin had a delightful weekend in Indianapolis where she saw Anne Fraser '99 and had tea at Caroline (Marmon) Fesler's charming home.

Katharine Griggs is now in New York representing Lingnan Univ. (formerly Canton Christian College). It is the first one of the Christian schools to place increased authority in the hands of the Chinese through the formation of a local board of directors. There is an article about this by Stanley High in the Apr. 14 issue of *The Christian Century*. The students at Lingnan Univ. have been loyal all through the unsettled period in China. Katharine's address is 150 Fifth Av., N. Y. C.

Bertha (Groesbeck) Haskell is so delighted with the junior year in France which her daughter Katharine has had, that she wants to urge every mother with a Smith daughter to try to get her daughter ready to have the same opportunity. Her two boys hope to be freshmen at Williams next year. The Haskell family will be in Rochester again for the summer, and will probably be in New York or Washington next fall.

Gertrude (Henry) Mead has spent twenty weeks studying problems in China with a class in international relations in connection with the Berkeley League of Women Voters and recently attended a Chinese-American conference in San Francisco. Mrs. Burton has been visiting her married daughter in Berkeley and Gertrude has met her there.

Aloysia (Hoye) Davis has been for six years very active in the Vermont Federation of Women's Clubs as finance chairman and legislative chairman. She and her husband had a delightful trip through New England, New York, and Virginia, being present at the opening of Congress. She is secretary of the program committee of the Windsor Celebration of the Vermont Sesquicentennial.

Dorcas (Leese) Boardman ('01) and nine directors and assistants have organized "Scientific Housekeeping Inc." at 158 E. 57 St., N. Y. C. The training of domestic employees will be carried on at her own home and, among other things, "the new organization will take over the entire opening of a home at the beginning of a season and bring a domestic staff to place the house in running order."

Miriam Loheed is regaining her strength after the accident in February.

Margaret Lyman is having a delightful trip. She was several weeks in Italy and had a driving trip with a party, visiting many villas and gardens. She had an audience with the Pope. In Rome she met Helen (Kerruish) Buffum and her daughter quite unexpectedly. She will return the latter part of August.

Clara Loomis, whose house and school were destroyed in the Japanese earthquake, says the school is carrying on in a portable building and a good dormitory with about 120 girls, "as fine a group as one could find anywhere." Clara has a sabbatical in 1929 and hopes to be at our next reunion. She saw Polly (Persons) Scott and her husband in Yokohama, and learned that Dr. Scott is to return to Honolulu to give a summer course in the University there. Florence (Brooks) Cobb is coming back in 1929 so we shall have her also at our reunion.

Charlotte (Marsh) Post's article in *Harper's* for June 1926, page 182, tells about her attitude toward life and her children. Her daughter Winifred intends to study singing instead of going to college. Her son Philip "is right-hand man to Mr. Harris in the Rosedale Nurseries, Tarrytown (N. Y.), and loves growing things as much as his sister loves music. It seems to me it would be hard to find two occupations more delightful than these. I enter into them with all my heart, and it's very nearly as good as being young again."

The Emogene Mahony Memorial Prize was awarded to Elizabeth Dresch '27 of Mishawaka, Ind., a member of Alpha, for her ability at the organ. The prize consists of the income from a fund of $500.

Virginia (Mellen) Hutchinson and her two daughters are traveling abroad. She says "her experience in raising money for Juniper Lodge has given her nothing but praise for Smith people, and 1900 in particular."

Mabel (Milham) Roys is back from her trip around the world and went at once to San Francisco to attend the Presbyterian Assembly where she made a number of speeches. She was in Northampton for Commencement.

Leslie (Mitchell) Poirier broke her leg and was laid up for three months. Though she says, "I have nothing for publication" she sounds like a very busy and useful person, with Library Board, Business and Professional Women's Club, Parent-Teacher Assn., and president of the Y. W. C. A. among other activities. Her mother died on Thanksgiving Day, 1926.

Sybil (Shaw) Trull's daughter was given honorable mention for the essay she wrote on a Shakespearean subject in competition for the Helen Kate Furness Prize at Smith.

Evelyn (Smith) Rolfe visited Florence (Whitin) Parsons and her interesting family in Washington. She had visits from Grace (Russell) Arnold and Katharine Lyman in her Newton home.

Marion (True) Redfern has been visiting Laura (Shedd) Schweppe for a fortnight and her visit was the occasion for several pleasant 1900 and 1901 luncheons. Her daughter Katherine is doing social service work in Portland, and her son graduates from Deerfield Academy and enters Amherst next fall.

Betty Whitney, after breaking up her old home in November, went abroad for several months, returning to a new home at 166 Edgehill Rd., New Haven. She has interesting plans for the future as she is going into partnership with Miss Katherine Jewell Everts in Camp Arden, near Brattleboro, Vt. It is expected that the Camp will be expanded into an eight months' school with music, art, drama, and other studies besides regular camp activities, for girls from 11 to 19. Betty is to be executive and business manager. In view of this responsibility, 1900 is most fortunate in having her as its representative

on the Alumnae Fund Committee and is very grateful to her for accepting the position and attending the meeting in June.

1901

Class secretary—Mrs. Sanford Stoddard (Hannah Johnson), 499 Washington Av., Bridgeport, Conn.

MARRIED.—Emma West Durkee to Colonel Chauncey Benton Humphrey. New address, East Patchogue, N. Y.

OTHER NEWS.—Agnes (Childs) Hinckley has been appointed class representative on the Alumnae Fund Committee to the great satisfaction of her classmates.

Maude (Miner) Hadden was a speaker at the International Relations session of the A. A. U. W. meeting in Washington this spring, where Agnes (Patton) Woodhull, Alice Wright, and Agnes Hinckley were delegates.

Ethel (Stetson) Bingham's daughter Katharine has added one more item of interest to her graduation this June. Laura Scales gave a tea for her in April to announce her engagement to Arthur Lee Kinsolving, Rector of Grace Church, Amherst, and Director of Religious Activities, Amherst College. Ethel was present to share in the hearty wellwishing. Katharine graduated *cum laude*.

Miriam Titcomb takes charge of the new Hillsdale School in Cincinnati this fall. It is a country day school for girls, of the newest type, providing courses of instruction for the six years previous to college entrance.

1902

Class secretary—Mrs. Henry Burr (Ursula Minor), 5515 High Dr., Kansas City, Mo.

For report of reunion see page 472. With the exception of the secretary, the class officers were reëlected.

Selma (Altheimer) Weil has been ill for a year with a severe nervous breakdown following influenza, and is not yet able to see her friends.

Achsah (Barlow) Brewster, who is still in Capri, sent an interesting collection of photographs of some of her pictures for the reunion exhibit.

Ethel (Barnes) Burns's younger daughter, Janet, who left Smith after her freshman year, is continuing her course at the Univ. of Southern California. The older has a tremendously successful hat shop in Los Angeles.

Ruth Benedict is collecting European experience and local color in Vienna and doing free-lance newspaper writing. Her father died this spring.

Rachel (Berenson) Perry has returned from Berkeley (Calif.) where she was unofficial assistant to her husband during his exchange professorship.

Edith Blanchard is running a clothespin factory in Montpelier, Vt.

Anna Maria (Bliss) Phelps's twelve-year-old daughter Barbara, who seems to have eluded the QUARTERLY, is headed for Smith.

Emma (Bonfoey) Ashe seems to be lost. Has anyone her address?

Jessie Brainerd is planning a trip to San Francisco and Seattle this summer.

Catherine Brannick is a psychiatrist in the Chicago public schools.

Helen Bryant is teaching in the Girls' High School of Brooklyn.

The class is very grateful to Carol (Childs) Haslam's husband for his help in song drill as well as his general usefulness.

It was a very welcome return to old times to have Florence (Clexton) Little leading the glee club at our Sunday night musicale.

Avis (Coburn) Churchill was one of the people who were back with a son as chauffeur.

Alice (Curtis) Steane was back for her daughter Catherine's graduation.

Julia (Davis) Richmond has graciously added another packing box to the 1902 accumulations in her attic where our belongings are beautifully cared for between reunions.

A picture of Florence (Dowling) Olp's daughter in her bridal dress was an interesting part of our reunion exhibit.

Helen (Durkee) Mileham's husband brought back some delightful movies of a wonderful New Brunswick trip. Helen is still painting miniatures.

Alice (Egbert) Howell was back in Northampton in February for a conference of the Institute for the Coördination of Women's Interests. She has a daughter in Smith.

Edith Fales is teaching a huge Sunday school class in Philadelphia and is more or less in politics.

Margery (Ferriss) Semple was unable to be here for reunion, as she was leaving for the Pacific Coast.

Catherine Fogarty has charge of the discipline in a large Brooklyn school where she is assistant principal.

Marion (Gaillard) Brackett's sailing for Europe prevented her from coming back for reunion.

Caroline (Gleason) Larkin took time out from reunion to see her daughter Margaret graduate *cum laude*.

Eugenie Hadd is teaching French from the kindergarten through the seventh grade in an experimental school in the Bronx.

Eda (Heinemann) Kuhn, who was back for reunion with her husband, has been playing in "Chicago," in a part second only to that of the leading lady. She will return to the company when the play reopens early this fall.

Blanche Hull hoped to be back from India in time for reunion, but to everyone's regret didn't make it.

Lillian Hull is running an Italian tea room in Rochester (N. Y.) and was too busy with the early tourist rush to get back for reunion.

Louise Irving has charge of raising money for the Staten Island Visiting Nurse Assn., whose staff, under her administration, has grown from three to twelve.

Constance Jones lost her father about a year ago.

Jean (Jouett) Blackburn and her husband are still teaching in Friends' School, Locust Valley (L. I.), and running a summer camp. From reunion they drove on to visit Alice (Egbert) Howell.

Helen (Kelley) Marsh had to leave reunion

early to see her son graduate from Princeton.

Alice (Kidder) Tuttle got our successful red hats for us, but failed to come back herself.

Margaret (Lusch) Allen's daughter Virginia graduated with the class of 1927.

Eloise (Mabury) Knapp is a Christian Science practitioner in California.

Sabina Marshall is director of the Girls' Bureau of Cleveland, formerly known as the Women's Protective Assn.

Grace (Mason) Young dropped in for a short stay at reunion on her way to Europe. She is taking only two of her eight children with her.

Ursula (Minor) Burr has just been appointed educational secretary for the Diocese of West Missouri.

Elizabeth Neal will study this summer at the Smith College School for Social Work.

Emma (Otis) Wilson's husband is mayor of Bangor, Me.

Helen (Pease) Wightman has recently moved to Watertown, N. Y. Her sixteen-year-old daughter Harriet hopes to come to Smith a little later.

Julia (Peck) Albee is a substitute teacher in Dobbs Ferry.

Helena (Porteous) Crosthwaite's daughter Helena, who is our class baby, was married May 16 to Henry Schroeder Jr. of N. Y. C.

Faith (Potter) Weed's daughter Phoebe was with us for reunion.

Martha (Riggs) Griffith and her daughter, Margaret (Truax) Hunter ex-'26, were both back for their respective reunions. Margaret received her degree from the Univ. of California.

Nann (Smith) Warner, temporarily free from the care of a house, is flitting back and forth between a daughter at Westover School and a husband and son in California. She is planning further travel.

Susan Smith lost her mother early this summer.

Ethel (Stratton) Pettingill's son Waldo graduated recently from a school of business administration and has made a most successful start in the motion picture business.

Gertrude Tubby has a book about her former chief, Dr. James Hyslop, in the press.

Louise Vanderbilt is a visiting teacher in the New York City Public Schools. Last year she handled over 500 cases.

The enthusiastic thanks of the class go to Ella (Van Tuyl) Kempton for her very efficient handling of pre-reunion arrangements.

Jessie (Wadsworth) Burns is chairman of Community Girls' Work in White Plains, and has charge of clubs of Italian, colored, high school, and business girls.

Eunice Wead is working this summer for her Master's degree.

Selma (Weil) Eisemann's daughter Ruth (Smith '26) delighted us at the picnic by her account of her experiences in Geneva, where she did secretarial work for the League of Nations.

Edith Wells sent from China the cunning red lions and the gorgeous lanterns that decorated our gatherings at class headquarters and elsewhere during reunion.

Louise Woodbury's lovely voice helped make our Sunday evening musicale memorable.

Ex-1902

Helen (Atherton) Govier's playing kept our Sunday evening entertainment from being purely vocal, and added greatly to everyone's enjoyment.

We welcomed Eliza (Atwood) Thompson back for her first reunion. She has a daughter in Vassar.

Kathrina (Condé) Knowlton was too busy helping her daughter Katharine graduate *cum laude* to give much time to reunion, but we were glad of the glimpses we had of her.

Wasn't it nice to have the Fishes back, and didn't you love the Campanari stunt?

It was fine to hear Marian Harris sing again. Having no family cares she has all the odd jobs on social service lines of the county given her.

Ada (Hilt) Street's son Julian Jr. was married Apr. 25 to Narcissa Vanderlip in the New Church, E. 35 St., N. Y. C. Ada's daughter Rosemary was one of the bridesmaids. He is on the staff of the *N. Y. Herald-Tribune.*

Lulie (Keith) Keith divided her time between reunion and Amherst where she had a son graduating.

Helen (Pease) Miller and Sue (Skinner) Raymond, with Helen's son as chauffeur, drove down to New Britain after Commencement to visit Augusta (Vibberts) Pelton.

Anna (Ripley) Ordway's daughter Dorothy (Smith '25) was married Apr. 9 to Vincent Farnsworth Jr. of Winchester, Mass.

Bertha Whipple is teaching domestic science in Univ. of Missouri, Columbia, Mo.

1903

Class secretary—Mrs. Francis W. Tully (Susan Kennedy), 3 Alwington Rd., Chestnut Hill, Mass.

NEW ADDRESS.—Mrs. Richard D. Logan (Florence Durflinger), 2220 Collingwood Av., Toledo, O.

MARRIED.—Caroline Bean, June 13, to Captain Algernon H. Binyon of London, England. Captain Binyon was born in Capri. He is a graduate of the Univ. of Naples and is an aviation and automobile engineer, having been for some years technical adviser to the Royal Automobile Club in London. During the war from 1915 to 1918 he was in this country, sent by the English Admiralty, to inspect all aero engines for war work at Hammondsport and Buffalo. Captain Binyon's mother, Signora Chiesa, lives in the Villa Bianca in Capri. He is a cousin of Lawrence Binyon, prominent in the artistic and literary world. Address for the present, 225 Kings Highway, Westport, Conn. Caroline had an exhibition of her portraits, paintings, and drawings in Washington recently and received many favorable criticisms of her work. The *Washington Star* says: "The majority of the exhibits were drawings in red chalk or in charcoal and colored chalks on tinted paper. There were two in red chalk, both extremely good, exquisite in line, very personal and vital. There were two of children in charcoal and colored chalks, just enough color being added to give vivacity, a suggestion of youth. There were one or two of young girls, sympathetically rendered. . . . Miss Bean also showed a lately completed portrait in oils in the style of the great English school, a decorative rendering." Caroline remained in Washington for some little time as she had a number of commissions to execute.

OTHER NEWS.—Alice Blanchard opened the Everyday Bookshop on June 15 at 184 Pearl St., Burlington, Vt. Her pamphlet says in part: "Here the booklover may browse undisturbed among the best books new and old. The shop is equipped to obtain any books desired whether or not they are upon its shelves. Mail orders will be answered the day they are received."

The following from the *Boston Transcript* is of interest as it concerns Dorothea (Burnham) Pond's daughter: "The fiftieth anniversary of the founding of the Mary A. Burnham School for Girls was observed in connection with the Commencement exercises, when a class of forty-one was graduated. One of the graduates was Mary Burnham Pond of Rutland (Vt.), a grandniece of the founder of the school. President William Allan Neilson of Smith delivered the address."

Myrtie (Booker) Robinson and her husband have been enjoying a trip through Europe. They planned to connect with Grace (Gilbert) Graff and her husband, last reported in Rome. Myrtie wrote from Paris that she had happened to run across Mabel Wilson and they had been in the midst of the great excitement over Lindbergh's arrival.

May and Maud Hammond have returned from their three months' Mediterranean cruise. They were heartbroken at being forced to leave Paris for the boat train just two hours before "Lindy" arrived.

Della (Hastings) Wilson writes, "Am doing private tutoring, along with care of home and one youngster." Della's address is 104 Bird, not Birch St.

Two tutors! For Betty (Knight) Aldrich reports: "I'm having a lot of fun with my tutoring. I'm busy every morning from 8.30 until 12, tutoring grammar school children who are behind for one reason or another—to say nothing of running a study class or two for grown-ups!"

Lilian (Lauferty) Wolfe wrote from 853 Seventh Av., N. Y. C.: "The chief news is that James Wolfe and I are going abroad on June 1. And I'm going as 'Mrs. Jimmy,' a name which my activities in club and newspaper life and magazines do not let me wear very often in New York. We shall be gone three months and friend husband will do a lot of concertizing—beginning in Riga (Latvia), his 'home town.' He has been singing around the U. S. A. in concerts this spring."

Frances Lawrence writes that they have moved their printing establishment to their home and, since January, she has been an "active partner" in the business as well as homemaker and "general utility" person. She says, "I feel much happier to have father directly under my eye."

Laura (Matthews) Sumner is a very busy woman for she not only teaches school but is the parish worker of the North Church, Portsmouth (N. H.), an important social service position.

Edith (St. John) Esty writes that her two sons are preparing for Yale at the University School, Cleveland.

Elizabeth (Strong) Hayden and her family sailed in June for a summer on the other side, mostly England and Scotland.

1903 children graduating from college this year: Our Class Daughter, Janet Olmsted (Marguerite Prescott's daughter) from Smith; Lucia (Bailey) Bliss's son Albert from Dartmouth; Julian Hargraves (Mabel Haberstroh's son) from Williams; and Leolyn (Smith) Morgan's daughter Leolyn from the Univ. of California. Janet Olmsted graduated *magna cum laude*, and the Class presented her with a hand-wrought silver pendant and chain at a 1903 supper at May Hammond's during Commencement.

Ex-1903

LOST! Chicago alumnae please take notice! Maude (Douglas) Hopkins, Mrs. James or Mrs. Douglas Hopkins. Had daughter Josephine at Mt. Vernon Seminary. Lived at 5430 Harper Av. and Chicago Beach Hotel. Has always been one of our loyal "Exes" so we are anxious to find her.

OTHER NEWS.—Mrs. James D. Adams (Isabel Gilson), 138 Brite Av., Scarsdale, N. Y. Isabel's daughter Katharine is at Abbot Academy in the class of 1928 and Isabel writes that she is so pleased with the school she will send her younger daughter there, but neither girl plans to go to college.

Florence (Strong) Wright's husband, Mr. Charles O. Wright, is the head of the West Side Branch of the Y. M. C. A. in New York.

Ex-1903 children graduating from college this June: Anne (Bullen) Gage's son, Joseph Albert Jr., and also Edward Sheridan, Anne's legal ward, from Bowdoin; Gilbert Ballantine (Yettie Du Bois's son) from the Univ. of California; James Harvey Winsor (Helen Howell's boy) from Yale; Josiah Waite Parsons Jr. (Lilla Stone's son) from M. A. C. at Amherst; and Lila (Towar) Irons's daughter Virginia from the Univ. of Nebraska.

1904

Class secretary—Eleanor Garrison, 99 Marion St., Brookline, Mass.

Anne Chapin expected to sail for England on the *Aquitania*, June 22, to be gone two months.

Mary (Comer) Lane's daughter Mary has been taken into Biology Club.

Hannah (Dunlop) Colt is a member of the Village Board of Education at Bronxville, N. Y.

Mary (Dutcher) Carroll was planning to be present at the marriage of Phila (Johnson) Burck's daughter Barbara, in Los Angeles, June 25. Barbara, born in 1908, is 1904's first bride.

Warren T. Newcomb, husband of Ruby Hendrick, died in an automobile accident in New Orleans, June 5.

A recent issue of the *Wesleyan University*

Alumnus says: "Among those of the Wesleyan community who are watching with pride the growth of the Olin Memorial Library perhaps none may with greater enthusiasm acclaim its progress than Miss Eugenia M. Henry, assistant librarian. To the undergraduates and faculty during the years of her work at Wesleyan she has become a well-known figure —thoroughly familiar with the resources of the library and cheerfully responsive to every request for assistance, intimately interested in Wesleyan life. She came to Wesleyan after having taken her Bachelor of Arts degree at Smith and the degree of Bachelor of Library Science at the Albany Library School. In the period of her connection with the Wesleyan Library the staff has increased from three to eight in number. An annual acquisition of five thousand books and pamphlets has raised the total number of volumes to the respectable figure of 150,000. Perhaps Miss Henry's greatest interest in the new library will be in the facilities afforded for the exhibition of art collections, a project from the growth of which she has derived much satisfaction."

Ellen Hildreth writes enthusiastically from Switzerland and Italy. "I tried to see Florence (Covel) Avitabile in Rome but we couldn't arrange it. Saw where she lives though, right near St. Peter's."

Adèle (Keys) Hull's husband died suddenly on Apr. 25. Adèle, with her daughter Posy, was on her way to Los Angeles via the Panama Canal. Her son Cameron has been spending the winter in California with Adèle's sister.

Frances Lockey motored from Leominster to Northampton last April to show the college to one of her sub-freshman pupils.

In the *Smith College Weekly* of Apr. 20, Helen (Peabody) Downing's Sally had a long article on the visit of the French students to the Grécourt Gates. "Just as we left the town hall a woman ran down the path and with tears streaming down her cheeks said, 'Même si nous vivions eternellement, nous n'oublierions jamais les dames de Grécourt et ce qu'elles ont fait pour nous.'"

Grace (Reynolds) Rice, formerly instructor in the Department of Chemistry at Barnard, has been made assistant professor. "I am thrilled by my job," she says, "and grateful that it is my privilege to be a member of the teaching profession."

Bertha (Robe) Conklin has accepted the chairmanship of the Alumnae Fund Committee for 1904.

Alice Morgan Wright returned to Albany in April after several months in New York. She says, "I am finding quite a lot of time to work in my little garret studio." Alice was in Northampton at Commencement time.

NEW ADDRESS.—Alice Martin Jones, 50 Locust Hill Av., Yonkers, N. Y.

Ex-1904

Grace (Buck) Stevens began her summer on Cape Cod in March. Her address is Rendezvous Lane, Barnstable.

Alice (Poore) Favinger's husband, Charles Luff Favinger, died suddenly, Apr. 5, in Waban, Mass.

Laura E. Smith, long on the Hide and Seek list of 1904, is Mrs. Harold White of Fitchburg, Mass. Laura entered with 1904 but continued with 1908. Her sister, Helen (Smith) Hamilton, graduated in 1901.

NEW ADDRESS.—Cornelia Le Roy, 424 E. 57 St., N. Y. C.

1905

Class secretary—Mrs. Frank Mansfield (Alice Curtis), 9 Salisbury Rd., Brookline, Mass.

BORN.—To Ruth (Bigelow) Christie a son, John Watson Jr., June 27, 1926.

OTHER NEWS.—Helen (Abbot) Lapham with her husband and children came East in June for the graduation from Hotchkiss of her oldest son, Lewis, who will enter Yale in the fall. They will spend a month with Edna (Capen) Lapham in New Canaan (Conn.) before returning home.

Flörie (Bannard) Adams's Jane will spend the summer in camp at Vergennes (Vt.) and Flörie will divide her summer between her father in Chicago and her uncle in North Carolina.

The following item from the *Boston Herald* should make us very proud of our class daughter: "Miss Nancy C. Barnett of Great Barrington, a member of the junior class of Smith College, has just been elected by the Student Council as head usher for next year. This position is one of great responsibility as well as honor. As head usher she will attend to the ushering at all concerts through the year, and will have charge of the ushering at Rally Day."

Grace (Beattie) Hardies's son is at the Lake Placid Club School where he is preparing to enter Williams in 1930. Her daughter will soon enter the Emma Willard School in Troy en route for Smith. Grace and her family spend much time at their summer home, "Woodholme," at Lake Pleasant, N. Y. Grace herself is active in the Amsterdam Women's Club and this past year has been taking courses in interior art decoration.

Ruth Blodgett plans to spend July in Thomaston (Me.) and the rest of the summer at Beach Bluff, where the latest attraction is a small nephew born June 5, John Henry Blodgett Jr.

Julia (Bourland) Clark's daughter Dorothy plans to go with the juniors to France this fall.

Grace (Brown) Higgins's husband, Willard Higgins, died suddenly in April.

Helen (Bruce) Loomis and her entire family left June 17, for Elkhorn Ranch, Bozeman, Mont., where they are to spend a month just "plain ranching."

Edna (Capen) Lapham writes: "We are at New Canaan (Conn.) for the summer; we have two boys in Hotchkiss, the older bound for Williams, the younger for Yale; and two daughters on their way to Smith. Our permanent address is 17 Battery Pl., N. Y. C."

Louise Collin attended the convention of the American Alumni Council held at Chapel Hill (N. C.) in April.

Edna (Day) Blakeslee and her family leave July 1 for Honolulu where her husband con-

ducts a round table conference at the School of Politics held there through July. Later Prof. Blakeslee is to spend some months studying conditions in the Far East.

Katharine (De La Vergne) Stevenson and her husband have recently taken over the management of "The Green Fish," a most attractive tea room in New Canaan, Conn.

After several months abroad Pauline Fullerton is back in her position in the art department of the N. Y. Public Library.

Evelyn Hooker returned June 12 from a year and a half of travel abroad, during which time she visited Italy and Southern France, England and Scotland, spent six months in Paris, and this spring went to Spain and Northern Africa.

Katherine (Irwin) Murray's youngest brother was ordained a Jesuit on June 23 by Cardinal O'Connell at Weston, Mass.

Alice (Lawlor) Kirby's daughter Teresa passed this year her examinations for the Sorbonne, but has decided to stay in Northampton.

Katherine (Noyes) McLennan came East this June for the graduation of her son Donald from Hotchkiss.

Blanche (Valentine) Haskell sends word that they are now established at Marblehead Neck for the summer. "We have a regular fleet in the family this year, as the four oldest children all have boats and are planning to enter the races this season."

Helen Wright is coming on from Santa Barbara (Calif.) to spend the summer in Northampton. Her address will be 249 Crescent St.

Ex-1905

Lucy Clark writes from Switzerland that she has had a splendid year abroad and has enjoyed especially the sports in that country.

Laura Copp went to London in May to study piano with Tobias Matthay through the summer.

Jessie (Girvan) Garlock's oldest son, Sprague, has just finished his freshman year at Cornell. He represents the third generation of Garlocks to attend Cornell.

Janette (Logan) Jacobs has been working with her husband who published this spring under the name of Charles Pelton, "The Old One Looks on," a novel dealing with Greenwich Village life. Her address is Washington, Conn.

1906

Class secretary—Mrs. Eben Atwood (Edith Moore), 2732 Irving Av. S., Minneapolis, Minn.

In response to a postal with "Please send summer plans NOW to your secretary" the following is submitted. Look in on each other.

Edith Battles has resigned her teaching position at Long Beach, Calif. She expects to be at her home in Brockton (Mass.) for the summer, and remain East this winter.

Nettie Baumann is on the Board of the Illinois League of Women Voters.

Marian (Beye) Hurlbut will be in Fairhope (Ala.) after Oct. 1. She will spend the summer at Lower Waterford, Vt., c/o Mrs. N. C. Beye.

Bernice Dearborn is supervising elementary and junior high grades at the summer school held in the Commerce High School building, Springfield, Mass.

Rosamond (Denison) McLean will take week-end trips with her husband and little boy, while her daughters are in camps. Last fall Rosamond had a trip to Bermuda, and looked up classmates in N. Y. City and Hartford.

Ethel (Gleason) McGeorge goes to a farm in Cuba (N. Y.) as usual. She will also motor through the White Mts. Ethel has become a director of the Buffalo College Club and is working in the League of Women Voters.

Florence Harrison says: "My plans for the summer include, I hope, a month in Minneapolis, and a chance to stay put. My present job keeps me traveling weeks at a time, and a nice spell of sitting is my idea of a vacation."

Anna Hastings will be at New Windsor, Md.

Caroline Hinman sails on Sept. 17 for a seven months' trip around the world. She is taking a small party—six at present, with room for two more—and they are going quite "off the beaten track." Sailing on the *Duilio* to Naples they will there take a Sitmar boat to Beirût, then cross Syria, Irak, and Persia, sailing from the Persian side of the Persian Gulf on Nov. 5 for northern India. They will motor in the Vale of Kashmir, look over the Khyber Pass into Afghanistan, spend Christmas in Darjeeling, travel through India to Ceylon, then sail to Java and motor through the interior, crossing over to the little, tropical, and seldom-visited island of Bali, then back to Singapore and through the Malay Peninsula to Bangkok in Siam. They will visit the ancient ruins of Angkor in Cambodia, then sail from Saigon to Japan, spending two weeks there in the early spring and returning to the States via Honolulu.

Margaret Hutchins is to teach at the Summer School for Librarians at Chautauqua (N. Y.) in Aug. Then she will hike in the White Mts., visiting around Lancaster and Randolph, N. H.

Edna (MacRobert) Morse and husband motored from Seattle to Santa Monica (Calif.) in May, to visit relatives. They return in July with their daughter after her College Board exams. She attends the Briarcliff School, Briarcliff Manor, N. Y. Edna highly recommends the new Redwood Highway, over which she traveled, to anyone going west.

Amy Maher has a little booklet called "Littlebrook." It describes her dreams come true of a little white house all her own, which she uses as a retreat. She purchased the place by correspondence, in a N. Y. village, making some alterations on arrival. There are ten acres of fruit trees, some flowers, and a running brook. In the brook are "charming little pools, which were soon haunted by water sprites" (in bathing suits). "Littlebrook" is on the side of a Berkshire hill.

Janet (Mason) Slauson will spend July and Aug., as last year, in the Thousand Islands

aboard their house boat, *Lysander*, at Alexandria Bay, N. Y.

Lucy Melcher will be at her home in Brunswick (Me.) where open house will be kept in June, on the occasion of her father's fiftieth reunion at Bowdoin College. He is secretary of his class. In July Lucy will be studying education at Harvard. She will then be ready for "the cool breezes and lazy life of Bustin Island, Me." 270 Maine St., Brunswick, Me., will always reach her.

Blanche (Millard) Parkin chooses home, in Niles (Mich.), after a winter in Calif. She, like many others, sends greetings to the class, and hopes to see us at her home.

Ethel (Monson) Holcombe and family plan a month on the Connecticut Shore, two or three weeks at their country place near Hartford, and some weeks at Kennebago Lake (Me.), at a camp near Rangeley, for fishing.

Clara (Newcomb) Back expects to spend Aug. as usual in the village of Chaplin, Conn. "Last year we built a new living-room and kitchen on to the old house." Clara is two hours' auto ride from her old home in New London. "Any 1906ers who want to hear quiet, and no telephone, COME!"

Margaret Norton will spend July in Chicago with her sister, at 1364 E. 58 St.

Esther (Porter) Brooks with husband and their two boys will camp in a cottage at the Cratts Club on Lake Champlain.

Florence Root is to have a delightful experience abroad as social director of the Westminster Student Tour. Florence says, "It isn't easy but tremendously interesting."

Theo (Sibley) Squire goes as usual to Cape Cod. In the winters she is in Florida.

Melinda (Prince) Smith was in Northampton at Commencement time. She has appointed Helen (Pomeroy) Burtis as our representative on the Alumnae Fund.

Josephine (Weil) Ryan writes a happy letter from Banff. She says: "As for my personal history, I married, of all people, a Royal Northwest Mounted Police Officer. I refer you to the movies. Clara Porter said she thought they only existed there, but I can assure you that they really exist. My husband is in command of the R. C. M. P. in the National Parks. Here in the Banff area of about 10,900 miles, he has a group of mounties and non-commissioned officers under him, whose red coats are one of the attractions of Banff to the tourists." Josephine has two small children. "Housekeeping, after one understands the conditions, is easy." For recreation Josephine skates, curls, dances, and plays bridge.

GET-TOGETHERS.—Marguerite(Dixon)Clark, Esther (Porter) Brooks, and Janet (Mason) Slauson had luncheons or picnics for our N. Y. classmates.

Your secretary's summer telephone is Minnetonka Beach 114–W. Or call Mr. Atwood, Geneva 1377.

Ex-1906

Helen (Block) Whittlesey will be in Pittsfield this summer, taking week-end trips to the shore.

Ruth (Durand) Lewis is moving to Easton (Pa.) where her husband has become President of Lafayette College. This summer she will be, as usual, at her summer home at Colebrook, Conn. Here, with her husband and 19-year-old daughter, they "live to the full our farm life of peace and quiet."

Gertrude (Fiedler) Mewborn will be in Canada for a few weeks. Gertrude has been made president of the Smith Club in Pittsburgh.

Jane Morey is driving with niece and nephew of college age through eastern Canada. Her pamphlet containing the 20th annual report of the Missouri Library Commission gives also a general survey of library conditions in the state at large. One needs to read such a report to get an idea of the comprehensive and extensive work of such a commission. Jane is secretary and has, besides routine office work, requests and talks.

1907

Class secretary—Mrs. James L. Goodwin (Dorothy Davis), 10 Woodside Circle, Hartford, Conn.

For reunion report see page 473.

Our new president is Muriel (Robinson) Burr.

BORN.—To Marian (Smith) Wallis a daughter, Margaret Orme, Jan. 23.

Sibyl (Buttrick) Gile conducts a gift shop on Washington St., Duxbury, Mass., called the Sibyl Shop. An unusual feature of this shop is her assortment of rare postage stamps for collectors.

Ernestine Friedmann is to be director of, and teach economics at, a new summer school for women workers in industry at Barnard College, for seven weeks this summer. Next winter she is to be head of the Economics Department at Wheaton.

Anna May has been in the U. S. Army for twelve years, being in charge of army libraries. The last five years she has been stationed in the Canal Zone. In the spring she resigned and has gone abroad for some months. Mail should be sent to her sister's address, 262 S. Second Av., Mt. Vernon, N. Y.

Mary (Ormsbee) Whitton's book on household electricity, entitled "The New Servant," was published in May. She has moved for the summer into the barn which last year she made over into a habitable dwelling. Summer address, R. F. D. 31, New Canaan, Conn.

Morley (Sanborn) Linton, after spending three years in this country, has rejoined her husband in Brazil. She sailed May 28 with her three little girls and her mother and sister. Address, Caixa 504, Rio de Janeiro, Brazil.

Ethel Woolf has been teaching in Atlanta ever since graduating from college. She is head of the History Department at the Girls' High School, faculty adviser for the Cum Laude High School Honorary Society and for the Dramatic Club, and is reported to be one of the most popular teachers in the school. Her new address is 1035 Peachtree St., Atlanta, Ga.

NEW ADDRESS.—Mrs. W. Paxton Cary (Jean Welch), 350 San Fernando St., Point Loma, Calif.

Ex-1907

NEW ADDRESS.—Mrs. T. H. Goodspeed (Florence Beman), 551 Santa Rosa Av., Berkeley, Calif.

1908

Class secretary—Mrs. James M. Hills (Helen Hills), 876 Carroll St., Brooklyn, N. Y.

Katherine Beane and her business partner have been managing a successful tea room called Ship's Haven in Quincy, Mass. They will open a second one by the same name in Plymouth this summer.

Harriet (Carswell) McIntosh's husband has been instrumental in promoting a college cruise around the world, to give students regular college courses while they enjoy the broadening effects of travel and gain international understanding. The cruise started Sept. 18, 1926, with a faculty of 50 and an enrollment of over 500. They were to be gone eight months, visiting 33 countries and 48 different ports. Real feats of pioneering lie behind these simple statistics, for there were no precedents to follow and it was necessary to plan a curriculum which was adapted to the limitations of shipboard. Many foreign universities entertained the students and, wherever practical, arrangements were made for seeing the native life on the trips ashore, rather than the standardized hotel life. It is hoped to make the tour a permanent institution. The shipping arrangements for the next cruise are with the Cunard Line.

Marjorie Henry became a Docteur de l' Université at the Sorbonne on May 20. She was the first to be granted the "Doctorat" this year. Her thesis, "Stuart Merrill, the Contribution of an American to French Symbolism," was received with the congratulations of the jury and with the mention *très honorable*. "In a style colorful, elegant, and precise Miss Henry has presented an analysis of the life and writings of Merrill, the first of such wide range to be written on this author. It takes its place among the best biographies and critical studies which have appeared during the last few years. Her information is based almost entirely on original documents."

May Kissock received her Master's degree in education from New York Univ. in June.

Betsey Libbey of The Family Society of Philadelphia conducted the Institute on Family Social Work held by the American Assn. for Organizing Family Social Work, in New York, May 23 to June 18.

1909

Class secretary—Mrs. Donald Pirnie (Jean MacDuffie), 138 Milbank Av., Greenwich, Conn.

Ding-a-dong, ding-a-dong, just a calm peaceful song, We are all on the job, and there's none raising hob, And we've medals on hand when the notables land.

Born, died, married. None. Just like Heaven.

OTHER NEWS.—Vera (Booth) Philbrick is to be in Groton Long Point (Conn.) this summer and is now a Smith Club Councillor from the Hartford Club.

Louise (Hennion) Fisher in April was re-

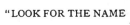

THE newest panorama of the Mode shows an endless succession of pleats and tucks stretching from here to Paris. . . . Crisp big pleats, clever little pleats, pleats with knife-edges that stay trimly in place.

Of all the modish fabrics, none pleats or tucks or stays in place better than Skinner's Crepes, made by the makers of Skinner's Satins. They have the *wearing quality* that has made the name Skinner famous, and are washable, with proper care.

Think of the colors you'll have to choose from in Skinner's Crepes . . . *eighty of them* . . . all the new, soft, delectable colors. . . . Think of the wear you'll get. . . . Then go to the nearest shop that sells these crepes — and when you ask for them,

"Look for the Name in the Selvage"

WILLIAM SKINNER & SONS, Established 1848
New York, Chicago, Boston, Philadelphia — Mills, Holyoke, Mass.

Skinner's Crepes

"LOOK FOR THE NAME   IN THE SELVAGE"

elected to the Hartford Board of Education, to serve three years. She says: "We are busy now planning for our grade school, which was voted on also at the April election. I am chairman of the Vocational Training Committee of the Hartford Board of Education."

Louise Elmendorf has come back to Hartford after a stay in New York and has resumed teaching in the high school.

Helen Marks writes that the Pennsylvania College for Women, of which she is Dean, has 350 students and has just completed a splendid year.

Gertrude (Schwarz) McClurg went abroad in May for a motor trip in Spain, returning to England in time for her sister's presentation at Court.

Edith (Scott) Magna attended 16 State Conferences of the D. A. R. in addition to all of the National Board Meetings in Washington. Beginning Oct. 5 in Connecticut, she went to the State meetings in Massachusetts, New Jersey, Indiana, Missouri, Oklahoma, Texas, Arkansas, Colorado, Iowa, Massachusetts, Maine, Mississippi, Illinois, North Carolina, and Georgia. She expects to spend the summer in the Rocky Mts., attending several State Conferences while there. She was invited to be present when Colonel Lindbergh received the Orteig Prize and was on hand for that and his final hop-off to St. Louis.

Colonel Walter Scott, father of Edith (Scott) Magna, and honorary member of the class, as one of the officers and trustees of the Orteig Prize presented Colonel Lindbergh with the Orteig Trophy on June 17.

Helen (Wing) Graves, director of the School Nature League of New York, had a public exhibition of the work of the League which was enthusiastically described by the *New York Times*.

1910

Class secretary—Alice O'Meara, 12 Keswick St., Boston, Mass.

BORN.—To Wilma (Ridgway) Perry a daughter, Judith Elizabeth, June 2.

MARRIED.—Marion Thomas to Frederic Willard Childs of Brattleboro, Vt., June 11. New address, Ames Hill, West Brattleboro, Vt.

NEW ADDRESS.—Mrs. H. P. Wherry (Esther Ann Smith), 26 E. 8 St., N. Y. C.

OTHER NEWS.—Marcia (Beebe) Flannery came to Boston to visit her mother last May, with Ida (Andrus) Williams as traveling companion. They both made· a pilgrimage to Northampton and had "a date" with each other for chapel.

They say that Lucile (Bradley) Paul's husband is much in demand as a public speaker. He is an enthusiastic Dartmouth and Thayer Academy man and is a vice-commander of the American Legion. He and Lucile are to be in Europe next September when the Legion goes over.

Besides caring for her three children, Helen (Gifford) Varnum is helping to establish a Mothers' Club in connection with the new school that her community is hoping to persuade Phelps Manor to build. She is also interested in the growth of a very young and struggling Episcopal Church and in the training of an active junior choir. She sees Bertha (Skinner) Bartlett on her summer trips through New London to New Bedford.

Edith Gill received her M.A. in English at Columbia in June 1925. During the summer of 1926, "to fix some of the learning ere it should all get away," she spent two months with a Columbia friend visiting literary shrines of Great Britain. They spent another month touring the Continent. This year Edith is keeping house for her father.

Florence (Hopwood) Judd sailed with her children June 28 on a North Cape Cruise, planning to stay in Europe until Oct. 1. She saw Edna Bunnell in Florida last winter.

Eva (Jenison) Pruyn's mother died very suddenly last spring.

Last May at the semi-annual Wisconsin Smith luncheon, at Madison, Erminie (Rost)· Sherman was elected president of the Club. There were 25 present, two members coming across country 70 miles for the gathering.

Mary Ann (Staples) Kirkpatrick was appointed last May chairman of the 1910 Committee for the Alumnae Fund. She attended in Northampton at Commencement time the first meeting of the class chairmen. You will hear from Mary Ann sometime soon. Be good to her. She thinks 1910 the best ever! We know what we think of her!

Ednah (Whitney) Gerrish writes that she has had a quiet year, her energy divided between "odd jobs around town of the sort that are always waiting for a shoulder to fall upon, a very active family," and about a trip a month from Boston to New York to keep her husband company while he is on business.

1911

Class secretary—Mrs. J. P. O'Brien (Margaret Townsend), 614 Madison Av., Albany, N. Y.

BORN.—To Mildred (Horton) Bonstein a second daughter, Marjorie Louise, Feb. 16, 1926.

OTHER NEWS.—A joint postcard from Gertrude (Lyford) Boyd and Joyce (Knowlton) Zinsser arrived from Scotland the last of May. Jake and husband spent several days with Gertrude and her family at Ayr.

Dr. Walter Adams Bradford, husband of Doris (Patterson) Bradford, died of pneumonia June 14, after an illness of only a few days.

Dorothy Pease is working as "laboratorian" in Mt. Vernon, N. Y. She has written an article on "Actinobacillus Meningitis" which appeared in the *American Journal of Diseases of Children* (32, 878–888) 1926.

Henrietta Scott is teacher of history at the Memorial High School for Girls, Boston. She is still working for an A.M. at Boston Univ.

Dot White is at home again after her trip to California following her mother's death.

NEW ADDRESSES.—Mrs. Pierrepont E. Grannis (Marguerite Miller), Glenville Rd., Greenwich, Conn.

Dorothy Pease, Ashfield, Mass. (Temp., 174 Archer Av., Mt. Vernon, N. Y.)

Henrietta Scott, 661 Hope St., Providence, R. I. (Temp., 19 Peterborough St., Boston.)

1912

Class secretary—Mary A. Clapp, Galloupe's Point, Swampscott, Mass.

For report of reunion see page 474.

BORN.—To Lucile (Buzzard) Flodin a daughter, Betsy Jean, Aug. 29, 1920.

To Alice (Casey) Dowd a first daughter and third child, Jeanne de Guise, Apr. 4. Alice is now living at 333 Central Park W., N. Y. C.

To Helen (Northup) Jackes a second daughter, Elizabeth Northup, Jan. 29, 1926.

To Ruth (Paine) Blodgett a first son and third child, John Henry Jr., June 5.

To Genevieve (Stockwell) Humphrey a second son and third child, Frederick G. II, Oct. 28, 1926.

DIED.—Agnes Aldridge, Apr. 9, in New York City, after a brief illness.

NEW ADDRESSES.—Mrs. William Head (Katharine Bradbury), Hooksett, N. H.

Mrs. Ralph Hayes (Helen Perkins), 752 Van Dyke Av., Detroit, Mich.

OTHER NEWS.—Ruth Lawrence is establishing a new world's record in traveling. After resigning her job with the New England Mutual Life Insurance Co. in February, she repaired to New Orleans with her parents, whence, after giving a blow of the eye at the Mardi Gras, and collecting a sister, a brother-in-law, and an automobile, she repaired to California, via every point of interest possible to be seen en route. Nine thousand miles they did in nine weeks; and then after seven days of—we were going to say "repose," but we think that "being" is better—at Medford, they all set sail for Ireland, Scotland, England, France, Switzerland, and way stations.

Ex-1912

Olive Barker is instructor in music at Iowa State Teachers' College.

1913

Class secretary—Mrs. Alexander Craig Jr. (Helen Hodgman), 314 E. 17 St., Brooklyn, N. Y.

MARRIED.—Mildred Tyler to Frank M. Van Schaack. Address, 184 Sigourney St., Hartford, Conn.

BORN.—To Agnes (Conklin) Mealand her first son and second child, Geoffrey Conklin, May 8.

To Florence (Dale) Walker a daughter, Natalie Sutherland, Mar. 24.

To Ruth (Ensign) Pease a second son, Frederic Arnold Jr., May 23.

To Helen (Kempshall) Pinneo a third child, in Feb. (Secretary can not decipher name!)

To Florence (Morman) Steele a daughter, Mar. 2. "She is my third daughter, but little Helen, the oldest, was killed over two years ago by an automobile."

To Miriam (Pratt) Gyger her second son and fourth child, John Thomas Jr., Feb. 10, 1926.

To Alice (Woodworth) Kiewit a third son, David Scott, Mar. 13.

OTHER NEWS.—Owing to the fact that most of 1913's loyal members stayed at home this year in order to be more sure of leaving home

next year for the 15th, the group of hardy perennials at Northampton in June was small, though, as usual, lively. See the 1913 Alumnae Registration for a roster of those who joined forces with 1776 to serenade and enjoy themselves in general. The Alumnae Fund was enthusiastically launched, and more of this anon. The President Burton Memorial was reported as nearing completion, with $27,500 in hand, about $3500 of which was contributed by 1914, about $1600 by 1913. Ideas for 15th reunion are now rampant, but always solicited, together with suggestions for committee chairmen, etc.

Barbara Bell: "After giving up my nice Pennsylvania Academy position, and playing last summer in Norway and Sweden and England with M. Booth '14, I have come home to roost. I have a studio in town where I am making children's portraits in pastel and crayon, and having a grand time; business is getting well started and I am very busy and working hard. While it is a bit early to say I am successful, I am satisfied so far."

Dot Brown: "I'm a realtor now." Boom Inc., 11 Church St., Montclair, N. J.

Emily Chamberlain has taken a degree at the Sorbonne. She writes, "I shall probably stay with the Division of University Extension teaching French correspondence and class work."

Sarah (Cheney) Despard: "My husband has business in Europe and Africa and we spend a good deal of time going abroad. Last year I was president of the Board of Trustees of the N. Y. Infirmary for Women and Children. This year we are trying to raise funds for a new hospital to be called the Gotham Hospital which is to be run by women and open to all women doctors who are grade A graduates. I also help to run in Huntington a fresh air home for children during the hot months."

Florence Cobaugh: "I am teaching English, and this year had the good luck to be placed in a beautiful new high school building. This is my third year in Johnstown, and I find it indeed the 'Friendly City' even if it was the 'Flood City.' This summer I expect to spend my vacation in foreign travel."

Alice (Cone) Perry: "Nothing spectacular to report except the boys' growth which is phenomenal." [See page 485.]

Eleanor (Cory) Leiper: "Henry (husband), the two youngsters, and I sail for France June 25. Henry goes in connection with his publicity secretary work of the Congregational Board and will be studying social and political conditions in the several capitals of Europe ending up at the Institute of the League of Nations in August. The children and I expect to bask on the shore of Brittany for two weeks, then on to Paris and Switzerland for over a month. We shall be in Geneva and Carol (daughter) who is an enthusiastic Girl Scout and myself as a Council member will attend the International Scout Conference. By the way, we go over on the boat with Prof. Harlow of Smith and a bunch of Smith girls."

Helen Estee expects to be in Paris next fall

THE SANTA BARBARA GIRLS' SCHOOL

Resident and Day Pupils. Eleven acres. Country life and sports. Sleeping Porches. Open-air rooms. Riding. Swimming.

Basis of work: **Clear Thinking.**

MARION L. CHAMBERLAIN, A.M., *Principal*

Post Office Box 548   Santa Barbara, Calif.

HILLSIDE
A School for Girls
NORWALK, CONNECTICUT

In a beautiful New England town, one hour from New York. Girls from all parts of the country. Four residences, schoolhouse, gymnasium. Extensive grounds. Preparation for all colleges. Special courses. Outdoor life. Catalog.

Margaret R. Brendlinger, A.B. (Vassar)
Vida Hunt Francis, A.B. (Smith)
Principals

GRAY COURT
A SCHOOL *for* GIRLS

Gray Court, beautifully situated at Stamford, Connecticut, fifty-two minutes from the Grand Central Station, New York, offers the unusual advantages of country and seashore.

Primary, Intermediate, College Preparatory, Secretarial and Cultural Courses, with opportunity for special work in Music, Arts and Crafts and Spoken English. Horseback Riding. All Athletics.

WRITE FOR ILLUSTRATED CATALOGUE

Jessie Callam Gray, A.B., Smith
Principal
STAMFORD · CONNECTICUT

HOWE-MAROT
COUNTRY BOARDING SCHOOL
College Preparation

Marot Junior College
Two-Year College Course

For Catalog address
MARY L. MAROT, Principal
THOMPSON, CONNECTICUT

The
Low and Heywood School
SHIPPAN POINT, STAMFORD, CONN.

A country School for Girls one hour from New York City. Thorough college preparation, also general and postgraduate courses. Separate cottages for younger girls. Sixty-second year begins Sept. 28, 1927.

MARY ROGERS ROPER, Head Mistress

MISS MADEIRA'S SCHOOL
1330 19th Street, N. W.
Washington, D. C.

A resident and day school for girls
LUCY MADEIRA WING, A. B., VASSAR

Mrs. David Laforest Wing
Head Mistress

Saint Margaret's School
1875   1927
A New England School for girls

Thorough Preparation for the Leading Colleges for Women.
Art, Music, and Special Courses.
New 20-acre country estate for recreation.
Well-organized athletic program.
Conveniently situated. Two and one half hours from New York City.
Catalog on request. Box C.
Alberta C. Edell, A. M., Principal, Waterbury, Conn.

studying at the Sorbonne. "I'm sailing the last of May and am planning to stay over until Aug. 1928—perhaps even longer."

Marian (Gardner) Craighill's mother writes the following news of Marian in China: "After the very serious fighting last fall, the city (Nanchang) gradually quieted down, and it seemed nice for them to stay. Soldiers quartered themselves in classrooms at the boys' school but not in the church, and they were able to keep on with work, though Unions and strikes and parades made difficulties. After the Nanking outrages, they knew they must leave. Word came at 6.30 A. M. March 26 and they packed hastily to leave in an hour, taking what they could. They are away from the river, so had several hours on the train to reach the boat. It carried 300 passengers, though designed for only 30, but they reached Shanghai safely and since then have been in a dormitory belonging to St. John's Univ. where they are glad to have a room. They expect to go to Urizese, Japan, later, and hope that by the end of the summer they can know whether they can go back to Nanchang, where they long to be. The latest news they had was that their house had not been occupied by soldiers, or looted, and they have been able to have some of their things sent to them. There is a very friendly attitude toward them in Nanchang and the people wish them to return. The baby was sick with bronchitis after their journey, but is well again."

Orpha (Gerrans) Gatch writes: "We have bought the old Gatch farm just outside of Milford (O.) that has been in the family seventy years or more, and we are going to move out there as soon as we have remodeled the old stone farmhouse which is nearly 100 years old. To-day I help start our first swarm of bees in a new hive."

Ada Leffingwell has "gone into the linen business: The Linen Chest, 950 Madison Av., N. Y. C. We sell everything from dish towels to banquet cloths, and we decorate bathrooms, linen closets, etc. If there are still any unmarried girls in 1913 besides myself they should see me about their hope chests!"

Edith Leffingwell, our artist, has been ill for many months with a trouble that has affected her arm.

Annie (Mather) Motheral: "The past year has been a very hard one. Just a year ago we lost my only brother, the next month my husband had a very serious operation from which he still feels the effects although he is gaining, and in March my father died suddenly and a month later my grandmother. Mother has come to live with us and we move to 137 DeVoe Av., Yonkers, the end of May."

Ruth McClelland: "I haven't a thing to report for school ma'aming isn't productive of glamorous tales of adventure. Of course I could compare notes with the best of you on the care of babies for I have taken care of three small nephews while their parents did a little vacationing."

Dorothy (Olcott) Gates: "We all hope to migrate along the last of May to our new house at Woods Hole, so tell any 1913s touring the Cape to look us up if they can stand the noise of five."

Nellie Oiesen returned from Denmark in May only to set sail for China in June where she will visit her mother and perhaps bring her back with her.

Nellie (Paschal) Metcalf lost her mother in Feb. after a short illness.

Aline (Smith) Ballard: "Having been very much married for twelve years I am going to forsake the family this summer to go abroad. Sail in June for France with my (much) younger sister. The two of us are going to have a good time all over Europe."

Margaret (Woodbridge) Price: "Arthur (husband) and I both holding down our church positions, studying with Prof. Olmsted and singing quite a lot."

NEW ADDRESSES.—Mrs. M. O. Kranstover (Martha Osborne), 105 Pinehurst Av., N. Y. C.

Marion Parker, 72 Lothrop St., Beverly, Mass.

Florence Seaman, 11694 Picturesque Dr. N., Hollywood, Calif.

Ex-1913

DIED.—Cecile (Vail) Follansbee, May 6, in California. Although Cecile was only in college one year she made many friends, and her bright, happy personality will be missed by many. She leaves three little children.

NEW ADDRESS.—Mrs. Sturgis Shields (Emma Clark), 310 W. 97 St., N. Y. C.

OTHER NEWS.—Helen (McBurnie) Bumpus: "My fond husband enclosed this [a clipping awarding Helen a prize for the best scenario for a picture taken in Rochester. This is now in the 1913 Scrap Book] but I'd really like it to go to Dot Brown. She always did make fun of my literary ability. Hurrah for English 13. You see what a college education can do!"

1914

Class secretary—Mrs. H. R. Miller (Dorothy Spencer), 120 Haven Av., N. Y. C. Tel. Billings 2414.

DIED.—Jeannette Heilbrunn, suddenly, May 4, in New York City.

ENGAGED.—Dorothy Thorne to George H. Fullerton. Mr. Fullerton is a manufacturer and is Stevens '12. They will be married probably in the fall and will live in Greensboro, N. C.

MARRIED.—Dorothea Simmons to Charles Cuthbert Harris, June 16, in Wilmington, Del. Portia Pratt and Madeleine (Rindge) Hands went down for the wedding.

BORN.—To Ruth (Brown) Harvey her first child, Joseph Larkin, June 10.

To Kathleen (Hosmer) Bowker her third child and second daughter, Ann Frances, Apr. 17.

To Fay (Kennedy) Mead her fourth child and second daughter, Rachel, June 13, 1926.

To Mary (Willard) Sawyer her third child and second daughter, Elizabeth Lane, Apr. 23.

NEW ADDRESSES.—Edith Bennett, to Oct. 1, 57 W. 58 St., N. Y. C.

Mrs. Royal Firman (Lillian Holferty), Port

Washington, N. Y. Her husband is with the Yale Press.

Mrs. J. H. Marshall (Louise Howe), summer, Box 24, R. F. D., Wakefield, R. I.

Elizabeth Roby, 220 E. 17 St., N. Y. C. Tel. Lexington 1435. "I am now doing vocational guidance work in the N. Y. schools and during the summer I shall continue working on a Vocational Guidance Research Study being conducted by Dr. Thorndike at Teachers College. Also studying some more."

Florence Root, Kwangju, Korea: "I am studying the Korean language preparatory to going into a girls' school here under the South Presbyterian Mission . . . and won't get home again until 1932, I suppose."

Mrs. E. W. Conklin (Dorothy Whitehead), 638 Lafayette Av., Buffalo, N. Y.

Mrs. H. P. Sawyer (Mary Willard), 68 Bigelow St., Fall River, Mass. They bought this house this spring. Two years ago they built a house in Touisset (Mass.) and are spending their summers there.

OTHER NEWS.—There were 33 members of 1914 at the spring lunch of the N. Y. Smith Club.

Barbara Addis and Jean Paton met accidentally on a steamer bound for Florida at Easter.

Next winter Dartmouth will be the hunting ground of Margaret (Alexander) Marsh. She will do research there from Monday to Friday and week-end with her husband in Amherst.

Margaret (Ashley) Paddock's father died in April while he was visiting her. Mr. Ashley's father introduced into Congress the bill for the Abolition of Slavery and the bill for the Impeachment of Andrew Jackson.

Eleanor Edson will study abroad this summer.

Marion (Freeman) Wakeman will transfer her teaching of art next winter to the Smith College Day School of which her husband is head.

Amelia (Gilman) Treadwell's father died May 29 in his eighty-first year. He was a member of the G. A. R. and had planned to march with them on Memorial Day.

Gladys Hall is found. She is now Mrs. Morris Ricker, Water St., Skowhegan, Me.

Norma Kastl is with Albert Frank and Co. advertising agency, writing copy and handling accounts.

Mabel (Kirley) Robinson and her baby will spend the summer at Vassar "to learn how to live. I am going to take the course in euthenics and shall put him in the nursey school."

We learned, via our St. Louis memory, that it was Kat Knight's uncle and cousin, Harry Knight Sr. and Jr., who backed Lindbergh.

Sophie (Marks) Krauss lost her father in May. He was eighty-one. Sophie made the trip from Memphis to New Orleans when the flood was at its height.

On June 18 Blanche Mitchell sailed to spend the summer studying in Italy.

A fourth member of the class, Agnes (Morgenthau) Newborg, lost her father this spring. Mr. Morgenthau, who was president of the Mirror Candy Co., died early in June.

Jean Paton will teach at the Hillsdale Day School in Cincinnati next winter.

Mary Olive (Phillips) Bailey has had a breakdown. She spent the winter in Ohio to regain her health.

Portia Pratt has taken a studio in Boston for next winter where she plans to do bookbinding.

Madeleine (Rindge) Hands's mother died suddenly in May.

N. Y. via Canal to California and back overland are Ruth Sawyer's summer plans.

Margaret Spahr has been made assistant professor at Hunter.

Rochester (N. Y.) opened its new $30,000 branch library on June 1 with Marjorie Taylor at its head. It is the only building there which was constructed for library purposes and has the greatest floor space of any in Rochester. Marjorie is also president of the Rochester Smith Club.

Molly Tolman after a two weeks' cruise to Jamaica will attend the Harvard Summer School.

Another 1914 S. C. president is Ruth Tomlinson of the Worcester Club, a very live organization.

Narka Ward will have a sabbatical year next year. She will attend the Ecole de Préparation à l'Etranger at the Sorbonne after a trip with Zoe this summer. Zoe will join her again the following summer when they will bury themselves somewhere and return with a very foreign accent. 11 rue Scribe, Paris, will reach her.

Carolyn (Welles) Ellis plans to open a school for girls and a baby clinic at Islampur, India. Her husband is opening up and developing a work for lepers. "There are a great many lepers about our district and they need treatment. A great number come to us and they bring their friends."

Ex-1914

BORN.—To Clarissa (Hall) Hammond her first child and son, Harold Atwater, May 8.

To Louise (Koons) Barnard her second child and daughter, May 7.

NEW ADDRESSES.—Mrs. Edmund Parr (Ruth Benton), Clinton, Conn. She has three daughters and one son.

OTHER NEWS.—Agnes Dowd is at the Institute of International Education, 2 W. 45 St., N. Y. C., doing secretarial work.

1915

Class secretary—Mrs. Dudley T. Humphrey (Marian Park), Loudonville, N. Y.

ENGAGED.—Mabel Marine to Cyril Backus Clark of Scarsdale, N. Y. Mabel is to be married Aug. 25, her address after Oct. 1 being 32 Walbrooke Rd., Scarsdale.

MARRIED.—Marguerite Kennedy to Denis Gerard Shea, Apr. 25.

Rebecca Painter to John McIntosh. Rebecca has been married some time and has three children. They are living on Third Av., Ford City, Pa.

Eleanor (Sackett) Cowles to Señor de Sureda, in Paris, May 17. Her husband is also an artist. Her new address is Señora

Eleanor de Sureda, La Garrigeta Rasa, Establiments, Majorca, Spain.

BORN.—To Ruth (Edwards) Meyer a third son, John Richard, Sept. 10, 1926.

To Marie (Graff) Carswell a second daughter, Cynthia, May 23.

To Anna (Jones) Mariette a son, Edward Ernest, June 20, 1926.

To Katherine (Nye) Gray a third child and first daughter, Apr. 27. Katherine said to report her anonymously as they had not decided on a name. K. B.'s mother died early in May after a long illness.

To Elsie (Swartwout) Whitney a daughter, Jane Swartwout, Oct. 28, 1926.

DIED.—Mildred Cross Fraser, May 1, after a week's illness. It is hard to realize Mildred's death—she was always such an active, alert person and her going is a great loss to the class. She hadn't been very strong since a nervous breakdown three years ago, but with her characteristic energy and pluck she had thrown herself into her work. Besides teaching in the Needham High School she had been working at Harvard for her Master's degree which she hoped to get this summer. Her character was an inspiration to those who knew her.

NEW ADDRESSES.—Mrs. Alexis A. Mahan (Olive Gauntt), 40 Madison Av., Newtonville, Mass.

Mrs. W. A. Lawrence (Natalie Grimes), 2488 Inagud Av., Coconut Grove, Fla.

Annie Minot, Vanderbilt Medical School, Nashville, Tenn.

Mrs. Neal G. Gray (Katherine Nye), 14406 Drexmore Rd., Cleveland, O.

Mrs. J. Kenneth Attwood (Evelyn Odlin), 3214 Riverside Av., Jacksonville, Fla.

Frances O'Connell, 246 Elm St., West Springfield, Mass.

Mrs. W. P. Hindman (Edith Tierney), 34 Walnut St., Milton, Pa.

OTHER NEWS.—There were eighteen of 1915 in Northampton during some part of Commencement. Marion Graves, Helen Flynn, Marion Fairchild, Frances O'Connell, and Marian (Park) Humphrey were there for the step sing Wednesday evening. Marion (Poole) Kidger came back for Burnham School's Fiftieth Anniversary and K. Boutelle for the Students' Aid meeting. Esther (Eliot) Forbes and Dorothy (Thayer) Greene dashed in for the Alumnae Parade and ten of us had dinner Saturday at New Allen Field Club House before joining the 1776 bat on Paradise, namely Helen (Safford) Reynolds, Jennette (Sargent) Drake, Amy Walker, Jennie McLeod, Florence Hanford, Charlotte Baum, Dorothy Davis, and the first three of the four Marions mentioned previously. Margaret Mensel joined us at the '76 bat and Esther (Mather) Phelps for the Illumination. Juliet couldn't be there for the meeting of the Alumnae Fund Representatives and Dorothy Davis took her place.

Dorothy (Adams) Eschweiler's winter has been given over largely to contagious diseases, majoring in four cases of measles first, and, this spring, scarlet fever. They are now on the ninth week of quarantine after a break of one week to disinfect and houseclean and fool themselves that they were through. D. reports that in spite of this they are really well and flourishing. "Sandy ready for second grade, John and Tom starting into first grade after a year of kindergarten, and 'Rubber' begging to go to school with the 'boyth.'" In the interstices, D. has run the Wisconsin Smith Club, which included a benefit concert for Juniper Lodge, and is interested in the shop for the occupational therapy work of the Junior League.

After a long search to locate Lydia (Avery) Olzendam and finally having found her, it's with a groan that I learn she has gone with her husband and three children to Switzerland for two years. Who knows her address?

Katherine Barnard's mother died recently and K. and her sister have rented their home and are living temporarily at 1776 Vista del Mar, Hollywood.

Agnes (Block) Bradley has taken a cottage at Palisades Park (Mich.) for August with her older sister, so that her two and her sister's four children will have a grand vacation together.

Anne Bridgers is working on another play. "Coquette," which she wrote with George Abbott, is to be produced by Jed Harris, producer of "Broadway," in October with Helen Hayes in the leading part.

Any Smithites will be gladly welcomed by Marian Chase at the "Ship's Cabin Gift Shop" at the Hotel Rockaway, East Gloucester (Mass.), during July.

Jessamy (Fountain) Haley is spending the summer with her parents in Conway, Mass.

Olive (Gauntt) Mahan's husband is assistant to the president of Ivers and Pond Piano Co. of Boston now.

Ever since Else (Goetz) Greene read the article on real household efficiency in a recent QUARTERLY she has felt that her efforts fall so short of that standard that they wouldn't interest anyone. She is gardening strenuously and obtaining excellent results with the help of two octogenarians, one of whom speaks French, the other German, and has amusing misunderstandings as a result.

Natalie (Grimes) Lawrence will probably be in Miami most of the summer while her husband, who is with the Florida Power and Light Co., plans ice plants and other refrigerating means for cooling off their fellow statesmen. Natalie is experimenting with tropical plants and trees, and squeezing her brain for story ideas while keeping the household going. They had a wonderful three weeks' cruise among the Florida Keys last winter in their catboat, the Sun-Hunter, and generally spend their week-ends on shorter cruises.

Hester (Gunning) Lord has been taking a most interesting correspondence course in writing with the Mawson Editorial School in Boston.

Florence Hanford received an M.A. in education at Columbia in Feb. and a diploma as teacher of kindergarten. During Feb. she did intensive work and study in the Nurs-

ery School at Teachers College, then taught in the Nursery School at the Iowa State T. C. for three months. She is to be a director at a camp for Settlement children near Montclair (N. J.) for the summer.

Lella May (Hunter) Clinger says her two lively daughters, aged nine and four, are her biggest job but mentions in passing that she is secretary of the Woman's Club, treasurer of the College Club, secretary of the Missionary Society, teaching a Sunday school class, a director of the Country Club, and chairman of the pre-school clinic of the Parent-Teacher Association.

Ann Minot is enjoying the same old game of research in a new locality. This summer she is driving to N. H. by Ford, hoping to survive to return to Tennessee in the fall.

Catherine (Okey) Geiger's husband left in March on three days' notice for a fascinating business trip to South America. Catherine spent six weeks in the balmy spring of southern Ohio and is now back in N. Y. indefinitely.

Louise (Porter) Dunn is grateful to the pleasant institution of a sabbatical year. With her husband and son, she left in January for a leisurely trip through Italy and France. They are to be in Edinburgh till July, then go on to Germany and other parts until November and home again. For anyone who likes dogs she recommends Edinburgh as the "doggiest" place she has ever seen.

Jennette (Sargent) Drake is to run their small summer camp in Thetford (Vt.) again this year. Families with children wanted.

Helen (Smith) Merriam has moved into a new home at Sylvan Shores with all the comforts—cat, dog, and garden—and is even now eating the melons that they have raised.

Edith (Tierney) Hindman's husband was appointed works manager of the American Car and Foundry Co. at Milton, Pa. They moved from N. Y. C. after William Jr. finished his second year in Lincoln School.

Marguerite (Tweedy) Biggs's family are all fine after measles which the whole family took and a bad scare when Barbara, her eldest child, was struck by an automobile. She is going to Professor Sleeper's camp at Vergennes (Vt.) this summer.

Katharine (Vermilye) Alford and her husband are to be at the White Mt. Camps, Tamworth (N. H.), again this summer. Her aunt, Jane T. Vermilye '97, is to be hostess at the adult camp. K. V. and her husband have been at the Edgewood School at Greenwich (Conn.) all winter, her husband teaching the junior high school group. K. V. took over his classes for a good part of the winter so that he would be free for camp business. She dreaded it as it was her first experience in teaching but soon became fascinated and wouldn't mind making it her life-work instead of editing. She adds, "Of course it was a progressive school which may make a difference."

Ruth (Wager) White's husband, Arthur H. White, died suddenly after an operation for appendicitis.

Edith (Waterman) Ten Eyck attended a Nursery School Conference and also the annual N. Y. Smith Club luncheon in N. Y. in April. She has just returned from a trip by motor to Washington (D. C.) and just missed Colonel Lindbergh there and in N. Y.!

Ex-1915

Born.—To Isabelle (Hoxie) Middleton a fifth child and first daughter, Janet Louise, May 21.

New Addresses.—Mrs. George H. Dwenger (Mary-Louise Alexander), 136 Linwood Av., Ridgewood, N. J.

Mrs. George P. Patteson (Joyce Bradt), 1272 Parkwood Blvd., Schenectady, N. Y.

M. Frances Hildreth, 71 W. 45 St., N. Y. C.

Mrs. Abram Berkowitz (Minnie Kroll), 44 Tarleton Rd., Newton Center, Mass.

Mrs. Henry B. Goodfriend (Jane Stone), 112 Walworth Av., Scarsdale, N. Y. Summer address, P. O., Sagamore Beach, Mass.

Other News.—Mary-Louise (Alexander) Dwenger has found the child psychology books on the directed reading list about the most helpful thing of college, in helping with the problem of an exceedingly active, energetic, and investigating young son.

Leonora (Boswell) Pardee's husband has completed his third year at the College of Physicians and Surgeons of Columbia. Lee is still teaching piano and directing the Music School of the Neighborhood House of the Central Presbyterian Church.

Frances Hildreth's business, the St. John Letter Co., which occupied 180 sq. ft. in 1919, now occupies 5000 sq. ft. All the officers of the company are women. Frances expects to go to the Coast this summer by way of Lake Louise and Banff, down the Pacific Coast, stopping at Grand Canyon and then spending two weeks at "Diamond G" Ranch in Wyoming.

Isabelle (Hoxie) Middleton took a hurried trip to California and Seattle this winter as her mother was desperately ill. She is better now. Isabelle stopped off in Chicago for five hours with Jeannette (Mack) Breed.

1916

Class secretary pro tem—Margaret King, 120 Bigelow Rd., West Newton, Mass.

Born.—To Mildred (Ackerman) Duryea a son, Robert, Dec. 21, 1925.

To Decia (Beebe) Veasey a daughter, Decia Beebe, Mar. 30, 1925.

To Dorothy (Furbish) Sharpa son, Jonathan, Nov. 16, 1926.

To Laura (Lewis) Norris a son, James King Jr., Dec. 18, 1926.

To Dorothy (Parsons) Boland a son, John Parsons, May 21.

To Ruth (Underwood) La Rue a son, John Carver, May 31.

To Cora (Wickham) Frazier a son, David, Nov. 29, 1919.

Died.—John Albert Malone, husband of Dorothy (Goode) Malone, Nov. 13, 1924. Dorothy's mother, Mrs. Goode, has adopted their daughter Kathleen whose name now is Kathleen Goode. Dorothy died in 1920.

New Addresses.—Mrs. Thomas L. (Mary Corbet), 3 Osceola Dr., Greenwich, Conn.

Mrs. Edward T. Willson (Ruth Rodgers), 15 Orchard St., Passaic, N. J.

Mrs. Herbert Watkins (Geneva Clark), Camp Marfa, Tex.

OTHER NEWS.—The following 1916ers were in Hamp at Commencement time and foregathered on Sunset Hill on Saturday night for an "elegant" bat: Dorothy (Eaton) Palmer, Mary McMillan, Priscilla (McClellan) Whelden, Marjorie (Wellman) Freeman, Helen (Strong) Belknap, Dorothy Buhler, Helen Cobb, Mildred Schmolze, Marguerite (White) Stockwell, Marie Gilchrist, Vera Montville, and Dorothy Ainsworth.

Dorothy Ainsworth sailed June 21 for Denmark where she is taking a course in fundamental gymnastics at the Niels Bukh School. She will resume her secretarial duties in the fall.

Helen Cobb is now assistant buyer of women's dresses at L. Bamberger and Co., Newark, N. J.

Augusta Patton received her M.A. from Columbia this June.

Eunice Stebbins has been appointed a fellow to the American School of Classical Studies in Athens, Greece, by Columbia Univ.

1917

Class secretary—Mrs. Theodore Z. Haviland (Esther Lippitt), 261 West End Av., Ridgewood, N. J.

For report of reunion see page 475.

New officers elected at class meeting are: president, Margaret (Alling) Sargent; vice-president, Catharine Weiser; secretary, Esther (Lippitt) Haviland; treasurer, Donna Couch.

ENGAGED.—Donna Couch to Dr. Richard A. Kern of Philadelphia. Dr. Kern was a senior lieutenant in the Medical Corps, U. S. N., during the War, and Donna met him when they both were in service overseas. They are to be married in August.

OTHER NEWS.—At Class Supper we learned that Flissie Smith was married in May and is living in Southern California. This piece of news is accountable for the scarcity of 1917 notes this issue, as Flissie is maintaining an impenetrable silence, even concealing the name of her husband. [The editor has just ferreted out the fact that Flissie is Mrs. D. E. Marquis, 140 S. Los Robles, Pasadena.]

Marion (Dakin) Burroughs's husband has been appointed junior minister of the Third Presbyterian Church in Rochester, N. Y. They expect to go to Rochester in August.

Dorothy (Hamilton) Brush has just lost her husband and her little girl, Jane.

Helen (Jones) Farrar came all the way from Honolulu for reunion—5000 miles!

Marion Sherwood has been awarded a Sterling Fellowship at Yale, 1927–28, for study in bacteriology, pathology, and public health.

Kitty (Wing) Williams has a new baby daughter, name and date unknown.

1918

Class secretary—Margaret Perkins, 3 Banks St., Chicago, Ill.

Replies from the February class letter are still drifting in and the secretary rejoices at each one, but urges that all questionnaires, not

yet returned, be speeded quickly on their way!

ENGAGED.—Thelma Woodsome to Theodore Plimpton Loring of Providence, R. I.

MARRIED.—Doris Devereaux to Norman Kennedy, last summer. They are living at 21 Chamey St., Cambridge, Mass.

Virginia Megeath to Captain Francis John Heraty, May 4. Captain Heraty is in the U. S. Infantry and is stationed at West Point in the department of tactics.

Jessie Thomas to Burnice Lincoln Rutt, in Oct. 1925. Jessie's husband is a Lieutenant in the Navy and has been stationed at Shanghai where Jessie went to join him in 1926. Address, U. S. S. Asheville, Asiatic Station, c/o Postmaster, Seattle, Wash.

Laura Wright to Van Dyke Wetmore of Centerbrook, Conn., in Oct. 1925.

BORN.—To Dorothy (Babcock) King a second son, Jerome Babcock, May 1. Address, Hemlock Rd., Short Hills, N. J.

To Vivian (Bell) Hanford a second child and first son, Edwin Signor, Apr. 7.

To Forence (Enderlin) Bartholomew a son, Lee Enderlin, Nov. 23, 1926.

To Mary (Hottel) Litsinger a second daughter who only lived three days, Apr. 14.

To Virginia (Lindeman) Ferguson a third child and first daughter, Mary Ann, Jan. 10.

To Adeline (Moore) McLinley a daughter, Adeline, Mar. 28.

To Katharine (Selden) McDuffie a third son, Charles Dennett, early in 1927.

To Charlotte (Weir) Jennison a daughter, Mary Gertrude, Apr. 11.

To Sally (Whitman) Henderson a third child and second daughter, Sylvia, Mar. 8.

OTHER NEWS.—Adah Attwood is head of the chart department of the National Industrial Conference Board.

Frances Bates is doing secretarial and readers' service work in the architectural department of the House Beautiful.

Theresa Boden is health supervisor in the New England Tel. and Tel. Co.

Elinor Curwen is with the Continental Cotton Co., N. Y., and is living at the Smith Club.

Clara Curtiss is doing high school library work in Rochester, N. Y.

Mary (Gazzam) Earling is in Fairbanks, Alaska, until October, when she will return to Cohasset, Mass.

Mary (Guerin) Wilson received her M.A. from the Univ. of Arizona last year.

Mary Frances (Hartley) Barnes is having published by Macmillan Co. a book entitled "Feeding the Child from Two to Six." Mary Frances has compiled the material for this book from six of the best authorities on child feeding in the country, and also the findings of the American Child Health Association. Mothers! You'd better take notice!

Chick (Hatch) Richards and Mildred Greene went on a trip to Porto Rico this winter.

Katharine (Howe) Torrey is assistant to the Good Looks and Fashion editors of the Woman's Home Companion. She says her work is mostly corresponding and investigating.

Katherine McGovern is teaching French

in the Julia Richman High School in N. Y. C.
She can be reached at 142 E. 33 St.

Margaret (Matthews) Otte writes that she
has two jobs—her home and children, and a
paid position with the Monroe County Children's Aid Society. She hopes the experiment
works for the sake of the Institute for the
Coördination of Women's Interests.

Esther Nichols writes that she received her
questionnaire when she was in Nice, France,
whence she and her mother had gone in search
of warmth and sunlight after a sojourn in
French Africa. They were returning to the
U. S. A. in April, but hope to go back to
France again in the near future.

Ellen Owen is doing medical social work
at the Blodgett Hospital in Grand Rapids,
Mich.

Elsie (Winneberger) Dietz and her family
expect to go abroad this summer for a stay of
fifteen months.

Dorothy Wolff is now assistant professor
of physiology at the North Carolina College
for Women.

Maude (Wooster) McDonnell writes from
China that a branch of the A. A. U. W. is
about to be started in Tientsin. As there has
never been a college club there she is much interested, and they hope to have from 30–50
members. Maude says she hopes to return
in 1928 for a visit to America, but it all depends upon conditions in China.

NEW ADDRESSES.—Mrs. C. H. Smith
(Dorothy Barnard), 137 Chestnut Av., Eden
Park, Cranston, R. I.

Mrs. A. C. Litsinger (Mary Hottel), 213
Catalina St., Burbank, Calif.

Katharine Johnson, 90 Second Av., Newark,
N. J.

Mrs. J. A. McLinley (Adeline Moore), 540
Laurel St., San Diego, Calif.

Mrs. C. M. Shull (Ruth Smith), 1183 Cook
Av., Lakewood, O.

Mrs. Richard T. McDonnell (Maude
Wooster), 53 Tyne Rd., Tientsin, China.

1919

Class secretary—Julia Florance, 161 Livingston Av., New Brunswick, N. J. Assistant
secretary—Eleanor Fitzpatrick, 141 E. Gorgas
Lane, Germantown, Pa.

DIED.—Helen (Walsh) Schein, Apr. 16, at
the birth of her second daughter, who survived.

MARRIED.—Betty Mangam to George
Warren Curtiss, May 14, in Paris.

ENGAGED.—Lois Allison to Reinhold Hell-
strom of Washington, D. C.

Hester Pratt to George Harry Richardson.

BORN.—To Adele (Adams) Bachman a
second child and first daughter, Susan, June
12.

To Ruth (Harris) Rivers a second child and
first daughter, Marian Bedell, Apr. 20.

To Katharine (Lamont) O'Donoghue a
second son, Derek, Apr. 19.

To Irene (Lord) Lane a son, Franklin, Apr.
29.

To Kathryn (Moyer) Gray a son, Donald
Alfred, Apr. 26.

To Ruth (Perry) Neff a son. For further
details the secretary awaits an official notice.

To Kitty (Wales) Haines a second son,
Samuel Browne, May 17.

OTHER NEWS.—As this is being prepared,
the class is in the midst of its "Informal
Eighth." We are dashing around in true
Hamp style with "that reunion gleam in our
eyes," and with at least a semi-suppressed
desire to be mistaken for seniors. Class supper
was great fun with Connie (McLaughlin)
Green as toastmistress and with thirty-seven
of us gathered around the "festive board."
See alumnae registration pages for names.
On Sunday evening, Connie entertained us at
her very charming home in Holyoke while her
"picture daughter" helped with all the dignity of her five years to serve a delicious
buffet supper. Do save the date for 10th, all
you good '19ers!

Miriam Berry is editing textbooks for Ginn
and Co. She says she "has found her niche
and is very happy as an editor."

Dorothea (Choate) Darrell has recently
visited Margaret (Woodwell) Johnston in
Ann Arbor where Peg and her husband have
"the cutest little English stone cottage in the
country with a Ford to get Peg to her lab, and
her husband to his classes."

Jean Dickinson writes a most interesting
"volume." We regret that we cannot print it
here. Jean is coming home for more training
in social work and if possible to get her Ph.D.
She hopes to come home via Russia, "politics
permitting."

Elsie (Finch) McKeogh is now selling real
estate, "or trying to," and asks for the names
of '19ers who want anything from an apartment to a factory!

Jane Griffin returned on Mar. 23 from almost a year in Europe. She spent some time
at the Sorbonne where she saw the Smith
juniors hard at work. Now she is back at her
old job with the Condé Nast publications.

Ruth (Hathaway) Swayze "spent fourteen
wonderful weeks at Miami Beach" where her
husband managed the brokerage office of the
Harris Winthrop Co. in the Roney Plaza
Hotel.

Mabel Lush is teaching. She writes,
"With a car, a dog, and the alluring state of
California to explore, the summer months
promise much."

Betty (Merz) Butterfield's operetta, "The
Widow of Wiles," was presented in Jamestown
this spring and was most enthusiastically
received.

Cornelia (Patterson) Spencer's husband
has been sent to Tokyo as assistant trade
commissioner under the Department of Commerce. "Pat" writes from Tokyo that she is
trying to learn Japanese, and in the meantime
is ordering the servants around by the sign
language.

Lois (Perley) Phelan and her husband are
planning a "poor-man's trip" to England and
France. Lois has a son, William Balfour,
born Dec. 22, 1925.

Mary (Rouse) Wilson is assistant librarian
in the new Scientific Library at Luxor, Egypt.
She and her husband expect to spend a month
or two at the Univ. of Chicago diggings in

Palestine, and then go to the cool of the Lebanon Mountains in Syria for the summer.

NEW ADDRESSES.—Mrs. J. P. Sedgwick (Isabel Emery), 54 Longfellow Rd., Wellesley Hills, Mass.

Mrs. Percy S. Johnson (Dorothy Marquis), 25 Hanover Rd., Pleasant Ridge, Detroit, Mich.

Dr. Edith Nicholls, 94 Howe St., New Haven, Conn.

Ex-1919

The secretary has just received notice of the death of Jerrine (Ramage) McDonald, May 4, 1924.

BORN.—To Olivia (Carpenter) Coan a daughter, Patricia, Mar. 15.

To Miriam (Lawrence) Tucker a son, Lawrence Stevens, Apr. 23.

To Honor (Marlow) Parry a daughter, Alicia Honor, Mar. 19.

OTHER NEWS.—Florence (Staunton) King writes that she expects to spend the summer on their farm near Pittsburgh after being in the South for most of the winter.

1920

Class secretary—Mrs. Arthur R. Hoch (Marian Hill), 312 N. Euclid Av., Oak Park, Ill. Assistant secretary—Josephine Taylor, 137 S. Scoville Av., Oak Park, Ill.

A REUNION IN 1928. Do You Want an Informal Eighth? Kay (Dickson) King is anxious to get the opinion of the Class in regard to such a reunion. The other classes seem to be trying it and so far though they have averaged smaller in attendance than the formal reunions there has been great fun. Do write Kay or add a note to your fall class response as to your sentiments. Come on, let's have some opinions!

BURTON MEMORIAL FUND.—The last report from our Chairman, Kay (Dickson) King, states that 1920 has so far contributed $813.50 to the Fund. 1920 has almost the lowest total gift of any class that was in college with President Burton. We can and will do better. The work of the committee is over but individuals may send in checks and send up the total! The scholarships that the money will supply will show our love and appreciation for our First Year President.

ENGAGED.—Harriet van Zelm to Ralph Wadsworth of New York City. They expect to be married early in the fall.

MARRIED.—Mary Martha Armstrong to Andrew Bishop McClary, June 15, at Indian Knoll, Osterville, Mass. Address after Sept. 1, Windsor, Vt.

Helen Cass to Ernest Leon Fisher, June 6. They will be at home after Oct. 1, 206 Nassau St., Princeton, N. J.

Agnes Dowd to Osborne E. Brown, May 10, in Minneapolis. Judith Relf '22 was her attendant. Catherine (Stickney) Relf '21 gave them a dinner party. They are to live in a little cottage on the banks of Lake Minnetonka. Address, Wayzata, Minn.

Helen Graves to Radcliffe Dann, Nov. 20, 1926. Address, 115 Norwood Av., Buffalo.

Carol MacBurney to Francis Fernando Storn Jr., June 1.

BORN.—To Viola (Aloe) Marx a second child and first son, Kenneth Aloe, Feb. 28. Address, 4950 Lindell Blvd., St. Louis, Mo.

To Catharine (Ashe) Brotherhood a first son, John Oliver Jr., last fall.

To Helen (Ayers) Maynard a second son, Robert Lowrey, May 19. Helen, Jean (Kimball) Tyler, and Helen (Howes) Barker '19 were all in the hospital at the same time.

To Alice (Beach) Murray a second son, Marshall, May 14. Address, 1702 W. 12 St., Des Moines, Ia.

To Helen (Field) Morse a third child and first daughter, Sylvia, Apr. 23.

To Ruth (Freimuth) Guthmann a third son, Edward James, Feb. 2. Ruth's husband is general manager of the Waller Mfg. Co., and they have just moved. Address, c/o Waller Mfg. Co., Waterloo, Ia.

To Helen (Hardinge) Robinson a first son, Dudley Bell Jr., Mar. 15. They expect to move from Cleveland back to Chicago in June.

To Margaret (Penney) Stewart a fourth child and second son, Thomas Penney, May 24.

To Wilhelmina (Schenck) Frederick a first son, William Schenck, Feb. 4. Address, Pinehurst Apts., 4515 Pine St., Philadelphia, Pa.

To Fannye (Wieder) Blumenthal a first son, Jesse Samuel Jr., June 8.

To Arva (Yeagley) Bergan a third child and second son, John Jerome, Apr. 4.

OTHER NEWS.—Rosalind (Bement) Porter has been studying violin with Frederic Hahn in Philadelphia the last two years and has played as violinist for the last two seasons in the Friday Chamber Music Society of Trenton. She writes, "We rehearse two mornings a week throughout the winter and give four recitals for the public." She also plays in church and has "even broken into radio."

Evelyn Bridger is doing amateur theatricals in New Rochelle. She was in the American Legion Follies given there in April. She is still society correspondent for the N. Y. Herald-Tribune for one half of Westchester County.

Mary Frances (Cathcart) Stevens was the Junior League delegate for Charleston for their convention in Boston.

Mary Louise (Chandler) Eagleton writes that they expect to be in Chicago again in the fall as her husband is to teach in the Law Department of the Univ. of Chicago.

Elizabeth Day has just returned from a trip to Europe.

The following report was received about Ruth (Dowell) Svihla. "In Dec. 1925, Ruth and her husband were living in the marshes of Louisiana. Their business was to pry into the private and public lives of muskrats and other fur-bearing animals, evidently to decide why furs are so expensive."

Rose (Foreman) Tishman is to move in the fall eight blocks from her present home to 888 Park Av., N. Y. C.

Gertrude Fuller is at present taking a secretarial course in Hartford.

Katherine (Graham) Howard's husband is Budget Commissioner of Massachusetts and chairman of the Massachusetts Commission of Administration and Finance.

Grace Hiller is just completing her third year at Rush Medical School. She took her pre-medic work at Tufts in 1923–24.

Constance Jones sends a new address, 1941 N. Delaware St., Indianapolis, Ind.

Ruth (Kirkpatrick) Evans writes that they have bought a new home. Address, Bates Av., R. 5, Olympia, Wash.

Rosalie (Morris) Voorhis's husband is Secretary of New York Univ.

Isabel (Painter) Wilson's husband is inspector of steel for "The Port of New York Authority." Address for a year, 7622 Waverly St., Pittsburgh, Pa.

Thelma Parkinson ('21), according to a clipping, has just been elected to the presidency of the Cumberland County Tax Board, of which she has been a member for one term previous. She is the first woman ever to be elected head of a tax board in New Jersey.

Harriet (Pratt) Lattin writes: "Moving. No permanent address till Sept." She has been a University Scholar this year and will be a University Fellow next year. Both Harriet and her husband played in a faculty recital at Ohio State in May.

Esther (Purrington) Jorgensen has a new address, 39 Flatt Av., Hamilton, Ont. Her husband is general manager of the Fuller Brush Co. Ltd.

Mildred Roe writes from Japan where she is doing Y. W. work: "Having a great time. Crazy about my work, the country (it's too beautiful for words in the springtime), and the people! Have been bicycling on several trips, skiing on 18 ft. of snow, and doing all sorts of interesting things in the same winter."

Sadie Saffian is still working as a statistician. She had an article on "Mentally Retarded Children" published in the *Jewish Social Service Quarterly* for March.

Violet Storey writes that D. Appleton and Co. are to issue a volume of her poems in the fall. She adds: "I believe this is the 'Class Book of 1920,' that is to say, the first book to be published by a member of the class. Since I have acquired no engagement or wedding ring to help swell the list of 1920's fiancées and wives, I can only offer this book as a token of my esteem for the best class ever! I hope it will be read and liked by all 1920s. My career has been rather checkered of late. After my father's death I had to go to N. Y. and act as vice-president of W. A. Brown and Co. It is a customs brokerage firm and, knowing nothing of the business, I had a great time. My father did all the Chinese importing in N. Y. and although I have known a great many Chinese socially, I found it difficult to do business with them. At night I worked on my book. I hope this week to go to 'Storeyland' in Mystic (Conn.)."

Virginia (Wiley) Price sends in the accurate news about her children: Andrew III, born Feb. 8, 1923; Barbara, Apr. 19, 1924; and Virginia, Oct. 5, 1925. Her husband is with the John E. Price Co., a bond house, and he is also president of the Marine National Bank.

Lois (Whitney) Perry sailed for Italy Apr. 14 to meet her mother.

Iris Williams's address is 118 N. Main St., Providence, R. I.

Ex-1920

MARRIED.—Jeannette Bruce to Marrs R. Gibbons, July 19, 1919. They have two daughters, Jean Jeffie, born Dec. 19, 1920, and Marjorie Bruce, Aug. 25, 1922. Jeannette's husband is a railroad contractor. She went to the College for Women, Western Reserve Univ., 1917–18 and Jan. to June 1919, and to Ohio State Univ., Sept. to Jan. 1918. Address, 3330 Maynard Rd., Cleveland, O. This is Jeannette's first letter.

Helen Lynch to William Rae Law, Oct. 16, 1926. Helen received her B.S. from Simmons in 1920. She is an advertising writer for R. H. Macy and Co., N. Y. C., and her husband is an interior decorator. Address, Fifth Av. Hotel, 24 Fifth Av., N. Y. C. Helen does not wish to be called a member of 1920.

Margaret Sparks to Jacob Hubert Roesgen, June 29.

Ethel Tye to a Mr. Gilchrist. Address, 5409 Blackstone Av., Chicago.

BORN.—To Dorothy (Funk) Guthrie a first child, Donald Bruce, May 20.

To Jean (Kimball) Tyler a second daughter, May 11. The baby had not been named when the news reached the secretary.

To Helen (McCann) Kinsman a fourth child and third daughter, Mary Ford, Nov. 12, 1926. Her husband is an engineer.

To Dorothy (Moore) Congdon a first daughter, Jean, Apr. 7, 1926. Dorothy's husband is an attorney. Her travels have included Europe in 1922, Alaska in 1922, and Bermuda in 1924. Permanent address, 807 Lonsdale Bldg., Duluth, Minn. Temporary address, 2130 Penn Av. S., Minneapolis. This is Dorothy's first letter.

To Jessica (Potter) Broderick a second child, Feb. 22, 1926. She gives no name for "it."

To Barbara (Seelye) Bottome a second child and first son, George Hill, Jan. 25, 1926. This is Barbara's first letter. Her husband is treasurer of the Good Luck Food Co.

OTHER NEWS.—Myrtle Bice writes that she has given several lectures on her tour to Europe.

Flora Eaton answers her first class letter but gives no especial news of herself. She was only at college three months. Address, 89 Prospect St., East Orange, N. J.

Margaret Fisk is gymnastic director for girls in the Glen Ridge (N. J.) High School.

Mary (Forker) Goodall answers her first letter. Her husband is with the National Marking Machine Co. Address, 3553 Holly Lane, Cincinnati, O.

Mildreth Gast is still teaching piano and organ. She gives recitals annually in Northampton.

Maxine Hilson says that she traveled in Europe in the summer of 1926 with Kathryn (Liebmann) Brannion. She wishes to be dropped from the class. Address, 114 E. 52 St., N. Y. C.

Elyzabeth (Huttig) Schell writes: "House-

keeper and bookkeeper for my husband's business. My husband is a breeder of thoroughbred Holsteins and Friesians. My travels include Hawaiian Islands, China, Japan, Korea, Philippine Islands, and throughout the Western and Middle Western States since the war." Address, Route 1, Liberty, Mo.

Helen (Job) Draper's husband is in the lumber business.

Allen (Johnson) Renick sends lots of news. Her husband is a lecturer and she writes that they have lived at least six weeks in each of the following places in the last three years—Cleveland, Toledo, Indianapolis, Cincinnati, St. Louis, Dallas, St. Paul, Minneapolis, Detroit, Kansas City, and Chicago. She spent July to Dec. 1923 in France and England and the work that she did in epidemiology was exhibited at the Strasbourg Centennial Exhibition in 1923. She attended Columbia for a while. Address, 39 Fifth Av., N. Y. C.

Elizabeth (King) Jones writes that her husband is a Captain of Field Artillery, U. S. A., and at present is detailed as coach of the West Point football team.

Sarah (Lownes) Conover is now assistant principal in a small private school.

Muriel (MacKenzie) Jager has a new address, 268 Prospect St., Northampton, Mass. She writes that they have traveled through the U. S. quite extensively from Maine to Florida and from Boston to San Francisco and in Canada they have "done" all the Eastern Provinces. For the last seven years they have motored 8–10,000 miles a year and last year were gone 4 months and did 14,000 miles. Muriel plays accompaniments in Hamp and the vicinity and is also teaching piano.

Marjorie (Marvin) Hartford is to be in Washington (D. C.) with her small daughter indefinitely. Her husband is an engineer in the International Paper Co.

Dorothy Moseley is secretary for the Union League Club in Chicago.

Frances (Newhall) Wright's son's name is Benjamin Mead. Address, 18 Wildwood Rd., Larchmont, N. Y.

Gladys (Nyman) Markward received her B.A. from the Univ. of Chicago in 1920.

Mary Orbison is continuing her work of school nurse. She went to Columbia in 1922–23.

Elizabeth (Pontius) Bloomstrom's address is 2674 Tuxedo Av., Detroit, Mich. Her husband is district manager for the Proctor and Gamble Co.

Thea (Schaefer) Dutcher's husband is a mechanical engineer.

Mildred Simpson is still doing her Wilmington Republican City Committee work, was executive secretary for two Delaware national committeemen in the 1924 campaign, is still doing her American Peace Foundation work, and was also secretary of the Philadelphia City Committee for the Pinchot Primary Campaign in 1926.

Ruth (Taylor) Anthony is studying this year at Teachers College in N. Y. and hopes to receive a degree next year. She expects to

motor south with her husband this summer.

1921

Class secretary—Mrs. E. Graham Bates (Dorothy Sawyer), 8 Maple St., Auburndale, Mass.

SECRETARY'S NOTE.—A few 1921 statistics may be of interest. There are 430 living graduates; deceased 6; engaged 3; married 213 or 49.5%; children 160, of whom 81 are girls and 79 boys; 15 are combining running a home with such professions as secretarial, teaching, music, or social work; 102 report having traveled outside the U. S. since 1921. The degrees are: M.A. 16; M.D. 1; B.Ed. 1; Ph.D. 3; M.Sc. 1. Since 1921 no news has been heard from 26 of our members, an unusually large number. At the present time Dorothy Bartlett, Clarinda Buck, and Dorothy (Butts) Gardner are lost to the class. Who can help locate them?

MARRIED.—Pearl Anderson to Harold S. McConnell, Aug. 1926. Pearl received her M.Sc. in entomology last June. She has continued her work this year as assistant professor of biology at the Univ. of Maryland. She has been discovering that a woman can keep house and have a career, "but she can't expect to do much else!"

Dorothy Knapp to Lawrence N. Thomas, June 4, in Greenwich, Conn. They will live in Wilmington, Del.

Marjorie Moulton to Donald Benner Hopkins, May 14. Grace Carver and Marion Bayer were bridesmaids and Barbara Winchester the maid of honor. They spent their honeymoon in Bermuda. Address, 70 Park Av., Bloomfield, N. J.

Ethel Phillips ('22) to Lindsley Hallock Noble, June 25. New address, 242 Billings Av., Paulsboro, N. J.

Nelle Rea to Frank Jeremiah Williams, Apr. 27. Address, 4122 Warwick Blvd., Kansas City, Mo.

Roberta Saunders to Curtis Franklin. Roberta's mother was her matron of honor and only attendant. Mr. Franklin is with the New York Trust Co. They are living in East Orange, N. J.

Marion Frances Smith to Joseph Wendell Putnam, Mar. 30. Address, 802 Campbell Av., Schenectady, N. Y.

Frances Treadway to James Lee Wallace, May 21.

BORN.—To Alice (Jaretzki) Cooper a daughter, Elizabeth Edna, May 8. Alice's summer address is Eastmeadow Rd., Westport, Conn.

OTHER NEWS.—Edith Betts is living at the Smith Club and working for Harper and Bros. on *Harper's Magazine*, running the "Where-to-Shop" section.

Mary Buchanan spent all last summer and fall abroad, living with her sister and brother-in-law in London.

Anne Coburn has been serving actively and helpfully on the Alumnae Fund Committee.

Berg Hooper sailed Apr. 16 for another visit to Sweden. She says she will be back in the fall.

Edith (McEwen) Dorian modestly writes in

a postscript to a fine newsy letter: "Think I forgot to mention last time that Columbia condescended to drop an M.A. in my lap last summer. The rest comes slowly—the rest meaning Ph.D.!"

Helen Pittman received her M.D. from Johns Hopkins in June.

We learn that Florence Richardson has done a little of everything since we left Hamp, but the most interesting things are in connection with newspapers and inns. She did all the advertising, shopping guide, etc., for Hearst in Atlanta for a year and then went back to Augusta (Ga.), where she helps run an exclusive winter tourist inn and does reporting (society chiefly) and interviewing for an Augusta paper. She has met and interviewed and golfed with everyone from Tilden to Belasco.

Outside of class secretarial duties and housework, Dorothy (Sawyer) Bates has been filling her time with dramatics and working with a church group of young people. This spring she played in "The Show-Off" and coached two smaller productions. She enjoyed the privilege of representing the class at Alumnae Council in February and June.

Barbara (White) Baker is living at 22 Pinckney St., Boston.

Blanche (Wiener) Diamond writes, "Living happily and raising a son who is now three years old and in good training to make a 'Y' at Yale." Address, 6451 Monitor St., Squirrel Hill, Pittsburgh, Pa.

1922

Class secretaries—A–K, Mrs. Francis T. P. Plimpton (Pauline Ames), 1165 Fifth Av., N. Y. C. L–Z, Mrs. Wallace W. Anderson (Constance Boyer), North Brookfield, Mass.

For report of reunion see page 476.

ENGAGED.—Julie Lincoln to Richard S. Hill, Cornell '24, a brother of Edith Hill '03 and Marian (Hill) Hoch '20.

MARRIED.—Margaret Humphrey to Richard Philip Windisch, May 28. Address, 52 Gramercy Park N., N. Y. C.

BORN.—To Louise (Townsend) Bethell a son, Richard Townsend, Mar. 16.

OTHER NEWS.—Helen Anthony received her M.A. in geology at Smith in June.

Miss Benedict, 1922's guardian angel, sails on July 23 for a trip around the world. She will return in February.

Laura Cabot is now staff assistant to the service superintendent at Filene's in Boston.

Eleanor Chilton was unable to autograph the copies of "Shadows Waiting" brought to Northampton by reuning classmates as she sailed for Europe just before Commencement.

Faith (Dudgeon) Taylor is moving to Merion, Pa.

Ruth (Ferguson) Vanderburgh spent last summer with her husband's family in Kuling. Their baby arrived there for they were delayed by the fighting around Hankow. After an exciting journey with baby, dog, boxes, etc., they are now in their first home in Hunan, China, where Dr. Vanderburgh is to do medical work in the Changteh Presbyterian Hospital.

"Kittle" Fisher met Caroline Schofield in Honolulu.

Sophie (Henker) Calhoun sends word of the death of her husband on Feb. 20. He was taken critically ill while on their honeymoon in Europe.

Marion Himmelsbach will spend the summer in Europe.

Mildred Lovejoy is very busy with Girl Scout work.

Mildred Mason plans to continue at the Strong Memorial Hospital in Rochester.

"Kippy" Murray will teach next year, continuing her work at the Donald MacKay Junior High School in Boston.

Wilhelmine Rehm ('23) has been continuing her work in applied arts at the Univ. of Cincinnati, and has the job of student assistant in the pottery department. In her course in pottery, she has made a sixteen-inch "Persian" vase.

Marguerite Rihbany ('23) sailed in May for Europe, to return in September.

Ruth Robeson will continue as assistant in the Rochester Public Library.

Caroline Schofield has just returned from a trip around the world. This is becoming nearly an annual affair with her.

Kay (Winchester) Wakeman has succeeded in raising a fund of $525, to be known as the Margaret Franks Gordon Memorial Fund, which was presented at the Alumnae Assembly to be used for experimentation in stage design under the direction of the Department of Art.

Marian Watkins is teaching English at the high school in Methuen.

NEW ADDRESS.—Mrs. John C. Esty (Virginia Place), rue Soloyns 43, Antwerp, Belgium.

Ex-1922

BORN.—To Adelaide (Armstrong) Sluiter a daughter, Eleanor Williams, Apr. 19.

1923

Class secretary—Mrs. Roswell C. Josephs (Frances Sheffield). Address after Sept. 1, Avon, Old Farms, Avon, Conn.

ENGAGED.—Mary Elizabeth Dunbar to John A. Kiggen Jr., a graduate of Harvard and Harvard School of Business Administration.

Edith Leach to Thornton Lorimer, a graduate of Amherst and Harvard Law School.

MARRIED.—Adeline Boyden to Clyde A. Horn, Apr. 23.

Isabelle McLaughlin to Rockwell Rittenhouse Stephens, May 12. Sydney (Cook) Brucker, Constance (McLaughlin) Green '19, and Esther (McLaughlin) Donahue ex-'21 were attendants. Their summer address will be 5609 Woodlawn Av., Chicago.

BORN.—To Louisa (Aldrich) Wilkins a second son, David Aldrich, May 27.

To Barbara (Barnes) Blodget a son, Donald McKelvey Jr., May 15.

To Barbara (Boyer) Chadwick a son, Thomas Lothrop, Feb. 14.

To Virginia (Browne) Slawson a son, Donald Gray Jr., May 5.

To Alice (Gould) Edman a son, Frank Talmage, June 14.

To Mildred (Miron) Schoenfeld a daughter, Janet, Mar. 20.

To Patience (Winchester) Sherman a son, Thomas Foster Jr., Mar. 29. Permanent address, American Consulate, Berlin, Germany.

OTHER NEWS.—A picture of Priscilla Capps in ancient Greek costume appeared in the *N. Y. Herald-Tribune* for Sunday, May 7.

Sara Cartmell won second prize in a contest conducted by *Scribners'* for the best list of 200 books written by American authors and published in America.

Phebe Ferris took her M.A. in geology at Smith in June.

Margaret Gantt received her M.D. from Cornell Medical this June.

Lois Rundlett has been teaching school for two years at the Shady Hill School, a private day school in Cambridge, open air and "progressive." Next year she will teach English and history in the 5th and 8th grades. From June to Sept. she will be traveling "every way from Shank's mare to char-a-banc in England and France."

Louise Russell took her M.A. in art at Smith in June.

Frances (Sheffield) Josephs's husband will teach math. and science next year in a new boys' boarding school at Avon (Conn.), twelve miles west of Hartford.

Ex-1923

MARRIED.—Ruth Burt to Lieut. Robert Tappam Chaplin U. S. A., May 24, in Honolulu.

1924

Class secretary—Marion Hendrickson, 548 Orange St., New Haven, Conn. -

For report of reunion see page 477.

New officers elected at class meeting are: president, Margaret Davenport; vice-president, Helen (Ferguson) Russell; secretary, Marion Hendrickson; treasurer, Elizabeth Mackintosh.

ENGAGED.—Muriel Crosby to Henry Lee Willet, Princeton '22.

Helen Crystal to Michael T. Gottlieb, a graduate of Columbia Law School.

Jane Griswold to John Sidney Judge of New York City. They expect to be married in September. Jane, having made a start in psychiatric social work as a visiting teacher for the Department of Child Guidance of the Newark public schools, expects to resume her position in October and see what can be done about coördinating women's interests.

Evelyn Hardy to Henry John Le Sbirel Kitchen, Esq., of "Jessops," Horley, Surrey. Evelyn is still in government service at the American Consulate General, London. She has poems appearing in "Home Book of Modern Verse," "The Art of Interpretation," and others. She has a novel appearing next winter.

Elizabeth McHarg to Edwin T. Holland of Norfolk, Va., Univ. of Virginia '26.

Paula Miller to Talbot Patrick, Yale '18, son of Dr. Hugh T. Patrick of Chicago.

Hartwell Wyse to A. J. Priest of Boise, Idaho, and New York City. He is Polly Priest's brother.

MARRIED.—Katherine Carpenter to William Stanley Patten of Philadelphia, Dartmouth '24, June 25.

Elizabeth Hawkes to Charles Willard Miller, June 20. New address, Bristol, Pa.

Margaret Litle to Colin Campbell, Apr. 24, 1926. They are living at 8758 Goethe Av., Detroit, Mich.

Barbara Nolen to David Fales Strong, June 14, in Vienna, Austria.

Mary MacBain to Edwin R. Match Jr., June 4.

Natalie Rogers to Thomas Dudley Green of New York, May 14.

BORN.—To Frances (Bragg) Eames a son, George Clifton II, Apr. 14.

To Elizabeth (Campbell) Greathead a son, Daniel McKenzie Campbell, June 16, 1926. He's a red-headed Scotchman, his mother writes.

To Marion (Clark) Atwood a second daughter, Natalie, June 2.

To Mary (Lightfoot) Milbank a daughter, Daphne, Apr. 12.

To Bernice (Millar) Church a daughter, Sally, Mar. 29.

To Selena (Reeder) Houston a daughter, Cynthia Jane, May 1.

To Hyacinth (Sutphen) Bowers a son, Fredson Thayer Jr., Apr. 7.

To Josephine (Wittmer) Hunter a daughter, Barbara Josephine.

OTHER NEWS.—Louise Barker became mental tester for the Women's Protective Assn. in Cleveland in January. Address, 320 Electric Bldg.

Esther Beckwith is director of educational research in the public schools of New Britain, Conn.

Ruth Bookheim has been teaching sixth grade in Albany.

Ruth Bugbee ('25) is teaching English in the Agawam (Mass.) High School.

Catherine Carlson has a secretarial position on *The Technology Review*.

Lois Cole is working in the college textbook department of Harcourt, Brace and Co., New York.

Dorothy (Crane) Vaughn wants anyone going to Spain to look her up at Apartado 753, Madrid.

Anna de Lancey is secretary to the assistant to the directors of the Fogg Art Museum at Harvard. Boston address, 28 Fayette St.

Helen Dexter is to teach in New Haven next winter at Mrs. Day's School. Her address will be 59 College St.

Rose Fitzgerald has been awarded a Yale Scholarship, 1927–28, for study in economics, sociology, and government.

Elizabeth Fogle has been taking a secretarial course at home in Canton, O.

Mary Foster is secretary to a statistician in Curtis and Sanger, a bond house in Boston.

Ruth Freer is still with the Curtis Publishing Co., Cleveland.

Ellen Gammack's father, Rev. Dr. Arthur J. Gammack, died Apr. 29.

Elizabeth Hall has had a varied winter, doing Americanization work, substituting in

the high school in New Haven, and doing secretarial work at the Yale Department of Health.

Dorothy Harris has been doing graduate work in French at Smith and working in the Smith Library.

Pauline Hayden has been teaching history and civics in the Westfield (Mass.) High School.

Peggy Hazen is the editor of the shopper's column of *Scribner's*.

Mildred Johnson received her M.A. from Cornell this year. She is a member of Pi Lambda Theta and Kappa Alpha Theta.

Marion (Knickerbocker) Palmer spent June and July in California visiting her family and showing the Pacific Coast to her husband.

Sylvia Leach has just been elected president of the Manchester (N. H.) College Woman's Club and secretary of the state Smith Club.

Marcia Lowd finished her two and a half years' training at St. Luke's Hospital in April.

Grace Lowe played the rôle of the queen in the Theatre Intime's (the Princeton undergraduate dramatic organization) production of "Hamlet." The play was given in its full form and extended over three hours with only three short intermissions.

Eleanor Mead graduated from the social service training course at the Univ. of California in 1926. After doing family case work for six months, she is now organizing a community center in Santa Rosa, Calif. Her address is Apt. 5, 733 Fourth St., Santa Rosa.

Emily Newman received her M.A. in art from Smith this June.

Elizabeth Noble is taking nurse's training at the Presbyterian Hospital, N. Y.

Anna (Otis) Duell is hiking and bicycling in England this summer. Her husband is teaching at Bryn Mawr next winter.

Ruth Present, after spending some time on the news staff of the *Rochester Times-Union*, has been made vicinity editor.

Ruth Raisler has been in New York this winter, having spent the two previous summers abroad.

Mary and Ruth Richardson are in Europe again. Mary is planning to take the Shakespeare course at Oxford.

Marian Ropes has been awarded a Trustee Fellowship by Smith for the study of medicine at Johns Hopkins.

Gertrude Ross keeps her position with the Teela-Wooket Camps.

Marguerite Schauweker has been traveling around the world for the past two and a half years. She and Olivia Bridges, who returned from a round-the-world trip last fall, spent several weeks together in China and again in Italy. Address, c/o American Express, Paris.

Janet Smith has completed her second year of teaching at Simmons College, Boston.

Marguerite Sowers had a four months' leave of absence from her job this spring to travel abroad.

Celia Spalter is teaching French and Latin in the Hartford (Conn.) High School and French, Spanish, and English in night school.

Evelyn (Thomas) McIlwain reminds touring classmates that her home in Hanover (Pa.) is only five miles off the Lincoln Highway.

Emily Wilson has decided to end her career as a teacher. She plans to enter Johns Hopkins Medical School in September.

Ex-1924

MARRIED.—Dorothy Casey to Don P. Moak. Her address is 90 Partridge St., Albany, N. Y. They have two children, Gertrude Virginia and Dorothy Prentice.

Sylvia Clark to Brayton Fuller Wilson, Harvard B.A. '20, M.A. '22, Nov. 13, 1925. They have a son, George Grafton II, Aug. 5, 1926. Address, 80 Spring St., Albany, N. Y. After Sylvia left Smith she went to Oxford and got her B.A. in the Honour School of English Literature and Language in 1925.

Grace Cutler to Beverly Smith. Address, 254 S. Whitney St., Hartford, Conn.

Pleasantine Doan to C. C. Thomas. Address, Highland Hospital, S. Av., Bellevue Dr., Rochester, N. Y.

Marion Giles to Burton Parker. Address, Rutherford Blvd., Passaic, N. J.

Evelyn Lucas to William Overton Jr. Address, 4517 Livingston, Highland Park, Dallas, Tex.

Eleanor Lyon to Sherman Baldwin, Dartmouth '23. They live at 34 Chiswick Rd., Brookline, Mass. Eleanor still has a studio at 44 Fayette St., Boston, and is attempting to do designing along with housework and golf.

Anna Paine to De Wolfe Barton, last Sept. Address, Witherbee Court, Pelham Manor, N. Y.

BORN.—To Olga (Merck) Wheeler a second child and first daughter, Polly, Mar. 4.

To Mary Allen (Northington) Bradley a son, in June 1926. The address of their new house which she and her husband built is 2844 Carlisle Rd., Birmingham, Ala.

To Augusta (Wales) Thomas a daughter, Mary Gwen.

To Pruella (Wallace) Foulke a second son, Frank Wallace. Pruella hoped to be able to register her baby for Smith '44, but is afraid the nearest he'll get will be for week-ends. Her address is 81 S. Carll Av., Babylon, N. Y.

To Olive (Webb) Winchester a son, Robert, Mar. 21, 1926. Her latest address is 29 Lexington Av., Waterbury, Conn.

NEW ADDRESSES.—Mrs. Robert H. Gries (Lucile Dauby), 11212 Euclid Av., Cleveland, O.

Mrs. James L. Brownlee Jr. (Kathleen Devlin), 160-15 Northern Blvd., Flushing, N. Y.

Mrs. Harris Frozier (Anita Haven), 2323½ Commonwealth Av., Chicago.

Mrs. Sydney M. Rosenthal (Dorothy May), 1225 Park Av., N. Y. C.

Estelle Rosenbloom, St. Regis Hotel, N.Y.C.

Mrs. Harry R. Fisher (Frances Schwartz), 1105 Jerome Av., N. Y. C.

Alice Siesel, Hotel Cambridge, N. Y. C.

Mrs. Whitney U. Seymour (Lola Vickers), 170 Sullivan St., N. Y. C.

OTHER NEWS.—Elisabeth (Blanchard)

Faber's daughter, Betty Lee, died Apr. 18.

Helen Garlinghouse's first letter since she left college deserves quoting: "In '24 I graduated, Phi Beta Kappa, from Syracuse Univ. Last year I spent reading English at Oxford and in London. Then a glorious spring in the south of France, Sicily, and Italy, and back to spend July at Toynbee Hall where the Sherwood Eddy group was studying strike conditions in London—and where I found 'thirt' material in midnight prowls around Wapping wharf and the Isle of Dogs, talking with river men and bobbies, or disguised with a torn dress and dirty face I became part of the scenery of East London pubs at closing time. All of which makes graduate work at Radcliffe this year all the more interesting."

Ruth Hamblett is at 129 Beacon St., Boston, as chaperon and dietitian at Miss McClintock's School.

Dorothy Hammett worked until the fall of 1925 and then started in college all over again, struggling with fifth year Latin and fourth year French. She is now in her sophomore year at St. Lawrence Univ., is a member of Kappa Kappa Gamma Fraternity, and is taking the combined College-Theological course (twenty or more hours of work). Her home address is 67 West St., Portland, Me.

Dorothea Hile received her degree at Teachers College, and has since been teaching physical education and dancing at Goucher. June 2 she sailed for Europe, where she is to spend three months, one of them in Vienna studying dancing.

Virginia Hill is teaching gym at Laurel School, 1928 E. 90 St., Cleveland, O.

Alice Holmes has had a very interesting job in a private library, which she is now giving up to be married to Shepard Dudley of Belmont, Mass.

Virginia Kingsbury worked as a reporter on a Syracuse paper until last year, when she went into a toy shop run by Eleanor Grant '25. She has now given that up, as well as the presidency of the Syracuse Smith Club, to gather a trousseau. She is to be married June 18 to John Thomas Gillespie Jr. of Morristown and New York.

Mavis (Kydd) Fenner moved last Sept. to an apartment at 430 E. 57 St., N. Y. C., which she describes as fairly sitting in the East River. She has been doing some publicity work, and acts as secretary for her husband. He is an architect with McKim, Mead, and White, and she writes out the specifications for his work.

Ex-'24 can now boast that over half its members are married, and there is a baby for every two married girls. Eight have two children apiece.

1925

Class secretary—Frances S. French, 165 E. 33 St., New York City.

BORN.—To Edna (Laurin) Hughes a son, Charles Ebbert, Apr. 25.

To Carol (Lyle) Fowler a daughter, Barbara Ellen, Mar. 26.

ENGAGED.—Clara Smith to John H. Field Jr.

Constance Walter to George Shelton Hubbell, a member of the faculty of the Univ. of California.

MARRIED.—Alice Garlichs to Herbert Whitton Sumsion, June 2, in Philadelphia.

Katherine Whitney to Dr. J. Malcolm Stratton, Apr. 20. Dr. Stratton graduated from the Univ. of California in '24, and from Harvard Medical School in '27. They will live at 55 Canyon Rd., Berkeley, Calif.

NEW ADDRESSES.—Alice (Bennett) Pynchon and her husband, George N. Pynchon Jr., are living at "Rocklea," Greenwich, Conn.

Mary (Joslin) Thorpe's new address is 40 S. Munn Av., East Orange, N. J. Her husband has recently been transferred to the New York branch of the Amer. Tel. and Tel.

Lucy Williams and her family have just moved into a new house at 116 Coolidge Hill, Cambridge, Mass. Lucy is studying landscape architecture and has a position with a landscape architect in New Jersey this summer.

OTHER NEWS.—Katharine Atwater received her M.A. in art from Smith in June.

Margaret Burnham has just returned from a trip abroad which began last September.

Kathleen (Grant) Van Wyck is still in Europe and can be reached c/o Brown, Shipley, 123 Pall Mall, London.

Caroline Jenkins has secured a B.S. from the Columbia School of Library Service, and has a temporary job at the Seward Park Branch of the Public Library. She wants to be in New York next year.

Josephine Setze received her M.A. in art from Smith in June.

1926

Class secretary—Gertrude E. Benedict, 8 Cabrillo Dr., Stanford Univ., Calif.

For report of reunion see page 478.

ENGAGED.—Elizabeth Bridges to Murvin A. French, Northeastern Univ. '25.

Marian Clow to Leslie S. Wilcoxson.

Eleanor Greco to John Carrere of New York.

Helen Houston to F. R. McDermand Jr.

Mary-Jane Judson to Kingsley L. Rice, Northwestern Univ. '20. They plan to be married next spring and live in Evanston, Ill. Mr. Rice is a brother of Elizabeth Rice '26.

Katherine Keeler to John E. Booth, Amherst '23.

Helen McNair to C. Howard Hook Jr.

Mary-Scott Ryder to William Mason.

MARRIED.—Frances Forbes to William Robert Taaffe, Apr. 2.

Kathleen Heile to Jean Reginald Stebbins, May 2. Address, 151 Mullin St., Watertown, N. Y.

Mildred Leak to Harold Schiffman, Apr. 21. Address, 310 S. Spring St., Greensboro, N. C.

Alma Murray to Hamilton Fish Potter, May 10. Mr. Potter was Harvard '24.

Dorothy Recht to Roy Plaut, May 26. They went to Europe for their honeymoon.

Dorothy Rinaldy to Theodor Carl Muller, Apr. 9. New address, 571 Horatio St., N. Y. C.

Esther Smith to Martin J. Lawrence, June 4, in the Naval Academy Chapel at Annapolis. Halo Chadwick was maid of honor. Address

after Sept. 1, c/o *U. S. S. West Virginia*, San Pedro, Calif.

Elizabeth Sweeney to Lieut. Richard B. Gayle, Apr. 2. Elizabeth White, Eleanor Golden, and Hope Palmer were among the bridesmaids. Address, Fort Washington, Md.

Alberta Thompson to Wyndham Kenneth Eaton, Mar. 19. Mr. Eaton graduated from the Univ. of Pennsylvania in '22· Their address is 62 E. Johnson St., Germantown, Pa.

Katharine Wiggin to Howard Hughes, May 28. They will live in Malden, Mass.

OTHER NEWS.—Ruth Abbott has a new address: 25 E. 86 St., N. Y. C.

Betty Alden is abroad for four months with her mother and two sisters. During the past winter she has been doing private library work for Miss Blodgett on Beacon Hill, studying rare editions and "caring for fine leather work with a secret lubricant that looks like axle grease but which works out wonderfully."

Eloise Anderson expects to attend the Lowthorpe School of Landscape Architecture for Women at Groton this summer.

Carolyn Case has been doing work as a member of the Junior League of Chicago.

Harriett Child has been working as a secretary for the Savings Bank Division of the American Bankers Assn. in N. Y. C.

Constance Chilton has been awarded a scholarship from the Students' International Union, enabling her to study international questions at the summer schools in Geneva and to take part in the activities of the Union.

Julia Church is taking a postgraduate course at Madison (Wis.) in landscape gardening and art. She has joined the Alpha Phi sorority.

Frances Cowles has gone to Europe for three months and expects to spend much time in Spain.

Anna Clark left in May for an eleven weeks' trip in France and Switzerland.

Eleanor Clark is studying piano and musical composition.

Mary Clark has been occupied as a laboratory worker, "being nursemaid to guinea pigs and white mice."

Janet (Eaton) Macomber is busy building a new house which she expects to occupy in October.

Alice Dolan will attend summer school at Cornell.

Edith Foshee left June 18 for four months' travel abroad.

Laurie Foster has been ill with mastoid trouble and has been forced to give up her work with *The Breath of the Avenue*. She is now convalescing at home.

Susie Friedlander is expected home from abroad by the middle of July.

Adele Goldmark has been "visitor" with the Charity Organization Society of New York.

Jane Greenough went to Italy in March and will spend the summer in England.

Marian Guptill plans to return soon from her year's study in Italy and Greece to work for an M.A. at the Univ. of Chicago.

Mary Jane Heath will be in La Fayette (Ind.) this summer and hopes anyone coming her way will look her up.

Betty Honess is in Europe with her family.

Ruth Hunter is spending the summer in the Sierra Mountains in Calif.

Jane Irving is working with the law firm of Ewing and Voorhees at 111 Broadway, doing stenographic work.

Margaret Kreuder and Louise McCabe are touring Ireland and England with a Ford and a moving-picture machine!

Betty Lewis expects to go to camp this summer after a busy year organizing a new library and teaching in Elizabeth, N. J.

Peggy (Lloyd) Aiken writes that she and Polly Winchester,· "the schoolmarms of the Rye Country Day Schools," were honored by a visit, lasting thirty minutes, from one of Mr. Harlow's classes which was on its way to study social problems in New York.

Janet McGee is working in the Public Library in Jackson, Mich.

Constance Mahoney has been elected director of the Holyoke (Mass.) Girl Scouts. She is now abroad and will attend the International Girl Scout camp in Geneva.

Ruth Montgomery has received her M.A. from Columbia in psychology.

Winnie Murfin has undertaken to superintend the Junior Sunday School in the neighboring church, now that art school is over.

Ruby Neal has a position with Lee, Higginson and Co. as a bond clerk.

Fanny Ottenheimer is doing social work in N. Y. C.

Janet Perry has finished her secretarial course and plans to work part of the summer in her father's law office.

Pauline Pierce, after a year as agent to the Massachusetts Mutual Life Insurance Co., has decided to see what policy the West has to offer, and is taking a Pacific Coast tour with an ever-open eye for opportunities Canadian, American, and Hollywood. Her New York address is 126 Claremont Av.

Jane Pither is traveling in Europe with her mother this summer.

Dorothy Rand has received a fellowship from Radcliffe for further study abroad. Her mother died June 3.

Henrietta Rhees has been traveling in Europe and the Near East.

Mary Robertson has been tutoring in a private school for little boys in Lakeville, Conn.

Ruth Rose expects to travel in Europe this summer.

Ethel Rothwell has been teaching English to sophomores, juniors, and seniors in Provincetown, Mass.

Frances Ryman plans to take a summer course at Teachers College with the aim of getting an M.A.

Genevieve Shepherd expects to teach French in Hempstead (N. Y.) next year.

Sylvia Shapiro has just returned from a six months' trip to California. She will study secretarial work this summer.

Dottie Spaeth plans to attend summer session at the Univ. of California.

The Flavor is Roasted In!

White House COFFEE

OF ADVERTISERS

Helen Spaidal has been traveling in Europe since the latter part of February and will return home about Aug. first.

Laura Stiehl finished her work for an M.A. at Columbia in May.

Ruth Strong plans to study at Harvard this summer.

Ruth Talbot is secretary to the superintendent-principal and part time teacher in the high school in Bound Brook, N. J.

Margaret Ward received her M.A. in sociology from Smith in June.

Louise Zschiesche's address is Stuart Club, 102 Fenway, Boston.

'26 will again be well represented in Europe this summer. The following plan to be there: Carolyn Case, Peg Bates, Betty Beam, Dorothy Garland, Millicent Hamburger, Virginia Heffern, Ruby Jordon, Jane Pither, Elisabeth Rice.

NEW ADDRESSES.—Evelyn Craig, 68 E. 92 St., N. Y. C.

Mrs. F. C. Davis (Lillian Davis), Westport, Conn.

Mrs. Leon Stern (Dorothy Regensburg), 1192 Park Av., N. Y. C.

Harriet (Wolcott) Works, 378 Lincoln Av., Salem, O.

Ex-1926

ENGAGED.—Esther Carver to Paul D. Standish. They expect to be married this fall.

Florence Heath to Theodore W. Koch. They will live in St. Paul after their marriage.

Helen Roberts to Robert Elliott McCormick. She planned to be married the latter part of June.

MARRIED.—Mildred Chichester to Turner Ashby Sims Jr., Aug. 31, 1926. Mr. Turner graduated fourth in his class at West Point in 1926 and is now in the flying corps at Kelly Field, Tex. Address until Sept. 1, 358 Kirk Pl., San Antonio, Tex.

Florence Draper to Otto Gray Lachmund. New address, 2521 E. 6 St., Duluth, Minn.

Harriet Moore to Boyle Owsley Rodes, Jan. 1. Address, 410 N. Newstead Av., St. Louis, Mo.

BORN.—To Nancy (Billings) Keeney a daughter, Margaret Morton, Sept. 5, 1926.

To Mary (Histed) Hughes a son, Hilliard Withers Jr., Apr. 5, 1926.

To Margaret (Stearns) Hauers a daughter, Nancy Winslow, July 21, 1926.

To Agnes (Janeway) Wise a son, William Theodore, Feb. 8, 1926. Agnes is a real estate saleswoman with Gaines, Van Nostrand, and Morrison in New York.

OTHER NEWS.—Elizabeth Cushman is studying singing with Mme. Caroline Mihr-Hardy in New York.

Elizabeth (Dickinson) Smith plans to come home from China in July.

Marie Drucker is vocational counselor on the Vocation Bureau of the Cincinnati Board of Education.

Inglis Griswold was an alternate to the Junior League Convention in Portland (Ore.) and is now in California.

Polly Marden graduated from Pratt Institute of Brooklyn in June after a two-year course in interior decoration and design.

Margaret Morgan has been temporary secretary in the Registrar's Office of Barnard College.

Elizabeth Muzzey is touring Europe for three months and will return the first week of Sept.

Virginia North graduated from the Law School of the Univ. of Wisconsin in June. She feels very proud at having just made the Order of the Coif.

Margaret (Truax) Hunter received her A.B. from the Univ. of California, Dec. 17, 1926.

Sallie (Wright) Grover lives at 177 Babcock St., Brookline, Mass. She has a son Richard, fourteen months old.

Suzanne Ziegler worked all winter for a business correspondence school. She has sailed for England and plans to attend the German music festivals in August.

1927

Class secretary—Catherine Cole, 17 Chestnut St., Dedham, Mass.

Other officers are: president, Amanda Bryan; vice-president, Harriet Mitchell; treasurer, Ruth Sears.

Notices

COLLEGE OPENS TUESDAY, SEPT. 27. COMMENCEMENT DAY IS MONDAY, JUNE 18.

All editorial mail should be sent to Edith Hill, College Hall, Northampton, Mass. Material for the November QUARTERLY should be typewritten and should reach College Hall by October 1. Please send subscriptions to Miss Snow at Rumford Bldg., 10 Ferry St., Concord, N. H., or College Hall, Northampton. Correspondence concerning advertising should be sent to College Hall. The dates of publication are November 20, February 20, May 20, and July 30, and subscribers failing to receive their copies within ten days after those dates should notify the business manager, as otherwise she cannot furnish free duplicate copies. The subscription price for one year is $1.50. Single copies 40 cents.

The New Hampshire Club And You At Juniper

The New Hampshire Club extends a cordial invitation to all Smith people to come to its August meeting at Juniper Lodge. Write Ruth Higgins, Manchester, N. H., telling her your address and she will notify you of the date.

Local Clubs

Owing to the pressure of Commencement material Club news was not included in this issue. It will appear in the fall *Register*.

Pictures In This Issue

Pictures in this issue were taken by Eric Stahlberg, Elizabeth Kingsley, and Marian Holden '29·

𝔖mith College

NORTHAMPTON, MASSACHUSETTS

WILLIAM ALLAN NEILSON, PH.D., LL.D., L.H.D., LITT.D., *President*

SMITH COLLEGE was founded by Sophia Smith of Hatfield, Massachusetts, who bequeathed for its establishment and maintenance $393,105.60, a sum which in 1875, when the last payment was received and the institution was opened, amounted to nearly if not quite a half million of dollars. The College is Christian, seeking to realize the ideals of character inspired by the Christian religion, but is entirely non-sectarian in its management and instruction. It was incorporated and chartered by the State in March 1871. In September 1875 it opened with 14 students, and granted 11 degrees in June 1879. In June 1927 the College conferred 464 A.B. degrees, and 20 A.M. degrees.

L. CLARK SEELYE, D.D., was the first president. He accepted the presidency in July 1873, and served until June 1910. He lived in Northampton as President Emeritus until his death on October 12, 1924. Marion LeRoy Burton, Ph.D., D.D., LL.D., was installed as president in October 1910 and served until June 1917. He left Smith College to be president of the University of Minnesota, and later was president of the University of Michigan. He died on February 18, 1925. William Allan Neilson, Ph.D., LL.D., L.H.D., Litt.D., came in September 1917 to be president of the College.

THE College opened its fifty-second year with an undergraduate enrollment of 2033 besides 34 juniors who are spending the year at the Sorbonne, 65 graduate students, a resident faculty of 203, and 9 chief administrative officers. There are 10,318 living alumnae exclusive of the class just graduated.

THE property owned by the College comprises 87.25 acres on which there are over a hundred buildings. There are botanical gardens and athletic fields, also a pond which provides boating and skating. There are 33 houses of residence owned or operated by the College besides 11 houses closely affiliated but privately owned. It is the policy of the College to give all four classes approximately equal representation in each house.

THE College fee for board and room is $500 per year and for tuition $400 for all students entering after 1925. Further details are published in the annual catalogs. The Trustees set aside approximately $100,000 for scholarships annually, besides which many special prizes have been established.

AMONG the distinctive features of the College are: (1) Junior year in France. A selected group of students majoring in French are allowed to spend their junior year at the Sorbonne under the personal direction of a member of the Department of French. (2) Special Honors. Selected students are allowed to pursue their studies individually during the junior and senior years in a special field under the guidance of special instructors. They are relieved of the routine of class attendance and course examinations during these two years. (3) The Experimental Schools: a. School for Exceptional Children. For public school children with special educational disabilities and retarded mental development. Conducted by the Department of Education in coöperation with the Northampton Board of Education. b. The Day School, an experimental school of the progressive type, also conducted by the Department of Education, offers instruction to children from five years of age through the work of the Junior High School. c. Nursery School, conducted by the Institute for the Coördination of Women's Interests in coöperation with the Department of Education. (4) School for Social Work. A professional graduate school leading to the degree of M.S.S. The course is fifteen months and comprises theoretical work in Northampton and practical work in the field.

FOR any further information about Smith College address the President's Office, College Hall, Northampton, Mass.

RUMFORD PRESS
CONCORD